# THE ROUTLEDGE COMPANION TO MOBILE MEDIA ART

In this companion, a diverse, international, and interdisciplinary group of contributors and editors examine the rapidly expanding, far-reaching field of mobile media as it intersects with art across a range of spaces—theoretical, practical, and conceptual.

As a vehicle for—and of—the everyday, mobile media is recalibrating the relationship between art and digital networked media and reshaping how creative practices such as writing, photography, video art, and filmmaking are being conceptualized and practised. In exploring these innovations, *The Routledge Companion to Mobile Media Art* pulls together comprehensive, culturally nuanced, and interdisciplinary approaches; considerations of broader media ecologies and histories and political, social and cultural dynamics; and critical and considered perspectives on the intersections between mobile media and art.

This book is the definitive publication for researchers, artists and students interested in comprehending all the various aspects of mobile media art, covering digital media and culture, internet studies, games studies, anthropology, sociology, geography, media and communication, cultural studies, and design.

Distinguished Professor **Larissa Hjorth** is a creative practitioner, digital ethnographer and Director of the Design & Creative Practice ECP Platform at RMIT University. Hjorth has published over 100 publications on mobile media studies—recent publications include *Haunting Hands* (with Cumiskey 2017), *Understanding Social Media* (with Hinton, 2nd Edition 2019), *Creative Practice Ethnographies* (with Harris, Jungnickel and Coombs 2020) and *Ambient Play* (with Richardson 2020).

Professor **Adriana de Souza e Silva** is the Director of the Mobile Gaming Research Lab at the Department of Communication at North Carolina State University (NCSU). Dr. de Souza e Silva is the co-editor and co-author of several books, including *Net-Locality: Why Location Matters in a Networked World* (with Gordon 2011), *Mobile Interfaces in Public Spaces: Control, Privacy, and Urban Sociability* (with Frith 2012), *Mobility and Locative Media: Mobile Communication in Hybrid Spaces* (with Sheller 2014) and *Hybrid Play* (with Glover-Rijkse 2020).

**Klare Lanson** is a performance poet and current PhD Candidate at RMIT University. Recent collaborative and interdisciplinary art projects are *#wanderingcloud* (2012–2015), *Commute* (2013–2016) and mobile art ethnography *TouchOn/TouchOff* (2017). Publications include *Digital Cultures & Society* (2019), *Min-a-rets Poetry Journal* (2018), *thephonebook.com* (2002), *Cordite Poetry Review*, *Overland Journal* and *Realtime Arts*, and she was also co-editor of the 40-year-old Australian literary anthology *Going Down Swinging*.

# THE ROUTLEDGE COMPANION TO MOBILE MEDIA ART

*Edited by Larissa Hjorth, Adriana de Souza e Silva, and Klare Lanson*

Routledge
Taylor & Francis Group
NEW YORK AND LONDON

First published 2020
by Routledge
605 Third Avenue, New York, NY 10017

and by Routledge
2 Park Square, Milton Park, Abingdon, Oxon, OX14 4RN

First issued in paperback 2022

*Routledge is an imprint of the Taylor & Francis Group, an informa business*



*Library of Congress Cataloging-in-Publication Data*
Names: Hjorth, Larissa, editor. | Silva, Adriana de Souza e, editor. | Lanson, Klare, editor.
Title: The Routledge companion to mobile media art / edited by Larissa Hjorth, Adriana de Souza e Silva, Klare Lanson.
Description: New York, NY: Routledge, 2020. | Includes bibliographical references and index.
Identifiers: LCCN 2019057235 (print) | LCCN 2019057236 (ebook) | ISBN 9780367197162 (hbk) | ISBN 9780429242816 (ebk)
Subjects: LCSH: New media art. | Digital media.
Classification: LCC NX456.5.N49 R668 2020 (print) | LCC NX456.5.N49 (ebook) | DDC 709.05/1—dc23
LC record available at https://lccn.loc.gov/2019057235
LC ebook record available at https://lccn.loc.gov/2019057236

ISBN: 978-1-03-239995-9 (pbk)
ISBN: 978-0-367-19716-2 (hbk)
ISBN: 978-0-429-24281-6 (ebk)

DOI: 10.4324/9780429242816

Typeset in Bembo
by codeMantra

# CONTENTS

# FIGURES

# COLOR INSERT FIGURES

# TABLES

# CONTRIBUTORS

**Matt Adams** co-founded Blast Theory in 1991, an artists' group making interactive work. Blast Theory is renowned for its multidisciplinary approach using new technologies in theatre, games, and visual art. The group has collaborated with scientists at the Mixed Reality Lab at the University of Nottingham since 1997. Blast Theory has shown work at the Venice Biennale, Sundance Film Festival, and Tate Britain. Commissioners include Channel 4, National Theatre Wales, and the Royal Opera House. Awards include the Golden Nica at Prix Ars Electronica, the Nam June Paik Art Center Award, and four BAFTA nominations. Matt has curated at Tate Modern and at the ICA in London and has taught widely. He has lectured at Stanford University, the Royal College of Art, and the Sorbonne. He was the Visiting Professor in Interactive Media at the Royal Central School of Speech and Drama from 2007 to 2014. He is an Honorary Fellow at the University of Exeter. www.blasttheory.co.uk/.

**Camille Baker** is a Reader for the School of Communication Design at the University for the Arts, Epsom, Surrey, UK. She is an interdisciplinary artist, curator, and researcher with a background of digital media practices and experience in wearable technology and e-textiles, mobile media art and performance, the body, VR/AR performance, digital art curating, video art, new media art, alternative music, interactive installation, and emerging technologies research and education. She explores new mechanisms to elicit engaging experiences using evolving approaches to participatory performance. Dr. Baker's first monograph is *New Directions in Mobile Media and Performance* (2018). This book features theory and practice on mobile devices, Augmented/Virtual/Mixed Reality, and wearable technology in various forms of artistic performance, especially since the release of the first iPhone. www.camillebaker.me.

**Will Balmford** is a Post-Doctoral researcher at RMIT University. His research involves exploring the impacts of domestic videogame usage within Melbourne households, an ongoing fieldwork for an ARC grant exploring mobile phone videogame practices around Australia, and the use of ethnographic observations to help a community health centre better understand the needs of clients. Recent publications appear in *Mobile Media & Communications* and a book chapter in *Refiguring Techniques in Digital Visual Research* (2019). Balmford is also currently co-writing a book (with Hjorth, Richardson, and Davies) on *Minecraft* at the intersection of education and creativity.

**Giselle Beiguelman** is a media artist and Associate Professor at the Faculty of Architecture and Urbanism of the University of Sao Paulo (FAU–USP). Her work includes interventions in public spaces, networked projects, and mobile art applications, which have been exhibited internationally in the main media art museums, research centres and contemporary art venues like ZKM (Karlsruhe, Germany), Gallery @ Calit2 (UCSD, USA), and the Sao Paulo Biennial. She is author of *Nomadismos Tecnologicos* (with La Ferla, 2011), *Possible Futures: Art, Museums and Digital Archives* (2014), and *Memory of Amnesia: Politics of Oblivion* (2019). Main research interests are in digital culture practices and memory studies. http://orcid.org/0000-0003-4812-5972; http://outrosurbanismos.fau.usp.br; http://www.desvirtual.com.

**Marsha Berry** is Senior Lecturer in the School of Media and Communication at RMIT University, where she teaches creative practice research methods. She is author of *Creating with Smartphones* (2017) and co-editor of two volumes on mobile media. Berry has published her research extensively in journals such as *New Media and Society* and *New Writing* as well as in edited books. She is an ethnographer, writer, and artist whose practice includes filmmaking, participatory art projects, and poetry. Her video art and photography have been exhibited in Australia and internationally in exhibition spaces such as the Directors Lounge in Berlin and the Queensland Centre of Photography.

**Joanna Bletcher** is a researcher and lecturer in Communication Design at the University of Dundee. Her main research interests include exploring the concept and process of innovation in design and craft, its public communication, and investigating the use of innovative practice-led research methodologies.

**Grant Bollmer** studies the history and theory of digital media. He is the author of the books *Inhuman Networks: Social Media and the Archaeology of Connection* (2016), *Theorizing Digital Cultures* (2018), and *Materialist Media Theory: An Introduction* (2019). He is an Assistant Professor of Communication at North Carolina State University and an Honorary Associate of the Department of Media and Communication at the University of Sydney.

**Matiu Bush** is the founder of *One Good Street*, a social networking platform to encourage neighbour-initiated care for older residents at risk of social isolation and loneliness. Matiu is Senior Strategist, Business Innovation at Bolton Clarke, driving innovation and creativity in the aged and community sector. Matiu has an MA in Public Health and broad clinical and managerial nursing experience including: working in Tijuana, Mexico with Nobel Prize Laureate Mother Teresa in international border aid, and as an emergency, oncology, intensive care nurse and as a sexual health Nurse Practitioner.

**Chelsea Butkowski,** MA, is a doctoral student at Cornell University where she studies gender representation and media technologies.

**Massimiliano Casu** is an architect, artist, and curator. He investigates public art and tactical urbanism and develops collective projects based on direct action, mostly using tools, tactics, and strategies that come from aural culture, music, and performance. Casu is co-founder of Grupal Crew Collective, an art group that explores the potential of party and soundsystem culture around the globe as a social laboratory. In the recent years, he has worked in Europe and Latin America developing art projects, workshops, and sound installations for art institutions such as Matadero Madrid, Medialab-Prado, Thyssen-Bornemisza Museum, the Spanish Agency for International Development Cooperation, Cervantes Institute, and Goethe Institute.

**Gretchen Coombs** is a Post-Doctoral Research Fellow in the Design & Creative Practice Enabling Capability Platform at RMIT. Her writing on socially engaged art and design has appeared in *Hyperallergic*, *The Brooklyn Rail* and *Eyeline* as well as academic journals and books. She is the co-editor of the journal, *Art & the Public Sphere.* Gretchen runs writing workshops ("Writing the Social") for artists who want to learn more about ethnographic and creative methods for their social practice. Her latest publication is an intimate and academic, personal and public creative ethnography: *The Lure of the Social: Encounters with Contemporary Artists* (2020).

**Saskia Coulson** is a research fellow at the University of Dundee, where she works on interdisciplinary projects that put design at the centre of collective enquiry. She works on projects that span both creative practices and geographical locations. Her primary research interest includes social innovation, environmental monitoring, and citizen sensing.

**Hugh Davies** is an interdisciplinary artist, curator, and scholar. His research sits at the intersection of game cultures and media archaeology with a focus on the Asia-Pacific Region. Hugh advocates interdisciplinary practice connecting industry arts and education. Previously, he was multiplatform producer at the Australian Broadcasting Corporation (ABC), senior lecturer at La Trobe University and Deputy Director of the Centre for Creative Arts. As an arts worker, Hugh has served as chair of the Australian Network of Art and Technology (ANAT), and was the inaugural chair of the Freeplay Independent Gaming Festival. He is currently a Post-Doctoral research fellow at RMIT University in the Design and Creative Practice Enabling Capability Platform.

**Adriana de Souza e Silva** is a Professor at the Department of Communication at North Carolina State University (NCSU) and Director of the Mobile Gaming Research Lab. Dr. de Souza e Silva's research focusses on how mobile and locative interfaces shape people's interactions with public spaces and create new forms of sociability. She teaches classes on mobile technologies, location-based games and internet studies. Dr. de Souza e Silva is the co-editor and co-author of several books, including *Net-Locality: Why Location Matters in a Networked World* (Blackwell 2011, with Eric Gordon), *Mobile Interfaces in Public Spaces: Control, Privacy, and Urban Sociability* (Routledge 2012, with Jordan Frith) and *Mobility and Locative Media: Mobile Communication in Hybrid Spaces* (Routledge 2014, with Mimi Sheller). She holds a PhD in Communication and Culture from the Federal University of Rio de Janeiro, Brazil.

**Paulien Dresscher** is, since 1994, an independent curator, researcher, writer and educator in the field of culture and digital media on the cross roads of theory and practice. Currently, she is part of the Steering Committee of PublicSpaces and curates the interactive programme of the Nederlands Film Festival and the art programme Into the Great Wide Open. Since 2015, she has been affiliated with Utrecht University, teaching Media Philosophy and Screen Cultures, and she joined the Fontys School of Fine and Performing Arts in 2018 as a researcher on Creative Industries. She is also part of the Advisory Board of the Dutch Literature Fund, Amsterdam Art Fund (AFK), and Stichting Cultuur Eindhoven. Dresscher has worked as a commissioner and curator with artists like Marshmallow, Laser Feast, Rosa Menkman, Theodore Watson, Emily Watson, Daito Manabe, Kyle McDonald, Ruairi Glynn, Chris Sugrue, Golan Levin, Zach Lieberman, and many others.

**Kate Durbin** is a Los Angeles-based artist and writer. She makes films, new media work, and does performance art in public spaces and online. Works include *Hello Selfie* (2012–2015), which she performed for the Pulse Art Fair in Miami with Transfer Gallery, in Union Square with Transfer Gallery, in Los Angeles with Perform Chinatown, and with Arts Queensland in Australia. Other recent work includes: *Unfriend Me Now!* (2019) about Facebook's rhetorical wars over the 2016 US Presidential election; *The Supreme Gentleman* (2015–2016) about Isla Vista shooter Elliot

Rodger; and *Cloud 9* (2015) about female artists and money, commissioned by New Hive. Publications include *E! Entertainment* (2014), *The Ravenous Audience* (2009), and experimental book *ABRA* (1913 Press). *ABRA* is also a free, interactive iOS app that is "a living text," which won the 2017 Turn on Literature Prize for electronic literature. https://www.katedurbin.la/.

**Marius Foley** is the Program Manager of the Master of Design Futures in the RMIT School of Design. The Master of Design Futures is grounded in the principles of human-centred design and the various practices that are emerging, such as Service, Strategic, Transdisciplinary, and Transition Design. Marius has an interest in what design brings to leadership in contemporary, networked, and multi-disciplinary situations. His research centres on co-creative and collaborative practices, innovation, and the influence of human-centred design across diverse sectors including design education; design engagements with aged care and approaches to death; and design and media innovation, especially in rural and remote communities.

**Ragan Glover-Rijkse** is a doctoral student in the Communication, Rhetoric, and Digital Media (CRDM) program and an affiliate of the Mobile Gaming Research Lab at NC State University. Her research focusses on the intersections between mobile media, mobilities, infrastructures, and space/place. She is the co-editor of the book *Hybrid Spaces: Crossing Boundaries in Game Design, Player Identities, and Play Spaces* (2020, with Adriana de Souza e Silva). In addition to her research, Glover-Rijkse teaches courses on mobile media, media history and theory, and media writing in the Department of Communication at NC State.

**Edgar Gómez Cruz** is a Senior Lecturer in Media (Digital Cultures) in the School of the Arts and Media at the UNSW in Sydney. He has published widely on a number of topics relating to digital culture, particularly in the areas of digital photography, digital ethnography, and visual methods.

**Helen Grace** established the MA Program in Visual Culture Studies at the Chinese University of Hong Kong and then moved to National Central University, Taiwan, where she taught cinema studies and new media studies. She is a photographer, filmmaker, and new media producer. Her books include *Culture, Aesthetics and Affect in Ubiquitous Media: The Prosaic Image* (2014) and she co-edited *Technovisuality: Cultural Re-Enchantment and the Experience of Technology* (2016).

**Jaz Hee-jeong Choi** is the Director of the Care-full Design Lab and Vice-Chancellor's Senior Research Fellow in School of Design, RMIT, Australia. As a transdisciplinary researcher, her approach to urban sustainability recognises play and care as the core of transformational encounters in cities as complex cyberphysical networks. Her current research and practice explore care-full design for liveable and equitable urban futures across three inter-related domains: self-care and mutual aid, creative and impactful research methods, and co-creative urban transformation. Choi has published in books and journals across disciplines, and given keynote presentations at major international conferences including the inaugural Global Social Economy Forum in 2013 and the 2010 UNESCO Creative Cities Conference.

**Leah Heiss** is a designer and RMIT researcher working at the nexus of design, health, and technology. Her wearable health technologies include Diabetes Jewellery, biosignal sensing emergency jewellery, and swallowable devices to detect disease. Facett, the world's first modular hearing aid that Leah designed for Blamey Saunder's ears won the 2018 Good Design Award and the CSIRO Design Innovation Award. Leah's work is part of Museums Victoria heritage collection, and she has exhibited at galleries locally and globally. She teaches at RMIT's Master of Design Futures, and her teaching practice focusses on health sector innovation.

**Drew Hemment** is an artist, designer, and academic researcher. He is a Chancellor's Fellow at Edinburgh Futures Institute and has been recognized by awards from the arts, technology, and business sectors including the STARTS Prize, Lever Prize and Prix Ars Electronica. He founded *FutureEverything* in 1995 and was Creative Director for 23 years. Drew develops collaborative and interdisciplinary forms for research, in which building communities of interest are integral. He is an Editorial Board member for *Leonardo* journal of art, science and technology, and member of the Citizens' Observatories Community Activity of the intergovernmental Group on Earth Observations (GEO), which is leading a worldwide effort to build a Global Earth Observation System of Systems (GEOSS).

**Julia M. Hildebrand** is an Assistant Professor of Communication at Eckerd College in St. Petersburg, Florida. She holds a PhD in Communication, Culture, and Media from Drexel University. Her research lies at the intersection of critical media studies and mobilities research with a special interest in visual communication and mobile technologies. She has published in journals such as *Media, Culture & Society, Digital Culture & Society* and *Mobile Media & Communication.*

**Sam Hinton** is a senior lecturer in digital media and runs the digital media program at the University of Canberra, Australia. With Larissa Hjorth, he is co-author of the second edition of *Understanding Social Media* (2019). His work relates to the social and technical aspects of games, game production and social media.

**Larissa Hjorth** is a digital ethnographer, artist, Distinguished Professor and director of the Design & Creative Practice ECP platform at RMIT University. Hjorth studies the socio-cultural dimensions of mobile media and plays practices in the Asia-Pacific region with an emphasis on interdisciplinary, collaborative, and cross-cultural approaches. She has published a dozen co-authored books, edited over a dozen Handbooks/Companions and has over 40 journal articles. Hjorth's books include *Creative Practice Ethnographies* (with Harris, Jungnickel and Coombs 2020), *Ambient Play* (with Richardson 2020), *Haunting Hands* (with Cumiskey 2017), *Screen Ecologies* (with Pink, Sharp, and Williams 2016), *Digital Ethnography* (Pink et al. 2016), *Gaming in Locative, Social and Mobile Media* (with Richardson 2014), *Understanding Social Media* (with Hinton 2013, 2019), *Online@AsiaPacific* (with Arnold 2013), *Games & Gaming* (2010), and *Mobile Media in the Asia-Pacific* (2009).

**Cat Hope** is a composer, sound artist, musician, and performance artist whose practice examines the corporeality of sound in different ways. Hope founded and co-edited *Sound Scripts: Proceedings of the Inaugural Totally Huge New Music Festival Conference* (2005), and her subsequent paper "Mobile Art/Sound Art" (2007) was one of the first on sound art in mobile media. Hope has also created a range of mobile media sound art works exhibited worldwide, as well as instrumental music works that engage digital graphic notations and related technologies that have been featured at ISEA and other festivals worldwide. Hope is the co-author of *Digital Art—An Introduction to New Media* (2014) and Professor of Music at Monash University in Melbourne, Australia. http://www.cathope.com/.

**Brian House** is an artist who investigates more-than-human temporalities. His work has been exhibited by New York's Museum of Modern Art (MoMA), Los Angeles based The Museum of Contemporary Art (MOCA), Cincinnati Contemporary Arts Center, Beall Center, Center for Art and Media Karlsruhe (ZKM), Ars Electronica, and Transmediale, among others, and has been featured in publications including *The New York Times* Magazine, *TIME*, *WIRED*, *Neural*, *Creative Applications*, *Hyperallergic*, and *Creator's Project*. He is currently a Mellon Associate Research Scholar at Columbia University's Center for Spatial Research. http://brianhouse.net.

**Erkki Huhtamo** is a media archaeologist, historian, and exhibition curator and works as a professor at the University of California Los Angeles (UCLA), Departments of Design Media Arts, and Film, Television, and Digital Media. He received his PhD in cultural history from the University of Turku, Finland. Huhtamo is an internationally renowned media historian and theorist and is also a specialist in the history and aesthetics of media arts. He is one of the founders of media archaeology. Recent books include *Media Archaeology: Approaches, Applications, and Implications* (edited with Jussi Parikka, University of California Press 2011), *Illusions in Motion: Media Archaeology of the Moving Panorama and Related Spectacles* (The MIT Press 2013), and *How to Dismantle a Fairy Engine? Media Archaeology as Topos Study* (forthcoming).

**Lee Humphreys**, is an Associate Professor of Communication at Cornell University where she studies the social uses and perceived effects of communication technology.

**Troy Innocent** is an artist, academic, and educator investigating playful wayfinding to reimagine cities. His non-objective art practice explores abstractions drawn from urban space expressed in works of code, sculpture, animation, sound, and installation. Innocent's interactive artworks use invented languages to create constructed worlds, exploring the potential of mixed realities to manifest new ways of being. This approach is also central to his public art practice through "urban codemaking"—a system he developed for situating play in cities such as Melbourne, Istanbul, Sydney and Hong Kong. He co-founded the digital arts collective Cyber Dada in 1989, and through pioneering works such as Idea-ON>!, has significantly contributed to the Australian new media arts practice during the 1990s. Innocent is represented by Anna Pappas Gallery.

**Kat Jungnickel** is a senior lecturer in the sociology department at Goldsmiths, University of London, where she teaches critical social theory, science and technology studies, and practises research methods. She codirects the Methods Lab and Digital World Making groups, which experiment with inventive ways of doing social research. Her research is concerned with invention, mobilities (particularly cycling), gender, DIY and DIT (do-it-together) technology cultures, and creative research transmissions. Recent publications include *Bikes & Bloomers: Victorian Women Inventors and Their Extraordinary Cycle Wear* (Goldsmiths Press 2018) and *Transmissions: Critical Tactics for Making and Communicating Research* (The MIT Press 2019). She is currently working on a five-year European Research Council funded project called Politics of Patents: Re-imagining Citizenship via Clothing Inventions 1820–2020. More about her research can be found at www.katjungnickel.com.

**Fumitoshi Kato**, is a Communication Professor at the Faculty of Environment and Information Studies, Keio University, Japan. His research interests include communication theory, media studies, socio-cultural impacts of new technologies, and qualitative research methods. He is especially interested in the use of camera phones in the context of place-making and community development. For the past 15 years, he has been conducting field research in various local communities in Japan, with a primary focus on the notion of mobile learning.

**Sybille Lammes** is a Professor of New Media and Digital Culture at Leiden University's Centre for the Arts in Society (LUCAS). She has been a visiting Senior Research Fellow at The University of Manchester and has worked as a researcher at the Centre for Interdisciplinary Methodologies at the University of Warwick, as well as the media-studies departments of Utrecht University and the University of Amsterdam. Her background is in media-studies and play-studies, which she has always approached from an interdisciplinary angle, including cultural studies, science and technology studies, postcolonial studies, and critical geography.

**Klare Lanson** is a performance poet and artist researcher. In the 1990s, Lanson was a curator of artist-run spaces, helped set up Australia's first internet café, worked on the visual arts program for the Adelaide Festival of the Arts, and directed the contemporary arts organization Umbrella Studios. Her PhD research at RMIT University investigates the mobility of digital parenting through speculative creative practice methods, mobile media studies, and the philosophy of sound and listening. Recent collaborative art projects are *#wanderingcloud* (2012–2015), *Commute* (2013–2017), and a mobile media art ethnography entitled *TouchOn/TouchOff* (2017). Publications include *Digital Cultures & Society* (2019), *Min-a-rets Poetry Journal* (2018), *thephonebook.com* (2002), *Cordite Poetry Review*, *Overland Journal*, *Realtime Arts*, and she was also co-editor of the 40-year-old Australian literary anthology *Going Down Swinging.*

**Amparo Lasén** is Professor of Sociology at the University Complutense de Madrid and member of the research group Sociología Ordinaria. Her research focusses on digital mediations, especially in relationship with mobile media, affectivity, the configuration of contemporary subjectivities, intimacies, and everyday life. Prior to her current position, she was the Vodafone Surrey Scholar at the Digital World Research Centre (DWRC) of Surrey University, where she conducted cross-cultural research on mobile phone uses and practices. She has been academic visitor at the Department of Sociology of the LSE and researcher of the CEAQ (Centre d'Études de l'Actuel et du Quotidien) Paris V-La Sorbonne.

**Jacina Leong** is an artist-curator. Over the past decade, she has worked in a range of hybrid new media spaces—to vision, develop, and deliver a diverse range of transdisciplinary engagement program via collaborative, experimental, and site-responsive processes. Most recently, Leong was curator for *Robotronica* (Brisbane), project lead and founding member (with Linda Knight) of the *Guerrilla Knowledge Unit* (Brisbane and Linz), guest facilitator of the *Future Innovators Summit* (Ars Electronica Tokyo Initiative 2018), and co-curator of the provocation, *Curating in the Age of Automation* as part of the Doing Digital Methods: Interdisciplinary Interventions Conference in Kyoto (2018). She is currently a PhD candidate at RMIT University.

**Golan Levin** is an artist, composer, performer, and engineer with an interest in new modes of reactive expression. Levin focusses on the design of systems for the creation, manipulation, and performance of audiovisual works, as part of his interest in formal languages of interactivity and nonverbal communication in cybernetic systems.

**Brian Massumi** is the author of numerous works across philosophy, political theory, and art theory. His publications include *99 Theses on the Revaluation of Value: A Postcapitalist Manifesto* (University of Minnesota Press 2018), *Semblance and Event: Activist Philosophy and the Occurrent Arts* (MIT Press 2013), and *Parables for the Virtual: Movement, Affect, Sensation* (Duke University Press 2002).

**Nancy Mauro-Flude** is an artist driven by the demystification of technology and the "mystification" that lie in and through the performance of the machinic assemblage. "Gray magics, hijackings, driftings and seizures of power are many of the sensitive and subversive subterfuges by which her projects urge, twist and explore the aesthetic politic of the open source spirit" (Goldenburg 2014). She has published, devised, and curated extensively within the field of experimental art. Mauro-Flude is also a founder of the feminist server stack *Despoinas Media Coven* and faculty member of the Digital Media programme at the School of Design, RMIT Australia. http://sister0.org/.

**Lauren McCarthy** is an LA-based artist examining social relationships in the midst of surveillance, automation, and algorithmic living. She is the creator of p5.js, an open-source programming language with over 1.5 million users, for learning creative expression through code online.

**Kelli McCluskey** and **Steve Bull** are co-artistic directors of pvi collective, founded in Perth, Australia in 1998. pvi is a tactical media art group that creates agitational participatory artworks intent on the creative disruption of everyday life. They use gameplay alongside emerging, familiar, and DIY technology to explore the social dynamics of the urban experience. Over the years, they have created playfully subversive performances and interventions that invite genuine engagement, transforming perceptions of space, cities, and environment. Recent artworks include *tiny revolutions* (2019) and *disobedience rules* (2018). https://pvicollective.com/.

**Caitlin McGrane** is a feminist researcher and activist. She is a PhD candidate in the Digital Ethnography Research Centre at RMIT University. Her research investigates the gendered uses, practices, and impacts of locative media for women's feelings around security. McGrane has previously researched how witnessing anti-feminist harassment can affect individuals' willingness to participate in online spaces and publicly identify as feminist. As an activist, she leads Gender Equity Victoria's *Online Active Bystander Project*, which helps to challenge gendered harassment and online abuse by encouraging bystanders to take an active role on social media.

**Shannon McMullen** and **Fabian Winkler** work as an artist duo whose collaborative art practice engages issues in contemporary culture at the intersection of nature, technology, and social enquiry. They combine their backgrounds in new media art and sociology to produce speculative social spaces and time-based installations. In 2016, Ars Electronica listed their collaborative practice in an international overview of artist working at the intersection of Art and Science. McMullen and Winkler are Associate Professors at Purdue University in West Lafayette, IN, USA, with appointments in the Department of Art and Design (McMullen, Winkler) and the American Studies Program (McMullen).

**Joshua McWhirter** is a writer, audio producer, and urbanist based in Brooklyn, NY. He is an editor for Failed Architecture, an independent foundation and digital publication seeking to reconnect architecture with the real world.

**Daniel Palmer** is Professor and Associate Dean of Research and Innovation in the School of Art at RMIT University, Melbourne. His books include *Photography and Collaboration: From Conceptual Art to Crowdsourcing* (Bloomsbury 2017); *Digital Light* (Open Humanities Press, 2015), edited with Sean Cubitt and Nathaniel Tkacz; *The Culture of Photography in Public Space* (Intellect 2015), edited with Anne Marsh and Melissa Miles; *Twelve Australian Photo Artists* (Piper Press 2009), co-authored with Blair French and *Photogenic* (Centre for Contemporary Photography 2005).

**Luisa Paraguai** is an artist and researcher at the Master Program in Language, Media and Arts, and faculty member at the Faculty of Visual Arts, Pontifical Catholic University of Campinas, Brazil. She studied Civil Engineering and Computing at the University of São Paulo and received her masters and doctoral degree at the Department of Multimedia, Institute of Arts, Unicamp, Brazil. Previously a post-doctoral Advanced Research Associate in the M-Node Planetary Collegium, NABA, Italy, Paraguai has also participated in many exhibitions such as *#EmMeio8.0 2016* and *#EmMeio10.0 2018*, *4D Interactive Computational Art* 2004, *Cinetic_Digital—Itaú Cultural* 2005,

Mostra SESC Artes 2010, *Mobility Futures* 2013, and the Cyber Fashion Show, *SIGGRAPH 2005*. http://luisaparaguai.art.br.

**Esther Polak** and **Ivar van Bekkum** are the artist-couple **PolakVanBekkum**. Routed in the history of the Dutch realistic landscape depiction, they express personal experiences of movement and space. Their projects are often informed by collaborations with participants, be it humans, animals or even the rays of the sun. Over recent years, the pair have developed a cinematographic method for synchronizing audio recordings with mapped routes. www.polakvanbekkum.com/.

**Gilbertto Prado** is an artist and coordinator of the Group Poéticas Digitais. He studied Engineering and Visual Arts at the University of Campinas, Brazil and in 1994 obtained his PhD in Arts at the University Paris I Panthéon-Sorbonne. Prado has participated in several art exhibitions in Brazil and abroad. Prizes include *9º Prix Möbius International des Multimédias* (Beijing 2001) and *6º Prêmio Sergio Motta de Arte e Tecnologia* (2006). He works with art in networks and interactive installations. Currently, he is Professor at the Post-Graduate Programs of Visual Arts at the Communication and Arts School at the University of São Paulo and Design at the University Anhembi Morumbi. www.gilberttoprado.net/.

**Ingrid Richardson** is Associate Professor in the School of Arts at Murdoch University, Western Australia. She has a broad interest in the human-technology relation and has published on the cultural and phenomenological effects of games and mobile media, digital ethnography and innovative research methods, urban screens, wearable technologies, virtual and augmented reality, remix culture, and web-based content creation and distribution.

**Martin Rieser** is both an academic and visual artist. His interactive film installations and mobile media works have been shown around the world, including *Understanding Echo* shown in Japan 2002, *Hosts* Bath Abbey 2006, *Secret Door* Invideo Milan 2006, *The Street* RMIT Gallery Melbourne 2008/ISEA Belfast 2009, *Secret Garden* Phoenix Square 2012/Taipei 2013, and RUR at Glyndebourne in 2014 for REFRAME at the University of Sussex. He has taught extensively since 1998 and was visiting Professor in the Digital Creativity Research Cluster at the University of the West of England 2012–2014, and Professor of Digital Creativity at De Montfort University's Institute of Creative Technologies 2007–2012. Rieser edited *New Screen Media: Cinema/Art/Narrative* (BFI/ZKM 2002), which combined a DVD of current research and practice in this area together with critical essays, and *The Mobile Audience: Media Art and Mobile Technologies* (Rodopi 2011). www.martinrieser.com

**Matthew Riley**, is a designer, researcher, and academic in animation, games, and interactivity at RMIT University, Melbourne, Australia who has received international and national recognition for his practice and research. Riley has exhibited at galleries and events including Australian Centre for the Moving Image, Monash University Museum of Art, Centre for Contemporary Photography, and Field 36. He been invited to speak at numerous conferences, festivals, and institutions including the London College of Communication (United Kingdom), xCoAx (Porto), the Society for Animation Studies (Melbourne), CODE (Melbourne), Digital Interventions (Perth), Freeplay Independent Games Festival (Melbourne), ISEA (Dubai and Hong Kong), NHK Japanese Broadcasting Corporation (Tokyo), Kajanni University of Applied Sciences (Finland), and the Milia Conference (Cannes).

**Teri Rueb** is an artist whose work combines sound and site using mobile media. She is best known for having established the form of GPS-based interactive installations, sometimes referred to as "locative media," as early as 1997. Rueb's work became a reference for generations of newer locative media artists interested in exploring the relationship between spaces, location-based technologies, and mobility. She has lectured and presented her work worldwide at venues including Ars Electronica, ISEA, SIGGRAPH, Transmediale, The New Museum of Contemporary Art, Kiasma Museum, and IRCAM. She has been nominated for numerous awards including the CalArts Alpert Award, Rockefeller New Media Fellowships, and the Boston ICA Foster Prize. Rueb completed her doctoral degree at the Harvard University Graduate School of Design in 2011, where her research addressed constructions of landscape and subjectivity in mobile network culture. She is currently Professor and Chair of the Department of Critical Media Practices at the University of Colorado, Boulder.

**Max Schleser** is Senior Lecturer in Film and Television at Swinburne University of Technology (Melbourne, Australia), Adobe Education Leader, Co-founder of the Mobile Innovation Network & Association (www.mina.pro), and Screening Director of the *International Mobile Innovation Screening & Festival*. Max's expertise is Immersive Media and Creative Arts 4.0 with a focus on Cinematic VR and interactive filmmaking. His research explores Screen Production, Emerging Media and smartphones for community engagement, creative transformation, and transmedia storytelling.

**Theresa M. Senft** is Senior Lecturer in Media, Music, Communications & Cultural Studies at Macquarie University. She founded the Selfies Research Network (selfieresearchers.com) and co-edited an issue of *International Journal of Communications* on global selfie culture (2015). Terri's next book, *Selfies: Drone Scholarship on Visibility as Power*, is scheduled for 2019 from Polity Press. Other books include *Camgirls: Celebrity and Community in the Age of Social Networks* (2008); *Routledge Handbook of Social Media* (2013); *History of the Internet: A chronology...* (1999); and an issue of *Women & Performance* on Sexuality & Cyberspace (1997). terrisenft.net.

**Mimi Sheller**, is Professor of Sociology and founding Director of the Center for Mobilities Research and Policy at Drexel University in Philadelphia. She is founding co-editor of the journal *Mobilities* and past President of the International Association for the History of Transport, Traffic, and Mobility. She helped to establish the interdisciplinary field of mobilities research. She is author or co-editor of ten books, including most recently *Mobility Justice: The Politics of Movement in an Age of Extremes* (Verso 2018), *Aluminum Dreams: The Making of Light Modernity* (MIT Press 2014), and forthcoming *Island Futures* (Duke University Press).

**Duncan Speakman** is a composer and sound artist based at the Pervasive Media Studio in Bristol. He creates narrative sound-led experiences that engage audiences in uncontrolled public and private space. He regularly creates bespoke work internationally including installations on trains in Guangzhou, loudspeaker symphonies in New Zealand, audio walks in Saitama, and sound installations in Porto; he has also recently developed a number of hybrid print/digital experiments. His current research is in the relationship between locative urban audio experiences and contemporary ecology, wrapping the questions in melancholy and romance. He set up and directed the arts collective Circumstance from 2010 to 2017 with Sarah Anderson and Emilie Grenier, later joined by Tom Abba. He continues now as a solo artist and researcher.

**Victoria Szabo** is an Associate Research Professor of Visual and Media Studies at Duke University. She studies and creates digital archives, apps, and extended reality experiences for cultural heritage and artistic applications. She is a member of the Wired! Lab for Digital Art History & Visual Culture, the Psychasthenia Studio art collective, and currently leads the ACM SIGGRAPH Digital Arts Community.

**Charlie Todd** is the director of Improv Everywhere in New York City, operating since 2001. The comedy performance collective has successfully energized thousands of performers with over 150 projects involving tens of thousands of undercover performers. Highlights include making time stop with the project Frozen Grand Central (2006), thousands of people listening to synchronized instructions over the years for The Mp3 Experiment (2004–), *The No Pants Subway Ride* (2002–), where participants become random passengers who board the New York Subway in winter without wearing any pants. Improv Everywhere also collaborate with industry, winning the Ex Award for their public artwork *The Giant Boombox* (2016), where unsuspecting New Yorkers who plugged it in were surprised by a massive holiday dance party with 100 acrobatic dancers, thousands of Christmas lights placed on historic ships and ten hidden snow machines.

**Nanna Verhoeff** is Associate Professor at the department of media and culture studies of Utrecht University. She specializes in screen and interface theory and has written on early cinema as well as mobile screens and media architecture. Her publications include "Urban Cartographies: Mapping Mobility and Presence" (2017); a special issue for *Television & New Media*, edited with Heidi Ray Cooley and Heather Zwicker; *Mobile Screens: The Visual Regime of Navigation* (Amsterdam University Press 2012); and *The West in Early Cinema: After the Beginning* (Amsterdam University Press 2006). With Sigrid Merx and Michiel de Lange she is co-editor of *Urban Interfaces: Media, Art, and Performance in Public Spaces*, a special issue for *Leonardo Electronic Almanac* (MIT Press 2019).

**Rowan Wilken**, is an Associate Professor in Media and Communication and Principal Research Fellow in the Digital Ethnography Research Centre (DERC), RMIT University, Melbourne, Australia. He has published widely on mobile and location-based media. His co-edited and authored books include *Cultural Economies of Locative Media* (forthcoming), *Location Technologies in International Context* (with Gerard Goggin and Heather Horst, 2019), *The Afterlives of Georges Perec* (with Justin Clemens, 2017); *Locative Media* (with Gerard Goggin, 2015), *Mobile Technology and Place* (with Gerard Goggin, 2012), and *Teletechnologies, Place, and Community* (2011). At present, he is preparing two co-authored books: *Digital Domesticity* (Oxford University Press) and *Wi-Fi* (Polity, under contract).

**Clancy Wilmott** is an Assistant Professor in Geography at UC Berkeley. Previously, she was a Lecturer in Human Geography at the University of Manchester. She has published widely on topics such as critical cartography, mobile media and spatial data, and is the author of *Mobile Mapping: Space, Cartography and the Digital* (2018) with Amsterdam University Press.

**Emile Zile** is an artist, filmmaker, and performer. In the darkly comic and critical re-use of online platforms, his work reflects a distributed humanity, a yearning for transcendence and the limits of language. Building on a background of live and single-channel video, his practice utilizes site-specific performance, photography, and filmmaking. Emile has an MFA degree from the Sandberg Institute and in 2012 completed a two-year studio residency at the Rijksakademie van beeldende kunsten, Amsterdam. In 2018, he commenced a practice-based PhD at Digital Ethnography Research Centre, RMIT Melbourne. His work is profiled in *Australiana to Zeitgeist: An A to Z of Australian Contemporary Art* (Thames and Hudson 2017). emilezile.com/.

# ACKNOWLEDGEMENTS

We would like to thank Routledge for the opportunity to publish a book on the many aspects of mobile media art as an exciting and developing field of research. We would also like to acknowledge Erica Wetter for her support in the early stages of the project, and Emma Sherriff and all production staff for their fantastic encouragement and help with the shaping of this Companion.

Larissa would like to thank her co-editors Adriana and Klare for their constant inspiration and collegiality, as well as RMIT's Design & Creative Practice ECP coordinators—Esther Pierini and Adelina Onicas—for their ongoing support. Adriana would like to thank Larissa and Klare for being the best co-editors they could be: always available, understanding, and providing great feedback. A special thanks to Klare, for your first-rate editorial work. In addition, Adriana is indebted to the Department of Communication at NC State University for providing Adriana the time and support to work on this project.

Klare would like to thank Larissa and Adriana for their gems of wisdom and unwavering guidance, Jacqueline Blanchard for her ongoing encouragement and friendship, and her free-running, mobile-friendly and tech-happy son Cooper, who is by far her favourite teacher. The editors would also like to acknowledge Jacina Leong and Mai Nou Xiong, for their very helpful editorial assistance towards final manuscript submission.

Finally, we give thanks and much gratitude to the incredible community of mobile media art—the artists, artist researchers, and scholars—who have meaningfully and generously contributed to this book.

# ABBREVIATIONS

| | |
|---|---|
| ABCD | Asset-Based Community Development |
| AI | Artificial Intelligence |
| ANAT | Australian Network for Art and Technology |
| AR | Augmented Reality |
| ARC | Australian Research Council |
| AIMIA | Australian Interactive Media Industry Association |
| AV | Audio Visual |
| CCTV | Closed-circuit Television |
| DARPA | Defence Advanced Research Projects Agency |
| DIY | Do it Yourself |
| DIT | Do-it-Together |
| dLux dLux | Media Arts |
| ERC | European Research Council |
| ETET | Every Thing Every Time |
| FM | Frequency Modulation |
| FSG | FutureEverything Singapore |
| GTT | Ghana Think Thank |
| GDPR | General Data Protection Regulation |
| GPS | Global Positioning System |
| GUI | Graphical User Interface |
| HCI | Human Computer Interaction |
| IoT | Internet of Things |
| ICT | Information Communication Technology |
| ISEA | International Symposium of Electronic Art |
| IRL | In Real Life |
| *keitai* | Mobile Phone |
| LAN | Local Area Network |
| LIDAR | Light Detection and Ranging |
| MCVR | Mobile Cinematic Virtual Reality |
| Mhz | Mega Hertz |
| MP3 | MPEG Audio Layer III |
| MR | Mixed Reality |
| MSRI | Media Society Research Institute |

| | |
|---|---|
| OP | Open Prototyping |
| PAR | Participatory Action Research |
| QS | Quantified Self |
| SI | Situationist International |
| SNS | Social Networking Sites |
| *shanzhai* | fake, copy |
| *sumaho* | smartphone |
| UCC | User Created Content |
| URL | Uniform Resource Locator |
| VOIP | Voice over Internet Protocol |
| VR | Virtual Reality |
| WAP | Wireless Application Protocol |
| Wi-Fi | Wireless Fidelity |
| WLAN | Wireless Local Area Network |
| XR | Extended Reality/*Crossing Reality* |

# MOBILE MEDIA ART

## An Introduction

*Klare Lanson, Adriana de Souza e Silva, and Larissa Hjorth*

Organizing *The Companion for Mobile Media Art* is a choreography of collaboration, process, and debate. It is a challenging endeavour, to say the least. Unpredictable connections occur when combining the fields of mobile media, creative practice, and contemporary art. With the continuing rise in artists turning towards social practice this century,[1] the role of mobile media as a vehicle for social and critical enquiry and intervention becomes heightened. Mobiles become a way not only to engage alternative publics but also as a way to intercept circuits of culture in which the digital is all-pervasive.[2] Through this turn, we can consider societal impacts on community, subjectivity, and environment. Art historian Claire Bishop considers the holistic role of the digital in relation to contemporary art practice:

> Performance art, social practice, assemblage-based sculpture, painting on canvas, the 'archival impulse,' analog film, and the fascination with modernist design and architecture … their operational logic and systems of spectatorship prove intimately connected to the technological revolution we are undergoing … the digital is, on a deep level, the shaping condition—even the structuring paradox—that determines artistic decisions to work with certain formats and media.[3]

Far from being a widely accepted and established term, mobile media art is an emerging field that over the years has received multiple overlapping and contradictory definitions. This process complicates mobile media art in ways that are invigorating, contested, and dynamic. The term mobile media art has gained popularity after the locative media boom in the early to mid-2000s. In 2004, Drew Hemment wrote the famous manifesto "Locative Dystopia" that popularized the term locative media, as the social and critical art movement that emerged with the use of positioning technologies—such as global positioning systems (GPS)—as interfaces for artmaking.[4] Followed by artists like Anne Galloway,[5] Marc Tuters, and Kazys Varnelis,[6] and a whole special issue of *Leonardo Electronic Almanac* in 2006,[7] locative media became a well-known and established term. Over the years, the term mobile media art slowly engulfed locative media as its subset and simultaneously developed to encompass art with diverse forms of mobile media—not only locative.

Mobile media art has relationships with, and genealogies within, other forms of media art—such as video art, electronic poetry and literature, internet art, sound art, film, performance art, game design, and locative media art. It emerges fundamentally from the use of different mobile media as interfaces for artmaking. However, as argued elsewhere,[8] defining mobile media art as art made with mobile technologies is to ignore its most important characteristics. In essence, mobile media art practices critique and support new social, political, cultural, and spatial relationships.

As Mimi Sheller points out,[9] mobile media art activates new practices that unfold in hybrid spaces,[10] that is, spaces that emerge when people, equipped with mobile technologies connected to the internet, are mobile and able to socialize with each other. In short, hybrid spaces blur the boundaries between the physical and the digital. But mobile media art—via its practices, artworks, and performances—also blurs boundaries and creates other types of hybrids and assemblages, such as bodies and information, playful/creative and ordinary spaces, creators and audiences, and public and private, to name a few. In this sense, following Sheller, we understand mobile media art as a way to explore how

> mobile medialities are creating new affordances for people to navigate public places and built or natural environments through hybrid socialites that are produced by a kind of 'moving with:' moving with connected technologies, moving with mobile social networks, moving with an awareness of locational relations.[11]

Just like mobile media, mobility is an essential part of mobile media art. Mobile media art as a creative practice can also be understood as mobility itself—having extensive mobility across many academic fields and disciplines of study.[12] However mobilities, as outlined by Sheller, Hannan, and Urry,[13] does not only mean constantly moving around—it includes immobilities, moorings, and the politics of mobility, that is, relationships of power and visibility over who moves and who is able to move.[14] As such, mobile media art is as much about movement and using mobile media, as it is about the lack of movement and access to mobile media. It is about understanding and forgoing our relationships with each other and with the spaces in which we live. It is also about questioning and understanding our relationships to the technologies we use and the power relationships that emerge from their production, use, and appropriation. Thinking through these relations is currently spotlighted by the global COVID-19 pandemic. As we navigate through mobile media practices to work remotely, home-school our children, and stay connected with family and friends during intense periods of physical lockdown, these questions around access and the digital divide become intensely more visible.

Mobile media seems to permeate all aspects of our lives today but interestingly, as media archaeologist Erkki Huhtamo notes,[15] the term mobile media has been absent from most media histories up to the twenty-first century. However, mobile media antecedents can be traced back to the nineteenth century and before. From portable cameras to pocket watches, media has been mobile much earlier than boom boxes, mobile phones, and GPS devices.

And so, what is different now? First, the way new mobile media is appropriated and repurposed for artmaking. Second, the way mobile media became the main interface to connect us to digital networks, and therefore embed digital information into physical spaces. And finally, the way that mobile media plays multiple roles in our lives, as devices used for communication, information access, interacting with urban spaces, and, of course, artmaking.

Mobile media art uses the vehicles of the "mobile" and "media" to frame art practice and intervention. As technologies emerge—from locative media to now automation—mobile media art is literally and metaphorically on hand to provide commentary, encounter the strange, and intervene in debates around intimacy, privacy, placemaking, and the ethics of communication, visibility, and careful practice. It provides both an intimate and public lens for contextualizing lived experience with speculative possibilities. It helps us navigate the uncertainties and ubiquity of networked media as indivisible from the social, material, and environmental. It highlights the role of art to provide a critical space for quotidian inquiry.

In recent decades, artists have continued to expand the boundaries of art as they experiment and engage with an increasingly networked, mobile, and copresent socio-material world. This pluralistic approach to artmaking entangles a range of environmental and political issues, many revealed within the pages of this book. It is the understanding of these issues through an intersectional and creative approach to sociality, mobility, and technology that enable us to understand how we can activate change and perhaps better prepare ourselves for the future—through process-based methods of seeing, listening, doing, and making. Importantly, artists are generating lively, playful, and imaginative ways of being in a digitally saturated world by performing and experimenting with the everyday; therefore, enhancing dialogue and creating new possibilities for making futures that move across—and through—creative disciplines, vibrant matter,[16] and the affective qualities of more-than-human relationships.

In the face of datafication, automation, and artificial intelligence (AI), mobile media art can provide us with a creative and critical space for reflecting on the role of quotidian agency. An example can be found in Trevor Paglen and Kate Crawford's *#ImageNetRoulette* (2019), which subverts a leading facial recognition database to remove more than half a million images. The project seeks to make people aware of the facial recognition biases and to change people's minds about AI.[17] The project resonates with a subgenre of artists working to creatively subvert social and mobile media technology to make more public awareness. Another example is Egor Tsvetkov's *Your Face is Big Data* (2016). In this project, Tsvetkov photographed strangers on St Petersburg's metro and then used facial recognition software (FindFace2) to identify them on social media.[18] Mobile media art, in this way, can be understood to highlight the social and cultural dimensions of new automation technologies in ways that put the everyday at the centre.

By collaborating with various forms of mobile technology, people, places, and things, mobile media art attempts to communicate the movement of particular forms of sociality in ways that are often multisensorial in nature, traveling through disparate fields of enquiry such as geography, environment, gender, computer science, sociology, and other areas of the digital humanities. Artists and writers continue to situate mobile media artmaking to be one composed of both material and virtual elements, seeking to create affective modes and alternative ways to consider how lifeworlds flow through a lively balance of social aesthetics and ideals.

Mobile media has also influenced art to shift away from the traditional gallery construct;[19] instead, it incorporates a more dynamic participation within an everyday sociality brought about by digital connectivity. Through playful mobile methods where "pre-existing cultural artifacts are remixed and reformatted, generating a *mise-en-abyme* of references to previous historical eras,"[20] it can also provide narratives of understanding the affective digital experiences of the past, present, and future. Our general understanding of how we participate temporally within, and over, mobile media platforms is being enhanced through the process of *making*, signalled through art as an active and mobile methodology. Due to obvious mobility in smartphone usage, no perceptual event or experience can be reduced to one category. Mobile media highlights this idea of diversity more than any other form of digital media because the smartphone is simultaneously co-existing and collaborative.

## Understanding the Companion

Mapping mobile media art reveals multiple contested histories, genealogies, and definitions. It is an interdisciplinary field shaped by different factors—cultures, societies, technologies, and practices to name a few. This Companion seeks to engage with some of the many complexities and intricacies as a starting point for further discussion. We have framed some key themes around mobile media art today in ten sections featuring writing from recognized scholars and practitioners in the field. Each section begins with an artist interview to situate and contextualize the key role practice plays in our understanding of mobile media art.

We begin with **Mobile Media Art Forerunners** in Section one. As stated above, mobile media art has many histories and this section includes relevant historical perspectives on the development of the field. It starts with Klare Lanson interviewing Golan Levin, who in 2001, developed and performed *Dialtones* at Ars Electronica. *Dialtones* is, up to this day, considered one of the first attempts to use mobile phones as interfaces for artmaking with a focus on sonic and visual patterning. Levin presents a critical view of his early work and looks forward, contemplating future directions for the field.

This interview is followed by media archaeologist Erkki Huhtamo, who argues that mobile media art can be traced through early mobile media interventions spanning a few centuries. He follows the archaeological trail of mobile media art back to portable, wearable, and vehicle-mounted media developed as early as the sixteenth century. Then, Giselle Beiguelman—considered one of the first mobile media artists in Brazil and in the world—takes us on an historical overview of Brazilian and South American early mobile media art in the specific context of emerging economies.[21] While Beiguelman's work is mostly visual, Cat Hope, in Chapter 4, maps the importance of sound in early mobile media art and how the escalating field of sound studies shifts our listening perceptions.[22] From the early recorded soundscapes of Canadian sound artist Barry Truax to the complex sound-based multimedia walks of British artist Janet Cardiff, Hope outlines early trends that established a path for the way sound is engaged in mobile media art today.

In Section two, **Practicing Mobile Media Art**, Rowan Wilken interviews Matt Adams from Blast Theory, exploring the affective tensions around being lonely in a crowd, feelings of togetherness and isolation, being drawn to interact with others while also desiring to break away, and how these tensions are enacted through mobile media art making with the aim of disrupting public space. For art collectives like Blast Theory, mobile media art is at the intersection of urgent interdisciplinary discussions we need to have about urban public life, surveillance, and agency. Disruption continues in Amparo Lasen and Massimiliano Casu's chapter that highlights the important role of shared listening practices in public art sound projects in Madrid, through a discussion of *La Romería de los Voltios* (The Pilgrimage of the Volts), an artist collective of collectives, band(width)ing together to celebrate the rise of the portable sound system. Subversion also features in Chapter 7, where Nancy Mauro-Flude turns up the tactics of an activist performance artist in *Bag Lady 2.0* (2007), who roams, collects knowledge and transmits data to an autonomous feminist server for realtime broadcasting. Caitlin McGrane continues the critique of technology in playing out biases and inequalities through an exploration of feminist locative art via the case study of Melbourne-based BE. collective's *Amplify Your Feminism* (2019) project.

In Section three, **Hybrid Realities,** authors consider the importance of hybrid spaces in constituting understandings and practices of mobile media art. Adriana de Souza e Silva interviews locative media artist Teri Rueb who has for decades made work around wayfaring, including locative media audiowalks that focus on bridging digital location information to physical environment—charting the vital act of listening to place and highlighting the importance of experiential soundings and the subjective "heard." In Chapter 10, de Souza e Silva and Ragan Glover-Rijkse analyse early telepresence and telecommunication-based art as predecessors of mobile media art practices that engaged the audience in the construction of hybrid spaces—before the emergence of locative media artworks.

In Chapter 11, Shannon McMullen and Fabian Winkler describe their evocative installation *Algorithmic Gardening* (2018) as a way to probe the hybrid infrastructural arrangements that emerge from nature/technology and humans/machines. As such, they speculate how hybrid ways of navigating spaces reveal insights into the future of algorithmic agriculture. Then, in Chapter 12, Joshua McWhirter presents alternative genealogies for augmented reality (AR) practices—from the *Situationist Internationale* (SI) to net art—as early experiments which sought to use geospatial technologies to interrogate the increasing mediation of urban space through networked technologies. McWhirter proposes an alternative view of "hybrid" cities composed of physical and digital elements. This section concludes with a chapter by Brian Massumi, who poetically recounts an experiment in urban *guerrilla* interventions that evolved around Rafael Lozano-Hemmer's large-scale projections on building façades, as part of his early millennial master workshop HUge and MObile (HUMO).

Section four takes us into the art of **Selfies**. As a key subfield of mobile media, selfies have highlighted the ambiguous role of social technology—both exploiting and empowering, both about individual self-expression and socio-cultural politics. This section begins with Lanson interviewing new media performance artist and writer Kate Durbin who takes a snapshot of *Hello Selfie* (2012–2015) and develops her intention to create a vehicle for critiquing the many gendered aspects of online behaviour and performance rhetorics in relation to social media. Chelsea Butkowski and Lee Humphreys continue the exploration around gender and representation by connecting self-portrait paintings and photographic self(ie) portraits as forms of qualified self. They emphasize the centuries-long process of self-editing and deliberate on the selfie development of "massified" app-based creative filtering in gendered ways, further problematizing visual representations of networked culture. The politics of representation, especially in light of facial recognition and its inherent bias, is powerfully situated in Theresa M. Senft's Chapter 16, which is a deep dive into Erving Goffman's "face-work," creative face mapping, meta-data up for grabs via Google Art, and the poignant case of how this type of face-work affects individuals who live with the condition of Autism. This section concludes with Grant Bollmer's fascinating investigation of selfies and drones, where the binaries of "figure-ground" and "transparency-obfuscation" are used to discuss how the visual culture of selfies emphasizes social forms of communication, and the material roles of digital culture.

In the next section we turn to **Play and Games**. Here, the role of mobile media art to push the social, cultural, and political dimensions of play is crucial. The chapters in this section reflect upon play as a multitude of possibilities from a mode of critical enquiry, a set of practices, performative cartography, and creative intervention. We begin with Lanson interviewing Kelli McClusky and Steve Bull from pvi collective, in which they discuss how playful agitation and participatory art can act as a tool for social change, which creatively challenges how power continues to impact society.

We then move to Sybille Lammes and Clancy Wilmott's considerations of the ongoing entanglement of art and mapping, with a particular focus on mobility. They argue that with the emergence of digital mapping technologies, such as GPS, satellite imaging, wearable interfaces, and Google Earth, there has been a cultural development of artistic mapping practices, embedded in situated locative art performances, and engaged by digital cartographic systems. In Chapter 20, Hugh Davies and Will Balmford tap into playful mobile media art in Australia, including artist workshops run by the Australian Network for Art and Technology (ANAT) and UK collective the-phone-book Limited. Set up in 2000, Ben Jones, Fee Plumley, and Ben Stebbing set about empowering artists, writers, and poets from around the world to come together and create work via their mobile phones.[23] Following this, Ingrid Richardson considers the notion of "ambient play" as a way to critically interpret the complex, creative, and diverse practices emerging from our use of mobile phones as portable game devices. The section ends with Matthew Riley, Troy Innocent, and Rowan Wilken, who invite us into the context of bushland (rather than the default urban setting) to extend the role of location-based augmented reality (AR) mobile gameplay.

Section six explores ideas around **Co-Design and Space** related to mobile media art. It begins with Lanson interviewing Duncan Speakman who articulately speaks to the poetics of combining narrative-driven sound works specifically composed for uncontrolled public and private spaces. Then, Jacina Leong, Larissa Hjorth and Jaz Hee-jeong Choi expand on debates around self-tracking practices by focussing on how creative interventions are addressing these concerns and changing the conversations. They focus on the work of pioneer locative media artist Hajime Ishikawa who began self-tracking nearly 20 years ago with the introduction of GPS devices.

In Chapter 25, Hemment, Joanna Bletcher, and Saskia Coulson discuss the role of mobile media art as a vehicle for Open Prototyping (OP) and innovation in smart cities. Then, Gretchen Coombs explores how Studio REV co-designs mobile media art projects with their communities, and how mobile apps are created and valued by the carers that use them. In doing so, she proposes an understanding of mobile media in terms of transport vehicles and explores how this changes the way we understand mobile media art. Further complicating the idea of more-than-human, this section concludes with Futomishi Kato's exploration of mobile media methods as a way for co-designing inventive social practice. For nearly two decades, Kato and his students have visited towns in rural Japan to co-design with older adults as a process of revitalization. Equipped only with the mobile phone for designing and editing purposes, the projects have evolved in sync with the technology.

In Section seven we turn to **Sensing New Visualities** to consider how mobile media art is changing how we feel about photography with the rise of quotidian visuality apps such as Instagram. Lanson interviews futurist Drew Hemment—one of the key figures to shape digital media and culture—who understands mobile media art as a critical response to phenomenon such as networked, locative media, and the rise of smart cities, and he heralds the crucial role of co-design and collaboration in relation to the innovation lab, FutureEverything. Daniel Palmer then walks us through the museum to reflect how networked media like Instagram are being deployed by artists for political intervention.

In Chapter 30, Edgar Gómez Cruz takes us to the street to consider the role of mobile media in street photography. For example, how does Instagram—and the "instagrammable" moment—change how we experience and see urban spaces? Helen Grace then transports us to the streets of Hong Kong and through the trope of the *shanzhai* (copy) she asks us to ruminate on the "affective assembly" of this "technovisuality." This section is concluded by an interview with video and performance artist Emile Zile, who waxes lyrical on the re-coding and re-performance of key works from art history through his dark and humorous breed of platform poetics.

Section eight, **Performing the Mobile,** takes us to the space of performance and the performative role of the mobile. Lanson interviews Charlie Todd, director of renowned New York-based urban comedy collective Improv Everywhere, who muses on the chaotic joy of unexpected public performance "missions" that amplify the importance of inclusivity. This is followed by discussions on film—Marsha Berry considers "Mobile Films as Mobile Art," asserting a more than representational experience, while Max Schleser brings us up to speed in relation to the Mobile Cinematic VR (MCVR). Then, in Chapter 36, Camille Baker discusses the paradoxical role of artists in designing around "wearing data" as both a source for inspiration and exploitation. Finally, Martin Rieser extends this line of proprioception by considering how the "networked experience" of mobile media art offers a space for "continual re-orientation."

In Section nine, we move towards the role of mobile media art in **Urban Interventions**. We begin with Leong interviewing artist Lauren McCarthy, who talks about her play with automated sensing technologies such as Amazon's virtual home assistant Alexa. This is followed by sound artist Brian House who critically reflects on his piece *Quotidian Record* (2013). In this work, House interprets a year's worth of his own geolocation data, gathered via the mobile phone, as a musical composition presented on a vinyl record.

In Chapter 40, artists Esther Polak and Ivar van Bekkum—who collaborate under the name PolakVanBekkum—develop a new lexicon to think through how film and mobile media art can transform the city into a performative object, a project they developed during 2016–2018 that focuses on the performativity of movement in relation to self. In Chapter 41, Luisa Paraguai and Gilbertto Prado consider the role of borders and mobility (and immobility) in understandings of place. They explore these ideas via their mobile media artwork *Encontros* (Meetings) (2015), inspired by the confluence of waters from the Negro and Solimões rivers that form the Amazon

River. To conclude this section, Victoria Szabo explores the affordances of AR technologies for urban experience design, drawing upon historic and current practices for urban exploration apps, as well as emerging possibilities for Digital Cultural Heritage.

We conclude the Companion with Section ten, **Critical Making and Future Directions**. In this section, authors explore how mobile media art can be both creative and critical, offering space for speculative and applied dimensions. We begin with Hjorth interviewing Kat Jungnickel who discusses how social research and creative practice synergies are being redefined as part of doing critical research, which has recently seen the role of creative practice (or "research creation") as central in doing impactful research within community and industry. Following this interview, Julia M. Hildebrand and Sheller contemplate the impact camera drones are having on the already contested field of mobile media art through the exploration of "Mobile LIDAR Mediality" as an "Artistic Anti-Environment." They use the film *Where the City Can't See* (2016) as a pertinent example of perhaps the first speculative fiction film shot entirely with Light Detection and Ranging (LIDAR) laser scanning technology, to bring their thinking around mediality home.

Nanna Verhoeff and Paulien Dresscher then explore how augmented reality (AR) projects publicly hack with the intent of "Artivism," and then encourage us to run full pelt into the space of extended reality (XR) or as they conceptualize, *crossing reality*, as a way to reimagine artistic media spaces. Then, Leah Heiss, Matiu Bush, and Marius Foley explore the role of mobile media art, through co-designed tactile tools, to offer ways to create and curate difficult conversations—especially around ideas of dying and grief. This section ends with the role of mobile media art to provide a space for critical intervention in and around datafication. As Hjorth and Sam Hinton investigate through the idea of "playful resistance" in "data futures," artists are using mobile media art to comment on quotidian technology phenomenon in ways that asks publics to reflect upon the ethical and social implications of being in the world.

This Companion does not seek to include every aspect constituting mobile media art. Rather, it seeks to provide a diversity of perspectives, disciplinary frames, practices, and theories from a variety of contributors spanning all continents across the world. We have sought to curate some of the key themes, approaches, practices, and philosophies informing this interdisciplinary area. And as mobile media goes forth in its ubiquity and pervasiveness, it provides new platforms and contexts for art to be expanded and extended across conceptual terrains, disciplines, modes of enquiry, and creative and critical practices.

## Notes

1 Claire Bishop, *Participation* (Cambridge, MA: MIT Press, 2006); Nicholas Bourriaud, *Relational Aesthetics* (Dijon: Les Presses du reel, 2009 [1998]).

2 Paul du Gay, Stuart Hall, Linda Janes, Hugh Mackay, and Keith Negus, *Doing Cultural Studies: The Story of the Sony Walkman* (London: SAGE Publications, 1997).

3 Claire Bishop, "Digital Divide," *Art Forum International* 51, no. 1 (September 2012): 435–41.

4 Drew Hemment, "The Locative Dystopia," 8 January 2004, https://nettime.org/Lists-Archives/nettime-l-0401/msg00021.html.

5 Anne Galloway and Matthew Ward, "Locative Media as Socialising and Spatialising Practices: Learning from Archaeology," *Leonardo Electronic Almanac* 14, no. 3/4 (2006), https://test.leoalmanac.org/wp-content/uploads/2012/07/Locative-Media-As-Socialising-And-Spatializing-Practice-Learning-From-Archaeology-Leonardo-Electronic-Almanac.pdf.

6 Marc Tuters and Kazys Varnelis, "Beyond Locative Media: Giving Shape to the Internet of Things," *Leonardo* 39, no. 4 (2006): 357–63, doi: 10.1162/leon.2006.39.4.357.

7 See *Leonardo Electronic Almanac* 14, no. 3/4 (2006), www.leoalmanac.org/leonardo-electronic-almanac-volume-14-no-3-4-june-july-2006/.

8 Larissa Hjorth, "Mobile Art: Rethinking Intersections between Art, User Created Content (UCC), and the Quotidian," *Mobile Media & Communication* 4, no. 2 (2015): 169–85, doi: 10.1177/2050157915619210; Adriana de Souza e Silva, Fernanda Duarte, and Cristiane S. Damasceno, "Creative Appropriations in

Hybrid Spaces: Mobile Interfaces in Art and Games in Brazil," *International Journal of Communication* 11 (2017): 1705–728.

9 Mimi Sheller, "Mobile Art," in *The Routledge Companion to Mobile Media*, edited by Gerard Goggin and Larissa Hjorth (New York: Routledge, 2014), 197–205.

10 Adriana de Souza e Silva, "From Cyber to Hybrid: Mobile Technologies as Interfaces of Hybrid Spaces," *Space and Culture* 3 (2006): 261–78, doi: 10.1177/1206331206289022.

11 Sheller, "Mobile Art," 202.

12 Klare Lanson, "Touch On/TouchOff: Mobile Media Art and Digital Wayfaring: Creative Practice Ethnography into Regional Mother's Commuting Practices," *Digital Culture & Society* 5, no. 1 (2019): 165–82, doi: 10.14361/dcs-2019-0110.

13 Kevin Hannam, Mimi Sheller, and John Urry, "Editorial: Mobilities, Immobilities and Moorings," *Mobilities* 1, no. 1 (2006): 1–22, doi: 10.1080/17450100500489189.

14 Tim Cresswell, "Towards a Politics of Mobility," *Environment and Planning D: Society and Space* 28, no. 1 (2010): 17–31, doi: 10.1068/d11407.

15 Erkki Huhtamo, "Pockets of Plenty: An Archaeology of Mobile Media," in *The Mobile Audience: Media Art and Mobile Technologies*, edited by Martin Rieser (Amsterdam, New York: Rodopi, 2011), 23–38.

16 Jane Bennett, *Vibrant Matter: A Political Ecology of Things* (Durham, NC: Duke University Press, 2010).

17 Naomi Rea, "How ImageNet Roulette, an Art Project That Went Viral by Exposing Facial Recognition's Biases, is Changing People's Minds About AI," 23 September 2019, https://news.artnet.com/art-world/imagenet-roulette-trevor-paglen-kate-crawford-1658305.

18 See Chapter 47 in this companion for a critique of Tsvetkov's project.

19 Mimi Sheller and Hana Iverson, "L.A. Re. Play: Mobile Network Culture in Placemaking," *Leonardo Electronic Almanac* 21, no. 1 (2015): 14–27, https://test.leoalmanac.org/wp-content/uploads/2015/12/LEAvol21no1_LA_Replay_Introductions.pdf.

20 Claire Bishop, "Against Digital History," *International Journal for Digital Art History*, no. 3 (2018): 122–31, 128, doi: 10.11588/dah.2018.3.49915.

21 Giselle Beiguelman's *#QR_Comms*, 2015, is featured on the front cover of this companion. Photography: Maya Messina.

22 See Marcel Cobussen, Vincent Meelberg, and Barry Truax, *The Routledge Companion to Sounding Art* (New York: Routledge, 2016).

23 Mark Frauenfelder, "Power to the Mobile People," 22 August 2003, http://thefeaturearchives.com/topic/Content/Power_to_the_Mobile_People.html.

# SECTION ONE

# Forerunning Mobile Media Art

# 1
# MAKING MOBILE CONNECTIONS

## *Golan Levin* in Conversation with *Klare Lanson*

Golan Levin is undoubtedly one of the front runners in mobile media art—he is as an artist, composer, performer, and engineer with an interest in new modes of reactive expression. Levin focusses on the design of systems for the creation, manipulation, and performance of audiovisual works, as part of his interest in formal languages of interactivity and nonverbal communication in cybernetic systems. With a variety of collaborators, Levin creatively adapts digital technology, to investigate human relationships with machines, making visible the ways we connect with each other.[1] He teaches at Carnegie Mellon University and also directs The Frank-Ratchye STUDIO for Creative Inquiry, a creative lab for "atypical, anti-disciplinary, and inter-institutional research at the intersections of arts, science, technology and culture."[2] In this interview, Levin begins by discussing *Dialtones (A Telesymphony)* (2001),[3] a large-scale live audiovisual performance, which used choreographed dialling and ringing of the audience's mobile phones, and then moves into his interests around artificial intelligence (AI), augmented reality (AR), and the importance of collaboration.

Firstly, I'm interested in your opinion on creating new fields of study, in this case mobile media art. Do you think that these categorizations are important?

The trend in emerging Media Arts is to have entire sub-fields that are based on the medium and not necessarily the concepts within it. I say this as a media artist and am painfully aware of it. So, you have bio art, or you have robotic art, or you have mobile media art. It's not too different in some ways, from when people talk about crafts, like glass art, or ceramic art. It's much more about the medium than it is about the ideas within it, as McLuhan would say.[4] Having said that, I think mobile media art is a little different. There are concepts that arise in mobile media to do with communication and networks, and I think the existence of these ideas characterize the medium in interesting ways.

What do you think about the artist "responsibility" to engage with new technologies, to interrupt/disrupt capitalist processes, and to consider the ethics around these processes when investigating and experimenting, even in the defining of mobile media art practice?

A simple answer is that one of the roles of contemporary artists is to engage with new technologies, in order to explore, understand and help others understand the impact of these technologies, and how they're transforming society. We are obviously in a period of tremendous social change owing partially to the technology, with both the social and technology in a feedback loop, and artists can help predict how the world is going to be and how it may take shape. Lauren McCarthy's work with the smart home is a good example of this—I think her work's amazing.[5] It has a great deal of acuity and is spot on in ways that are really important. There are tons of other examples of artists being the sort of distant early warning system, or the bellwether or the canary in the coal mine, or the person who's wanting to cry wolf—to explain the problem perceived that may not be obvious to others.

As humans, we are both incredibly sensitive and socially perceptive beings. Also, we're able to make powerful work and communicate messages that contain these things. So, I think that the job of the new media or emerging artist is to help explore the meaning of and meanings made with new technologies. And that can take wider forms, a kind of critical approach and surfaces too. We can question the downside to all these technologies that are being put into use or take a purely aesthetic approach. What new sorts of aesthetics are possible? I'm fascinated with new technologies, in the ways that technology and art have always worked together—whether it was through optics in the seventeenth, eighteenth and nineteenth centuries, or whether it was the invention of the paint tube and other kinds of readymades—all helping artists transform their practices.

Technology has always had a big role in shaping how art is done, and now it's really become a key subject of art itself. When I made *Dialtones* in 2001, a critic at the time called it a "loss leader for the tech industry." I think as time goes on—not that that's the only way of perceiving the piece or that it's the only correct way of understanding it—I do see more and more the ways in which that statement is true of the project that I developed back then. I don't think that project was especially critical. I think when we made it, I was in this camp of exploring the aesthetics and making a kind of spectacle. Trying to make a new kind of sound that no one had ever heard, making a new kind of situation that no one had ever been in. People who were actually there and part of it said it felt magical, although within the 40 minutes of the recording, there's probably only three minutes that I think genuinely sound pretty amazing. For it to happen at all, at the time, cost a quarter of a million dollars—I had to get the technological support and assistance from so many large tech companies (Figure 1, color insert).

Ars Electronica helped with that, didn't they?

Yes, they were the venue that commissioned it. Technologically, Ars Electronica bridged us to the mobile phone provider in Austria, who provided critical technical support. They introduced us to A1 Telecom Austria, who installed special antennas in the venue to allow for more signalling channels, without which the project wouldn't have worked. They also gave us a direct T1 line, actually it was two E1 lines, special kinds of ISDN (Integrated Services Digital Network) lines to connect into their systems, so that we could launch the calls.[6] So essentially, they gave us digital access to a tool for calling people.

Nowadays, you could do a concert in any modern city for basically a few dollars of credits and probably a ten-line script to launch all the phone calls, but at the time in 2001, there was no other way to have these unique forms of access—there weren't readymade ways of launching automated phone calls. So, to do this, we had to get into bed with the big mobile companies. And furthermore, to do the testing—remember we were going to perform this with the audience's mobile phones—we actually had to compose and test it first. So, to do that we had to borrow or get donated, dozens, scores of phones, so that we could test the project.

You had over 70 phones for testing, didn't you?

Yes! So, again, we had to persuade mobile companies—whether it was service providers, phone or handset manufacturers—to provide us with support (see Figure 1.1). For them, it was an opportunity to get their logo on something and support local culture and community in general. I think the critic's comment I mentioned earlier about being a loss leader for technology has more truth to it than I acknowledged at the time. All media art has to deal with the extent to which any given media or work is, in some sense, a loss leader for whatever tech industry it is incidentally promoting for technology at the moment.

Also, in some ways, creative engagement with these mobile companies could be seen as a form of intervention?

I think that if you're using new technologies, as a new media artist, then you are part of the problem, perhaps a particular problem. Even if you're critical of the technology, you're still glorifying it. There might be a way in which this is tolerated in capitalism by playing a kind of court jester role. You know, it's ok to be critical, as long as you're generating a buzzy press event.

I'm almost 20 years older now than I was when I did the *Dialtones* project. I now see the ways in which we need to be more critical of technologies. This is truly obvious to us now—certainly not the case in 2001—with the influence of social media and the rise of technofascism in the West. Remember in 2001, we were still just coming off this kind of 1990s good feeling about the internet.

Yes, and for me, what's interesting about your work at this time has more to do with the sociality and pattern making that occurred in *Dialtones*—not so much the composition of the sounds per se but rather the emphasis on hearing and listening as part of mobile technology engagement. Perhaps one of the most important aspects of *Dialtones* is the idea of performing

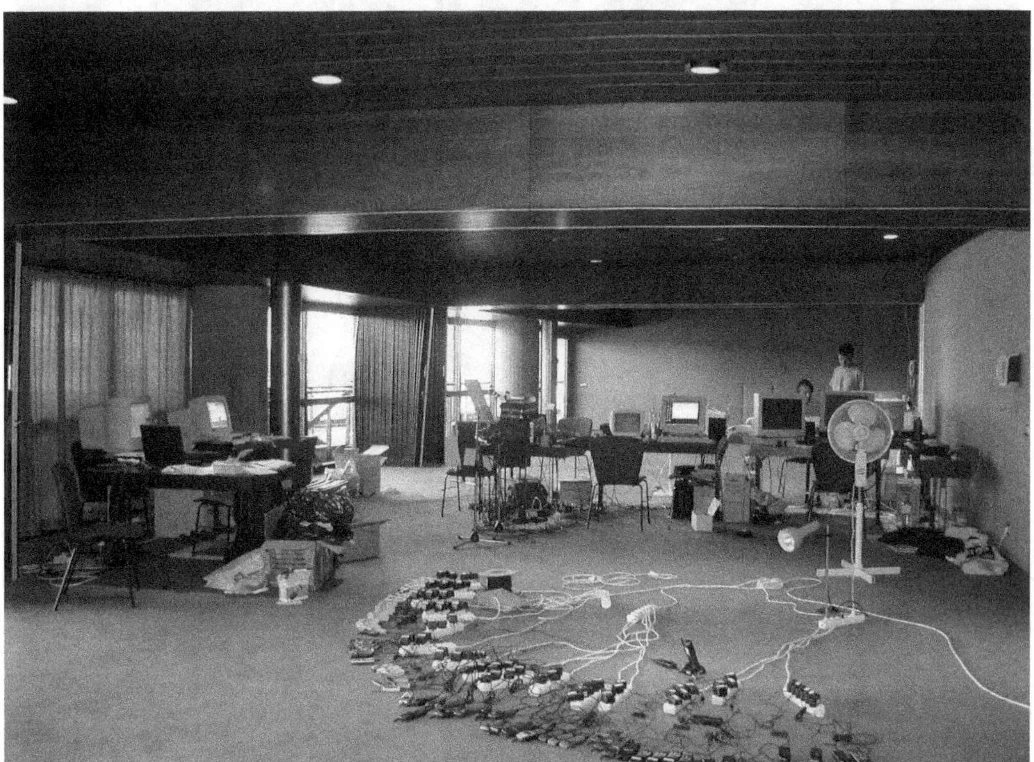

*Figure 1.1* Testing the means by which the audience's mobile phones were computationally dialled (and thereby performed) for *Dialtones* (2001). Photo credit: Golan Levin

the network. And performing the network is vital, obviously, in relation to social media and platformativity. I'd love to hear your thoughts on that.

At the time, that wasn't the vocabulary I was using but, yes, in hindsight I suppose it was kind of performing the network. I hadn't really thought of it that way, at least when I had the idea. First of all, I'm a recovering formalist, you know, the work I had done prior to this was an audiovisual environment suite at Ars Electronica 2000, which was a set of synesthetic, audiovisual performances involving the realtime control of sound and graphics.

There was a project called *Scribble*,[7] a performance that I'd done the year before at Ars Electronica that formed the basis for convincing them to allow me to do the *Dialtones* project. And when *Dialtones* was conceived, I was partly thinking about the nature of the audience as a kind of "audiovisual pixel," because there was a very significant visual element as well.

The idea with *Dialtones* was that each person in the audience would make sound with their phone, but they would also light up. They actually lit up in two different ways. The first way was through projection, a spotlight, just on the individual audience member (Figure 1.2). So that when your phone was ringing, you were synchronized with this gigantic overhead projection that was aligned with your seat. When your phone rang, you had your very own personal spotlight. This was quite extraordinary when there were very few phones ringing because the audience could look up into this giant mirror and we could look out across the stage. And you could see whose phones were activated.

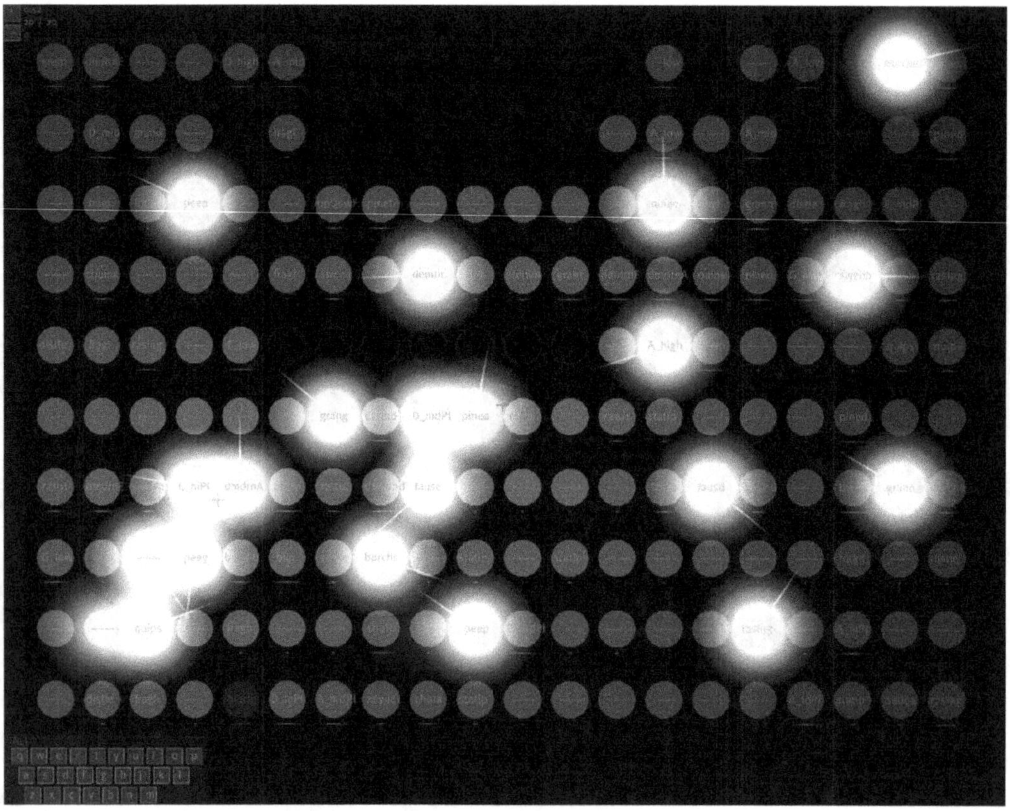

*Figure 1.2* Performance computer with grid-based visual interface permits conductor to dial audience phones in deliberate patterns, *Dialtones* (2001). Photo credit: Golan Levin

Poetic too—the idea of isolating an individual within the network is beautiful. The audience arrival was also interesting: the process to register their mobile number, the exchange of ringtones and seat allocation, an engagement in actions before the performance experience.

Yes. Another idea was in the little devices that we handed out that had an attached LED that would light up. They were very popular in Japan at the time, like a little keychain fob. Japanese business people would use them to mute the ringer on their phone. They would have the keychain nearby, and when the radio waves on the phone would broadcast, the LED would blink. When people came into the theatre, we gave them one of these and so there were lots of tiny blinking lights everywhere—that would be activated with your phone, and the people next to you (Figure 1.3). This was one part of the audiovisual aspect of the piece.

There was also another aspect; the distributed sound field of Iannis Xennakis,[8] where he stated that the problem with electronic music is that it always comes out of the same two speakers. This notion in relation to *Dialtones* was enacted by making diffuse sound where sound was coming from all around us—there were hundreds of speakers. I loved the idea of performances being made up of hundreds of distributed objects. I was looking at, for example, Laurie Anderson's *Car Horn Symphony* in the early 1970s. There was also a performance in 1965 for the Swiss National Expo that involved hundreds of typewriters.

Even John Cage, with his compositions to make heard environmental sound.

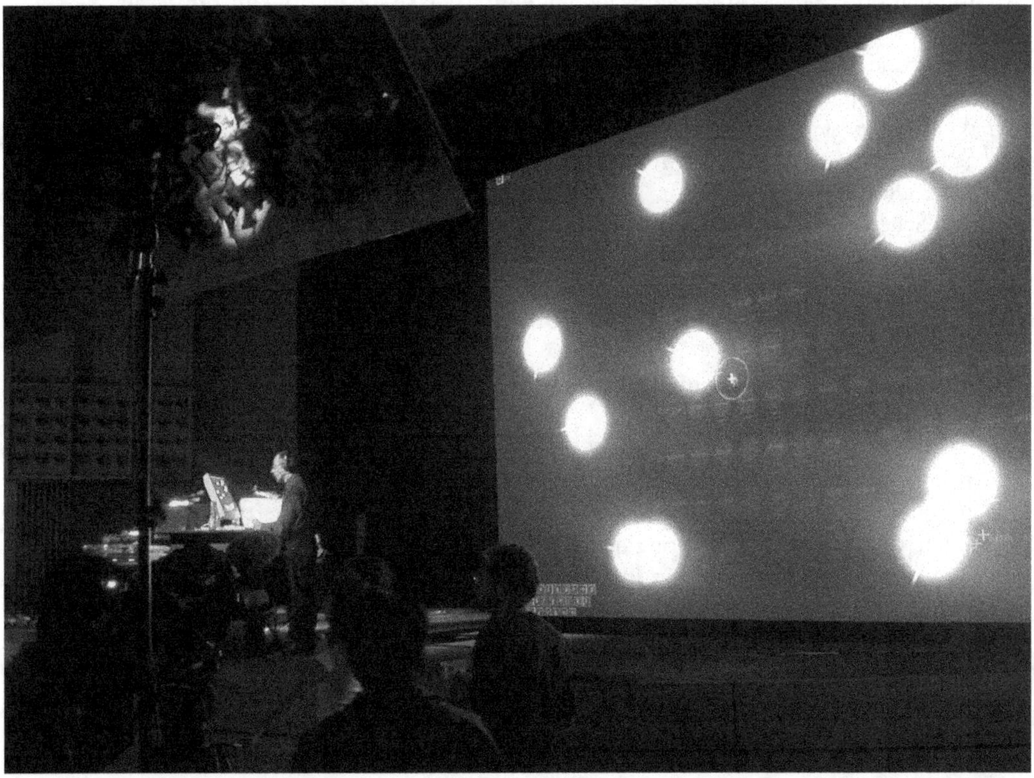

*Figure 1.3* One of the optical subsystems of *Dialtones* (2001): a vertically suspended video graphics projection system, which beamed individualized spots of light onto audience members to coincide with the ringing of their phones. Photo credit: Golan Levin

Right, and the idea of getting a huge orchestra of people, all of whom have an unconventional object, well not conventionally thought of as musical. And then to think okay, now that we have an orchestra of these then... GO. For me, it was special that it was the audience bringing that to the project, it was an interesting condition of people arriving with the instruments from off the street.

Which brings us to the everyday, where mobile media is very much about the social. I think in a past interview you've said that what you found exciting as an outcome of *Dialtones* was the idea of being personally connected to the mobile?

It was the idea around making and receiving calls which was important, especially back in the early 2000s, when people still actually made phone calls. Nowadays, we all have mobile phones and we're even more physically attached to them, yet we make fewer phone calls per se. We don't call as much. Back then, especially when your phone rang, it wasn't just like, "Oh, this device that I have, is making, you know, a sound." It was actually this little thread in the back of your head saying, "Oh, someone's trying to reach me." Putting that idea into the minds of hundreds of people hundreds of times within one hour was quite funny to me.

There were other people making art with mobile phones at this time too, both related and different. I remember we had just performed *Dialtones* on the 2 September 2001, nine days before 9/11. I had literally just returned to my home in New York City when it happened. It was quite a shock. As we were preparing the piece—I remember we had a week to go—I suddenly heard of two different other projects that were close enough to make me weirdly uncomfortable.

One was by Tobias Trier called *MobilSymfoni* (2001)[9] in Aarhus, Denmark. He had 20 mobile phones suspended from a ceiling and ringing, dialled by a live performer. The other was more of a promo piece where there were seven phones making an event, interoperating together musically to make one experience. This was in Germany, Berlin. They were both really close by—I was in Austria. So, I almost felt like if I didn't do it, then someone was going to beat me to it (laughs). There was a lot of pressure to do it, it was all happening in late 2001. There was Peter Hrubesch and Dirk Scherkowski who made a work called *Handywolke* (2001),[10] a cloud of 1200 phones that reacted sonically to movement and dialling from the museum crowd below, and *Sky Ear* (2004)[11] in London, by Usman Haque, which visualized electromagnetic transmissions in the atmosphere using helium balloons and mobile phones.

One might say that what's important now in terms of mobile media art is the multi-sensorial approach to making. Thoughts?

This is not a particularly surprising piece of information, but what has surprised me is the extent to which the mobile has surpassed the desktop, as the primary aperture through which we experience the internet. I had thought that desktops and laptops would be around longer. The extent to which mobiles are becoming our lens for understanding the physical world, in ways that laptops and desktops are not—because of augmented reality (AR)—is going to be very significant. Assuming we're all around to enjoy it, I think it's going to allow us to see layers on the world that have not been part of computing yet. That's where I think mobile art is heading now. A lot of my students are enjoying making AR, and for them, it's not the AR goggles, it's the mobile phone.

Mobile media is increasingly employing AR and also artificial intelligence (AI). As an algorithmic engineer, do you have any thoughts on the future in terms of mobile media and AI, in how these algorithmic transformations impact us?

There's absolutely an extent to which there's been a very significant transformation. We've certainly rounded a corner in terms of using machine learning, both generally and in the arts. It's impacted our ability to understand some things about the world that we couldn't understand before. That's really changing how machines know about the world around us and can give us information that's contextual.

> Ethics are important too right now, in the way we behave with machine learning and the way that the machine learns from us. The way we interact with technology (for example, the way that people are treating their smart technology at home, swearing etc) and how this affects the environment. I think ethics is a bit of a key at the moment?

I'm painfully aware of this. Unfortunately, we're not all painfully aware of it. There are people who I think have written about this in really intelligent ways that are much smarter than me. For example, there is Dan McQuillan's take on AI's ability to hide situational politics,[12] and Nabil Hussein, who writes about the positives of AI not being able to recognize black people.[13] There's also Kate Crawford—she's really on top of it—as the Co-founder and Director of Research at the AI Now Institute at NYU.[14]

I'm not an AI expert. Although, like a lot of new media artists, I'm using it in my practice. I'm trying to stay current, partially because I have to teach my students, partially because AI can do some really interesting things—I've gotten some ideas from it. Partially, I'm also following it with a lay person's interest because I think it's altering the world around us. I wouldn't say that AI is central to my practice, at least as a subject, as much as it's a tool for me.

> Could you speak to how you're thinking about making at the moment? What sort of future projects are you thinking about?

I'm directing a lot, now that I'm mostly guiding students and the people at Carnegie Mellon (University) to make their projects. I have a few research projects ongoing that continue to deal with my interest in hands and interactive projects that are concerned with tracking the hand and defamiliarizing our own hands. Dealing with the uncanny, I'm working on some games because I think games are really interesting cultural expressions.

> A large component of your practice is in connection to the body. The Opto-isolator work that you've done focuses on light and the eye. You seem to be slowly moving through different body parts. Is it about haptics or gestural aspects?

Gestural I suppose, I have a project called the *Augmented Hands Series*,[15] which I completed in 2014 (see Figure 1.4). But I had been working on it for 11 years, starting the project in 2003. It took a long time because of a very hard technical problem that I didn't know how to solve. The very first attempt to realize that project actually manifested in a project called *The Manual Input Workstation* (2004), or *Manual Input Sessions* (2004) with Zach Lieberman.[16] It was all about hands. But that was just a partial attempt towards realizing what was the project that I finished in 2014, and I'm now continuing our project into the mobile space. We're trying to work on the mobile phone because I want to be able to share it in ways that a kiosk in a festival can't.

> Collaboration is important in your work. It can be about like-mindedness, support, and the skills and knowledge that individuals bring to any project. Do you think it's important to make visible skills that may not be driven by technology but are instead driven by technological thinking?

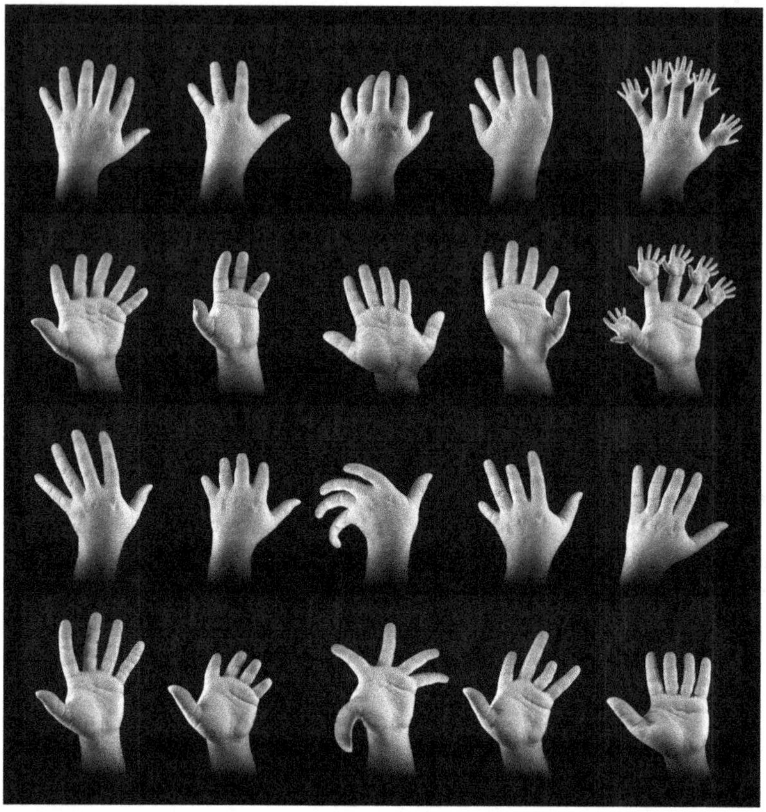

*Figure 1.4* The *Augmented Hands Series* (2003–2014) by Golan Levin, Kyle McDonald, and Christine Sugrue. Photo credit: Golan Levin

I'm more interested in my teaching, for example, teaching people to be able to do it all. I think that's more unusual and scarcer than the kind of corporate model where you work in teams. You know, this person is a designer, and that person is an engineer, the producer, etc., defined roles like that. The idea of a collective is important at the moment. It could just be two people working on something together because it's fun. It's easier to do if you live in a city with a lot of density, where you can more easily see your collaborators. When you're at certain life stages where you can hang out as late as you like working with your collaborators away from home. I think that collaboration is great. I collaborate all the time—it takes many different forms as well. I hire my students, I give them credit, or I bring in a friend and put them up for a week, and we have an intensive work focus on a hard problem. This is very important. I'm not saying everyone has to do everything themselves. Certainly, my bigger projects like *Dialtones* were accomplished with teams.

There are different ways to collaborate too, not everything is about sitting in a room together. I'm very richly connected through Twitter, for example—there's very high bandwidth sharing of links and resources and new ways of working. To the extent that we're all sort of working in related ways, or on similar problems, and sharing information and tools. Open source is a big way of sharing things, where you're not necessarily working on an artwork together, but you're working on tools that can leverage our artworks.

Could you speak more to the idea of open source software? The collaborative process certainly provides tools to enable other people to work together.

If there's one big thing to come out in the new media arts in the last 15 years, it's been the development of robust open-source cultures. We're making tools for ourselves because no one else is going to do that. We don't have the money to buy the commercial tools, and the commercial tools often don't address our needs anyway. You make it your own when you make your own tool, something that isn't circumscribed by the possibilities and limitations of commercial software.

Open source has been massive in terms of transforming education in media, so that we can have more media artists, and also so that we can make our work more easily. We can share techniques with the community: this is big. Many people who don't necessarily collaborate on artworks nevertheless contribute to the open-source toolkits that exist. In my laboratory, I try to help support those toolkits by providing money and support in different ways to help improve those kits.

Finally, do you have any thoughts on how mobile media art is recalibrating audience engagement with art?

New York's Museum of Modern Art (MoMA) has done a few AR exhibition projects over the years, extending the gallery and artworks via the mobile phone.[17] There's also MoMAR, a non-profit artist group's app called *Hello, we're from the internet* which is basically augmented reality in MoMA. There's a Jackson Pollack with a bench in front of it, and if you sit down and point your mobile phone at the Pollack, it uses it as an anchor for mounting an exhibition of virtual artworks contributed by artists not represented in MoMA.[18] It's a nice way of going to a gallery and seeing works that you wouldn't normally see. Augmented reality allows us to put a layer of information on the world, in as much as that it aligns with artists' desire to comment or critique—to point out observations or to change how we see the world. Augmented reality is going to be a significant part of mobile media art because of the way it works that way. It's literally a layer of commentary that alters, transforms and re-contextualizes the world. That's an artistic practice right there.

## Notes

1 See Golan's website, http://flong.com/
2 See http://studioforcreativeinquiry.org/
3 See http://flong.com/projects/telesymphony/
4 Marshall McLuhan, *Understanding Media: The Extensions of Man* (New York: McGraw-Hill, 1964).
5 Lauren McCarthy's interview introduces Section 9 of this book.
6 T1 is the North American term that refers to the digital carrier that transmits a digital signal. E1 is the European term, which was used for *Dialtones*. Each E1 line has 32 channels at the speed of 64 Kbps, with two channels reserved for (1) signalling and (2) controlling. The rest are used to carry simultaneous voice calls; therefore, allowing for 30 voice calls or data to be transferred simultaneously.
7 See http://flong.com/projects/scribble/
8 See www.theguardian.com/music/tomserviceblog/2013/apr/23/contemporary-music-guide-xenakis.
9 See Golan Levin's, "Informal Catalogue of Mobile Phone Performances, Installations and Artworks," http://flong.com/texts/lists/mobile_phone/
10 Ibid.
11 See www.haque.co.uk/skyear.php and archive site http://www.haque.co.uk/skyear/ for full project description.
12 Dan McQuillan, "Towards an anti-fascist AI," *Open Democracy*, 25 May 2019, www.opendemocracy.net/en/digitaliberties/towards-anti-fascist-ai/.
13 Nabil Hassein, "Against Black Inclusion in Facial Recognition," *Digital Talking Drum*, 15 August 2017, https://digitaltalkingdrum.com/2017/08/15/against-black-inclusion-in-facial-recognition/.

14 Kate Crawford and Vladan Joler, "Anatomy of an AI System: The Amazon Echo as an Anatomical Map of Human Labor, Data and Planetary Resources," 2018, https://anatomyof.ai/
15 See http://flong.com/projects/augmented-hand-series/
16 See www.flong.com/projects/miw/
17 See for example, Sander Veenhof and Mark Skwarek, MoMa NYC augmented reality exhibition, 9 October 2010, http://sndrv.nl/moma/
18 Catherine Ollinger, "Augmented Reality 'Gallery' at MOMA Allows Viewers to Virtually Alter Art," 3 August 2018, www.psfk.com/2018/03/momar-augmented-reality-gallery-moma.html.

# 2

# MAGIC SPECTACLES AND PORTABLE BOXES

## Notes toward a Media Archaeology of Mobile Media

*Erkki Huhtamo*

Mobile media is often considered a recent phenomenon, conditioned by industrial strategies, technological breakthroughs, social needs and trends. Although yesterday's new devices rapidly become obsolete and fall out of fashion, more than a 25-year perspective to account for their history may seem far too long, not to mention anything about a century or even a millennium. It is obvious that if assessed solely from the perspective of engineering and industrial developments, the habit of using mobile technological devices for remote communication cannot be extended very far into the past.

Yet, media archaeology claims that there are other layers, other histories, other forms in which mobile media has existed much longer.[1] These layers must be dug out and released from oblivion where they have fallen. Such an archaeology has to take into consideration both media machines that were realized, marketed and used, and those that remained drafts, intentions or even daydreams. All are essential to form a general picture. As this tentative media archaeology of mobile media will demonstrate, portable and wearable devices for instant communication were anticipated in the cultural imagination long before they became technically feasible. Many more examples, beside the ones discussed in this text, could likely be discovered.

For the sake of clarity, I will divide mobile media into three categories: *portable*, *wearable*, and *vehicle-mounted*. Portable refers to a device that is carried around, for example, in a bag, whereas a wearable device is body-mounted: strapped to the body, pressed against the skin. The dividing lines are anything but absolute: this is a model only. In actual practice, constant overlapping and switching of roles happens: a mobile phone can be said to be a wearable when it is carried in a container on the belt, but it turns into a portable when it is kept in a bag or held in hand while walking.

Vehicle-mounted devices, which are not discussed in this text, can be permanent features of the vehicle, but also portable/wearable devices given a temporary role as its fixtures. This happens when a mobile phone is placed in a holder by the car's dashboard to be used as a navigational and communication device by the driver. This model is not historical. It is only a tool to help us make sense of the topic. The designs and uses of mobile media devices also raise other issues such as the relationship between being in motion and in stasis. They are often, but not always, used during a momentary stop.

In this chapter, I will explore mobile media from a media archaeological perspective, suggesting that it makes sense to penetrate beyond contemporary forms to gain insights about the slow unfolding of media culture. The basic premise is that media cultural processes are layered constructs. Not all the layers have developed simultaneously or along parallel lines. Neither have they been equally visible for earlier observers. Much remains hidden, waiting to be brought back to light and connected with forms that are remembered and already acknowledged by media historical scholarship. Uncovered in the hidden layers, forgotten devices and unaccounted for discourses should be brought into dialogue with later forms, inciting all to explain each other. The media archaeologist functions as a catalyst helping to make it happen.

## From Magnetic Needles to Pocket Communicators

The discursive history of mobile media goes back at least to the early modern era; depending on approach, it could probably be extended further. Communication by means of vibrating magnetized needles was suggested by the Italian Jesuit Famiano Strada (1572–1649) in his book *Prolusiones Academicae* in 1617.[2] It was not a book of science; rather, it presented a series of rhetorical exercises featuring human characters familiar from classical antiquity. Strada's description became well-known in the English-speaking world because Joseph Addison adapted it for *The Guardian* in 1713.[3]

In Strada's text, an impersonation of the Roman poet Lucretius, known for the epic cosmogonical poem *De rerum natura*, explains how "a certain loadstone" that touched "two several needles" could make them move "in the same manner." Two friends, each in the possession of such a needle, "made a kind of dial-plate, inscribing it with the four and twenty letters, in the same manner as the hours of the day are marked upon the ordinary dial-plate." The needles were fixed to the dials so that they could freely point at any of the letters. A wireless personal communication device, albeit an imaginary one, had been created. It could be put to test when the friends moved to distant countries.[4]

Although it may seem very early, Strada's idea was hardly original—similar fantasies about the occult powers of magnetism were already circulating. In his *Magnes sive De Arte Magnetica* (1641), another Jesuit, Athanasius Kircher, poked fun at them, telling a story about two dear friends who—as Joscelyn Godwin explains it—"tried to communicate with each other by pricking themselves in numbers corresponding to the letters of the alphabet. When the other friend felt the sympathetic pricking in his own flesh, he could decode the message by counting the pricks."[5] Such ideas were presented as curiosities without associating them with "serious" social, economic, or political applications.

Communication at a distance was normally associated with personal needs such as uniting separated friends or lovers—emotion and longing played roles. This may, however remotely, be associated with cultural developments and the mentalities of the era. Although traditional modes of mobility had not yet radically changed, the voyages of discovery and colonialism had begun to crack the patterns of age-old lifestyles based on proximity and immobility. Some people travelled far away, never to return. Perhaps we could say that the movement from the village to the "global village," to refer to Marshall McLuhan's familiar ideas from the 1960s, had started.

The first permanent systems of telecommunications for expressly official purposes were over a century away. The optical telegraph, which was introduced in the late eighteenth century, and the electrical telegraph, which came some decades later, made the technical presence and institutional use of remote communication palpable. The infrastructures were permanent and fixed rather than mobile. Still, continuities with ideas about magic or telepathic communication by means of portable devices (manifested also by devices like religious travel altars and wearable talismans) persisted.

Strada's description recalls in an almost uncanny manner the nineteenth-century spiritistic seances where messages from afterlife are said to have been received by the Ouija transmission board, a common "magical device" used in esoteric practices.[6] There does not seem to have been a concerted desire for portable media until the late nineteenth century. This had to do with the persistence of stationary lifestyles prevalent in local communities where most of the humankind still lived. As tokens of emerging modernity, colonialism, immigration, international trade, urbanization, industrialization, organized tourism, and related social and economic forces began questioning such age-old patterns on a scale not seen before. New means of transportation like the train and the steamboat made it easier to move from place to place, challenging prevailing coordinates of time and space.[7]

The changing modes of mobility, the speeding up of lifestyles, and the fears caused by the increasing social polarization within developed industrial societies brought about an increasing need to stay in contact.[8] It manifested itself in different forms such as the popularity of letter writing, the habit of using the telegraph not just for official but increasingly also for private communication, telephony, and—last but not least—the new craze of sending picture postcards, which began in the 1890s and burst into full bloom around 1900.[9]

The idea of scribbling one's private thoughts on a piece of card, which allowed potentially anyone to read then would have been considered impossible only a few decades earlier. The picture postcard habit, which even became a mania, broke the taboo. The picture postcard joined the plethora of mass-(re)produced visual formats that had begun proliferating in the nineteenth century. It gave rise to a massive expansion of visuality. Pictures were reduced to lilliputian scale and associated with the actions of the human hand (where the mobile phone would be put a century later). Although the picture postcard has been neglected by academic scholars, it is a complex cultural object—a portable entity, a challenge for graphic design, a collectable, a vehicle for virtual travel, a means of connecting people, a passing of visual information, and entertainment.[10]

Anticipations of portable technical media appeared in this environment. Albert Robida's *Le Vingtième Siècle* (*The Twentieth Century*, 1883), an imaginative forecast of the media culture of the future, was mainly occupied with stationary devices. An audiovisual media machine named *Téléphonoscope*—an extension and improvement of the telephone—was omnipresent and had many uses.[11] It transmitted real time or recorded theatre performances to homes, allowed private two-way conversations "suppressing the absence," and even served the need of surveillance.[12]

Robida's vision also included a portable version, the "pocket telephonoscope." However, it was reserved for professionals only.[13] The roaming reporters of the telephonographic newspaper *L'Époque* used it to transmit live news on a gigantic telephonoscope "screen" flanking its headquarters along the Champs-Elysées, while another glass disc on the other side of the building presented advertisements.[14] An illustration of a camel-mounted war correspondent shows that Robida still imagined the pocket telephonoscope as a wired tool. [15] Wireless telegraphy was "in the air"—the existence of Hertzian waves was confirmed soon after the book was published—but the first practical public demonstrations by the Italian Guglielmo Marconi were more than a decade away.

## Prophesies and Parodies

Much has been written about Marconi—it is not worth repeating it here. Instead, it is worth looking at a less well-known prophesy, which was presented in February 1897, while Marconi was in England performing demonstrations of his wireless communication system for the British government to convince the authorities of its usefulness. The prophecy quickly went "viral" and was reprinted in numerous magazines both in England and in the United States (and probably elsewhere).

Years later, this vision of the future was still routinely quoted in the concluding chapters of books on wireless telegraphy as well as in technological journals.[16] The density of references confirms the pregnancy of the idea—a desire for wireless communication had been ignited. The prophecy in question had its origin in a lecture titled "Sixty Years of Submarine Telegraphy" by the British scientist William Edward Ayrton, delivered at the Imperial Institute in London on February 15, 1897. *The Electrician* published a lengthy abstract four days later.[17] Most publications, including not only scientific journals, but also religious and theosophic ones, were content with relaying the following extract, which must have stirred the imagination of countless readers:

> Well, there is no doubt the day will come, maybe when you and I are forgotten, when copper wires, gutta-percha coverings and iron sheathings will be relegated to the museum of antiquities. Then when a person wants to telegraph to a friend, he knows not where, he will call in an electromagnetic voice, which will be heard loud by him who has the electromagnetic ear, but will be silent to everyone else, he will call, 'Where are you?' and the reply will come loud to the man with the electromagnetic ear, 'I am at the bottom of the coal mine, or crossing the Andes, or in the middle of the Pacific'... Or perhaps, no voice will come at all, and he may then expect the friend is dead. Think what that will mean. Think of the calling which goes on from room to room, then think of that calling when it extends from pole to pole, a calling quite audible to him who wants to hear, absolutely silent to him who does not.[18]

It is likely this formulation was not entirely original. Discovering its antecedents is a task for other media archaeologists. Yet, another widely relayed prophesy was made by Nikola Tesla, a Serbian inventor who emigrated to the United States, becoming the nemesis of Thomas Alva Edison. Whether he was a genius or not, Tesla was certainly an eccentric thinker and a ferocious self-promoter. He famously wrote in an article published in 1905:

> Within a few years, a simple and inexpensive device, readily carried about, will enable one to receive on land or sea the principal news, to hear a speech, a lecture, a song or play of a musical instrument, conveyed from any other region of the globe.[19]

The moment when Tesla first voiced this idea is difficult to determine because he wrote many articles and comments to the popular press and charmed both admirers and interviewers with his visions.[20]

In the previous year, the *International Wood-Worker* quoted a different version about Tesla's "world telegraphy" in the context of "The Newspaper of the Future," a topic that had already occupied Robida and others. After describing how he would place a number of plants in strategic locations around the Earth to transmit "individualized signals to the utmost confines of the earth," Tesla said:

> A cheap and simple device, which might be carried in one's pocket, may then be set up somewhere on sea and land, and it will record the world's news or such special messages as may be intended for it. Thus, the entire earth will be converted into a huge brain, as it were, capable of response in every one of its parts.[21]

Tesla's vision was not pure speculation. It grew from his pioneering work on the wireless (for which he tried to claim primacy) and high-intensity electrical currents. The mobile device Tesla envisioned was part of his all-embracing scheme for a "World-System," a total solution to global energy needs and communications purposes. He began propagating it around 1900 in a sensational article in the *Century* magazine, where he mentioned "the idea of effecting communication to any distance through the earth or environing medium [...]."[22] Tesla tried to convince the reader that "in a time not very distant most telegraphic messages across the oceans will be transmitted without cables."[23]

The "World-System" was a mixture of scientifically tested ideas and wild fantasy. Its fate was to remain a noted but unrealized discursive system. The only materialized part was an unfinished power station and transmission tower built in Shoreham, Long Island with venture capital funding from the banker J. P. Morgan. By creating a global network of similar plants, Tesla intended to charge the Earth with electrical energy. Combining this with his theories of "standing waves," he intended to provide free energy and communications for the entire humankind. In addition, the system was also going to be used to communicate with extra-terrestrials.

How original were these—and other—prophecies of portable media? Further excavations are needed to give more precise answers, but it is likely that many of their components were provided by tradition, which became coated in contemporary attire. With eager support from the international press, they certainly had a broad influence on cultural imaginaries. The ideas were stretched in different directions, depending on the writer's ideological leaning. The theosophical publication *Century Path* connected Ayrton's prophecy of wireless person-to-person communication with thought-transference in the following manner:

> This recalls the fact that all our mechanical inventions are, after all, mere imperfect copies of what we have inside of us. The human machine is the best machine known, mechanically, chemically, in every way. May it not be that there have been people—perhaps still are—able to accomplish without machinery results we can only accomplish with it? If so, then the proficiency in mechanical arts is no absolute measure of capability.[24]

The writer claimed that it was "no more difficult to explain how I can send a thought to China than how I can send it into my arm."[25] Such ideas about magic media resonated widely—perhaps we could add, wildly—within esoteric and even scientific circles of the time.

Cartoonists were abreast of the times. In England, the satirical journal *Punch* published in 1906 a "forecast for 1907," where an elegant couple is shown spending their time in Hyde Park with antennas protruding from their hats. Both are holding portable wireless devices on their laps. [26] The caption specifies the situation: "These two figures are not communicating with one another. The lady is receiving an amatory message, and the gentleman some racing results." Both are sitting on their own chairs apart from each other and facing different directions. They are utterly lost in mediated reveries that have carried them far away from the natural beauty of Hyde Park. The cartoon indicates that social discontents associated with portable media, which are routinely associated with much later developments, were already felt. There are also other cartoons that depict solitary human beings surrounded by fantastic communication devices, alienated from direct proxemic contacts with other humans.[27]

However, the alienating effect of increasing media use was not necessarily associated with portable devices only. As the home became conceived as a "media center," connections with the outside became increasingly mediated. How the "home audience" in front of the radio or the television set was affected is an important and complex issue but belongs to a different trajectory of enquiry that I discuss in a forthcoming book on the media archaeology of the screen.

## Between the Discursive and the Material

In the early twentieth century, the discourse on imaginary portable devices began gaining material forms, although not in straightforward one-to-one relationship. Readers were informed that devices like the "pocket wireless" had come to existence.[28] Of course, few of them were in a position to verify what was actually meant and how the new technological wonders functioned. The relationship remained mainly discursive.

In October 1900, the *Electrical World and Engineer* wrote about a "pocket telephone" invented by Evan Shelby, the manager of Lafayette Telephone Company in Indiana.[29] It was said to be a small receiver and transmitter that could be folded together and "conveniently carried in the pocket." The plan was to equip every policeman with one, enabling them "to hold communication with anybody in the city who has a telephone." The device could not be wireless because the possibility of wireless telephony was only beginning to be investigated. The idea was to place connection boxes on telephone poles here and there in the city. Each was going to be equipped with a battery and an automatic connection to the central office. Similar devices were also designed for the linemen maintaining telephone lines and even used at the Harlem Jockey Club's racetrack in Chicago.[30] All were initially meant for professional use.

The emergence of the pocket telephone reflected the need to maintain the increasingly complex technological infrastructures in developed societies, but also highlighted fears of crime and subversive actions. Its adoption by police departments was related with other developments such as the installation of street lighting in cities to eliminate dark spots where crimes could occur.[31] A pocket telephone network that operated in Berlin, Germany, received much attention.

In 1912, the Chicago-based *Telephony* explained its principles, publishing an eerie photograph of an undercover woman detective dressed in black posing while "calling patrol wagon."[32] It was said that the system was built because "[i]n consequence of the enormous expansion of the German capital, there are many outlying districts which are rendered unsafe through insufficient policing." Contact devices were said to have been installed practically everywhere: "They are fastened to walls, doors, trees, lampposts or other convenient places." Even parks and forests had them, allowing "a long walk through the woods and still be in touch with the city at all times."

Portable telephones, which could be "carried in a pocket without inconvenience, or in a lady's hand bag," were claimed to be available for anyone to purchase in Germany.[33] Similar devices seem to have been introduced elsewhere as well. The August 1912 issue of *Popular Mechanics* wrote about the "Watch-Case Telephone" or the "sanitary vest-pocket telephone transmitter," which could be carried like a standard pocket watch.[34] Pushing a button released the lid of the case, making a spiral spring push the collapsible mouthpiece out "into operative position." The case had sockets to connect it with "special terminals on the stationary telephone instrument or the desk stand."

Instead of being an independent self-supporting unit, the device was meant to be attached to public telephones, obviously to defend the user from contagious infections.[35] The idea made sense, but for widespread adoption, the infrastructure would have had to be modified. The Watch-Case Telephone required "that all public telephone instruments be equipped with extra terminals."

In spite of the technical limitations, efforts were made to turn portable media into more than a figment of the cultural imagination. The Watch-Case Telephone was not the only device that was modelled on the pocket watch, a familiar and proven object that is easy to store on the body (in a pocket or hung from chains) and pull out and use. The pocket watch became a model used in ever-new contexts. A Swiss clockmaker even produced a peep watch, which functioned like a normal pocket watch, except that it had round picture windows at the front and back for rotating circular picture discs, often with semi-clad women.[36] Cameras were fashioned on pocket watches and other everyday objects, partly as a reaction against the hostile attitudes towards photography in public places. In France, Georges Demeny designed a pocket *Fonoscope* for both taking and viewing moving pictures, while the *Mikiphone* was also identified as Pocket Phonograph, likely the smallest mechanical portable record player ever made.[37]

Against this background, it is interesting to try assessing the originality of yet another prophesy made by David Sarnoff (1891–1971), a Marconi wireless telegraph operator who became the CEO of the powerful Radio Corporation of America (RCA). He presented the evolution of radio in three stages. From professional uses by "radio men," it had been extended to "nonradio persons" at homes. The third stage would bring it "not only to the home but to the individual, whether he be within or outside of a fixed place."[38] Sarnoff presented specific plans detailing how this could be achieved. The main issue for him was reception, "developing a suitable receiver in such compact and efficient form as to enable an individual to conveniently carry it on his or her person and to satisfactorily receive such broadcasted material."[39] Not surprisingly, the model was "the watch carried by a lady or a gentleman, which is not only serviceable but ornamental as well."[40]

Sarnoff's ideas about the design of what he called "Radiolette" are highly interesting and resonate with discussions ignited in our time by devices like Google Glass and the Apple Watch. Sarnoff acknowledged that the Radiolette "should first be developed with the utilitarian view in mind." The battery was a major concern—as it still is.[41] However, Sarnoff also suggested that the combined effect of the radio tube ("lamp") and the battery could be used to turn the device into a flashlight, "to show the way in dark place," and that other extra functions might also be possible. The combined uses "would ultimately create in the individual a real desire to possess a Radiolette."

What Sarnoff wrote next pre-echoes the industrial voices resounding in the media cultural discourses of the early next millennium. For a comparison, it would be instructive to revisit the articles, press releases, and videos released by the Apple Corporation to accompany the launch of the Apple Watch in 2015. If we focussed on the discursive aspects and forgot the purely technological developments for a moment, it would seem that little has happened during the century in-between.

As Michael Brian Schiffer demonstrated in his pioneering and still relevant book *The Portable Radio in American Life*, the introduction of radio broadcasting inspired many imaginative designs for portable or wearable radio sets. Many of them were more or less impractical—pinkie ring radios, billfold radios, purse radios, bicycle radios, wrist radios, etc.[42] As Sarnoff predicted, inventors combined different media functions in the same package, anticipating the way smartphones and smartwatches embody and combine the functions of earlier separate devices. This burst of sometimes wild and out-of-control creativity was not unexpected as perusing popular scientific publications from the late nineteenth century onward easily demonstrates.

The innovative imagination became even more agitated as media culture's grasp as an industrial endeavour became stronger. In the coming decades, many varieties of portable and wearable devices appeared in both material and discursive forms that influenced each other. Only a fraction became successful. The piles of accumulated ideas were revisited over and over again. So, the first portable transistor radios, introduced in the mid-1950s, may have seemed a breakthrough, but the phenomenon had been gathering force for decades. Yet, contemporary social, cultural, and economic factors—youth subcultures, consumerism, wider personal mobility—also mattered, contributing to the illusion of mobile media as a novelty and cultural rupture.

## The Magic Spectacles

One of the current grand narratives of mobile media, beside the ubiquity of the smartphone, is the idea of wearing the device on the head. Google Glass was a short-lived and failed effort to transfer remote communications into the user's field of vision, associated with voice commands.[43] What can be said about the archaeology of media worn in front of the eyes? Many early portable devices—both real and imaginary—were used to listen to sounds, send voice messages or snap pictures, so they did not involve continuous viewing with or through the device. The watch is not a perfect comparison because it is mainly used for glancing at visual information rather than staring at it for an extended amount of time.

However, from a behaviouristic point of view, the wearable clockface is a relevant reference for devices like the smartphone and the smartwatch. Especially in the case of the latter, rapidly glancing at what it displays is common and represents a continuity from earlier forms of using both pocket watches and wristwatches. The smartphone seems to encourage both repeated glances and intensive staring, both of which are predefined modes of use "preprogrammed" by manufacturers and contents providers (we can claim that Twitter is for glances, Facebook with its "infinite scrolling" for extended gazing).

The spectacles as a mobile media interface may not have been as common as other alternatives, but examples can be found from Western cultural traditions. "Magic (or magical) spectacles" is a popular topos evoked at least since the eighteenth century in numerous texts, and it still persists. Its origins may have been inspired by the coming of the enhancement of vision by means of eyeglasses, which is a historical traceable development. The eyeglasses or spectacles became gradually more common as a utility since the sixteenth century. Their evolution had to do with the refinement of the art of lens grinding, but also with the new emphasis on literacy and individual reading (an issue with many implications, including changing religious conventions brought by reformation movements and the establishment of the bourgeois domesticity and public sphere).[44] In the cultural imagination, the "magic" qualities of the eyeglasses with their artificial magnifying lenses were extended beyond the immediate physical reality. They became a means of looking into "augmented" or even "virtual" realities (to use anachronistic points of comparison), empowering the mental abilities of the person who wore them. The use of lenses in devices like the telescope and the microscope may well have contributed to this imaginary extension of vision.

A common context for "magic spectacles" was the fairytale. To mention just one example among many, in Chauncey Giles' *The Magic Spectacles* (1870), two children, a brother and sister, encounter a mysterious old man, a street crier selling spectacles.[45] In an amusing anticipation of the parody videos inspired by the Google Glass, the man says he has "a pair of spectacles which enables me to see the names of everybody I wish to know."[46] In exchange for their lives, he gives the children spectacles that are "not worn on the nose, but on the inside of the eyes."[47] The story has a moral: wearing the virtual spectacles persuades the restless children to become good and to concentrate on their studies. They are a metaphor of inner motivation: "The spectacles will never help you to see anything that you can see well enough without them. Nor will they help you in anything, unless you try to help yourself."[48]

No matter how vacillating the discursive origins of magic spectacles may have been, their emergence was also associated with concrete circumstances. It may be imposing to merge all their manifestations within one topos tradition because magic spectacles appeared in many contexts, including satires about the future.[49] The saying "putting on the magic spectacles" signified a deeper look into something not immediately visible, such as unfolding political events. The expression was related with another topos: looking into a magic mirror.[50] The gaze through the magic spectacles was explained to penetrate beyond the surface, allowing the user to read minds. Among many others, this commonplace was put into words by the actor Charles Dibdin, who rhymed about light-hearted women in one of his popular songs: "I put on my spectacles, look mighty wise / Read her warm yielding heart through her cold frigid eyes."[51]

More precise discursive, and—in a still minimal way, material—foundation for the coming of media goggles were laid in the 1930s, in the era when the television had just reached the stage of experimental broadcasting. Hugo Gernsback (1884–1967), a well-known popularizer of science and science fiction, who became a household name for American boys and men through his publications, had presented the idea of "television spectacles." He first wrote about them in 1936.[52] Gernsback revived the idea in 1938 in *Radio-Craft*, explaining that in the future every radio set would be equipped with television. He then asked: "[H]ow will I be able to see a television program by means of a vest-pocket set?"[53] The answer was to "wear a pair of 'spectacles' which have a twin television receiver built right on the eye-glass frame."[54]

Gernsback admitted that the images would be small, "but they need not be large, because they are right up close to your eye; indeed they will be sharper in this manner."[55] He suggested that "the frame of the television set on the bony part of your nose will also, by molecular vibration, transmit the sound to your ear-drums in a most realistic fashion."[56] Gernback returned to the idea once again in 1949 in the *Radio-Electronics* magazine, now calling the device Tele-Eyeglasses (or "television eyeglasses" and even "teleyglasses").[57] He had toned down his predictions, perhaps because television was now becoming common in living rooms. The device would not be "at least for years to come, a complete self-contained television receiver." Rather, it would be a plug-in accessory, "particularly useful for invalids and for those who wish to relax without having to sit rigidly in front of the television receiver for hours."

The fourth time Gernsback got an opportunity to stir up the public imagination with television goggles came in 1963 when the *Life* magazine published a feature about his career.[58] Perhaps because of his age (he had four more years to live), or because of his observations of technological developments, Gernback (or *Life*?) decided to give the glasses a prominent role. Thanks to "thin, inch-square cathode tubes" and "low-voltage current from very small batteries," his "New Deal era concept" was said to be no longer impractical. The reservations he had sounded over a decade earlier were gone. The user would be able to "take them out of his pocket anywhere, slip them on, flip a switch and turn to his favorite station."[59]

With *Life's* photo session in mind, Gernsback had "ordered some of his employees to build a mock-up." A photograph shows him posing wearing a device which has a V-type aerial protruding from the top. The reporter found the site "neo-Martian." Today, the picture has gone viral on the internet. It has become a reference point for those trying to demonstrate what gadgets like Google Glass did not come from. I will discuss this issue in a forthcoming study about its rise and fall.

In the article in *Life*, Gernsback proclaimed that "since there will be a picture for each eye, the glasses will make a stereoptical view possible." It is interesting to note that Gernsback envisioned 3-D television without glasses by suggesting that a polarizing optical film would be stretched across its screen. Like any technology popularizer and enthusiast, Gernback must have been following what engineers and inventors were doing, adding occasionally an insight of his own in his comments. He certainly knew that the Scottish television pioneer John Logie Baird had demonstrated a mechanical stereoscopic television as early as 1928 and presented an electronic version in the early 1940s.[60]

Gernsback may have been familiar with a patent that was granted posthumously to the American inventor Henry J. De N. McCollum in 1945. Under the heading "Stereoscopic Television Apparatus," it described wearable 3-D "spectacle frame viewing apparatus."[61] The system recalls the one Gernsback described in 1949, without mentioning stereoscopy. Collum had suggested—like Gernsback—that "several viewing spectacles may be connected in parallel to the same switch device."[62] Both explained that the device "permits the spectator to recline in a comfortable chair and to view the object being televised without sitting in some certain position relative to a screen or other fixed surface upon which the images are shown."[63] This evokes a remarkably low-tech wearable device, which had been introduced by the British optician Theodore Hamblin in 1936. The spectacles—still known as "Hamblin glasses"—were equipped with mirror prisms. The user could therefore lie on his/ her back on the bed facing the ceiling while reading a book placed standing on the belly—perhaps the same thing could be used to watch the television in the other end of the room.[64]

Whether Gernsback was ever alone with his ideas is doubtful. In 1963, it was certainly no longer the case. Wearable media glasses had been created by others. In 1960, the Californian inventor and filmmaker Morton Heilig patented a "Stereoscopic-Television Apparatus for Individual Use."[65] His main ambition at the time was to create totally immerse multisensory experiences inspired by Cinerama, a novelty ultra-widescreen cinematic spectacle.[66] Heilig's main claim to fame is the Sensorama Simulator, an ingenious but commercially failed single user arcade machine that combined vision and audio with aromas, wind, vibrations, and other sensory experiences. His glasses or "television viewing mask" was also meant for immersive experiences. Therefore, it also belongs to the prehistory of virtual reality as a head-mounted display. Another interesting device was the "TV Monocle" introduced in *Popular Mechanics* in October 1962.[67] It had been developed by Hughes Aircraft Co. for pilots, who would, "[w]ithout being distracted from flying duties," see "a television picture of air-traffic information and ground conditions through a lightweight electronic-optical viewer." The picture seen with the "TV Monocle" was projected "onto a transparent-mirror monocle positioned in front of the eye." It was said to appear "as large as eight feet," and also be suited for surgeons, who could "monitor a patient's pulse rate while performing an operation." The idea of the monocle was adopted by Google's experimental Google[x] unit, when it began developing its Google Glass around 2010. Whether a display, which was only seen hovering in front of the user's right eye was technological necessity or the goal of Google's design efforts, has not been fully verified. In Google's promotional videos, a hypothetical fully augmented field of vision was presented (something which Google Glass could not deliver, contributing to disappointments and the speedy demise of the device).

The choice between binocular and monocular wearable interface is important because it affects the relationship between the real world seen through glasses and digital realms overlaid in the field of vision. Rather than Gernsheim or Heilig, the traditional topos of the magic spectacles is a more relevant point of comparison here. The pioneering virtual reality head-mounted displays of Ivan A. Sutherland, constructed in the late 1960s, belonged to the "see-through" type. Opaque versus see-through models are still the two types of VR goggles.

However, in the technological imagination of the 1960s, mobile media technology does not seem to have played a very prominent role. The field that gets closer to mobile media is medicine, where "long-distance heart checks" will be performed. A miniature transmitter, "[l]ittle larger than a nickel," would be attached to the patient's chest and its signals "received by an electrocardiograph machine in the doctor's office or hospital."[68] Rocket-propelled jet packs will be used by soldiers and perhaps even by others to "Get to the Office."[69] The overall vision is surprisingly stationary, location based. Finding out how representative this idea is requires further excavations.

## Conclusion

This short and tentative archaeology of mobile media has not told the entire story of devices associated with it. Very likely, the full story can never be told. Another task is to extend the "excavation zone" examined in the preceding pages towards more recent developments, such as the discourse that surrounded Google Glass, which was a failed but nevertheless interesting effort to promote see-through wearable media interfaces as a potential model for the mobile media culture of the (near? far?) future. Google Glass may have seemed a futuristic effort, but in fact it did not emerge from nowhere.

As we have seen, "magic spectacles" was an established topos, but even more short-term developments deserve attention. For example, the artist and tinkerer Steve Mann had not only built devices that anticipated Google's project, but developed a pervasive years-long practice of wearing them in public. The efforts of Mann, Thad Starner, and many others—including media artists like Janet Cardiff, the pioneer of sound walks, and Masaki Fujihata, the pioneer in using GPS as a tool for mobile art—were involved in extending the realm of mobile media deserve to be included in future media archaeological excavations of the field. The ancient and the recent can be put in dialogue with each other to reveal the logics of rupture and continuation, repetition and rediscovery, underlying obvious, and overt manifestations of media culture.

## Notes

1 See Erkki Huhtamo, "Pockets of Plenty. An Archaeology of Mobile Media," in *The Mobile Audience: Media Art and Mobile Technologies*, edited by Martin Rieser (Amsterdam; New York: Rodopi, 2011), 23–38.

2 Famianus Strada, *Proclusiones Academicae, Oratoriae, Historicae, Poeticae* (Audomari: Carolus Boscardus, 1619); Patrice Flichy, *Une histoire de la communication moderne. Espace public et vie privée* (Paris: Éditions de la Découverte, 1991), 17–18.

3 *The Guardian*, no. 119 (Tuesday, July 28, 1713), in Alexander Chalmers (ed.), *The Guardian; a New Edition, Carefully Revised, in Two Volumes; with Prefaces Historical and Biographical*, Vol. II (London: F. C. and J. Rivington, et al., 1822), 161–65.

4 Ibid., 164.

5 Joscelyn Godwin, *Athanasius Kircher's Theatre of the World: The Life and Work of the Last Man to Search for Universal Knowledge* (Rochester, Vermont: Inner Traditions, 2009), 194. Godwin reminds that this theme inspired Umberto Eco's *The Island of the Day Before* (note 11, 214).

6 See introduction, "The Coming of Jap Herron," in the extraordinary *Jap Herron: A Novel Written from the Ouija Board* (New York: Mitchell Kennerley, 1917), 7–8, 11. The work is claimed to be a post-mortem work by Mark Twain. Another book purportedly "received" with a Ouija board is Katherine Mardon Davis, *Light from Beyond as Taken Over the Ouija Board* (New York: W. J. Watt & Company, 1919).

7 Wolfgang Schivelbusch, *The Railway Journey: The Industrialization of Time and Space in the Nineteenth Century*, trans. (Berkeley: The University of California Press, 2014); Stephen Kern, *The Culture of Time and Space 1880–1918* (Cambridge, MA: Harvard University Press, 1983); Claude Pichois, *Vitesse et vision du monde* (Neuchatel: Éditions de la Baconnière, 1973).

8 John Urry, *Mobilities* (Cambridge: Polity Press, 2007).

9 For telegraphy as a private means of communication, see Carolyn Marvin, *When Old Technologies were New: Thinking About Electric Communication in the Late Nineteenth Century* (New York & Oxford: Oxford University Press, 1988), 94–95.

10 Various visual formats that preceded the picture postcard have been discussed by Frank Staff, *The Picture Postcard and Its Origins* (London: Lutterworth Press, 1979 [1966]); Martin Willoughby, *A History of Postcards* (London: Bracken Books, 1994); George and Dorothy Miller, *Picture Postcards in the United States 1893–1918* (New York: Clarkson N. Potter, Inc., 1976). The Chicago World's Fair (1893) and the Paris Universal Exposition of 1900 were important in popularizing the postcard as a medium. The remarkable interactive installation *The Postcard Trail* (1996) by George Legrady was a kind of archaeology of postcard culture.

11 Albert Robida's, *Le Vingtième Siècle*, facsimile edition (Genève and Paris: Editions Slatkine, 1981 [1883]), 55.

12 Ibid., 72–73.

13 Ibid., 200.

14 Televisual media was not ubiquitous in Robida's vision. An imbalance prevailed between Paris and the provinces. Although *l'Époque* had mostly abandoned paper editions, special typographic and photographic paper editions were published for provincial readers. Ibid., 201–02.

15 Ibid., 201.

16 Charles R. Gibson, *Wireless Telegraphy and Telephony without Wires* (London: Seeley, Service & Co, 1914), 140. The author used the expression "pocket telephone." Ernst Ruhmer bundled Ayrton's and Tesla's prophesies together in *Wireless Telephony in Theory and Practice*, trans. James Erskine-Murray (New York: D. van Nostrand Company, 1908), 196–97.

17 William Edward Ayrton, "Sixty Years of Submarine Telegraphy," *The Electrician: A Weekly Illustrated Journal of Electrical Engineering, Industry and Science* XXXVIII, no. 17 (No. 979) (Feburary 19, 1897), 545–48.

18 Ibid., 548.

19 Nikola Tesla, "The Transmission of Electrical Energy Without Wires as a Means for Furthering Peace," *Electrical World and Engineer* (January 7, 1905): 21–24. Reprinted in facsimile in: *Tesla Said*, ed. John T. Ratzlaff (Millbrae, CA: Tesla Book Company), 82. Photocopy of the book manuscript in author's archive.

20 Tesla is reported to have told his admirer Katharine Johnson:

> The time will come when crossing the ocean by steamer you will have a daily paper on board with the important news of the world [...] and by means of a pocket instrument and a wire in the ground, you can communicate from any distance with friends at home through an instrument similarly attuned.

Quoted by Cheney & Uth (49) from Robert Johnson, *Remembered Yesterdays* (1923). In his autobiography Tesla quoted this from a "technical statement" about the "World-System." Nikola Tesla, *Moji pronalasci/ My Inventions*, ed. Branimira Valic (Zagreb: Skolska Knjiga, 1987), 66. The quotation appeared in an article (from a series the autobiography was based on), "My Inventions: The Magnifying Transmitter," in *Electrical Experimenter*, June 1919.

21 "The Newspaper of the Future," *The International Wood-Worker* 14, no. 6 (Chicago, June 1904), 244. The publication referred to *Scientific American* as the source.

22 Nicola Tesla, "The Problem of Increasing Human Energy, With Special Reference to the Harnessing of the Sun's Energy," *The Century Magazine* LX, no. 2 (June 1900), 207 (article 184–211). The expression "World System" is not yet mentioned. In their *Tesla: Master of Lightning* (New York: Fairfax Publishers/

Metrobooks, 1999) Margaret Cheney and Robert Uth erroneously claim that Tesla included television and telephone in the *Century* text (99). They must have quoted a later source. Tesla wrote about "Television" as a possibility to "see as well as hear by means of electricity" in his contribution to "Famous Scientists Forecast Future of Wireless" in the 50th Anniversary Issue of *Popular Science Monthly* 100, no. 5 (May 1922), 28. He did single out portable devices, although he wrote that "[i]t will be possible to see as well as to hear either by wireless telephone or over the regular wire circuits" (ibid.)

23 Tesla, "The Problem of Increasing Human Energy," 209.

24 Student, "Wireless Telegraphy and Thought Transference," *Century Path* (Point Loma, San Diego, CA), ed. Katherine Tingley 10, no. 33 (June 23, 1907), 17.

25 Ibid.

26 Lewis Baumer, "Development of Wireless Telegraphy: Scene in Hyde Park," *Punch, or the London Charivari* CXXXI (26 December 1906), 451.

27 See Harry Grant Dart's cartoon, "We'll All Be Happy Then" in the cover of *Media Archaeology*, edited by Huhtamo and Parikka. Originally published in *Life* LVIII, no. 1591 (7 December 1911), 1007. Another example of the discontents of new technology is the "wrong number" topos that appeared in connection with the Telectroscope in Robida's *Vingtième siècle* (75) and later in another cartoon by Dart, "A Possible Drawback of Television," *Judge*, 1929 (issue not known). The gender roles have been reversed: in the former, a group of men peep at a woman dressing up, while in the latter a modern woman surprises a man taking a shower after having been given a wrong connection by the operator.

28 For a detailed discussion, see Grant Wythoff, "Pocket Wireless and the Shape of Media to Come," *Grey Room* no. 51 (Spring 2013), 40–63.

29 "Pocket Telephone," *Electrical World and Engineer* XXXVI, no. 15 (13 October 1900), 579.

30 "Racing Horses by Telephone," *The American Telephone Journal* VII, no. 25 (18 June 1903), 398–99; "A New Type of Pocket Telephone," *Popular Mechanics* 24, no. 2 (August 1915), 162; ad for the "Pocket 'Phone'" for linemen, *Telephony* 66, no. 18 (2 May 1914), 11.

31 Wolfgang Schivelbusch, *The Disenchanted Night. The Industrialization of Light in the Nineteenth Century* (Berkeley: University of California Press, 1988), 133–34.

32 "The Pocket Telephone in Germany," *Telephony* 62, no. 9 (2 March 1912), 280. Some sources that relayed this information said that similar systems operated in other German cities too.

33 Although "one misses the privacy of the telephone booth ... the pocket telephone is so delicately constructed that one need speak in only a very low tone of voice" (ibid.). The receiver and transmitter fit into a circular nickel case two and half inches in diameter and three-quarters of an inch thick.

34 "Watch-Case Telephone Transmitter," *Popular Mechanics*, 12 August, 243.

35 See examples such as "Hall's Standard Lung Tester" (1886) in, Richard M. Bueschel and Steve Gronowski, *Arcade 1. Illustrated Historical Guide to Arcade Machines*, Vol. 1 (USA: Hoflin Publishing Ltd, 1993), 45, 116, 138–40, passim.

36 C. 1902. The author's example bears the patent numbers 24792 (Swiss), D. R. G. M. 192177 (German) and S.G.D.G. (French, no number given). According to Christie's, the Swiss patent refers to "Exposé d'invention, brevet No. 24792, A[rnold] Schweizer-Schatzmann, Chaux-de-Fonds, 22 juillet 1902." [Earlier patent, 24340, Dec. 23, 1901]. Another portable device in the shape of the pocket watch, "The Panorama Watch," was sold in France by M. L. Bienfait, 7 Place de la Nation, Paris. It contained a rotating disc with 12 minuscule photographic images (Stephen Herbert, "Nouvelles Scientifiques," *The New Magic Lantern Journal* 6, no. 1 (January1989), 7. The information is from the supplement to *La Nature* between 1891 and 1907 (exact issue unknown). An example marked "Montre 1900 Diorama, K.B.B. SGDG" was sold on eBay France in February 2005. The glass disc had ten tiny photographs of nude or scantily dressed ladies, some on bicycles.

37 The pocket Fonoscope recorded a short moving image sequence on a rotating sensitized disc and could also be used for viewing developed (positive) discs. The only known example is in the collection of the Musée du Cinéma of the French Cinématheque. Mikiphone was patented by Vadász brothers, Génève, in Nov. 1924 and manufactured in 1926–1927 by Paillard in Ste-Croix, Switzerland, www.portable-gramophone.com/mikiphone_gramo.ws. Last accessed 25 August 2015.

38 Ibid., 45.

39 Ibid.

40 Ibid.

41 Hugo Gernsback imagined in 1938 a portable radio in the shape of the pocket watch, which would have instead of batteries a "watchspring-driven electric generator." "Radio in the Future," *Radio-Craft* IX, no. 9 (March 1938), 613. In the same article, he suggested that portable radios would be used as pagers that would allow "physicians, contractors, business men, and others" reach the user (613).

42 Michael Brian Schiffer, *The Portable Radio in American Life* (Tucson & London: The University of Arizona Press, 1991).
43 I am working on a study on the rise and fall of Google Glass.
44 Raimonda Riccini, *Taking Eyeglasses Seriously: Art, History, Science, and Technologies of Vision* (Cinisello Balsamo: Silvana, 2002); Wolfgang Winkler, *A Spectacle of Spectacles*, exhibition catalogue (Leipzig: Edition Leipzig, 1988); *La lente. Storia, scienza, curiosità attraverso la collezione Fritz Rathschüler*, exhibition catalogue (Genova: Edizioni Culturali Internazionali Genova, 1988), 25–27. An early study is Emil Bock, *Die Brille und ihre Geschichte* (Wien: Verlag von Josef Šafár, 1903).
45 Chauncey Giles, *The Magic Spectacles. A Fairy Story* (Edinburgh: William Oliphant & Company [1870]). Educational stories with "magic spectacles" in the title are still published. See, for example, Rachel FreierMiller Sivek's children's book *Zachary and the Magic Spectacles: A Book about a Boy Who Learns to be Nice* (Bloomington, IN: AuthorHouse, 2012).
46 Ibid., 18. For examples of such parody videos, search "Google Glass" on YouTube.
47 Ibid., 39.
48 Ibid., 29–30. The topos of the magic mirror also appears, 137, 144.
49 "The Magic Spectacles. A Peep into a Possible Future," *Punch* LXXXIV (9 June 1883), 265.
50 Old Statesman [David Williams], *Lessons to a Young Prince on the Present Disposition in Europe to a General Revolution*, 7th ed. (London: H. D. Symonds, 1791), 114.
51 Charles Dibdin, "Magic Spectacles," in *A Collection of Songs, Selected from the Works of Mr. Dibdin* IV (London: Printed for the Author [1790], 127–29.
52 In *Short Wave Craft*, October 1936.
53 Hugo Gernsback, "Radio in the Future," *Radio-Craft* IX, no. 9 (March 1938), 590–91, 613.
54 Ibid., 613.
55 Ibid.
56 Ibid.
57 Hugo Gernsback, "40 Years of Television," *Radio-Electronics*, March 1949. www.antiqueradios.com/features/40years.html. Last accessed 25 August 2015. In the same article, Gernsback writes about "Multiperception," which we would now call multitasking, anticipating media practices of much later times.
58 Paul O'Neil, "The Amazing Hugo Gernsback, Prophet of Science. Barnum of the Space Age," *Life*, 62–69. Photo of Gernback wearing his glasses was published on page 68. ETSI.
59 Ibid., 69.
60 Picture of Baird with the 1928 stereoscopic television was published in "Television Scanning and Synchronizing by the Baird System," *Popular Science Monthly*, February 1932, 84. It used a standard Victorian Holmes-type stereoscope as the eyepiece! See also Tom McArthur and Peter Waddell, *The Secret Life of John Logie Baird* (London: Hutchinson, 1986), 151, 230. Baird also worked on 3D radar.
61 Henry J. De N. McCollum, "Stereoscopic-Television Apparatus for Individual Use," US Patent 2,388,170, filed April 15, 1943, granted October 30, 1945. McCollum had several other patents. He was from Chicago, and the executrix was his widow Thelma McCollum.
62 Ibid., 1.
63 Ibid.
64 In our time, devices like the Supine Reading Glasses or the Lazyglasses (sold by ThinkGeek) re-embody the same idea. According to *Daily Mail*, "'Lazyglasses' allow apathetic telly addicts and lethargic book worms to kick back and watch their favorite shows lying down." "A Couch Potato's Dream," *Daily Mail*, 16 August 2013.
65 Morton Heilig, "Stereoscopic-Television Apparatus for Individual Use," US Patent 2,955,156, filed May 24, 1957, granted 4 October 1960. The prototype and much related documentation was salvaged in November 2018 by Scott Fisher and the author, together with surviving Sensorama Simulators and other Heilig items, and placed in the collection of the University of Southern California, Los Angeles.
66 Morton L. Heilig, "Enter the Experiential Revolution. A VR Pioneer Looks Back to the Future," in *Cyberarts. Exploring Art & Technology*, edited by Linda Jacobsen (San Francisco, CA: Miller Freeman, Inc., 1992), 293 (article 292–305).
67 "TV Monocle," *Popular Mechanics* 118, no. 2 (October 1962), 96.
68 Ibid., 134.
69 Ibid., 100.

# 3

# MOBILE ART

## From the WAP Promises to the App Bubbles

*Giselle Beiguelman*

The launch of the first cell phones with an internet connection in the early 2000s came with promises of technological nomadism that would soon be possible. With wireless connections and the first WAP (Wireless Application Protocol)[1] cell phones, triple-A (Anywhere, Anyone, Anytime) technology would finally make sense. Before that, online banking, e-commerce site purchases, email reading, and news demanded that people return to a specific point connected to a computer terminal and a modem. This situation was, of course, a paradoxical experience of mobility. It was a necessary step in being a technological nomad.

It is true that all this, a decade later, proved to be a techno-nightmare of exploration 24/7[2] and burnout society.[3] However, at first, for artists and activists of the southern cone,[4] this technological turnaround carried with it a series of expectations. Unlike the countries in Europe and the United States, where telecommunications infrastructure was already settled in the 1990s, the absence of landlines was the first barrier to accessing the internet for countries like Brazil. The deployment of cell towers would eventually circumvent a shortage of landlines—which were considerably more costly and complicated to install—allowing a significant increase in the number of people connected to the internet. In 2005, only 21% of the Brazilian population used the internet.[5] In 2017, the number of internet users in Brazil reached 120.7 million, representing 67% of the population above ten years old. Of these, 96% used the internet by cell phone, with 49% using the network only through this device.[6]

It is undeniable that the internet, with the expansion of mobile telephony, had ceased to be a resource solely for the more affluent classes in Brazilian society—it was now becoming accessible to the new urban middle class. This new middle class emerged in the early 2000s and was immediately above the 50% poorest and the 10% richest. At the turn of the century, it became the most important social group in the Brazilian internet.[7] However, these new users had limited digital skills.[8]

Internet access via cell phones in Brazil now concentrates on social media (77%) and messaging services (90%)—especially WhatsApp, followed by Facebook Messenger. As such, its use is relatively uninventive and restricted to corporate internet environments for communication and download. The expectations that the spread of the mobile internet would entail the consolidation of the Knowledge Society—a society based on broadening the channels of participation in democratic societies via open channels and based on open-source technologies[9]—have not been fulfilled. This reality is not very different from the global spectrum as a whole, which is almost absolutely dominated by mobile internet use for pure consumption, communication, and entertainment activities.

In the early days of the internet, the Deleuzian rhizome was considered to be the icon of the web. We must remember that in the 1990s, when the internet was no longer exclusive to military and academic circles and became accessible to any consumer, it indicated the possibility of a full revolution in orbit culture. Although new control and power systems emerged with the Domain Name System (DNS) model,[10] there was a cut in the hierarchical form of knowledge production based on the decentralized structure and the link-based architecture, which could be done without prior authorization or licensing systems. However, the walled gardens of social media platforms made the rhizomatic association meaningless.

Mobile media art, in turn, anticipated issues that became central to the understanding of contemporary cultures such as behavioral transformations, new perception regimes, and the conversion of the city into an interface. Mobile media devices are tools specially developed for adaptation to traffic and displacement situations. Those devices answer to an urban universe of continuous acceleration and entropy, which alters and adapts itself to new forms of perception, visualization, and reading. Their interfaces are mediators of environments of constant flow and to situations that involve interaction with multiple and non-correlate tasks (such as speaking on the phone and driving, checking emails and eating, or watching films privately and being in a line.) In this chapter, I review some mobile media artworks from the turn of the millennium, so as to envision other possible future uses of mobile technologies and alternatives to "app bubbles."

## Art to Experience in-between While Doing Other Things

In 2001, when I created my first mobile artwork, *Wop Art [wap + op art]*, designing art for portable devices meant considering a whole new set of conditions for artistic fruition.[11] Using a mobile device involves interaction with different technologies and combining previously unrelated tasks (such as speaking on the phone and driving, checking emails and eating, or watching films privately and standing in a line). Creating for those conditions of saturation and entropy implies rethinking the nature of artistic realization and communication's conventions in the range of a culture of ubiquity in which contemplation vanishes. How can we think of an art form that may be read "in between" among varied and simultaneous but not synchronous activities and interfaces?

I expanded those arguments in a series of urban interventions I did between 2002 and 2004 (*did you read the east*, *egoscope*, *Poetrica*, and *esc for escape*), combining electronic billboards and user interactivity via desktops and cell phones. Those projects explored the emerging context of mixed realities since they assume the interconnection of on- and offline networks and informational and urban spaces as their realms of action.[12] Based on fragmented and distributed interfaces, all of these works discussed nomadism, de-territorialization, and the discontinuous integration of mediums through multi-authorial operations in open public streaming environments.

These concepts are at the core of *Poetrica* (2003–2004), the most complex project of these early years. In the beginning, it was a series of visual poems made of system fonts and dingbats (Unicode encoding of non-textual symbolism) conceived for Palm Tops. In the second stage, *Poetrica* became an urban intervention or, more precisely, a "teleintervention" that began in São Paulo and ended in Berlin.[13] *Poetrica* investigated the rise of a new cultural experience related to entropic situations and distributed aesthetics, exploring the features of the cell phone as an urban remote control (Figure 3.1).

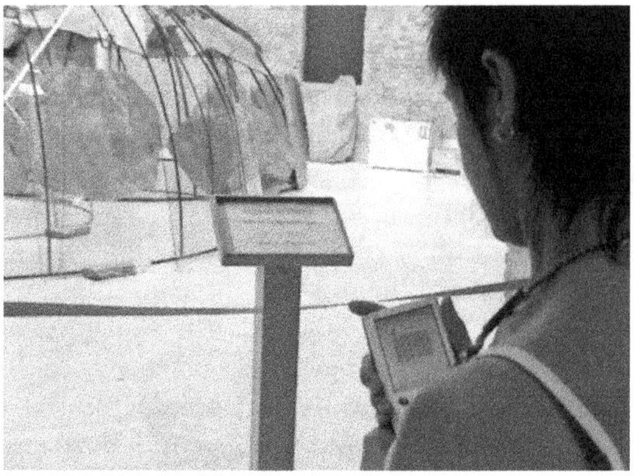

*Figure 3.1* *Poetrica Palm Version* (2002). Photo credit: Giselle Beiguelman

## The City as an Interface

The *Poetrica* teleintervention in São Paulo allowed anyone to submit messages, via web and SMS, to three electronic billboards located in downtown São Paulo. Messages were transmitted from 4 to 8 pm for ten seconds, every three minutes, following the order of ads scheduled to be broadcast in the same billboards. Three billboards transmitted those messages simultaneously and converted them automatically to dingbats and systems. A projection inside Galeria Vermelho (an art gallery in São Paulo) sent back to visitors all the webcam images of the action in the electronic billboards. All contributors were notified by email or SMS about the transmission schedule. On the website, it was possible to check all messages converted into images with captions that identified the original text before its conversion into an iconic font family, revealing a community of poetic hackers of the telecommunication system[14] (Figure 3.2).

Because of the resources commented above, it is possible to say that *Poetrica* configured a proto-social media network. Besides being able to communicate with each other, empowered by the project interface, this community subverted the limits imposed by the screen and acted in public spaces by using the feedback provided by the billboards and the images streamed via their webcams. As the Brazilian semioticist and theoretician Lucia Santaella stated, *Poetrica* was "an expansive ecosystem of subcultures that blend into micro, macro, and megacommunities."[15]

*Poetrica* stressed the logic of cloning, which permeates digital culture in the mobile age, with a myriad of contents, like news, images, social media stuff, which are replicated in different platforms. Despite being the very same in format and informational content, messages produced in the scope of *Poetrica* are not identical concerning their reception backgrounds. The messages created on the web or cell phones were read in a completely different way, depending on their reception context (electronic billboard, video documentary, website, or exhibition room). This is not a result of the screen size nor the kind of surface on which images and texts shortly adhered. It is the result of what Peter Lunenfeld defines as a "mutable aesthetics" that accommodates the contemporary phenomena of the "second-hand original."[16] Peculiar to this nomadic public art is that it's clonable and disconnected from the support, dematerializing the medium to make the interface become the actual message.

The questions posed by *Poetrica* were consistent hypotheses based on artistic thought long before the industry was able to systematize them. Today, responsiveness has become very important for web design.[17] The *Poetrica* project also fundamentally problematized the transformation of the cell phone into an urban remote control and the emergence of the city as an interface. This issue was already pertinent to projects such as the seminal *Blinkenlights* (2001) of the German collective

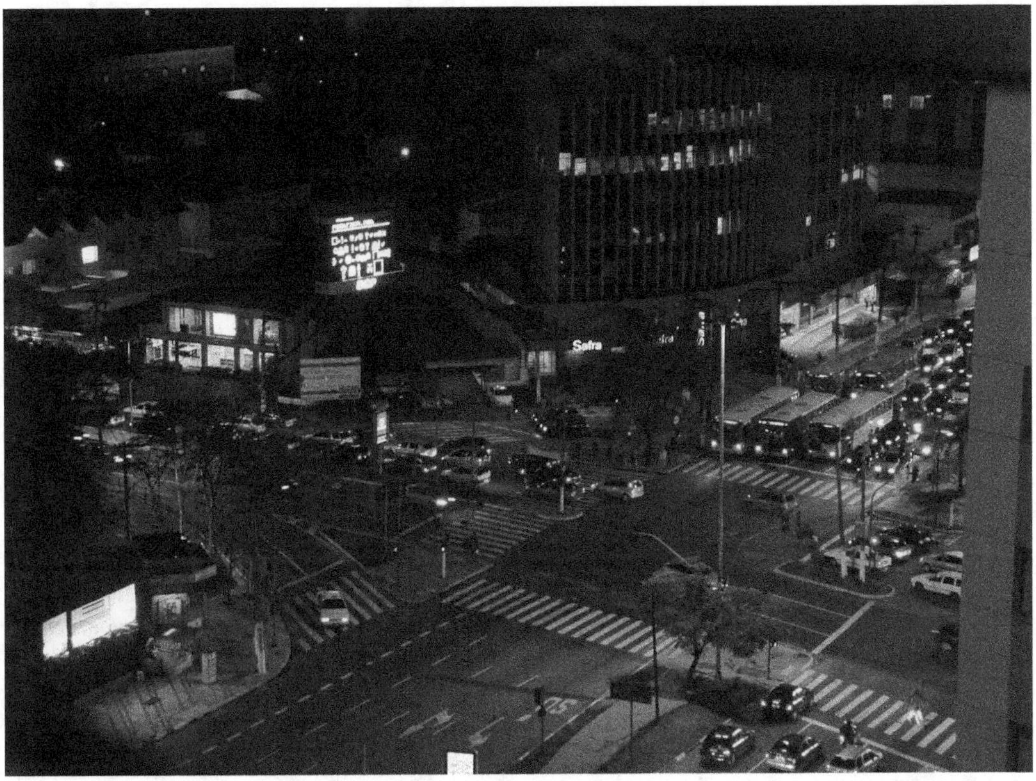

*Figure 3.2* *Poetrica*, urban intervention using electronica billboards in Sao Paulo (2003). Photo credit: Helga Stein

Chaos Computer Club (CCC) and *Amodal Suspension* (2003) by the Mexican-born artist Rafael Lozano-Hemmer. In the case of *Blinkenlights*, CCC converted the façade of the Haus des Lehrers building at Alexanderplatz, Berlin, into an interactive screen. The audience could generate content via the internet and play *Pong* on the building façade using cell phones.[18] *Amodal Suspension* empowered the text-messaging feature, turning it into the agent of a public light spectacle. As Lozano-Hemmer describes on his website, "Rather than being sent directly, the messages are encoded by robotically-controlled searchlights, similar to Morse code. Messages 'bounce' around from searchlight to searchlight, turning the sky into a giant switchboard."[19] Key to these works is the exploration of the expanded use of architecture conceived as an informational layer of a new type of urban space. In this space, what matters is "to work with technological images as constituent elements of urban spatiality, having as the most relevant principle the stimulus to interactions among users."[20]

The popularization of the cellular phone announced at that moment the possibility of redesigning urban landscape and the understanding of public space as *datascape*. On the one hand, mobile phones opened new constructive and cognitive horizons for buildings that can now function as a platform for urban activity and interaction. Electronic façades open to social activity via user generated content uploaded by cell phones and connected to apps that can inform, for example, about the climate and air quality conditions.[21] On the other hand, they pointed to the rupture of the boundaries between the real and the virtual, irreversible in the post-digital context in which we live.

Through expansion by digital technologies, cities have become unprecedentedly complex networks that entangle data from different backgrounds. There is plenty of evidence of this process, aside from the occupation of the façades with LED signs. Traffic information is available in real time by webcams all over the planet. Mobile apps, such as Waze, monitor traffic trends from drivers who share information on the streets. The urban equipment is increasingly reactive to our copresence. It is true that all these examples together have shown, as their counterpoint, a significant increase in the ability of public and private powers to monitor and track our actions. Yet, it is patent that they urge us to think on how to explore architectural relationships with data-rich environments and to ask: how do these *dataspheres* complement the construction of richer urban experiences?

This type of questioning, which is central today, has been the benchmark of several artworks since the early 2000s. Projects like *SPECFLIC 1.0* (2003) by Adriene Jenik and *Manifeste-se: todo mundo artista* (*Speak Out: Everybody Is an Artist*, 2006)[22] by the Brazilian artists Milena Szafir and Mariana Kadlec integrated mobile technologies into social forms and redirected data mediation in new ways to exercise citizenship and further understand the public space via artistic practice. For example, Jenik proposed integrating cell phones and other electronic gadgets into the cinema experience, working in public space. To this end, she carried a live telematic performance using pre-recorded media elements and the audience's social activity to create a multi-modal story event. As Anne Balsamo states: "the design of these public interactives encourages people to contemplate the nature of digitally augmented relationality that is not simply about accessing information from digital networks, but rather about engaging in embodied conversations with others in a specific context."[23]

In the case of Szafir and Kadlec, there was a whole new political pedagogy via the field of audiovisual production, which the first camera phones promised to make central in the contemporary world. Assuming that "the audience is as active as the message emitters"[24] and heavily impacted by the launch of the video-sharing website YouTube, they understood that the social response, at that moment, was coming not from the urban situation of São Paulo but from the internet, which had become a place of mutual recognition via video. They were aware of the power of the web to give a voice to all was not socially inclusive.

To this end, it is worth remembering that in 2006, the cell telephone in Brazil was still a luxury object with high operating costs restricted to 46% of the population, 90% of which used prepaid cell phones.[25] Internet access via mobile telephony, due to the high cost of the connection and access infrastructure, summed up to 5% of the total users. Moreover, 52% of access to the internet was dial-up.[26] Aiming at circumventing the gap between the technological potential and its reality, Szafir and Kadlec built a portable studio, inspired by the equipment of street vendors, which offered camera phones and a streaming system. On the streets, they invited the audience to express themselves in video by recording and learning how to stream their material, and, therefore, become more familiar with the possibilities paved by the medium.

Another artist who was notable for projects that proposed new formats for the use of audiovisual resources combined with mobile technologies—oriented to citizen use based on artistic methodologies—was the Spanish Antoni Abad with the megafone.net project, which has been in progress since 2004. As Abad states in the project website, "megafone.net invites groups of people marginalized within society to express their experiences and opinions." He distributes mobile phones to sex workers of Madrid, gypsies in Leon, motorcycle couriers in São Paulo, and people with limited mobility in Montreal, among others. Those groups use mobile phones to create different contents (like audio recordings, videos, text, and images) and publish them on the web. By doing so, "participants transform these devices into digital megaphones, amplifying the voices of individuals and groups who are often overlooked or misrepresented in the mainstream media."[27]

## The Third Eye in the Palm

The introduction of camera phones radically changed the contemporary visual culture and quickly became a kind of third eye in the palm. It would be no exaggeration to say that we can periodize the history of the production of the images in BC and AC (Before Camera phone and After Camera phone). After all, the process of production and transmission of images after the popularization of the smartphone was no longer exclusive to large-scale communication groups. Images became a kind of Sanskrit of the twenty-first century—a common language transversal to different social groups—and this implied a profound reconfiguration of our daily life.

The first camera phones appeared in Brazil in 2004. At the invitation of the artist and curator Lucas Bambozzi, I developed ***//Code_UP* (2004), a project entirely based on the use of the camera phone for the Life Goes Mobile exhibition by Nokia Trends.[28] Nokia was then the largest cellphone company and hosted an annual event—aptly titled Nokia Trends—in which the company commissioned artwork based on their conceptual devices. In *// ** Code_UP* (2004), the audience takes photos with their cell phones and sends them via Bluetooth to large screens in the exhibition room. There, they are transformed into mobile matrices that can be manipulated by keyboard and mouse commands, acquiring variable movement and density as a result of a program that converts the RGB color numeric values in height measures. It was possible not only to take photos and send them to the screens but also to interact with the images created by other people.

The title of the artwork is a reference to Michelangelo Antonioni's film *Blow Up* (1966), one of the most profound discussions ever made about the nature of the image and the ways we deal with the visible and the invisible. The film tells the story of a photographer (Thomas, interpreted by David Hemmings) who may register, by chance, a crime in a park. Upon developing his pictures, he is startled to find what appears to be a man with a gun in the bushes and, in a later shot, a body. Rushing back to the park in the middle of the night he finds the body, but on his return to the studio, all his pictures have disappeared. When he returns to the park in the morning the body, too, has gone and Antonioni seems to say: it all might never have happened.

His investigation about the crime is made through successive magnifications of the photographic registers he shot accidentally. In this process, the picture appears in its essence, reduced to its materiality: nitrate of silver grains on paper. In other words, the image was not there, and Antonioni now seems to ask us: what you see is what you get? In short, we can say Thomas could not interpret images. His superficiality allowed him only to see the material photographs. He trusted the technical devices (which are tools) but could not deal with technology as the production of knowledge.

In *//**Code_UP*, I reproduced Thomas' movements by working on the same images he developed in the film, blowing them up using programs that perform algorithmic zooms, allowing manipulation of the RGB values, exploration of the pixel and screen structure and their translation into different numeric systems, and codes (hexadecimal, binary, ASCII). Reproducing Thomas' procedures in his investigation, but reverting his point of view, paying attention to the invisible dimension of the image, establishes the conceptual dialog with Antonioni. At the same time, it opens the possibility to interrogate the image construction in the context of new technologies of seeing and perceiving.

The project investigated what could change in the cultural repertoire with the dissemination of image production processes. The mobile camera not only tends to be in everyone's pocket, but the mobile image is produced to be immediately shared. Another aspect of the project discussed the role of code in the construction of meaning since with the mobile camera, digital images become the norm.

At the time of developing ***//Code_UP*, I presumed, by the connections of the public with their self-portraits—which would become an axis of contemporary visuality with the selfie—that the cell phone camera would radically affect our ways of seeing and perceiving our everyday worlds, becoming a kind of membrane through which we would see the world. It was precisely this new image status that anchored the trilogy *De vez em sempre, De vez em nunca, De vez em quando* (*Sometimes Always, Sometimes Never, Sometimes* 2005/2006), now part of the ZKM (Center for Art and Media Karlsruhe) collection.[29]

The work reflects on the world seen through screens where every moment of the day looks like a film, which goes out and consumes itself as it is shot, responding to the dynamics of fragmentation and acceleration that produce them. Technically, it consists of an interactive projection, based on generative systems, which allows the audience to shoot images with the cell phone video cameras and send them, via Bluetooth, to big screens in the exhibition space. If one draws the computer mouse across the screen, the video then fragments into single pictures, which can then be recombined by a renewed movement of the mouse. By using the keyboard, the interactors introduce colored filters on the new images. When someone ceases to move the mouse, the original film restarts over the layers built by the public on the screen. By stopping the action, the videos resume without erasing the mosaic of scattered images that formed on the screen. The result is a dynamic palimpsest that consumes itself following an entropic logic. Here, saturation produces erasure and fluid memories mediated by experiences of difference and repetition (Figure 0.3, color insert).

*Sometimes...* highlights the haptic relation with the image that became paradigmatic with the touch screens that succeeded the iPhone in 2007. It also explores the context in which the cameras would become a sort of "exo-retinae" of the contemporary eye. These trends have become our reality. With social networks, the camera, which traditionally was just a capture device, "turns into a social projector rather than a recorder," as pointed out by Steyerl.[30]

## Drawn to the App Bubble

The contemporary visual culture is inseparable from the production of imagery in social networks. Daily, 55 million photos are uploaded to Instagram. Every two seconds, people all over the world take more pictures than were taken in the first 150 years of the history of photography.[31] The relevance of this phenomenon is not its quantitative strength, more importantly it points to qualitative transformations. On the one hand, what is at stake here is the process of appropriation of the image by new social profiles that have no antecedent. On the other hand, a new context of algorithmic domination standardizes the gaze and imposes a regime of confinement in the bubbles of the applications, which have uses conditioned to its rules.

The social history of photography and audiovisuals shows that from its beginning, image production, in its content and form, relates directly to instances of class, gender, and political power, being reserved first to sacred figures, kings, aristocrats, and popes, and then to wealthy politicians and bourgeoisie. Throughout the twentieth century, mass communication expanded this radius. However, it is only in the twenty-first century, with the digital cameras and the internet that one can discuss multiple social spectrums of imagery records.

In a very positive way, the internet and the camera phone cannibalized the screen. Over there, on YouTube, Instagram, Snapchat, etc., other aesthetic regimes flow and break canons of style and market. The impacts are significant. On the one hand, we see new social characters and themes occupying all screens, like the funk masters of ceremonies (MCs) from the favelas of Rio and the hip-hop of the Brazilian urban centers.[32] On the other hand, a phenomenon as Brazilian as it is global, a lens-mediated way of life has become commonplace. Everything can be recorded and tubed, even before it exists. The camera, through its constant companionship, seems to justify being in place and on the scene. These two aspects are essential in the documentary *Pacific* (2009), made by Brazilian filmmaker Marcelo Pedroso.[33]

Created using images recorded by the passengers of a cruise (Pacific itself) that makes the Recife-Fernando de Noronha route, *Pacific* appropriates the "school" of Do It Yourself Hollywood, of the image "produsers"[34] of the Web 2.0. The production team traveled on the ship and, at the end of the trip, approached the passengers requesting their recorded material. At the opening of the film, we see/hear, between the screams of a euphoric crowd waiting for "more than 50 years," according to a lady in the documentary, for the appearance of the dolphins. "Filmed?" one asks. The other replies: "But of course..." What would it have been worth if it was not recorded—even if compulsory recording robbed the privilege of seeing? The film reveals the textures of these randomly produced images in the eagerness to record everything. At the same time, it is feed-backed by the neo-panoptic surveillance state that "results in an almost compulsive—one might say fetishistic—desire to make virtually everything available in the form of an image."[35]

We are amidst an overproduction of images, but, despite the plurality of emitters, it does not result in diversity. The liberal economy of "Likes" and the algorithmic regimes of digital cameras and hashtags modulate the ways of seeing and constructing images. This set of factors standardizes angles, frames, scenes and styles, and tends to homogenize everything we see on the web.

This sense of *dejà-vu* is the reason behind the creation of the *Insta_Repeat* (2018) project by the Dutch artist Emma Scheffer.[36] The project confronts us with zillions of travel photos. They are all practically identical with countless girls on their backs looking at gorges and roads seen from the windshield. Scheffer collects these images in several profiles from searches for specific hashtags and organizes these photos as mosaics. The result resembles a strategy used by Natalie Bookchin in the video *Mass Ornament* (2009).[37] The title of her work makes a direct reference to the work of the German cultural critic and sociologist Siegfried Kracauer (1889–1963), who coined the term in an essay on the famous troupe of choir dancers Tiller Girls. Kracauer interpreted the syncopated choreography of the chorus girls in the light of Taylorism. For him, the workers' hands in the factories corresponded to the legs of these dancers. The mass ornament was "the aesthetic reflex of the rationality to which the prevailing economic system aspires."[38]

In her work, Bookchin appropriates hundreds of YouTube videos of people dancing in front of the camera in synchronized gestures, which is a product not only of editing expertise but also of an adjustment of the bodies to a particular type of image. In this limit, these bodies are trained not only by the image that should reflect them but also by the keywords that will give them visibility. This is a phenomenon that the Brazilian artist Denise Agassi explored in works such as *Monument Online* (2007–2011), which is centered on Christ the Redeemer and *Rising Eiffel Tower* (2009–2015), videos produced in real time from searches for "tags" related to these monuments.[39]

Scheffer updates these questions, highlighting the standardization of the gaze that fits the parameters of the cameras. Her mosaics with a series of 12 sequenced travel photos that circulate on Instagram show the same landscapes and situations. It is difficult not to agree here with Jacques Rancière when he says that "the complaint is then no longer that images conceal secrets which are no longer such to anyone, but, on the contrary, that they no longer hide anything."[40] In this context, they substantially reduce the possibility of betting on a visual culture capable of engendering dissonances and ruptures concerning the images that the political and economic powers project in the public sphere.

The explosion of the cell phone market, instead of directing us to other forms of cognitive exercise and citizenship, has turned the internet into a space populated by fortified citadels. In these citadels, people live within a few popular social media applications such as WhatsApp, Twitter, Instagram, or Facebook. In them, anyone can take part, but only according to the rules prescribed by the algorithms previously programmed.[41]

*Unlooping Film* (2014), an artwork I developed by invitation of The Webby Awards,[42] approaches the ambivalences of the culture of mobility that are reflected in the production and circulation of images, exploring the universe of hashtags. The starting point was common hashtags used by groups with radically different ideological aspirations, like #macho (used by gay people and homophobes) and #WorldCup2014 (used by fans and protesters against the World Cup in Brazil).

The result is an endless slideshow based on automatic searches in the Instagram database, revealing the way the web recovers data. By doing so, *Unlooping Film* disclosed the Darwinist engine that rules social networks and paves the hashtagged app culture. As in the process of "natural selection," the strongest (most mentioned) is always the winner, the one who has more visibility.

In a countermovement to this status quo, I developed the *#QR-Comms* project in 2016. The *#QR-Comms* distribute the ten commandments for artistic creation in the network age that Mark Amerika and I created for the Buenos Aires Biennial (2002), both a remixing and redistribution of the biblical commandments.[43] At this time, we were investigating the fluidity of network identity and the narrative potential of open-source code and social software for new forms of intersubjectivity.

Embedded in QR codes, the "Comms" were projected on the vast building's LED facade of 92 meters high with an area of 3.7 thousand meters squared. The public used an app specially developed for the project to capture and decipher the QRs and share beautiful ready-to-go digital stickers with *#QR-Comms* via Twitter, Facebook, Instagram, WhatsApp, messaging, etc. The urban intervention was a commission of Galeria de Arte Digital SESI-SP and occupied the façades of the Federation of Industries of the State of São Paulo (FIESP) building in São Paulo, an icon of Brazilian architecture located at one of the city's main landmarks, Paulista Avenue (Figure 3.3).

It was rather strange to have an intervention with an open-source call and then to paradoxically have to cross all the tolls of the app stores to make available a free application with specific versions for iOS, Android, and Windows that would self-install on the devices as the camera pointed

*Figure 3.3* The *#QR_Comms* intervention at Galeria de Arte Digital do Sesc, FIESP building at Avenida Paulista, Sao Paulo (2015). Photo: Maya Messina

out to the building. Moreover, the FIESP building became the concentration point of the right-wing in the public protests that culminated with President Dilma Roussef impeachment (2016).[44] However, considering the ease with which the public interacted with the project, it confirmed the hypothesis that the cell phone would become the primary urban remote control of contemporary society and a bet in the future of open-source culture.

## Conclusion

I believe that by deconstructing the market models and risking proposals for civil and cognitive emergencies, the projects discussed herein repurpose, through art, the city as the main interface of contemporaneity. Fostering the appropriation of urban equipment, electronic panels, as in *Poetrica*, or city architecture as in *#QR-Comms*, and the establishment of new uses for camera devices, as in *// ** Code_UP* or the *Sometimes* trilogy, problematizes the ways of use and reinvents the rules of creation and distribution of images beyond the programmed circuits of social networks. Through it, we can think of new forms of public space, considering its informational territories as constitutive of the public sphere. Through this review process and upon further reflection, mobile media art could enable a re-think toward an old Aristotelian idea that man is a political being. His place is the polis (the city), not the app bubble.

## Notes

1 Wireless Application Protocol (WAP) is a technical standard for accessing information over a mobile wireless network. Introduced in 1999, it had been superseded since 2010.

2 Jonathan Crary, *24/7: Capitalismo tardio e os fins do sono [24/7: Late Capitalism and the Ends of Sleep]*, tran. Joaquim Toledo Jr. (São Paulo: Cosac Naify, 2015).

3 Byung-Chul Han, *Sociedade do cansaço* [*The Burnout Society*] (São Paulo: Editora Vozes, 2015).

4 The Southern Cone is a macro region of Latin America and includes Argentina, Brazil, Chile, Paraguay, and Uruguay. The concept of Global South, despite being known since the late 1960s, was popularized after the first decade of 2000. In 2004, the term "Global South" appeared in just 19 publications in the humanities and social sciences, but by 2013, the number had grown to 248. See Heike Pagel, Karen Ranke, Fabian Hempel, and Jonas Köhler, "The Use of the Concept 'Global South' in Social Science & Humanities," in Symposium *Globaler Süden / Global South: Kritische Perspektive*, Institut für Asien & Afrikawissenschaften, Humboldt-Universität zu Berlin, 11 July 2014, www.academia.edu/7917466/The_Use_of_the_Concept_Global_South_in_Social_Science_and_Humanities; Andrea Wolvers, Oliver Tappe, Salverda Tijo, and Schwarz Tobias, "Concepts of the Global South—Voices from Around the World." *Global South Studies Center, University of Cologne, Germany*, 2015, https://kups.ub.uni-koeln.de/6399/1/voices012015_concepts_of_the_global_south.pdf.

5 Instituto Brasileiro de Geografia e Estatística—IBGE, "Acesso à Internet e posse de telefone móvel celular para uso pessoal 2005," *IBGE*, (2007): 35, https://biblioteca.ibge.gov.br/visualizacao/livros/liv33982.pdf.

6 Núcleo de Informação e Coordenação do Ponto BR. *Survey on the use of information and communication technologies in Brazilian Households: ICT households 2017* (São Paulo: Comitê Gestor da Internet no Brasil, 2018).

7 Marcelo Neri, *The New Middle Class* (Rio de Janeiro: FGV/IBRE, 2008); Google, *Os novos donos da internet: Classe C, de conectados* (Google. Março 2015), https://think.storage.googleapis.com/intl/ALL_br/docs/novos-donos-internet-classe-c-conectados-brasil_research-studies.pdf.

8 Marcelo de Henrique Araújo and Nicolau Reinhard. "Who are the Brazilian Internet Users? An Analysis Based on Digital Skills," in *Survey on the use of information and communication technologies in Brazilian Households: ICT households 2017*, by Núcleo de Informação e Coordenação do Ponto BR, 157–67 (São Paulo: Comitê Gestor da Internet no Brasil, 2017), 160–63.

9 Jorge Werthein, "A sociedade da informação e seus desafios," *Ciência e Informação* 29, no 2 (maio-agosto 2000): 71–77.

10 Alexander R. Galloway, *Protocol: How Control Exists After Decentralization* (Cambridge MA: MIT Press, 2004).

11 Giselle Beiguelman, *Wop Art [Wap + Op art]*, 2001, http://desvirtual.com/wopart/.

12 For a detailed description and comments about the projects, see Giselle Beiguelman, "Public Art in Nomadic Contexts," in *Urban Screens Reader*, edited by Scott McQuire, Meredith Martin and Sabine Niederer (Amsterdam: Institute of Network Cultures, 2009), 179–89.

13 In Berlin, *Poetrica* was presented indoors at the digital poetry exhibition P0es1s, at Kulturforum, and in open space. In the museum space, *Poetrica* consisted of a set of large dimensions prints, a video projection, and a website. In public space, *Poetrica* was displayed on the Kurfürstendamm (Kudamm avenue) electronic billboard and in the movies, in trailer format, announcing the P0es1s exhibition through the series "ad_oetries" (ads + poetry) conceived specially for this venue by invitation of Friedrich Block, P0es1s curator. See Giselle Beiguelman, *Poetrica*, 2003, http://desvirtual.com/poetrica/.
14 See Giselle Beiguelman, "For an Aesthetics of Transmission." *First Monday*, February 2006, doi: 10.5210/fm.v0i0.1553.
15 Lucia Santaella, *Linguagens líquidas na era da mobilidade* (São Paulo: Paulus, 2007), 349–50.
16 Peter Lunenfeld, "Art Post-History: Digital Photography and Electronic Semiotics," in *Photography after Photography: Memory and Representation in the Digital Age*, edited by Hubertus Von Amelunxen, Stefan Iglhaut, Florian Rötzer, Alexis Cassel, Aktiengesellschaft Siemens, and Aktionsforum Praterinsel (Amsterdam: G+B Arts, 1996), 92–98.
17 The responsive design responds to the needs of users and their devices. The layout changes according to the screen size and device features, adapting "to the media that renders them." See Ethan Marcotte, "Responsive Web Design," *A List Apart*, 25 May 2010, http://alistapart.com/article/responsive-web-design/.
18 Katia Kwastek, *Aesthetics of Interaction in Digital Art* (Cambridge, MA: MIT Press, 2013), 107.
19 Rafael Lozano-Hemmer, *Amodal Suspensionin*, 2003, www.lozano-hemmer.com/amodal_suspension.php.
20 Fábio Duarte and Polise De Marchi, "Fantasmagorias, vitrines, infiltrações: ensaio sobre as tecnologias e a cidade," in *Mediações, tecnologia e espaço público: panorama crítico da arte em mídias móveis*, edited by Lucas Bambozzi, Marcus Bastos and Rodrigo Minelli (São Paulo: Conrad Editora do Brasil, 2009), 58.
21 See, for example, the *Light Creature* project by Brazilian architect Guto Requena that changes color as noise increases on a major avenue in São Paulo, allowing to interpret through a mobile application those colors as information about environmental pollution. The higher the number of cars, the greater the intensity of the sound, which corresponds to higher air pollution: Guto Requena, *Light Creature*, 2015, https://gutorequena.com/light-creature.
22 Milena Szafir, and Mariana [mm não eh confete] Kadlec, *MANIFESTE-SE [MOBILE WEBTV LIVE BROADCAST]*, Manifesto 21, 2006, www.manifesto21.com.br/manifestese2006/.
23 Anne Balsamo, "The Cultural Work of Public Interactives," in *A Companion to Digital Art,* edited by Christiane Paul (Oxford: Willey Blackwell, 2016), 341. For the artwork documentation, see Adriene Jenik, *Specflic*, 2003, www.specflic.net/
24 Lucia Santaella, *Pesquisa: mestrado e doutorado* (São Paulo: Hacker, 2001), 22.
25 Cetic. BR, "Destaques: TIC Domicílios 2007 Uso e Posse de Computador e Internet, Barreiras de Acesso, Uso do Celular, Intenção de aquisição." (Cetic.BR, 2008), 55, https://cetic.br/media/analises/destaques-tic-2007.pdf.
26 Ibid.
27 Antoni Abad, *megafone.net*, 2003, http://megafone.net/site/index.
28 Giselle Beiguelman, *//**Code_UP*, 2004, http://container.zkm.de/code_up/web/english/index.htm.
29 See Giselle Beiguelman, "Sometimes Always/ Sometimes Never/ Sometimes," 2005, www.desvirtual.com/sometimes-always/.
30 Hito Steyerl, "Proxy Politics: Signal and Noise." *e-Flux*, no. 60 (December 2014), www.e-flux.com/journal/60/61045/proxy-politics-signal-and-noise/.
31 Rose Eveleth, "How Many Photographs of You Are Out There In the World?" *The Atlantic*, 2 November 2015, www.theatlantic.com/technology/archive/2015/11/how-many-photographs-of-you-are-out-there-in-the-world/413389/.
32 Ivana Bentes, *Mídia-multidão: estéticas da comunicação e biopolítica* (Rio de Janeiro: Mauad, 2015), 105–18.
33 Marcelo Pedroso (dir), *Pacific*, www.youtube.com/watch?v=bY-nRNBZNTs. 2009.
34 Axel Bruns defines the users of web 2.0 as produsers because they are producers and users. See Axel Bruns, "From Prosumer to Produser: Understanding User-Led Content Creation," *Produsage.org*. 30 August 2009, http://produsage.org/node/67.
35 French philosopher Michel Foucault used the panopticon to explain, in *Discipline and Punishment* (1975), how the disciplinary model developed to control society in the nineteenth century. In this control system there is an asymmetrical system of surveillance where the subject is seen, but never sees who watch him/her. In the neo-panoptical system described by Timothy Druckery, there is a compulsory desire to watch and being watched. Timothy Druckrey, "Instability and Dispersion," in *Overexposed: Essays on Contemporary Photography*, edited by Carol Squiers (New York: The New York Press, 2000), 94, 93–104.
36 Scheffer, Emma, *Insta_Repeat*, Instagram Art Project, 2018, www.instagram.com/insta_repeat/

37 Natalie Bookchin, *Mass Ornament*, Natalie Bookchin, 2009, https://bookchin.net/projects/mass-ornament/, accessed 1 June 2019.

38 Siegfried Kracauer, *The Mass Ornament: Weimar Essays/SiegfriedKracauer, translated, edited, and with an introduction by Thomas Y. Levin* (Cambridge, MA: Harvard University Press, 1995), 79.

39 Denise Agassi, *Vista On, Vista Off*, midiamagia.net, 2012, http://midiamagia.net/projetos/vista-on-vista-off/

40 Jacques Rancière, *The Future of the Image*, trans. Gregory Elliott (New York: Verso Books, 2009), 22.

41 Martin Warnke, "Databases as Citadels in the Web 2.0," in *Unlike Us Reader: Social Media Monopolies and Their Alternatives*, edited by Geert Lovink and Miriam Rasch (Amsterdam: Institute of Network Cultures, 2012), 86, 76–88.

42 *Unlooping Film* (2014) presented at The Web at 25, an exhibition organized by the Webby Awards, was sponsored by Sesc-SP and exhibited as an installation in the Multitude show, curated by Lucas Bambozzi. See Giselle Beiguelman, *Unlooping Film,* 2014, http://desvirtual.com/multitude/.

43 The 10Comms are: I am the Net who linked thee out of the purgatory of thy Interface; Thou shalt have no other Net before me; Thou shalt take every name in vain; Honour thy codes and thy sources, that thou mayst be longlived upon the no-man's-land which thy Web will give thee; Thou shalt kill all spam; Thou shalt adulterate everything; Thou shalt not be inspired; Remember that thou keep thy passwords that thou mayst be logged in thy network; Thou shalt not bear false consciousness in all media environments; Thou shalt covet thy neighbors' source code. See Giselle Beiguelman, *#QR-Comms*, Vimeo, 2015, https://vimeo.com/136340534.

44 The impeachment of President Dilma Roussef was a controversial process that resulted in a coup d'etat widely publicized in the international press. See, for example: Amanda Taub, "All Impeachments Are Political. But Was Brazil's Something More Sinister?" *The New York Times*, 31 August 2016, https://nyti.ms/2loe5b0.

# 4

# FROM EARLY SOUNDINGS TO LOCATIVE LISTENING IN MOBILE MEDIA ART

*Cat Hope*

Sound has been an ongoing concern in mobile media art, where listening, speaking and the creation of music and sound art have been pivotal drivers for the ongoing development of the form. From the early recorded soundscapes of Canadian sound artist Barry Truax to the complex sound-based multimedia walks of British artist Janet Cardiff, early trends that established a path for the way sound is engaged in mobile media art today are outlined. The key traditions of mobile sound art are established around the locative and public aspects of works, but also the way sound is engaged artistically and conceptually in respect to mobility, tracing this back to early radio and the nexus of music and sound.

Mobile technologies have created new ways to expand our understanding of sound in urban public spaces and the natural environment through the use of internet connectivity, compact data storage, and access to high quality, portable recording, and playback equipment. Using our voice to control the light switches in our home, or having directions spoken to us by John Cleese as we navigate remote road and cycle ways, were the stuff of science fiction not so long ago. Yet, it is not only electronic technologies that have changed the way we become mobile—an ever-developing understanding of our bodies has seen art embedded in and shared between us. Mona Hartoum's performance art work *Look No Body!* (1981) filmed audiences in the bathroom with small cameras after she had them drink water. Eduardo Kac's *Time Capsule* (1997) has the artist embed an Radio-frequency identification (RFID) chip into his body and Zoran Todorovic's *Algama* (2002–2005) involved washing of people using soap made from the artists body fat.

The burgeoning area of sound studies has expanded our understanding of sound as artwork by considering sound as relevant to space, materiality and recording, focussing on what Salomé Voegelin calls "the transient ephemerality of sonic materiality and subjectivity."[1]

This chapter discusses the way this materiality and subjectivity is facilitated and highlighted through mobile media art practices, beginning with a brief examination of tools that have enabled sound to become mobile via recording, playback, and transmission. This is followed by a discussion around the importance of the work of soundscape artists and how the miniaturization of technology assisted artists to get out of the studio and into landscape. The importance of telecommunications and mobile telephony is then examined, leading to a discussion of tools that have facilitated sound mobility. This is proceeded by an examination of the relationship between sound and space in sound-based artworks, given the impact of mobile technologies and their ability to transform listening practices. It then goes on to propose that the engagement of sensors, locative, and mapping technologies have revolutionized the way we listen to music.

## Recording, Playback and Transmission

Music has itself been mobile for hundreds of years, with travelling minstrels, processions and other music productions performing on portable instruments as part of most cultures worldwide. What signals modern mobile sound art and music making, however, is the engagement of tools not designed specifically for that purpose. Mobile phones, for example, were designed to expedite phone calls, not to create artworks or act as musical instruments. Further, the invention of new ways of disseminating music and sound, beginning with radio broadcasting and later audio recording, has changed the way we engage with music significantly. Our voices and designed musical instruments are no longer the only way to create or reproduce a musical idea, and music welcomes all possible sounds as part of its construction—reproduced and shared in an unlimited array of different methods and locations.

The development of the radio from a large piece of wooden furniture with a speaker inside, to the handheld plastic portable transistor device with headphones connected, into the internet streaming medium we see today, has provided an important foundation for the development of mobile sound art. Radio maps a trajectory from fixed to mobile reception, as well as the impact of hard media storage moving to cloud computing. The disembodied voice and music performances broadcast over radio are instantaneously dislocated from their physical location of production, to floating in the "ether" of wireless communication. This provided a fundamental change to the way people engaged with listening and performance. Broadcasts from a location situated hundreds of miles away being transmitted to any place or space has seen opportunities for interactivity, mobility, and an important disassociation from music and sound art "belonging" to anywhere—concert halls, music studios, or even site-specific locations.

Radio art continues to flourish with artists such as New Zealand's Sally Ann McIntyre, who uses narrowcast[2] transmissions via portable transistor radios to create installation pieces such as *Twin signals at Silver Stream (fragments of a landscape for specimens #50.766 & #50.767)* (2016–2018), a narrowcast work for field recordings, small radius Mini-FM transmissions and archival materials.[3] The work features the transmissions of a recording made while visiting male and female examples of taxidermized, extinct New Zealand birds in a museum in Vienna, Austria—referred to in the title as "specimens #50.766 & #50.767." The artist calls these recordings "recorded silences," that she then transmits to portable radios (see Figure 4.1) into the original habitat of the bird and again later

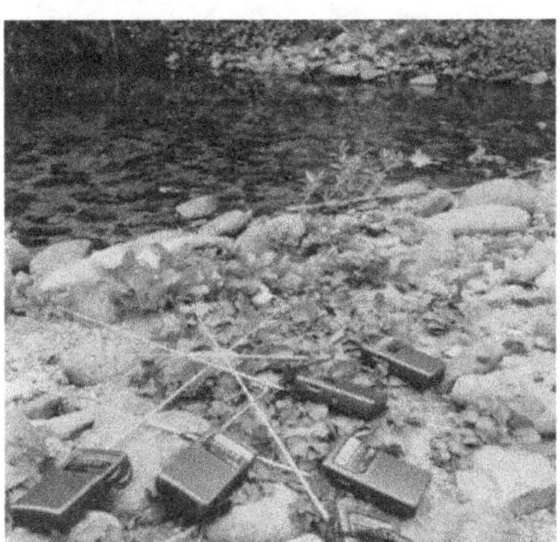

*Figure 4.1* Portable radios by Silver Stream, South Island, New Zealand, as part of Sally Ann McIntyre's radio work, *Twin signals at Silver Stream (fragments of a landscape for specimens #50.766 & #50.767)* (2016–2018). Photo credit: Sally Ann McIntyre

to a gallery setting where radios are installed alongside other archival components. The work interleaves the ghostly and airborne presence of radio by re-iterating the absence of another once airborne species of bird, creating a delicate commentary on time, place, and the nature of experience.

The advent of audio recording, similarly, expanded upon this separation of the creator from its output, and led to a range of mobile media devices. Electrical recording, as opposed to the previous acoustic methods developed in the late nineteenth century, saw sound recorded and reproduced with ease, and developed hand in hand with telecommunications technology that saw a range of tools and media developed for the storage and reproduction of recordings.

The Boombox, a portable music playback station with radio but also music media such as tapes and Compact Discs, grew even more opportunities to bring the human voice and music out of concert halls and into public space, with powerful speakers spilling sounds into the environment on battery power. Just as radio playback devices shrunk in size as technology developed, the rather cumbersome Boomboxes invented in 1966 transformed into more personal playback systems, epitomized in the original tape Walkman, leading to the iPod, and onto a music listening experience where a dedicated playback device is no longer really necessary.

## Portable Tools, Expanded Listening

This development of portable playback mirrored advancements in the technology for mobile recording where compact high-quality recording equipment and media could be easily transported to remote locations. This facilitated the soundscape movement as led by Canadian artists such as Barry Truax and Hildergard Westerkamp. "Soundscape" is a broad term that can refer to any recording that creates the sensation of a particular acoustic environment, or a composition made from sounds of an environment.[4]

The *World Soundscape Project*[5]—initiated by Truax, Westerkamp, R. Murray Schafer, and others in the late 1960s—played an important role in comprehending the sounds around us through a dedicated listening experience, bringing environmental sounds into the realm of musical understanding, and thus the entire landscape to the materials of composition. It also played an important role in drawing attention to urban development and its impact on the sounds of our daily lives. These soundscape recordings were a key development in the appreciation of "found sounds" as music, which opened the way for a range of sound art where many defining parameters of music—such as pitch, formal structure and harmonic considerations—were no longer necessary components in sound-based artworks.

The miniaturization of consumer electronics, including the increasing capacity of digital storage, has seen small but powerful audio players and applications for the composition of music. The mobility of much sound generating media was driven by the invention of the computer microprocessor that first appeared in telecommunication devices in 1971[6] and sparked a range of digital developments that enabled a rapid growth in mobile sound art and music. This new smaller computing component facilitated the digital compression, storage, and distribution of audio files, which saw a plethora of works using portable consumer-level playback devices.

Janet Cardiff's *Forest Walk* (1991),[7] a 12-minute piece that accompanies a walk through a planned forest pathway, is an early example of a sound work dependent on mobile media. Cardiff's transmission of found sounds, voice, and composed music via headphones that travel with the participant creates an intensely personal experience that would be impossible if large speakers placed in the forest were disseminating the same audio. For Cardiff, this piece began a long trajectory of works known as "sound walk" that explore the landscape and the displacement of time within them, creating remote and transient experiences that play the present against the past and engaging with technology as it develops. More recent works by Cardiff, such as *The City of Forking Paths* (2014)[8] with collaborator George Bures Miller, engage portable vision as well as sound as the artists include fictional scenes depicted on mobile phones together with the actual physical locations the participants journey through.

## Beyond Telecommunications

The development of mobile telecommunications, including mobile phone handsets, powerful communication networks, the internet and the Global Positioning Systems (GPS), has revolutionized the possibility for media to be mobile. The evolution of the mobile phone, since it first entered the consumer market in Japan in 1979, has seen the voice disembodied in other ways such as connection to the internet and texting in the 1990s and video calls in the 2000s. Mobile phone handsets offer a range of functionalities that augment radio, walkie-talkies, and landline phones in the making and distribution of what Frank Popper calls "communication art," defined by six characteristics—staging physical presence at distance; telescoping the immediate and the delayed; focussing on the playfulness of interactivity; combining memory and real time; and promoting planetary communication and the encouragement of a detailed study of human social groupings.[9] In 1969, the Chicago Museum of Contemporary Art staged an exhibition called *Art by Telephone* where 36 artists were asked to call the museum via telephone with instructions regarding their contribution to the show.[10] While the telephone at this stage was not itself mobile, it mobilized the artist voice in a new way.

British art collective The Disembodied Art Gallery created a range of works that explored conceptual telecommunication-based art. *Babble* (1993) is a work where over 70 different contributions were "phoned in" from around the world and recorded on an answering machine that began playing when people entered the gallery. This work exemplifies the use of telephones to explore "absent presence," where the voice is removed from and repositioned in space and time, making it mobile.[11] Linking the world through powerful satellite communications, the evolution of the telephone to be truly mobile has facilitated a playful interactive element to artworks, using a tool available to most people. Mobile phones have assisted in the creation of hybrid public spaces, where the development of technological systems has seen sound facilitate a transformation of our perception of reality to some extent.

Telecommunications technology has enabled the creation of other devices that are not network dependent in the way as the telephone. Handheld voice recorders, tablet computers, and Personal Digital Assistants (PDAs) feature technology similar to those found in mobile phone handsets that have also been adapted and engaged as controllers for audio, at times augmented by hacking firmware and software in a search for extended functionality. Sound artist Atau Tanaka created an accelerometer-based custom-made augmented PDA to control streaming audio, used in participatory works such *Malleable Mobile Music* (2004),[12] where dynamic location-based and peer-to-peer networked remixing are facilitated, creating what the author calls a "social remix."[13] The author's work *Pickpocket* (2005) featured 40 handheld voice recorders mounted in a frame, featuring modified software that enables the devices to record and playback intermittently (Figure 4.2). The work "listens" and "speaks" using the portable voice recorder technologys as situating the recorders into the large gilt frame highlights the emphasis on looking in the gallery space.

However, it is the mobile phone that has been consistently featured in the domain of music. Golan Levin's *Dialtones: A Telesymphony* (2001) is one of first works to use mobile phones in a concert setting, engaging audience members' mobile phones to contribute parts to a musical work. In this piece, a computer would "call" the phones so that a range of custom ringtones installed earlier could be heard, turning the mobile phones into musical instruments in their own right.[14] Works like this, in conjunction with a range of software developments, have led to the formation of a plethora of repertoire-based mobile phone orchestras, starting with American artists' Ge Wang's *MoPho Orchestra*, founded at Stanford University in 2007.[15] These orchestras engage a wide range of approaches to music making, often engaging with external computer's driving behaviours.

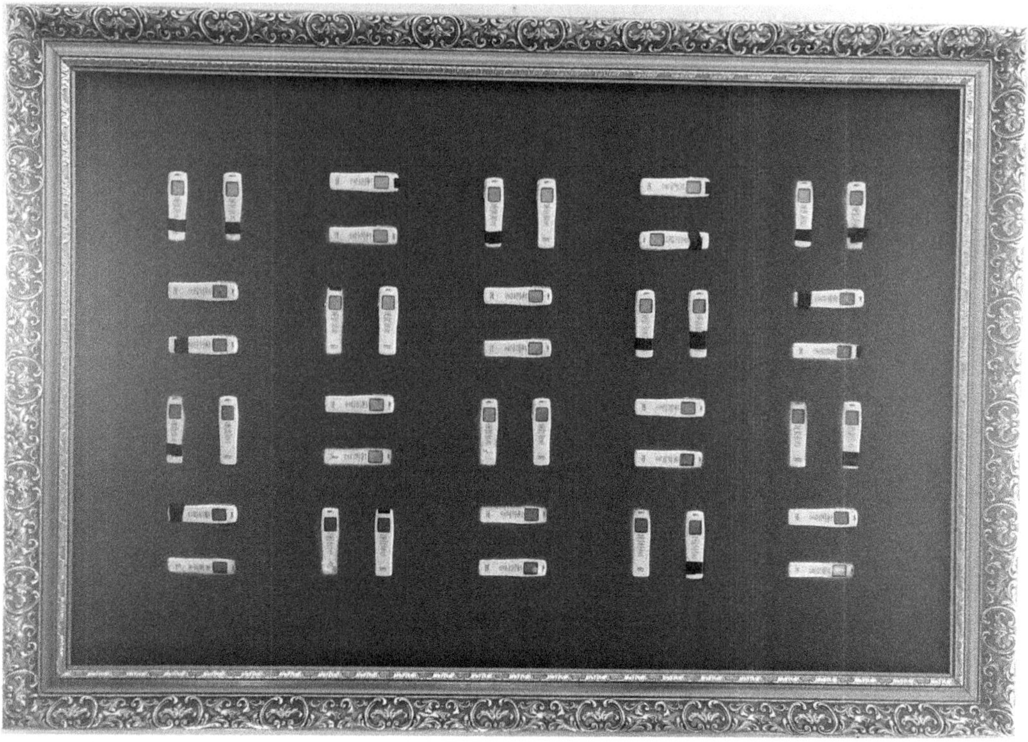

*Figure 4.2* Cat Hope's *Pickpocket* (2005) at the John Curtin Art Gallery, as part of the Biennale of Electronica Art Perth (BEAP), Australia. Photo credit: Cat Hope

Acoustic music compositions including mobile phone "parts" in scored music compositions continue to be made. Chinese composer Tan Dun's *Passacagilia: Secret of Wind and Birds* (2015), for mobile phones and orchestra, features audiences' and orchestra members' phones playing back birdcalls imitated by Chinese traditional instruments. The audience, accesses parts as streaming audio from a web site hosted by the publisher by using instructions outlined in the concert programme. The audience is "called upon" at the appropriate moment in the piece to contribute. Australian composer Miriama Young's *Grey Ghost* (2017) is a composition for piano and electronic media where the audience download a mobile phone application *SyncSound*[16] to find and stream their "part" (Figure 4.3) of the composition that consists of field recordings of endangered bird calls mixed with music created by the composer. Works like these can be stymied by issues around compatibility with different mobile phone operating systems. For example, the *SyncSound* application is only available for iPhone operating systems at the time of print, so any phones using other operating system are not supported.

Greg Schiemer's *Pocket Gamelan* (2003) is a performance interface for mobile phones and is an early example of a work where musical interaction between players is facilitated via wireless Bluetooth communication.[17] The introduction of wireless technologies such as Bluetooth were key to the development of devices being able to communicate between each other in physical space, permitting free movement within the range of Bluetooth casting. *Pocket Gamelan* is designed for performance of microtonal music by large ensembles of non-expert players, and works in conjunction with a computer that sends audio to the different mobile phones. Microtonal music is usually considered difficult to perform by traditional instruments, so this work creates an alternative approach to creating microtonal sound worlds. Participants are encouraged to wave their mobile phones in the air during the work creating a unique spatial quality to the sound created by the constant

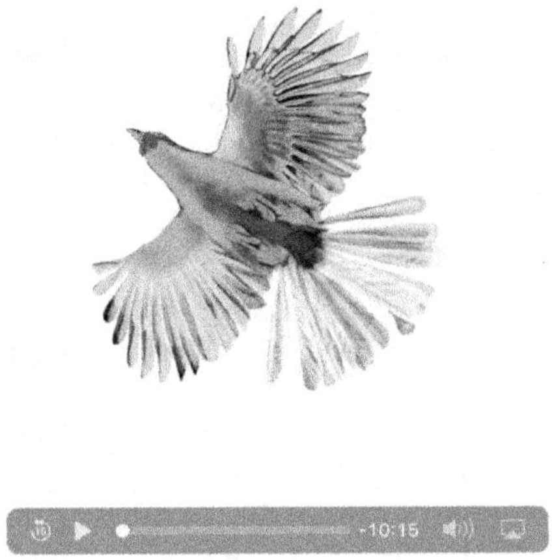


*Figure 4.3* A screenshot of the interface for the *SyncSound* application used to playback audio as part of Miriama Young's composition *Grey Ghost* (2017). Photo credit: Miriama Young

motion of the handsets. As in the Dun and Young works, the positioning of the handsets—by performers or audience participants—creates a way of spreading multiple low-volume sounds over a large space, creating a detailed multi-speaker system with a unique audio quality defined by the small speakers typical of mobile phones.

The audio quality of mobile media playback—often a result of miniaturization—has been a defining challenge for sound artists. Therefore, the most successful projects are those where the limited frequency range of the small speakers and microphones common in devices are used deliberately. The speakers on mobile devices still provide relatively poor sound recording and reproduction, limited largely by the size of the speaker. While speaker technology is constantly evolving, many artists have made this poor quality a feature, rather than a lack. *Sky Ear* (2004) by Usman Haque was a one-night event in which a glowing "cloud" of mobile phones attached to helium balloons was released into the air. Audiences call the cloud using numbers provided, enabling them to listen to the sounds of the sky that includes sounds of the atmospheric electromagnetic phenomena that are the audible equivalent of the Northern Lights.[18] The frequency range of the sounds fits comfortably into the limited and high-frequency centric range of mobile phone speakers.

## Tracking Mobility

In addition to standardized audio signal input and output access on most mobile phones, sophisticated sensor technologies such as cameras, microphones, accelerometers, GPS, and multi-touch screens have become common. These technologies enable in new ways of seeing, sensing, and listening to the world around us. Mobile phones are almost considered musical instruments and digital audio workstations in their own right by providing highly programmable multimedia platforms where the composition, arrangement, and interpretation of sound can be undertaken and reproduced.

Some artists use the mobile phone's microphone as a way to "listen" to the environment, creating an augmented listening experience for users. British company Reality Jockey Ltd (2008–2013) claimed to develop a new genre of non-linear music called Reactive music, where music is affected by events occurring in the real life of the listener. Their software application, *RjDj*, adapts to a listener and their environment utilizing the built-in sensors of mobile phones.[19] Similar to the way the structure of video game music is determined by choices made in the game, the software creates and plays music compositions that are influenced by real-time user data collected through these sensors.

Some mobile phone applications mirror compositional processes that exist on other platforms. The mobile phone application *Bloom* (2008), created by ambient composer Brian Eno and Peter Chilvers, is a generative music application that uses the touch screen of the phone or tablet computer to create a melody that plays back in a loop. As Eno points out, "You can play it, and you can watch it play itself."[20] Instruments can also be emulated on mobile phones, leading to use in concert performances.

The Theremin, an electronic musical instrument developed in 1919 that relies on the hand movements of the performer, is adapted to the phone by using the built in accelerometer to interpret gesture into pitch and volume much like the original instrument. The now defunct *ThereminVox* application[21] used different tilt angles to control volume on one axis and pitch on the other. Creating a portable Theremin alternative with a sound quite similar to the original, the application was used in the recreation of some of the first music written for the Theremin, by Australian composer Percy Grainger. *Free Music 1* (1936) and *Free Music 2* (1937) were performed by the Australian new music ensemble Decibel first on mobile phones plugged into external speakers, then on iPads using inbuilt speakers.[22] The performance was facilitated by the reworking of the score, enabling it to be put into motion and read on networked tablet computers, using the *Decibel ScorePlayer* (2013) application developed within the ensemble.[23]

In addition to the plethora of keyboard, synth, and drum machine applications and instrument emulations, there have also been numerous projects to turn mobile phones into original instruments in their own right. Ge Wang's *Ocaraina* application[24] uses breath on the microphone of a mobile phone as a trigger for pitches selected on the mobile phone screen. A synthesized "wind instrument" sound is created but the experience of playing it aims to resemble the playing an actual wind instrument (Figure 4.4).

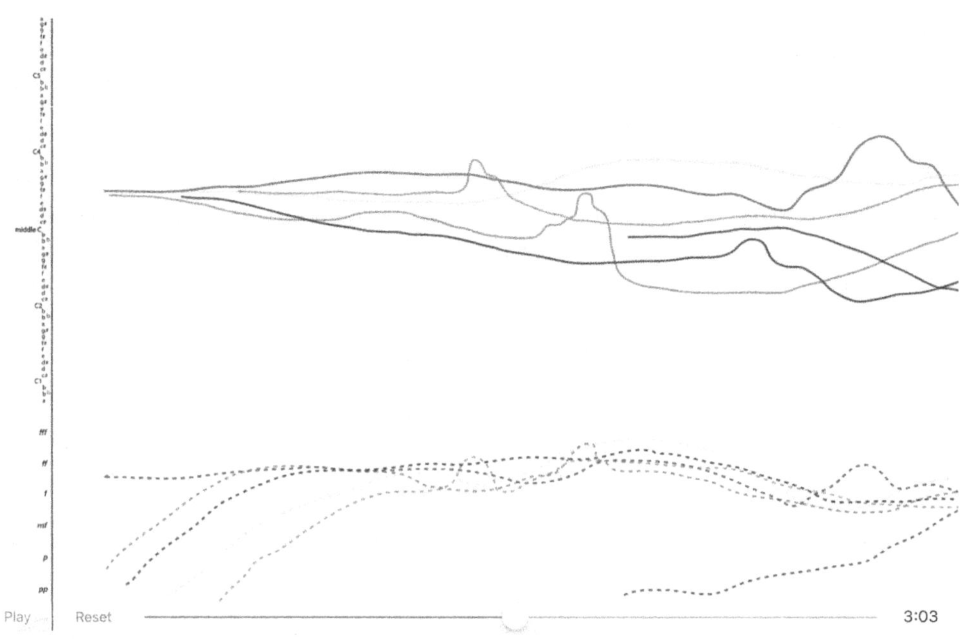


*Figure 4.4* An iPad screenshot from the reworked score of Percy Grainger's *Free Music No. 2* (1937), presented to performers in motion. Each "part" is in a different color, the top group of notation representing pitch and the bottom representing volume. The score moves past the vertical key on the right, which is the point of performance.

## Participation via Sound in Space

Mobile phones highlight the potential of human computer interaction in the creation of new works and have played a key role in the proliferation of what has become known as "mobile music."[25] The internet and other ad hoc peer-to-peer and distributed networks have enabled groups of users—artists, participants or audiences—to work together with music and sound art irrespective of location, creating a tension between sound and space that was originally hinted at in the soundscapes mentioned earlier.

The sound and space tension can be engaged to draw attention to sounds from far away, in order to increase understanding and empathy for environmental concerns. Leah Barclay's augmented reality project *Aurality* (2017) uses a downloadable phone application that engages with GPS to access 100 soundscapes from rainforests, rivers, and reefs in Queensland, Australia (Figure 2, color insert). The phone becomes a sonic compass, where the sounds are updated through time to reflect environmental change.[26]

British group Blast Theory has created a significant body of work focussed on audience participant networks and has relied on handheld computers and wireless devices to facilitate game play in public spaces. Their first collaboration, *Can You See Me Now?* (2001), featured participants from anywhere in the world playing online games with members of Blast Theory, using tracking satellites but also handheld walkie talkies to communicate with the network of participants. Walkie-talkies were later replaced with mobile phones in works such as *I Like Frank* (2004), where players in the real city chat with players in a virtual one as they search for the character Frank.[27] These works test the possibilities of hybrid spaces by juxtaposing photographs and sound recordings against real places and sounds.[28]

Audience participation and collaborative music making are aspects strongly supported by engagement with mobile media. While Blast Theory explores the juxtaposition of real and virtual locations in works such as *I Like Frank*, mobile listening and sharing are explored in Mark Shepard's *Tactical Sound Garden* (2009). This work uses an open-source software platform for cultivating public "sound gardens" in contemporary cities, drawing from the culture of urban community gardening to encourage a participatory environment where degrees of privacy and publicity are explored.[29] It uses gardening terminology—words such as planting and pruning—to describe audio functions and editing for a collaborative community of audio editors and listeners, who create what Shepard calls a "sonic topography of urban public space."[30] Mobile media has enabled this kind of collaborative music making in more traditional music formats. *Cellphonia* (2006) is a locative-based karaoke opera devised by Steve Bull, Scot Gresham-Lancaster, and Tim Perkins, where participants choose a song to sing from music delivered to their mobile phone in styles that have been algorithmically generated. The libretto is delivered via RSS newsfeeds to participants' mobile phones, and a variety of versions of the work have been created.[31]

*Cellphonia* aims to enable a participatory operatic experience, irrespective of audience location. Sound can provide listens with a less literal description of experiencing place. Jessica Thompson's *Triangulation Device* (2014–2015) is an Android application that invites a pair of mobile phone users to collaborate and generate improvised networked soundscapes by translating the physical distances between users into atmospheric soundscapes. These scapes unfold and change in response to the users' movement in relation to their original position, creating recognition of location change.

## Sensing, Sounding and Mapping

American composer Alvin Lucier used handheld eco-location devices for his 1967 work *Vespers*. The devices, known as *Sondols*, are held by participants who wander through space. They send out streams of crisp electronic clicks that are designed to echo against objects and were originally designed for underwater use. The work creates what Lucier calls "very slow audio photographs of that space,"[32] where the sound can describe aspects of our environment.

Wearable and sensor technology has also introduced exciting possibilities to sonic works created while moving through space. *Sonic City* (2003), was created by Lalya Gayle, Lars Erik Holmquist, Ramia Mazé, Margot Jacobs, and Daniel Skoglund at the Swedish Institute of Computer Science, and it uses a wearable system for creating electronic music by sensing bodily movement and environmental parameters. The sensors were built into clothing, enabling the passive listening experience to become more active and relative to physical experiences.[33]

Mobility has also informed audio speaker design with most surfaces able to be turned into speakers with the addition of surface transducers. These are transducers that when attached to objects or surfaces activate them to create sound; whereas, speakers, use a built-in cone to do so. American artist Spencer Toepel's sound installation *Listening Glass* (2014) explores the sonic reproductive quality of twelve surfaces by attaching transducers to them. Visitors experience a continuous live audio stream from a nature reserve via the filtering properties of these different surfaces. *Slab* (2010), by Adriano Abbado and Stefanie L Ku, features six vibrating plexiglass slabs that are activated by transducers, turning the slabs into interactive musical instruments as they respond to audience proximity.[34]

The Raspberry Pi, introduced to the market in 2012, provides an example of how miniaturization of computing can be engaged for mobile audio reproduction. Not much larger than a credit card, the Raspberry Pi is a computer powered by a standard nine-volt battery running similar software to that of a basic laptop computer. The Bicrophonic Research Institute—consisting of British artists Kaffe Mathews and David Griffiths—conceived of the *Sonic Bike* project in 2006. The project started with a fleet of bicycles fitted with speakers on the front that face the rider, which went on to play audio "found" by a GPS tracking audio via the Raspberry Pi3 computer on the back. Compositions are mapped to this system at different locations, and as the bicycle is ridden through the locations, different sounds or instructions are transmitted to the bicycle. As a networked, internet free project, it has evolved to include further iterations such as the *Buzz Bike* (reclining, vibrating bikes) and the *Sensory Bike* (which includes live music interaction).[35]

Quick Response (QR) codes have been another facilitator of mobile art. These are images that virtually "point" to sounds hosted elsewhere from anywhere, an image can be shared. QR codes are widely used to convey URLs and other short texts through camera-based smartphones. A variety of free tools exist to generate and read these codes that are presented as a black on white graphic. German artist Akutsk creates graffiti QR codes, which the artist names "fonografitti," to link to recordings of an improvisation that occurred at that location, in a project entitled *Ceci n'est pas une pub* (2012).[36] The codes are adorned with colourful graffiti, often suggesting visually what may be pointed to aurally.

QR codes help us to find sound in unexpected places, but there is also sound art that is built into the most personal of mobile media, our own bodies. Performance artist Stelarc's project *EAR ON ARM* (2008) has seen him construct an extra ear on his forearm that intends to transmit as well as listen to sound, with potential to connect to the internet.[37] Rich Lee, as part of the US-based collective Grindhouse Wetwares, prototyped the first "internal headphones" in 2013 by embedding magnets in each ear enabling listening using electromagnetic signals via bone conduction.[38] Implant technologies will see the possibilities of mobile media expand further, which could signal another new generation of mobile sound works.

## Conclusion

Without a doubt, mobile media has revolutionized sound art and music for both practitioners and listeners: it has enabled it to reach beyond a single source of sonic reproduction and be shared beyond and between audiences across distances that can be difficult to comprehend. It has challenged how we understand music. It has created a thriving culture of interactive practice and grown the possibilities for audience interaction. It has democratized music making in the Western world, offering up tools that most people can access, enabling the sense of play music can bring. Sound promises to hold more influence in contemporary life than the visual media that has saturated it in recent times. Mobile media has brought us closer to the sounds of the world and will continue to enable us to reconsider our experience of it with the very tools we use to navigate our way through.

## Notes

1 Salomé Voegelin, *Sonic Possible Worlds: Hearing the Continuum of Sound* (London and New York: Bloomsbury Academic Publishing, 2014).
2 Narrowcasting, as opposed to broadcasting, is the transmission of information to a niche or smaller audience, rather than the broader public at large, usually facilitated by small transmission units.
3 Sally Ann McIntyre, Twin signals at *Silver* Stream (fragments of a landscape for specimens #50.766 & #50.767), artwork, http://radiocegeste.blogspot.com/2018/11/twin-signals-at-silver-stream-fragments.html.
4 Barry Truax, "Electroacoustic Music and the Soundscape: The Inner and the Outer World," in *Companion to Contemporary Musical Thought*, edited by John Paynter (Routledge, 1992), 374–98.
5 Barry Truax and Hildegard Westerkamp, *The World Soundscape Project*, artwork, https://www.sfu.ca/~truax/wsp.html.
6 Cat Hope and John Charles Ryan, *Digital Arts: An Introduction to New Media* (New York: Bloomsbury Academic Publishing, 2014).
7 Janet Cardiff, *Forest Walk*, artwork (1991), www.cardiffmiller.com/artworks/walks/forest.html.
8 Janet Cardiff and George Bures Miller, *The City of Forking Paths*, artwork (2014), www.cardiffmiller.com/artworks/walks/forking_paths.html.
9 Frank Popper, *Art of the Electronic Age* (New York: Harry N. Abrams, 1993), 127.
10 Adriana de Souza e Silva, "From Cyber to Hybrid: Mobile Technologies as Interfaces of Hybrid Spaces," *Space and Culture* 9, no. 3 (2006): 261–78, doi: 10.1177/1206331206289022; Adriana de Souza e Silva, "Art by Telephone: From Static to Mobile Interfaces," *Leonardo Electronic Almanac* 12, no. 10 (October 2004), https://test.leoalmanac.org/wp-content/uploads/2012/07/LEA-v12-n10.pdf.
11 Ibid., 47.
12 Atau Tanaka, *Malleable Mobile Music*, artwork, (2004), http://ataut.net/site/Malleable-Mobile-Music.
13 Atau Tanaka, "Mobile Music Making," NIME 04, Proceedings of the *2004 Conference on New Interfaces for Musical Expression* (Hamamatsue, Japan, 2004), 145.
14 See Golan Levin's interview in this Companion, introducing this section.
15 Ge Wang, Georg Essl and Henri Pentinnen, "MoPhO: Do Mobile Phones Dream of Electric Orchestras?" in *Proceedings of the International Computer Music Conference* (Belfast, Northern Ireland: ICMC, 2008).
16 SyncSound, software application, https://apps.apple.com/nz/app/syncsound/id1249173344.
17 Greg Schiemer and Mark Havryliv, "Pocket Gamelan: Tuneable Trajectories for Flying Sources in Mandala 3 and Mandala 4," in *Proceedings of the 2006 Conference on New Interfaces for Musical Expr*ession (Paris, France, 2006), 37, www.researchgate.net/publication/221164883_Pocket_Gamelan_Tuneable_trajectories_for_flying_sources.
18 Cat Hope, "Sound Art/Mobile Art," in *Proceedings of the Inaugural Totally Huge New Music Festival Conference* (Perth: Tura New Music, 2005), 42–48, https://ro.ecu.edu.au/csound/7/.
19 David Barnard, Joachim Bondo, Dan Burcaw, Tim Novikoff, Craig Kemper, Chris Parrish and Keith Peters, *iPhone User Interface Design Projects* (New York: Apress, 2009), 235–38.
20 Brian Eno, *Bloom*, Software Application (2008), https://itunes.apple.com/us/app/bloom/id292792586?mt=8&ign-mpt=uo%3D6.
21 Paisley Shirt Applications, *ThereminVox*, Software Application (2012).
22 Cat Hope, "Reading 'Free Music:' Adapting Percy Grainger's 'Free Music' Scores for Live Performance," In *Proceedings of the 2015 WA Chapter of MSA Symposium on Music Performance and Analysis*, edited by Jonathon R. Paget, Victoria Rogers, Nicholas Bannan, Paul HopWood, and Krista Low (ECU Books, 2017), 140–52, http://ro.ecu.edu.au/cgi/viewcontent.cgi?article=1005&context=ecubooks.
23 *Decibel ScorePlayer*, Software Application (2013), https://apps.apple.com/au/app/decibel-scoreplayer/id622591851.
24 Wang "MoPho," 493.

25 Layla Gaye, Ramia Mazé, and Lars Erik Holmquist, "Sonic City: The Urban Environment as a Musical Interface," in *Proceedings of the Conference on New Interfaces for Musical Expression*, (Montreal, Canada, 2003), 109–15.
26 Leah Barclay, "Aurality," AR Sound Project, www.auralitylab.com/.
27 Blast Theory, *I Like Frank*, artwork, (2004), www.blasttheory.co.uk/projects/i-like-frank/.
28 Please see Blast Theory interview in section two of this Companion for further project discussion.
29 Mark Shepard, *The Tactical Sound Garden*, sound installation, (2009), www.leoalmanac.org/leonardo-electronic-almanac-volume-14-no-3-4-june-july-2006/.
30 Ibid.
31 Steve Bull, *Cellphonia*, artwork (2006), http://cellphonia.org/listen/.
32 Mathew Guererri, "Sound Is Messenger for Composer Lucier," *The Boston Globe*, 28 October 2011, www.bostonglobe.com/arts/music/2011/10/28/sound-messenger-for-composer-lucier/oONV-JVKa1wdVB7pfc2fTpM/story.html.
33 Gaye et al., *Sonic City,* 1.
34 Adriano Abbado, *Slabs*, AudioVisual installation (2010), www.noisegrains.com/?page_id=5.
35 Ibid.
36 CasperHerdanezCordez,"Cecine'sunepub:ThisIsNotaCommercial."Building*SoundCollectives*.30August 2012, https://cultural-sustainability.eu/2012/08/30/ceci-nest-pas-une-pub-this-is-not-a-commercial/.
37 Stelarc, *EAR ON ARM*, artwork (2008), https://stelarc.org/?catID=20242.
38 Leslie Katz. "Surgically Implanted Headphones Are Literally 'In-Ear,'" *C|Net*, 28 June 2013, www.cnet.com/news/surgically-implanted-headphones-are-literally-in-ear/.

# SECTION TWO

# Mobile Media Art Practice

# 5

# UNCOMFORTABLE INTERACTIONS

## *Blast Theory's Matt Adams* in Conversation with *Rowan Wilken*

Blast Theory is an internationally renowned collaborative art group based in Brighton, England, led by Matt Adams, Ju Row Farr, and Nick Tandavanitj.[1] The group has a long-standing interest in examining issues of alienation and otherness through their work—exploring and fostering "uncomfortable interactions"[2] between relative and complete strangers (Figure 5.1).

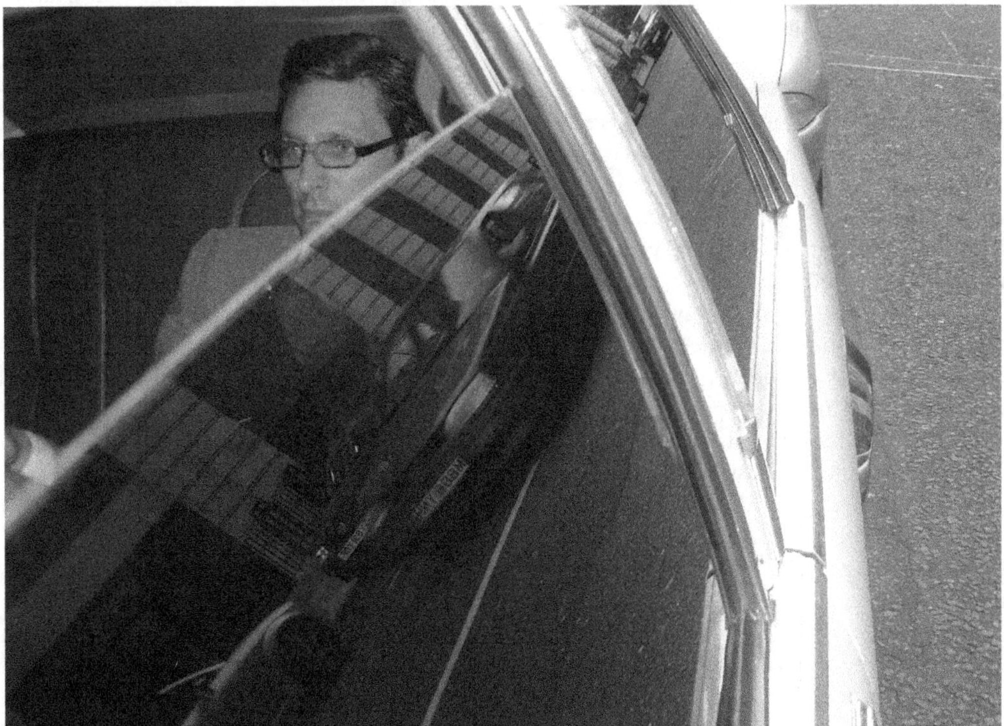

*Figure 5.1* Blast Theory, *Uncle Roy All Around You* (2003). Photo credit: Blast Theory

One of the reasons Blast Theory's work has proven so successful, and continues to resonate so strongly, is that it often speaks to—and provokes reflective critical engagement with—longstanding tensions within urban social life and technology use between the paradoxes of loneliness/togetherness, alienation/proximity, and of the desire for avoidance of others and/versus possibilities for encounters with others. In social theory, for example, we see a particular tension between, on the one hand, the characterization of city life as marked by anomie and alienation, as the very epitome of "loneliness in togetherness,"[3] and where the urban subject falls silent and withdraws,[4] and, on the other hand, a view of the city as a "productively heterogenous space"[5] where it is possible for the urban dweller to take pleasure "in being drawn out of oneself."[6] A similar tension is repeated in early scholarship on mobile phones and mobile media where these devices are characterized as "technologies of separation"[7] that facilitate forms of "psychic cocooning"[8] that enable subjects to simultaneously "retreat from urban space" by "neutralizing it"[9] while also holding potential for "reconfiguring urban encounters."[10]

As pioneers of mobile storytelling, dramaturgical play, and location-based gaming, Blast Theory have "sought to transform urban spaces into playful places,"[11] and have often used mobile technologies (both cutting edge and mainstream) as a means of probing the aforementioned tensions and engaging with them critically. This chapter—which draws from two long interviews conducted with Blast Theory's Matt Adams in London and via Skype—explores how the group came to be interested in these issues, and how they are taken up within specific projects.

To begin, on your website it states that across your projects, you have sought to pose and explore, "important questions about the meaning of interaction," both technological and interpersonal, "and, especially, its limitations."[12] Can you speak to those broad motivations, and what brought you as a group to focus on that particular set of questions?

Yeah, I think culture has always been intensively interactive, but went through an interesting period in the mid-twentieth century where it became an industrialized process of production, where the rise of recorded music, film, television really suggested that there was a very clear mechanism for how culture was to be created and distributed. I think you can include visual art in that, in terms of the rise of a globalized art market and the modernist movement where the suggestion was that Picasso sits and makes it, and everything goes out globally and is transmitted to the rest of us. And, of course, you know, if you go back to a pre-industrial period, culture was never really like that. I think we are in some ways still heavily within that.

But, we've also, I think, been in a period for a couple of decades where the cracks are really starting to blow wide open in the sense that culture is now much more participatory and made with people as much as *for* people. My background is in theater, and I was very, very interested in the fact that theater is a live medium. Its only ace card was to destroy the fourth wall, you know. As a young, enthusiastic theater practitioner, the biggest problem was the architecture of theaters—that's just deathly, this kind of mock cinema kind of structure. So, I became very interested in how and what a theatrical moment would look like if you and I are face-to-face as that theatrical moment takes place. The very first works we made were around thinking about those sorts of questions.

And then, in the very first project we did, we stumbled onto a developer who was working with video processing on an Omega, and he was like, "I can do this thing," and we were like, "fuck, that is brilliant!" That immediate opening that technology was going to be the way in which we could orchestrate affirmative interactions kind of came through, and then our work has really been fuelled by that set of possibilities ever since. I'm not a technologist. My primary interest in technology is as a sort of social and cultural phenomenon, rather than as an artistic medium, although it clearly is an artistic medium; it is, in itself, very, very rich, and fascinating.

> Sociologist Georg Simmel famously wrote that "one nowhere feels as lonely and lost as in the metropolitan crowd."[13] I am wondering what your thoughts are on that statement in light of Blast Theory's work?

I sometimes say, kind of slightly jokingly, but you know I think there's truth to it, that our work is a way of orchestrating opportunities for me to talk to strangers, from a completely selfish point of view. That clearly has a very strongly political set of ramifications because the ways we are kind of atomized and segmented by the society we live in is a key way in which we are manipulated and controlled. And so, to try and find ways to make random bridging between strangers has always been fascinating to Ju, Nick, and me. That politics of how you deal with a woman struggling with a push chair on the bus, as much as what chant you use at a demonstration—I think it's something we feel very passionately about. And technology has transformed how we come into contact with strangers, and who a stranger is in any case, and that's a really fascinating set of negotiations.

Again, the debates have shifted, but the internet was really considered a Wild West of pedophiles, Neo Nazis, people committing suicide, renegades, drug dealers, spies, al-Qaeda operatives, you know, the narratives in the press around the internet for many years were about that over and over and over again. It's only around Facebook and Twitter, since big brands started to own that space, that the conversation shifted in terms of how these places were talked about. To try and explore what community means online, what relationships mean that are electronically mediated, has become something that we've looked at over and over.

> One of the striking features of your work is that you are actually encouraging others who are engaging with your work to do the same, to interact with strangers in a variety of ways.

Yeah, and to try and find a politics in that moment, to try and find different ways for these platforms to create interactions between strangers, so that you can potentially talk to a stranger in a way that you could not talk to someone that you know. That's one of the amazing potentials of strangers: they are not friends you haven't met yet. They are something more existentially profound, which is people who have no idea about you and potentially no real lasting interest in you, and, sometimes, that enables conversations to happen or connections to happen in very, very particular ways.

I was very, very deeply influenced by being on the Poll Tax Riot in 1990, where, in the course of that day as it unfolded, I was often in environments where I was surrounded by 15 or 100 peoples who I'd never met before and people were discussing together what should be done and what was acceptable behavior and so on. Someone throws a rock at a policeman on a horse and someone else is completely outraged that they're throwing rocks at horses and you're having these kinds of discussions, but there's a shared sense of common purpose and a very mercurial and interesting set of exchanges going on between people who are in some ways total strangers and in some ways totally united. In some ways, they're kind of driven to be a kind of mob of people behaving as one, and in other ways completely nuanced and individualized in terms of our own approaches and with respect to what is and is not acceptable behavior, and what should and should not be done.

In addition, traditions of pot luck or pot latch and all of those street processions, street carnivals, public spaces as places that are wild and ungoverned, etc., have all really informed the work we've made. You see that in the Shakespearean period, about how culture is done and moved around and toured and presented, through to the sort of big processions and public works in the immediate post-revolutionary period in Soviet Russia in the 1920s. Those things are all kind of strands and threads that run through our work.

I think the thing that anchors our work is: how can you provide a platform for people to be changed through their engagement with one another, even if that engagement is very thin or occasional or random? In some ways, there's a kind of hippy history to this, there's random acts of kindness and these various ways of trying to think about how we can change our feeling about the people around us. These, I think, are the things that are of perennial concern to us.

> The project that springs to mind for me in relation to these issues is *Uncle Roy All Around You* (2003),[14] which seems to be quite explicit in its focus on these forms of interactions. As you've described it in the summary of the project online, the core artistic theme of the work is trusting strangers, whether they be remote players, Uncle Roy, or passers-by. It's interesting that all three are incorporated in that. How did you arrive at this issue as a core one for that game, particularly the idea of the postcard and the paid stranger in the car?

We had a residency at The Banff Centre in Alberta, Canada, in the development of this project, and, at one point, Ju wrote a questionnaire for all three of us to fill in, that was maybe 100 or 150 questions about the city and the street and the pavement, and it was filled with very prosaic kinds of questions. It asked things like: Which part of the pavement do you tend to walk on? If it's late at night, how aware are you of people around you? How do you observe that? And so on. But it was one of those things that, as you read the three sets of answers back, it became clear that we all have these intensely worked out strategies for how to deal with shaded doorways where you can't see whether someone has stood in that doorway or not and all of that, and it just seemed to us at the time, based in London, that we all had this incredible kind of set of antennae that we employed in navigating and negotiating the city around us.

At the same time, there were suggestions that there was no such thing as community online and constant scare stories about people who get chatting, and then it turns out one of them is a cannibal, and he kills and eats the person he's been chatting to. Those sorts of stories were just recurring over and over again. So, I think those sort of things merged together with the fact that *Uncle Roy All Around You* was developed for the Institute of Contemporary Art here in London, and that area of the city has been used in a thousand espionage films—there are three police forces who deal with that area because of all the royal sites there, and because of the royal parks, and because it's filled with embassies. One of the squares in which *Uncle Roy All Around You* was first shown is where Yvonne Fletcher, a female police officer, was shot dead by a gun from the Libyan embassy, and there's a memorial that marks where she fell. And, so, you've got all of these rich cultural and political histories.

While the title came very early, it was quite late in the process that the project kind of crystallized. It was maybe only two or three weeks before we first showed that work that we sat together on one Sunday and, suddenly, this thing about who this Uncle Roy character is and why came to us. There was also the realization that, well, Uncle Roy is actually never found, he is a stranger, he is an absence, and we can make it work where you are looking all the time for someone who you never find. And, in fact, one of the things that's amazing about Uncle Roy is that no one comes back going "where the hell is Uncle Roy?" People never do, despite the fact that they start off with that one goal. They get to the end and they've forgotten about it.

> These sorts of questions around the issue of the stranger seem implicit in the way in which *Rider Spoke* (2007) unfolded.[15] I'm wondering if this was part of your intention when making it?

There were a couple of really curious ironies around *Rider Spoke*, and one is that, quite late in the process, it became clear that we were never going to be able to do live uploads of the recordings, and we weren't even going to be able to do timely uploads of the recordings. In fact, the only way we could do it was that, each night, when all of the writers were back, all the devices plugged in and on charge, and we could suck the recordings off, then we could put them out into the world for the following day. And we had this real moment, this terrible realization, that, you know, because one of them is going to be doing it, their friends will be doing it, and I'm going to be going, "oh great, I wonder where my friends' recordings are," and I'm going to cycle around and go, "oh, that's weird, my friend doesn't seem to record anything," or, "there's my friend over there recording something, and why can't I hear what he's saying?" But, for a number of reasons, people don't notice that at all. They don't perceive that. They are actually listening to kind of 24 hours out-of-date version of the work.

For those of us who are not very technical, that's a process that's going on a thousand-fold everyday—even latency, even these simple things about communication networks. When you look at them, you realize these are profound things. Latency is not just like, "oh well, it just gets it a few seconds later or a few milliseconds later." Actually, with latency, fundamental trade-offs are being done in all sorts of ways to enable those communications to happen, and live is rarely live, and so on.

So, I think, that's one of the interesting contradictions in *Rider Spoke*. The other is that we all sat in that room deciding which recordings go through to the following day. We listen to every recording every night, and we're essentially scoring it from 1 to 5. There's a series of protocols about how we do that and try and do that in particular ways. But, essentially, it's in, out, out, in. So, we're grading the quality of the recordings, even though it appears to be a kind of open place in which each recording counts (Figure 5.2).

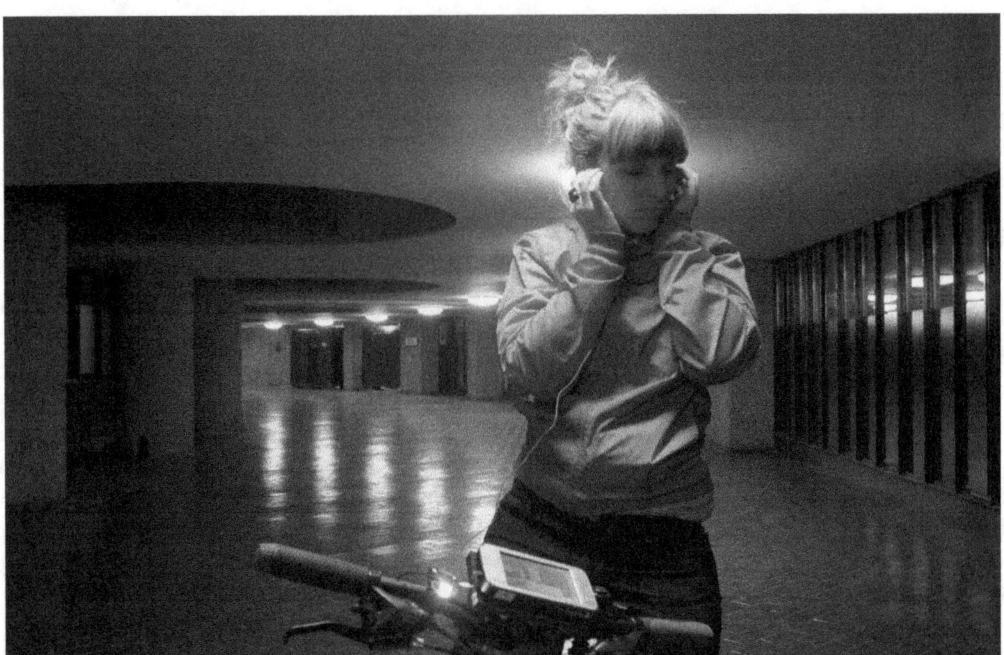

*Figure 5.2* Blast Theory *Rider Spoke* (2007). Photo credit: Blast Theory

Some of that is to do with how you invite people to interact, and how you give them a platform for self-expression. And, part of that is about looking a lot in our work at what it is to make a declaration of any kind, within an artwork, or within a software platform, or within both of those at once. And, so, in *Rider Spoke*, in a way, it's kind of a traditional Hollywood type of narrative, in that you come out of it changed by the experience in some way. We really tried to look at lot at how you invite everyone to speak, not just bubbly, garrulous, matey, socialized people, not just people who've got an axe to grind—how do you invite people who speak in an awkward register, or are uncomfortable speaking, or are tangential to the mainstream, or who aren't good at building conversations, or don't have witticisms. How can we create works that invite those people and ensure that their integrity is retained?

And, so, the promise at the end of *Rider Spoke* is that sense where it's really for you to frame what that promise might be. One of my real concerns as we went into the later stages of making that work was, this is going to be a big kind of United Colors of Benetton sort of thing, of like, hey, everyone come and speak, everyone can chat in there in a large embracing world where we all share stuff. How do we do that, how do we create a specific tone of voice to this work that enables you to speak in a way that is not just like some kind of schleppy thing, and it was a worry then, and today it's ten times worse because every brand on earth wants you to chat and share....

> ... to "join the conversation"...

Yeah, have a profile. Exactly! And so, what we've learned through that work was that cycling alone at night in the city gave it an incredibly specific context where people spoke in very particular ways. But, nevertheless, if you look at the questions that you're asked in *Rider Spoke*, they are generally very open, and especially the initial ones have that tremendous breadth, to try and invite people to speak in very particular ways.

> In projects such as *Rider Spoke, Uncle Roy,* and *I Like Frank* (2004),[16] are there specific things that you are trying to do in terms of location? I mean, is it a case of you've been invited here, to a particular festival, so, therefore, you work within the constraints of that? Or, were there other underlying issues and concerns around location that you're trying to explore?

I think we've been on an interesting journey where the first time you come across a Global Positioning System (GPS), and I think this is sort of a common thing, you think "oh wow, a computer that tells you where you are, and it's accurate to within a metre, that's amazing." Now, I've got the entire planet and I know exactly where anyone is, and I can provide them something based on precisely where they are. And, then, of course, *Can You See Me Now?* (2001)[17] was our process of learning just how wrong that was, and we were incredibly lucky that some of the idiosyncrasies of design of *Can You See Me Now?* enabled us to get away with some of the inefficiencies of GPS, or the idiosyncrasies of GPS. Especially in those early days, we worked really hard even just to get the satellite readings working correctly. It was a much more flawed system, and the algorithms for interpreting the data from satellites were much weaker than they are these days. And, then, realizing that, of course, there is no XY certainty around GPS, it's a much more elastic and unstable thing.

And, then, also realizing that this idea of a kind of Cartesian landscape in which you would imprint experience is also very weak. It can be good for some things, but all the rhetoric around GPS in those days was about detours, where you walk to a street corner and it pops up and tells you stuff. It's strange how weak most of that stuff is, that actually you might as well have a book. To walk into this courtyard and go, "Welcome to the British Library," all of that stuff, it's like, actually, you don't really care. So, around *Rider Spoke* we got interested in context. What we have suddenly realized is that it's much more fluid. Being roughly here in this part of London [near to the British Library, where we are talking], with its history of the railway station, the fire here where 30 people were killed in the Underground, prostitution and drugs, which are rife in these areas, this intersection. These are the things that are really interesting. So, it's then about the … and, I don't know if you're aware of the kind of location system that underpins *Rider Spoke*, it's a Wi-Fi fingerprinting system.

> Wasn't it the case that you were quite determined *not* to have a particularly precise location system?

It wasn't a determination on our part, but it kind of came about that way. We've always tried to stay open to ways in which we can engage with broader concerns. One of the broader concerns at that time was that GPS still was very rare on electronic devices and that you couldn't do location experiences without it, and, so, therefore, the whole thing was stillborn. It was a chicken and egg kind of situation. So, we set about to say, well, "I'm sure you could use Wi-Fi to do that," and that's where the Wi-Fi fingerprinting thing came from.

Originally, we were working with a PlayStation Portable, then for all kinds of tedious production reasons we moved to working with a Nokia N800. I met one of the scientists who we were working with on that project just last week, and we were joking about the fact that we were, like, "this thing is so useless, all it, is a thing that connects to the internet with a screen on it, it's like a phone with no SIM, why would anyone ever want this." And, of course, we now realize that we were looking at a tablet. <laughs> We completely missed a multi-billion-dollar business: having worked with this thing for a couple of years, we still thought that it was a useless and pointless device. It's always a good, humbling kind of lesson.

So, yeah, I don't really have a neat way of framing all of this because *A Machine To See With* (2010)[18] and *Ulrike and Eamon Compliant* (2009)[19] are again very precise about location, and they direct you turn by turn through the city. I'm not a believer that you can't do interesting things with that. But, *A Machine To See With*, in particular, is a kind of return to something where the walk is the narrative driver, and you have this kind of slight sense that someone puts their hand on your lower back and is constantly pushing you because you cannot stop, you cannot break, it's a phone call, and there's no pause (see Figure 21, color insert). It absolutely propels you. Obviously, for the people who don't like *A Machine To See With*, that's one of the things they hate about it: it brooks no argument or deviation, and if you get a bit lost, you have to call back in and reset and so on. But, of course, it's a work about the financial crisis, so to me it feels appropriate that it has that quality of being unarguable, and in a way it's a work about the dictatorship of technology, a sense that I sit down and make my apology to you before we begin speaking. It's like that device [points to my audio recorder] has already cast a kind of frame over our conversation, establishing that you and me interacting is contingent on other things (Figure 5.3).

> I would also like to ask you about *Ulrike and Eamon Compliant* (2009). Compared to some of Blast Theory's other projects, in *Ulrike and Eamon Compliant* you do not just encourage an interaction with strangers, what you are proposing is an interaction with the Other, in the capital "O" sense of that word. How did this project come about?

Well, I can't avoid tidying it up in retrospect, so I'm sure it was a much more fragmentary process than this will make it sound. But, essentially, around the time of developing *Ulrike and Eamon Compliant*, there was a desire on our part to make work that was more politically engaged again, because I think we felt that, you know, in 2008–2009 it felt like, okay, we're now in a moment of real possibility again, we're now in a moment where the entire kind of Blair/Bush era has really cracked open, its bankruptcy has been absolutely laid bare, and there's a moment where we now

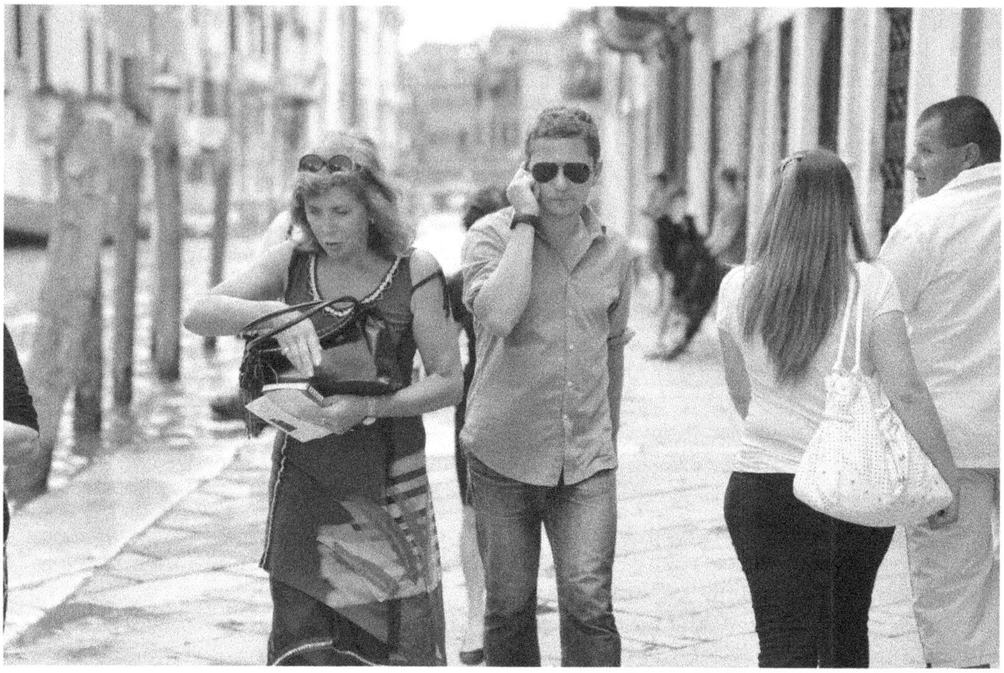

*Figure 5.3* Blast Theory, *Ulrike and Eamon Compliant* (2009). Photo credit: Anne Brassier

need to really talk explicitly about the social gist of things. And enough time had passed I think since 9/11 to start saying, well, this constant refrain about terrorism, which is also linked to the Other culturally, religiously, and racially. Let's go back to the period where terrorism wasn't anything to do with those things: it was politically Other, and in no other way.

Ulrike Meinhof and Eamon Collins were white middle-class people who were bombing their way around Europe. So that seems to me a very critical moment. The entry point into it was coming across Eamon Collins' book, *Killing Rage*, which is an astonishingly honest and self-lacerating memoir of his journey toward Republicanism and toward the IRA, and it tracks how it took him ten years to get there.[20] He was not a joiner in any way at all. Very, very slowly did he come to the idea. So, I just felt that was a really interesting story. And, then, we were put off using Ulrike Meinhof because it was such a well-trodden story, and we felt that people have been here many, many times, and there's a sort of terrorist chic around Ulrike Meinhof that I was a bit uncomfortable with. But, ultimately, the quality of her writing was so strong and her biography[21] was so strong that we had a variety of those two things.

In addition to these things, I also came across the work of Philippa Foot, an English philosopher, who, in the late 1960s, was the first person to devise the trolley problem, in which an individual meets a kind of hypothetical, ethical dilemma.[22] Once I came across the branch of philosophy from which that had originated, I had this sudden moment of a real realization of, like, if you're making each member of the public the protagonist within a work, as we had begun to do, then the really interesting thing is to give them an ethical situation. We spend 80% of the work trying to make that as finely balanced and as complex and well attuned as possible, and then you drop someone into a situation and go, "okay, now what, what do you want to do?" So that's really where *Ulrike and Eamon Compliant* came from. Formally, we started from the interview. We were like, "okay, let's do a work where every single person who comes through the door is interviewed by us. So, we can only do that for a few minutes. So, how can we make those few minutes really count?" And, then, kind of track backwards from that, to say, "yeah, we want to try and establish everything we possibly can."

The work had a fairly strongly scripted narrative running through it. Do you think it would have worked in a less scripted, looser way, or was that pivotal to its success?

I think it had to be that way because, you know, once you've chosen to be Eamon or Ulrike, every call you receive treats you as Eamon or Ulrike. You are bombarded with this sense in which you are being put into this position. I think one of the engines of that work is either you are going, "alright, cool, right, I'm Eamon, then fine." Or, you're going, "what is this work that treats me as if … I'm not adopting this role of a terrorist from the 1970s!"

And what was the response?

Well, the great thing is that you don't have to make up your mind. You can be blurring backwards and forwards across those two responses all of the time. But, then, you come in and you are seated in the room and the first thing that person says to you is, "what would you fight for?" And so you see people hesitate for a second, like, "well, am I Eamon now, or am I Matt now?" You are not clear how you are to answer. Some people begin with fiction, and then usually collapse because it's very hard to have a moral and philosophical debate in character, and some people drop straight off it. But, that sense in which there's a hesitation, there's an ambiguity about context within which you are being asked that question. To me that's very important.

So is the fact that you've had this kind of strong biographical trajectory that has brought you to that point. The narrative is very, very carefully written to demonstrate the moral compromises that were made, without in any way condemning them for the route that they take. My perspective is to say, these were intelligent, thoughtful brave people who did what they thought was absolutely the most important thing on earth at that time, and both were willing to pay for it with their lives from that conviction. Which is not in any way to defend them, it's to try and bring people into a position where you can hold those contradictory positions, where you can encourage uncomfortable interactions.

## Notes

1 For further detail on Blast Theory and their activities, see: www.blasttheory.co.uk/
2 Steve Benford, Chris Greenhalgh, Gabriella Giannachi, Brendan Walker, Joe Marshall, and Tom Rodden, "Uncomfortable Interactions," in *CHI'12 Proceedings of the SIGCHI Conference on Human Factors in Computing Systems*, May 5–10 (2012), Austin, TX, http://dl.acm.org/citation.cfm?id=2208347.
3 Georg Simmel, *The Sociology of Georg Simmel*, edited by Kurt Heinrich Wolff (New York: The Free Press, 1950), 119.
4 Richard Sennett, *The Conscience of the Eye: The Design and Social Life of Cities* (New York: Alfred A. Knopf, 1990).
5 Iris Marion Young, *Justice and the Politics of Difference* (Princeton, NJ: Princeton University Press, 1990).
6 Marion Young. For discussion, see Alice Crawford, "Taking Software to the Streets: Mobile Cocooning and the (An-)erotic City," *Journal of Urban Technology* 15, no. 3 (2008): 79–97, doi: 10.1080/10630730802677970.
7 Michael Bull *Sound Moves: iPod Culture and Urban Experience* (London: Routledge, 2007), 28.
8 David Morley, "What's 'Home' Got To Do With It? Contradictory Dynamics in the Domestication of Technology and the Dislocation of Domesticity," *European Journal of Cultural Studies* 6, no. 4 (2003): 435–58, doi: 10.1177/13675494030064001; Joachim R. Höflich, "Part of Two Frames: Mobile Communication and the Situational Arrangement of Communicative Behaviour," in *Mobile Democracy: Essays on Society, Self and Politics*, edited by Kristóf Nyíri (Vienna: Passagen Verlag, 2003), 33–51.
9 Bull, *Sound Moves*, 28.

10 Mimi Sheller and John Urry, "Introduction: Mobile Cities, Urban Mobilities," in *Mobile Technologies in the City*, edited by Mimi Sheller and John Urry (London: Routledge, 2006), 1–17; Jason Farman (ed.), *The Mobile Story: Narrative Practices with Locative Technologies* (New York: Routledge, 2013).
11 Larissa Hjorth and Ingrid Richardson, *Gaming in Social, Locative, and Mobile Media* (Houndmills, Basingstoke, Hampshire: Palgrave Macmillan, 2014), 7; Adriana de Souza e Silva and Larissa Hjorth, "Playful Urban Spaces: A Historical Approach," *Simulation & Gaming* 40, no. 5 (2009), 602–25, doi: 10.1177/1046878109333723.
12 Blast Theory, "Our History and Approach" (2019), www.blasttheory.co.uk/about-us/.
13 Simmel, *The Sociology*, 418.
14 See: www.blasttheory.co.uk/projects/uncle-roy-all-around-you/.
15 See: www.blasttheory.co.uk/projects/rider-spoke/.
16 See: www.blasttheory.co.uk/projects/i-like-frank/.
17 See: www.blasttheory.co.uk/projects/can-you-see-me-now/.
18 See: www.blasttheory.co.uk/projects/a-machine-to-see-with/.
19 See: www.blasttheory.co.uk/projects/ulrike-and-eamon-compliant/.
20 Eamon Collins with Mick McGovern, *Killing Rage* (London: Granta Books, 1997).
21 Ulrike Meinhof, *Everybody Talks About the Weather ... We Don't: The Writings of Ulrike Meinhof*, edited by Karin Bauer (New York: Seven Stories Press, 2008).
22 The trolley problem is generally framed in the following terms. There is a runaway trolley speeding along railway tracks. In the path of this runaway trolley, five people are tied to the tracks. You are standing some distance away, next to a lever. If you pull the lever, the trolley will switch tracks, where it will now be in the path of one person. You are faced with a choice: do nothing, and the trolley kills five people; or, pull the lever, diverting the trolley away from the five, where it will kill one person. This is the ethical dilemma: Which is the correct choice? See: Philippa Foot, "The Problem of Abortion and the Doctrine of the Double Effect," *Oxford Review* 5 (1967), 5–15.

# 6

# MOBILE LISTENING, DISRUPTIVE AMBIENT MUSIC, AND PUBLIC ART PROJECTS IN MADRID

*Amparo Lasén and Massimiliano Casu*

This chapter draws on current research about the Madrid public art scene and their use of mobile loudspeakers, following the more or less visible and audible threads connecting recent art projects with ordinary social practices enacted in the city. The public art projects that we discuss are inspired by the mundane collective music listening in urban spaces with mobile phones and Bluetooth loudspeakers.

These practices connect with a long history of mobile listening and sounding in the city mediated by music reproduction technologies (record players, boomboxes, portable radios, etc.) and sound amplification devices. They increase the sonic presence of people playing and holding these devices and mobilize a shared, relational, and contextual agency, which contributes to the shape of urban spaces, ambiances and experiences, revealing how they are sound spaces as well. They are examples of the intersection of musicking[1] and spacing, where music and spaces are understood as verbs rather than nouns. Therefore, these mobile listening practices are complex choreographies involving people, devices, multiple materialities, senses and regulations, producing spaces and temporalities within the city, as well as eliciting different kinds of attunements, affects and intensities, from pleasure and joy through to annoyance and disgust.

Popular and media framing of these practices attribute them to a manly and thuggish version of territorial tactics, labelled as *sodcasting*, where mobile listeners are considered as "tomcats that spray their audio wee around" because they are defiant and want to be noticed.[2] This claim is frequently attributed to working-class migrants and youngsters, yet the relation between mobile listening and territoriality cannot be reduced to this aspect. Making and unmaking territories relate not only to enlarging one's personal space, imposing one's sonic presence on others, but are also ways to inhabit the city spaces to make oneself at home within public places, as well as experiencing them as more pleasant and less hostile, creating a place and moment, an environment, to share music sounds, gestures and moves with those in our surroundings, to make playful and pleasant encounters possible: with people, with songs, with sounds, with different materialities to share music sounds, gestures and moves with those in our surroundings, to make playful and pleasant encounters possible with people, with songs, with sounds, and with different materialities. This is a sonic island which is part of the sonic cartography of simultaneity that makes up the city.[3]

Different types and degrees of listening attention prompt forms of dancing, singing, and humming in public. This shared mobile listening can then be considered a kind of disruptive ambient music,[4] susceptible of eliciting controversies and territorial conflicts around whether playing music, singing and dancing are suitable and expected public behaviour or not, revealing the inherent contentious politics of urban public space, made of plural and divergent practices, concerns, tastes, and sensitivities.[5]

Our chapter is structured in four parts, echoing the four phases of *Romeria of the Volts* (2018), one of the art projects discussed. The first section encompasses the "meeting," where we discuss the articulation between ordinary practices and art projects. We show how music enjoyment has become a way to produce the urban social space through these encounters between different sounds, technologies and people, ordinary mobile listening and sounding, and finally artistic interventions.

The second section is the "tune-in" and looks at how the attunement of people, technologies, and places happens. Through the investigation of how sounds and songs are selected and played, we understand how mobility is enacted, and how these shared, contextual, and relational agencies are deployed—by highlighting the entanglements between the technical, the aesthetic and the affective in these choreographic performances. In the third section, the "parade," we discuss how bodies affect and are affected, move and are moved through the practice of mobile listening, which increases their sonic presence and the display of diverse subjectivities. Finally, the "herald" focusses on the conclusions related to this interaction between ordinary popular practices of music enjoyment and public art projects that are mediated by technology, market, and urban regulations.

## The Meeting: Human and Nonhuman Encounters in a Context of Constraining Sound Regulations

A Romeria is a religious festival where participants receive the name of *romeros*. They carry an image—very often a Virgin—from one church to another in order to make a plea, or as a celebration of devotion. Romerias are also festive rituals where music is played, people listen, sing and dance, drink and eat, and enjoy the company of other participants, in the temporary and repeated experience of becoming *romero*. The *Romeria of the Volts* is something between a street carnival parade, a protest, and a collective art performance. The organizers, a network of more than 30 Madrid collectives connected to public art, music and dance, describe it as:

> a celebration with no roots in tradition, bound to no one or nothing. It calls a diverse crowd of Madrid *fiesteros* (partygoers), brought together by a common desire to transform the world through music and dance. In short, a noisy proclamation and expression of our rights to use our city's streets and public spaces as places for fun and enjoyment.[6]

The 2018 edition of the *Romeria of the Volts* was scheduled to start at 6pm on a Friday afternoon of early September in Legazpi, a working-class area at the border between the wider centre and the periphery of Madrid. Outside EVA (*Espacio Vecinal Arganzuela*), a self-managed neighbourhood centre, about 50 people were holding banners, wearing kerchiefs on their necks and waiting in anticipation under a late-summer cloudy sky (Figure 6.1). They looked like something in between a crowd of protesters waiting for a demonstration and churchgoers waiting for the procession to start.

Some of them brought mobile music devices: cheap plastic loudspeakers, small battery-powered handmade sound systems, tiny FM transistor radios or medium-sized PA speakers, like the ones often used by street musicians. This technological compilation is just a small example of the vast collection of popular devices for mobile music listening that we can find all around our city.

With the commercialization and adoption of personal stereos, Walkmans, and MP3 devices, the habit of collective music listening in urban public spaces in Madrid seemed to disappear, until the emergence and massive adoption of smartphones and portable speakers with Bluetooth. After the consolidation of MP3 as the dominant music format around the globe[7] and the growth

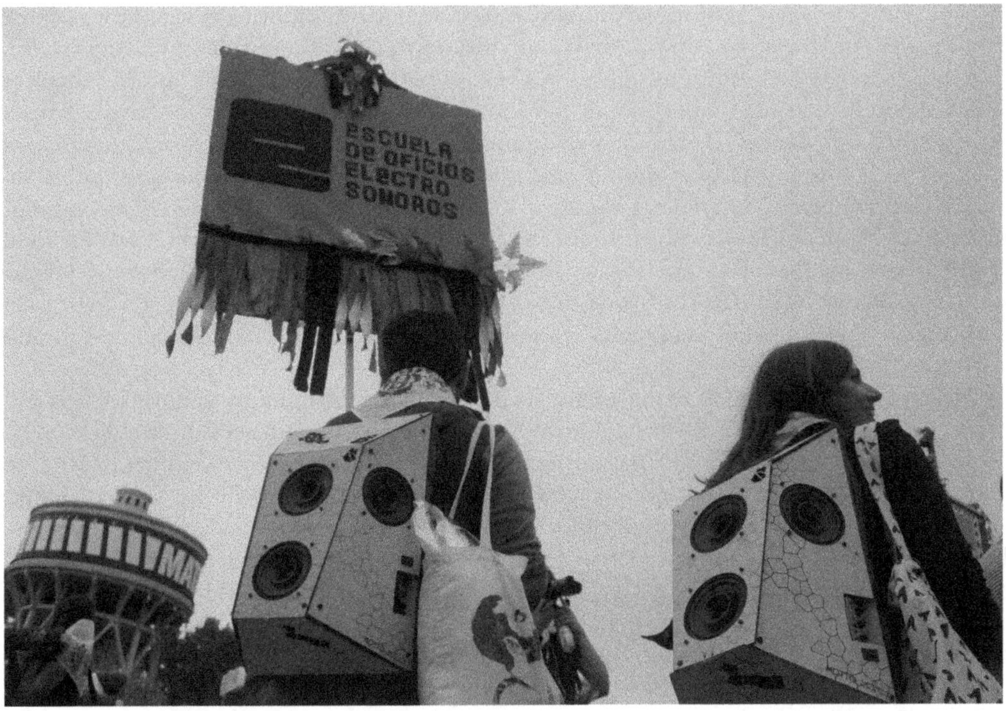


*Figure 6.1* Participants of the *Romería of the Volts* waiting for the procession to start. Photo credit: Irene Zótola

of smartphones as the most common environment for music listening—especially in association with music streaming services—portable Bluetooth loudspeakers became the core of a complex *apparatus*. It joins together the musical services and databases (Spotify, YouTube, Soundcloud, Bandcamp, and a multitude of other services), the audio player (mainly a mobile phone), the portable speakers and people listening to the music played (often in groups).

Collective music listening has always been part of shaping shared subjectivities. The new possibilities of listening (for free or affordably) to a limitless song database, everywhere and anytime, has led to specific uses of public space and public atmospheres and ambiences.[8] Today, we observe a rise of these practices throughout the city and the ubiquitous presence of this new kind of portable loudspeakers in shops windows and online catalogues, from cheap technology bazaars to the showrooms of luxury technological and fashion brands. Not only does almost every company related to sound technology have a portable Bluetooth speaker in their catalogue (even the more audiophiles-oriented) but also a great number of fashion and design labels have also started selling their branded models.

This commercial boom is due to several factors: the decrease of technology's prices, the improvements in the relationship between portability and sound power and quality, the enhancement of batteries duration and, most importantly, the formerly mentioned integration with smartphones (and broadband technologies), giving access to the global music catalogue. While in the last decades portable music devices such as boombox were often expensive, even a status symbol,[9] today's cheapest mobile loudspeaker available in online catalogues costs less than a metro ticket. Therefore, if for over a decade people were suddenly surprised by a loud drumbeat sounding from a customized car stereo—which is quite common—then today in Madrid, as in other cities throughout the world, it is also frequent to hear the same kind of sound coming from the backpack of a delivery biker or from a small group of teenagers walking by the street.

Though the commercial imaginary related to the first portable musical devices, such as suitcase record players and transistor radios, was strongly related to a middle-class leisure imaginary such as countryside trips and vacations, their actual use was more often related to urban subcultural communities. It was in the late 1970s in the United States when television commercials started to locate their boomboxes in the urban environment, and for the first time depicted their target customers as young people from the suburbs, quite often groups of black teenagers, rather than middle-class families. The previous idea of "doubling the thrills of your travels and outings," suggested by a famous Philco advertising mentioned by Gopinath and Stanyek[10] was embodied by urban working-class youngsters who enhanced their urban experience and sonic presence through collective listening. This made the emergence of sonic territorial disputes inescapable, as pictured by Spike Lee through the adventures of Radio Raheem, main character of the 1989 movie *Do The Right Thing.*[11]

The lasting thrilling appeal of shared mobile listening for contemporary young people is at the origin of the project *Semilla Boombox.*[12] It developed a mobile app connected to a sound system placed in a public urban space, the Relampaguito park in Villaverde, in the summer of 2013. It is both an artistic intervention and a citizen collaboration project following the initiative of designer Sergio Galán, Intermediae, a laboratory for the production of projects and social innovation of the Madrid arts centre Matadero and the grassroots association Semilla, a group fighting youth exclusion in Villaverde, a working-class neighbourhood in the south of Madrid.

Semilla and Intermediae organize courses and activities for youngsters and teenagers. In collaboration with Galán, they organized a workshop for Villaverde teenagers, where the designer presented several of his projects. Among them a public installation of a sound system was connected to a mobile app, allowing users to select and play songs in the urban public space where the installation was situated. Due to the youngsters' wish to produce something similar in their neighbourhood, the workshop focussed on this project, teaching the participants to build an app specific to meet the project's co-designed brief.

With a long track record of collaboration with the local council, Semilla obtained council approval to make the sound system work during the summer. Local authorities were worried by the image of insecurity and danger that some recent incidents have given to the parks in the area and they liked the idea of a convivial activity as a form of community engagement and to change the perceived mood and ambience of the public park. Through negotiations, new requirements were added to the design, regarding both the sound volume and the hours when it could be used, in order to fulfil the urban regulations and not disturb the neighbours.

## The Tune-in: Negotiating our Sonic Appearance in Public Space

The recent story of Madrid's urbanism, like in many other global cities, is the scenario of a confrontation between a centralized model of urban design and grassroots practices like tactical urbanism, informal architecture, and public art. In this scenario, both right-wing strategies and more progressive ones have in common the necessity of regulating sound pollution and noise. All mechanical sounds of the contemporary world tend to generate a social problem, as pointed by Bijsterveld[13] and Labelle.[14] However, music emissions, with roots stemming from busking and gramophones, have always been considered one of the main social problems affecting urban co-existence. Therefore, when digital mobile media affords the ability to listen to every song ever recorded and when people with their portable devices occupy public spaces for collective listening and music playing, conflict begins to surface.

Therefore, while the market for Bluetooth loudspeakers in Madrid grew exponentially, the public administration reacted by explicitly prohibiting their use in several parts of the city. This was achieved by defining zones of special acoustic protection (ZPAE)[15] and to the launch of public campaigns such as *Diviertete sin molestar* (Have fun without disturbing)[16] and *Salimos sin molestar* (We go out without disturbing).[17] This presented the ultimate paradox: while the devices for amplified sounding—allowing collective listening—became more and more popular, their use was banned in many areas of the city.

The political and legal control on the use of mobile loudspeakers in the public space of the city suddenly transformed these practices into everyday forms of resistance. This was enacted by communities that have limited options for gathering and listening to music together such as migrants and young people. The conflict generated by this situation recently opened a wide field for critical art practices in the public space of Madrid, as shown by the initiatives described in this chapter, as well as by collective exhibitions such as *Post-it City*[18] (2011) and *Pop Politics*[19] (2012). The first one—curated by Giovanni La Varra, Martí Peran, Filippo Poli and Federico Zanfi, that was exhibited in the Madrid council venue CentroCentro Cibeles—explored the connections between art and popular ordinary practices in pop-up urbanism such as barbecues in urban empty lots or small street parties. The second one—which took place in Centro de Arte 2 de Mayo and was curated by Iván López Munuera—investigated the relationship between pop music culture and everyday resistance.

In 2012—a year before *Semilla Boombox*—when the council was developing the first ZPAE, architecture collective Todo por la Praxis developed a project called *Soundsystem Guerrilla* in collaboration with the same local council art centre Matadero Madrid.[20] They built open prototypes of cheap battery-powered speakers that were installed, without any authorization, for free collective utilization in Madrid Río, a park situated along the Manzanares river.

According to Todo por la Praxis, the practice of social music listening was a way to produce important forms of placemaking and site-specific community building, empowering those communities that were more vulnerable to expulsion from public space. We find here similar goals as with *Semilla Boombox*: to help people make certain public places their territories and to enlarge the possibilities of such public places and equipment by the gestures, practices, and pleasures of mobile listening.

This idea was one of the main topics of *Charivaria*, an exhibition opened at the end of 2017 in Madrid's art centre CentroCentro Cibeles, defined by curators José Luis Espejo and Andrea Zarza as "an exhibition about how people assume a position in public space through sound."[21] It was a historical display of both ordinary practice and art making that used sound in the public space as a critical tool for protests and collective actions, containing documents, paintings, sculptures, and sound art pieces (Figure 6.2). The exhibition's catalogue joined together the work of art

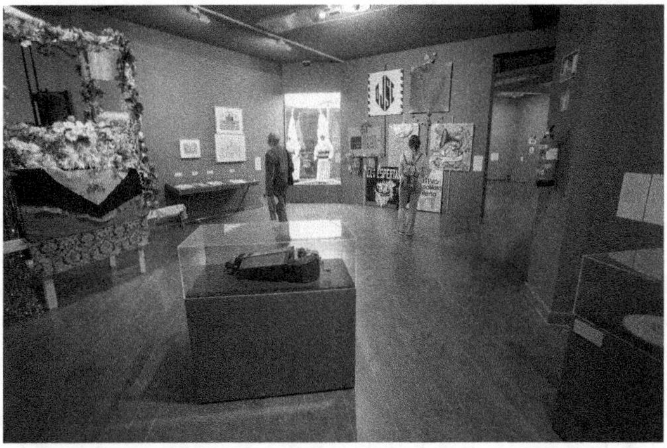

*Figure 6.2* A section of *Charivaria* exhibition, CentroCentro Cibeles. Photo credit: Lukasz Michalak

activists like Infernal Noise Brigade and Ultrared with several local artists, such as Krapoola and Chi_lo_sá, authors of the controversial performance *Amplified Procession* (2007)[22] that was strongly criticized by conservative media for mocking Catholic rituals.[23]

The exhibition's starting point addresses the fundamental mobility of sound, as it cannot be spatially delimited. It crosses the boundaries between communities as well as the private and public divide. One section of the exhibition was specifically dedicated to sonic disobedience and displayed some of the banners created for the *Romeria of the Volts*, next to examples of traditional carnivals and other practices related to political demonstration, popular festivals and art performances. The audience engagement programme[24] of *Charivaria* was directed by artist and curator Ruben Coll, consisting of guided tours and workshops entitled A Sonic March.[25] This was developed by Massimiliano Casu. The participants produced geo-located audio pieces hacking the main platforms for mobile-based urban audio guides in order to reproduce a virtual street parade that joined together dance and protest.

Shared music listening has the power to activate urban conflict like no other forms of sound or noise does because music plays a key role in subjectivation and belonging.[26] This can explain how ambient music becomes disruptive, when it does not fit with the music tastes of those in the surroundings. This disruptive ambient music mobilizes atmospheric attunements, an "intimate, compositional process of dwelling in spaces," where "things matter not because the form they are represented but because they have qualities, rhythms, forces, relations, and movements."[27] Following Stewart's notion, we can understand this mediated attunement as a temporary effect, not always conscious, involving human and non-human entities. Recently, in one of the discussion panels of Ciudad Bailar,[28] an art festival focussed on the relation between dancing communities, the urban space and art practices, a street b-boy called Music explained how street dancers regulate their musical and sonic coexistence: "our spaces are open for anyone who wants to dance, but sometimes we have to ask someone to leave because the music he's playing is not appropriate."[29]

Through mundane ways of music listening via mobile media, the selection of the tunes played, and the configuration of the playlists results from the shared agency between users' decisions, following their particular tastes and curiosity, and the selection algorithms of the different platforms. The workings of these opaque algorithms draw on vast amounts of data about user behaviour, listening preferences and histories, how tunes and users are classified and defined by these algorithmic procedures, the music content available, and importantly the commercial interests of the platforms.

The projects discussed above propose particular modes to select, curate, and decide which songs are going to be played and listened to. This is also part of the collective attunements embedded in these practices. *Romeria of the Volts* prepare their own playlist every year. This is also a collective and participatory process realized the week before the event, drawing on music choices resulting from a callout to potential participants through collective emails and social media platforms. This procedure extends the temporality and participation beyond the festival event, as it happens in the ordinary preparation of playlists and music selection to be shared.

For the *Semilla Boombox* project, the young participants who designed the mobile app introduced modifications to manage the disparity of music tastes of the potential users. The app allows users to select songs available online and to vote for the songs selected by others, in order to democratically create the playlist played through the loudspeakers of the sound system. In the artist's original version, the playlist order depended on the number of votes. Songs no one voted for were not played and dismissed.

However, the young women and men from Villaverde decided against this idea, as it could be seen as an affront to people, causing conflict and disquiet. Alternatively, they decided that all the songs chosen should be played, where the number of votes was instead used to create the song order within the playlist. In this case, the shared agency between the technical features of the device and the collective interests and concerns of the people using it informed the design process. In both projects, the technical affordance of automated music selection of current mobile media was downplayed. Instead they accommodated the diverse music tastes and choices of all participants, no matter whether they would be congruent or not with conventional or algorithmic forms of knowledge about music tastes and genres.

The contextual agency in the music selection of *Semilla Boombox* produced a controversial situation. The technical availability of all kinds of songs colluded with the lack of collective copresent control, at the time of the day when the heat was highest. In August, at siesta time early in the afternoon, when the park was deserted, someone used the app to play a fascist hymn and other similar tunes. Some neighbours heard it and posted about it in the blog of the National Federation of Forums for the Memory, an association for the rights of the victims of the Franco regime.[30] This is a very sensitive and controversial topic in Spain. Local media covered the incident, stating that a council sound system was playing fascist songs. Thus, local authorities stopped the project, until the designers could assure them that something similar won't happen again.

As a result, Galán and the young participants workshopped and modified the app's functionality. They learned how to create and install filters in order to avoid the selection of polemic songs and to allow for less disruptive attunements. The user "failure" of *Semilla Boombox* in this way can be seen to be highly positive because it created further iteration, giving the lead artist and workshop participants further learning opportunities related to rolling out and maintaining public art projects.

The atmospheric attunement of the Romeria project involved further forms of tuning and modification. Back at the meeting point outside the doors of EVA, while the typical soundcheck noise begins to play from inside the neighbourhood centre, the crowd starts tuning their devices to the frequency of 88.5 Mhz, as the organizers of the meeting told them to do. No radio stations broadcasted on that frequency, so it began with an unwanted white noise-orchestra concert. This is the very reason why the organizers chose it: it's the only blank space in the FM spectrum that can be (almost) legally occupied by a playlist. The music was transmitted over a 200 meters range by a self-constructed pirate radio antenna. The song *Cumbia de la Romeria*, played by the Mexican band *Grupo Macao* begins to play simultaneously through this network of FM devices. The gates of EVA open and one palanquin was welcomed with the applause of the waiting crowd.

The idea of building a mobile pirate radio station came a few years ago to a group of Madrid artists searching for a technical solution to synchronize many portable loudspeakers, when they found the website of *Tom and Gary's Decentralized Dance Party* (2009–), a performative project started in Canada ten years ago, consisting of hundreds of party people carrying boomboxes and a DJ wearing a backpack with an FM radio transmitter. All the boomboxes are tuned into the DJ's master FM broadcast, resulting in a mobile, synchronized sound system, defined by the organizers "a Portable Dance Party lasting all night long, blurring the boundaries between participants and performers."[31]

These music and dance activists successfully found a way to produce a powerful acoustic swarm. In some way, this resonated with the mass social protests and occupations[32] that, since 2009, were about to grow in northern Africa and Spain, and afterwards, in the global Occupy movement. As all of them are enactments of hybrid rhythmic crowds, inhabiting public spaces and making people's presence and issues public. These collectives are entanglements of human and non-human agencies, enabled by the mediations of different digital and sound technologies, developing particular political aesthetics, and collective urban experiences in which the body and the sharing of affects are central.[33]

## The Parade: Moving Bodies and Augmented Sonic Presence

In Madrid, as in the whole Iberian Peninsula, there is a very strong and extended tradition based on the act of walking together. Both religious practices, as the formerly mentioned *Romerias*, processions, pilgrimages, *cabalgatas* (the Three Wise Men parade that take place on the 5th of January in every Spanish city) or civil and secular traditions. From local festivals to collective actions or just mundane leisure activities such as military parades, the parades of Moors and Christians in local festivals of the Valencia region and the South-East of Spain, protest marches, or even the mundane *tapeo*, which implies the practice of walking from bar to bar with friends.

People gathering, walking through the city in groups, displaying symbols, shouting slogans, but also getting in contact with the materiality of the city at the sidewalk level, crossing streets, squares and parks. They enacted a collective *flânerie*, a direct experience of the urban soundscape and landscape from the body's scale as Careri described through the concept of "transurbance."[34] In these gatherings, they re-territorialize the urban. Solnit wrote: "Only citizens familiar with their city as both symbolic and practical territory, able to come together on foot and accustomed to walking about their city, can revolt."[35]

Many of the mentioned traditions add sonic elements to the walking experience, amplifying the sonic presence of the participants and generating what Kassabian defines as a dynamic and distributed subjectivity with the human and non-human participants and surroundings, which joins together the people and devices generating the sound who are part of this aural space.[36] As Balliger observed, "Sound or P.A. systems may create an internal spatiality or 'temporary autonomous zone,' but through them music can traverse and challenge spatially organized social divisions."[37]

The *Romeria of the Volts*, as a hybrid experience between a procession, a protest, and a carnival parade, explores the intersection between collective mobility and movement, adding the element of dance and its bodily power. The gathering of dancing bodies, digital and urban materialities, and their performativity[38] can produce other meanings beyond what is explicitly said. This is, an atmospheric attunement where the sense of what happens, and the sense that something is happening, results from the rhythms, gestures, movements, and affective intensities elicited. This performativity, powered by the music experience, generates a dense entanglement between the inside of the procession and the environment.

Brought by eight people and filled with plastic flowers, the palanquin of the *Romeria of the Volts* looks like the ones used in the Spanish Holy Week processions However, instead of the statue of the Virgin Mary or Christ, it brings a portable sound system named Saint Soundsystem I (Figure 6.3).

The volume of the music is turned up. Some volunteers push the people in line, and the *Romeria* begins for its third edition led by its secular and technological Saint. "Soundsystem The First," a battery-powered loudspeaker, appeared for the first time in the art centre Matadero Madrid one night in August 2015. It was the first prize for a dance contest organized by Madrid-based art collective Grupal Crew, with the purpose of reclaiming the right to dance in public space. After the official end of the dance battle, which counted 250 participants and an audience of 1,500 peoples, the winner of the contest turned on the loudspeaker he won. He connected it to a mobile phone and went dancing in the streets around Matadero. He was followed, like as a kind of Pied Piper of Hamelin, by a crowd of 150 people like an improvised rave party.[39]

Crossing the borders of the art centre with their sound system, this crowd of dancing bodies followed the drumbeat. They not only crossed the limit between the protected space of the art centre and the streets, but also the line that delimits where playing music through a speaker is permitted and where it is illegal. Like in a spontaneous Reclaim The Streets protest, the crowd went on dancing and defying the possibility of a police intervention until late hours. Participants remember it as a significant collective liberation.

> It's a little difficult to explain … it was an energy that came from the group, people were putting on music and we all seemed to acquire the code of the dance, a feeling of abandon,

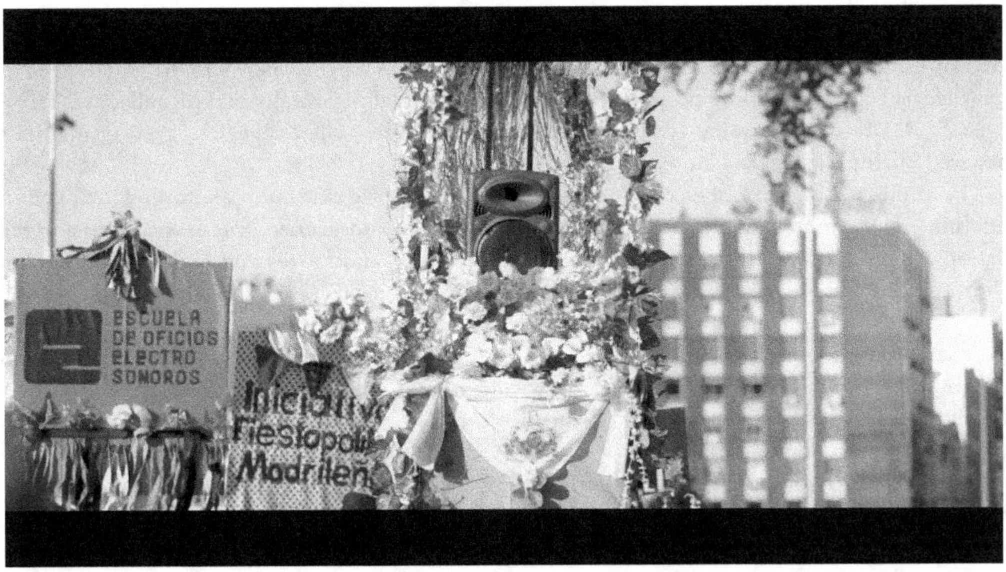


*Figure 6.3* The palanquin of San Soundsystem I, a snapshot from the short movie *La Romería de los Voltios* (2017), by Grupal Crew Collective (2017). Photo credit: Grupal Crew Collective

> of being in the street, of taking off our clothes, thinking "this can't stop here," a moment of collective ecstasy. I remember the police passed by several times, but they didn't say anything, and we stayed there until 3 o'clock playing great music and not so great music and dancing like crazies.[40]
>
> I danced and rubbed up against other sweaty people. It seemed like my body was set free ... as if my body lost its limits and merged with all the other bodies and through the music became one pulsating body unified by one marvellous and improvised choreography.[41]

Since then, the annual *Romeria of the Volts* remembers and re-enacts this experience every summer. Through a two kilometres path, it claims the right to the city's public space for those who are often considered outside normativity: LGBTIQ+ activists, ravers, associations for conscious club culture, or even rarer ones, like the church of Nicholas Cage's worshippers or the "DJs without a booth" association. The parade celebrates this diversity and demands spaces for its expression by dancing in the streets to a collective playlist played randomly by mobile devices.

*Semilla Boombox* in the Relampaguito Park was a great success and attracted many people of all ages, producing and enjoying a very heterogeneous playlist and revealing the appeal of collective mobile listening and music sharing. Conversely, the atmosphere created in the park bothered some of the neighbours, who did not like how this familiar place sounded now. The area near the park is a relatively gentrified zone of white national middle-class people who did not appreciate the attendance of people from other areas of Villaverde, especially youth. They complained to the council about the noise. In this case, bearing in mind the low volume due to the urban regulations and the distance between the park and the closest houses, it was not the music sound but the augmented public presence of those others, in what they perceive as their territory, that was noisy. Thus, *Semilla Boombox* was involved in that inherent contentious politics of the urban public spaces,[42] making visible and audible the different social fabric of the neighbourhood regarding class, age and ethnicity, and their territorial controversies.

## The Herald, or a Tentative Conclusion

After one hour and a half into the parade, with frequent stops for the dance and the ritual speeches, the *Romeria* gets to its ending point, where the party goes on informally and illegally, as it started in 2015. Before its end, every year, a herald is chosen to give a last speech, a kind of manifesto prepared during the weeks before the event.

The projects discussed here are choreographies of spacing and mutual tuning in involving different people, mobile media such as mobile phones and loudspeakers, and institutions and regulations. They show ways of sharing personal music tastes and moves and making them public. Thus, they contribute to making people public through their increased visual and sonic presence. Both, human and non-human participants affect and participate in making the public, revealing and challenging the politics of the ordinary. These collective ways of sound spacing and mobile listening reveal how public space is a paradoxical space of controversies and negotiations due to the heterogeneity of the subjects and objects involved. In performances and enactments that are territorial displays and negotiations as well, we modulate our visual and sonic presence.

These spacing choreographies entail different temporalities. The *Romeria* has a ritualistic vocation and is repeated every year. The *Soundsystem Guerrilla* was deemed to last and go viral, even if the illegality of the interventions proposed limited its expansion. And the *Semilla Boombox* worked for several hours every day during August 2013. Since then, it has been re-enacted in festivals organized by Intermediae, such as the youth event FESTeen, as the technical equipment (mobile app and loudspeakers) can be easily moved.

Due to current urban noise regulation, urban segregation, gentrification, and social inequalities and prejudices, the mobile musicking possibilities afforded by mobile media become more disruptive. Public art initiatives, often hosted and invited by local institutions, facilitate the emergence of these choreographic performances, increasing sonic presences and encounters. The examples discussed presented themselves as straightforward forms of reclaiming the streets and of fostering mobilities between art and the ordinary with the help of mobile media.

However, the artistic and institutional framing of these mobile media practices entails its own pitfalls regarding this claim. First, they often fail to call and assure the participation of those excluded from the usual artistic audiences. For instance, every year, the *Romeria of the Volts* gathers a diverse crowd regarding gender, sexuality and age, but it is mostly white and middle-class. Second, in spite of the wish of becoming viral or replicated, these projects often are single events, raising ephemeral awareness in the best of cases, as in the example of *Soundsystem Guerrilla,* and are hardly replicated due to financial, technical, or regulatory issues such as the case of *Semilla Boombox*. This project succeeded in assuring the participation of people and spaces outside the usual artistic realm, but also revealed the weakness of the artistic frame to counteract social prejudices and inequalities out of the art centres. The re-enactment of these choreographic performances is only assured in the spatial and temporal boundaries of artistic events or youth festivals with mostly white and middle-class participants. It is as if the "art" in the expression Public Art was at the same time a condition and limitation of its public vocation to reach and affect the public. These projects are not only collective experiences but they are also experiments aiming to make issues, claims, and presences public beyond the artistic realm.

We conclude here with an extract of the text that closed the first edition of the *Romeria of the Volts*, written and read by the performer and cultural agitator Jesús Bravo:

> Romeros, neighbours, friends and dancers, bodies full of desire and passion, groups and collectives here in front of me, welcome to the *Romeria of the Volts*. We come from the streets and we live in the streets. Madrid depends on its plazas and its streets. For a few hours we'll take back these spaces for the people. For those who are cheerful and willing. So that we don't lose our sense of illusion and keep enjoying life.

Volts are units of electrical measurement, volts are basically an excuse to talk about batteries, which are in effect a form of electrical autonomy. "Give yourself a volt" [go for a stroll] is an expression that has fallen into disuse, but it gives off an air of the sense of abandon that impregnated the roguish enthusiasm of the eighties. The *Romeria of the Volts* attempts to bring those words and traditions back to life to create something new. To reclaim the importance of the Volts. Autonomy. To take as our own what is relevant from the expression. The Street. To give ourselves a volt with these containers of volts, these speaking objects, in a festive and beautiful way, the streets are ours. They belong to the people that inhabit them that walk them and that dance in them, and we're not dependent on anyone to demonstrate it.

Although these enormous speakers have 4 hours of autonomy, our flesh and our spirit is unlimited. We don't need electricity to feed the energy that flows through us. It connects us, it brings us together today, in this plaza, in this neighbourhood, in this city.[43]

## Notes

1 Christopher Small, *Musicking: The Meanings of Performing and Listening* (Hanover: Wesleyan University Press, 1998).
2 Pascal Wyse quoted by Dan Hancox, "Mobile Disco: How Phones make Music Inescapable," *The Guardian*, 12 August 2010, www.theguardian.com/music/2010/aug/12/sodcasting-music-in-public-mobile-phones.
3 Carmen Pardo Salgado, "Cartographies of Simultaneity," *International Journal of Art and Art History* 3, no. 2 (2015): 17–29, doi: 10.15640/ijaah.v3n2a2.
4 Amparo Lasén, "Disruptive Ambient Music. Mobile Phone Music Listening," *European Journal of Cultural Studies* 21, no. 1 (2018): 96–110, doi: 10.1177/1367549417705607.
5 Andres Jaque, "15M and YES WE CAMP. Controversy as Urbanism," *Domus*, 20 July 2011, www.domusweb.it/en/op-ed/2011/07/20/15m-and-yes-we-camp-controversy-as-urbanism.html.
6 Grupal Crew Collective, *La Romería de Los Voltios*, 2017, https://vimeo.com/277509064.
7 Jonathan Sterne, *MP3 The Meaning of a Format* (Durham: Duke University Press, 2012).
8 Lasén, "Disruptive ambient music."
9 Joseph Schloss and Bill Bahng Boyer, "Urban Echoes: The Boombox and Sonic Mobility in the 1980s," in *The Oxford Handbook of Mobile Music Studies Volume 1*, edited by Sumanth Gopinath and Jason Stanyek (Oxford: Oxford University Press, 2014), 399–412.
10 Sumanth Gopinath and Jason Stanyek, "Anytime, Anywhere? An Introduction to the Devices, Markets, and Theories of Mobile Music," in *The Oxford Handbook of Mobile Music Studies Volume 1*, edited by Sumanth Gopinath and Jason Stanyek (Oxford: Oxford University Press, 2014), 1–34.
11 *Do The Right Thing*, directed by Spike Lee, 1989.
12 Sergio Galán, *Semilla Boombox*, 2013, http://sergio.eclectico.net/portfolio/semilla-boombox.html.
13 Karin.Bijsterveld, *Mechanical Sound: Technology, Culture, and Public Problems of Noise in The Twentieth Century* (Boston, MA: MIT Press, 2008).
14 Brandon Labelle, *Acoustic Territories. Sound Culture and Everyday Life* (New York: The Continuum International Publishing Group Inc, 2010).
15 Ayuntamiento de Madrid, *Zonas de Protección Acústica Especial*, 2019, www.madrid.es/portales/munimadrid/es/Inicio/El-Ayuntamiento/Publicaciones/Listado-de-Publicaciones/Zonas-de-proteccion-acustica-y-ambiental-de-Madrid/?vgnextfmt=default&vgnextoid=5b34198f267cc410VgnVCM1000000b205a0aRCRD&vgnextchannel=f1aebadb6b997010VgnVCM100000dc0ca8c0RCRD.
16 Ayuntamiento de Madrid, *Diviértete Sin Molestar*, 6 July 2016, www.madrid.es/portales/munimadrid/es/Inicio/Actualidad/Noticias/Diviertete-sin-molestar/?vgnextfmt=default&vgnextoid=87eca077d6f-b5510VgnVCM2000001f4a900aRCRD&vgnextchannel=a12149fa40ec9410VgnVCM100000171f5a0aRCRD.
17 Ayuntamiento de Madrid, "'Salimos sin molestar' o cómo conciliar el ocio nocturno y el descanso vecinal," 24 April 2019, www.madrid.es/portales/munimadrid/es/Inicio/Actualidad/Noticias/Salimos-sin-molestar-o-como-conciliar-el-ocio-nocturno-y-el-descanso-vecinal/?vgnextfmt=default&vgnextoid=7c1a112128f4a610VgnVCM1000001d4a900aRCRD&vgnextchannel=a12149fa40ec9410VgnVCM100000171f5a0aRCRD#.

18 *Post-it City*, 2013, www.ciutatsocasionals.net/.
19 Centro de Arte 2 de Mayo, *Pop Politics*, 30 November 2012, http://ca2m.org/es/historico/item/1363-pop-politics-4.
20 Todo Por la Praxis, *Soundsystem Guerrilla*, 2013, https://todoporlapraxis.es/048-soundsystem-guerrilla/.
21 CentroCentro Cibeles, *Charivaria*, 24 November 2017, www.youtube.com/watch?v=rtY-armtLos.
22 Ars Herejé, *Iª Procesión Amplificada*, 20 September 2007, www.youtube.com/watch?v=3ACFyL-m3Vk.
23 "Carmena alberga la exposición de unos 'artistas' que ridiculizan las procesiones en Semana Santa," *Ok Diario*, 4 December 2018, https://okdiario.com/espana/carmena-alberga-exposicion-unos-artistas-ridiculizan-procesiones-semana-santa-1577869.
24 CentroCentro Cibeles, *Charivaria. Actividades Y Visitas Comentadas*, 15 November 2018, www.centrocentro.org/programa-publico/charivaria-actividades-y-visitas-comentadas.
25 Massimiliano Casu, A Sonic March, 2018, https://sonicmarch.tumblr.com/.
26 Simon Frith, *Taking Popular Music Seriously* (New York: Routledge, 2016); Pablo Vila, "Identidades, narrativas y música. Una primera propuesta para entender sus relaciones," *Revista Transcultural de Música* 2 (1996): 1–27.
27 Kathleen Stewart, "Atmospheric attunements," *Environment and Planning D Society and Space* 29 (2011): 445, doi: 10.1068/d9109.
28 Intermediae, Ciudad Bailar, 23 October 2018, www.intermediae.es/agenda/ucmm-ciudad-bailar-cuerpos-calles-pistas-de-baile.
29 Intermediae, *UCMM—Ciudad Bailar/ mesa 4_ Ciudad Pista de Baile 27.10.2018*, 2018, https://vimeo.com/303119713.
30 Foro por la memoria de la Comunidad de Madrid "Vecinos de Villaverde Alto (Madrid capital) denuncian que el 'Cara el Sol' suena por megafonía en una pista deportiva municipal," *Foros por la memoria*, 28 August 2013, www.foroporlamemoria.info/2013/08/vecinos-de-villaverde-alto-madrid-capital-denuncian-que-el-cara-el-sol-suena-por-megafonia-en-una-pista-deportiva-municipal/. See also the comments to the same post shared in this other website, where some of the participants ask for content moderation in order to prevent this kind of songs to be played: www.meneame.net/story/vecinos-villaverde-alto-denuncian-cara-sol-suena-megafonia-pista.
31 "Who Are Tom and Gary and What Is This Thing," The Official DDP Website, www.decentralizeddanceparty.com/faq/about/.
32 Some of the tactics used during these social protests, such as the "Human Microphone," where people listening to a speaker loudly repeat each sentence, or the *caceroladas* in which gatherings of protesters hitting cooking pots are based on the same idea: decentralize the sound emission in order to avoid law restrictions and to strengthen the protester's active role.
33 Amparo Lasen and Iñaki Martínez de Albeniz, "'An Original Protest, at Least': Mediality and Participation," in *Cultures of Participation: Media Practices, Politics and Literacy*, edited by Hajo Greif, Larissa Hjorth, Amparo Lasen and Claire Lobet-Maris (Berlin: Peter Lang, 2011): 141–58.
34 Francesco Careri, *Walkscapes, el andar como práctica estética* (Barcelona: Editorial Gustavo Gili, 2002).
35 Rebecca Solnit, *Wanderlust: A History of Walking* (New York: Penguin Books, 2001), 402.
36 Anahid Kassabian, *Ubiquitous Listening. Affect, Attention, and Distributed Subjectivity* (Berkeley: University of California Press, 2013).
37 Robin. Balliger, "Sounds of Resistance," in *The Global Resistance Reader*, edited by Louise Amoore (New York: Routledge, 2005), 434.
38 Judith Butler, *Notes Toward a Performative Theory of Assembly* (Cambridge: Harvard University Press, 2015).
39 These moments are depicted in the first 5 minutes of Grupal Crew Collective's short film, *La Romería de los Voltios*, 2017, https://vimeo.com/277509064.
40 Pablo Durango, from the film *La Romería de los Voltios*, 2017.
41 Eva Zaragoza, from the film *La Romería de los Voltios*, 2017.
42 Jaque, "15M and YES WE CAMP."
43 Jesús Bravo, from the film *La Romería de los Voltios*, 2017.

# 7

# PERFORMING WITH THE AETHER

## An Aesthetics of Tactical Feminist Practice

*Nancy Mauro-Flude*

This chapter describes the application of networking technology as an artistic medium and reconsiders mobile media art practice through introducing the concepts of the feminist internet and the *oimai*, an antediluvian term that unravels the processual marvels of wandering through the labyrinth of the world.[1] When we navigate through the *cosmographia* of analog and digital networks in our passing, we leave a variety of tracks inadvertently when encumbered with electronic devices and mobile gadgets these traces become substantial.[2] The digital—as technically defined—is abstracted symbols such as letters, numbers, incremental units, or instruction sets irreconcilable to multifaceted analog signals that vary on scale, such as a "sound wave, a light wave, a magnetic field, the flow of electricity in any circuit including a computer chip," including, but not limited to footprints and scent.[3] Thus, many of us unwittingly disclose information that can be analyzed to a disconcerting level of accuracy with publicly available forensic tools.

Paradoxically, in 2019, it is a typical condition that citizens possessing mundane consumer mobile devices also intentionally engage in the media practice of perpetual recording and sending of data through third-party social media platforms.[4] For two decades, business services harness "users" through digital technologies to link their daily activities by providing interfaces between mobile devices and internet-based applications for archiving digital imagery and blogging activities. Consummate research on facilitating real-time documentary has been delivered by Gordon Bell's/ *MyLifeBits/* (2001) project, while a menacing counterpart to this work was initially formulated in the Defence Advanced Research Projects Agency's (DARPA) concept of a "Total Information Awareness Office."[5]

There is no doubt that ubiquitous computing has altered archiving and storing practices. Whereas conventional archiving implied curation, selection, and maintaining processes, documentation in the digital age is often reduced to recording and storing simply everything with the benevolent, benign, or malignant possibility of future selection. Colossal databases of information collection frequently result in unregulated trade by brokers. This unearths complex political issues around ownership, access and control over the data generated in the aether, notwithstanding the issue of who finances and profits from said data. Nevertheless, the transmission of information has never been, nor is simply neutral, reminding us how war does not end but instead evolves, as does our fundamental experience of communication design.[6] Aesthetic developments in design, art, and fashion arbitrations of knowledge transmission in mobile media in the context of war are docilely domesticated.

Extensively, mobile media has facilitated the art of map making, a significant military technology enabling colonial pursuits. Artisanal open hardware experiments in mobile media art and design share commonalities with emergent systems in the professional telecommunications industry—they bring a paradoxical return of Renaissance tactics of wartime espionage. This reaches back to Galileo who taught private courses on fortification (1592–1609) where the practical discipline of military architecture, geometry, and drawing techniques revolved around a distinctive compass kit developed for students.[7] Early obsessions with *machinic* fortification connect directly into the cybernetic reveries of World War II and advances in military device automation—shadowed by the 1950s concentration on satellites and intergalactic navigation. Aesthetic concerns and encryption are never far from the military objectives of exploration into ways to protect or deceive—where the figure of the "other" emerges as an enemy or a projected threat and often sways the inventions of new media.[8]

In contrast to expedient narratives of technocratic progress, this chapter enquires how a situated engagement with bespoke hardware, creative code, aesthetical computational media, and electronics can further explore the ingenuity behind our fascination with a force that connects us all—*the aether.*[9] An elusive medium that dwells in the interstices between the particles of matter embracing innumerable resonances and rays. *The aether,* understood as incorporeal but not merely celestial, is a part of cultural lore for many who hold dear to the world view that embraces "a deep understanding … of sites that hold … subtle feelings that resonate through the bodies…."[10] Tuning into rarefied elements and realms in order to augur, translate, manoeuver and/or transmit indeterminate gems assisted by an assemblage of minerals consisting of custom-built code, and electronics is addressed in this chapter.[11]

## The Tactical Spectrum

A period of widespread media diversification was enabled most dramatically through the rise of the internet of networked cultures. The term "tactical media" was conceived by David Garcia and Geert Lovink in 1997 stating, "The artist needs to learn how to operate as a nomadic sophist in a migrant polis."[12] The philosophical and political problems of such a proposition were outlined in their manifesto, *The ABC of Tactical Media* proposed to remedy to the media autocracy that Peter Lamborn Wilson intriguingly described as "The enemy … the unopposed rule of money over human values."[13] The domination of commercial stakeholder interests over "user" well-being plugged into the heart of wider societal systems and mechanisms. The nemesis of broadcast media corporations funded by stakeholders endorsed gratuitous consumption through ruthless target marketing.

In reaction "tactical media" as a subculture made on-the-fly speculative interventions to "an antidote to newly emerging forms of technocratic scientism which under the banner of posthumanism tends to restrict discussions of human use and social reception."[14] Critical perspectives generated by alternative symposiums acted to unravel nascent techno utopian transhuman narratives spawned by Silicon Valley computer culture.[15] The "tactical media" concept was expressed in opposition to the enemy, that is, formations of hierarchical power (the Nation State, the Mass Media) and congealed notions of class, gender, bloodline, status, occupation, ethnicity, and other variants of colonial dominance and privilege. It also referenced the theories of Michel de Certeau whose "Tactics" encouraged diverse forms of knowledge through variegated resources and self-reflexivity in everyday life (in an invigorated and performative manner) to challenge centralized mass concentrations of power structures.[16]

The "Information Superhighway" is the epitome of such futuristic tendencies for which the internet is colloquially described.[17] Consequently, such adversary "tactics" were also influenced by avant-garde experimentation with mediums, including the historical and intellectual context of the Situationist International (SI) movement.[18] Simultaneously, "tactical media" harks back to Walter Benjamin's Marxist plea for more rigorous attitudes in creation, in order to perceive the nascent conceptual languages of emergent industrial culture and production in order to turn consumers into prosumers.[19]

A thread common in twenty-first-century art practices influenced by "tactical media" is to conduct creative exploits of command and control matrixes.[20] The onset of the internet was always predicted to behold potential perverse elements that are "...woefully inadequate for the extremely large number of often complex trades that will be required."[21] With this background in mind, we may now be able to examine a tactical feminist media practice through the context of *Bag Lady 2.0* (2007), a bespoke apparatus for creative acts of cosmographic cartography. Bestowing alternate modes of engagement, the artist investigates how we habitually document, record, encode, broadcast, and transmit data emissions in our daily lives through commercially available off-the-shelf products.

In contrast, appraising artisanal custom design as critical theory and practice, Hanna Musiol writes that

> We owe, in many ways, the very practice and metaphors of digital encryption and decryption not only to the military but also to LGBTQ+ innovators to forgotten female laborers, whose removal from that history is paralleled by the erasure of the work of ethnic or indigenous Navajo, Choctaw, or Comanche coders.[22]

Exemplified by women "computers" who were tasked with providing computers instructions via cryptic machine code in places such as Monterey, Australia's own Bletchley Park, the British Government Cypher code-breakers' headquarters during World War II.[23] Remarkably cracking the Enigma cipher system and changing the course of the conflict for Europe—and the Pacific region—it is astounding that after 60 years in 2017, Joan Fairbridge was able to discuss her role as "the cream of Australian, American and British code-breakers, code-readers a small army of young women specialising in processing and analysing intelligence ... worked covertly on 'sigint' (signals intelligence) in Melbourne...."[24] Engendering the complicated ways and means, the gap between production and consumption feeds into concealed machine labor is worth coming to terms with and comprehending, albeit exceeds the bounds of this chapter. Yet, the necessity for feminist voices to clarify and reify a diversity of perspectives, challenging conventional methods thus requiring a restructuring of institutional, educational, economic, corporeal, and cultural barriers, is undeniable.

Performing directly and repetitively with more-than-human entities—such as systems and networks—intersections and tangential assemblages are formed with corporeally distant and local actants. Addressing computational media as a processual medium where wired terrestrial and wireless extra-terrestrial communication takes place gives rise to the notion that "the greater the dependence on a technology the greater the need to study and expose its inner workings ... expand[ing] 'machine' to describe interrelationships encompassing devices, bodies, agents, forces and networks."[25] This suggests that as a species we are assemblages of elements, notwithstanding our computational media mother boards as new temples in which we pay reverence to the stones, elements, particles, and molecules from which they draw.

Alluding to issues around technological power relations of computational provenance, commodity electronics through implementation of alternative networking technologies as artistic mediums by their very nature challenges official modes of knowledge production and dissemination, especially an opaque internet infrastructure sanctioned by state and commercial interests. A position is articulated through means of the author's peripatetic project *Bag Lady 2.0* (2007) (Figure 7.1a and b) by way of investigating and intervening into the Wireless Fidelity (Wi-Fi) spectrum, introducing custom hardware and rigorous techniques for a psycho-geophysical comprehension of the zone around us.

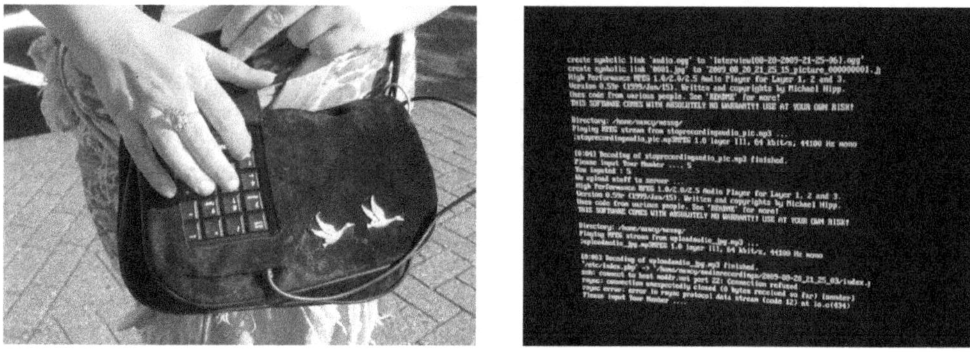

*Figure 7.1* Left: *Bag Lady 2.0* Performative Transmission; Right: Software Encryption Screengrab. Photo credits: Nancy Mauro-Flude

## Bag Lady 2.0 and the Feminist Internet

*Bag Lady 2.0* is a custom-built computational tool conceived in order to reflect on the aesthetics of poetic computation and signal communication more broadly. An expressive communications device, this autopoietic machine has more than a broadcast function, which Turkle describes as "intimate machines" that are "experienced as both part of the self and of the external world."[26] Baring the testimony to tactility and making, transmitting glimpses and aspects of the world in motion including abrasions and smudges, the output is not a hi-res graphical masterpiece of immersive visual sublimation—instead the aesthetic embraces "the capacity to capture a moment and contribute to the ongoing constitution of nonunified collective intelligence outside and in between the blind alleys of the silicon age."[27] Reaching beyond archival telos the interdisciplinary project forecasts that networking technology could be *something other* than an "Information Superhighway," a thinly veiled data harvesting system operating on the ground in the guise of *The Cloud.* At the Australian Linux conference in 2009, the intentions of the hardware experimentation was

> ...intended as an artistic and political statement ... it contains a Linux-based system with wireless networking ... The immediate-upload feature ensures that the data gets out, even if the device is discovered—at least, in places where an open access point is available. The subversive possibilities of such a device are clear; so are the potential privacy problems. Nancy was clearly aware of those issues ... Others will certainly follow this particular artist's lead; expect to see more mobile devices which record their immediate environments and put the results on a server for all to see. It is going to be interesting.[28]

Typically, "users" access the internet amid heavily prescribed trajectories navigating through distended Graphical User Interface (GUI) applications. In contrast, envisioning the internet as feminist, means it is scalable and lovingly hand coded, beckoning deeper understandings of the computational medium and the underlying directory structure encouraging adeptness in digital literacy through the practice engagement. Providing documentation of design specificities, the *Bag Lady 2.0* website is a crucial aspect of the work to reduce technical asymmetry.

Experimentation with a network of internet servers is not possible without an autonomously maintained server which confers agency to a community of users for testing. A server is a computer program that provides services to users and other computer programs in the form of local or remote computers including processing requests from client programs. Thus, a feminist server aims to provide a safe space for experimentation with internet protocols, for an intimate community who are considered "prosumers," instead of "clients" who have limited webserver access and permissions antithetical to archetypes of supremacy.[29] Running on an Apache webserver and a Debian operating system—an open source Linux distribution—means that the source code is made available for users to modify and extend upon.

Hence, a conflict between experimentation and a need for dependability arises. Experimenting with custom tools in ubiquitous computing and mobile media art means digital literacy practices and infrastructures are inherently self-led, chaotic, and locally shaped. The tension between ideals and action does not have effortless solutions for complex systems.[30] Tiziana Terranova explains "it is not enough to demystify the Internet as the latest capitalist machination against labour ... it is ... an immensely complex range of cultural and economic phenomena."[31] Thus, the "feminist internet" is a nascent pioneering form of knowledge transformation, experientially learning about system maintenance with peers as an alternative mode of exchange in post-industrial network society.[32]

Working against the grain of an internet that casts its web as a homogenizing technology eradicating difference and giving users a finite set of choices for interaction, if the artist should take responsibility as system administrator of her own computer server, the act abandons deterministic systems deeply informed by malefic conditions of colonialism. Dubbed as the "great digital swindle," Mark Fisher catechizes "how has this model of progress, in which history culminates in the glorious invention of iPhones and apps, become so uncontested? ... old forms of exploitation are obfuscated by the distracting urgencies of digital communication."[33] This recognizes how "users" have little choice but to conform to the existing laws and regulations applicable within national jurisdiction. Commercial models prey on the unsuspecting users, especially those with rudimentary digital literacy, and thus exceedingly complex to countenance.

## The Technical Anatomy of Bag Lady 2.0

We can consider the *Bag Lady 2.0* scenario as follows:

> In the new dark ages after "The Crash," of capitalism, a bag lady lives in the wreckage. In the spirit of a bricoleur weaving through the discarded wardrobe of industrial waste lands, she scans, tracks, wanders and plays with what is encountered; throwing coins, analyzing motherboards, scrying through the dense layering of small cell chemical and electromagnetic content passing through both body and air, navigating via constellations, auguring mythologies from circuit assemblages. Tuning in, redirecting and distributing signals, by conducting tactical magic faerie circuits. She travels light, embellished with a black suede bag, embedded with a keyboard, microcomputer and antennae, probing the aether. Pirating open WiFi networks with her autopoietic machine, she archives and broadcasts her on-the-fly encounters.

*Bag Lady 2.0* (2007) is a net.art performance of indeterminate wanderings with a customized electronic tool, a small bag with an antenna and an embedded board, programmed for live transmission of sound, digital image, video, and text. The device probes for open Wi-Fi access points connected to the internet, so as to transmit real-time image and audio feeds onto a webserver. A first-person point-of-view, the artist as "nomadic sophist" collects fragments that she considers worthy of transmission (Figure 6, color insert) to a designated.html webpage.

The project has at times appeared simultaneously as an installation in a gallery space. In 2010, an iteration of *Bag Lady 2.0* was exhibited for four months in Hobart at the Tasmanian Museum and Art Gallery. Pictured in Figure 7.2 (left) we see the bag and its contents along with a small laptop featuring the project website—in front of a gaffer-taped map of Hobart. At times, the artist took the handbag and its electronic components for a walk in the streets, secretly capturing images of the local environment. Photographs were printed and stuck to relevant points on the map to

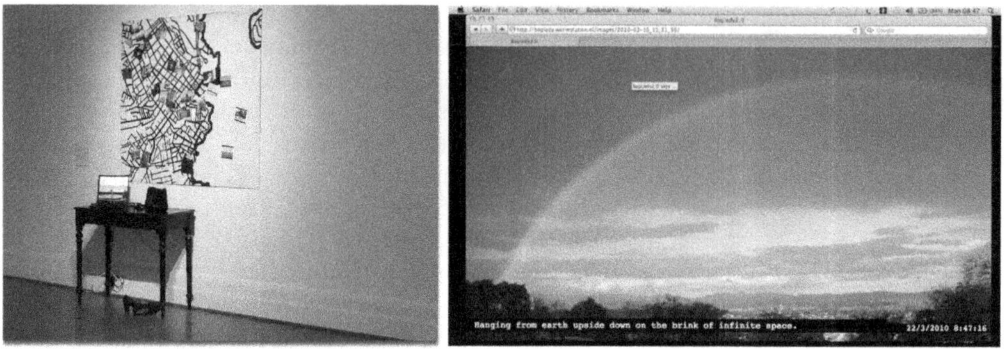


*Figure 7.2* Left: *Bag Lady 2.0* Tasmanian Museum and Art Gallery (2010). Right: Screen shot *Bag Lady 2.0* Browser transmission. Photo credit: Nancy Mauro-Flude

accompany the moving footage captures updated on the *Bag Lady* website. Daily RSS (Rich Site Summary) news feeds from local newspaper *The Mercury* flashed constantly at the bottom of the screen, emphasizing the works immediate relationship to time and locality.[34]

The small bag holds an antenna, an embedded board 500 mhz with an 8GB flash card, a small numeric keypad programmed for live wireless broadcasting of a sound, digital image performance event, as seen in Figures 1–4. A web camera takes an image 1 x frame every 5 seconds which is then uploaded to the server (Figure 7.2, right). Audio is captured via a cortado player and embedded as both an audio and image series onto the server, where requested.html files from the web server are executed, thus exhibited in a browser (i.e. Firefox, Chrome). As soon as the files are uploaded and double checked for errors, they are deleted from the bag's hard drive. The collected data is encoded to only take up the least amount of bandwidth and hard drive space. Not only does this method appreciate file collection as a dynamic process rather than one of sedimentary accumulation, it is the effervescent manner of processing that eludes any possible interception on the local drive, in the case sensitive information has been collected.

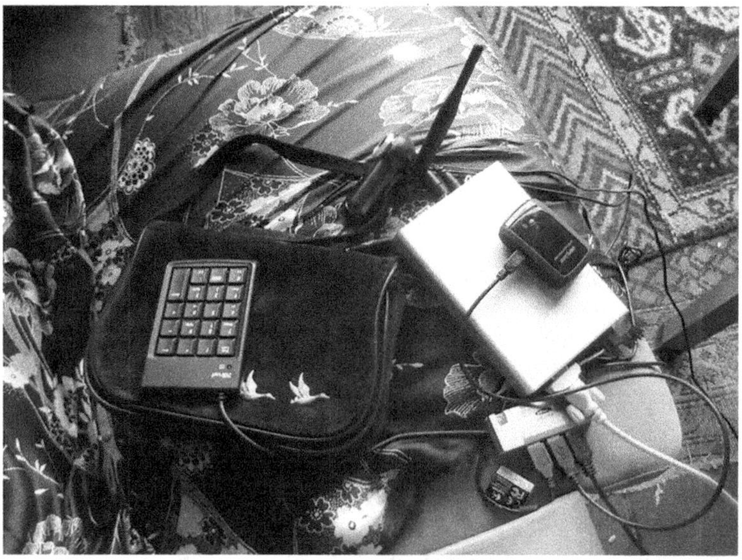

*Figure 7.3* *Bag Lady 2.0* Hardware: Photo credit: Nancy Mauro-Flude

Hardware, as seen in Figure 7.1 and 7.3:

1x Alix3c3 mini euro-card format with Audio, VGA and Award-BIOS [super expandable] 500 MHz Processor[35]
1x wireless card 1x mini pigtail for external antenna
1x Battery Power 12 V
1x 8 Gb Cf card
1x USB webcam Logitech CamPro 9000 is 1600x1200 (HD-TV)
1x 4 port mini-min USB hub
1x numeric keypad
1x external battery power for 12 v 800ma and recharger
1x Black Handbag.
Software—some of the file parsing is seen in Figure 6
Bash script command syntax
LFS Linux from scratch
KNOPPIX kernel
Audio streaming darkice as client. Encoding ogg vorbis
Webcam UVC video module

The performer need not look at a screen in place of the typical computational user paradigm of a GUI one often encounters to capture, edit, and share digital audio and video (AV). Instead, the operation of the device occurs through a numeric USB controller where audio is the interface. The artist receives a series of sound prompts via headphones to operate the microcomputer through a small numeric keyboard that triggers auto functions (i.e. press: 1# Scan for network | 2# Connect | 3# Start AV | 4# Stop recording AV. 5# Upload to a server | #666 Reboot, and so on). A script paired with the number keypad both records and streams AV data to the server, as seen in Figures 2, 3 and 5. A bash script command processor makes this possible through running on a microcomputer installed with Linux from scratch, KNOPPIX kernel, audio streaming, darkice as client, encoding ogg vorbis, and employing a Webcam UVC video module. The front-end of the website is coded with .html and javascript where the images are provided as a composite—when clicked on, a moving image feed shows embedded texts from the performer, interspersed with subjective aphorisms and an "off beat news" RSS feed—into the browser (Figure 7.2b).

What is often not examined is the tactical friction inherent within these systems that make the seamless vision of being able to truly customize such a device quite unattainable. The design, production, and deployment of this kind of system involves extensive time on technical forums, testing and simply the hands-on coding and coordination between many different software packages and firmware—with each having their own dependences. The process of trying to link together the many layers of technology using a "bricolage of component middleware," none of which is initially optimized for the task.[36] The mobile media art project is first and foremost a provocation because, as a group of artifacts, *Bag Lady 2.0* is a volatile, material residue of critique on commodity electronics.

## Feminist Encryption

The foremost principles of networked art are acknowledging the internet as a cultural apparatus, the browser as a canvas is a place where art can also happen (rather than merely a mercantile or military matrix). Feminist tactical media practice stretches interfaces and technologies into the realm of dreams and the imagination, ripping them from their function of a commonplace commodity or military inspired tool. The author was active in many grassroots digital literacy projects, including creative research into ubiquitous wireless public surveillance systems, specifically how they could be decrypted and used for alternative kinds of experience beyond that of control. Mirko Tobias Schafer noted that,

> As an artist and a designer she forges the raw materials of her art to fit more than just the work of art itself. Basic research, appropriation of electronic consumer goods and applied technological design constitutes a work of art that consequently questions the apparatus of production and opens a range of unknown possibilities for others to employ and extend upon. Instead of creating yet another black box that just blinks, sounds or does something funny, Nancy Mauro-Flude provides a literally open bag full of possibilities.[37]

One instance of this is commonly known in computer hacker circles as "Video Sniffing," stemming from the practice of picking up signals broadcast by wireless CCTV networks using a cheap video receiver. Empirical research questions were asked, such as: *What do the cameras see?; Is the data simply recorded via automated process and stored?; Is there an alert system?; How is this information interpreted?* Consequently, the practice of analyzing and evaluating the aether through experientially working with wireless phenomena based on these questions foregrounded that we need further articulation of conflicts in knowledge production. Bringing to the fore the possibility of reconfiguring data capture as processes of control, to a process of release, which generates further visibility in how the cultural politics in these lines of thought acquired its concrete materiality in *Bag Lady 2.0.*

Thus, awareness of the control codes hardwired into conceivable interactions with our environs is "a mutation that is totally immanent to late capitalism..."[38]—that is, the software actants that orientate, nudge, and configure our perception. Corporations make *de jure* decisions on the software we use every day, creating a one-way system where the vast majority of us have no control over indispensables means of communication. As an alternative, *Bag Lady 2.0* envisaged a hopeful trajectory for a "feminist internet" and to the diverse ways of how we may experience a repository of knowledge. To reconsider, *what if* the internet was a place of engaged autonomy and not a place of malign ubiquitous surveillance? Reaching beyond standard applications of surveillance that typically fall into two camps. On the one hand, there is the Michel Foucault model that presents surveillance as a disciplining force and focuses on the loss of individual privacy.[39] On the other hand, surveillance through uniformed consent is often embraced by consumers. For instance, the gestural act of scrolling and swiping one's consumer mobile phone is not only the recuperation of free time by capitalism, masked as leisure it turns *free* work into labor where the conflation of *fun* and profit is perfectly executed. It is often referred to as "voluntary servitude," a term initially explained by Etienne de la Boëtie (1577).[40] This catchy notion is dismissed by Pierre Bourdieu who deduced this as essentialist and simplified evidencing the nebulous aspects at play in submission and domination.[41] In line with Terranova's point on how "the deepening exploitation based on free labour..." is "an intensification and therefore a mutation, of a widespread cultural and economic logic,"[42] Foucault and Bourdieu advocate for nuanced reflection of the patterns that trap our perceptions and desire since to not recognize these results is akin to being enslaved by alien habits and conventions.

By tinkering into systems for other kinds of experience than one of control but as a release, radically aims to challenge the restrictions brought about by reductionist systems that ignore the complexity of actants in human and non-human relationships that nest, recur, and repeat beyond the initial adoption of a technological solution. Aberrant behavior opens up entirely new sets of possibilities towards that which we develop habitual use patterns. Exploring the unintended by-products of wireless emissions—specifically the porosity of borders and rarefication—opens up confined technical knowledges from centralization and standardization. This creates alternative spaces for corporeal and cultural politics that exist beyond the shadow of sovereignty even the possibility of digital literacy acquisition.

Tactical feminist practices of decryption transfigure the way we understand the world, mutating and exploring new ways of *doing* change and including diverse personhood such as the poor, imperiled, terrified, and the supposedly dangerous. The dull ceremonies of direct action in protest are easy to grasp, but poetic application in "designing dissent"[43] through technical performances of mutant radical subjectivity, allows for a deeper capacity to start atypical conversations that resonate and ripple beyond initial intent. As Musiol explains,

> Perhaps more vitally, technology itself becomes a medium of critical theory. Thus, it is important to recognize the role and the work of programmers and designers as potential allies of social justice practices, and as creators of critical theory ... This, in turn, requires that we recognize "design" not only as a tool of "social dreaming" ... but also as a vehicle for a radical critical and political practice ... and often as a remedy to legal and political disempowerment.[44]

The aesthetic processes are far-reaching when mobile devices are understood as talismanic paraphernalia, not slick lifestyle products. Analyzing the connection between the accoutrement of the hand-fan and the mobile phone device, Hugh Davies explains the affordances of how these "deeply intimate objects" are simultaneously ubiquitous accessories that convey "expression personal styles, values, politics, and beliefs." In this way, the hand-fan, or handbag can convey volumes of communicative capacities that far exceed their utilitarian function as a fashion item or artifact.[45]

The conception of *Bag Lady2.0* was inspired by the bewitching ingenuity and aesthetic of the underworld milieu. Containing within this function is the ability to be deployed as a fortification tool for grassroots journalists operating under the conditions of oppression. In particular, the character Carla Aulaulu performs this with a bag in *Gods of the Plague/Götter der Pest* (1970) by Fassbinder.[46] Portraying the "Noiry" netherworld character, Carla Aulaulu trades purloined information from out of her wicker handbag (Figure 7.4).

A recurring motif in literature is a character who carries a bag with narrative content that is rather mysterious, unknown or of a shady nature, perhaps counterfeit items, illegitimate material or objects with transcendental power. The ambivalence expressly points to human existence outside the peripheries of dominant culture, and other collective laws and regulating systems in existence, such as, subculture lore, and/or ancestral customs that have no regard for nation state

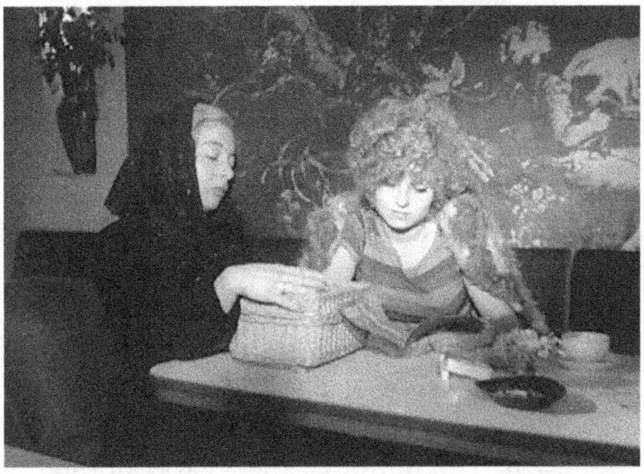

*Figure 7.4* Carla Aulaulu earns money by giving clues from her bag. Screenshot *Gods of the Plague/Götter der Pest* (1970)

meddling in their affairs. These experiential ways of being characteristically evade captivity. Their lack of formal codification allows such knowledges to exist beyond jurisdiction.[47] Acknowledging those who live on the peripheries, in this nonetheless disregarded realm, it is not a matter of choosing to struggle. Rather, it is the inevitability that many people are born who exist under the radar, outside the fold of the imperial establishment. Geert Lovink reminds us, "It must therefore be understood that tactical media never reaches a state of perfection; it is constantly changing, because it constantly needs to question the system under which it operates."[48] It is vital that we continue to read and share such subjugated knowledges, encrypt their secrets, relate it to their interiority, and seek them for such wisdom. In this way, it was intended that *Bag Lady 2.0* goes forth, finds and share meanings from found objects, gestures, signs on the street, and makes connections with them and through them.

## A Peripatetic Stance

> Of these events from somewhere, O Muse, daughter of Zeus, speak also to us.
>
> *(Book 1, line 10)*[49]

The practices of capture and control played out in strategies of consumer electronics raises structural and philosophical issues of the mechanisms that enable mobile media art. Entering into a mobile phone contract, we become a client to a commercial telecommunications platform. The agreement enables us, potentially, to seamlessly receive and transmit data. There is no doubt that most mobile consumer products seem well-made at first (although many have obsolescence built-in). Communicating with ease, we are enrapt (and entrapped in the digital labor of responding, typing, searching, swiping, downloading, reviewing, endorsing, managing accumulations of data, and multi-tasking as an endless administration task). Some of us may even assume the benefits of time saving our data management and opt in to the in-built "cloud storage" the mobile operating system encourages, such as: Google, Samsung, Android, or iPhone. Eventually, we may adjust our settings and endeavor to avoid reductive tedious infrastructures that nudge us to reify our definition of what constitutes reality. Some of us may eventually come to the realization that we have limited permissions to be able to truly customize our consumer device because any deep reconfiguration would void the warranty. All the while this device enables the manipulation of our sensory habitat by machine learning and analyzing our use patterns in order to pipe through notifications and neuromarketing adds.

Taking a cue from the hackneyed maker culture adage "if you can't open it, you don't own it," Kristina Anderson explains how and why we need to develop tools according to our own subjective experience. She writes, "we are re-inserting ourselves into a process that we are otherwise excluded from ... Maybe we can say, we are making technology in order to understand it, and understanding technology in order to make our own."[50] We are not in control of our data if it is stored on a commercial server, nor do we own our software or hardware if it is proprietary. If we can truly choose how we transmit and receive information, it seems consistent that we are granted the freedom to communicate in a diverse and creatively potent manner idiosyncratic to our own predilections. Without having the choice of interface, front end design, presentation modality, and adaption of backend code, as we please, making do with over bloated applications that use far too much bandwidth or content management software templates offered by third-party providers reifies the aesthetic decisions that these carry in their wake.

We must seriously consider the current direction of network topology, global flow and retention of data, and what little control and understanding the typical end-user has of the process of data exchange. As the next wave in mobile 5G wireless technology breaks, satellite cognitive radio's dynamic spectrum access will enable widespread new in-body applications which will alter people's lives worldwide.[51] Ground-breaking communication systems based on biology and chemistry are emerging, encoding bits and bytes through molecules enabling signal transfer, editing and storage in a vast range of new small cell, micro and macroscale applications. This raises serious ethical questions around the impact of corporeal, political, and geographical policies, if biosemiotics becomes a consumer product, rather than a process of emergence.

The reach of computational media is changing the ways we understand and receive knowledge of habitats. Wayfarers could move across lands—their journey was never set in stone but always open to change. Uncovering alternate cartographies brings new insights into familiar routes. John Miles Foley explains how:

> The ancient Greek bard navigates through the maze of traditional story, Homer also speaks of pathways (which he calls *oimai*) "...the Muse has taught the pathways, for she loves the singers' tribe."[52]

This is of interest. Pathways are about how to navigate and plot things as such, the poetic possibilities, "the Homeric *oimai* are parallel to links on the Internet."[53] Reminiscent also Aristotle's peripatetic practice of walking to and from while teaching. Guided by imaginative parables radically beholds the possibility internet as a labyrinthine network of poetic potentials, a public medium, a meeting place and deep information source, along with its tactical aspect such questions-of-presence emphasizes the importance of the *oimai*. The maundering that a peripatetic stance generates is acquiescent to such contingencies. Many people have an emergent ongoing relationship to place—for some it is especially a source of information.

Once our tools took on forms of ritual significance—for instance, talisman and other such paraphernalia objects—that serve the purpose of deep contemplation can become highly customizable. In a world obsessed with convenience and economic expedience, perhaps the ceremonious connection to the mobile device, as an artifact to interface with the aether, can be rethought, revisited, and revived. Musiol elucidates upon how "one's unique 'mobility traces'—cellphone geo-spatial pings, credit card swipes, browsing data—is the most ubiquitous form of collective human–machine scripture, with astounding profit-generating and behavioral-modeling capabilities."[54] Leading to the suggestion upon how provenance of mobile media operations and their production and consumption truly necessitates a rethink. Historically, traces left on stones, plants, rocks, or by rivers, or mountains can be extended to graffiti, public monuments, found objects in the street, as texts, responses, and silent demonstrations. Katherine Hayles forewarns that "An important assumption underlying code's supremacy is the idea that information can be extracted from its material substrate."[55]

The thorough entanglement in the contemporary networked culture of the datasphere is exemplified in *Bag Lady 2.0's* continuous performative exchange. The interjection of sophist visual tableaux that interrupts the otherwise steady image flow act like *thoughts for the day.* These phrases juxtaposed with the textual insertion recording the transmission's time and date stamping (see Figure 7.2, right). Ephemeral thoughts and impressions provide a tone that embellishes these "slices of life" as existing somewhere in between the interstices of ritual and routine and the happenstance of mundane reality and nocturnal reverie.

By tapping into these diverse "other" knowledges in circulation, the *oimai* is only at the scale of our embodied interactions with the place around us that we can aptly observe and sensorially reply to the needs of the unfolding world. For those of us in the metropoles, many of us are becoming unable to discern with any clarity the manner in which we embodied cognition—our memories, perceptions, and thoughts are being overshadowed and shifted by our sensory involvement with consumer electronic technologies. Sincerely being present is intrinsic to the notion of *oimai*, tuning in corporeally to the power of navigation through the aether and other networks of possibilities, which are to be sure not secured or closed:

> What the Muse teaches, we should notice, isn't texts—that is, items supporting the twin illusions of object and stasis—but rather routes, avenues, means for getting there. She is represented not as lending volumes from an immense story-archive, but as providing links for the performing bard (and his audience) … Her repository of traditional oral epic consists not of scrolls shelved in an Alexandrian Library, but rather of a web of pathways that give users access to the stories via a pre-textual analogue to our Internet.[56]

Often certain knowledges exist only in corporeal transmission, the *oimai*, an experiential performance that is perpetually shapeshifting. The *oimai* exists in stark contrast with commercial digitization that promotes a top-down knowledge system that emphasizes individual positivistic reasoning incongruous to alternative knowledge systems which promote communal wisdom, community, and collectivity.[57]

## Future Recommender Systems

It has been established that new modalities of tactical feminist practice and radical subjectivation in network culture topologies do not end at the borders of visible reality. It is no secret that fortification and artillery are fundamental to modern states and nations, which—like most powerful technologies—enable further centralization and increasingly global forms of governance.[58] An increasing population obtaining mobile devices in everyday life results in a dense layering of chemical and electromagnetic content passing through both air and bodies on route to its target. We are not just senders and recipients but also carriers of signals. Despite the logistical snags posed by the technical literacy of the apparatus when revisioning feminist internet, including the promiscuity of mycelial networks, an amalgam of material, and immaterial distributions, there is no doubt that contributing to the homebrewed server community and scripts enact maintenance. These human and non-human actors (actresses) have an innate ability to decant the power of a data storeroom. Actants play their part in the unraveling of orthodox dynamics between reception and participation; reader and writer; programmer, maker and user; performer, object and audience; and non-human and human.

*Bag Lady 2.0* (2007) anticipated the supremacy of a network society dominant in our mobile media habitus, an elaborate communication device, demystifying, reprogramming, rethinking, and redesigning tools of production and transmission. The hardware-software application was custom built and designed to accompany the *oimai*, urban wanderings and wonderings, and encourage a more haptic engagement with the aether. Transgressing inbuilt features of slick mobile design functions that inscribe our consumer experience, the work instead inhabits a hybrid space, enabling room for new design approaches and hence new (and neglected) modes of creatively fertile spaces to unfold.

Through an analysis of how deeply we share the *aether*, validating the process of poetic possibility that has always been contingent on not only what is made, but also *how* and *why* it is made in a shared adaptable environment that is accessible, flexible, and responsive. Present attempts to democratize computational media are gradually acquiring aesthetic ambitions, which allows us to reflect on complex genealogies and traditions which many have perceive to be abandoned. Mark Fisher once noted the absurdity of just how insidious the reach of mobile media has become "Who could be so self-important as to believe that they needed to be contactable everywhere and anywhere? Now, everyone is required to act like some cross between a hustler always on the make and an addict jonesing for contact."[59] Experimenting with mobile media is in a way just like developing radar systems, artillery, or propaganda as it performs in the nexus between innovation, technology, and war: we must not forget how mobile objects are deceptively inconspicuous. Beyond the imaginary enemies of yore, these investigations also set in motion the rasp one may encounter when experiencing the rub between material and immaterial experience. This paradigm is one we need to interrogate, and a possible start could be an active attempt toward understanding the paradox of how computing and electronics are material and political while increasingly are also aesthetic expressions of our insights into *routes, avenues, means for getting there* truly embodying our place in the cosmos.

## Notes

1 According to Foley, Homer referred to the term *oimai* to speak of pathways, in his presentation of "Oral Tradition and the Internet," 157, www.dspace.cam.ac.uk/handle/1810/229725. A further definition of *Oimai* is explained to be "Imagine (be of the opinion) to suppose, to think, to look for a possible contingency; to hope, fear, to deem, and conceive," in *A Greek-English Lexicon* with a Revised Supplement, 1996: Ninth Revised Edition, edited by Henry Liddell and Robert Scott (Oxford: Oxford University Press 1982), 1093.

2 Cosmography is the knowledge and study of the universe especially important for this chapter is "its simultaneous embrace of terrestrial and celestial subjects ... the theatre of Nature, the local scale of individual experience, and the universal scale of the divine plan ... descriptions ... often demand simultaneous attention to different scales," Jeremy Kargon, "One City's Urban Cosmography," *Planning Perspectives* 29, no. 1 (2014): 103–20, doi: 10.1080/02665433.2013.860880.

3 For the pertinence of such analog and digital modalities and the way they are addressed in post digital culture, see Florian Cramer, "What Is 'Post-Digital'?," in *Postdigital Aesthetics*, edited by D. M. Berry and M. Dieter (London: Palgrave Macmillan, 2015), 15–8, doi: 10.1057/9781137437204_2.

4 James D. Walsh, "Ten Years On, Foursquare Is Now Checking in to You: Even the Company is Still Trying to Figure Out Whether that's 'Cool or Creepy'," *Intelligencer*, 27 August 2019, http://nymag.com/intelligencer/amp/2019/08/ten-years-on-foursquare-is-now-checking-in-to-you.html.

5 Mark Williams Pontin, "The Total Information Awareness Project Lives On," *MIT Technology Review*, 26 April 2006, www.technologyreview.com/s/405707/the-total-information-awareness-project-lives-on/.

6 Beatriz Colomina, "Domesticity at War," *Assemblage* no. 16 (1991): 14–41, doi: 10.2307/3171160.

7 Eileen Reeves, "Galileo, Oracle: On the History of Early Modern Science," *I Tatti Studies in the Italian Renaissance* 18, no. 1 (2015): 7–22, doi: 10.1086/680483.

8 For further elaboration on communication technologies relationship to necessity as mother of invention Doug Kahn describes "The British forces called the helter-skelter results of such makeshift means *cosmic airlines*". *Earth Sound Earth Signal: Energies and Earth Magnitude in the Arts* (Berkeley: University of California Press, 2013), 78.

9 Containing atmospheric substances, Aether αἰθήρ (aithēr) means "pure, fresh air" or "clear sky" akin to the air we breathe, a mixture mainly of oxygen and nitrogen; for the Homeric Greeks it "was thought to be the pure essence that the gods breathed, filling the space where they lived, analogous to the air breathed by mortals," in "Aether," www.greekmythology.com/Other_Gods/Aether/aether.html.

10 George C. Morris, "An Approach to Ensure Continuity and Transmission of the Rainforest Peoples' Oral Tradition," in *An Identification of Problems and Potential for Future Rainforest Aboriginal Cultural Survival and Self-Determination in the Wet Tropics*, edited by H. Fourmile, S. Schnierer, and A. Smith (Cairns, Centre for Aboriginal and Torres Strait Islander Participation Research and Development, 1995), 71. The aether is "subtler than light," See Robert Fludd, *Mosaical Philosophy* (London: Humphrey Moseley, 1659), 221.

11 The literature on rays, light metaphysics, and light speculation is important but immense and beyond summary for this chapter, for a general treatment, see N. H. Clulee, *John Dee's Natural Philosophy, Between Science and Religion* (London, New York: Routledge, 1988).

12 David Garcia and Geert Lovink, "The ABC of Tactical Media," <*nettime*> 16 May 1997, www.nettime.org/Lists-Archives/nettime-l-9705/msg00096.html.

13 Peter Lamborn Wilson, "Media-Space! Opening Speech Public Netbase Media-Space!", 28 February 1997, https://hermetic.com/bey/pw-opening/.

14 David Garcia and Geert Lovink, "The ABC of Tactical Media." *<nettime>*, www.nettime.org/Lists-Archives/nettime-l-9705/msg00096.html.
15 An exemplar of this is the "singularity" movement, see Paul G. Allen and Mark Greave, "The Singularity isn't Near," *MIT Technology Review*, 12 October 2011, www.technologyreview.com/s/425733/paul-allen-the-singularity-isnt-near/; Geoffrey Winthrop-Young, "Silicon Sociology, or, Two Kings on Hegel's Throne? Kittler, Luhmann, and the Posthuman Merger of German Media Theory," *The Yale Journal of Criticism* 13, no. 2 (2000): 391–420. doi: 10.1353/yale.2000.0027.
16 Michel de Certeau, *The Practice of Everyday Life*, translated by Steven Rendall (Berkeley, University of California Press, 1984).
17 In this context, the word internet refers specifically to its role as a communication technology. For further reference see Lorenzo Cantoni, and Stephano Tardini, *Internet* (London; New York: Routledge, 2006).
18 Sadie Plant, *The Most Radical Gesture: The Situationist International in a Postmodern Age* (London: Routledge, 1992), 38–74.
19 Walter Benjamin, *The Rigorous Study of Art: On the First Volume of Kunstwissenschaftliche Forschungen*, translated by Thomas Y. Levin (October 47, 1988), 84–90.
20 Ensuing the constant interrogation of infrastructural paradigms, *The Critical Engineering Working Group* (2011–2019) point out "...with each technological advance our techno-political literacy is challenged," *Critical Engineering Manifesto*, Berlin, October 2011–2019, http://criticalengineering.org.
21 See Paul Resnick, Richard Zeckhauser, and Chris Avery, "The Working Paper No. 179," in *Roles for Electronic Brokers*, 1994, http://ccs.mit.edu/papers/CCSWP179.html.
22 Hanna Musiol, "Metaphors of Decryption: Designs, Poetics, Collaborations," *Decrypting Power, the Global Critical Caribbean Thought Series*, edited by Ricardo Sanín-Restrepo (London: Rowman & Littlefield International, 2018), 157–78.
23 Nancy Mauro-Flude, "A Commentary on the 3rd European Symposium on Gender & ICT: Working for Change in Manchester," February 2005, https://networkcultures.org/blog/2005/02/18/a-commentary-on-the-3rd-european-symposium-on-gender-ict-working-for-change-in-manchester/.
24 It is important to note that it is mentioned that "no such gesture of thanks has come from the Australian authorities to those numerous souls" who partake in the role of "computer." See Tony Wright, "The Modest Spy and Monterey, Australia's Bletchley Park," 6 July 2017, www.smh.com.au/opinion/tony-wright-column-the-modest-spy-and-monterey-australias-bletchley-park-20170706-gx5mxu.html.
25 The Critical Engineering Working Group, *Critical Engineering Manifesto*, Berlin, October 2011–2019, http://criticalengineering.org.
26 Sherry Turkle (ed), *Evocative Objects: Things We Think With* (Cambridge, MA: The MIT Press, 2007), 5–9.
27 Terranova, "Free Labor: Producing Culture for the Digital Economy," *Social Text* 18, no. 2 (2000): 33–58.
28 Jonathan Corbet, "Mobile Linux at linux.conf.au," 21 January 2009, https://lwn.net/Articles/315705/.
29 One version of the feminist internet was proposed by Nancy Mauro-Flude, "Feminist Internet Lore Manifesto: 10 working points for the twenty-first century, Rehearsal of a network,"*–empyre–*, 5 June 2018, http://lists.artdesign.unsw.edu.au/pipermail/empyre/2018-June/date.html, proceeding a Feminist Internet Art workshop 18 December 2017 facilitated by Nancy Mauro-Flude as part of Favour Economy's residency "Doing Feminism / Sharing the World," symposium at Melbourne University, drawing upon "The Feminist Principles of the Internet," an evolving document initially developed in 2014 by the Association for Progressive Communications. Another version of "The Feminist Internet Manifesto" was collectively created during a Feminist Internet workshop in September 2017, https://feministinternet.com/manifesto/.
30 The function of such peer production is still not well understood beyond mainstream art world discussions around participation and relational aesthetics that are completely disarticulated from net.art and other twenty-first-century mediums. For a comprehensive discussion of Net Art, see Josephine Bosma, *Nettitudes: Let'sTalk Net Art* (Rotterdam: Institute of Network Cultures, NAI, 2011).
31 Tiziana Terranova, "Free Labor: Producing Culture for the Digital Economy," *Social Text* 18, no. 2 (2000): 54.
32 Manuel Castells, *The Rise of the Network Society, the Information Age: Economy, Society and Culture. Vol. I.* (Cambridge, MA; Oxford: Blackwell, 1996).
33 Mark Fisher, *The Great Digital Swindle* (London: Repeater, 2016), https://repeaterbooks.com/the-great-digital-swindle-by-mark-fisher/.

34 "Lookout," Tasmanian Museum and Art Gallery, 13 March–4 July 2010, www.contemporaryarttasmania.org/program/lookout.
35 See http://pcengines.ch/alix3c3.htm.
36 Mike Crang, and Stephen Graham, "SENTIENT CITIES: Ambient Intelligence and the Politics of Urban Space," *Information, Communication & Society* 10, no. 6 (2007): 789–817. doi: 10.1080/13691180701750991.
37 Mirko Tobias Schaffer, "The Bag Lady: Trading secrets, spreading news," August 2008, http://mtschaefer.net/entry/bag-lady/.
38 Tiziana Terranova, "Free Labor: Producing Culture for the Digital Economy," *Social Text* 18, no. 2 (2000): 54.
39 Michel Foucault, *Discipline and Punishment: The Birth of the Prison*, translated by T A. Sheridan (London: Penguin Books, 1977); Michel Foucault, *Two Lectures: Power/Knowledge: Selected Interviews & Other Writings 1972–1977*, edited by C. Gordon (New York: Pantheon Books, 1980), 78–108.
40 This was initially in a clandestine publication, for further elaboration see Michel de Montaigne, *The Essays: A Selection*, translated by M.A. Screech (London: Penguin Books, 2004).
41 Pierre Bourdieu and Loic J. D. Wacquant, *An Invitation to Reflexive Sociology* (Chicago and London: University of Chicago Press, 1992), 24.
42 Tiziana Terranova, "Free Labor: Producing Culture for the Digital Economy," *Social Text* 18, no. 2 (2000): 54.
43 Ana María León, *Designing Dissent: Architecture and the Paradox of Dissidence*, edited by Ines Weizman. (London: Routledge, 2013), 1.
44 Hanna Musiol, "Metaphors of Decryption: Designs, Poetics, Collaborations," 166–67, www.researchgate.net/publication/324780732_Metaphors_of_Decryption_Designs_Poetics_Collaborations.
45 Hugh Davies, "Fanology: Hand-Fans in the Prehistory of Mobile Devices," *Mobile Media & Communication* (July 2019), n.p., doi: 10.1177/2050157919846181.
46 *Gods of the Plague* [*Götter der Pest*], directed and written by Rainer Werner Fassbinder, 1970, www.imdb.com/title/tt0065808/?ref_=nm_flmg_act_15.
47 There are many exemplars of cultural traditions beyond imperialist law. See, Bruce Pascoe, *Dark Emu, Black Seeds Agriculture or Accident?* (Broome: Magabala, 2014); Alexei Plutser-Sarno, "The Language of the Body and Politics: The Symbolism of Thieves' Tattoos," in *Russian Criminal Tattoo Encyclopaedia* edited by Honey Luard (Göttingen: Steidl/Fuel, 2003), 26–55; Julius S. Scott, *The Common Wind: Afro American Currents in the Age of the Hattian Revolution* (London; Brooklyn: Verso, 2018); Maya Deren, *Divine horsemen: The living Gods of Haiti* (London; New York: Thames and Hudson, 1953).
48 Geert Lovink, *Dark Fiber: Tracking Critical Internet Culture* (Cambridge, MA: The MIT Press, 2013), 394.
49 Cited in Foley, *Oral Tradition and the Internet*, 163.
50 Kristina Anderson, "Making Your own Hardware," *Digital Artists Handbook* (Lancaster: Folly, 2009), 208, https://monoskop.org/images/4/47/Digital_Artists_Handbook_2009.pdf.
51 Andrea Goldsmith, "The Future of Wireless and What It Will Enable," in *ACM Learning Webinar*, 3 April 2019, www.youtube.com/watch?v=nfNR6nvmWJ4.
52 Foley, *Oral Tradition and the Internet*, 157.
53 Ibid., 158.
54 Musiol, "Metaphors of Decryption," 166.
55 N. Katherine Hayles, *My Mother Was a Computer: Digital Subjects and Literary Texts* (Chicago; London: The University of Chicago Press, 2005), 320.
56 Ibid.
57 Munyaradzi Murove and George Mukuka, "The Dominance of the Spirit of Neo-Liberal Capitalism in Contemporary Higher Education Practices in Post-Colonial Africa: A Reconstruction of an African Ethic of Indigenization," *Indilinga* 6, no. 1 (2007): 14–25.
58 For further detailed discussion on cartography's relationship to expressing ideas of nation state through mobile media see Larissa Hjorth, "It's Complicated: A Case Study of Personalisation in the Age of Social and Mobile Media," *Communication Politics and Culture* 44, no. 1 (2011): 45–9.
59 Fisher, *The Great Digital Swindle.*

# 8

# *AMPLIFY YOUR FEMINISM*

## Social Media and Feminist Locative Art

*Caitlin McGrane*

While locative media art is well-documented in its overt social and political aims,[1] investigations into the role of intersectional feminism and locative art practices on social media have yet to receive much scholarly attention.[2] Social media feminism, in part popularized by celebrity culture, has made space for re-examinations of feminist thought, particularly around notions of intersectionality.[3] Recent scholarly work suggests that while consciousness-raising and debate are occurring, there is scope for further analysis of the power dynamics and surveillance practices that these platforms enable and encourage. For International Women's Day 2019, Melbourne-based creative hub BE Collective Culture (hereafter BE) installed a billboard mural outside Bakehouse Studios calling on passers-by to *AMPLIFY YOUR FEMINISM* (see Figure 8.1) and featuring a portrait collage of prominent local activists. The installation was accompanied by an Instagram post on the collective's page that argued "Your Feminism Isn't Feminism Unless It's Intersectional."

As images of artworks posted on social media can reach a much larger audience than works only displayed in galleries, this chapter critically reviews three of BE's social media posts of the installation as a case study for how locative media and social media feminist activism are colliding to reinvigorate debates about intersectional feminism in Australia. An ethnography of BE's Instagram page investigates how feminist artists from marginalized communities are utilizing the locative capabilities of social media to create intimate copresent galleries with audiences and thus bring attention to power imbalances. Employing social media to create copresence between

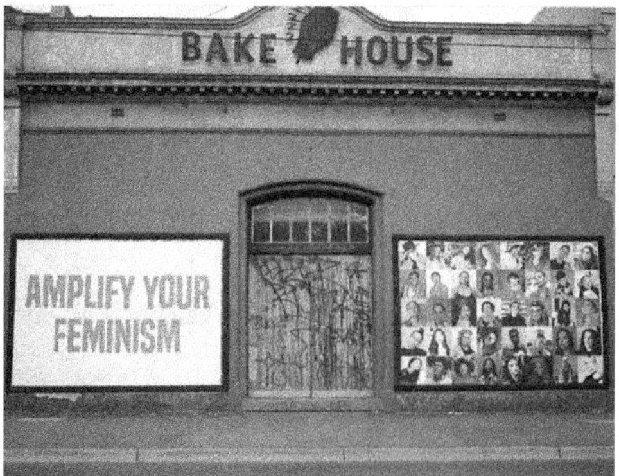


*Figure 8.1 International Women's Day Billboards* (2019). Photo credit: BE Collective Culture

audiences and artists also allows for greater distribution of the artwork and increased mobility for artists and audiences. Curated copresence with artworks suggests mobile media artists might use social media to create broader community access to politically engaged artworks, which, in turn, can advance intersectional feminist politics.

## BE Collective Culture

Melbourne-based art and culture collective BE is utilizing social media to create a community of activists and artists committed to bringing about effective social change. Their work spans artwork, events, publications, and collaborations.[4] Founded as a collective for young people to connect, create, and inspire change in popular culture and their peers, BE is passionate about creating lasting social change and amplifying marginalized voices.[5] While not a specifically feminist organization, the collective has engaged in feminist activism, particularly for International Women's Day 2019. As social media feminism is sometimes critiqued for being too individualistic, BE is taking a community-centric approach to engage with their audience. Conceptions of community and the fostering of intimacy are central to effective locative media art. In the late 1990s, Ben Russell predicted that "local communities can be brought closer together if common interest is allowed to intersect with location in a more efficient way."[6] The convergence of mobile media art and locative media brings to mind artworks that are functionally bound to a location or that have the capacity to move or be carried by the artists or the audience. By utilizing social media to communicate and create intimacy with audiences, artists are able to engage and motivate their audiences to participate in politically engaged reflexive processes.

The locus for this case study is the social media image-sharing platform Instagram. Used for sharing user-generated photographs, images, graphics, and text, the platform is key for artists and activists to promote and distribute their work. Instagram allows for an analysis of the ways social media imagery has been used to, as Barthes argued, "animate" the viewer. Barthes also further described how "a specific photograph, in effect, is never distinguished from its referent (from what it represents)."[7] Photographs are always representative of and about the objects of the photograph, and that they can cause affective or emotional arousal in the viewers.

Sontag articulates the relationship between the photographed world and the "real" world as one where the photograph is a simulacrum of the physical world being photographed: "Photographed images do not seem to be statements about the world so much as pieces of it, miniatures of reality that anyone can make or acquire."[8] Both Barthes and Sontag seem to suggest that the photograph enables the viewer to experience the world being photographed as if they were really there. An intimacy is created between the audience and photographs, or in this case, images.

Advances in digital technologies have deepened and thickened the relationships between audience, artwork and artist, where the uptake of digital communication technologies like smartphones enable copresence. As Leorke argues, "a rhetorical positioning of locative media as the 'forefront' of new media art, embracing new devices and taking interactive art out into the streets, in contrast to net arts 'confinement' to the gallery and computer screen."[9] Traditional galleries confine art to a particular space while socially mediated artworks allow the artist to take the works and their messages out into the streets. As locative media art has always-already been politically engaged, the mobility of artworks enabled by social media suggests not only copresence but also the opportunity to subvert and challenge normative power structures. Putting the political call-to-action in the hands of the audience through social media asks the audience to critique their subjectivity and engage in a reflexive praxis that challenges what their assumptions means now that the forefront of locative media art is now on social media. The imbrication of locative and social media such as Instagram brings audiences into close proximity with socio-political concerns such as intersectional feminism and surveillance.

Social media—particularly the ways it reflects both the mundane and the profound aspects of one's life—enables audiences to challenge their own thinking. These calls to action can be seen as a reflection of recent interest of intersectional feminist politics and thought, which can also be seen in contemporary popular culture.[10] Intersectionality requires an ongoing interrogation of privilege and power and communal efforts to engage in a deliberative and continuing discussion of these issues ought to be supported. By employing community mobilization, copresence and intimacy, the collective is able to question the ways in which feminism has been co-opted into an individualistic, neoliberal framework.

Locative media has a historical association with challenging surveillance practices. Sousveillance, or "surveillance from below" has been utilized by many activists to challenge hegemonic power structures, such as the police.[11] When employed in community settings with an intersectional feminist lens, the effect is to ask the audience to critically engage with themselves and their fellows. This enables sousveillance to be practiced at an intra-group level, thus keeping activists mobilized and engaged.

The activism and artistic work practiced by BE are at the forefront of contemporary intersectional feminist discourse, which they advance by utilizing social media copresence to engage their audience and encouraging sousveillance of one's own personal politics. In advancing intersectional feminist discourse, the collective is also reshaping the ways we might deploy mobile media artworks for effective social change.

## Locative Media Art: Social and Political Aims

Socially and politically engaged art practices are characteristic of locative media and indeed are deeply embedded within the history of locative media studies. This is particularly true when following Zeffiro's argument that locative media is a field of cultural production.[12] Early locative media workshops were directly engaged with "appropriating and retooling surveillance and control infrastructures."[13] By reconfiguring the ways location data is used to monitor and control populations, locative media art practitioners have been able to disrupt these mechanisms and provide a critical lens on their uses.

These reconfigurations are reflective of the ground-up revolution predicted in Ben Russell's *headmap manifesto*.[14] Twenty years ago, Russell envisioned a world in which everyone and everything would be located and locatable with ongoing political and social implications. Some of the practices predicted by Russell such as tagging physical locations and sharing this real-time data with others have become commonplace with everyday ways for users to create intimacy with audiences. While the text is not without its limitations (particularly around the way it envisioned equitable access and use),[15] it is worth considering how the radical potential of *headmap* reverberates today.

As Leorke argues, "*headmap* ... focused on users' appropriation of [information] technologies, envisioning that most applications of location-aware devices would emerge through grassroots experimentation with them."[16] While Leorke establishes that imagining locative media to be primarily used by grassroots organizations for subversion is somewhat naïve, importantly, he also notes that *headmap* functions as an optimistic prediction of future engagement with locative technologies. These predictions are currently being partially realized by activists in order to expose and critique surveillance of overly policed bodies and communities.

The populations most likely to be surveilled and overly scrutinized are marginalized communities including people of color, queer folks, and women. Simone Browne has argued that surveillance, particularly of African American communities, is a manifestation of the systematic anti-black racism that pervades the United States that must be seen as distinct from the technologies that enable surveillance:

> rather than seeing surveillance as something inaugurated by new technologies, such as automated facial recognition or unmanned autonomous vehicles (or drones), to see it as ongoing is to insist that we factor in how racism and antiblackness undergird and sustain the intersecting surveillances of our present order.[17]

To see surveillance as a supporting mechanism for intersectional oppression is to acknowledge and accept the experiences of marginalized communities in relation to the state and corporate forces. Surveillance is arguably perceived as a constant for these communities[18] and so attempts must be made to expose and circumvent these mechanisms. One response to surveillance has been for journalists[19] and activists[20] to utilize surveillance tactics and mechanisms in an attempt to undermine and subvert the problematic frameworks that keep them under intense scrutiny. These practices are an attempt to run counter to the prevailing logics of "surveillance capitalism"[21] in which monitoring is enabled through the omnipresent and continuous gathering of personal usage data. By undertaking forms of surveillance from below, or "sousveillance," activists are then able to promote their work and ideas. As social media, notorious for gathering and using user data, has become a site of political subversion and activism,[22] the importance of Instagram as a site for sousveillant activism through intimacy and copresent art practices has yet to be investigated.

## Social Media Feminism and Locative Art Practice

Mobile media enables intimacy and copresence among users. Image-based sharing platforms in conjunction with the rise of high-quality cameras built into smartphones has enabled new levels of intimacy among users, what Larissa Hjorth terms as "mobile intimate publics."[23] Intimate publics enable the connection between artists and audiences through mobility that "overlay[s] the geographic and physical space onto an electronic position and relational space."[24] Because smartphones travel with users wherever they go, they are their own form of locative media.[25] Further, as the haptic is so closely associated with intimacy and copresence, the smartphone can, through its intimate physicality, become a proxy for something or someone we wish to touch.[26]

As location data is gathered by an increasing array of smartphone applications, not just those directly related to locating the user like mapping services, it is important to expand the notion of what might be considered locative media.

Moving beyond this definition allows us to challenge and question the materiality of the locative technology and consequently understand some of the social and political implications for locate-ability.[27] When everything is located or locatable in geographic space, mobile-enabled artworks can be distributed through networks on social media, reaching larger audiences than would many static, less mobile artworks. This expansion therefore enables a consideration of how artworks promoted through Instagram can bring their audiences into contact with accounts that disrupt or dismantle normative ideas and politics. This is not to say that this is a universal ideal, but it suggests that these practices can be utilized to promote positive social change and critical engagement with existing norms and structures.

Instagram is an important site of feminist activism, yet its significance has yet to be fully acknowledged among scholars.[28] The image and video-sharing social media platform has become increasingly popular for activists to promote their work, exchange ideas and connect with their audiences. Feminist Instagram accounts enable activists, artists and publics to intimately connect around emotive and personal issues like restrictive and dominant beauty narratives and standards.[29]

Accounts such as @effyourbeautystandards and @i_weigh have been celebrated as a way for Instagram users to critically engage with the media they might otherwise passively consume and the socio-political messages embedded within them. It is also possible to think of these sites as creating an intimate public space for social and political engagement by allowing the user to view, like, comment, and share the post with their followers. While these accounts enable intimacy with publics, with the rise in importance of intersectional feminism, these accounts are also now at the forefront of incisive political movements.

## Intersectionality in Feminism and Artwork

Intersectionality has become something of a feminist buzzword in recent times. The resurgence of feminism in popular culture has arguably reinvigorated debates among scholars about how to reckon with intersectional feminist theory. Intersectionality, the history of which stretches back to the late nineteenth century,[30] argues that it is impossible to separate the categories of one's identity from the way oppressions are experienced. Law scholar Kimberlé Crenshaw is credited with bringing the term back into contemporary discourse when she argued in the late 1980s that black women experience the oppressions of the laws in the United States as *black women*. That is to say, they are discriminated against under law on the basis of being both black and women. This theory of what Patricia Hill Collins calls the "matrix of oppressions" is highly influential on social media today.[31] As Gines argues, however, caution must be exercised to not equivalate all oppressions as the same, and that power dynamics must be considered in the context of practicing intersectional feminism.

Intersectional feminism has been at once criticized for being both too thick and too thin, which Gines argues suggests feminists must critique and grapple with what intersectionality means and how it is practiced in order to challenge existing power dynamics.[32] Others have critiqued the promotion of feminism through individualistic, consumerist and celebrity cultures as a stand-in for feminism that seeks to deconstruct power relations.[33] These critiques of the application of intersectional feminism also suggest ways in which the theory can be effectively applied to practices. For instance, Brown et al.'s study of the #SayHerName hashtag on Twitter found that this hashtag was very effective in raising consciousness and awareness of black women victims of police brutality in the United States.[34] The authors argue that the mechanisms of social media for awareness raising should be utilized to understand the effects of other social movements.

As Australian activists such as BE are engaged with activist practices on social media, it seems that these predictions can be applied in contexts outside of the United States. In Australia, intersectional feminist activism through social media has received scant scholarly investigation. This is not to suggest there is an absence of interest, rather that there is more work that needs to be done to explore the practices and effects of intersectional feminism. Engagement and awareness raising on social media are essential parts of doing activist work, and indeed work in other contexts has highlighted the importance of collectively working together to achieve common aims.

Collaboration, connection and community are essential parts of feminist work, in both online and offline contexts. Existing research suggests that feminist social media collectives are engaging in consciousness-raising, but that these practices are at risk from anti-feminist surveillance.[35] However, the importance of intersectionality and the power dynamics involved in surveillance must also be taken into account.[36] Marginalized communities utilize the mechanisms of social media, such as public sharing, geotagging, and hashtags to conduct their activist work. These efforts are challenging and require intensive effort. As Mohammed writes of online feminist activism in Ghana, "for online activism to gain traction, it cannot be just a one-woman job: it requires several heads to work relentlessly and post meaningfully but excessively to get the attention needed from the relevant power players."[37] BE's initiative and ongoing engagement activities are evidence of this and will be analyzed using an ethnographic social media analysis (Figure 8.2).

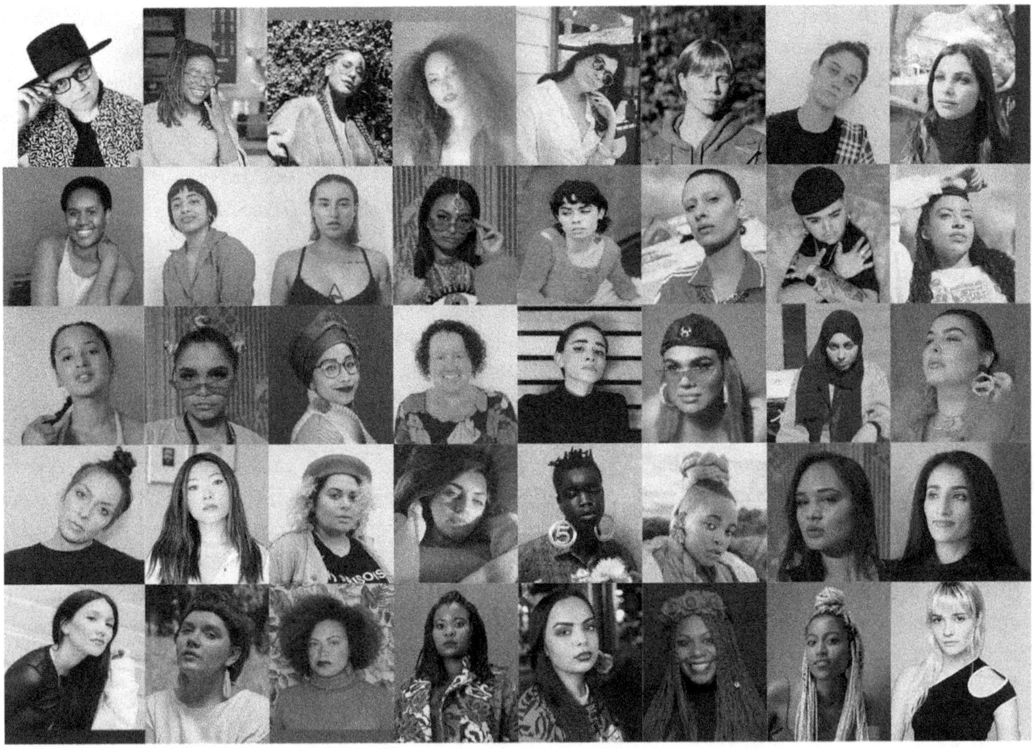

*Figure 8.2 International Women's Day Portraits* (2019). Photo credit: BE Collective Culture

## Ethnographic Analysis

The method used in this study is an ethnographic analysis of BE's Instagram feed in the lead up to and immediately following the unveiling of the billboards. Utilizing digital ethnography allows for the researcher to remain unobtrusive while observing the ways the community uses Instagram.[38] The observations are less about the people liking, commenting and reposting the artwork but are instead showing how the use of social media mechanisms such as image sharing, hashtags, and geotagging create copresence, community, and solidarity among activists. This then consequently allows the community to advocate for intersectional feminism through their artworks, events and social media posts.

Due to the ethical constraints of this project and a desire to advocate for further support of BE.'s work, only the publicly available images and their captions posted by BE will be analyzed in this chapter. As Murthy argues, "though the internet projects an air of neutrality, it is a space of power relations."[39] The subjective nature of social media ethnography means that while it is possible to observe the work on Instagram without obtaining formal ethics approval because the subjectivity of the researcher is always a potential ethical risk factor. As a white, middle-class, cis-gender woman, it is essential for me to acknowledge that in analyzing these images there is the potential for me to bring an unintentionally "othering" view of any subjects in the images.

It is also important to note that any members of the public engaged with the posts have not consented to being observed. Therefore, in order to avoid misrepresenting individuals or the meanings and messages in these posts, all the observations and analyses have been reviewed by BE. prior to publication. Further, only three public posts have been analyzed in order to limit the frame to only the installation that was available to the public and two accompanying images that complement the installation.

The first post is dated 7 March 2019 and is a series of three images showing the billboards in situ on a busy Melbourne street. The second post is dated 8 March and is an image of yellow text on a pink background that states *YOUR FEMINISM ISN'T FEMINISM UNLESS IT'S INTERSECTIONAL.*[40] BE's logo is at the top of the third post, dated 12 March. It is another text post of yellow text on a pink background that states *AMPLIFY YOUR FEMINISM,*[41] which is then followed by a Melbourne musician's logo. These three posts are just a selection of the Instagram posts made during the installation of the billboards, and the analysis presents a snapshot of the work the collective is doing to dismantle, disrupt and challenge normative power structures.

The digital ethnography conducted in this case study involved the researcher "following" the collective on numerous social media channels and viewing the Instagram posts as they unfurled throughout the two weeks the billboards were in situ. The location of the billboards—on a busy 8-lane road close to the center of Melbourne—suggests that these billboards were intended to cause mobile and incidental physical engagement, with the majority of the engagement seeming to be through Instagram and a live event to celebrate International Women's Day. By sharing the billboards on Instagram however, the photograph creates a counter-narrative to traditional notions of photography, which Barthes describes as "what could never be repeated existentially."[42] That is, while the billboards were intended to be publicly available for a finite period, through social media sharing the artworks are able to be repeatedly viewed, discussed, and disseminated. Sharing the artworks in this way creates intimacy between audience and the artwork.

## Intimacy between Audience and Artwork

Intimacy is an important part of politically engaged locative artworks because it enables the audience to feel like they are active participants in critiquing and disrupting the status quo. Through the creation and maintenance of intimacy between audience and artwork, the socio-political messages of the art are able to be absorbed and digested by the public. As Sontag argues, "a photograph passes for incontrovertible proof that a given thing happened."[43] While Instagram as a platform is well known for the proliferation of its filtered images, they still visually represent an event or moment as having taken place.

The first BE post under analysis here contains three images of the billboards. The first is a front-on view of them where they are situated in front of Bakehouse Studios in Melbourne's east. The brightly colored imagery of the billboards is juxtaposed against the grey Melbourne sky and the graffiti covering the doors to the studios. The second image is of the billboard on the left Bakehouse Studios—pink block lettering on a yellow background states *AMPLIFY YOUR FEMINISM.* It is only in this close-up that the audience notices the word *INTERSECTIONAL* sits behind the main text. The third image in the slideshow is of the billboard on the right of Bakehouse Studios—a collage of portraits of local and international activists, artists, creators, and disruptors. The post is geotagged to Bakehouse Studios, which can then be opened for viewing in a Maps app. Geotagging in conjunction with the three images demonstrate how Instagram helps the artist recreate the experience of being present with the artwork. This kind of "intimate public"[44] generates what Barthes describes as a feeling of animation in the audience. It is as if the audience is invited to be there.

The intimacy of this invitation is reflective of the critical nature of intersectional feminist politics. The post text also offers a provocation and an invitation to the audience to engage with the artwork and therefore "redefine feminism as something that advocates for all marginalised identities."[45] Advocacy for marginalized communities and identities is part of the discursive politics of intersectional feminism. In presenting it as an action for the audience, BE is able to raise awareness of the actions required to consider oneself an intersectional feminist. This text also suggests that the collective work of intersectional feminism is being undertaken by the collective in conjunction with the audience, thereby creating intimacy and shared understandings.

A second consequence of creating intimacy between public and artwork is that the post offers an accessible way for the audience to "unpack, check [their] bias and understand and acknowledge that history and pave the way for a new standard."[46] As Hjorth has argued, "intimacy has always been mediated,"[47] and so BE has used Instagram to create a space for deliberative thought and self-criticism. Whether this provocation has produced the kind of self-reflexive praxis that the collective intended is not the focus of this analysis. Rather, the mere invitation to self-critique, reflect, and contribute ideas to a new standard of feminism is indicative of the ways in which activists can use social media to encourage sousveillance and activism. Before reflecting on how the artworks encourage this though, the importance of the audience being copresent with the artworks through the locative capabilities of Instagram needs to be considered.

## Copresence between Audience and Artists

The use of camera phones for intimacy and copresence is a well-documented phenomenon. Activists use smart and camera phone photography to hold authorities to account and conduct vital activist work. The BE case study offers a chance to explore two elements of visual activism that have yet to be sufficiently understood and explored: the importance of copresence for feminist work and the use of visual media for spreading intersectional feminist messages and information. The haptic has been a key element of fostering intimacy and copresence.

As Palmer argues, "the iPhone, held in the palm of the hand, reintroduces a visual intimacy to screen culture that is missing from the larger monitor screen."[48] Using smartphone photography and associated image-sharing apps such as Instagram can thus be seen as a form of visual intimacy that enables the audience to feel connected to the work in their hand. In the case of BE, this can be demonstrated through the images of the billboard projects, which might be inaccessible or unreachable for many of the social media audience members. These images can, through Instagram and the smartphone, be accessed and appreciated.

Copresence can thus reduce the distance between intention and action. As Palmer argues, "the iPhone signals a shift in thinking about photographs as being primarily about *representation* to thinking about photographs as *information*."[49] As audiences feel closer and more connected to artworks, they are much more empowered to take action on political or social issues that concern them. Locative media has historically been utilized as a way of engaging in political agitation and activism.[50] Social media, used as a tool to document both the mundane and the profound, enables a reflection and interpretation of the world they are recording. Measurement mechanisms and clear calls to action therefore enable practitioners to document and record the impact of the art even after it has been dismantled.

## Instagram Artwork for Sousveillance and Activism

There is a long history of activists using photography to document and illuminate injustices. In *On Photography*, Sontag writes, "photographs are as much an interpretation of the world as paintings and drawings are"[51] in that photographs capture the world yet also bring a particular perspective or lens to it. In BE's work around International Women's Day, there is a perspective that calls on the audience to see and critique the world as it is presented to them. While sousveillance has previously been used to describe activist surveillance practices that bring attention to and challenging the surveillance state.[52] The BE posts invoke sousveillance as a way of challenging normative feminist power structures (colloquially known as "white feminism"). Feminist movements are not immune to power differentials, and indeed contemporary feminist movements have been shown to exclude or malign whole swathes of the population including women of color, women with disabilities, transgender women, and gender diverse folks.[53] Calling on feminists to explore their prejudices and subjectivities by proclaiming "your feminism isn't feminism unless it's intersectional" in the second Instagram post under analysis brings a particular lens to social media sousveillance as something that needs to occur as much within activist communities as outside of it.

Sousveillance within activist communities is a new frontier for effective social and political movements. Previous research into sousveillance suggests that watching from below and engaging communities through social media have been effective for raising awareness about social issues.[54] The second and third BE posts—calling on the viewer to be reflective of their own work, attitudes and practices—demonstrate how individuals can contribute to and be responsible for community safety.

Intersectional feminism is partially about amplifying the voices of those without sufficient power to be able to hold space for themselves. It is about giving up power in order to make space for others. BE encourages the audience to reflect on whether they are achieving this within their own lives, thus enabling critical self-reflection.

## Conclusion

Deliberation, discussion, critique, and reflexivity are all essential for conducting intersectional feminist activism. BE takes a communal, critical, and mobile approach to these issues by creating intimacy among their social media audience. They have achieved this by sharing their artworks and provocations on Instagram, thus inviting the audience to engage in critical reflection on their own practices.

In a highly mediated world, this intimacy and deliberative discussion space is also reflective of the copresence generated between audience and artists, which also contributes to an intersectional feminist forum. The locate-ability of these artworks, enabled by Instagram's affordances, creates a simulacrum of a gallery for copresent audiences to reduce the distance between the audience and artwork. Practices of mobility—through transport or on foot—are engaged through the use of billboards, thus bringing in additional audiences and creating a highly mobile and intimate mediated space.

## Notes

1 Andrea Zeffiro, "A Location of One's Own: A Genealogy of Locative Media," *Convergence: The International Journal of Research into New Media Technologies* 18, no. 3 (2012): 249–66, doi: 10.1177/1354856512441148; Suneel Jethani and Dale Leorke, "Ideology, Obsolescence and Preservation in Digital Mapping and Locative Art," *International Communication Gazette* 75, nos. 5–6 (2013): 484–501, doi: 10.1177/1748048513491904.

2 Raz Schwartz and Germaine R. Halegoua. "The Spatial Self: Location-Based Identity Performance on Social Media," *New Media and Society* 17 (2015): 1643–60, doi: 10.1177/1461444814531364.

3 Akane Kanai, "Between the Perfect and the Problematic: Everyday Femininities, Popular Feminism, and the Negotiation of Intersectionality," *Cultural Studies* (2019): 1–24, doi: 10.1080/09502386.2018.1559869.

4 "BE Collective Culture, be.collectiveculture Instagram post," 7 March 2019, www.instagram.com/p/Bus437Undly/.

5 "BE Collective Culture, From the Founder," 7 March 2019, https://becollectiveculture.com/from-the-founder/.

6 Ben Russell, "Headmap Manifesto," (1999), www.technoccult.net/wp-content/uploads/library/headmap-manifesto.pdf, 24.

7 Roland Barthes, *Camera Lucida: Reflections on Photography* (New York: Hill and Wang, 1981), 5.

8 Susan Sontag, *On Photography* (New York: Rosetta Books, 1977), 2.

9 Dale Leorke, "'Know Your Place': Headmap Manifesto and the Vision of Locative Media," *The Fibreculture Journal* 216 (2017): 10, doi: 10.15307/fcj.29.XXX.2017.

10 Kanai, "Between the Perfect."

11 Jan Fernback, "Sousveillance: Communities of Resistance to the Surveillance Environment," *Telematics and Informatics* 30, no. 1 (2013): 11–21, doi: 10.1016/j.tele.2012.03.003.
12 Zeffiro, "A Location of One's Own."
13 Ibid., 252.
14 Russell, "Headmap Manifesto."
15 Leorke, "Know Your Place."
16 Ibid., 6.
17 Simone Browne, *Dark Matters: On the Surveillance of Blackness* (Durham: Duke University Press, 2015), 9.
18 Laurence Kirmayer, Cori Simpson and Margaret Cargo, "Healing Traditions: Culture, Community and Mental Health Promotion with Canadian Aboriginal Peoples," *Australasian Psychiatry* 11 (2003): 15–24, doi: 10.1046/j.1038-5282.2003.02010.x; Stephen Green, "A Plague on the Panopticon: Surveillance and Power in the Global Information Economy," *Information, Communication & Society* 2, no. 1 (1999): 26–44, doi: 10.1080/136911899359745.
19 Bora Ataman and Barış Çoban, "Counter-Surveillance and Alternative New Media in Turkey," *Information, Communication & Society* 21, no. 7 (2018): 1014–29, doi: 10.1080/1369118x.2018.1451908.
20 Lina Dencik, Arne Hintz and Jonathan Cable, "Towards Data Justice? The Ambiguity of Anti-Surveillance Resistance in Political Activism," *Big Data & Society* 3, no. 2 (2016): 1–12, doi: 10.1177/2053951716679678.
21 Shoshana Zuboff, "Big Other: Surveillance Capitalism and the Prospects of an Information Civilization," *Journal of Information Technology* 30, no. 1 (2015): 75–89, doi: 10.1057/jit.2015.5.
22 Jessalynn Keller, Kaitlynn Mendes and Jessica Ringrose, "Speaking 'Unspeakable Things:' Documenting Digital Feminist Responses to Rape Culture," *Journal of Gender Studies* 27 (2018): 22–6, doi: 10.1080/09589236.2016.1211511.
23 Larissa Hjorth, "Frames of Discontent: Social Media, Mobile Intimacy and the Boundaries of Media Practice," in *New Visualities, New Technologies: The New Ecstacy of Communication*, edited by J. Macgregor Wise and Hille Koskela (Farnham, England: Ashgate Publishing, 2013), 99–118.
24 Hjorth, "Frames of Discontent," 102.
25 Jordan Frith, *Smartphones as Locative Media* (Cambridge: Polity Press, 2015).
26 Daniel Palmer, "iPhone Photography: Mediating Visions of Social Space," in *Studying Mobile Media: Cultural Technologies, Mobile Communication and the Iphone*, edited by Larissa Hjorth, Jean Burgess, and Ingrid Richardson (New York: Routledge, 2013), 85–97.
27 Eric Gordon and Adriana de Souza e Silva, *Net Locality* (Oxford: Blackwell Publishing, 2011).
28 Frances Shaw, "'Bitch I Said Hi:' The Bye Felipe Campaign and Discursive Activism in Mobile Dating Apps," *Social Media + Society* 2, no. 4 (2016): 1–10, doi: 10.1177/2056305116672889.
29 Sofia P. Caldeira, and Sander De Ridder, "Representing Diverse Femininities on Instagram: A Case Study of the Body-Positive @effyourbeautystandards Instagram Account," *Catalan Journal of Communication & Cultural Studies* 9, no. 2 (2017): 26–43, doi: 10.1080/02560046.2018.1447592.
30 Kathryn Gines, "Black Feminism and Intersectional Analyses: A Defense of Intersectionality," *Philosophy Today* 55 (2011): 275–85, doi: 10.5840/philtoday201155Supplement68.
31 Patricia Hill Collins, *Black Feminist Thought: Knowledge, Consciousness, and the Politics of Empowerment* (New York: Routledge, 2000).
32 Gines, "Black Feminism."
33 Kanai, "Between the Perfect."
34 Melissa Brown, Rashawn Ray, Ed Summers and Neil Fraistat, "#sayhername: A Case Study of Intersectional Social Media Activism," *Ethnic and Racial Studies* 40, no. 11 (2017): 1831–46, doi: 0.1080/01419870.2017.1334934.
35 Jessica Megarry, "Under the Watchful Eyes of Men: Theorising the Implications of Male Surveillance Practices for Feminist Activism on Social Media," *Feminist Media Studies* 18, no. 6 (2018): 1070–85, doi: 10.1080/14680777.2017.1387584.
36 Green, "A Plague on the Panopticon."
37 Wunpini Fatimata Mohammed, "Online Activism: Centering Marginalized Voices in Activist Work," *Ada: A Journal of Gender, New Media and Technology* 15 (2019): n.p., doi: 10.5399/uo/ada.2019.15.2.
38 Sarah Pink, Heather Horst, John Postill, Larissa Hjorth, Tania Lewis, and Jo Tacchi, *Digital Ethnography: Principles and Practice* (London: Sage, 2016).
39 Dhiraj Murthy, "Digital Ethnography: An Examination of the Use of New Technologies for Social Research," *Sociology* 42 (2008): 837–55, 840, doi: 10.1177/0038038508094565.
40 *YOUR FEMINISM ISN'T FEMINISM UNLESS IT'S INTERSECTIONAL!* BE. Collective Culture. 2019. be.collectiveculture Instagram post, 8 March 2019, www.instagram.com/p/BuuN24gHv-D/.

41 *#amplifyyourfeminism*. BE. Collective Culture. 2019. be.collectiveculture Instagram post, 12 March 2019, www.instagram.com/p/Bu5lhQVHeV5/.
42 Barthes, *Camera Lucida*, 4.
43 Sontag, *On Photography*, 3.
44 Hjorth, "Frames of Discontent," 101.
45 "We did a thing for International Women's Day! *AMPLIFY YOUR FEMINISM* – Your Feminism Isn't Feminism Unless It's Intersectional." BE. Collective Culture. 2019. be.collectiveculture Instagram post, 7 March 2019, www.instagram.com/p/Bus437Und1y/.
46 Ibid.
47 Hjorth, "Frames of Discontent," 108.
48 Palmer, "iPhone Photography," 88.
49 Ibid.
50 Jethani and Leorke, "Ideology, Obsolescence."
51 Sontag, *On Photography*, 4.
52 Fernback, "Sousveillance."
53 Susana Loza, "Hashtag Feminism, #solidarityisforwhitewomen, and the Other #femfuture," *Ada: A Journal of Gender, New Media and Technology* 5 (2014). doi: 10.7264/N337770V.
54 Brown et al., "#sayhername."

# SECTION THREE

# Hybrid Realities

# 9
# SOUNDING PLACE

## *Teri Rueb* in Conversation with *Adriana de Souza e Silva*

Teri Rueb is an artist whose work combines sound and site using mobile media. She is best known for having established the form of Global Positioning System (GPS)-based interactive installations, sometimes referred to as "locative media," as early as 1997. Rueb's work became a reference for generations of newer locative media artists interested in exploring the relationship between spaces, location-based technologies, and mobility.

In this conversation, Rueb begins by talking about her artistic background and the main inspirations for her work. She also addresses the relationship among her GPS-sound installations, such as *Drift* and *Itinerant* and the concept of hybrid spaces, that is, how the participant interacts with the landscape via location-based technology in a constant process of becoming. Finally, she shares her thoughts about the current and future landscape of mobile media art (Figure 9.1).

> Can you tell me a little bit about your background, your main inspirations, and how you became interested in locative media art?

I grew up along the front range of the Rocky Mountains in Colorado where it was common for us as children to be allowed to explore the countryside for hours on end, unattended. We would go walking and telling stories and building imaginary worlds that were often derived from features in the environment. An evocatively shaped rock formation, a wandering creek bed, or an abandoned dwelling—any of these might invite us to pause and wonder who passed through here before, how did they live, and what marks did they leave, visible or invisible?

The sense of being a tiny figure traversing a vast landscape, in a moment that was a mere dust mote in the realm of geologic time, was captivating. Growing up in this place gave me a powerful grounding in the land and has shaped my practice at a deep level. My work is land-based and ultimately concerned with exploring the relationship between place and people. As a sculptor, I initially worked in clay and later found myself drawn to working in a more conceptual way with communities, public, art and site-specific installation. My mentor when I was a student at Carnegie Mellon University, Conrad Atkinson, inspired a political impulse in my work and introduced me to the work of artists like Joseph Beuys, Martha Rosler, and Tim Rollins + KOS.

After graduating, I was living in New York City and the lack of a studio allowed me to embrace the challenge of working informally in public settings outside of the gallery and museum system. Instead of using singular materials such as clay, glass, or textiles to define my work, I now saw my palette as the whole site, as the community and shifting conditions over time, and even as the geological scales of time. I went to graduate school at NYU in 1996 where, instead of joining

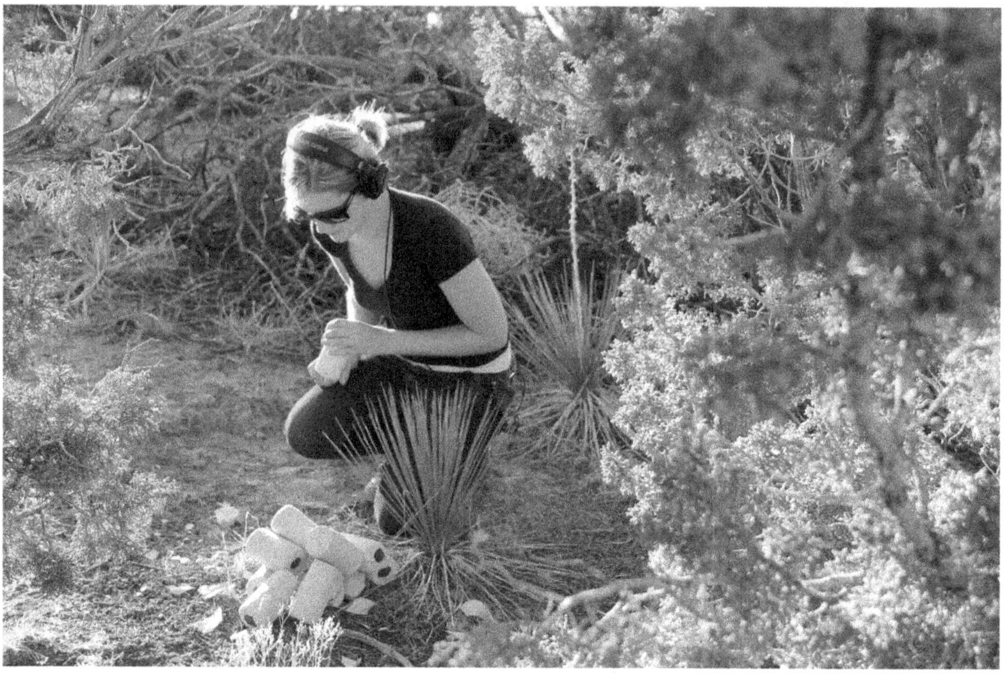

*Figure 9.1* Teri Rueb in collaboration with Larry Phan and Carmelita Topaha (Navajo), *No Places With Names* (2012). GPS-based responsive sound installation set on the campus of the Institute of American Indian Arts, Sante Fe. Photo credit: Teri Rueb

the momentum that was fueling screen-based works from interactive video and Net Art to CD-ROMs and websites, I found in GPS and mobile media an emerging means to transform the land itself into a kind of canvas without making any marks on the land or leaving any trace of my presence. My interest in public art was also reinvigorated by this emerging network space that offered another domain in which to explore negotiations of meaning in the public realm.

Land speaks in so many languages, a voice heard through layers and layers of time and material. Using mobile media as a means of directing our attention back to the land, I have attempted to create a space for dialog between people and place, one that is anchored in individual curiosity and exploration, a journey that begins with listening to the land.

How do you see yourself contributing to the production of hybrid spaces and hybrid realities?

My first impulse as an artist was always to make things in three dimensions. Whether building things with wood or metal, fashioning a form in clay, organizing a little parade with my neighbors, or rearranging the furniture in my room, I have always been compelled by the dialog between my body, other collaborators and materials of all kinds, and through their interaction, the remarkable capacity we have to understand and co-author the world around us, at least in little moments and proximal localities.

The concept of hybrid spaces and hybrid realities begins first with the recognition of ourselves as agents in processes that lead to becomings of all kinds. Transformation from one state of being to another involves the material and the immaterial. As a sculptor and installation artist weaving responsive sounds into the landscape, I see my work as forming layers of latent strata waiting to be revealed through the movement of the participant. *Core Sample* is perhaps the most overt example of this design concept in that it draws upon the metaphor of a core sample, layering sound regions and locating them at elevations that correspond to the past, present and future material processes that make up Spectacle Island. Visitors move through these layers, activating sound playback as they pass through them. The fundamentally mobile and kinesthetic nature of mobile media speaks to the mutability of place and our own materiality as an active force in shaping its permutations.

In other moments, I have written about this condition of agency and mobile subjectivity in terms of *everyday practices*, the *lived* and *perceived*, as *kinaesthetic attunement*, and as flows of *forces*, and *intensities*.[1] To me, each of these frameworks, like different sculptural media, suggests a way of understanding what we know and how we know through the body through technological prosthesis and through our sense of place and interaction with the world. With any medium, certain epistemological assumptions and proclivities are expressed over others, depending on how it is used. I am interested in media that hold the potential to reveal the confluences of all that we perceive as flow in a moment of time unfolding in dialog with physical movement, whether it be the tiniest movement of the gaze or the act of walking, the solitary trajectory of a single person or the movement of crowds, the perambulations of the body and the magnetic propulsion of the earth.

I think this is why I first recognized the technology of global positioning satellite receivers as a sculptural and ultimately temporal medium. Rather than becoming slave to its conventions and explicit affordances as a technology of control, I came to GPS as a sculptor and composer discovering a new means of addressing the body in space, bound up in techno-cultural webs of relations. In adapting these tools to an unexpected use, I discovered an endlessly compelling medium with which to explore and create hybrid spaces and realities. In the same way that the variously fluid and fixed properties of clay and glass originally fascinated me, I gradually found in digital media another domain in which to explore the point of transition where a medium or technology shifts and becomes something other than what we assume it to be, and in that, we may find a reflection of our own mutability and empathy with the sentient and non-sentient. For example, in many of my works recorded sound blurs with environmental sound, such that spatial and temporal properties of sound that we typically take for granted become confused or "out of phase" with one another. *Fens* is perhaps the richest and most dense of these works, in this respect, and the piece that most directly evokes a blurring of human and non-human, sentient and non-sentient.

> Several of your pieces strongly connect natural landscapes, cultural history, sound, and location-aware technologies. Can you explain why you choose to focus on natural landscapes, such as beaches and rivers, versus more commercial locative media apps that are clearly developed to be used in dense urban centers? How do you see the tension between technology and nature in the production of hybrid spaces?

With each piece, I have sought to be attentive to the particularities of a given site, as well as to the many places that exist within a site as echoes and reverberations that link one place to another in a network of relations. In coming to a site, I try to resist the tendency to associate it with any specific category or typology (park, city, natural, constructed, wild, domesticated, human or non-human, etc.), but instead approach it as a confluence of forces and influences that can be discovered by pulling on one thread of its identity and watching the others respond.

So while I haven't chosen to focus on particular types of places, several of my early works were set in non-urban locations, such as beaches and mountainous areas (*Drift*, *Trace*) or large urban parks (*Surfacing*, *Itinerant*, *Core Sample*), partly because I was inspired by those places—I am drawn to remote expanses, edge conditions and littoral zones, as much as urban wilds and disturbed landscapes—and partly because I had opportunities to work in them for an extended period of time with the support of residencies or fellowships. Before location tracking was commonly supported on mobile phones (most of which now draw upon a variety of wireless networks for geo-location), reception was limited to the performance of GPS unaided by other transmissions and was therefore much more constrained to line of sight.

As such, large open spaces were more conducive to optimal reception. Because of this, my early work was especially sensitive to the variations of GPS reception at a site, especially since the interactive sound relies upon a consistent flow of frequent and accurate GPS readings to control not just playback, but modulation of volume.[2] Rather than triggering momentary isolated events after which location sensing can "idle," I'm typically using a constant flow of GPS data to track location and determine sound playback, as well as fades and mixing of multiple "tracks" which exist as (sometimes overlapping) spatial regions through which participants will wander in different directions and at different speeds. Variations in temporality and speed (in *Drift*, for example, where standing still is as effective as walking to trigger the sounds which move with the tides), as well as the itinerary of the participant and environmental forces such as weather and social patterns of use, interact to produce complex interaction schemes and compositional conditions. I enjoy drawing upon these transits and exchanges between the designed and discovered, the "natural" and "cultural," and the constraints held within each site which act as cues to poetic invention.

While it might seem that most of my works are sited in remote or pastoral settings, the majority are actually urban, though they often are set in parks or urban wilds, and sometimes shipping lanes, freeways and parkway systems that blend motorized and pedestrian traffic. My interest in these peri-urban sites is often focused on their complex entanglements of social, physical, technological and biological forces. *Drift*, *Core Sample* (see Figure 12, color insert), *Other Order*, *Grimpant*, *Fens*, and *Times Beach*, for example, are all concerned with the complex infrastructural concatenations of the urban environment and the extraordinarily resilient natural processes that survive and continue to shape these landscapes, even in the midst of often radical disturbances (informal dumping, dredging, waste containment facilities, landfills, transportation and communication infrastructure, pollution and run-off, the channelization of waterways, etc.).

All of these processes point to the broader conditions of hybrid spaces and hybrid realities which are part of our daily experience, even if we aren't consciously aware of them. Consider, for example, that a walk through Bussey Brook Meadow, such as in my work *Other Order* (2014), which to the uninformed appears as a lovely path through open meadows and wooded hollows, takes one from a subway station, across a busy street, over a hill that is actually a massive constructed berm, to a pathway that follows the above ground railway and the channelized section of Bussey Brook, to ultimately passing by a landfill and massive buried sewer pipe that lies below a now healthy functioning wetland.

My work seeks to draw attention to these overlooked aspects of the "natural" or "urban" and raise awareness of our own embeddedness in these processes. Formally, I often blur the registers of environmental sound and pre-recorded sound (often recorded on site), linking the virtual and the real to physical environment and movement. For me, sound is the perfect modality for exploring the inherent intersubjectivity of these relationships. Broadly understood as vibration, sound holds the potential to upend our assumptions about subject and object, self and other, fixed and mutable, visible and invisible. The tactility of sound, combined with its fleeting and ephemeral nature, make it an apt metaphor for exploring the paradox of witnessing our own continual emergence and dissolution.

> You are considered to be one of the pioneer locative media artists, and you've been there since the beginning. Looking back, what are some of the defining moments in the mobile media art field for you?

Certainly, the most memorable shifts for me happened when the term "locative media"[3] emerged roughly around 2004 along with the proliferation of the technology in the readily available form of smart phones (this happened earlier in Asian countries and Northern European countries like Finland and Norway, while the United States lagged behind due to competing technology standards and corporate pricing models). At this time in the art world, there was a burgeoning interest in critical and collaborative cartography and situated narratives, as well as an interest on the part of museums and cultural heritage institutions to seize on the technology as a means of providing alternative modes of interpretation and to reach new audiences. This moment placed me in dialog with an entirely new set of practitioners (prior to this moment I had found company mostly with artists working in site-specific, community-based or performative veins, whether or not they were interested in extending those practices to include new technologies).

Now that the medium had been given a name, the rush to codify it and declare its "proper" use was on, making what had been a rather wide open, though sometimes lonely field of experimentation, suddenly feel like a suburban housing development with neighborhoods divided up according to political, ideological, or aesthetic leanings. The most liberating aspect of this moment was that now I could easily reference what I was doing without needing to provide background information or explanations of how the technology worked. It was also a thrilling moment of exchange with a new group of makers and thinkers working across the domain of critical spatial practices.

This was a watershed moment for me in that increasingly the work could be received by general audiences as one among many different kinds of artistic genres where the concept and composition could be foregrounded, rather than the "magic" or curiosity of a technological novelty. It also created a space of differentiation across commercial and independent or experimental applications, which was useful to the evolution of critical discourse in the field.

> We've been talking about mobile media art as if it is an undisputed term, but there are some competing and often times contradictory definitions of it. How do you define mobile media art?

This picks up on an interesting theme anticipated by my response to the last question. When I first started working with GPS to activate media, around 1996–1999, my work was often referred to as Augmented Reality (AR), a term that I was somewhat ambivalent toward, given that I had arrived at my practice through a rejection of Virtual Reality as an apparatus and a cultural construct (the use of the term reality in this context always struck me as hyperbolic and hubristic). I preferred to think of my work as sound installation at the time, and I still do, though an explicit reference to the mobility and responsive / interactive behavior inherent to the form is lost in this term. Around 2004, the term "locative media" emerged, as I said before, and with it came debates about the nuances of its meaning versus "location aware," "mobile," "location sensing," "context aware" media, etc.

Later, around 2010, I recall the term AR came back into common use, likely as a result of the emergence of more user-friendly platforms for the creation of augmented reality experiences (LayAR, etc.). The term "apps" also became a more commonplace term around this time, and before long modifiers were added such that we now commonly refer to "mobile apps," "mobile media art," and "location aware apps." These terms, when combined with the word "art," can sometimes have the effect of diminishing the status of the work as art. Why do we need to modify the word "art" which should be sufficient on its own to signify a creation that exceeds the utilitarian, regardless of medium?

Why do we not feel the need to refer to "oil painting art," for example, or "marble art," yet we seem to need terms like "sound art," "digital art," "performance art," and even "media art"? A cell phone novel may be thought of as a form of mobile art, especially if it is meant to be read in situ or in an itinerant fashion, but it may also be consumed in a sedentary fashion as if it were a book.

Does that make it fundamentally different than mobile media art? I'm not sure, since even in my work I can think of examples of mobile media art, such as *Drift*, which can be equally appreciated while walking or standing still.

The work I'm doing now takes up this early interest, exploring it in an entirely different form where the sound is meant to be appreciated while moving very slowly. In this work participants are invited to attend to their own hearing and listening practices through exploring a sound field in relative states of motion or stillness. While these works may be closer in form to gallery-based sound installation where sound is delivered via loudspeakers that fill the room with sound, to me they are still every bit about the subjectivity and performativity of movement and perception as any of my prior works which may fit more conventionally within the definition of "mobile media art."

Imagine, for instance, a standing wave field with varying "pockets" of sound differentiated by pitch and volume with a spatial granularity ranging from 12 cubic inches to 3 cubic inches. Now place yourself in this field and imagine a low light condition that affords just enough visibility for you to move safely, but cautiously, forcing a slowing down, even to stillness, as you begin to acclimate to the subtle changes in sound as you tilt your head or crouch down toward the floor. This is the basic framework for a series of acoustic experiments that my collaborator, David Anderson, and I are calling "sounding situations."

In my view this new work is a form of mobile media art that operates at different scales, speeds, and temporalities than we conventionally associate with the genre. Though contained to a room, they are often perceived as topographies, each with their own signature contours depending on the series of pure tones used and the acoustic properties of the space in which the sounding apparatus (a flat panel loudspeaker) is installed. In the end, I'm intrigued by these shifting terms and definitions, but equally compelled to challenge and redefine them in the interest of continuing to interrogate the embodied, kinesthetic, proprioceptive, acoustic, and relational dimensions of experience, perception, and interaction.

> Who are some of the most exciting and influential practitioners in the field for you today and why?

More recently, I have turned my attention to everyday listening and hearing practices and the continuum that exists between movement and stasis and the perceptual awareness that resides in the transition between the two. Still fascinated by the ways we hear and listen with apparatuses of all kinds, I think I am currently most fascinated by the listening experiences of long-term meditators, minimalist dancers and users of assistive hearing technologies, whether they are public figures in speaking about these experiences or not.

I am also interested in people with unique listening and hearing abilities, including the hearing and hard of hearing, especially when we are attending to the particularities of what it is to listen in a manner that engages the whole body and the space and time around it. The acoustic properties of everyday spaces, both indoor and outdoor, also interest me as a kind of architectural concern, as much as a rich domain for inquiry around the construction of subjectivity through spatial and sonic experience. The apparatus of mobile media (mobile phone, tablet, Walkman, laptop, etc.) are still of great interest to me in these current inquiries, particularly because they have proliferated to a point that we can no longer comprehensively account for everyday listening and hearing practices without considering their influence.

Specifically, I have an abiding interest in the research of Douglas Kahn, in particular his investigations into what he calls the "aeolectrosonic," a blending of acoustic and electrosonic sound and transmission that concerns the spectrum of wavelengths from natural radio to microwaves.[4] Examples of this may be found in radio astronomy transmissions or the interference of lightning on telephone or broadcast radio transmissions. For myself, I enter into dialog with this work with the question, "What might a minimalist GPS art look like? One that could reveal transits across time and space, elucidating the relationship between satellite transmissions (GPS is radio, after all), planetary movement, natural radio, and human movement?"

How do you think mobile media art has the potential to transform audience engagement, public encounters, and mobility?

I'll pick up on just one point which is the "problem" of distraction. Most of us assume mobile media have created a culture of attention fragmentation to the point that we now fetishize the "unplugged" moment, and seek technology free spaces as a luxury. While I fully understand and appreciate this perspective, I'm currently interested in how the constant abiding presence of our mobile phones can be used to draw our awareness to the relativity of moment, place, and time in everyday situations. That is, what if the impulse to pick up the phone, for whatever reason, could be transformed into being a moment of awareness where we might feel a sense of calm in a storm, or alternatively, the sense of being jolted awake with a vivid sense of being here and now? What if this could lead to a heightened sense of being attuned to each other across space and time, and to the universe and our simultaneous vulnerability and agency in the grand scheme of things? Again, the simple observation that GPS is radio writ at a planetary scale suggests a rich opportunity for designing for a much longer longitudinal sensibility.

What do you see as the future for mobile media art?

Looking to the future from the perspective of the past, it strikes me as worthwhile to acknowledge and carry forward historical and contemporary non-Western and indigenous peripatetic practices, from Aboriginal walkabout to situated oral traditions such as oral epic poetry, rhapsody, and land-based narratives (e.g. Icelandic oral epic saga, Native American origin stories that are anchored to land, orientation to the cardinal directions and the movement of planets and stars). These mobile media practices continue to echo in our fundamentally corporeal modes of encoding place, story, and memory today. I feel these resonances, still latent in our contemporary mobile media art forms and what we now see in the "sonic turn" and "spatial turn" in cultural thought.

While I hesitate to predict the future, I might express the hope that we may find in mobile media art, or whatever terms we use to locate these practices and techniques in the future, the potential to create forms that enhance our sense of synchrony with rhythms and forces of all types and kinds, both human and non-human. Ultimately, I would hope mobile media art forms could return us to a genuinely land-based way of knowing, one that draws upon the wisdom of cultures and peoples who have passed this way before and recognized and revered the tiny place we hold in the universe and the precious responsibility implied by a relational view of all things.

## Notes

1 See prominent thinkers Lefebvre, de Certeau, Heidegger, Merleau-Ponty, Deleuze and Guattari, Grosz. I have referenced their work in various publications including my unpublished dissertation (Harvard archives); Teri Rueb, "Restless: Locative Media as Generative Displacement," in *Mobility and Locative Media: Mobile Communication in Hybrid Spaces*, edited by Adriana Souza e Silva and Mimi Sheller (New York; London: Routledge, 2015), 241–58; Teri Rueb, "This is (Not) a Map," in *Locative Media*, edited by Katherine S. Willis and Regine Buschauer (Bielefeld: transcript Verlag, 2013), 137–50.

2 As the years unfolded, I could increasingly create reliable responsive sound works in dense urban areas, but other factors also determined the form and location of the work. For example, even in 2009 it was

still too soon to assume that visitors would commonly have a smartphone with location services in their pocket, which meant that there needed to be some central point where they could go to borrow equipment. While this didn't dictate that I work in urban or non-urban areas, it did shape the context of interaction and accessibility of the work, making it a more rarefied experience than what has now become reduced to the banal launching of an "app." The particular set of contemporary design conventions and expectations of what an "app" is as a typically commercial entertainment experience has radically re-shaped the mode of distribution, reception and interpretation of my work, which is now largely delivered as free "apps" that can be downloaded from two primary commercial platforms. This, along with the proliferation of associated headphone and earbud listening practices and cultures, has become reified to the point that I am currently focused on making "mobile media art" that defies these conventions and expectations, directing our attention to collective listening experiences and invitations to slow down, observe and reflect upon the movements held within stillness.

3 See Drew Hemment, "Locative Arts," *Leonardo Electronic Almanac* 39, no. 4 (2006): 348–55, doi: 10.1162/leon.2006.39.4.348.

4 See Douglas Kahn, *Earth Sounds, Earth Signal: Electromagnetic Arts* (Berkeley: University of California Press, 2013).

# 10

# HISTORICIZING HYBRID SPACES IN MOBILE MEDIA ART

*Adriana de Souza e Silva and Ragan Glover-Rijkse*

We live in hybrid spaces. And our hybrid spaces are a part of us. Hybrid spaces emerge when people, carrying mobile technology devices, are able to communicate and interact with others while mobile in urban physical spaces.[1] As such, hybrid spaces occur across the physical and the virtual and, in turn, unfold when different contexts (digital and physical, remote and contiguous) are embedded into each other. This embedding asks us to account for, and be accountable to, the properties of plural contexts which merge as one.

Responding to this phenomenon, mobile media artists have often inquired about the relationships between physical and virtual spaces by exploring how our interactions in and between these spaces are shaped by a diverse range of mobile technologies, including mobile phones, proximity sensors, and wearable devices. However, while these particular mobile technologies are relatively new, the inquiries that they provoke are not. A look back at early telecommunications-based art, also known as *telepresence art*, demonstrates that efforts to merge physical and virtual spaces were already occurring long before contemporary mobile electronic media and its array of sensing technologies. Such art can be viewed as the first examples of creating a hybrid space, prior to the widespread diffusion of mobile phones as easily portable, information-networked devices.

Early telecommunications-based art made use of such technologies as telephones, satellites, and videophones to achieve the sensation of human presence at a distance (i.e. telepresence). While, today, telepresence may exist as a norm for creating closeness or intimacy between geographically dispersed individuals, Stephen Wilson points out that "some earlier observers of the telephone were so unnerved by the unnatural presence afforded by the disembodied voice that they ran frightened from the room."[2] In this sense, the term telepresence precedes digital technologies and computer networks, yet it has still served as a fruitful site of artistic inquiry. Artists like Kit Galloway and Sherrie Rabinowitz, Douglas Davis, Keith Sonnier, and Roy Ascott—among others—are considered pioneers in the exploration of telepresence art. Collectively, their works have used telecommunication technologies to experiment with concepts like collaboration, communication, aleatory encounters, and consciousness in public places—much like the work of many contemporary mobile media artists. As such, we acknowledge the persistence of artistic inquiry into the development of sociability in urban public spaces, human mobility, and the possibilities for creating hybrid spaces. We also observe today the residual qualities[3] of telecommunications technologies, that is, how they remain a part of our communicative landscape and influence our communicative practices in hybrid spaces.

In this chapter, we therefore historicize hybrid spaces by examining how early telecommunications-based art has reinterpreted public places, using telecommunication technologies (e.g. satellites, telephones, videophones, flip phones) as interfaces for artmaking and the city as a canvas for artwork. In doing so, we situate telecommunications-based art in relation to mobile media art, emphasizing telecommunications-based art as a foundation for mobile media art. We argue that the artists who created these works transformed sociability and human interaction in urban places and spaces.

Our goal is to analyze the hybrid space-making practices of early telecommunications-based artists in relation to current practices of contemporary mobile media artists. Through this analysis, we hope to better understand how hybrid spaces are formed and transformed by mobile media art, that is, what happens to public spaces when artists create situations in which participants can communicate and interact via mobile technologies. We proceed by first considering how early experiments with telecommunications technologies created hybrid spaces. Following this, we consider mobile media art works that use the city as a canvas to create hybrid spaces. Through this consideration, we discuss how, similar to telecommunication-based art, mobile media art allows for collaboration, communication, and aleatory encounters but also allows the unique possibility to transform the space of the city.

## Early Experiments with Telecommunications

For a long time, telecommunications technologies have been explored as a means to create connectivity by merging physical and virtual spaces. Steve Dietz, curator of the itinerant show *Telematic Connections* that took place in 2001,[4] suggests that the first telepresence instrument was the synchronous telegraph, created by the Greek Aeneas around the year 350 A.D. The synchronous telegraph used visual cues to communicate information within line-of-sight range. Much later, the modern electric telegraph was able to transmit messages at a distance, greatly speeding up information transmission time. The electric telegraph was the first telecommunication technology to drastically alter people's perception of time and space. For instance, at a December 1868 banquet held for Samuel Morse (one of the inventors of the electric telegraph), Morse was toasted for having "annihilated both space and time in the transmission of intelligence."[5] Since then, the fascination with telecommunications technologies' influence on our perceptions of time and space has endured.

Nevertheless, it was not until the twentieth century, when telephones became a common reality in people's households, that artists started using telephones for artmaking with the particular goal of connecting remote contexts and creating new spaces for sociability. For instance, in 1969, the Chicago Museum of Contemporary Art organized an exhibition called *Art by Telephone*, which considered the telephone as both the medium for artistic practice and a source of inspiration. Reflecting on this exhibition, Eduardo Kac tells us that in one of the more creative uses of the technology at that time, artist Robert Huot;

> potentially involved all visitors of the museum and attempted to generate unexpected first meetings by employing chance and anonymity. Twenty-six cities in America were chosen, each starting with a letter of the alphabet, and twenty-six men named Arthur were selected, one in each city. Each Arthur's last name was the first listing under the initial letter of the city (Arthur Bacon, in Baltimore, for instance). The Museum displayed a list of all cities and names, and invited visitors to call and ask for "Art." The work was the unexpected conversation between "Art" and the visitor, and its development totally up to them.[6]

Huot's piece presents the artist as the creator of a context, in which the visitor participates in the creative process. Here the telephone was used to turn artmaking into a social experience and to expand the museum space into other urban spaces.

A few decades later, artists began exploring the possibilities for connecting with people in public places by dialing pay phones. These artists include Heath Buntin, Stephen Wilson, Ian Pollock and Janet Silk, among others. For example, Heath Bunting, a member of the British group Disembodied Art Gallery, created a piece that incorporated the internet to reach a more spatially distributed audience. In this piece, entitled *Kings Cross Phone-in* (1994), he scattered the phone numbers of the Kings Cross British railway station's telephone kiosks across several online newsgroups and list-servs. He then asked those who found these phone numbers to choose one, call it at a specific time, and chat with whomever picked up the phone. This piece experimented with disrupting the rhythms of a public place by creating opportunities for spontaneous encounters with remote, unknown others.

Likewise, Stephen Wilson created a telephone-based project called *Is Anyone There?* (1992), which took place during one week in San Francisco. In the project, a computer-based system with digitized voice capabilities made hourly calls to five payphones with the aim of involving whomever answered the call in a conversation about life in the city. The system used intelligent response programming to engage passersby in a short dialog. The conversations were then stored in a digital database and made accessible as part of a more complex gallery installation. Specifically, the installation would change, at random, from presenting visitors with prerecorded conversations to, suddenly, allowing viewers to hear calls to the pay phones, as they were happening in real time. Wilson tried to explore random communication between unknown people, designing the user as content creator. Furthermore, he looked into possible developments for Artificial Intelligence (AI) systems by analyzing dialogs between computers and humans, much like what has been common with some chat bots, like Eliza or Julia.[7]

The above-mentioned artworks, through attempts to enfold local and remote contexts and create new social situations, mostly explored one-to-one conversations, which was the original intention for telephones. The works made use of urban spaces as a backdrop, but these spaces did not really influence how the piece unfolded or shaped specific aspects of the interaction. However, with satellite-based art we can appreciate a more ambitious use of urban space—one that allows the enfolding of both the visual and aural properties of multiple contexts.

The year 1977 was crucial for telecommunication-based arts, specifically artworks employing satellites as interfaces for artmaking. Satellites can be considered a particular kind of mobile media—they are in constant movement, but they are not personal devices like telephones. Nevertheless, they are part of the hybrid spaces assemblage, by connecting two or more remote contexts.

In 1977, the *Documenta 6*[8] art show in Kassel, Germany, featured the first live international telecast by artists. Performances by Nam June Paik, Joseph Beuys, Charlotte Moorman, and Douglas Davis were transmitted to over 25 countries via satellite. While Paik and Joseph Beuys played instruments and performed theatrically in Kassel, Douglas Davis streamed live from Caracas, Venezuela, to discuss his ideas about art as well as the distance between himself and the audience. Collectively, the performances dealt with the parameters of global media communication and the idea of telepresence by connecting both remote audiences to *Documenta 6* performers and, likewise, remote performers to the *Documenta 6* audiences. Furthermore, the satellite transmission of the three performances to other countries created an additional layer of meaning by interrogating what it meant to experience something at the same time but not in the same place as others.

In the same year, a collaboration between artists Keith Sonnier in New York and Liza Bear in San Francisco resulted in *Send/Receive Satellite Network: Phase II* (1977). The collaboration included a 15-hour, two-way, interactive satellite transmission between the two cities that was broadcast on TV, reaching an audience of 25,000 people. Using an experimental satellite, co-owned by NASA and the Canadian Government, artists in both cities discussed people's rights to access satellites by specifically questioning "the shifting balance of power between government and industry and the limits of citizen access."[9]

Thus, even in its earliest instantiations, telecommunications-based art considered the sociopolitical stakes of telepresence. However, the project also experimented with the possibilities for telepresence. Notably, two dancers (Nancy Lewis who was in New York and Margaret Fisher who was in San Francisco) performed together via the satellite transmission, altering their dance moves in response to what the other was doing. This, among other performances during the broadcast, demonstrated the possibilities for virtual collaboration using telecommunication technologies.

In a similar vein, Kit Galloway and Sherrie Rabinowitz organized an interactive dance via satellite, which involved performers on the Atlantic and Pacific coasts of the US *Satellite Arts Project* (1977) (see Figure 10.1).[10] Similar to *Send/Receive Satellite Network: Phase II*, the dancers responded to one another's dance moves. For the first time, however, several performing artists could appear and perform together in the same image, even if they were not in the same physical place. Accordingly, the artists referred to the space occupied by the performers as "a space with no geographical boundaries"[11] and considered *the image as a place*. From these initiatives we realize that the ability of having people to occupy the same "virtual" space, at the same time, is older than the World Wide Web. Further, we recognize that occupying the same "virtual" space offers opportunities for real-time collaboration in the same medium, which prior to telecommunication technologies, required geographic contiguity.

Following the *Satellite Arts Project*, in 1980 Galloway and Rabinowitz developed *Hole in Space*,[12] which also utilized satellite technology. In this work, one life-size video projection screen was placed in a shop window in New York, while the other was located in a shop window in Los Angeles. As the New York screen projected Los Angeles and the Los Angeles's screen showed New York, they functioned as "windows" or "holes" to the opposed city (Figure 10.2).

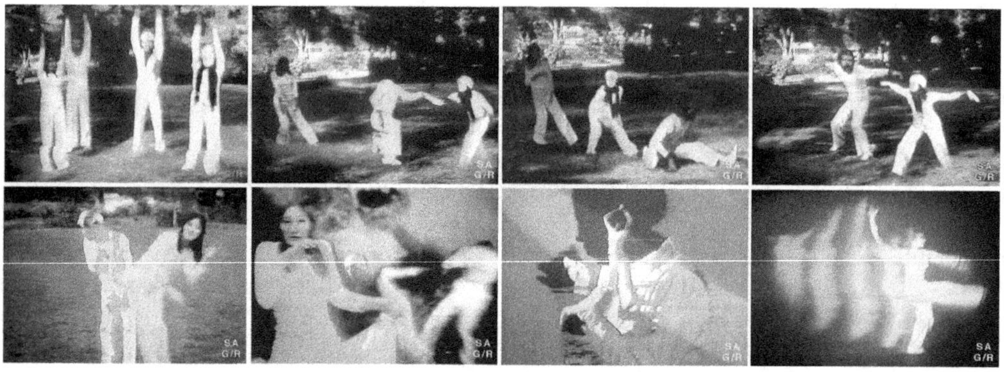

*Figure 10.1* Screenshots of live interactive dance on the Atlantic and Pacific coasts of the US *Satellite Arts Project* (1977). Photo credit: Kit Galloway

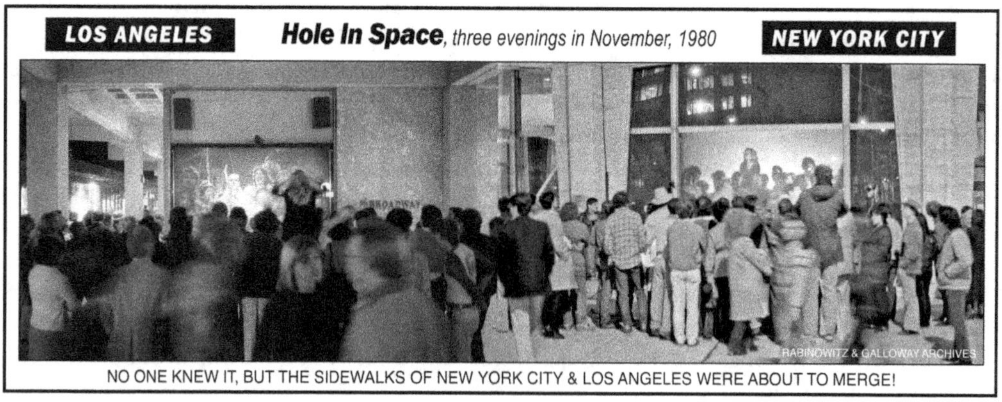


*Figure 10.2* Documentation video of *Hole in Space* (2003) in the shop windows of New York and Los Angeles. Photo credit: Kit Galloway

The video documentation of the piece shows passersby simultaneously amazed and incredulous about the screens. At that time, no signs, sponsorship logos, or credits were posted, and many people thought that what they could see was a fake image or a recorded video—they did not believe they were seeing the other city in real-time.

On the other hand, some perceived that the project could become a powerful communication tool in real-time between both cities. In the documentation video, people wave at each other, make plans to meet again the following day, and meet long-time-no-see friends and family, developing a "network through the virtual space created by the satellites."[13] Ultimately, the piece became a very strong communication device between the two cities. In addition, it fundamentally changed the urban physical space in which citizens were used to passing by every day. The addition of another "layer of space" changed the characteristics of the public space of both cities for three days, transforming the circulation space of the street into a gathering and communication place.

With *Satellite Arts Project* and *Hole in Space*, Galloway and Rabinowitz focused on creating hybrid spaces when developing telecommunications artwork, primarily through the connection of people in specific locations across large distances, using the available telecommunications technology. *Hole in Space*, for example, created a hybrid space between the two cities, in which communication would occur. Placing one screen in Los Angeles and another one in New York, people would gather on the streets to see and contact other people across the screen. While these people would not be sharing the same physical place, communication was happening between them and directly influencing all other passersby. Galloway and Rabinowitz claim that they have always been interested in creating a communication context by connecting physical places, rather than creating a simulated world in which communication could occur, as is the case with the virtual reality (VR).[14] *Hole in Space* is significant, among other reasons, because it foresaw more than 20 years ago the power of using mobile media to communicate in public places.

Another important project, beginning in the 1990s, is Paul Sermon's *Telematic Dreaming*. In 1992 the artist created a "virtual bed" that could be shared by people that were not actually in the same physical place. The installation artwork consisted of two physical beds in two remote locations. Then, an image of a remote person laying on the remote bed was projected onto the nearby bed. In this kind of responsive environment, participants could then interact with each other "as if" they were sharing the same place. *Telematic Dreaming* used an ISDN digital telephone network to connect remote places, which functioned as a video-conferencing system. One of the beds was located in a dark space, while the other was placed in a bright space. The bed in the bright location had a camera situated right above it, which sent the live video image from a person that laid on the bed across the network and projected it onto the dark bed. There was also a second camera located in the dark bedroom that captured the virtual image of the two people on the bed and sent it to the series of televisual monitors that surrounded the installation. When one watched the TVs, it seemed that the two people were actually sharing the same space. According to Sermon, "The ability to exist outside of the user's own space and time is created by an alarmingly real sense of touch that is enhanced by the context of the bed and caused by an acute shift of senses in the telematic space."[15]

In the following year, Sermon replaced the bed with a sofa, creating *Telematic Vision*. One person would sit on a sofa in front of a TV. The TV then showed an image of the sofa in which the participant was seated, with the difference being that there was somebody else sharing the sofa with them. This "someone" was a remote person, seated on a distant sofa, whose image was transmitted via a telephone network, simultaneously visualized as occupying the same living room and watching the same doubled image on the TV. As such, in both *Telematic Dreaming* and *Telematic Vision*, Sermon explores the possibility for telecommunications technologies to produce a sense of intimacy between remote individuals by sharing a responsive environment—one which, according to Söke Dinkla, reacts to users' actions by means of sensors and other interfaces, such as video cameras, to create the sense of being together in time and space.[16]

Myron Krueger's *Videoplace* (1974)[17] and David Rokeby's *Very Nervous System* (1986–90)[18] also offer examples of responsive environments. Responsive environments, in a sense, are controlled hybrid spaces. They include communication, sociability, and the enfolding of contexts, but lack the larger experience of urban spaces. However, when mobile technologies started being used as interfaces for artmaking, entire cities, buildings, or outdoors spaces could be used as the "responsive surface," as we will discuss next.

## The City as a Canvas

By using the city as a canvas, mobile media art reconfigures several relations. First, like in telecommunication-based art, mobile media art transforms the relationship between artwork and the audience by connecting art and mobile technologies. As such, it positions the audience as no longer an observer, but an active participant. Furthermore, mobile media art reconfigures cities as hybrid spaces by enfolding multiple contexts as individuals move through the city with their mobile devices. As an early form of mobile media art, in 1991 Canadian artist Janet Cardiff began creating audio walks, which utilized a portable cassette player with prerecorded cassettes to aurally direct individuals through a particular space. Discussing Cardiff's work, Lev Manovich considers how the audio walks augment the space of the city itself.[19] He states, that Cardiff:

> creates her pieces by following a trajectory through some space and narrating an audio track that combines instructions to the user ('go down the stairs;' 'look into the window;' 'go through the door on the right') with narrative fragments, sound effects and other aural data.[20]

Accordingly, these audio walks not only produce particular pathways through a space but transform the user's relationship with space as they experience the narrative fragments, sound effects, and other aural data. That is, by means of words and sounds, the artist overlays another conceptual meaning onto a physical space, thereby embedding a different context in the urban space while the user moves through it.

Comparably, we might consider the Walkman experience in the 1980s, in which individuals carried around a portable media player to listen to their personal music collection while mobile. Noting this experience, Hosokawa suggests that the Walkman mixed the present context of the urban environment with a soundtrack that did not belong to it, but was particular to the person who wore the device.[21] Similarly, Bull has argued that the Walkman allowed users to manage their experience of the city, by listening to sounds not natural to it.[22] Unlike the Walkman effect described by Hosokawa and Bull, however, Cardiff's audio walks did not depend only on the user but were the product of the interaction among the participant, the artist, and the environment itself. Cardiff's guided tour would create a hybrid space, except for the fact that the tour, like the Walkman, isolated the user from other people and, thus, it did not create a social environment.[23] According to Hosokawa,

> The practical meaning of the Walkman is found in the distance that it creates between the reality and the real, the city and the urban, and mainly between the other and the self. The Walkman destroys the context of the city, and promptly places any incoherent situation in its context.[24]

Cardiff's walks do not destroy the context of the city, however. Unlike the Walkman effect, they create new kinds of connections to the city and attribute new meanings to urban spaces.

These new ways of experiencing mediated connection is exactly what happens with Rafael Lozano-Hemmer's large-scale installations in public spaces. Mexican-Canadian media artist Raphael Lozano-Hemmer's pieces interfere with the city spaces, causing people to experience public spaces in a different way. In addition, some of his installations succeeded in using digital spaces to transform the actual space of the city, thus connecting distant and "digital" users to passersby. Lozano-Hemmer creates public installations that change how people behave in and perceive public spaces.

His work *Amodal Suspension (Relational Architecture 8)* (2003) used searchlights in the public space setting of the Yamaguchi Center in Japan. However, instead of displaying online drawings, as it was the case with his previous installation *Vectorial Elevation* (1999), the searchlights "caught" unread SMS sent among users via the amodal.net website or their cell phones. The messages were then encoded into a sequence of flashes and displayed in the sky around the Yamaguchi Center for Arts and Media (YCAM) in Japan. *Amodal Suspension* was hybrid in a double sense: first because it connected over 400,000 users from 94 different countries who were not physically copresent[25] and second because it displayed text messages before their actualization. Interestingly, it caught SMS in a potential (virtual) state, before they had been read, and transformed them into visible (actual) light that illuminated a public space. This hybrid space that encompasses SMS messages, people sending and receiving messages, search lights, the Yamaguchi Center in Japan, and mobile phones is a powerful assemblage that reconfigures people's relationships to the city and to each other in a mobile media artwork setting.

Beyond using the streets like Cardiff, or using the plaza like Lozano-Hemmer, other mobile media artists have considered the physical architecture of the city as a canvas for creation. For instance, the German group Chaos Computer Club transformed a whole building façade into a responsive environment in their iconic project, *Blinkenlights* (2002), which used mobile phones as a remote control to intervene in a public space. In 2002, they transformed an eight-story building in Berlin's Alexanderplatz into the world's biggest interactive computer display. One hundred forty-four lamps were arranged behind the building's front windows, which were independently controlled to produce a monochrome matrix of 18 x 8 pixels. Users could "control the building's façade" either via their mobile phones or internet, creating animations, playing *Pong*, or sending love letters. For example, people could use their mobile phones to call a specific number in order to play *Pong* against the computer. At first, they would hear some instructions like "use the 5 to move the paddle up and 8 to move it down." If a second person called in the system simultaneously, they would play against each other.

*Blinkenlights* could also be used to send love letters. Users could create an animation with the software "blinkenpaint," which could be downloaded from their website, and then e-mailed to the Club. The movie with the love letter would then be queued in the system, and the user would then receive an access code. With the code, the user could call the system, as when playing *Pong*, and, when the game showed up on the "screen," dial the access code, which would release the animation (Figure 5, color insert).

As showed in their documentation video, many Berliners would use that to send a letter to a loved one who was passing by Alexander Platz—they just had to know when. Similarly, people could create a picture to display on the building just by using ASCII characters (0 and 1) in a text file. For example, the pattern below makes a heart (a pulsing heart) that contracts (left) and expands (right):

| *@200* | *@800* |
|---|---|
| 000000000000000000 | 000011100011100000 |
| 000011100011100000 | 000111110111110000 |
| 000111110111110000 | 001111111111111000 |
| 000111111111110000 | 001111111111111000 |
| 000011111111100000 | 000111111111110000 |
| 000000111110000000 | 000011111111100000 |
| 000000001000000000 | 000000111110000000 |
| 000000000000000000 | 000000001000000000 |

When the project was running, the *Blinkenlights* website[26] provided all kinds of tools and software to facilitate the interaction with the system. The project also kept a database with the best animations created by users who had participated in their contest. *Blinkenlights* brought a great number of people to Alexanderplatz and later to Paris when the project expanded.

*Blinkenlights* was one the first art projects to transform mobile phones into gaming devices, bringing the game board/screen outside into urban spaces. With that, it also transformed sociability into these newly created hybrid spaces by connecting remote and contiguous people. The enlargement of the game board to the size of a building façade immersed large numbers of players and passersby into the game, transforming physical space into the game board. The possibility of carrying around the game control (i.e. the mobile phone) allowed people to interact with the screen and with each other in an open and public space. *Blinkenlights* explored the mobile phone's potential to engage large groups of urban users and viewers in a hybrid space configured by Alexanderplatz, *Blinkenlights'* website, mobile phones, Chaos Computer Club, and Berliners.

*Blinkenlights* and *Amodal Suspension* are examples of mobile media art projects that transformed urban circulation spaces, through which people pass by but no longer stop, into public places where people gather. In doing so, the mobile media art transformed the spaces through which people move into a space that facilitates social interaction. These large-scale mobile media art installations intervened in public spaces, inviting citizens to stop, perceive, and engage in urban spaces in a different way.

While mobile technologies of various sorts can be used to create hybrid spaces, networked mobile media add an important feature to hybrid spaces, because they allow coordination among various people and systems. Whereas using a static interface fixes the user in a specific location, mobile interfaces allow users to gather and disperse, bringing new meanings to tele- and close communication. For example, Mark Shephard, in collaboration with several programmers, created *Tactical Sound Garden* (2006),[27] a project that allows users with Wi-Fi-enabled mobile devices to digitally layer sounds onto specific locations in the city. In turn, other users can later access those sounds by traveling to the location in which the sound was layered. According to the documentation video, the project attempts to create a participatory culture in which individuals can contribute to the meanings of locations by adding digital information to them. However, the project also contemplates the politics of access in participatory culture, since users in spaces with high degrees of network access have more opportunities to participate than those who are in spaces of limited access. As such, *Tactical Sound Garden* is an important project for recognizing that mobile media art can open-up the possibilities for meaning-making in networked spaces while simultaneously furthering the disparity felt in non-networked or poorly networked spaces.

Yet, another example of the powerful and innovative artistic uses of networked mobile media to create hybrid spaces was by British group Blast Theory in conjunction with the Mixed Reality

Lab at the University of Nottingham. Their pioneer work focused on developing games that happened in hybrid spaces by integrating players who walked on the streets as well as online players. In their games / artworks, an action in the physical space could influence a decision in digital space and vice versa.

Their first collaboration, *Can You See Me Now?* (2001)[28] resembled a traditional *Pac-Man* game played in hybrid space. The game was played on specific days in Sheffield (United Kingdom) in 2001, in Rotterdam (the Netherlands) in February 2003, and in Oldenburg (Germany) in July 2003, among other cities.[29] During the gameplay, online players from anywhere in the world could play against the members of Blast Theory who were positioned in the streets of the city (Figure 10.3, left). Tracked by satellites, Blast Theory's runners appeared on a virtual map of the city center next to a silhouette of online players. Street runners were equipped with handheld computers connected wirelessly to the internet, Global Positioning System (GPS) receivers, and walkie-talkies to communicate with other users. They could also track the positions of online players on their mobile devices. Up to 20 people could be online simultaneously. Online players ran away from street players in order to elude capture. Likewise, street runners could catch an online player if they managed to get within five meters of the online player's position on the map of the city. If a street runner caught a virtual player, they were supposed to take a picture at the place where the chase ended, which was obviously an empty space like the one shown in Figure 10.3 (right). The game demonstrates the potential to use the city space as a gameboard, interacting with those in the streets and influenced by the interactions of online users. *Can You See Me Now?* emphasizes the potential of hybrid spaces as spaces for coordination and cooperation, as well how digital information co-constructs the physical space of the city.

Collectively, we see that mobile media, when used as interfaces for artmaking, has the potential to transform people's experience of spaces by transforming whole cities into responsive environments. Implicit within works like Cardiff's audio walks, Lozano-Hemmer's large-scale installations, Chaos Computer Club's *Blinkenlights* (2001), and Blast Theory's art / games is the idea that through mobility and the use of mobile media, we constantly experience new connections, meanings, and encounters as we traverse urban spaces. Rather than finding ground in the relative stability of place (insofar as any place can be stable), these mobile media artists have adopted instability and flux as both the means of artistic practice and the art itself.

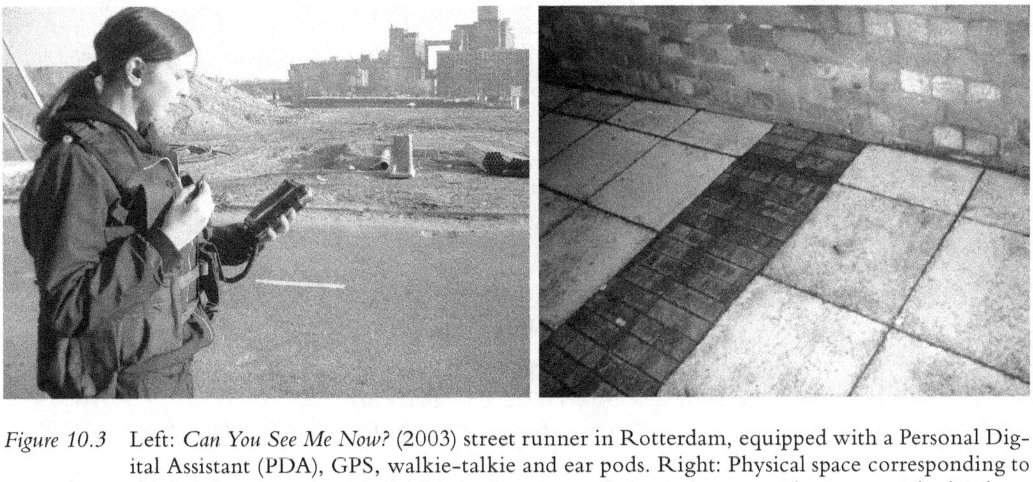

*Figure 10.3* Left: *Can You See Me Now?* (2003) street runner in Rotterdam, equipped with a Personal Digital Assistant (PDA), GPS, walkie-talkie and ear pods. Right: Physical space corresponding to the place where the online player was in the digital simulation, in the moment she has been caught. Photo credits: Blast Theory

## Conclusion

When our (tele)communication media becomes mobile, they become more than two-way communication devices. As we have seen with early telecommunication-based art, these works employed satellites and pay phones to change how people experienced their city spaces, creating unexpected social interactions with (known and unknown) others. In these works, people were often moving around urban spaces, but the artwork was restricted to specific locations. When these devices are released from a fixed location, so is the artwork. As a result, whole cities (or at least larger areas) are used as interfaces for artmaking.

Henry Jenkins has suggested that "games have been to the PC what NASA was to the mainframe—the thing that pushes forward innovation and experimentation."[30] From this summation, we might add: mobile media art has driven innovation and experimentation with a whole range of devices, including PCs, phones, and music players. By placing mobility at the center, these artists have explored the power of communication and community formation when mediated by mobile technologies. They have also transformed the possibilities for creating new encounters with a space.

Mobile media art, especially art that uses urban spaces as a canvas, helps make us aware of the hybrid space in which we live. While digital technologies in the 1990s have been mostly criticized for disconnecting us from the physical world and focusing our attention on simulated / digital spaces, telecommunications-based art and mobile media art have brought social and playful experiences to physical spaces, encouraging users to interact with others. They have also embedded familiar spaces with new meanings.

Today, the emergence of 5G networks, Internet of Things (IoT) devices, neural networks, and ambient intelligence promotes increased connectivity and mobility for many in urban spaces. On the flipside, the pervasiveness of these digital technologies also amplifies the issues of power disparity and exclusion for those who do not have access to these technologies. As these new mobile technologies inform artistic practice, we recognize an increased artistic focus on issues of power, surveillance, and exclusion that arise with their increased use—instead of a primary focus on experimentation with the technology itself. For example, early telecommunications-based art experimented with copresence, aleatory encounters, and collaboration. However, with satellite-based art such as the previously discussed *Send/Receive Satellite Network: Phase II*, we begin to see a transition to discuss the politics of technology access.

This transition has continued in recent years as hybrid spaces have become a norm, allowing artists to focus less on the novelty of hybrid spaces and more on the politics of these spaces. For example, Blast Theory's work is highly political. One of their recent works, *Ulrike and Eamon Compliant* (2013) uses location-based technology to guide the audience through the city in an audio walk that asks people to reflect upon terrorist attacks in urban space. While the work makes use of mobile technology, it more importantly asks audiences to critically reflect on social issues. From this perspective, mobile media artists help us to challenge these hybrid spaces as spaces embedded not only with digital information, but also with complex social, cultural, and political relationships.

## Notes

1 Adriana de Souza e Silva, "From Cyber to Hybrid: Mobile Technologies as Interfaces of Hybrid Spaces," *Space and Culture* 3 (2006): 261–78, doi: 10.1177/1206331206289022.

2 Stephen Wilson, *Information Arts: Intersections of Art, Science, and Technology* (Cambridge, MA: MIT Press, 2002), 526.

3 Charles R. Acland, "Introduction," in *Residual Media*, edited by Charles R. Acland (Minneapolis: University of Minnesota Press, 2007), xiii–xxv.

4 Telematic Connections: The Virtual Embrace, Online Exhibition, curated by Steve Dietz, http://telematic.walkerart.org/.
5 Tom Standage, *The Victorian Internet: The Remarkable Story of the Telegraph and the Nineteenth Century's on-Line Pioneers* (New York: Walker & Company, 2007), 90.
6 Eduardo Kac, "Towards Telepresence Art," *Interface* 4, no. 2 (1992): 48–72, http://ekac.org/telepresence.art._94.html.
7 Janet H. Murray, *Hamlet on the Holodeck: The Future of Narrative in Cyberspace* (New York: Simon and Schuster, 1997).
8 Joseph Beuys, Douglas Davis, and Nam June Paik. "Documenta 6 Satellite Telecast," 1977, Germany, Electronica Arts Intermix, www.eai.org/titles/documenta-6-satellite-telecast.
9 Lisa Bear and Keith Sonnier, "Phase II: Send/Receive," artists' description, 1977. Arts and Electronic Media, 28 August 2009, www.artelectronicmedia.com/artwork/sendreceive-satellite-network.
10 "Satellite Arts Project 1977," Los Angeles Olympic Arts Festival, www.ecafe.com/getty/SA/index.html.
11 Ibid.
12 "Hole in Space, 1980," Los Angeles Olympic Arts Festival, www.ecafe.com/getty/HIS/index.html.
13 Ibid.
14 Personal communication with Adriana de Souza e Silva in the Electronic Café in Santa Monica, California, 15 November 2003.
15 Paul Sermon, "Telematic Dreaming Statement," Media Art Net, www.medienkunstnetz.de/works/telematic-dreaming/.
16 Söke Dinkla, "The History of the Interface in Interactive Art," (Paper presented at the Proceedings of the 1994 International Symposium for the Electronic Arts (ISEA), 1994).
17 "Myron Krueger Videoplace," Media Art Net, www.medienkunstnetz.de/works/videoplace/.
18 "Interactive Installations: Very Nervous Systems (1986–1990)," Rokeby, 17 September 2019, www.davidrokeby.com/vns.html.
19 Lev Manovich, "The Poetics of Augmented Space," *Visual Communication* 5, no. 2 (2006): 219–40, doi: 10.1177/1470357206065527.
20 Ibid., 226.
21 Shuhei Hosokawa, *Der Walkman-Effekt* (Berlin: Merve Verlag, 1987).
22 Michael Bull, *Sounding out the City: Personal Stereos and the Management of Everyday Life*. Oxford: Berg, 2000.
23 For additional discussion on the Walkman Effect and mobile media art, see Drew Hemment's interview in this collection.
24 Hosokawa, *Der Walkman-Effekt*, translation to English by the authors. Original: *Die praktische Bedeutung desWalkman besteht in der Distanz, die er zwischen der Wirklichkeit und dem Realen, der Stadt und dem Urbanen und insbesondere zwischen den Anderen und dem Ich entstehen lässt. Er zerstört den Kontext des bestehenden Textgefüges der Stadt und stellt gleichzeitig jedwede zusammenhanglose Situation in einen Kontext.*
25 Rafael Lozano-Hemmer, "Amodal Suspension: Relational Architecture," Amodal Suspension, www.amodal.net/intro.html.
26 "Welcome to Project Blinkenlights." Project Blinkenlights, http://blinkenlights.net/.
27 "Tactical Sound Garden," Mark Shepard, www.andinc.org/v4/tactical-sound-garden-tsg/.
28 "Can You See Me Now?" Blast Theory, www.blasttheory.co.uk/projects/can-you-see-me-now/.
29 *Can You See Me Now?* was nominated for an Interactive Arts BAFTA in 2002 and has won the 2003 Prix Ars Electronica Golden Nica for Interactive Arts.
30 Henry Jenkins, "Games, the New Lively Art," in *Handbook of Computer Game Studies*, edited by Joost Raessens and Jeffrey Goldstein (Cambridge, MA: MIT Press, 2005), 175–92.

# 11

# ALGORITHMIC GARDENING

## Questions of Mobility, Hybridity, and Infrastructure

*Shannon McMullen and Fabian Winkler*

### A Robot Escape Story

A *Soybot* is a robotanic hybrid, consisting of a sensor-enhanced mobile robotic platform and a planter box containing a soybean plant. *Soybots* are programmed to navigate to optimal light conditions in an effort to provide the best environment for their soybeans. A trio of *Soybots* were installed by a trio of humans in Paris at the VISAP'14 art exhibition located in a lobby area of the basement level of the Hilton Hotel.

In order to confine the robots to their assigned location, a virtual enclosure was defined by a perimeter of battery-powered infrared light beams. Though not visible to human eyes, infrared light is "visible" to *Soybot* sensors, constantly scanning local light conditions. When it came time for the human trio to eat lunch, they left the *Soybots* to seek out the best light conditions within their enclosure. Upon return from their lunch adventure, the humans discovered that all three *Soybots* had escaped from their assigned territory. Two robots had come to rest around a corner just a few steps away and were easily recovered. However, by the time the third robot was discovered, it was one move away from ascending the escalator to the first floor where it would have been wholly possible for this self-driving plant to exit the building and wander around Paris in its search for sunlight.

As it turned out, the infrared virtual barrier devices had automatically shut off (an inconvenient habit occurring automatically after two hours). Thus, freed from their spatial confinement, the *Soybots* were attracted to the more alluring light conditions coming from a skylight between the exhibition space and the central escalators. Do robots dream of electric sheep?[1] We don't know, but it was amusing to learn that *Soybots* have desires and will act on them, if given the opportunity (see Figure 11.1).

We begin with this story in order to explain why edible plants, robotic mobility, and algorithmic perception of the world are equally important in our contribution to this section on mobile media art and hybrid realities. Cultivated plants, particularly those developed for industrial agriculture, occupy a critical space at the intersection of environmental challenges, national policies, and emerging technologies. For nearly a decade, we have engaged in an artistic practice that we define as "critical gardening," often aimed at questioning the relations of nature and technology and the inherent values expressed in monocultural farming. For example, our new media art installation, *Algorithmic Gardening*, discussed on the following pages, employs soybeans to imagine an agricultural future that is autonomous, botanical and robotic. The installation's key works—*Soybots: Robotanic Micro-Gardens* (the small fleet of light-seeking soybean plants introduced in the

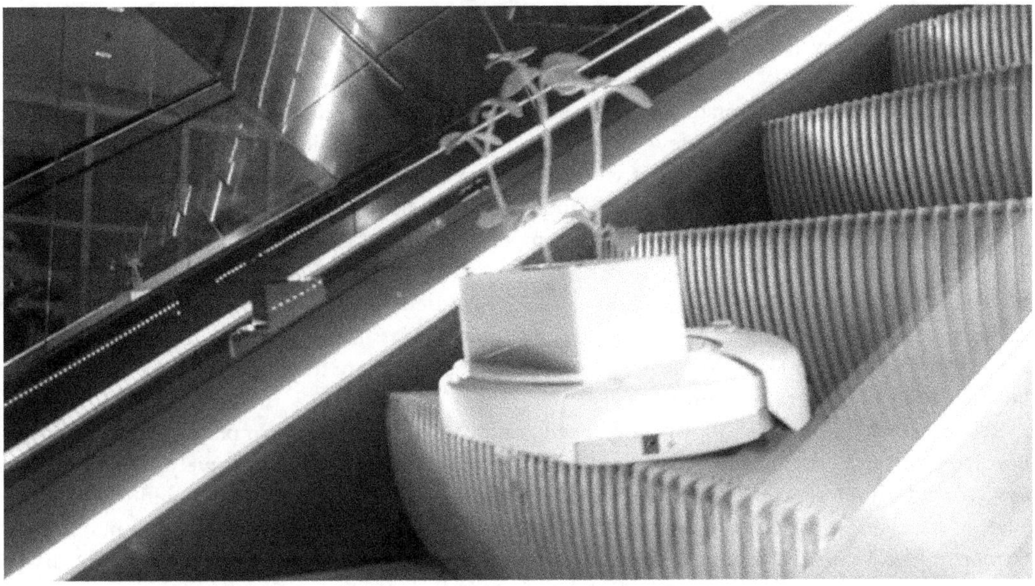

*Figure 11.1* Video still from the recreation of the *Soybot* escape in the Paris Hilton Hotel, November (2014). Photo credit: McMullen_Winkler

preceding robot escape story) and *The Algorithmic Gardener: Tales of Future Natures and Code* (a weed-picking robot with computer vision capabilities)—elicit questions of mobility, infrastructure, and hybridity. The subsequent sections of this chapter take up each of these themes in more detail, reflecting on what we have learned in the process of creating sentient machines, and taking a closer look at machinic perception of the world. We conclude with a discussion of artistic strategies for visualizing or materializing technological interventions in "nature" and their possible application in future work.

## Critical Gardening as Artistic Practice

Our path to the art practice of critical gardening began in 2006, when we moved from Pittsburgh, PA to Lafayette, IN. Living in the heart of industrial farmland, we became intrigued by soybeans, a crop that initially we neither recognized, nor had given any thought to before our relocation, despite its ubiquity. Our fascination for the soybean plant intensified when colleagues in Horticulture explained the contemporary international importance of soybeans as animal feed, food ingredient and biofuel. They also introduced us to their historical significance in farm to factory utopias such as Henry Ford's chemurgy and his plans for a soybean-plastic car.[2] These discussions coincided with an October 2008 *The New York Times Magazine* article written by journalist Michael Pollan. Addressing his letter to the as yet to be determined president-elect as "Farmer in Chief,"[3] Pollan urged the next US President[4] to prioritize agricultural resources as potential assets for national security.

Thus, we began to comprehend that the soybean plant formed the center of a dense web of interrelated global scale concerns in politics, agriculture, the environment, and technology. And yet, soybeans had become a "naturalized" part of the regional landscape. Within this context, and inspired by the research of science studies scholar Chandra Mukerji, we initiated artistic experiments that led to an emerging art practice we termed "critical gardening." In her cultural and political study of the gardens of Versailles in the seventeenth century, Mukerji analyzes gardens as sites where art and technology produce material realities and social narratives with political consequences. She writes:

> Gardens are complex laboratories, where new cultivation techniques are explored, new approaches to engineering entertained, new aesthetics mobilized, and new demonstrations/ representations of power tendered; they are places where human will and the natural order are co-constructed. Gardens address, in other words some fundamental ties between human action and the material, "natural" world, so they have surprisingly important tales to tell about human societies.[5]

This view of gardens—and by extension other cultivated sites such as fields—highlights their political nature. Gardens, groves, and fields can and do express ideas, support ideologies, and relay narratives. At the same time, Mukerji makes clear that gardens are technological and often rely on human engineered infrastructures to exist.

Plants are technological too. In the United States, 94%[6] of the soybean plants grown on farms have come from genetically modified seeds. Engineered for genes that positively influence plant growth and oil content, they provide resistance to unfavorable climatic events and create tolerance of herbicides such as glyphosate. While this may be common knowledge and practice for farmers in the Midwest, genetically modified monoculture is largely invisible and tends to disappear into the agricultural landscape. With this in mind, the question for us became, how do we create evocative visual metaphors? And, how can they help us contemplate the kind of natures or nature-technology hybrids enabled or discouraged by human interventions? In response, we see critical gardening as an artistic practice to explore the relationships and tensions between recent or emerging technologies and natural environments shaped by human agency. Additionally, critical gardens are a creative method to initiate public conversations around the ideologies, values, and possible futures of nature-technology hybrids.

## Mobile Gardens as Conceptual Art

Gardens, fields, or individual plants are rarely considered to be independently mobile in the same ways that human bodies (or as an extension robots) are. Although natural environments are constantly shifting and changing, the temporalities involved can be radically different. The human experience is often perceived as immediate and the standard by which "real-time" is measured.

Real time implies a relationship between technology and humans that favors a human sense of time as we live and experience it day by day, minute by minute. In contrast, geologic time or "deep time" represents a timescale measured in eons, mountains, and glacial periods.[7] In between these scalar extremes, is the Anthropocene, a recently proposed era that refers to the measurable long-term effects of industrial production and human influences on the environment. The conflicting environmental perspectives inherent in incongruous temporalities have been a rich source of inspiration for contemporary art from the mid-twentieth century to the first decades of the new millennium within Western art. Here, we offer three examples that we find insightful for the ways they think of nature, culture and their often-competing temporal perspectives together.

Polish artist Maria Loboda's contribution to dOCUMENTA (13) was motivated by the witches' prophecy in Shakespeare's tragedy *Macbeth*: "Macbeth shall never vanquish'd be until/ Great Birnam wood to high Dunsinane hill/ Shall come against him."[8] Loboda's *This Work is Dedicated to an Emperor* (2012)[9] consisted of 20 cypress trees in planters placed in military formation on a vast lawn.

Over the 100 days of the dOCUMENTA exhibition, the artist moved the trees according to a "plan of attack" toward the orangery in the Kassel Auepark, a Baroque garden. Her artwork was informed both by the assault on Macbeth's castle by soldiers camouflaged with branches and twigs in Shakespeare's drama, and by the military strategy, appearance, and deception illustrated in Roman writer Vegetius *De re militari* (around 400 AD). Executing strategic movements following literary instructions, as if an algorithm, the trees in Loboda's work addressed mobility in surprising ways. By fusing soldiers and their camouflage—producing soldier-tree hybrids—Loboda raises questions about the nature of enemies and the role of the environment in military conflict. She gives the trees agency through their movement, but what would be aggressive formations and movements by human soldiers reads differently with trees and planter boxes. The interdependence of humans, gardens, and woods is highlighted through this absurd gesture.

*Portable Orchard* (1972),[10] part of the *Survival Pieces* series by US ecological artists Helen Mayer Harrison and Newton Harrison, speaks to the idea of mobility in plants within a different context: connections between (sub)urban sprawl, environmental urgency, and food production. Haunted as the Harrisons were by Rachel Carson's *Silent Spring* (1962) and informed by California counterculture, art historian Amanda Boetzkes argues, "...their work aimed to reclaim technological development for a democratic future."[11] The *Portable Orchard* installation consisted of citrus and avocado trees planted in hexagonal boxes, illuminated from above by hexagonal light boxes in a museum gallery. The indoor orchard was prompted by the disappearance of citrus groves in Orange County, California due to environmental factors, specifically pollution and suburban sprawl.[12]

The Harrisons talked then of the work as the "last orange orchard in Orange County."[13] Although in actuality citrus groves did not disappear from Orange County until the mid-1990s,[14] their prediction was indeed correct. *Portable Orchard* and the other works included in *Survival Pieces* grappled with questions of scale, technology, and ecological ethics.[15] By highlighting the dependence of citrus trees on highly engineered environmental conditions, the installation asked viewers to consider the complexities of food production and urban development in 1970s California.

Yet another approach to mobile gardens exists in the work of Austrian artist Lois Weinberger. *The Mobile Garden,*[16] a publication of essays, poetry and documentation, presents thought-provoking ideas dealing with the mobility of plants, emphasizing what such mobility has to say about the cultures, political systems and environmental conditions in which they reside. In works such as *Portable Gardens* (1994–2008), *What is Beyond the Plants / Is at One with Them* at *documenta X* (1997) and *Empty Garden* (1998), Weinberger highlights infrastructures that help in the dissemination—ultimately the mobility—of plants. For example, shopping bags which imply human agents, railway systems which transport not only people, but also seeds and plant matter, or winds that spread plant seeds to remote locations: these are all vegetal modes of travel.

What is interesting to us about the artworks outlined above is the conceptual use of mobility to reveal larger social, political, or environmental issues. Audiences encountering these projects are invited to contemplate, question, and imagine. Furthermore, in these examples, the plants involved were carefully chosen by the artists, creating a close connection between their cultural importance and the added element of mobility. Our own artistic experimentation with these issues can be found in the two related projects: *Soybots* and *Algorithmic Gardening.*

## Soybots: Robotanic Micro-Gardens

Much like the works introduced in the preceding section, the idea for *Soybots* came from a desire to work conceptually with the mobility of plants in an artwork. The resulting nature-technology hybrids consist of an iRobot Create autonomous robot platform and custom-designed planter boxes big enough to hold up to three soybean plants. Each robotic platform is further augmented with three infrared distance sensors around the front bumper as an obstacle detection and avoidance system. Two light-dependent resistors (LDR), one on the left and one on the right side of the robot, form the basis of a phototropic navigation strategy. Information from the sensors are used to track and follow sunlight intensity, to locate LED grow lights, or travel to the brightest artificial light conditions in a space.

While traversing through architectural space, each robot transmits both sensor data and positional coordinates to a visualization window in the gallery. The upper half of the window plots position data in real-time as lines: dense in areas of high light levels and sparse in darker areas. This part of the visualization connects architectural space to movement and light, while the lower part of the window displays statistical information that compares average light values and distance traveled over the course of each day. Soybeans are significant in this work for their reference to industrial scale agriculture and for their hybridity between nature and technology—in this case, as a result of biotechnological strategies for increasing crop yields through genetic modification. As self-pollinating organisms paired with a light-seeking mobile platform, *Soybots* become metaphors for plant and robot desires that are independent of human need.

## *Algorithmic Gardening*

*Algorithmic Gardening* combines documentary fiction and speculative design. While *Soybots* move soybean plants to locations of maximum sun (or indoor light) exposure, the two-armed Taurus dexterous robot in the *Algorithmic Gardener* works to identify and pull weeds from the *Soybots*' micro-gardens (see Figure 11.2). The video depicts a robotic gardener roughly the size and shape of a small human upper torso. Its head is equipped with a stereoscopic camera weeding the *Soybots*. The *Algorithmic Gardener* video suggests that a robot can identify a weed and successively plan its motion to navigate to the identified plant and pull it from the garden. Humans have difficulties

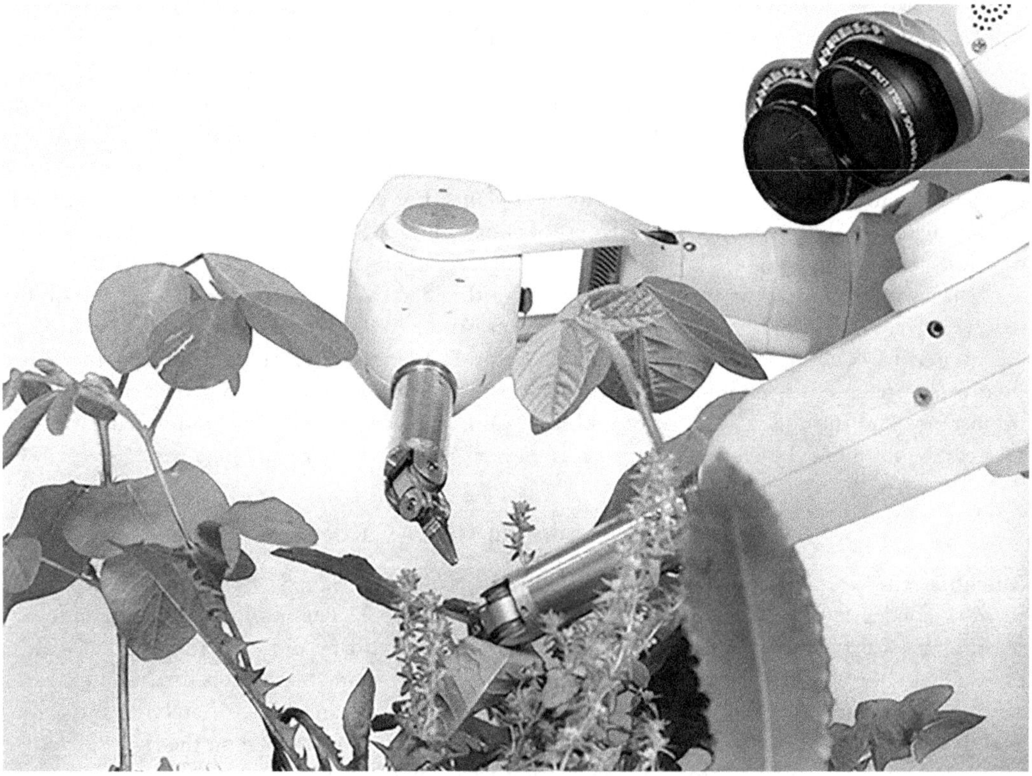

*Figure 11.2* Taurus dexterous robot as *Algorithmic Gardener*, weeding a patch of soybean plants, Summer (2015). Photo credit: McMullen_Winkler

determining what exactly a weed is—definitions shift based on context and culture. How could this cultural concept be translated into a machine algorithm?

Given the dexterity of its grippers and the mobility of its arms the Taurus robot seemed to be an ideal experimental platform for precision gardening work and addressing this question.[17] The choice of an ambiguous concept, such as "weed" rather than a functional agricultural application, was deliberate. Possible divergent outcomes of the weeding process, including what might be construed as mistakes and failures, were desired as speculative acts that could reveal the relationship between culture and code.

Soybeans are an agricultural monoculture in Indiana, and they are the first logical step in identifying weeds seemed straightforward: everything that is not a soybean is automatically a weed. This was a manageable computer vision task. Still the similarity of foliage colors and leaf shapes made the discrimination non-trivial: often plants other than a soybean would be identified correctly and removed, but sometimes parts of a soybean plant would be misidentified and clipped, or in other instances only parts of a weed would be pulled. Furthermore, the translation of the computer vision classification into actual movement code for the gardener's arms and pincers resulted in imprecisions due to the complexity of the physical environment of the plants. Crooked growing patterns, one plant growing behind the other and changing light conditions are just a few common conditions that make the coding task and execution challenging.

Rather than pursue perfection, we thought of code as similar to the sets of instructions in the conceptual art of Sol LeWitt[18] and Yoko Ono.[19] We embraced the idea of the *Algorithmic Gardener's* algorithm as a set of instructions for visual classification and physical movement that would intentionally reveal imprecisions and possibilities for variation. To make this critical component of the project legible, we developed a set of instructions written in a narrative "pseudo-code" that could be exhibited alongside the weed-picking Taurus robot. Opening the algorithmic "black box" was an important decision because it allowed us to draw attention to the subjective and culturally inflected parts of computer vision algorithms. This can be seen clearly, for example, in the early stages of the weed identification process when researchers point out some of its falsely classified results.

## Visual Sentience and Hybrid Realities

With continually increasing computational power being housed in ever smaller processing units, there will likely be an explosion of independently mobile devices (from toys to social robots, self-driving cars and trucks) equipped with an advanced visual awareness attempting to read and classify the environment around them. Already now, algorithms looking at the world create a surplus of unseen images "by-machines-for-machines."[20] The training of these visually sentient devices will be an essential process for coding responses to culturally ambiguous concepts as the *Algorithmic Gardener's* pseudo-code illustrates.

The development of advanced artificial intelligence systems is based on an important negotiation between humans and code before these algorithms can function as desired in a real-world environment. It is exactly at this interface between humans and algorithms in the training process where a plurality of perspectives and cultural backgrounds need to be discussed by developers and conveyed to a computer algorithm, often in the form of annotated images. Yet, these processes happen too often in closed environments without the participation of a diverse group of designers or communities. The consequences are often much less poetic, ranging from inconvenient to harmful as recent research has shown.[21]

While the *Soybots'* visual sentience is quite limited in its readings of brightness values to the right and left of the soybean plant, it can reveal interesting insights about the relationship of the plant to the environment it is looking at. The *Soybots* transmit data about local light conditions in real time to a visualization window in the gallery along with the coordinates of their current position in the space. The visualization of the robots' movements together with their light sensor readings recorded along the paths they travel create intricate light architectures, revealing how light shapes spaces.

During an exhibition, light densities emerge on the control monitor over the course of the day materializing the quality of natural and artificial light in the gallery. Without the data visualization, the subtle changes in light quality in a space over the course of a day easily goes unnoticed to a human observer. Providing this information to visitors inspires thought about energy demands, consumption, and balance—comparing forms of sun and electrical energy. As one reviewer of the work observed, this graphical representation suggests that

> the process of photosynthesis is more deeply entangled with technology and cultural-based ecologies than perhaps previously imagined. Rather than being simply a translation of light into plant matter, photosynthesis extends through food webs to include the relationship between humans and technology.[22]

Both the *Soybots* and the *Algorithmic Gardener* use mobility and hybridity to ask questions about how these concepts in material objects reveal non-human agency: What can their mobility tell us about their perception of and reflection on the environment they inhabit? How does a technological awareness of space (through complex computer vision or simple brightness values) compare and contrast with the human experience of that space?

And, at the same time, what can the design and appearance of the environment tell us about the capabilities and limitations of the machines that interact with it? The first two questions reflect on the machines' sentience and interpretation of their spatial context creating hybrid realities in which humans have varying degrees of access and, therefore, awareness. The latter question inspires thought about how autonomous devices influence and shape the spaces around them, something we would like to discuss in the final section of this chapter.

## Making Visible: Manifestation through Infrastructures

While it is the ultimate goal of industrial engineering to create robots that work with high precision in environments that are constantly changing, certain technological and architectural infrastructures usually need to be in place to help the robots perform their tasks. Specifically, in the context of mobile robots, a physical space provides clues about machine habits and capabilities, limits, and peculiarities of seeing the world.[23] For example, in the case of the *Soybots*, we carefully set up infrared (IR) light barriers to keep the robots in designated areas. Although in general quite reliable, this method of containment can still fail. However, in the process the robots' intentions are revealed in even stronger ways, as the anecdote in the introduction to this chapter illustrates.

Furthermore, the relatively low-profile mobile platform and sensors in combination with the height of soybean plants means that the *Soybots* prefer spaces in which obstacles can be detected a few inches above the ground and where two feet of "head room" exists. And although their wheels are equipped with rugged treads, *Soybots* navigate best on flat, even indoor surfaces. The Taurus robot in the *Algorithmic Gardening* installation on the other hand prefers the objects it interacts with in close proximity. Although the robot's arms are almost the same size as human arms, their reach is much more confined, to a small approximately 12 × 18" space in front of it—much smaller than the range of garden dimensions that humans navigate. For a fixed installation of the weed picking robot, small planter boxes or mobile gardens that can be delivered to the *Algorithmic Gardener* were ideal. This observation resulted in the specific interactions between the Taurus dexterous robot and the *Soybots* in the video component of the *Algorithmic Gardening* installation.

These observations and reflections—a result of what Mukerji terms "material thinking"—allow us to imagine future artistic installations that explore the relationship between mobile sentient machines and plants. In their most radical form, these installations might only suggest the presence of the machine through a careful design of the environment. For example, an inexpensive approach to indoor positioning of robots is the use of AprilTags,[24] a system of visual markers placed in the environment that allows a robot to determine its position by a visual analysis of the markers' orientation and distance from it. The AprilTag markers are computer generated and resemble QR code. In contrast to an analysis of naturally occurring features in computer vision, AprilTags are based on artificial features (known as fiducials) to create a more controlled environment.

As a result, they deliberately look "alien" in a space, carrying little visual information for humans. Plants arranged in the shape of fiducial markers (there is a peculiar resemblance to the layout of hedges in formal gardens) might be combined with other design interventions in a future installation. We can also imagine infrastructural features like vertical gardens extending in height far beyond a human's reach, plant-specific light conditions emphasizing the red and blue spectrum, and a visualization of plant features in a computer vision algorithm: a constellation that could provide a glimpse of a future garden assemblage.[25] Such a work could evoke certain images of robots and sentient machines in the context of gardening without ever physically introducing the machines. The machines and their forms of mobility would reside in the minds of the audience members who would be encouraged to create their own speculative fictions about the shape, function, capabilities and limits of such algorithmic gardeners, and how they might help shape future understandings and experiences of gardens.

## Acknowledgments

Work on *Algorithmic Gardening* was made possible by funding through a Purdue College of Liberal Arts Transdisciplinary and Interdisciplinary Research Grant and Purdue's Office of the Vice Provost for Research Laboratory Research Equipment Program. Professor Juan Wachs generously gave us access to his industrial engineering lab and enthusiastically supported our art and technology experiments. Early algorithms for the project's synthetic vision and robot control were developed by Arjun Narang (Masters student in Electrical and Computer Engineering, Purdue University) with the support of Tian Zhou (PhD candidate in Industrial Engineering, Purdue University). Finally, we would like to thank Industrial Engineering PhD student Glebys Gonzalez for her expert industrial engineering knowledge and command of the Taurus robot and for her ability to explain complex engineering processes in terms that allowed us to write robotic instructions in prose.

## Notes

1 A reference to speculative fiction writer Philip K. Dick's 1968 novel, which became the basis for the film *Blade Runner.*

2 William Shurtleff and Akiko Aoyagi, "Henry Ford and His Employees: Work with Soy," *Soyinfo Center*, www.soyinfocenter.com/HSS/henry_ford_and_employees.php.

3 Michael Pollan, "Farmer in Chief," *The New York Times Magazine*, 9 October 2008, www.nytimes.com/2008/10/12/magazine/12policy-t.html.

4 Democratic candidate Barack Obama would defeat Republican candidate John McCain to become the President-Elect in November 2008.

5 Chandra Mukerji, *Territorial Ambitions and the Gardens of Versailles* (Cambridge: Cambridge University Press. 1997), 35.

6 US Department of Agriculture, Economic Research Service, "Adoption of Genetically Engineered Crops in the United States, 1996–2018," www.ers.usda.gov/webdocs/charts/58020/biotechcrops_d.html?v=7149. According to the same source, the percentage for Indiana in 2018 was 91%.

7 Jussi Parikka, *A Geology of Media* (Minneapolis: University of Minnesota Press, 2015). As media archeologist Jussi Parikka explains, this does not mean that geologic time has no connection to technology. Through a "geology of media," he argues that the seeming immateriality of digital media relies extensively on the geologic materiality of metallic ores like Coltan which resulted from deep time processes. Furthermore, the breakdown of electronic devices that contain elements extracted from Coltan (e.g. tantalum), plastics and the "after products"—many environmentally hazardous—resulting from extraction and production will only progress at a geologic scale of time.

8 William Shakespeare and Eugene M. Waith, *The Tragedy of Macbeth* (New Haven, CT: Yale University Press, 1954), 67.

9 Eva Scharrer, *dOCUMENTA (13) Catalog 3/3: The Guidebook* (Ostfildern, Germany: Hatje Cantz, 2012), 274.

10 "Portable Orchard, 1972–73," *The Harrison Studio*, http://theharrisonstudio.net/portable-orchard-1972-73.

11 Amanda Boetzkes, "Techniques of Survival: The Harrison and the Environmental Counter Culture," in *West of Center: Art and the Counterculture Experiment in America, 1965–1977*, edited by Elissa Auther and Adam Lerner (Minneapolis, MN: University of Minnesota Press, 2011), 308.

12 Through this work, the Harrisons created a provocative image for environmental degradation by making the disappearing citrus trees in the California landscape reappear in an indoor gallery setting. However, if looked at critically, this project considers ecological questions in a narrow historical scope—not addressing how orange trees were imposed onto an ecosystem prone to water shortage or the politics of industrial agriculture.

13 Neil Genzlinger, "Helen Mayer Harrison, Leader in Eco-Art Movement, Dies at 90," *New York Times*, 13 April 2018, www.nytimes.com/2018/04/13/obituaries/helen-mayer-harrison-leader-in-eco-art-movement-dies-at-90.html.

14 Doug Smith, Emily Foxhall and Sandra Poindexter, "Orange County's Vanishing Oranges," *L.A. Times*, 16 January 2015, www.latimes.com/visuals/graphics/la-me-g-the-decline-of-the-orange-20150116-htmlstory.html.

15 Boetzkes, "Techniques of Survival."

16 Lois Weinberger, *The Mobile Garden*, ed. Claudia Zanfi (Bologna, Italy: Damiani editore, 2009).

17 This act of automated gardening work also raises provocative labor issues. After all, we see a shift in the use of robots in factories and fields: while robots once have assisted humans in their work, humans today (at least the few that kept their jobs) are more likely to support the robots in their work (see: Sheelah Kolhatkar, "Dark Factory: The Robotics Revolution Is Changing What Machines Can Do. Where Do Humans Fit In?" *The New Yorker*, 23 October 2017, 70–81.). In addition, we were also intrigued by the metaphorical complexity of the word "weed" that can range in its scope from undesired plants to undesired humans. These issues may be explored in a separate discussion, in the scope of this essay they unfortunately needed to be relayed to a footnote.

18 "Catalogue # 1971.18: Work from Instructions," *Sol LeWitt Prints Catalog Raisonné*, www.sollewittprints.org/lewitt-raisonne-1971-18.

19 Yoko Ono, *Grapefruit* (New York: Simon & Schuster, 2000).

20 Jörg Heiser, "Safety in Numbers," *Frieze*, 12 March 2014, www.frieze.com/issue/article/safety-in-numbers.

21 See, for example, the following: Joy Buolamwini's *Algorithmic Justice Project*: www.media.mit.edu/people/joyab/overview/; Cathy O'Neil, *Weapons of Math Destruction: How Big Data Increases Inequality and Threatens Democracy* (New York: Crown, 2016); Safiya Umoja Noble, *Algorithms of Oppression: How Search Engines Reinforce Racism* (New York: NYU Press, 2018).

22 Anonymous reviewer, SIGGRAPH Art Gallery, 2015.

23 In a related context, New Aesthetic is grappling with increasing manifestations of the visual language of digital and virtual worlds in the physical world. In works such as *Activations* and *Autonomous Trap* (both 2017) artist and writer James Bridle shows the unique visual perception of self-driving cars and manifestations of their flaws in the physical world. In the context of architecture and urban architecture, see, for example: Guillermo Fernández-Abascal and Urtzi Grau, "Becoming Digital—Learning to Live Together," in *e-flux architecture*, www.e-flux.com/architecture/becoming-digital/248074/learning-to-live-together/.

24 "April Tags," April Robotics Laboratory, https://april.eecs.umich.edu/software/apriltag.html.

25 For a discussion of assemblage in the context of gardens see: Graham Livesay, "Assemblage Theory, Gardens and the Legacy of the Garden City Movement," *ARQ* 15, no.3 (2011): 271–78, doi: 10.1017/S1359135511000819.

# 12

# BACK INTO THE LOCATIVE

## Theory and Practice in Urban Augmented Reality, 1999–2016

*Joshua McWhirter*

> "I guess you could say it started on the first of May 2000," Alberto said.
>
> "What did?"
>
> "Geohacking. Or the potential thereof. The government announced then that Selective Availability would be turned off, on what had been, until then, strictly a military system. Civilians could access the GPS geocoordinates for the first time."
>
> . . .
>
> Odile squinted over the rim of her white breakfast bowl of café au lait.
>
> "Cartographic attributes of the invisible," she said, lowering the bowl. "Spatially tagged hypermedia."
>
> This terminology seemed to increase her fluency by a factor of ten; she scarcely had an accent now.
>
> "The artist annotating every centimeter of a place, of every physical thing. Visible to all, on devices such as these." She indicated Alberto's phone, as if its swollen belly of silver tape were gravid with an entire future.
>
> —William Gibson, *Spook Country*[1]

The above passages—excerpted from a chapter called "Into the Locative" from William Gibson's novel *Spook Country*—adopt a surprisingly exotic tone to describe what, at least from the vantage point of the twenty-first century's third decade, would appear a common confluence: geolocation and art. Gibson's dialog suggests that the granting of public access to Global Positioning System (GPS) coordinates is an event still pregnant with possibility (and danger): "spatially tagged hypermedia," imbued with a sense of futurity and mystery become almost mythic "cartographic attributes of the invisible." For Gibson's eager, art world characters, annotation of the physical world by digital means is poised for an astonishing ubiquity.

Published in 2007, *Spook Country* is a story about a journalist whose exposure to locative art gradually leads to the discovery of a global political conspiracy. At the time of the novel's writing, the still-uncommon use of mobile, digital interfaces to overlay information (in this case, visual art) onto specific geospatial coordinates presented Gibson, an acclaimed speculative fiction writer, with an effective plot device for a bleeding-edge political thriller. Gibson's prose references to locative media were also an early signal of his own developing understanding of cyberspace (a term he had himself helped popularize in the 1980s) as a virtual landscape which had "everted" into the real world and "colonized the physical."[2] Yet, for its intimations of an experimental medium "gravid with an entire future,"[3] *Spook Country* contains perhaps some of the final words on locative media as a distinctly subcultural art form. Released just days after the first generation of iPhone, the book's image of locative media would be gradually supplanted by a different sort of imaginary, cultivated by large tech companies in the wake of a smartphone revolution.

Currently, outside of a small niche of media scholars and practitioners, it may appear that locative media has evolved into something largely synonymous with one particular location-based, augmented reality game: *Pokémon GO*.[4] The arguably mixed success of *Pokémon GO*, for perhaps millions of people, implies an unchallenged trajectory for locative media (broadly defined) as a form of mass entertainment, molded by the commercial sensibilities of existing media franchises. At this critical moment, then, in which locative media's possibilities seem new and pliant to mainstream audiences, and perhaps also (once again) to curious artists and technologists, it becomes urgent to revisit and critique locative works that explored ways of enriching public spaces with non-normative information and narratives—and that, by extension, explored alternative modes of participating within the public realm.[5] Likewise, it becomes just as important to resurface the theory that informed early locative media and to unpack many of the common conceptual touchstones animating scholarly work surrounding the medium.

In an attempt to provide some much-needed historical context in a discursive climate of ahistorical "innovation," this chapter presents an overview of some of locative media's forgotten genealogies. By highlighting early experiments with geospatial technologies that sought to interrogate the increasing mediation of urban space and subjectivity through—to borrow theorist Anne Galloway's inclusive criteria for "ubiquitous computing"—technologies that "[comprise] any number of mobile, wearable, distributed, networked and context-aware computing devices, applications and services."[6] Looking past locative media art's supposed mid-aughts peak, this survey also includes a few recent projects that have taken up the mantle of exploring the medium's potential to challenge dominant spatial narratives and propose alternative visions of "hybrid" cities composed of material and virtual elements.[7]

By going back "into the locative" I hope to retrieve something of locative media's subversive, creative past—dating back nearly 20 years—from the recent commercial recuperations that have shaped current perceptions of what the medium has been and could be. Furthermore, I hope to provide an interpretive lens, rooted in locative media art, that might be promiscuously applied to the form of locative media that has most captured the popular imagination today. Though location-based gaming has its own particular histories outside the scope of this chapter, perhaps some insight into the mass-mediation of urban space and subjectivity through something as innocuous (yet widespread) as *Pokémon GO* can be inferred from this brief—and far from complete—glimpse into the theory and practice of locative media art.[8]

## Roots and Recuperations

Locative media's history threads through multiple and sometimes contradictory vectors of development—the military origins of the GPS, the synthesis of location-based gaming and entrepreneurial tech, and the eventual use of locative technologies as platforms for critically examining social and political issues. However, it would be remiss to begin any investigation into these genealogies outside the practice of new media and experimental art.

Many of the earliest and most influential, *cultural* uses of GPS, mobile telephony, and other "smart" interfaces emerge out of projects that deliberately probed the ontological, material, and social implications of such technologies. The proliferation of early locative works, starting in the late 1990s, can be situated within a broader historical confluence of art and network technologies that emerged out of the gradual popularization of the internet and "net art." Net art, according to critic Josephine Bosma, has often concerned itself with "the public domain as a virtual, mediated space consisting of both material and immaterial matter," indicating a conceptual and ethical foundation for locative media's radical leap from the space of the screen to mediated "hybrid space."[9]

Locative media artist Teri Rueb convincingly argues that the "land art" of practitioners such as Robert Smithson and Richard Serra have also had a large influence on the development of the medium. Speaking particularly to Smithson's "earthworks," such as the well-known *Spiral Jetty,* Rueb states that this form of art practice "can be seen as providing an historical precedent and theoretical lineage to locative media, especially as the performer/participant is framed as a kinesthetic agent in the construction of the work and its meaning."[10] Earlier, analog soundwalks predating access to and use of GPS, such as Janet Cardiff's *Forest Walk* (1991),[11] similarly anticipated what Adriana de Souza e Silva describes as a "layer of information on top of physical space, which influences the way we move through space ..."[12] Rueb and de Souza e Silva identify the critical potential of locative media as a phenomenological mediator of spatial experience—a concern echoed through other locative projects.

This phenomenological emphasis and the tensions produced by it became a recurring theme during the early years of locative media theory and practice, as exemplified by Rueb's own locative work. *Trace* (1999), one of the first documented locative media projects ever, was a "memorial environmental sound installation" that was site-specific to a network of trails in Yoho National Park in British Columbia. Participants were sent wandering through a mountainous landscape with a backpack containing a computer and GPS unit. According to Rueb, various audio artifacts (poems, stories, songs, and other compositions)

> are played back in response to each hiker's movement and position in the landscape, which is detected by a computer/ GPS unit in the hiker's knapsack. Recordings are heard through open-cel headphones and playback is at low volume so that memorials intermingle with ambient sounds of the natural environment.[13]

Another often cited, and perhaps obvious, influence on locative media art is the work of the Situationist International (SI)—in particular, the Situationist concepts of "psychogeography" and the *dérive* (briefly cited in this chapter's introductory epigraph by SI founding member Guy Debord). Kazys Varnelis and Marc Tuters recognized early on the impact these practices had on locative media:

> Broadly speaking, locative media projects can be categorized under one of two types of mapping, either annotative—virtually tagging the world—or phenomenological—tracing the action of the subject in the world. Roughly, these two types of locative media—annotative and tracing—correspond to two archetypal poles winding their way through late 20th century art, critical art and phenomenology, perhaps otherwise figured as the twin Situationist practices of *détournement* and the *dérive.* Annotative projects generally seek to change the world by adding data to it, much as the practice of *détournement* suggested... Similarly, in adopting the mapping-while-wandering tactics of the dérive, tracing-based locative media suggest that we can re-embody ourselves in the world, thereby escaping the prevailing sense that our experience of place is disappearing in late capitalist society.[14]

The SI, nominally a group of artists and theorists producing a wide range of place-based multimedia from psychogeographical maps and speculative urban sculpture to revolutionary graffiti and literature, serves as a helpful and practical analog model for later digital interventions in urban space through locative media. Moreover, the Situationist concept of *détournement*—which McKenzie Wark defines precisely as an "act of unauthorized appropriation" treating culture as "an active place of challenge, agency, strategy, and conflict"[15]—would seem to be something of a guidepost for locative media's subversion of the normative, surveilling logics deployed through the GPS. Like the Situationists' appropriations of aerial surveillance photography for use in psychogeographical mapping, locative media would appear to create new possibilities for political life within a control society.

However, beyond these formal similarities in concept and execution, the SI's leftist political praxis, alongside their collective body of work's recuperation into more institutionalized canons of art history and popular culture, serves as more ironic precedents to the cultural dispositions of much locative media art.[16] Locative media projects, in adopting the formal techniques of *dérive* and *détournement* bereft of political content, have often recuperated not just Situationist practice, but many other ideas and tactics gleaned from radical and critical urbanism at large into circuits of cultural and financial capital via institutional and corporate sponsorships, or otherwise commercial aims.

A characteristic shared by some of the projects presented in this chapter, abetting such recuperations, is a propensity to focus on the purely phenomenological aspects of a psychogeographical practice (what Debord calls "unities of ambience") at the expense of a more politicized understanding of urban space, which Debord perceived as a crucial outcome of the *dérive* in particular, and psychogeography in general ("principal axes of passage... exits and... defenses").[17] On the other hand, other projects described here preserve and even expand upon the radical and subversive potentialities of the *dérive* and *détournement*.

Despite this spectrum of intended political engagement and affect, the "pervasive and ubiquitous computing" that enables locative media. According to Galloway, this is done by default to "create unique forms of inhabitable space and means of habitation, and therefore raise issues not only of spatialization, but also of temporalization and embodiment."[18] I would argue, by extension, that locative media's foregrounding of space, time, embodiment, and inhabitation—either intentionally or unintentionally—begets questions of spatial inclusion and exclusion.

The intertwined genealogies explored through the projects featured in this chapter produce a portrait of locative media's development as a sometimes messy and conflicted, and at other times synergistic, recombination of art, media, political, and spatial practices. It should also be acknowledged that, though outside the scope of this chapter, the relatively "modern" media and spatial practices discussed here—embodied by such projects as *Border Memorial: Frontera de los Muertos* (2012) discussed later in the chapter—have deeper historical roots in oral monolog, ritual pilgrimage, theater, and many modes of non-Western, non-"modern" uses of space—monologue forms which have been too often relegated to the "deeper past" through colonial discourses (Figure 12.1).

## Dialectical Interfaces

The notion of "making the invisible visible" has long been a major concern of modern urban and cultural theory. Its currency can be traced, in large part, directly to the work of Walter Benjamin in general and his *Arcades Project* in particular. In this famous, unfinished work of historical materialism—an experimental, Marxist exploration of the origins of Western modernity through the socio-material urban fabric of nineteenth-century Paris—Benjamin employs a historiographic method which collapses past into the present, in part, through a recognition that "... image is dialectics at a standstill."[19] He operationalized this method through "literary montage," a collage-like assembling of different texts into "large-scale constructions out of the smallest and most precisely cut components... to discover in the analysis of the small individual moment the crystal of the total event."[20] Furthermore, he claims:

> In the dialectical image, what has been within a particular epoch is always, simultaneously, 'what has been from time immemorial.' As such, however, it is manifest, on each occasion,

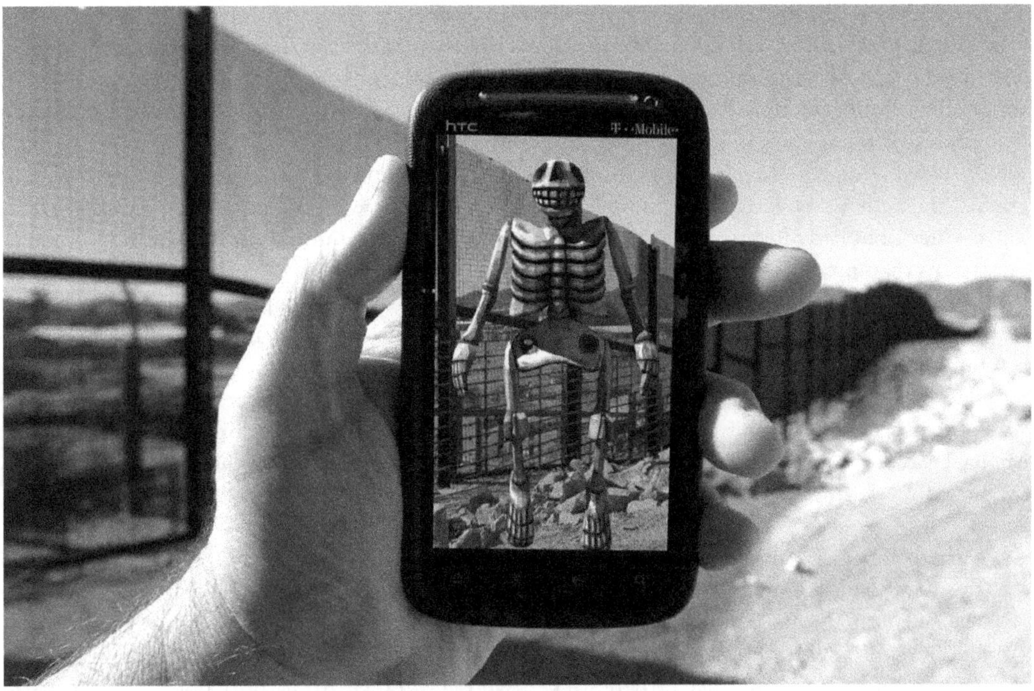


*Figure 12.1* John Craig Freeman, *Border Memorial: Frontera de los Muertos*, Lukeville border crossing, Arizona (2012). Augmented reality public art. Photo credit: John Craig Freeman

> only to a quite specific epoch—namely, the one in which humanity, rubbing its eyes, recognizes just this particular dream image as such. It is at this moment that the historian takes up, with regard to that image the task of dream interpretation.[21]

Seventy-one years after Benjamin's untimely death, digital humanities scholar Brian Greenspan, describing his locative, text-based storytelling project *StoryTrek*—in which pieces of a larger "spatial narrative" were geotagged to specific coordinates, and read with a mobile application capable of generating different narrative devices depending on a user's movements along a spatial path—writes in a similar vein:

> We are using the city streets as a *dialectical interface* that layers residual social structures onto emergent configurations, and links historical images and accounts of social migration. upheaval and urban renewal to more recent cartographies of uprise. If locative media 'involve persistent tensions between pasts, presents, and futures that make certain identities and objectives possible or probable, and others impossible or improbable' [Galloway 2010, 32], then they also present the opportunity to contour those possibilities toward social progress.[22]

Both dialectical image and interface share a similar logic (perhaps deliberately so on Greenspan's part) in treating the process of layering time and space as a politicized, deliberate act of radical history, and future-making. Locative media, in this sense, extends Benjamin's "literary montage," beyond text, into sound and image. It also extends the "site" of layering from the space of the book to the space of the city. Along with the transposition of addressable "metadata" from screen space to "hybrid space," this conceptual migration of montage from the book to the interface characterizes the annotative impulse inherent to locative media from its earliest stages.

The variety of information one can overlay onto space with a digital interface distinguishes it from other, more purely visual, analog mediums of urban annotation, such as graffiti or signage. But given the capabilities of available locative interfaces during the medium's emergence at the very end of the 1990s (i.e. GPS-enabled, pre-smart mobile devices), annotation and augmentation first expressed themselves in locative media as primarily audio and textual elements. Increasingly sophisticated augmented reality imaging has expanded possibilities for a kind of locative, digital graffiti (the ability to overlay live mobile-phone camera feeds with 3D graphics via *Pokémon Go*, for instance), but early locative media projects share more in common with Benjamin's "literary" evocations than merely an act of (geo)tagging.

Two early locative works that exemplify this critical annotative impulse are *[murmur]* (2003) and *The Yellow Arrow Project* (2004). *[murmur]* was an (initially) Toronto-based project led by collaborators Shawn Micallef, Gabe Sawhney, and James Roussel, in which participants would use mobile phones to call a number posted on green ear-shaped signs, scattered across the city, to access site-specific audio histories.[23] Meanwhile, *The Yellow Arrow*, developed by Brian House, Michael Counts Christopher Allen, and Jesse Shapins, was predicated on the not-yet-ubiquitous act of text messaging:

> Participants place uniquely-coded Yellow Arrow stickers to draw attention to different locations and objects—whether a back-alley mural, a favorite dive bar, or a new perspective on a classic landmark. By sending an SMS from a mobile phone to the Yellow Arrow phone number beginning with the arrow's unique code, Yellow Arrow authors essentially save a thought on the spot where they place their sticker. Messages range from short poetic fragments to personal stories to game-like prompts to action.[24]

While *[murmur]*'s creators framed their project as technologically assisted oral history, *Yellow Arrow*'s more explicit references to street art and psychogeography hinted at slightly subversive agenda. At one point, *Yellow Arrow* even served as a platform for a tour of Washington D.C.'s famous punk rock scene, curated by members of some of the city's most notable, politically charged bands, as well as a Berlin-based project documenting "vanished nightlife."[25] However, *Yellow Arrow*, produced by Counts Media—an "arts-driven entertainment company"[26]—ultimately embraced more (albeit small-scale) entrepreneurial uses of its platform and took an entrepreneurial turn itself in eventually collaborating with travel guide publisher Lonely Planet on a book entitled *Experimental Travel*.[27]

On the one hand, this tendency to discursively employ critical theory, and on the other hand, to partner with more normative institutions, is shared by Proboscis' *Urban Tapestries* (2002). The more ambitious of these annotative "montage" projects, *Urban Tapestries* (originally *Social Tapestries*) was launched in 2004 as a "a research project and experimental software platform for knowledge mapping and sharing" oriented toward establishing a "public knowledge commons:"

> *Urban Tapestries* investigated how, by combining mobile and internet technologies with geographic information systems, people could "author" the environment around them; a kind of Mass Observation for the 21st Century. Like the founders of Mass Observation in the 1930s, we were interested creating opportunities for an "anthropology of ourselves"—adopting and adapting new and emerging technologies for creating and sharing everyday knowledge and experience; building up organic, collective memories that trace and embellish different kinds of relationships across places, time and communities.[28]

*Urban Tapestries* lasted three years. In addition to the platform itself (built for "personal digital assistant" devices), this project resulted in the release of a number of related essays, reports, videos, workshops, and installations. All requiring the technical and financial support of a number of partners, including the London School of Economics, Birkbeck College, Orange Telecom, Hewlett-Packard Labs, France Telecom R&D UK, and Ordnance Survey—a robust mix of educational and governmental institutions and private technology firms.[29] Thus, the project's goal of establishing a "public knowledge commons" was, from the beginning, diluted by an uncritical examination of such partnerships and their implications. Tuters and Varnelis acknowledged this type of contradiction as a "central question for locative media." As locative media relied (and in many respects, still rely) on proprietary technical knowledge and data infrastructures, several artists working within the medium adopted a "research and development" framework amenable to corporate sponsorship and venture capital.[30]

## Locative Praxis

This parsing of language and references to critical theory matters insofar as we begin to recognize the ways in which locative media art's avant-garde inspirations serve as both a fountain of re-appropriated ideas (both in a positive and negative sense) and a limitation. *Urban Tapestries*, in one of their foundational reports written in 2004, explicitly model their project on the theories and practices of Benjamin, the Situationists, Michel de Certeau, and Georges Perec.[31]

Meanwhile, Rueb, writing in 2016, draws from Deleuze and Guattari's *A Thousand Plateaus* to describe how "mobile media, and the mobilities they engender, make legible… spatialities and temporalities," which "challenge the totalizing view of GPS or surveillance technologies as the solely instrumental apparatus of control societies that would employ them as tools of oppression in the regulation of power and knowledge via language, code, and prosthetic agency."[32] Rueb's assertion serves as useful summation of the strategic referencing of critical theory made by locative media artists, and many others—and does so tactfully I might add.

What these artists draw upon from urban theory, in particular, is a critical understanding of subject positionality within space: bodily and socially, and, in more sophisticated iterations, culturally and politically. Though this is an important facet of understanding how space is produced, and many locative media artists have expressed a comprehension of critical phenomenology as one facet among many in the production of urban space. Many locative media artworks themselves often fall short of wholly connecting this scale—that of the subject—to larger social, political, and economic dynamics through which urbanity is produced.

This emphasis on phenomenology (i.e. urban experience) may be a limitation, then, but one which, I believe, is due more to a lack of direct engagement with locative media by contemporary urbanists than any shortcoming on the part of locative media artists. Locative media discourse is, itself, located within the scalar purview of the interface, centered around individual subject positionality, and, crucially, with the concept of "everyday life" as an object of critical thinking. Art discourse, for good reason, privileges the subjective, the individual, the personal. It is at this scale that human sensuality, out of which much of art history has, by necessity, evolved. But the interfacing of an individual with space, and, thus, society, is an unfurling assemblage of events, involving senses, yes, but also other modalities of knowledge and knowledge-making. Such an assemblage—which one could identify as "public space"— involves systems and rhizomes that connect the "everyday" (i.e. at the scale of individual human experience) to larger social (and physical) infrastructures and political economies.

Certain strains of locative media theory and practice have, to be sure, interrogated the production of public space at larger scales, often adopting explicitly political terms of engagement in the process. Contemporaneous to the medium's earliest experiments, pseudonymous author and technologist Ben Russell released *The Headmap Manifesto* (1999)—a radical vision of locative augmented reality with a wide variety of references, from Australian aboriginal songlines to occult tomes, and pulling heavily from cybernetic theory and the Temporary Autonomous Zones of Hakim Bey. At turns both wildly hypothetical and eerily prescient, this chapter explored the implications of "location-aware" augmented reality as a kind of "parasitic architecture" affording ordinary people the chance to re-script and re-interpret their physical environments in socially and politically radical ways.[33]

Following the release of the first iPhone and subsequent advancements in mobile-phone cameras and imaging, such "parasitic architectures" have been deployed, in practice, to address specific issues and injustices. *Tiananmen Squared* (2011), created by art collective 4 Gentlemen (a politically motivated group of exiled Chinese artists), featured 3D digital recreations of icons from the 1989 Tiananmen Square protests—the famous "Tank Man" image and "Goddess of Democracy" statue—geotagged to the specific locations where these real events had occurred 22 years prior.[34] That same year, a locative, augmented reality tribute to the Occupy Wall Street protest movement, organized by the anti-capitalist Manifest.AR collective, included *Tiananmen Squared* alongside other 3D locative works, geotagged to the facade of the New York Stock Exchange.[35] Members of the Manifest.AR collective, whose manifesto included a vision to "install, revise, permeate, simulate, expose, decorate, crack, infest and unmask Public Institutions, Identities and Objects previously held by Elite Purveyors of Public and Artistic Policy in the so-called Physical Real," would continue to experiment with socially conscious, location-based augmented reality art in the ensuing decade.[36]

Two of the group's alumni, in particular, have worked to establish locative augmented reality as a bonafide genre of critical public art. John Craig Freeman—currently a professor at Emerson College—has developed a number of provocative, location-based public works such as *Border Memorial: Frontera de los Muertos* (2012), a project highlighting the deaths of migrant workers who have attempted to illegally cross the border between Mexico and Arizona. In this project, 3D renderings of a skeleton effigy, based on a traditional form of Oaxacan wood-carving, were geotagged to thousands of precise coordinates where the remains of migrants have been recovered.[37] Tamiko Thiel, meanwhile, has created multiple augmented reality installations exploring the impacts of climate change on specific landscapes. Thiel's *Gardens of the Anthropocene* (2016), for instance, is a speculative work tailored to Seattle's Olympic Sculpture Park (Figure 12.2) which

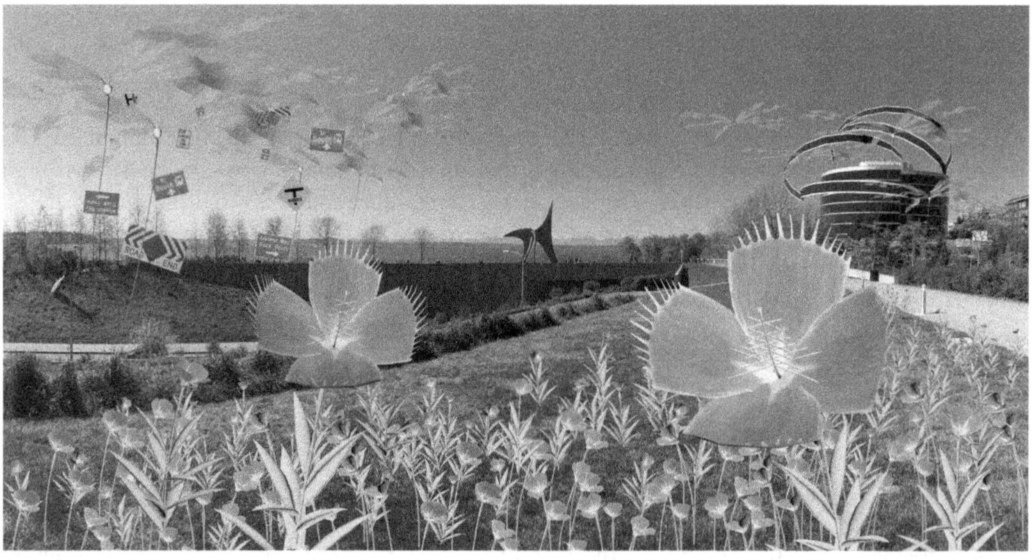

*Figure 12.2* Tamiko Thiel, *Gardens of the Anthropocene*, Seattle Art Museum Olympic Sculpture Park, Washington (2016). Augmented reality installation. Photo credit: Tamiko Thiel

"posits a science fiction future in which native aquatic and terrestrial plants have mutated to cope with the increasing unpredictable and erratic climate swings."[38]

## Conclusion

In a recent article for *Drain* magazine, media artist Jessica Thompson observes that:

> if we examine locative media through the lens of technological innovation, it is reasonable to ascertain that locative media lost its operative power when all media became locative, and when user-generated content could be used to form relational affiliations between places, networks, and individuals.[39]

As even more recent technological innovations have ushered in visually driven locative works, it is not difficult to imagine more immersive futures for the medium as a whole which too, in time, might lose some form of operative power with ubiquity.

In the short film *Hyperreality* (2016), designer and filmmaker Keiichi Matsuda crafts a speculative scenario (set in Medellín, Colombia) in which locative mixed-reality, enabled by granularly context-specific augmentation through wearable interfaces, is truly oppressively ubiquitous.[40] Here, locative media's annotative and phenomenological impulses are put into overdrive. Cleverly shot from a first-person perspective (the embodied perspective of the user), the perceptual field is overrun with immersive, audiovisual advertisements, signage, games, music videos, bizarre animations, virtual renderings of fake architecture and fake nature, and social media platforms. Urbanism in this world simply *is* interfacial: in one scene, the film's protagonist ("Juliana") becomes confused, even anxious, by a technical glitch which forces a reboot of her device while shopping for food, showing us a brief glimpse of an un-mixed reality. *Hyperreality* offers a glimpse of a radically accelerated locative imaginary—to which *The Yellow Arrow Project* or *Trace* or *The Headmap Manifesto* might be some distant ancestor—stretched completely over the urban environment.

This vision, like William Gibson's early speculations of an everted cyberspace, may one day become quaint, particularly as locative media migrates across interfaces. But as all media continues to become locative—perhaps indistinguishable from everyday life itself—intimations of "dialectical interfaces" and "parasitic architectures" may seem less like techno-historical curiosities and more like bold socio-technological predictions. In any case, it will be useful to preserve and continue considering the modes (and modes of thought) by which practitioners and theorists have, since the early years of geolocative interfaces, sought to stake a claim to mobile media art as something that challenges and (re)mixes, not capitulates to, dominant social realities.

## Notes

1 William Gibson, *Spook Country* (New York: Viking Press, 2007), 29–31.

2 William Gibson, "Google's Earth," *The New York Times*, 31 August 2010, www.nytimes.com/2010/09/01/opinion/01gibson.html?_r=1.

3 Gibson, *Spook Country*, 31.

4 Nicole Pacampara, "How the Tech Behind 'Pokemon Go' Has Been Powering Games for Decades," *Vice*, 15 November 2016, www.vice.com/en_us/article/9bkgaz/how-the-tech-behind-pokemon-go-has-been-powering-games-for-decades.

5 Eric Gordon and Adriana de Souza e Silva, "Mobile Annotations," in *Net Locality* (Boston: Blackwell, 2011), 40–58.

6 Anne Galloway and Matt Ward, "Locative Media as Socializing and Spatializing Practices: Learning from Archeology," *Leonardo Electronic Almanac* 14, no. 3 (2006), n.p., www.leoalmanac.org/wp-content/uploads/2012/07/Locative-Media-As-Socialising-And-Spatializing-Practice-Learning-From-Archaeology-Leonardo-Electronic-Almanac.pdf.

7 Adriana de Souza e Silva, "From Cyber to Hybrid: Mobile Technologies as Interfaces of Hybrid Spaces," *Space and Culture* 9, no. 3 (2006): 261–78, doi: 10.1177/1206331206289022.
8 Adriana de Souza e Silva, "Hybrid Reality and Location-Based Gaming: Redefining Mobility and Game Spaces in Urban Environments," *Social Psychological and Personality Science* 40, no. 3 (2009): 52–59, doi: 10.1177/1046878108314643.
9 Josephine Bosma, "Constructing Media Spaces," *Medien Kunst Netz*, 15 February 2007, www.medienkunstnetz.de/themes/public_sphere_s/media_spaces/.
10 Teri Reub, "Restless: Locative Media as Generative Displacement," *Leonardo Electronic Almanac* 21, no. 1 (2016): 220–34, www.leonardo.info/sites/default/files/leavol21no1_la_replay_teri-rueb.pdf.
11 Janet Cardiff, "Forest Walk 1991," Project notes and photographic documentation, www.cardiffmiller.com/artworks/walks/forest.html.
12 Gordon and de Souza e Silva, "Mobile Annotations."
13 Teri Rueb, "Trace," project notes and video documentation, http://terirueb.net/trace/.
14 Marc Tuters and Kazys Varnelis, "Beyond Locative Media: Giving Shape to the Internet of Things," *Leonardo* 39, no. 4 (2006): 357–63, doi: 10.1162/leon.2006.39.4.357.
15 McKenzie Wark, *The Beach Beneath the Street: The Everyday Life and Glorious Times of the Situationist International* (London: Verso, 2015).
16 McKenzie Wark, *50 Years of Recuperation of the Situationist International* (New York: Princeton Architectural Press, 2013).
17 Guy Debord, "Theory of the Derive," in *Situationist International #2* (Paris, December 1958), translated by Ken Knabb in 2014, www.bopsecrets.org/SI/2.derive.htm.
18 Anne Galloway, "Intimations of everyday life: Ubiquitous computing and the city," *Cultural Studies* 18, no. 2–3 (2004): 384–408, doi: 10.1080/0950238042000201572.
19 Walter Benjamin, *The Arcades Project*, translated by Howard Eiland and Kevin McLaughlin (Cambridge, MA: The Belknap Press of Harvard University Press, 2003).
20 Ibid.
21 Ibid.
22 Brian Greenspan, "The New Place of Reading: Locative Media and the Future of Narrative," *Digital Humanities Quarterly* 5, no. 3 (2011), n.p, www.digitalhumanities.org/dhq/vol/5/3/000103/000103.html.
23 Chris Eaket, "Project [Murmur] and the Performativity of Space," *Theatre Research in Canada* 29, no.1 (2008): 29–50.
24 Brian House, *Yellow Arrow*, project documentation, http://brianhouse.net/works/yellow_arrow/.
25 Jessica Thompson, "Beyond Beyond Locative Media: Art, Data and the Politics of Place." *Drain* 15, no.1 (2018): n.p., http://drainmag.com/beyond-beyond-locative-media-art-data-and-the-politics-of-place/.
26 CommForum, "Branding the Urban Landscape," *MIT Communications Forum*, 31 August 2016 [2005], https://commforum.mit.edu/branding-the-urban-landscape-b30e8d5f5f82#.ivw5fw9wb.
27 "Follow the Yellow Arrows: An Interview with Michael Counts," *Confessions of an AcaFan*, http://henryjenkins.org/2007/02/follow_the_yellow_arrows_an_in.html.
28 *Urban Tapestries*, http://urbantapestries.net/.
29 Ibid.
30 Tuters and Varnelis, "Beyond Locative Media."
31 Giles Lane, "Social Tapestries: Public Authoring and Civil Society." London: Proboscis, July 2004, http://proboscis.org.uk/publications/SNAPSHOTS_socialtapestries.pdf.
32 Reub, "Restless."
33 Ben Russell, "Headmap Manifesto." *Technoccult*, 23 April 2010, www.technoccult.net/wp-content/uploads/library/headmap-manifesto.pdf.
34 About 4 Gentlemen, *Diary in Exile*, http://fourgentlemen.blogspot.com/p/about-4-gentlemen.html.
35 "AR Occupy Wall Street," accessed 28 July 2019, https://aroccupywallstreet.wordpress.com/.
36 "Manifest.AR," accessed 14 April 2019, https://manifestarblog.wordpress.com/.
37 John Craig Freeman, *Border Memorial: Frontera de los Muertos*, Artwork, 7 March 2016, https://johncraigfreeman.wordpress.com/border-memorial-frontera-de-los-muertos/.
38 Tamiko Thiel, *Gardens of the Anthropocene*, Artwork, http://tamikothiel.com/gota/index.html.
39 Thompson, "Beyond Beyond."
40 Keiichi Matsuda, *Hyperreality*, Vimeo, directed by Keiichi Matsuda, Medellín: Fractal, 2016, http://hyper-reality.co/

# 13

# URBAN APPOINTMENT

## A Possible Rendez-Vous with the City (HUMO)

*Brian Massumi*

To catch the city in a different light, the Situationists recommended making virtual appointments.[1] A group member was asked to show up at a certain corner at a predesignated time. Neither party knew who the other was. Steeped in uncertainty, the encounter was destined to remain merely a possibility. Merely a possibility? *Fully* a possibility.

Think of what it feels like going to meet someone you have never seen before in a public place. Every person walking by might be about to step into your life. The slightest of gestures amplifies into an emergent sign of recognition. The space around is no longer a neutral frame. It is charged with anticipated gazes leading potential approaches.

> *Arrival supplants departure; everything arrives without necessarily having to depart.*
>
> (Paul Virilio)[2]

Your peripheral vision sharpens to catch the subtlest flutter of arrival at every angle all around, giving a much more palpable sense of immersion than you normally feel. Space thickens, liquefies and stirs. Wavelets of possibility fill it like a fourth dynamic dimension.

> *Transitions and arrivals are the only events that happen, though they happen by so many sorts of path.*
>
> (William James)[3]

The device of the virtual appointment is designed to make possibility movingly palpable, in a city space now defined as much as an overcharge of potential paths of human encounter as by its geometrical and geographical properties.

> *The experience says 'more,' and postulates reality existing elsewhere.*
>
> (William James)[4]

### Relationship-Specific Art

The HUge and MObile (HUMO) workshop made a virtual appointment—not between individuals in the city but between a collectivity and the city. Twelve artists[5] were invited to Linz, Austria, for the week of February 3–7, 2003. Waiting for them was the world's most powerful projector mounted with a power generator on a 12-ton truck. The projector is capable of throwing an image over 60 by 60 meters, large enough to cover the façade of a large building.[6] "The project," Rafael Lozano-Hemmer's call for participation announced, "will consist of rapid deployment of strategic images to transform urban landscapes. Logos, emblematic buildings, quotidian spaces, suburban malls, advertising billboards, etc., will be the targets of unannounced, unregulated ephemeral interventions ... below the radar of potential regulators." The Ars Electronica FutureLab was placed at their disposal for the preparation of digital images and their transfer to acetate slides for rapid-fire open-air projection.

Like the Situationist *dérive*, or experimental urban "drift," for which the possible rendez-vous was one tactic, HUMO was a plan to exceed the expected. A truck-borne band of artists would roam the city making stealth image attacks on buildings, factories, fields, and highway underpasses, onto anything and everything. The locations would be scouted ahead of time or chosen on the spur of the moment in passing. They would be as central as a main plaza or as marginal as an industrial slag heap. In either case, art would leave the walls of the gallery behind to flit for a moment on the periphery of official urban vision, out of place, out of scale, out of nowhere. The image's arrival would momentarily alter the perceptual conditions of the local space, crystallizing at least a vague sense of the unaccustomed possibilities it enfolds. Even if no legible message were sent, the anomaly of the image's very presence would signal a "more" postulating the existence of an *elsewhere*, beyond the conventional logic of that place.

In the everyday course of things, the sites of the city can be trusted to keep their appointments. A skyscraper can be counted on to be in the right place at the right time in order to serve as a landmark. A train station or government building will faithfully fulfill its promised function, on schedule. There are regions of known possibility surrounding each of the building types or infrastructural elements composing the city—ways of featuring in the lives of those who enter them or pass them by that are as conventionalized as the types are generic. For each generic, there are regulated rhythms of passage into and out, more or less predictable patterns of circulation around, and strict zoning and ownership limitations on what can affix to the external envelope that stabilizes its public mode of appearing. The regularity of a building's regime of transition creates a backdrop against which any unexpected arrival will stand out.

The background, however, does not simply disappear under the weight of the anomaly. In fact, it rises to the surface and reasserts itself in and through, in addition to, the unaccustomed gesture. For example, projecting an inside scene on an outside wall actually strengthens the feeling of exteriority. Nobody is fooled into thinking that it is no longer a façade. But few seeing it will be untouched by the strangeness of seeing the inside out. The uncanniness of the feeling brings a sharpened awareness of the façade's exteriority, but with a twist: not as it normally presents itself. Exteriority reasserts, with new and added effect: in a special effect.

When an artist makes an appointment with the urbanly unexpected, this must be taken into account. There is no simple displacement or replacement. There is no straightforward inversion, contradiction, or even combination. The accustomed persists in background conditions contributing to a special effect which is not reducible to a logical operation on the generic type, a message about it, or even a visual recontextualization of it. This is because the *sensori*-motor specifications of the human body are built into the city on several registers at every site. The city's amenities offer what James J. Gibson calls "affordances" and Arakawa and Madeline Gins, "landing sites."[7]

Landing sites are offers of useful connection and platforms for possible action pre-fit to the needs and capacities of the human body. Each landing site offers the body one of its own functions, stored in objective form. A park bench, for example, is a storage of repose. It has been sculpted to that function. Its objective form *is* that function in urban reserve: an available mold for its civil reliving. Each landing site beckons the body from a particular angle of its unfolding experience, to which it affords a response. The park bench beckons the body from the angle of its city-caused exhaustion, affording rest in response. For the foot-weary, the sight of a bench is not just a visual image of a recognizable object. Compressed into the visual image is a palpable anticipation of the additional steps it will take to reach the state of rest, a pre-sensation of knees flexing and body plopping at destination, an advance on the pleasure of tired muscles relaxing throughout the body—already tempered by the coming hardness of slats against vulnerable bones.

The landing sight already includes an anticipatory feeling, stretching across perceptual registers other than vision, of the experience of affording oneself of the offered function. The sight of the bench invokes movement-feeling (or kinesthesia) as well as postural feeling (or proprioception) and tactile sensation (texture, pressure, hardness). These other-than-visual sensings are included in the image, in nascent form, as inklings or pre-feelings of a promise kept. They inhabit the sight and are as present in the recognition of the object as its properly visual form. The recognition is not a merely cognitive act triggered by visual form. It is a veritable pre-living of the process leading to the enjoyment of the promised function. Fused into the visual presentation of the object are nascent experiences in other sense registers whose pre-feeling compresses into the presence of the image their own unfolding over time. The bench sighting is *fusional* (an integral experience whose overall quality is attributable as much to touch and other senses as to vision) and *durational* (presenting not just an object but an unfolding).

The façade of a building is also an affordance. Enfolded into the sight of an apartment complex is the feeling in the legs of winding down corridors and the drop in the stomach of ascending in elevators and the touch of a doorknob and the slip of a key and a swaddling in warmth and artificial light: a nascent, multi-registered experience of arriving home, already presented, in fusional duration, in the façade's visual attributes of flatness, and verticality. We cannot not experience home arrival, from one angle actually and integrally in potential, at the sight of the apartment façade. It is built into our learned relationship to that generic building type. Every city sight, at any moment, is an arrival of this kind without, as James would say, any necessity of departure.

Because there is perceptually built into every city feature an acquired relationship that has taken time to develop and takes time to unfold, Lozano-Hemmer emphasizes that urban art is not site-specific but *relationship-specific*. The relation always arrives, coming to us through a leading perceptual edge—usually visual—in advance of its next sequential unfolding. In other words, its arrival is a promised *event* that has yet to occur: an appointment with a known but not yet actually afforded outcome. To afford oneself of the outcome is to eventuate the relationship, to *perform* it: to follow through with its actual step-by-step unfolding.

Urban art, as a relationship-specific practice, approaches the external surfaces of urban elements such as buildings as *performance envelopes* already presenting potential events. It *suspends* the unfolding of those events for its own duration. For example, as long as a citizen has stopped to experience a strange art image on a familiar façade, he is not affording himself of home. The promised home-appointment is still perceptually enfolded in the façade, but its step-by-step fulfillment is temporarily suspended. For that duration, the event is held in its potential: the appointed outcome remains virtual. In place of the beckoning event, what unfolds is an unsought art experience. The art *parasitizes* the expected event with its own happening. The Situationists also had a name for this practice of inserting unexpected encounters-with-potential into existing landing sites: *détournement* (hijacking or detouring).

## Special Effect

Urban art intervention involves holding virtual appointments in a parasitic event. It affords a temporary detour from accustomed paths leading to known landing sites. The detour, like the unfolding it suspends on arrival without erasing, is not a merely cognitive act. Even though it always involves a combination, displacement, or replacement of forms, and these procedures often suggest inversions or contradictions of message and meaning, the art event cannot be reduced to its formal procedures or semantic content. The accustomed event it detours is a fusional duration that is irreducibly experiential, in that it compresses into itself perceptual continuations that are really, if nascently, lived. In order to effectively substitute its own event for the expected event, the art intervention must be of the same nature as the event. It is also a fusional duration, compressing in itself multi-register experiential potential.

But since there is no expected outcome in particular, what that potential might unfold as remains unspecified. The already known, normally expected event is thus wrapped in a parasitic *indeterminacy*. The art intervention's *special effect* is an added parasitic twist to the pre-fit experience habitually associated with the site type and the promised outcomes its form generically enfolds. This special indeterminacy effect is *felt* without being recognized.

In the example of an interior scene projected onto a façade, the nascent other-sense experiences of being inside are already elicited on the outside that normally promises them only after an unfolding. Their arrival comes too soon. The spatial displacement of the interior and its combination with the exterior presents a temporal distortion whereby two unfoldings find themselves occupying the same surface. The presence of the disjoint durations produces interference between the multi-sense patterns each enfolds. It is this excess of interference that is felt as the event's added special effect: a surplus of undefined potential. This extra indeterminacy effect has its own experiential quality arising from the coming-together of its component durations: the feel of unaccustomed potential taking up residency in the joints of the familiar. More other-sense nascencies pack in, less distinguishably affording: the promise of more promise, without landing. A performance envelope has been differently activated, without however anything in particular eventuating.

The felt suspense of this eventuating of a public nothing in particular could be the whole art event. Or it could just be a first phase. The event can be framed in such a way as to invite its viewer to become a participant. Platforms using motion detection, tactile interface, or sound activation may offer actual other-sense opportunities to interact with a hijacked visual surface as well as with other participants. This actuates unaccustomed intersense linkages, which may crystallize into suggestions of as-yet unrecognized affordances inhabiting landing sites to come. Rather than re-experiencing a generic type, the participants will have performed a *prototype* of experience. And they will have done it together. From the leading edge of a perception, the event has drawn the participants into a collective unfolding, however vague to begin with, of their own *sociality* as such.

Urban art intervention is not best fit to reflect the reality of the city—for the simple reason that is better suited to revise it. It has its sights more immediately on the augmentation of urban reality than its representation. It is a *social laboratory*: a performative platform for provisional group definitions of potential, in a public innovation of affordance.

The setting in place of a provisional performance envelope is complicated by the fact that the relations which the art event parasitizes always in fact include a *nonlocal* dimension: all the more reason why the intervention cannot be site-specific. Every generic type composing the city is iterative and distributive. Home buildings, for example, repeat themselves at any number of sites, with variation, in an ever-developing distribution, as houses sprout, and apartment complexes are razed and rebuilt. The same applies to storage tanks, highway underpasses, industrial slag heaps, and museums; to every urban element. The art intervention pertains as much to this process of elemental distribution and variation inherent to the city, on which its ability to regenerate itself is based, as it does to any particular si(gh)ting. The art event is addressing not just the specific site, but through that site a general urban dynamic, a way the city has of being and rebecoming itself—a city *mannerism*.

Urban art intervention addresses *citiness*, the city itself, from the mannerist angle of one of its constitutive self-iterations. That is why whatever kind of interaction eventuates from the art event's special activation of a performance envelope is prototypical. If distributive conditions are right, the parasitism may inherit the host-site's potential to repeat elsewhere with variations. The design of the event platform can take measures to accommodate this mannerist possibility. This is the role of *documentation*.

Documentation is the art event's park bench: the form in which it rests. Except that documentary rest is *transport*—since it is in documentary form that the event may *move* from one "park" to another. Documentation as vehicular event benching. To vehiculate the event, the documentation cannot be conceived merely as reflecting or representing it. It must be thought of as, and designed to be, the event in seed form. If the documentary germ falls on fertile urban ground, the performative prototyping may well resprout. *Documentary design* is an integral component of urban art as ongoing *process* dynamically addressing the city from a local angle on its generality (its translocal iterability). It is the event's way of angling itself, or generally affording its own rehappening.

## Effraction

There is another way in which nonlocality features in an urban art event, in particular one employing the strategy of image projection. The urban surface is itself a generic type. Every surface in the city onto which an image might be affixed or projected already affords a recognizable, nonlocal function: advertising. An urban art event cannot avoid being, simply by virtue of deploying *public* imagery, an engagement with *publicity*. Advertising makes every urban surface a potential billboard. And every urban volume can now be transected in a way that resolves it into a configuration of newly available surfaces. Any and every city space can in principle be sliced into so as to multiply indefinitely the number of publicity surfaces it can host.

This is the leading edge not just of a perceptual mode—visuality—but in the same stroke of a global system—capitalism. Through the ubiquity of advertising, capitalism is continually breaking and entering the lived volumes of urban experience, parasitizing them in its own profitable way. This public breaking and entering of the city by visible expressions of capital is what Paul Virilio calls *effraction*.[8] It "overexposes" the city to capital-intensified sight. New digital technologies have provided advertising with effraction tools of inestimable power. They offer previously unseen possibilities: variations of scale, from the smallest of miniaturizations to a new gigantism, in addition to new dimensions of mobility and angles of attention-getting. The logo is as much a component part of the urban landscape as the apartment block.

An advertising image brings *transnational* arrivals to the city. The logos more and more attach to multinational companies of global reach. Their presence betokens connections between each city locale and local sites across the globe. As Saskia Sassen argues, the contemporary city is a global city in the sense that it connects outwardly and horizontally, through or beneath its vertical integration in a nation-state, to form an economic and social network filigreeing with other far-flung urban centers and their associated rural reaches. Cities are part of a "new geography" that "links subnational spaces across borders ... This is a space that is both place-centered, in that it is embedded in particular and strategic locations, and transterritorial, because it connects sites that are not geographically proximate yet are intensely connected to each other."[9]

Not all the finely webbed connections are made visible in the advertising image. There are many its sponsors have an interest in *not* envisioning. The arrivals to the global city are not only consumer goods bringing purchase choice, but also people bringing labor power. Immigrants of all kinds, including political and economic refugees, flow into and out of the cities as part of a mass human migration of unparalleled magnitude. Their life histories, memories, and maintained economic and cultural links connect back to areas of the world where the structural effects of nineteenth-century European colonization are still playing themselves out, as new forms of imperialism daisy-chain with them. The sweat-shops and child-labor practices targeted in recent years by boycott campaigns are emblematic of the kind of operative imperialist connections that go unsighted by advertising.

A giant Nike ad that recently occupied the entire multi-story façade of a large building in the center of Rotterdam is a case in point. Featuring Edgar Davids—a Dutch soccer star of African ancestry born in Suriname—it makes visible a structural effect of colonial history that can be publicly and profitably affirmed (the cosmopolitanism and increasing ethnic and cultural diversity of global cities that makes them a social factory for the creative emergence of new skills, styles, and modes of expression that are then subject to appropriation and logoing) while backgrounding others that are troubling (the increasingly unequal distribution of wealth in the global economy and the dependence of companies like Nike on exploitative labor practices in other corners of the world in order to maintain their profitability in an intensely competitive transnational economic environment). Like all urban perceptual events, an advertising display presents in the now of the moment another duration, and in the here of that now a potential unfolding elsewhere. The desired unfolding from the Nike ad is toward the elsewhere of a shoe store and the time of a purchase. It is not a step-by-step retracing of the connections leading to sweat-shops, possible labor action in Asia, and domestic boycott.

An urban art event employing image projection engages with this dimension of advertised nonlocality in the global economic environment, whether it wants to or not. Consciously or not, it will embed decisions about how it can or will deal with that engagement in the very form of the platform it designs for itself, the performance envelope it actuates, and the documentary follow-up tactics it adopts. Will it ignore it, at the peril of further blurring the boundaries between art and advertising, already called into question by the cannibalizing of what were once avant-garde artistic strategies by an increasingly style-savvy public relations industry? Will it consciously try to suspend the consumer unfolding for a moment by producing perceptual interference patterns that detour participants' actions and deflect attention toward other unfoldings? Or will it exploit its parasitizing of potential advertising sites to ironize or explicitly comment upon the kinds of connections that the advertising normally occupying and multiplying urban surfaces makes a concerted practice of not envisioning? Or will it combine strategies, either in different phases of its eventuating or integrated into each phase as different levels of itself (giving it a multilayering effect, like an event-depth or spacing proper to the time of its performance)?

## Two Poles

The strategy of explicitly displaying unvisualized connections suggests a second pole or orientation of urban art intervention. The first orientation was the perceptual/experiential pole tending toward a prototyping of sociality as a self-disseminating process that is itself essentially urban in nature. The second orientation is ideological, asserting missing logical connections and transmitting a message that is not urban itself but is rather *about* the city and its elsewheres, "speaking" from a principled distance on them.

Every urban art project operates at both poles, to different degrees or intensities. Every such intervention must prepare the perceptual conditions for its own occurrence and at least momentarily suspend site-specific affordance, and, to the degree that it does, it operates at the experiential pole. Every intervention is also a comment on generic urban practices like advertising, if only by virtue of unexpectedly occupying a city surface, and thus carries a certain weight of ideological analysis and comment. It is a question of emphasis, or what is preponderately conveyed. If what is vehiculated is primarily an idea or message content about the city and the connections between the local and the global, the conveyance is *communicational* or informational and parks itself toward the ideological end of the urban art spectrum, toward the iteration of a principle. If what is mobilized is primarily a self-seeding performance of sociality, it is preponderately *contagious* or mimetic, and parks itself at the perceptual end of the spectrum, toward the iterative dissemination of a new experience-type.

The work of a given artist is likely to tend more toward one pole or the other. Lozano-Hemmer's work tends toward the social contagion of experience pole, while that of Krzysztof Wodiczko tends to the ideological communication of a message pole. In most instances, to the extent that an urban art practice operates at one pole, it backgrounds or disengages from the other. If it emphasizes one pole, it is because it has set specific mechanisms in place to uphold that orientation. Every practitioner or project will display a selective emphasis or signature mixture of these tendencies. Either tendency may be staged in a way that empowers participants to appropriate the event's outcome for themselves, toward their own ends.

The perceptual/experiential pole was presented above as the base state or default setting of urban art intervention not because the genre in any way excludes communicational strategies, but because the communicational function it can play is not unique to it but is shared with other arts (and can be practiced in print, online, and in the gallery). It is through its communicational aspect that urban art intervention itself communicates with other arts, and through its necessary treatment of perceptual/experiential urban landing sites that it drifts off on its own as an autonomous art practice.

## Frictions

The members of the HUMO workshop came from a variety of art practices and represented a healthy mix of these strategies. The broad range of participant approaches and disciplines was essential to the workshop conception. The exceeding of the expected was meant to be part of the workshop experience itself, and to feed forward into the on-site projections. Group heterogeneity can produce positive feedback fostering the emergence of unplanned synergies. This notably occurred in the HUMO workshop, at least in part in response to other contingencies. As with the Situationists, chance and constraint were not considered contraries. The attitude was that they could work hand in hand, as in the tactic of the possible rendez-vous where the arbitrary imperative of being at a particular time and place for an imposed purpose gives rise to an intensified living of potential. Working under unchosen imperatives, friction in the procedural machinery, and obstacles encountered *en route* can gel perceptions that might otherwise remain peripheral and crystallize creative tactics that might have been overlooked.

Sure enough, obstacles began to be encountered almost immediately. It soon became clear that in order to hijack a city site with an image, you have to deal with the possibility that the image might be hijacked by the site. There is no such thing, the group soon learned, as a simple 2-D projection on a found city surface. A building is not just a bigger screen. Its surface has a shallow depth of its own due to the texture of its construction materials, which can give the image a strange, almost tactile thickness. The building also imposes in places its own form and configuration. Windows, for example, can swallow pictorial elements like black holes, significantly altering the overall visual effect, to the point sometimes of undermining the comprehensibility of the image. Just the fact of being blown up in scale can turn some images monstrous while neutralizing others. Which way a given image will go is not as easy a call to make as one might expect. Scale comes into its own as a problem. Unpredictable plays of ambient light and weather conditions can also significantly affect image quality (Figure 13.1).

Further, a building in its urban context, unlike a screen or canvas, is essentially unframed. It is impinged upon, even visually altered, by its surroundings. The presence of neighboring buildings, for example, may impinge upon an image by casting shadows, and even alter its perceived form by peripherally entering into a gestalt with it. Street and security lights dapple the scene. Trees grow, sometimes in the vicinity of fences, in league with which they can make finding an optimum line of sight—or even any line of sight—difficult. Visibility can be hard to format. This was brought

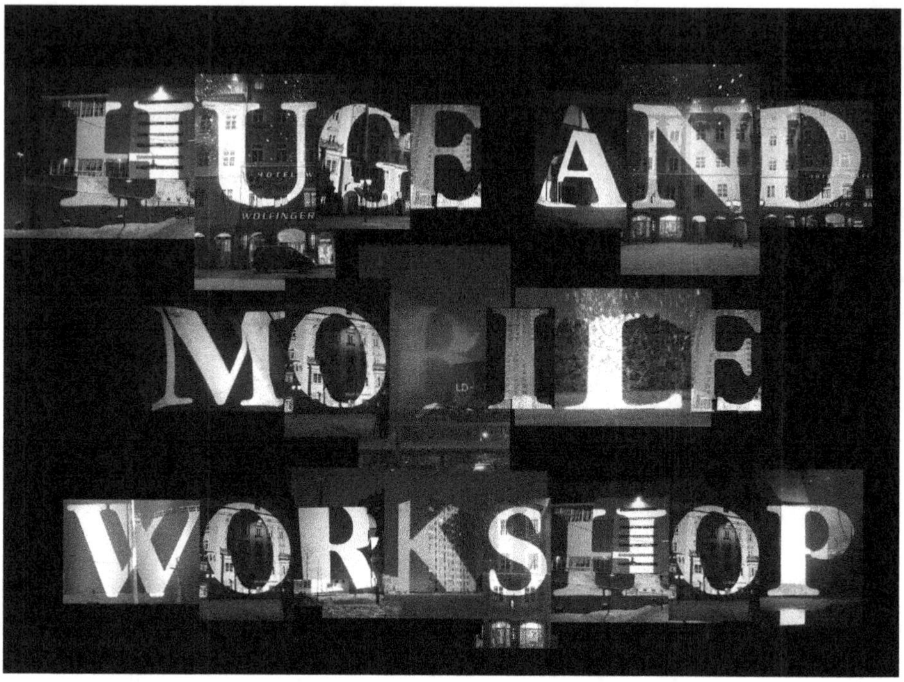


*Figure 13.1* Rafael Lozano-Hemmer, *1000 Platitudes* (2003) as part of the HUMO workshop, Ars Electronica Festival, Linz, Austria, 2003. Photo credit: Antimodular Research

home to the group when it realized that the first projections, which were barely discernible on site, had been so striking a mile away that people driving on the highway had started to pull over in large numbers to watch. Participant Johannes Gees summed up the general group feeling following the first projections: "It's amazing how a building can get in the way of an image."

There are two responses to this indiscipline of buildings. One is to learn how to gain a measure of control over site-interferences by developing a sensitivity to them and a feel for assessing their parameters, and then adopting or inventing technical procedures to eliminate contingencies where possible or, for those that cannot be eliminated, to minimize their impact. The second response is to embrace the unpredictability of the context as a collaborator, treating the contingencies as nonhuman image co-authors. The accidental swallowing of the pictorial element of an eye by a window, for example, can produce a strikingly unplanned effect of face and façade morphing into each other. Projecting onto a highway underpass fractures an image onto disjunct surfaces at different depths from the projection point, creating an eery amalgam of surface and volume that gives a sense of motion in stillness that cannot be achieved in a non-urban medium. When on top of this the image is of a building interior or a human body, the scene is weirdly, almost ineffably, affecting. The strongest image-enfoldings of multisense feelings, and the most intensely suspending special indeterminacy effects, seemed often to arise at fortuitous conjunctures.

The HUMO group developed both the control and embrace responses. On the control side, composition and printing techniques were found to sharpen image resolution to withstand certain ambient interferences. Devices were employed to enable the artist to fit the image precisely to a site configuration. One device was a preparatory trip during which a coordinate grid composed of white lines on a black background was projected onto the site. The resulting site map was then digitally photographed. This created a digital template. Back at the lab, an image could be superimposed upon the template, allowing it to be scaled to the site with its constituent elements exactly positioned. This control device actually yielded chance results of its own, as the group started spontaneously responding to certain grid projections as works of arts in themselves. Templates were also produced manually using a camera obscura to outline the scene in perspective. In the lab, the perspective outline was scanned into the computer to be used as a template in a similar fashion to the gridded photograph.

Once these control procedures had been perfected, the workshop members could go back out into the field with a mix of controlled and uncontrolled images to test at different sites under variable conditions. A spirit of image experimentation effectively took hold. Group members no longer felt that the buildings necessarily got in the way. But they also did not necessarily feel a compulsion to prevent them from doing so. There was a creative margin of play between the image hijacking the site and the site hijacking the image, in which the group quickly learned to operate artistically.

## Arrival and Transition

The overall response of the workshop members to the barrage of obstacles they encountered in the beginning was to rally around each other, and each other's images, facilitated in large measure by the expert motivational orchestration of Lozano-Hemmer. Participants worked together around the clock to respond to the challenges. A mutual aid ethic took hold. One form it took was an informal assembly-line set up to shepherd each artist's images from screen to acetate to projector to landing site. The collaborative nature of the work loosened somewhat proprietary feelings of individual authorship. By the last night, the mood had upturned to euphoria, despite the accumulated exhaustion of a week of sleeplessness and endless hours huddled around the truck late into the night in subzero temperatures. Some participants were already talking about bringing urban art intervention techniques back to their home terrain, in the hopes of seeding a translocal community of inquiry and experimentation into the practice. If the seeds grow, the virtual appointment with the city will have been kept, by many and multiplying paths.

The experience says "more" ...

## Acknowledgement

An extended version of this chapter appeared in *Making Art of Databases*, edited by Joke Brouwer and Arjen Mulder (Rotterdam: V2 Organisatie/ Dutch Architecture Institute, 2003), pages 28–55. The HUMO Masterclass was part of the "Interfacing Realities" project, a series of four masterclasses organized as part of the European Culture 2000 program. It was realized in cooperation with ENCART (European Network for Cyber Arts). Partners: V2_Organisatie (Rotterdam), ZKM (Karlsruhe), C3 (Budapest), and Ars Electronica Center (Linz). The workshop was directed by Rafael Lozano-Hemmer and Brian Massumi; produced with the Ars Electronica Center / Futurelab: Eva Luise Kühn, Martin Honzik, Stefan Mittlböck-Jungwirt, Magnus Hofmüller, John Gerrard, Rüdiger Weibold; commissioned by V2_Organisatie: Boudewijn Ridder, project manager and was supported by PANI Projection and Lighting Vertriebs GmbH (Bernhard Höfert, lead technician) and Hartlauer Handelsgesellschaft m.b.H. Participants: Julie Andreyev, Noel Douglas, Rainer Eisch, Johanne Gees, John Gerrard, Peter Grünheid, Martin Honzik, Maya Kalogera, Anya Lewin, Stefan Mittlböck-Jungwirt, Harald Schmutzhard, Flavia Sparacino, and Lorenzo Tripodi.

## Notes

1 Guy Debord, "Theory of the Dérive," in *Theory of the Dérive and Other Situationist Writings on the City*, edited by Libero Andreotti and Xavier Costa (Barcelona: Museu d'Art Contemporani, 1996), 26.
2 Paul Virilio, "The Overexposed City," *Zone1/2* (1987), 19.
3 William James, "The World of Pure Experience," *Essays in Radical Empiricism* (Lincoln: University of Nebraska Press, 1996), 63.
4 Ibid., 67.
5 See acknowledgment above for full list of artists involved.
6 The HUMO workshop utilized the BP12 projector from PANI Austria. This projector has a 12,000-Watt HMI lamp that can produce images with over 100,000 ANSI lumen intensity.
7 James J. Gibson, *The Ecological Approach to Visual Perception* (Boston: Houghton-Mifflin, 1979), 127–43; Madeline Gins and Arakawa, *Architectural Body* (Tuscaloosa: University of Alabama Press, 2002), 5–22.
8 Virilio, "The Overexposed City," 25.
9 Saskia Sassen, "Geographies and Countergeographies of Globalization," in *Anymore*, edited by Cynthia C. Davidson (Cambridge, MA: MIT Press, 2000), 137.

# SECTION FOUR

# Selfies

# 14
# SALUTATIONS TO THE SELFIE

*Kate Durbin* in Conversation with *Klare Lanson*

Los Angeles-based artist, writer and filmmaker Kate Durbin has a keen interest in how societal forces behind technological development shape human experience.[1] Her performance art projects include *Hello Selfie*, *The Supreme Gentleman* and *Cloud 9*, which investigate the many gendered aspects of online behavior and performance rhetorics in relation to social media and the internet. Durbin's book *ABRA* is a "living text" experiment of twenty-first-century bookmaking—winning the 2017 Turn on Literature Prize for electronic literature—and she was a Digital Studies fellow with Rutgers-Camden University in 2018. With the social very much embedded in her practice, Durbin is arguably one of the first artists to start working with the phenomenon of selfies. To introduce this section, we focus on *Hello Selfie*, an iterative public performance art intervention (2012–2015), which coincided with the word "selfie" being dubbed the 2013 Oxford word of the year. Durbin ends with her most recent work *Unfriend Me Now!* (2018–2019), which features a Facebook clown and explores political polarization during the US presidential election campaign.[2]

How do you define mobile media art when thinking about your *Hello Selfie* project?

*Hello Selfie* takes place in the physical public square (such as an outdoor shopping center) and in the online public square, on the Facebook event wall, where performers post their selfies in real time. People say that the IRL (In Real Life)/URL (website address) divide no longer exists, but I don't think that is entirely true. I see a lingering gap between these spheres, and gaps are interesting places for art to inhabit. One of my intentions with *Hello Selfie* was to defamiliarize what has now become ubiquitous—the selfie. Most people have phones with little cameras on them now, and the impulse is to turn them back on the self, to engage with one's public, At the time, an audience. I wanted *Hello Selfie* to encourage people to think more deeply about the mediated self, particularly in this moment where we are constantly presenting aspirational, digital versions of ourselves to the world (Figure 14.1).

> I totally agree. The "iPhone moment" made self-imaging so much more accessible, a weird kind of hyper polaroid. Maybe the selfie is the stereotypical polaroid, or everyday Kodak moment of the female self Portrait in the twenty-first century?

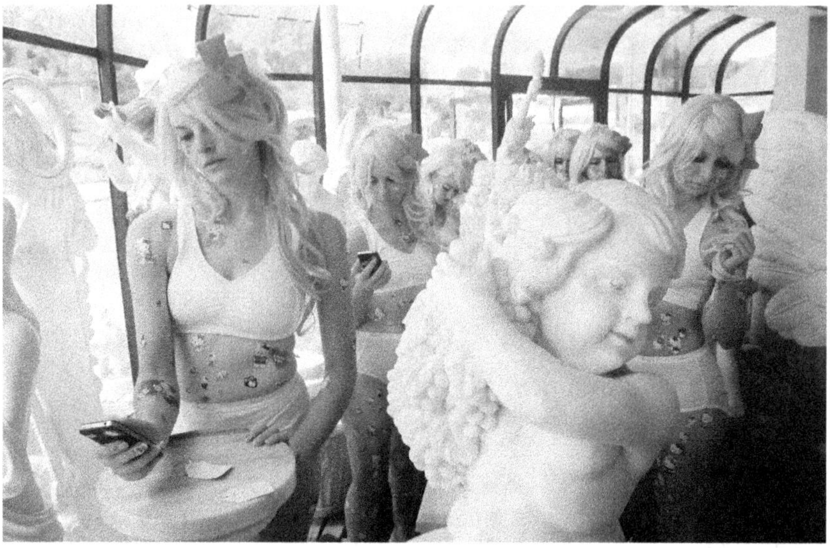

*Figure 14.1* Kate Durbin, *Hello Selfie Los Angeles* (2014). Photo credit: Kate Durbin

I like that idea.

> Using the Hello Kitty girl "power" stickers in your performance certainly highlights ideas around visibility. What was your initial intention?

The Hello Kitty stickers and rainbow wigs served two purposes. Practically, it helped draw attention to the piece because a large group of people taking selfies is a rather mundane activity. I needed to ensure the audience knew an artwork was "happening." It was also an aesthetic choice. I wanted to play with the *hyper-femme*, an aesthetic young woman performs for her own pleasure that is not intended to attract others sexually but rather to signal to other women. As a girl, I often covered myself in stickers, in a kind of meditative, trance-like state of pleasure. I saw young people on Tumblr doing the same. As a result, I developed this specific look for *Hello Selfie*, since the piece is about the female gaze.

> What for you are some of the defining moments in the field of mobile media art, or more specifically artists working with aspects of social media?

Ann Hirsch's *Scandalishious* project:[3] it was one of the early YouTube intervention projects that explored the performance of gender and the trope of the young girl. I love this project for being one of the pioneering explorations of how young girls' identities are formed via socialization with an audience on the web. Another project I love is from the 1990s, Josh Harris' project *Quiet: We Live in Public.*[4] He placed more than 100 volunteers in a human terrarium under New York City, with webcams capturing every move they made. He really anticipated the advent of reality TV and our current surveillance culture, with all of the ethical problems and complex power dynamics it involves. I love that reality TV started as an art project.

> Could you comment on these moments of intervening the private "self" in public? I'm thinking here of *Hello Selfie's* white underpants and girls playing dress-up or putting on makeup together. Your work could perhaps even be seen as a form of activism too. Thoughts?

I'm pretty careful to distinguish between art and activism, as I think there's been a kind of collapse in people's minds of these two spheres in the past few years that I find troubling, both for what bizarre pressures it puts on art and how it weakens activism. Activism has very clear parameters and functions in a specific way to make tangible change and that is not the purpose of art, which is by nature contemplative.

To answer your question about the private self, you nailed it—I was thinking a lot about how much of our formerly private lives is shared online now. For *Hello Selfie*, I was specifically thinking about how girls were using the internet in 2011–2014, sharing these types of very tender images and diary-like posts with one another on Tumblr, forming a public community that felt private. Later, as Tumblr became a kind of increasingly corporatized, aggressive and mean-spirited space, I realized even more deeply how vulnerable that early Tumblr community had been.

> So true, these online social spaces have definitely become less authentic and more performative ten or so years down the track... I suppose this kind of platform usage is now so normalized.
>
> Your 3rd iteration of this project entitled *Hello Selfie Men* was staged in Brisbane, Australia in 2015. This experiment with reorienting the "gaze" was interesting, and also the "meta" aspects of the public taking selfies of the performers taking selfies and all then uploading to social media. What specifics motivated this gender flip of Hello Selfie?

I came across this meme online that said REAL MEN DON'T TAKE SELFIES. I saw that as a challenge, to get the men to take selfies and to do it in public and shirtless to boot! I was thinking of how gendered the selfie is. There was that photo being passed around online at that time, of a group of girls taking selfies at a sports game. Everyone was making fun of it, saying look at those silly girls taking selfies. And yet, of course, young women are taking selfies and thinking of themselves as objects, because they are objectified by the culture. For the men, I also wanted to bring their insecurities about their bodies out in the open. Not in a cruel way, but a way that was honest and refreshing (see Figure 14.2). In the time leading up to *Hello Selfie Men* I walked around Brisbane a lot and noticed how few images of men there were on the billboard advertisements.

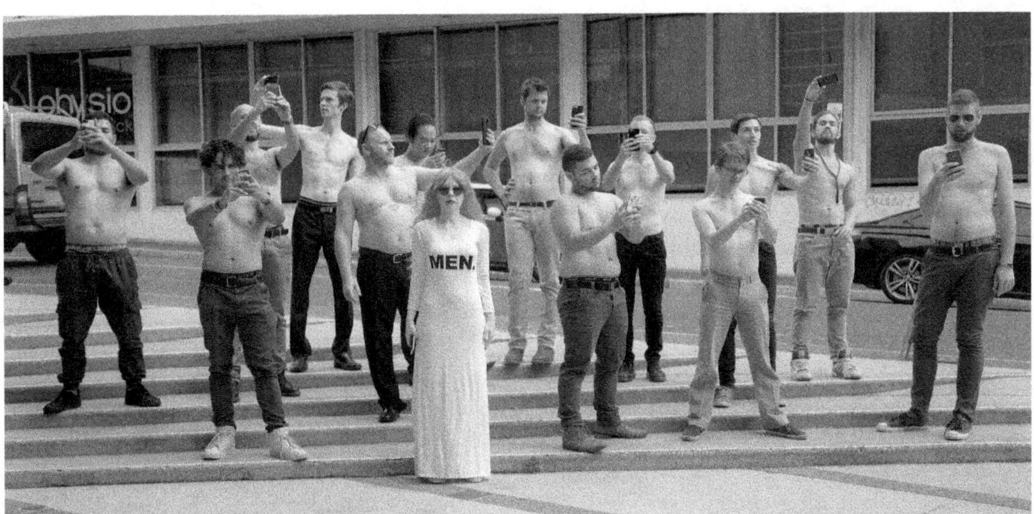


*Figure 14.2* Kate Durbin, *Hello Selfie Men* (2015). Photo credit: Kate Durbin

The few men that were there were depicted as exercising or camping, and oddly there were quite a few silhouettes of men but no full color images. That was interesting. The heterosexual male selfie was invisible. I wanted to render it visible.

Tell us more about your practice and how it intercepts with mobile media art?

My art is first foremost experiential and intuitive. However, my work also shares affinities with social science fields such as anthropology and archeology. My practice engages with popular digital culture, whether that be social media, reality TV, or political talk shows. I am particularly interested in how quickly the world is changing as mobile digital technologies evolve. We spend so much of our time on our phones, online, staring down, scrolling, absorbing. What is this doing to our minds and bodies? To our politics, communities and societies? These are simple questions, but I think about them a lot and they inform my work.

What about the participatory elements of your work?

The role of spectatorship is important in much of my work, as I think a lot about how the creation of culture is a participatory act, and how our technologies facilitate this process. Sometimes I explore the role of spectatorship through direct audience collaboration. For example, in both *Hello Selfie* and *Cloud 9*, the audience's participation was an essential part of the work and the pieces would not have existed without the audience playing their "roles." *Cloud 9* (2015) was a live stream project named after the common cam girl name and focused on the ways in which late capitalism impacts women and women artists in particular. The audience participation was crucial.

Other times, I explore the role of spectatorship without active audience participation, and through other means such as moving material from one medium to another. For example, in my book *E! Entertainment*, which is a book of short stories created from material I transcribed from reality TV shows, my hope is that the reader becomes more aware of their judgments of reality TV and the women on these shows, through the process of reading. I have taken what is usually on-screen and turned into literature, defamiliarizing it. Reality TV is a common theme in a lot of my work, as I see it as our cultural condition (and this was the case even before Donald Trump, a reality TV star, was elected President of the United States).

How do you think mobile media art projects such as *Hello Selfie* recalibrate audience engagement and public encounters?

*Hello Selfie* receives a wide variety of audience responses. The performance in Union Square had the strongest audience engagement, with the audience loudly dissecting the work, and getting up in the women's spaces (uncomfortably so). I think this is due to the culture and energy of New Yorkers—how they embrace art, are very talkative and spend a lot of time outdoors in crowds. At the Pulse Art Fair in Miami, the piece was viewed by some as being in "the way" of the "real art" (the paintings and sculptures), while others understood it as both a work of art and a spectacle (see Figure 14.3 and Figure 22, color insert). It inhabited a nervous space between those interpretations. And of course, the IRL audience are taking pictures, and staging selfies with the piece, so the work's meaning is mirrored in their engagement, and they become a part of the work. It then becomes a sort of hall of mirrors, or a hall of selfies.

Ha! A disorienting situation to say the least. Although, I find it strangely comforting that audience reactions to *Hello Selfie* are still very much governed by place and not homogenized

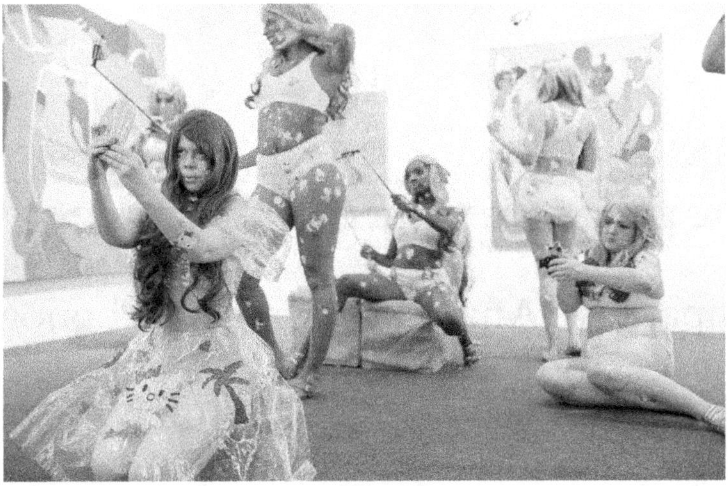

*Figure 14.3* Kate Durbin, *Hello Selfie Miami* (2015). Photo Copyright: Kate Durbin

like some of the design aspects of Web 2.0, especially when thinking about social media. So where to now for you?

I just completed a new project called *Unfriend Me Now!*, which is about the rhetorical wars on Facebook over the 2016 election of Donald Trump. I perform real Facebook posts from the right and the left of the political spectrum in the United States in the piece, as a character called Facebook Clown. There are two versions of *Unfriend Me Now!*: a narrative film and a three-channel video installation that plays continuously on loop, with clowns screaming "unfriend me now!" eternally in a Facebook hellscape void. The clown is inspired by the ancient art of the jester, a figure who speaks uncomfortable truths to power. The piece explores the role of the Facebook algorithm in increasing political polarization, promoting hyperbolic rhetoric and soapboxing and shutting down dialog. It's about how corporations like Facebook benefit from feeding the continuous cycle of rage.

Recently my work about the networked self has definitely taken a darker turn, as the web has become a more frightening place, with the rise of hate forums, the alt-right, clickbait, fake news, Russian interference, the spread of group-think, data mining, and so on.

True enough, but at the same time we've always had the deep dark web, haven't we? As you've said, it's just surfacing more and more algorithmically, more easily witnessed in mainstream culture… Do you have any final thoughts on the future for mobile media art?

I'm very strict about not predicting the future. As an artist, I can only respond to the present and try to understand it more clearly.

## Notes

1 See www.katedurbin.la.
2 www.katedurbin.la/unfriend-me-now/.
3 See http://archive.rhizome.org/anthology/scandalishious/.
4 See short clip from Ondi Timoner's documentary *We Live in Public* (2009), IMDB, www.imdb.com/title/tt0498329/.

# 15

# GENDERED ART, WORK, AND SELF-REPRESENTATION

## A Comparative Analysis of Camera-Phonographic and Painted Self-Portraits

*Chelsea Butkowski and Lee Humphreys*

When Kim Kardashian released *Selfish*—a hefty photography book compiling nearly a decade's worth of her selected selfies—the public responded with a mixture of disdain, elation, and bafflement. Amidst speculation that the 2015 book was a vapid money-making ploy or an expertly honed post-modern critique of contemporary American celebrity, journalist Laura Bennett encapsulated one of its most arresting qualities.[1] Of Kardashian, she writes, "Clearly this is someone who has spent her life devising elaborate ways to get herself seen, and it's mesmerizing to see the full arc of her self-actualization so vividly on display."[2]

This desire to be seen, which permeates Kardashian's book and much of her wider presence in our image-saturated celebrity culture, resonates historically across centuries and, in particular, the lives of many women. It reflects a politics of visibility that is inevitably governed by questions of identity and exclusion.[3] Who is permitted to be visible or invisible? How should we see them? Who may control our visions of others? The ways that we answer these questions have changed over time with shifting social and economic tides, as well as changing media technologies. However, from the earliest paintings to today's mobile phone photos, a tradition of self-portraiture has persisted over the course of Western history that enables people to gain a measure of control over their own representations.

In this chapter, we consider self-portraits within a theory of media accounting.[4] We describe them, regardless of their medium or creation date, as media traces that "indicate our presence, existence, or action through media" and facilitate connection between people.[5] We also understand them through an art worlds perspective, recognizing that the designation of *art* is not determined by the object itself but rather by the actors, structures, and systems within which that object is situated.[6] Finally, we maintain that qualified self-making—a process of understanding ourselves through the media traces we create and revisit—is driven by enduring self-representational practices that persist despite changing media technologies.[7] To illustrate the longstanding nature of self-representational strategies in historical and contemporary self-portraiture, we compare the work of two prolific and controversial self-portraitists: French court painter Élisabeth Vigée-Lebrun (1755–1842) and reality television star and celebrity mogul Kim Kardashian (b. 1980). What follows is a visual discourse analysis of self-portraits by Élisabeth Vigée-Lebrun and Kim Kardashian that draws on the intertextual connections between their art, autobiographical writings, and the larger conversations surrounding their work.[8] We ground this comparative analysis by positioning self-portraits more concretely as media traces and describing the evidentiary nature of identity work.

## Self-Portraits as Media Traces

Scholars and journalists have characterized the rise of the selfie disparately as a phenomenon, a movement, and even a pathology.[9] However, selfies can be understood as a form of self-portraiture. *The Oxford English Dictionary* defines self-portrait as "a painting, photograph, piece of writing, etc., depicting the person who created or produced it."[10] Within a media accounting framework, self-portraits are fundamentally media traces that serve as indexical markers of a person's place in the world. This implies that self-portraits are both self-representational and relational objects.[11] To create a self-portrait is to create a mediated text that reflects only a limited and edited portion of our lived experiences while concurrently enabling future reengagement with them.[12]

By making representations of ourselves and the world around us, we are also representing others. Senft and Baym explain that "selfies are not just photographic objects of self-representation, but importantly also practices that emote different relationships and meanings as well."[13] They share this quality with pre-existing modes of self-portraiture, which mutually suggest relationships between the people depicted and other individuals, groups, and communities as we invoke systems of shared meaning for them to read and interpret.[14] Self-portraits also constitute identity performances, carrying over the tensions that govern our ongoing constructions of identity into representational, mediated form.

Despite similarities that unite self-portraits, the affordances of media technologies can impact how we create and consume them differently. These differences become especially pronounced when comparing the selfie with previous painted or sketched modes of self-portraiture. For example, painting a self-portrait requires training, time, and monetary resources, all dedicated to producing a singular self-representation. Selfies, however, are defined in part as fundamentally digital traces which bring unique affordances to the mediated textual object.

As Paul Frosh argues, the selfie's "distinctiveness from older forms of self-depiction seems to derive from *nonrepresentational* changes: innovations in distribution, storage, and metadata that are not directly concerned with the production or aesthetic design of images."[15] Selfies are situated in larger sociotechnical systems that promote sharing with networked audiences. Despite technological differences in nonrepresentational form, self-portraiture spans media technologies as well as historical epochs in its representational and fundamentally relational nature. Importantly, media traces are read as evidence of people and their identities. The self-portraits of both Kardashian and Vigée-Lebrun serve as important indexical evidence of who they are as women.

## The Qualified Self as Identity Work

The problem of coming to know people by their media traces is that they are always already incomplete. Self-portraits, like all media traces, are subjective and partial, but nevertheless are read as representing an identity. Therefore, any understanding of a person through their media traces is qualified. The qualified self is that which can be read through one's personal media representations.[16] In particular, we focus on the *work* that Kardashian and Vigée-Lebrun undertake in negotiating and representing selves across media contexts. Self-portraits are rooted in identity work because they enable us to control the mediation of our own identity performances.

Furthermore, this work of representing the self can create value for individuals. Though the practice may be pleasurable or enjoyable, it is also often necessitated by some sense of duty, self-promotion, or self-improvement fulfilled through self-representation. Therefore, in historicizing self-representational practices, we examine and compare specific and situated manifestations of identity work. Camera-phonographic selfie or painted self-portrait, identifying the shared practices between these media highlights how identity work strategies can endure and facilitate communication within and between time periods.

## Historicizing Creative Self-Representational Practices: A Visual Discourse Analysis

We begin our comparative analysis by providing background information on Élisabeth Vigée-Lebrun and Kim Kardashian to highlight the distinct tensions of their respective time periods and the similar privilege and visibility that typify both of their careers. Élisabeth Vigée-Lebrun strove to become a financially self-supporting, publicly recognized artist during the eighteenth and early nineteenth centuries when women artists were rare, and gendered respectability politics designated them as amateur hobbyists.[17] The daughter of a moderately successful bourgeois portraitist who died when she was young, Vigée-Lebrun was a largely self-taught painter. Nevertheless, she quickly gained critical acclaim for her many contemplative self-portraits and luxurious paintings of French elites. By age 28, she was appointed as Marie Antoinette's court painter and admitted to the foremost French art institution, the *Académie Royale de Peinture et de Sculpture*.[18] Despite Vigée-Lebrun's professional success, her step-father and, later, her art dealer husband legally controlled her property and squandered her income. Vigée-Lebrun fled her home country in 1789 to seek asylum from certain imprisonment for her conservative views and political status at the start of the French Revolution. Even after she returned in 1801, the patriarchal structure of post-revolutionary France prevented her from fully regaining her previous standing.[19]

Despite this political turmoil, Vigée-Lebrun has an uncommonly well-preserved legacy for a woman artist of her era.[20] This is due, in part, to how prominently the artist features in her own work. Vigée-Lebrun was one of the first women artists to publish an autobiography, and her prolific painted self-portraits have always been among her most famous works.[21] However, historical accounts of Vigée-Lebrun's art often dismiss it as shallow, self-absorbed, and hyper-feminine.[22] Only recently have some historians come to recognize Vigée-Lebrun's self-portraits as visual navigations of a rift between the clashing expectations of her public persona, which required her to perform competence in a traditionally masculine career while remaining safely within the boundaries of Enlightenment-era feminine respectability and modesty.[23] We analyze Vigée-Lebrun's self-portraits along with her 1835 autobiography, *Memoirs of Madame Vigée-Lebrun*, to examine the career of an artist who negotiated conflicting identities through her self-representational practice.

Kim Kardashian is a reality television star, model, entrepreneur, and beauty mogul who has constructed her celebrity brand through the imaginaries of "glam" and "luxury" that have become associated with her image. Having grown up in a wealthy, famous family, she began her career in the Hollywood socialite scene of the early 2000s, working as a stylist and assistant to Paris Hilton. In 2007, a leaked sex tape of Kardashian and famous former boyfriend Ray J brought her to the center of celebrity gossip. That same year, the E! reality show *Keeping Up with the Kardashians* propelled the entire Kardashian family to stardom with Kim at its helm. Concurrent with her television career, Kardashian has developed several successful businesses, including boutiques, fragrances, fashion and beauty brands, and mobile apps. Kardashian's fame grew further when she married rapper Kanye West in 2014. By 2015, she was among *Time* magazine's 100 most influential people and had an estimated net worth of $52.5 million.[24]

Kardashian has long been emblematic of the celebrity category reserved for those deemed too untalented to be deserving of their fame and wealth, "famous for being famous."[25] She simultaneously challenged and poked fun at this notion in 2015 by publishing *Selfish* with the prestige art press Rizzoli. It compiles over 400 of Kardashian's selfies, culminating with her wedding to West. Each year from 2006 to 2014 is designated as a chapter, and the pages are filled with brief, mundane captions printed in a font that appears to imitate the author's handwriting. We analyze *Selfish* as a curated visual archive, tracing a celebrity career unapologetically founded in leveraging Kardashian's glamor, sexuality, and everyday experiences.

## Tracing Self-Representational Practices

Viewed in aggregate, Élisabeth Vigée-Lebrun's self-portraits and Kim Kardashian's selfies chronicle the identity work of two polarizing women creators as they navigate the gendered tensions of their respective time periods. Despite the centuries that separate these women's lives, we argue that Vigée-Lebrun and Kardashian's creative self-representational practices share important similarities that transcend media technologies. These four practices—self-portraits at/as work, indexing visual craftsmanship, leveraging the aesthetic body, and conveying the relational self—contribute to the distinctive identity work of both women as artists and, in turn, to constructing their qualified selves.

## Self-Portraits at Work; Self-Portraits as Work

Both artist and celebrity are careers and states of being that have long been driven by mystified cults of identity. For roles entangled with conflicting expectations of "authentic" creativity and requisite self-promotion—the visionary, entertainer, or even entrepreneur—creative labor blends with creator selfhood to fuel career prestige and financial success.[26] This is evident in Vigée-Lebrun and Kardashian's self-portraits, which tend to portray them as creators at work while presenting creative work as a fundamental component of their identities. Self-portraits are also valuable properties in themselves that demonstrate skill and technique while enabling the career advancement of both women.[27] After all, the fusion of work and self is the cornerstone of Kardashian's "famous for being famous" career.

In *Selfish*, she is almost perpetually engaged in the work of celebrity—staring in the mirror as someone does her make-up, being on set for a photoshoot, or posing with Snooki and Jennifer Lopez at promotional events. Selfies capture Kardashian's appearance while also allowing her to oversee it. Beneath a spread of nearly identical photos, she writes, "I always take some pics at a photoshoot before I go out on set to make sure my glam is on point."[28] These selfies provide a peek into the typically hidden "behind-the-scenes" process of Kardashian's luxurious celebrity work, sometimes generating more buzz than the intended products of this work, as in the viral selfie reproduced in Figure 15.1 (Right). Then, amassed on her social media profiles and compiled in her book—both sources of income and brand prestige for Kardashian—selfies help to propel her career.

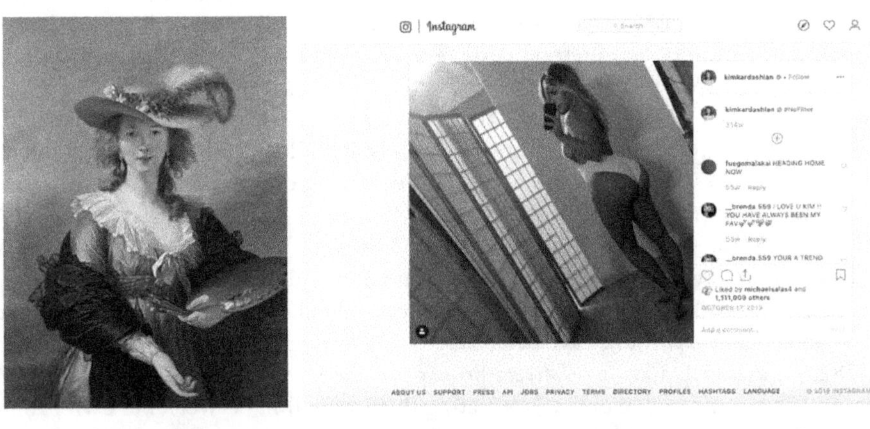

*Figure 15.1* Left: *Self-Portrait in a Straw Hat*, Élisabeth Vigée-Lebrun (1782). Photo credit: Wikimedia Commons, PD-US. Right: "I was doing a photoshoot. I took a selfie before I went out. Who knew it would get more attention than the actual shoot. #PowerOfTheSelfie," Kim Kardashian (2016), *Selfish: More Me! With New Selfies 2015–2016*, 322–23. Fair Use

For Vigée-Lebrun, whose income was dependent upon portrait commissions from conservative French aristocrats, self-portraits were a means of making the same assertion that Kardashian's selfies take for granted. They enabled Vigée-Lebrun to ground her identity in her work despite cultural dictates that the designation of artist was against the essential nature of woman.[29] In *Self-Portrait in a Straw Hat* (1782), depicted in Figure 15.1 (Left), she asserts her artist role by presenting herself holding the tools of her craft, paintbrushes and a palette. With an additional level of detail, she also subtly affirms that she is not just an artist, but *the* artist who painted this canvas. The paint blots covering her palette specifically match the colors in the painting, especially the flowers adorning her hat. In this self-portrait, Vigée-Lebrun asserts control over her own likeness and argues that her art should be taken seriously.

Ultimately, *Self-Portrait in a Straw Hat* brought the artist some of the widest commendation of her career. The painting played a major role in her nomination to the prestigious French academy, an institution for master artists that traditionally prohibited woman entrants. Of it, she wrote, "I feel free to confess that it added considerably to my reputation."[30] For Vigée-Lebrun and Kardashian, self-portraits entangle individual identity with work. This connection has led both women's public personas to be criticized as self-absorbed and self-promotional while at the same time facilitating their career advancement.

## Indexing Visual Craftsmanship

For Western women in the eighteenth century, a traditional artistic education was difficult to come by. Professional training of the era was fundamentally founded in copying renowned paintings by famous master artists of the past. Due to restrictions on women's public movement and independent travel, their access to such models was limited.[31] Vigée-Lebrun, most likely because of her family's bourgeois status, had the privilege of visiting private art collections from adolescence. She wrote of one such visit, "I at once became exactly like a bee, so much useful knowledge did I eagerly gather while intoxicated with bliss in the contemplation of the great masters."[32] She would later go on to incorporate elements of these masterworks directly into her own self-portraits.

*Selfish* is also preoccupied with notions of creative mastery. Rizzoli's official marketing description for the book discusses Kim Kardashian as a "trailblazer of the selfie movement," informing readers that she "has *mastered the art* of taking flattering and highly personal photos of herself."[33] But Rizzoli never explains what actually constitutes mastery of this art, which, seemingly by design, requires almost no training to produce. In labeling her as a master, however, Rizzoli endows Kardashian's photos with a sense of authority and prestige derived from its institutional credibility, just as the French Academy recognized Vigée-Lebrun. Through their self-representations, both Vigée-Lebrun and Kardashian visually align themselves with traces of creative skill in their respective media, demonstrating their artistic credibility to suspicious audiences. By indexing visual craftsmanship, the women assert that their professional skills and outputs are deserving of consideration and support.

Vigée-Lebrun was a woman artist living in a society that rated women's capacities for artistic skill and thought as fundamentally subordinate to men. However, this society also valued the observation and imitation of revered male artists as a currency signaling artistic training and lineage. Vigée-Lebrun pulls from this currency in her self-portraits, which explicitly reference canonized masterworks for audiences that would have been fully aware of them. For example, *Self-Portrait in a Straw Hat* (1782, Figure 15.1, Left) pays direct homage to Peter Paul Rubens' *Chapeau de Paille* (1622), a portrait of a young Dutch woman. In creating this iconic link between her own painting and the work of a "great master," Vigée-Lebrun indexically demonstrates her artistic ability and demands authority as a skilled artist in her own right. More importantly, she inserts herself into the narrative of the original painting, transforming it from a portrait of a women created by a male artist into the portrait of a woman created by the woman herself.

In contrast, much of the conversation surrounding *Selfish* questioned whether Kardashian could be creating art at all. This opposition stems from her celebrity status, stereotypical public image, and choice of medium: a genre of photography derided for its narcissism and superficiality.[34] While the book's sheer size indicates that Kardashian is a prolific selfie-taker, the photos within it subtly demonstrate her distinct skill in capturing mobile phone self-portraits. As we observe her rising fame, her selfies take on a parallel air of intentionality. This is most apparent in the ways that Kardashian engages and positions her mobile phone camera.

For example, capturing self-portrait photos with mobile phones presents distinctive challenges of gaze. Front-facing cameras, also known as selfie cameras, have a lens mounted above the touch-screen on most smartphones. They enable users to see themselves on the phone screen so that they can position themselves in frame, check the background, and manage their facial expressions. But, in order to look at themselves, users are forced to look away from the camera lens, directing their gaze slightly lower instead. Gunther Kress and Theo van Leeuwen maintain that images in which represented figures make direct eye contact with viewers "demand" a connection or "imaginary relation" between the two parties.[35]

In contrast, images where this contact is broken or disengaged "offer" the represented figure to be gazed upon.[36] In the case of selfies, looking at the screen causes the represented figure—the user—to serve as the gazer and gazed upon, witnessing their own self-representation. Kardashian deliberately negotiates these gaze relations throughout *Selfish*. She gazes directly at the lens in some images and looks away to watch herself on screen in others. In Figure 15.1 (Right), a swimsuit mirror selfie, the audience observes Kardashian's reflection in the mirror as she offers herself to be gazed upon, watching her own image on the mobile phone screen. Through these subtle indexes of medium- and context-dependent visual craftsmanship, Kardashian, like Vigée-Lebrun, uses self-portraiture to align her own subjectivity with artistic credibility and notions of creative mastery.

## Leveraging the Aesthetic Body

Though selfies enable a wider array of people to engage in networked self-representation than pre-existing media, this broadened access does not necessarily bring about changes to the ideals of media content.[37] They can allow for identity play and experimentation, but adopting normative self-representational styles also presents tangible advantages.[38] Conforming to feminine imperatives allows Kardashian to reach mass audiences. Her entire multi-million-dollar brand is based in post-feminist logics of an empowered, sexualized consumer-self, and her selfies are styled to match.[39] Even in an era when public self-representation was limited to those with the necessary connections, tools, and training, Vigée-Lebrun also leveraged normative conceptions of femininity in constructing her artist identity. Her conformance to these standards may have been the key to her status as an artist in the first place. Kardashian and Vigée-Lebrun both visually position their bodies in relation to societal imperatives of normative feminine aesthetics as a means of bolstering their success.

Roughly three-quarters of the way through *Selfish*, the pages change from white to black. This shift marks the start of a 43-page spread of Kardashian's explicit and presumably personal photos. She poses naked in bed and stands before full-length mirrors in lingerie, informing readers, "6 months after baby and I'm feeling sexy again."[40] As a celebrity whose fame was initially built on the mass sexualization of her body without her consent, some of Kardashian's most publicized acts continue to be risqué photoshoots and playfully sexual social media posts. There is more to this connection than sexualization, however. She openly acknowledges that her selfies are objectifying, saying "There's power in that. There's a control."[41]

Kardashian negotiates the prominent gendered tensions between self-objectification and self-love, self-expression and self-absorption that have come to dominate the conversation around women's selfies. Her self-objectification can be framed as conformance or rebellion from these perspectives, but it remains undeniably feminine. Over the course of the book, readers witness telling changes to Kardashian's body that illustrate her alignment with feminine selfie ideals. She shares bikini selfies, wedding dress selfies, "glam" and #nomakeup selfies, a perfunctory spread of gym selfies, and a handful of pregnancy selfies. Beyond the most controversial and sexual of her self-representations, these pictures document her everyday displays of a femininity that is noticeably informed by the selfie genre.

Vigée-Lebrun wrote openly about how her beauty as a young woman aided her in building an artistic career. She recounts resisting suitors who hired her to paint their portraits from a young age:

> It may be readily guessed that some admirers of my face gave me commissions to paint theirs. They hoped to get into my good graces this way. But I was so absorbed in my art that nothing could take me away from it. Then, besides, the moral and religious principles my mother had instilled me with were a strong protection against the seductions surrounding me.[42]

In this passage, Vigée-Lebrun presents herself both as a "virtuous" woman and a dedicated artist. The balance she strikes between non-threatening lady and competent painter was fundamental to her success as a woman in a traditionally masculine career. The same positioning is also made visible in her self-portraits. In comparison to the Ruebens painting on which the self-portrait in Figure 15.1 is based, Vigée-Lebrun raises the neckline of her dress to minimize her cleavage. She extends her hand toward the viewer in a welcoming gesture, staring out at us with a small smile to convey her cordial and welcoming personality, a mandate of Enlightenment-era femininity and an asset to portrait painters who spent hours in sittings with clients. As Vigée-Lebrun demonstrates her modesty and Kardashian displays her sexuality, both women create self-representations that characterize their bodies as sites of gendered social imperatives.

## Conveying the Relational Self

During the early years of Vigée-Lebrun's career, a new convention emerged in the self-portraits of professional women artists. They began painting themselves alongside their husbands and relatives—the people who enabled them to pursue artistic careers—in what art historian Frances Borzello calls "support-system self-portraits."[43] She classifies this style as "a particular property of women," citing the challenges that women faced and the financial and social support they required to pursue artistic work professionally.[44] Initial reviews of Kardashian's book express surprising parallels to these texts. Journalist Sarah Begley called *Selfish* "anything but," describing Kardashian's selfie compilation as "an ode to the people around her."[45]

Indeed, embedded within and implied beyond Kardashian's selfies are her famous husband and siblings, along with the stylists and make-up artists whose combined presence make her the icon she has become. Nevertheless, the most essential presence in *Selfish* is that of its readers. On the dust jacket of the book's extended edition, Kardashian describes it as "a candid tribute to all of my fans, who were with me the entire time."[46] *Selfish* presents Kardashian's fans with yet another, more tangible display of intimacy in her already very public life by sharing personal, presumably once-private photos drawn mostly from her own cellphone. Kardashian and Vigée-Lebrun represent themselves both in relation to their loved ones and the broader audiences who will observe their self-portraits.

Despite the rise of support-system self-portraits during her lifetime, the only person that Vigée-Lebrun painted herself alongside was her daughter, Julie. She painted two mother-daughter self-portraits within three years of one another in 1786 and 1789. The first of these portraits is

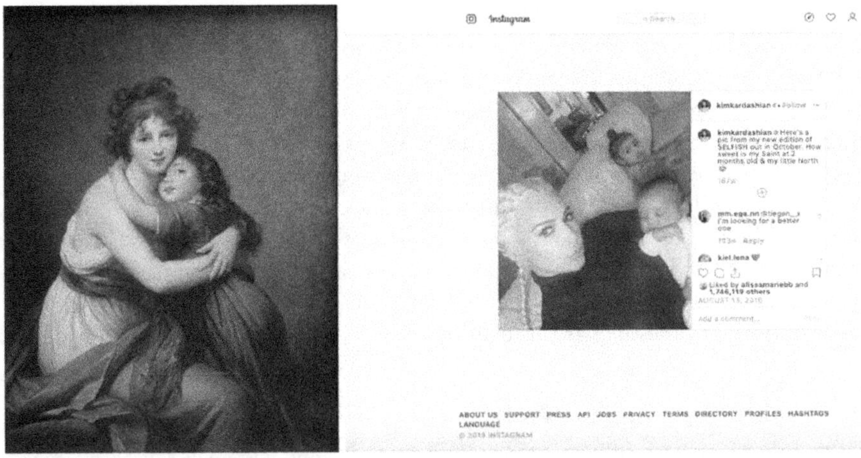

*Figure 15.2* Left: *Self-Portrait with her Daughter, Julie*, Élisabeth Vigée-Lebrun (1786). Photo credit: WikimediaCommons,PD-US.Right:"My<3,"KimKardashian(2016),*Selfish:MoreMe! WithNewSelfies 2015–2016*, 501. Fair Use

represented in Figure 15.2 (Left), with Vigée-Lebrun wrapping her arms around a white-dress-clad Julie and softly resting a cheek in her daughter's hair. She directly borrows the composition for this portrait from the *Madonna Della Seggiola* (1514), a Renaissance-era painting of the Virgin Mary protectively holding the Christ child by famed "master" artist Raphael. However, Vigée-Lebrun substitutes herself for the Virgin and her daughter for Christ in this image. Art historians speculate that Vigée-Lebrun painted this mother-daughter self-portrait in response to scandalous rumors that she was romantically involved with one of her upper-crust male portrait clients.[47] By creating a parallel between herself and the Virgin Mary in this image, the artist aligns herself with the purity and moral standing of saintly motherhood.

Kardashian's children also appear in her self-portraits like the one depicted in Figure 15.2 (Right). The original edition of *Selfish* featured only a handful of photos of her eldest daughter, North. However, when she published an extended edition with two new chapters to cover 2015 and 2016, several pregnancy selfies and pictures of Kardashian alongside her kids filled the added pages. Her children pop up in the backseat of the car, trying on her make-up, and sleeping in her arms. Unlike Vigée-Lebrun's carefully honed motherhood self-portraits, Kardashian captures an everyday, intimate picture of motherhood for her already over-exposed audience. In visually representing themselves, both women use their relational identities as mothers to convey traditional norms of femininity.

While still considered self-portraits, the presence of others in the photograph or painting reinforces the necessary relational identity of women, that is, their identity is not singularly theirs, but tied to those who women ostensibly care for. Of course, neither woman spent her days caring for her children as their privilege and professions meant that others likely did much of that work. Nevertheless, the visual representations of these women with their children serve as important identity markers of their womanhood.

## Conclusion

It seemed easy to dismiss *Selfish* as a narcissistic cash grab or a ploy for attention in a culture where Kim Kardashian is already a household name. Many people did dismiss the book, and in a way, it is both of those things. A number of historians have similarly discounted Vigée-Lebrun's self-portraits as uninteresting and self-absorbed for decades. However, both women's self-portraits are more than they seem. They are mediated means for performing and documenting identities, connecting with others, and advancing careers. We view both Kardashian's camera-phonographic selfies and Vigée-Lebrun's painted self-portraits as visual archives of the identity work involved in the project of being seen, as they build and share qualified selves for others to read.

In constructing these archives, we observe both women navigating gendered and situated tensions of skill, labor, respectability, credibility, normativity, and intimacy that do not discount their shared status as very privileged, white, cisgender women. It is not necessarily for us to judge whether these practices and their outputs constitute art. Rather, we read and compare both women's qualified selves to examine how they, and their self-portraits, fit into the complex technological and social systems within which they are embedded.

## Notes

1 Allison Flood, "Kim Kardashian's Selfish Book Snapped Up by Thousands," *The Guardian*, 18 May 2015, www.theguardian.com/books/2015/may/18/kim-kardashian-selfish-book-selfies.
2 Laura Bennett, "Self-Publishing: Kim Kardashian Just Wants To Be Seen. This 445-Page Book of Selfies Might Be Her Masterpiece," *Slate*, 6 May 2015, https://slate.com/culture/2015/05/selfish-kim-kardashian-wests-book-of-selfies-reviewed.html.
3 Jane L. Parpart, "Choosing Silence: Rethinking, Voice, Agency, and Women's Empowerment," in *Secrecy and Silence in the Research Process: Feminist Reflections*, edited by Róisín Ryan-Flood and Rosalind Gill (London: Routledge, 2010), 15–29, 15–16.
4 Lee Humphreys, *The Qualified Self: Social Media and the Accounting of Everyday Life* (Cambridge, MA: MIT Press, 2018), 9.
5 Ibid.
6 Howard S. Becker, *Art Worlds: The 25th Anniversary Edition, Updated and Expanded* (Oakland: University of California Press), 5.
7 Humphreys, *The Qualified Self*, 18.
8 Gillian Rose, *Visual Methodologies: An Introduction to the Interpretation of Visual Materials*, 2nd ed., (London: Sage, 2007), 141.
9 Derek Conrad Murray, "Notes to Self: The Visual Culture of Selfie in the Age of Social Media," *Consumption Markets & Culture* 18, no. 6 (2015): 490–516, 490–93, doi:10.1080/10253866.2015.1052967.
10 "Self-Portrait," Oxford English Dictionary, www.oed.com/view/Entry/175392.
11 Humphreys, *The Qualified Self*, 52.
12 Nancy Thumim, *Self-Representation and Digital Culture* (Basingstroke: Palgrave-MacMillan, 2012), 7.
13 Theresa M. Senft, and Nancy K. Baym, "What Does the Selfie Say? Investigating a Global Phenomenon," *International Journal of Communication* 9 (2015): 1588–1606, 1589, https://ijoc.org/index.php/ijoc/article/view/4067/1387.
14 Humphreys, *The Qualified Self*, 53.
15 Paul Frosh, "The Gestural Image: The Selfie, Photography Theory, and Kinesthetic Sociability," *International Journal of Communication* 9 (2015): 1607–28, 1607, https://ijoc.org/index.php/ijoc/article/view/3146.
16 Humphreys, *The Qualified Self*, 26–28.
17 Frances Borzello, *Seeing Ourselves: Women's Self-Portraits* (New York: Thames & Hudson, 1998), 100.
18 Mary Sheriff, *The Exceptional Woman: Élisabeth Vigée-Lebrun and the Cultural Politics of Art* (Chicago, IL: University of Chicago Press, 1996), 4.
19 Gita May, *Élisabeth Vigée Le Brun: The Odyssey of an Artist in an Age of Revolution* (New Haven, CT: Yale University Press, 2005), 175.
20 Sheriff, *The Exceptional Woman*, 7.
21 Ibid.
22 Rozsika Parker and Griselda Pollock, *Old Mistresses: Women, Art, and Ideology* (London: L.B. Tauris, 1981), 96.
23 Sheriff, *The Exceptional Woman*, 189–99.
24 "The 100 Most Influential People," *Time*, http://time.com/collection/2015-time-100/; Vanessa Page, "Kim Kardashian: Net Worth," Investopedia, www.investopedia.com/university/kim-kardashian-biography/kim-kardashian-net-worth.asp.

25 Bryan Moylan, "Kim Kardashian's Butt is an Empty Promise," *Time*, 12 November 2014, http://time.com/3581618/kim-kardashian-butt-paper-magazine-empty-promise/.
26 Sarah Banet-Weiser, *Authentic$^{TM}$: The Politics of Ambivalence in a Brand Culture.* (New York: NYU Press, 2012), 91.
27 Borzello, *Seeing Ourselves,* 28.
28 Kim Kardashian West, *Selfish* (New York: Rizzoli, 2015), 247.
29 Catherine Montfort, "Self-Portraits, Portraits of Self: Adélaïde Labille-Guiard and Elisabeth Vigée-Lebrun, Women Artists of the Eighteenth Century," *Pacific Coast Philology* 40, no. 1 (2005): 1–18, 2, www.jstor.org/stable/25474166.
30 Élisabeth Vigée-Lebrun, *Memoirs of Madame Vigée Lebrun*, trans. Lionel Strachey (New York: Doubleday, 1903), 34.
31 Borzello, *Seeing Ourselves,* 100.
32 Vigée-Lebrun, *Memoirs*, 9.
33 "Selfish: More Me! With New Selfies 2015–2016," Rizzoli Bookstore, www.rizzolibookstore.com/selfish-more-me-new-selfies-2015-2016.
34 Murray, "Notes to Self," 491. See also Megan Halpern and Lee Humphreys, "Iphoneography as an Emergent Art World," *New Media & Society* 18, no. 1 (2016): 62–81, doi: 10.1177/1461444814538632 for a discussion of how artists must actively justify cameraphone photography as art.
35 Gunther Kress and Theo van Leeuwen, *Reading Images: The Grammar of Visual Design*, 2nd ed., (London: Routledge), 118.
36 Ibid., 120.
37 Stephen Barnard, "Spectacles of Self(ie) Empowerment? Networked Individualism and the Logic of the (Post)Feminist Selfie," *Studies in Media and Communications* 11 (2016): 63–88, 66, doi:10.1108/S2050-206020160000011014.
38 Alice Marwick, "Gender, Sexuality, and Social Media," in *The Routledge Handbook of Social Media,* edited by Theresa Senft and Jeremy Hunsinger (New York: Routledge, 2013): 59–75, 61.
39 Banet-Weiser, *Authentic$^{TM}$*, 56.
40 Kardashian West, *Selfish*, 293.
41 Tai Trachtman Alroy, "Kim Kardashian: My Selfies Give Me Power," *CNN*, 3 July 2015, www.cnn.com/2015/07/03/living/selfies-kardashian-empowerment-feat/index.html.
42 Vigée-Lebrun, *Memoirs*, 11.
43 Borzello, *Seeing Ourselves*, 69.
44 Ibid.
45 Sarah Begley, "Kim Kardashian's *Selfish* is Anything But," *Time*, 7 May 2015, http://time.com/3849456/kim-kardashians-selfish/.
46 Kim Kardashian West, *Selfish: More Me with New Selfies* (New York: Rizzoli, 2017).
47 Montfort, "Self-Portraits, Portraits of Self," 11.

# 16
# WHEN THE FACE IS DATA

*Theresa M. Senft*

For a recent installation at the Cincinnati Art Museum, British artist Gillian Wearing included a video made by "swapping" her face onto the bodies of strangers, who volunteered to be part of the project.[1] Created with ad agency Wieden+Kennedy, the video was described by museum directors as "a creative way to market [Wearing's] work, as well as a statement on her need to do so in the first place."[2] Wearing explained that she was drawn to face-swapping in the context of autobiographical art-making because of the "feeling of un-realness" the technology evokes.[3]

Reading reactions to the project online, I was struck by the contrast between the largely positive reception to Wearing's video and the anxiety voiced by most press coverage of "deep fake" technologies. The coverage is by now formulaic, where we are shown a video featuring someone recognizable, like Mark Zuckerberg, after which we are informed that what we just witnessed was the work of an artificial intelligence (AI) program trained to search online for images and sounds of targeted individuals and stitch these into representations of actions that never actually occurred. "The most chilling realization about the rise of deep fakes is that they don't need to be perfect to be effective," explained a recent article. "They need to be just good enough that the target audience is duped for just long enough."[4]

While there are certainly important differences between videos depicting news stories that never happened, and art projects created with willing volunteers, I'm more interested in their similarities. As creative practice, deep faking contains a range of sub-genres, including audio swaps, lip-synching, body puppetry, and others. Of all these, creative and critical focus tends to linger on face-swapping: the practice of inserting a recognizable face into fictional contexts. In *Face Politics*, Jenny Edkins suggests that contemporary anxiety over the face masks a larger unease over the changing nature of political personhood.[5] At the very moment our belief in the power individual agency seems to be on the wane, "the face remains of haunting significance and political consequence." [6]

If Edkins is correct (and I think she is), it's worth asking: which faces haunt us? Are they the ones in live bodies; are they representations of those faces; are they alterations to those representations? And what of duping? What is the relationship between being tricked through manipulation of the material features of the face (e.g. eye color, or width of smile) and coming to the wrong conclusion about an intention, or state of mind? Is the capacity of technology to deceive us our predominant concern, or are we more anxious over the shift in social status that comes from being contextualized by others as inappropriate, unacceptable, or illegal?

What does it mean to speak of the face as data? In the pages that follow, I draw on theories about the face from the fields of clinical psychology, sociology, philosophy, and art history. These are interwoven with stories about faces drawn from the seemingly distant worlds of digital application development, autism studies, and live performance. I do this to demonstrate the range of needs that faces currently service. The face offers a site of social recognition; it also serves as a source of representational power and pleasure. The online circulation of faces works both as a site of capital accumulation and as a means to accelerate capital flows worldwide. Although it is by now a commonplace argument that the face is especially vulnerable to state control, I am just as interested in how certain types of faces get categorized as social problems to be solved. The display of the face, and the data derived from it, are today regarded as premier markers of identity, truth and reality. Who benefits from this way of thinking? Who does not?

## Face-Data and the Face of the Data

"When we meet someone face-to-face, do we try to read their face in the same way as we might read a face in a photograph?" asks Edkins. "Or is something rather different happening?"[7] The answer is hard to give without a clear understanding of what is meant by "face." As a noun in the English language, the word links to materiality and abstraction. As a verb, it designates position ("face the back of the room") and/or cognition ("face the facts"). These meanings overlap in curious ways.

In art, representations of the face often serve as shorthand for humanity itself; yet in language we often reference pets, clocks, and even situations by the face. Two humans meeting online might desire face-to-face interaction as concrete proof of existence or intention. During the meeting, they scan the face of their partner as if it were an object under inspection, usually search for indicators of their own social success or failure. Afterwards, they may describe their encounter by using abstract references to faces lost—or saved.

In 2014, researchers from CUNY University posted the results of a project they called *Selfie City*.[8] As one of the first scholarly efforts to apply a "big data" approach to online selfie culture, the project involved scraping Instagram for photos posted with the hashtag #selfie geotagged in five different cities around the world. After collection, the photos were classified by categories like gender and angle of head tilt, and the data was presented using a range of impressive visualization techniques on the *Selfie City* website. The site invited users to "play" with the collected data on their own through a series of prompts, such as "Do angry people tilt their heads more strongly? And what is a characteristic mood for people in Moscow? Find out!"[9]

Projects like *Selfie City* are reminders that just as faces contain data, data has a face—which is to say, it appears as unmediated representation, but is better understood as a narrative that frames information in specific ways. Annette Markham observes that there are at least two ways to understand what data is, and what it means. The first, articulated through references to "the data," present it as something concrete, derived through impartial observation and/or controlled experiments. Yet the notion of "data-driven solutions" shows data as ideological abstraction: the belief that data solves problems.[10] Are the perceived emotions derived from an analysis of faces of Instagram enthusiasts in one city, using one hashtag, a problem to be solved, or an expression already formulated? Here, it seems worth remembering that when it was imported into English from Latin in the sixteenth century, the word "data" referenced not facts, but incontrovertible beliefs, mostly in mathematics and religion.[11]

The practice of using facial expressions to deduce personality traits is known as physiognomy. Theorizing about physiognomy began in ancient Greece with Aristotle and continues in cognitive psychology labs around the world, where "considerable experimental evidence suggests that people can and do infer personality traits from faces," explain clinical psychologists Ran and Trope.[12] In their summary of face-reading dynamics observed in laboratory settings, Ran and Trope identify a dialectical relationship between what they term "reading *from* faces" and "reading *into* faces."

When we read from a face, we observe the movement facial muscles, and use these observations to draw inferences about whether someone is truthful, trustworthy, and so forth. When we read *into* a face, we modify our perception so that what we see in the face in front of us corresponds to what we have been told about the person in front of us. In laboratory settings, they note, it is clear: "data about 'the person behind the face' may be used in the perception and interpretation of the face."[13]

## Face as Work, Portraits as Capital

The driving engine of face-based big data projects is arguably a culture that encourages users to continuously upload multiple images of their face, shot from slightly different angles, for the purposes of "being themselves." In the West, the portrait has long served as the link between representational practices and claims to identity. That link was cemented in in eighteenth-century Europe, when a rise in commissions for painted portraits featuring non-royal subjects both reflected and shaped the outcome of what was at the time a radical philosophy: individualism. By the nineteenth century, the bourgeois craze for painted portraits had democratized via photography. "We were all individuals now, or at least almost all," notes Edkins, explaining that the same camera technology used to celebrate individuality through portraiture was also used to document (and thus create) categories like the criminal, the poor, the foreign, the mad.[14]

By the late-twentieth century, efforts were already underway to digitally supplement analog bio-policing practices that began with the mug shot and the patient photo. The introduction of facial recognition software is one example of this effort; the biometric passport is another; the development of privately owned and networked databases offering worldwide access to images of surveilled workers, patients, cases, and "offenders" is still another. In technical terms, facial recognition software is designed to detect a face in an image, develop a "face-print" out of what it deems are the face's unique features and attempts to match this face-print to an existing data set. One reason face recognition gained popularity worldwide as a biometric technology of choice is because it is capable of recognizing faces as people "normally do, at a distance, without the knowledge or consent of the subject."[15]

In 2018, an app called *Google Arts & Culture* surged in popularity after it added a feature called Face Match.[16] Pitched with the slogan, "Is your portrait in a museum?" the feature encouraged users to upload a selfie, which was then scanned using facial recognition software, and matched against *Google Arts & Culture* database, which currently houses more than 70,000 museum images. Those of us without a portrait of ourselves hanging in a museum cataloged by Google were offered "near match" choices from their database that was delivered in an easy to share format, with a link that encouraged others to upload their photos, and share their results.[17]

In an interview about the app, *Google Arts & Culture* president Amit Sood extolled the Face Match feature's capacity to democratize the experience of art appreciation. Growing up in Mumbai, India, he explained, he was taught to view museums as "a posh experience, and not something that was for me or for my people."[18] When *New Yorker* reporter Adrien Chen tried the app, he was pleasantly surprised to be matched with a painting by the twentieth-century Japanese artist Ryusei Kishida, especially given the "current state of facial-recognition algorithms, which are famously bad at parsing nonwhite features."[19] *Tech Crunch* reporter Catherine Shu reported different results, noting complaints from non-white users that their matches tended to feature "stereotypical tropes that white artists often resorted to when depicting people of color: slaves, servants or, in the case of many women, sexualized novelties." [20] When asked comment to comment, Google replied that "Historical artworks often don't reflect the diversity of the world," and "we are working hard to bring more diverse artworks online."[21]

Shortly after the Face Match sharing trend went viral, I started to see posts from users outside the United Sates requesting "work-around" suggestions that would allow them to download the app. Some quick questioning revealed that most users outside the United States (and some within the country) were blocked from accessing *Google Arts & Culture*, due to concerns that Google's face-data-harvesting practices were in potential violation of most biometric privacy laws around the world.[22]

To understand better why some users were hell-bent on accessing the app anyway, the work of sociologist Erving Goffman can be of help. In his 1967 book, *The Presentation of Self in Everyday Life*, Goffman analyzed how personal trust and political order adhere by way of a social glue he called "face-work."[23] Face-work refers to the labor it takes to make our bodily actions consistent with our self-image in society, including vigilance against "interactions [that] threaten face."[24] In digital contexts, face-work is used to generate cultural and social capital for users, as well as economic capital for platforms. We use representations of the face to engage in digital face-work when we submit a photo of ourselves for verification; when we wonder which selfie to use on a dating profile; when we distort our faces with filters to make our friends laugh.

When we apply theories of face-work to Face Match, its appeal to users makes perfect sense. For the smallish price of signing away the rights to biometric data (which to many users, already feels relinquished), we are offered the pleasure of circulating images of ourselves through their networks, in ways that accrue both cultural capital (see which work of art you match!) and social capital (can you believe what they matched me with?!). For the platforms providing environments where results are circulated, there is economic capital to be gained from each click, share, and save, which can be packaged and sold to third parties interested accruing target markets for political persuasion, sales, and/or surveillance purposes. Platforms can also present this data in aggregate form to substantiate arguments made (to investors, to the press, to governments) about the nature of their consumer base, or their future viability as money-making operation—essentially, to back up their "brand face."

## The Face and Its Other: From Faciality to Autism

"The face is a particular politics, and dismantling the face is also a politics," writes Edkins.[25] The term used by Deleuze and Guattari to encapsulate this argument is *faciality*.[26] The paradox of the face is this: we experience our own face (and narrate the faces of others) as expressions of interiority, yet to function in society, we rely on shared social codes that translate the meaning of every face we encounter, including our own. In cognitive psychology labs, it has been demonstrated that in everyday interactions, we judge our own faces, and the faces of others using interpretive processes not unlike the "search and match" patterns of facial recognition systems. When we are asked to make a judgment about the emotion someone is feeling, or if they are truly feeling it, we rationalize our judgments using these codes, making statements like, "Look, his expression changed."[27] Thus, argue Deleuze and Guattari, "the signifier is always facialized,"[28] and "faces are not basically individual."[29]

For Emmanuel Levinas, the only thing the face truly represents is "our inability to fully capture and control the Other."[30] As Daniel Black explains, "For Levinas, the face represents the paradox of imagining that the Other experiences an inner life like one's own while simultaneously only being able to interact with the Other as a sealed exteriority."[31] Perhaps nowhere is this argument given deeper consideration than within the field of autism studies where political narratives about the face and the Other dominate.

Consider how childhood autism is usually diagnosed. It often starts with a caregiver's inability to get a child to pay attention; that is, to face them, to meet their eyes. In cases where inattention is coupled with an observation that the child's speech is not developing at the pace of peers (or is non-existent), the worry is for the child's presence. In cases where the child has learned to speak but communicates in a way that indicates no interest in social cues (which tend to be exchanged as unspoken "looks"), the worry is for the future. When their beloved child seems unwilling or unable to mirror the expressions of others (the first step of face-work), the caretaker starts to fear they may wind up classified as humanity's Other: living among us, yet not truly one of us.

When the caretaker has the time and money to do so, the child is taken to a clinic for diagnosis and treatment. There, trained professionals guide the child through a series of tests designed to assess reactions to face-related data. The first involves the child's ability to distinguish between individual faces. As Edkins points out, although "face-blindness" frequently occurs among people with autism, it also affects up to 2% of the general population, including renowned portrait photographer Chuck Close.[32] Another set of tests is designed to assess what philosopher and autism activist Erin Manning labels "mind-blindness": the mistaken belief that people who struggle to mimic the facial cues of others do so because they lack the capacity for social connection and empathy.[33]

## Is there an App for that? Autism Meets Artificial Intelligence

Although there is evidence that early care can be beneficial to children on the autistic spectrum, there is currently a "detection gap" in diagnosis and treatment. Many signs of autism can be spotted in children as early as age two, but the average age of diagnosis in the United Sates is four.[34] The current model is especially unsuited to serving children from poor and rural areas who often go unscreened. In the scientific community, there is great interest in seeing whether an Artificial Intelligence (AI)-based methodology called "deep learning" might help overworked health care professionals with autism screening and diagnoses processes.[35] Although there is understandable concern about the ethics of misdiagnosing a child via computer, there is also evidence that in some fields, the accuracy of predictions made via deep learning algorithms matches the accuracy of humans, sometimes even exceeding them.[36]

One example of an autism-oriented deep learning project involves a free iPhone app designed by researchers at Duke University. The app is designed to access the phone's selfie video camera feature to collect a child's facial reactions while watching short movies. Once they've created their videos, caregivers are asked to complete a questionnaire about the child, upload the questionnaire and the videos, and consent to be part of an ongoing study at Duke. The selfie videos are then subjected to a series of facial recognition algorithms designed to quantify the child's capacity for attention and emotion. "For example," explains a recent article, "in response to a short movie of bubbles floating across the screen, the video coding algorithm looks for movements of the face that would indicate joy."[37] The first year the app was introduced, it was downloaded 10,000 times, and 1756 families participated in the study. Participating families received some feedback from the app about what the child's apparent risk for autism might be, including advice to seek further consultation with their health care providers.[38]

Regardless of how Duke's app fares with caregivers, it has already been declared a success from a machine learning perspective, providing up to 88% "usable data" on uploaded videos.[39] This matters, explains *Spectrum* writer Jeremy Hsu, since "to learn new tasks, [computers] 'train' on datasets that typically include hundreds or thousands of 'right' and 'wrong' examples—say, a child smiling or not smiling—manually labeled by people."[40]

Earlier this year, autism advocacy blogs were filled with discussions of a project called "Super-Power Glass."[41] The project, aimed at developing social skills of children with autism, combines Google Glass eyewear with software for face and emotion recognition. While wearing the glasses, children are taught to recognize facial expressions of others, by way of an emoji display and a robotic voice naming the emotion. The glasses, meant to be worn all day (presumably also transferring data all day to the project developers) also feature game modes, such as "guess my emotion," in which "a parent acts out a facial expression that corresponds to one of the app's eight core facial expressions, and the child tries to identify the emotion."[42]

Cognoa, the California healthcare company behind SuperPower Glass, claims to have already raised more than $20 million in venture capital funding—a figure some find perplexing, given how Cognoa's autism diagnosis app came under criticism a year earlier.[43] Researchers provided evidence that the product's effectiveness noted high rates of user abandonment in the studies conducted and expressed concern about the way positive parent feedback was evaluated.[44] Notes Neuroscience professor Rebecca Jones, "It's possible that simply by parents seeing their children were wearing the glasses, that changed their perception of their child's behavior."[45] It's not hard to understand why. Too often, parents experience the diagnosis of their child on the autistic spectrum as "the death knell of the potential for a meaningful relationship," explains Shannon Manning.[46] "Of course, we will see a lot of advances. We will also see a lot of snake oil," explains pediatrics professor Fred Stiz. "So, we've got to be vigilant and suspicious and critical like we've been about everything that comes up; just because it's couched in mathematics doesn't mean it's more real." [47]

## Facing the Battle: The Face in Live Performance

Interestingly, at least one autism expert argues that projects like SuperPower Glass target the wrong problem. Connie Kasari, a professor of human development and psychology, argues that most children with autism do in fact know how to recognize emotion from faces. "What they don't understand is how to take the emotion from the context [they are in] and know what to do about it."[48] Kasari makes it plain: for some of us, the war over what a face should mean, and what data from faces should do, is not a new one.

If we wish to do battle in this war—on our own behalf, or as a gesture of solidarity with others—it seems worth asking which direction seems the most productive to face. Here, "old fashioned" live entertainments such as museum installations and staged plays can become surprisingly useful venues. In lived experience, the face isn't a set of data points on a screen, but exists on a body "which is never fully fixed, grasped or possessed by the viewer of that face."[49] Perhaps one reason Wearing's face-swapping video "worked" with audiences was because it was designed to be viewed not in privacy on a device, or even in a darkened cinema, but as part of an exhibit in a museum. Watching Wearing speak about the discomfort of looking at her own face, viewers were free to notice other faces in the space. Perhaps some of these were attached to bodies in agreement with the sentiment Wearing was voicing; perhaps others were not.

In 2017, the stage play *Uncommon Sense* made its New York premier at the Sheen Center for Thought and Culture.[50] Created by members of the Tectonic Theater Project after intensive fieldwork in the autistic community, the play focused on the lives and families of four adults representing a range positions on the spectrum. In her review, autism researcher Rebecca Jone shared, "As someone who studies face processing, I was thoroughly entertained when a facial emotion detection video played as backdrop during a complicated social interaction." [51] She explains one scene in the play in which a character named Jess narrates an argument with her teacher, while a video makes clear to the audience that Jess "was not picking up [the teacher's] facial cues."[52] Over the course of the play, however, it is made plain that Jess is as perfectly capable of engaging with social cues—provided they occur outside the face.

## Unmaking the Face: Selfies, Sidekicks, Maps

"In painting, photography, and the digital arts, practitioners are exploring what it might be like to think differently about the face, and to see differently, as a result," writes Edkins.[53] Media theorist Jodi Dean makes a similar argument about a contemporary communications practice she terms "selfie communism."[54] Dean begins with comparing the rise of photography in the nineteenth century to the development of selfie culture in the twenty-first century. Borrowing terminology from Marxist critic Walter Benjamin, Dean explains that although the democratization of photography moved art spectatorship from cult value to exhibition value (that is, out of the church and into the museum), one practice still clung to quasi-religious notions of aura: the photo portrait.

Enter the selfie. Earlier, I used the work of Erving Goffman to characterize selfie creation and circulation as a sort of "portraiture meets face-work." Dean sees things differently. "When we upload selfies, we are always vaguely aware that someone, when it is least opportune, may take an image out of its context and use it to our disadvantage," she explains.[55] "But we make them anyway, as part of a larger social practice that says a selfie isn't really of me; it's not about me as the subject of a photograph. It's my imitation of others and our imitation of each other."[56] For Dean, selfies present themselves and circulate, as neither unique, nor irreplaceable, but rather "an instance of how one is like many, equal to any other."[57]

Dean maintains that "when photography starts to feature images without people, exhibition value trumps cult value." Rather than representing an assumed ideological position on the nature of identity, the selfie represents instead "a kind of evidence, an accompaniment to stories and texts."[58] Dean's arguments can be very useful for understanding online autobiographical photography practices that don't quite fit today's conceptualizations of the self-portrait. One example would be the rise of so-called "faceless selfies" that clearly foreground the perspective of the photographer, but focus on body parts beyond the face, possessions, pets, views, landscapes, and so forth. Another example would be an online status update that couples the face of well-known celebrity or meme figure, with the message, "Me right now."

## From Traps to Maps

At the end of their review of the influence of physiognomy on behavioral psychology, Ran and Trope posed the question: "Are we trapped in our faces?"[59] They respond with the reassuring thought that "it is possible that, in the long run, verbal and nonverbal information might change the physiognomic information conveyed by one's face and, hence, 'untrap' it."[60] In the meantime, we might take to heart Manning's argument that "autistic perception, in its divergent, complex, and continually evolving forms, may open the way for an ethic of the more than human urgently needed today."[61]

I recently watched a film called *Life Animated*, based on 2014 memoir of the same name by Ron Suskind.[62] In the film, Suskind describes how he and his wife learned to connect with their autistic son Owen through his singular passion: Walt Disney films. In autism advocacy communities, Suskind's film spurred a renewal in what is termed usually called "restricted interests" of those on the spectrum (Suskind calls them "affinities"). At the request of families, Suskind began to work with one of the inventors of Apple's Siri on a personal assistant app called *Sidekicks*, which uses child-selected cartoon avatars to share the child's special interests with a parent or therapist.

"The face does not reflect a natural state of things. It is not a natural object. Rather, the face is produced… and it is contested," insists Edkins.[63] As we move through this moment in history, we could all stand to face away from our culturally inherited fixation on displays of data on and through the face. In a recent essay, Suskind used the example of a map to describe how identity needn't be restricted to faces, or even humans. "A map is not only geography and topography—it is also identity, it's where you sit in the world." Suskind believes a family with a "map kid" can tap this affinity, if they "learn to speak the map."[64] Faced away from our faces long enough, we might one day learn to use these maps as technologies to access landscapes of identity, cognition, politics, art, and ethics so rich and vast, they make the ground on which we currently stand seem barren and lifeless. When we reach these places, they will probably strike us as fresh, contemporary, and for a long time, foreign. To those with the wiring (or the courage) to listen to the world before looking at it, they probably feel like home.

## Notes

1 Jillian Wearing, "Life: Jillian Wearing." Exhibit at Cincinnati Art Museum, 5 October–30 December 2018. For more information, see www.cincinnatiartmuseum.org/wearing.
2 Jeff Beer, "This New Deep Fake Video Is Both Advertising and a Work of Art," *Fast Company*, 12 November 2018, Online at www.fastcompany.com/90279597/this-new-deep-fake-video-is-both-advertising-and-a-piece-of-art.
3 Ibid.
4 Sabena Siddiqui, "AI Is Leading Humanity into Unknown Territory," *Asia Times*, 16 January 2019, www.asiatimes.com/2019/01/opinion/ai-is-leading-humanity-into-unknown-territory/.
5 Edkins, *Face Politics*, 3.
6 Ibid.
7 Edkins, *Face Politic*, 55.
8 *The Selfie City* web site can be found at http://selfiecity.net. The methodology used is discussed at http://selfiecity.net/#findings.
9 See http://selfiecity.net/#selfiexploratory. In fairness, the research team did include critical reflections of their work from academics outside their own team. See Elizabeth Losh, "Beyond Biometrics: Feminist Media Theory Looks at Selfiecity," 2014. *Selfiecity.Net*, http://selfiecity.net/#theory.
10 Annette Markham, "Troubling the Concept of Data in Qualitative Digital Research," in *The Sage Handbook of Qualitative Data Collection*, edited by Uwe Flick (London: Sage Publications, 2018), 511–23.
11 Daniel Rosenberg, "Data before the Fact." In *Raw Data Is an Oxymoron*, edited by Lisa Gittleman (Cambridge: MIT Press, 2013), 20.
12 Hassin Ran and Yaacov Trope, "Facing Faces: Studies on the Cognitive Aspects of Physiognomy," *Journal of Personality and Social Psychology* 78, no. 5 (2011): 837–52, 839, doi: 10.1037/0022-3514.78.5.837.
13 Ibid., 840.
14 Edkins, *Face Politics*, 2.
15 Ibid., 16.
16 The Google Arts & Culture web site can be found at https://artsandculture.google.com/. The app can be downloaded for the iPhone at https://apps.apple.com/au/app/google-arts-culture/id1050970557.
17 Amy Held, "Google App Goes Viral Making an Art out of Matching Faces to Paintings." NPR, 15 January 2018, www.npr.org/sections/thetwo-way/2018/01/15/578151195/google-app-goes-viral-making-an-art-out-of-matching-faces-to-paintings.
18 Brad Stone, "Google Figures Out How to Make People Care About Art: Selfies," *Bloomberg* (blog) 28 January 2018, www.bloomberg.com/news/articles/2018-01-22/google-figures-out-how-to-make-people-care-about-art-selfies.
19 Adrian Chen, "The Google Arts & Culture App and the Rise of the 'Coded Gaze,'" *The New Yorker* (blog) 26 January 2018, www.newyorker.com/tech/annals-of-technology/the-google-arts-and-culture-app-and-the-rise-of-the-coded-gaze-doppelganger.
20 Catherine Shu, "Why Inclusion in the Google Arts & Culture Selfie Feature Matters." *TechCrunch* (blog), 20 January 2018, https://techcrunch.com/2018/01/21/why-inclusion-in-the-google-arts-culture-selfie-feature-matters/.
21 Ibid.
22 See Gabriela Barkho, "Google Arts and Culture Face Match: Why It Doesn't Work in Two States," *Inverse* (blog), 18 January 2018, www.inverse.com/article/40288-google-arts-culture-face-match-app-biometric-privacy-laws.
23 Erving Goffman, *Interaction Ritual: Essays in Face-to-Face Behavior* (New York: Routledge, 2017).
24 Michael Hviid Jacobsen and Soren Kristiansen, *The Social Thought of Erving Goffman* (London: Sage Publications, 2014), 12.
25 Edkins, *Face Politics*, i.
26 Gilles Deleuze and Félix Guattari, *EPZ Thousand Plateaus* (London: A&C Black, 2004), 127.
27 Ibid.
28 Ibid.
29 Ibid., 186.
30 Daniel Black, "What Is a Face?" *Body & Society* 17, no. 4 (2011): 1–25, 20, doi: 10.1177/1357034X11410450.
31 Ibid.

32 Edkins, *Face Politics*, x.
33 Erin Manning, *Always More Than One: Individuation's Dance* (Durham, NC: Duke University Press, 2013), 149.
34 Karl Bates, "Mobile App for Autism Screening Yields Useful Data Pilot Study Finds App Easy To Use, Liked by Parents," *Duke Today*, 1 June 2018, https://today.duke.edu/2018/06/mobile-app-autism-screening-yields-useful-data.
35 Jeremy Hsu, "Can a Computer Diagnose Autism?" *Spectrum | Autism Research News* (blog), 11 July 2018, www.spectrumnews.org/features/deep-dive/can-computer-diagnose-autism/.
36 Ibid.
37 Bates, "Mobile App for Autism," n.p.
38 Ibid.
39 Ibid.
40 Hsu, "Can a Computer Diagnose Autism?" n.p.
41 Hannah Furaro, "Tech Firm's 'Superpower Glass' for Autism Not So Super, Experts Say," *Spectrum | Autism Research News* (blog), 2 May 2019, www.spectrumnews.org/news/tech-firms-superpower-glass-autism-not-super-experts-say/.
42 Ibid.
43 Hannah Furaro, "Doubts, Confusion Surround Cognoa's App for Autism Diagnosis," *Spectrum | Autism Research News* (blog), 27 June 2018, www.spectrumnews.org/news/doubts-confusion-surround-cognoas-app-autism-diagnosis/.
44 Bates, "Mobile App for Autism," n.p.
45 Ibid.
46 Manning, *Always More Than One: Individuation's Dance*, 151.
47 Ibid.
48 Ibid.
49 Black, "What Is a Face?" 21.
50 Anushka Paris-Carter and Andy Paris, *Uncommon Sense*. Presented by Tectonic Theater Project at Sheen Center, 25 October–26 November 2017. For more information, see www.sheencenter.org/shows/uncommon-sense-2017-10-26-2/2017-10-26/.
51 Rebecca Jones, "Review: 'Uncommon Sense' Exquisitely Explores Autism's Sensory Experiences," *Spectrum | Autism Research News* (blog), 5 December 2017, www.spectrumnews.org/opinion/reviews/uncommon-sense-exquisitely-explores-autisms-sensory-experiences/.
52 Ibid.
53 Edkins, *Face Politics*, 4.
54 Jodi Dean, "3. Images without Viewers: Selfie Communism," *Fotomuseum* (blog), 2016, www.fotomuseum.ch/en/explore/still-searching/articles/26420_images_without_viewers_selfie_communism.
55 Ibid.
56 Ibid.
57 Ibid.
58 Ibid.
59 Ran and Trope, "Facing Faces," 850.
60 Ibid.
61 Manning, *Always More than One*, 156.
62 Claudia Wallis, "An Oscar-Nominated Film Inspires a New Approach to Autism." *Scientific American*, 2017, www.scientificamerican.com/article/an-oscar-nominated-film-inspires-a-new-approach-to-autism/.
63 Edkins, *Face Politics*, 3.
64 Ron Suskin, "Animated Sidekick Connects Parents to Children with Autism," *Spectrum | Autissm Research News (blog)*, 21 February 2017, www.spectrumnews.org/opinion/viewpoint/animated-sidekick-connects-parents-to-children-with-autism/.

# 17

# SELFIES AND DRONIES AS RELATIONAL POLITICAL PRACTICES

*Grant Bollmer*

This chapter, drawing on a prior essay written by Katherine Guinness and myself,[1] elaborates *figure and ground* as a binary that describes specific, formal relations in technologically mediated images—in particular, the digital self-portraits popularly termed "selfies" and the drone-assisted selfies often referred to as "dronies." In so doing, I work to position selfies following the arguments of Ariella Azoulay on the politics of photography and the distinction between "the aesthetic" and "the political" in contemporary art. For Azoulay, all images are both aesthetic—in that they relate to the senses and sensation—and political, where "every image results from the actions of multiple participants who play various roles in its production and dissemination. It is the relations between such participants in the world of action that create a political space."[2]

In contrast with theorists who suggest the task of the political is merely to acknowledge, chart, and/or assemble these intertwining relations,[3] my interest is in how the formal properties of selfie and dronie photography are themselves differential and "mobile." By this, I mean the politics of these images must be contextually articulated to the variable actions of taking a picture, disseminating it, and viewing it, and it is in these material practices that conflicts and oppositions—conflicts which are central to the task of politics—manifest themselves as "things" that can be debated and contested. Even though I argue that specific formal relations characterize all selfies and dronies, there is no singular articulation of these relations that determine their political "content" or social significance. This contextual mobility is a problem for a range of artistic interventions into digital visual culture, or at least the uneven politics of the digital cannot be remedied through the advocacy of particular tactics and strategies without considering a wide range of other, situated relations.

As Katherine Guinness and I have argued, selfies are ontologically dependent on a figure-ground relation in which the figure of a "self" is rendered distinct from a "background."[4] This occurs in two ways. First, in the experience of taking a picture one's perception focuses on the "self" rather than the environment within which one is located, in which the environment is obscured as background, vanishing from the perception of the one taking a picture. This means, as we suggest, a selfie should be considered to be an autopoietic distinction between self and environment that works to literally produce the "self" of the selfie.

Second, this distinction occurs in the image itself, the figure is located in front of its background, and the relations obscured to perception in the act of taking a picture may reappear, relations that are nonetheless oppositional and differential. The politics of this distinction are ambivalent—the forgetting of a background in favor of a "self" is not inherently an act of self-absorption akin to colloquial uses of "narcissism" as a pejorative, but a relational act, the effects of which depend greatly on context. Nonetheless, all selfies can be described as producing and documenting a relation between self and background, in which the background disappears in relation to the self.

As I argue here, the relational politics of figure and ground are made more overt when contrasting selfies with examples of drone photography, which locate a figure within—and as part of—a larger environment. If in a selfie a figure is *in front* of a background, then in a dronie a figure is located *within* the ground of the image. This does not inherently speak to a kind of superiority of drone imagery, however. Drone photography has a deeply troubling genealogy given the strong links between drones and military visuality.[5]

I should note, my understanding of both selfies and dronies is indebted to some of the claims of cybernetics, and the troubling implications of drone photography are further problematized given the implications of cybernetics. As Peter Galison has suggested, cybernetics is marked by an "ontology of the enemy" in which aberrant patterns are identified specifically for their destruction, thus achieving homeostasis.[6] The militaristic use of drones seems to follow this ontology, identifying bodies within environments specifically for their elimination.[7]

The remainder of this chapter moves from a discussion of my larger political framework, to the figure-ground relation in selfies and dronies, and concludes with a brief turn to artistic, political interventions into digital surveillance and visuality. Again, the point here is to define figure and ground as ontologically constitutive of any understanding of selfie-type photography, but also to suggest that any "politics" of selfies must articulate this binary within specific conjunctures. Thus, "interventions" into digital visual culture that suggest there are an inherent politics to a particular, formally-derived visual tactic are misguided.

## Photography and Political Relationality

Theorist Ariella Azoulay provides us with an understanding of photography and visual culture that foregrounds the political and the relational, in part because she argues for the necessity of a "political imagination," or "the ability to imagine a political state of being that deviates significantly from the prevailing state of affairs."[8] Today, she claims, this political imagination must be relational, it must suggest a "form of imagination that exceeds the grasp of the individual mind—it is a form of imagination that transcends the single individual alone and exists *between* individuals and is shared by them."[9] Photography, in documenting relations between a range of individuals—both human and technological—provides a means for visualizing a kind of collective body. With the circulation of an image, the possibility a photograph has for "assembling" a collective that exceeds the individual expands.

Yet the judgment of an artwork as "political" or "aesthetic"—which, Azoulay suggests, is itself an aesthetic judgment—forecloses the role of a photograph or an artwork as participating in this kind of political imagination. This leads Azoulay to rethink the very definitions of both politics and aesthetics. There are two dimensions of Azoulay's arguments I want to stress here. The first of which is derived from Hannah Arendt's discussion of politics and political life, the second emerges from an engagement with Walter Benjamin's distinction between aestheticization and politicization in the final paragraphs of his "Work of Art" essay. I then want to supplement Azoulay's claims with a more agonistic definition of the political than the one on which she seems to rely, turning to some arguments of Jacques Rancière.

Azoulay's understanding of the political is deeply indebted to Arendt and her framing of *action* and the *vita activa*, or active life, as "the political activity par excellence..."[10] As Arendt states, action "gives birth," or demonstrates the essence of politics as "natality," which only emerges from interaction. "Politics arises *between* men," she argues, "and so quite *outside of man ... politics arises in what lies between men* and is established as relationships."[11] Arendt, however, circumscribes what she means by this domain of action, differentiating the political from the social and the public from the private.[12] Action that is political, then, is a particular kind of public activity that has a narrow definition. Arendt privileges speech as an ideal of political action, excluding "private" or "social" activities, such as labor—which she defines as an animalistic capacity of bodies—and work—or the instrumental fabrication and craft with the human hand and tools. Arendt also excludes the visual gaze from the public space of politics. She thus renders aesthetic fabrication completely within the domain of work, and relegates the contemplation or experience of art outside of public, political action since the gaze is not "public" as speech is.

Azoulay follows Arendt's definition of political action but refuses her placement of art and the aesthetic completely outside of public politics, instead stressing the publicity of seeing and being seen. Azoulay suggests that the task of the political—in Arendt's sense—is essentially aesthetic:

> Human beings look at one another, speak and act in spaces always populated by others. By virtue of this fact, they can never wholly control the outcome of their actions, nor wholly determine the outcome of their confrontations with others, or the interventions of others with respect to them.[13]

Azoulay suggests that first, the political is something that exists wherever human beings are acting, and, second, much of this action is about becoming sensible toward another. "Action" cannot be reduced to speech alone, and the act of taking a photograph, for her, is about documenting a particular set of visible political relations, perpetuating them as visible. Through the circulation of the photograph, this space of politics is enlarged by increasing the number of bodies in contact, disseminating knowledge about an event and the relations needed to "produce" a particular image. A photograph, for Azoulay,

> is a platform upon which traces from the encounter between those present in the situation of photography are inscribed, whether the participants are present by choice, through force, knowingly, indifferently, as a result of being overlooked or as a consequence of deceit.[14]

The politics here, more than simply one of documentation and inscription,[15] come from the public circulation of an image, which reveals and makes sensible the relations existent at a particular moment in time:

> ...photographer and photographed subjects are to be found together, present in different ways, capable of leaving traces on the basis of which different utterances can be extracted, articulated and connected to one another, or to other kinds of utterance, in a manner that allows them to continue to participate not only in the act of photography, but also in the political space that the photograph elicits, in accordance with the principles by which it operates.[16]

Or, apropos of transformations in the public/private distinction that have been ongoing since at least the last decades of the twentieth century,[17] Azoulay refuses the distinction that renders some bodies and some activities beyond the political because they do not manifest sensibly, publicly as speech. This not only radically expands the domain of the political (and political action) but also seems to follow the very definition that Arendt gave for the political (though it also erodes the distinction between political and social Arendt wanted to maintain).

The distinction between the aesthetic and the political—a distinction today that I think Azoulay is correct in suggesting characterizes judgments of particular kinds of art and their existence as "political" or "not political"—descends not entirely from Arendt, but also from Walter Benjamin's final paragraphs of his "Work of Art" essay. There, Benjamin offers his famous proclamation,

> *All efforts to aestheticize politics culminate in one point. That point is war* ... Humankind, which once, in Homer, was an object of contemplation for the Olympian gods, has now become one for itself. Its self-alienation has reached the point where it can experience its own annihilation as a supreme aesthetic pleasure. *Such is the aestheticizing of politics, as practiced by fascism. Communism relies by politicizing art.*[18]

Azoulay argues that the vast majority of art criticism inspired by this quote is guided by a misreading, one that differentiates aesthetics and politics rather than the distinction Benjamin actually makes, which is between *aestheticizing* and *politicizing*.[19] Essence and process are conflated, and the actual point of critique Benjamin was working to make—which refers to kinds of art, like that of Marinetti and the Futurists, or the *Gesamtkunstwerk* of Wagner, which move from total sensory experience to, say, a spectacular glorification of war, delighting in death through an "immersive" sensory overload that only exists because immersion and alienation exist together in a specific range of material forms of spectatorship—ends up reduced to a form of judgment in which something "aesthetic" cannot be political and something "political" cannot be aesthetic.[20] The point Azoulay is making is, then, not a rejection of Benjamin per se, but rather an acknowledgement that the distinction between aesthetics and politics circumscribes the boundaries of "political art" in a way that refuses the ability of photography, *in general*, to document and circulate relations and encounters, producing new relations and encounters in the process of circulation.

The politics of photography theorized by Azoulay shares many affinities with the arguments of Jacques Rancière, though she tends to stress the capacity of a work of art to either reveal relations or produce them in circulation and consumption, which can be seen in how she defines the political as a space of action through encounter. Rancière, while he also argues for the necessity of this kind of aesthetic and sensory space for political encounter, defines politics as the contestation of boundaries, of the "policing" of a "distribution of the sensible":

> The distribution of the sensible reveals who can have a share in what is common to the community based on what they do and on the time and space in which this activity is performed. Having a particular "occupation" thereby determines the ability or inability to take charge of what is common to the community; it defines what is visible or not in a common space, endowed with a common language, etc. ... Politics revolves around what is seen and what can be said about it, around who has the ability to see and the talent to speak, around the properties of spaces and the possibilities of time.[21]

What is *political* here is the boundaries that limit the ability to be speak, to be seen, to be heard. Thus, politics involves an aesthetic dimension, as it relates to the boundaries set around who or what is permitted to enter into public space as one who has a stake in "the political."[22]

I think Rancière and Azoulay would agree on the aesthetic dimension of the political and the necessity of expanding the distribution of sensibility beyond that of speech. But there's a point of distinction between them that allows us to have a broader, multifaceted definition of political relation than we would get from each alone. Where Azoulay sees the political as a space of aesthetic encounter that can be revealed and expanded by photography, Rancière sees politics as a contestation over who and what can become sensible at a particular moment in time. Or, politics, for both, is about the potential of sensing a particular relation—Rancière, however, stresses that the debate over the relations that are seen (or not seen) is itself political.[23]

## Figure and Ground in Selfies and Dronies

The politics of selfies—following the lessons of Azoulay and Rancière—are found in the particular ways that relations are made sensible and documented. Why I stress linking these two theorists is, in part, because I think Azoulay's stress on relationality often underemphasizes how particular relations are *not* experienced at particular moments. As Rancière highlights, the boundary between what can and cannot be experienced is itself political. At the same time, I think Rancière's focus on the contestation of boundaries tends to sideline the politics that stems from encounters that *are* sensible, which is what Azoulay theorizes. Admittedly, I think both acknowledge each of these aspects, but they each tend to foreground either relationality or boundedness in how they define the political. So, we must maintain the definition of the political that both theorists offer—both the politics of relational encounter and the politics that defines boundaries that either allows for or excludes particular experiences from encounter.

Selfies are often either dismissed as deeply "narcissistic" or are thought of as an example of phatic communication that announces one's presence for another. While dismissals of selfies as narcissistic are exceptionally common, one of the more nuanced versions of this claim comes from Henry Giroux, who sees selfies as an expression of internalized, neoliberal surveillance that

> are not only an indication of the public's descent into the narrow orbits of self-obsession and individual posturing, but also good for the economy ... The unchecked rise of selfishness is now partly driven by the search for new forms of capital that recognise no boundaries and appear to have no ethical limitations.[24]

While Giroux sees some hope in the possibility of redrawing the boundaries between public and private, personal and political, he nonetheless understands the vast majority of selfies (and the forms of "narcissism" they express) as an extension of a relentless drive toward extracting maximum economic value from body image, inducing a variety of emotional and psychological disorders (that can be "solved" through plastic surgery, therapy, and consumerism) in the name of an idealized, public body image.[25]

While I think Giroux is generally correct in diagnosing the relationship between selfies, image, and capital (though I find his definition of "narcissism" as self-absorption to be lacking, for reasons I'll note momentarily), many other authors writing about selfies tend to stress the positive possibilities that he briefly acknowledges, even when they also emphasize how selfies can perpetuate varieties of surveillance capitalism.[26] Some authors suggest selfies are an expression of an eternal desire to document and share images of the self to others, part of a genealogy of self-portraiture more broadly, expressive of an artistic agency to become present and engage in intimate self-fashioning and self-presentation for others.[27] This argument tends to foreground a politics not unlike the one described by Azoulay.

Selfies provide a means for a "citizenship" that comes from placing photographs of intimate spaces and private bodies into the public sphere, reshaping who (and what) can enter into "the political" through images that document and announce one's presence to another. Selfies, in visualizing and displaying a self, is a hailing of an unknown, networked audience, producing an encounter in the circulation of a photo, opening and remaking the possibilities of "private" bodies to enter into public visibility.

But, as is the case with the limitations of encounter that are often deemphasized by Azoulay, these arguments tend to only acknowledge the relationship between the viewer and viewed, rather than the relationships constitutive of the image itself, the relationships sensible in the act of taking a selfie rather than viewing one of another over social media. This is a problem, as it neglects the boundedness—and exclusion—of particular relations from sensation in the actual taking of a photograph. While it's true that the dissemination of a selfie may induce a political encounter by enabling forms of networked contact through visual representation, it's equally important to acknowledge the boundaries of sensation that come from both taking a picture and viewing one. This is one of the points Guinness and I derive from our phenomenological analysis of selfies. A selfie is

> about the distinction made between the assemblage that is the self (which isn't inherently about a single body) and the background upon which it appears (which recedes in the actual act of taking a selfie). A selfie involves locating the body in space, but locating that body as differentiated from and outside (or in front of) that space ... While the intent may be to document, to mark one's presence in a specific location at a specific time, this documentation occurs only through a means that differentiates figure and background—setting them in relation, but a relation in which the background recedes from awareness in the act of taking a picture.[28]

Or, the literal act of taking a picture of oneself, of viewing one's own body on a screen, requires a visual orientation toward an image of one's face and away from the specific place within which one's body is situated.

As we see it, the common dismissal of selfies as narcissistic misses the point, focusing on a colloquial (and non-theoretical) fear of self-absorption rather than the necessity of bodies and their orientations in particular situations, one which permits experience to be directed toward some things but not others. Following the history of narcissism as a form of subjectivity—through Freud, Lacan, Bernard Stiegler, Joan Copjec, Marshall McLuhan, and others—we suggest that narcissism can be theorized as either a self-reflexive pointing back to the self, producing it, prior to opening into relations with others, or as a numbing that negotiates self with environment, protecting the self. These positions are not mutually exclusive, and, thus, self-absorption is not an end, but rather a beginning that directs one elsewhere.

The problem with selfies, then, would be when they *cease to be narcissistic* and fail to produce a "self" that can then be directed elsewhere—when turning back on the self forecloses relations, between self and environment, between self and other.[29] This is the problem Giroux highlights—but we would suggest that it is not that selfies are narcissistic, but that they are *not narcissistic enough*, in that no "self" is produced that can engage with other relations that enable it to direct desire elsewhere.

So, any discussion of selfies as a form of relational image must stress two separate moments that have quite different political implications. First is the taking of a picture, in which perception of a self is turned inward, in which the relation between a body and itself is foregrounded in sensation, but the relation between the body and the space in which it is located is bracketed and excluded. The boundaries of perceptibility differentiate the body from its environment but reduce (and exclude) the environment to that which only exists as the space behind one's back. Second is the circulation and examination of the selfie, in which the background from the initial act of taking a picture becomes sensible to the one viewing the image, though the space of sensation is again bracketed as attention is directed toward the image.

In each stage, the experience of what is observed (one's self, the selfie) produces a system of relations that differentiates a particular "body" from the environment in which it is located at the time of viewing. This permits the opening of specific relations—between viewer and self, viewer and selfie—but also forecloses particular relations that do not enter into perception.[30] Figures (and "selves") only emerge through the perception of relations that remove a background from sensation.

The relational politics here become even more overt when we contrast selfies with "dronies," or self-photography taken with drones. In my opinion, Anthony McCosker has advanced the most sophisticated understanding of drone photography as the product of a relational, more-than-human assemblage that links the human body with a range of often invisible technological sensors that, often autonomously, help a drone navigate space beyond the direct agency of its pilot.[31] "The image *of* drone vision emphasises the spatial relations and the camera's semi-subjectivity, its motility," says McCosker, drawing on William James' radical empiricism, "And the image-experience is bound up in this relational movement."[32]

While photography, in general, should be theorized as a form of augmented or "nonhuman" perception, with the digital it seems that forms of photographic perception are, as Joanna Zylinska claims, "increasingly decoupled from human agency and human vision."[33] McCosker argues that drone photography—given its necessary reliance on technical processes of movement and environmental sensation that, while processed by drone sensors, never enter into human perception—induces a form of "camera consciousness" that highlights the relational intertwining of human sensation with its technical prostheses.

McCosker's claims highlight one articulation of the necessary relationality of any photographic image, and how forms of relationality are marked by particular relations into sensation, but not others. Again, we can see how imagery is inherently relational (and therefore political), but the boundaries between what can be sensed and what remained beyond sensation is how this political space is circumscribed. Here, what remains beyond sensation are the technical actors and processes that permit drone imagery to become possible in the first place. As McCosker and Bradley L. Garrett elaborate, the specifics of drone imagery depend on the material capacities of particular models of drones:

> The DJI Mavic, for example, incorporates a 4K high-definition movable camera for recording and FPV, in addition to two fixed forward-facing stereo vision cameras and a sonar system. In combination with computer vision, object recognition, and machine learning processing, these are used to track objects in 3D space, detect and avoid obstacles, and track and follow chosen subjects on the move.[34]

Or, seeing through drones relies on a massive assemblage of sensory technologies, not all of which correspond in any direct way to human sensation.

Additionally, I want to highlight how drone photography also rearticulates the figure-ground relation we see in selfies. This is perhaps most overt in critiques of drone visuality that stress the militaristic (rather than consumerist) applications of drone vision. As Grégoire Chamayou claims, in what may be one of the most comprehensive accounts of how drones have reinvented the very meaning of war and the ethics of sovereignty, military drones, which are essentially flying video cameras with missiles attached, introduce the logic of telepresence into war and make it so the "primary task is no longer to immobilize the enemy but to identify and locate it."[35]

This "vertical mediation" of war, as Lisa Parks describes it, requires a relational understanding of infrastructure and environment,[36] but also produces a particular sense of top-down visuality that *locates a figure within its environment*. If, in a selfie, the figure is in front of a background, then in drone photography, the vertical scale of the image places that figure in relation to the space it is in, but also alienates the figure from the viewer of the image. This has clear implications for the definition of politics we've been working through within this chapter.

As both Parks and Chamayou argue, there's an ethical distancing that happens via the drone, which permits the consumption of images of death. As Parks explains, via an analysis of user comments on aerial assault videos, there's two coherent tendencies in how viewers contextualize images of death mediated via drones:

> The first approaches these videos' depiction of the killing or death of people on the ground as a source of entertainment and visual pleasure such that these sequences function as a kind of *aerial snuff*. The second tendency is to use the videos to scrutinize US military policies, actions, or violence, so that they function as *aerial exposés* that question the rules of engagement or condemn specific attacks.[37]

The figure is placed within its environment—which, in the militaristic use of drones, is to eliminate it as an "aberration" or something "improper" to the space in which the figure is located—as the image is disseminated any affective dimensions of relation and contact are subsumed into pleasure and dispassionate analysis. While there's still a potential "politics" here, the actual mobilization of political investment seems undermined by the distance of verticality.

Self-photography using drones induces a rather different set of relations from those we understand in a selfie. One's body is placed into an environment—figure is located within the ground of the image—but the scale of the image is alienating, in which one's self is viewed and consumed from a distance. And, if discussions of selfies tended to stress the kind of relationality that followed Azoulay's claims about photography, while neglecting the politics that required specific relations to be excluded from perception, with dronies this, too, is inverted. The relationship between viewer and viewed, the "intimacy" transmitted through the image, wanes, while the space of relations made visible to the observer is expanded as the photographer places themselves within a larger environment.

## Conclusion: Figure and Ground, Transparency and Obfuscation

I want to conclude by pointing elsewhere. If understanding the political relationality of these different modes of photography requires a specific, differential understanding of how relation is articulated, then political interventions into selfies (and dronies) need a nuanced understanding of the specificity of visual and relational politics. This doesn't seem to be what's happening currently. Rather, artistic interventions into digital visual culture tend to merely stress a different binary: that of transparency and obfuscation. This binary may help theorize the intent of artists working to challenge a visual culture of surveillance that demands complete visibility and—often through computer-aided vision—"transparently" discerns knowledge of interior states from visible evidence of facial expression.

Trevor Paglen, Jemima Wymen, and Adam Harvey, among others, use practices of obfuscation to make a figure disappear to particular (usually automated) viewers. Harvey's *CV Dazzle*, or "Computer Vision Dazzle," for instance, refers to a technique from World War I developed by the British, where ships were painted using conspicuous, abstract shapes in order to interfere with the targeting of the ships by German U-boats (Figure 17.1). Using conspicuous makeup and hair styling, Harvey proposes a model in which fashion can be used to disrupt and hide from systems of facial recognition, including those used in CCTV surveillance and the kinds of facial detection used widely in the automated social media analysis of selfies. While visible to other *people*, employing the techniques of *CV Dazzle* obscures one's face from *computer* vision.[38] While I generally agree with the intent of these artists, one of my goals here has been to set up a definition of aesthetic politics that questions the intent of acts of obfuscation, instead looking to a politics that is more situated and invested in *particular relations* that emerge from *formal generalities*. Practices of obfuscation make sense in the context of the militarized logic of drone photography—and, likewise, can be seen to descend from militaristic techniques of camouflage—refusing (and preempting) the location of a figure in an environment for its elimination. Yet these practices can be seen to valorize individualized acts while neglecting systemic intervention.[39] More importantly, any emphasis on obfuscation as a means to resist digital surveillance presumes only one variant of figure-ground relation in these images.

Working through the limitations of obfuscation will be a task I will take up in a future essay. For now, I merely wish to emphasize that any political theory of selfies and dronies must acknowledge, first, the politics of relationality and the boundedness that limits specific relations from entering into experience and, second, how different variants on self-photography today, including, but not limited to, selfies and dronies, require us to think through how the relation between figure and ground in these images is enacted.

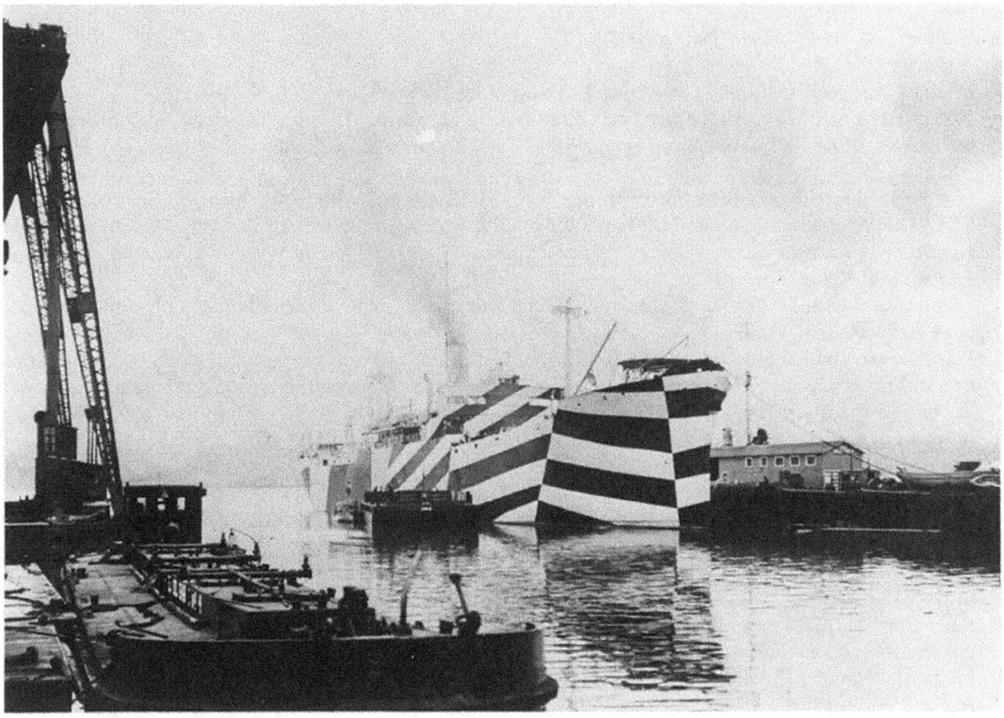

*Figure 17.1* The USS West Mahomet, circa November 1918, painted with Dazzle camouflage. Photograph from the Bureau of Ships Collection in the US National Archives, Photo #: 19-N-1733. Photo credit: US National Archives; Public Domain

## Notes

1 Grant Bollmer and Katherine Guinness, "Phenomenology for the Selfie," *Cultural Politics* 13, no. 2 (2017): 156–76.
2 Ariella Azoulay, *Civil Imagination: A Political Ontology of Photography*, translated by Louise Bethlehem (London: Verso, 2012), 55.
3 Bruno Latour, "From Realpolitik to Dingpolitik: Or How to Make Things Public," in *Making Things Public: Atmospheres of Democracy*, edited by Bruno Latour and Peter Weibel (Karlsruhe: ZKM|Center for Art and Media Karlsruhe, and Cambridge, MA: MIT Press, 2005), 4–31; Jane Bennett, *Vibrant Matter: A Political Ecology of Things* (Durham, NC: Duke University Press, 2010). Also see Grant Bollmer, *Materialist Media Theory: An Introduction* (New York: Bloomsbury Academic, 2019), 141–71.
4 Bollmer and Guinness, "Phenomenology."
5 The use of drones in everyday life perhaps challenges this legacy, though the modes of visuality that characterize drones are bound up with a larger history of imperial and militaristic vision. See Grégoire Chamayou, *A Theory of the Drone*, translated by Janet Lloyd (New York: The New Press, 2015), 78; cf. Caren Kaplan, *Aerial Aftermaths: Wartime from Above* (Durham, NC: Duke University Press, 2018).
6 Peter Galison, "The Ontology of the Enemy: Norbert Wiener and the Cybernetic Vision," *Critical Inquiry* 21, no. 1 (1994), 228–66.
7 Cf. Chamayou, *A Theory*, 34.
8 Azoulay, *Civil Imagination*, 3.
9 Ibid., 5.
10 Hannah Arendt, *The Human Condition*, Second Edition. (Chicago: University of Chicago Press, 1958), 9.
11 Hannah Arendt, *The Promise of Politics* (New York: Schocken Books, 2005), 153.
12 Arendt, *Human Condition*, 22–78.
13 Azoulay, 99–100.

14 Ibid., 24.
15 Bollmer, *Materialist Media Theory*, 51–78.
16 Azoulay, 60.
17 Michael Warner, *Publics and Counterpublics* (New York: Zone Books, 2002), 21–63.
18 Walter Benjamin, *Selected Writings*, vol. 3, edited by Howard Eiland and Michael W. Jennings (Cambridge, MA: Harvard University Press, 2002), 121–22. Italics in original.
19 Azoulay, 35.
20 For the aesthetic demands of Futurism, see F. T. Marinetti and Fillia, *The Futurist Cookbook*, edited by Charlotte Birnbaum, translated by Barbara McGilvray (Berlin: Sternberg Press, 2014); On the *Gesamtkunstwerk* and spectacle see Matthew Wilson Smith, *The Total Work of Art: From Bayreuth to Cyberspace* (New York: Routledge, 2007).
21 Jacques Rancière, *The Politics of Aesthetics*, edited and translated by Gabriel Rockhill (London: Bloomsbury Academic, 2004), 8.
22 Rancière distinguishes between the "politics of aesthetics," which, properly speaking, refers to what is or is not judged as "art," and what I've suggested here—which is that the political inherently involves an aesthetic dimension. "Politics" refers less to an ontological domain (like "the political") than to a process of setting, regulating, and debating the boundaries of particular domains or spaces. See Grant Bollmer, *Theorizing Digital Cultures* (London: Sage, 2018), 155–73.
23 Admittedly, I think Azoulay is making a very similar point in her discussion of judgment, though her comments are more about what Rancière would think of as the politics of aesthetics rather than the aesthetics of politics.
24 Henry A. Giroux, "Selfie Culture in the Age of Corporate and State Surveillance," *Third Text* 29, no. 3 (2015), 158.
25 I see some similarities here with Eva Illouz's arguments about therapy and the commodification of emotion. See *Cold Intimacies: The Making of Emotional Capitalism* (Cambridge: Polity Press, 2007).
26 See, for instance, Adi Kuntsman's edited volume *Selfie Citizenship* (Cham, Switzerland: Palgrave Macmillan, 2017).
27 Adam Levin, "The Selfie in the Age of Digital Recursion," *InVisible Culture* 20 (2014), http://ivc.lib.rochester.edu/the-selfie-in-the-age-of-digital-recursion/; Derek Conrad Murray, "Notes to Self: The Visual Culture of Selfies in the Age of Social Media," *Consumption Markets & Culture* 18, no. 6 (2015), 490–516.
28 Bollmer and Guinness, 166.
29 Ibid., 170. Similar arguments to ours have been advanced by Ana Peraica, in her *Culture of the Selfie: Self-Representation in Contemporary Visual Culture* (Amsterdam: Institute of Network Cultures, 2017).
30 The arguments here are strongly influenced by Sara Ahmed's *Queer Phenomenology: Orientations, Objects, Others* (Durham, NC: Duke University Press, 2006).
31 Bradley L. Garrett and Anthony McCosker, "Non-human Sensing: New Methodologies for the Drone Assemblage," in *Refiguring Techniques in Digital Visual Research*, edited by Edgar Gómez Cruz, Shanti Sumartojo and Sarah Pink (Cham, Switzerland: Palgrave Macmillan, 2017), 13–23.
32 Anthony McCosker, "Drone Media: Unruly Systems, Radial Empiricism and Camera Consciousness," *Culture Machine* 16 (2015), 14.
33 Joanna Zylinska, *Nonhuman Photography* (Cambridge, MA: MIT Press, 2017), 2.
34 Garrett and McCosker, 16.
35 Chamayou, 34.
36 Lisa Parks, *Rethinking Media Coverage: Vertical Mediation and the War on Terror* (New York: Routledge, 2018), 143–89.
37 Parks, 154.
38 For extensive information on Harvey's project, and images of the *CV Dazzle* project, see https://cvdazzle.com/. On the relation of these artists to the history of masking, see S. Yiğit Soncul, "Facial Politics of Images and Media: Mask, Body, Immunity" (Doctoral Thesis, University of Southampton, 2019).
39 Torin Monahan, "The Right to Hide? Anti-Surveillance Camouflage and the Aestheticization of Resistance," *Communication and Critical/Cultural Studies* 12, no. 2 (2015): 159–78.

# SECTION FIVE

# Play and Games

# 18

# MOBILIZING AUDIENCE AND PLAYFUL DISOBEDIENCE

*pvi collective's Kelli McCluskey and Steve Bull* in Conversation with *Klare Lanson*

Based in Perth, Australia since 1998, pvi collective have been creatively disrupting everyday life through performance-based participatory works that playfully agitate and mobilize audiences around the world. Using gameplay alongside emerging, familiar and DIY technology to explore social dynamics, they're passionate about using art as a tool for social change, challenging the way that power and privilege impact modern society.

Firstly, twenty years is a fantastic achievement for an art collective! The whole idea of mobilizing audience as one of the aims listed on your website is very appealing, could you start by speaking to common interests within your practice as a whole?

SB: pvi has been making work for a quite a while now and we're constantly looking ahead. We look at different subject matter—what makes us anxious, what concerns us as global citizens. You can see that with the works we've made over the years; around terrorism, or surveillance, or disaster capitalism, and the potential threat of another global economic collapse. So, while these things don't inspire us, they certainly drive us to creatively make work in response. We like to make immersive experiences for our audiences, and at the back of our heads is a desire for the experience for the audience to be in some ways both difficult and empowering.

KM: That's always a tricky balance. With our practice, it's about putting the *audience* front and centre. It's taken us a while to figure out how we should go about doing that. We have done, and still do, work in black box spaces—gallery spaces—but there's always this sense of frustration, of being locked into that black or white cube. We'd always find a way to pick up the phone or open the doors and get out. In wanting to get out onto the streets and into the real world, the next challenge was how to take the audience with us. Once we'd figured that out, then the question was: what's their experience out here, and how can we help facilitate? Our practice has transitioned. It is still very much performance based; we still talk about making performance work, but there's not as much performativity—the audience are becoming the performers. The idea that the audience becomes an activist within the work is certainly something that we're pushing harder now. That's where the challenge lies.

SB: What we've started to openly acknowledge is the element of gameplay in our work. Over the years we didn't really acknowledge that; it was more thought about in terms of role playing for our audiences, they had a particular role in our work. Increasingly, there has been a game theory structure to a number of works that we've made, *deviator* is a good example of this, which blends radically altered versions of children's games with subtle live performance in order to alter the narratives of place.[1]

KM: In a way, that's very much a tactic. Play is a very loaded word. It's automatically associated with childhood and frivolity. We try to talk about serious play, ways to play with what frightens us. The mechanics of play, or game structure, is a way of levelling the playing field for audience members as well, so that they understand that structure and become familiar with it.

> It gives people agency too, and a kind of nostalgia, where they simultaneously reminisce about their childhood, which is kind of captivating.

KM: You start to think about things differently, you behave differently, become competitive and less inhibited. You have permission to misbehave and become a lot more creative if you're embracing a game structure.

SB: What changed my definition of mobile media art was going to South Africa, a developing country. Historically, my mind set had always been that the mobile phone is a ubiquitous device, everyone's got one. In a developing country, it doesn't quite work like that. People use their phones in a different way, they use more free apps to save costs, and communicate differently to how we do.

So, tactically, thinking about another experience not mediated by technology that enables participation and a different sense of mobility, or a journey, or a narrative in a public space became really interesting. After that, we adapted our work to a new model of making, where we'd combine a series of workshops with a public outcome at the end. In this case in Bloemfontein, South Africa, we made an outdoor public board game that had the one-on-one levelling of the playing field with audiences. The work was called *transformer* (Figure 18.1) and it was a cooperative

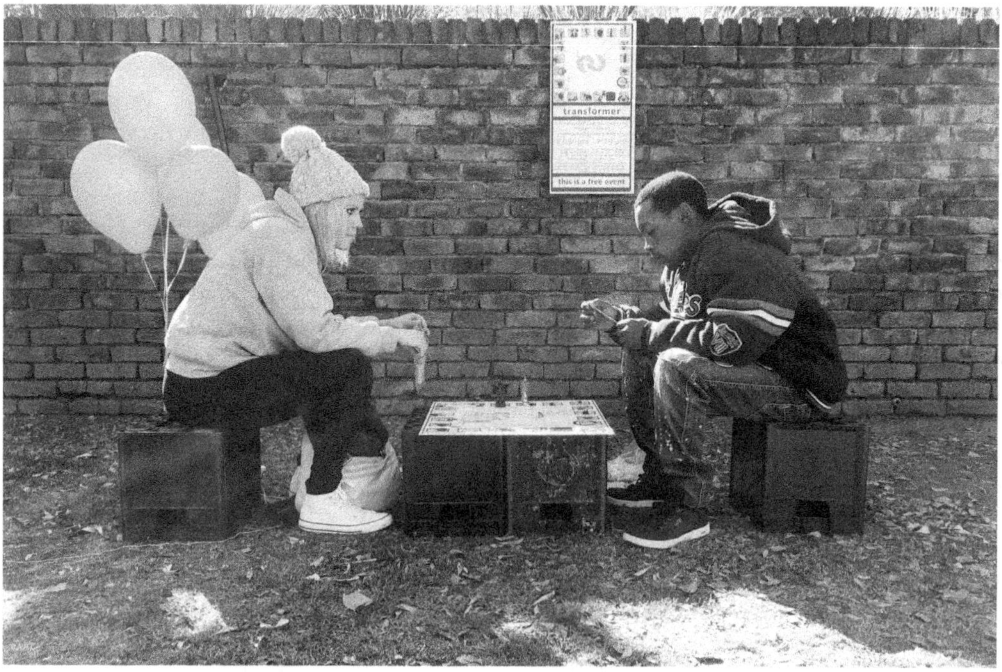


*Figure 18.1* *transformer* (2016). Vrystaat Art Festival, Bloemfontein, South Africa. Photo credit: pvi collective

one-on-one game where you rolled a dice and moved a figure around the board. When you landed on a particular square you received a card that gave you a playful instruction to initiate an action. The whole game was played in a public space.

KM: This relates to *disobedience rules* and how we developed that project. We played so many board games! It's so funny, the one we kept coming back to was not one of the classics; it was a really cheap board game from the second-hand shop, called *Lizzie McGuire: What Would Lizzie Do?* Lizzie McGuire was a Disney TV show in the 1990s. Actress Hillary Duff played the character, and what was lovely about the game was that it set physical challenges and asked the players to role play her. It was kind of embarrassing to role play a teenage character, but there was something appealing in the mechanics of the game, and in the difficulty level; having to embrace the discomfort of it (Figure 18.2).

SB: We played another game that was very significant too, called *Pank-a-Squith Oh! The Suffragettes*. This is a very old board game from 1909 and what really stood out was that there was one square that you land on that asks you to make a donation, so it actually takes you *out* of the board game back in the real world. That was our trigger for *transformer*,[2] the one-to-one tactical intervention work that we did for the 2016 Vrystaat Art Festival in Bloemfontein, South Africa.[3] We've been back every few years, it's unfinished business really, as much of our work is. *transformer* looked at how to play a board game where the audience can have a temporary impact on the public space around that board game, so it inspires them to undertake actions in their immediate surroundings.

KM: And to transform the space that you're actually occupying. In the judicial capital of South Africa, Bloemfontein, the festival was keen to bring us into the city centre. There's still a massive racial divide, this weird inversion, where the city centre itself is quite ghettoized, and all the wealthy white South Africans are in the suburbs and don't make their way into the city. So, it was important to hold the festival in the city and do a lot of things outdoors to bring people

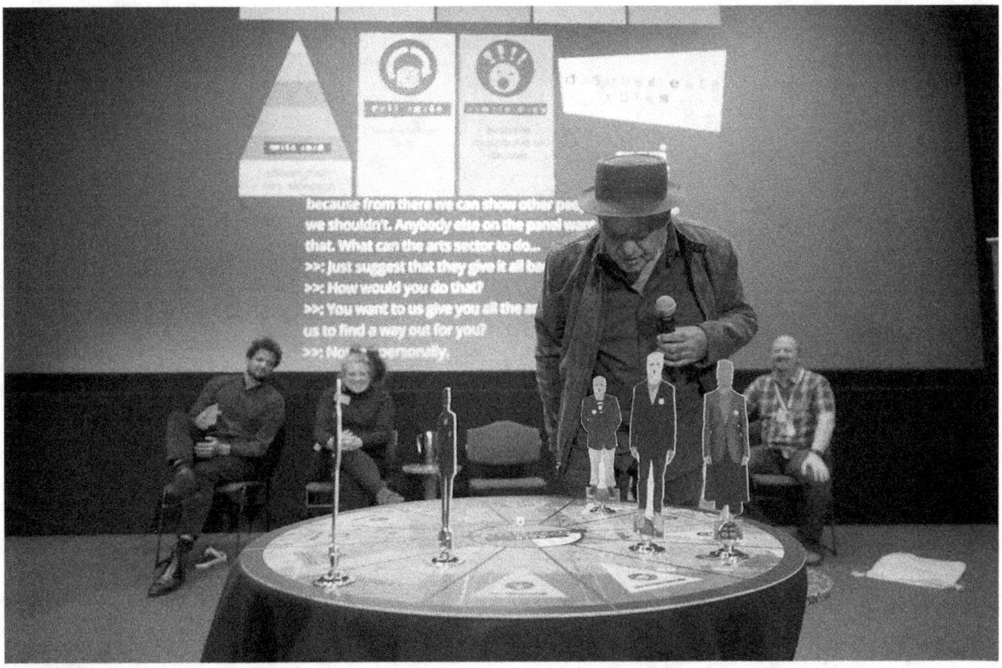


*Figure 18.2* Art game *disobedience rules: the policy edition* (2018). NAVA Future Forward Summit, Parliament House, Canberra, Australia. Photo credit: Zan Wimberley

in, an attempt to improve the perceived fear of the city as a "dangerous place." We were given a space that was a little park with this massive hideous colonial statue of Hertzog, who was one of the founders of Apartheid. He's there waving his finger in this park in this really ugly overt way.

The park itself well, there's a homeless community there, and the board game for us was about trying to find ways of bringing people together, while transforming this urban space at the same time. So, we asked, what can we do within the timeframe of an hour a day, to actually make some tiny transformations? How can we use the board game as a vehicle or tool to do that, together? The project kind of worked, bits of it certainly … but going back a second time we developed our ideas further with *disobedience rules* (Figure 18.3), which was a follow-on board game.[4] This game was looking at the philosophies of civil disobedience. 2017 was the 50-year anniversary of Howard Zinn, who famously wrote seven guidelines for civil disobedience. It was written at the time of the Vietnam War, and he gave a very famous lecture, which has been performed time and time again by lots of Hollywood stars, I think Matt Damon even does a version of it! Zinn says, "the problem is not civil disobedience, the problem is civil obedience." We held on to that, and 50 years on we were questioning what has changed.

Alongside that, we were reading Micah White's *The End of Protest*.[5] He's one of the co-creators of the Occupy Movement, and really honestly wrote about the failure of Occupy Wall Street and how those old traditional paradigms of protest—of taking to the streets and occupation—don't work; we need to invent new modes. So, we carried that with us, and *disobedience rules* was an invitation to bring together community leaders who were perhaps quite agitational or changemakers within their own fields—not artist practitioners—and actually challenge them, ask them questions about the role of civil disobedience in a creative context. You roll the dice—and there are various card categories which all relate to creative forms of disobedience. So, there's a card and a question that's posed to you, and what we loved was that it wasn't just a bunch of people sitting around playing this game. Players are actually filmed—televised live—then screened out into a public square.

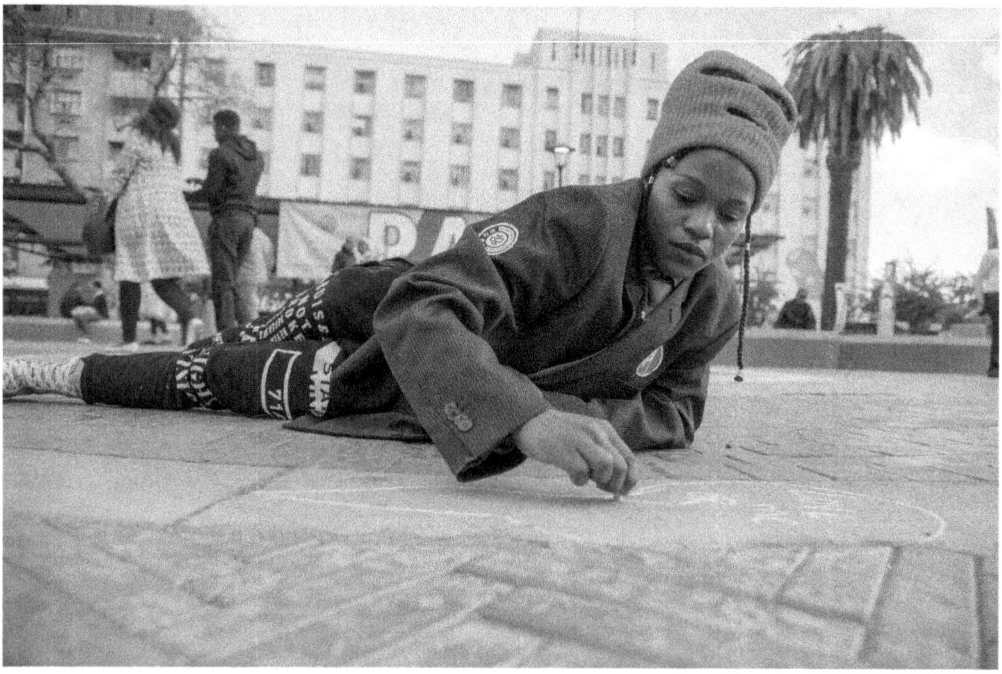

*Figure 18.3* *disobedience rules* (2018). Bloemfontein, South Africa. Photo credit: Francois Iflair

In that public square we have four local artists who specialize in different artforms (such as a street artist, sound artist, dancer) all watching the screen and referred to as the Uncivil Servants. Flipping the bureaucracy on its head, we also had the Mistress of Disobedience hosting the game. The answers that participants were giving when they played the game, if at any point their answers had a sense of clarity that could take them forward, would then be taken to the streets. So, then the artists would try to respond to what the answer was, and actually try out that idea. It didn't quite work, and we're still grappling with it, but there was a beautiful sense of urgency that was coming from within the community, pushed back out again and then responded to. We were just facilitating the process.

> Ah, mistakes we make. I love it when things don't quite work. One of the most beautiful things about play is this idea of failure—to label it failure is fantastic in terms of art making and the learning process embedded in play. All of your projects are so well thought out and collaborative in thinking, with lots of different people informing the work. Could you speak to the idea of collective art making?

KM: One of the unspoken rules we have when we are developing new work is that when we come to the table to start to discuss things, the ideas really need to be unresolved, or at least half thought out—it could just be a quote. With *disobedience rules*, we knew that quote was the anchor point to hold onto.

SB: Yes, and I think what we learned over a 20-year history, is that it's ok to disagree. Collectively, if you want to discuss your point of view, or forward it, everyone else in the group will have to listen.

> Active forms of listening are so important … groups need that sense of contemplation.

SB: Interesting things happen when we bring an expert or another artist into the mix. *disobedience rules* came out of working with a UK artist that we met the first time we were in South Africa, a guy called Alex Rinsler,[6] who makes large-scale temporary outdoor sculptures. We had similar social and political leanings, were really interested in his work, and also in how he galvanized such huge audiences. It was great to work with him and also to discover new ways to grow our audience scale.

KM: In terms of collectivity, there is a real belief that the *work* will be better because of the collective brain power. Collectivity is always stronger and more rigorous than just the one person. We always hold onto that—it might be because of our performance background, where you're very used to working with groups of people, as opposed to working in isolation. Different perspectives will always make it a stronger piece.

> More democratic too I suppose, that micro-level practice of social interaction is key. In terms of recalibrating audience through mobile media such as social media platforms through the smartphone, do you use mobile media as a tool for artmaking, alongside engaging new audiences?

KM: Mobile media has definitely been used as a tool, and we've explored this over the years, but we've also made a conscious decision not to be locked down by it. But what we *have* learned in making work with mobile phones is the need to work with programmers who also have an artistic voice in the process. We were very lucky to collaborate with Steve Berrick[7] and Chris McCormick,[8] two programmers that have their own arts and music practices, so it wasn't a process where we have the idea and hand it over to "make it work on the phone." Instead, it was a very iterative process where we figured things out together. This process also takes a lot of time, and we've always felt that we were too slow. But Kate (our producer) was like, "No, no, it's rigour!" It is difficult to know when to stop researching and make it come out of the brain, and into the world. Working with mobile media really stretches out the development process.

> The creative methods that you're applying in the collective practice with audience is so mobile too.

KM: What we loved about working with mobile phones was the potential for mixed realities and the blurring of how what you're hearing and what you're seeing through your phone is actually very different from the world that you're in. It is almost like inhabiting a movie set. We did *black-market*[9] in Kings Cross, Sydney, which was the perfect spot for that work, with real-life drug deals going on and cops everywhere, you were never quite sure what was part of the work and what was not. Actually, I think *tts:australia*[10] taught us that; audiences on the bus, with us orchestrating these little interventions that they would see driving by or get out and take part in it. People would come away from it saying, "Oh, when that person was doing that, was that part of the work?" I loved that slippage, it was really juicy.

> Yes, that ambiguity is so beautiful. And pvi also really owns that idea of "Artivism" too.[11] In terms of social change, could you speak to the role of art and activism in the work?

KM: This is interesting because at the moment we're developing a new work called *tiny revolutions*,[12] which looks at—going back to the very beginning of our conversation—the overwhelming sense of *so* many catastrophic crises coming our way for global humanity. It looks into issues like climate change, rapid technology advancement, minority rights, and the status of women. Everything feels way too big, that rising sense of anxiety that we carry within us. Is there a way that we can take those massive issues and have a tiny response to it, something that's bite sized? Something that matters, that's still meaningful.

The *tiny revolutions* work (see Figure 23, color insert) is an invitation for people to submit their anxieties. We invite them to give us a paragraph based on one of 15 global issues that have been researched by the UN, framed as the most pressing crises we currently face. The lists include things like energy, education, wealth inequality, and rapid technology advancement. We'll then have a really fast and deep conversation about how we transform that anxiety into an action. We have a thinktank—some specialists coming in to give talks—and then we have a "do-tank," to process that massive issue into something tiny, like a giant funnel. Then we ask people to pick an intervention tactic, so we bring a bit of game mechanics into it. For example, someone might write a paragraph about climate change, and the tactic they choose is "public disrobing." So, all these intervention tactics throughout the course of each individual story that have been used non-violently by activists, and we're like "Ok, so we've got to fit this issue with this tactic, we have 30 minutes, how can we go deep with this quickly? keeps its substance and create an action that can be undertaken in public?"

SB: Look at its potential, the new reinvention of that tactic, and where it could possibly go.

> Anxiety is a great way to move forward, and in terms of the tiny narrative aspects too, short texts and short forms of multisensorial communication relate well to mobile media art, changing the way we operate socially.

KM: Yes! "Your tiny little revolution is being processed." We're all so used to that disaster narrative now, we just really feel the need to feed in some hope and some positivity. The potential for everyday activism is huge, that's what we're tapping into there.

SB: *tiny revolutions* is also very much a response to the fact that a lot of our works take a good while to manifest. Some may take two–three years, and we're constantly thinking we need to be more responsive; something like *tiny revolutions* allows us to do that. It also extends our audience base from not just the gallery inhabitants, or someone who might sign up to a newsletter, but those armchair activists who may want to communicate to us in another way. Working with people in a new way, they may not be an actual participant, but they could be a global participant in terms of giving us an issue and provocation. Their experience would be through digital means, the process and through the documented outcome that we send to them.

## Notes

1 See *deviator* project description at https://pvicollective.com/project/deviator/.
2 pvi collective, *transformer*, 2016, live art performance work, https://pvicollective.com/project/transformer/.
3 Vrystaat Art Festival, website, www.vrystaatkunstefees.co.za/en/home/.
4 pvi collective, *disobedience rules*, 2018, live art performance work, https://pvicollective.com/project/disobedience-rules/.
5 White, Micah. *The End of Protest: A New Playbook for Revolution* (Toronto: Knopf, 2016).
6 See http://alexrinsler.com.
7 See http://steve.berrick.net.
8 See https://mccormick.cx/.
9 pvi collective, *blackmarket*, 2015, live art performance work, https://pvicollective.com/project/black-market/; see also http://steve.berrick.net/blackmarket for video documentation.
10 Christmas, Pip. "PVI's Terror Australis," *realtime arts*, 1 February 2005, www.realtime.org.au/pvis-terror-australis/
11 See Chapter 45 within this Companion for a curatorial discussion on artivism.
12 pvi collective, *tiny revolutions*, 2019, live art performance work, https://pvicollective.com/project/tiny-revolutions/

# 19
# MOBILE MAPPING AND PLAY

*Sybille Lammes and Clancy Wilmott*

Art practices, mapping and play have a shared history that harkens back to the creation of the earliest maps, from more recent examples across the playful symbolism of pictorial cartographies, the cartographic play of the *Situationiste Internationale* (SI) to the maps used in geographic board games from the early modern period.[1] However, the beginning of this millennium signalled a new turn in this relationship, as digital mapping technologies became more widespread, reshaping mobilities and offering alternative modes of play using wayfinding and digital location. Mobile mapping practices leveraging locative technologies (such as global positioning systems) became a field for experimentation by artists such as Esther Polak, Blast Theory and Mark Hansen using GPS traces to make images from the urban form.

These artists were seen as a new wave of so-called locative artists[2] that used *mobile* digital media in new inventive ways and experimented with the new affordances of mobile mapping. In particular, as the hybridization of maps, spaces and bodies was enabled through GPS location by linking the physical location of the user with a near-real-time digital coordinate, the possibility of putting the moving user *in* the map *in situ* became a key site of exploration either using mobility to affect the map, or the map to affect mobility. As MacDonald has argued, such artistic practices often reflected upon the temporality of movement of the user, whether as artist or invited participant.[3] For example, Polak's and Kee's 2002 project Amsterdam Real Time (with Waag Society), mapped the traces of way-finders in Amsterdam, rendering a colourful image that highlighted how movement through the inner city takes on the shape of a spider-like web.[4]

Since then, many creative experiments have become part of mainstream platforms, as people make their own figures with running apps (such as Strava), leave their traces on OpenStreetMap while participating in amateur mapping parties or use bespoke maps for catching Pokémon. Yet with the proliferation of popular mobile mapping practices, the relation between art and mobile mapping has not ceased to exist but instead has just become more dispersed to a more general user population, and out of the confines of the art gallery. As this chapter discusses, we now see mobile mapping used in playful ways in a wide range of creative cultural practices.

In this chapter, we consider such practices through the lens of mobile mapping as play. Central to our argument is that digital mobile mapping has rather literally brought play into the map object itself. Through the reciprocal movement of map user and of the map image, we foreground the playful affordances of the map and mobile mapping interfaces as central to artistic mapping practices.

Play is, as Huizinga[5] claimed, one of the main forces of the human creative condition. Huizinga was also a technological pessimist, believing that with the advent of mechanization, play would disappear, and "civilization" would be consequently doomed. Yet, what we have seen instead in this millennium is not so much a decline of play, but rather a dispersion of play and a hybridization of play with (post)digital technologies such as smart watches, phones and tablets. This has become even more apparent since the emergence of mobile and ubiquitous technologies that allow us to engage with play "on the go," whether it concerns travelling to work, waiting for a bus or running through a park. This intermingling of spatiality, mobility and play comes as no surprise as play is predominantly about the spatial exploration of and moving through space.[6]

Thus, play and mobility have the affordances to merge easily, and this connection has been promulgated since the emergence of wearable and mobile technologies. Also related to this potential of play to invite experimental spatial exploration is the close relation between mapping and play. As we have argued elsewhere—and counterintuitive to the belief that play is frivolous and mapping rational—mapping and playing have always been practised together, whether in analogue activities such as board games, orienting or geo-caching, or other forms of digital location-based games.[7]

In this chapter, we focus on how ludic mobile mapping can be understood as a creative practice, drawing on an approach to play as fostering creativity.[8] As Sutton-Smith argues, play and playthings (toys, materials) are often the instigators of creative thinking and problem solving.[9] Maybe through its ambiguity play can be a lever to make mapping into simultaneously a playful and mobile practice, while setting up an assemblage in which artistic relations between mapping, mobility and play are explored.[10] Play, in the words of play-scholar Miguel Sicart, "is brought by people to the complex interrelations (...) between things that form daily life," and "to play is, then, to assemble a number of actors to re-create a world."[11, 12] It is therefore a state of being, doing and knowing that we can bring to many cultural settings, including that of mobile media art and mapping.

In a similar vein, mobile mapping can be broadly understood as a situated, interpretative practice of working between cartographic, spatial and embodied knowledge.[13] Specifically, mobile mapping refutes the easy distinction between maps and mappers, and underscores the roles that relationality, movement and entanglements play in the process of navigation, exploration and wayfinding. In doing so, it understands both space—in the form of materialities, flows and processes—*and* maps—in the form of representations, symbology and data—to have *a priori* political impacts which are engaged, rearranged, reformed or transformed through moments of mapping. For instance, a person opening a geolocative mobile phone app at a particular point in space and time might simultaneously entangle the spatial politics of where they are (e.g. dispossession, gentrification), the technological politics of what they are mapping with (e.g. data ethics, infrastructures), and the bodily politics of who they are (positionality, experience, embodiment, memory). In this entanglement, mobile mapping can be understood as a relatively radical move away from classic post-structuralist cartographic theory towards an account of mapping which is more performative, material and more-than-cartographic.[14, 15, 16]

Analysing mobile mapping is crucial to understanding mobile media art, which often engages the embedded, spatial, and movement-oriented aspects of artistic practice. The framework of mobile mapping offers the theoretical and critical ability to extend analysis beyond the artwork into the geographical and historical situatedness of the project: if mobile media art comes into being through movement and location, then where, when and who also matter. In short, the same mobile media artwork performed in two cities might be engaged differently because of their architectural, spatial and cultural specificities. At the same time, the same artwork performed across the same city by different people at different times will also emerge differently due to shifts in weather, light, social crowds, personal histories, memories, technological ability, mood, etc. Thus, no two entanglements are ever fully the same—even where continuous threads of dissent, resistance and hegemony may be traced through multiple spaces and times.

Furthermore, the emphasis on arranging and moving within a mobile mapping framework underscores the playful affordances of mapping itself.[17] Play, in this context, does not diminish the political nature of space and spatiality, but rather opens up the possibility for radical reimaginings and wanderings through everyday spaces. The assembling and reassembling of actors in mobile, situated and mediated ways is precisely where mobile mapping and play begin to intersect. Arguably, mapping is always potentially playful and mobile as it is a practice of drawing things, objects, lines and spaces together.[18]

In addition, play reveals the affordances of the technological, social, and spatial entanglements within mobile mapping, as objects break or are repurposed, people learn, unlearn, remember and re-envision, and materialities weather, morph, or disrupt. Here, Serres' notion of the quasi-object becomes a crucial theoretical tool to both comprehend the relationship between mobile mapping and play.[19] The quasi-object becomes through its relationality with other things and other actors. Thus, mobile mapping and play as situated, performative and disruptive bedfellows open up possibilities for engaging with mobile media art in unexpected, unanticipated and often transformative ways.

In this chapter, we consider how technological affordances and the quasi-object might render a critical reading of mobile mapping and play. We will do so first by outlining some of the nuances of Serres' theory of the quasi-object, as well as how it sits within the concept of relationality that is widely under debate in science and technology studies, new media studies and geography. Then, we unpack our reading of mobile mapping and play through the quasi-object by closely analysing two case studies: *Bee in the City*, created by Wild in Art and Manchester City Council in 2018, and the *Wayfinder Live* project, created by Troy Innocent in 2019—are specific cases of large-scale public artworks requiring mobile phones. Because of their public appeal, their technological (rather than say, solely critical or artistic) distinction and their eschewal of traditional gallery spaces, these two cases provide concrete examples of both mobile mapping and playful affordances in public, as objects that sit in place, yet invite certain actions from passers-by, while also being mapped as specific routes through which to navigate the city.

## Serres and the Quasi-Object

> Being or relating, that is the whole question.[20]

As the above quote suggests, the quasi-object is neither really object or subject and goes beyond this dichotomy. A subject, writes Serres,[21] acts and moves objects along. An object, in comparison, is enclosed, absolute and defined. The quasi-object dismantles these Cartesian distinctions, by inviting activity, but not being made only from it.

The ball is perhaps the most recognizable example of how Serres understands quasi-objects. It is also an interesting example in the context of this chapter, as it is at once a playful and mobile "thing." In Serres' estimation, the ball on its own is "dumb" and still, it has no purpose and no action. Yet, when engaged in a team sport or collective activity, it restructures social relations, charged with immense capacity and agency for action through the affordances that it contains. The player who has the ball is marked as having a special status in the game, either as a subject to attack or defend, as does the next subject/player to whom the ball travels next and is invited by the ball travelling to it to be picked up. As it moves, the subjective social relations between players become shaped by the location, possibilities or affordances of the ball, where it goes and where it has been, and where it might go next.

Thus, the ball becomes directly responsible for the framing of social relations or, in Serres' words "[t]his quasi-object that is a marker of the subject is an astonishing constructer of intersubjectivity."[22] Crucially, Serres makes the case that the ball and the players shape, if not entirely construct, each other in tandem, and so, object and subject cannot be disentangled. The ball becomes, or is, a quasi-object, one that both defines and is defined by its relations with subjects and objects around it.

Interestingly, while Serres illustrates what a quasi-object is by referring to a ball, Latour takes a map as his prime example to explain his concept of an immutable mobile.[23] Immutable mobiles are a collection of things that retain their structure and shape while moving through spaces-times. These two figures merge in the case of mobile mapping, when we are dealing simultaneously with a mutable mobile and a quasi-object. Through the affordances of the map, an assemblage is formed that depends on fluctuating translations and relationalities. Here, the map becomes the ball. In other words, the map invites us to engage with mobile practices to produce spatio-temporal imaginative relationalities.

So mobile maps are quasi-objects with particular mobile and relational affordances. As such, they are also *navigational* interfaces that invite us as users to produce mobile spatio-temporal relationalities as "micro practices of power."[24] Furthermore, in the case of mobile mapping as creative practice, the ludic affordances of the navigational interface are foregrounded, inviting us to produce an assemblage of quasi-objects—for example, GPS trackers, things on our path, mobile phones.[25] If we work from the understanding that a ball is an interface that is designed to interact with, and possesses certain stimuli to explore further, we can define ludic interfaces as quasi-objects that invite us to play with them and give meaning to them within a larger network which is both material and immaterial.[26, 27, 28] The playfulness of such interfaces is intricately connected to their mobility and interactive transformability, as such interfaces invite users to visually move, perform and play with them. Furthermore, their playful agency is related to their ambiguity—as a term resonating with quasi—in which a mobile map can take on multiple and paradoxical meanings, and, for example, a bridge (as urban interface) can invite you to walk over it, but also to become part of an imaginative mobile mapping practice.[29, 30]

In the case of mobile mapping and play, all parts of the entanglement are quasi-objects. From the phone, either as a whole or a conglomerate of component parts, to the player (as bodied and virtual at once), or the material world such as architecture, green public spaces or the digital and cartographic structure of the map with its words, codes and numbers. As tendrils come together, these quasi-objects of mobile mapping make and remake, afford and designate, mark and remark in thoroughly playful ways, putting play in this assemblage.

When technologies are new, their ludic qualities are often emphasized. Whether we look at the story of the X-ray, colour cinema or more recent technologies like the Apple Watch, play often wears off after this so-called domestication of technologies.[31, 32] As observed by both Tuters and MacDonald, a similar tendency can be seen in relation to play and mobile mapping art.[33] Around the millennium a surge of artists, designers and performers engaged with the creative and playful affordances of newly widely available technologies like GPS tracking, Google Earth, OSM, or tagging. As the newness has somewhat waned, they have become part of more mundane practices that are embedded in quotidian life, as the case of *Pokémon Go* so clearly shows.[34] Yet that doesn't mean that the relation between artistic and mobile mapping practices has been severed altogether. As the cases below show, they have taken different forms and have hybridized to a greater extent with daily routines, in particular traversing urban environments.[35] In a subtle way, they augment quotidian mobility and experiences, inviting citizens to move differently through public environments and to be moved differently by them and create different relationalities.[36]

## Bee in the City: Walking, Mapping, Playing

In 2018, the Manchester City Council in partnership with Wild in Art, ran a major public art project to fundraise for the victims and families of victims of the 2017 Manchester Arena bombing. The project, which ran for two months, saw the construction and emplacement of over 100 large sculptural bees throughout Greater Manchester. Each bee was partnered with a local artist and sponsored by an initiative, organization or company (usually located near to the location of the bee). These artists were then asked to paint or decorate the bee as to depict a specific tenet of

Manchester's heritage, along themes as diverse as labour movements, gay rights, industrial innovation, health and well-being, or the advertisement of the sponsor's brand.

Mobile mapping and playful experiences were central to the project. The design and placement of bees was accompanied by the production of the *Bee in the City* (2018) app, which enabled users to pinpoint the location of bees, unlock them, find out further information about the design, collect rewards, count steps, donate to the funding drive, and link to social media (see Figure 19.1). Importantly, in order to unlock the bees on the app, a four-digit code was required, a code that could only be found on the physical bee sculpture itself. Users had to be *in place* in order to mediate between the materiality of the bee and its virtual counterpart.

In doing so, mobile media like phones affords a hybridity between map and object, what de Souza e Silva has called "hybrid space."[37] The sculpture and the app can be connected through a shared location, semiotic codes, and copresence.[38] Yet, what Serres' theory of the quasi-object offers is insight into how and through what this hybridization occurs—or, how things are (re) arranged. In the case of *Bee in the City*, hybridization is enabled by the technological capabilities of the mobile phone, specifically, its geo-location and software applications. As people use the (m)app to identify, locate, plan, and guide their route through the city, mobile media playfully produce opportunities for new paths and tours through the city. Holding the phone in your hand, deciphering which locations have been visited and unlocked and which haven't, deciding on the simplest, shortest, fastest, or most pleasant path to take, the phone becomes a quasi-object as it structures and restructures relations between people, objects, spaces and software.

Yet, in investigating the playful arrangement of things and the way in which they come together through mobile mapping, it is also possible to identify a multitude of quasi-objects, and so, multiple sites of hybridization. In *Bee in the City*, the bee sculpture also operated as a quasi-object, inviting different kinds of play and playful activities. Children could be seen looking around for it—and upon seeing it, letting out a squeal of delight and then climbing upon it or dancing around it. Groups would take photos (selfies or of each other) with the bee. The Queen Bee in the Royal Exchange Arcade, for example, often had queues of people waiting around for the opportunity to have a photo taken with a large bee sculpture with the face and Tudor clothing of Elizabeth I.

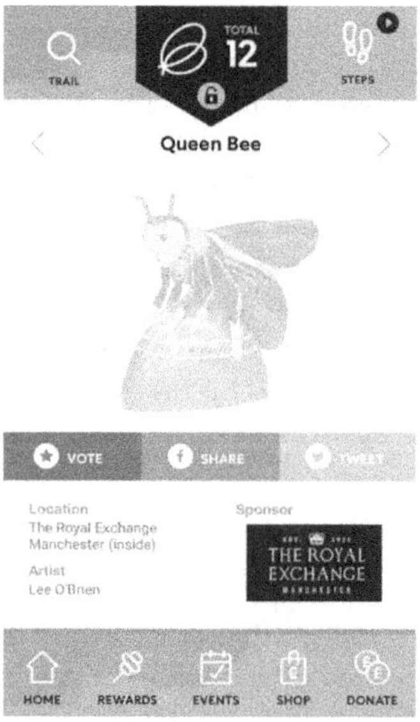


*Figure 19.1* *Queen Bee (locked)*, found in the Royal Exchange Arcade in central Manchester (2018). Photo credit: Wild in Art

The app, which at first was the key guide in the search by pinpointing a location and helping a person navigate to it, becomes subordinate to the material presence of the sculpture itself. Now, the bee becomes a social *and spatial* constructor of intersubjectivity—also a quasi-object within itself. But, when the code is found on the bottom ledge of the sculpture, the (m)app is re-engaged again. The addition of the (m)app extends the network—or "tesserae"—of quasi-objects and demi-quasi-objects: on its own the app is nothing, combined with sculptures and users it becomes part of a playful mobile mapping process, assembling and reassembling urban mobilities and flow.[39]

In addition, with digital-material interactivity, it becomes even more playful, producing different relations in time and space between spaces and subjects, as well as quasi-objects. The bee, the app—the entire mobile media artwork—in this way becomes a constructor of intersubjectivity. Thus, the bee sculptures as immutable and immobile, become both mobilized and mutable through the interfaciality of both the urban landscape and the mobile application. In short, *Bee in the City* shifted how people interacted with each other, as well as with technologies, urban materialities and artworks.

Under the gaze of the impressive neo-Georgian architecture of the library, Dazzle Bee was a relatively adorned bee, fashioned with sparkling faux jewels glued to the exterior of the sculpture. In the words of the artist, Liz Faram, it was designed so that it "sparkles and dazzles like the Manchester spirit—hard working people with energy and fire in their veins."[40] It was an easy bee to find, with heavy foot traffic as bee hunters and everyday urban walkers intermingled across its path. In summer, the reflective light on its jewels made it somewhat easier to find. The four-digit code for the bee was located on the square foundation of the sculpture.

As well as the further information about both the bee and its sponsor, Daylight, the code also allowed access to the *Bee Gallery*, an archive of photos taken by other bee hunters. These photos usually feature images of people (and their dogs!) standing with the bee in different poses, some touching the bee, others standing loosely beside it. Here, play and the quasi-object once again become folded into mobile mapping via the artwork. The bee itself is a quasi-object, but also, so is the app: the bee gathers urban walkers towards it, through visuality, touch and location. Then, it becomes the centre-point of photographic practice, which passes engagement from the bee towards the phone and the app. A photo is taken and uploaded, which sits hybridized between the sculpture and the app, until someone else finds or comes across the bee.

Here, the playful construction and reconstruction of spatial as well as social relations becomes a central tenet of the mobile mapping practices afforded by *Bee in the City* (see Figure 19.2, left). At the same time, there is also space for critique of both play and mobile mapping practices as lubricants smoothing over critical concerns over the commercial and political interests of the city. The bee itself stands as an unofficial, but collectively acknowledged symbol of Manchester's industrial history and can be found repeated on the urban landscape from bollards to the architecture of the Town Hall. Following the Manchester Arena attack, 22 bees were painted in a large mural on a wall in the Northern Quarter as a memorial to the 22 people who were killed. There are multiple interpretations of the meaning of the bee symbol: from economic productivity, unionism and workers, community harmony, and more recently, innovation, creativity, and entrepreneurialism. Thus, the symbolic status of the bee—even as a quasi-object—is quite elastic and its politics, contingent on the arrangement of urban interfaces (see Figure 19.2, right).

This is apparent in subtle advertising throughout both the app and the sculptures. The sponsorship and placement of the bees are foundational to the arrangement of quasi-objects Play and mobile mapping unfold together in the exploration of space, but are also entangled in the political economy of the city itself. There was a vast range of sponsors: the National Health Service (NHS), for instance, sponsored several bees placed closed to health care providers; the LGBTIQ+ community sponsored a bee in the Gay Village. Bees were also sponsored by large corporations, such

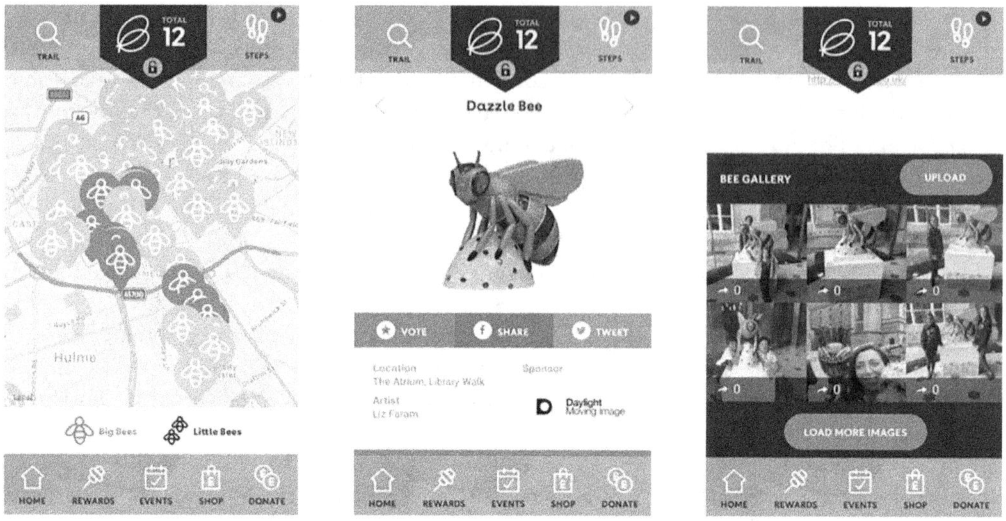


*Figure 19.2* Screenshots from *Dazzle Bee.* Left showing the map interface, center with the unlocked bee and further information, and right showing selfies and photographs uploaded by others (2018). Photo credit: Wild in Art

as Deloitte, who have been key participants in the state-led spatial restructuring of Manchester's infrastructure along economic, rather than, say, social, lines.[41] Thus, within the arrangement of quasi-objects (from the sculptures themselves to the interface and where they are placed), the politics of sponsorship—and specifically, *who* is sponsoring the decoration of sculptures—becomes flattened by the (m)app: community and local organization sponsors are placed with ambivalence alongside major international investment, financial and development firms that have contributed to increasing inequality within the city.

The *Bee in the City* project overall raised £1.1 million. Wild in the City, the creative partner in the project, has replicated similar public art installations in cities across the world—Bristol, São Paulo, and Melbourne.[42] The assembly and arrangement of quasi-objects through combinations of sculptures and mobile apps is formulaic but works precisely—as described above—because of the relationship between mobile mapping and play.

Yet, crucially, if mobile mapping is a situated practice, and play is about re-creating worlds, then the material, spatial and political specificity of the project matters. Like play itself, the symbolic meaning of the bees is ambiguous and elastic. Their status as quasi-objects lead to further ambiguity, interpreted and re-interpreted by sponsors, artists, and (m)appers. Thus, play at once opens up the creative re-exploration of the city through hybridizations of moving and looking but also might minimize or even obscure the political structures encompassed within that hybridization.

## *Wayfinder Live*: Ambiguities, Affordances and Post-Gallery Art

In 2016 the Melbourne based artist Troy Innocent developed the Augmented Reality (AR) game *Wayfinder Live*, which has since been played in diverse urban environments like Bristol, Tampere, Taipei, Barcelona, and Melbourne. Dispersed through an urban environment, colourful small "tokens" or tags can be found and photographed with an app. Here the tags are foregrounded more than those on the bees in *Bee in the City*. Placed in sight are little panels "stitched" together in beautiful geometrical shapes attached to walls and other urban interfaces.[43] Their bright colour and style contrasts with the red and grey hues of urban materials and clashes in style with fading graffiti tags.

Similar to the bees in Manchester, this transforms the city into a playground, but also into a curated space akin to a post-digital museum.[44] Also similar to *Bee in the City*, one does not need to engage with the sculptures via a mobile app. As these tags or codes are attached to walls and other city surfaces, even before taking our mobile devices out of our pockets or bags, we are already encountering a hybridized quasi-object of wall and visual thing which includes urban, aesthetic and playful affordances. On its own, the wall is inviting us to stop or diverge and to *move* in another direction. But the striking tokens—which almost look like mini-pictures on a museum wall—entice us to stop and stand still. Thus, the clashing aesthetics and affordances of the token and the wall produce a new relationality for the passer-by. Together the wall and the tag, in themselves motionless and dumb, entice us to look and pause, before continuing our journey, whether as part of the *Wayfinder* "tour" or as a person on our way to work, or a *rendezvous*. In a subtle but more explicit way the tokens are quasi-object, ones that augment and aestheticize the relationality of the urban environment.

*Wayfinder Live* adds another mobile dimension to this playful experience. Now we have the graphic user interface (GUI) on our phone screens and are invited to turn our phones into the direction of walls and tokens. A series of translations or relationalities are set in motion, which the navigational and ludic interface on our screen—again, similar to *Bee in the City*, where players cross the city in different ways—create micro spatial stories through stitching the tokens together, thus creating imaginary spaces that go beyond the functionality of urban environments. Instead, the wall becomes a beacon that nudges you to a different way of traversing the urban environment and creates a new world of augmented interrelationality that the maker calls *Ludea*.

While *Bee in the City* is developed as part of a series of interactive objects whose sculptural forms are specific to the identity and culture of the city where each project is located, the *Wayfinder Live* artworks are portable from city to city. Arguably, the *Wayfinder Live* tokens are comparable to immutable mobiles. Much like Lt Cook's maps on the desk of La Perouse, their immutable form renders a continuity across time and space and between distinct urban environments. The project works based upon commonalities of the built environment, urban experience and city life. However, reconceptualizing the tokens as quasi-objects allows us to understand how the same objects become embedded and re-embedded in urban environments in ways that are both similar and unique to that city. The token is only part of the object—it is only "quasi," in that it requires the wall or the urban fabric to realize its affordances. At the same time, the wall itself is augmented by the tokens, and new affordances are generated, new possibilities explored and new situations anchored through their repositioning in different spaces and times. The mobile device is pivotal to becoming playful in the network of tokens across the city. Or as Innocent and Leorke write:

> [t]he ways in which they influence walking, navigation, and exploration of the city; [...] is a way of decoding the city so as to perceive it as a process or system, leading players to reimagine or reinvent the city through their play experience.[45]

They emphasize the way in which the processuality of the city as a system is laid bare via the playful *Wayfinder* app. The figure of the quasi-object adds yet another layer to this analysis as it allows us to understand the mobile device, or more precisely the GUI of *Wayfinder*, as not only inviting us to decode and reimagine the city, but also to produce new relationalities in which both the tokens and the app figure as quasi-objects, inviting us to spin micro stories that are assemblages of all kind of stuff.[46] Crucial to this is that the tokens and the app do more than just adding another layer to urban interfaces such as walls: they transform them into ludic *and* navigational interfaces, thus inviting us to approach them as ambiguous in use (is it a wall or a plaything?) and inviting us to produce new mobilities and spatial stories. This is where mobility, play and mapping forge new and creative relationalities.

## Conclusion: Hope and Failure

This chapter has considered how the relationship between mobile mapping and play affords possibilities for reassembling social and spatial relations in mobile media art. Using Serres' concept of the quasi-object, we map how the hybridization of both mapping and play has resulted in an extensive collection of actors—from technologies to users, material objects and architectures. Artworks that leverage the combined act of looking at shifting maps on mobile interfaces while touring around the city offer the opportunity to restructure urban relations, even if only temporarily, creating different navigational practices and spatial engagements. Furthermore, reading these formulations through the lens of the quasi-object, it becomes clear that mobile media art projects that use the combination of play and mobile mapping have the potential to turn the city into a playground through the hybridization of touring and looking.

We have explored the relation between art and mapping, especially in relation to play and mobility. We have argued that mapping and creativity have always had an intricate compatibility and share a long history, which has often been denied in the past in a bid to propagate the idea of maps as objective or serious, thus denying both an understanding of mapping as a hybrid and mobile practice, and being blind to the seriousness that play can harbour.[47] The intimate connection between mapping, play and mobility is in particular foregrounded in artistic mapping practices like locative art.

At the same time, following Sutton-Smith, we argue that the ambiguity of play may act as a force that de-politicizes, re-politicizes, or erases critical concerns about those social and spatial relations within mobile mapping and urban navigational mobilities.[48] This is hinged on precisely how different quasi-objects are arranged and formed through mobilities, interactions and explorations. In the case of *Bee in the City*, the bee sculptures invite a re-engagement of urban touring through locating and unlocking bees, participating in divergent urban practices on a social scale, uploading and sharing experiences generated through the artwork via the app. Yet, these playful mobile mappings also smoothed over the economic structure of sponsorship that enabled the project to come into fruition. In doing so, it also smoothed over the economic and political inequalities embedded in Manchester's urban processes and development, flattening large corporate interests into the same level as local community organizations through the linguistic, semiotic and spatial arrangement of the interface and the sculptures. Thus, play at once makes visible the presence of these corporate interests within the city through branding, but also makes them invisible by relegating them to the edge, and obscuring urban economic inequalities.

Comparably, in the example of the *Wayfinder Live* app, the clandestine, hidden and mundane parts of the city become key spaces in hybrid play. Yet, *Wayfinder Live* engages far more directly and critically with the already existing material architectures of the city. Compared to the symbolic decoration of the bees as facets of Manchester's identity, the geometric tokens invite various kinds of urban engagement. Tokens can be found on walls of different textures and materials, requiring users to directly engage with the multitude of materialities, spaces and places of the city.

Using two case studies we have identified how mobile media art playfully uses complex arrangement of quasi-objects to open up opportunities to remap and reencounter urban environments. We argue that while the assembly and arrangement of quasi-objects is playful, how these quasi-objects are arranged is often intensely political in ways that are deeply contingent on the mobilities, technologies and socio-spatial relations involved. Therefore, when we consider how play and mobile mapping may operate in post-digital environments, we argue that it is absolutely crucial to consider how digital and material politics become folded into how quasi-objects are arranged.

The hybridization of quasi-objects, or even their arrangement, while also allowing a plurality of interpretation and action, may also present only a singular or partial interpretation, stripped of political, situated or cultural meaning. Thus, in analysing the political and social consequences of mobile media art using mobile mapping and play, the way in which quasi-objects are assembled—and the limitations placed on their affordances—is crucial. This is magnified by the ambiguity of play itself.

Moving away from the notion of maps as being too static a notion to analyse such practices, we wanted to emphasize the "ings of things" in this chapter and focus on processes of translations and processuality that are pivotal to such artworks.[49] In the same vein, we approached artistic mapping practices as a network of quasi-objects with particular mobile and relational affordances that are both playful and mobile. Their mobility lies in their capacity to invite users to move in different ways and their navigational affordances to produce micro spatial narratives as assemblages. Their playfulness is related to their ambiguity in which a bee can become simultaneously a sculpture, playful beacon, and advertisement or a tag on a wall, transforming its surface in a more ambiguous urban interface with more than one meaning. Thus, new interrelationalities are spun that are situated and work between different planes of (urban) environments. That is, if the passer-by wants to pick up on this. Otherwise there is nothing and mobility and play do not bring a collective into being.

Here, we make a final argument: in mobile mapping and play, politics are played out through relations and relationality. Furthermore, the quasi-object is neither political nor apolitical. Instead, it is both at once: it holds numerous possibilities for action and for structuring intersubjectivities—all, some or none of which may be realized. This realization is dependent on the collection of other objects, subjects or quasi-objects that come into contact with the quasi-object. This is evident in the similarities and disparities of both the case studies discussed: the urban, social, spatial and economic contexts, where and how sculptures are placed, what the app invites or asks, all shape the broader consequences, social impact, and engagement of mobile media art.

## Notes

1 Brian Quinn and William Cartwright, "Geographic Board Games," *Proceedings of the 2014 Geospatial Science Research 3 Symposium (GSR_3)*, 2–3 December 2014 Melbourne Australia.

2 Marc Tuters and Kazys Varnelis, "Beyond Locative Media: Giving Shape to the Internet of Things," *Leonardo* 39, no. 4 (2006): 357–63. doi: 10.1162/leon.2006.39.4.357.

3 Gavin Macdonald, "Traces, Tiles and Fleeting Moments: Art and the Temporalities of Geomedia," in *Time for Mapping: Cartographic Temporalities*, edited by Alex Gekker, Sam Hind, Sybille Lammes, Chris Perkins, Clancy Wilmott, and Daniel Evans (Manchester: Manchester University Press, 2018), 138–53.

4 Ester Polak, Jerome Kee and Waag Society, *Amsterdam Real Time: a Diary in Traces*. 2002.

5 Johan Huizinga, *Homo ludens: proeve eener bepaling van het spel-element der cultuur* (Amsterdam: Amsterdam University Press, 1938), 199.

6 Sybille Lammes, "Destabilizing Playgrounds: Cartographical Interfaces, Mutability, Risk and Play," in *Playful Disruption of Digital Media*, edited by Daniel Cermak-Sassenrath (Singapore: Springer, 2018): 87–98.

7 Sybille Lammes and Clancy Wilmott, "The Map as Playground: Location-Based Games as Cartographical Practices," *Convergence: The International Journal of Research into New Media Technologies* 24, no. 6 (2016): 648–65, doi: 10.1177/1354856516679596.

8 Mihaly Csikszentmihalyi, "Play and Intrinsic Rewards," *Journal of Humanistic Psychology* 15, no. 3 (1975): 41–63, doi: 10.1177/002216787501500306.

9 Brian Sutton-Smith, "The Epistemology of the Play Theorist," *Behavioural and Brain Sciences* 5, no. 1 (1982): 170–71.

10 Brian Sutton-Smith, *The Ambiguity of Play* (Cambridge, MA: Harvard University Press, 2001).

11 Miguel Sicart, *Play Matters* (Cambridge, MA: The MIT Press, 2014), 2.

12 Miguel Sicart, "Quixotean Play in the Age of Computation," *American Journal of Play* 10, no. 3 (2018): 262.

13 Clancy Wilmott, *Mobile Mapping: Space, Cartography and the Digital* (Amsterdam: Amsterdam University Press, 2019).

14 J. B. Harley, "Deconstructing the Map," *Cartographica* 26, no. 2 (1989): 1–20.

15 Chris Perkins, "Performative and Embodied Mapping," in *International Encyclopedia of Human Geography*, edited by Rob Kitchin and Nigel Thrift (London: Elsevier, 2009), 126–132.
16 Clancy Wilmott, "In-Between Mobile Maps and Media: Movement," *Television & New Media* 18, no. 4 (2016): 320–35.
17 Sybille Lammes and Chris Perkins, "An Introduction to Playful Mapping in the Digital Age," in *Playful Mapping in the Digital Age*, edited by Playful Mapping Collective (Amsterdam: Institute of Network Cultures, 2016), 12–27.
18 Sybille Lammes, "Digital Mapping Interfaces: From Immutable Mobiles to Mutable Images," *New Media & Society* 19, no. 7 (2017): 1019–33, doi: 10.1177/1461444815625920.
19 Michel Serres, *The Parasite* (Minneapolis: University of Minnesota Press, 2007), 224–35.
20 Ibid., 224.
21 Ibid.
22 Ibid., 227.
23 Bruno Latour, "Visualization and cognition: Drawing things together," *Knowledge and Society* 6 (1986): 1–40, doi: 10.22394/0869-5377-2017-2-95-15.
24 Kim Dovey and Stephen Wood, "Public/Private Urban Interfaces: Type, Adaptation, Assemblage," *Journal of Urbanism: International Research on Placemaking and Urban Sustainability* 8, no. 1 (2015): 1–16, doi: 10.1080/17549175.2014.891151.
25 Sybille Lammes and Clancy Wilmott, "The Map as Playground: Location-based Games as Cartographical Practices," *Convergence* 25, no. 6 (2016): 648–65, doi: 10.1177/1354856516679596.
26 James Gibson, *The Ecological Approach to Visual Perception* (New York: Psychology Press, 2015); Donald Norman, *The Design of Everyday Things, Revised and Expanded Edition* (Cambridge, MA: The MIT Press, 2013).
27 Mathias Fuchs, "Ludic Interfaces. Driver and Product of Gamification," *G | A | M | E The Italian Journal of Games Studies* 1, no. 1 (2012): 19–26.
28 Latour, "Visualization and Cognition."
29 Sutton-Smith, *The Ambiguity of Play*.
30 Dovey and Wood, "Public/Private Urban Interfaces."
31 Clancy Wilmott, Emma Fraser and Sybille Lammes, "'I Am He. I Am He. Siri Rules': Work and Play with the Apple Watch," *European Journal of Cultural Studies* 21, no. 1 (2017): 78–95, doi: 10.1177/1367549417705605.
32 Jean Burgess, "The iPhone Moment, the Apple Brand, and the Creative Consumer: From 'Hackability and Usability' to Cultural Generativity," in *Studying Mobile Media: Cultural Technologies, Mobile Communication, and the iPhone*, edited by Larissa Hjorth, Ingrid Richardson and Jean Burgess (London: Routledge, 2012), 28–42.
33 Marc Tuters. "From Mannerist Situationism to Situated Media," *Convergence* 18, no. 3 (2012): 267–82, doi: 10.1177/1354856512441149; Gavin MacDonald, "Moving Bodies in the Inhabitable Map: The GPS Trace in New Media Art," PhD Thesis, Manchester Metropolitan University (2012).
34 Larissa Hjorth and Ingrid Richardson, "Pokémon *GO*: Mobile Media Play, Place-Making, and the Digital Wayfarer," *Mobile Media and Communication* 5, no. 1 (2017): 3–14, doi: 10.1177/2050157916680015.
35 Adriana de Souza e Silva and Larissa Hjorth, "Playful Urban Spaces: A Historical Approach to Mobile Games," *Simulation & Gaming* 40, no. 5 (2009): 602–25, doi: 10.1177/1046878109333723.
36 Monika Büscher, "Moving Methods," in *Routledge Handbook of Interdisciplinary Research Methods*, edited by Celia Lury, Rachel Fensham, Alexandra Heller-Nicholas, Sybille Lammes, Angela Last, Mike Michael, and Emma Uprichard (London: Routledge, 2018), 167–82.
37 Adriana de Souza e Silva, "From Cyber to Hybrid: Mobile Technologies as Interfaces of Hybrid Spaces," *Space and Culture* 9, no. 3 (2006): 261–78, doi: 10.1177/1206331206289022.
38 Mizuko Ito, Daisuke Okabe, and Misa Matsuda, *Personal, portable, pedestrian: Mobile phones in Japanese life* (Cambridge, MA: The MIT Press, 2005).
39 Serres, *The Parasite*, 233.
40 Wild in Art and Manchester City Council, *Bee in the City*, Manchester, 23 July to 23 September 2018, https://beeinthecitymcr.co.uk/.
41 Mike Hodson, Simon Marvin and Andy McMeekin, "The Amenable City-Region: The Symbolic Rise and the Relative Decline of Greater Manchester's Low Carbon Commitments, 2006–2017," in *Rethinking Urban Transitions: Politics in the Low Carbon City*, edited by Andrés Luque-Ayala, Simon Marvin, and Harriet Bulkeley (London: Routledge, 2018), 91–106.
42 Wild in Art, 2018.
43 Dovey and Wood, "Public/Private Urban Interfaces."

44 Lissa Holloway-Attaway and Rebecca Rouse, "Designing Postdigital Curators: Establishing an Interdisciplinary Games and Mixed Reality Cultural Heritage Network," in *Advances in Digital Cultural Heritage*, edited by Marinos Ioannides, João Martins, Roko Žarnić, and Veranika Lim (New York: Springer, 2018), 162–73.

45 Troy Innocent and Dale Leorke, "Heightened Intensity: Reflecting on Player Experiences in Wayfinder Live," *Convergence* 25, no. 1 (2019): 18–39, doi: 10.1177/1354856518822427.

46 Michel de Certeau, *The Practice of Everyday Life* (London: Routledge, 1984).

47 Huizinga, *Homo ludens.*

48 Sutton-Smith, *The Ambiguity of Play.*

49 Celia Lury, Rachel Fensham, Alexandra Heller-Nicholas, Sybille Lammes, Angela Last, Mike Michael and Emma Uprichard (eds), *The Routledge Handbook of Interdisciplinary Research Methods* (London: Routledge, 2018).

# 20
# TAPPING IN
## Playful Mobile Media Art in Australia

*Hugh Davies and Will Balmford*

In the early stages of the new millennium, the mobile phone—like the equally new internet—had in short time become a storied medium. Rumors of the emergent fields of mobile media art trickled through to Australia from abroad. Whispers of immersive new possibilities with tantalizing labels such as "mixed reality gaming,"[1] "locative literature,"[2] "mobile dramas,"[3] "MS storytelling"[4] and "microcinema"[5] were being generated for and with the increasingly ubiquitous mobile phone—a device shrouded in technology but bristling with potential. Alongside a growing ubiquity in writing, rhetoric and communication,[6] mobile media opened up new avenues within the creative arts. Paradoxically, these tiny portable devices appeared to allow for a scale of arts practice previously unrealized, existing throughout and between the everyday lives of mobile users. The rise of smartphones in the late 2000s marked a dramatic shift in how arts practitioners created through mobile devices. Accordingly, the design limits of creative practice were rearticulated for the new platform.

This chapter recalls the emergence of playful mobile media art in the Australian context. We explore the pioneering efforts of key artists, arts organizations and community-based programs to promote new forms of creativity by exploring the potential of mobile media games and playful interventions. We discuss the work of Australian arts organizations such as dLux Media Arts based in New South Wales and the Australian Network for Art and Technology (ANAT) based in South Australia, who each facilitated and presented mobile media workshops for artists, technologists and youth. These key organizations formed the creative center of mobile art games in Australia. By recognizing the impact and possibilities of mobile devices, these groups aimed to empower creators by providing necessary skills and technical literacy to create personal narratives via the mobile phone. Offering neither a complete survey of the era or of the field, instead we aim to highlight a series of pioneers, developments, artworks and, moments in the establishment of mobile art in Australia.

Beginning with several early examples of mobile media art projects from around the world, this chapter considers key theories and examples of mobile media art and playable content prior to the meteoric rise of the smartphone. The first section shows the variety of mobile-inspired work that proliferated in the early 2000s and the creative energy the technology provoked. The second and major section focuses on the Australian context, detailing how mobile phones were ingratiated into creative practice by exploring the growth of mobile games and art in Australia from the early 2000s onwards. Our exploration here traces the shifting contours of design and creative practice within the Australian mobile art discipline, using mobile media art to explore how design practices have reformed around changing criteria. We conclude with insights into potential futures and offer questions for future research into the intersections between mobile art and the Australian media landscape.

## Early International Mobile Media Art Experiments

Through the early 2000s, technical improvements in mobile devices were constant. New models brought dramatic reductions in device size and ever impressive expansions of screen space, storage capacity and processing capability. The growth in ubiquity and increasing intrusion of mobile devices in social spaces and interactions became a central point of discussion. Deep human relationships developed with these portable technologies that were carried close to one's body at all times, even during the night, provoking new levels of technological intimacy. Mizuko Ito, Daisuke Okabe and Misa Matsuda's edited volume *Personal, portable, pedestrian: Mobile phones in Japanese life*[7] pioneered research into the integration of *keitai* (mobile phone) in Japanese daily life, defining mobile technology internationally as a personal accessory allowing for ongoing social connection. The dramatic social and societal changes of mobile phones Ito and others detail evidenced a medium rich with creative potential. Much of the innovative work was pioneered internationally in Vodafone's now defunct *Receiver* magazine—specifically Mimi Ito's work on mobiles and the appropriation of place[8] and danah boyd's discussion of digital socialization.[9] These texts spread discussion of mobile phones as an important spatial and social medium and expanded academic engagement with the burgeoning technology.

In the field of arts, mobile devices were also making a sizable impact. In the United States, Golan Levin had created *Dialtones, A Telesymphony*[10] a concert piece that riffed on annoying mobile phones in theater settings. With attendees providing their mobile phone numbers at the beginning, the concert involved the choreographed calling and ringing of audience members' mobile phones to create the musical performance. Levin's work built a collective narrative through its engagement and distortion of social conventions, playfully tapping into the shifts and expectations of intimate mobile usage. In his artist's statement, Levin contends that: "Caught between adoration and irritation, we have come to regard our intimate communications apparel with a deep ambivalence."[11] This recognition of "intimate communications" was an ongoing focus of early mobile media art experiments and their artists, who were grappling with a changing social narrative of communication and interaction.

In the United Kingdom, artist Tim Etchells pioneered creative work using mobile communication with audience members. His work *Surrender Control* saw 75 text messages sent to participant players over five days with compelling commands such as:

> Write the word SORRY on your hands. Leave it there until it fades.
> Change something no one will notice.
> Call someone you hardly know.[12]

Existing somewhere between a game and a set of dares, *Surrender Control* opened up intimate spaces and situations in the everyday. Meanwhile in Berlin, the Chaos Computer Club had transformed a dilapidated office building in Berlin's Alexanderplatz into a giant interactive screen. Each of the building's windows was rendered into a pixel using lights turned on and off by computer. Passers-by were able to send text messages or play "pong" on the massive screen accessible via mobile phones. *Blinkenlights* created a deep sense of local pride in the downtown Berlin area, and a huge party was held to farewell the beloved installation in 2003.[13]

For some, these works represented something radically new in that they "explore the simultaneously public and intimate characteristics of mobile messaging. They scratch the surface of what's possible with mobile phone art and related technologies."[14]

For others, they recalled the interpersonal ambitions of 1960s' social performances albeit through digital technologies. This social/technological juxtaposition evoked and invited Relational Aesthetics in their understanding of "how communication technologies have created a series of fissures in everyday life, a series of moments when some small act—a phone call, text message or a letter—creates the possibility of stepping into someone else's world."[15] As seen in the examples above, many of these works also facilitated playful and game-like interactions with mobile technology.

The broader cultural impact of mobile devices was articulated at the introduction of the 2004 International Symposium of Electronic Art (ISEA) at which it was declared that "mobile devices are turning from communication media to become expressive media, sites for arts, social engagement, and … entertainment."[16] By this time, mobile phones were not just a portable device, they signaled a technology revolution.

## Australian Mobile Media Art in the Early 2000s

Meanwhile in Australia, the cultural implications of mobile devices were also gaining momentum. While advances in mobile technology typically arrived 12 months behind Scandinavia and Europe and ran on a different system to those in Japan, nonetheless local artists created their own mobile expressions. Notable pioneers were Lucas Ihlein and Jane Simon who developed *KeyPadPomes*[17]— a collection of hundreds of SMS poems and haiku. These micro poems were transcribed, typeset and silk-screened onto cardboard, before being cut into postcards and distributed by hand with an accompanying mobile phone number to ensure more submissions could be collected toward a growing archive of intimate prose.

The capacity for deeply personal, intimate and sensorial gestures that the mobile phone enabled recalled previous handheld media such as the letter,[18] the postcard,[19] and the hand-fan.[20] Mimi Ito initiated discussion around the intimate and ubiquitous dimensions of mobile media, especially in terms of intimate copresence.[21] Likewise, Dean Keep and Marsha Berry observed that, in its ubiquity and intimacy, the mobile phone had become "an extension of the self."[22] Mobile devices had enabled viewers to interact with story content and influence the direction of the interactive narrative of their own lives.

It was increasingly understood by arts organizations that in order to embrace this global mobile revolution locally, they had to be responsive by advocating and educating on the creative possibilities of this new medium. Leadership was taken up by two Australian digital arts organizations: the Australian Network for Art and Technology (ANAT) and dLux MediaArts (dLux). From its inception as the Sydney Super 8 Group in 1982—through to the Sydney Intermedia Network in the 1990s—dLux has been committed to supporting the development, engagement and experience of Australian screen and digital media culture.[23] ANAT, conversely, had established more recently in 1988 with the remit of connecting artists with emerging science technologies and research.[24] For those in the arts community, science and technology represented potent mediums of creative expression for artists to employ. Much of dLux and ANAT's prior activity through the 1990s had already been focused toward facilitating workshops, masterclasses and other training events that skilled-up artists in new digital technologies. To deliver similar skills development in the technicalities and affordances of the mobile platform, ANAT and dLux, along with the support of Australian Interactive Media Industry Association (AIMIA) and the Australia Council for the Arts formed the *Mobile Journeys* Consortium—a national group of not-for-profit bodies collaborating to promote and facilitate explorations of the creative potential of mobile devices.[25] This national initiative would see a broad gamut of training, industry collaboration, creative activity and exhibition outcomes that reverberated for many years to come.

Projects begin in January 2004, with a four-day FutureScreen Mobile masterclass titled *Aware: shared mobile experience(s)* held at dLux Media Center in Sydney. The workshop featured Finnish-based artists John Evans and Andrew Gryf Paterson. The pair presented how mobile phones manifested in performances, poetry, and social experiments as well as tactical architectures and playful storytelling with an awareness of local socio-economic conditions. The workshop also introduced the Aware platform, a prototype media blog, design tool and a production environment that existed between 2003 and 2005, constituting arguably the most sophisticated platform for publishing and syndicating of mobile media at the time. During its existence, Aware enabled and hosted experimental arts content for mobile and was featured as part of the International Symposium of Electronic Art (ISEA) in 2005.

The second iteration of *Mobile Journeys*—also in 2004—invited UK-based collective the-phone-book Limited as facilitating artists. The-phone-book Limited had been established in 2000 by Ben Jones, Fee Plumley and Ben Stebbing as a tactical gesture to define what kinds of art can be made for and by mobile media. In a strident anti-corporate stance and DIY ethic, the-phone-book Limited were determined not to let commercial interests monopolize the mobile revolution. Their explicit mission was to educate nonconformists, students, youths, artists and activists on how to create innovative content for mobile phones and basically to "get in quick before the telcos do and make a balls of the whole thing."[26] These workshops cultivated a deep sense of play. As one participant recalls: "I remember Fee telling us that the challenge for the morning was to 'crash our phone.' The point being to demonstrate these devices weren't delicate, that we should be playful and experimental with every aspect of the creative process."[27]

One of the-phone-book Limited's key tenets was that the mobile platform heralded a new interactive display format different from cinema, television, video and computers— it called for new content and screen vernacular created specifically for its parameters. "It just doesn't make sense to re-purpose old materials," said Ben Jones of the-phone-book Limited, "mobile video must have its own grammar!"[28]

For example, the 140-character limit of SMS mobile phones recalled the formal restraint of poetry forms such as *haiku*—whereby design limitations compelled readers to read between the lines. This ethos was augmented through the online micro-writing project *the.phone.book.com*, a Wireless Application Protocol (WAP) site that supported publication of SMS writing, capped at "the Mini Story (150 words or less), the Micro Story (50 words or less), and the Short Micro Story or SMS (15 characters or less)."[29] Through this WAP platform, authors were able to have their work published and hosted in a free and open mobile space (Figure 20.1).

The WAP design and micro-writing model offered by the-phone-book Limited presented an important new publishing model. Accessible for writers, poets and artists the WAP model enabled the SMS novel trend, a collective approach to micro-writing that mirrored similar mobile literature trends occurring in Japan with *Koizora* having 12 million readers in 2005.[30]

The-phone-book Limited became deeply ensconced in Australia's early mobile creative content development, becoming key partners with miniseries and the aforementioned *Mobile Journeys* to run workshops as well as to document the ideas that emerged with ANAT and dLux. They also did much to promote ethical business models to protect the rights of content developers within a commercial framework. Through the-phone-book Limited and Aware workshops, participants learned more than technical and creative skills but also developed literacy around the importance of free and open platforms, with each facilitator offering their own version—the-phone-book Limited's WAP and the Aware mobile publishing platform. Both the-phone-book Limited and Aware also keenly advocated local artists emulating their example by building and hosting mobile content from the ground up.

In Adelaide, throughout 2004, ANAT facilitated public programs exploring radical new possibilities of the mobile platform in locative art. ANAT invited UK groups Blast Theory and Mixed Reality Lab into the Adelaide Thinkers in Residence Program in partnership with Adelaide Fringe 2004. ANAT encouraged Blast Theory and Mixed Reality Lab to run a locative play masterclass that invited participants to consider the pervasive and locative affordances of mobile devices and how they could be used to create new playful and sensorial experiences of people and

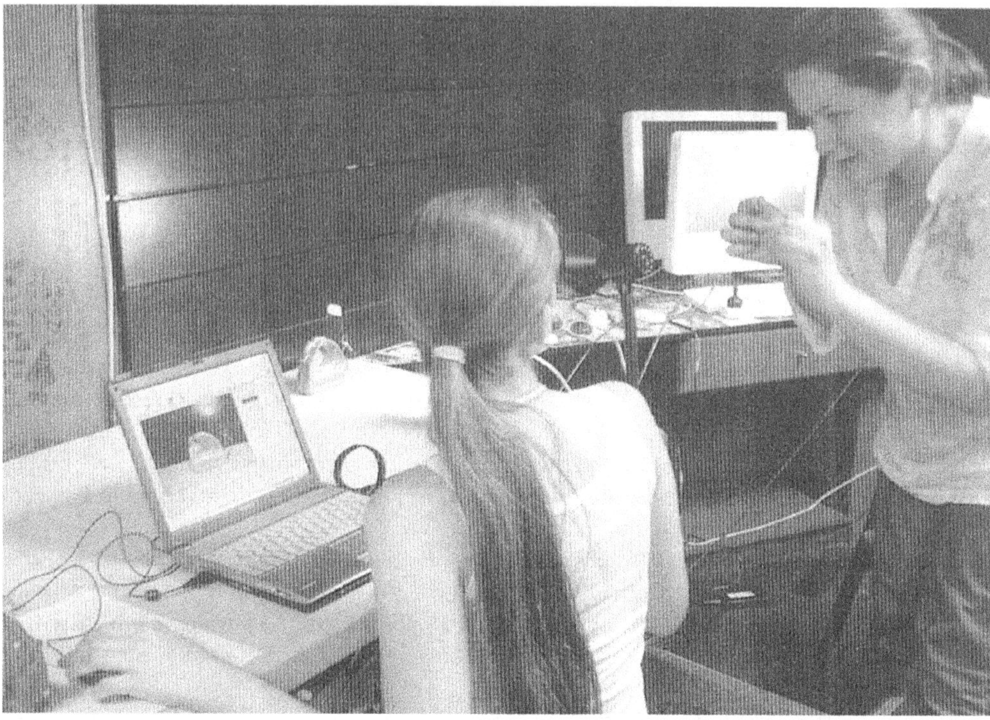

*Figure 20.1* Image from the-phone-book Limited workshops. Photo credit: ANAT, *Filter* Magazine

place. Blast Theory and Mixed Reality Lab also ran a mixed reality game titled *I Like Frank* on the streets of Adelaide that invited participation from the general public and involved several of their masterclass participants. The masterclass and mixed reality game would shape and inspire artists—both attending and otherwise—to pursue the creation of hybrid reality game experiences. The possibilities of mobile play had expanded out of the mobile interface and into city streets (Figure 20.2).

If 2004 had seemed on the verge of a mobile revolution, then 2005 was the year that mobile phone creativity exploded across Australia. The detonation occurred with the latest must-have consumers gadgets; 3G mobile handsets designed to receive and send high-speed multimedia. The sudden upsurge in 3G phones and other technologies—mobile media devices such as PDA's, iPod's, MP3 Players, PSP (Play Station Portable)—allowed easy creation and publication of media and sparked a phenomenon of *moblogging* or *life caching*, activities defined by Trendwatching as: "collecting, storing and displaying one's entire life, for private use or for friends, family, even the entire world to peruse."[31] More broadly, mobile phone uptake and popularity increased as handsets became cheaper, featured larger screens, improved cameras, multimedia content, and storage capability. Film festivals began to feature mobile-movies in their programs (e.g. Adelaide and St Kilda Film Festivals) and the numerous "mobile media" art exhibitions, festivals and "locative media" events being held worldwide began to appear in Australia.[32] The mobile phone handset was becoming recognized as a site for both production and exhibition.

In the wake of the Blast Theory residency and the *Mobile Journey* masterclasses a year earlier, the locative potential of mobile technologies flourished. For example, Blast Theory participant Megan Heyward's *Traces*, a fusion of video documentary and emerging social media that revealed intimate secrets and shared moments from a range of iconic Sydney locations, was invited into the

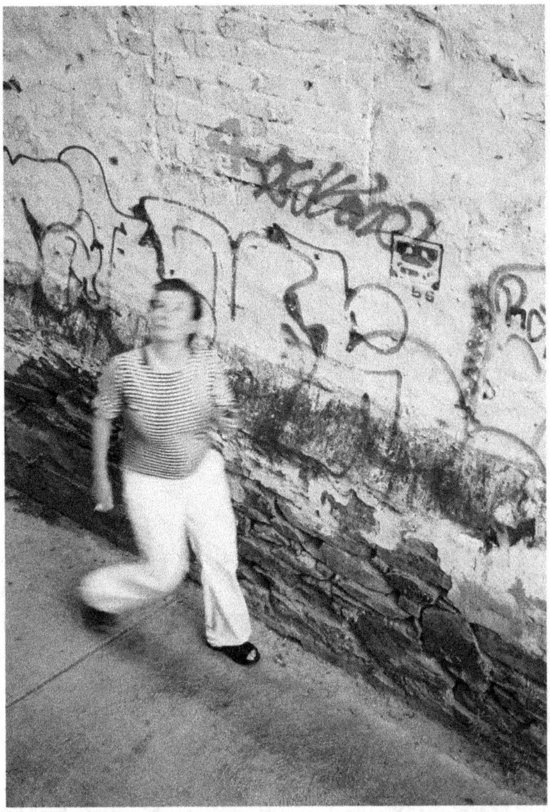

*Figure 20.2* *I Like Frank* in Adelaide (2005). The world's first 3G mixed reality game. Photo credits: Blast Theory

international program of the Pocket Film Festival at the Center Pompidou, Paris. *Mobile Journeys* alumni Hugh Davies created *Yestercry*, a pervasive game that led players to hidden locations via SMS messages and hand-drawn maps, an experience that would go on to be presented in Adelaide, Sydney and New York. Blast Theory participant Deb Polson created *Scoot*, a location-based game exploring mobile phones as tools of play. With support from the Victorian Government, *Scoot* would go on to be presented at the Australian Center for Moving Image in collaboration with National Gallery of Victoria, State Library of Victoria, the Arts Center and Melbourne Museum. Fellow Blast theory participant Troy Innocent would increasingly include locative and pervasive games in his urban code-making practice for the decade to come beginning with the *Micronation of Ludea* that first emerged in 2005 (Figure 20.3).

The miniseries initiative to support the development of creative applications for mobile devices kicked off in February 2005. It commenced a series of workshops, a forum program and the announcement of a production initiative that assisted digital media practitioners, film and video makers to develop works for delivery via mobile phone. Miniseries also involved a showcase of international programs for mobile phones at the Adelaide Film Festival 2005. The miniCinema—Australia's first mobile phone booth cinema—provided a viewing space for audiences to watch movies made specifically for mobile phones. Two programs of international short films were curated for miniCinema by Dooeun Choi from Art Center Nabi (Korea) and Fee Plumley (United Kingdom) from the-phone-book Limited.

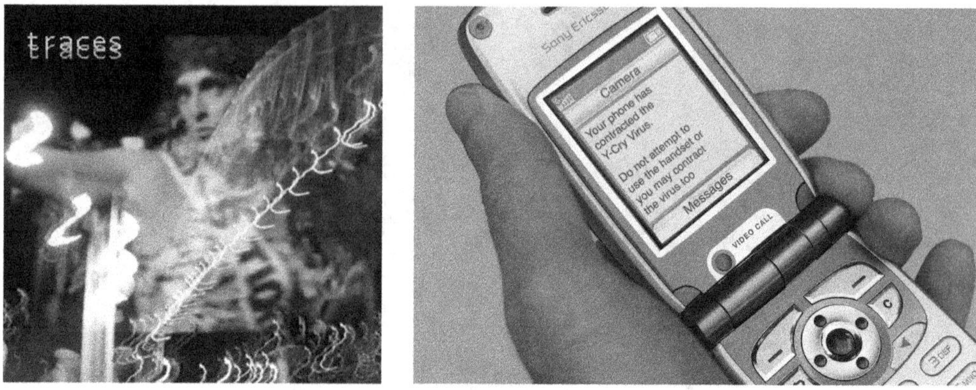


*Figure 20.3* Left: Image from the locative experience *Traces* (2006). Photo credit: Megan Heyward. Right: Images from the pervasive game: *Yestercry* (2005). Photo credit: Hugh Davies

In parallel, 2005 marked the appearance of artworks for mobile devices in major institutional spaces across Australia. The National Gallery of Australia presented the exhibition *Fullscreen: Explorations in digital media* which included both mobile phone works and a mobile content workshop presented by Ian Andrews. Not only did the *Mobile Journeys* workshops, masterclasses and professional forums continue, but the initiative also commissioned 14 Australian artists to create new games, videos, social networks, and interactive installations for mobile devices. A selection of these works was presented as part of D>Art.05 Exhibition at the Sydney Opera House in 2005, and then at the State Library of South Australia as part of ANAT's *Media State* program.

The exhibition featured works by Ian Andrews, Rebecca Cannon and Karen Jenkins, Chris Fullham, Tina Gonsalves, Ian Haig, Shane Ingram, Megan Heyward and Mark Simpson, all Australian artists growing in acclaim for their experimentation with the small screen. The conceit of the exhibition was that the art works were portable to the point that viewers were able to port them to their own mobile devices in an effort to inspire and challenge the way audiences thought about their phone and art (Figure 20.4).[33]

Beyond its embrace in the arts domain, 2005 also signaled the moment at which mobile content creation went commercially mainstream. This phenomenon was easily identifiable in the sudden emergence of the *mobisode*, a neologism conjoining the mobile delivery platform with the televisual episodic drama. However, vast differences in mobile platforms, devices and operating systems (OS) of the leading device manufacturers (Motorola, Nokia, Sony Erikson) meant that delivering video content across multiple handsets was almost impossible, rendering commercialization fraught. As a result, entire companies were set up and survived on "porting" or transcoding mobile content from one operating system and handset to another.

The mobile soap *Random Place* exemplified the limited possibilities of creating mass media for the micro screen.[34] At this time, ANAT Director Julianne Pierce noted of the Vodaphone delivered series;

> ...it has no sound and is delivered as a series of still images. Mainly comprised of close ups and big facial expressions, the dialogue is delivered via text captions embedded into the image. So, in an ironic twist for the expansion of high-tech gadgetry, Australia's first mobile phone soap opera is experienced in the form of a comic strip.[35]

But while this operating system competition created limitations that proved challenging for commercial enterprises, these challenges left ample room for creative experimentation.

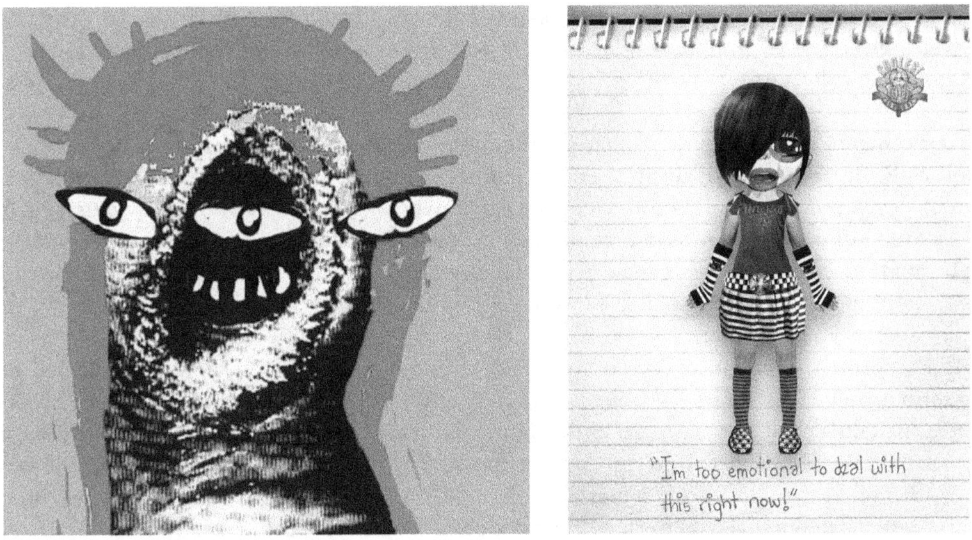


*Figure 20.4* Left: Ian Haig's possessed mobile phone in *Liberv rel reguli* (2005). Photo credit: Ian Haig, and Right: Avatar from Owen and Lanthois' *Coolest Girl in School* (2006) mobile game (Emo). Photo credit: Holly Owen and Karyn Lanthois

For example, Adelaide-based makers Holly Owen and Karen Lanthois created the mobile game *Coolest Girl in School.* To overcome the technical challenges of the platform, the game play utilized simple multiple-choice questions, which Owen described as "the type usually found in teen girl mags."[36] The game drew instant controversy with a tagline that invited teenage girls to "lie, b★★ch and flirt your way to the top of the high school ladder."[37] While parental, religious and feminist groups piled on to condemn the game, most did so without ever having played it—due to its limited availability on devices.

With increasingly popular games content emerging on the mobile platform, calls for publishing models that ensured the financial security and artistic integrity of creators grew. As Paul Daly, director of innovation of M.Net Consortiums whose 3G test bed played a key role in *Mobile Journeys*' experiments, commented:

> It is critical that experimental pioneers in this field — are in the position to assert creative control and expect solid remuneration from the consumers and from the telecommunications companies that profit from their work.[38]

Practitioners such as Larissa Hjorth whose activities straddled arts and academia began to investigate how users of mobile devices were playfully integrating these technologies into their everyday interactions and ways of being. Hjorth's exhibitions *Snapshots of Almost Contact* (2005) and *Snapshots: Portrait of the Mobile* (2006) drew attention to the increasing ubiquity of mobile devices and their deep yet intimate impact on the lives of users. Indeed, mobile phones were beginning to lose their veneer of newness. Just as mobile phones had permeated across all public and private spaces, likewise the production of artwork for mobile devices was increasingly seen as an established creative medium. In a 2006 government report into media arts activity, the authors stated:

> Artists are pushing the boundaries of everyday technologies as ubiquitous as the Internet, or the mobile phones and iPods people carry around in their pockets. Inherent within such

> experimentation are new ways to engage audiences, including possibilities to disseminate work direct to the public, which will have long-term implications for artists, arts organizations and galleries.[39]

Further cementing the institutionalization of mobile creative content, the Australian Film, Television & Radio School (AFTRS) began to run short courses, workshops and masterclasses on content development for mobile devices. Other universities and education providers began to follow suit. Although the ambitions of producing sophisticated games and interactive cinema lay just beyond the capability of the majority of handsets, it was widely understood that the platform would continue to develop rapidly, as would growing audience numbers for the content these mobile devices could deliver.

As is common with the uptake of any new technology, among the most curious and most contentious audiences for the mobile were youth. While children could not afford the new devices, parents began purchasing mobile phones for their children who took serious interest in the capabilities of these new devices. Against the duality of mobile content fever and the severe limitations of its actuality, former participants of ANAT and dLux workshops began running mobile content making classes to share knowledge of mobile content production to new generations of makers, specific to primary and secondary school-aged children. The most prominent of these was pixel.play.

Presented by ANAT, pixel.play was a digital media education program targeted toward youth. Developed by artist Sasha Grbich within the ANAT organization, pixel.play manifested as a series of touring workshops that aimed to "develop creative and digital literacy skills in youth participants. Young artists were skilled up to make short screen works (animations/films/images/logos and ringtones) for their mobile phone."[40] Between 2006 and 2008, pixel.play toured across regional South Australia delivering tactical media workshops ranging from three hours to five days in length. These projects also supported young artists by creating mentoring, arts festival participation, and online exhibition opportunities.

A collection of student and youth works from the pixel.play program were launched on the NOISE (National Youth Media Festival) website in January 2007.[41] Pixel.play won the Innovation in Digital Media award at the 2007 SA Short Screen Awards. Children were now developing and sharing sophisticated content from animations to short films in classroom and playground settings. Meanwhile the success of the *Mobile Journey* initiative had resulted in many artists incorporating mobile content into their practice, indeed so many that a number of exhibitions were held to showcase theirs works. The first of these was Portable Worlds, born in 2006.

Portable Worlds offered a survey of contemporary Australian new media artists working specifically for the mobile platform. The curated works reflected on the changing nature of communication, community, and creativity enabled by the mobile phone and explored the intimate viewing space of the hand-held device. Curated in late 2006 and touring in different versions over the following two years, the exhibition included works by Larissa Hjorth, Lisa Harms, Geraldine Bigelow, Christopher Fulham, Blaide Lallemand and Hilary Cuerden-Clifford, the Lycette Bros, Anita Bacic and Natalie Woodlock, Nicola Moore, and Lawrence English. Portable Worlds also incorporated a two-day workshop developed to complement the exhibition that sought to engage young artists aged 13–19 years to develop and execute their own creative works.

The Portable Worlds exhibition and education program confidently signaled the extent to which Australia had embraced the mobile phone as a creative platform. Arts content for portable devices appeared as established, nuanced and evolving, within a distinctly Australian context. Australia's leadership position was further bolstered by the 2007 Mobile Media conference in Sydney; the first international conference to focus on the social and cultural aspects of mobile phones, convergent media, and wireless technologies. Featuring leading scholars from across the globe, the conference brought comprehensive analysis and debate to mobile platforms, exploring emerging structures, practices, producers and audiences, and delving into its social, cultural and commercial implications.

By the time of the Mobile Media conference in 2007, rumors of the imminent iPhone had eventuated. Amid what had become an intensely complex and competitive ecology of smartphone technologies, platforms, and operating systems, the iPhone was keenly anticipated for its promise of introducing a unifying standard for mobile technologies. Indeed, in the United States, the enormous expectation of the device saw it bestowed the moniker: "The Jesus Phone" which became a frequent characterization of the product in blogging, tech reviews and ultimately the mainstream press.[42, 43] But the iPhone's walled garden and pay up-front publishing model represented a total inversion of the ideals set out by artists, trainers and developers in Australia only a few years earlier. The cost of publishing to mobile thinned the field of creative practitioners producing art for the platform but saw an increase in the number of commercial games developed for mobile by Australia's emergent community of independent game makers. Several artists continued to develop content in browsers and as apps, among them were the tactical media artworks by pvi collective,[44] the pervasive games of Troy Innocent and Hugh Davies,[45, 46] and the spatial and locative works of Megan Heyward. The mobile revolution was over, the platform having become invisible in its ubiquity.

It can be argued that the mobile development activities enabled by arts organizations in collaboration with industry partners entirely saved Australia's games industry, given that between 2005 and 2015, almost all of the major Australian-based game studios closed (KMM Brisbane, Pandemic Studios, Krome Studios, THQ, Visceral Games and 2K Australia). It was only due to the successes of the growing community of independent game developers, developing largely for mobile, that Australia's gaming industry survived. By October 2015, half of the top ten mobile games in the Apple App Store were Australian made.[47] Significant instances include *Fruit Ninja* (Half Brick Studios 2010), *Crossy Road* (Hipster Whale 2014) and *Florence* (Mountains 2018).

Today, Australian mobile creativity takes on dramatically different forms with the device, a conduit to more granular phenomena. The vast majority of activity occurs within global social media platforms that were all but non-existent in the country's pioneering days of mobile creativity. Yet not everything has changed. Mobile cinema remains an enduring, if niche form, with several organizations gathering together annually to recognize and reward its exponents. Most notable is MINA, the longest running film festival dedicated to celebrating mobile and smartphone film-making. The ubiquity and technical capability of mobile devices has also resulted in their recognition as a major games platform, to which many Australian game developers have contributed.

## Conclusion

Detailing several key moments and initiatives in Australian mobile art development from the early 2000s, we have explored how design literacy and creative practice for hand-held devices was pursued through community-based programs and spread across the country after the turn of the millennium. Looking into the future, it is interesting to note where mobile art and games may be headed. Recent work has shown a shift toward tablet usage in youth mobile device engagement,[48] with the increasing creation and distribution of mobile games. However, thanks to the rise of mobile-based streaming, creative practice through mobile devices is in no danger of elimination.

On the contrary, the new scenarios of use engaged by today's youth encourage further remediation of mobile media. Future research into this area might benefit from examinations of how changing mobile literacy levels alter the way design workshops take place, or the growing consideration of industry in best design and technology literacy. Such research could uncover further changes, offering alternative key moments to those we have outlined in this chapter. Alternatively, future research may uncover a decentralizing design focus as designers become increasingly adept at circumnavigating distribution guidelines or designing specifically to oppose them.

Throughout this chapter we have shown how the work of organizations such as dLux Media Arts and the Australian Network for Art and Technology were crucial in forming the creative center of mobile art in Australia. These organizations educated and enabled makers to extend public perceptions of new media technologies. Through workshops such as Mobile Journey, pixel. play, and the-phone-book Limited, particular emphasis was placed upon how education and playful engagement resulted in a proliferation of mobile art in a variety of manifestations. We have argued that such a manifestation of design has in part contributed to the productions of new forms of playful creative practice that highlight and unpack the potent capacity of mobile media as well as to lay the groundwork form the mobile game development industry that followed in its wake.

## Notes

1 Adriana de Souza e Silva and Daniel Sutko, *Digital Cityscapes: Merging Digital and Urban Playspaces* (New York: Peter Lang Publishing, 2009).
2 Anders Løvlie, "Locative Literature: Experiences with the Textopia System," *International Journal of Arts and Technology* 4, no. 3 (2011): 234–48, doi: 10.1504/IJART.2011.041479.
3 "Mobile Drama Round-Up," Christy Dena, www.christydena.com/2006/06/mobile-drama-round-up/.
4 Jennifer Stein, Scott Ruston and Scott Fisher. "Location-Based Mobile Storytelling." *International Journal of Technology and Human Interaction* 5, no. 1 (2009): 41–50. doi: 10.4018/jthi.2009010104.
5 "Tiny Art, Big Experience," Rhizome, https://rhizome.org/editorial/2006/mar/31/tiny-art-big-experience.
6 John Tinnell, *Actionable Media: Digital Communication Beyond the Desktop* (Oxford: Oxford University Press, 2018).
7 Mizuko Ito, Misa Matsuda and Daisuke Okabe, *Personal, Portable, Pedestrian: Mobile Phones in Japanese Life* (Cambridge, MA: MIT Press, 2005).
8 Mizuko Ito. "Mobiles and the Appropriation of Place" *Receiver* 8, 1 (2003), 4 September 2019, www.academia.edu/2717464/Mobiles_and_the_appropriation_of_place.
9 danah boyd. "Socializing Digitally," *Receiver* 18, no. 1 (2007), 4 September 2019, www.danah.org/papers/VodafoneReceiver.pdf.
10 Golan Levin, "Dialtones, A Telesymphony: Final Report," www.flong.com/storage/pdf/reports/dialtones_report.pdf; See also interview with Levin in Section 1 of this volume.
11 Golan Levin, "Dialtones," 5.
12 Tim Etchells, "Surrender Control", 27 July 2019, http://timetchells.com/projects/surrender-control/.
13 Chaos Computer Club, "Project Blinkenlights," http://blinkenlights.net/project.
14 Anna Davis, "Mobilizing Phone Art," 28.
15 Matt Locke, "Are You Awake? Are You In Love?", https://test.org.uk/2003/07/09/are-you-awake-are-you-in-love/.
16 Anna Davis, "Mobilizing Phone Art," 28.
17 Ibid.
18 Esther Milne, "The Art of Mobile Phone Empathy," *Realtime* 75 (2006): 34.
19 Larissa Hjorth, "Postal Presence: A Case Study of Mobile Customization and Gender in Melbourne," *Knowledge, Technology and Policy* 19, no. 2 (2006): 29–40, doi: 10.1007/s12130-006-1022-6.
20 Hugh Davies, "Fanology: Hand-Fans in the Prehistory of Mobile Devices," *Mobile Media & Communication* 7, no. 3 (2019): 303–21, doi: 10.1177/2050157919846181.
21 Mizuko Ito, "Mobiles and the Appropriation of Place."
22 Dean Keep and Marsha Berry, "Narratives in Miniature: Aesthetics for Mobiles," Paper presented at *Vital Signs: Creative Practice and New Media Now, Australian Center for the Moving Image*, September 2005. https://search.informit.com.au/documentSummary;dn=040824247239881;res=IELHSS.
23 See dLux MediaArts, www.dlux.org.au/history.
24 Mike Leggett, "The science and Art Synapse," *Realtime* 61 (2004): 38, www.realtimearts.net/article/issue61/7461.
25 ANAT, *Annual Report 2004* (Australia: Australian Network for Art and Technology, 2004).

26 Darren Tofts, "Dead to the World: The Future of Hand-Held Art," *Scan Journal* 4, no. 3 (2007), http://scan.net.au/scan/journal/display.php?journal_id=102.
27 Hugh Davies, interview with former phone-book Limited participant.
28 Ben Jones in Anna Davis, "Mobilizing Phone Art," 28.
29 Klare Lanson, "Q&A with Ben Stebbing," last modified 20 January 2004, http://cordite.org.au/guncotton/klare-lanson-interviews-ben-stebbing/.
30 Larissa Hjorth, "Stories of the Mobile: Cartographies of the Personal through a Case Study of Mobile Novels in Japan," in *Mobile Media Narratives*, edited by Jason Farman (Minnesota: University of Minnesota Press, 2013), 238–48.
31 "Lifecaching," Trendwatching, https://trendwatching.com/trends/LIFE_CACHING.htm.
32 Anna Davis, "Mobilizing Phone Art."
33 Sue Ballard, "dLux media arts—D>art05: Distributed Art and MobileJourneys," Filter, ANAT, issue 61 (2005).
34 Julianne Pierce, "The Fourth Screen," *Off the Air: Screenrights Newsletter* (2005), www.joemiale.com/press/screenrights_01.pdf.
35 Ibid.
36 Chloe Lake, "Aussie Game Creator Blasts Sex Critics," *News.com.au*, 23 October 2009, www.news.com.au/technology/aussie-game-creator-blasts-sex-critics/news-story/0ff588867b70e87f3013d4fbe66188d2?sv=a78bca39530a3ea8352908d058b54a8.
37 Ibid.
38 Samara Mitchell, "Miniseries: Episodic Adventures for Mobile Phones," *Filter Magazine* 59, no. 1 (2005), https://filter.org.au/issue-59/miniseries-episodic-adventures-for-mobile-phones/comment-page-1/.
39 Andrew Donovan, Sarah Miller and Elaine Lally, "New Media Arts Scoping Study Report to the Australia Council for the Arts, Report," September (2006), 13, https://apo.org.au/node/1672.
40 "Pixel Play," ANAT, www.anat.org.au/2010/06/pixel-play/.
41 Kirsten Krauth, "Noise: Youth Art, Making Links," *Realtime* 46 (2001): 17. www.realtime.org.au/noise-youth-art-making-links/.
42 Hugh Davies, "Religious Devices: A Survey of Technologies of Worship," *Communication +1* 7, no. 2 (2019): 5, https://scholarworks.umass.edu/cpo/vol7/iss2/5/
43 Heidi Campbell, *When Religion Meets New Media* (London: Routledge Palgrave Macmillan, 2010).
44 PVI Collective, "PVI Collective," https://pvicollective.com; see also the artist interview introducing this Section.
45 Hugh Davies and Troy Innocent, "The Space between Debord and Pikachu." *DiGRA '17—Proceedings of the 2017 DiGRA International Conference* 14, no. 1 (July 2017): www.digra.org/wp-content/uploads/digital-library/88_DIGRA2017_FP_Davies_Debord_and_Pikachu.pdf. Melbourne, Australia: Digital Games Research Association.
46 Matthew Riley, "The Augmented Bushwalk: Contemplative Play Across Digital Systems and Natural Worlds," 2018, https://commons.swinburne.edu.au/items/2bf17d21-d618-498a-8e7d-670847dfb364/1.
47 "Video games industry records $1.161 billion sales in 2012" Computer World, 13 February 2013, www.computerworld.com.au/mediareleases/15759/video-games-industry-records-1161-billion-sales/.
48 Will Balmford and Hugh Davies, "Mobile Minecraft: Negotiated Space and Perceptions of Play in Australian Families," *Mobile Media & Communication*, February 6 (2019). doi: 10.1177/2050157918819614n.

# 21

# AMBIENT PLAY AND BACKGROUND GAMING

## Reflecting on Quotidian Creative Practices

*Ingrid Richardson*

Mobile media interfaces have seen the rise and proliferation of new modes of digital and creative play, as mobile apps, services and games have become increasingly embedded in the interstices of our day-to-day lives. This chapter considers the notion of *ambient play* as a way to critically interpret the complex and diverse practices emerging from our use of mobile phones as portable game devices. Conceptually, ambient play takes a versatile and open approach to the experiential significance of mobile games and playfulness as fundamental creative practices, and aptly conveys the way mobile media are more broadly part of a manifold lusory and creative sensibility in contemporary culture. In particular, the chapter focuses on the way people frequently engage in playful mobile media practices in between other activities and in the moments of *waiting* that are peppered throughout urban life—in the many minutes spent on public transport, or while taking a short break from work or domestic tasks. The necessity of waiting has provided one of the experiential contexts for a new genre of videogame play that is especially popular on mobile platforms: the idle or background game.

The chapter begins with a critical overview of background games in the broader context of casual mobile games and identifies other nomenclature that is used to describe similar games within mobile media and game studies literature. Toward the end of this first section, it is argued that the concept of ambient play provides some insight into the way such games are perceived, experienced, and creatively enacted by players. The discussion then focuses on the way background games intersect with quotidian creative practices,[1] both in terms of players' productive management of time, and as an expressive and personalized form of playful labor. This interpretation of gameplay as labor also explores some of the negative effects of background games as theorized by both game critics and scholars alike.

In the final section, the chapter turns to ethnographic fieldwork to identify and describe some of the diverse ways people incorporate background games into their everyday lives. The scenarios described are representative of a subset of the data gathered in 2017–2018 through the *Games of Being Mobile* Australian Research Council (ARC) project, the first national study into mobile gaming that sought to explore Australian usage of mobile games around three major themes: place, space and practice. Participant engagement consisted of home visits and interviews to establish the household's history of mobile media usage and mobile gaming. Subsequent meetings were adapted around the particular routines and practices of a household, which included active sessions with participants and observations of daily household life through "home tours" and enactments of play.

## Background Games: Idle, Incremental, Interstitial and Interpassive

Mobile media, especially smartphone devices, are enabling users to engage in many kinds of digital play. They are used to socialize, to be antisocial, to experience mediated copresence, to be in the moment. The paradoxes and ambiguities surrounding creative practices, digital media and its playful capacities are often intensified by mobile games and the perception that they are trivial, pointless ways to spend one's time. In discussions with our participants, for example, many expressed a sense of ambivalence around the purposefulness of games. For example, Trish from Adelaide felt guilty playing *Tiny Tower* (NimbleBit 2011) at home while her girlfriend did more "worthwhile," productive and materially creative activities like knitting.[2] To counter this feeling, Trish would often get her mobile gaming "fix" during periods of waiting throughout her day—what Shira Chess refers to as *interstitial time*—when on public transport or while standing in line at a cafeteria.[3] Filling otherwise empty moments with mobile gameplay, Trish explained, was "somehow okay, because I'm not doing anything else, so I'm not actually *wasting* time." As this chapter suggests, background games such as *Tiny Tower* challenge and complicate existing understandings of "play" and "labor" around digital and mobile games.

In contrast to the enduring time and labor commitments of console or desktop computer games, smartphones have become home to a range of "casual" game genres that promote quick and flexible engagements. People frequently play mobile games while doing other things—waiting at the bus stop or for a friend to arrive, in the moments between household chores, or in conjunction with watching the "lean back" medium of television. This phenomenon has seen the increasing popularity of what are referred to as idle games,[4] interpassive or incremental games,[5] interstitial or invest/express games,[6] and background games.[7] Such games are particularly organic to mobile interfaces because mobile screens are typically engaged with intermittently, while the user is waiting for something to happen or arrive, or in between everyday activities.[8]

As Alharthi et al. explain,[9] idle games are those which require limited player interaction—where the player sets up the conditions for game progress that occurs even when the game is not being played. Such games, they claim, shift the player's focus from playing to *planning*, and question dominant assumptions about the nature of gameplay. Sonica Fizek's insightful analysis of incremental games and interpassivity suggests that self-playing or clicker games—games characterized by nominal participation and automated gameplay that requires the player to perform the minimal task of clicking—exemplify the "joy of delegated play" and challenge the way we think about games as fundamentally interactive media forms.[10]

Chess examines the industry category of "invest/express" games such as *Farmville* (Zynga 2009) and *Clash of Clans* (Supercell 2012), which draw players into a repetitive cycle of investment (of both time and money) through mechanisms of personal expression and affect (e.g., via individualized arrangement and decoration of the game space). Invest/express games focus "less on social gaming and more on temporal gaming aspects… best characterized by the push and pull of time."[11] That is, the player is "pulled" by the necessity of attending to the game at regular intervals, but time-based parameters on resource acquisition are "pushed" away after a short duration of play. For example, *Farmville* progresses with the aid of virtual currency that must be accumulated over time in order to play. Akin to these forms of gameplay, and especially idle games, background games are those that require the player to set up a series of tasks which are carried out "in the background" while the player goes about their day, occasionally checking into the game to reap its rewards and queue up new tasks. Mobile games such as *Tiny Tower*, *Simpsons: Tapped Out* (EA Mobile 2012), *Godus* (22cans 2014) and *Fallout: Shelter* (Bethesda 2015) fall into this category, as they all involve player-initiated tasks that can take anywhere from a few minutes to days of real time to complete.

While these game genres have some variations, all point to the way that the social, material and economic contexts of mobile phone practices have given rise to genres of digital play based not around playing but around *waiting* to play. Whereas mobile play has been previously theorized as part of social practices of waiting, mobile games are commonly played intermittently in between daily activities.[12] These background, idle and interstitial games formally integrate the *necessity of waiting* into their mechanics. They accommodate the fact that players typically play mobile games for a few minutes at a time, yet they effectively instill a sense of progression reward and achievement over a much longer duration. They are also mostly repetitive and endlessly cyclic, with no specific goal or end, and in this way they play into existing economic pressures faced by mobile game developers in designing "freemium" games; instead of paying for the game at the outset, players who prefer not to wait (for free) are given the option to progress instantly via in-app purchases or micro-transactions, and they can continue doing so perpetually.

Background games are also a subset of the broader genre of mobile casual games, but importantly complicate how such games are often conceptualized. Casual games first received committed scholarly attention by Jesper Juul in *A Casual Revolution*,[13] but have also been a popular topic in mobile media and game studies, in part due to their prolific rise and substantial capture of the global game market. Often, the temporal and spatial flexibility, and the low-barrier mimetic and haptic features of many mobile touchscreen games, are contrasted against console and desktop computer games that demand higher-level skills and deep involvement in elaborate storyworlds. This flexibility is partially due to an effect of the familiar and haptic intimacy of mobile screens. That is, once a player is familiar with the "feel" of a mobile game, they have an intuitive sense of the cadence of play—what hand movements are required, when eyes must focus on the screen, when there are gaps in the play—that allows for oscillation between the background and foreground of visual, aural and embodied attention. And yet as mobile games become more sedimented in our quotidian lives, this notion of casual play doesn't fully address the complex and diverse ways in which time, labor and presence are framed within that engagement.

The term casual game problematically suggests that the labor of casual players is somehow less committed or less significant than those of non-casual or "hardcore" gamers, an assumption that has been critiqued by both game developers and researchers within mobile media and game studies. Larissa Hjorth and Ingrid Richardson suggest that the alternative term "ambient play" is better able to account for mobile play as "thoroughly embodied, situated, and social."[14] Drawing from the work of Paul Dourish[15] and Paul Roquet[16] on ambient media, ambient play

> enables a flexible and open approach to games and playfulness more generally, as it effectively incorporates the various ways we engage with and embody mobile games in our everyday lives, deliberately moves beyond the problematic ascription of the term 'casual' to mobile games, and conveys the way mobile media are part of a lusory sensibility in contemporary culture.[17]

Like casual, ambient accounts for the flexibility required by certain kinds of digital games, especially those on mobile devices. Unlike casual, however, ambient does not suggest the same sense of triviality or lack of commitment. An ambient game may be only played for five minutes at a time, but importantly, it can also be imbued with a sense of ever-presence, filtering into numerous quotidian contexts as the player goes about their day, like a low hum in the background. They can therefore be understood as conduits of modalities of play that hold cultural significance in terms of our critical understanding of everyday life practices.

In definitional terms, there is also considerable overlap between background games and what have been defined as "social games," or games that are played through social networking sites (SNS) such as Facebook. Many social games, specifically those that involve resource or time management (such as *Farmville*) also require background activities such as daily "checking in," periodic resource management, rewards for mini-game achievements, waiting for tasks to complete, and intermittent attendance to and maintenance of a simulated environment. In this way, social games, like background games, quite deliberately "accommodate real life necessities"[18] by allowing players to embed gameplay in the routines and habitudes of everyday life. As Christopher Moore comments, we no longer "consciously take games with us in order to access diverse ludic experiences"; rather, our play operates across work and leisure domains, and domestic and public spaces, following us "in new ways, through digital distribution services, across social networks and over cloud-based applications."[19] This aptly describes how contemporary game practices are enactments of ambient play.

In their embodiment of ambient play, background games invert the relationship between mobile play and practices of waiting as it is commonly understood. Instead of games that are played while the player is waiting, these are games that the player *waits to play*. While most of the time they are situated in the background of awareness, at various intervals they make themselves known according to real-time progression, thus demanding a certain rigidity and *inflexibility* typically understood as the inverse of good casual or ambient design. Participants in our study described how they would deliberately plan the task-setting in their background games to ensure ongoing progression and achievement, effectively enacting a *correlation* between gameplay and everyday life activities. In a very real sense, this kind of play is not actually playing, but *waiting*. Players are aware of the time-sensitive actions required in the game and will often arrange their daily activities in ways that permit checking-in to assess the status of various tasks; this involves making subtle changes to their temporal routines. In the following section, the discussion further explores the way background games are embroiled with practices and perceptions of productivity, the experience of waiting and the everyday management of time.

## Playing or Not Playing: Labor, Temporality and Play in the Quotidian Context

Conversations among social and media researchers concerning affective labor and playful creativity have often been contentious, with some arguing for the subversive potential of play,[20] while others emphasize the corporate exploitation of users and players.[21] However, in everyday life these divisions, as Judy Wajcman identifies,[22] are blurry and more uncertain. Indeed, spatial and temporal boundaries between public and private, work and leisure have often been unclear—a characteristic that mobile games exploit.

Time has also become a key question for many contemporary theorists of digital media. In *Social Acceleration,* Hartmut Rosa argues that the temporal fabric of society has changed.[23] He identifies three categories of change: technological acceleration (manifested in transportation, communication and production); the acceleration of social change (as witnessed in the cultural, social and interpersonal domains) and acceleration in the pace and temporal demands of life (despite the expectation that technological change should increase free time, as first heralded in the 1980s). In particular, Rosa notes that media practices are marked by a "shrinking" of temporal and spatial perception whereby the relationality between the past, present, and future diminishes.[24] For feminist scholar Wajcman, many of the paradoxes associated with time and leisure are interwoven with our understandings of technology.[25] Arguing that it is indeed humans not technologies that expand and blur priorities and parameters, Wajcman observes that "being busy" has become a key performance indicator of our productivity and task driven culture.[26] In this context, enforced periods of waiting and inertia, however short, are experienced as moments of bodily agitation, frustration and lost productivity.

Yet importantly, waiting can be conceptualized in other, more productive and affirmative ways. In the discerning historical exploration of the cultural and experiential modalities of waiting,

*Delayed Response: The Art of Waiting from the Ancient to the Instant World,* Jason Farman[27] argues that despite the desire and promise of immediate fulfillment that predominate in the digital age, waiting is a crucial part of our communicative lives and collective ways of knowing, and fundamental to our well-being:

> Waiting shapes our social lives in many ways, and waiting is something that can benefit us. Waiting can be fruitful. If we lose it, we will lose the ways that waiting shapes vital elements of our lives like social intimacy, the production of knowledge, and the creative practices that depend on the gaps formed by waiting.[28]

As will be discussed in the following section, many of our participants described how idle and background mobile games were deployed in positive, reflective, expressive and mindful ways. In this way, we might consider how such games are part of the broader spectrum of vernacular or quotidian creativity[29] and innovative everyday praxes that typify our engagement with contemporary media.

Mobile games and gameplay are often indicators of perceptions of time due to their intimate connection with our mundane temporalities, yet their use in transient moments means that they are also considered of little significance in terms of their impact on everyday life practices.[30] As indicated above, although mobile games have been called casual, this designation doesn't address the complex, diverse and often inventive ways in which time, labor and presence are framed and negotiated within that engagement. As Juul noted in his interviews with casual game players in the late 2000s[31] (before the widespread popularization of mobile casual games), casual games offer players a temporal and portable flexibility that console and desktop computer games do not. Indeed, the activity of casual mobile gaming often becomes a way of managing the corporeal agitation of impatience, aloneness, and boredom in public, effecting a mobilization of private space that can be deployed *in situ* while "being-with-others." This temporary scaffolding is achieved through the ambient affordances of mobile media. Chess suggests that mobile devices now commonly fill these spaces of interstitial time, and that invest/express, idle and background mobile games are specifically designed to inhabit these in-between periods of idleness or "tiny excesses of time"[32]—that is, they are specifically targeted as time-fillers to fit in with the temporal constraints and mobilities of urban dwellers.

Significant criticism has been leveled at social games, idle games, background games, and some resource and time management games more generally, in terms of their status "as games," due to the way they require what some regard as a facile form of resource acquisition, and because they actively prompt users to "pay to not play." In his critique of social games such as *Farmville*, Ian Bogost[33] argues that the manner in which they turn "friends" into useful game elements is an instance of "enframing" (*das Ge-stell*) in Heidegger's sense;[34] that is, social games are exemplars of the "essence" of modern technology within which the world (and our place in it) is translated as "standing-reserve" or in terms of its (and our) function as resources. Bogost created the game *Cow Clicker* (Bogost 2010) as a deliberate deployment of enframing, and as a derisive parody of such games:

> It's partly a satire, and partly a playable theory of today's social games, and partly an earnest example of that genre. You get a cow. You can click on it. In six hours, you can click it again. Clicking earns you clicks. You can buy custom 'premium' cows through micropayments (the *Cow Clicker* currency is called 'mooney'), and you can buy your way out of the time delay by spending it.[35]

As *Cow Clicker* sardonically exposes, playing is itself optional, as rote play acts (that is, clicking) can be skipped or avoided by buying clicks (or other actions or objects) with real money. In a very literal sense, for Bogost, these are games that you don't have to play, and thus not really games at all.

In addition, they do violence by their persistent incursion upon our time even when we are not playing, through reminders and updates, arbitrary wait-times for recharging energy, and an underlying compulsion to accumulate clicks, points, resources, or virtual currency. Moreover, as Bogost[36] and Mejia and Bulut[37] argue, the industry practices surrounding "clicker" mobile and social games seek to translate the labor of play—a form of toil that collapses the work-leisure binary, reconceptualized as the portmanteau *playbour*[38]—into profitable data and intricate metrics. That is, such game applications and their platforms gather information about players' usage, social networks and location, and so "should be understood as playful spaces for the valorization of surveillance and psychosocial resource extraction."[39] In this view, idle, background and incremental games are far from spaces of vernacular creativity[40] and personal expression.

Background games also raise questions regarding the very definition of games as interactive media that enable personal expression and creativity. In her work on interpassive games, Fizek[41] argues that

> we have arrived at a point where interactivity alone does not suffice anymore as a predominant conceptual framework. Idle games... seem to be the first video game genre to epitomize the delegation of pleasure and embody the interpassive relationship between players and the game.[42]

Interpassivity—where the effort of participation is removed or delegated to the game itself—sits in contrast to interactivity, which has been deemed one of the primary distinguishing features of games. The player engages not in gameplay but in a perpetual state of idling, escaping "the pressure of actual play, giving up their agency, and delegating it to the clicker algorithms."[43] In this analysis, too, regardless of the pleasures we might take in delegation, background games constitute the very antithesis of creativity and personalized playfulness.

Upon posting his rationale for the *Cow Clicker* game on his blog, Bogost received numerous comments that were deeply critical of his elitist approach to game development and design, many in defense of the way games such as *Farmville* can provide "tiny slices of pleasure" and relief from the daily grind. In the words of one commenter:

> As a human, I'd *much* rather push a happy button for 3 minutes (and then get on with my day), than mash controller buttons in noisy, heart-pounding, adrenaline-pumping fear for 3 hours... *FarmVille* is *fun* because you get to have a *farm*. People—every day normal regular people—actually *like* the idea of having a farm. It's part of our agrarian heritage. It's comforting. It's heartwarming. It's a nice little dream. And *FarmVille* lets you do it. And decorate it. With friends. Again and again.[44]

As Michele Willson[45] has argued, despite the denigration they receive from both game critics and researchers, social games are also spaces of personal expression. They are networked environments that facilitate the sharing of everyday creativity, generating forms of *playbour* that can promote social connection and positive affect. Despite the sometimes-vitriolic criticism these games garner, and the consequent shame and guilt that their players experience, it is salient to remind ourselves of the value ascribed to them by the people who play them, and of the need to critically interpret such play *in situ* through the ethnographic study of players. The debate is a useful one, however, as it forces us as cultural and media critics to unpack the complex fiscal and social relations that reside in mobile game ecologies, and to carefully articulate the various trajectories of the "playful attitude"[46] in contemporary cultural practices.

In what follows, through the stories of our research participants, I consider how mobile games are used to manage and navigate the interstices of everyday life, and identify some of the ways in which temporality, playfulness, mindfulness and creativity are experienced with and through the ambient play of background games.

## Negotiating and Reflecting on Everyday Life: Participant Stories of Background Games

With the rise in quantified self (QS) apps that measure and quantify our daily activities and routines, there has been much discussion about how this drives us to be more mindful with our time, to be more productive, both at work and at leisure. Participants often spoke of the need to *feel* that their time was used purposefully, and coopted mobile gaming as a way to play more efficiently, filling the in-between moments with a form of playful productivity. This need for all our activities to have constructive purpose is of course not specific to games, but such play practices spearhead a more general societal imperative. As scholars such as Wajcman,[47] and more recently Farman,[48] have highlighted, time has become a pivotal and yet elusive obsession in contemporary culture.

As our participants revealed, mobile games have many affordances, depending on the game and the context of play, enabling diverse modalities of play across a spectrum of attentiveness—from the intermittent and ambient flexibility of background games to the more demanding requisites of racing, adventure and strategy games. Jenny, a young mum from Perth, described how the characteristics of some mobile games created a particular relationship between time and context. She explicitly preferred clicker and city-building games as an effortless way to manage and orchestrate interstitial time:

> I play the *[The Simpsons] Tapped Out* game during ad breaks, when I'm just sitting on the couch watching TV. I'll pick up my phone and make sure there are no tasks that have to be started or if some have just finished. Other games make you focus your attention and are very time critical, but with *Tapped Out* I can just click on something, look away, come back, click on something, and it doesn't matter if you're not even looking at the screen. Nothing is going to happen. If I took my eyes off *Jetpack Joyride*, I would crash. Game over. Whereas this I can put down, go grab a coffee, come back, and click away. It's stress-free.

Similarly, for Sydney-based freelancer and seasoned RPG gamer Natalie, casual mobile gameplay enacted a deliberate well-being strategy intimately tied to her sense of identity as a gamer, allowing her to fit "ambient" play practices into her increasingly busy life:

> I tend to be on trains a lot, or driving to pick someone up and waiting in a carpark, or waiting for an appointment, so I've got lots of little pockets of free time. I've been a gamer forever, so I find ways to sort of sneak that into my life no matter how busy it is, even if it's for a few minutes. Mobile games are perfect for that.

For Efthimiou,[49] the gamer as a "mindful and creative practitioner" is a phenomenon emerging in mobile, networked and social spaces, as players leverage gameplay to "generate novel products or outcomes, originality and effectiveness," demonstrating varying degrees of intentionality and mindful attention.[50] Mark, an office worker from Adelaide encapsulates the practices of the mindful gamer who uses mobile play as a way to manage workplace stress more effectively. Mark quite strategically deployed mobile games as a way to step back from difficult work situations, allowing him to reassess the situation and think through his responses with more clarity:

> Sometimes work can get complex with people issues... I find it's good not to react impulsively. Mobile games help me, sometimes I'll take a walk and play a quick few quick levels for ten minutes or so. I know some people use games to escape reality, but I find they allow me a space to reflect. I'm more present when I finish and then I can resolve the problem.

In this way, mindfulness is linked to practices of resilience and creative problem-solving *around* the game, achieved by deliberately carving out interstitial time *as* a moment of incremental play, enabling reflection and a gathering of the self. As Efthimiou's work and Mark's experience suggests, understanding practices of mediated attention, mindfulness and presence, and the creative deployment of mobile game spaces as reflective "time-outs"—including the place of idle and background games in this process—requires a more open and non-judgmental perspective about what constitutes "real" gameplay.

Several of our participants played *Godus,* a world-building game that positions the player as a "god" who breeds builders, farmers and miners to accumulate resources and "belief" (also acquired in exchange for gems which can be purchased with real money). Players also sculpt a layered landscape, which costs increasing amounts of "belief" the higher the altitude. Jamie, a 38-year-old screenprinter from Perth, commented:

> I've actually steered clear of games with in-app purchases, as I don't like the way they make you wait. But *Godus* was genius, you could create entire landscapes, islands, mountains and towns by sculpting these colored layers on the touchscreen. Really satisfying in a tactile way, and creative and beautiful, and people would upload screenshots of their amazing creations. I never paid for gems... It was a bit frustrating but also felt somehow right that your workers took hours and sometimes days to build and harvest.

Jamie's *Godus* play exemplifies what Chess[51] identifies as particular to invest/express games, that is, those that allow for personalization or creative expression (in the design or decoration of the game space) and involve some form of time management (or investment in terms of labor, waiting or microtransactions to further the goal of resource accumulation). The expressive labor of world-building games such as *Godus* and *SimCity*—games that require significant periods of waiting and reside ambiently in the background of everyday life—reveal how such modalities of play have the potential to engender forms of vernacular creativity, produsage,[52] and imaginative artistry that are enthusiastically shared by communities of players. Playing background mobile games is also a productive, creative, and intentional *handling* of the temporal and spatial dimensions of interstitial waiting. Indeed, many of the play scenarios revealed through our ethnographic fieldwork directly challenge the view that mobile games are trivially "casual," and more specifically, counter the common perception that background games are insignificant, exploitative and manifestly non-creative.

## Conclusion

Throughout this chapter, it has been argued that mobile games reside at the crossroads of labor, leisure, creativity and play. More specifically, the discussion focused on background games that embed extended periods of necessary *waiting* into the gameplay and showed how such games—like many mobile games—are easily incorporated into the temporal rhythms, routines, and habitudes of everyday life. Through anecdotal insights gleaned from a three-year ethnographic study of mobile game practices, the chapter explored participant experiences of background games across a diverse spectrum of engagement.

As the chapter suggests, these modalities of play can be considered "ambient" as they become seamlessly part of players' quotidian existence. Unlike the term casual, ambient play does not imply the same sense of triviality or lack of engagement that is frequently ascribed to mobile games, particularly incremental, interstitial, idle, and background games. Such games generally involve minimalist player engagement—typically, checking in at various intervals and clicking to begin a new task—and in this way might be regarded as the least imaginative of mobile game genres. Yet as I have argued, the play practices involved in background gaming can be broadly interpreted as "artful" or creative in terms of their ambient play modalities, as players co-opt the games into their creative management and use of time, their mindful approach to the stresses of work, and in their negotiations of aloneness in public space. In this way, as a form of ambient play, background games are an integral aspect of the creative media practices that are diffused throughout everyday life via the ubiquity of mobile apps and games, and are consequential to the *playful attitude*[53] that now thoroughly permeates contemporary culture.

## Acknowledgments

The *Games of Being Mobile* project was funded by the Australian Research Council (ARC) Discovery Scheme.

## Notes

1 Larissa Hjorth, "Mobile Art: Rethinking Intersections between Art, User Created Content (UCC), and the Quotidian," *Mobile Media & Communication* 4, no. 2 (2016): 169–85, doi: 10.1177/2050157915619210.
2 All ethnographic participant names used in this chapter are not their own.
3 Shira Chess, "A Time for Play: Interstitial Time, Invest/Express Games, and Feminine Leisure Style," *New Media & Society* 20, no. 1 (2018): 105–21, doi: 10.1177/1461444816660729.
4 Sultan A. Alharthi, Olaa Alsaedi, Zachary O. Toups, Joshua Tanenbaum and Jessica Hammer, "Playing to Wait: A Taxonomy of Idle Games," *CHI2018*, 1–15, doi: 10.1145/3173574.3174195.
5 Sonia Fizek, "Interpassivity and the Joy of Delegated Play in Idle Games," *Transactions of the Digital Gams Research Association* 3, no. 3 (2018): 137–63, doi: 10.26503/todigra.v3i3.81.
6 Chess, "A time for play."
7 Brendan Keogh and Ingrid Richardson, "Waiting to Play: The Labour of Background Games," *European Journal of Cultural Studies* 21, no. 1 (2018): 13–25, doi: 10.1177/1367549417705603.
8 Larissa Hjorth and Ingrid Richardson, "Playing the Waiting Game: Complicating Notions of (Tele) presence and Gendered Distraction in Casual Mobile Gaming," in *Cultures of Participation Media Practices, Politics and Literacy*, edited by Hajo Greif, Larissa Hjorth, Amparo Lasén, and Claire Lobet-Maris (New York: Peter Lang Publishing, 2011), 111–26.
9 Alharthi et al., "A Taxonomy."
10 Fizek, "Interpassivity," 137.
11 Chess, "A Time for Play," 107.
12 Hjorth and Richardson, "Playing the Waiting Game."
13 Jesper Juul, *A Casual Revolution: Reinventing Video Games and their Players* (Cambridge, MA: MIT Press, 2010).
14 Larissa Hjorth and Ingrid Richardson, *Ambient Play* (Cambridge, MA: MIT Press, 2020), n.p.
15 Paul Dourish, "The Culture of Information: Ubiquitous Computing and Representations of Reality," in *Designing Ubiquitous Information Environments: Socio-Technical Issues and Challenges IFIP—The International Federation for Information Processing,* Springer, no. 185 (2005): 23–26, doi: 10.1007/0-387-28918-6_4.
16 Paul Roquet, *Ambient Media: Japanese Atmospheres of Self* (Minneapolis: University of Minnesota Press, 2016).
17 Hjorth and Richardson, *Ambient Play.*
18 Valentina Rao, "Facebook Applications and Playful Mood: The Construction of Facebook as a 'Third Place'," in *Proceedings of the 14th International Academic MindTrek Conference: Envisioning Future Media Environments* (New York: ACM, 2008): 8–12, 9.
19 Christopher Moore, "The Magic Circle and the Mobility of Play," *Convergence: The International Journal of Research into New Media Technologies* 17, no. 4 (2011): 373–87, 374, doi: 10.1177/1354856511414350.
20 Mary Flanagan, *Critical Play: Radical Game Design* (Cambridge, MA: MIT Press, 2009); Miguel Sicart, *Play Matters* (Cambridge, MA: MIT Press, 2014).
21 Ian Bogost, "Cow Clicker: The Making of Obsession," *Videogame Theory, Criticism, Design*, 21 July 2010, www.bogost.com/blog/cow_clicker_1.shtml.
22 Judy Wajcman, *Pressed for Time: The Acceleration of Life in Digital Capitalism* (Chicago, IL: University of Chicago Press, 2015).

23 Hartmut Rosa, *Social Acceleration: A New Theory of Modernity* (New York: Columbia University Press, 2015).
24 Ibid., 99.
25 Wajcman, *Pressed for Time.*
26 Ibid., 71.
27 Jason Farman, *Delayed Response: The Art of Waiting from the Ancient to the Instant World* (New Haven, CT: Yale University Press, 2018).
28 Ibid., 18.
29 Tim Edensor, Deborah Leslie, Steve Millington, and Norma Rantisi, *Spaces of Vernacular Creativity: Rethinking the Cultural Economy* (London: Routledge, 2009). Hjorth, "Mobile Art."
30 Hjorth and Richardson, "Playing the Waiting Game."
31 Juul, *A Casual Revolution.*
32 Chess, "A Time for Play," 111.
33 Bogost, "Cow Clicker."
34 Martin Heidegger, *The Question Concerning Technology and Other Essays*, translated by William Lovitt (New York: Garland Publishing, 1977).
35 Bogost, "Cow Clicker," n.p.
36 Ibid.
37 Robert Mejia and Ergin Bulut, "The Cruel Optimism of Casual Games: Neocolonialism, Neoliberalism, and the Valorization of Play," *Critical Studies in Media Communication* 36, no. 2 (2019): 156–70, doi: 10.1080/15295036.2019.1566626.
38 Julian Kücklich, "Precarious Playbour: Modders and the Digital Games Industry," *Fibreculture*, 5 (2005), http://five.fibreculturejournal.org/fcj-025-precarious-playbour-modders-and-the-digital-games-industry/.
39 Mejia and Bulut, "The cruel optimism," 162.
40 Jean Burgess, "Remediating Vernacular Creativity," in *Spaces of Vernacular Creativity: Rethinking the Cultural Economy*, edited by Tim Edensor, Deborah Leslie, Steve Millington, and Norma Rantisi (London: Routledge, 2009), 116–26.
41 Fizek, "Interpassivity."
42 Ibid., 151.
43 Fizek, "Interpassivity," 155.
44 Bogost, "Cow Clicker," n.p.
45 Michele Willson, "Social Games as Partial Platforms for Identity Co-Creation," *Media International Australia*, no. 154 (2015): 15–24.
46 Sicart, *Play Matters.*
47 Wajcman, *Pressed for Time.*
48 Farman, *Delayed Response.*
49 Olivia Efthimiou, "Heroic Play: Heroism in Mindful, Creative and Playful Participation," *IM: Interactive Media,* 11 (2016): 1–18, https://researchrepository.murdoch.edu.au/id/eprint/32455/1/IM11-heroism-article-efthimiou.pdf.
50 Ibid., n.p.
51 Chess, "A Time for Play."
52 Axel Bruns, *Blogs, Wikipedia, Second Life and Beyond: From Production to Produsage* (New York: Peter Lang Publishing, 2008).
53 Sicart, *Play Matters.*

# 22

# RE-IMAGINING BUSHLAND SETTINGS THROUGH LOCATION-BASED AR MOBILE GAMEPLAY

*Matthew Riley, Troy Innocent, and Rowan Wilken*

How can mobile gameplay connect two seemingly disparate systems—the naturally occurring system of the bush, with the artificially constructed system of a mixed reality—to create new experiences of traversing a bushwalk? "The bush," the favored term for describing the elusive concepts of "nature" and "wilderness" in Australia, remains an enduring source of fascination, debate and significance, and is subject to diverse interpretations, practices and associations. Given its harsh environment, many may not relate the bush with play.

However, play has always shaped our engagement with the world in expressive ways, with games providing systems and rules for the construction, interaction, and traversal of our physical environment. Existing work on play has focused predominantly on urban spaces, from children inscribing neighborhood lanes and streets with outdoor games, the art tactic of the psychogeographic *dérive* in radically navigating the city in different ways, to the playing of mobile augmented and mixed reality games that playfully connect urban spaces, people, and digital systems.[1] Shifting our experiences of place, these activities aim to transform the way we relate to particular city locations by re-imagining their familiar social, temporal, physical, and situated contexts through play.

With respect to bush settings, scholars such as Richard White and Caroline Ford[2] and Melissa Harper[3] have recently drawn attention to the history of bush-based recreation with nature-play, bushwalking, birdwatching and wildflower hunts forming outdoor ambulant and playful relationships with these settings. Camera traps, drones, data sensors, biotechnologies, and monitoring tools have recently mediated our experience of natural places for scientific and information purposes. This chapter, however, examines how digital systems can invite people to engage with a bush setting in playful and expressive ways. Exploring how these apparently disparate and complex worlds can intersect, it reflects on the motivations, design, and evaluation of *Epiphyte*, the experimental mobile AR game that places players within an augmented bush setting.

*Epiphyte* (2016–2017) was developed as a collaboration between Matthew Riley and Troy Innocent. The game's aim was to engage players in a form of contemplative interaction and play in a natural setting, through creating and sustaining an artificial ecology; the mechanics of the game and how it operates are detailed later in this chapter. Before turning to consider *Epiphyte* in detail, we first delineate what we mean when we speak of the Australian "bushland," the setting for the *Epiphyte* game. We then consider a number of artistic precedents that explore related concerns to those taken up within *Epiphyte*. In the remainder of the chapter, we describe the *Epiphyte* game and its constituent elements.

## The Australian Bush Setting

Given the diversity of bush settings—from patches of urban bushlands on suburban fringes to the expanses of the Australian outback—definitions of the bush encompass multiple contexts and understandings constructed through varying perspectives, ideologies, and interpretations. While referring to sparsely inhabited or rural settings outside of cities, Bidwell and Browning[4] recognize that understandings of natural places also encompass social and cultural meanings, and characteristics that emerge in and through their use. While sometimes associated with notions of an unadulterated "wilderness," vast areas of the bush have been subject to care, cultivation and maintenance by indigenous Australians for thousands of years.[5] More recently, European settlers have manipulated the natural environment through agriculture and habitation with large areas of bush being cleared or altered.

The bush setting of *Epiphyte* is not a remote or untouched location. Rather, it is situated in Sherbrooke Forest, a small national park within the Dandenong Ranges on the eastern outskirts of Melbourne, Australia. It is a site that is increasingly surrounded by peri-urban development and one that is managed in order to protect and regenerate precious flora and fauna. While there are salient sensory and situated characteristics of this site that differ from a built or city context, the Forest is nonetheless closely entwined with people's activities and interactions.

## Location-Based Augmented Reality Mobile Games

Augmented reality (AR) systems are also interconnected, complex systems that commingle and switch between seemingly divergent modes of experience, encompassing subject and object, presence and distance, nature and artifice. This coalescence has opened up new opportunities for multi-layered experiences of our surroundings via technological mediation. With their ability to construct and traverse real-world spaces in new ways, AR systems have often been modeled as pervasive, mobile games that attempt to re-shape customary relations with the physical world.[6] Jessika Weber defines location-based AR mobile games as

> outdoor games that make use of the player's physical location via the [Global Positioning System] GPS sensor, accelerometer, compass and camera to project virtual 2D and 3D objects in real time onto the device interface in order to facilitate gameplay activities. The player interacts with the virtual and physical environment (movement).[7]

Mobile AR platforms have recently provided a playful interface for pervasive games to connect, transition between, and negotiate with these multiple worlds.[8] Within these games, players navigate city locations (the streets, laneways and public spaces of our actual environment) while simultaneously engaging with a game world and its rules of engagement, systems for play and modes of interaction.

Location-based AR mobile games have predominantly been situated in urban contexts, with systems for implementing AR largely suited to small indoor environments[9] or city locations, where networking, mobility and displays can be more tightly controlled. AR games designed for contexts outside of built locations or urban settings have been uncommon, with theoretical and practical knowledge on the potential and implications of this practice in natural environments comparatively under-represented.

*Epiphyte* can be understood as a location-based AR mobile game. It is, however, distinct in two ways. First, while *Epiphyte* accords in almost all respects with Weber's earlier definition of a location-based AR mobile game, it uses physical markers in the landscape (rather than GPS or internal device sensors) to determine a player's position in the field of play. Second, unlike many other AR

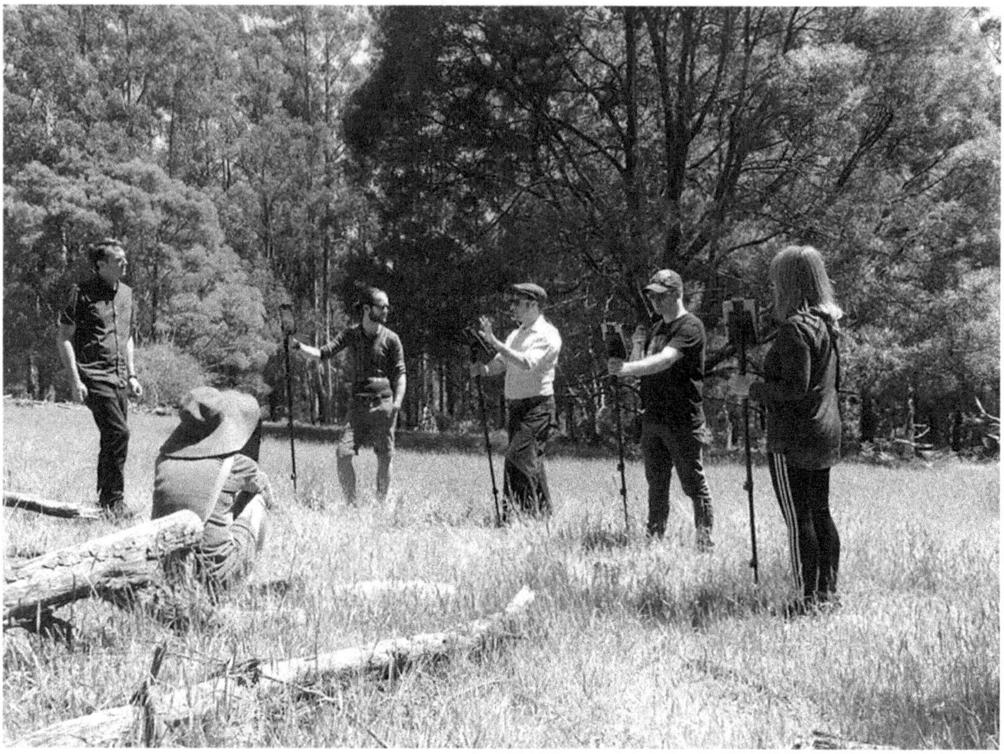

*Figure 22.1* *Epiphyte*: players starting the game. Photo credit: Kate Baker

mobile games, *Epiphyte* is designed specifically for a non-urban, bushland setting (see Figure 22.1). *Epiphyte*, then, is firmly anchored within the specific context of location-based AR mobile gaming.[10] It does, however, draw inspiration from, and thus ought to be also understood within, the broader contexts of media arts,[11] locative media arts,[12] and other established landscape-based art practices, such as the Land Art movement.[13] In order to explain fully what we have tried to achieve with *Epiphyte*, it is first necessary to consider some of its key precedents within these wider artistic fields.

## Precedents: Locative Media Arts and/in "Natural" Settings

Natural settings have long been contexts for creative and cultural forms of expression. Journeys on foot by indigenous Australians along Dream Tracks, or "Songlines," are one of the most ancient and poetic forms of navigation. Knowledge and beliefs of plants, animals, stars, forests, terrain, and routes used to safely traverse the land were shared through dance, painting, singing, and ceremonies, knowing the song allowed you to know the landscape. Using natural materials such as soil, water, rocks, and twigs, artist Andy Goldsworthy has, throughout his career, staged contextually subtle and sensitive site-specific interventions in landscapes to activate, abstract, or amplify their geographic, spatial, and aesthetic characteristics.[14] Goldsworthy draws attention to not only the visual forms, qualities, lines, and colors of nature but also their processes and relations. Richard Long's practice interprets remote and rural locations through walking, his ambulant interaction and navigation of an environment ultimately captured through photography, maps, sculpture, and text.[15] Long's walks are an aesthetic process for understanding and perceiving these landscapes and the time, pace, and characteristics of his walks through them.

A creative practice has also emerged exploring digital systems and technologies that are situated in or that respond to natural, wild, or remote settings. These have taken a variety of forms. For example, the outdoor treasure-hunt activity of geocaching (2000–) is one of the earliest games bringing together the outdoors, play, and technology, where players use GPS devices to locate hidden containers embedded in unexpected or remote sites. Analyzing this treasure-hunt game, Jason Farman describes the player experience as involving "proprioceptive-semiotics."[16] Here the game space is created by the proprioception of the self in relationship to an augmented landscape, with digital information integrated into the physical environment. Space is not seen as a pre-existing entity for geocachers, Farman argues. Rather, it is produced through our embodied engagement. We move through the physical environment and its augmentation—guided by the digital system of the mobile device and where the social and technological come together in geocaching to establish a playful experience in outdoor settings.

In addition to geocaching, artist Teri Rueb has created innovative GPS-driven audio walks, such as *Trace* (1999), *Core Sample* (2007), and *No Places with Names* (2012), where participants move through expansive outdoor landscapes with headphones to experience location-specific narratives that attempt to alter sensory, perceptual, and cognitive engagements with a site.[17] Brett Stalbaum has generated alternative engagements and relationships with remote locations through employing a range of Geographic Information Systems (GIS) data sets, visualization tools, GPS, and Application Programming Interfaces (API) that relate data and human movement together.[18] The *Walking Tools* (2008–) project he leads enables people to create and share GPS-navigated walks through a set of open-source tools and APIs for mobile phones, encouraging others to produce their own kinds of mediated experiences with the landscape.

Scott Hessels' artwork blends sculpture, the moving image and the environment together where natural forces—wind, erosion, temperature, water, and so on—are detected as data by computational sensors and become an agent in the construction and experience of the work.[19] Informed by the temporal and process-driven affordances of nature harnessed in Land Art, his *Mediated Earthworks* (2011) prototypes are similarly open to the forces of the environment. This series utilizes computational sensors in dynamically shaping Hessels' kinetic artworks, often translating natural elements into data to drive how the piece is experienced. Describing his practice as "partnering with wildness,"[20] Hessels' work—like that of Cameron Robbins, which connects weather system sensors with drawing equipment[21]—can't exist without this input from the environment.

In an Australian art context, Mitchell Whitelaw has examined the disjuncture between the persistent "heavy slowness" of the physical Australian landscape and the immaterial "fast lightness of data."[22] In works such as *Watching the Sky* (2007), which reinterprets weather and day/night cycles into abstract data visualizations, he explores the changes to and patterns of the outdoor landscape and its occupation, and the complex processes and cycles of the material world.[23] In Whitelaw's writing, he points to another Australian artist, Jon McCormack, who has also explored "computational nature studies"[24] in creative practice that is informed by the processes, behaviors, and aesthetics of Australian landscapes and ecosystems.[25] McCormack's *Eden* (2002–2010) was an installation that featured a self-generating, artificial ecosystem inspired by the layered and distinctive sounds of the "top end" of Australia. Sound indicates how creatures of this ecosystem adapt to their environment and the human participants within it—the creatures' sonic behavior encouraging people to remain in the space with their food supply tied to visitors' movement and presence.

In addition, Perdita Phillips, who is known for her photographic, sound, and installation work situated in remote parts of Australia, has employed digital technologies to investigate specific locations that invite reflection on their history and potential impending climatic and social changes.[26] In *The Sixth Shore* (2012), she created a GPS-driven 3D soundscape that was experienced by walking around Lake Clifton in Western Australia, demonstrating how digital technologies can be employed to understand the complex and dynamic ecologies of specific locations. These works form both important precursors to, and valuable sources of inspiration for, *Epiphyte*.

## Epiphyte

*Epiphyte* is a location-based AR mobile game staged within Sherbrooke Forest, which forms part of the Dandenong Ranges on the eastern outskirts of Melbourne, Australia. Sherbrooke Forest is a site with a complicated, multi-layered history: it has been shaped by thousands of years of indigenous culture and was later subject to various forms of farming before being restored and protected as bushland by its National Park status.[27]

The work aims to encourage an affinity with the Dandenong Ranges and is structured around a mediated bushwalk within Sherbrooke Forest. The bushwalk is remapped via the positioning of 39 AR markers that were temporarily integrated in the bushland near features of the walk—trees, ferns, grasslands, streams, and rocks. Held in place using natural cotton rope, knots and pegs these AR markers are both familiar and unfamiliar in the bushland context. They are familiar as environmental signage but have their own unique code that draws on existing practices and signs in non-urban environments such as geoglyphs, orienteering guides, and topographic symbols. The AR markers serve a number of purposes: redefining the space with signs to establish a cross media ecology; distinguishing the species within this ecology; acting as navigation landmarks to guide players as they traverse the space; and, finally, serving as readable signs. They also trigger changes in the on-screen digital content of the Apple iPad minis carried by players. The game begins when a player finds the first marker in the bushland and scans it with the mobile device, collecting a digital seed to activate the next site.

Players have two main motivations for connecting with the work. For many video game players who have grown up in the artificial nature of virtual worlds, outdoor nature spaces are unexplored environments worthy of investigation. For those that already enjoy nature walks, the work sought to explore how a digital intervention could invite different modes of experience and traversal in these settings. Initiated from a collaboration with Troy Innocent, this work was inspired by a series of Innocent's mixed realities titled *noemaflux* (2010–2011) in which players were encouraged to explore the city with mobile devices to activate custom-designed AR markers situated within streets and laneways.[28] Using the metaphor of pollination, players carried "seeds" from one site to the next to evolve the visual and sonic properties of digital entities: this mechanic linked the temporal behavior of *noemaflux's* artificial world with the physical space of the city.

## Seeds

Given its relevance to bushlands, the "seed" motif of *noemaflux* was considered a meaningful one to explore further and in different ways within *Epiphyte*. Players set out to find the aforementioned fiducial markers (see Figure 22.2, right) that they use to evolve an artificial ecology on their mobile device. When a marker is discovered and scanned, a digital "seed" is stacked vertically on the screen and interacted with in different ways by the players via rule-based organizing principles that determine how the seeds behave (see Figure 22.2, left). The collection of seeds acts as a dynamic and expressive mapping[29] of the bushwalk that develops in subtlety and complexity as the site is explored.

There are three different types of seeds—orange, green and blue—that interact with one another in different ways. The goal with this interaction is to enact a generative system resulting in different animated, abstract visual forms, and musical scores based on these interactions. The places players visit when playing generate different outcomes; the data collected as they walk will

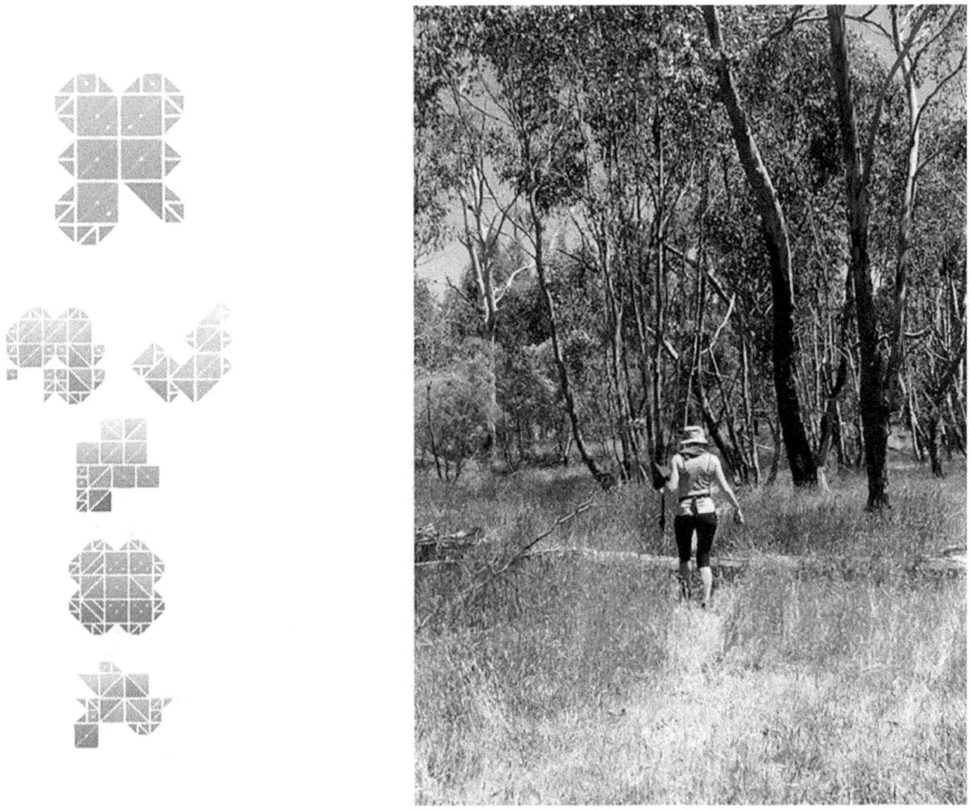

*Figure 22.2* Left: *Epiphyte*: digital "seeds"; Right: searching for AR markers. Photo credits: Matthew Riley

be visualized through this process in terms of their individual map or cartography. Seeds have a lifespan, slowly fading over time. Their lifespan may be extended by scanning "water" markers or their power increased by scanning "sun" markers.

At the completion of the walk, each player's collection of seeds comes to life and transforms into a composition of sound and image that reflects their particular navigation and interactions in the setting. After each staging of *Epiphyte*, players take turns to "play" this unique artificial ecosystem collected on their device—or, alternatively, this ecosystem can be interacted with as an audiovisual instrument by tapping the on-screen seeds.

## Games in Urban and Bushland Settings

Several accounts of location-based games link them back to subversive play in urban environments, such as parkour (free running through urban space) and the Situationist International activity of dérive (drifting through the city inspired by emotional rather than functional responses to urban space).[30] Furthermore, numerous pervasive games emphasize adrenaline-inducing running, speed, and pursuit through city streets.[31]

Games in non-urban settings tend to cultivate alternative modes of engagement. *Epiphyte*, for instance, invites players to engage with its bushland and forest surroundings, and the game itself, through forms of play and interaction that speak to understandings and histories of bushwalking as something that is generally undertaken as a solitary activity or in a small group, and where the goal typically is immersion in nature and in contemplation.[32] While games scholars have pointed to the ways that many pervasive games engage forms of ambient play within the context and routines of everyday life,[33] the aim of *Epiphyte* is to foster interactions that specifically encourage contemplative interaction and play within bushland settings. The term "interaction" implies active involvement rather than quiet or sustained reflection. Contemplation, however, is not necessarily an escape or passive introspection: it can support a close and attentive way of relating with and to the world.[34] In *Epiphyte,* the augmented bushwalk is staged as an exploratory, reflective, and subtle experience.

The challenge of contemplative interaction—in the perceived conflict between the slow, quiet reflection typically expected of the bushwalk, and the fast, intensive play usually associated with location-based augmented reality games—is indicative of broader concerns in pervasive, location-based AR mobile game design. Central to these concerns are the affordances and design baggage that come with mobile devices such as phones or tablets. They typically absorb the attention of players completely, at the expense of the environment in which the player is situated, whether it be city or bushland.

The constraints and affordances of location-based AR games are critical in shaping the design[35] and getting players off the screen and into the world is a key challenge in the city and in non-urban contexts. These games offer the opportunity to connect players with their environment in new ways; however, games such as *Pokémon GO* present views of the world that are detached from the world—they recode rather than decode the places in which they are situated.[36] A key difference between *Epiphyte* and *Pokémon GO* is that, in the former, the gameplay is driven by interactions with physical artifacts that are placed *in* the landscape at different heights and distances from the player, whereas, within the latter, artifacts appear as overlays on a landscape. Moreover, while *Pokémon GO* encourages urban explorations that hold potential for, among other things, facilitating parochial (subtle, fleeting) interactions between players,[37] *Epiphyte* seeks to facilitate more individualized contemplative reflections *in* and *on* place.

## Adapting Technologies for Bushland Settings—Constraints and Opportunities

Bush environments introduce new constraints and opportunities for game design. Many of these are practical concerns such as catering for extremes in weather or dealing with slow or intermittent mobile data coverage (a known issue in regional and remote Australia,[38] as elsewhere). These were significant considerations in the development of *Epiphyte.* For this game, a customized set of technologies was provided to players to experience the work. This included portable batteries and anti-glare surfaces on the iPad screens to minimize reflection from the sun. All data for the experience was stored locally on the device so that no connection to mobile data was required. iPads were mounted on repurposed monopod selfie sticks that were the same size as sticks often used by bushwalkers when following a trail. The markers themselves were made of Tyvek so as to be waterproof and were mounted using camping gear (rope and tent hooks) to minimize impact on the environment and allow them to be adapted to a range of different sites (see Figure 22.3).

*Epiphyte* also exploited a key difference in the way that sound in bushland environments tends to be experienced from how it is in urban-based games. In urban environments, it is often desirable for players to wear headphones so that they may block out city noise—what Michael Bull refers to as the process of "sounding out privatized space" while navigating the space of the city[39]—in order to be more deeply immersed in the gameplay experience. In a bushland setting, our experience of sounds is often quite different. The natural environment provides a rich, spatial soundtrack that shifts between different ambient moods and that is punctuated by the sounds of birds, running water and other environmental sounds. In *Epiphyte,* we used portable Bluetooth speakers—also mounted on the selfie/multi-functional walking stick—so that the sound design of the game blended environmental sounds and could be experienced as one cohesive experience.

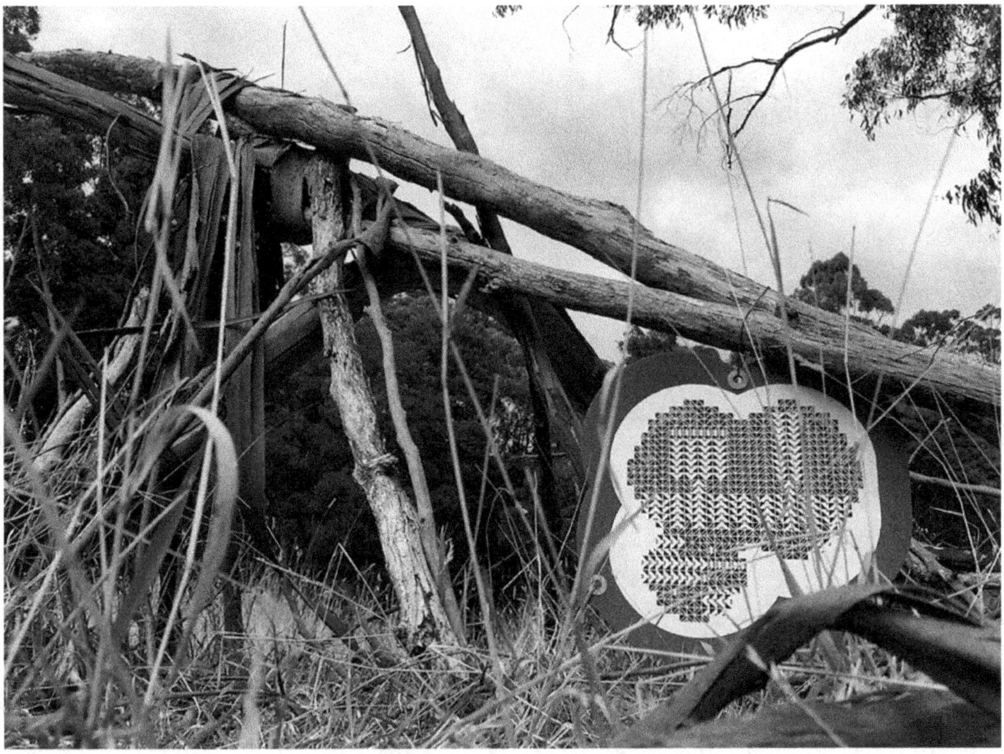

*Figure 22.3* *Epiphyte*: AR marker. Photo credit: Matthew Riley

## Contemplative Interaction and Play

With all these design considerations in place, *Epiphyte* uses strategies developed in Innocent's *noemaflux* (2010–2011)[40] and *Wayfinder Live* (2016–),[41] such as using material objects situated in the environment to shift players attention from the screen to their environment. In this way, the main activity is walking, exploring, and looking, punctuated by intense encounters with augmented reality experiences—forms of interaction that Larissa Hjorth and Sarah Pink refer to as "digital wayfaring."[42] *Epiphyte* responds to the affordances of the bushland environment to create an experience that is slower and more reflective in comparison with those typically associated with urban-based mobile AR games. "Playing the forest" involves balancing the distraction of screen time of the mobile device with immersion in the "natural" setting. Our game design involved three modes of interaction that responded to the bushland environment and that aimed to encourage contemplative interaction and play.

First, when scanning a fiducial marker, the augmented reality encounter was designed to be intense in order to concentrate the attention of the player. Second, and in contrast, while walking, the screen content is largely static, inviting players to explore their environment to find more physical markers in the space. Third, the overall experience has a fixed point in time when it ends, and players gather together at one location to collectively share the audiovisual composition of their individual walks, creating moments of social engagement to end the experience (see Figure 22.4). Although the mobile device is a key component enabling the gameplay, the interaction is not device-centric but more importantly experienced as a combination of the entangled and complex assemblage of the bushland setting, augmented reality encounters and social interaction.

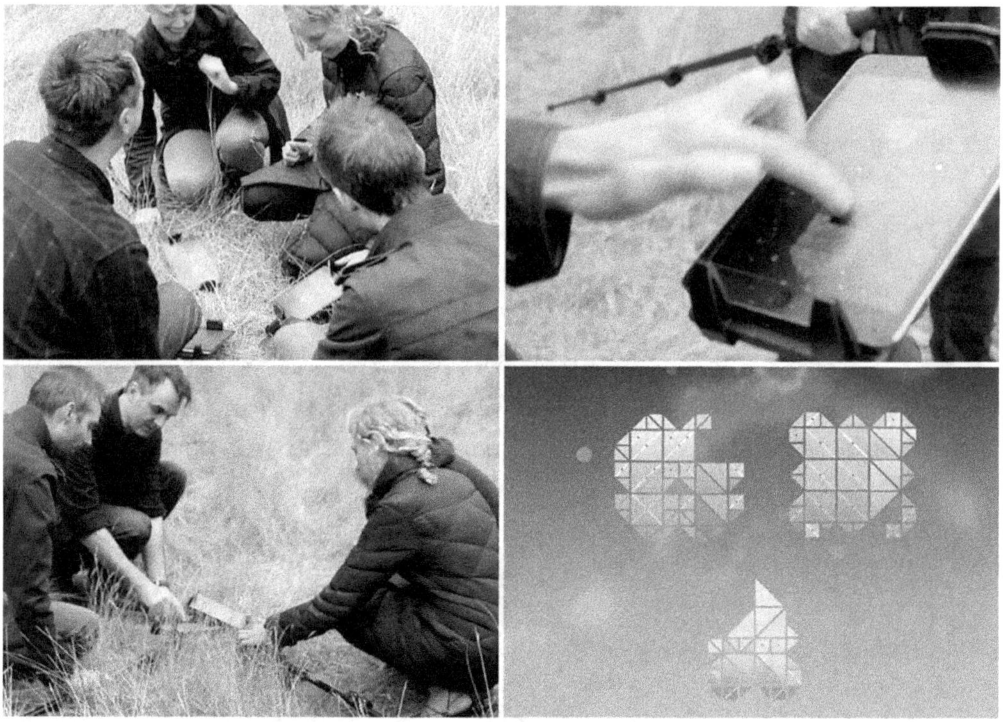

*Figure 22.4* *Epiphyte*: players sharing the audiovisual composition of their individual walks. Photo credit: Steve Jennings

Through the design of play experiences that balance the affordances and constraints of location-based game design in a bushland setting, opportunities for contemplative interaction became possible. The design of *Epiphyte* shows that these two seemingly incongruous elements may co-exist and benefit from one another. Players who may usually engage with urban environments may be drawn into a bushwalk—perhaps their first for some time—and those who are regular bushwalkers may experience social encounters or a renewed engagement with bush settings by "playing the forest."

While *Epiphyte* is a prototype and had to overcome many physical challenges associated with its bushland setting—the elements, lack of infrastructure, adaptation of game design—it demonstrates the rich potential of exploring these environments for location-based augmented reality games. Moreover, further themes and opportunities are revealed, such as the potential for this practice to engage with place-making and broader conversations around our relationship to the "natural" environment. Further discussion will focus on this potential and will encourage a movement toward contemplative interaction as expressed through experiences of "playing the forest."

## Conclusion

*Epiphyte*, a location-based AR game staged in the Sherbrooke Forest in the Dandenong Ranges near Melbourne, Australia, was developed in order to investigate how contemplative interaction and play could be adopted in a bushland setting to relate people, technologies, spaces, and objects within a mixed reality. What the development, staging, and analysis of *Epiphyte* have revealed is that it is possible to re-conceptualize the experience of the bushwalk through play. *Epiphyte* worked to shift the way players engaged with the bush by fostering contemplative experiences of place that led to the creation of new site-based associations and meanings, and which introduced alternative social and physical interactions within the site.

*Epiphyte* also offers a model—that can productively form the basis of future work—for how an AR platform can expressively depict bushland. Nature, however, was not depicted within the game as a static representation. Rather, through its simple abstraction, the game attempted to dynamically convey the complex, temporal and dynamic qualities of the bushland setting. The representation of the bushland was performative and shifting, with players constructing and sharing their playful mappings of their bush walks via the game. As such, *Epiphyte* makes a valuable contribution to present understanding of how bushland settings, digital systems, and players can be connected via contemplative play and interaction, and how location-based AR games can interpret and alter our engagement with the bushwalk.

As *Epiphyte* reveals, by marking the landscape with physical and virtual signs and codes to augment natural settings, mixed realities can be generated that invite novel and alternative experiences of and engagements with settings outside of urban contexts. Reflective modes of interactivity can encourage slower, attentive, and subtle experiences of mixed realities in these environments and set the conditions for contemplative forms of playful engagement in this context. Situating mobile AR in expansive outdoor, bushland spaces offers new opportunities for the exploration of natural places, where game worlds, physical places, and mixed realities can be simultaneously engaged.

## Notes

1 Jane McGonigal, *This Might Be a Game: Ubiquitous Play and Performance at the Turn of the Twenty-First Century*, PhD Dissertation, University of California, 2006; Mary Flanagan, "Locating Play and Politics: Real World Games and Activism," *Leonardo Electronic Almanac* 16, no. 2–3 (2007): 1–13; Adriana de Souza e Silva and Larissa Hjorth, "Playful Urban Spaces: A Historical Approach to Mobile Games," *Simulation & Gaming* 40, no. 5 (2009): 602–25, doi: 10.1177/1046878109333723; Michiel de Lange, "From Always On to Always There: Locative Media as Playful Technologies," in *Digital Cityscapes: Merging Digital and Urban Playscapes*, edited by Adriana de Souza e Silva and Daniel M. Sutko (New York: Peter Lang, 2009), 55–70; Markus Montola, "A Ludological View on the Pervasive Mixed-reality Game Research Paradigm," *Personal and Ubiquitous Computing* 15 (2010): 3–12, doi: 10.1007/s00779-010-0307-7; Ingrid Richardson, "The Hybrid Ontology of Mobile Gaming," *Convergence: The International Journal of Research into New Media Technologies* 17, no. 4 (2011): 419–30, doi: 10.1177/1354856511414797; Dale Leorke, *Location-based Gaming: Play in Public Space* (Singapore: Palgrave Macmillan, 2019); Troy Innocent, "Play and Placemaking in Urban Art Environments," MAB '16, Proceedings of the *3rd Conference on Media Architecture Biennale*, 1–4 June 2016, Sydney, Australia, doi: 10.1145/2946803.2946805.

2 Richard White and Caroline Ford (eds.) *Playing in the Bush: Recreation and National Parks in New South Wales* (Sydney: Sydney University Press, 2012).

3 Melissa Harper, *The Ways of the Bushwalker: On Foot in Australia* (Sydney: University of New South Wales Press, 2007).

4 Nicola J. Bidwell and David Browning, "Pursuing Genius Loci: Interaction Design and Natural Places," *Personal and Ubiquitous Computing*, 14 (2010): 15–30, doi: 10.1007/s00779-009-0217-8.

5 Bruce Pascoe, *Dark Emu* (Broome, WA: Magabala Books, 2014).

6 Pervasive games have been defined as games that "extend the gameplay out into the real world—be it on city streets, in the remote wilderness, or in the living room." Steve Benford, Carsten Magerkurth, and Peter Ljungstrand, "Bridging the Physical and Digital in Pervasive Gaming," *Communications of the ACM* 48, no. 3 (March, 2005), 54, doi: 10.1145/1047671.1047704.

7 Jessika Weber, *Designing Engaging Experiences with Location-based Augmented Reality Games for Urban Tourism Environments*, PhD Dissertation, 2016.

8 Here we are thinking of games such as *Wayfinder Live*, *TimeWarp*, and *Viking Ghost Hunt*, as well as commercially available games such as *Ingress Prime*, *Harry Potter: Wizards Unite*, and, of course, *Pokémon GO*.

9 Iman Zendjebil, Fakhr-Eddine Ababsa, Jean-Yves Didier, Jacques Vairon, Luc Frauciel, Martin Hachet, Pascal Guitton, and Romauld Delmont, "Outdoor Augmented Reality: State of the Art and Issues," in *Proceedings of the 10th ACM/IEEE Virtual Reality International Conference (VRIC 2008), Laval, France,* 2008.

10 See: Leorke, *Location-based Gaming*; Larissa Hjorth and Ingrid Richardson, *Gaming in Social, Locative, & Mobile Media* (Houndmills, Basingstoke: Palgrave Macmillan, 2014); Tama Leaver and Michele Willson (eds.), *Social, Casual and Mobile Games: The Changing Gaming Landscape* (New York: Bloomsbury, 2016).

11 Darren Tofts, *Interzone: Media Arts in Australia* (Fishermans Bend, Victoria: Craftsman House, 2005).

12 Andrea Zeffiro, "A Location of One's Own: A Genealogy of Locative Media," *Convergence: The International Journal of Research into New Media Technologies* 18, no. 3 (2012): 249–66, doi: 10.1177/1354856512441148.

13 Jeffrey Kastner and Brian Wallis, *Land and Environmental Art* (London: Phaidon, 1998).

14 See, for example, Andy Goldsworthy, *Rain, Sun, Snow, Hail, Mist, Calm: Photoworks by Andy Goldsworthy* (Leeds: Henry Moore Centre for the Study of Sculpture, 1985); Andy Goldsworthy, *Andy Goldsworthy* (London: Viking, 1990); Andy Goldsworthy, *Andy Goldsworthy: Ephemeral Works: 2004–2014* (New York: Harry N. Abrams, 2015).

15 William Malpas, *Richard Long in Close Up* (Maidstone, Kent: Crescent Moon Publishing, 2008).

16 Jason Farman, "Locative Life: Geocaching, Mobile Gaming, and Embodiment," Proceedings of the Digital Arts and Culture Conference, 2009, https://escholarship.org/uc/item/507938rr.

17 See: http://terirueb.net/; Teri Rueb, "Restless: Locative Media as Generative Displacement," in *Mobility and Locative Media: Mobile Communication in Hybrid Spaces*, edited by Adriana de Souza e Silva and Mimi Sheller (New York: Routledge, 2015), 241–58.

18 See: https://visarts.ucsd.edu/people/faculty/brett-stalbaum.html.

19 See: http://scotthessels.com/.

20 D. Scott Hessels, "The Dumptruck Interface: Earthworks and Interactive Art," *Interactive Environments, UCLA DIMA* (2004), http://classes.dma.ucla.edu/Winter04/256/projects/scott/report.html.

21 Cameron Robbins, *Field Lines* (Hobart: Museum of Old and New Art, 2016).

22 Mitchell Whitelaw, "Landscape, Slow Data, and Self-revelation," *The Teeming Void*, 15 May 2009, http://teemingvoid.blogspot.com/2009/05/.

23 Whitelaw, "Landscape."

24 Mitchell Whitelaw, "Computational Nature Studies," *The Teeming Void*, 2 April 2007, teemingvoid.blogspot.com/2007/04/computational-nature-studies.html.

25 See: http://jonmccormack.info/artworks/.

26 See, for example: www.perditaphillips.com/current-projects/the-sixth-shore/.

27 Helen Coulson, *Story of the Dandenongs* (Melbourne: F.W. Cheshire Publishing, 1968); see, also, the Sherbrooke Forest Area's Statement of Significance in Heritage Council Victoria's Victorian Heritage Database: https://vhd.heritagecouncil.vic.gov.au/places/70375/download-report.

28 See: http://troyinnocent.net/noemaflux.htm.

29 Nanna Verhoeff, "Urban Interfaces: The Cartographies of Screen-based Installations," *Television and New Media* 18 (2016): 305–19, doi: 10.1177/1527476416667818.

30 de Souza e Silva and Hjorth, "Playful Urban Spaces;" Adriana de Souza e Silva, "From Cyber to Hybrid: Mobile Technologies as Interfaces of Hybrid Spaces," *Space and Culture* 9, no. 3 (2006): 261–78, doi: 10.1177/1206331206289022; Jaako Stenros and Markus Montola, "Historical Influences on Pervasive Games," in *Pervasive Games: Theory and Design*, edited by Markus Montola, Jaako Stenros, and Annika Waern (Burlington, MA: Morgan Kaufmann, 2009), 53–70; Flanagan, "Locating Play and Politics;" see also, Leorke, *Location-based Gaming*, 4.

31 Here we are thinking of games such as Blast Theory's *Can You See Me Now?* (2001), among others, and *Botfighters* (2001) and *Zombies, Run!* (2012). See: Adriana de Souza e Silva and Jordan Frith, *Mobile Interfaces in Public Spaces: Locational Privacy, Control, and Urban Sociability* (New York: Routledge, 2012), 89–96; Jamie Henthorn, "Rewriting Neighbourhoods: *Zombies, Run!* and the Runner as Rhetor," in *Social, Casual and Mobile Games: The Changing Gaming Landscape*, edited by Tama Leaver and Michele Willson (New York: Bloomsbury, 2016), 165–77.

32 See: John Ryan, "Not a Bush Flaneur? The Convergent Typographies of Recreational Bushwalking, Floristic Appreciation and Human Embodiment in the Southwest of Western Australia," *Colloquy: Monash University Postgraduate Journal* 20 (2010): 5–32; Melissa Harper, *The Ways of the Bushwalker: On foot in Australia*, Sydney: University of New South Wales Press, 2007). And, outside the Australian bush context, on walking, immersion and contemplation more broadly, see: Rebecca Solnit, *Wanderlust: A History of Walking* (Harmondsworth, Middlesex: Penguin, 2001); Jean-Jacques Rousseau, *Reveries of a Solitary Walker*, translated by Russell Goulbourne (Oxford: Oxford University Press, 2011).

33 Thomas Apperley and Kyle Moore, "Haptic Ambience: Ambient Play, the Haptic Effect and Co-presence in *Pokémon GO*," *Convergence: The International Journal of Research into New Media Technologies* 25, no. 1 (2018): 6–17, doi: 10.1177/1354856518811017; Hjorth and Richardson, *Gaming in Social, Locative, and Mobile Media*, 59–75.

34 Rebecca Krinke (ed.), *Contemporary Landscapes of Contemplation* (London: Routledge, 2005); Alex Soojung-Kim Pang, "What is Contemplative Computing?" *Deliberate Rest*, May 31 2012, www.deliberate.rest/?p=1755; Timothy Morton, *Realist Magic: Objects, Ontology, Causality* (Ann Arbor: Open Humanities Press, 2013), 128–36.

35 Leorke, *Location-based Gaming*.

36 Hugh Davies and Troy Innocent, "The Space Between Debord and Pikachu," *DiGRA '17—Proceedings of the 2017 DiGRA International Conference*, Melbourne, Australia.

37 Lee Humphreys, "Involvement Shield or Social Catalyst: Thoughts on Sociospatial Practice of *Pokémon GO*," *Mobile Media & Communication* 5, no. 1 (2017): 15–19, doi: 10.1177/2050157916677864.

38 See, for instance, pages 12–13 on questions of geography in *Measuring Australia's Digital Divide: The Australian Digital Inclusion Index 2018*, https://digitalinclusionindex.org.au/wp-content/uploads/2018/08/Australian-digital-inclusion-index-2018.pdf.

39 Michael Bull, "'To Each Their Own Bubble': Mobile Spaces of Sound in the City," in *Foundations of Mobile Media Studies: Essential Texts on the Formation of a Field*, edited by Jason Farman (London: Routledge, 2017), 154.

40 See: http://troyinnocent.net/noemaflux.htm.

41 See: http://troyinnocent.net/wayfinder_live.htm.

42 Larissa Hjorth and Sarah Pink, "New Visualities and the Digital Wayfarer: Reconceptualizing Camera Phone Photography and Locative Media," *Mobile Media & Communication* 2, no. 1 (2014): 40–57, doi: 10.1177/2050157913505257.

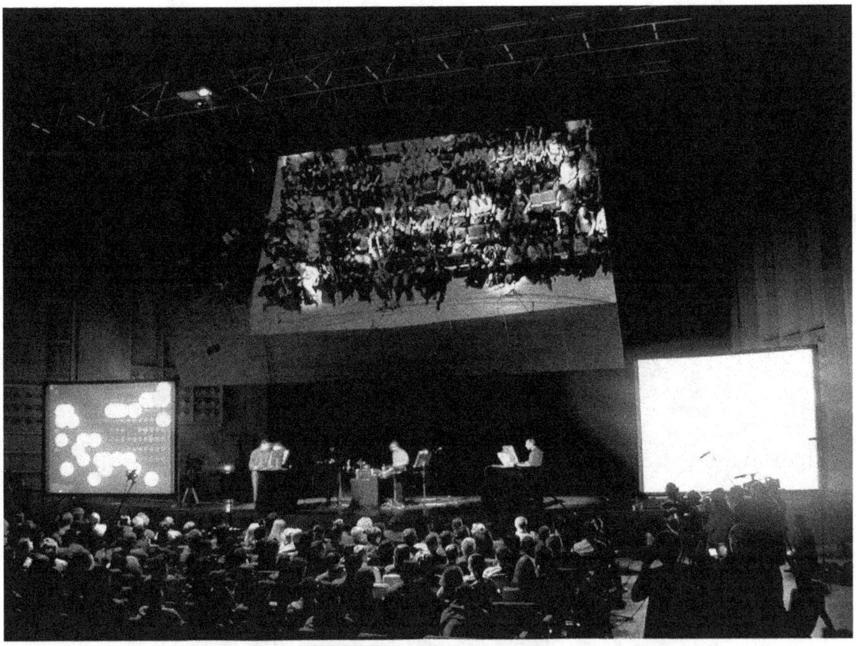

*Figure 1* Golan Levin, *Dialtones (A Telesymphony)* (2001). Photo credit: Golan Levin

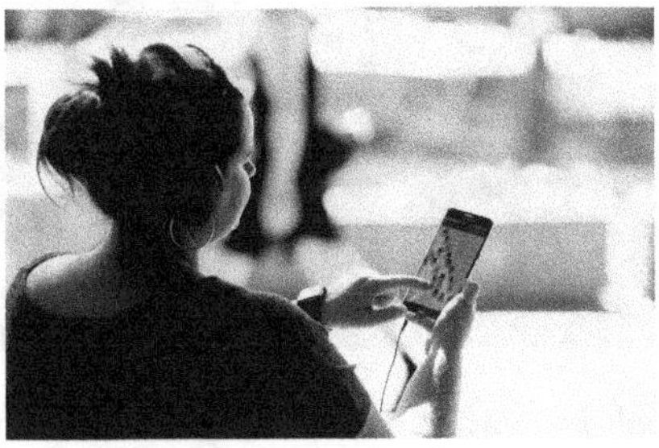

*Figure 2* Leah Barclay, *Aurality* (2017). Photo credit: Greg Harm

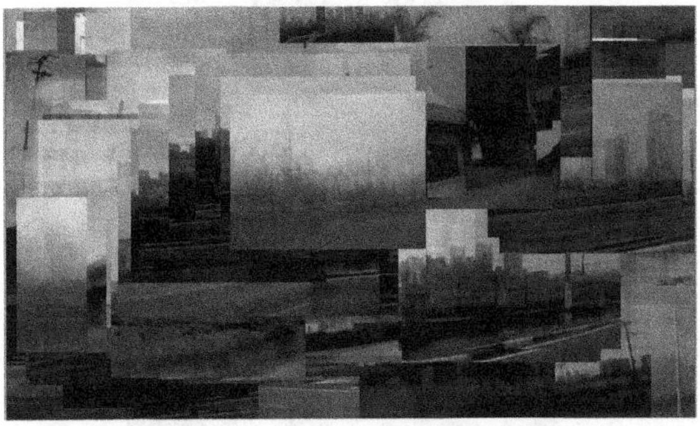

*Figure 3* Giselle Beiguelman, *Sometimes (De Vez em Quando)* (2006). Photo credit: Giselle Beiguelman

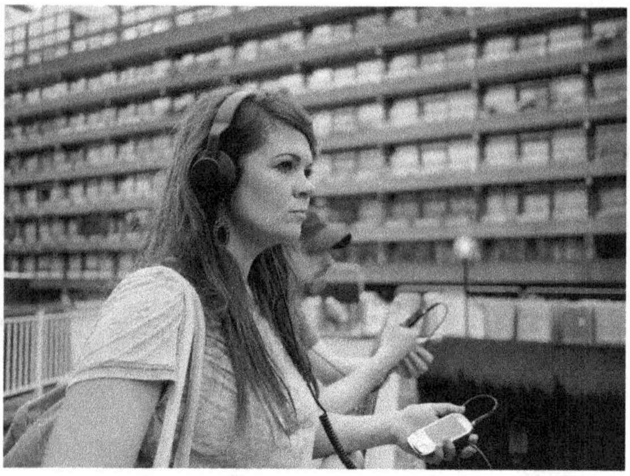

*Figure 4* Circumstance, *A Hollow Body* (2014). Photo credit: Duncan Speakman

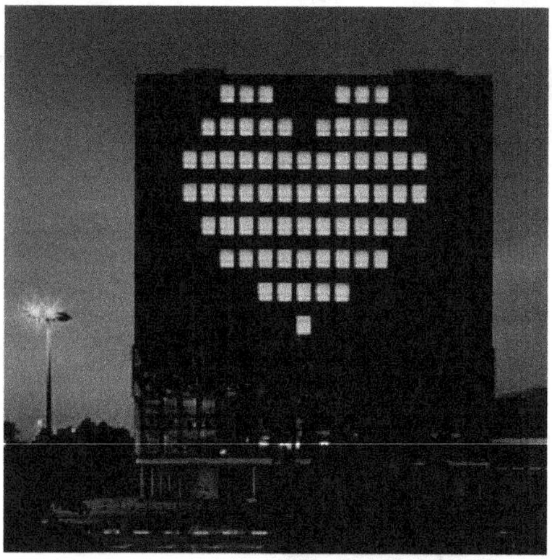

*Figure 5* The façade of *Blinkenlights* with love letter (a pulsing heart). Photo credit: Chaos Computer Club

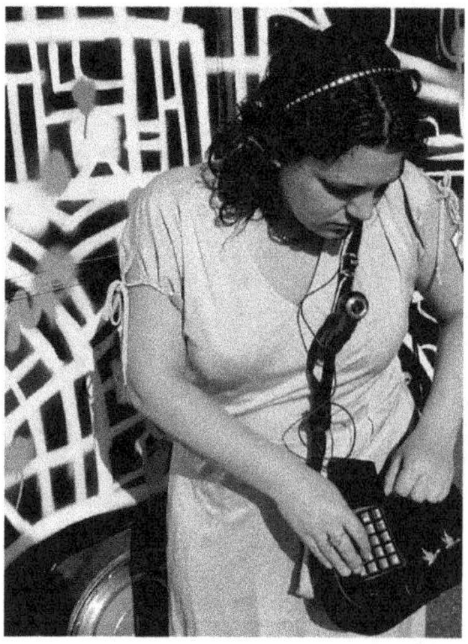

*Figure 6* Nancy Mauro-Flude, *Bag Lady 2.0* (2007). Photo credit: Nancy Mauro-Flude

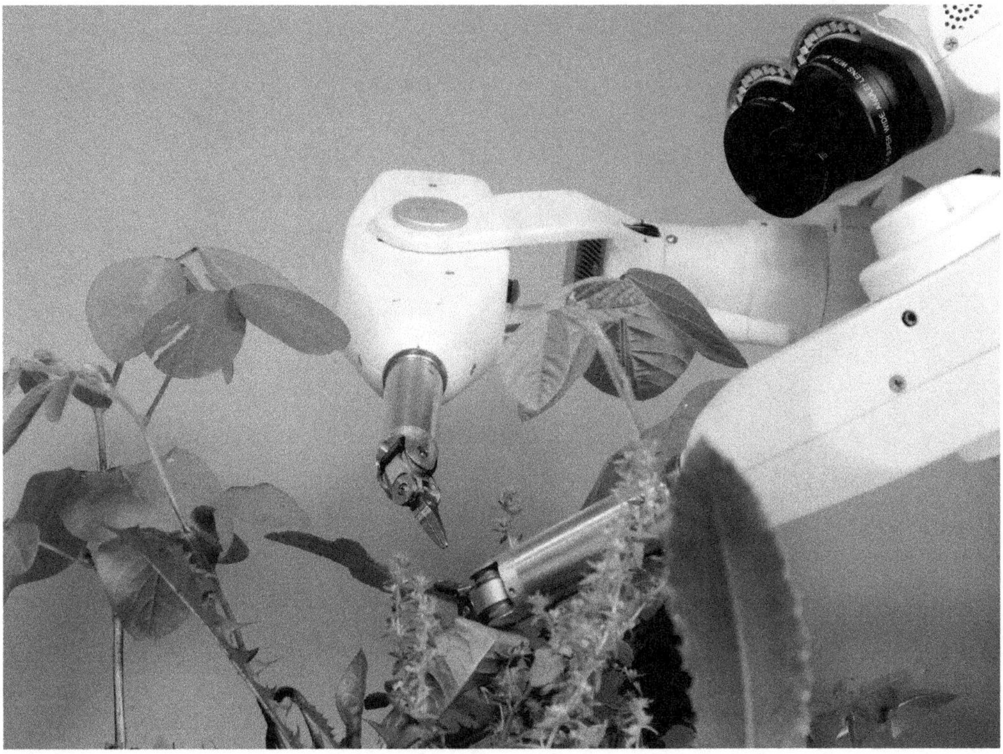

*Figure 7* Shannon McMullen and Fabian Winkler, *Algorithmic Gardener* (2015). Photo credit: McMullen_Winkler

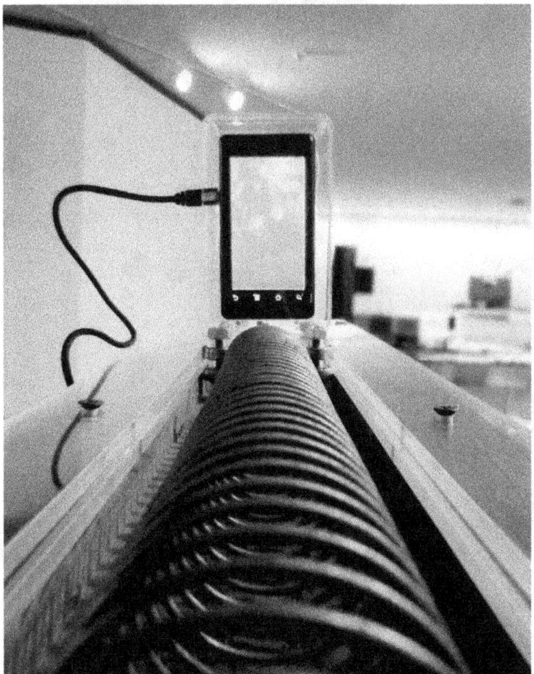

*Figure 8* Gilberto Prado, *Encontros* (2012). Photo credit: Gilberto Prado

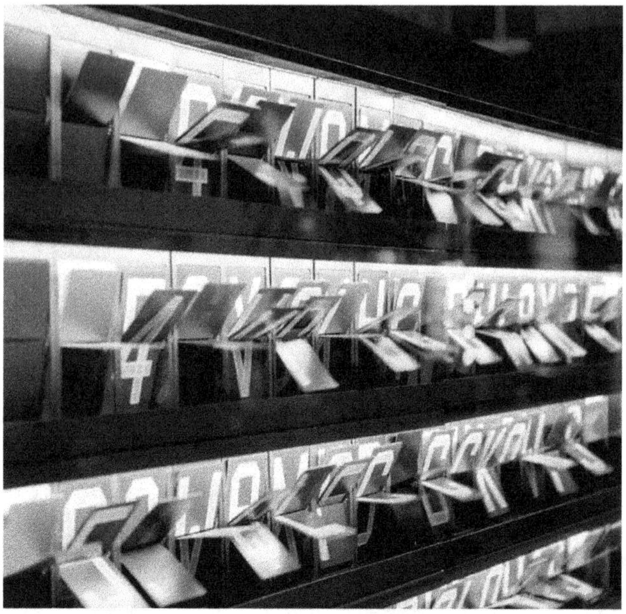

*Figure 9* *Every Thing Every Time* by Naho Matsuda (2017), as presented at Great Exhibition of the North (2018). Produced by FutureEverything. Open Prototyping Case Study. Image courtesy of Naho Matsuda

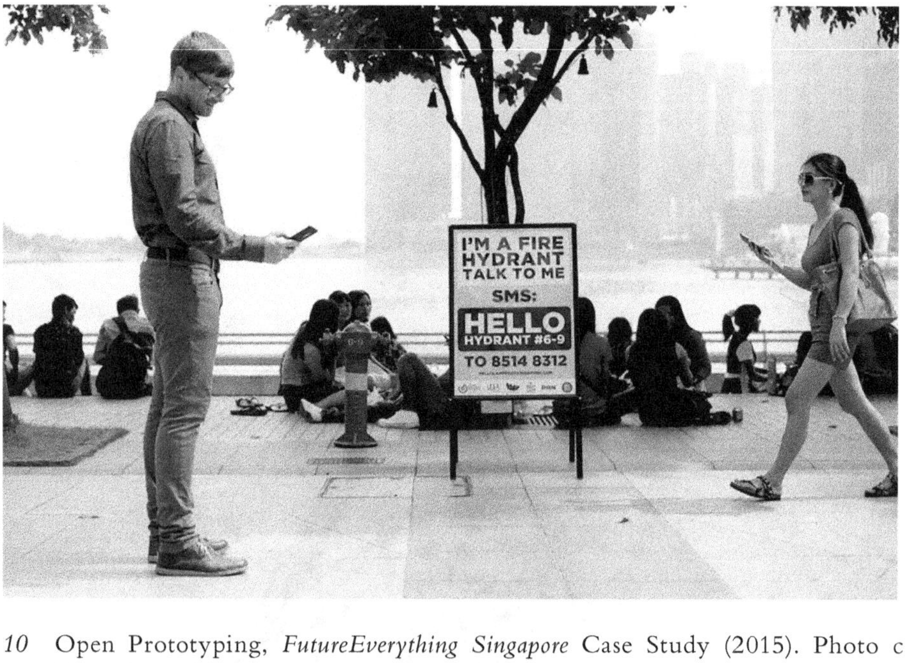


*Figure 10* Open Prototyping, *FutureEverything Singapore* Case Study (2015). Photo credit: FutureEverything

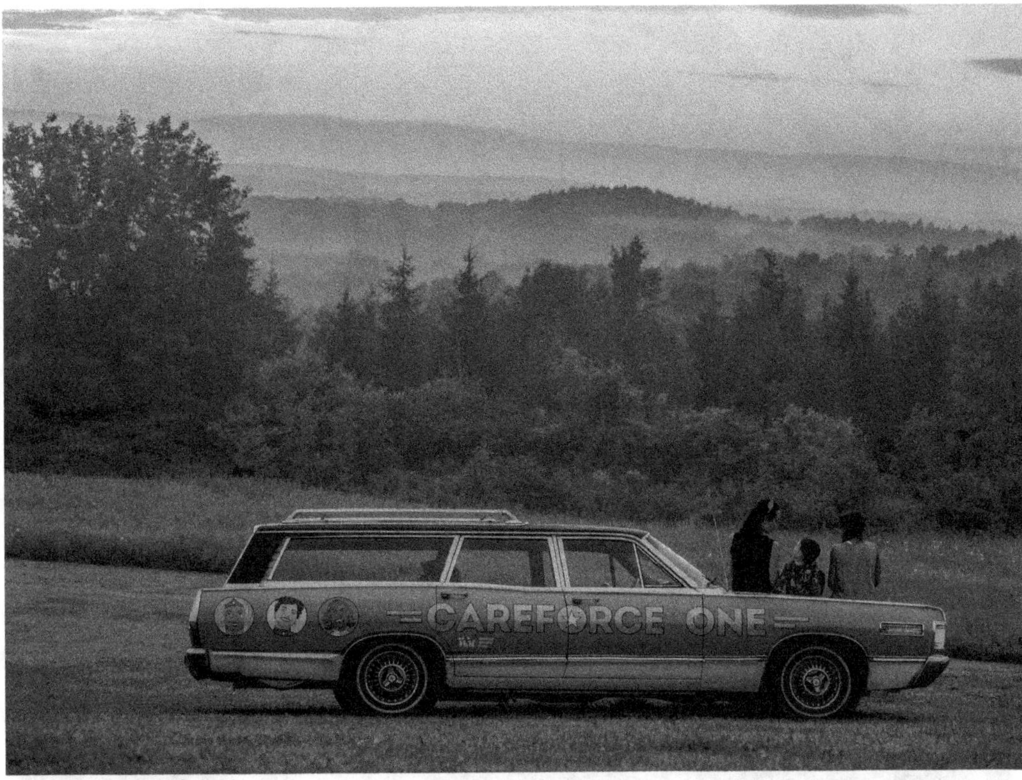


*Figure 11* Marisa Morán Jahn (Studio REV), *CareForce One* (2017–2019). Photo credit: Marisa Morán Jahn

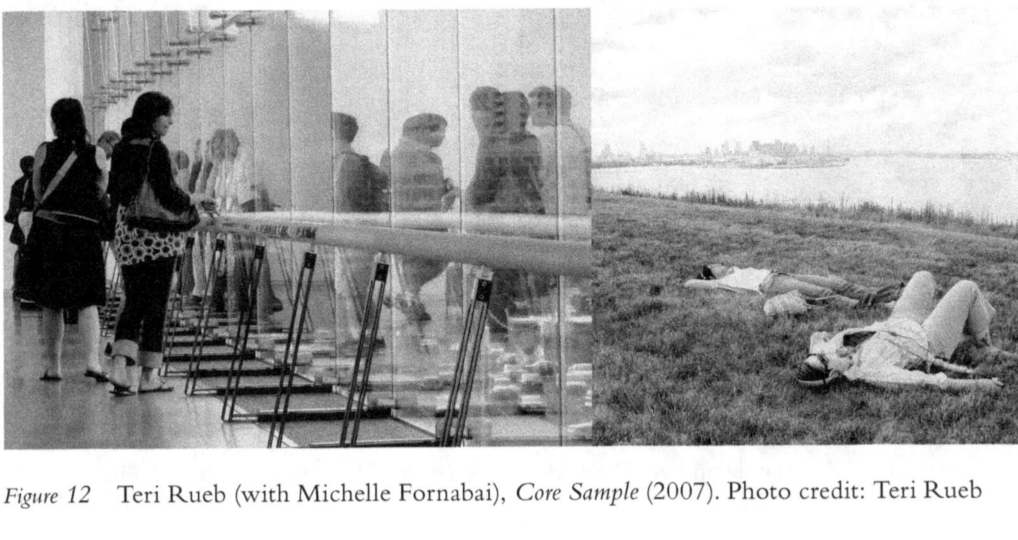

*Figure 12* Teri Rueb (with Michelle Fornabai), *Core Sample* (2007). Photo credit: Teri Rueb

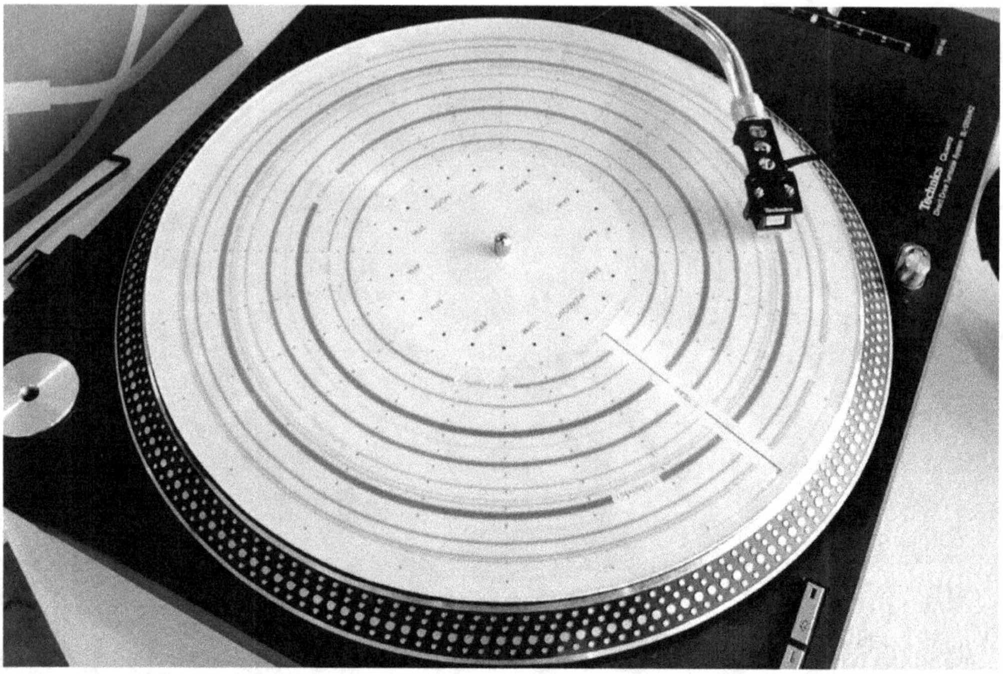

*Figure 13* *Quotidian Record* exhibited. Photo credit: Brian House

*Figure 14* Rafael Lozano Hemmer, *Body Movies, Relational Architecture 6* (2002). Photo credit: Antimodular Research

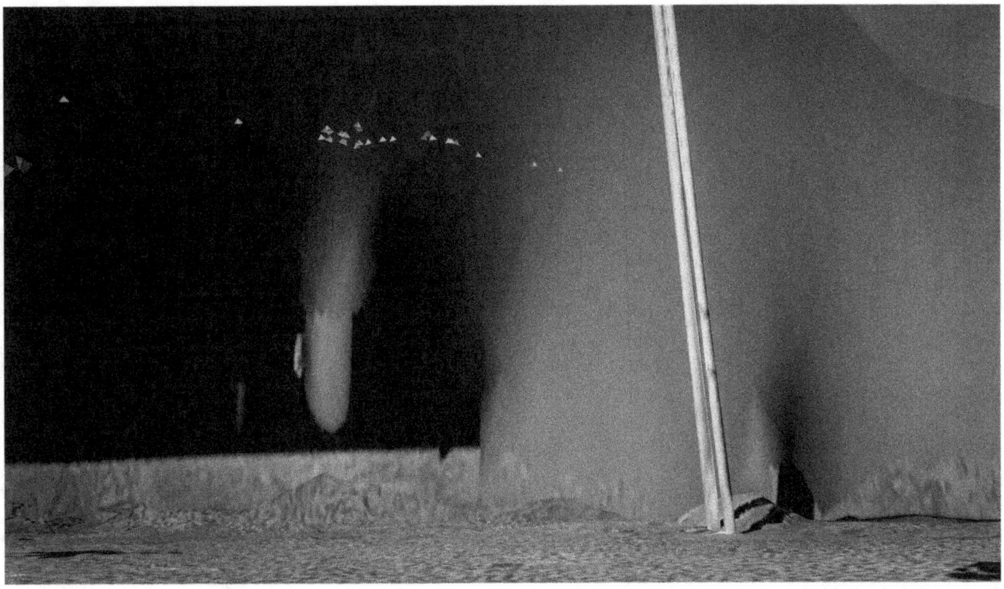

*Figure 15* PolakVanBekkum, *GoMoveBe revisited* (2019). Photo credit: PolakVanBekkum

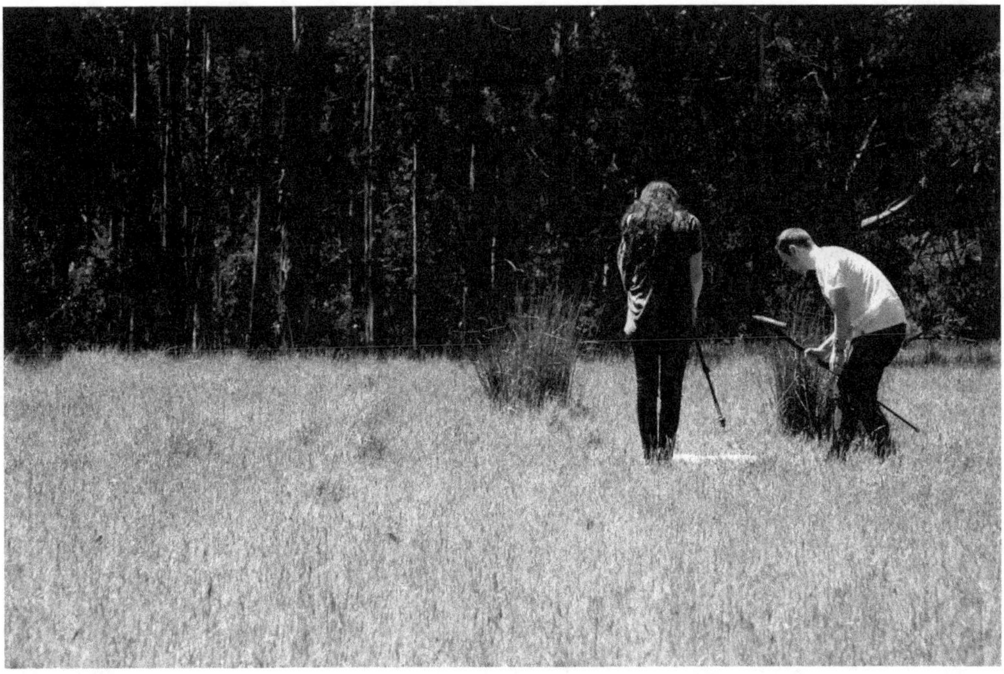

*Figure 16* Matthew Riley and Troy Innocent, *Ephiphyte* (2017). Photo credit: Kate Baker

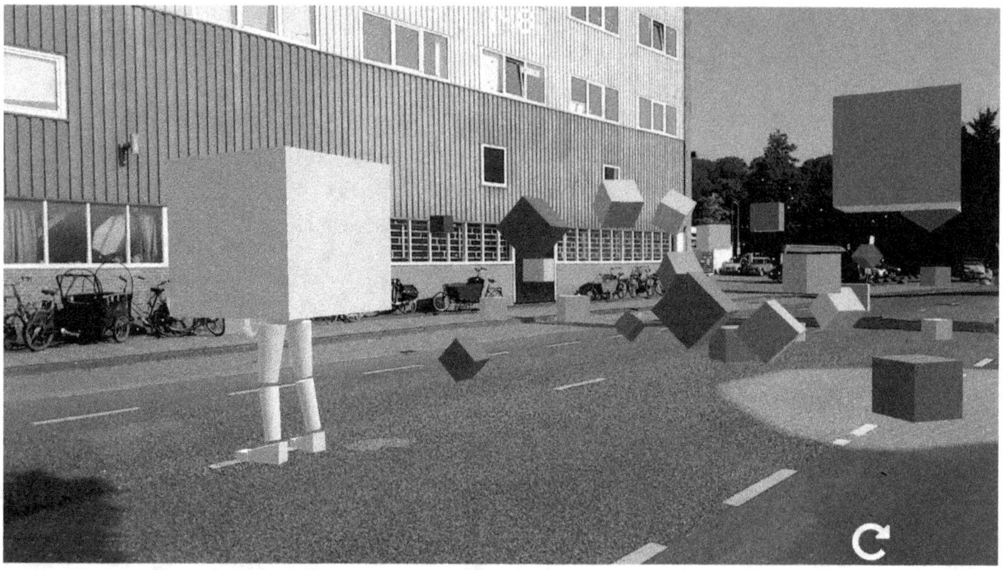

*Figure 17* Sander Veenhof, *Avatar Says No* (2019). Photo credit: Sander Veenhof

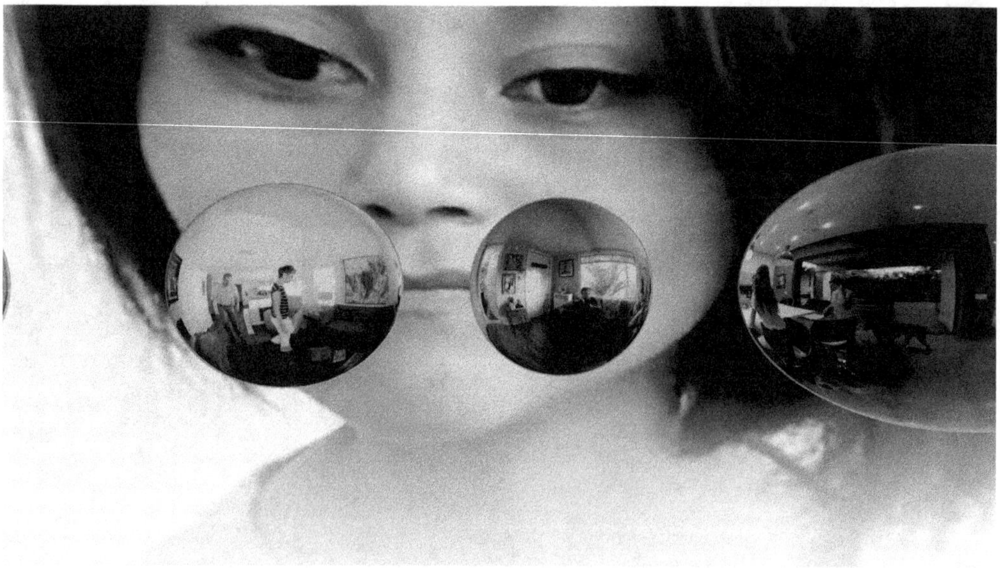

*Figure 18* Lauren McCarthy, *LAUREN* (2018). Photo credit: Lauren McCarthy

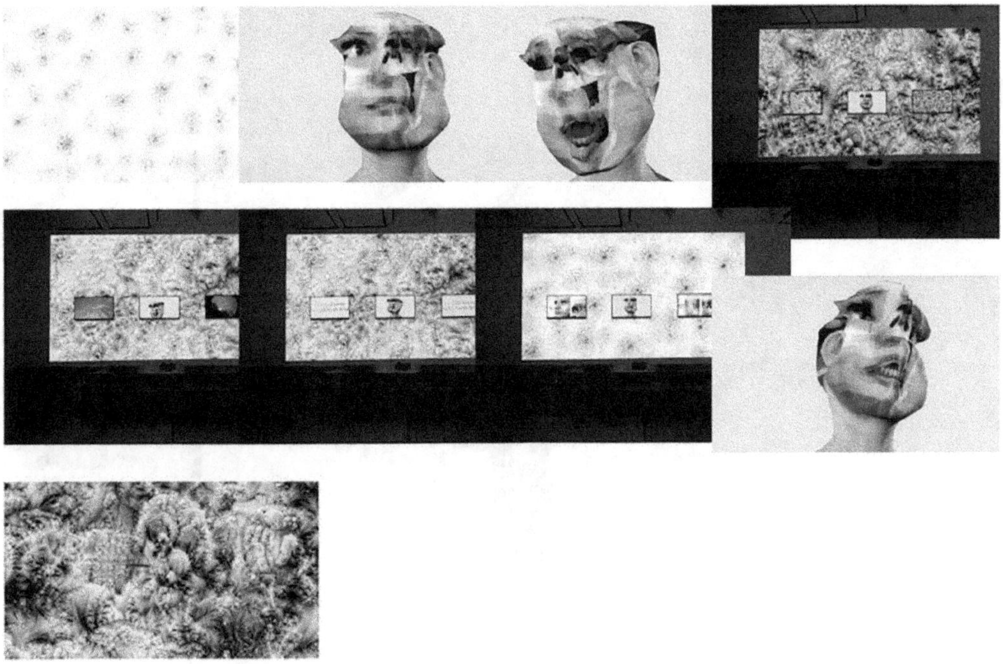

*Figure 19* Zach Blas, *im here to learn so* ☺ (2017). Photo credit: Zach Blas

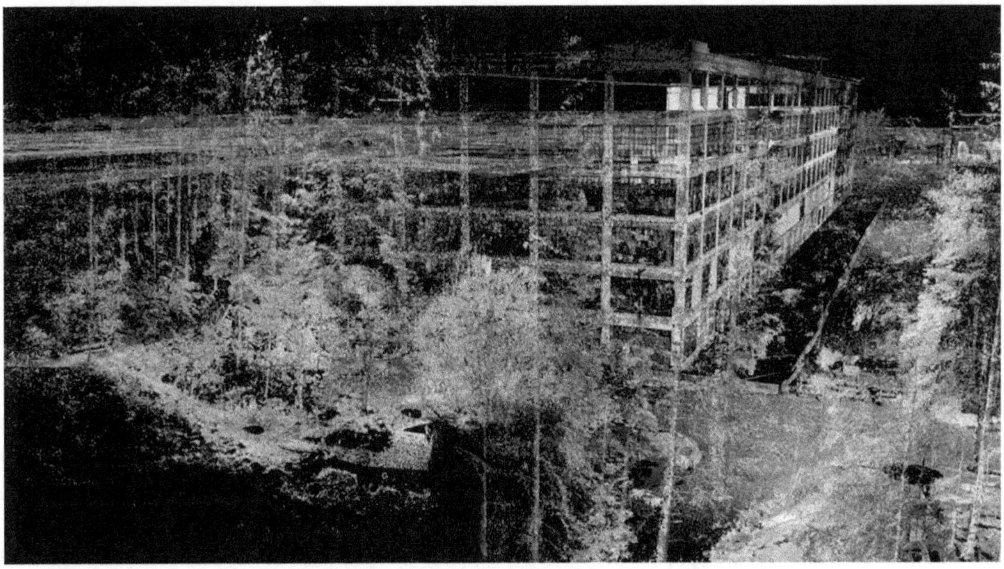

*Figure 20* Liam Young, *Where the City Can't See* (2016). Photo credit: Liam Young

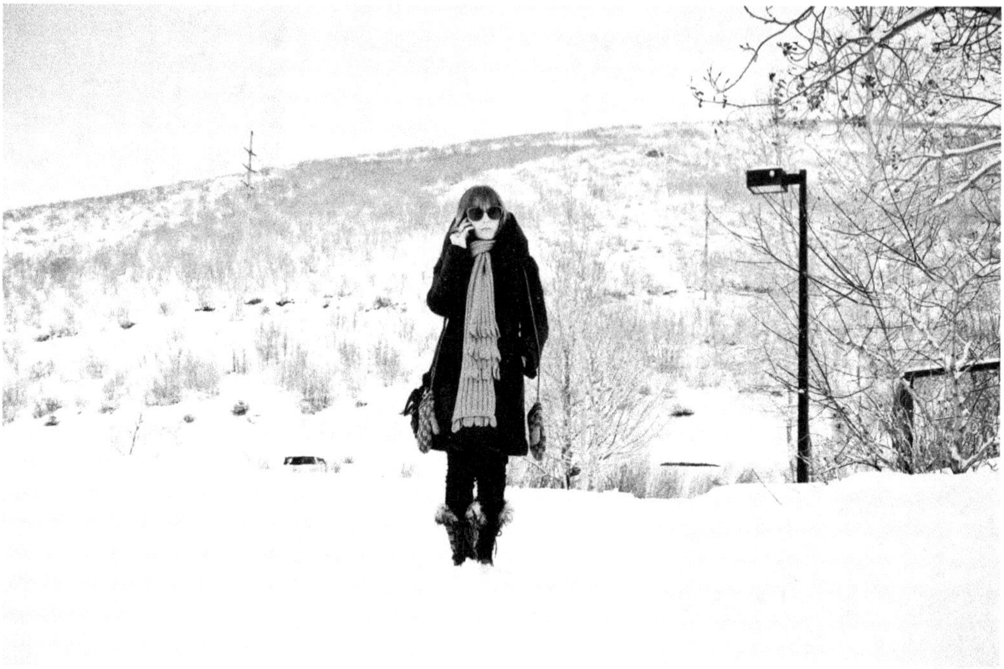

*Figure 21* Blast Theory, *A Machine to See With* (2010). Photo credit: Blast Theory

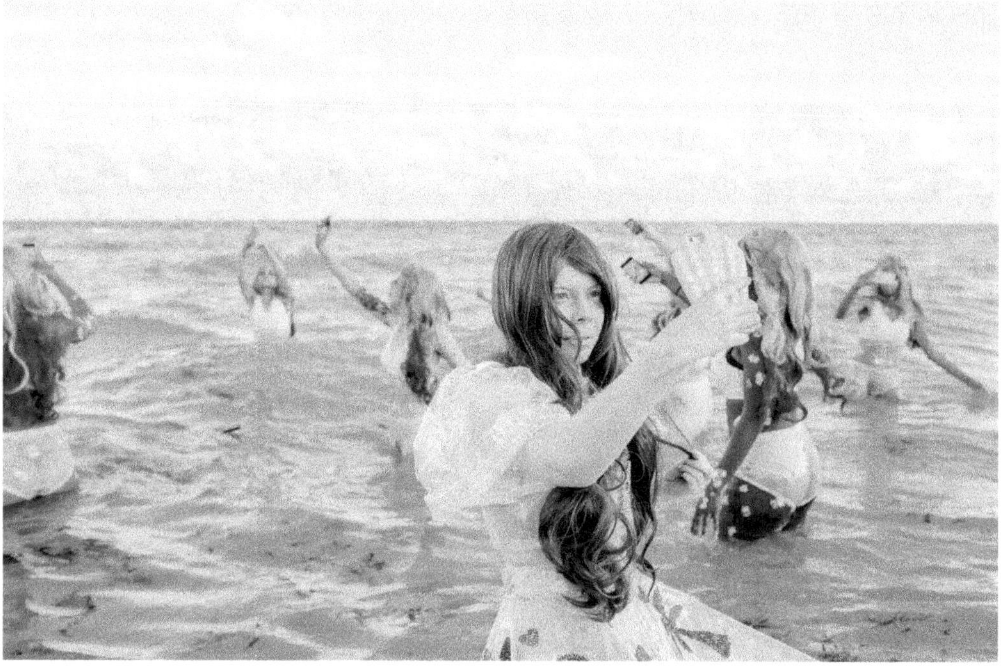

*Figure 22* Kate Durbin, *Hello Selfie Miami*. Photo credit: Kate Durbin

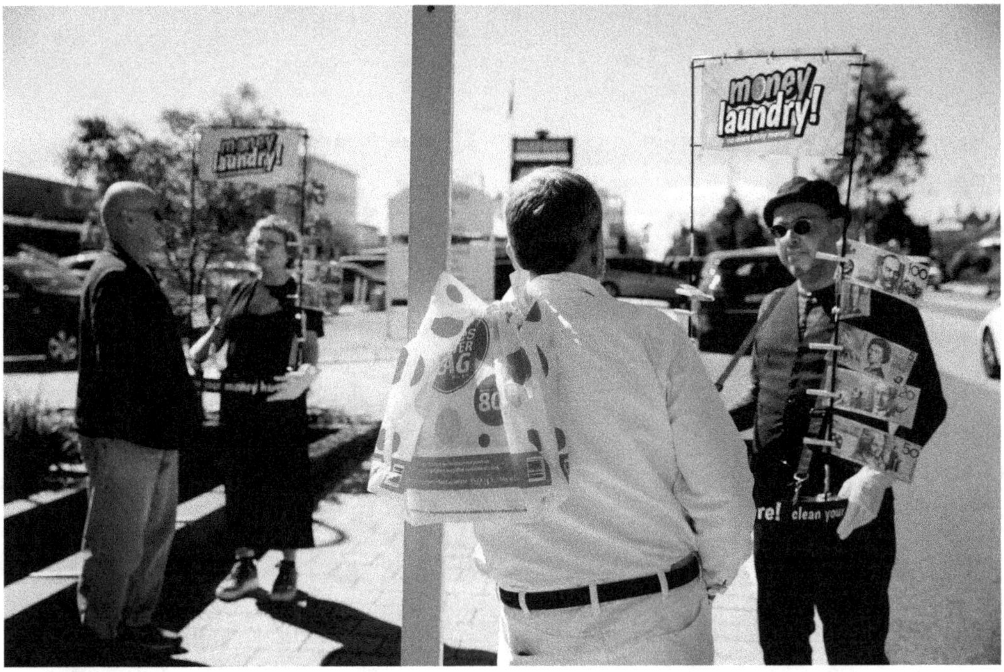


*Figure 23* pvi, *tiny revolutions* (2019). Photo credit: David Cox

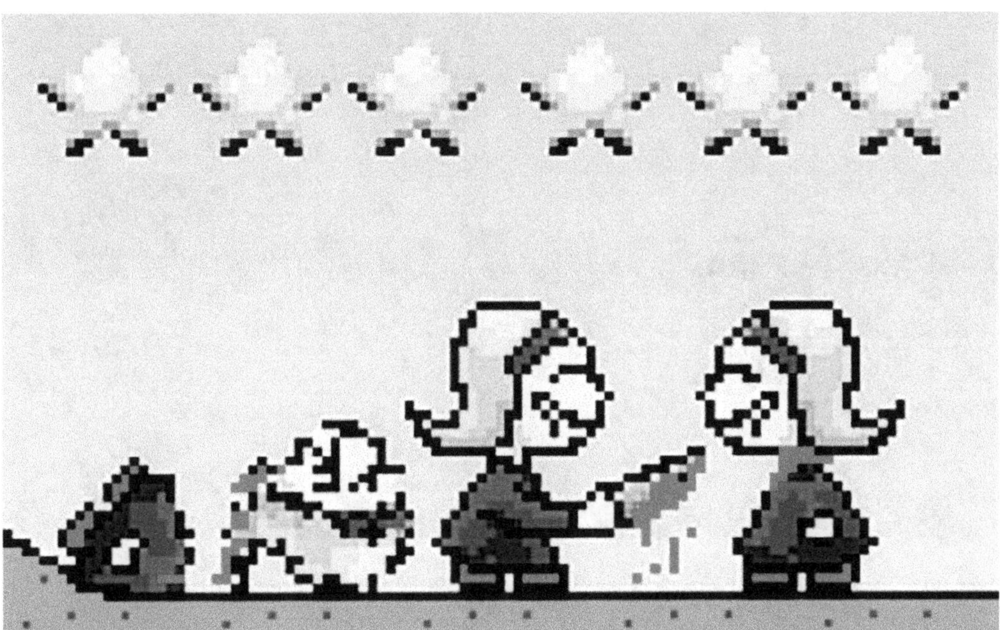

*Figure 24* Rebecca Cannon and Karen Jenkins, *Kill Yourself Game* (2005). Photo credit: Rebecca Cannon and Karen Jenkins

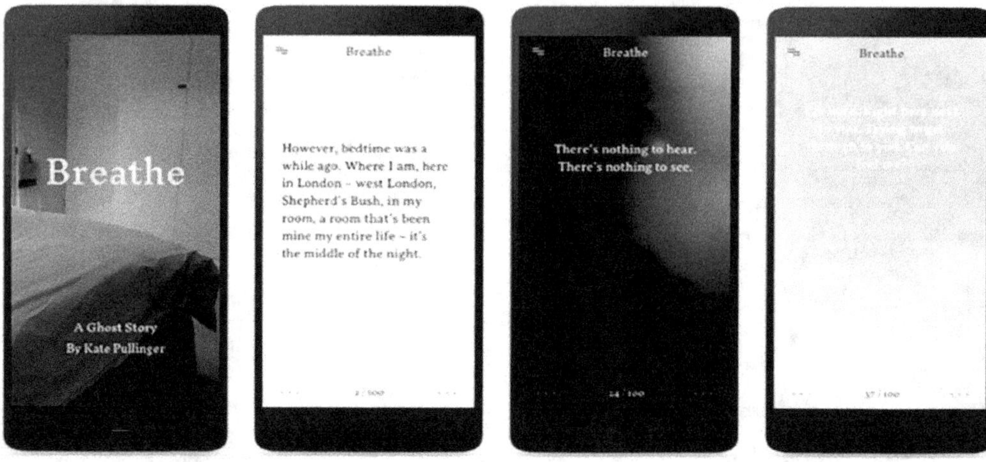


*Figure 25* Screenshot of Kate Pullinger's Breathe (2016) Photo credit: Kate Pullinger

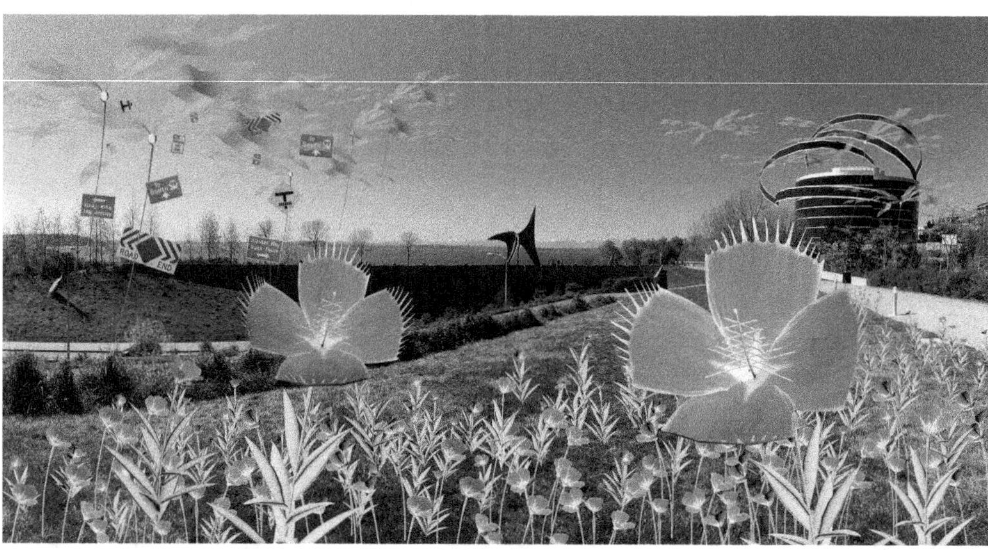

*Figure 26* Tamiko Thiel, *Gardens of the Anthropocene* (2016). Photo credit: Tamiko Thiel

# SECTION SIX

# Co-Design and Space

# 23
# LISTENING TO CIRCUMSTANCE

*Duncan Speakman* in Conversation with *Klare Lanson*

Duncan Speakman is a composer and sound artist based at the Pervasive Media Studio in Bristol.[1] His work creates narrative sound-led experiences that engage audiences in uncontrolled public and private space, in often cinematic and poetic ways. He makes art internationally including installations on trains in Guangzhou, loudspeaker symphonies in New Zealand, audio walks in Saitama, and sound installations in Porto. He set up and directed the arts collective Circumstance from 2010 to 2017 with Sarah Anderson and Emilie Grenier, later joined by Tom Abba (Figure 23.1).[2]

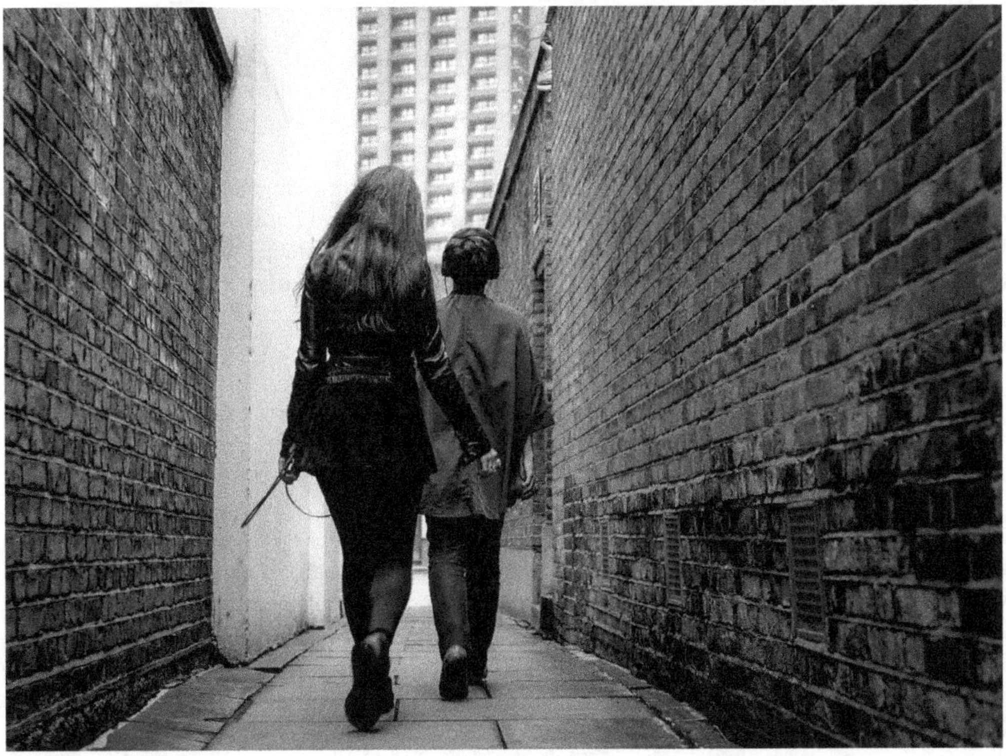

*Figure 23.1* Circumstance—*A Hollow Body* (2014). Photo credit: Duncan Speakman

How do you define mobile media art in relation to the performance within your projects?

For me the use of mobile tools as a performative device was always led by my feeling that while these devices were excellent at connecting us to remote people and places, they had a tendency to distance and separate us from our immediate surroundings. To this end, I always sought to think about how I could use these devices, so that they actively encouraged audiences to engage with their environments, in both physical and social ways. It was about using them to change our sense of place. There was also an agenda for me in terms of using tools that people already had in their pockets. So, while I have used and built bespoke systems, I really like using things that are already part of the everyday.

What for you are some of the defining moments in the field of mobile media art you have experienced?

In terms of defining moments for me, the epiphany came through a commission from the Mobile Bristol research group set up by Hewlett Packard Labs in Bristol. Up to this point, I hadn't really been a mobile device user, not even using a Walkman, but I had been involved with the pre-YouTube online videoblogging community. In that field, I tended to make short observational documentaries, often unedited single shot film for which I would compose music scores. HP asked me to make something using their new locative media system, so as an early test I loaded some of my soundtracks onto it and took a walk. At this moment, I essentially saw the films I had been making played out in real life, the music score silencing the world and creating the same aesthetic feeling, so from that point on I pretty much stopped making films and began treating everyday uncontrolled environments as my visual material for sited listening experiences.

Can you speak to what inspired you to create a collective based around mobile media art?

Circumstance was originally created as a kind of thought experiment. As a solo artist I had been collaborating regularly with the same people (at that time Emilie Grenier and Sarah Anderson) and had become a bit tired of seeing the pieces credited as Duncan Speakman with etc. I wanted to work under a group name to both emphasize the collaborative nature of the work and move the focus away from the makers and onto the work itself. The challenge was of course that I still sort of remained the creative director (and only full-time member), instigating and leading all the projects, so in the end the logistical burden of running it became too much, and I've gone back to working under my own name, but often still collaborating with the same people!

Your work is a fascinating way to question the collective experience of public spaces, where sound and listening are integral to work such as your 2014 projects *Periphery Songs, A Hollow Body*, and the pedestrian symphonies. Can you elaborate on these projects?

There's an important categorization to make here, works like *Periphery Songs* are a solo audio walk for one audience member to experience in isolation. *A Hollow Body* is a more performative audio walk, designed for a pair of listeners, each one receiving different instructions, so they become performers for each other, cast as figures in the city landscape that they both look at. The pedestrian symphonies were the pieces *Vicinity Songs* (2011), *Of Sleeping Birds* (2012) and *A Folded Path* (2013), these pieces use a system of 40 portable speakers, each one has a geolocated mobile phone in, and each speaker plays a different instrumental element of the composition (e.g. one might play a violin part, another a voice, etc.). They are carried by the audience to create the pedestrian symphony, and the geolocation software triggers different parts of the composition depending on the physical location of the audience. We act as conductors for the audience, three of us would each guide a different group through the city and because we knew where the geo triggers were, we could shape the pace and dynamics of the piece. Also, we would choreograph the three groups so at times they would meet and visually/sonically overlap.

This project developed as a direct response to the solo and mass participation audio walks I'd been making. In those projects, I was making the city into a cinematic experience by framing it with a music soundtrack. In the mass participation "subtlemobs" this space was shared by everyone taking part, but they existed in a kind of separate layer to everyone else in the environment and were also isolated from the acoustic environment. So, I wanted to explore what happened if you turned the concept inside out, have a music score that frames the city, but that is shared by the participants, passers-by, and the sound of the environment.

The other aspect of these pieces I really like is something I called *social composition*. Because each speaker played an individual musical element the physical dispersion of the audience would change the sound mix. For example, if everyone was sticking close together you would get a really dense sound; if there was one person straggling at the back you might get a distant trumpet solo. Equally because of the vagueness and drift of Global Positioning System (GPS) signals, different speakers would trigger at different times. What this means in practice is that even though as conductors we know what section would be triggered, we wouldn't know exactly which musical voices would enter first or last.

The thing I never fully resolved with this work is the "ask" for the audience. Essentially, we're making the audience complicit in playing "our" music out into a public or uncontrolled space, and somehow taking responsibility for a sonic intervention that they may not want to actually be responsible for. We tried to alleviate this partly by always making sure that the conductor and an usher following the group wore hi-vis coats. This was so that if a passer-by had some issue or problem with what was happening, they were more likely to challenge one of the hi-vis "organizers" rather than an audience member. It was a kind of protective buffer for participants.

In your opinion, who are some of the most exciting practitioners in the field and why?

Things I have enjoyed over the years have been *And While London Burns* (2007) by Platform Arts[3] and *Core Sample* (2007) by Teri Rueb.[4] I'm always a big fan of Ant Hampton's work, which while not so "mobile" I think does fit into the category.[5] Plan B Performance have always had a combination of conceptual rigor and aesthetics that I love.[6] I think Sander Veenhof has been making interesting works in AR for a long time[7].

Your work radiates ideas around cartography and mapping. Can you speak to this element within your projects?

It's changed historically. It's not amazing to be walking around with mobiles now, but in the legacy of making work in this area, the idea of having a live updated map on your phone is something that first appeared over the time of making this work. It wasn't there to start with. When we were making those early GPS-based pieces, we were using those car systems that were being adapted to mobile phones. What was interesting about the linearity during that time was that the audience were presented art works where you'd see a region on a map, and you'd know that there'd be some kind of media content there, and you'd walk there, and you'd hear it. However, the problem I think for me, as a composer, was that it took away this sense of composition that happens over time. As you'd walk somewhere, because people were choosing their places, rather than having a continuous furred experience. In the end, I'd just end up making audio-only pieces that didn't give you that digital interface at all. Then a few years ago, making *It Must Have Been Dark by Then* (2017) (Figure 23.2), a lot of the narratives were about borders and migration, especially the

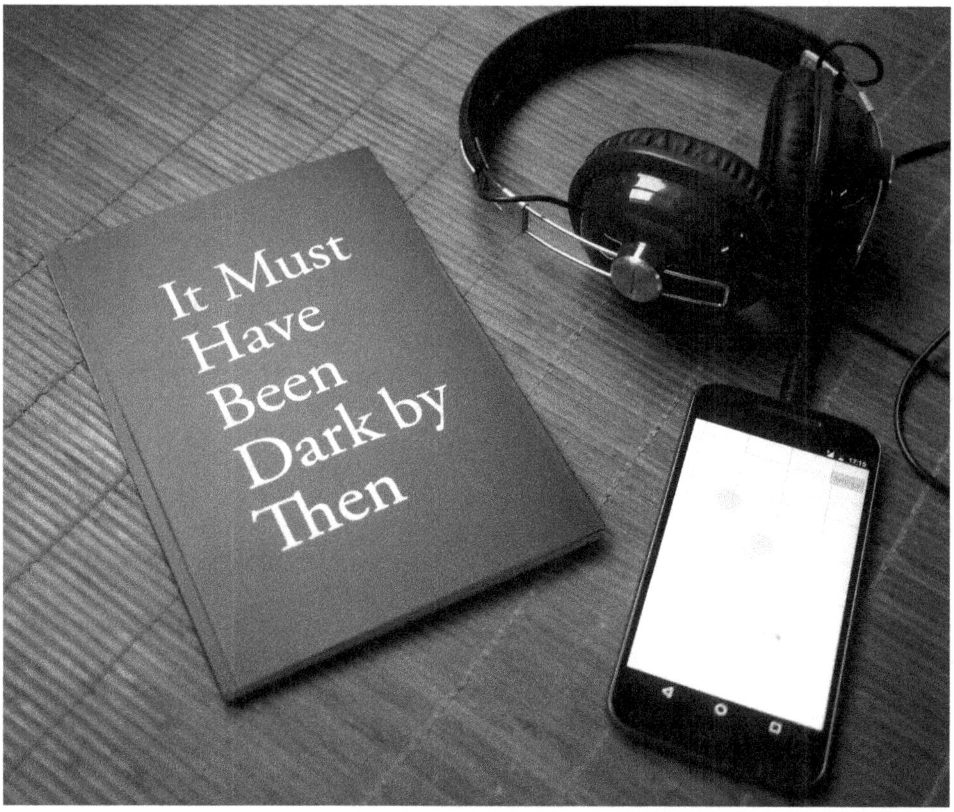


*Figure 23.2* Mapping place with *It Must Have Been Dark by Then* (2017). Photo credit: Duncan Speakman

history of maps. The permeance of physical maps as opposed to the continually updating digital map; the idea that with a digital map you are constantly erasing history—someone knocks down a building or changes a territory or a border, that updating doesn't give you the context that change has happened. Whereas if you look at physical maps, whether it's an old physical projection by some colonialist explorer, it's going to be a very different map, but it's going to be dated and it has a time, and you can see how these things have changed. So, in *It Must Have Been*, we use the map without markings on it; you have the grid and you have the flashing blue dot that's ever present, but there's no physical markings.

In our everyday life we're so used to the digital map now (so that part of the excitement is gone) but my feeling was that we pre-plan our journeys through the city because it shows us where everything is. In the project we took all that away, just leaving the blue dot, so you've got to get *there*, but not telling you what's in between. You have to physically engage with the place. For me, the exciting thing about mapping is actually undermining it and sort of taking away the safety net of the onscreen map and forcing you back into the wayfaring approach, where you've got to constantly sense and deal with what's around you.

> The idea of erasure in a poetic sense is nice, a kind of minimalism. Your method of "literal" erasure of the map highlights the flux of geography too.

I think one of the challenges is how you make that sort of erasure visible in a sense. I know there's some geography research into how to make maps more temporal. I like *showing* erasure. There's a piece I make in collaboration with a theater company called Uninvited Guests, it's called *Give Me Back My Broken Night* (2010)[8] and one of the sections of that piece is that we take the audience on a guided tour. Sometimes it's pre-recorded and sometimes it's a live performer walking ahead of you speaking to everyone through a radio transmitter. What you're hearing is a description of your surroundings in the past tense. So, we've always called that "the erasing moment." As you're walking along it might say "There used to be cars driving up and down this street, there used to be a building here that people lived in, there used to be a library here..." It's amazing, this kind of melancholic sense it brings to the looking of something, being told that what you're looking at is a sort of ghost image that won't be there some day.

> A lot of your work has a haunting quality, very cinematic. You've got a background in sound and composition, can you speak to the idea of sound as mobility in terms of your projects?

There are two aspects. First is the making process, it's really iterative. It usually starts with a music sketch, a theme or idea for the work. Then I go out and walk with that music, that selection of sketches, and see what that leads to. So, I start by being in that cinematic space from the get-go, seeing what it directs my attention to, how it makes me feel—kind of auto-ethnographic. Second, I'll start collating, editing into a shape, thinking how the text might work, and just keep adding to it. It often starts from listening to music in situ.

With *It Must Have Been Dark*, there was a research component to the making process, which was about traveling to different places—even though the piece wouldn't actually happen in those places—it was important that the process started with the wandering mindset. I stole a technique from the Australian sound artist Oren Ambarchi,[9] where I made a slowly developing 40-minute rhythm track and gave it to Sarah my collaborator, who then performed an improvisation with it, transforming it to a 40-minute piece of rhythm and tone. I took that with me on my research trips, driving across a desert in an empty building in Latvia. Whenever I was making field recordings or choices about sites, having the music playing gave a sense of cohesion for me across all the places—an underlying sense of tonality and the idea of searching was based on the idea of disappearance and looking.

I'm really interested in Salome Voegelin's ideas about sound crossing borders,[10] the impermanence of borders through sound. I think there are a few conceptual challenges with that, but I like it. There's this blurring and bleed that happens with sound that maybe more explicit or understandable to people than visuals? The idea of hearing a voice from another room works a lot more with everyday understanding, than being able to see through a wall.

> I like that way Voegelin critiques sound too, her thinking around listening is great well, a mobile connection to the world...

There's also that idea that when you're listening to a soundscape, you're always contributing to it as well. That relates to the newest pieces I've been making with augmented audio systems, really trying to think through those ideas. Of course, one of the issues with headphone work is that I'm really isolating people, I've chosen to do that. I still think there's something really powerful that happens in that moment where you're in the uncontrollable everyday world and experiencing it in an unnatural or mediated way (Figure 23.3).

> What about the flipside of that, where your use of the mobile as a tool for hacking public space actually changes the environment for the audience?

One of the projects that does this was the subtlemob *As If It Were The Last Time* (2009).[11] One of the problems is that there's an issue around the language of making work for public space.

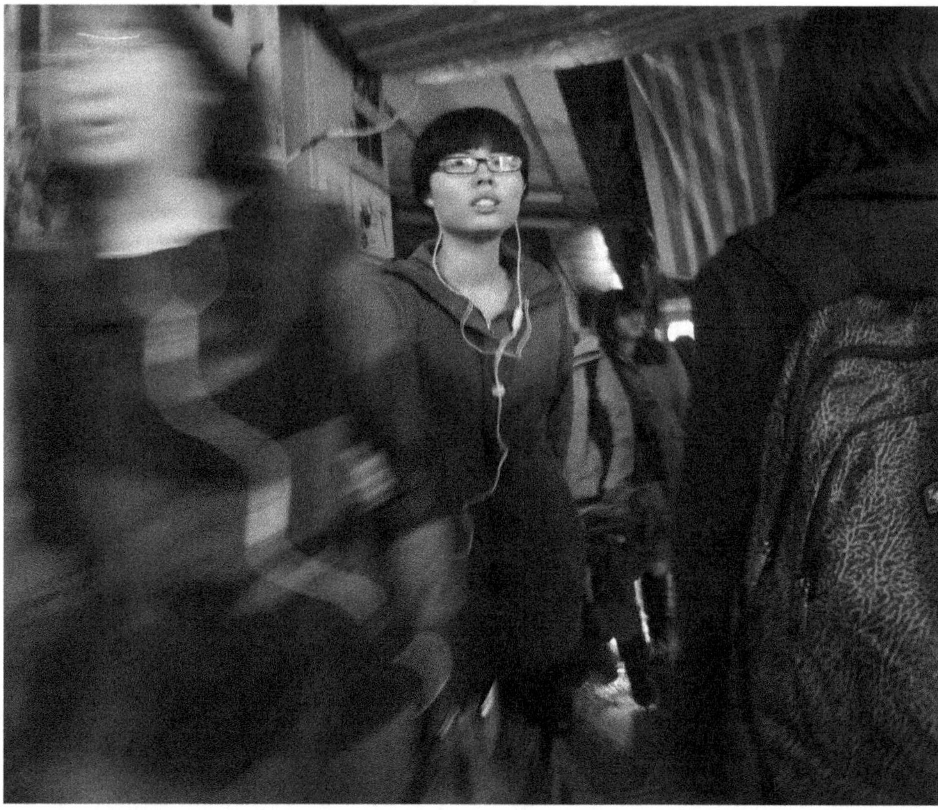

*Figure 23.3* Subtlemob *As If It Were The Last Time* (2009). Photo credit: Duncan Speakman

Public space is a legally defined term, and one of the problems we have in Europe is that what happens increasingly is that public space is disappearing, replaced with privately owned spaces that are made to look like public spaces. For example, in *A Hollow Body* (2014)[12] there's a situation in the piece where it points out the copper studs in the ground—in the pavement—and those studs actually mark the division between private and public land. No one tells you that, there's no acknowledgment, but in *Hollow Body*, it explicitly makes you aware of the boundary, that edge. Part of the intent here is to make people conscious of what their rights and roles are within the space.

For me, *As If It Were The Last Time* was more interesting because the goal with those was always to embed them in the everyday. To really make them totally invisible—we never had to ask for permission, which would mean we'd be changing the way the space was being used. Our second subtlemob *Our Broken Voice* (2010)[13] had a bit more of a fictional narrative, it was set in a train station and based around a terrible event, suggestive of a bombing but never really spoken about. We staged that in a number of train stations, and to research that we spoke to police and security teams, to find out what were the actual ways people moved that would alert them to security services. We learned what it is to be "normal" and unnoticeable in a train station and built this into the instructions that the audience received. They were really performing the everyday.

One of the times we staged it was in Edinburgh, normally we had no venue or meeting place—it's entirely run by the audience—but this time the piece was *so* depressing, where the ending sent you out on a solo, isolated walk. Because of this, we felt it was only fair to let people have some sort of decompression chamber, so there was an option to meet at a bar at the end of the piece. Someone came to it and said their battery ran out on the mp3 player, so they had to stop taking part in the piece, and they started taking photos in the train station instead. Well, the police pulled them up and asked them what they were doing, and the person said "Oh, well I'm in this show..." and showed the police all the photos.

Well, the police thought he was drunk or on drugs and escorted him out of the train station, and made him delete his photographs. While they were doing this there were 300 people performing in the same train station around them, including taking pictures on their mobile phone. We'd designed this piece, so it was interesting to realize that the work really had integrated with the world. It doesn't always work, but sometimes it does, and for me that sort of blurs the way you can intervene. The work becomes about those sorts of environments ones that we're in all the time. If you're taking part in it, you're hyper conscious of the mechanics of those spaces and the way people interact. If you're not taking part you never really know what's happening, so you never really feel exposed as a participant.

There's a duty of care to the audience for these kinds of works as well. Because you've added to their experience, and you're somehow framing it. There is a sense of extra responsibility. If people have to cross the road, we'll doubly emphasize this, even put fake car sounds into it. With the subtlemobs, we pick a location that has lots of pedestrian traffic, and we'll plot the site carefully, but while it's happening, we have no control.

In China, we do ask for permission. The relationship between public gatherings and the police is really difficult. If we get the mapping wrong, miscalculate the number of people coming into the area, it can become a crowd. If we make that mistake, it's entirely our fault. In that situation, we're essentially creating a public disturbance, somewhere that is incredibly strict.

> It can be very dependent on the politics in relation to location, which hasn't really been discussed that much in terms of location-based mobile media art?

Yes, it's interesting. I don't know if it's been published yet, but there's a collection of writing around audio walking for people of color. What the general sense of it was that these pieces work in urban contexts, but they're not made in suburban contexts. The audience and the makers tend to be white and privileged. The whole socio-cultural relationship of what you're putting your audience into is not considered.

> What direction are you heading towards now?

At the moment I'm focusing on the expansion of eco-critical augmented audio works. Partly because there's less text. I'm really enjoying getting into the sonics again and being able to use live audio and bringing the sound world around people into the piece. Also, I'm finishing my PhD at the moment, which is in compositional methods for mobile media art, and has a focus on time. How do we compose temporally for location works that are mainly discussed in terms of spatiality?

## Notes

1 http://pmstudio.co.uk/.
2 http://duncanspeakman.net.
3 https://platformlondon.org/p-multimedia/and-while-london-burns/.
4 http://terirueb.net/core-sample-2007/.

5 www.anthampton.com/about.html.
6 https://planbtheatre.org/.
7 See http://sndrv.nl/.
8 http://uninvited-guests.net/home.
9 https://orenambarchi.com/.
10 http://salomevoegelin.net.
11 http://wearecircumstance.com/as-if-it-were-the-last-time/; www.youtube.com/watch?v=FY6S4GkCZ9c.
12 http://wearecircumstance.com/a-hollow-body/.
13 http://wearecircumstance.com/our-broken-voice/.

# 24

# INVENTIVE APPROACHES TO DATA TRACKING IN MORE-THAN-HUMAN WORLDS

*Jacina Leong, Larissa Hjorth, and Jaz Hee-jeong Choi*

> Sit less. Move more. Get some exercise, persuades a health app on my smartphone. It is 12.45PM and according to the app, I have walked 1,190 steps (0.75km) or the equivalent of two flights of stairs; 10,000 steps is my daily target. But the app is not telling the truth. It has not considered the steps I walked earlier, with a friend and their dog, without my phone in hand. I am disappointed—not with the app, but because of the steps that remain invisible and unaccounted for by the surveillance of my phone. I remind myself that I can make up for it tomorrow; the app is always tracking.[1]

Personal data tracking practices (like those described in the opening vignette) have gained momentum in recent years, giving rise to terms such as the "Quantified Self,"[2] "self-tracking,"[3] and "life-logging."[4] While the act of monitoring, measuring, and tracking is not new—people have kept track of their movements, emotions, interactions, growth, and weight changes through analog devices for centuries[5]—technological advancements have ushered in a new generation of tools (for example, smartphones and wearable self-tracking devices) with which humans (and non-humans) can be digitally or biometrically tracked in real-time and in formats that can be "captured, archived, and retrieved indefinitely."[6]

However, as a new and evolving practice, the espoused benefits of personal data tracking such as self-care and the redistribution of expertise[7] remain largely speculative and promissory.[8] There are also parallel concerns in scholarly literature about the relationship between *voluntary* and *private* modes of self-tracking, and a growing awareness of the ways in which humans and non-humans are being *unknowingly* or *involuntarily* surveyed, more than in any other time in history, by security, government and commercial organizations[9]—often by the same technologies that purport self-care.[10] This chapter expands on these debates in and around personal data tracking practices by focusing on how experiments in the space are addressing and exploring these concerns, especially around providing more complexity around discussions that consider human and non-human digital entanglements.

In doing so, we acknowledge that the significance of human and non-human, or more-than-human, relations has been the focus of many Indigenous knowledges and ontologies for millennia[11] and more recent multispecies theorists including Donna Haraway,[12] Anne Galloway,[13] Matthew Calarco,[14] Anna Tsing,[15] Elaine Gan,[16] Zoe Todd,[17] Hanna Wirman[18] and others. Much of this work problematizes human-centric approaches to ontology, agency, design, and ethnographic research and also speaks to a broader turn in the digital humanities around critiques of the concept of the Anthropocene[19]—in itself a human-centric term—as framed by Joanna Zylinska: "a geo-historical period, in which humans are said to have become the biggest threat to life on earth."[20] Digital technologies (as non-humans invented by humans) are often seen as a mirror of humanity, highlighting our many limitations. And yet, if we shift the focus away from an exclusively human experience, *what might other-than-humans teach us about being in the world and ways to critically-creatively and inventively engage with the complexities and potentialities of data tracking practices?*

This chapter engages with the rubric of mobile media art by beginning (and predominantly focusing) with a pioneer in the space of locative media, Hajime Ishikawa, who began self-tracking 20 years ago with the mainstream introduction of Global Positioning System (GPS) devices. Ishikawa—who was interviewed by the authors on 5 July 2018 via Skype—not only uses his data tracking to think creatively about his surrounds but also, by tracking his cat, he began to think differently about how he and his non-human companions move in and through the environment. We then briefly explore other examples of animal tracking experiments and conclude our chapter with several questions to go beyond animals and attune to the complexity of human and non-human digital entanglements.

## Case Study: Hajime Ishikawa and The Cat

Hajime Ishikawa is a landscape architect and mobile sociologist, based at Keio University (Tokyo), who for 20 years has tracked his daily movements using multimodal GPS devices. Ishikawa first purchased a GPS at the start of the new millennium, around the same time the technology entered the domestic car market, beyond its more traditional use in military tracking and navigation systems. He has tracked his movements ever since. He states, "whenever I go out, I have a GPS. I even return home if I happen to forget it." [21] While he does not describe himself as a "digital geek,"[22] Ishikawa's enthusiasm for developments in locative technologies has not diminished since his first purchase:

> My first GPS purchase was in 2000. At that time the locative media was used for car navigation systems. Also, there was a jam as America had not opened that technology completely at the time. So, it wasn't accurate at all. At the time the technology was used to locate yourself within a map—where you are now. And after that, locative media devices became part of the mobile phone. We started sending photos and texts with location data. It was revolutionary. I remember how excited we were about that... It was a big deal at the time. And then, we became able to send those data to Social Networking Sites (SNS) and share. The locative media became share the location and time with others. It was a big change. After the start of Google Maps, the location became like an address ... like a URL. So, every single location became a universal address. I think that enabled a sense of location to me—because when I stand at the bus stop for example at the university campus, and I open Google Maps, instantly I know where I am.[23]

These unique experiences and the data collected over the course of Ishikawa's ongoing experiments with GPS devices have revealed to Ishikawa a number of insights. Described as the "patterns and shapes"[24] of the places he inhabits, the areas he regularly frequents and the infrastructures (footpaths, traffic and road conditions) that influence the walkability of an area, or lack thereof. As Ishikawa mentions, "in Tokyo, my walking pattern is not that visible in the centre of the city because we use the subway a lot."[25]

Visuals of his data tracking sometimes look like unstructured and abandoned spiderwebs (see Figure 24.1)—without Ishikawa's accompanying narratives, as told during our interview over Skype, it is difficult to situate his movements and make sense of the traces his GPS devices have captured. Other visuals, however, show Ishikawa's tracings overlaid onto more recognizable satellite images making it easier to discern motorways from suburban streets and in some cases,

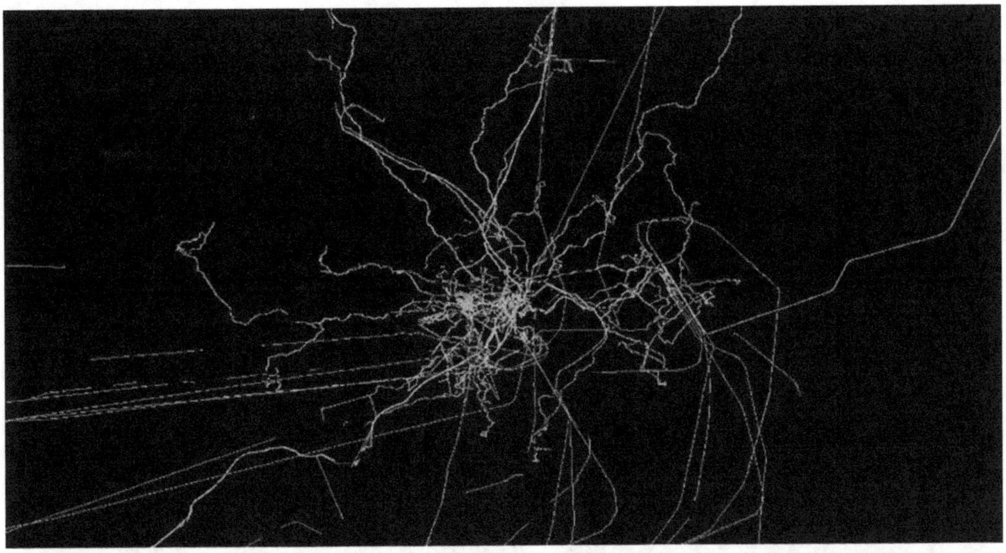

*Figure 24.1* *Track Log Around Tokyo, Rendered with Kashmir 3D* (2014). Photo credit: Hajime Ishikawa

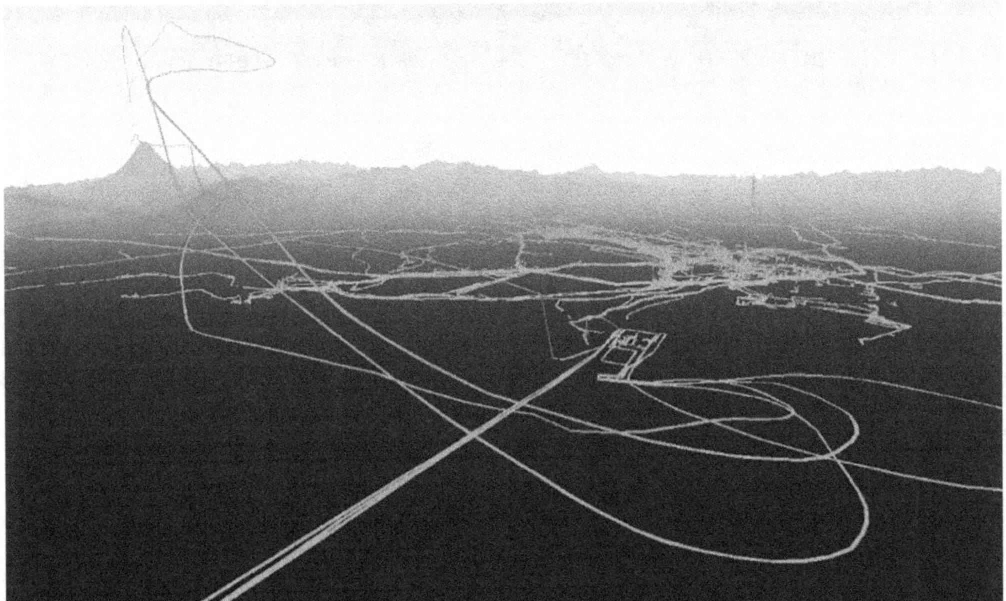

*Figure 24.2* *14 Years of Track Log, Rendered with Kashmir 3D* (2014). Photo credit: Hajime Ishikawa

instances where Ishikawa has traveled by air (see Figure 24.2). Where the GPS log appears to have lost connection illustrates occasions when Ishikawa has likely caught an underground train, or where the device has dropped out. Like the micro-nudging functions of many mobile health apps, which persuade you to *sit less* and *move more*, his data tracking practices have prompted Ishikawa to become more curious and active with his movements (Figure 24.3). He cites artist Jeremy Wood as an inspiration,[26] and like Wood, uses his GPS-enabled body as a pencil to draw snails, pigs,

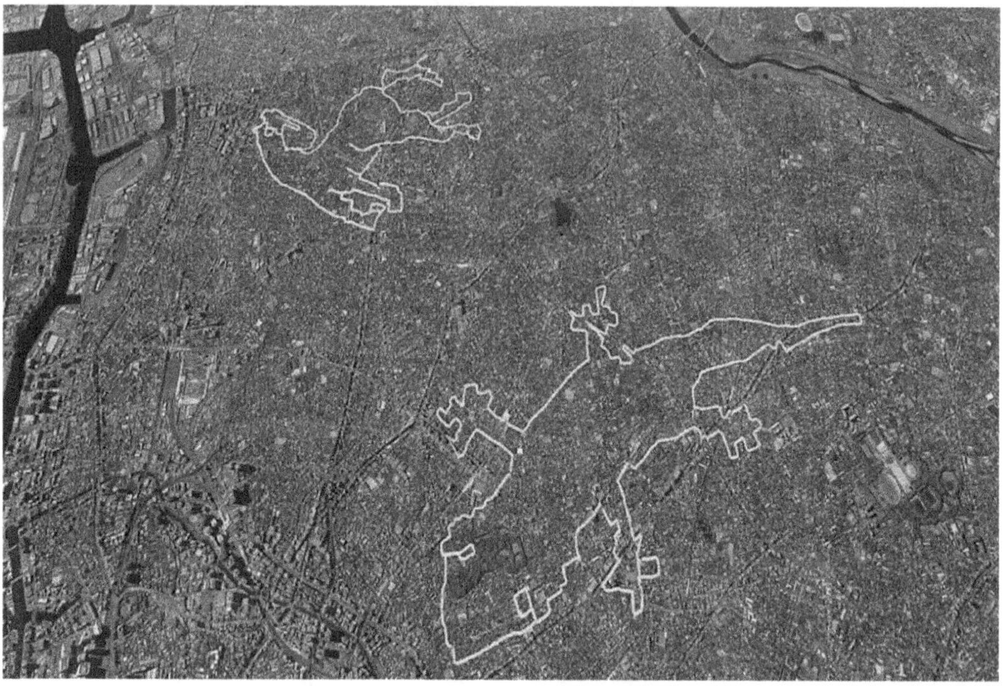

*Figure 24.3* *GPS Drawing Shown on Aerial Photo, Rendered with Kashmir 3D* (2014). Photo credit: Hajime Ishikawa

ducks, elephants, horses, or lizards (see Figure 24.3). Such curiosity can be motivating for him to make more—traces of—movements: "half of my day I spend on the train. In the morning, I usually go straight to the office from the station, whereas on the way back returning home, I try to walk."[27]

While mindful of the "sense of crisis"[28] surrounding tracking technologies, Ishikawa remains optimistic about the potentials of self-tracking practices, adding he is "on an experiment. I do not know how it affects society level behavior but it affects how we see things, big time, I think. I am using myself as an experiment."[29] This experiment, however, also includes his non-human domestic cohabitant: his cat.

## The Cat

> This is the cat that we have as pet. It was a stray cat, and it settled down at our place, and we could not just keep it inside the house. The cat tends to be asleep all day, but we could never find out where it was during the day. Nowadays, you can have these very compact GPS receivers. We have mounted it on the cat, and the results turned out to be quite surprising.[30]

For almost a decade, Ishikawa tracked or "cat logged"[31] the daily movements and interactions of his female house cat using a compact GPS and video camera attached to its collar. The accompanying visuals of his cat's movements, similarly to Ishikawa's tracings, have been overlaid onto satellite images—revealing concentrated areas of seemingly unstructured, chaotic but also cautious movements. For example, where the cat appears to avoid expansive, open spaces such as the neighboring sports field (Figure 24.4).

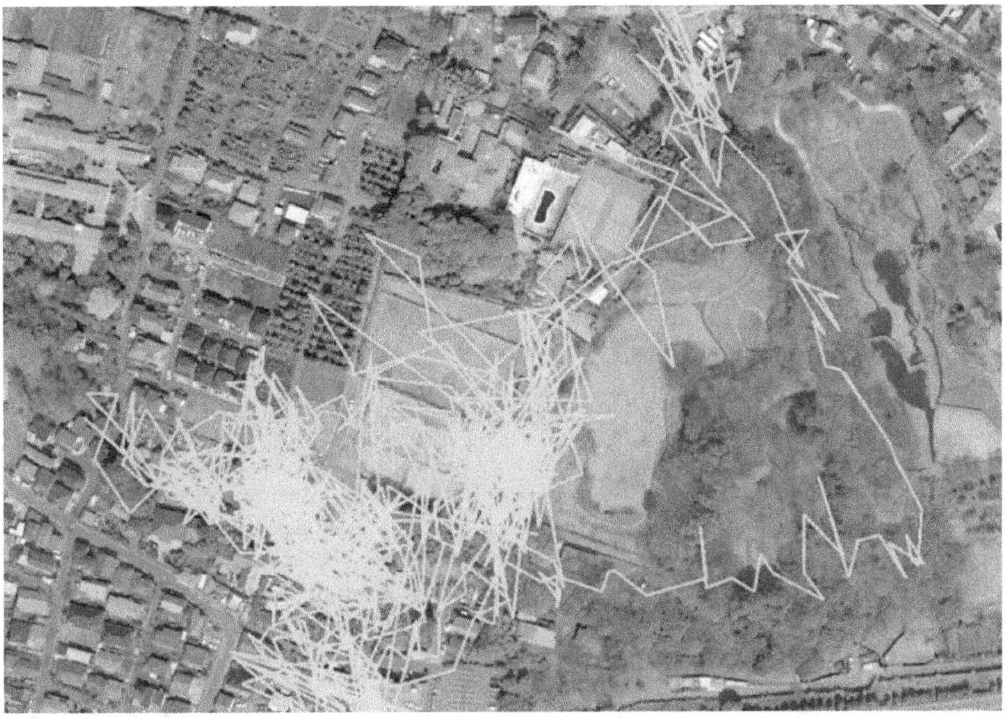

*Figure 24.4* *The Cat Log, Drawn with Google Earth* (2012). Photo credit: Hajime Ishikawa

For Ishikawa, "cat logging" revealed several other insights described as follows:

> I learned about the sorts of hidden structures of (my local) residential area. For example, I (had) seen it but I didn't recognise it that way, the backyard was continuous. But it's divided by fences and walls, so we do not see a continuous open space. But for a cat, height, like 1m high, that's not (an obstacle). They just go through it, jump it or walk under it. It's not (a problem) for them. So, looking at the cat's movements, those backyards are like continuous large open space(s) and I didn't see that potential until I saw the cat's movements.[32]

Ishikawa became fascinated by the cat's seemingly unlimited and free movement in comparison to his own, enabling a more augmented understanding of "the whole landscape of my neighborhood from the street view."[33] The GPS tracking of both human and non-human successfully highlighted these navigational differences, where cats improvise their movement based on their senses, avoiding streets, and larger open spaces. "They don't like to be exposed in a space like that, so they go through, underneath parked cars, or behind the wall, or behind the air conditioning machine."[34] It is these alternative methods of wayfaring that provide a richer understanding of our in-situ environments and how *all* beings choose to move through them.

> I also started seeing other animals like sparrows, pigeons or house dogs, or other wild small animals, which I sometimes observe in residential area[s]). For them, the landscape of the area is totally different, and they see the houses, electric poles or lines as part of their natural environment.[35]

When asked about the *Hiroshima Cat Street View*, a Google Maps-inspired interface designed to boost the local tourist economy by inviting e-visitors to explore the Hiroshima prefecture from the perspectives of cats, Ishikawa is skeptical of the project's ability to represent the animal.

> [Cats] do not move as I expect. They take the course which we do not know or do not expect because there is no street there or no road there, or it's divided by fences or someone else's property. It's different. But in the case of the Hiroshima project, that's just a simulation of the animal, very low angle of a video camera, because they are moving via the street and the cat doesn't move like that. I know how they move. [The Hiroshima project] is just an experiment to expand the human view a little bit, but there's no unexpected move there.[36]

## Mapping More-Than-Human Cartographies

Ishikawa's exploration of cat tracking is not unique—nor is it a recent development, with technologically enabled animal tracking experiments dating back almost 50 years.[37] Recent examples include *Crittercam*, an ongoing project initiated by National Geographic in 1986, whereby small tracking devices are secured to marine and terrestrial wildlife to capture sound, video, and other information, providing rare insights into the "private lives of animals" that help researchers "solve scientific mysteries (to) protect the animals that wear them."[38] Similarly, *Ocearch* tracks the movements of white sharks, dolphins, whales, seals, alligators, and turtles to help scientists collect previously unattainable data about these animals and the environmental changes impacting their migratory habits. *Ocearch* is also an advocate for scientific communication and outreach, using Twitter to upload the movements of many of the animals its researchers survey.[39]

Since 2015, park rangers and researchers from the *Voyageurs Wolf Project* have also been studying seven different wolf packs (including their prey: moose, deer and beavers) located in and around Voyageurs National Park, northern Minnesota. The project, a collaboration between the park and the University of Minnesota, collects location and video data from the wolves every 20 minutes and like *Ocearch* has established a Facebook account to share (occasional) GPS mappings of each pack's movements. Another example is *Movebank*, an open portal online database hosted by the Max Planck Institute for Ornithology, which helps animal tracking researchers to manage, share, protect, analyze and archive their data. A search of the current public database reveals tracings of everything from yellow-eyed penguins (New Zealand) and swamp wallaby (Australia), to Mongolian gazelle and domestic dogs and cats.

Human-animal-tracking entanglements have also been taken up by a group of local residents in the remote area of the Faroe Islands, Denmark. Dissuaded by the lack of interest shown by Google to map the islands, working alongside a local shepherd, the group fitted specially designed harnesses with cameras to five resident sheep. As the sheep walk and graze, the cameras capture geo-located videos and still images, which are then uploaded by the group onto Google *Street View*. They have also released panoramic video footage through the *Sheep View 360* website, allowing visitors to explore the island quite literally from the view of a sheep.[40] The project is part of a local campaign, similarly to the *Hiroshima Cat Street View*, to boost tourism to the area, which boasts 80,000 sheep to 50,000 humans, and convince Google to complete the mapping project.[41]

In *Staying with The Trouble*, Haraway[42] surfaces another experiment taken up by artist-researcher, Beatrix da Costa, who used racing pigeons as "living co-producers"[43] to monitor air pollution in Southern California—recognized as an area with some of the poorest quality air conditions in North America. Professional air monitoring devices are often fixed and placed at higher altitudes than areas typically inhabited by humans and non-humans and are also be expensive. By equipping pigeons, traditionally and extensively used during the World Wars for surveillance and communication purposes, with a small backpack (combining GPS, pollution and temperature sensors), da Costa's *PigeonBlog* tracked and collected data in real-time from various vantage points (on-ground through in-flight)—sharing findings via an online blog.

Following Lury and Wakeford[44] and Marres, Guggenheim and Wilkie,[45] such relationality, between humans, non-humans and technology, can inspire *inventive* situations and methods, whereby "diverse ways of knowing and co-creating in a world where the humans alongside the land, forests, rivers, and non-human animals can become our ever-present teachers and interlocutors."[46] Indeed, experimentations and animal-tracking initiatives such as those canvassed in this chapter so far can be critical for establishing broader comparisons across studies, species, geographical range and years,[47] to understanding the ecology of animal species and its impact on the environment,[48] and also the impact of human-made efforts on the environments animal species inhabit.[49]

Animal-device interactions also remind us that processes of social and technological change are not only tied up in relations between technologies and humans, but part of assemblages of a myriad of human and non-human relations. While this observation is the key starting point for specific sub-disciplines such as Animal-Computer Interaction (ACI), it rarely features in more "traditional" research and remains a subfield of HCI (Human Computer Interaction), rather than core to understanding the dynamic relationalities of being in the world that is, more often than not, more-than-human.

## The Art of Feeling Data

Toward the end of our interview, Ishikawa informs us that he has recently upgraded to a Narrative Clip worn (not unnoticeably) around his neck. This device, developed in 2012 and known for use in lifelogging, captures geo-located images every 30 seconds and when tapped can record up to 12 seconds of small-file video and sound—revealing in greater detail, *how* and *who* he spends his time with, and *what* he spends his time doing. Similarly to Steve Mann's concept of *sousveillance*, whereby surveillant technologies are reclaimed from their use in top-down practices with the goal of helping one's self and others to "see, understand and recall the world,"[50] Ishikawa refers to this as the collection of "meaningful data"[51]—that is, data that is collected by being in and with the world. He demonstrates how the device works, suggesting that we too have now been "captured" by the Narrative Clip: "so tomorrow, when I check my record (you) will also appear."[52]

When asked about the ethical implications of involuntarily capturing others (both human and non-human), Ishikawa acknowledges that it is a concern he frequently grapples with. While keen to open source his data, he is also mindful that much of this data contains images, conversations, locations, and other sensitive information about his family, friends, colleagues, strangers, and neighbors (most notably and recorded unknowingly by his cat): "My sharing (of images) is very limited. I am still trying to figure out the best way to share. I show them in academic conferences, but I avoid showing at general public lectures or on social media."[53] (See also Mann on the privacy, legal and ethical issues that sousveillance practices have and continue to raise.)[54] And, while Ishikawa has stopped "cat logging," he remains curious of the movements and behaviors of the many humans and non-humans he encounters—mindful of how paying attention can attune him toward different ways of being in his "surrounding landscape," as Ingold eloquently expresses in his discussion around wayfaring.[55]

This is what curiosity can do. It allows us to torque our imaginaries to other possibilities, "uncovering realities previously unseen or unimagined, even across seemingly exhausted grounds."[56] Curiosity unfolds potential and can inspire experimentations and creative interventions that are fluid and open, allowing the opportunity for change. However, while curiosity can create new possibilities, Maria Puig De La Bellacasa[57] also reminds us that etymologically, curiosity shares its Latin origins with *care*. Indeed, as tracking technologies and locative media are constantly improving, enabling more technically accurate tracking, over larger distances and areas, and for longer periods of time,[58] we argue that such practices necessitate an ethics of care and attention to the *neglected* or *hidden* aspects of data tracking in a more-than-human world, to ensure that those with who we share our "cartographic terrain,"[59] both humans and non-humans, are not inadvertently compromised, placed at risk or made more vulnerable. Inventive approaches to data-tracking require careful balancing of creativity and criticality.

For example, Kate Crawford, Jessa Lingel and Tero Karppi,[60] in discussing the widespread proliferation of wearable self-tracking devices remind us that the data produced, aggregated and interpreted by wearables like the *FitBit* are also being used and on-sold to a diverse range of intermediaries—from parent companies to third parties, health insurers and employers. While for intermediaries, such devices document a wealth of data and patterns of activity "across geography, class and gender,"[61] "well beyond the control of the user, and sometimes in direct contravention of (their) interests,"[62] only a "small fraction of the potential and value of this data is returned to the user."[63] The implications of the "lack of control that users have over the flows of that data,"[64] are also surfaced in the recent work of Virginia Eubanks,[65] who offers a significant perspective around complex questions of agency, privacy and consent, particularly around the impacts of how big data mining, such as those collected from self-tracking devices, is coalescing with policy algorithms and predictive risk models on poor and working-class people in America.

The ethical implications of monitoring, surveillance, and power has also been taken by many creative practitioners including artist Lauren McCarthy.[66] Works such as *LAUREN* (2017), *FOLLOWER* (2016), *SOMEONE* (2019) and *LOVEINT* (2014)—a collaboration with artist Kyle McLachlan—explore McCarthy's interests in reclaiming and enacting the practices and technologies of locative media, as a way to reveal the "inherent contradictions, ambiguities, gaps, blind spots, and limitations"[67] of such devices (see interview this edition). This includes how "product promises"[68] used to sell wearable, smart home assistants (for example, Amazon's *Alexa*), and other tracking and surveillance technologies figure into consequential reports of connected home devices and cases of domestic violence,[69] surveillance infrastructures and cyber-stalking.[70] Shannon Mattern similarly acknowledges the importance of paying attention to the many other bodies (humans and non-humans) tracking and surveillance practices involuntarily keep track of—suggesting that "making entities" (including endangered and vulnerable species, persons and habitats) "visible and locatable can, in some cases, represent a threat or a breach of necessary anonymity."[71]

Researchers and practitioners exploring data-tracking could therefore do well by recognizing how our attempts to data track fit into these broader socio-technical, ideological, and political agendas, practices, discourses, ideas, and other related terrains that are (in)visible to us at various temporal-spatial points. As tracking devices infiltrate the spaces and experiences of human and non-human life, there is an imperative for more rigorous examinations and experimentations[72] to better understand how the methods, technologies, processes, and practices we use, both enable the tracking of these and other data[73] and enmesh with complex and potentially consequential outcomes.

Data tracking can be transformative but only if we also engage with what slips through the "product promises" of technological innovation. In discussing the role of critical interventions in this field, as Jenny Pickerill suggests: "This involves staying with the mess, working with experimentations over longer timeframes and critically reflecting on failure, who is included, who and what is being transformed,"[74] and as with any form of experimentation, asking "to what ends?"[75]

## Conclusion

This chapter is by no means an exhaustive coverage of understanding data tracking in a more-than-human world. It is only a small contribution to a larger and ongoing field of inquiry. We have probed at what is "mobile art" through engaging with one history of inventive uses of locative media. We suggest more critical reflection is needed around mobile art and its ethical dimensions, especially in terms of the complex ways data entangles human and more-than-human subjectivities, by asking questions such as: how do tracking technologies produce, document, and aggregate data about those they survey—and according to whose logic, and for whom? How do our attempts to data track extend the possibilities of this work, rather than simply feed into broader political, ideological, and socio-technical agendas and concerns? How and what new knowledges might be forged by coalescing human and non-human ontologies in our interpretations of data tracking practices? In the pursuit of open sourcing data, what are the ethical implications of rendering something or someone visible? Who or what is considered to have a right to privacy? Whose privacy is not a concern and why? How do we coalesce our own data tracking pursuits with the needs and well-being of others? How do we enact care-full encounters with human and non-human others in these transactions?

Asking these questions has sought to be a provocation to thinking about the history of locative media as complex and multilayered—and also, crucial to thinking through the ethics of mobile art and mobile media practice more generally. As Ishikawa's pioneering work illustrates, we need more critical-creative debate around the ethics of data—an issue which mobile art is far from immune. There is a distinct need for inventive research-practitioners to further push conversations and provocations around data tracking and how we inhabit the multispecies dimensions of worlds, in ways that are both careful *and* full of care.

Inventive approaches engendered by curiosity, creativity, and criticality must also commit to understanding our implications in these and other questions as a place to begin to pay attention to the ways in which humans, non-humans, and technologies coalesce. In our quest for more inventive approaches to data tracking, as co-inhabitants of more-than-human worlds, we must remain vigilant to the matters that slip through, ensuring such curiosity reflects a practice that is also (and necessarily) critical and careful, not just another form of reckless innovation for innovation's sake.

## Acknowledgments

The research in this chapter was funded by the Australian Research Council Linkage grant, *Locating the Mobile* (LP130100848). The authors wish to thank Hajime Ishikawa (and cat) for generously sharing his human and more-than-human data tracking experiences.

## Notes

1 Jacina Leong, personal experience.
2 Gary Wolf, "Know Thyself: Tracking Every Facet of Life, from Sleep to Mood to Pain, 24/7/365," *Wired*, 22 June 2009, www.wired.com/2009/06/lbnp-knowthyself/.
3 Gina Neff, *Self-tracking* (Cambridge, MA: The MIT Press, 2016).
4 Stefan Selke, *Lifelogging: Digital Self-tracking and Lifelogging – between Disruptive Technology and Cultural Transformation* (Wiesbaden: Springer, 2016).
5 David Beer, "The Biopolitics of Biometrics: An Interview with Btihaj Ajana," *Theory, Culture & Society* 31, no. 7–8 (2014): 329–36, doi: 10.1177/0263276414546380.
6 Ian Kerr, Carole Lucock, and Valerie Steeves, "Lessons from the Identity Trail: Anonymity, Privacy and Identity in a Networked Society," in *Feminist Surveillance Studies*, edited by Rachel E. Dubrofsky and Shoshana Magnet (Durham, NC: Duke University Press, 2015), 4.
7 Dana Greenfield, "Deep Data: Notes on the n of 1," in *Quantified: Biosensing Technologies in Everyday Life*, edited by Dawn Nafus (Cambridge, MA: The MIT Press, 2016), 156–79; Minna Ruckenstein and Natasha Dow Schull, "The Datafication of Health," *Annual Review of Anthropology*, no. 46 (2017): 261–78, doi: 10.1146/annurev-anthro-102116-041244.
8 Kate Crawford, Jessa Lingel, and Tero Karppi, "Our Metrics, Ourselves: A Hundred Years of Self-tracking from the Weight Scale to the Wrist Wearable Device," *European Journal of Cultural Studies* 18, no. 4–5 (2015): 479–96, doi: 10.1177/1367549415584857; Tamar Sharon, "Self-Tracking for Health and

the Quantified Self: Re-Articulating Autonomy, Solidarity, and Authenticity in an Age of Personalized Healthcare," *Philosophy & Technology* 30, no.1 (2017): 93–121, doi: 10.1007/s13347-016-0215-5; Ruckenstein and Schull, "The Datafication of Health."

9 Deborah Lupton, *The Quantified Self: A Sociology of Self-tracking* (Cambridge: Polity Press, 2016); Helen Nissenbaum and Heather Patterson, "Biosensing in Context: Health Privacy in a Connected World," in *Quantified: Biosensing Technologies in Everyday Life*, edited by Dawn Nafus (Cambridge, MA: The MIT Press, 2016), 79–100.

10 Crawford, Lingel, and Karppi, "Our Metrics, Ourselves."

11 Zoe Todd, "An Indigenous Feminist's Take on the Ontological Turn: 'Ontology' Is Just Another Word for Colonialism," *Zoe Todd*, 24 October 2014, https://zoestodd.com/2014/10/24/an-indigenous-feminists-take-on-the-ontological-turn-ontology-is-just-another-word-for-colonialism/.

12 Donna Haraway, *Staying with the Trouble: Making Kin in the Chthulucene* (Durham, NC: Duke University Press, 2016).

13 "Who We Are," More-Than-Human-Lab, http://morethanhumanlab.org/who-we-are/.

14 Matthew Calarco, *Thinking Through Animals: Identity, Difference, Indistinction* (Stanford, CA: Stanford University Press, 2015).

15 Anna Lowenhaupt Tsing, Heather Swanson, Elaine Gan, and Nils Bubandt, *Arts of Living on a Damaged Planet: Ghosts of the Anthropocene* (Minneapolis: University of Minnesota, 2017).

16 "Elaine Gan," NYU Arts & Science, http://as.nyu.edu/content/nyu-as/as/faculty/elaine-gan.html.

17 "About," Fish Philosophy, https://fishphilosophy.org/about/.

18 Hanna Wirman, "Nonhuman Animal Players: Overcoming Speciesism in Cultural Studies of Digital Game Play," *Crossroads Conference of Cultural Studies Conference 2012*, Sorbonne Nouvelle University and UNESCO, 2–6 July 2012; Hanna Wirman, "Games for/with Strangers: Captive Orangutan (Pongo Pygmaeus) Touch Screen Play," *Antennae*, no. 30 (2014): 105–15, doi: http://hdl.handle.net/10397/7611.

19 Joanna Zylinska, *Minimal Ethics for the Anthropocene* (Michigan: Open Humanities Press, 2014); Larissa Hjorth, Sarah Pink, Kristen Sharp, and Linda Williams, *Screen Ecologies: Art, Media, and the Environment in the Asia-Pacific Region* (Cambridge, MA: The MIT Press, 2016).

20 Zylinska, *Minimal Ethics for the Anthropocene.*

21 Jacina Leong, interview with Hajime Ishikawa, July 5, 2018, Skype.

22 Ibid.

23 Ibid.

24 Ibid.

25 Ibid.

26 Hajime Ishikawa, "Drawing Lines with Moving Experiences," International Convention for Media Arts, Tokyo, 2014, 73.

27 Leong, interview with Hajime.

28 Ibid.

29 Ibid.

30 Hajime Ishikawa, "Drawing Lines."

31 Ibid.

32 Leong, interview with Hajime.

33 Ibid.

34 Ibid.

35 Ibid.

36 Ibid.

37 Bart Kranstauber, Alison Cameron, Rolf Weinzierl, Tony Fountain, Sameer Tilak, Martin Wikelski and Roland Kays, "The Movebank Data Model for Animal Tracking," *Environmental Modelling & Software*, no. 26 (2011): 834–5, doi: 10.1016/j.envsoft.2010.12.005.

38 "Crittercam Education," National Geographic, www.nationalgeographic.org/education/crittercam-education/.

39 See, for example, the individual Twitter accounts of @MissCostaShark and @Jefferson_Shark.

40 See https://visitfaroeislands.com/sheepview360/.

41 A petition was launched by the Faroe Island residents with the hashtag #wewantgooglestreetview to promote the case. Google responded to the petition commenting that anyone is able to create their own *Street View* experiences and apply to borrow Google's camera equipment.

42 Haraway, *Staying with the Trouble.*

43 Ibid., 22.

44 Celia Lury and Nina Wakeford, *Inventive Methods: The Happening of the Social* (London; New York: Routledge, 2012).

45 Noortje Marres, Michael Guggenheim and Alex Wilkie, *Inventing the Social* (Manchester: Mattering Press, 2018).
46 Richa Nagar, "Hungry Translations: The World Through Radical Vulnerability: The 2017 RGS-IBG Lecture," *Antipode* 5, no. 1 (2019): 20, doi: 10.1111/anti.12399.
47 Ran Nathan, Wayne M. Getz, Eloy Revilla, Marcel Holyoak, Ronen Kadmon, David Saltz and Peter E. Smouse, "A Movement Ecology Paradigm for Unifying Organismal Movement Research," *Proceedings of the National Academy of Sciences* 105, no. 49 (2008): 19052–59, doi: http://www.pnas.orgcgidoi10.1073pnas.0800375105/.
48 Kranstauber et al., "The Movebank data model for animal tracking."
49 Ibid.
50 Steve Mann, "Wearable Technology," *Ethics Quarterly* 97 (2014): 13–15.
51 Leong, interview with Hajime.
52 Ibid.
53 Ibid.
54 See for example: Steve Mann, "Big Data Is a Big Lie Without Little Data: Humanistic Intelligence as a Human Right," *Big Data & Society* 4, no. 1 (2017): 1–10, doi: 10.1177/2053951717691550; Steve Mann, "Veillance: Beyond Surveillance, Dataveillance, Uberveillance, and the Hypocrisy of One-Sided Watching," in *Uberveillance and the Social Implications of Microchip Implants: Emerging Technologies,* edited by M.G. Michael and Katrina Michael (Hershey: Information Science Reference, 2014), 32–45.
55 Ingold, *The Life of Lines.*
56 David Hamers, "To Walk, Stumble, Hesitate and Listen to Practice Participation," in *Trading Places: Practices of Public Participation in Art and Design Research*, edited by David Hamers, Naomi Bueno de Mesquito, Annelies Vaneycken and Jessica Schoffelen (Spain: DPR Barcelona, 2017), 59.
57 Maria Puig De La Bellacasa, "Nothing Comes Without Its World': Thinking with Care," *The Sociological Review* 60, no. 2 (2012): 197–216.
58 Christian Rutz and Graeme C. Hays, "New Frontiers in Biologging Science," *Biology Letters* 5, no. 3 (2009): 289–92, doi: 10.1098/rsbl.2009.0089; Martin Wikelski, Roland Kays, Jeremy N. Kasdin, Kasper Thorup, James A. Smith and George Swenson, "Going Wild: What a Global Small-Animal Tracking System Could Do for Experimental Biologists," *The Journal of Experimental Biology*, no. 210 (2007): 181–86.
59 Shannon Mattern, "Mapping Intelligent Agents," *Places Journal*, September 2017, https://placesjournal.org/article/mappings-intelligent-agents/#0.
60 Crawford, Lingel, and Karppi, "Our Metrics, Ourselves."
61 Ibid., 494.
62 Ibid., 490.
63 Ibid., 494.
64 Ibid., 490.
65 Virginia Eubanks, *Automating Inequality: How High-Tech Tools Profile, Police, and Punish the Poor* (New York: St. Martin's Press, 2018).
66 See interview with Lauren McCarthy which introduces Section nine of this Companion.
67 Gary T. Marx, *Windows into the Soul: Surveillance and Society in an Age of High Technology* (Chicago, IL; London: The University of Chicago Press, 2016), 143.
68 Crawford, Lingel, and Karppi, "Our Metrics, Ourselves."
69 Nellie Bowles, "Thermostats, Locks and Lights: Digital Tools of Domestic Abuse," *The New York Times*, 23 June 2018, www.nytimes.com/2018/06/23/technology/smart-home-devices-domestic-abuse.html.
70 Andrea Peterson, "When NSA Officers Use Their Spying Power on Love Interests," *The Washington Post*, 24 August 2013, www.washingtonpost.com/news/the-switch/wp/2013/08/24/loveint-when-nsa-officers-use-their-spying-power-on-love-interests/?noredirect=on&utm_term=.b07279efa913.
71 Shannon Mattern, "Mapping Intelligent Agents," *Places Journal*, September 2017, https://placesjournal.org/article/mappings-intelligent-agents/#0.
72 Stefan Selke, *Lifelogging: Digital Self-tracking and Lifelogging – Between Disruptive Technology and Cultural Transformation* (Wiesbaden: Springer, 2016).
73 Jen Jack Gieseking, "Digital," in *Keywords in Radical Geography: Antipode at 50,* edited by the Antipode Editorial Collective (New Jersey; Oxford: Wiley Blackwell, 2019): 85–89, https://onlinelibrary.wiley.com/doi/pdf/10.1002/9781119558071.fmatter.
74 Ibid., 121.
75 Jenny Pickerill, "Experimentations," in *Keywords in Radical Geography: Antipode at 50,* edited by the Antipode Editorial Collective (New Jersey; Oxford: Wiley Blackwell, 2019): 120, https://onlinelibrary.wiley.com/doi/pdf/10.1002/9781119558071.fmatter.

# 25

# OPEN PROTOTYPING

## A Framework for Combining Art and Innovation in the IoT and Smart Cities

*Drew Hemment, Joanna Bletcher, and Saskia Coulson*

We are living in an era when cities have become sites for the creation of big data. Widening access to mobile, wearable, and ubiquitous technologies has led to an unprecedented capacity for people to be constantly connected to the internet, and each other. Recent developments in big data, cloud computing, and artificial intelligence (AI) profoundly shape the human condition today, often in ways that are neither transparent, nor accountable. At the same time, a tradition of art practice has developed over recent decades in which artists experiment with these technologies, and the social context in which they are situated. Crucially, this practice speaks to, and participates in, wider debates and developments surrounding emerging socio-technological constructs. Such practices cross disciplinary boundaries, and, as a consequence, have an uncertain relationship to both the wider arts sector and the technology industry.

This chapter presents a guide to understanding this practice and a framework for devising and evaluating such boundary-spanning works. We look at the role artists can play in producing hybrid realities, bridging the space between technology and society, and contributing to city and technology innovation. We present a framework, titled "Open Prototyping" (OP), for creative practice which experiments in, makes tangible, and reflects on the social and material conditions of a digital society. OP can be understood as the formalization of a set of artistic practices that involve experimentation with mobile, locative, and urban technologies. The framework has been iteratively developed within programmes led by Drew Hemment introducing art to the major Smart City and Internet of Things (IoT) Programs of the United Kingdom, Europe, and Singapore. Case studies include the first art commission in the United Kingdom's national IoT demonstrator and the first cultural programme in the Singapore Smart Nation initiative. These are examined using the OP framework to understand how they operate as boundary objects across domains. The outcomes for both artists and technology programmes have been assessed, and this chapter reports on research conducted across these contexts. OP points to a space where cultural policy and industrial policy meet. This is about both enabling significant art, and a novel dimension to ethical and responsible technology development. The chapter concludes with reflections on the potential of such practice to shape the direction of future technology development.

### Art, Innovation, Participation

OP is a framework and process model for innovation through artistic creativity and participation. As first proposed by Hemment, the framework describes a co-creation process, involving people from different backgrounds, and participation of communities and audiences at different stages.[1]

It involves experimentation or play, and a culmination in some form of public experience. The key offering of the OP process model is the way in which it proposes a scaffold for people to combine art, participation, and ICT.[2]

OP is grounded in both theory[3] and practice[4] of new media art, and, specifically, in digital art practices that work with emerging science and technologies[5] and creative practice that makes ideas about the future tangible.[6] The term "open prototyping" was originally introduced by Bullinger et al. to describe a co-creation process involving external inputs,[7] and the OP framework is also informed by the new materialism of Barad and the relational turn in cultural theory.[8] OP evolved from over 20 years of art curation and social innovation within the FutureEverything festival and organization, under the creative direction of Drew Hemment (1995–2018).[9] It can be seen as a culmination of a curatorial and research trajectory from artworks on social and political aspects of technology,[10] experiments in mobile and urban technologies,[11] social innovation around open data[12] to the combination of art and ICT in large-scale technology demonstrators.[13, 14, 15] In these later iterations, OP sits between art, design and industrial technology innovation.

One period that illustrates how art, technology, and society can converge is the period between 2002 and 2004, when the field of locative media came to prominence through a series of cultural and technology initiatives, and accompanying academic reports.[16, 17, 18] These initiatives built on ideas from the Headmap Manifesto,[19] and formed a community that first convened at a workshop in Karosta during 2003. This moment and community helped give rise to the Mobile Connections[20] and ISEA2004[21] cultural programmes, the Open Street Map[22] platform, and, later, the Pervasive and Locative Arts Network funded by the UK EPSRC. The social, political, and methodological consequences of location-aware mobile technologies were variously addressed.[23, 24, 25] Coming before the emergence of the smartphone and digital mapping services such as Google Maps, this moment had influence across a number of domains including the arts, mobile communications, cartography, urban studies, and human-computer interaction, and prefigured and helped to shape fields that followed, notably IoT and Smart Cities.

Today, the combining of art, creativity and technology innovation continues at Ars Electronica, Eyebeam, Waag Society, MIT, YCAM, MediaLab Prado, Pervasive Media Studio, FutureEverything and similar organizations and festivals worldwide. These sites encourage creative endeavours which are participatory, socially innovative or have a vigorous research dimension. There are limitations in scaling this approach however, as there is currently no defined method or process to refer to when applying this way of working. Scholarship has for over 15 years addressed the challenges of curating art and creative technology; these include, for example, its iterative, distributed and participatory character.[26] Nevertheless, it can be difficult to know how to initiate and deliver such transdisciplinary projects, particularly at scale, or how to frame and evaluate impact. Attending to this gap, the OP framework has been developed through the theory and practice noted above, and through involvement in new media art over two decades.

## Methodology: Open Prototyping Case Studies

The OP process has been built and evaluated using a case study methodology with combinations of six qualitative methods: direct and participant observation, semi-structured interview, workshops with project partners, document analysis, focus groups/workshops with audiences, and audience surveys or questionnaires. We use social science researcher Bent Flyvbjerg's[27] broad definition of case study research as "an intensive analysis of an individual unit (as a person or community) stressing developmental factors in relation to environment." The individual unit of analysis is the art project or commission in question, which is outlined via the case studies below.

Those studies chosen for reporting in this chapter are drawn from a number of programmes, including FutureEverything's festival of art and digital culture,[28] pilots in the Smart Nation programme of the Singapore Government,[29] *CityVerve*, the United Kingdom's IoT Smart City Demonstrator,[30] and *FAULT LINES*, a talent development programme supported by Arts Council England.[31] A brief outline of each case study is offered below, followed by an analysis of each phase of the OP process model. This analysis brings in evidence from each case study, to pull out key insights that indicate the forms of value the OP model brings as a scaffold for combining art, participation and ICT.

## CHATTR, 2013[32]

*Chattr* was an art installation and speculative design fiction that shared the private conversations of participants online, forever. Visitors to the FutureEverything and TodaysArt festivals were invited to sign up to a new service, gaining access to the luxury of the *Chattr* lounge. Spoken conversations of those who agreed to *Chattr's* "Data Use Policy" were recorded, transcribed, and published as indelible text on the internet.

*Chattr* questioned our life online and the trade-offs in future digital services: how much of our data are we willing to leak into the public online domain? Participants were able to confront the trade-off between granting access to information online and a physical denial of service, that is, being denied access to the use of the *Chattr* lounge. The infrastructure was made tangible and visible by encasing the recording devices carried by participants in toy guinea pigs, performing the speech to text algorithm using human stenographers visible to the audience, and showing conversations on displays around the venue. By creating an immersive scenario, together with experts to contextualize the work, participants explored, interpreted, and evaluated current concerns about privacy, ownership, and data sovereignty.

## FUTUREEVERYTHING SINGAPORE, 2015[33]

FutureEverything Singapore (FSG) was a nine-day festival of digital culture, featuring city-wide art and design installations, a conference and innovation lab. It made ideas about the future of Singapore tangible with talking street furniture and a public sleep lab. FSG was the flagship digital culture component of SG50, the year-long celebrations that marked the 50th anniversary of the founding of Singapore and the first cultural activity within the Singapore Government's preeminent technology programme, the Smart Nation initiative (Figure 25.1).

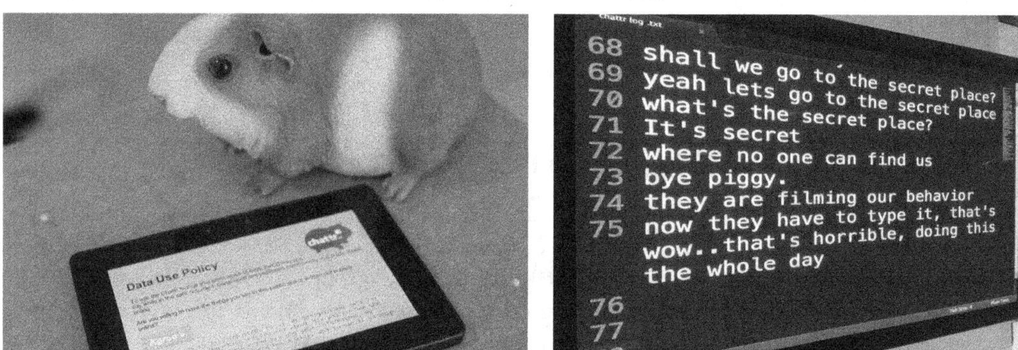


*Figure 25.1* *Chattr* (2013). Open Prototyping Case Study. Image courtesy of FutureEverything.

FSG explored near future scenarios for Singapore's ambition to become a "Smart Nation," and how smart technologies and artificial intelligence (AI) are reshaping the fabric of cities. More than 50 artists and designers made these scenarios tangible as experiences including commissions from Loop. pH and Pan Studios FSG was attended by 60,000 people, and announced by Prime Minister David Cameron in three major policy speeches during his 2015 trade mission to Asia. Thousands of people taking part were able to share their data which was analysed to generate insights into the concept of a Smart Nation.

## EVERY THING EVERY TIME, 2017[34]

The first iteration of *Every Thing Every Time* (ETET) was as a piece of digital writing or poetry, generated in real-time from publicly available city data and displayed on custom-made flipdot displays across Manchester. A tailor-made data platform gathered various data streams from sensors and data sources measuring variables such as weather, traffic, and travel. As Manchester's citizens interacted with the city, these data streams were turned into an ephemeral, poetic narrative that gave a glimpse into the ubiquity of technology in the urban space. Wraparound activity included an artist-led walking tour on the history and future of innovation in Manchester, a rule-based poetic writing workshop and an artist-technology discussion forum (Figure 25.2).

ETET was a meditation on the "Smart City," the data that passes through the fabric of the city each day, the use and value of those data, and how they create a lens to visualize the urban landscape differently. The artwork was envisioned by the artists and lead technology partner Cisco to be the first implementation of the *CityVerve* API, or "platform of platforms"—seen as one of the Smart City demonstrator's most significant dimensions. Due to delays in its development, the artists instead developed their own IoT infrastructure and adopted a modular

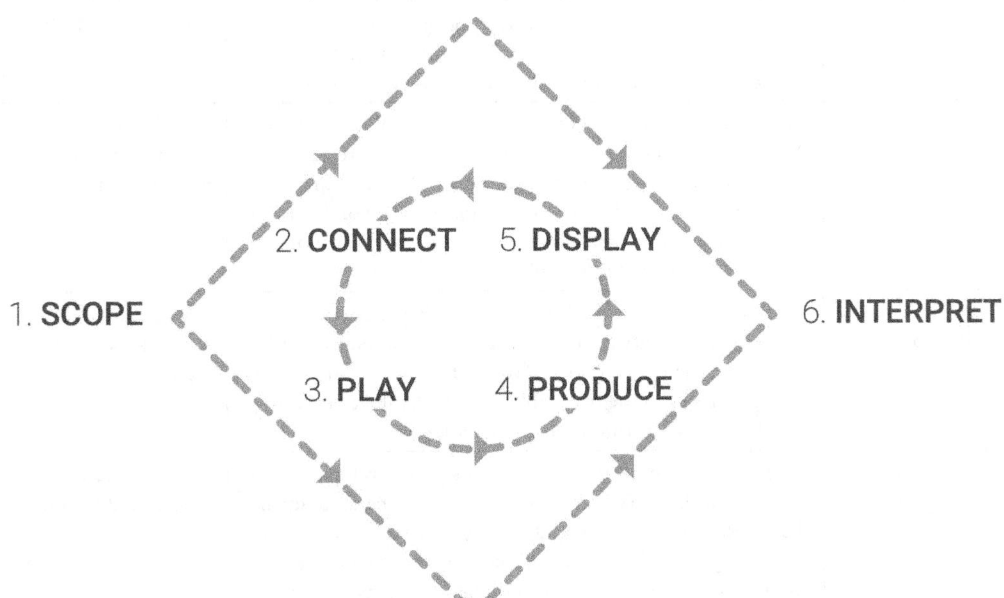


*Figure 25.2* Open Prototyping Process Model V2.0 (2017). Image courtesy of Drew Hemment.

approach to aggregating datasets that were used to generate over 150,000 unique poems, one of which is as follows:

the sun rises
the streets are empty
today is the last day of the term
the car park is almost empty
the traffic light turns green
the cleaning shift starts
the bus is on time
and it is colder than yesterday

## The OP Process Model

Continued development, delivery and analysis of the case studies above has resulted in the current OP framework, comprising both a visual representation or "process model" (Figure X), and a written "step by step" process (See Table 25.1). The process model is a visual representation that frames and formalizes the dimensions of a typical OP process. This is made up of a concentric

*Table 25.1* A description of the OP process model

| *OP Stage* | *Methods* | *Deliverable* |
|---|---|---|
| 1. SCOPE | Research undertaken to map, identify, and frame emerging issues: e.g. literature reviews, interviews, surveys, networking, attending events, devising workshops. | Concept Note / Artist Brief. |
| 2. CONNECT | Creation of artistic/transdisciplinary team, roles defined. Engage communities and stakeholders, a strong collaborative approach to build ownership and trust. Co-creation of shared, flexible, and realistic objectives and goals. | Shared goals and indicators / Stakeholder map. |
| 3. PLAY | Exploring technologies and entanglements of people, data and machines. Prototyping early concepts with hardware, software and data. Testing of artistic concepts with stakeholders, community engagement where appropriate. | Documented prototype and/or Production plan. |
| 4. PRODUCE | Artist(s) and production team produce/install the artwork. Wrap-around engagement activity devised to create opportunities for reflection and impact. Project team plan and launch press and marketing. This is a core preparation stage for evaluation activities, to capture targeted audience response and gather actionable insights. | Installed work; Communication materials / plan. |
| 5. DISPLAY | The artwork/experience is launched with associated engagement activity at city scale, engaging audiences with the art experience, and testing the technologies and concepts (as appropriate) in the live public setting. Evaluation tools are used to gather data with target audiences. | System and audience data; Press/media report. |
| 6. INTERPRET | An evaluation phase, triangulating insights developed throughout the project, analysing the data generated during the Display phase. Debrief interview held with Artist(s) and Technology/City Partners. A report can be produced that communicates high level and actionable insights. Other communications can be produced to disseminate results of the project to broad and specialist audiences. | Documentation; reports and papers. |

circle and diamond, and both lines are broken indicating porosity. It can be positioned alongside other visual representations of a design or innovation process such as the Design Council's Double Diamond[35] and IDEO's Design Thinking Process Model.[36]

The process model is intended as a tool or lens to design, deliver and evaluate these cross-sector collaborations. It is not intended to be prescriptive or a formula to follow, and is primarily for use by researchers or intermediary organizations. Many artists would not use such a design tool, and may even find it could distract from or inhibit their creative process. It may, however, be useful to artists to reflect on the scaffolding of collaborative projects, especially those for whom research and discourse plays a significant part of their practice. The OP process model represents this duality through the inner circle and exterior diamond, and steps that can be delivered by the intermediary in a non-intrusive way.

Six dimensions or steps are defined: Scope, Connect, Play, Produce, Display, and Interpret. The OP process can move successively through the six stages, although more commonly there is some cyclical movement around certain groups of stages, such as between Scope, Connect and Play. In these early exploratory phases, scoping takes different forms, depending on the practice of the people undertaking the activity (e.g. the curators, artists, technology partner or other stakeholders, including citizens).

In the visual representation, the outer line is a diamond to represent movement between divergence and convergence. The inner line is a circle, indicating the steps are on a continuum and can be approached in various ways. The outer line represents activity to inform, frame, analyse and build on a creative project, that contributes to a research dimension. The inner line represents aspects of artistic practice that are typical whether there is a research dimension or not, such as making, invention, teamwork and audience participation. Taken together they represent an artistic practice in which research plays a significant part, or a research practice in which experience, creativity and participation are integral.

Table 25.1 gives an overview of a typical OP process, providing examples of methods that can be used and "deliverables" that can be generated at each phase.

In the following section, we discuss each stage through examination of the case studies and explore the phases in more depth..

## Discussion: The OP Framework and Phase Analysis

Examination of the case studies allows outcomes and themes of interest to emerge. Below we offer insights that connect to each of the six stages of OP, notably relating to how the collaborative effort can fuel or shape the artistic practice, the innovation process, the various outcomes, and the interaction with audiences.

### *Scope*

This phase elicits themes and questions for exploration through curatorial, artistic, and other research on emerging technologies and future scenarios. For artists and cultural organizations, this may take the form of the development of a theme and trajectory in a body of work, addressing, say, the social and material conditions of technologies, practices, and ideas. It can entail an element of advocacy, as in FSG and *CityVerve*, where Hemment developed the case over several years for the incorporation of art and artists in the flagship technology programmes.

In FSG, interaction between the curator and the Singapore Government moved the event concept from a technology conference to a cultural festival. The ambition and assumptions inherent in the narrative of the Smart Nation were examined through the lens of the critical new media art community. Through curatorial research, city-wide art and design installations were selected to respond to challenges facing Singapore today: urban density, ecology, and pace of life.

In ETET, provocations were developed as part of an artistic brief, synthesizing the ongoing research of the FutureEverything curators, insights from *CityVerve* Community Forums and engagement with technology partners. These aimed at ensuring the interests and concerns of all actors would be available for artistic interpretation. A second phase of scoping by the artists then looked at available city data sources, APIs and displays, and connected their concerns, which ranged from power relations to formal possibilities, to the IoT demonstration technologies.

We see from examining these case studies how the SCOPE phase can integrate curatorial and artistic research to build on, extend or contest the innovation project themes. A key insight suggests artistic research and critical thinking can reframe technology concepts, and also to broaden the frame of technology innovation to address cultural, political, and ecological concerns alongside the functional and technical.

## Connect

This phase creates a constellation of people and things that all agree is worth building and defending. It identifies a promising collaboration and constructs the collaborative team. The case studies emerged as a result of the interaction of the actors in the "network" each collaborative project constituted.[37] In each network there were artists, engineers, curators, innovation managers, city officials, service users and citizens, and also, data, algorithms, standards, devices, buses, buildings, streets, and situations.

*Chattr* was presented at the FutureEverything and TodaysArt festivals where there is an existing openness among the audience to being data subjects in provocative experiments. FSG created a space where senior Government officials, figures from international art and design communities, and local community actors in urbanism, architecture, data science, entrepreneurship, circular economy, and the literary scene came together for an open and critical debate in a way that was unprecedented for Singapore. ETET has been presented internationally, including at Great Exhibition of the North 2018, SXSW 2019 and Qatar British Festival 2019 following the first presentation as part of *CityVerve*. In *CityVerve*, a design canvas was used with artists and Cisco's global head of APIs to develop a shared set of goals. This also served to exchange a rich set of concepts between the artist, curator, and technology partner. The connections between artists and engineers were, furthermore, seen to be significant by the technology partner:

> I think the interface with … the artists, is a new thing, that I think they [technology partner engineers] find a lot of value out of this. And working together, even working together trying to represent this, it's an interesting concept, a very interesting concept.[38]

Nonetheless, the collaboration at times came under strain. The alignment was undermined by a delay in the wider *CityVerve* project timeline. This limited the artists' access to data and technologies, although they were able to develop their own bespoke, creative solutions within the artistic team.

An insight here is that all parties to such cross-sector collaboration can benefit, but the relationships can be asymmetrical, and there can be marked differences in cultures and language. A brokering role is required to negotiate these fault lines and to sustain common purpose, commitment, and trust.

## Play

This phase creatively explores a field of possibilities through experiments in technique, concept, materials, and technologies. *Chattr* included experimentation in the service architecture and governance model for the fictional future service. Principles for the engagement of people and data were made explicit to participants performatively by the *Chattr* team, who were dressed in uniform and presented the research ethics statement on a tablet. In FSG, the artists experimented in imaginative interfaces to the city and cross-disciplinary workshop teams explored future scenarios on how technology will impact urban living. The teams also made ideas tangible through artefacts presented at Singapore's ArtScience Museum. In ETET, the artists experimented in tangible interfaces to data, hacking together flipdot displays reclaimed from buses. Their iterative development of data infrastructure raised questions around availability, licensing, and security when aggregating multiple data sets. The technology partner noted:

> we are now at the point that we have all these tools in our hands, what can we do with them? And artists could provide this kind of evolution, the next step, what is possible....[39]

The findings highlight the ways that artists can apply their creative skills to test the limits of technologies, ideas, materials, and applications. Artistic experiments can integrate knowledge and methods from different disciplines to address themes ranging from data aesthetics to regulatory frameworks. Artists can apply their creative skills to explore the social and material conditions of technologies, practices, and ideas.

## *Produce*

This phase involves the resolution of the field of conceptual and aesthetic possibilities into a concrete work. The artistic works in the case studies each configure systems, data, displays, people, and situations to produce IoT infrastructure and experiences, of very different kinds. In FSG, two large-scale art installations created interfaces to data, generated by participants as they interacted with objects around the city. The works were conceived as experiences of future scenarios concerning urban living in Singapore. Of the art installations in FSG, one participant reported that "It felt like a sci-fi movie, like I was about to go into cryogenic sleep and ready to be blasted into space."[40]

Likewise, ETET represented city data as lines of digital poetry on flip-dot displays installed in locations around the city (or split-flap displays in later versions of the work). Poems created unusual and interesting representations of city interactions that were based in live and existing city data. For the artist, the physical realization of the site-specific work gave new meaning to this data where "to have a sign situated there and to see the data stream of the city was kind of eye opening, I think."[41]

In *Chattr*, components of the system were performed by humans, to make those tangible and visible to the audience, in a reversal of the Wizard of Oz approach from human-computer interaction, where a seemingly autonomous system is operated by unseen human hands. This included the use of human stenographers in place of a speech-to-text algorithm, to generate the digital writing that was then published in an open format and as an indelible record online.

The artists in *CityVerve* are seen by the technology partner as credible technologists, creating robust technology solutions:

> In almost every one of the proposals [the artists] had a very clear technical understanding of what they were trying to do. None of them came as vague or impossible or unfeasible.... [With the artist's work] there is a very kind of robust technical interface behind it, which is brilliant.[42]

In examining these case studies, we see that novel interfaces and open infrastructures reorder and add imaginative dimensions to the IoT and Smart City.

## *Display*

This phase engages an audience in experiences, situations, narratives, and artefacts that enact local determinations of things, boundaries, and meanings in the world. The presentation of an artwork to an audience in some form of public setting is an integral dimension of each case study. This mode of participation, emerging from an art tradition, has parallels to and yet is distinct from the engagement of service users in participatory design.[43]

In the case of FSG, a high-profile public debate was generated around the project themes. Sixty thousand people experienced the programme (230,000 including the online audience), and one art installation generated 18,000 digital interactions with nearly 700 smart objects across Singapore. It was covered by press in the United Kingdom, Singapore, China, Hong Kong, the United States, Bahrain, Malaysia, Indonesia, Spain, Egypt, Australia, Canada, Brunei, and the Philippines. In ETET, the work was conceived by the artist as an object for reflection on ethical questions surrounding data systems where "removing the human out of it makes it really difficult also to make it where the responsibility lies."[44]

The art was seen by the technology partner to have engaged more people than any other of the City Verve activities to date and generated awareness and literacy among non-technology audiences: "It is making them aware; this is the big one. This is the most powerful element of all this. Engaging people that would not naturally engage. I think it's brilliant."[45]

Audience feedback similarly suggested such artworks and experiences can make city data infrastructure visible and tangible, and also build data literacy, with one audience member commenting, "Data and the infrastructure that makes it possible is invisible in most instances and by making it visible I think it increases digital and data literacy."[46]

This was supported by a survey of the general public audience, 70% of whom learned of at least one type of city data they did not know was collected. In this case study, the artwork and its use of data made 83% of people question how information is generated and where it comes from. Respondents reported the experience led them to question how their interactions with the city generate information/data, for whom, for what purpose, and what it is used for.

We see through evaluation of the DISPLAY phase in the case studies are that art can make visible and legible systems that are hidden or complex. Conversely, artists sometimes choose to obscure and create hidden depths. The artworks also enable a wide audience to experience future scenarios.

## *Interpret*

This phase translates the data and insights generated during deployment into knowledge, practices and things. Outputs can include artistic documentation, research reports, technology, datasets, algorithms, and new artist commissions.

In Chattr, people taking part could reflect on the experience as it was happening, in debates and forums at the festival, and in conversation with the project team, who recorded observations and feedback. In Figure 25.1, we see the venue display commentary of the stenographers captured by one of the recording devices, creating a reflective dimension within the artwork itself. This speaks to contemporary debates around 'ghost workers' in automated systems: "wow... that's horrible, doing this the whole day." The criticality of the work engendered reflection among members of the audience, such as "I think that's the whole thing, it's the google glass discussion isn't it … and the insidious way it just gets in there without you realising…."[47]

Other insights concerned the experience of the data subject, and the way participants were able to game the system, while one participant reported more concern for the reputation of their online persona than for the privacy of their private conversations: "Well I think the thing that would frustrate me the most is that the version would come out with loads of spelling mistakes … and put my pseudonym to it!"[48]

In ETET, the capacity of the artwork to stimulate ideas and shape technology development was highlighted by technology industry respondents. Though based on a small sample (11 respondents), 82% of ETET industry respondents reported the artwork showed them a new way of representing multiple datasets, and 64% would be more likely to engage with similar data via a single access point. One commented: "yes of course! I am experimenting already with other APIs."[49]

In the case studies, we also see how participation in the works can stimulate a critical approach to data systems, equipping people to better navigate this complex landscape. In ETET, central to the artistic concept, was that the artwork lead people to reflect and ask questions about information systems in the city, where the data comes from, the algorithms operating on it, and if it can be trusted:

> I think it might make people question also, other signage and other types of information in the city … the next time someone comes across a sign that informs them, they [might] ask questions of where that comes from.[50]

Significantly, the value of asking questions about data systems was embraced as a key insight by the technology partner, who stated that "More people will see these signs and hopefully more people will question what the signs are all about … You don't need the answer, just the questions."[51]

The key finding from evaluation of the INTERPRET phase is that OP can contribute to greater transparency and criticality in technology development and new pathways in the way people interact with data systems. Our research suggests impacts include contributions to ethical consideration in technology development and agency for people whose data is captured and acted on.

## Insights: Key Contributions of OP

Table 25.2 offers a summary of these findings, and also suggests key benefits that have emerged from the research for artists and stakeholders (understood to include technology and city partners, as well as citizens).

The implementation of the OP framework directly led to the integration of the major technology programmes in the United Kingdom and Singapore. This, in turn, generated artistic commissions, generating income for artists from outside the arts sector. The work generated engagement across the arts, science and industry in critical debates around IoT technologies. In Singapore, this shaped the language of Government. The Singapore Government Minister speaking at the FSG festival opening asserted that bringing art into the Smart Nation programme can inform the direction of technology development: "Art is an expression of human creativity. It inspires us to imagine a different reality, and challenges technology to find ways to bring those imaginations to life."[52] In *CityVerve*, likewise, the Cisco Project Lead through participation in the cultural programme came to champion a more questioning outlook in technology innovation.

We have seen that various dimensions of such cross-sector projects can be represented using the stages of the OP process model. OP provides a scaffold for eliciting insights during the development and reception of the work. The findings suggest ways in which OP can support a collaborative exchange between sectors, activating art, creativity, and participation in the pursuit of ethical innovation in IoT technology development. In addition, a number of cross-cutting themes or principles can be discerned: reframing technology concepts through artistic research; brokering cross-sector engagement; creative experimentation in data systems; adding imaginative dimensions to city infrastructures; making future scenarios tangible as experiences; and nurturing a more informed relationship to technology among various publics.

Our findings suggest three key contributions of the OP process:

*Table 25.2* Findings of the case studies—dimensions of OP framework and perceived benefits to artists and stakeholders through OP

| *OP Stage* | *Action* | *Key Insight* | *Benefit for Artist(s)* | *Benefit for City or Technology Partner(s)* |
|---|---|---|---|---|
| 1. SCOPE | Develop a theme and trajectory through practice and discussion on emerging technologies and future scenarios. | Artistic research and critical thinking introduce a novel framing of a problem, concept, challenge or capability. | Provocation, jumping off point. | Domain & problem characterization. |
| 2. CONNECT | Mobilize people and resources around a premise all agree is worth building and defending. | OP builds connections, interchange, and trust through continued negotiation of the fault lines between domains. | Build cross-disciplinary team & network. | Community links & creative talent. |
| 3. PLAY | Creatively test the limits of technologies, ideas, materials, and applications. | Artists can apply their creative skills to explore the social and material conditions of technologies, practices, and ideas. | Concept & technical development. | Creative experiments & artistic user testing. |
| 4. PRODUCE | Produce and install an artistic work by configuring systems, data, displays, people, and situations. | Novel interfaces and open infrastructures reorder and add imaginative dimensions to the IoT and smart city. | Work realized, supporting infrastructure. | New expressions, interfaces & experiences. |
| 5. DISPLAY | Present to an audience an experience, narrative, or artefact that reorders the world and our knowledge of it. | Art makes visible and legible systems that are hidden or complex, and enables a wide audience to experience future scenarios. | Work presented, audiences engaged. | Visibility, attention & participation. |
| 6. INTERPRET | Translate insights into knowledge, practices, and things, through documentation, reports, and new versions. | OP can contribute to transparency, criticality, and new pathways in the way people interact with data systems. | Develop a unique voice on technology & society. | Elicit requirements, build trust. |

## *Create legibility*

Public participation in such artworks can enable people to look past the veneer of technology and see the electronic components and human interventions at play. This can make visible the implicit rules for exchanges in these new spaces.

## *Build agency*

The introduction of art to technology innovation can generate wider civic participation in social and ethical questions surrounding the IoT and Smart Cities. Such art practices and the works that result can stimulate a more critical approach to data systems and enable people to question what is either, or both, acceptable, and desirable.

### Stimulate innovation

We have seen the introduction of art in technology innovation can stimulate new ideas about technology development and possibilities for data use. The input of artists and designers can help to both identify inherent limitations and also create insights to feed into the design and development of the technologies.

## Conclusion

OP walks the fault lines between art, design, and technology innovation. Through reflection on the case studies, the authors have scrutinized a set of practices that create experiences around important social constructs and the consequences of technology. This can help to foster greater transparency and criticality in the way people interact with data systems, among the general public, artists, and also employees at technology vendors. Embedding art in the IoT and Smart Cities offers one way to broaden participation in technology development, enable people to see and understand systems that are often complex and hidden, encourage ethical consideration in technology development, and, occasionally, stimulate the innovative aspects of the technologies. The OP framework can be used to map and analyse outcomes and impacts of work that crosses boundaries that may otherwise be hard to represent across disciplinary borders. Longitudinal studies, beyond the scope of the case studies reported here, are necessary to determine the long-term outcomes and impacts of the reorderings of concepts, situations and materials that result. Future work will further assess how the application of such a framework to cross-sector collaborations can cultivate ongoing ethical consideration in technology innovation and provide a route to impact for critical artists.

## Acknowledgments

Thanks to Naho Matsuda, Dan Hett, Peter J. Evans, Loop.pH, Pan Studios, Ben Dalton, Elliot Woods, Mel Woods, Joel Porter, Lara Salinas, and all the team at FutureEverything.[53] *FAULT LINES* was funded through Ars Council England's Ambition for Excellence Programme. *CityVerve* was funded by InnovateUK. Chattr was funded by the Creative Exchange (AHRC). FutureEverything Singapore was funded by the Singapore Government.

**Authors' Notes:** An earlier version of this paper was presented at the World Creativity Forum 2017 in Aarhus, Denmark.

## Notes

1 Drew Hemment, "Open Prototyping," 2015, https://futureeverything.org/news/open-prototyping/.

2 Drew Hemment, Joanna Bletcher and Saskia Coulson, 2017, "Art, Creativity and Civic Participation in IOT and Smart City Innovation through 'Open Prototyping'" Paper presented at *Creativity World Forum*. Aarhus, Denmark.

3 Drew Hemment, "Reordering the Assemblages of the Digital through Art and Open Prototyping," *Leonardo*, (2019): 1–12, doi: 10.1162/leon_a_01861.

4 Drew Hemment, *The FutureEverything Manual* (Manchester: FutureEverything, 2011). https://futureeverything.org/news/futureeverything-manual/.

5 Stephen Wilson, *Information Arts: Intersections of Art, Science, and Technology* (Cambridge: MIT Press, 2001).

6 Stuart Candy, *The Futures of Everyday Life: Politics and the Design of Experiential Scenarios*. University of Hawaii, Honolulu, PhD Dissertation, doi: 10.13140/RG.2.1.1840.0248.

7 Angelika Bullinger, Holger Hoffmann and Jan Marco Leimeister, "The Next Step—Open Prototyping," (2011) *ECIS Proceedings* 150, https://aisel.aisnet.org/ecis2011/150.
8 Karen Barad, "Posthumanist Performativity: Toward an Understanding of How Matter Comes to Matter." *Signs: Gender and Science: New Issues* 28, no. 3 (2003): 801–31, doi: 10.1086/345321.
9 From 1995 to 2018 Hemment was Creative Director of FutureEverything, before leaving to help establish Edinburgh Futures Institute.
10 Broken Channel, 2001, a FutureEverything project. Creative Director: Drew Hemment, https://futureeverything.org/archive/brokenchannel.
11 *Loca*, 2006. A project by John Evans, Drew Hemment, Theo Humphries, Mika Raento. https://futureeverything.org/archive/loca.
12 Open Data Cities, 2009. A FutureEverything project. Creative Director: Drew Hemment, https://futureeverything.org/archive/opendatacities.
13 Smart Nation, 2014–ongoing, www.smartnation.sg.
14 CreateIoT, 2016–2018, https://european-iot-pilots.eu/project/create-iot.
15 *CityVerve*, 2016–2018, https://cityverve.org.uk.
16 Drew Hemment, "Locative Dystopia 2," in *Acoustic Space: Transcultural Mapping*, edited by Rasa Smite and Marc Tuters, (Latvia: RIXC; The Centre for New Media Culture, 2004), 156–61.
17 Drew Hemment, "Locative Arts," *Leonardo* 39, no. 4 (2006a): 348–56, www-jstor-org.ezproxy.lib.rmit.edu.au/stable/20206267.
18 Drew Hemment (ed), "Locative Media—Guest Editorial," *Leonardo Electronic Almanac* 14, nos. 3–4 (June–July 2006b), www.leoalmanac.org/leonardo-electronic-almanac-volume-14-no-3-4-june-july-2006.
19 Ben Russel, "HeadmapManifesto," 1999, https://dpya.org/en/index.php/1999_-_Headmap_Manifesto_(1)_-_Ben_Russell.
20 Mobile Connections, 2004. A FutureEverything project. Creative Director: Drew Hemment, https://futureeverything.org/archive/mobileconnections.
21 12th International Symposium on Electronic Art (ISEA2004), Helsinki, Finland, and Tallinn, Estonia, 2004, www.isea-archives.org/symposia/isea2014.
22 Open Street Map, 2004–2019, www.openstreetmap.org/#map=5/54.910/-3.432.
23 Drew Hemment, "The Mobile Effect," *Convergence: The Journal of Research into New Media Technologies. Special Issue: Mobile Phones* 11, no. 2 (Summer 2005): 32–40.
24 Drew Hemment, "Loca: Location Oriented Critical Arts," in *The Hothaus Papers: Paradigms and Perspectives in Media Arts*, edited by Joan Gibbons and Kaye Winwood (ARTicle Press, 2006), 163–66.
25 Monika Büscher, Paul Coulton, Drew Hemment and Preben Holst Mogensen, "Mobile, Experimental, Public," in *Mobile Methods*, edited by Monika Büscher, John Urry, and Katian Witchger, 119–37. Oxon: Routledge, 2010.
26 Beryl Graham and Sarah Cook, *Rethinking Curating: Art After New Media* (Cambridge: Leonardo, 2010).
27 Bent Flyvbjerg, "Case Study," in *Strategies of Qualitative Inquiry*, edited by Norman K. Denzin and Yvonna S. Lincoln (Thousand Oaks; London; New Delhi: SAGE, 2013), 169–204.
28 FutureEverything, 1995–2018. Creative Director: Drew Hemment, https://futureeverything.org.
29 Smart Nation, 2014–ongoing, an initiative of the Singapore Government, www.smartnation.sg.
30 *CityVerve*, 2016–2018, Innovate UK £10M. Delivered by a consortium including Manchester City Council, Cisco and FutureEverything. Theme Lead for Culture and Public Realm: Drew Hemment. https://cityverve.org.uk.
31 *FAULT LINES*, 2016–2019, A FutureEverything project supported by Arts Council England Ambition for Excellence. Creative Director: Drew Hemment, https://futureeverything.org/art/entry/fault-lines.
32 *Chattr*, 2013. A FutureEverything and Creative Exchange project by Ben Dalton, Drew Hemment, Elliot Woods, Mel Woods, Joel Porter, Lara Salinas, https://futureeverything.org/archive/chattr; http://thecreativeexchange.org/projects/chattr.html.
33 FutureEverything Singapore, 2015, A FutureEverything project commissioned by the Singapore Government. Creative Director: Drew Hemment, https://futureeverything.org/event/futureeverything-singapore-signals-of-tomorrow.
34 *Every Thing Every Time*, 2017. A FutureEverything project by Naho Matsuda commissioned by *CityVerve*. Supporting Artists: Dan Hett, Peter J. Evans. Creative Director: Drew Hemment. Technology Partner: Cisco. First presented: Manchester public realm, 22 June–9 August 2017, www.futureeverything.org/projects/every-thing-every-time-naho-matsuda.
35 Design Council, "Eleven Lessons: Managing design in eleven global brands," Last modified 2007, www.designcouncil.org.uk/sites/default/files/asset/document/ElevenLessons_Design_Council%20(2).pdf.

36 d.school, “Introduction to Design Thinking Process Guide,” n.d., https://dschool-old.stanford.edu/sandbox/groups/designresources/wiki/36873/attachments/74b3d/ModeGuideBOOTCAMP2010L.pdf?sessionID=573efa71aea50503341224491c862e32f5edc0a9.
37 John Law, “Notes on the Theory of the Actor-Network: Ordering, Strategy, and Heterogeneity,” *Systems Practice* 5, no. 4 (1992): 379–93, https://link.springer.com/article/10.1007%2FBF01059830.
38 ETET, Technology partner respondent, 1.
39 Ibid.
40 FSG, General Audience Respondent, 1.
41 ETET, Artist.
42 ETET, Technology Partner Respondent, 1.
43 Erling Björgvinsso, Pelle Ehn and Per-Anders Hillgren, “Design Things and Design Thinking: Contemporary Participatory Design Challenges.” *Design Issues* 28 (2012): 101–16, doi: 10.1162/DESI_a_00165.
44 ETET, Artist.
45 ETET, Technology Partner Respondent, 1.
46 ETET, Technology Industry Audience Respondent, 1.
47 Chattr, Audience Respondent, 1.
48 Chattr, Audience Respondent, 2.
49 ETET, Technology Industry Audience Respondent, 2.
50 ETET, Artist.
51 ETET, Technology Industry Audience Respondent, 1.
52 ETET, Government Minister, Singapore.
53 See http://futureeverything.org/.

# 26

# TROJAN HORSE

## An (Incomplete) Lexicon of Art on Wheels

*Gretchen Coombs*

### The Myth and the Movement

The exact height of the Trojan Horse is unknown, but estimates place it at 3x7x7.5 meters. What is known about this mythological equine is it did not have hooves but wheels—most depictions show very small wheels, no more than a foot across. The wheels were dwarfed by the horse's wooden body, put together in a patchwork fashion, which was said to be "of mountainous size," over three meters wide, enough to hold an army of Greek soldiers.[1] Against the warning of the Trojan priest Laocoön, this symbol of subterfuge was activated when it crossed into the city of Troy, and undercover of the night, an army was unleashed.[2] Whether symbolic, metaphorical, or a true Greek war tactic, the Trojan Horse myth can be traced to this day.

Art critic Lucy Lippard describes the Trojan Horse myth as the first activist artwork.[3] She considers the subversive and empowering elements of it and relates it to the power of political art. Writing in the 1980s, she describes how activism must often cloak itself in aesthetics as a way to pass, to get through the barriers, to cross into unfamiliar territory so that later, once trusted or accepted into the context in which it entered, the political could undress into something more explicit.[4] Or, once inside it would create chaos and challenge social and political structures and otherwise surprise and upend those who encounter it.

Lippard's hope for the more politicized art practices rang true to artists in the 1980s and 1990s as they began their resistance to the culture wars and efforts to dilute the United States's multicultural landscape by promoting homogenous cultural dominance. As a challenge to then president Ronald Reagan's values, Lippard's characterization of political/activist art and the Trojan Horse were to be subversive—not didactic, necessarily—in order to counter the dominant political spectacle with "alternative images, metaphor, and information formed with humor, irony, outrage, and compassion, in order to make heard and seen those voices and faces hitherto invisible and powerless."[5] For her, activist art is always in process: not only does it include formal properties but also takes into account "*how* this art will reach its audience and *why*."[6] It is this "how"—through mobility—that organizes this (incomplete) lexicon.

The Trojan Horse metaphor for activist and political art remains to this day. In the context of art and design social practices, the methods, materials and forms of art, and design projects are increasingly interpolated. It's common to refer to socially engaged art as process oriented, based on relationships and encounters designed to ultimately effect change, yet the material object—the moveable feast so to speak—can reframe these artworks away from the process itself to *how* the works move through the world and what comes from this movement. Current aesthetic tactics are responsive to new subjectivities stemming from neoliberalism, a shrinking social safety net, and the continued marginalization and oppression of certain social groups and cultures. As a consequence, artists have amped up the subterfuge in order to trespass into sometimes-hostile territory—metaphorical and literal. As such, its different affective registrar has no less of the impact of unleashing artistic encounters to unsuspecting publics. Depending on the site, inserting these activities into the everyday blurs the distinction between art and life.

Since mobility characterizes the modern age, it is no wonder that artists acquire various types of vehicles in their work to circulate information, reach beyond urban hubs, parade sites, libraries, museum forecourts, parks, suburban neighborhoods, community centers, and other sites not otherwise visible.[7] Each project activates engagement with a temporary mobile structure that addresses its diverse and provisional publics in these sites. *Mobility* becomes *performative*: smuggling ideas through real or perceived barriers which pass as an everyday experience. Some are mobile design labs; some attempt social inclusion and unleash radical pedagogy.[8] Each in its own way interrogates their surroundings, physical or discursive, and raise questions about how we live together—about democracy, social justice, race, ethics, and the use of public space. Through this form of mobility, artists are able to place their ideas into actions through performance, intervention, information, deception, and humor.

The designs of the vans or trucks are based in a redesign—an industrial readymade repurposed for its new use in public space. The readymade then shuttles political and social art from the outside into the inside (the art world, politics) as something aesthetic or masquerading as art to be unleashed when unsuspected. My (incomplete) lexicon describes selected projects to show the scope of possibility they offer in the public realm. These art projects can be framed in several ways, but I'd like to focus on how the vehicle acts as a subterfuge, whether as a way to smuggle ideas, get people involved in their own representation, or offering tools that help empower a particular community.[9] When publics form around these vehicular projects, and when information and participation are extended through this form of mobility, they can contribute to active citizenship and reshuffle the way we interact with each other.

What connects these art projects is the ability to infiltrate imaginations and drive the Trojan Horse myth into contemporary art practices. They are placed in alphabetical order and are tagged to themes which characterize the types of *mobile tactic* used. The hashtags anchor them to archival tendencies, and the lexicon offers a loosely contained collection as a contribution to mobile art history.

## Agit-Trains #propaganda #visualcommunication

The agit-trains consisted of 16–18 cars—often brightly decorated by Russia's finest artists of the time such as Vladimir Mayakovsky, El Lissitsky, and Kazimir Malevich.[10] Between 1918 and 1922, these trains (and their cousins the agit-boat and agit-cars) set out to "educate" and agitate for revolution to the far-flung countryside of the Russian peasantry.[11] As a propaganda tool of the Bolsheviks, one train, the *Lenin Train* as it was also known, had 15 cars and was decorated with brightly colored paintings with revolutionary inscriptions based on the principles of Russian Constructivism, a darkroom, a projector, a screening room, a bookshop, and a branch of the telegraph bureau.[12]

Everywhere the trains passed, leaflets, and revolutionary pamphlets were handed out, socialist and revolutionary literature distributed, lectures held, while propaganda instructed and galvanized the masses. About 90,000 workers, peasants, and soldiers from the Red Army attended the meetings and conferences. Some of these activities helped boost morale of the Red Army soldiers engaged in hostilities and importantly built support for the revolution in populations living near the front. The notable *October Revolution* agit-train was popular with Bolshevik leaders and offered

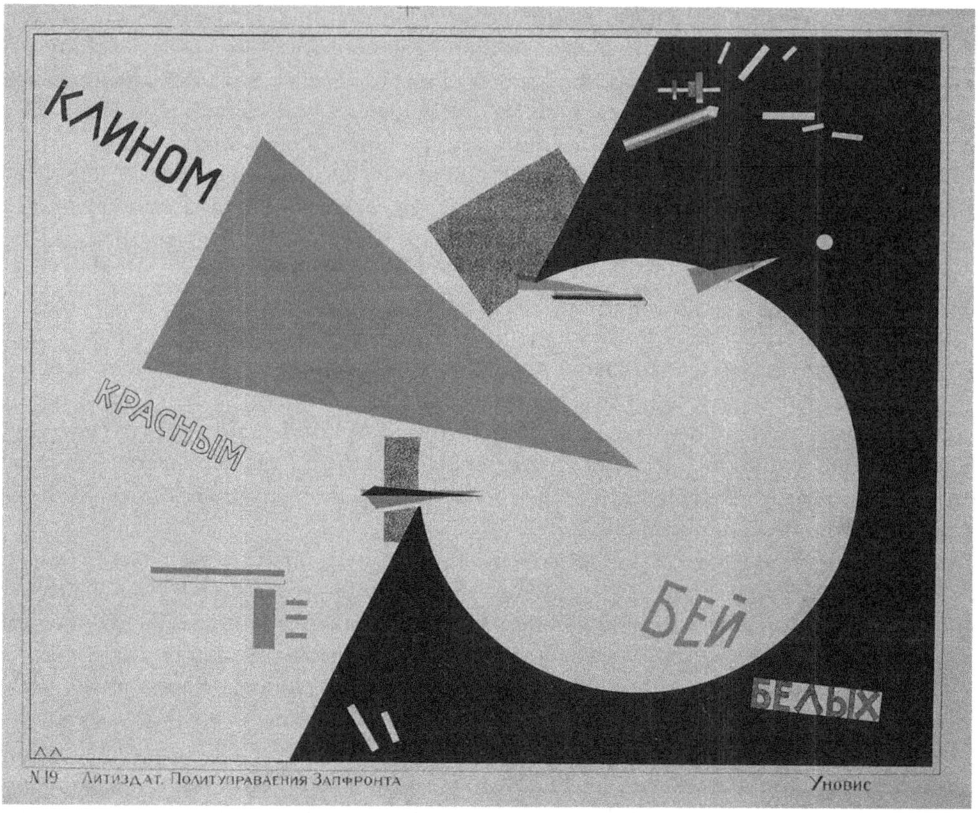


*Figure 26.1* Propaganda Poster *Beat the Whites with the Red Wedge* (1919) by El Lissitsky. Photo credit: Fair Use

them a way to maintain activities in the countryside. This train made a dozen trips in 1919, each averaging about three weeks and is estimated to have shown over 430 films, many to peasantry who had never encountered the medium and was a simple way to deliver a powerful message.[13]

The agit-trains demonstrate the power of mobilizing diverse forms of visual communication media into areas unfamiliar with the urban center. Russian Constructivist El Lissitsky's famous propaganda poster, *Beat the Whites with the Red Wedge* (1919) (see Figure 26.1), represented the strength of using visual communication to "educate" the peasantry. The work's "red wedge" symbolized the Boshleviks, emphasized the revolutionary's dominance over the "white" Russian army in simple graphic terms.

## The Black Factory #blackness #crossingborders #designtrace #civicengagement

Performance artist William Pope L.'s *The Black Factory* was a seven-meter-long paneled truck, a slow-moving vehicle averaging three miles per gallon. Constructed in a GMC 1989 Step van[14] at the conclusion of the hiatus project, retitled *PULL!* (2013), the truck was donated to 2100 Lakeside Men's Shelter in Cleveland, Ohio.[15]

*The Black Factory* roamed around the United States "collecting and distributing" items of black origin and parked in front of museums, alternative art spaces, and community service agencies. During this time, members of *The Black Factory*—community members and art students—hosted the sale of objects and interacted with the public who came to visit *The Factory*. At the back end of the truck was the "Igloo Archive Inflatable (IAI)," which carried donated black objects. For Pope L., "a black object is anything, anything! a person believes represents blackness to him or her."[16] A gift shop sells such Factory-altered items (with a Black Factory label) as canned foods, bottled water, t-shirts, and American flags.[17] Objects like "black sambo" figurines revealed racialized material culture, while others were associations of blackness—the queen of spade card, a jar of chocolate syrup, and the items like W.E.B Du Bois' *The Souls of Black Folk* and Motown records underscored Black America's contribution to American culture.

As a mobile performance installation, it engendered interactions with imagery, objects, and ideas and encouraged reflection on one's racial assumptions and desires, with the goal of challenging the representation of what constitutes "black." The collective experience of the project demonstrates how a *public can be mobilized* in different contexts to consider how race operates at nearly every point of exchange in America. In the words of Pope. L:

> The Black Factory does not make blackness, it makes opportunity; the chance to imagine a future we'd like instead of one imposed on us. *The BlackFactory* is a conversation piece on wheels. It's a chance for folks to open up their hearts and minds, laugh and talk freely, maybe even disagree about what brings us together as well as what divides us.[18]

By presenting and discussing the experience around these objects in the many sites, *The Black Factory* became a way to "trace" of blackness and open a platform for the public to discuss race based on material culture in America.

## Dialog in Transit #crossingborders #agency #civicengagement

The cog★nate cruiser leads the pack. This 1987 Chevrolet Cavalier (Station Wagon) is white with big black bold designs on its hood and doors. The hood has lotus flower. The lotus was flanked on either side by two figures—one more European-looking, the other more indigenous (depicting the figure wearing a ski mask in reference to the Zapatista movement).[19] Rising from their mouths are stylized speech glyphs, borrowing their iconography from Pre-Columbian codices.

On the driver's side is a bull-design, which artist Peru Dyer painted in reference to the act of ramming the border. He added the phrase "Amor Sin Barreras" (love without borders/barriers). This hood piece would serve as a platform for dialog and conversation, while moving through spaces of encounter/negotiation/confrontation.[20] Artists painted the car at the San Ysidro Port of Entry (between San Diego and Tijuana—Baja California) as the cruiser waited in line to cross the border.[21]

In 2014, the Cog★nate Collective staged this series of dialogs which became "an ongoing series of conversations inviting artists, researchers and activists from Los Angeles, San Diego and Tijuana."[22] The cog★nate cruiser flirted with trans-border dynamics to better understand what was shaping the lives of communities in the greater Baja/Alta California border region. These recorded conversations also took place as the group waited to cross the border and was live-broadcast over pirate radio at the San Ysidro Port of Entry on 87.9 FM.

## Free Mending Library #civicengagement #socialinclusion #agency #icecream

Artist Michael Swaine repurposed an ice cream cart and mounted it with a treadle-operated sewing machine. He wheeled it to Cohen Alley in the Tenderloin District of San Francisco on the 15th of each month from 12 to 6pm. During this time, Swaine would mend holes, darn socks, and share stories with people in the neighborhood. He had pushed this cart around other areas of the city as part of a "social sculpture"—a way of fabricating experiences instead of objects—but found that the folks in the Tenderloin District—the largest percentage of immigrant families in the city, many of whom remain marginalized because of race, sexuality, and gender—engaged more with the readymade, so he remained.

In a world where everything is thrown away, many people want to keep things and mend or fix them instead. For Swaine and many residents of this neighborhood, this project would help them resist being a part of the throw away culture. Instead, it would give clothes a second life. Over the years, he transformed this into a mending library by setting up several sewing machines, so neighborhood residents could learn to sew and mend their own clothes. Swaine wanted to meet people and exchange life stories, and is what has happened, with a community growing around his encounters. He found that despite the sewing machine's unlikely presence on the street, that it was familiar to most people and encouraged them to stop and chat.

Swaine considers "the project a collaboration between himself and those whose clothes he patches, mends, hems, and darns—an opportunity to create social interaction where there would otherwise be none."[23] The sidewalk where Swaine keeps his machine cultivates a social ritual for the residents of the Tenderloin. These social rituals revolve around the machine and influenced the tenor of the streets, subverting common media representations of this district, repeated behavior loaded with emotional, and social value. The coming together becomes and physical and psychological act performed at the same time and place each week, giving way to a sense of ownership and belonging.

## FREEmobile #social inclusion #crossingborders #civicengagement #icecream

During the summer of 2003, artist Jon Rubin drove the *FREEmobile* into the residential neighborhood of Hillman City, Seattle, home to many new immigrant communities living alongside long-time residents. Based on a readymade ice-cream truck, Rubin's modified 1976 Chevy Van traversed the neighborhood, stopping whenever it was hailed. This gesture based on free exchange allowed participants to come together around similar hobbies and personal histories. He also offered residents an opportunity to sign up to have use of the vehicle for a day.

During that time, they could exchange products and services with neighbors, familiar and unfamiliar. Some of the exchanges included hair braiding, psychic readings, bike repairs, dance lessons, crotchet bookmarks, drumming lessons, and religious rants. The truck also became the stage for a weekly interactive performance where people's amateur talents were elevated to the public realm and "created a system that publicly celebrates the hidden talents and resources of the neighbourhood."[24]

*FREEmobile* challenged the traditional forms of exchange, activated relationships in new and different ways, and shifted proximities through this movement across the town. The publics formed through this exchange, and movement created a provisional, yet potent, counterpublic that broke through barriers for those unsure about the changes occurring in their area. The legacy of Chevy Van has a long road ahead.

## Homeless Vehicle Project of 1987–1989 #codesign #agency #agency #shelter

It's not all art! Design also plays a big role in mobile structures. After consulting with homeless people in NYC, Krzysztof Wodiczko created a homeless vehicle—a cart to transport a small number of belongings, provide space for the collection of bottles, and could be used as a simple shelter. This would

> redirect attention from the work of art as dissent to the work of art as social action: in this case, the discussions and design collaboration with members of the homeless community to develop both a physical object and a conceptual design that would make their participation in the urban economy visible and self-directed.[25]

Wodiczko states,

> [...] the aim of critical public art is neither a happy self-exhibition nor a passive collaboration with the grand gallery of the city, its ideological theatre and architectural social system. Rather it is an engagement in strategic challenges to the city structures and mediums that mediate our everyday perception of the world; an engagement through aesthetic-critical interruptions, infiltrations and appropriations that question the symbolic, psycho-political, and economic operation of the city.[26]

*The Homeless Vehicle Project*, like many of Wodiczko's designs, wasn't necessarily about subterfuge. The critical component of this work comes with its focus on humanizing and giving agency to those living on the urban fringe.

## Mexico Border Project #crossingborders #codesign #participatoryactionresearch #agency

At the border sits a brightly colored cart with green and blue wheels, and red and purple pivoting seats under a shade structure. Attached to each seat was an iPad—an invitation to interact. The cart was equipped with a modified winch controlling the spikey wheels that slowly advanced people along the pedestrian line at San Ysidro Point of Entry. The design and color were based on "Tablitas," a folding wooden block toy, which is similar to a Jacob's Ladder toy. The cart was designed to fold and stack up flat like these toys, and then pop open. And while people sat and crossed the border, they dealt with contentious issues directly across from each other.

Everyone in line had the same goal—moving across that border—but were separated by many other aspects of that border they crossed together. This project responded to contemporary debates about immigration in the United States. In particular, understanding the area's congestion—with over 12 million crossing a year, 300,000 daily commuters often with four to five hours of waiting. The double register of mobility at the border—one that uses mobility, a slow-moving cart, offers a border crossing in an easy and efficient way. At the same time, the cart offered those in line an opportunity to interact.

As part of their art practice, Ghana Think Thank (GTT) uses mobile structures to move through different areas, country towns, urban centers, and border crossings. The group realized that when they started working on issues related to the border, that mobility (or lack of) was built into the flow when crossing between Tijuana and San Diego. The pedestrian line can take several hours to cross. During workshops GTT used Participatory Action Research (PAR) techniques in collaboration with the Tijuana-based art collective Torolab and several think tanks in Mexico to develop the cart.

GTT's horizontal research approach incorporates community feedback, reflection, and then further action based on the discussions with community. GTT used this cart as a collection point for people to submit problems about immigration (if they are "American") or solve those problems (if they are "immigrants"). GTT's readymades traverse visible and invisible borders to remote towns or villages often associated with the developing world or represent contentious geopolitical sites like the US border. The collective is invested in the way their vehicles become *tools for the artistic process*. Moving through a neighborhood—between several communities of participants—improves communication and increases the complexity of each project and also enables it to be highly responsive to local contexts.

## NannyVan and Careforce One #hiddenlabor #codesign #digitalagency #icecream #designtrace #accessibility

The dimensions of the 1976 Chevy Van are 175x74x74 inches. Available to this third-generation Chevy was full customization, one of the more popular options was shag carpet, others included red-orange flames on the outside, rotating seats, and side pipe exhaust. Such van comforts would eventually stimulate an entire subculture of custom van enthusiasts.

Already an icon in American car culture, Chevy Vans also ushered in a new film genre: *vansploitation*. Beyond offering a vehicle for teen comedy antics and sexual experimentation popular in 1970s, the vans were integral to the plot—they had to move the plot forward; they were key to the story and how it would unravel and flow. But a new use of the Chevy Van has found its way into contemporary visual culture: *NannyVan*.

A refurbished 1976 Chevy Van is rechristened *NannyVan*. It's painted burnt orange and emblazoned with "NannyVan" and graphic cut-outs of domestic workers: one hailing the public "get on board" and the other "fair care = quality care." And on the other side of the van it says, "accelerating the movement for domestic workers rights." Cut-outs of stars have transformed this humble Chevy Van to one of superhero transport with a pop-art aesthetic (Figure 26.2). The van traveled around American cities stopping at various locations—museums, libraries, or other sites frequented by domestic workers, their employers, and other advocates. When parked, out of the van jump two women with matching orange aprons. They push out two portable orange carts containing bins of art supplies, fliers, recording equipment, and speakers to form a mobile art design unit, part recording studio, but all advocacy.

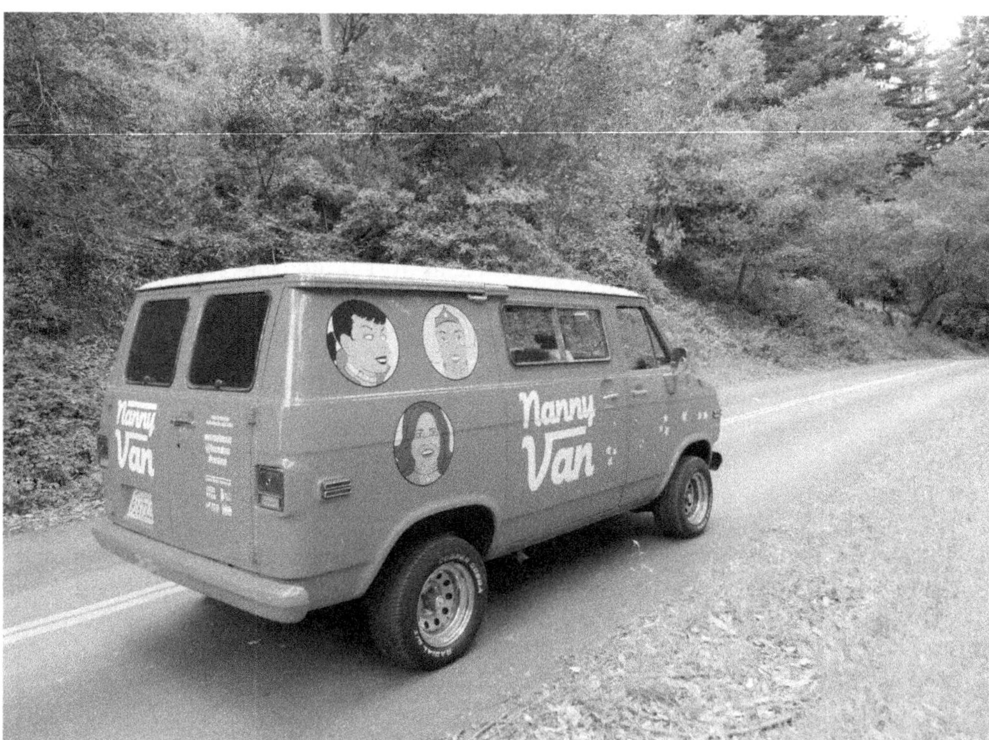


*Figure 26.2* Marisa Morán Jahn (Studio REV), *NannyVan* (2013–2016). Photo credit: Marisa Morán Jahn

In the driver's seat of *Studio REV-* ("as in, to 'rev' an engine") is Marisa Jahn—an artist, activist, and media scholar. The projects *Studio REV-* blur the boundaries between art and design and engage mobile media in their formation to engage—and advocate for—the increasing class of domestic, elder, and childcare workers. *NannyVan* worked to improve how information about domestic labor is given to carers and domestic laborers. It has helped to energize the Domestic Workers Rights' campaign through storytelling, drawing, brainstorming, charades, and mobile media applications. In one instance a phone app was co-designed with domestic workers to help other workers know their rights (Figure 26.3).

Inspired by *NannyVan* came *CareForce One*, a 1967 Mercury Colony Park station wagon modified with more superhero graphics (Figure 11, color insert). This larger project traverses across the United States to advocate for carers' rights. Participants get involved in activities based on their personal experiences as house cleaners, nannies, elder caregivers, or as other domestic employees, and then contribute to new creative outputs. Visitors to the *CareForce One* can point their phones at the vehicle's graphics to activate videos, animations, and danceable songs that feature the stories of caregivers and care-receivers, as well as collectible playing cards that use an augmented reality app to trigger 30-second animated videos.[27]

On the subject of ice cream, Jahn and her collaborators made *A La Carte* (2004), a repurposed ice cream cart. Known as "a roving exhibition of art for popsicle prices,"[28] the group rolled it around the Mission District of San Francisco, offering visitors inexpensive items (under $5) such as collages, knitted goods, and fabric. For Jahn, the cart was a way to "bring art into everyday contexts."[29]

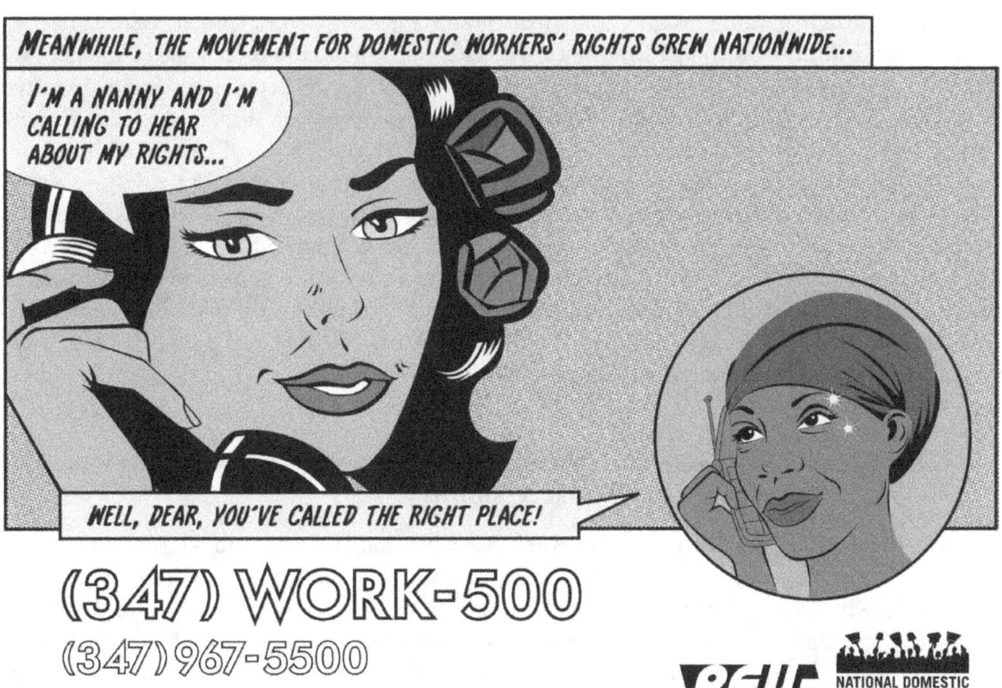


*Figure 26.3* Marisa Morán Jahn (Studio REV), *Domestic Worker App* (2011–2015). Photo credit: Marisa Morán Jahn

## The Natural History Museum #subterfuge #publicpedagogy #accessibility

Part pop-up museum, part "toxic" tour guide vehicle, and all activism, The Natural History Museum epitomizes the spirit of Lucy Lippard's hope for the activist art through subterfuge. Not An Alternative (Beka Economopoulos and Jason Jones) is part of a larger movement of artists and art collectives working to get cultural institutions to divest from fossil fuels. The group targeted corporate sponsorship in an American context by calling out museum board members (The Koch brothers at the American Museum of Natural History (AMNH), for example). In addition, to "get on the inside" and effect change, the group joined the American Alliance of Museums and the Association of Science and Technology Centers.

The Natural History Museum is itinerant with a 15-passenger mobile museum, a 2006 Ford E-350 cab complete with Glavel conversion, a former airport shuttle bus which runs off bio-diesel. There's bench seating that allows people to face each other, so it's conducive to group conversations. They have used the bus for "toxic tours" led by scientists and community groups, and for roving discussion sessions with speakers and small groups.

Not An Alternative took the pop-up museum to the floor of the American Alliance of Museums' annual convention in 2015, in Atlanta, Georgia, as part of an exhibition where they re-created dioramas such as the David H. Koch Dinosaur Wing (from the AMNH), but instead of dioramas of dinosaurs in their habitat, a lone human skeleton stood in front a large vitrine pointing to a large dinosaur skeleton. The title was chilling: *Will the Story of the Sixth Massive Extinction Ever Include the Story of Its Sponsors?* Another diorama featured a large polar bear in the midst of tires, mufflers, and an oil pipeline attributed to Koch Industries titled, *Our Climate, Whose Politics?*[30]

These dioramas draw attention to how economic, social, and political forces shape our understanding of—or even what we understand as—nature through their exhibition displays. The critical installations function as a backdrop for conversations with museum professionals, conducting stakeholder research, gaining insights, and identifying sympathetic allies who, if collectivized, can help push for institutional change from within.[31] These pop-up exhibits appeal to audiences who already enjoy this type of museum but may not know the extent of corporate sponsorship or their board affiliations, or how this might affect what and how things are displayed in the museum. They use aesthetics, public pedagogical models, and presentation forms of natural history museums in order to support a perspective that regards nature as a commons.[32]

As they travel to different venues, the bus reinforces the narrative of NHM as a traveling, pop-up museum, at a time when the museum sector is very intrigued by and interested in the pop-up model and the idea of a museum bus. It suggests a cool, edgy pop-up version of a natural history museum that would appeal to younger audiences, including the museum sector's Holy Grail demographic: millennials and Gen Z.[33] For the artists, these tactics may resemble institutional critique, but they focus on institutional liberation.

## The School of Panamerican Unrest #publicpedagogy #crossingborders #accessibility

Pablo Helguera's 2006 road trip began in Anchorage, Alaska, and ended in Tierra de Fuego, the tip of South America, and made 29 stops along the way. He and his Chevy Van navigated the Americas in what was to become one of the largest public art projects ever realized. The van stopped in plazas and museums, where Helguera would install a pop-up schoolhouse: a "nomadic think tank" with films, performances, and discussions about often-charged issues such as immigration, nationalism, and regionalism as they related to the 19th notion of "Panamericanism."[34]

Based on the nineteenth-century premise that the Americas (North, Central, South) would connect through social, economic, cultural activities, and would be reinforced through declarations, treaties, and alliances, Panamericanism faded with the wars of the twentieth century and continued with the United States' imperial activities in the region. Helguera wanted to reignite the dialog about some of these ideals in the context of current political and social environment in order to better understand the hopes and concerns of artists and citizens along the way.[35] He documented these personal encounters through his blog, which highlighted regional issues as well as larger art world concerns (for example, the artist intentionally visited cities and towns off the art world radar), as well as the challenges he faced along the way, whether the challenge to connect disparate communities across thousands of miles, the car trouble he had, or the low attendance at his events. This exercise in public pedagogy traversed and crossed borders through space and time, pulling past ideals into current contexts, and intersecting geopolitical histories with artistic encounters.

## The Social Mirror #hiddenlabor #choreography

If you happen to live in New York during the late 1970s, when public services and public works transformed parts of the city into a garbage heap, a free for all for rats, for opportunists, and anarchists. As New York slowly pulled itself together in the early 1980s, a few years shy of the now disparaged yuppie culture, artists began to weave the social tapestry back together. But it was the sanitation workers who cleaned up the mess.

Then imagine that you found yourself standing at the front of a four-person deep crowd lining the streets of one of New York's main streets. As you stood, a 15-cubic meter garbage collection truck decorated with hand-tempered glass mirrors with smoke Plexiglas mirror trim passed you by. You saw yourself, you saw others, you saw how the city worked and lived together, all reflected on the sides of a garbage truck.

Mierle Laderman Ukeles' *Social Mirror* was part of the 1983 grand finale of the first New York City Art Parade.[36] The reflecting truck was a metaphor for the interrelationship between "us" whose images get caught in the mirror and "those" who collect our garbage. The goal was to get the public—parade goers—to "reflect" on their disposal habits to consider the lifecycle of their consumptive behaviors and those who are hidden in this cycle. In much of Ukeles' work, the vehicle figures prominently, whether it is in her engagement with NYC sanitation workers or the choreographing of a ballet of snowplows.

The mirrored sanitation truck moved through time, and in 2017, its truck showed up on the forecourt of the Queens Museum so that Open Engagement conference goers could see their reflections. However, the truck remained stationary throughout its time in the forecourt, perhaps highlighting the ongoing paradoxical situation around waste removal, stalling its once potent mobile action for a contemporary art audience.

## The Tactical Ice Cream Unit #icecream #surveillance #subterfuge #propaganda

*The Tactical Ice Cream Unit* (TICU), a 2006 project by The Center for Tactical Magic, is a large white van reminiscent of a communist-era spy vehicle—a "bastard lovechild of an ice cream truck and a S.W.A.T. van."[37] Pasted on the side are two menus on the van: an ice-cream menu and a propaganda menu, yet the ice-cream flavors have vaguely political names such as "da bomb." Rather than asking if someone wants information with their ice cream, a man donning a black uniform and mirrored sunglasses asks: "What flavour of propaganda would like with your ice cream?" The public is given a choice of flavors, but not a choice of whether or not to make choice—it is assumed they want both. The public leaves with a "treat for the streets" and "food for thought," and some "righteous propaganda."[38]

TICU roved from place to place, functioning differently in each context—an art exhibition or a political rally, for example. Arriving as an ice cream truck disguises The Center for Tactical

Magic's (CTM) dual purpose: the truck is equipped to support protest and has within it the tools the capacity to support activists with a legion of surveillance cameras that can monitor police activity. Aaron Gach, CTM's director of operations states, "in each case—a museum or a protest—we are providing a set of services that can be measured concretely; yet, we are also presenting familiar cultural forms combined in an unfamiliar way."[39] The result of mixing elements of popular culture with satire is disarming. They link media and political propaganda to an everyday pleasure—ice cream—drawing in the unassuming public and sending them away with new associations and more information before the "bastard love child" rolled onto the scene.

## #trojanhorse #movingon

The Trojan Horse may be an ancient myth, but its trace helps us understand how mobile contemporary art practices perform social and political activism in the public realm. The manner in which these are performed are diverse. Readymades such as Ghana Think Tank's Mexican Border Project and Cog*nate Collective's Dialogue in Transit cross literal and metaphorical borders to instigate dialog and reflection; *The Natural History Museum* performs deception to bring awareness to the hidden economic dimensions of climate change: The *Tactical Ice Cream Unit* and FREEmobile engage neighborhoods and give new meaning to being in place: Agit-trains educate peasantry through graphic propaganda; or a more measured pedagogical approach to geopolitical history with Helguera's *School of Transamerican Unrest* offers a more measured pedagogical approach to geopolitical history; and co-design with the *NannyVan* of CareForce to be aware of rights and improve labor conditions.

In contrast to stationary artworks, or even short- or long-public art projects, the #trojanhorse projects are distinctive in their mobility. They move in or across, they arrive and leave; publics form and disperse. What is left in their wake are new associations with the world, with their environment, and with issues of concern. Lucy Lippard's 1980s Trojan Horse may have been more metaphorical than its application today, but the aim continues: if the unassuming public encounters a vehicle disguised as art, it allows for the unexpected to be unleashed. This is the power of art—its indeterminacy instigates wonder, its rhizomatic tendencies infiltrate the imagination, unmoored from any site and made mobile, this power becomes exponential. This (Incomplete) Lexicon allows space for additions, for new interpretations, for accessing new and different audiences, and innovative mobile art.

## Notes

1 Virgil: Book 2, *The Aeneid*, www.glyniliffe.com/2013/10/a-few-facts-about-the-trojan-horse/.
2 Ibid.
3 Lippard, Lucy, "Trojan Horses: Activist Art and Power," in *Art After Modernism: Rethinking Representation*, edited by Brian Wallis (New York: New Museum of Contemporary Art; Boston: D.R. Godine, 1984), 341–58.
4 Ibid.
5 Ibid, 342.
6 Ibid, 343, "how" emphasis author; "why" emphasis Lippard.
7 This chapter is also inspired by the important work of Mimi Sheller. In particular, "Mobile Art: Out of Your Pocket," in *The Routledge Companion to Mobile Media*, edited by Gerard Goggin, and Larissa Hjorth (New York: Routledge, 2014, 197–205. In this chapter, Sheller calls for a more expansive understanding of mobile art, one that encompasses socially engaged public art (among other forms such as performance). She sees this, along with Claire Bishop's "relational antagonism" as critical elements to expanding and interpreting mobile art in the public realm.
8 The art collective Temporary Services compiled a "mobile resources" collection on their website. In it they detail structures ranging from mobile art galleries, lending libraries, services for homeless people and architectural services. This resource provides an extensive archive and exemplifies the proliferation of mobile projects in social and public practice. Please visit the site for a more thorough overview of

this type of work. My purpose is to extend them within Lippard's Trojan Horse activist art framework. www.temporaryservices.org/mobile_struct_rsrce.html, accessed June 2019.

9 Other notable conceptual frames include interventionist art, made famous through the groundbreaking exhibition and its accompanying publication: Nato Thompson, Arjen Noordeman, and Massachusetts Museum of Contemporary Art, *The Interventionists: User's Manual for the Creative Disruption of Everyday Life* (Boston: MIT Press, 2004).

10 Lidiia V. Maksakova, *Agitpoezd "Oktiabr'skaia Revoliutsiia" (1919–1920 gg.)* [The "October Revolution" Agit-Train (1919–1920)], (Moscow: Moscow: Nauka, 1956), 11.

11 Szymon Boyko, "Agit-Prop Art: The Streets Were Their Theatre," in *The Avant Garde in Russia, 1910–1930: New Perspectives*, edited by Stepahanie Barron and Maurice Tuchman (Cambridge, MA: Los Angeles County Museum of Art/MIT Press, 1980), 76.

12 Jonathan Smele, *The "Russian" Civil Wars, 1916–1926: Ten Years that Shook the World* (New York: Oxford University Press, 2015), 248.

13 Ibid, 196.

14 Model: forward control, body type: P3500, vehicle ID# 1GDHP34R0K3501306, as of June 2013 the most recent odometer reading was: 214,398 miles.

15 See www.theblackfactory.com/truck.html.

16 "Overview," *Black Factory*, www.theblackfactory.com/town_11.html.

17 See www.moma.org/learn/moma_learning/william-pope-l-the-black-factory-archive-2004-ongoing/.

18 William Pope. L quoted in www.absolutearts.com/artsnews/2007/03/19/34409.html.

19 Email correspondence with the artist, Misael Diaz, 20 June 2019.

20 Ibid.

21 Ibid.

22 Cog•nate Collective, www.cognatecollective.com/dit-en.html.

23 Michael Swain, "KQED Spark," 2005, https://ww2.kqed.org/spark/michael-swaine/.

24 Jon Rubin, "Project Histories," in *What We Want is Free: Generosity and Exchange in Contemporary Art*, edited by Ted Purves (New York: SUNY Press, 2004), 129–30.

25 Kathleen MacQueen, *Tactical Response: Art in an Age of Terror* (New York: Agon Press, 2014), 103–71.

26 Krzysztof Wodiczko, *Critical Vehicles: Writings, Projects, Interviews* (Cambridge: MIT Press, 1999), 27.

27 See www.studiorev.org.

28 Slaton, Joyce. "Merrily We Roll Along," San Francisco Weekly, June 2–8, 2004.

29 Ibid.

30 Author's correspondence with the artists, July 13, 2019.

31 Ibid.

32 Marisa Mazria Katz. "Clearing the Air: Artists Take on Corporate Influence in Natural History Museums," Creative Time Reports. September 2, 2014, http://creativetimereports.org/2014/09/02/not-an-alternative-natural-history-museum/.

33 Author's correspondence with the artists, July 13, 2019.

34 Elyse Gonzales and Sara Reisman, eds. 2019. *Mobilizing Pedagogy*, Art, Design & Architecture Museum, University of California, Santa Barbara.11.

35 http://pablohelguera.net/2006/06/the-school-of-panamerican-unrest/.

36 www.citylab.com/life/2016/11/the-artist-who-made-sanitation-workers-worthy-of-a-museum/508862/.

37 Leah Modigliani, "Behind the Curtain: Leah Modigliani Interviews the Center for Tactical Magic," *C Magazine* 106 (2010): 4–9, 8.

38 www.tacticalmagic.org/CTM/project%20pages/TICU.htm.

39 Ibid, 9.

# 27
# UNDERSTANDING MOBILE METHODS THROUGH CO-DESIGN WORKSHOPS

*Fumitoshi Kato*

Over the past ten years, smartphones (*sumaho*)—as a key portal for social media—have been playing an increasingly visible role in the relationship between sociality and place in Japan. Importantly, mobile phones (*keitai*), alongside current *sumaho* users are now "matured," in the sense that they are well trained in using digital media technologies, and in handling various types of information over Social Networking Services (SNS). Therefore, notions of "friend" and "family" are continuously negotiated through how we connect each other via mobile media technologies.[1]

This chapter draws from 15 years of using mobile media to co-design with regional communities for revitalization. Over this period, just as the media had developed, so too have the possibilities for collaboration, connection, and sustainability. This chapter is particularly interested in how mobile media can be understood as equipment for methods that enhance our creativity and enable a variety of design practices. In this chapter, I begin with a contextualization of mobile media in Japan and discuss possibilities in the context of art and design. In promoting the discussion, I will introduce the cases of participatory learning projects using mobile media as practical examples.

## Indispensable Media

As mentioned, smartphones have become an integral part of our everyday mundane environments. According to a survey by the Mobile Society Research Institute (NTT DoCoMo), smartphone ownership in Japan is over 70%, and their use by children and the elderly is also increasing on the rise.[2] One of the most popular reasons that elderly people purchase *sumaho* is that it is often recommended by family members for communication with grandchildren, or for confirming their safety by staying in touch with family members. The structure of the family is diversified. The so-called "nuclear family" has been the social model for a while, but in Japan over the last 25 years, "couples only" and "single-parent families" have increased. Concurrently "couple and child" households are decreasing year by year.

The style of living together with a large family has become unusual with family members often living apart. Mobile media play an increasingly important role in maintaining contact and care at a distance. In particular, social media platforms such as LINE—especially if they are geographically distanced—have become pivotal in maintaining the relationships via exchanging text, photos, and videos.

Various social problems are emerging as smartphones have become an integral part of our everyday life. In Japan, natural disasters are frequent—escalating in recent years. In response, there has been a movement to use SNS in an emergency situation, or to utilize apps for disaster prevention. In the case of the earthquake and tsunami known as "311" in 2011, information on safety status and traffic damage were exchanged via SNS. After that experience, we came to understand SNS as a mechanism for confirming everyday safety and security. It can be said that the role of mobile media such as smartphones is significant in that they can be reassured by being always watched by people.

Given the variety and intensity of this problem, everyday life in Japan will increasingly rely on smartphones and related social networks for support and to stay connected during times of crisis. The *sumaho* is an individual's intimate companion, an extension that amplifies one's creativity, imagination, and expression in day-to-day activities. It is important that we develop creative and critical ways to engage with mobile media as a vehicle for social inclusion and enhancement as society changes. The co-design workshops I discuss below address these concerns.

## Exploring the Power of Places

Asset-Based Community Development approach (hereafter referred to as the ABCD approach) aims to understand the nature of local "assets" and to discover their possibilities, rather than to follow the well-trodden pathway of "problem-solving." In other words, the ABCD approach is an attempt to shift our research emphasis from the "needs-driven" approach to "capacity-focused" approach.[3] A relatively familiar approach for us would be to identify the problems in the local community and to explore solutions for them. For example, we typically begin with the mapping of the problem situations within the area, then go on to examine the priorities among those problems and possible solutions for them. Further, we estimate necessary costs and make allocation plans.

Kretzmann and McKnight suggest that "needs-driven" approach may serve to create client neighborhoods. That is to say, many urban neighborhoods are becoming "environments of service where behaviors are affected because residents come to believe that their well-being depends upon being a client."[4] Once the "problem" in the local community is identified and shared among community members, the participants involved, and their expected roles tend to become fixed. As a result, community members become *consumers* of service, rather than *producers*. In addition, when the problems are described and delivered in a fashion aimed to the general public, regardless of them being local issues, community members may begin to understand the problems as somebody else's business.

In contrast, the ABCD approach provides a mapping based on a different idea. Community "assets" are mapped with regard to gifts of individuals, citizens' associations, and local institutions. For each of the categories, various local "assets" are identified as strengths of the local community. By doing so, a series of "assets" becomes visible and at hand for our further explorations. Community members become co-designers.

As mentioned, the uses of mobile phones are changing the ways in which we shape and reshape our day-to-day activities. With the ubiquity of mobile media—and its ability to take, edit, send, and publish photos—they become key vehicles in increasing one's opportunity to generate quotidian "life documents." It is suggested that a new mode of more pervasive photo taking is emerging through the use of mobile phones, and it contributes, to some extent, to change the ways in which we record and preserve our "life documents" on a daily basis.

The role of mobile media in qualitative research projects is complex. It can be the researchers' tool, the research, the participant's tool, subject, and object. It can provide intimate understandings into quotidian life. Given these factors, how does the use of mobile media change our mode of knowing, especially in terms of ethnographic research method? What are the possibilities of "mobile methods" to preserve and share public images of the community? How do they contribute to further expand our knowledge about the power of places?

In order to examine these issues, I will refer to cases of co-design workshops, both conducted as a part of class assignments in a Japanese university setting. These workshops are examples of the synthesis between research and teaching, whereby teaching probes inform research frameworks and vice versa.

## Case 1: Designing Mobile Kit (Stay Mobile and Carry On)

Designing Mobile Kit was devised to explore the ways in which various "good places" are shaped and reshaped through our communication processes. Acknowledging that we are always "in-communication," our research design begins with a series of critical observations of our day-to-day activities.

Initially, we conduct field research to identify *when, where,* and *with whom* our "intimate moments" are organized and shared. Based on ethnographic findings, we designed a set of "mobile kits" that enabled us to promote our communication while we were on the move. Somehow, many things did not work out naturally, as expected. Our day-to-day mundane is full of happenings and messiness. However, we continued to resolve these worries and stresses through engagement and communication. Thus, we began to speculate upon the notion of place-making due to the basic idea in relation to the organization of our use of time and space—to get together.

We further attempted to utilize various tools in the process of place-making by understanding the given situation. What are the tools that we select and carry around? What are the important aspects of realizing our "precious moment"? As part of the iterative design process, we recognized the variety of tools and artifacts available on site, so much so that we did not have to prepare and carry everything, instead utilizing existing elements of place. We often attempted to organize time and space based on our past experiences and expertise. And if we were to get together with close friends, for instance, we acknowledged that it could be anytime and anywhere, so that we do not have to worry about a series of adjustments and preparations in advance. It may suggest that, eventually, place-making can be realized even when we are empty-handed. There is no doubt that we will feel more comfortable when we are empty-handed, freed from thinking about time, space, and other tools/artifacts.

In understanding how we go about place-making activities, we are gradually preparing to let things go and to stay mobile. We developed relationships with others in which we could "make moves" spontaneously.

In a co-design project called "Stay Mobile and Carry On," five groups of students attempted to design a "mobile kit" for place-making activities.[5] That is, to envision and identify when, where, with whom, and how our "intimate moments" could be realized. From a carry cart to a bicycle, each group tried to modify and redesign a range of selected items (vehicles) based on their own issues at hand.

### *Learning through Design*

In the project, I prepared a series of "vehicles" in advance and allocated one of them to each group. There were various shapes and sizes, such as kickboards, carry carts, and bicycles with electric assistance.

Students worked on the design of a "mobile kit," one that facilitates place-making and promotes communication while considering the specific situation of when, where, with whom, and how long they want to spend within it. As a class project, students were told that the "vehicles" devised, as prototypes, must be taken out to the town at least once and practiced (to conduct field experiments). Above all, it was important not to keep the "vehicle" in the classroom or laboratory, but rather to take it out to a more realistic site and think through the practice. These challenges were quite difficult. Once a specific "vehicle" (artifact) is given, the consciousness tends to turn to creation rather than its' active process. Thinking too much about making things makes it difficult to think. In order to prevent this from happening, I attempted to urge students to forefront thinking about what kind of communication is created by the "vehicle" (Figure 27.1).

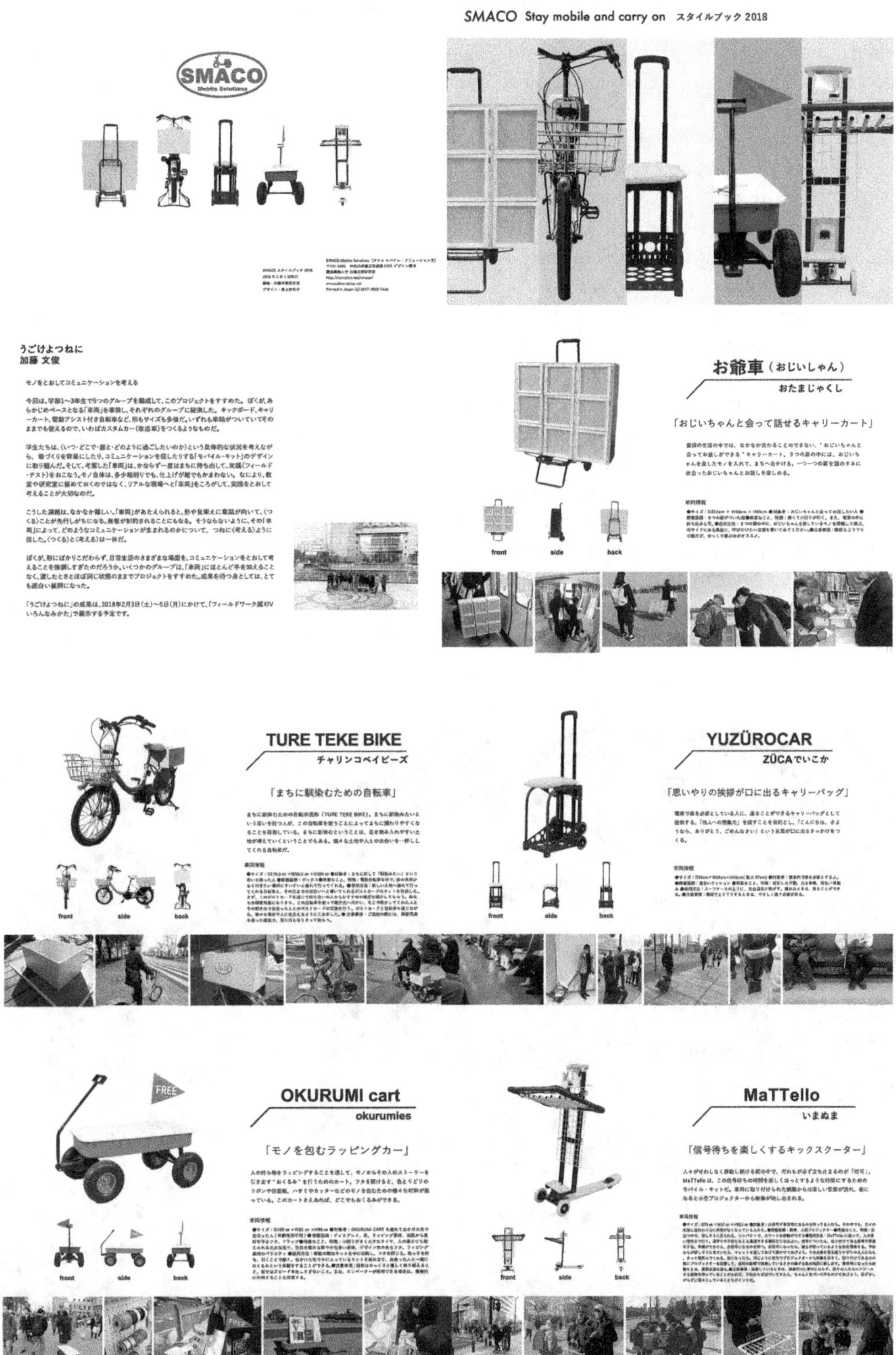


*Figure 27.1* Style book from the *Stay Mobile and Carry On* project (2018). Photo credit: Fumitoshi Kato

## *Returning the Results Back to the Community*

This project sought to produce repeated engagements—rather than a parachute study it provided sustained activities that could be deepened over time and reproduced in different contexts. It is designed in a way that one has to have a relationship with the local community more than once as a "repeater," rather than just a one-time visitor. It is a mechanism whereby students not only develop experiences in the local community, but also return something back to the community.

As I have introduced, each "mobile kit" can be understood as a "media" through which communication within the local community is facilitated. Particularly, when the artifact is designed and tested in public places, it may raise community members' awareness about their commitment to the local community, and to gradually foster a sense of "civic pride." For this project, an exhibition was held to publicize the results of the project and return it widely to the local community (Figure 27.2).

Again, from the "capacity-focused" perspective, what stands out is not the idea of marketing. Needless to say, it is always important for us to think about the "readers" of our papers and reports. When we consider the possibilities of social contributions of the research, we should have a clear idea about our audience and how the research will be communicated and adopted by them. We need to have more rigorous questioning of what constitutes a market or industry, and how we can deepen our engagement and impact with—and for—communities.

When we reflect upon the nature of our social relationships, being with someone or being on-site (at the time of the event) is becoming more and more important. It points to the pivotal role of design in sharing and co-designing to find the best pathways to communicate and embed

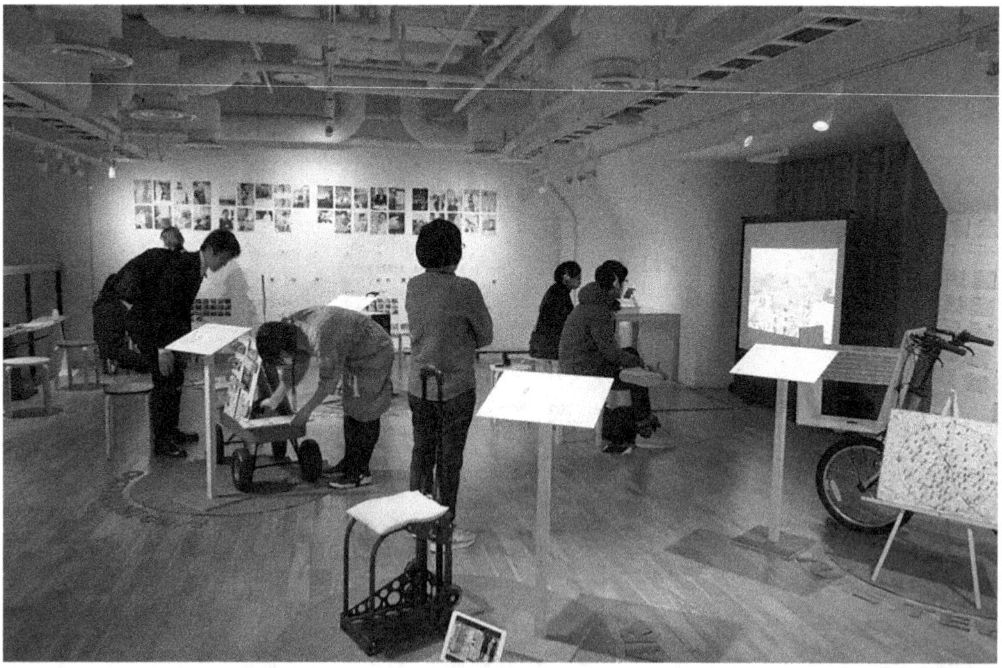

*Figure 27.2* Exhibition in Yokohama (February 2018). Photo credit: Fumitoshi Kato

findings. The *Stay Mobile and Carry On* project is an attempt to promote a sense of belonging to the community and the nature of human relations in the region.

## Case 2: Poster Project

Over the past ten years, I have been exploring the use of camera phones and other mobile media technologies for qualitative research methods—with a particular focus on a participatory mode of learning. Guided by the idea of an alternative classroom, these projects were designed to create experiential learning opportunities outside the university campus. By incorporating the ideas of experiential learning, our projects consist of field research and interviews, together with collaborative co-design workshops, and debriefing sessions. Such a mode of learning can be characterized as a "camp," in that participants seek to understand the resources available and attempt to expand their capacities to organize their ideas within given situations. Currently, *sumaho* plays an important role as a device to facilitate communication among participants and thereby stimulate their creativity.

A "camp" is an attempt to design a place at which we can reflect upon things that are regarded as "taken-for-granted" in our day-to-day activities. I suggest that such a form of learning may promote communication among participants, through the set of goals, roles, and rules that constructs the situation. As a mode of learning, the program consists of three closely interrelated steps. Each step has its emphasis in terms of our process of knowing as iterative. The design of the learning process is primarily based on the theory of experiential learning, and it unfolds as three steps. These three steps of the "camp" create a cyclic process (Figure 27.3).[6]

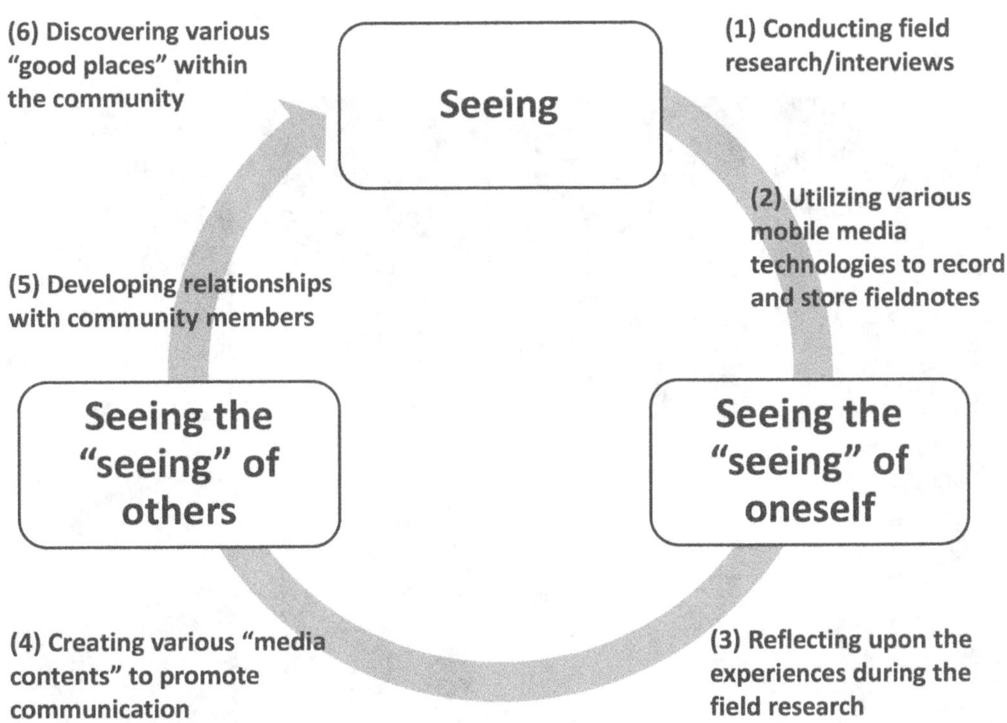


*Figure 27.3* Process of the co-design workshop. Photo credit: Fumitoshi Kato

## *Getting in Touch with People*

In the first step, we conducted interview sessions with members of the local community. Typically, participants worked in a pair, in that one concentrated on taking photos while the other worked on generating fieldnotes. A primary purpose here was to listen to the "real" voices of the ones who live their lives in the community, and to collect and compile data (i.e., including photos, voice recordings, sketches, and other forms of fieldnotes). This process can be understood as collating a pile of life documents with which one can begin to weave a story about his/her experiences in the area. Through this phase, participants learnt about how he/she could get closer to the interviewee and develop the relationships with her/him particular to each given situation.

## *Making Sense Out of Interview Sessions*

The next step of the program was to reflect upon the interview session and to think about the person interviewed, and her/his day-to-day activities within the community. After the fieldwork, participants were asked to select photos and to come up with a catch copy, phrases, and short texts to illustrate the situation created simultaneously by both the interviewers and the interviewee. As a way to organize and present this process of understanding, we created a set of posters. Through this process, one had to distance oneself from the situation within which he/she was embedded. It triggered a mode of self-reflection, in which one had to look back and attempt to make sense of things and events he/she observed during the fieldwork.

For example, in the recent project conducted in Okayama, Japan (June 2019), we created eight posters out of interview sessions (Figure 27.4).[7]

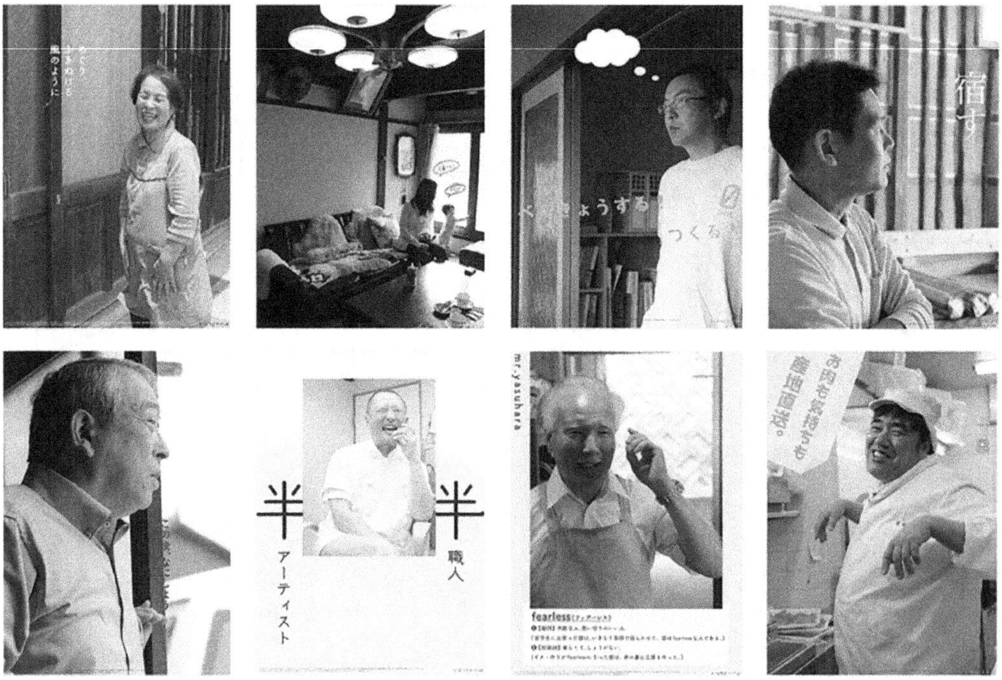


*Figure 27.4* Posters created during the workshop (June 2019). Photo credit: Fumitoshi Kato

### *Sharing Posters with Interviewees*

When conducting field research in a local community, it is essential to deliver the result of the research back to the community members. As mentioned, as a way to distribute the images of the person (that is, in fact, the images of the community) the photos, phrases, and texts are organized into a set of posters. I suggest here that a poster is a distinct, useful medium for presenting one's experiences in the field. By delivering and sharing these posters, one can begin to further develop a relationship with the interviewee. We held the presentation session of the posters during our stay. This phase of the project may further develop the relationship between the interviewer(s) and the interviewee while also promoting one's self-reflection. This process is one of initiation: to pursue additional interviews, as well as to incorporate new participants for future research activities. Also, this cyclic process may expand the scope and perspective of the research itself.

## Conclusion

As highlighted throughout the case studies discussed in this chapter, mobile media plays an essential role in every phase of the participatory workshop. In addition to recording photos, videos, audio, etc., LINE, Messenger, and Slack were also used for communication between participants. When multiple participants are scattered in the field at the same time, and each act autonomously, various unexpected things occur even if they are carefully planned. Mobile media is always on hand to improvise and choreograph.

The facilities used for the design workshop were fully equipped with Wi-Fi and could be recharged without difficulty. Without such an environment, the design workshop would not have progressed well. As for the printing of posters, I always use printers that support large format printing during the community residency period. This allows for many variables. However, during our coding workshop I prepared for the related variables, but the printer broke down by accident. In the end, we were able to print and open a presentation session using a copy machine at a convenience store. The utilization of equipment found on site can often strengthen relationships between researcher and participant.

One of the important features of the co-design workshop was to leave our experiences of the research site with the community members, immediately after the interview session. That is, we try to meet the interviewees again on the next day. It is iterative and ongoing. We work overnight to create a set of "small media." Here, the notion of "small media" refers to forms of presenting the results of interview sessions, such as postcards, posters, zines, flyers, booklets, podcasts, and video clips. Here too, with the capacity of mobile media technologies, they are relatively easy to create and deliver back to the residents. A piece of "small media" transforms a dyad relationship into a triad relationship during the second meeting, and thereby facilitates our conversations. It also alleviates the pressures associated with face-to-face communication that the participants encountered during the day before. By having a set of "small media" in-between, both the students and residents can talk and reflect upon the session together.

In relation to the context of conducting research with mobile media, one of the functions considered was to be hyper aware of the directions of "externalization" and "embodiment," which may also be called the "monitoring function." As "externalization" progresses, "camera eyes" will see us in various situations. The media "embodied" also has the identical functions. As noted earlier, we are always moving with camera phones and constantly uploading various images to the SNS. These "monitoring functions" of media devices have been critically argued in the initial stage of workshop discussions. However, it is also possible to use such a "monitoring function" itself in our social science approach, especially in the context of "mobile understanding" and mobile methods.[8]

With the advent of smartphones, our social media usage has increased significantly. As mentioned above, with the help of operability, mobile media has become an integral part of our daily lives. It has already been about ten years since the appearance of smartphones, and now many models have smartphone-like specifications. With the rise of the "always on" dimension of mobile media, there is an opportunity to develop co-design projects that enhance and enable better social inclusion and connection. There are generations of mobile media literacy on hand that we should engage with in critical and creative ways.

## Notes

1 Kana Ohashi and Fumitoshi Kato, "Lines for Connectedness: A Study of Social Media Practices in Japanese Families," in *Routledge Handbook of New Media in Asia*, edited by Larissa Hjorth and Olivia Khoo (London: Routledge, 2016), 199–208.
2 Mobile Society Research Institute (MSRI), *Keitai riyou Hakusho* (Trends in the use of keitai and sumaho), (Tokyo, Chuokeizai-sha, 2018).
3 John P. Kretzmann and John L. McKnight, *Building Communities from the Inside Out: A Path toward Finding and Mobilizing a Community's Assets* (Skokie: ACTA Publications, 1993).
4 Kretzmann and McKnight, *Building Communities*, 2.
5 See https://vanotica.net/smaco/ for details.
6 Fumitoshi Kato, "Seeing the 'Seeing' of Others: Environmental Knowing through Camera-Phones," in *Mobile Understanding: The Epistemology of Ubiquitous Communication*, edited by Kristof Nyiri (Vienna: Passagen Verlag, 2006), 183–95.
7 The project was held in Tamashima, Okayama, Japan (June 2019). For an illustration, a digest video is available at: www.youtube.com/watch?v=Mn4hWFKUAIw.
8 Monika Büscher, John Urry, and Katian Witchger (eds.), *Mobile Methods* (London: Routledge, 2011).

# SECTION SEVEN

# Sensing New Visualities

# 28
# FUTUREEVERYTHING, ALL THE TIME

## *Drew Hemment* in Conversation with *Klare Lanson*

As artist, designer, and academic researcher, Drew Hemment wholeheartedly advocates creative and collaborative forms of future thinking and making. Over 25 years, he has been one of the key figures who has shaped the field of digital art and culture, with a track record of leadership roles in domains including open data and human-centered smart cities. In 1995, Drew founded the renowned innovation lab and festival FutureEverything, directing continuously for 23 years the United Kingdom's annual festival of digital culture and numerous innovative co-design programs spanning science, society, technology, and the arts. As lead artist on many projects, he speaks on location media art and the ongoing importance of embodied and participatory experience (Figure 28.1).

This Companion highlights the cultural consequences of enhanced mobility due to technological developments. Your projects have a fantastic approach to the art of collaboration, where multisensorial forms of experience are key to complex ways of making ideas and things more visible. What inspired you to develop this work and create FutureEverything?

I've long been fascinated by the way in which technology, culture, and urban spaces collide. This goes back to 1982, when I visited Japan while my father was there for work. I was mesmerized by the flows of humanity on the subway, the density of electronic displays, the futurity of the shinkansen, the iconography of *anime*, all rubbing up against another age of temples and tea rooms. Then, in my late teens at the end of the 1980s, I was involved in electronic music and dance culture and witnessed how a new constellation of media, technology, beats, and bodies could profoundly shift the cultural and urban landscape. In the early 1990s, while doing a master's in continental philosophy at University of Warwick, I stumbled across the Virtual Futures conferences and got involved as an organizer and speaker. I then started Futuresonic in 1995, renamed FutureEverything in 2010.

How do you define Mobile Media Art in relation to the performance/participation of the smartphone? What for you are some of the defining moments in the "field" of Mobile Media Art you have experienced?

I'd point to the emergence in 2003 of what we called back then *locative media*. It was something of a movement, with a group of people all collaborating on something we felt was really important.

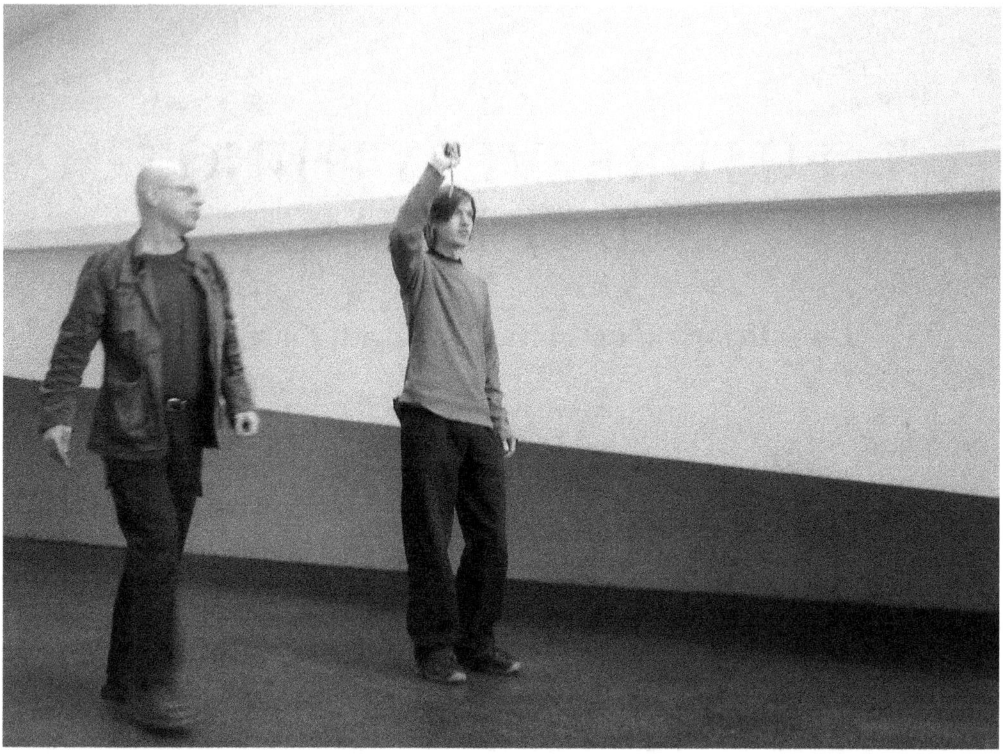

*Figure 28.1* *Loca: Set To Discoverable* (2006)—"Please hold your networked device in the air." Photo credit: Drew Hemment, Mika Raento, John Evans, Theo Humphries

Rasa Smite and Raitis Smits at RIXC organized a mapping workshop in Latvia that year. I was working on a project on mobile phones and surveillance as part of an Arts and Humanities Research Council Creative Fellowship. I met Ben Russell who had published the hugely influential *Headmap Manifesto* in 1999,[1] and connected with artists making really interesting work at this time using GPS and collaborative cartography. These included Teri Rueb's *The Choreography of Everyday Movement* (2001) and Esther Polak's *Amsterdam RealTime* (2002). Together with Mark Tuters—and a traveling band of artists, thinkers, and developers—we organized a series of events through 2003 and 2004, at events such as Next5Minutes in Amsterdam and Transmediale in Berlin. This captured an upcoming wave of change, prefiguring smart phones and Google Maps, and bringing together the champions of bottom-up alternatives, such as Steve Coast, founder of OpenStreetMap[2] and Julian Priest of Free Networks (Figure 28.2).[3]

What interests you about mobile media and how it is used by artists? Can you elaborate on a few projects in terms of the experiential elements utilizing mobile media to realize them?

Two years after I wandered the streets of Tokyo as a 12-year-old, Shuhei Hosokawa published an essay that had an influence on me many years later, "The Walkman Effect."[4] This was in 1984, soon after the introduction of the Walkman by Sony. Hosokawa challenged the idea that the mobile user is disconnected and isolated from the world around them. He does not deny that there is a separation or solipsism but argues that there is a doubling between the experience of private listening and the experience of embodiment in social and physical space. The mobile experience for Hosokawa is one of negotiating the seam or interface between these two spaces. Just as in the

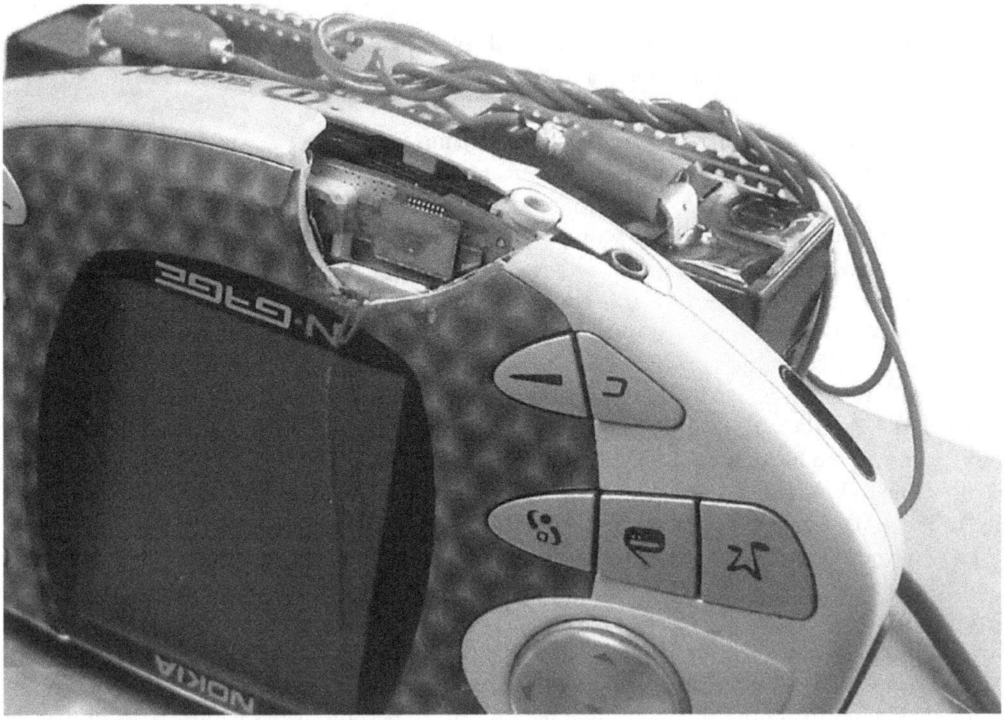


*Figure 28.2* *Loca: Set To Discoverable* (2006)—Modified phones running Loca software. Photo credit: Drew Hemment, Mika Raento, John Evans, Theo Humphries

1980s people were concerned about the isolation of Walkman users in their own private sound bubble, so too today we are concerned about people glued to the mobile screen, eroding the public sphere, and posing a danger to themselves and others at street crossings. Giving the example of a boy and a girl at a party who are too shy to talk and only manage to connect by sharing a Walkman, Hosokawa shows us how nonetheless new kinds of encounter arise where media and physical spaces meet.

In 2003, we were interested in something very similar. The internet was widely seen to make place and geography irrelevant. Locative media presented another view and pointed to the way that mobile media can reconfigure urban space. This to me was the key insight that opened a world of possibilities.

This was the focus in Mobile Connections at the Futuresonic festival in 2004[5]—the first major conference and exhibition on mobile and locative arts. This included a number of artworks and talks looking at the intersection of telecommunication space and the physical, embodied space of the user. It also presented works that were not networked, but highlighted the phenomena Hosokawa had written about such as *Sonic Interface* by Akitsugu Maebayashi.[6] Mobile Connections looked at how mobile media would reconfigure geographical, cultural, and perceptual space, and transform the nature of the art object and the art event. Mobile Connections sought to sketch the outlines of emerging artforms that were coalescing around artists, programers, and DIY technologists who responded to new technical tools by asking what can be experienced then that could not be experienced before. These experiments in mobile media art prefigured much about the mobile experience of today.

You mentioned earlier that you were interested in surveillance. How have the politics of mobile media featured in your work as a curator and artist?

I'd looked at how artists intervene in surveillance in an exhibition, Broken Channel, in 2001. Then I'd started working on mobile phones and surveillance in 2002 and had connected with people such as Steve Wright and Duncan Campbell who had revealed the ECHELON surveillance program in 1988.

What captured my imagination was that it was so Janus faced. The capacity to locate and connect in digital and physical space was opening the door, at the same time, to some incredibly exciting new design concepts and to an unprecedented potential for surveillance. There was a community hugely positive about the, frankly, mind blowing possibilities. And there was increasing awareness of the potential for coercive control. Shoshana Zuboff would later claim that "surveillance capitalism" was invented in this same period—in 2001.[7] For my own part, I shared my own misgivings in January 2004 in the Locative Dystopia, first published on the nettime.org mailing list.[8]

I channeled this into an artwork, *Loca: Set to Discoverable* (2006).[9] In this Mika Raento, John Evans, Theo Humphries, and I set up our own surveillance network across downtown San Jose as part of the ZeroOne festival in 2006. Customized phones were installed on lampposts and in flowerpots, encased in concrete, and with a production line to keep them charged over the festival. We used bluejacking to send messages to devices we recognized to engage people in chatter about the "urban semantics" of the places they visited.

The conversations became increasingly sinister and invited people to visit us at the exhibition stand, where people were given a print out of their movements during the festival, some of which were up to 200 m long. The goal was to spark a debate on how mobility can be traced as we move through a networked space.[10] The project was given extra bite when one of our nodes was confiscated by the police the same weekend that three Palestinian men were arrested in possession of mobile phones in another US State. We felt conflicted because we as white artists in that moment embodied the uneven playing field that Silicon Valley represents (Figure 28.3). This project

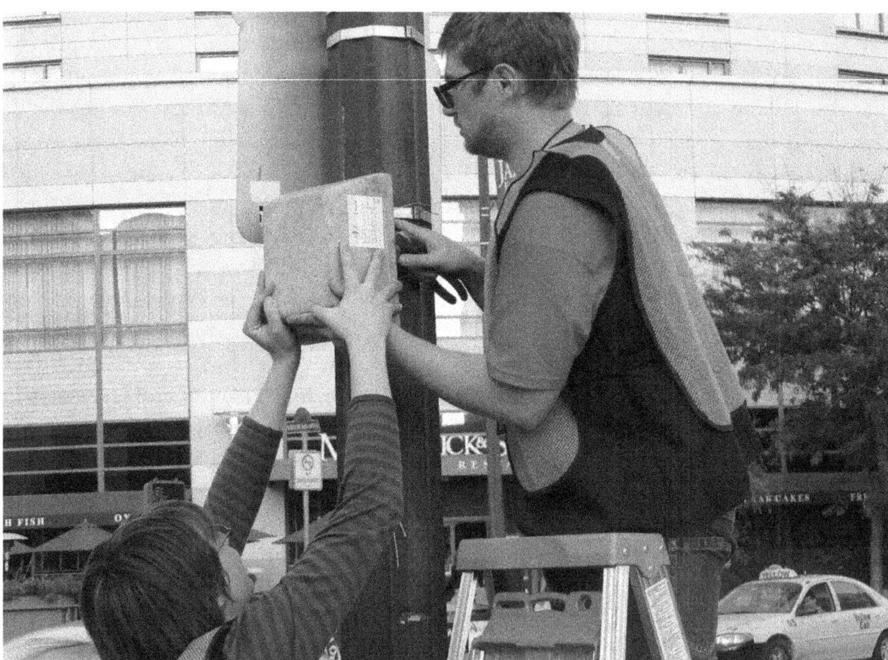

*Figure 28.3* *Loca: Set To Discoverable* (2006)—Hemment and Raento deploying the Loca network in San Jose. Photo courtesy of Drew Hemment, Mika Raento, John Evans, Theo Humphries

has new relevance now at a time when population scale contact tracing is being proposed due to COVID-19.

In your view then, was the positivity misplaced? You have written elsewhere on participatory mass observation. The paradox here is that whilst we can utilize mobile media for creative projects, the technology we use to move around the world could be seen as one of the main causes of environmental damage. We can easily engage in lived experiences that open our eyes to the global impact of ecological decay. What reflections do you have on this paradox and how do your projects embody this?

Zuboff shows us how many of the behaviors that have emerged with mobile media are not an inevitable result of the technology but are driven by a new form of capitalism.[11] The early positivity of digital culture today looks quaint and naive in the extreme. But again, it's Janus faced. There is an enabling, emancipatory side which can be very powerful, and this can be applied to positive ends.

One area I've spent a lot of time on is the scope to drive positive social change around the environment. From 2006 to 2009, I ran a project called *Environment 2.0*.[12] This included some experiments in generating novel data sets to science through participatory gaming with the Met Office and culminated in an art exhibition in 2009. A concept that emerged in this project was the idea of a "global observatory of one billion eyes."[13] This, in turn, inspired the GROW Observatory, a project funded by the EC in 2016, which is mobilizing communities of growers and scientists around Europe to regenerate soils and improve the accuracy of climate information on floods, fires, drought, and agriculture.[14] In another project, *Making Sense*, we released the Citizen Sensing Toolkit to empower others to run their own campaigns.[15]

What is the legacy of this work today?

Over this period there were a number of outcomes. I edited a special issue of *Leonardo Electronic Almanac*, which included an editorial, a double issue of papers, an online Gallery of artworks, a collaborative bibliography, and a curriculum section on new teaching by course leaders. In research, the fields of locative, pervasive, and ubiquitous computing and media conversed in the PLAN: Pervasive and Locative Arts Network—led by Steve Benford at the University of Nottingham, Ben Russell, and myself.[16] In terms of technologies and platforms, the one that best represents the spirit and ethos of the period is Open Street Map, which Steve Coast founded in 2004.[17]

There was a lot of writing and exhibitions that came in the years that followed, such as Off the Map at Futuresonic in 2006, and I wrote about Hosokawa in a paper, "The Mobile Effect," in a special issue of *Convergence* on Mobile Phones during 2005.[18] For me, this period set the groundwork for the next 15 years working on art, technology, and cities. The interesting thing has been across the faultlines between those spaces, bringing art into the Internet of Things (IoT), and championing bottom-up strategies for the ways that cities are constantly made and remade.

I think what's also interesting about technology and the rise of Mobile Media Art was—and still is—its socio-political impact and experimentation with the everyday. Increased gender visibility, technology devices became co-present, and there are many women artists weaving social participation, performance poetics and sound making into work that is becoming more openly entangled with a consideration of feminist ethics. You've not mentioned gender, I'm interested to hear your thoughts on that, as well as any final thoughts you may have on the collective experiences of DIT co-design, the ethics of making with mobile media, and of course, the not too distant future of FutureEverything and Edinburgh Futures Institute.

Gender and aspects of representation more broadly have been a real concern over this period. There's been a concerted effort to address representation in new media arts, with female practitioners and feminist theory at the forefront in that. In the tech industry, on the other hand, it's still depressingly common to see all male conference sessions. Beyond this, we are in an interesting moment if you look at gender ambiguity, say. In an exhibition I've curated this week, Preternatural, one work by Jake Elwes addresses lack of representation by retraining a machine learning model on faces of drag performers and gender fluidity. Critical art and critical theory—including feminist, queer, and post-colonial theory—have a vital role to play as we continue to grapple with our entanglement in control technologies.

As for the future of FutureEverything, that's a chapter for someone new to write. After 23 years at the helm, I've handed over to the inspirational Irini Papadimitriou. I'm proud to say that as of the last Board Meeting, the CEO and Chairperson were both female, as were 85% of the team. I've moved on to help set up Edinburgh Futures Institute. My work there is very much in this same spirit. I'll still be experimenting, trying out new things, but I'll also be consolidating. I hope to build on past learnings to work on a more strategic level, scale up, and help more people navigate uncertain futures.

## Notes

1 Ben Russell, *headmap manifesto* (1999), http://technoccult.net/wp-content/uploads/library/headmap.pdf.
2 Steve Coast, *openstreetmap*, 2004. www.openstreetmap.org/.
3 Julian Priest, Website, http://julianpriest.org/.
4 Shuhei Hosokawa, "The Walkman Effect." *Popular Music* 4 (1984): 165–80. doi: 1017/S0261143000006218.
5 See https://futureeverything.org/portfolio/entry/mobile-connections/.
6 See https://v2.nl/archive/works/sonic-interface.
7 Shoshana Zuboff, *The Age of Surveillance Capitalism: The Fight for a Human Future at the New Frontier of Power* (New York: PublicAffairs, 2019).
8 See http://amsterdam.nettime.org/Lists-Archives/nettime-l-0401/msg00021.html.
9 See www.youtube.com/watch?v=pCX7A6kir78.
10 See http://news.bbc.co.uk/1/hi/technology/6677683.stm.
11 See https://shoshanazuboff.com/.
12 Drew Hemment, "Environment 2.0: Participatory Mass Observation." *Leonardo* 43 no. 2 (2010), 104. doi: 10.1162/leon.2010.43.2.104.
13 Ibid.
14 See https://growobservatory.org/.
15 http://making-sense.eu/publication_categories/toolkit.
16 https://www.wired.com/2005/01/the_locative_ar/.
17 Coast, *openstreetmap*.
18 Drew Hemment, "The Mobile Effect." *Convergence* 11, no. 2 (2005): 32–40, doi: 10.1177/1354856505 01100204.

# 29

# MOBILE PHOTOGRAPHY AND ARTISTIC ACTIVISM IN THE "INSTAGRAM MUSEUM"

*Daniel Palmer*

The significance of the mobile phone as a tool for activism has been widely recognized.[1] Most obviously, mobile media has been embraced by activists as a way to organize rallies, protests, and advocacy campaigns. While telephones have long been used for political organizing and polling, digital phones can more quickly and easily draw people together around an issue or campaign (as "flash mobs" also playfully demonstrate). Mobile phones also facilitate logistical communication within a protest situation. Hardware, as Zeynep Tufekci notes, "has its own affordances: a mobile phone is always connected and easy to carry around and thus creates differently structured opportunities for activists."[2] For instance, the cameras embedded in mobile media have, through the opportunities opened up by social media, made them indispensable devices for the promotion of activism. The ubiquity of mobile phone cameras means that they are now widely employed to identify and draw attention to social and environmental issues. From grassroots photo-mapping of climate change impact, or the identification of poorly designed bicycle lanes, from the exposure of working conditions in global garment factories to the monitoring of pollution, every activist campaign now has its corresponding social media accounts and hashtags centered around an accumulation of photographic evidence. At the same time, mobile photography provides an on-the-ground witness-based visual record of activist events as they occur, for immediate circulation via global social media networks.

Protests and marches trade in visual symbolism, as the conventions of the banner and poster suggest.[3] From Soviet agitprop to the contemporary *gilets jaunes* ("yellow-vests") movement in France, protestors of all political persuasions have long utilized images and choreography as a way to achieve maximum visual impact. Today, political protests take place in the context of always-on mobile media, enabling a proliferation of so-called "citizen journalism." Rather than the classic model of photojournalism, which hungered for single iconic image designed for mass circulation within broadcast media, phone cameras generate more ephemeral photo-sketches, designed to be proliferated by many.

Moreover, activists now habitually stage scenes for maximum visual impact and viral potentiality *within* social networks, rather than simple mass-media newsworthiness. Photographers operating within this environment—whether citizen or professional—are not simply documenting a pre-existing action as a complete statement. Instead, they are involved in the generation of a complex set of performative visual utterances. In other words, the proliferation of mobile cameras enmeshed in activist events is influencing both the nature of documentation and also the activism itself.

This chapter explores the use of mobile media photography by the Melbourne-based collective the Artists' Committee, and specifically a series of protests staged in 2017 at the National Gallery of Victoria (NGV), arguably Australia's most prestigious art museum. The Artists' Committee are "an informal association" of artists and arts workers who make "collaborative public work around the intersection of money, ethics and culture."[4] Their work sits on the border between activism and art, and can be conceived as a sub-genre of *artistic activism* (or *artivism*[5])—activism through art, informed by an artistic logic, specifically concerned with the real-world impact of how the artworld operates.[6]

This chapter is inspired by a photograph that documents a single moment within a series of protests directed against Wilson Security as the then security provider for the NGV—the same company who were also responsible for providing security services on Manus Island and Nauru, as part of the Federal Government's so-called Pacific Solution approach to border security (see Figure 29.1). The photograph itself was not taken by a mobile phone but by a professional photographer involved in the Artists' Committee. Nevertheless, its literal depiction of people using camera phones in the image speaks directly to the role of mobile media in the event. By first addressing a brief history of the camera as a witness to art events, and then turning to the use of mobile photography in the art museum, I consider the Artists' Committee's intervention as an exemplary illustration of the potential role of mobile media within museum activism. The methods of the Artists' Committee, I argue, offer a counterpoint to the primary tendency of art museums to orient mobile photography within an entertainment and marketing loop.

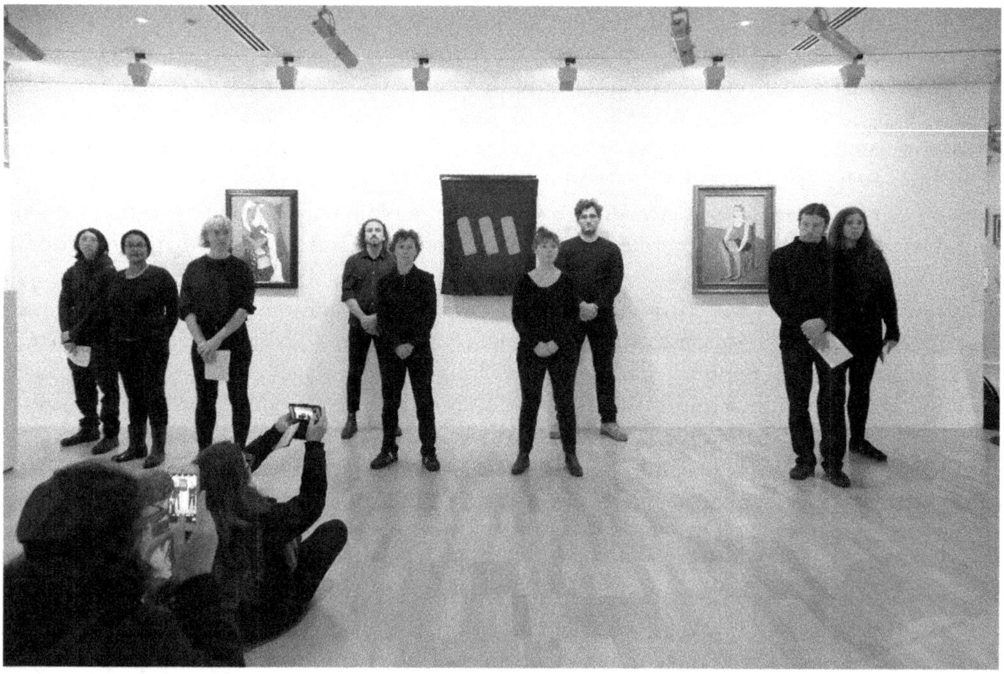

*Figure 29.1* Artists' Committee, *Weeping Woman* (2017), performative intervention at the National Gallery of Victoria. Photo credit: Tatjana Plitt for the Artists' Committee

## The Camera as a Witness to Art

The term mobile photography refers to images made with a camera phone. However, the camera has been physically mobile since it was released from the shackles of the tripod in the late nineteenth century, thanks to faster film speeds and smaller, handheld cameras. Following the release of the Kodak box camera in 1888, which came pre-loaded with film in a leather carrying case, ordinary people could easily carry cameras as they ventured on their travels. Kodak's early advertisements routinely featured cars and bicycles and other modes of transport to underline this sense of physical freedom. Smaller pocket cameras also gave rise to fears of voyeurism in public places, a fear recently revisited with the arrival of camera phones.

Equally importantly, the advent of print journalism and professional "miniature" (35mm) film cameras in the 1920s—embodied by the Leica—opened up the world to photojournalistic witnessing. This mobility of witnessing has been equally important to art, as art practice and its photographic documentation increasingly converged over the course of the twentieth century. Advanced art practice has very frequently involved performative, ephemeral and site-specific elements, rendering its documentation crucial for dissemination to secondary audiences (and sometimes replacing primary audiences entirely). Many of the most influential works of art in the late twentieth century are known almost entirely by their documentation, such as Robert Smithson's iconic but rarely visited *Spiral Jetty* (1970), whose documentation is itself highly mobile (a film made from a helicopter echoes the organic spiral form of the earthwork itself). Site-specific art—often remotely located, not transportable or easily replicated—has relied on photography to ensure its dissemination.

Photography's function as a publicity and memory machine for art is closely linked to institutional, curatorial and art market imperatives. The more event-like the artwork—the more impermanent and public—the greater the importance of the documentation. Performance art, which become central to contemporary art in the 1970s—like so many efforts since the 1960s to move away from the autonomous and timeless art object—is almost unthinkable without the machinery of photographic documentation. Photography and performance operate in an inseparable relationship, but photographs of performance art are not merely *indexical*, offering us a trace of the past and pointing to something absent: they are also *performative*, bringing a world into being.[7]

Thus, photography emerges as not only crucial to the artwork's afterlife, to the formation and maintenance of its official public memory but is also in many cases entirely bound up in its production. Consider American artist Vito Acconci's work *Following Piece* (1969) that saw him following one randomly chosen stranger each day for nearly a month through the streets of New York until he or she entered a private location. The photographs that make up this work are not taken by the artist but show him trailing his prey as a looming figure. Acconci used photography to provide evidence of the execution of a preconceived action and specifically his body's occupancy of public space. Avant-garde practices such as these and many others by conceptual artists since the 1970s hint at the transactional and collaborative photographic practices that are now commonplace following the rise of mobile phones and social media, as the brief fad for "planking" (c. 2008–2012) underlined.[8]

The importance of the mobile phone camera only became fully apparent once it was widely connected to the internet in the 2000s. Networking the camera has had significant and ongoing implications for the documentation of artistic events and interventions, and the promotion of art practice itself. One early artwork exploring the growing ubiquity of mobile media photography was Australian-born Chinese artist Michael Yuen's 2007 work *Follow*, in which he hired 50 people in Seoul, South Korea, to follow him for a day as he went about his usual activities in the city. Yuen had the people follow him throughout his daily routine as he met with friends, artists, curators, shopped, and visited the bank—gently mocking the logic of the artist as a celebrity. In 2008, Yuen staged another version of *Follow* in Shanghai. As a newspaper reported: "The museum sponsoring the event told him to halve his desired 100 participants for fear it would be mistaken as a 'gathering,' dangerous when the state was cracking down on anything that might interrupt the glorious Olympics."[9] Nevertheless, the group steadily grew to 100 followers as curious bystanders joined the pack. As Yuen has written: "It was a pilgrimage, a protest, bought stardom, a human roadblock, a labour strike, a fanatical pack, a mob, and a march. *Follow*, for me, is foremost a public action resonating throughout a city. It is the hiring of a crowd's services."[10] That crowd, of course, obliged by taking photographs.

It is no accident that the artwork celebrated as the "first Instagram masterpiece," *Excellences and Perfections* (2014) by Argentinian artist Amalia Ulman, also drew upon the notion of celebrity, namely the micro-celebrity culture enabled by selfies. Ulman created an Instagram feed as a work of art in itself, creating a fictional persona as a Los Angeles "it girl." For months, Ulman pouted and posed for the mirror, attracting 80,000 followers. The diaristic performance takes the immediately recognizable tropes of Instagram perfectionism and effectively embodies them, curating the photogenic life of an innocent and attractive blonde who moves to LA and develops a drug addiction. Ulman bragged about her supposedly enviable lifestyle in LA, as she attended pole-dancing classes and underwent breast-enlargement surgery.

However, Ulman's final post revealed the whole thing as a fabrication—an Instagram hoax designed to draw out the gendered nature of Instagram performances and their link to the attention economy. Effectively, then, *Excellences and Perfections* comprised a durational feminist performance piece, hosted unwittingly as a visual diary by Instagram. Critiquing the narcissism of exhibitionists and the voyeuristic dimension of viewers, the work was also an exemplary illustration of the complex conditions of viewing art practice today—namely, that it relies on both actual and virtual viewers, who assume the roles of primary and secondary audiences. Ulman's production of enlarged fine art prints of the Instagram posts for art gallery viewers could be viewed as wholly unnecessary, since the work occurred in real time on Instagram, but also operates in the same way as any performance art documentation—both as a market necessity for the artist and a reminder that the museum is, at one level, a kind of mausoleum for art. As a secondary audience, the museum viewer is given glimpses of an original but staged event, which they must re-imagine.[11]

## Mobile Phones and the Art Museum: The Performance of Viewing Art

In key respects, the whole sphere of museums and galleries now operates as a promotional performance platform. Social media—Instagram in particular—is now central to the promotional machinery of the artworld, far supplanting the role newspapers and glossy art magazines once held. With artists, curators and collectors embracing Instagram as platform for the circulation and display of contemporary art, the resulting demand for photogenic art is influencing not only the forms of art practice that are privileged and gain visibility, but also its mode of display (right down to the lighting conditions of commercial galleries).

Simultaneously, public art museums have dramatically altered their relationship to visitor photography. Until recently, it was rare to see ordinary people photographing inside museum spaces. Photography was either prohibited, or prohibitively expensive in the film era. Only the most dedicated or naïve would risk wasting expensive film inside the gallery space with its artificial light sources that rarely produced satisfying results (before digital cameras and their automatic white balance, color casts posed a particular technical challenge). Permission was often required for the use of tripods, and so on.

Today, by contrast, art museums actively encourage audiences to use their cameras—perhaps initially because of the impracticalities of physically preventing people from using their phones,

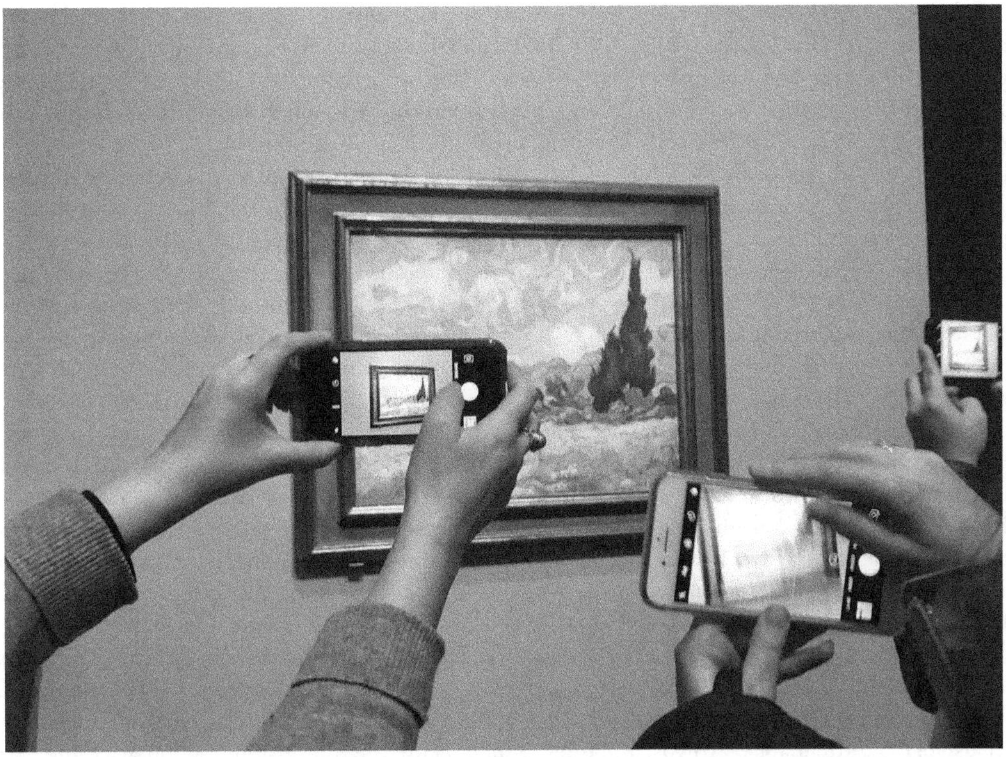

*Figure 29.2* Visitors using mobile phones to photograph a Vincent van Gogh painting at the National Gallery of Victoria (2017). Photo credit: Daniel Palmer

but more importantly because museums have come to understand the marketing power of positive experiences being channeled to social media networks. Thus, in a remarkable departure from the era of "photography not permitted," since at least 2012 the NGV have been encouraging viewers to "snap and share," promoted via signage in the gallery with the now recognizable social media icons for Twitter, Facebook and Instagram. This shift has coincided with a more general turn from the art museum as a hushed place of rarefied contemplation into a popular place of entertainment, characterized by blockbusters, events, and crowds.

The experience of viewing a blockbuster exhibition is an experience of jostling with crowds and mobile phone cameras competing for the best view, a development not without its critics. A common complaint is that excessive mobile phone photography detrimentally impacts on the art viewing experience. At the NGV, blockbuster exhibitions, such as Vincent van Gogh in 2017, led to complaints—published in the newspaper—that selfie seekers, in particular, were preventing others from seeing the paintings (Figure 29.2).[12] Clearly a degree of snobbery is involved in such criticism, which seems implicitly directed at young women.

Nevertheless, one wonders about the desire of visitors to take mobile phone images of paintings such as Mark Rothko's *No. 3/No. 13 (Magenta, Black, Green on Orange)* (1949), viewed at the NGV in 2018 on loan from the Museum of Modern Art in New York. Quite aside from the fact that Rothko's dynamic rectangular zones of color are best encountered in the flesh, a simple Google search reveals that a high-resolution image is available online. Which raises the question: what purpose do these low-quality mobile phone images of the painting serve? What motivates the photographer? Evidently, in this case the act of taking the photograph may be more important than the resulting photograph itself.

Mobile phone photography of art in museums would appear to support Susan Sontag's insight that, as a mass art form, photography "is mainly a social rite, a defense against anxiety" in the face of the unfamiliar.[13] This seems especially true in contemporary art exhibitions. Mobile phones allow visitors to "participate" in difficult but visually striking art—photographing it, commenting on it, sharing and posting the results on social media for friends and followers to see—bringing it into the visual orbit of one's social life. As Rob Horning suggests, social media in the art museum "offers an 'arena of exchange' on a scale that makes the ambitions of relational aesthetics seem mundane."[14]

One logical extension of mobile photography in museums is that art has become something to be posed in front of. For Horning, the art museum becomes a place not only for "photo-ops" but also for "personal branding opportunities." From this perspective, social media produces a new museum experience: "Museums are no longer spaces in which to experience art, but rather spaces in which to *perform the self having art experiences*."[15] Indeed, the NGV's official Instagram feed regularly features people in the act of photographing visually spectacular artworks with their mobile phones. A typical promotional photograph features a young woman inspecting an oversized and/or sublime and/or mysterious artwork with her phone held up in front of her. Taken from behind, the glowing screen of her phone at once highlights the liveness of the experience (the need to be there in the flesh), and how Instagramable the moment is (the opportunity to circulate the experience to a social network). These are instructional images, offered as prompts to invite others to do the same, updating the touristic convention of camera icons at "scenic viewing spots."

From the museum's perspective, all of this is perfectly understandable. Art is now an integral part of spectacle culture, and art museums compete for attention in the experience economy as one among other urban pleasure grounds. In this context, "Museums now aspire to be inclusively exclusive: large attendance, crowds, and lines, which secure the impression of popularity and scarcity in transmitted images from the scene."[16] Yet despite the crowds, this form of self-conscious mobile phone photography is consistent with an individualized viewing experience of art. Visitors become "brand ambassadors," whose diaristic photography follows a consumption logic that ensures a social practice—visiting the art museum—is experienced as a private encounter. Aside from anything else, the interventions of the Artists' Committee are notable for activating mobile photography in the museum in a more collective manner.

## Activism in the Art Museum: The Artists' Committee

In 2017, the Artists' Committee commenced a project involving a series of unsanctioned performative interventions to "highlight the National Gallery of Victoria's connection with the immigration detention industry."[17] Specifically, the collective sought to end the NGV's contract with Wilson Security, a commercial company "known to have committed human rights abuses against asylum seekers and refugees" held on Manus Island and Nauru. The approach adopted by the Artists' Committee—notably in "scale, impertinence and embodied presence"—took inspiration from the British art collective, Liberate Tate, founded in 2010 to explore the role of creative intervention in social change.[18] Liberate Tate aims to "free art from oil" with a focus on the Tate art museum ending its corporate sponsorship with BP, as set out in an open letter to Tate director Nicholas Serota in 2011.[19] Toward this goal, Liberate Tate undertook various unauthorized performative interventions, including a performance in Tate Britain on the anniversary of the Deepwater Horizon explosion, *Human Cost* (2011), when a naked member of the group had an oil-like substance poured over them on the floor; and *The Gift* (2012), in which over 100 members carried a mammoth wind turbine blade into Tate Modern's Turbine Hall. This work was later submitted to be part of Tate's permanent collection as a "gift to the nation" under the provisions of the Museums and Galleries Act 1992 from which Tate's mission is drawn. All of these guerrilla interventions were meticulously documented and widely promoted, and all involved human bodies—from the dramatic performance of a person curled up and covered in oil, to circles of bodies around a turbine blade, to a final 24-hour endurance performance of people scrawling messages about climate change in charcoal on the floor. The campaign was successful: in 2016, BP announced it was ending its Tate sponsorship after 26 years.[20]

Since the 1960s, a whole tradition of contemporary art practice has focused on the museum and gallery as a site for political provocation and intervention. Such practice, now broadly known as "institutional critique," has its own canon of practitioners who have approached such questions as the logic of the white cube and other conventions that dictate modern art's reception (Daniel Buren, Michael Asher, Brian O'Doherty, et al.), the biases and gaps in museum collections (Fred Wilson, The Guerrilla Girls, et al.), the funding and sponsorship of museums and the discursive framing of art (Hans Haacke, Andrea Fraser, et al.). Some of these practices have themselves been surveyed in major museum exhibitions, such as *The Museum as Muse: Artists Reflect* at the Museum of Modern Art in 1999, curated by Kynaston McShine, which among other things explored artist's appropriation of museum practice as a conceptual or formal strategy. Crucial to that exhibition, as the press release stated, were "works that reveal how artists have interrogated and challenged the museum's political, bureaucratic, and corporate dynamics."[21] The exhibition even included a museum shop with a sales counter in the shape of a dollar sign (by the art collective General Idea). In other words, critical practices associated with institutional critique have found themselves easily incorporated into the museum's overall logic, as a form of self-critique that does little to undermine its authority. In light of this, and inspired by Liberate Tate, the Artists' Committee determined that "unsanctioned performative interventions" were necessary to force the issues it wanted to address into public debate.[22]

Let us now return to the photograph that inspired this chapter: a documentary image inside an unremarkable gallery space at the NGV (see Figure 29.1). The image depicts a set of three paintings on a white wall, spot-lit by ceiling lights. The central painting—Picasso's *Weeping Woman* (1937)—is covered with a piece of black cloth, affixed with black tape to the wall, featuring three diagonal red marks. The red marks could be mistaken for an abstract painting but are in fact a version of the Wilson Security corporate logo, whose three white marks on a red background are a common urban feature in Melbourne thanks to Wilson's carpark business. Standing in front of the paintings on a blond parquetry floor are nine young adults dressed in black, men and women, mostly white, their legs apart and hands clasped. Several of them are holding pieces of paper and all are facing forward toward the camera. Evidently, this particular arrangement of bodies is no accident. As Gabrielle de Vietri, one of the key members of the Artists' Committee, has written:

> ... we wanted to test the limitations of our bodies in creation as well as in resistance. We planned a series of unsanctioned performative actions in response to the Gallery's collection, program and building. Our bodies were to deliver our voices, perform our opposition and enact change.[23]

Given the issue at stake involved the abuse of asylum seeker's bodies, this attention to embodiment in the Artists' Committee's intervention is double-edged. Two further interventions in the following weeks underlined this. The first involved an action of using an artificial dye to turn red a famous water wall (as well as the surrounding moat) at the entrance to the NGV—loved by visitors and often used as a photogenic backdrop for snapshots. A third intervention took the form of a solo cello performance blockading the front entrance of the gallery, circled by members of the Artists' Committee attached by long streams of red ribbons. The cellist performed a song by Kurdish-Iranian journalist and writer Behrouz Boochani, an asylum seeker imprisoned by the Australian Government on Manus Island (itself relayed by mobile media).[24] All of these interventions by the

Artists' Committee establish a link between the architecture of the NGV and the exclusion of certain bodies from space.[25]

The decision to veil *Weeping Woman* by Picasso was entirely strategic. The painting is the most famous work of modern art in the NGV and gained notoriety in 1986 when it was stolen from the NGV and held to ransom by a group that called itself the Australian Cultural Terrorists, as a protest against the state of arts funding. Although the painting was eventually found in a train station locker, the details of the theft are shrouded in mystery and nobody was ever charged. Most importantly, *Weeping Woman* was chosen for its symbolically charged depiction of human suffering. The painting is linked to Picasso's commitment to the pain endured by ordinary civilians during the Spanish Civil War. As de Vietri notes, citing Gene Sharp's 1973 treatise "198 Methods of Nonviolent Action:"

> We shrouded Picasso's famous *Weeping Woman* in reference to the abuse, and the cover-ups of abuse, committed by Wilson Security (Method #29. Symbolic reclamations). With the painting veiled in a black cloth, we silently stood guard. Management panicked around us, shutting down the galleries. What a troublesome paradox that this painting—one that was designed to remind us of the suffering of families torn apart—is watched over by the same company that oversees the torture of children, women and men in Australia's offshore prisons.[26]

The Artists' Committee's action also echoed another famous instance of a Picasso being veiled: a tapestry reproduction of his most famous anti-war painting, *Guernica*, was notoriously covered by blue fabric outside the Security Council chamber at UN headquarters when US Secretary of State Colin Powell addressed the media in 2003 to make his case for the invasion of Iraq.

In the media commentary around the Artists' Committee's intervention, and in the published reflections by those involved, the role of mobile media and photography passed unmentioned. Nevertheless, it is my argument here that mobile media photography helped to make the intervention effective, allowing the group to use the spectacle logic of the museum's own mobile media marketing strategy to pressure change within the museum. How? At one level, professional photography was more important to the communication of the event. For instance, in *The Age* newspaper published the following day, an image by the photojournalist Eddie Jim was published of *Weeping Woman* as it was being covered.[27] The Artists' Committee had notified a handful of trusted journalists before the action, including Hannah Francis from *The Age*, who sent the photographer.

Likewise, the photograph that inspired this chapter was taken by a professional photographer, Tatjana Plitt, using a digital SLR camera. An artist, Tatjana Plitt had volunteered her services with the Artists' Committee, but she also describes herself on LinkedIn as "a commercial lifestyle and architectural photographer," which might explain the formal quality of the interior composition.[28] Two people are seated in the foreground, taking photographs of the event, their thumbs pressed to their glowing iPhone screens.

The covering of *Weeping Woman* was a carefully choreographed event, for which reconnaissance was simple. Given the institutional blessing for photography noted earlier, members of the Artists' Committee could take mobile phone photographs as close to the Picasso as they wished. The Committee also created a series of diagrams showing the positioning of people and their roles.[29] The diagram shows "paired documenters," including social media documenters, responsible for photographs and video, and professional photographers. The mobile phone users are crucial, to effectively network the gallery space. Their phones turn the museum into what media theorist Adriana de Souza e Silva influentially calls "hybrid space"—a mixture of physical and digital space.[30] Indeed, the two mobile phone users pictured in Plitt's photograph function as embodied interfaces.[31]

Since security guards at NGV closed the galleries as soon as the painting was covered, the role of these embodied cameras was to relay images out of the gallery space. Another Artists' Committee member was stationed at the entrance of the gallery to receive images and quickly frame messages to send out to social media. This continued for approximately two hours, after which time the Artists' Committee left the space freely of their own accord, and after another few minutes, the security guards took away the fabric veil. The interventions attracted significant attention, as well as solidarity from international artists exhibiting in a major exhibition at the NGV. Soon after, in early 2018, the NGV changed security providers.[32]

## Conclusion

The ubiquity of mobile digital devices coincides with the increasing circulation of user-generated image testimonies. As media theorist Paul Frosh states, the increasing ubiquity of mobile devices makes "ordinary individuals always already witnesses-in-potential in their everyday lives."[33] Frosh also makes a link between the importance of embodied presence—so critical to activists—and the new potential of perpetually networked mobile media. Beyond a new infrastructure for circulating messages, he describes the intimate scales of bodily action registered by live networks of perpetual presence as "a radical intensification of the possibilities for witnessing" and an *existential* condition involving "responsiveness to others."[34]

Live networks are always open to abuse, as the 2019 Christchurch shooter dramatically demonstrated via Facebook. However, the intensification of witnessing brought on by mobile phones also open up creative possibilities of resistance. Frosh writes about the Israeli artist Noa Jansma, who adopted what he calls a form of "digitized flesh-witnessing" by turning the mobile camera on men who "catcalled" her in the street and inviting others on Instagram to do the same, thus producing a catalog of visual evidence of sexism in the public sphere which was then exhibited in a gallery.[35] Jansma, like the Artists' Committee, appears to intuitively understand the importance of the *collective* witnessing body.

The interventions of the Artists' Committee are far from an obvious example of "mobile media art." However, as Mimi Sheller has written, mobile art "is not simply a matter of viewing digital imagery using new apps, but involves phenomenological experiments with experiential happenings and performative interactional events."[36] Mobile phones are now enmeshed within almost every art experience. While this condition has given rise to criticisms, sometimes for good reason, of the "Instagram-friendly museum" as merely the latest site of popular spectacle, it also opens up opportunities for the museum as a site of creative networked visual protest.[37]

The ubiquity and perpetual presence of mobile phone visuality also provides another angle to what Ariella Azoulay calls "the civil potential of photography," in which photography shifts from a documentary role to a co-constitutive agent of activism. The work of the Artists' Committee is testimony to this potential, in which the bodies of artist-activists operate as embodied interfaces to mobile networks that extend the power of individual action and fuse the individual with the collective. Underlying all of this, as one of the activists observed, "the spectacle of the image allows people to organise and mobilise."[38]

## Notes

1 See, for instance, Arnau Monterde and John Postill, "Mobile Ensembles: The Uses of Mobile Phones for Social Protest by Spain's Indignados," in *The Routledge Companion to Mobile Media*, edited by Gerard Goggin and Larissa Hjorth (New York: Routledge, 2014), 429–38; Nicholas Mirzoeff, *How to See the World* (Harmondsworth: Penguin Books, 2015); and Zeynep Tufekci, *Twitter and Tear Gas: The Power and Fragility of Networked Protest* (New Haven, CT: Yale University Press, 2017).

2 Tufekci, *Twitter and Tear Gas*, 125.

3 Tim Alves, "Contemporary Art and Images of Protest in the New Millennium," unpublished PhD Thesis, Monash University, 2017.
4 "About Us," Artists' Committee website, www.artistscommittee.com/about.
5 Artivism is associated with the playwright and performer Eve Ensler; see, for example, the site https://urbanartivism.wordpress.com.
6 On the distinction between art and activism, see Alana Jelinek, *This is Not Art: Activism and Other 'Non-Art'* (London: I.B. Tauris, 2013).
7 David Green and Joanna Lowry have argued that the photographic documentation of performance art, ordinarily conceived as secondary, "is both additional *and* integral, both marginal *and* central, both outside *and* inside, and both superfluous *and* necessary." See David Green and Joanna Lowry, "Splitting the Index: Time, Object and Photography in the Work of Joseph Beuys and Yves Klein," in *Sculpture and Photography: Envisioning the Third Dimension Photography*, edited by Geraldine A. Johnson (Cambridge: Cambridge University Press, 1998), 160.
8 In canonical critical accounts of participatory and collaborative art practice, such as Claire Bishop, *Artificial Hells: Participatory Art and the Politics of Spectatorship* (London: Verso, 2012), photography is positioned as a passive medium of documentation, and its role as an enabling medium of participation and collaboration is rendered invisible. See Daniel Palmer, *Photography and Collaboration: From Conceptual Art to Crowdsourcing* (London: Bloomsbury, 2017).
9 Brendan Shanahan, "Beijing Calling," *The Australian*, 4 June 2011, www.theaustralian.com.au/arts/beijing-calling/news-story/c328ba01d257ba03a59eed2302dcaa33.
10 Michael Yuen, "Follow," *Broadsheet: Contemporary Visual Arts+Culture* 37, no. 4 (December 2008).
11 On secondary audiences to art via its documentation see Bishop, *Artificial Hells*.
12 Michael Scammell, "When Did an Art Exhibition Just Become an Opportunity for Selfies?" *The Age*, 12 July 2018, www.theage.com.au/national/victoria/when-did-an-art-exhibition-just-become-an-opportunity-for-selfies-20180712-p4zr0c.html.
13 Susan Sontag, *On Photography* (New York: Farrar, Straus and Giroux, 1977), 8.
14 Rob Horning, "The Price of Shares," *Even Magazine* 10 (2018) http://evenmagazine.com/the-price-of-shares.
15 Ibid.
16 Ibid.
17 www.artistscommittee.com/about.
18 Gabrielle De Vietri, "Protest as Practise," *The Dancehouse Diary* 10 ("The Many & The Few—Assembling the political" (June 2018), www.dancehousediary.com.au/?p=3398.
19 "Liberate Tate," www.liberatetate.org.uk.
20 Benjamin Sutton, "Liberate Tate Activists Look Back on Six Years of Fighting BP Sponsorship," *Hyperallergic*, 4 April 2016, https://hyperallergic.com/288254/liberate-tate-activists-look-back-on-six-years-of-fighting-bp-sponsorship/.
21 Press Release for *The Museum as Muse: Artists Reflect* (1999) available on the Museum of Modern Art's website: www.moma.org/documents/moma_press-release_386995.pdf.
22 See Penelope Benton, "Q&A with the Artists' Committee," NAVA, 30 January 2018, https://visualarts.net.au/news-opinion/2018/q-artists-committee.
23 De Vietri, "Protest as Practise."
24 As de Vietri notes, mobile media has also allowed the calls from people detained on Manus Island and Nauru "to compel us to see their humanity, their resilience and act to change things where we are in accordance with their wishes, and for us to communicate our actions back to them," including Behrouz Boochani's song used in the cello intervention (personal email 6 March 2019).
25 This link between the architecture of the NGV and "carceral logic" is explored in a critical reflection on the interventions by one of the participants, Carol Que, in "Securing the State Art Museum," *Overland Literary Journal,* 232, Spring 2018, https://overland.org.au/previous-issues/issue-232/feature-securing-the-state-art-museum.
26 De Vietri, "Protest as Practise."
27 Hannah Francis, "NGV dumps Wilson Security after Artists Protest against Detention Links," *The Age*, 28 February 2018, www.theage.com.au/entertainment/art-and-design/ngv-dumps-wilson-security-after-artists-protest-against-detention-links-20180228-h0wsnk.html.
28 Tatjana Plitt on Linked in, https://au.linkedin.com/in/tatjana-plitt-1365a25.
29 Personal email with De Vietri, 6 March 2019.
30 See Adriana De Souza e Silva, "From Cyber to Hybrid: Mobile Technologies as Interfaces of Hybrid Spaces," *Space and Culture*, vol. 9, no. 3 (2006): 261–78, doi: 10.1177/1206331206289022.

31 Mimi Sheller, "Mobile Art: Out of Your Pocket," in *The Routledge Companion to Mobile Media*, edited by Gerard Goggin and Larissa Hjorth (New York: Routledge, 2014), 197–205.
32 Steph Harmon, "National Gallery of Victoria dumps Wilson Security over Offshore Detention," *The Guardian*, 28 February 2019, www.theguardian.com/australia-news/2018/feb/28/national-gallery-of-victoria-dumps-wilson-security-over-offshore-detention.
33 Paul Frosh, "Eye, Flesh, World—Three Modes of Digital Witnessing," in *Image Testimonies: Witnessing in Times of Social Media*, edited by Kerstin Schankweiler, Verena Straub and Tobias Wendl (New York: Routledge, 2019), 121.
34 Frosh, "Eye, Flesh, World," 121–35.
35 See the 2017 exhibition by Noa Jansma at Kuli Alma Gallery in Tel Aviv, Israel. Jansma's work has a precedent in Laurie Anderson's remarkable photo-narrative installation *Fully Automated Nikon (Object/Objection/Objectivity)* (1973). In that work, Anderson took pictures of men who made unsolicited sexual comments to her on the streets of Lower Manhattan over the course of a single day.
36 Sheller, "Mobile Art," 201.
37 Sam Eicher, "Lights, Cameras, Action: The Rise of the Instagram-Friendly Museum," *The Daily Beast*, 25 August 2018, www.thedailybeast.com/lights-cameras-action-the-rise-of-the-instagram-friendly-museum.
38 Que, "Securing the State Art Museum."

# 30

# MOBILE STREET PHOTOGRAPHY

## Continued, Collective, and Contested Decisive Moments

*Edgar Gómez Cruz*

Street photography, as a photographic genre, is experiencing a renaissance at the beginning of the twenty-first century. While contested in definition, *street photography* consists of images taken candidly in public places. As Howarth and McLaren defined it following Walker Evans': "the impulse to take candid pictures in the stream of everyday life,"[1] or, as David Gibson points out, photos of "ordinary people going about their everyday life."[2] While street photography has clear connections with documentary photography and certain forms of the snapshot, the genre is recognizable as increasingly used by photographers to define their work.

In the last decade, a number of volumes have documented this rise—from overviews of the genre[3] and manuals on how to do street photography[4] to self-published books engaging with the genre produced by serious enthusiasts.[5] All these volumes sit along new discoveries of unknown "masters" on the genre such as Vivian Maier and revised editions of specialized books about the topic.[6] A number of online courses taught by professionals have popped-up with massive success, as well as workshops sponsored by camera brands, cultural centers, or self-organized ones all over the world. New photo contests, focusing on street photography or including it as a category, are constantly joining those already consolidated.

All this landscape speaks volumes on the vibrancy and interest on street photography by both photographers and publics. Some of the most replicated and commercially successful photographic phenomena of the new millennium are projects that could be considered street photography such as the "Humans of" series—originally set in New York[7] but now reproduced or imitated in dozens of cities. While these projects are discussed in several different terms—for example as a new journalistic approach[8]—they do have a clear street "flavor."

At the same time, several collectives such as in-Public, Observe, Burn My Eye (BME), Un-posed, Women in Street, etc., combining professional photographers and committed amateurs, have gained visibility internationally while local and national collectives are everywhere. Finally, a horde of enthusiasts and amateurs are developing their own courses, blogs, websites, constantly feeding their Instagram, Tumblr, and Pinterest accounts, as well as self-publishing photo-books, advice and tips' guides,[9] and "point of view" videos. This panorama of street photography discourse highlights it as one of the most successful photographic subfields in the digital age.

This chapter explores street photography at the intersection between art, photography studies and mobile media. I focus on the role mobile phones have played in challenging, developing, expanding, and changing discourses and practices of street photography. Using a digital ethnographic approach that comprises participant observation, interviews, both online and offline, and analysis of images online, the ultimate aim of the text is to present a commentary on the role mobile phones have had in the revitalization of street photography as a field. This commentary could serve as an example, a case study of sorts, of how digital cameras in general—and cameraphones, mobile phones and, especially smartphones in particular—have expanded and transformed the practice, reception and consumption of photography in the digital age.

I suggest that, along with expanding the sociotechnical assemblage formed by cameras, connections and social media platforms, mobile phones have increased and coalesced an audience and a market for street photography while also reinforcing the platforms where street photography is learned, practiced, and shown. One direct consequence of this emerging phenomenon is the energizing of the genre with new sociotechnical possibilities that have opened controversies, as we will see in the final section of the chapter, which are redefining the limits of photography, both as a practice and as a discourse.

## The Best Camera Is the One That's with You

Almost every account of the history of photography begins with the introduction of the Leica camera in the 1920s as a milestone and a starting point for street photography as we recognize it today.[10] The small size of the Leica, its portability and its unobtrusiveness, provided photographers with "much readier access to his (sic) subject, to both the everyday moment in life and also the 'action', the big events. It took photographers into areas that, while not absolutely impossible, were so much more difficult for larger cameras."[11] This access was, in part, because the camera size allowed photographers to carry it constantly, for long periods of time without assistance or an exhausting effort. The camera became an extension of the photographer.

The relationship between the photographer and camera has always been special: for street photographers it is unique. Henri Cartier-Bresson, perhaps the most important street photographer of all times, once said that "the camera is for us a tool, not a pretty toy."[12] This almost symbiotic relationship between photographer and camera creates a sense of belonging, an identity, photographer, and camera working together. There is, however, a constant tension that arises from this connection because, while photographers are proud of their gear, they rely on it, trust it, and love it, at the same time they actively own their images regardless of the equipment they have used to produce them. A street photographer once wrote on her Facebook timeline: "If someone else asks me again what camera do I use I'll punch him in the face."[13] This signals the importance that authorship and copyright struggles still have for photography, not only for images made on the streets.

The process of "getting to know" and "understanding" the camera is an important one. It is very common to hear photographers saying things like: "this lens invited me to photograph this," or "having this feature on the camera allowed me to do that." There is a symbiotic and complementary relationship but, at the end of the day, the photographer claims authorship of his or her images. Therefore, the equipment, albeit treasured, still seems secondary to the author's vision.

Since the camera is one of the main instruments for the production of images (there are others such as the darkroom or photo-processing software), there are certain affordances and photographs to be favored by certain combinations of camera, lenses, software, connections, etc., both technically and discursively. In the case of street photography, the Leica became historically the quintessential tool to photograph in the streets, not only because of its size and portability but because it was unobtrusive and discreet.

Another key feature of the camera was its rangefinder system. The rangefinder cameras are usually regarded as the best cameras for street photography because they allow photographers to "predict" when a situation will unfold. Traditional SLRs have the viewfinder above the lens (so the mirror can reflect the image that is coming directly from the lens). This forces the photographer to close her left eye since it is pretty much blocked by the camera body anyway. Rangefinders in contrast have the viewfinder on the upper left edge of the camera, allowing the photographer to have both eyes open, one looking at the frame, the other being aware of what's happening in the surroundings. This allows the photographer to be able to foresee things that can potentially become part of the frame and act fast to make it happen. This action forms a continuous gaze that allows the photographer to imagine and anticipate the composition even before it occurs inside the frame, what Cartier-Bresson famously called the decisive moment: "putting one's head, one's eye, and one's heart on the same axis."[14]

Key photographers in the genre of street photography have used a Leica, from Robert Capa to Bruce Gilden, from Walker Evans to Garry Winogrand. As Henri Cartier-Bresson noted of his Leica—"it became an extension of my eye, and I have never been separated from it since I found it."[15] The features of the camera allowed street photography to thrive. This sense of technical innovation and game-changing technologies has been a constant in the history of photography, and it happened again, in a very similar fashion, with the cameraphone (see Figure 30.1).

In 2009, Chase Jarvis, a photographer and entrepreneur, launched an iPhone app called *Best Camera*. The app was one of the first third-party apps for photography to be launched on the iPhone, pioneering, among many things, the taking, processing, and sharing of digital images as part of the same practice that, up to that point, still required different technologies.[16] Another technical innovation of the app was the use of pre-determined filters to post-process photographic images, one of the features that would become key on Instagram, the first app that successfully reached a global audience for mobile photography.

Along with the app, Jarvis published a photobook with pictures taken with his iPhone, entitled: *The Best Camera Is the One That's With You*.[17] This catchy phrase became widely cited and paraphrased—becoming a recognizable element in the emerging discourse of what mobile

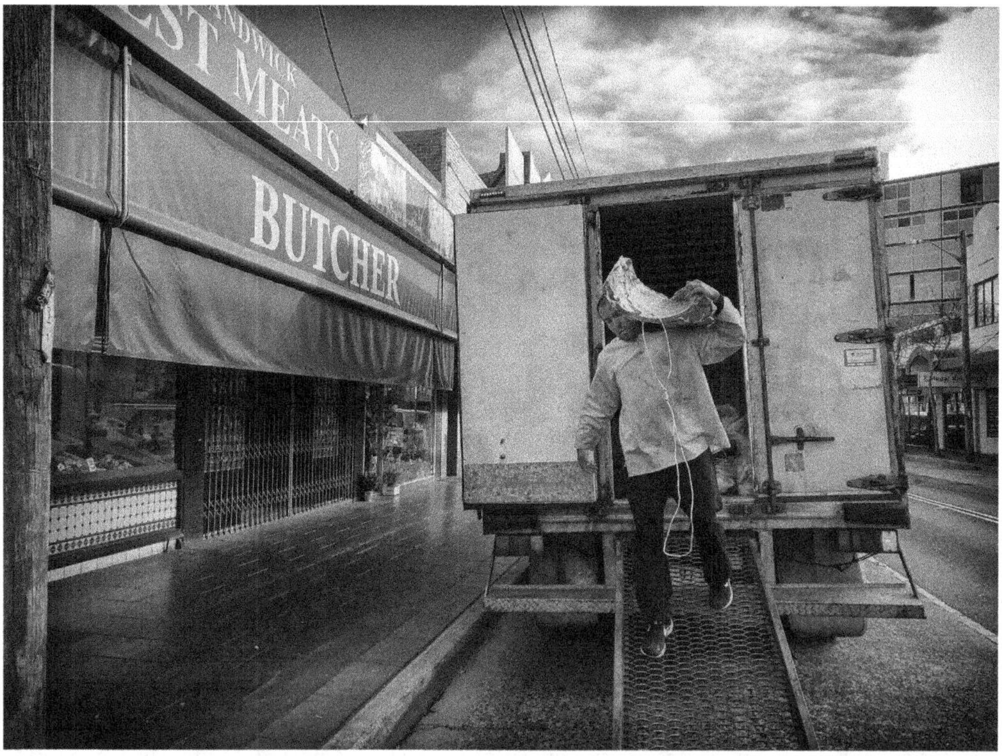


*Figure 30.1* An example of street photography made with an iPhone. Photo credit: Edgar Gómez Cruz

photography could be and what creative directions it may take. This idea, I suggest, encapsulated the main advantage of using a camera that, at the time, was technically very limited (as the Leica was in comparison with larger cameras commonly used at the time): it was the camera that was always available because you had to carry it anyway and all the time since it was *also* your phone. This awareness was historically aligned with what happened with the introduction of the Leica, it was the trade-off between portability and quality that allowed new photographic forms to emerge. Perhaps not in the kind of images that were possible, but in how they were produced and therefore the way photography was practiced. This connection became more solid when Steve Jobs introduced the iPhone 4 by saying it was "like a beautiful old Leica camera"[18]—hinting not only at the design of both technologies but to the way they were both used.

Early accounts on cameraphones made similar claims on the importance of mobile phones in the expansion of the objects and uses of photography, particularly connected to the easiness of image-sharing. None of the early cameraphones attracted as much attention and caused more excitement when discussing photography as the iPhone. A number of photographers embraced the idea that the iPhone represented a new photographic tool and heralded it by pushing the concept of "iphoneography," not only as a valid form of photography[19] but as a cutting-edge, hip and *avant garde* form of photographic art. Several publications, collectives, and blogs contributed to this idea by publishing a number of manuals on how to do good 'iphoneography.'[20]

In the early days of the smartphone, the iPhone became synonymous with emergent photographic practices. This way to do photography is still echoed by Apple's campaign "shot with an iPhone"—a series of visually astonishing images taken by common users and displayed in giant billboards around the world[21]. While many important competitors (with perhaps better lens quality in their phones) have risen since 2009, the iPhone became the paradigmatic camera in the digital era. In Flickr, for example, the main online platform during the consolidation of digital photography, the iPhone was the "most used camera."[22] Still today, in what remains of Flickr, the most used camera is by far the iPhone in its variety of models, with the iPhone 6 as the ultimate camera used to take 889,307,155 photos uploaded to the site.

This constant availability of a camera in everyday life became central for a group such as street photographers that have this availability as one of the central elements in their practice. Street photographers embraced cameraphones because it was the camera that was always with them, in their pocket, purse or backpack. Many texts about street photography recognized this:

> Most of us carry a camera without even subconsciously thinking we are, in the form of our mobile phone. It might not conform to the traditionalistic viewpoint of street, but as basic as the camera may seem, phone photography (iphoneography) is an ever growing and popular form of the art.[23]

But there is another important element that has not been discussed as important in the literature but nonetheless is key to understanding the expansion of street photography practice: the touchscreen. Understood quite rightly as pioneering technology, in the early days of the smartphone there were multiple texts discussing the relationship between the iPhone and photography, where the majority of these texts focused on the relationship between the camera as an image-producing device and its sharing capabilities. While this combination is undoubtedly at the core of the iPhone success, the touchscreen has been strangely under-theorized, although it has been an essential part of the consolidation of the smartphone and a key element in expanding the field of photography.

Daniel Palmer already signaled to this different and equally compelling element in the equation: "in the process of seamlessly melding mobile, computing and internet cultures, the iPhone turned the phone into an attractive display device."[24] He continues: "the iPhone is carefully designed to make viewing photographs an emotionally satisfying experience."[25] The touchscreen, first introduced by the iPhone, made possible—as the rangefinder system did before—to see and also to experience the production of photography differently. It also opened up the path to the constantly affective look of photographs while in motion. I want to suggest that, in the case of photography in general and street photography in particular, the screen, as an emotional interface to see (and touch) images, has played a key role in expanding the reach of photography by rearticulating the photographic assemblage.

## (Mobile) (Street) Photography as an Assemblage

In my previous work, I have developed the idea of photography as a socio-technical assemblage,[26] that is, as a production practice, a combination of skills, knowledge, technologies and discourses. What photography is or could be is not and has never been fixed; it is in constant motion depending on new elements becoming part of the assemblage. While this idea was applied to photography as a practice regardless of the specific genre, I want to focus my lens (pun intended) to discuss street photography.

By briefly tracing the emergence of this new assemblage we call digital photography, we could observe the importance the mobile phone has had in restructuring it. I suggest that, similar to what happened with the introduction of the 35 mm and the rangefinder system, mobile devices have contributed to the revitalization of the genre by shaping new ways of seeing, navigating, thinking, perceiving, experiencing, representing and behaving in the urban environment. Two particular features are key.

On the one hand, the possibility to take, process and share images almost in real-time and without limitations (once a data plan, enough battery, storage and a platform account are part of the practice), and, on the other hand, the possibility to view and observe images taken by others all the time. Mobile phones opened a new way to see/take/share photographs. Life became more photographable, and photographs became more alive. In his blog, Eric Kim, a commentator on photography, stated, "Perhaps the future of disruption in photography is this: cameras that also happen to be phones."[27] This constant sharing has opened a new scale in producing and looking at photography within the digital realm.

Street Photography is perhaps one of the traditional photographic genres that have had a boost with the digital and particularly the mobile phone. Not only are there more and more people interested and practicing the genre but also the number of images taken with a street style have increased exponentially with camera phones, precisely because those candid moments *hunted* by street photographers became more *capturable* with the camera that was available all the time. To give a sense of this growth, Flickr, the flagship of the consolidation of digital photography, had large groups devoted to street photography—the largest, by the number of photos posted to the group is Just Street Photography that has 2.7 million images.

Instagram, the platform that has become the main sharing platform for mobile photography, is organized not by groups but by hashtags. Hashtags are used as a metadata tag that allows content from different users to be aggregated. In mobile media platforms such as Instagram and Twitter, there are no groups (as were common in web-based platforms), therefore the only way to connect users and content is by using a hashtag. The hashtag #streetphotography has 51 million entries. This clearly signals the important relationship, in scale and reach, between the use of mobile phones and street photography. Mobile phones are not necessarily the camera used for taking all these images, but they certainly are one of the main technologies for consuming them. Street photographers are using mobile phones not only to take street images but also to access the platforms where street photography can be viewed. The mobile phone screen has become the window to think about the world *photographically* but also to *observe the photos* of the world, street by street.

## Reconfiguring the Limits of Street Photography? The Fall of the in-Public Collective and the Rise of Algorithmic Images

Street photography, as a genre, has always been contested, at least to some extent. While the cameraphone has revitalized the practice, it has also opened a path for the potential to completely reconfigure its meaning. In a key text to define the genre, Westerbeck and Meyerowitz traced the history and development of street photography, pointing out that: "Street photography has often had more than just a history. It has represented a culture in the true sense of people bound to one another by common interests, beliefs, and practices."[28] This collective sense has always been essential for the definition of street photography, paradoxically since photography tends to be practiced somewhat in isolation. In introductory books to the genre such as *The Street Photographer's Manual* by David Gibson[29] the definition of what street photography is seems to involve a collective sensibility that is particularly important in the digital age.

With the use of social media platforms, the practice is reinforced by people who are constantly questioning and experimenting with its limits as a genre. Photographers continually state that their practice can be improved thanks to the constant sharing and looking at images, and the collective feedback, support and criticism of fellow photographers. One female street photographer that is part of a photographer's collective told me, in a personal communication, that their goals were: "to spread street photography, to incentivise the consolidation of emergent photographers, and to learn from each other." These collectives, most of them online-based, have become the public face of street photography for the digital age and there are several that are recognized worldwide.

One of the most prominent of these collectives is In-Public. Funded in 2000 by Nick Turpin, In-Public was defined as an "international group of street photographers that operates as a collective." Their website, the quality of the photographers included in the group and their online presence cemented a reputation as the reference for street photography for the digital age (despite the fact that many of them still shoot film regularly). The demise of this collective can tell us an interesting story about how mobile phones have revitalized the practice of street photography while, at the same time, disrupted its limits. If you visit In Public's website, you will face this sign on a pop-up square:

> in-public was the first Street Photography collective, it was founded in 2000 and ran for 18 years until October 2018. A disagreement between the members made it impossible for the group to continue in its present form. The site is now archived as a resource as it was just prior to the end and will no longer be updated.[30]

What was the disagreement that ended this successful collective? It was a photograph made with a mobile phone. A photo taken with the *pano* (panoramic) feature of the iPhone by Blake Andrews (see Figure 30.2) was chosen as "Picture of the month" in August 2018. Picture of the month was a monthly contest among members. It was a clever way to maintain the engagement of both the members of the collective and the audience of the site. Nick Turpin, the founder member of the collective wasn't happy with the decision calling the photo a "computational image," criticizing the entry that, according to him, challenged traditional understandings of street photography "where an algorithm written by Apple engineers invents reality."[31] People took sides and, at the end, Turpin, as the administrator of the site, decided, almost dictatorially to "archive" the site. The collective was officially over.

John Berger, in his extraordinary book with Jean Mohr and Nicolas Philibert, *Another Way of Telling* stated that: "In a photograph, time is uniform."[32] That doesn't seem to be the case anymore and emerging features such as the panorama or portrait modes in contemporary mobile phones seem to be challenging not only this statement but several ones related to photography

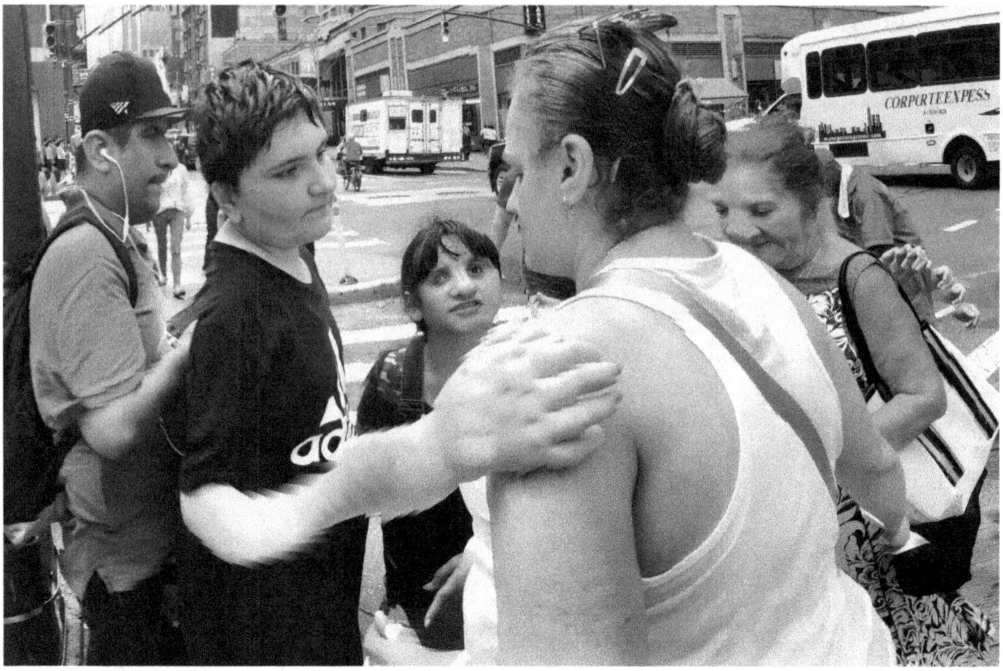

*Figure 30.2* Picture of the Month by Blake Andrews, In-Public collective, August 2018. Photo credit: Blake Andrews

(photography as a memory device, as a representation). Mobile phones and digital cameras are pushing the definition of what photography is, since the digital sensor can indeed do different things than just produce a photographic image,[33] alternatively photographs can indeed be produced without a sensor or combining several different images.[34] These variations in how we think about digital photography suggest the emergence of a non-human turn in photography.[35] Zylinska, in her book *Nonhuman Photography* discusses this turn in terms of images involving "the execution of technical and cultural algorithms that shape our image-making devices as well as our viewing practices."[36]

Rubinstein and Sluis[37] clearly synthetized these ideas by saying that: "the digital image is an image/software machine that operates on several levels at once, some visual, others computational, operating within media ecologies involving both human and non-human actors."[38] In the strict sense therefore, all digital images are "computational images." Why then, can an image taken with an algorithmic feature become the center of such a controversy? Annie Leibovitz, for example, while not a street photographer per se but one of the most recognized and respected photographers within photographic art practice, commonly used the merging of images as part of her workflow, even before the contemporary digital realm.[39]

On the one hand, there is a tension between traditional understandings of photography as a representational form of "truth" that have been deluded even further with the arrival of the digital and the possibilities to manipulate images digitally. Now, an emerging tension is gaining further traction. Yet on the other hand, digital technologies have opened "new ways of representing and seeing the world, ways dependent on algorithmic interventions between the viewing subject and the object viewed," [40] what Uricchio calls an algorithmic turn. New algorithmic possibilities (low light performance, panoramas, time-lapses, filters, film simulation, variable depth of field, etc.), are increasingly included as features in camera phones, extending the traditional limits of photographic genres that were coined during the analog era.

Cameraphones, therefore, are at the center of these tensions, not only because they are technically advancing these algorithmic affordances but also because adopters have normalized their use within the same platforms where "purists" are showing their work. This is one example of how the digital image produced with smartphones is challenging traditional understandings of what photography is, what photography should be and further possibilities for the role of the photograph. Photography has never been exempted from controversies and the struggle over meaning has been a constant feature surrounding the technology, the practice and the reception of it. Photography as a technology has never stopped introducing new features and new terms such as iphoneography, algorithmic photography, or lens-based art are increasingly pushing the limits while expanding the reach, and sometimes reconfiguring well-known practices to the point of turning them into something completely new (as in the case of selfies and self-portraits). As a growing art form, street photography is still very much in motion.

## From Street Photography to Mobile Media Street View

I want to conclude this chapter by taking the controversy about the nature of algorithmic images even further—as discussed in the In-Public group—while responding to the title of the book.

Street photography has been commonly defined as "the impulse to take candid pictures in the stream of everyday life."[41] As I mentioned when discussing the role of the screen, the stream of everyday life is increasingly visible, experienced, and embodied precisely through the mobile screen. Gary Winogrand, one of the most important street photographers used to say that he photographed things "to see how they look like photographed." Adding, "through the screen" could be an accurate update. Screens are becoming the interface between looking, taking, and experiencing images. It is therefore logical to think that the street mindset can indeed be translated to this new form of mobility represented by the screen.

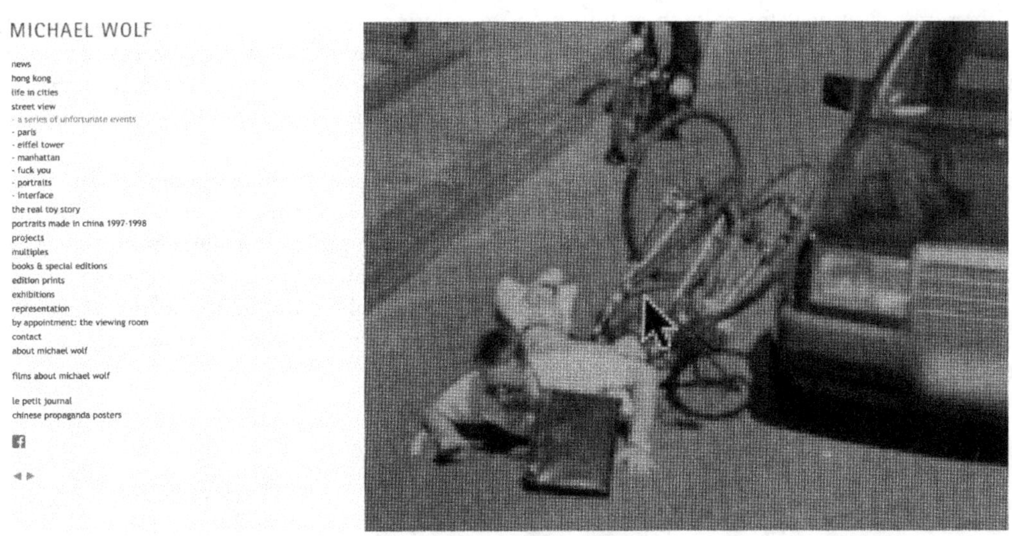


*Figure 30.3* Michael Wolf's *A Series of Unfortunate Events*, http://photomichaelwolf.com/#asoue Photo credit: Screenshot of Michael Wolf's website

One of the most innovative takes on the street photography genre in the last decade has been not by shooting photos on the street with a camera but instead by "framing" images using Google street view. Howarth and McLaren go as far as saying that Google street view is "the most prolific street photographer today."[42] While the system is certainly an endless flow of images of and in the street, they are produced automatically. Nevertheless, as aforementioned, intentionality and authorship are still central to many photographers' motivations. Given that rationale, I want to briefly discuss the work of two photographers that have created artistic work by spending hours wandering the streets of the world looking for interesting and candid scenes to photograph... using their computer screens. Michael Wolf's series *A Series of Unfortunate Events*[43] (see Figure 30.3) was awarded a honorable mention at the prestigious Word Press Photo competition in 2011.[44] Wolf found, as the name of the series suggests, moments such as a car on flames, people falling to the ground, or people kissing, captured by the seamless stream of the Google Street View technology system. He framed those moments on screen and then photographed them. They had all the traditional elements of street photography: candid images taken in a public space, showing "decisive moments."

The second body of work is by Jon Rafman,[45] which follows the same idea, however, it uses screenshots instead of shooting the screen. While these two projects are not new and they are not strictly connected to mobile phones, I want to make the point that the screen—as an interface to experience the world, normalized and integrated in our lives through our mobile phone screen—is expanding even further the limits of how we see and what can be seen by pushing the limits of what could be considered street photography. These works expanded the definition opening exciting and still to discover paths. Street photography is becoming a mobile media art made in the streets.

## A Note about Method

Amateur photographers, as discovered during my PhD fieldwork, are highly reflexive people that enjoy and invest time, money, and effort documenting their own practice, researching it and learning it collectively. They are heavy producers of information on social media platforms, blogs, websites, and they are increasingly finding spaces to show their work that are aligned with more traditional forms such as books and exhibitions. While clearly there is an aspirational component to it, it is also a way to document, share, and feel part of a larger community. As Jurguenson, talking about how a photo becomes a "social photo" points at "the degree to which its existence as a stand-alone media object is subordinate to its existence as a unit of communication."[46]

Photography can become a lonely practice without reaching out to other photographers. Social media creates a space for sharing an abundance of information and reflexive thoughts about photography practice. As in the case of Wolf and Radman, my empirical engagement with photography has decreased in face-to-face interactions but exponentially grow by following blogs, sites, social media accounts and being in touch with street photographers around the world. They offer a great deal of ethnographic information on how practitioners, professionals, and amateurs understand, live, and experience contemporary street photography.

## Notes

1 Sophie Howarth and Stephen McLaren, *Street Photography Now* (London: Thames & Hudson, 2010).
2 David Gibson, *The Street Photographer's Manual* (London: Thames & Hudson, 2014), 9.
3 Jackie Higgins and Max Kozloff, *The World Atlas of Street Photography* (New Haven and London: Yale University Press, 2014); Sophie Howarth and Stephen McLaren, *Street Photography Now* (London: Thames & Hudson, 2010); Stephen McLaren, *Magnum Streetwise* (London: Thames & Hudson, 2019).

4 Valérie Jardin, *Street Photography: Creative Vision Behind the Lens* (PLACE: Focal Press, 2017); David Gibson, *The Street Photographer's Manual* (London: Thames & Hudson, 2014); Brian Lloyd Duckett, *Mastering Street Photography* (London: Ammonite Press, 2019).
5 Andrew Funderburg, *Street Photography: Document Your World* (Buffalo, NY: Amherst Media, 2019); Priya Ranjan, *Street Portrait Photography: How To Make Stunning Street Portraits* (2019), www.portraitofhumans.com.
6 Colin Westerbeck and Joel Meyerowitz, *Bystander: A History of Street Photography* (London: Lawrence King, 2017).
7 Brandon Stanton, *Humans of New York: Stories* (London: Macmillan, 2015).
8 Jessica Roberts. "From the Street to Public Service: 'Humans of New York' Photographer's Journey to Journalism." *Journalism* (2017): 1–17, doi: 10.1177/1464884917698171.
9 Duckett, *Mastering Street.*
10 Gerry Badger, *The Genius of Photography: How Photography Has Changed Our Lives* (London: Quadrille, 2007).
11 Ibid.
12 Henri Cartier-Bresson, *The Mind's Eye: Writings on Photography and Photographers* (New York: Aperture, 1999, 38).
13 Facebook post, September 2017, collected by the author.
14 Cartier-Bresson, *The Mind's Eye*, 16.
15 Ibid., 22.
16 Edgar Gómez Cruz and Eric T. Meyer, "Creation and Control in the Photographic Process: iPhones and the Emerging Fifth Moment of Photography," *Photographies* 5, no. 2 (2012): 203–21, doi, 10.1080/17540763.2012.702123.
17 Chase Jarvis, *The Best Camera Is The One That's With You: iPhone Photography by Chase Jarvis* (New Riders Publishing, 2019).
18 See https://youtu.be/Gb1AzheeYiU.
19 Megan Halpern and Lee Humphreys, "Iphoneography as an Emergent Art World," *New Media & Society* 18, no. 1 (2016): 62–81, doi: 10.1177/1461444814538632.
20 Michael Clawson, *IPhoneography: How to Create Inspiring Photos with Your Smartphone* (New York: Apress, 2015).
21 www.apple.com/au/newsroom/2019/01/share-your-best-photos-shot-on-iphone/.
22 www.flickr.com/cameras.
23 Tanya Nagar, *The New Street Photographers Manifesto: Any Camera, Anywhere* (London: Ilex Press, 2017), 14.
24 Daniel Palmer, "iPhone Photography: Mediating Visions of Social Space," in *Studying Mobile Media. Cultural Technologies, Mobile Communication, and the iPhone*, edited by Larissa Hjorth, Jean Burgess, Ingrid Richardson (New York: Routledge, 2012), 93–105, 87.
25 Ibid.
26 Asko Lehmuskallio and Edgar Gómez Cruz, "Why Material Visual Practices?" in *Digital photography and Everyday Life: Empirical Studies on Material Visual Practices*, edited by Edgar Gómez Cruz and Asko Lehmuskallio (London: Routledge, 2016), 1–16.
27 See http://erickimphotography.com/blog/2019/05/07/a-camera-that-also-happens-to-be-a-phone/.
28 Westerbeck and Meyerowitz, *Bystander: A History.*
29 Gibson, *The Street Photographer's Manual.*
30 https://in-public.com/.
31 http://blackkamera.com/interview-nick-turpin-founder-public-collective/.
32 John Berger, Jean Mohr, and Nicolas Philibert, *Another Way of Telling* (New York: Pantheon, 1982), 95.
33 Edgar Gómez Cruz, "Photo-genic Assemblages: Photography as a Connective Interface," in *Digital Photography and Everyday Life: Empirical Studies on Material Visual Practices*, edited by Edgar Gómez Cruz and Asko Lehmuskallio (London: Routledge, 2016), 228–42.
34 Asko Lehmuskallio, "The Camera as a Sensor: The Visualization of Everyday Digital Photography as Simulative, Heuristic and Layered Pictures," in *Digital Photography and Everyday Life: Empirical Studies on Material Visual Practices,* edited by Edgar Gómez Cruz and Asko Lehmuskallio (London: Routledge, 2016), 243–66.
35 Joanna Zylinska, *Nonhuman Photography* (Cambridge: MIT Press, 2017).
36 Ibid., 2.
37 Daniel Rubinstein and Katrina Sluis, "The Digital Image in Photographic Culture: Algorithmic Photography and the Crisis of Representation," in *The Photographic Image in Digital Culture* (London; New York: Routledge, 2013), 36–54.

38 Ibid., 25.
39 Annie Leibovitz, *Annie Leibovitz at Work* (New York: Random House, 2008).
40 William Uricchio, "The Algorithmic Turn: Photosynth, Augmented Reality and the Changing Implications of the Image," *Visual Studies* 26, no 1 (2011): 25–35, doi: 10.1080/1472586X.2011.548486.
41 Howarth and McLaren, *Street Photography Now*, 9.
42 Ibid., 10.
43 Michael Wolf, Marc Feustel, and Steven Harris. *A Series of Unfortunate Events* (Berlin: Peperoni Books, 2010).
44 www.worldpressphoto.org/collection/photo/2011/30133/1/2011-Michael-Wolf-CIS-HM-AL.
45 https://9-eyes.com/.
46 Nathan Jurgenson, *The Social Photo: On Photography and Social Media* (London: Verso, 2019).

# 31

# SHANZHAI

## Affective Assemblages and Technovisuality

*Helen Grace,* 葛海崙

### Introduction

This chapter explores the affective spaces of technology, using research on plastic camera production in Hong Kong in the 1960s and the context of technology production and consumption in southern China. The work builds on research on the aesthetics of camera phone pictures and the impact that proximity to the global production base of mobile media has on the understanding of technology and aesthetics in this region. As a photo essay, it reflects on the fragile sites of artistic/new media production, especially the repurposing of industrial buildings for creative use in Hong Kong.[1]

To do this, I "walk through" some of these areas, reflecting on the appearance and disappearance of assembly processes and of the emergence of "assemblage" as a mode of understanding neo-industrial reality in a city, coming to terms with the fragility of the future itself. I suggest—following the brief speculations on the phenomenon of *shanzhai* by Byung Chul Han—that creativity itself must be rethought beyond the notion of the discontinuity and suddenness of a new creation, completely breaking with the old, toward a more playful pleasure in recombination, modification, and variation.

In Chinese, the neologism *shanzhai*, 山寨, often understood to mean "fake," literally refers to the "mountain stronghold" of a warlord, and it invokes unregulated cottage industry, "grassroots innovation," as well as cheap knock-offs and here, it is used to suggest a more ambivalent sense of the improvised nature of innovation.

### Accumulating the Particles

> *... the slow shaping of daily life is of equal importance to the explosions of history; for in the anonymous life, the particles accumulate into an explosive force.*[2]

> *The more abstract the space, the more important the image becomes ... and the more dominant becomes the visual as a mode.*[3]

Reaching the street from the MTR, our warm breath vaporizes in the cold air of this chilly Hong Kong winter morning. We've come looking for that which cannot be easily located: the spirit of *shanzhai* and its traces in derelict and abandoned spaces, now taken over by the contemporary spirit of property speculation, as manufacturing moves across the border to southern China's "special economic zones".

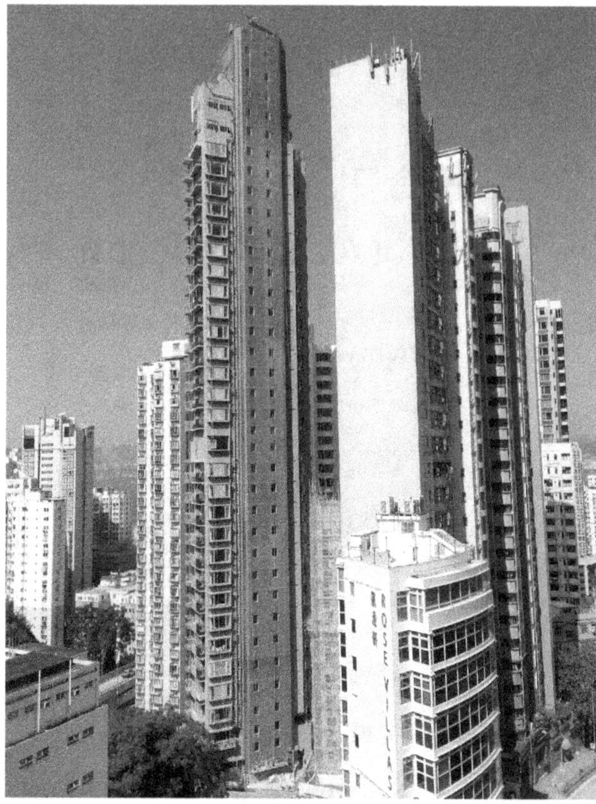


*Figure 31.1* Shek Tong Shui, 5 February 2016, 1.33pm

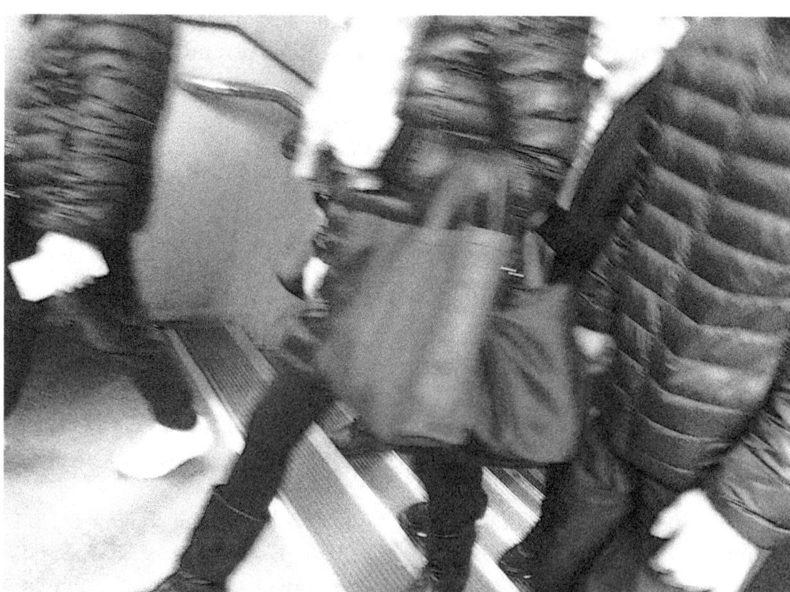

*Figure 31.2* Kowloon Bay, 16 February 2016, 9.23am

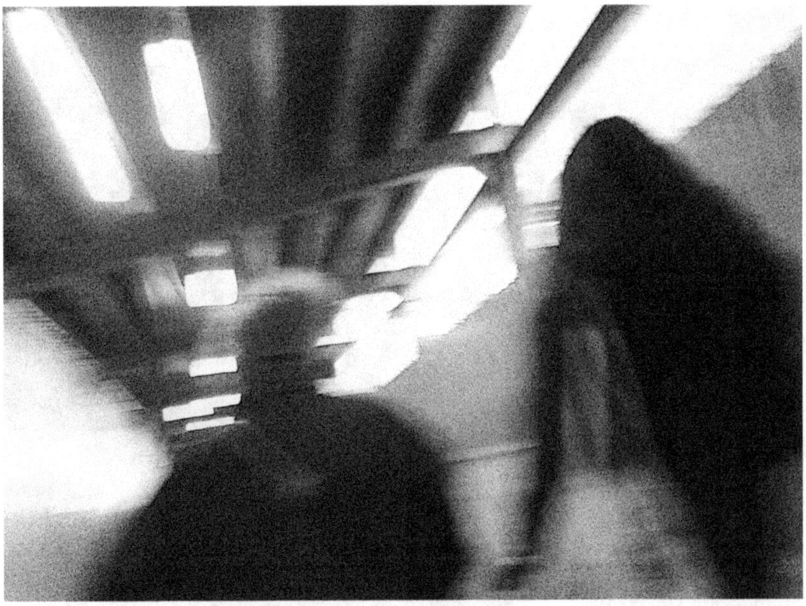

*Figure 31.3* Kowloon Bay, 16 February 2016, 9.53am

We're on a ghost hunt, searching for shadows—the remnants of toy camera production in 1960s Hong Kong, the precursors of contemporary ubiquitous devices. So, we're using toy-like technology to capture the invisible as ephemeral images: a Google Map of our location, an activity tracking app that charts our path, producing rough "drawings" of our meandering walks, a small "body-cam" called a Narrative Clip, 35 square millimeter, recording the journey. Designed in Sweden, made in Taiwan, a market failure, no longer produced. The device unobtrusively images what we fail to notice, randomly capturing moments and movement, giving us date, time, and GPS co-ordinates, so we can retrospectively animate our odyssey.

Our heartbeats, our emotional states recorded, we are present here, feeling our way, motion registering emotion. We are tracking the remnants of small factories where toys and toothbrushes and plastic flowers and chopsticks were once made, and where new "creative industries"—as ephemeral as their precursors—are emerging in the city's former factory buildings. The experience of these spaces is lost in totalizing narratives of "outsourcing" of "supply chains" and "cheap labour," of "economic miracles"—rather than human labor—taken for granted and erased in global "development" processes, the mere effects of World Bank and IMF policy thinking.[4] Local history gathers up the details, trying to remember: "not the return of past memory, but the return of memory to the past."[5]

We're searching here for what we might call the authentic memory of the "fake" or *shanzhai* object. Byung Chul Han suggests the phenomenon of *shanzhai* challenges us to rethink creativity itself beyond the notion of the discontinuity and suddenness of a new creation, completely breaking with the old, toward a more playful pleasure in recombination, modification, and variation.[6] A movement in this direction requires a plasticity of thought, a means of "grasping in a speculative way the process of the self-determination of substance"[7] and we think this *shanzhai* spirit can be understood, not only in terms of the philosophy of neuroplasticity—Malabou's focus—but also by looking at the more mundane plastics industries of East Asia in the 1950s and 1960s.

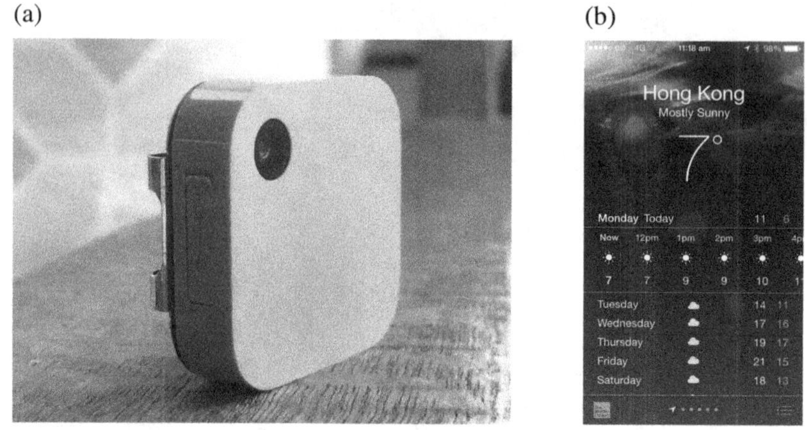


*Figure 31.4* (a) Narrative clip camera. (b) iPhone screenshot

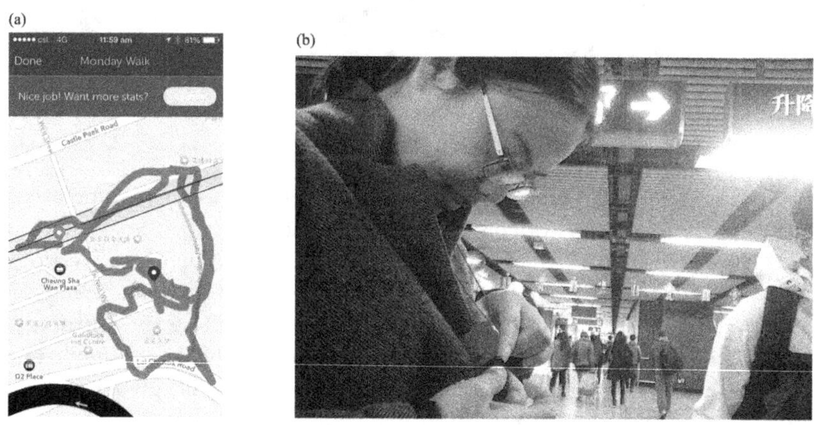


*Figure 31.5* (a) Runkeeper walktrack. (b) Kowloon Bay, 16 February 2016, 9.15am

Mobile media art challenges us to entirely rethink what has become the default position of art and creativity: that unique works emerge from global "centres," like—let's say—New York, Berlin or Silicon Valley, and find their way to various "peripheries" such as Taoyuan or Shenzhen in emulated and copied forms. This default enhances the fantasy of a seminal originality and singular creative genius: of design preceding fabrication. The assembled technologies that enable so much contemporary art now are much more dispersed in their genesis and involve specific innovations in production processes that happen, not only in the design process, but especially in the fabrication—in machinic and bodily encounters with materials that are plastic (and plasticized) in all senses.

If a global art superstar releases an image into the Instagram flow, it is not an act of originality. Instead it is more like a *shanzhai* gesture, returning the ephemeral object back into the stream of things that began in the streets we are walking, in the post-war outsourcing of assembly processes from western industries to East Asian "guerrilla capitalist" production processes.[8]

In a kind of cosmic journey, we're heading to Cheung Sha Wan: 長沙灣—"long sandy bay," once the home of Tanka fisherfolk, now, on reclaimed land, the location of Cosmos Machinery Trading Company, parent company of Great Wall (Optical) Plastic Works Limited, where

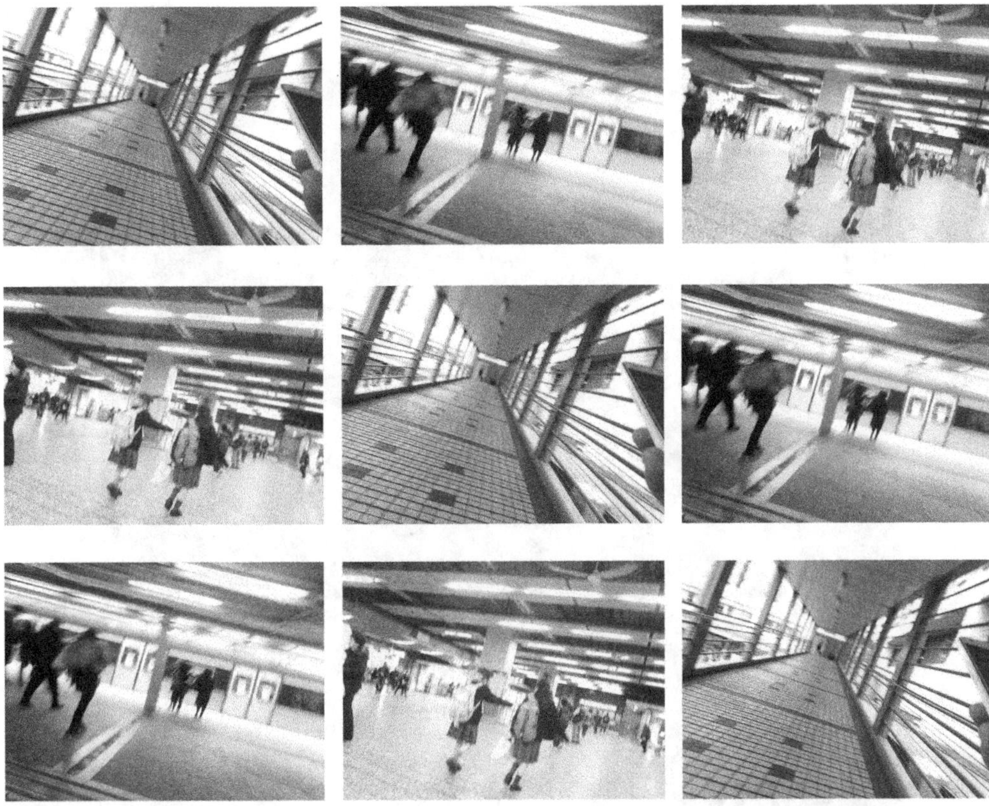

*Figure 31.6* Kwun Tong, 10 March 2016, 1.42pm

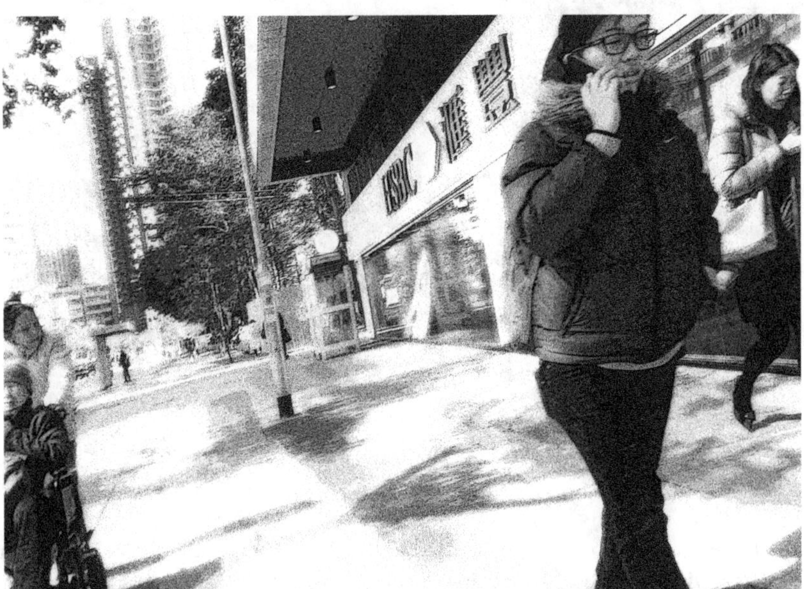


*Figure 31.7* Cheung Sha Wan, 25 January 2016, 10.50am

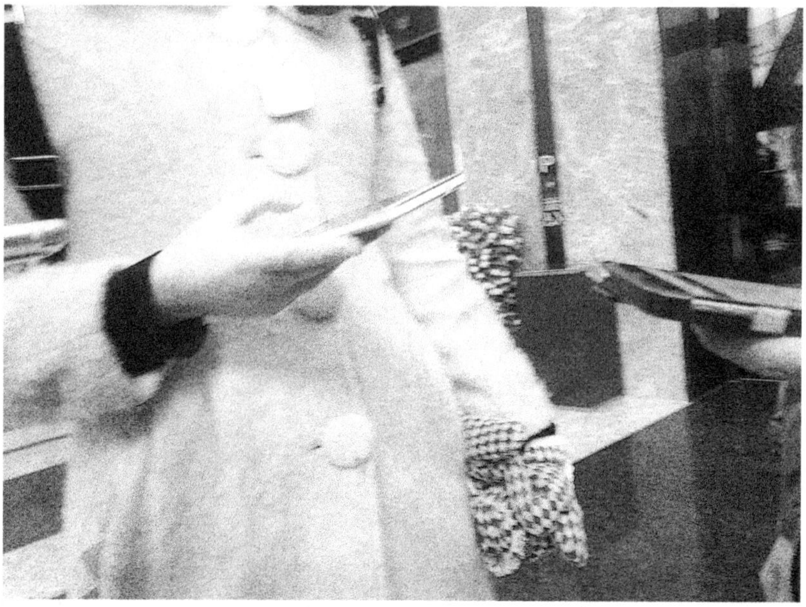

*Figure 31.8* Cheung Sha Wan, 25 January 2016, 11am

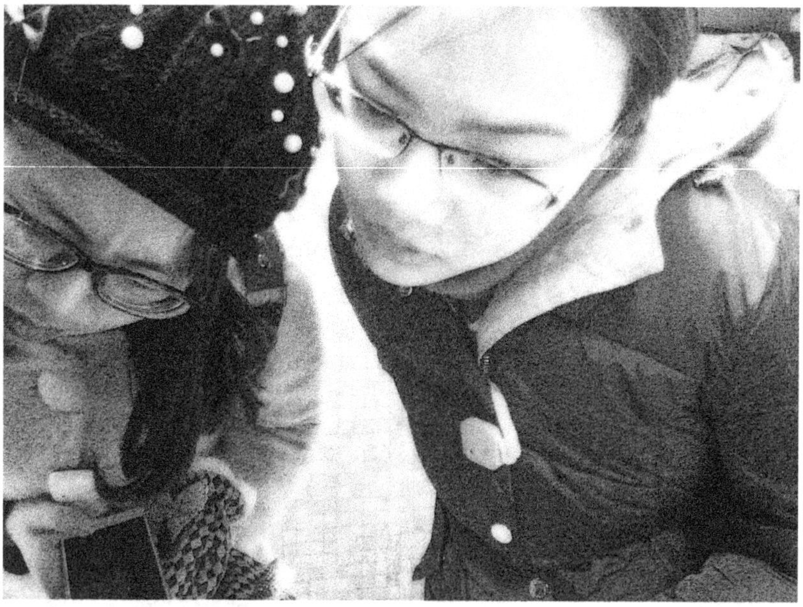

*Figure 31.9* Cheung Sha Wan, 25 January 2016, 10.32am

ostensibly, the Diana camera, one of the earliest and most iconic plastic cameras, was once made in its thousands. The Diana—one of hundreds of models of differently "branded" (and unbranded) plastic cameras produced in Hong Kong from the late 1950s–early 1960s—became famous in part because of its use from the late 1960s in American art photography.[9]

In the genesis myth of the Diana, the factory was said to be in Kowloon Bay. A historical search of the Hong Kong Stock Exchange Companies list produces dozens of companies called "Great Wall," so it is impossible to link this particular device to any individual factory, in a city where production of bits of plastic was so dispersed. The Diana has no individual birthplace: "The origin turns out to be a *retrospective construction*."[10]

American art photography invents its precursors at the very point that US assembly processes are outsourced to East Asia, frequently as part of economic development schemes and an extensive military procurement network during the Vietnam War. Even toys are weapons. In the 1960s, Hong Kong becomes production location for the *heads* of GI Joe—the Hasbro toy ("action figure") that gets boys playing with dolls while coming into their being as patriots.[11] The other body parts of the figures will be made somewhere else, another factory, another country, wherever the contract price is lower and labor can be squeezed a little more.

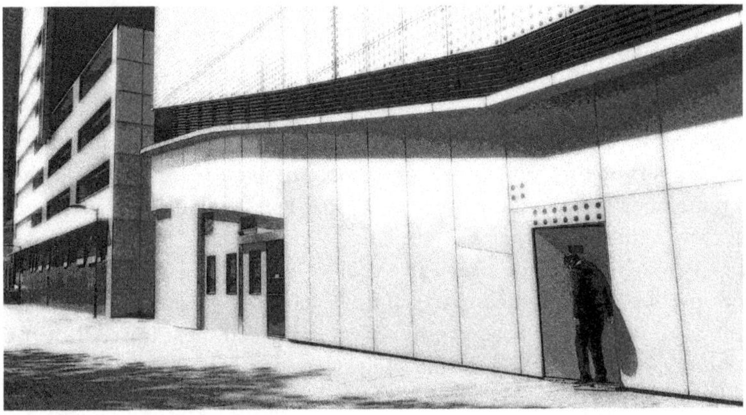

*Figure 31.10* Cheung Sha Wan, 25 January 2016, 10.51am

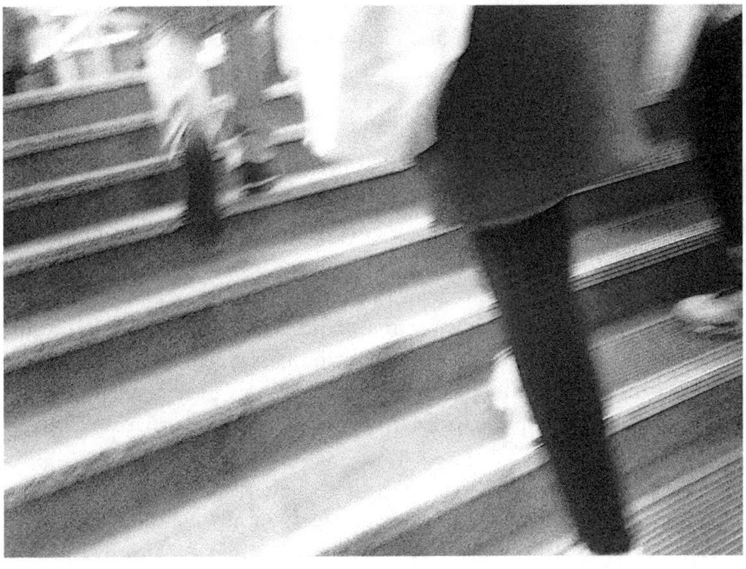

*Figure 31.11* Kowloon Bay, 16 February 2016, 9.56am

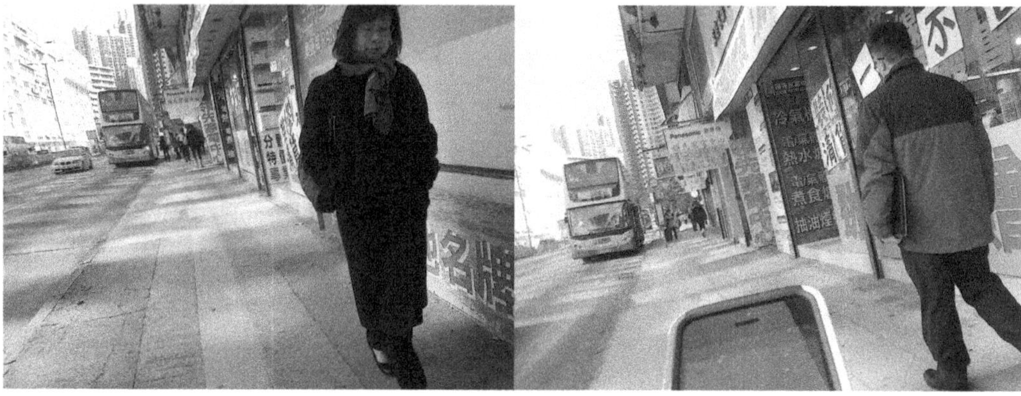

*Figure 31.12* Cheung Sha Wan, 25 January 2016, 9.49am.

At the Cosmos Head Office (the factories have moved to the mainland), no one has heard of the Diana camera, everyone from those days is gone, but even if we *could* find them, it's unlikely anyone would remember because these products of small plastics injection molding factories probably left the factory as unbranded parts.

The brand is that which comes after the event of production and assembly. Production no longer produces products: it produces parts. The "whole" is a fantasy, imagined in marketing, consisting not only of the designed object, but of its enhanced meaning. All over these old Hong Kong factory estates, built near the housing estates, small factories made parts, which were frequently assembled and packed in piece work in the housing estates, built near here in the aftermath of the Shek Kip Mei squatter settlement fire in 1953.[12] Architecturally, the modernist blocks of the factory estates and the housing estates were of the same design and used the same concrete construction methods so they could be hastily built.

The brand is the attempt to turn the generic low-value modular and mass-produced object into a unique "original" item, like a work of art. The *shanzhai* object is closely linked to this process and the brand could not exist without it; the *shanzhai* version is both precursor and successor to the brand. To trace out its pathways involves entering the rabbit-hole of patent filings, observing the tiny incremental changes that are registered in the development of models. But this will fail to note the tiniest of fabrication adjustments that are not registered as patents: the changes that make all the difference.

Our "aesthetic" research for forms and precursors to contemporary ubiquitous devices uncovers the very pathways that explain to us in concrete terms the nature of networks—social, economic, communicative and technological. For my students—local Hong Kong students with, for example, Hakka village backgrounds, or mainland students, the single children of Cultural Revolution parents—these walks are media-archeological: we discover the origins of everyday devices, exploring a kind of "techno-biography" that locates everyday life in technological developments. It is through the complete ordinariness of banal things that we engage with personal and national histories.

Stoneman identifies what he calls *soft innovation* (i.e., a form of innovation related to the non-functional or aesthetic dimension of new products or product variants launched onto the market),[13] but what we are dealing with here is a type of "super soft innovation"—the very low-level improvisations and fabrications of materials, used to solve technical problems at a micro-level.

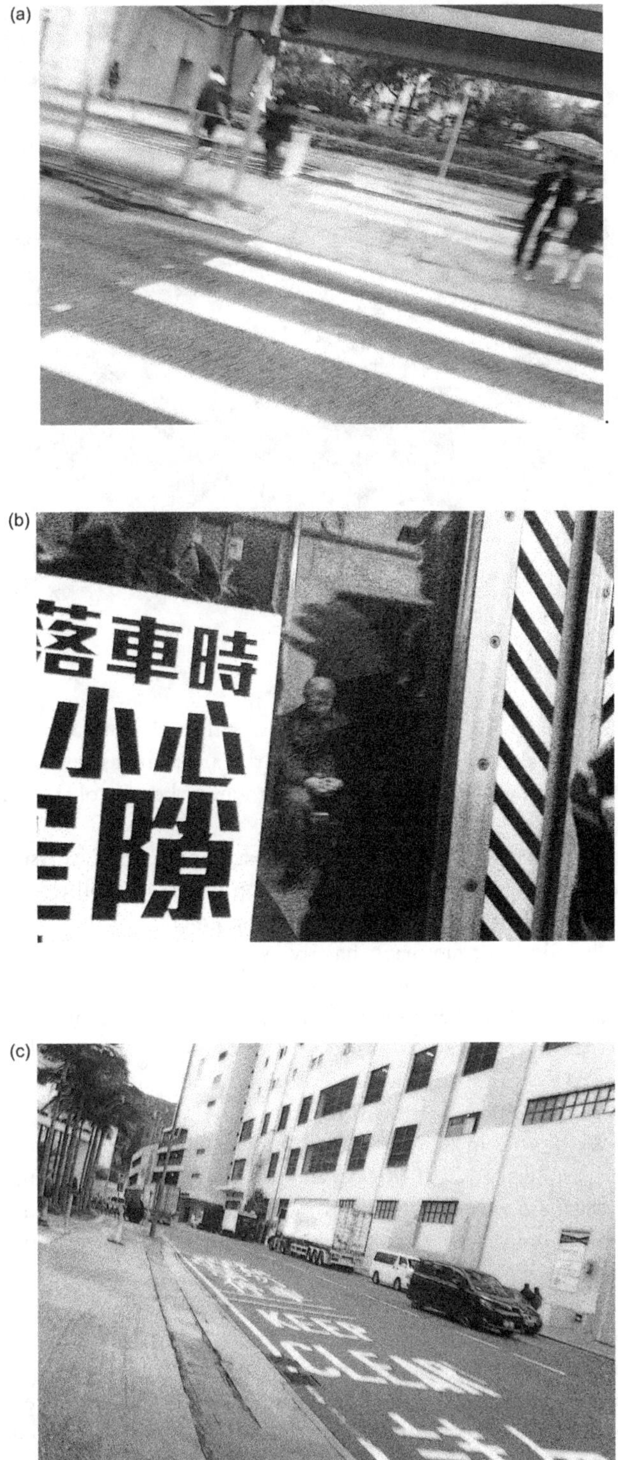


*Figure 31.13* (a) Kwai Chung, 10 March 2016, 2.27pm. (b) Kwai Chung, 10 March 2016, 2.45pm. (c) Kwai Chung, 10 March 2016, 2.15pm

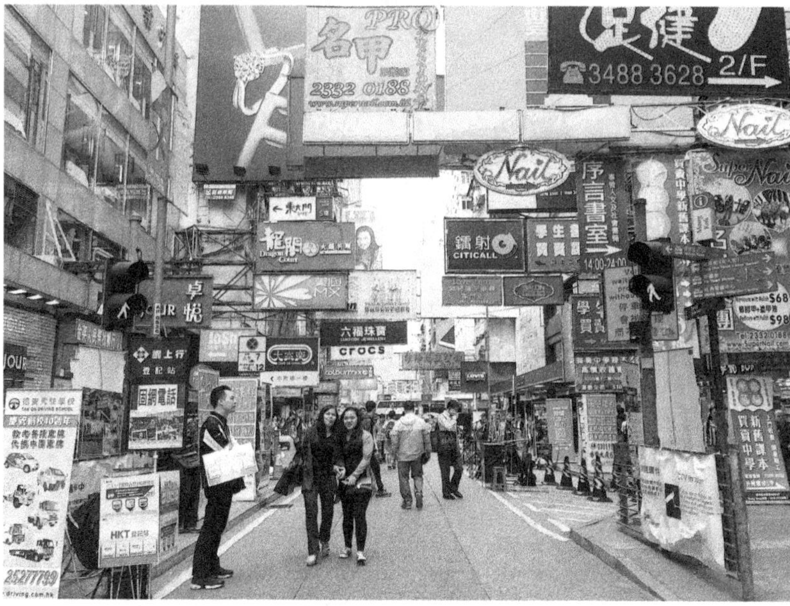


*Figure 31.14* Mongkok, 6 March 2016, 2.01pm

These types of changes have transformed industries within the dynamic structures of small—indeed micro—businesses, although these processes are hard to measure on scales of technological innovation, so they tend to be overlooked, especially when they involve such mundane things as toys, toothbrushes, and plastic flowers.

These are the types of businesses characterizing the economies of East Asia and especially Hong Kong in the 1960s to the 1980s, a feature of adaptation to the instabilities of war-time displacement leading to a biopolitical situation of general *experimental life*. Living takes place in hastily built shelters for refugees, hastily built factories, hastily assembled shops and services catering to very basic needs, where people are left to themselves to survive. Self-help communities thus form to mitigate the generalized context of exploitation in which participants are immersed. The colonial government realizes that, in the interests of social cohesion to preserve market advantage, housing needs to be built close to factories, so that the economic benefit of "Empire made," "British Hong Kong" goods can continue to flow past tariff barriers.

Time moves on. We're now in Kowloon Bay, in search of the Holga shop, base for Universal Electronics Industries, established by TM Lee, the inventor of the Holga, another plastic camera, serving a new analog nostalgia movement for film cameras in the time of digital images. Nostalgia has been monetized by Lomography, established by a group of Austrian students seeking to revive an old Soviet-era camera they've discovered in a Prague camera store, on a summer holiday after Central Europe is opened up by the collapse of the Berlin Wall.[14]

Lee's biography is a geopolitical narrative: he trains in engineering in Beijing before the Cultural Revolution, translating Russian technology on transistors.[15] He returns to Hong Kong in 1966–1967, the time of the riots,[16] and establishes a factory to produce transistor radios and then flashguns for cameras. He's contacted by a Japanese manufacturer, looking to expand their business. Later, in the 1980s, in developing the Holga, he hoped it would be popular in China, but it turns out his markets are in Europe and the United States because the expanding Chinese consumer market is more interested in expensive European brands.

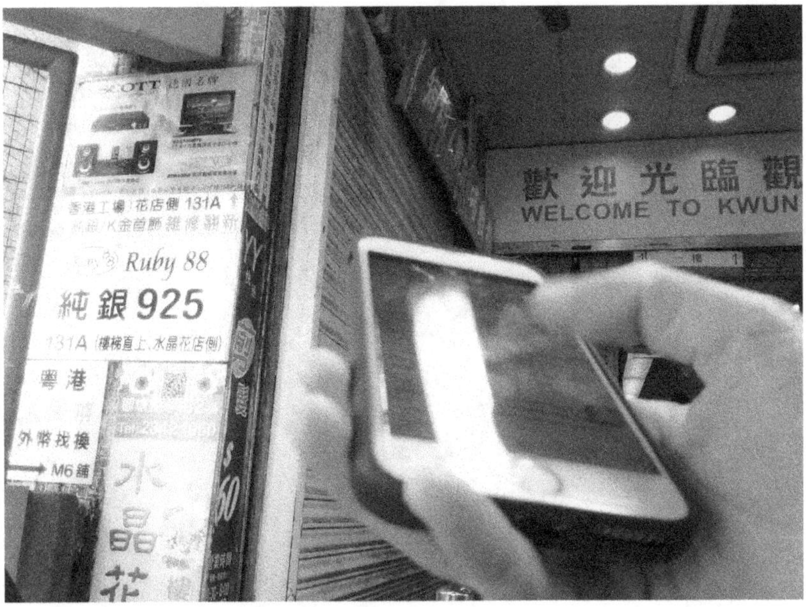


*Figure 31.15* Kwun Tong, 16 February, 2016, 10.08am

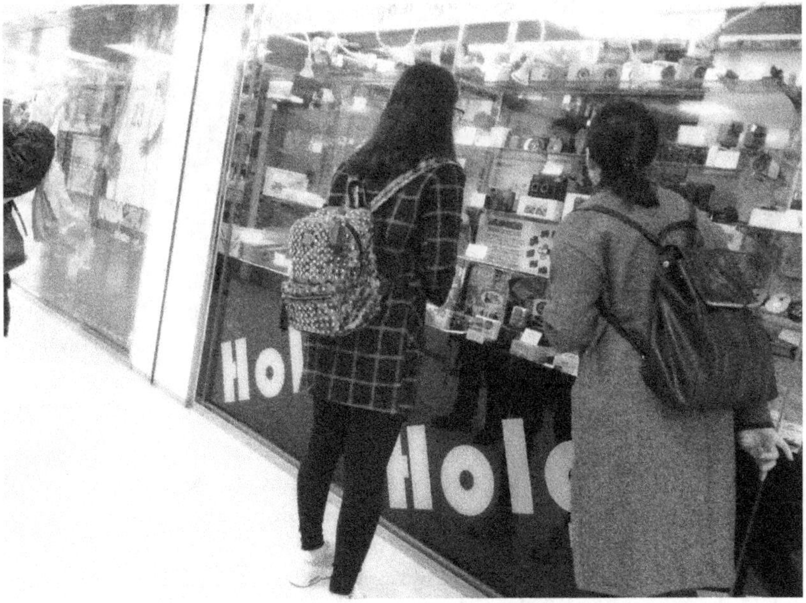


*Figure 31.16* Kowloon City, 16 February 2016, 9.23am

Although there is a shop in a Kowloon Bay shopping centre, the Holga too has stopped production in Hong Kong and a second retail outlet in Kwun Tong has closed, just a month before we visit. The shelves are still there, empty, and it's still possible to buy a few camera things at one of the other small stores in this arcade, which is closing down, slated for demolition.

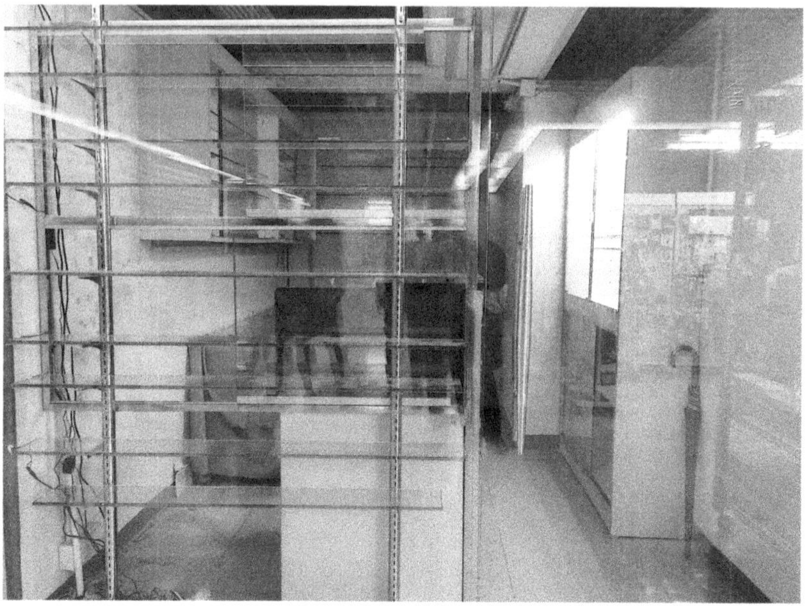

*Figure 31.17* Kwun Tong, 16 February 2016, 11.11am

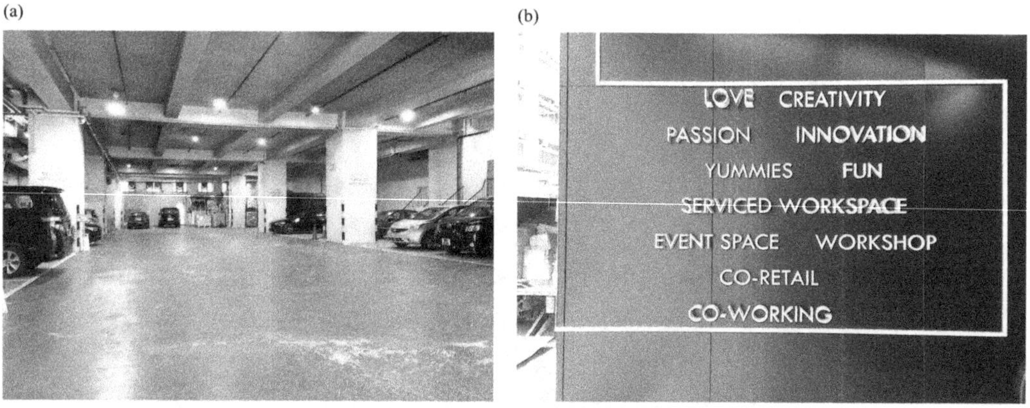


*Figure 31.18* (a) Kwun Tong, 16 February 2016, 11.36am. (b) Kwun Tong, 16 February 2016, 11.31am

Kwun Tong—one of the most intensive factory districts in the 1960s and 1970s—is being redeveloped and the old factory buildings are being pulled down and replaced by expensive apartments. Those that remain are being repurposed as boutique fashion outlets, creative industries, cafes and art galleries, as small car repair businesses, textiles, and old industries are replaced, though still glimpsed on the way to the lift that takes you to the café or art gallery.

We map in this visual-algorithmic way, randomly generating aggregations of data that form themselves into lo-res pictograms, patterns that are sometimes blurred but a recognizable everyday through miniaturized plastic lenses. Hito Steyerl has written of the qualities of the "poor image," this "copy in motion," this "itinerant image," the "lumpen proletarian in the class society of appearances," that can create "disruptive movements of thought and affect"—but above all giving us a link to the present.[17] The poor image, as an ensemble of heterogeneous elements, as a configuration of components that are interchangeable is itself an "assemblage."[18]

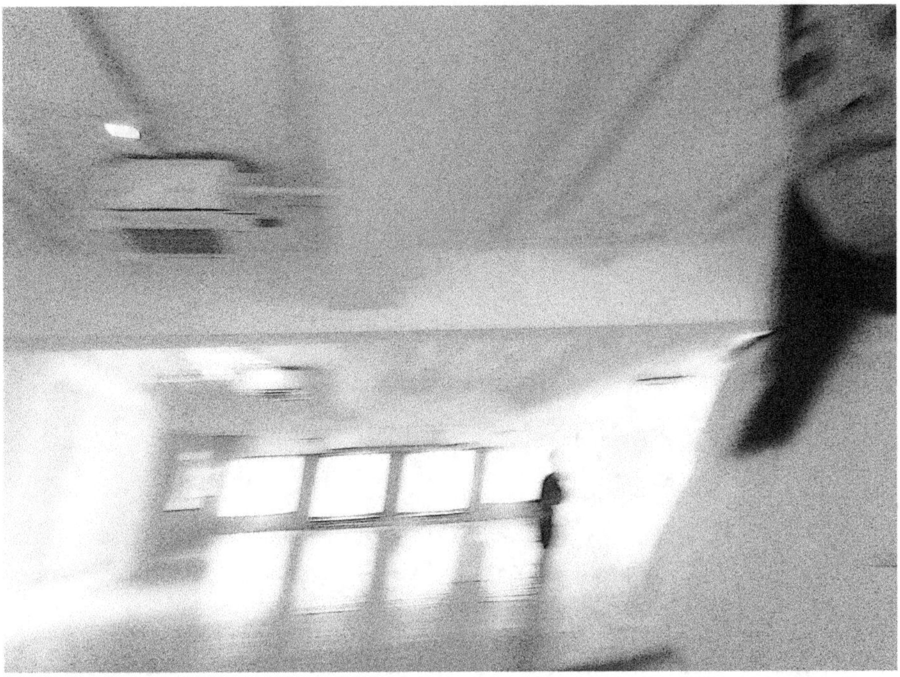

*Figure 31.19* Kwun Tong, 16 February 2016, 9.36am

For humans to be able to act freely, Byung-Chul Han points out that the future has to appear to be open, unpredictable. Big Data closes off that possibility by aggregating and then predicting human behavior, so that the future ceases to be uncertain. Rather, it becomes controllable and calculable—and a world in which there are persons who possess "free will" comes to an end.[19]

It is a situation that creeps up on us, as we embrace charismatic new technologies, like new religions. We are less likely to object because our new state of subjection comes with a set of devotional objects that materialize and stabilize the new dominion, distracting us from our subjugation. Mobile phones are "*the devotional objects of the Digital*," and the smartphone, as a "subjectivation-apparatus," acts like a rosary, another handheld device for self-monitoring and control.[20]

In our ambivalence, of course we do not wish to believe this gloomy view, preferring to see emancipation in our devices, in the energetics of our divagation through these streets. And we know all the ways that social media mobilizes crowds. In 2014, these streets were mobilized by the Umbrella Protests, a time of profound intellectual decolonization. The leaders of the movement have recently been convicted and now face prison.[21]

The "poor image" in particular takes the pulse of the population, embodying, as Steyerl reminds us, its "opportunism, narcissism, desire for autonomy and creation, its inability to focus or make up its mind, its constant readiness for transgression and simultaneous submission."[22] We are left with uncertainty, complexity.

In our research on Hong Kong mobile media images, we noted the repetition of images of bright blue sky, of brilliant white cloud patterns, deep blue water and the rich greenery of country parks. We asked people what they considered the constituents of a "good image" and the most common response was to say that a picture needed to be "clear."[23] We can call these clichés—or we can see them as the projections of hopes for the future, as yet unrealized, in a city where the future is certainly unclear.

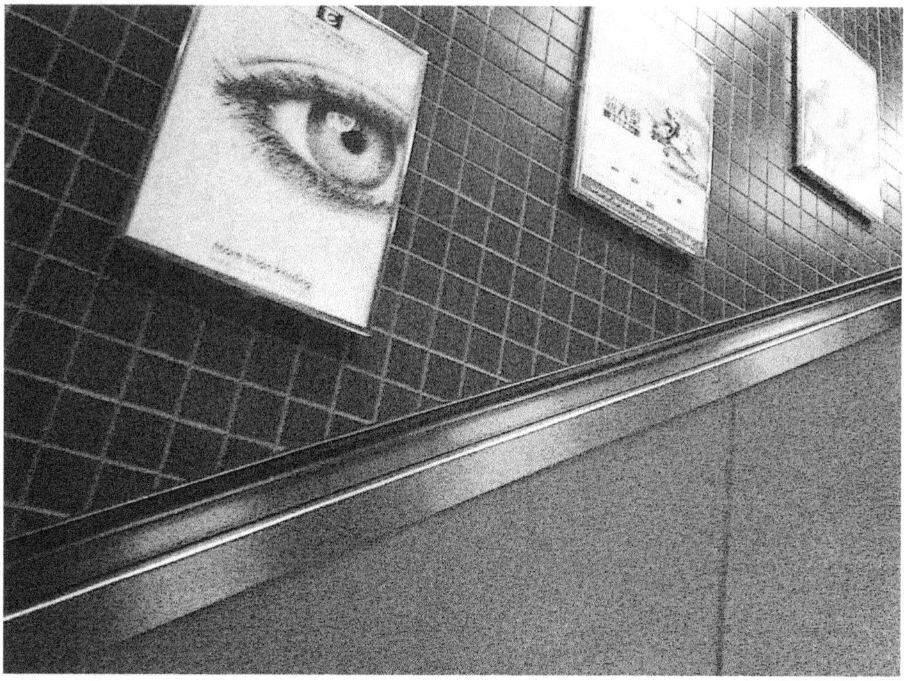

*Figure 31.20* Kwun Tong, 10 March 2016, 1.51pm

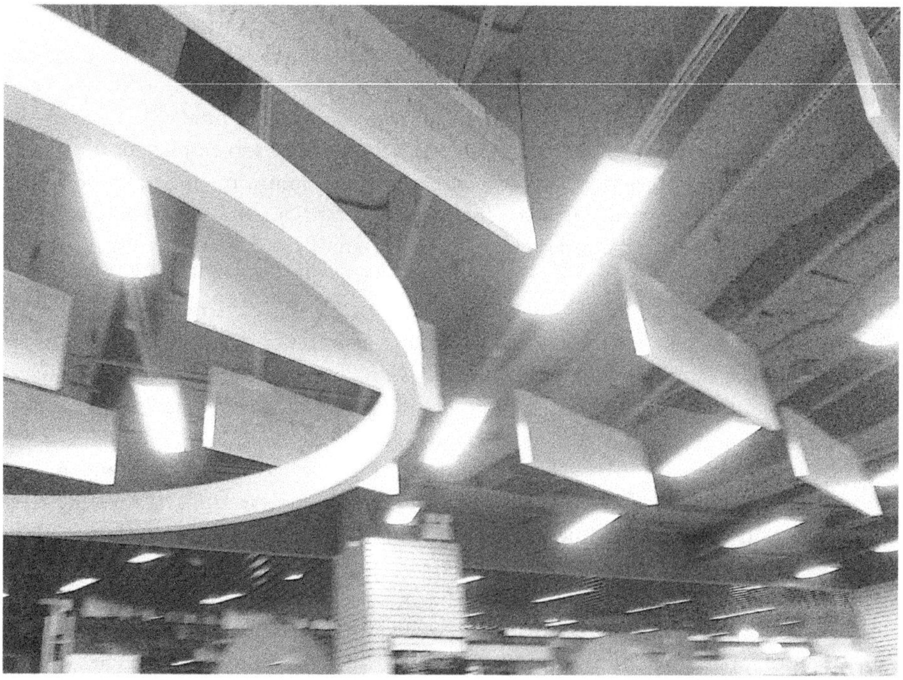

*Figure 31.21* Kwun Tong, 10 March 2016, 1.29am

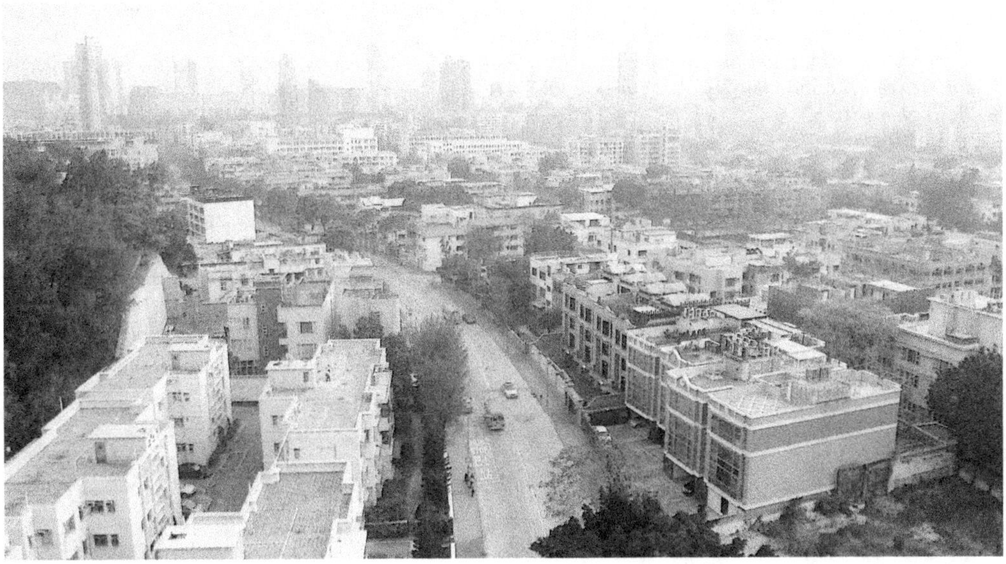

*Figure 31.22* Kowloon Tong, 24 March 2016, 4.37pm.

## Notes

1 All images within this chapter are courtesy of the author.
2 Sigfried Giedion, *Mechanization Takes Command: A Contribution to Anonymous History* (Oxford: Oxford University Press, 1948), 3.
3 Ackbar Abbas, *Hong Kong Culture and the Politics of Disappearance* (Hong Kong: Hong Kong University Press/University of Minnesota Press, 1997), 9.
4 Robert Wade, "The Role of Industrial Policy in Developing Countries," in Calgano et al., *Rethinking Development Strategies after the Financial Crisis: Volume 1: Making the Case for Policy Space* (UNCTAD/ United Nations Conference on Trade and Development, 2015), 67–80; Robert Wade, "East Asia's Economic Success: Conflicting Perspectives, Partial Insights, Shaky Evidence," *World Politics* 44, no. 2 (1992): 270–320, doi: org/10.2307/2010449.
5 Abbas, *Hong Kong Culture*, 98; see Hong Kong Memory site: www.hkmemory.hk/index.html; for a more contemporary "recovery" see Hoi Shan Anson Mak, ed. *From the Factories* (Hong Kong: kaitak, Centre for Research and Development, Academy of Visual Arts, Hong Kong Baptist University, 2014).
6 Byung-Chul Han, *Shanzhai: Deconstruction in Chinese* (Cambridge, MA: MIT Press, 2017).
7 Catherine Malabou, "Deconstructive and/or 'Plastic' Readings of Hegel," *Bulletin of the Hegel Society of Great Britain* 21, no 41/42 (2000): 132–41, doi: 10.1017/S0263523200007448.
8 Danny Kin-Kong Lam and Ian Lee, "*Guerrilla capitalism* and the Limit of Statist Theory: Comparing the Chinese NICs," in *The Evolving Pacific Basin*, edited by Cal Clark and Steve Chan (Boulder, CO, LynneReiner Publishers, 1992), 107–24.
9 Michelle Bates, *Plastic Cameras: Toying with Creativity* (Second Edition, Waltham: Focal Press, 2010).
10 Han, *Shanzhai,* 13.
11 On the Hong Kong toy industry, see Sarah Monks, *Toy Town: How a Hong Kong Industry Played a Global Game* (Hong Kong: Toys Manufacturers' Association of Hong Kong, 2010).
12 See www.youtube.com/watch?v=evIwMJRVoHQ.
13 Paul Stoneman, *Soft Innovation: Economics, Product Aesthetics and Creative Industries* (Oxford: Oxford University Press, 2010).
14 Helen Grace, "A Sentimental Bond with the Product: The Veneer of Time," *Sturgeon* 2, June (2014), 52–59.
15 Shi Chi Leung, Interview with Lee Ting-Mo (李定武), Hong Kong, April 2016.
16 Gary Cheung, *Hong Kong's Watershed: The 1967 Riots* Hong Kong (Hong Kong, Hong Kong University Press 2010).

17 Hito Steyerl, "In Defense of the Poor Image," *e-flux journal* #10, November (2009), www.e-flux.com/journal/10/61362/in-defense-of-the-poor-image/.
18 Aiwha Ong and Collier Stephen J. eds., *Global Assemblages: Technology, Politics, and Ethics as Anthropological Problems* (London: Wiley-Blackwell, 2006).
19 Han, *Shanzhai*, 5.
20 Ibid.
21 Chris Lau and Lam Jeffie, "Occupy Leaders Found Guilty over Role in Hong Kong's 2014 Umbrella Movement," *South China Morning Post*, Tuesday 9 April 2019, n.p. www.scmp.com/news/hong-kong/law-and-crime/article/3005312/occupy-leaders-found-guilty-over-role-hong-kongs-2014.
22 Steyerl, "In Defense of the Poor Image."
23 For more detailed discussion see Helen Grace, *Culture, Aesthetics and Affect in Ubiquitous Media: The Prosaic Image* (London: Routledge, 2014), 187–90.

# 32
# PLATFORM POETICS

## *Emile Zile* in Conversation with *Klare Lanson*

Emile Zile is an artist who has performed the network since the early noughties, using moving imagery, live art and mobile communication tactics. With dark humor and critical re-use strategies, Zile occupies the creative spaces of gesture, live video and improvised site-specific work to analyze digital culture's role in our increasingly amplified everyday sociality. Reflecting back to us "a distributed humanity, a yearning for transcendence and the limits of language,"[1] through re-coding and re-performance, Zile's most recent performance was for UK arts organization Modern Art Oxford's project *This Image is No Longer Available* (2019)—a set of artist works, live-streamed performances, screenings and an open talks program by researchers, artists, curators and visitors to discuss digital space and online presence (Figure 32.1).

What for you were some of the significant "moments" in the field of mobile media art?

Discussion of a category of art which has such strong links to industrial production of consumer goods means I cannot separate significant moments of art from significant moments of technical/commercial innovation. The artist is a parasite who uses what is around to build their reality, not unlike a hermit crab scavenging for appropriate plastic shelter at the bottom of the sea floor. I could talk about miniaturization of technology being a pivotal moment in the freeing up of image-making, I could talk about the Sony PortaPak™ which brought electronic moving images to artists hands, I could talk about the development of always-on networked devices that further reduced the size and increased the scope of communication. In each wave of miniaturization of image making there is an amplification in the velocity and circulation of imagery.

How then do you define mobile media art in terms of your practice?

I define mobile media art as a flexible method which responds to, and is based in, the world in which it is located. I am solely interested in it because it is a medium used by the mass of society to conduct its most intimate and most commonplace interactions. Papyrus, Stone, Stained glass; these communication technologies precede us. I am attracted to the vernacular of networked speech as it is the primary site of communication, miscommunication, intimacy, and power.

This constant circulation of images and networked vernacular you speak of. Could you expand on this in relation to how you make mobile media art?

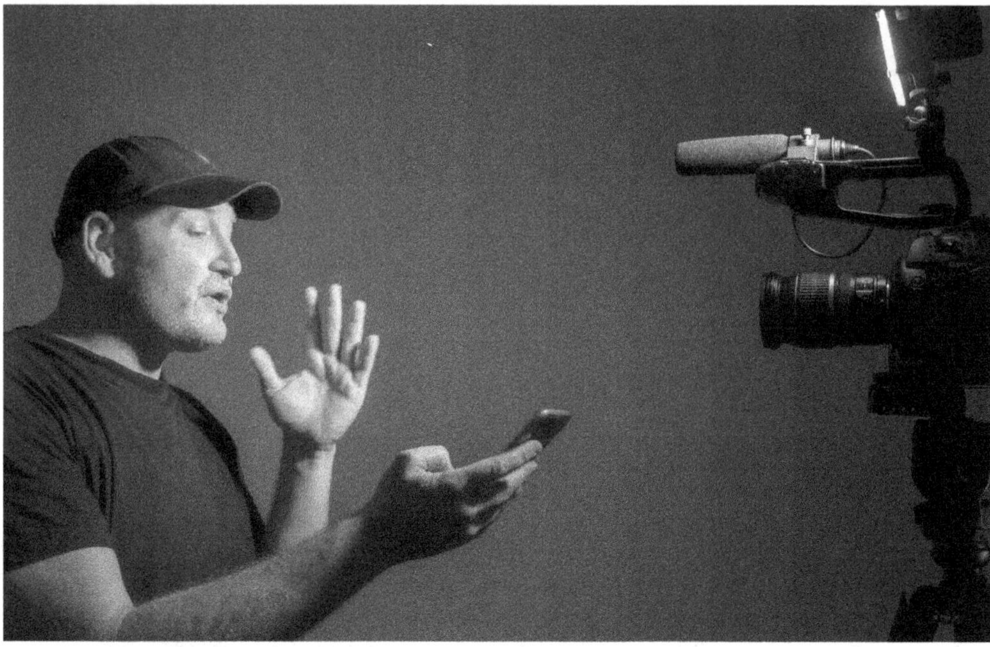

*Figure 32.1* Emile Zile. Photo credit: J. Hall

We are all producers and consumers within Communicative Capitalism. The platforms require our cultural capital to gain authenticity and a critical mass of participation. I am as much an avid consumer of user-generated content as I am a distanced critical observer. By shifting a medium, a tempo or a tone, energy can move between readings and evolve into a new meaning. Nudging a context can be all that's required to destabilize a text and offer a new perspective to an audience. Perhaps we can talk about neuro-chemical states: the compulsive, addictive feedback flow that is nurtured by the more aggressive platforms of mobile social media. These can be halted, transported to an art context, laid bare and under a different neuro-chemical state assessed and dissected. We are moving from an era of visual culture studies to what Warren Neidich[2] describes as neuroaesthetics.

> The use of gesture in your creative work over the years is interesting in terms of embodied language and its performativity, stemming from Larry Emdur's Suit (2002).[3] Could you speak generally to how this method has developed within your practice before we delve into a couple of your more recent works?

Gesture releases itself through the short-circuiting of spoken forms of language. When words are not enough gesture returns. As concise packets of embodied sense-making, gesture is a universal language. Many projects of mine have utilized gestural performance—the hand can become an animated Hollywood logo, a mask, a portal, a transmitter of energy. In regard to this approach as method, the reduction of energy into the gestural movement is the barest and most refined form of communication. Reduced to the body, at the ground zero of existence, poetry can be made. Discarding the apparatus and superfluous trinkets, the body can speak.

> Definitely, embodiment is intrinsically front and center in your work. What previous mobile media art projects inspire your thinking?

Spat + Loogie's *NEW!SHOP 2006*[4] was an open-ended site-specific performance which emulated the socio-commercial linguistic structures of the supermarket experience. Embracing the efficiencies of Point-Of-Sale sales infrastructure and bending it to serve artistic ends, it generated a reality that rode our expectations of the shopping experience and detoured them convincingly. Nikolaus Gansterer's *TransLectures* 2000-ongoing[5] consist of a live-camera on a tripod pointing at a blackboard table. Gansterer then uses this universe, platform, stage to elaborate on scientific and relational concepts that incorporate gesture, narration, and spatio-linguistic performance. Both of these projects inspired my thinking on ways to bend the tools of modern communication and semio-capital[6] to serve artistic outcomes.

> You use multisensorial forms of language in your work and I'd like to hear your thoughts on how network cultures such as how social media platforms could be seen to be evolving new forms of paralinguistics.

It's not too difficult to foresee a mode of gestural twitch response to visual communication in the near future. A straight and brutally efficient line from visual input, to muscle responses in the hand, to credit card details shared with commercial entities. Facebook's newly announced plan for its online currency Libra is one such method to remove any hesitation from stimulus to sale. Muscle memory to bypass critical faculties. This has already been the case within the Chinese model of siloed social media WeChat Payment, which incorporates a tradable currency, your social media profile, purchasing history and social-engagement record. It is unsurprising that addiction engineers are working in all these companies to make their offerings "sticky" and "unputdownable." Of course, this overwhelming push toward a streamlined algorithmic logic will bring about its explosive opposite, namely, individuals thirsty for experience and physical exertion in the other world (non-screen). Remote digital detox centers, extreme gyms, and the temporary autonomy and anonymity of the nightclub (with its drug experiences) will only increase in relevance (Figure 32.2).

> Agreed, it's interesting how new visualities such as emoji, emoticons and stickers in our daily communication act as a weird kind of de-evolution back to hieroglyphics. Perhaps there are positives too, in terms of crossing global language barriers?

THERE IS NO BARRIER TO LANGUAGE WHEN EVERYONE SPEAKS SILICON VALLEY AMERICAN ENGLISH—WE LEARN FROM YOUTUBE TO SPEAK FACEBOOK-ACCENTED.COMLISH.

> Are you flaming me right now? ;-)
>
> Your live performance of dictation software in *I Follow Yoko and Yoko Follows Me* (2014)[7] harnesses the improvised comic nature of your work and also speaks to various forms of social media produsage.[8] Could you tell us about how that project rolled out, and what's interesting to you about all the word hacks that come out of this performance work?

I was invited to respond to a survey exhibition of Yoko Ono's career at the Museum of Contemporary Art (MCA) in Sydney, Australia. Rather than using a Fluxus script of hers to remake an old performance, I instead took her current day twitter feed as an impromptu data set to create a new live performance in the MCA cinema. Inviting network effects into my work destabilizes my presence as a performer of the work; by rinsing energies through the network, I accept machine translation as an auto-poetic co-author of meaning. The audience can be heard riding the potential for chaos and collapse, giggling along and engaging with the results. In one sequence, I take a Granny Smith apple, a stand-in for the one seen in Yoko Ono's sculpture *Apple* (1966)[9] and

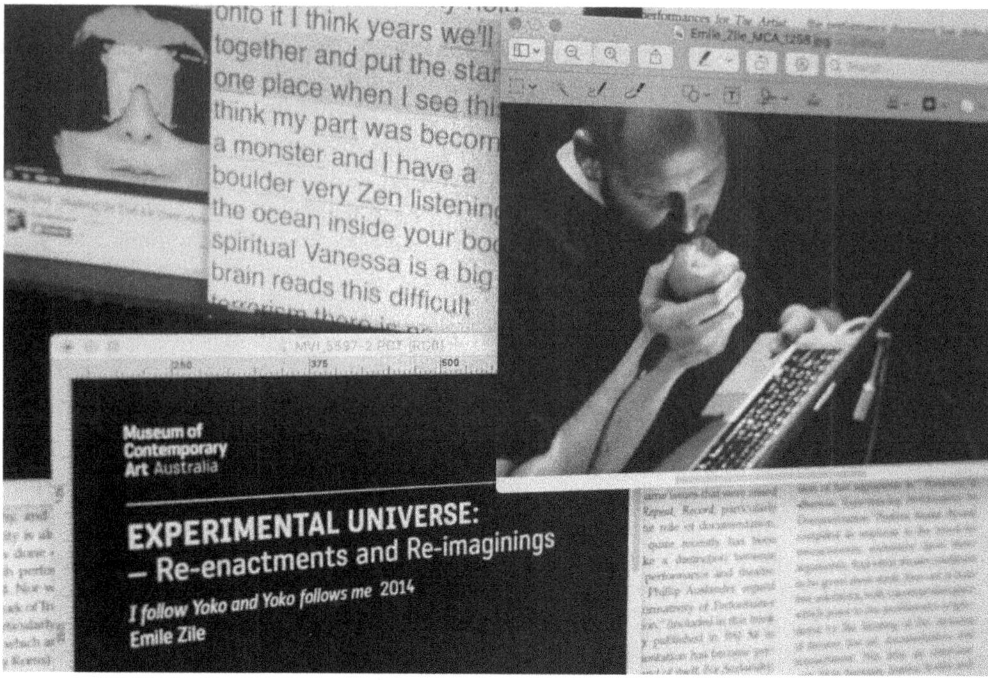


*Figure 32.2* *I Follow Yoko and Yoko Follows Me* (2014), performance at Museum of Contemporary Art (MCA), Sydney. Photo credit: Emile Zile

proceed to eat it on-stage through the speech-to-text function of the TextEdit application. The apple passes through my body as the sound of the apple is passing through the network.

The results are displayed onscreen for the audience to see live. The transportation of energy and the dissolving of matter into language are key here. These purposeful mistranslations allow me to shepherd a meaning through different states of matter, while holding an audience's attention. There is a pleasurable adrenaline rush from inviting both the cloud and the crowd to participate. Layered states of liveness. We are familiar with these moments of language collapse—using these modes of desktop office surrealism and machine-aesthetic absurdism is a contemporary folk art (Figure 32.3).

> In relation to the performance of the smartphone within your projects, for example the mobile's co-performance in your re-performance of Dan Graham's famous Performance/Audience/Mirror work,[10] could you speak to the shift in harnessing and activating more receptive roles for the collective audience?

I have undertaken a number of live performances that incorporate a media-streaming component. Occasionally, the streaming dynamic is more pronounced, at other times it is less so. But it is always implicit that we exist in a network society, and distinctions between a flesh audience and a streaming audience are becoming less and less relevant. The tension between addressing multiple versions of audience is important here. By talking to my phone, I am also talking to each one of those live audience members directly. The phone is a portal to talk to a disembodied tele-present audience, and it is also a prop that activates the "in the room" audience, allowing me to strategically place myself between them and their highly personal relationship to their phone/social universe.

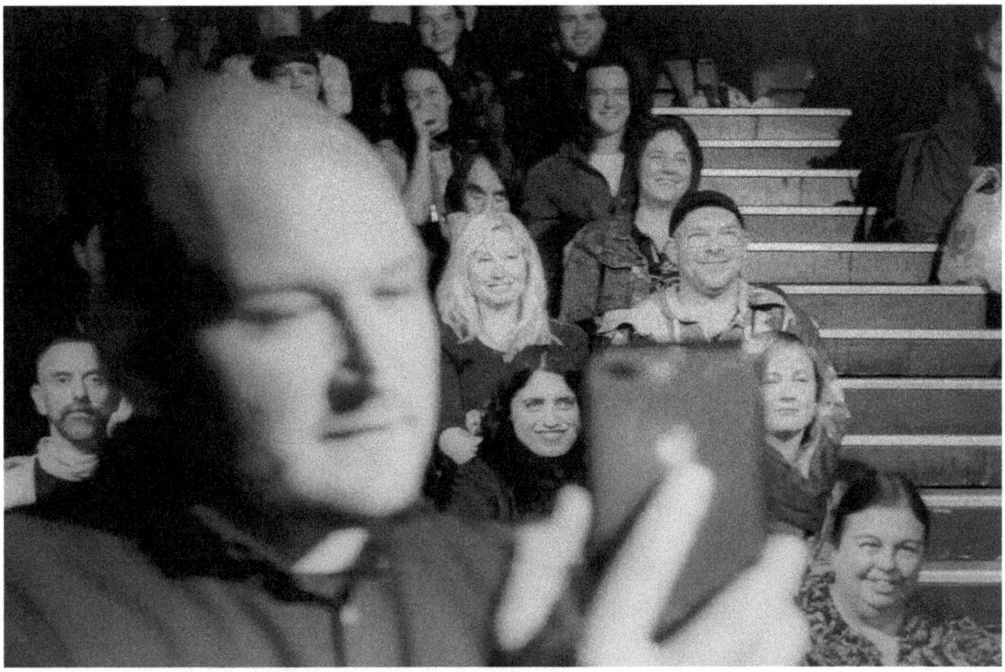

*Figure 32.3* Performance *Audience/Performer/Lens (After Dan Graham)* (2018). Photo credit: Emile Zile

Yes, it could also be an interesting networked play on Lucier's sound art piece *I Am Sitting in a Room* (1969). What's important to you about re-performing art from the 1970s era?

I am talking in highly simplified terms to say that the 1970s were a moment of return to the body, the self, and individual after the failure of 1968 and radical social movements. The return to the body in the seventies coincided with a growth in new-age spirituality, aerobics, and personal development. The nature of always-on networking in the present time, the cheapness and availability of powerful mobile computing and the failure of anti-globalization movements such as Seattle in 1999, S11 in Melbourne with the collapse of the future brought on by the New York terror attacks in 2001, and subsequent unending wars have led to this present moment where an interest in personal subjectivity accelerated by technology is prevalent. Political impact is impossible, so we go inside. It is no coincidence that psychedelic experimentation such as the use of DMT/Ayahuasca or LSD micro dosing is appealing to people as a proactive and protective strike against semio-capital, which encroaches on the imagination in deep and profound ways.

The implosion of humanity becomes a new form of Artivism in a way. So, where to now? What excites you about the future of mobile media art and are there any new works developing in the horizon?

Akin to an addict, I am always situated between submission and removal. Between being submerged and dry land. I let the codes and language of mobile media wash around me, finding excruciating moments of life framed in new ways. I remove myself again, delete accounts, dislodge apps in a futile attempt to salvage my attention span. Moments break free and exist as memories, then return to be incorporated as notes toward an artwork.

Presently, I am working with dancer Lilian Steiner[11] on a new traditionally staged dance work that explores political speech, political dress, gesture, and folk tradition. Within it, I am activating my entire body and extending from hand gesture to full body movement. Working with dancers is a consistent pleasure and offers innumerable insights, often in the downtime away from the rehearsal room. They are inevitably, exquisitely conscious of their bodies at all times. A return to the body is imminent.

Fantastic. The body as media in all its mobility... Thanks Emile.

## Notes

1 https://emilezile.com/about.
2 See www.warrenneidich.com/.
3 See https://emilezile.com/selected-work/larry-emdurs-suit.
4 See www.realtimearts.net/article/issue73/8104.
5 www.gansterer.org/translectures/.
6 https://libcom.org/book/export/html/45057.
7 https://emilezile.com/selected-work/i-follow-yoko-and-yoko-follows-me.
8 Axel Bruns, *Blogs, Wikipedia, Second Life, and Beyond: From Production to Produsage* (New York: Peter Lang, 2008).
9 www.artsy.net/artwork/yoko-ono-apple.
10 https://emilezile.com/selected-work/performer-audience-lens.
11 www.liliansteiner.com/about.

# SECTION EIGHT

# Performing the Mobile

# 33
# COLLECTIVE CHAOS AND JOYFUL MOBILITY

*Charlie Todd* in Conversation with *Klare Lanson*

Improv Everywhere is a New York City-based comedy performance collective created by Charlie Todd and operating since 2001. Over the years they have staged over 150 unexpected performance "missions" and public art projects in urban public places, often surprising audiences with what they define as "positive pranks." Situated within the realm of *détournement* and employing methods of instruction, these performative jokesters' experiment with the mobility of mundane city life, often utilizing the mobile phone to creatively hijack public space. The collective has successfully energized thousands of performance art special agents to cause hysterical scenes of chaos and feelings of well-being throughout the everyday of the city-scape (Figure 33.1).

Improv Everywhere is a bit of an institution in terms of a collective approach to improvisation, live performance and technology use. How do you define mobile media art in relation smartphone use within your projects, and what for you are some of the defining moments for mobile media art?

It's interesting because Improv Everywhere started in 2001—long before the smartphone. I had only owned a cell phone for 1 month before starting the collective. Therefore, the mobile phone did not play much of a role in our work in the very early years, instead we were focused on public art works that connected in both funny and inclusive ways. As technology has evolved over the years, it has inspired many of our projects.

In 2006, I realized that nearly everyone had a cell phone from one of a few major brands (Samsung, Nokia, and Motorola) and that these phones all had stock ringtones. So, in 2006, I created a project called *Cell Phone Symphony* where 50 people placed their cell phones inside backpacks and entered The Strand bookstore in Manhattan that had an enforced bag check policy.[1] So these 50 bags were hanging out by the register with phones inside, and then I had 50 other people out in the park start calling them simultaneously. We "conducted" this orchestra of phones by calling different phone brands at different times. "OK, now let's call the Motorola group!" We got kicked out of the store, but not before eliciting some incredible reactions from employees and customers.

After publishing this project, people started sending me links to Golan Levin's *Dial Tones* project from 2001, which similarly created orchestrated music out of ring tones.[2] I think this era of the early to mid-2000s was a defining moment where cell phone ownership had reached a saturation point and suddenly you could rely on nearly everyone having this tool in their pockets. And that's what phones are—a tool. A mobile tool that can be used to create art, comedy, and participatory experiences for all of us.

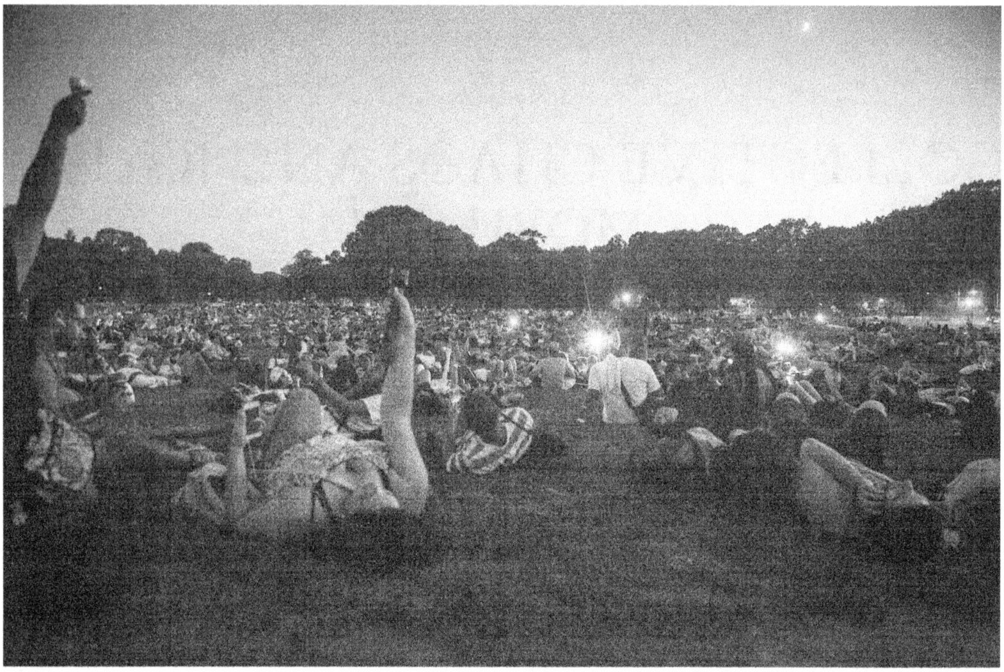

*Figure 33.1* Improv Everywhere, *Mp3 Experiment 12* (2012). Photo credit: Arin Sang-urai

Another defining moment for mobile media art was the iPod. In 2004, the iPod reached a similar saturation point. Almost everyone had an iPod or comparable mp3 player. All of a sudden you could be on a subway car and look around and everyone around you had white headphones on. This inspired us to create the *Mp3 Experiment* (2004), an interactive participatory project where large crowds of people collectively listen and respond to the same mp3 file at the same time.[3] That project has been happening annually ever since, and it's been fascinating to see how it's evolved with technology.

In the early days you needed to download an mp3 file to your computer and transfer it to your iPod. Back then you needed to wear a watch to synchronize time (flip phone clocks were not always in sync). And you'd need to bring your digital camera if you wanted to document it. Now all you need is your smartphone and our app. Instead of three devices in your pocket and a watch on your wrist, you just need one.

> The *Mp3 Experiment* is a successful project, now in its 15th year and counting (see Figure 33.1), what exactly do the participants listen to, how interactive is it? How did the project change over the years?

The *Mp3 Experiment* is 100% interactive. It was actually originally developed as a stage show at the Upright Citizens Brigade Theatre, a comedy theater in New York. The idea was to create a show that had no performers. The audience members were the only performers. There was a countdown clock projected onto a screen and when it got to zero, everyone pressed play on their mobile device. One of the first instructions was for everyone to leave their seats and get on stage. The audio file is a mix of original music and a narrator telling people what to do. So, we had people do simple, fun things. Dancing, blowing bubbles, hitting balloons in the air.

At the end of the show, the narrator asked people to go outside to meet a special guest. An actor dressed as Santa Claus met everyone on the street and handed out candy. I realized that people out in public made it much more provocative because it had the added element of other people not understanding what was happening and reacting, which, in turn, had an interesting impact on the performance itself. All subsequent experiments have been outdoors in public spaces.

> Social participation is a method that can be difficult to roll out, do you consider this method to democratize the art making process, and could you speak to how this may change the final project outcome?

Our projects have always been participatory from the start, so it's hard for me to answer this with nothing to compare it to. Over the years we've really come to value the unexpected element participation brings to our ideas. We design things in a specifically open-ended way so we can account for the unexpected (Figure 33.2).

> The nostalgic connections made between the blur of private/public, work and the defunct space of the phone box in *Phone Box Coworking* (2018) is funny, also ecologically important, in terms of using recycling strategies when designing space for future urban planning. Could you expand on this project when thinking about the mobility of work, labor, and its shift due to mobile technology?

I hate phone booths. In New York, there are still about eight thousand phone booths on the streets, and almost no one uses them. They take up valuable real estate on our crowded sidewalks for no reason other than to house outdoor advertising, a blight on our streets. So, we wanted to do something with these useless structures and make them more useful for a day. By the way, their

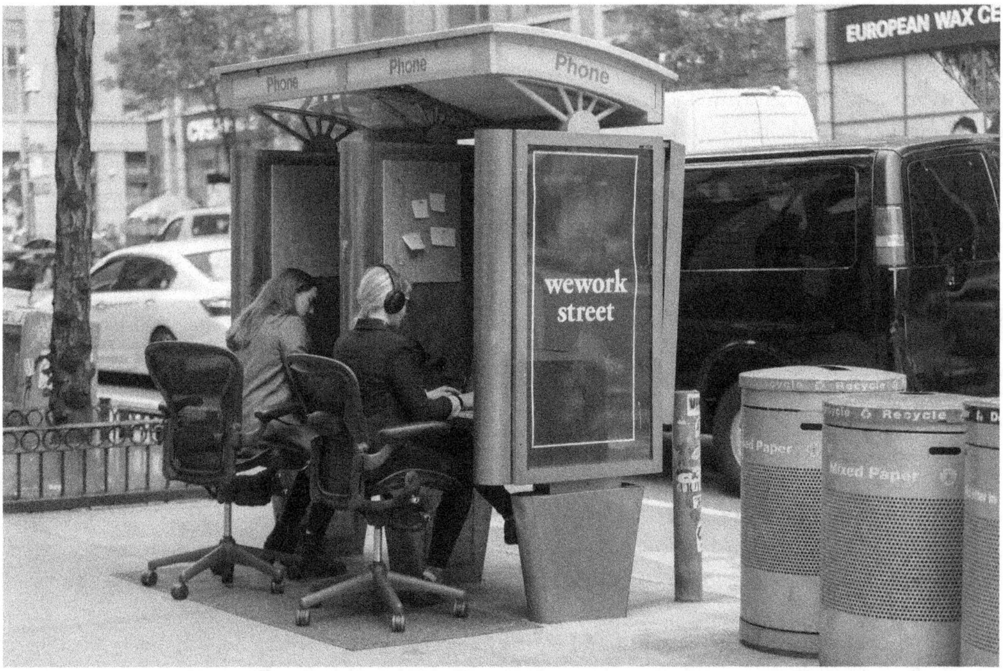


*Figure 33.2* Improv Everywhere, *Phone Box Coworking* (2018). Photo credit: Arin Sang-urai

replacements, the LinkNYC Wi-Fi kiosks are better in some ways as they provide fast Wi-Fi and free VoIP calling, but their bright video advertisements feel like pop up ads—and are even tackier. In terms of the co-working component and the satire of We Work, we wanted to poke fun at how coworking has exploded in recent years. We Work is now the #1 real estate tenant in New York City.[4] It's a little out of control. It's also interesting how the concept of an office has gone completely mobile. With our phones and our laptops, we really can truly work anywhere.

Mobile technologies have definitely changed our experience of work and how we play. We've been listening to music on the move for a while now, via the ghetto blaster and the Walkman stemming back from the late 1970s. *The Giant Boombox* project steps sideways from your usual impro work. It highlights how over time we develop the ways we listen, hear, and experience the city physically. Thoughts?

One thing that makes *The Giant Boombox*[5] so alluring to the public is that while these days you very rarely encounter a "boombox," everyone instantly knows what it is and how to work it, which I find fascinating, a weird innate behavior related to technology, especially the young kids. As all things have transitioned to the digital space, there is a kind of universal love and nostalgia for the old analog tools. You see these tools represented as icons for smartphone apps all the time. They have become the shorthand for technology even though no one uses them in real life. So, it was fun to work with an 18-feet wide boombox and celebrate it in a way.

Indeed, audiences wouldn't have needed to use an Instagram filter when sharing photos of that artwork! How do you think mobile media art shifts audience engagement and public encounters? It doesn't have to be about the smartphone, in fact *No Pants Subway Ride (2002)* amplifies aspects of playful performance work that highlights diversity and difference. Or is it just about having fun with the "mobile public?"

Improv Everywhere was created primarily as a vehicle for fun. I wanted to bring fun, excitement and surprising things to public spaces. I remember sitting on the subway commuting to and from work every day and thinking about all of the interesting people connected by proximity but who shared no real connection. I got really excited about the idea of causing undercover "scenes" that would give people a chance to connect over a shared experience. Typically, these types of shared experiences on public transportation or in other public spaces are a negative one. You commiserate with a fellow passenger when there is a delay, for example. I wanted to see if we could create experiences that were positive in nature that would still break through and cause people to connect.

Who are some of the most exciting practitioners in the field and why?

I'm a fan of Ji Lee's *Bubble Project* (2002–) from many years ago, where he essentially hacked public advertising with blank speech bubble stickers.[6] I'm not sure if it qualifies as mobile media art or not, but it was a very clever way to initiate a dialog with random strangers in public spaces. I'm also a big fan of Steve Lambert and his creative activism projects. His work prompts incidental conversation between strangers. His *Capitalism Works for Me True/False* (2011) project is a great example of this, where he offers members of the public a very simple binary choice, but in doing so it sparks dialog. It provides an accessible way to think about Capitalism while moving through the city.[7]

Yes, Steve Lambert mashes art and activism very well. I also love the way Ji Lee re-appropriates famous paintings with mobile technology in his *If it were Today* project.[8] Do you see artist-as-activist as an important role for Improv Everywhere and mobile media art?

I've steered clear from mixing activism and Improv Everywhere. On a personal level though, I've been involved in activism campaigns over the years. I played a small part in the *Fake New York Times* project put on by The Yes Men and Steve Lambert back in 2008.[9] I've also been part of some direction action events for the safe streets' activists Transportation Alternatives.[10] I think creativity and humor are key ingredients that are often missing in activism. They are effective tools to getting a message seen and heard, and more importantly remembered. Improv Everywhere has been largely apolitical, maybe that's why we've been around so long. We focus on comedy for comedy's sake, though sometimes my personal opinions on public space can't help but seep through...

How could they not? So, Charlie, what does the future bring for Improv Everywhere?

Last year we shot a 12-episode series with Pixar. It's called *Pixar In Real Life*, and it involves us bringing elements from Pixar films to life in unexpected places around New York. It's being released over the course of this year on the Disney+ platform. In the meantime, I'm waiting for it to be safe for crowds to gather in public again. I'm also starting work on the next *Mp3 Experiment*, which should happen next summer.

## Notes

1 See https://improveverywhere.com/2006/02/18/cell-phone-symphony/.
2 For more on *Dial Tones*, see Golan Levin's interview in the first section of this book.
3 See https://improveverywhere.com/2018/06/28/the-mp3-experiment-fifteen/ for the latest iteration.
4 See https://www.wework.com/l/new-york-city—NY.
5 See https://improveverywhere.com/2018/12/17/the-giant-boombox/.
6 More info on Ji Lee's *Bubble Project* can be found at https://pleaseenjoy.com/#/bubble-project/.
7 See Steve Lambert's project at https://visitsteve.com/made/capitalism-works-for-me-truefalse/.
8 See https://pleaseenjoy.com/if-it-were-today/.
9 www.theyesmen.org/tags/new-york-times.
10 https://www.transalt.org/.

# 34

# MOBILE FILMS AS MOBILE ART

## More than Textual

*Marsha Berry*

My discussion of mobile media art and creative practices involved in the making of mobile art is filtered through the lens of non-representational theory. Non-representational theory in essence is concerned with the background, the often invisible and slippery aspects of the enacted: the embodied, animate, and dynamic dimensions how we do things in our lifeworlds.[1] The more than textual, more than representational, material, and corporeal experiences are important to how we imagine and theorize creative art making practices with mobile media. I am concerned to address how we can better understand the dynamic processes and actions associated with creating films and video art works with smartphone assemblages, which themselves are constantly evolving due to the rapid advancement of technology.

In previous research on mobile media,[2] I issued a provocation to imagine a world without smartphones in order to highlight the extent to which smartphones are enmeshed in our everyday lives. This chapter develops this provocation further. Our use of social media is entangled in our everyday movements and routines to the extent where people in Australia are proposing legislation to fine people for looking at their smartphones if they are crossing a road.[3] The use of smartphones has visceral implications and consequences, some of which can be tragic. Smartphones, their use and the effects of their use are integral to our lifeworlds. Since their inception, a little over a decade ago, smartphone assemblages have inspired new and emergent forms and contexts for film and video art. Smartphones have given impetus to many creative impulses and have provided the means to make these expressions visible to a wide audience through social media.

This chapter is arranged into three sections—lifeworlds of mobile films, making stories, and creating and reflecting spaces through mobile art projects. Smartphones are deeply embedded in our lifeworlds made up of social interactions and physical and material environments. The first section provides a discussion of the lifeworlds of mobile films. The second section explores how stories are made in mobile media lifeworlds. The conditions of possibility for making stories are ever expanding in tandem with the changing our lifeworlds. Traditional ways of making stories through filmmaking have been disrupted through the development of mobile media interfaces and platforms. The third section interrogates the relationship between participatory cultures and how these can support mobile media art. Each section shares a common concern with the vitality, liveliness, and fluidity of mobile media.

I take a non-representational approach to filmmaking and video art, so that I can begin to account for the complex background aspects including mobility, emplaced visuality, and participation in order to theorize mobile media art. Through this approach we can observe how the internet's inherent logics around participation, sociability, and replicability[4] may provide people with easy access to audiences and the means of production to make mobile media art.

## The Lifeworlds of Mobile Films

The idea of a lifeworld presupposes the material, the physical, the embodied and the temporal. A lifeworld is dynamic and mobile through time and space, where places are never understood to be static. A lifeworld may be explained empirically and scientifically as well as experientially and socially. Edmund Husserl in the ground-breaking philosophical treatise *The Crisis of European Sciences and Transcendental Phenomenology*, explains that the "world exists as a temporal, spatio-temporal, world in which each thing has its bodily extension and duration and, again in respect to these, its position in universal time and space."[5] He further develops the idea of a lifeworld by placing ourselves within this world so that "we are ever conscious of the world in waking consciousness, as such it is valid as universal horizon."[6] The notion of a universal horizon carries within itself the possibility of relational aesthetics as propounded by Nicolas Bourriaud because the idea of a universal horizon lends itself to things and phenomena being open to intersubjective shared experiences and perceptions, which, in turn, are open to various representations and interpretations through social interactions.

The entanglements of smartphones and the everyday help shape our lifeworlds and expand the opportunities for creative practices and art making that draws on intersubjective experiences within collective everyday activities and interactions. Bourriaud has conceptualized these intersubjective and often collective experiences as relational aesthetics.[7] He describes how relational aesthetics come into play in contexts where the artist attempts to catch "the world on the move"[8] whereby each offering becomes a proposal to live in a shared world."[9] There are a plethora of mobile film works that self-consciously seek to draw on relational aesthetics emphasizing the intersubjective and the shared. I discuss some illustrative examples of such works later in this chapter.

Mobile media ecologies are part of our contemporary lifeworlds. Copresence now traverses time zones, geographic locations, and distance—relational aesthetics can frame and, in turn, be framed by these. Further, these, in turn, may become conditions of possibility for mobile media art projects. So, can mobile media art be theorized through mobile media interfaces being implicated in the process of making an artwork? Are mobile media artworks defined through participatory and social relations to either mobile media content or context? These two questions refer to things, processes and phenomena that lie in the background and in the lifeworld of an artwork rather than what it represents aesthetically. In her recent book, *New Directions in Mobile Media and Performance*, mobile media scholar Camille Baker[10] explores the liveliness of mobile media and notices that "mobile video has always been associated with an inherent embodied expressivity."[11]

Non-representational theory provides an interesting way to move beyond representation and its politics to better capture and understand the fluidity, vitality and liveliness of mobile media as well as mobile art making practices.

## Making and Performing Stories

Smartphones continue to disrupt traditional ways of making films and there are clear indications that mobile filmmaking is starting to become more and more acceptable to the mainstream. Indicators of this wider acceptance include the rise of film festivals (see, for example, Disposable Film Festival,[12] Cinephone International Smartphone Shortfilm Festival,[13] iPhone Film Festival,[14] Mobile Innovation Network Australasia Film Festival);[15] and the fact that films made on mobile devices are now included in prominent film festivals such as Sundance (for example, *Tangerine* was a hit at Sundance in 2015 and was shot on an iPhone 5S).[16]

Making stories in mobile media contexts is removed from traditional modes of filmmaking and broadcasting with their binaries of producer and consumer. Screen production, storytelling, and script development have far more informal and spontaneous relations than mainstream production processes in mobile interfaces and platforms. Filmmaking may take on both performance and performative qualities. Other indicators of these tendencies towards performance that sits in the background of mobile media are the popularity and evolution of episodic web series, now created for, distributed and enhanced through mobile platforms such as Instagram. Web series have been around since the mid- to late 1990s and really started to become a force in the 2000s.[17] Initially, web series were an alternative to mainstream screen production and broadcasting. Their attraction lay in that they were less expensive to produce and could be made available online rather than aired at specific times on specific network channels. They have provided fertile environments for innovative script development because they were not subject to the kinds of normative constraints and commercial imperatives of mainstream television.

In an interview about the second season of her popular web series *The Out There*, Hannah Lehman describes how she adapted standard script development to the very short form afforded by the Instagram platform. She said,

> I was forced to really strip back all of the dialogue and land only on the 'selected reality' (or moment in time) that would drive the story and characters forward in a way that an audience would still be able to understand.[18]

She goes on to discuss the processes involved in keeping takes under one minute which meant dialogue needed to be carefully considered from the performance perspective—"We had to time the takes to make sure they were coming in under a minute! On the day, we would sometimes strike dialogue that ended up being too long once the actors performed."[19] The delivery of the artwork here is an obvious constraint and is arguably shaping the emergent forms that web series are now taking.

Over the past decade or so, mobile media has completely changed our social, emotional and cultural cartographies in ways that we now take for granted. In his review of a decade of filmmaking with mobile devices, Max Schleser argues that the accessibility to filmmaking technology has clearly increased through the ubiquity of mobile phones and smartphones and that this, in turn, is "shaping not only new modes of film production but also modes of consumption, distribution, and exhibition, by embedding these digital stories in network media."[20] Schleser concludes his survey of mobile filmmaking saying that mobile devices have provided people in the twenty-first century with new opportunities to make cultural contributions in movie making and storytelling.

Filmmaking, video art, and photography have been pushed into terrains where the old ways of working are being challenged profoundly. The relations and interdependencies associated with mobile media assemblages and interfaces underpin the story-making practices of Adam Kossoff, an artist filmmaker. He suggests that the mobile phone "allows us to imagine that we are part of the flow of everyday life" and argues that mobile phones may now be seen as an "inherent part of the event, as theorized by Alain Badiou,"[21] where the event is tied to a *zeitgeist* or spirit of the times. He sees mobile phones as double-edged where they are both "an object of desire"[22] that can give us a type of agency in the world yet at the same time they are "a fetish that obscures us from the world."[23]

In his film, *Moscow Diary* (2011), Adam Kossoff revisits the streets and buildings in Moscow, which Walter Benjamin mentions in his famous diary from his visit to Moscow in 1926–1927. The film—shot on a mobile phone camera—engages with the modernist notion of a *flâneur* as an "urban wanderer who individualizes time and space by remaining outside of the metropolitan crowds and the cut and thrust of the city."[24] Kossoff's conceptual mobile art seeks to connect the past with the present through two sets of lived experience—he retraces Benjamin's steps and reflects on Benjamin's perceptions of the streets and buildings—both accounts focus on the dynamic flux of the lifeworld experienced. Kossoff's work has elements of auto-ethnography through the reflexive conversations his mobile art video has with thick descriptions of Moscow street life and culture documented in Benjamin's diary. Kossoff's complex lifeworld—where the past and the present fuse—become manifest through the vitality, liveliness and fluidity of mobile media.

Mobile interfaces and contexts also figure prominently in the filmmaking and story making of Leo Berkley—who started experimenting with mobile media in the early 2000s. His initial forays into mobile media art and filmmaking included making machinima to be viewed on mobile phone screens; however, what is pertinent here is his short film titled *57 Tram* (2013). This is a self-referential essay film that underlines the idea of mobility, experience, and presence. The story making in this film focusses on mobile media and smartphones as "portable and accessible motion picture technology"[25] to offer "a personal, reflective style of documentary filmmaking such as that modelled by the essay film."[26]

Berkley suggested that there were some similarities to amateur still photography in that his improvised shooting process on the number 57 tram in Melbourne was "impressionistic, opportunistic, and fragmented."[27] This similarity freed up his practice so that he took advantage of the emergent aesthetics of mobile phone cameras. He extended his practice into new directions where he was able to film moments that captured his attention. Yet, this very ability left him with a new dilemma that was "how to structure the mass of fragmented material collected in a way that conveyed the complexities of the lived experience while still being sufficiently coherent to interest the proposed audience."[28]

Berkeley rethought the implications of the accessibility of portable and potentially invisible movie cameras in the form of camera phones through the experience and process of shooting footage for the film. When he reflected on his unwillingness to document "the rowdy men who were almost always at the back of the tram,"[29] he touched upon a really interesting aspect of mobile media art that is becoming increasingly complex. This concerns the ethics of improvised filmmaking in public spaces. For him, the extreme accessibility of a mobile phone camera did not create the sense that "it was possible to film anything at any time"[30] but, rather, it led him to think deeply about whether or not to distort an experience by conforming to the traditional conventions of filmmaking, for example, to include dramatic action as a part of a narrative.

The mobile interface led to a new way of approaching story making for Berkeley. His *57 Tram* has the distinct voice of a lyrical essay, there are no turning points; rather, it is a sophisticated and nuanced unfolding of lived experience tracing the natural contours of the tram route and journey—deeply shaped by the mobile interface and context. The film is also an extension of his research into the possibilities of smartphones as a production device for filmmakers with limited resources and is an eloquent demonstration of how smartphones take filmmaking into new poetic forms such as the lyrical essay film.

Notions of mobility, performance, and the mobile interface itself also shape the work of video artist and scholar, Gerda Cammaer. Her travel film *Mobilarte* is another poetic example of how smartphones and iPads have shifted filmmaking and story making into new contexts creating new vernaculars[31] that engage with both the tropes and the corporeal dynamisms of mobility as conceived by Cresswell,[32] a human geographer who theorized mobility as three entwined threads—movement through the physical world, representations of movement and practice as an embodied phenomenon. Cammaer has extended the form and contexts for travel video with her film *Mobilarte.* The blurb on her Vimeo profile describes the film:

> Mobilarte is based on a video recording of a tuktuk ride through the city of Maputo (Mozambique) filmed on an iPad. The piece explores the particular qualities of iPad moving images (ghost frames, pixellation), as well as various ways to represent quick impressions and fleeting memories of life in Maputo. The video is edited following the workings of associative memory and change blindness, the fact that if movement and action remain constant, viewers don't perceive continuity errors in film. The sound is constructed by creating four different musical tones of short tuktuk sounds, which were each attributed to one of the national colors of Mozambique: yellow, green, red and black. The actual sound track is the result of applying a computer program to the image that scanned it for those four colors and translated this into music. The video has three parts that each have a different emotional character: Maputo Alto, Maputo Baixa and Maputo Praia.[33]

Cammaer's oeuvre embraces mobility and pushes the boundaries of filmmaking through poetic juxtapositions of visual and sonic imagery. She exploits the characteristics of video shot on mobile devices to emphasize aspects of mobility. A more recent work, *Kinetic Travel Memories #1,*[34] also shot with an iPad, plays with the new contexts of mobile media further and is described by Cammaer as

> an experiential representation of the experience watching both the view out of the window and the iPad's rendering of that view at once. The video is meant to evoke the sensation of speed and (cosy) displacement when traveling in this case by train.[35]

Cammaer's story making has a direct relationship with her networked mobile device—an iPad—and is conceptually informed by the Slow Media movement as articulated in the Slow Media Manifesto by David et al.[36]

Cammaer's autobiographical travel video has some strong resonances with the themes and tropes of Keep's mobile art exploring mobility. While her work is primarily concerned with travel stories using slow media aesthetics, Dean Keep is a mobile media artist researcher who over the past decade has been making short evocative stories that draw connections to places to create new spaces using mobile media. He has argued that the absence of established conventions "promotes a culture of creative experimentation and presents new ways to view our world."[37] The interplay of mobile technology and social practices native to camera phones is central to Keep's notion of a liquid aesthetic and his experimental video art.

In recent work, Keep has suggested that smartphones act as repositories for the ephemerality of everyday life and expands on how this feature informs his practice as a mobile media artist. His work *Decombres*[38] was made using material stored on his smartphone comprising video shot out of a train window capturing the countryside between Melbourne and Bendigo and text messages between himself and a friend. As an example of mobile media art, *Decombres* (2014) pushes documentary and film essay into poetic forms through the juxtapositions of material that sits within the memory archives of smartphones. He further experiments with this form in a work called *Remembering Hiroshima* (2016). In his research statement about the making of the story for this documentary (Figure 34.1), Keep proposes

> that the smartphone is more than a dynamic networked media tool, rather it is a 'digital *Wunderkammer*', a portable database to aid the storage and retrieval of captured moments that can be later used for the production of a wide range of documentary stories.[39]

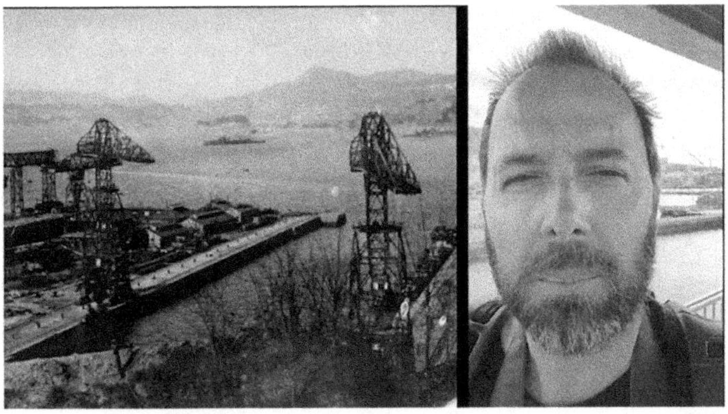

*Figure 34.1* Screenshot of *Remembering Hiroshima*. Photo credit: Dean Keep

## Creating Spaces with and for Mobile Media Art

Co-creation, co-design, and participatory culture provide the background for filmmakers and video artists creating mobile media art that seeks to produce new kinds of spaces for both making and exhibiting films and video art. Two examples of projects that take advantage of the participatory cultures associated with social media are Max Schleser's *24 Frames 24 Hours*,[40] and Iceberg Fernandez's *Now + Here = Everywhere*.[41] Both projects illustrate how social media participation serves as a source of inspiration for mobile media art that provides a way to socialize through emplaced visuality. Pink and Hjorth theorize such social phenomena as "a shift from networked visuality to emplaced visuality and sociality."[42] Briefly, emplaced visuality refers to a shared social practice whereby location-based services are in combination with smartphone camera applications to overlay images with a time and a place. Hjorth and Pink later expand this idea in relation to camera phone photography and locative media.[43] Anyone can easily observe networked and emplaced visualities on his or her social media timelines where people post, share and "like" each other's visual images. Each project is conceptually informed by participatory culture and social media. Schleser's project had an educational focus as well as a creative one. Fernandez's, on the other hand, engages with conceptual art and audience participation and plays with the notion of time zones and geographic locations being collapsed together through mobile media. Schleser aimed to capture life and a perception of place in different cities over a 24-hour period and then developed this further through a dynamic website.[44] Visitors were encouraged to contribute their work and are provided with a tutorial so they can access clips from parts of the world that interest them. Whereas Fernandez regularly invited mobile filmmakers to participate in a collaborative project using the social media platform Facebook[45] where they were asked to upload video shot at a specific time on a set date to her project website. In these two projects, mobile media interfaces as well as a participatory relationship where mobile lifeworlds performed through video clips provided a *raison d'etre*.

To further unfold how participatory culture can help understand mobile media art, I turn to the work of digital ethnographer Didem Özkul. If we take Özkul's framework[46] derived from Sheller and Urry's discussion of the mobilities turn,[47] we can begin to see how everyday smartphone usage increases our understandings of being present in a place and how they can create new spaces. In turn, this has a profound influence on mobile media art and related practice. Özkul draws on Sheller and Urry to shift how we understand mobile communication from its spatial organization to mobility itself "in a mobile world, where social life revolves around one's presence or absence, communication technologies, especially mobile modes of communication, gain fundamental importance in everyday life."[48]

As Özkul's asserts, mobile media "alter our experience of a place, not only because they are portable, but also because they provide a connected form of presence that can help their users establish new relationships and maintain old ones."[49] The illustrative examples presented above may be understood as manifestations of how mobile media art is defined through a participatory relationship to geographic place, where presence and place start to become altered through the spaces generated by Schleser and Fernandez for their respective film projects.

Creating spaces with mobile media is premised on

> the idea that there is value in standing at the site where an event took place; far more than simply reading about an event, being in the place where that event happened offers an experiential value that gives us a deeper sense of the story and the ways that story affects the meaning of the place.[50]

Also embedded in this idea is the proposition that "mobile media offer the possibility to layer multiple—even conflicting—stories onto a single space"[51] in a way that is simply not possible in non-digital forms.

In a recent book chapter discussing art making practices with mobile media, Jess Kilby and I[52] suggested that the ability to record the complex and subtle movements through everyday activities and routines changes the ways film and photography are conceived. Traditional media distribution and attendant power relationships have been disrupted through mobile media. New expressive potentials opened up as they wrestled with what networked copresence and virtual proximity could mean in and to everyday social activities and routines. Through their mobile media art making, they created spaces where they could interrogate what it means to be a digital wayfarer[53] in the second decade of the twenty-first century. We argued that our methods and methodologies using walking to make mobile art resulted in works that extend screen production into new and emergent forms.

As a digital wayfarer, Kilby created a game without rules between the city and herself by leaving small objects as interventions using her smartphone camera as an intermediary, while I sought to address new forms of screen production through my video poem, *Wayfarer's Trail*.[54] My process was inspired by Zen philosophy and walking meditation techniques drawn from yoga and meditation practice—I set my intention to simply walk and to notice my surroundings and sensations without any particular intention. I had my smartphone with me and used it to photograph and video things that caught my attention. I present a vignette of my method of wayfaring with my smartphone as an illustration of how mobile media interfaces shaped the processes and methods behind my mobile media art work (Figure 34.2):

> So many footprints on the path—human and animal—piping seagulls, a counterpoint to the restless sea. A perfect moment—I post photos of various details of sandy path on Instagram and Facebook with short evocative captions. A left-behind skirt flaps helplessly on the fence bordering the path. Backstories about how the skirt came to be there beckon enticingly, so I almost lose my place on the path … I sidestep the temptation and take a short video of it instead. I post it to Instagram and Facebook.
>
> I continue to shoot video with my smartphone while walking—posting the snippets to Instagram and Facebook—I work intuitively, intentionally without any specific intention other than to simply notice as much as possible whilst walking along a coastal trail. When my thoughts drift, I ground myself back into the present by listening to the sound of my footsteps on the downbeat—thunk, thunk, thunk.

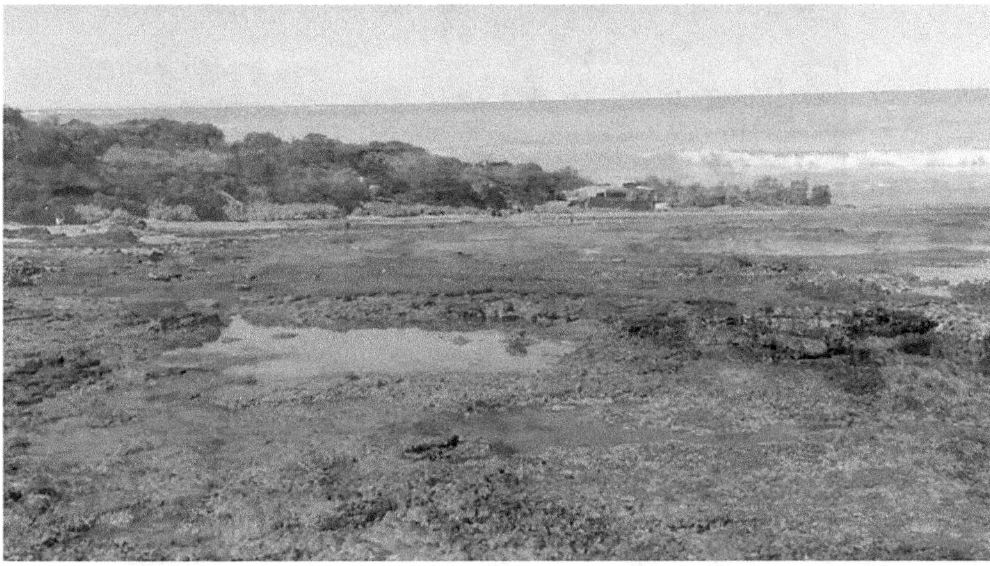

*Figure 34.2* Screenshot from *The Wayfarer's Trail*. Photo credit: Marsha Berry

> I check Facebook. The comments on my posts show me that people are with me; we are walking together, experiencing the coastal path. I notice that my interlocutors are pulling my images into a virtual trail of their own, but theirs is a narrative, a guided tour rather than a sequence of moments in the lifeworld of a coastal path. The seed for a film is sown.

Digital wayfaring also plays a part in Patrick Kelly's mobile media art. He used the mobile video-sharing platform Instagram to reflexively engage with his experiences while moving through Melbourne as a juxtaposition of moments. Kelly suggests the "portability and high-functionality of both the device and the platform mean that images can be captured promptly and inconspicuously, and therefore offer a more personal experience for the capturer"[55] so mobile filmmakers "might discover the emergence of even more contexts and auratic experiences."[56]

Smartphone camera apps enable artists to share any resulting moving images through social media with location-based overlays. This facility of mobile media generates new ways of communicating visually using smartphones and other networked mobile devices in our everyday social interactions. In a conversation about his film *Give Me Faces Give Me Streets*,[57] Kelly mentioned that his ideas for filmmaking were inspired by the idea of enacting and re-presenting emplaced visualities. The work is auto-ethnographic in that it uses lived experiences reflexively to engage with well-trodden path of the dichotomy between the urban and the rural.

The project itself arose out of collaboration between Kelly and another filmmaker Kelly Shanahan, where she challenged him to explore the urban/rural dichotomy through sound. He used his iPhone voice memo app to record and juxtapose sounds in the city and in the country. The country sounds include the crunch of footsteps on gravel and wind distortions. The city sounds include voices, traffic, and building construction. He then overlaid an audio track of himself reflecting on Walt Whitman's poem *Give me the Splendid, Silent Sun*. Kelly recorded the visual material using Google Street View within the Google app on his smartphone. The work extends both the forms of mobile filmmaking and has created a new context for creative practices with smartphones. The film was selected through a double peer-review process for MINA, which

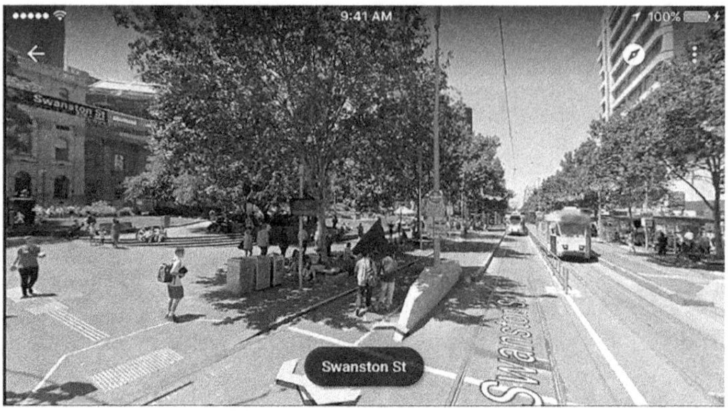


*Figure 34.3* Screenshot from *Give Me Faces, Give Me Streets* (2016). Photo credit: Patrick Kelly

showcased mobile filmmaking projects from around the world in Melbourne (Lido Cinemas, 1 December 2016) and Wellington (Ngā Taonga Sound & Vision, Te Anakura Whitiāhua, 1 December 2016; Figure 34.3).

The filmmaker and screenwriter, Bettina Frankham also uses juxtapositions as a conceptual frame for her own creative practice with smartphones. She describes this as *cinécriture* following Agnés Varda by saying that the "phone is my notebook, my mood board, the memory folder where I gather video, sound, still images and jottings of ideas, all to be worked further at a later date."[58] Frankham argues that the lines between writing for filmmaking and filmmaking itself become blurred when working with a smartphone. Rather than writing being something that happens away from the filmmaking process, making videos can instead become a way of writing or composing a script. The contrasts and connections that occur through the search algorithms in data storage systems such as the cloud or in content folders have become integral to Frankham's creative practice. She concludes her argument for the need to rethink writing for screen works because "literacy in these new territories of creative practice enables a considered and deliberate approach to forms of interhuman and human/algorithm collaboration."[59]

## Conclusion

I commenced this chapter advocating a non-representational theory approach to filmmaking as mobile art. The appeal of everyday occurrences is manifested on our social media timelines and reflected in much of the material we post. Locative, mobile, and social media have converged to form a universal horizon[60] within which we enact creative, communicative, and social impulses.

Returning to the questions I proposed at the beginning of this chapter, I conclude that non-representational theory with its focus on the embodied, multisensory, and background phenomena has provided me with a useful way to examine the practices of several mobile filmmakers in order to address questions about what constitutes mobile media art, and its relation to participatory culture and platforms or affordances. Non-representational theory provides a way to theorize mobile media art that places attention on verbs rather than nouns—the process of the doing and the making of mobile media art rather than what it represents as a cinema or static cultural studies object. By focussing on the actions and practices of the filmmakers in each of the previous, examples I have aimed to make visible the intrinsic relationships that foreground mobile media art, in particular relation to moving imagery and mobile filmmaking.

Furthermore, the techniques taken from non-representational theory with their focus on dynamic aspects offer practical as well as evocative ways for creative practitioner scholars to engage in conversations about how theory and practice inform each other to contribute and expand knowledge about mobile media art as a field of enquiry. New mobile media art will continue to emerge, and flourish that are inspired by creative vernaculars and nourished by the impulses and interplays between artists, writers, filmmakers, and photographers. New forms and genres of mobile media art will continue to evolve through creative actions and practices in response to hybrid screen ecologies that merge the physical and the digital, the material and the immaterial, the tangible and the intangible.

## Notes

1 Philip Vaninni, "Non-representational Ethnography: New Ways of Animating Lifeworlds," *Cultural Geographies* 22, no. 2 (2015): 317–27, doi: 10.1177/1474474014555657.
2 Marsha Berry, *Creating with Mobile Media* (New York: Palgrave Macmillan, 2018), xi.
3 Ella Donald, "It May Soon Be Illegal to Text and Walk in Australia," *Smith's Lawyers*, 10 October 2018, www.smithslawyers.com.au/post/it-may-soon-be-illegal-to-text-and-walk-in-australia.
4 Limor Shifman, "Humor in the Age of Digital Reproduction: Continuity and Change in Internet-based Comic Texts," *International Journal of Communication* 1 (2007): 187–209, https://ijoc.org/index.php/ijoc/article/viewFile/11/34.
5 Edmund Husserl, *The Crisis of European Sciences and Transcendental Phenomenology* (Evanston: Northwestern University Press, 1954 [1970]), 63.
6 Ibid.
7 Nicolas Bourriard, *Relational Aesthetics*, trans. Simon Pleasance and Fronza Woods (Dijon: Les presses du reel, 2002).
8 Ibid., 14.
9 Ibid., 15.
10 Camille Baker, *New Directions in Mobile Media and Performance* (London; New York: Routledge, 2019).
11 Ibid, 4.
12 Disposable Film Festival, https://en.wikipedia.org/wiki/Disposable_Film_Festival.
13 Cinephone International Smartphone Short Film Festival, https://worldfilmfair.com/screening/cinephone-international-smartphone-short-film-festival.
14 iPhone Film Festival, https://iphoneff.com.
15 Mobile Innovation Network Australasia Film Festival, https://mina.pro.
16 Casey Newton, "How One of the Best Films at Sundance Was Shot Using an iPhone 5S," *The Verge*, 28 January 2015, www.theverge.com/2015/1/28/7925023/sundance-film-festival-2015-tangerine-iphone-5s.
17 Alec McNaryr and Robert Gustafson, "A Brief History of the Web Series," 12 August 2010, www.scriptmag.com/news/a-brief-history-of-the-web-series.
18 Hannah Lehman in Liz Nord, "Instagram Series Are a Thing Now—Meet One of the First Creators," No Film School, 21 June 2018, https://nofilmschool.com/2018/06/instagram-series-are-thing-now-meet-one-first-creators.
19 Ibid., n.p.
20 Max Schleser, "A Decade of Mobile Moving-Image Practice," in *The Routledge Companion to Mobile Media*, edited by Gerard Goggin and Larissa Hjorth (London: Routledge 2014), 155.
21 Adam Kossoff, "The Mobile Phone and the Flow of Things," in *Mobile Media Making in an Age of Smartphones*, edited by Marsha Berry and Max Schleser (New York: Palgrave Macmillan 2014), 35–44.
22 Ibid., 43.
23 Ibid.
24 Ibid., 39.
25 Leo Berkeley, "Tram Travels: Smartphone Video Production and the Essay Film," in *Mobile Media Making in an Age of Smartphones*, edited Marsha Berry and Max Schleser (New York: Palgrave Macmillan 2014), 27.
26 Ibid.
27 Ibid., 30.
28 Ibid., 31.

29 Ibid., 32.
30 Ibid.
31 Jean Burgess, "Hearing Ordinary Voices: Cultural Studies, Vernacular Creativity and Digital Storytelling," *Continuum: Journal of Media & Cultural Studies* 20, no. 2 (2006): 201–14, doi: 10.1080/10304310600641737.
32 Tim Cresswell, "Towards a Politics of Mobility," *Environment and Planning D: Society and Space* 28, no. 1 (2010): 17–31, doi: 10.1068/d11407.
33 Gerda Cammaer, *Mobilarte*, Mobile Film, http://gerdacammaer.com/?myportfoliotype=mobilarte).
34 Gerda Cammaer, *Kinetic Travel Memories #1*, Mobile Film, https://vimeo.com/181436263?from=outro-embed.
35 Ibid.
36 Gerda Cammaer, "Creating an Experiential Narrative: The Making of *Mobilarte*," in *Mobile Story Making in an Age of Smartphones*, edited by Max Schleser and Marsha Berry (New York: Palgrave Macmillan 2018), 94.
37 Dean Keep, "Artist with a Camera-Phone: A Decade of Mobile Photography," in *Mobile Media Making in an Age of Smartphones*, edited by Marsha Berry and Max Schleser (New York: Palgrave Macmillan 2014), 19.
38 Dean Keep, "Smartphones and Evocative Documentary Practices," in *Mobile Story Making in an Age of Smartphones*, edited by Max Schleser and Marsha Berry (New York: Palgrave Macmillan, 2018).
39 Dean Keep, "Remembering Hiroshima," *Sightlines Journal*, 2 (2017): n.p. www.aspera.org.au/research/remembering-hiroshima/.
40 Max Schleser and Tim Turnbridge, "24 Frames 24 Hours," *Ubiquity: The Journal of Pervasive Media* 2, no. 1–2 (2013): 205–13, doi: 10.1386/ubiq.2.1-2.205_1.
41 Iceberg Fernandez, *Now + Here = Everywhere*. Mobile film, 2013, www.now-here-everywhere.org.uk.
42 Sarah Pink and Larissa Hjorth, "Emplaced Cartographies: Reconceptualising Camera Phone Practices in an Age of Locative Media," *Media International Australia* 145 (2012): 145–55, 145.
43 Larissa Hjorth and Sara Pink, "New Visualities and the Digital Wayfarer: Reconceptualizing Camera Phone Photography and Locative Media," *Mobile Media & Communication* 2, no. 1 (2014): 40–57, doi: 10.1177/2050157913505257.
44 Max Schleser, *24 Frames 24 Hours,* Mobile documentary, www.24frames24hours.org.nz.
45 Fernandez, *Now + Here = Everywhere.*
46 Didem Özkul, "Placing Mobile Ethnography: Mobile Communication as a Practice of Place Making," in *The Routledge Companion to Digital Ethnography*, edited by Larissa Hjorth, Heather Horst, Genevieve Bell, and Anne Galloway (London; New York: Routledge 2017), 221–31.
47 Mimi Sheller and John Urry, "The New Mobilities Paradigm," *Environment and Planning A* 38 no. 2 (2006), 207–26, doi: 10.1068/a37268.
48 Özkul, "Placing Mobile Ethnography," 222.
49 Ibid., 230.
50 Jason Farman ed., *The Mobile Story: Narrative Practices with Locative Technologies* (New York: Routledge 2014), 7.
51 Ibid., 8.
52 Jess Kilby and Marsha Berry, "Wayfaring, Creating and Performing with Smartphones," in *Mobile Story Making in an Age of Smartphones*, edited by Max Schleser and Marsha Berry (New York: Palgrave Macmillan 2018), 42–51.
53 Larissa Hjorth and Sarah Pink. "New Visualities and the Digital Wayfarer: Reconceptualizing Camera Phone Photography and Locative Media," *Mobile Media & Communication* 2, no. 1 (2014): 40–57, doi: 10.1177/2050157913505257.
54 Marsha Berry, "Wayfarer's Trail," *Sightlines Journal* 2 (2017): n.p., www.aspera.org.au/research/wayfarers-trail/.
55 Patrick Kelly, "Slow Media Creation and the Rise of Instagram," in *Mobile Media Making in an Age of Smartphones*, edited by Marsha Berry and Max Schleser (New York: Palgrave Macmillan 2014), 135.
56 Ibid., 136.
57 Patrick Kelly, *Give Me Faces Give Me Streets*, 2016, https://vimeo.com/168155426.
58 Bettina Frankham, "Writing with the Small, Smart Screen: Mobile Phones, Automated Editing and Holding on to Creative Agency," *Journal of Writing in Creative Practice* 9, no. 1–2 (2016): 50, doi: 10.1386/jwcp.9.1-2.47_1.
59 Ibid., 55.
60 Husserl, *The Crisis of European Sciences.*

# 35
# *MOBILE CINEMATIC VR*—MCVR

*Max Schleser*

While the idea of VR is not new and has been surfacing since the 1990s, accessible omnidirectional video cameras that integrate with standard video production workflows launched in 2016. One of the new VR enterprises is Humaneyes, who believes that virtual reality will "become a major communication platform in a 'VR echo system.'"[1] Beyond online viewing experiences, film festivals, independent exhibition, and art spaces are adjusting to the 360° and cinematic VR domain. VR can be created in entirely digital environments ranging from computer-generated imagery (CGI) in animations to games to *Mobile Cinematic VR,* where the focus is on live action and 360° videos. As there are a number of different interpretations and understandings of what Virtual Reality (VR) is, this chapter will define cinematic VR as a VR/360° video camera that can be operated or synced via mobile apps or are add-on cameras onto the smartphone itself. This chapter looks at small-scale VR cameras[2] that can be compared to mobile, smartphone, and pocket filmmaking's mobility and accessibility. By embracing these qualities and mobile specific media practices over technical video standards and camera resolution choices, MCVR reveals one of the possible creative futures of smartphone filmmaking. The innovative element is twofold: it includes the participatory element of mobile media art and gives independent filmmakers and anyone with a smartphone[3] and a 360° video camera the opportunity to create stories and experiences. Furthermore, this chapter links early mobile media art aesthetics[4] to the realm of MCVR and mobile media art more generally.

This chapter explores *Mobile Cinematic VR* (MCVR) in the context of mobile art and examines the directions that this dynamic field is taking. In an MCVR environment, viewers are performing the mobile. *Mobile Cinematic VR—MCVR* creates synergies between the aesthetics of mobile media art[5] and MCVR. In 2018, the *SF3 Smartphone Flicks Fest*[6] in Sydney and the *8th International Mobile Innovation Screening*[7] in Melbourne introduced *mobile cinematic VR* categories and showcases to their festivals. SF3 finalists *Vega Island*[8] and *[Mynd] Journey*[9] premiered at the Sydney Opera House. At MINA *Before I Sleep,*[10] *PND,*[11] *A Little Negor Boy's Prayer,*[12] and *Interwoven: Veganism, Ethics, Economics*[13] were featured as part of the longest running mobile and smartphone film festival with a focus on mobile (moving-image) art internationally. This chapter discusses MCVR projects in the context of mobile media art and explores the relationship between mobile, pocket, and smartphone filmmaking's specific qualities and MCVR's emerging characteristics. *Mobile Cinematic VR—MCVR* outlines intimacy, presence, and imaginative encounters as key considerations and characteristics for MCVR.

A proliferation of scholarship re-engaged with this new cinematic form and format—including Rose (2018),[14] Nash (2018),[15] McRoberts (2017),[16] and Ross (2018)[17] among others.[18] In addition, there are a number of industry-led investigations such as *Storyliving* by Google News Lab[19] or research labs engaging in this domain such as Columbia Journalism Review,[20] MIT Open Doc Labs *Virtually There*[21] conference, or *Virtual Realities Immersive Documentary Encounters*[22] research project. While all of these initiatives bring very relevant work to this emerging field, one gap appears in the form of MCVR.[23] Furthermore, the context of creative arts and mobile media arts is not well represented. Bucher's *Storytelling for Virtual Reality* (2017)[24] only very briefly references "Experimental Art Installations" as a storytelling principle for Immersive Space, and *Virtual Reality Filmmaking* (2016)[25] provides a summary of the alternative approaches to VR through immersive theater, dance, or sculpture. This chapter will explore Cinematic VR in the context of mobile art, with a particular focus on experimental mobile, pocket, and smartphone filmmaking as well as mobile moving-image arts.[26]

## Cinematic VR

When Cinematic VR appeared on the horizon of the mediascape in early 2016, Werner Herzog was quite critical of this new cinematic form, stating in a *New Yorker* interview, "in this case, we do have a technology, but we don't have any clear idea how to fill it with content."[27] In the same year, a number of leading film festivals started to display and exhibit VR dedicated cinematic programs.[28] In addition, a number of new festivals with dedicated Cinematic VR programs were established internationally.[29] While Herzog's criticism is understandable for someone who has produced an extensive list of feature works,[30] there are only few VR pioneers who engaged in Cinematic VR and 360° video production. Here, one could point at the work for Jessica Brillhart for the Google VR Team. As one of the early cinematic VR works in 2015, Brillhart and her team used a 16-camera live-action virtual reality rig and workflow now known as Google Jump.[31] Her work *Deep Dream* (2016)[32] in partnership with AMI[33] explored the imaginative experimental capacities of experimental film and video. Another filmmaker that is often cited in the context of Cinematic VR is Chris Milk. In 2013, he created a 360° interactive video of Beck's performance of 'Sound and Vision.'[34] More recently, he demonstrated the capacity for creative enterprise and immersive entertainment as CEO and founder of the VR platform Vrse in 2014, which re-launched as Within in 2015 or the virtual reality production companies as Here Be Dragons (formerly Vrse.works).

These early Cinematic VR works required a quite sophisticated technical workflow. Following the introduction of the Nokia Ozu 360° video camera in the end of 2015, a number of omnidirectional video cameras appeared on the market that integrate with smartphones in one way or another, as previously mentioned.[35] Simultaneously, the leading video platforms YouTube,[36] Vimeo,[37] and Facebook[38] integrated 360° videos. With the launch of Adobe Premiere Pro CC 2017,[39] 360° videos and cinematic VR could be edited in standard production workflows. Prior to this integrated production process, 360° video production cameras required a complex workflow including custom-made rigs for GoPro cameras and dedicated video stitching software (such as Autopano giga, VideoStitch, or the open source software PTGui Pro). Now a number of 360° video cameras can be synched, attached to, or are even integrated with smartphones.[40] Next to the creative filmmaking process, which is exemplified through the works discussed later in this chapter that screened at SF3 and MINA, the dissemination via head-mounted displays (HMDs) links smartphones to VR.

HMD headsets are available for all budgets, ranging from Google Cardboard paper folding VR headsets to Samsung's Gear VR[41] or Google's Daydream,[42] which makes VR accessible to anyone with a smartphone. "Google Cardboard (or Oculus Thrift as it is affectionately called) has ushered in the democratisation of VR filmmaking."[43] When using a VR headset, viewers need to perform movements in order to view the entire film scale or panoramic view. Proprioception, the awareness of one's body in space, is central to a cinematic VR experience. In *Mobile Cinematics*, Enberg and Bolter argue that proprioception contributes strongly to the sense of immersion and presence (Figure 35.1).[44]

*Figure 35.1* Cardboard VR at the #MINA2018 MCVR showcase (www.mina.pro). Photo credit: Mobile Innovation Network & Association

## *Mobile Cinematic VR*

The 69th Berlinale (2018) featured two smartphone feature film productions in its program,[45] and Hollywood *Unsane*[46] premiered smartphone filmmaking in the world of the blockbusters. In 2015, *Tangerine*[47] gained substantial attention at independent film festivals such as Sundance. Mobile artists and smartphone filmmakers have paved the way for the contemporary understanding of mobile, pocket, and smartphone filmmaking. A number of publications have outlined this development and discussed mobile filmmaking from a number of different viewpoints. *A Decade of Mobile Moving-Image Practice* outlines how mobile filmmaking evolved from the "underground" and "art-house" into an egalitarian moving-image practice.[48] *Making Films and Video Art with Smartphones*[49] explores evolving practices, emerging forms and changing contexts of this dynamic form of mobile media art. In particular, *Mobile Aesthetics and Criticism* points out that "many of the new mobile creative practices merge, sample or hybridize particular forms, and have prompted scholars to assess whether a new aesthetic language may be needed in order to articulate these outputs."[50] This argument very much translates to the development of MCVR. While smartphone filmmaking is in the process of establishing itself as a film form, early creative practices bear a particular significance in understanding the developments in mobile art and in particular MCVR. The three qualities that characterize early mobile phone films and contemporary smartphone films are presence, intimacy, and imaginative encounters. These characteristics are also key considerations for MCVR.

## Presence

In *Vanishing Point: Spatial Composition and the Virtual Camera*, Jones investigates presence as a unique VR experience by explaining it through the a novel camera technique. In this (VR) logic, the camera no longer represents an authorial perspective. It does not communicate a story through the logic of "this is what happened." Instead it communicates in the present, "this is happening."[51] The experience of presence as communicated by a camera—and respectively the filmmaker—resembles similarities to established qualities of early mobile phone filmmaking that are still characteristic for contemporary smartphone films. The *Aesthetics of mobile media art* embraces presence. The aforementioned connection between camera technique and the captured experience at a certain location is key for mobile and smartphone filmmaking. The limitation of the camera phone or smartphone means that filmmakers need to be close to the action. The device's mobility can afford to capture these unique experiences (in a way this could not be achieved by broadcast or DSLR cameras):

> This aesthetic emphasises the importance of location, space and also non-space—*being here,* being anywhere, but here is where the phone is and not any fixed place, via immersion. The individuals' experience of the *space*, or *state* of being is located within their own *bodies*. This is expressed as a haptic aesthetic, rooted in an embodied affectivity, manifested through gesture and movement of the device while documenting or "videoing" innate performativity or movement, which is afforded by the phones themselves.[52]

In a similar way VR films—therefore also MCVR films—are experienced by viewers through their decisions to engage with the work. Especially in interactive cinematic VR, viewers make choices while navigating and performing in the story space. Deniz Tortum defined this as "embodied montage," which creates new meanings through viewer's performance as a montage. The viewer presence and thus movement define the decision and also the meaning making process.[53]

## The Viewer as Performer in MCVR

While Saker and Frith argue that Mobile Virtual Reality (MVR) interrupts the established discourse on copresence[54] in the field of Mobile Communication Studies (MCS), I provide an alternative way to explore MVR and "a third stage of mobile media theory." I argue that the context of mobile media art with attention to the novel experience in the VR (story or dream) worlds (rather than the location of the VR experience) facilitates copresence[55, 56] in the mobile performance of the viewer. As a viewer in a MCVR experience, one is asked to perform a movement to engage with the (story or dream) world. Interactive VR, such as MCVR produced with WondaVR,[57] also enables choices for the viewer made via performance. With current developments toward location-based VR, which also implements performative elements in the space of the VR experience itself, the notion of immersion is further defined. For example, the MVCR work *[Mynd] Journey* asks viewers to lay down while experiencing the work, and the recent Cinematic VR work *Metro Veinte: Cita Ciega* requires viewers to sit in wheel chair.[58] This development in Cinematic VR and MCVR is in synch with the presented analysis of the intimate and phenomenological mobile aesthetic in Baker's *New Directions in Mobile Media and Performance.*[59]

## Intimacy

The notion of intimacy resonates in mobile media art and is also of key significance in MCVR. Baker notes that mobile media affordances encourage a high degree of intimacy due to the size of the smartphone, which

> encourages complexity and freedom, not to mention an uninhibited quality in what one can represent to others, with an immediacy and accessibility that enables participation and intimacy, as a sense of privacy, unlike other media production tools.[60]

This argument translates to and can be used to describe MCVR cameras, which as mentioned earlier are not much bigger than smartphones. The MVCR examples discussed later in the chapter will pin point to this specific notion of intimacy. The experimental MCVR works are characterized by a personal and private encounter. One element that highlights a drastic difference is the change from the close up or the super close up in mobile and smartphone filmmaking to the super long shot and panoramic video utilized in MCVR. Next to the production, the viewing

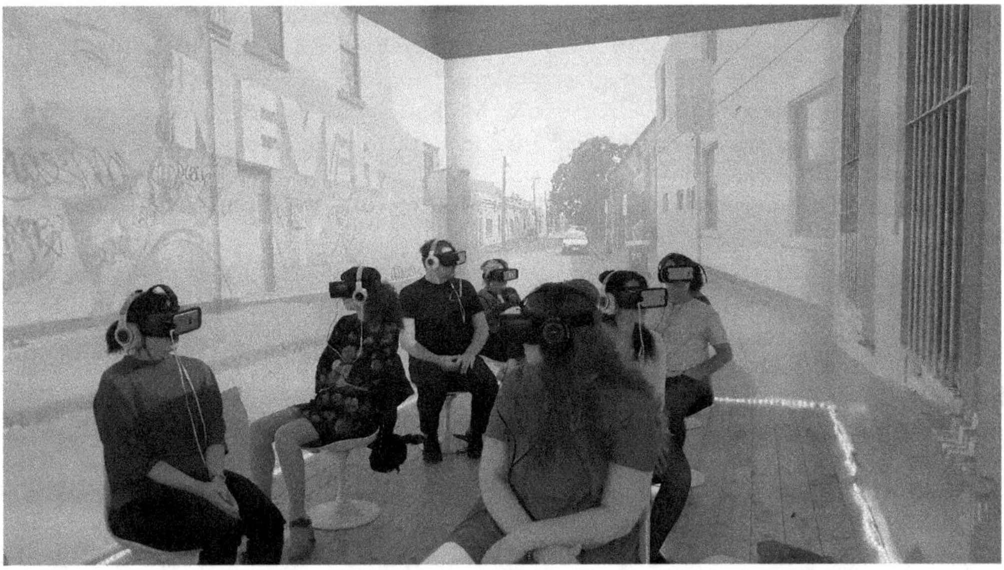

*Figure 35.2* Virtual Reality Cinema in Melbourne (Australia). Photo credit: Virtual Reality Cinema

experience also incorporates these qualities of mobile media. As aforementioned, Engberg and Bolter note that mobile VR is "intimate, close to the body, in a way that IMAX, or even conventional film or television viewing, clearly are not (Figure 35.2)."[61]

## Independent Art Space for VR

The *Virtual Reality Cinema*[62] in Melbourne is an independent space hosting events like *The Digital Underground Festival*,[63] the Virtual Reality Fringe Film Festival 2017, and cinematic VR works by independent VR filmmakers such as Lester Francois' *Rone*.[64] The Virtual Reality Cinema provides a space for filmmakers, artists, and viewers to discuss their experiences and facilitates a shared experience, very much like a cinema. The independent spaces and festivals such as SF3 and MINA are key for creatives to connect and for audiences to engage. With the increasing development of location-based VR, independent spaces and forums become even more significant. A successful VR experience is more similar to a Gallery visit than browsing a website. The locative aspect becomes part of the experience.

*Electric South* runs grassroots VR workshops, new dimensions VR labs, and VR hackathons in Africa.[65] Their 2017 program included productions on Afro-Futurism like *The Other Dakar* by Selly Raby Kane or *Spirit Robot* by Jonathan Dotse, and the 2018 program featured stories from Zimbabwean, Nigeria, and South Africa.[66] Electric South is run by Ingrid Kopp and Steven Markovitz, and their work opens up spaces for original voices and underrepresented narratives, allowing African VR filmmakers to have their work featured at Tribeca Film Festival, pitched at IDFA (International Documentary Film Festival Amsterdam) or Gap Financing Market at the Venice International Film Festival.

In the context of community engagement, the work of Empathic Media showcases how to engage communities through MCVR. In partnership with the European Journalism Centre, El Pais (Spain) and Die Zeit Online (Germany), Empathetic Media created *Schuften für fast nichts: Inside the Garment Industry in Bangladesh*, *La Paz en 360* (Peace in 360 Degrees), and *The Baltimore Sun: Inside a Home with 20 Code Violations*. In order to create a link to established theoretical frameworks, their MCVR projects can be characterized as following the observational and, with key significance to this chapter, the performative documentary mode.[67] Nichols defines the latter as affective and situated, which engages one through experiential encounters. One of the central characteristics of the observational mode that is relevant for MVR is the willingness to let audiences decide for themselves about what they see and hear[68] and focus their attention on. By placing a relatively small camera into factories, houses, dumps, streets, and various other locations, viewers are exploring several environments that they would otherwise most likely never encounter in a full panoramic or 360° view. MCVR's "noninterventional approach" and "unobtrusive recording" create a unique notion of presence in *Schuften für fast nichts: Inside the Garment Industry in Bangladesh*[69] and *The Baltimore Sun: Inside a Home with 20 Code Violations.*[70] In the case of *La Paz en 360,*[71] the performative element is even further established through the introduction of the protagonists Adriana and Numar in their Columbian villages. The autobiographical and "affect-laden" engagement of the viewer, in which one experiences the protagonists' environment in the Columbian conflict and reconciliation, is driven by the viewer's performance in the MCVR documentary.

Reports such as *Walking in another's virtual shoes: Do 360-degree video news stories generate empathy in viewers?*[72] confirm the creative choices of a narrator and/or protagonist to produce immersion in the form of engagement and empathy as affective creative strategies. Furthermore, the report by *Columbia Journalism Review* argues that "VR formats prompted a higher empathic response than static photo/text treatments"[73] and points out that "there is a negligible difference in perceived levels of interactivity between the head-mounted (HMD) and desktop-based virtual reality treatments."[74] Through focusing on the experimental and poetic domain, this research explores questions relating to imaginative spaces, similar to surreal experiences or memory scapes.

## Imaginative Encounters

While the area of MCVR is an emerging creative practice, one can position these works historically through experimental film and moving-image arts. In this context, one could explore the work of Maya Deren or Chris Maker as a precedent. *La Jetée*[75] intertwines the past, present, and future, where the prisoner/time traveler is witness to his own execution through the various shifts in temporality. If one considers the time traveler as a memory-traveler, the entire project is based in the present progressive or continuous time.[76] As a voice-over in *La Jetée* says, "nothing distinguishes memories from ordinary moments. It is only the later that they claim remembrance. By their scars," the time traveler wears a face mask that bears some resemblance to HMD. While *La Jetée* demonstrates conceptual ideas of VR time, *Meshes in the Afternoon*[77] can be used to explain spatial considerations in VR experiences. In this film by Maya Deren, the notion of dream stage and actual events are intertwined and twisted. The non-linear drifting in and out of dream worlds can provide some inspiration for more performative, reflexive, and poetic MCVR experiences. The following examples that screened at the MINA screening were curated with the intention to explore the mobile media art capacities of MCVR.

## #MINA2018 & SF360

MINA is the longest running film festival internationally dedicated to mobile and smartphone filmmaking with a focus on moving-image arts, documentary, community engaged film productions, experimental films, and emerging film production forms and formats such as drone videos, AR, and *Mobile Cinematic VR*. In 2018, accessible and *mobile cinematic VR* projects were introduced in the program. Very much in alignment with experimentation in mobile, smartphone, and pocket filmmaking, four mobile cinematic works were selected and presented at the Smart Storytelling Day.[78]

*Before I Sleep* by Dawn Chan takes the viewer into her bathroom. Edited as a 180° split screen, one side shows the filmmaker's face in the mirror, and her mind is identified in blue subtitles as her "head." In another mirror, the other side is the back of the filmmaker, and her "heart" is identified with a red subtitle. The audio emerging from the two opposite sides (right and left audio channel in stereo) asks viewers to perform a movement to follow the conversation between mind and body. The internal argument takes an unexpected twist when we see the heart turning around and showing her face. The head and the heart have an open-ended discussion that is interrupted by the voice-over (shifting through left and right audio channels) of the filmmaker herself acting as a referee and reminder of the diametric opposites. The location of the bathroom amplifies the intimate, where inner conversations could not be more private. We are invited to listen to this internal dialog and take a hybrid position. While we can look the filmmaker in the eye, we are doing so through the third-person perspective. As an imaginative encounter, we experience the state of mind, rather than a narrative. The filmmaker Dawn Chan founded *Studio 0*, a boutique multi-media digital arts studio based in Los Angeles.

Miram Ross' *PND* is a surreal exploration of spaces and viewpoints. We experience a stroboscopic light experiment, where a pregnant woman performs some kind of abstract ritual, being trapped in an animal container with a cat circling us. We then explore multiple experimental and poetic perspectives, such being in a car by the beach, seeing animals behind a window, hanging on a flag pole, being placed in an egg container, being in a box with a cat, or being in an aquarium. The filmmaker Miriam Ross describes her work as:

> an autobiographical exploration of antenatal experience which is taken as an alienating period where the pregnant body is measured and constrained in ways that seem at odds with the public emphasis on both the "naturalness" of the event and "pregnancy glam." However, it is not a documentary of how pregnancy should be perceived but rather a phenomenological inquiry into this experience that will resonate with some viewers and open up different perspectives in others.[79]

The MCVR work also challenges our well-known perspectives and provides surreal and imaginative encounters. The intimate quality is expressed through the filmmaker's antenatal experience (Figure 35.3).

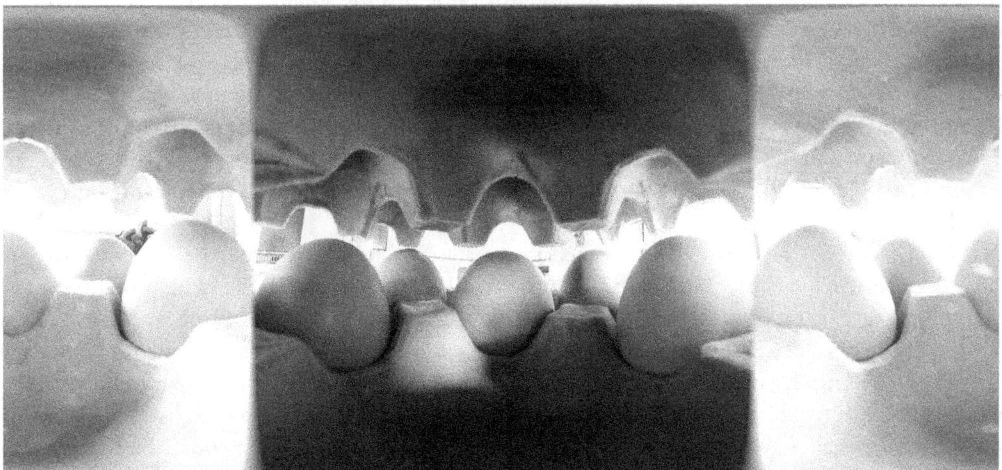

*Figure 35.3* PND MCVR at #MINA2018 (www.mina.pro). Photo credit: Miriam Ross

Eric Adelheim is the founder of production/digital communication company Defocus Films. In his cinematic VR work, he combines landscapes in Guadalupe (French Caribbean) with effectively simple and imaginative animation. The voice-over features Guy Tirolien's poem *A Little Negro Boy's Prayer* (1943), which is also the name of the MVR project. Guy Tirolien was part of the *Négritude* movement of the African Diaspora. The presence is established through the viewer following the boy's movements, while the intimate world of his thoughts is revealed. As a viewer, we walk with the boy who shares his troubles about his struggle with the school and the colonial way of life that is forced upon him as the voice-over narration reveals in the closing sequence "an African Caribbean child that does not want to go to a colonial school, run by gentlemen who cannot walk with their flesh on their feet and who no longer know how to tell stories."[80]

In *Interwoven: Veganism, Ethics, Economics,* Michaela Lucas and Raul Ramirez discuss the connections between veganism and everyday life in a MCVR experiential documentary. We are greeted by Raul who introduces Michaela at a beach in Vancouver. The two launch into a conversation by sitting opposite each other, and the view becomes part of the conversation. During their dialog, the two protagonists reveal that they are vegans and discuss environmental issues in relation to sustainable business models and the contemporary political economy more broadly. It is interesting to note that one can engage in their line of reasoning and follow the argument, which after a short time becomes very persuasive. As a viewer, it feels as if we are a participant in the conversation and get to know the two activists. One leaves the MCVR experience with a better understanding of the discussed environmental issues and may reflect on their debate and perhaps even some lifestyle choices.

SF3 provides "a platform for budding, emerging and professional filmmakers to bring their ideas to life and have their films seen by a global audience, without the need for lots of fancy equipment or a big budget."[81] The Smartphone Flick Fest believes in the democratization of filmmaking. In 2018, they premiered SF360 at the Sydney Opera House.[82] In its fifth program, SF3 announced its second round of *SF360* as "short films, amazing locations and life's simplest moments created in 360 so you can experience each moment as if you were there."[83] The SF360 2018 finalists were *Vega Islands* by Keith Mellingen from Norway and *[Mynd] journey* by this author.

*Vega Islands*, the tranquil cinematic VR experience, starts with a journey on a fishing boat to the Vega Islands. A voice-over narrates life on Norwegian islands. We meet the protagonist preparing fish for her coffee break, enjoying the landscape and heading out on a fishing boat. The personal commentary is linked with memories of childhood and romantic and idealist notions about the Vega island. While there are no more inhabitants, some people come to watch and protect birds. The commentary talks about the silence on the islands and ends with a view from a mountain over the coast line. In a filmic context, the mobile cinematic work *of* the *Vega Islands* is reminiscent of the well-known Flaherty documentary *Man of Aran*.[84] We get to know a remote location and live in this environment through a personal connection with the protagonist and, thus, the islands. The MVR projects let viewers explore the environment as if one was on the island.

*[Mynd] journey* is a journey into a meditative state of mind. We see the filmmaker in the MCVR experience in a dream chamber, similar to a Japanese capsule hotel. The protagonist talks to a computer-generated voice and is sent on a journey. One sees a coast line in New Zealand, and similar to the meditative experience, it allows viewers to drift into the unconscious mind. The journey along the coastline uses abstract colors and sounds to further drive the experience, which is unexpectedly interrupted by a computer error message. As an imaginative encounter, the MCVR work challenges one's time and space continuum as the abstract sound circulates across the panoramic ocean road. The traveling shots reveal a panoramic road between the ocean and the mountains that is intercut with color. The MVR project creates an immersive experience through placing the viewer in a dreamscape and on an imaginative journey (Figure 35.4).

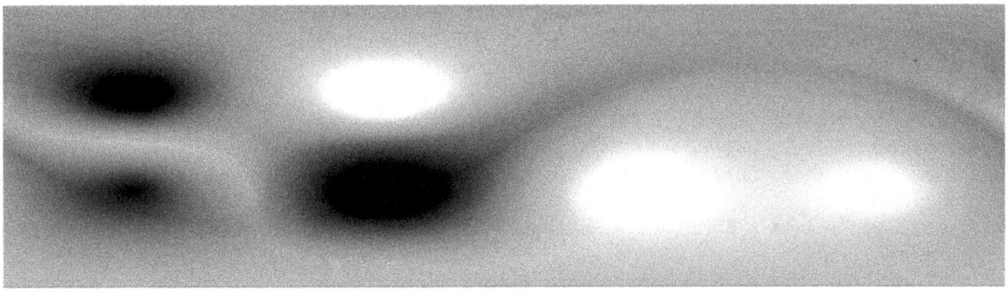

*Figure 35.4* *MCVR* [Mynd] Journey at SF3. Photo credit: Max Schleser

The SF360 program embraced presence through the displayed locations in Norway and New Zealand "as if you were there." Both experiences use a protagonist to welcome viewers into a story or dream world. Once viewers entered this imaginative stage, they are engaged in performing the mobile with their bodies and minds.

## Conclusion: Toward MCVR

As a mobile artist, filmmaker, or maker, one does not need a high res cinematic VR camera to produce experimental work. Mobile media art is a means to experiment with and engage in a myriad of stories, experiences, and dream worlds. The MCVR works discussed in this chapter highlight the qualities of early mobile media art aesthetics. Intimacy and presence can be explored as both a creative strategy and conceptual framework for analysis. Furthermore, the MCVR works either engage in discussion about important issues such as the environment and colonialism or enable us to understand the world in many different and complex ways, through letting viewer experience intimate situations, such as the antenatal experience or one's inner thoughts.

Within these MCVR worlds, viewers are performing the mobile as a form of meaning-making. Mobile media art augments experimental film, video, and moving-image utilized within performative and visual art projects. MCVR makes VR accessible for anyone with a smartphone and 360° video production camera. Most filmmakers discussed in this chapter used their own personal experiences or themselves as protagonists to make these MCVR works happen. MCVR provides an opportunity for creative experimentation similar to early mobile films. At this point in time, a window for mobile media art opened. In the same way as with early mobile films, creatives', makers', and filmmakers' experimentations are in the process of developing into a specific art and film form before industry standards and distribution channels are defined. In order to understand questions concerning MCVR specificity, mobile art will provide the answers through experimentation. This chapter initiated a debate on one of the sub forms and formats for Cinematic VR that will establish itself in the VR ecosystem.

## Notes

1 www.humaneyes.com/.
2 www.threesixtycameras.com/360-degree-camera-comparison/.
3 As an entry point one could consider the free Google Cardboard Camera app, which creates 360° pictures with audio or apps like Pie (www.pie.video/) for sharing short ten second or less 360° videos or pictures.
4 Camille Baker, Max Schleser, and Kasia Molga, "Aesthetics of Mobile Media Art," *Journal of Media Practice* 10, nos. 2–3 (2009): 100–22, doi: 10.1386/jmpr.10.2-3.101_1.

5 Ibid.; Khatib, Lina. "A Decade of Media Practice: Changes, Challenges and Choices in the Digital Age," *Journal of Media Practice* 10, nos. 2–3 (2009): 97–99, doi: 10.1386/jmpr.10.2-3.97_2.
6 "SF3 SmartFone Flick Fest" website, www.sf3.com.au/.
7 www.mina.pro.
8 *Vega Island*, directed by Mellingen (9th International Mobile Innovation Screening, 2018), www.mina.pro/screenings.
9 *[Mynd] Journey*, directed by Schleser (9th International Mobile Innovation Screening, 2018), www.mina.pro/screenings.
10 *Before I Sleep*, directed by Chan (9th International Mobile Innovation Screening, 2018), www.mina.pro/screenings.
11 PND, directed by Ross (9th International Mobile Innovation Screening, 2018), www.mina.pro/screenings.
12 *A Little Negor Boy's Prayer*, directed by Adelheim (9th International Mobile Innovation Screening, 2018), www.mina.pro/screenings.
13 *Interwoven: Veganism, Ethics, Economics*, directed by Ramirez (9th International Mobile Innovation Screening, 2018), www.mina.pro/screenings.
14 Mandy Rose, "The Immersive Turn: Hype and Hope in the Emergence of Virtual Reality as a Nonfiction Platform," *Studies in Documentary Film* 12, no. 2 (2018): 132–49, doi: 10.1080/17503280.2018.1496055.
15 Kate Nash, "Virtually Real: Exploring VR Documentary," *Studies in Documentary Film* 12, no. 2 (2018): 97–100, doi: 10.1080/17503280.2018.1484992.
16 Jamie McRoberts, "Are We There Yet? Media Content and Sense of Presence in Non-Fiction Virtual Reality," *Studies in Documentary Film* 12, no. 2 (2017): 101–18, doi: 0.1080/17503280.2017.1344924.
17 Miriam Ross, "Virtual Reality's New Synesthetic Possibilities," *Television & New Media* (2018): 1–18, doi: 10.1177/1527476418805240.
18 Here one could point toward Rasa Smite and Raitis Smiths, *Experiences, Art and Ecologies in Immersive Environments* (RIXC Publisher: Riga, 2019).
19 https://newslab.withgoogle.com/assets/docs/storyliving-a-study-of-vr-in-journalism.pdf.
20 Walking in another's virtual shoes: D 360-degree video news stories generate empathy in viewers. Columbia Journalism Review, www.cjr.org/tow_center_reports/virtual-reality-news-empathy.php.
21 http://opendoclab.mit.edu/virtually-there/.
22 http://vrdocumentaryencounters.co.uk/.
23 One exception is Miriam Ross's article about her MCVR work *PND*, which is discussed later in the chapter. Miriam Ross, "PND: Autobiographical Performance for Virtual Reality Film," *International Journal of Performance Arts and Digital Media* 14, no. 2 (2018): 130–38, doi: 10.1080/14794713.2018.1505384.
24 John Bucher, *Storytelling for Virtual Reality: Methods and Principles for Crafting Immersive Narrative* (Routledge: London, 2017).
25 Celine Tricart, *Virtual Reality Filmmaking: Techniques & Best Practices for VR Filmmakers* (Routledge: London, 2017).
26 Max Schleser, "A Decade of Mobile Moving-Image Practice" in *The Routledge Companion to Mobile Media*, edited by Gerard Goggin, and Larissa Hjorth (New York: Routledge, 2014), 158.
27 www.newyorker.com/tech/annals-of-technology/werner-herzog-talks-virtual-reality.
28 For example, Cannes Marché du Film's *NEXT* (France), HotDocs (Canada), Toronto IFF POP programs (Canada), DOK Leipzig VR screenings (Germany), Melbourne IFF (Australia), RIDM (Canada), Festival du nouveau cinéma—FNC (Canada), Dubai IFF Different Reality (U.A.E.), European Film Market (Berlin IFF), VR Theatre (Venice Film Festival), FIVARS (Canada), Screen4all (France), RAINDANCE (UK), TAMPERE FILM FESTIVAL (Finland), Atlanta IFF and SXSW (USA).
29 See KALEIDOSCOPE VR (Online network) http://about.kaleidoscope.fund/, Steamer Salon (Israel), EMC VR Film Festival (Russia), MIXAR VR Film Fest (Russia), VR FEST|Stockholm (Sweden), VIR: Cinema VR Day within LISTAPAD IFF (Belrus), LICHTER Filmfest (Germany), CINEQUEST (USA) and Geneva Tous Ecrans (Switzerland).
30 On ImdB Herzog has 71 Director credits, 55 Writer credits and 36 Producer credits. www.imdb.com/name/nm0001348/.
31 https://vr.google.com/jump/.
32 www.youtube.com/watch?v=Ahonv4cNvgc.
33 https://ami.withgoogle.com/.
34 www.wired.com/2013/02/beck-360-degree-online-video/.
35 For example, the Samsung 360 gear was launched in 2016 and updated in 2017. The Samsung 360 gear integrates with the Samsung Galaxy S9, S9+, Note8, S8, S8+, S7, S7 edge, Note5, S6 edge+, S6, S6 edge, A8 (2018), A8+ (2018), A5 (2017), A7 (2017) *Android 5.0 or later.

36 www.youtube.com/channel/UCzuqhhs6NWbgTzMuM09WKDQ.
37 https://join.vimeo.com/360/.
38 www.facebook.com/Facebook360/.
39 www.youtube.com/watch?v=KV6hEQnCPAc&t=1195s.
40 https://techlog360.com/first-smartphone-built-360-degree-vr-camera/.
41 www.samsung.com/us/mobile/virtual-reality/.
42 https://vr.google.com/daydream/.
43 Camille Baker, *New Directions in Mobile Media and Performance* (Routledge: London, 2019), 111.
44 Maria Engberg and Jay David Bolter, "Mobile Cinematics," in *Compact Cinematics: The Moving Image in the Age of Bit-Sized Media*, edited by Pepita Hesselberth and Maria Poulaki (Bloomsbury: London, 2017), 165–73.
45 *Selfie*, directed by Agostino Ferrente (Italy, 2018). www.berlinale.de/en/archiv/jahresarchive/2019/02_programm_2019/02_Filmdatenblatt_2019_201916356.html?openedFromSearch=true#tab=film-Stills, www.berlinale.de/en/programm/berlinale_programm/datenblatt.html?film_id=201916356 and *Midnight Traveler*, directed by Hassan Fazili (USA / United Kingdom / Qatar / Canada, 2019) www.berlinale.de/en/programm/berlinale_programm/datenblatt.html?film_id=201913468.
46 *Unsane*, directed by Steven Soderbergh (USA, 2018), www.imdb.com/title/tt7153766/.
47 *Tangerine*, directed by Sean Baker (USA, 2015), www.imdb.com/title/tt3824458/?ref_=fn_al_tt_1.
48 Max Schleser, "A Decade of Mobile Moving-Image Practice," 131–53.
49 Marsha Berry, "Making Films and Video Art with Smartphones," in *Creating with Mobile Media* (Cham: Palgrave Macmillan/Springer Nature, 2014), 131.
50 Sylvie Prasad, "Mobile Aesthetics and Critism," in *Creative Mobile Media* (London: World Scientific Publishing, 2017), 25.
51 Mike Jones, "Vanishing Point: Spatial Composition and the Virtual Camera," *Animation: An Interdisciplinary Journal* 2, no. 3 (2007): 225–43. doi: 10.1177/1746847707083420.
52 Camille Baker, Max Schleser and Kasia Molga. "Aesthetics of Mobile Media Art," 119.
53 https://cmsw.mit.edu/wp/wp-content/uploads/2016/10/326754928-Deniz-Tortum-Embodied-Montage-Reconsidering-Immediacy-in-Virtual-Reality.pdf.
54 Michael Saker and Jordan Frith, "From Hybrid Space to Dislocated Space: Mobile Virtual Reality and Third Stage of Mobile Media Theory," *New Media & Society* 21, no. 1 (2019): 214–28. doi: 10.1177/1461444818792407.
55 Larissa Hjorth, *Games and Gaming: An Introduction to New Media* (Oxford: Berg, 2011); Larissa Hjorth and Ingrid Richardson, "Pokémon Go: Mobile Media Play, Place-Making, and the Digital Wayfarer," *Mobile Media & Communication* 5, no. 1 (2017): 3–14, doi: 10.1177/2050157916680015.
56 In the context of co-presence, the work of Larissa Hjorth is a key reference; Larissa Hjorth and Sun Sun Lim "Mobile Intimacy in an Age of Affective Mobile Media," *Feminist Media Studies* 12, no. 4 (2012): 477–84. doi: 10.1080/14680777.2012.741860; Larissa Hjorth and Sarah Pink, "New Visualities and the Digital Wayfarer: Reconceptualizing Camera Phone Photography and Locative Media," *Mobile Media & Communication* 2, no. 1 (2014): 40–57. doi: 10.1177/2050157913505257; Kathleen Cumiskey and Larissa Hjorth, *Mobile Media Practices, Presence and Politics: The Challenge of Being Seamlessly Mobile* (Routledge: London, 2013). The scope of this chapter and its focus could not facilitate the detailed discussion, but its references are key. As mentioned in this chapter, Michael Saker and Jordan Frith discuss the relationship between co-presence in mobile communication studies (MCS), while this chapter approached the discussion from a mobile media art perspective.
57 www.wondavr.com/.
58 https://vimeo.com/311346686.
59 Baker, *New Directions*.
60 Ibid., 12.
61 Maria Engberg and Jay David Bolter, "Mobile Cinematics," in *Compact Cinematics: The Moving Image in the Age of Bit-Sized Media*, edited by Pepita Hesselberth and Maria Poulaki (Bloomsbury: London, 2017), 169.
62 http://virtualrealitycinema.com.au/.
63 http://thedigitalunderground.com.au/.
64 It is a prominent example of VR's capacity to capture scale and the large dimensions of the distinctive street artist Rone. The cinematic VR doc reveals the abandoned spaces in which he creates his street art and murals such a paper mill, a theater, or a house set for demolition. See www.ronevr.com/.
65 www.electricsouth.org/.
66 www.electricsouth.org/production/2018-productions/.

67 Bill Nichols, *Introduction to Documentary* (Indiana University Press, 2017).

68 Ibid., 109.

69 *Schuften für fast nichts: Inside the Garment Industry in Bangladesh*, directed by Empathic Media (Bangladesh, 2017), www.empatheticmedia.com/360-video/.

70 *The Baltimore Sun: Inside a Home with 20 Code Violations*, directed by Empathic Media (USA, 2017), www.empatheticmedia.com/360-video/.

71 *La Paz en 360 (Peace in 360 Degrees)*, directed by Empathic Media (Columbia, 2017), www.empatheticmedia.com/360-video/.

72 Dan Archer and Katharina Finger, "Walking in Another's Virtual Shoes: Do 360-degree Video News Stories Generate Empathy in Viewers?" *Columbia Journalism Review Online*, 2018, www.cjr.org/tow_center_reports/virtual-reality-news-empathy.php.

73 Ibid., n.p.

74 Ibid., n.p.

75 *La Jetée*, directed by Chris Maker (France, 1962).

76 The present progressive or present continuous is used for actions or events in progress, being repeated, or of a temporary nature or to express the future. This has some similarities to VR experiences. Present continuous is used for "storytelling, something which is changing, growing or developing, something which is new and contrasts with a previous state or something which we think is temporary," see https://learnenglish.britishcouncil.org/english-grammar/present-continuous.

77 *Meshes of the Afternoon*, directed by Maya Deren (USA, 1943).

78 www.swinburne.edu.au/events/departments/research/2018/11/mina2018-towards-a-theory-practice-of-smart-storytelling.php.

79 www.mina.pro/screenings.

80 Voice-over in *A Little Negor Boy's Prayer*, directed by Adelheim (9th International Mobile Innovation Screening, 2018), www.mina.pro/screenings.

81 www.sf3.com.au/Aboutinner/1.

82 www.sydneyoperahouse.com/events/past-events/films/2018/sf3-gala-tickets.html.

83 www.sf3.com.au/Aboutinner/12.

84 *Man of Aran*, directed by Robert Flaherty (Ireland 1934).

# 36

# WEARING DATA

## Intentions and Tensions of Art and Design in Performance using Wearables

*Camille Baker*

Wearable technologies have evolved over the last few decades, with 2014 known as "Year of Wearables"[1] in *Forbes* and other media outlets. As noted by Elizabeth Wissinger, "There are many kinds of technologies that can be deemed 'wearable.' From smart fibers and tattoos, biosensing devices and implants, networked jewelry, or an LED encrusted dress, what, exactly, we mean when we say 'wearable tech' is in flux."[2]

*Wareable* online magazine stated in 2015 that 84 million wearable devices were sold that year, and by 2019 that figure would be 245 million wearable fitness bracelets and other devices. However, a recent report from *Statistica*, an online business data analysis platform, suggests that the number is actually closer to three times that amount, roughly 742 million.[3] Such reports show how the industry has grown especially in the last five to ten years. Many tech companies and start-ups have been vying to make the next great wearable device or "killer app" for body-data tracking. Physiological, body-based, sensor devices, and electronic technologies have become cable-free, Wi-Fi-enabled,[4] smaller, more powerful, and sewable, using smart or electronic textiles, conductive fibers and other smart materials. Hardware is increasingly smaller, less visible, and more widely connected; data is more seamlessly and ubiquitously harvested. There has been concurrently rapid and extensive explosion in the development of electronic materials, conductive inks and threads, and new smart materials, fabrics, and textiles for use in various fashion, sports, fitness, medical, military, and governmental projects, as well as for artistic and performance projects such as those by artists like Kasia Molga's *Human Sensor* project for the Invisible Dust organization.

In this chapter, I provide an overview of the complex concerns around wearables that draw on datafication and privacy such as using people's physiological data to sell to health insurance companies to make money off our body data. I begin by discussing the politics of datafication and privacy. I then move on to focus on art, performance, and design with wearables and e-textiles, giving examples of my own collaborative wearable performance work and research, to reflect upon some of the novel and productive ways we might think about wearables for future directions in the design of wearables and in the marketplace.

### The Politics of Datafication and Privacy

Wearable devices collect users' personal body (physiological) data for medical or fitness monitoring, and this data is owned by the technology companies who make the devices who then send it into the cloud to physical server farms. Most wearables connect to multiple sensors on the body, via tracker applications on smartphones, facilitating and integrating all data collection. The wearable companies then analyze it, store it, and/or sell it, frequently without overt user consent. For example, personal fitness activity data has been used in numerous cases to monitor workers' health for job-worthiness.[5]

The exponential rise of wearables has had diverse ramifications. Yet in recent years, increasingly more people, including politicians, have had concerns about the amount of personal data that wearable technology companies harvest and sell as their business model. Corporate data harvesting activity reveals a unique set of insidious problems emerging from controversial practices,[6] not to mention related poor labor practices in manufacturing, and mineral sourcing issues existing from electronic technology development and in the supply-chain, including for wearable devices. For example, at a wearables networking event I attended in July 2015, at the Business Design Centre in London, industry representatives were asked to envision future wearables. One representative from one of the world's dominant fast-food chains was interested in ways to track and monitor their employees,[7] ostensibly to improve their employees' efficiency and make money from their data. Another participant wanted all employees to have devices implanted into their brains to enforce improved eating habits, increase exercise, and change or stop their chemical dependencies, which impede worker efficiency.[8] Moore and Robinson state:

> The [monitoring of employees' data at work] is thus part of managerial efforts to control and extract value from creative as well as physical labour in more precise, quantified ways. [Wearable Self-tracking Technology] raises new demands on workers, potentially intensifies workloads, and leads to rationalization of staff, whilst displacing accountability. The measure of physiolytics is a way to extract information from wearables data 'to improve performance' [...] While physiolytics is predominantly used in sport it is 'spreading to workers in factory and office settings as well.'[9]

Physiological data can also be used against those employees in performance reviews.[10] Moore and Robinson point out:

> [...] quantification helps corporations and self-employed precarians to keep up with cutthroat competition [...] the spread of wearables in the workplace may be seen as an extension of a control society [...] and a subordination of precarious workers' qualitative being to capitalism in the form of a Taylorism which reaches into the body [...] Against a new regime of quantification, social movements can be expected to seek new forms of refusal and exodus, which must increasingly take the form of a refusal of data—a refusal to track the body, a refusal to subordinate the qualitative to the quantitative, a refusal of surveillance, a refusal to share data with corporations and the state.[11]

While corporate data collection has become more regulated since the roll out of the European General Data Protection Regulations (GDPR) in May 2018,[12] similar laws do not seem equally in place across the world or in the United States, in particular, where Facebook, Apple, Google, Amazon, and other big corporations who harvest and use personal data operate. With little ethical oversight, many companies try to find work-around for these recent regulations: they continue to develop new ways to use our data to increase their profit margins.[13] Ethics are of no interest to Google, Apple, Amazon, and wearables tech companies. We are just data to harvest. We are the business model. As Garrett quotes others:

> Facebook knows your friends, what information you provide about them, what they say about you, what other sites you visit (if they include a Facebook 'like' button, which most do), what you bought, what device you used to access Facebook, and much more.[14]

> Apple collects phone data which they say is collected anonymously while users have no opt out clause.[15]

Yet, respecting privacy and security issues for personal data related to fitness logging activities is increasingly being highlighted by users, researchers, and journalists, more notably due to the growing Quantified Self QS Movement community;[16]

> [...] individuals have become information hungry. What started as a slightly awkward hobby in the 80s, the quantified self has now become mainstream with people self monitoring anything from sleep to eating habits, from sport activities to mood [...] uploading intimate details such as heart-rate, sleep patterns and whereabouts to corporate servers in order to improve their performance.[17]

Even though more people are becoming aware of how corporations and governments are collecting and using their data,[18] with complex world concerns such as combating cyber criminals and terrorism, governments are using security and terrorist events to rationalize and legislate for more control, access, and powers to gather increasing amounts of personal data from all citizens. Without their knowledge and awareness of where and how their personal data is being collected or who owns their data, consumers are left unprotected against corporate and government surveillance. In China, facial recognition software and Artificial Intelligence (AI) are now being used across the country as an overt totalitarian form of social control,[19] which is also being trialed in the United Kingdom, Germany, and around the world, in so-called democratic countries.[20]

We are in a time of public cynicism around mass surveillance, privacy and unethical data collection, as highlighted by Edward Snowden, Wikileaks, as well as the popular TV series *Black Mirror*[21] and *Mr. Robot*.[22] More profoundly, the Cambridge Analytica[23] scandal involving Facebook and Russian interference impacted two countries' elections—with wide-reaching political outcomes. Users now want to better understand and articulate their rights to access, own, control, and use their body data and need to play a more active role in interpreting or reinterpreting this data however they choose. Companies usually sell personal data to insurance or healthcare companies, rarely—or not at all—allowing users to access their data. However, they should be regulated to provide users with open-access and ownership of their own physiological data and enable ways for the public to use these devices and garments for their own personal benefit, rather than for the benefit of the company. As Garrett states:

> Haraway proposed that the 'proper state for a Western person is to have ownership of the self, to have and hold a core identity as if it were a possession,' and that 'not to have property in the self is not to be a subject, and so not to have agency.'[24]

What are the consequences of giving away all your private body data in exchange for free services? Can we somehow own our own data? According to *Wired* writer, Gregory Barber,[25] we can own our own data, with great effort and expense (almost as a fulltime job), but we will not make much money from it as the profit is only made in aggregate as huge datasets, not for an individual's data.

Data privacy aside, the significant ethical issues around social, environmental, labor, and supply chain concerns in the wearable and broader tech industry still need to be addressed. We are moving into a time of ever increasing miniaturization of microchips and sensing devices, worn, embedded, or ingested within the body itself.[26] In addition, with the increased sophistication of electronics and smart-e-textiles[27] in our clothing, cars, homes, and ubiquitously in our lives, gathering our physiological, biometric, DNA/Genomic,[28] or other personal data, there will be major implications for increased surveillance with increased corporate and government control over our lives, from inside our bodies. As Pedersen suggests, there are already

> [...] networks of wireless sensors that can be sewn into clothing, placed directly on the skin, or implanted into the body. Human Body Communication (HBC) or intrabody communication uses the body itself rather than air for wireless transfer.[29]

All this with well-meaning intentions: to keep us, or our children, or elderly parents safe; to prevent or solve crime; for our comfort, or any number of "good" reasons.

As Daniel Howe points out, "[...] there are a multitude of vectors by which corrupt advertisers, repressive governments, and other malicious players can [...] identify its user and access valuable personal data without consent."[30] Pedersen demonstrates how the focus in tech industries is now on embeddable, injectables and ingestibles,[31] as well as brain-computer interfaces,[32] to predict our moods, desires, and impulses in order to match with AI and machine-learning algorithms to capitalize on everything we do. She stresses:

> [...] new embodied technologies may make people vulnerable to datafication [...] I define "datafication" as using devices, networks, and sensors to track human behaviours and responses, monitor them, store them, and control them using algorithms to orient or persuade people (prod them) in a desired direction.[33]

Based on this, what difference will General Data Protection Regulation (GDPR) legislation make? What does ethical data collection mean in the context of such pervasive surveillance? Many companies, such as 23andme—and now governments—have obtained DNA data[34] from a huge number of people who have given their data away in search of their ancestral heritage. In this context, what does privacy actually mean today? As Pedersen points out,

> The belief is that emerging technologies, network culture, and human and non-human processes of datafication will revolutionize healthcare and everyday life *by directly sensing the body's core through passive monitoring.*[35] To meet such a speculative scenario, brain, heart, skin, skeletal, and other topological and visceral sensors would need to track biometric data continuously through biomedical telemetry. The bio-surveilled body would be datafied in—numerous ways.[36]

*What a terrifying prospect.* This outlook upsets many, alongside the impending climate apocalypse—the future indeed looks dark. What happens when there is no privacy and we are nothing but a dataset to be learned and replicated by machine learning algorithms? Some of these questions pose key ethical issues not only for our present, but also for the future.

## Art, Performance, and Design with Wearables and e-Textiles

People are becoming more aware and educated about the dark side of wearable and mobile technologies, cloud computing,[37] Big Data, and smart/electronic textiles that include not only data privacy issues but also labor ethics and the environmental impacts of these technologies.

While there are well-intentioned efforts to protect and treat the aging population and cure medical conditions and diseases, there are simultaneously advertisers, politicians, and malicious hackers trying to monetize, manipulate, and control our bodies and minds. For this reason, artists, activists, and philosophers are increasingly necessary because in making critical work, they educate the public and become a source of resistance, awareness, and change. For example, artist Jennifer Morone has made a performance out of harvesting her body data and making it for sale to anyone to buy, incorporating her body as a business to make a political statement of controlling the sale of her data rather allowing others to exploit it as *Jennifer Lyn Morone™ Inc.*[38]

We are all involved in giving our data away, from the QS movement and health apps installed on our phones, selfie-fixation for Instagram self-promotion to become "influencers," or the TikTok frenzied youth absorbed in making their own live-streamed video blogs of everything they do every day.

Artists, social scientists, philosophers, data privacy activists, and others have been asking questions about the use and deployment of the wearable devices and related apps. There are now many artists and theorists exploring methods, not only to educate the public to be more aware and wary of government and corporate pervasive surveillance, but also how not to be complicit through self-monitoring and "sousveillance."[39] As Garrett mentions,

> Ippolita, a group of activists and writers, warned how social media promotes emotional pornography, where our feelings are exploited by click baits in exchange for our personal data. We are a rich source of data-mining material.[40]

Meanwhile, facial recognition surveillance is more commonplace (especially in China) and even more invasion of personal intimate privacy is taking place in ever-surreptitious ways.[41]

Wearables and smart or e-textiles are increasingly part of a more self-contained system of body-based, skin-like bio-textiles or other forms of mobile, and wearable technologies that are finding new roles and manifestations in artworks, performance, fashion, and entertainment industries such as Virtual Reality games. There are now amazing biotech/biofabric projects and research, such that of Victoria Geany's bioluminescent dress, or Suzanne Lee's biocouture, and Guilia Tomasello's Alma, where designers and artists are growing new materials and blending them with (or trying to) conductive and/ or electronic textiles to transmit data (ideally not collecting it), while being recyclable and/ or biodegradable. This is the new direction for new materials and technologies that I have hoped for.

In my recent book, *New Directions in Mobile Media and Performance*, I discuss how mobile phones are used performatively as tools, content, guides, and also as collaborators within immersive theater, live art, dance, music and other creative projects.[42] I also provide examples of art and performance work using mobile phones and wearables as a subset of the larger mainstream fashion and technology industry. While wearable devices and smart or e-textiles do not strictly use the mobile phone, they are mobile media and are used in performance more and more, usually tethered to or linked to mobile applications or laptop computers to enable the embedded devices[43] to "work," but also to become artistic collaborators in the piece.

How do data surveillance issues discussed herein impact the arts? What can artists understand and effectively question of the relationship between data, wearables, and the body in their work for public discussion? How can artists be the watchdogs or ombuds[wo]men around ethics, the body, and data privacy for the public? I'm grappling with these questions in my own creative practice and research while encouraging other artists to explore and tackle them pro-actively within and through their work.

In recent years, my own practice goals have moved to initiate more collaboration between artists and performers with wearable technologists and companies. This creates a mutually satisfactory way forward—to demonstrate how art and performance can influence the research and development in Human Computer Interaction (HCI), interfaces, and data collection, not to mention as a means to create more ethical, environmental, and sustainable technologies and interfaces for the future.

## *Hacking the Body 2.0*

*Hacking the Body 2.0 (HTB2.0)*, my main artistic project using wearables in performance, was the second iteration of an ongoing collaboration between choreographer/media artist Dr Kate Sicchio and myself since 2012. It was born of a need to explore and critique how wearable technology can extend our senses, and also from the concern of how personal/physiological data identity can be revealed and understood through layers of "known-ness,"[44] which also exposed personal data privacy and vulnerability issues.

The project focus has been on identity and how body data ownership in performance might manifest (if possible). As such, *HTB2.0* uses the latest off-the-shelf wearable electronics and smart materials, alongside "hacked" corporate fitness wearable tech garments to explore identity and privacy issues within the wearable technology, e-textiles, and smart fashion industries while adding to performance and technology development and discourse.

During our research we observed how self-monitoring and quantified-self activities lead to narcissism, while enabling corporate and government exploitation of private, personal data. As Ridgway (2015) stated in her online article "Personalisation as Currency,"[45]

> [...] we govern ourselves through our 'behaviours' being captured and cultivated in 'personalised machines, sharing everything we do as huge amounts of data, surrendering our privacy for free services and participation in the attention economy.

Our focus, however, was on interpreting inner physiological states and processes, interpreted as unique personal identity signatures that may (or may not) influence one's movement, gestures, expression, and interaction with others. As researchers and artists for *HTB 2.0*, we questioned data collection agendas and sought ways to access body data locally (not "in the cloud"). Performers co-create and explore how their own physiological changes and movement style uniquely demonstrates who they are, like a new language.

Our primary questions were: can people be empowered by allowing them to access and use their own personal data as a means to express and perform their own identity?[46] Can we create new forms of non-verbal interaction and communication during performance, using this data and unique data expression? This was intended as a performative confrontation of corporate and government surveillance and data control. The aim was to critically and artistically challenge the control of and patenting/copyrighting of people's body data from wearables, to expand the concept of the body as part of greater social, political, and technological (opensource) network, and for body data rights, as individuals who give consent only to those who ask and respectfully utilize it for non-profit and artistic purposes.

These concerns, as well as the curiosity about how biofeedback data might be used to create a personal bio-signature, led to several iterations and performance outcomes, bespoke costumes embedded with wearable tech, and new research insights (Figure 36.1).

## e-stitches *and* WEAR Sustain

The *WEAR Sustain*[47] project was an off-shoot of an in-person bi-monthly meetup group at the Victoria & Albert Museum in London, which I started in 2014, called *Stitch, Bitch, Make, Perform.*

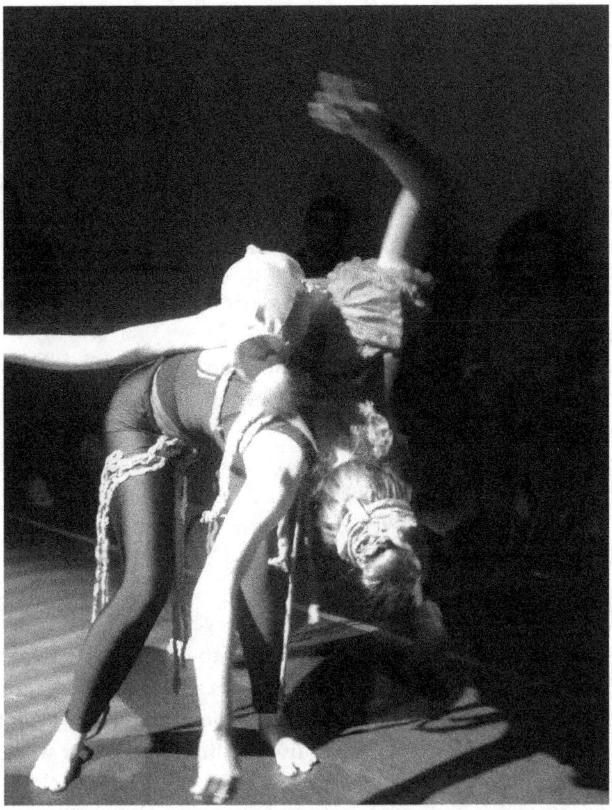

*Figure 36.1* *@ Hacking the Body 2.0* (2012–). Photo credit: Kate Sicchio and Camille Baker

It's still running and now called *e-stitches* with now over 160 members of which about 10–15 attend at each meetup. *e-stitches* initially aimed to address issues of data harvesting, privacy and the sale of personal data by corporations and governments, and to scrutinize poor data ethics, labor, and environmental ethics and practices. When starting the *e-stitches*, the intention was to bring women artists, performers, and designers together to critically discuss these issues and be involved in making changes in an evolution toward a more critical making[48] and design practices for ethical ends.[49]

*WEAR Sustain* was developed to build and extend the European dialog on these ethical and sustainability issues. It reached out and engaged a wide range of stakeholders with an emphasis on collaborations of artists and designers with engineers and technologists. It focused on creating a pan-European network, funding 48 example projects and developing a sustainable strategy that included ethical employment of labor and waste management processes. It also focused on creating and sharing methods for designers and manufacturers on how to source ethical minerals and materials and locally made components.

*WEAR Sustain* brought together wearable technology industry experts, technologists, tech companies, and entrepreneurs in an effort to work with designers and artists across Europe. The aim was to shift the methods of development within the EU wearables industry and draw on the extensive landscape of designers and smart textile stakeholders, to further address critical, ethical, aesthetic, and environmental issues head on at the initial research and development stages.

We were motivated by a passion to change the way that the electronics and technology industry and its supply-chain, as well as the fashion and textiles industries, work and how they make their products. We wanted these industries to stop harming the environment with mountains of electronic waste, to limit or stop all surveillance of wearable users, and to generally contribute to better ways of making products. We aimed to contribute to innovation with a purpose, with a soul, and aim to build a network of like-minded pioneers. We felt it important to have industry to take responsibility for itself and to give something positive back for consumers and society.

*WEAR Sustain*'s aims were to:

1 Engage with alternative discourses in the conceptualization and design of wearables and e-textiles by promoting artist-technologist synergies and catalytic thinking;
2 Address issues of sustainability and life-cycle design in both production and end-of-life of wearables and e-textiles;
3 Foreground the ethical issues of privacy and ownership of personal and embodied data, as well as the appalling labor practices in African mines and Asian PCB and component factories; and
4 Build a network of 1475+ like-minded actors in the sustainable and ethical wearable space from hubs to individual artists and technologists, creating a unique and compelling cross-section of the community and the experts who aim to shape a more sustainable and responsible future for wearables and e-textiles.

*WEAR Sustain* also examined the recycling and/or upcycling of both non-electronic and electronic parts and how to avoid waste by fabricating made-to-measure wearables, economical application of new materials replaceable components, and the careful separation of new and traditional materials, with lifespan considerations. It encouraged new and more established companies to employ strategies for recycling or disposal and to use modular system for wearable hardware to ensure not only that the garment/device can be worn longer and be washed, but also that electronic technology and carrier material can be separated once one of them outlives the other, as well as other sustainable and end-of-life/life-cycle approaches.

The *WEAR Sustain* partners ensured that the funded teams were supported by matching them with experts, mentors, local hubs, and services providers during the development of their prototype(s) and encouraged them to implement their novel solutions to sustainable and ethical innovation. In addition, partners conducted large-scale knowledge exchange activities, gathering experts, mentors, and service providers in ethical and sustainable wearable and e-textile design, manufacturing business services, legal support services, as well as other support services to help them with the whole life-cycle of the design from production to the commercialization of the products. This led to the development of the first version of the *Sustainability Strategy Toolkit* (SST).

The goal of the SST developed best methods for enabling, facilitating, and connecting future collaborations, designers, resources, experts with development, production, manufacturing, and end-of-life / waste management solutions for wearable technology and smart/e-textiles, built on ethical and sustainable foundations. The *SST* was based on the UN's Sustainable Development Goals and was expanded into a toolkit for partners to use to advise teams and provide access to online resources, a bespoke knowledge base, for mentors, hubs, and services that focus on the environmental and socio-cultural impacts of wearable technologies. More specifically, the strategy aimed at providing a position on sustainability and ethics with detailed recommendations, resources, best-practice examples, case studies, and real-life outcomes in relation to sustainable materials, energy sourcing, ethical data choices and data security, sustainable financing and funding, privacy, ownership, and control of data. Labor conditions and mineral sourcing were essential aspects addressed in the innovation process.

The *SST* and *Wear Sustain Knowledge* platform was built to cater to these challenges and provide e-textiles and wearable technologists with sustainability and ethics resources, techniques and tools, a viable network of peers, and thematic hubs to provide hands-on support for design and development teams. Their aims are to support design efforts and advise, inform, and empower artists, designers, and technologists to implement a more sustainable and ethical approach to their practice.

The *WEAR Sustain* database is an expanding through user sourced resource from the online *WEAR* community. There are over 1687 design and development resources, from which 1435 are uploaded just for the teams themselves and 152 available to the public (as of this writing), such as local legal or IP adviser, living labs and hubs for design projects, articles on the processes, and much more. It also includes a guided self-assessment tool, along with a comprehensive flowchart and decision-making-tree. This helps current and future design teams to identify areas for improvement in their design and manufacturing processes and suggest to the team members how they might identify next steps necessary in the design process.

The project funding ended in April 2019, but several of the consortium members are now carrying on with the work started, as a non-profit ethics and sustainability consulting, training, advisory, and brokerage firm, in which I will continue as an academic advisor.

## Conclusion

If Petersen's forecast does become true, the world of wearables will soon disappear, and we will all have embedded, ingested, and injected technologies along with brain-computer interfaces. At that point, if we are not all controlled by AI-driven social media messages, we will be presented with consumer products just as we begin to form thoughts about or desire them. All diseases will be cured as they begin to manifest via nanobots delivering medicine to us as we start to develop symptoms, and if we *do* live 50 years longer, we may feel we have nothing else left to live for, apart from virtual reality dreams. If the planet can still support us, we will be continuously surveilled in every breathing moment.

In this scenario, the natural world will have entirely collapsed, and we will no longer go outside due to extreme weather and climate collapse. We will barely be able to feed ourselves, as there will be no animals left and food will no longer grow. This is not the future I want, but this vision is now a real possibility unless humanity takes a stand. Artists have a role to play in changing this scenario, and I am now focused on this agenda too. I highlight the dangers of wearables data collection, as one way to achieve this goal. Making work that impacts others is another way to change the future. It is vital that we make and use wearable technologies—smart/e-textiles in design, art, performance in order to provide the catalytic creative and critical thinking necessary to experience more in life and the planet than consumption. Our technologies and artworks need to be more ethically, sustainable, and critically designed if we want a brighter future. In the words of Greta Thurnberg, Swedish teen environmental activist, "our house is on fire,"[50] and we need to radically change the way we do things in every sphere of our lives. We need to do it now! As artists, we have a huge role to play in creating the future we want to live, or any future, really.

What are the intentions and tensions around art and design for performances and wearables with regards to data? Artists are now shining light on the issues, creating more awareness, and actively encouraging the public to demand more transparency in corporate and governmental practices. Artists need to find new ways to work with data instead of treating it as the "new oil," a commodity to be excavated regardless of all the dirty polluting and environmentally devastating connotations. We must turn to "good data," using data for good, rather than through exploitation, or to be sold useless goods and services, or to control us.

My own efforts are just at the beginning of what I hope to achieve, as I become clearer about how to make direct changes and impact, along with the efforts of other artists and designers,[51] in our own practices while educating the public on stewardship of the Earth and influencing others to make critical changes to secure a better future.

## Notes

1 See Ewan Spence, "2014 Will Be The Year Of Wearable Technology," November 2, 2013, https://www.forbes.com/sites/ewanspence/2013/11/02/2014-will-be-the-year-of-wearable-technology/#72cdb205c466; Grace College (no author), "Rapid Growth: The Past, Present and Future of Wearable Technology," November 17, 2016, https://online.grace.edu/news/business/the-past-present-future-of-wearable-technology/.
2 Elizabeth Wissinger, "Wearable Tech, Bodies, and Gender," *Sociology Compass* 11, no. 11 (2017): n.p., doi: 10.1111/soc4.12514.
3 See Sophie Charara, "245 million wearable devices will be sold in 2019," *Wareable*, 1 Septermber 2015, https://www.wareable.com/wearable-tech/245-million-wearable-devices-sold-2019-1606; Statistica Research Department, "Number of connected wearable devices worldwide from 2016 to 2022, February 19, 2020, https://www.statista.com/statistics/487291/global-connected-wearable-devices/.
4 Isabel Pedersen in her article, "BodyNets: Datafied Bodies and Critical Approaches to Body Area Networks" (February 2019, 4) points out:

> Depending on your viewpoint, Bluetooth is either the invisible lifeline or the prison chain between people, embodied devices, and highly profitable corporations [...] Embodied communication is on the brink of exponential change and moving toward networking the body directly to the cloud.

5 Information can be found on for-managers.com and personneltoday.com.
6 More on the terrible practices of data collection in Silicon Valley: "Data spies: The dark and shady practices of Silicon Valley with Roger McNamee," *Big Think*, 15 March 2019, 2:13, https://youtu.be/C2Ag1iQKWeM.
7 Phoebe Moore, and Andrew Robinson, "The Quantified Self: What Counts in the Neoliberal Workplace." *New Media & Society* 18, no. 11 (December 2016): 2774–92, 2776, doi:10.1177/1461444815604328. They note,

> ABI Research predicts 13 million wearable fitness devices in workplaces by 2019 [...] more than 13 million fitness tracking devices will be incorporated into employee wellness programs by 2019 (Nield, 2014) [...] in order to 'learn how human behaviours impact productivity, performance.'

8 Moore, and Robinson, "The Quantified Self," 2277. They *also say*

> Amazon and Tesco [UK] warehouses monitor every minute zero-hour contracted workers spend on the performance console using arm-mounted terminals. The 'wearable terminal' is in effect a streamlined replacement for the clipboard [...] Information from barcodes, or location information is listed on the upper section of the terminal that is strapped to the forearm.

9 H. James Wilson, "Wearables in the Workplace," *Harvard Business Review*, September 2013, https://hbr.org/2013/09/wearables-in-the-workplace cited in Moore, and Robinson, "The Quantified Self."
10 Ian Forrester, "Quantified self and the ethics of personal data," *BBC Research and Development Blog*, 23 June 2014 (updated 17 March 2017), http://www.bbc.co.uk/rd/blog/2014/06/qs-ethics-ofdata.
11 Moore, and Robinson, "The Quantified Self," 2281.
12 A GDPR explanation can be found here https://gdprexplained.eu; https://publications.europa.eu/en/publication-detail/-/publication/3e485e15-11bd-11e6-ba9a-01aa75ed71a1/language-en.
13 Data Collection is a multi-billion-dollar business in the US according to Nick Routley in the *Visual Capitalist* (14 April 2018), www.visualcapitalist.com/personal-data-ecosystem/.
14 Garrett, as cited in Moore and Robinson, quotes Mark Hachman, "The price of free: how Apple, Facebook, Microsoft and Google sell you to advertisers," *PCWorld*, 1 October 2015, www.pcworld.com/article/2986988/privacy/the-price-of-free-how-apple-facebook-microsoft-and-google-sell-you-to-advertisers.html.
15 Garrett, as cited in Moore and Robinson, quotes Meg Marco, "Privacy Change: Apple Knows Where Your Phone Is And Is Telling People," *Consumerist*, 21 June 2010, https://consumerist.com/2010/06/21/privacy-change-apple-knows-your-phone-is-and-is-telling-people.
16 This worldwide community that uses wearable devices monitor their own health and bodily functions, as a way to improve fitness and health, as a hobby, or as a narcissistic preoccupation. Official definitions can be found here https://quantifiedself.com; https://qsinstitute.com/about/what-is-quantified-self/.
17 de Valk, 2016 in Garrett, 2017, 7.
18 See Endnote 6.
19 This is paired with social media tools to "out" or shame citizens into good behavior (like in Netflix' *Black Mirror* Season 3, Episode 1, "Nosedive," 2016, written by Charlie Brooker) and discussed in Wired UK (Oct 2017) www.wired.co.uk/article/chinese-government-social-credit-score-privacy-invasion.

20 More on Chinese facial recognition technology in *Business Insider* (July 2018) www.businessinsider.com/china-facial-recognition-limitations-2018-7?r=US&IR=T and *The Economist* (October 2018) *China: facial recognition and state control* mini-documentary on YouTube https://youtu.be/lH2gMNrUuEY. See activities being trialed in the UK and Germany, discussed in *Politico* magazine online (September 2018). www.politico.eu/article/berlin-big-brother-state-surveillance-facial-recognition-technology/, in *Wired* UK magazine www.wired.co.uk/article/face-recognition-police-uk-south-wales-met-notting-hill-carnival, and *The Independent* newspaper online www.independent.co.uk/news/uk/home-news/facial-recognition-cameras-london-met-police-suspects-arrests-identity-a8687481.html.

21 Charlie Brooker, *Black Mirror*, Miniseries, 2013–2018, Netflix.

22 Sam Esmail, Rami Malek, Christian Slater, Jimmy Ryan, Carly Chaikin, Portia Doubleday, and Martin Wallström. 2016–2018. *Mr. Robot.* Universal Pictures.

23 As explained in the Guardian online March 17, 2019: www.theguardian.com/technology/2019/mar/17/the-cambridge-analytica-scandal-changed-the-world-but-it-didnt-change-facebook.

24 Garrett, 2017: 16.

25 In his article, "I Sold My Data for Crypto. Here's How Much I Made," in *Wired Magazine Online* 17 December 2018, www.wired.com/story/i-sold-my-data-for-crypto/.

26 "Ingestible devices, for example, are being developed to travel inside the body, collect information, and send it to servers to report on an individual [...] They are intended to visualize, monitor, and diagnose internal processes such as blood pressure, PH balance, core body temperature (Nikita, 2014), and ultimately report to an external receiver." (Pedersen, 2019, 21).

27 The definition of "e-textiles" from WEAR glossary, https://legacy.wearsustain.eu/about/wearables-e-textiles/.

28 See Institute of Network Cultures on *The Goodness of Genomic Data and other concerns*, Barbara Dubbeldam, 22 January 2019, http://networkcultures.org/blog/2019/01/22/not-as-good-as-gold-goodness-of-gnomic-data/.

29 Pederson, "BodyNets", 12.

30 Daniel C. Howe, "Surveillance Countermeasures: Expressive Privacy via Obfuscation," *APRJA* 4, no. 1, (June 2015): 88–99, https://aprja.net//issue/view/8402/894

31 "[...] ingestible technology is a new frontier under much development in the sphere if visceral computing [...] The idea of swallowing a computer device, allowing it to either act on or surveil the body from within [...]" (Pedersen, 2019: 28) The European Commission wrote a paper in December 2016 on this and a feedback paper in 2017, confirming these insights by Pedersen, found here https://ec.europa.eu/digital-single-market/en/news/feedback-stakeholders-smart-wearables-reflection-and-orientation-paper.

32 "Cognitive experiences will not only be used for digital telepathy (i.e. moving computer interfaces with the brain), they could be stored by third parties, or they could be used in predictive models to draw conclusions about thoughts and feelings (Nick, Berman, and Barnehama 2015)." (Pedersen, 2019: 24).

33 Ibid, 11.

34 Bruce Baer Arnold and Wendy Elizabeth Bonython discuss Genomic/DNA Data and what might constitute the "good data" in this context in their chapter "Not As Good As Gold? Genomics, Data and Dignity."

35 Hernandez 2014, my italics.

36 Pederson, "BodyNets", 5, my italics.

37 Taken critically, personal cloud computing involves a depoliticized ideology that rhetorically justifies bodily surveillance and [...] the "the subjugation of the body through the acquisition and assimilation of data." (Manley et al. 2012, 313 in Pedersen, 2019, 11).

38 Ibid Garrett 2019 and see the work of Morone here http://jenniferlynmorone.com.

39 'Sousveillance' is a term coined by wearable-computing pioneer Steve Mann in 2004 to describe inverse surveillance [...] Mann suggests that societies may employ sousveillance "as a way to balance the increasing (and increasingly one-sided) surveillance." More on this here http://wearcam.org/acmmm2004sousveillance/mann.pdf.

40 Sulleyman 2017, cited in Garret, 2017, 6.

41 "Seamless interaction with cognitive processes, if networked, would *risk parasitic relationships where humans (i.e., thoughts, ideas, memories, lies, etc.) are the source for data*, rather than positioning humans as the benefactor of (seamless) services," (Pedersen, 2019, 26, my italics).

42 Camille C. Baker, *New Directions in Mobile Media and Performance* (Oxford, New York: Routledge), 2018.

43 Pedersen points out that:

> Connecting wearables, implantables, and ingestibles, through body networks would eventually treat them as one data system [...] that would funnel data to and from the body to third parties. It would

> also require human users committed to the practice of sharing bodily data in everyday life (e.g., working, staying healthy, playing, shopping, dating, etc.).
>
> (February 2019, 10)

44 This concept is unpacked well by Slavoj Zizek in his book, especially the about the concept of unknown knowns in *How to Read Lacan*, London: Granta Books, 2006, 52–53.

45 In *A Peer-Reviewed Journal About … Datafied Research*, Vol 4 (1) ed. Christian Ulrik Andersen and Geoff Cox, www.aprja.net/personalisation-as-currency/.

46 Originally, this concept was inspired by Judith Butler in *Gender Trouble: Feminism and the Subversion of Identity* (New York: Routledge, 1990).

47 See the full *WEAR Sustain* project website here https://wearsustain.eu/dashboards/home about the project https://wearsuitute Good Data in this stain.eu/static/about and the legacy website http://legacy.wearsustain.eu/.

48 Term and practice instigated by Matt Ratto as described here https://current.ecuad.ca/what-is-critical-making.

49 Baker, *New Directions*.

50 Greta Thunberg, "'Our house in on fire': Greta Thunberg, 16, urges leaders to act on Climate," www.theguardian.com/environment/2019/jan/25/our-house-is-on-fire-greta-thunberg16-urges-leaders-to act-on-climate.

51 Such as the work of the WEAR Sustain funded teams, artist Kasia Molga kasiamolga.net, designers CuteCircuit https://starts-prize.aec.at/en/soundshirt-2-0/ and non-wearables focused data artists, such as Ciutat Vella https://starts-prize.aec.at/en/ciutat-vellas-land-use-plan/, Kate Crawford AI Now Institute and Vladan Joler https://starts-prize.aec.at/en/anatomy-of-an-ai-system/, Leon Baauw, Marcha Schagen https://starts-prize.aec.at/en/project-kovr/, James Bridle https://jamesbridle.com/works/citizen-ex-installation and Julian Oliver https://julianoliver.com/output/category/projects.

# 37

# NETWORKED EXPERIENCE AND CONTINUAL RE-ORIENTATION

*Martin Rieser*

In 2006, while developing a taxonomy of mobile artworks, Tuters and Varnelis[1] identified two types of locative mapping: annotative and phenomenological. The first tags the world virtually, while the latter traces the actions of people in the world. To extend this taxonomy of mapping through to the mode of the performative, they postulated a performative mapping practice that tracks participants' actions but doesn't trace them in order to create a map. The map is not an empty canvas to be painted, instead it is part of a dynamic process negotiated by collective participants. Locations become events that cause the map to perform in certain ways. The concept of "performative mapping" relied on dynamic processes set in motion by the participants' movements and the spaces that evolved between them.

Since the early days of mobile play in 2001, games such as *Botfighters* and *Can You See Me Now* have been overlaid on real cities, demanding physical engagement from players as they chase one another through the streets. Other mobile experiences have drawn on the pure pleasure of physical exploration to find digital or physical resources, such as in Geocaching. Educational experiences engaged learners in simulations that overlay the real world such as *Savannah*.[2] Location-based technologies have also enhanced Live Action Role Play by enabling the creation of fantasy artifacts. Finally, artists have combined digital media with physical locations, props, and players on the city streets to create performances that draw on the everyday world as a theatrical backdrop, such as in the work of Duncan Speakman.[3]

Thus, mobile devices appear performative in their nature, with public space interpenetrating our private concerns, so that any conversation has its willing or unwilling eavesdroppers. If one adds to this the potential for social interaction, demonstrated by mobile gaming, you have a case of new technology creating adaptive social behaviors that contain strong performative elements. These new kinds of free movement refer back to the idea of mobility, which some theorists have started to term "hypermobility," informed by what Virilio in philosophical terms calls the "third interval":

> The third interval is the space of hypermobility. It is a third place made of time and space. Hypermobility is something not so new for us, it is already known as physical mobility, that of flight, of train travel, and that of voice communications. This is what is usually considered as mobility by the tradition of studies by architects, urban planners and sociologists from the rising of the industrial age until now. The dimension of hypermobility works in addition to other levels of known mobility, opening up to a symbolic kind of interaction between human actors and 'real space'. The real space of communication roads splits open to communication

> means and now wireless mobility gives birth to a new form of mobility where urban space of cities represents an accelerated dimension of everyday life, an ongoing witness probably reshaped by what is happening in its different aspects and declinations of social, private, public, material.[4]

An early locative project, which epitomized these emergent qualities of performative mapping was *MILK*, winner of a Golden Nica at Ars Electronica. With *MILK*, the artists Esther Polak and Leva Auzina used Global Positioning System (GPS) to trace routes to create a form of landscape art for a networked society.[5] *MILK* was based in part on a project by Polak and the Waag Society: Amsterdam Real Time, in which GPS transponders mapped cyclists in Amsterdam on their traffic routes by the aggregation of their travel measured over a period of weeks. *MILK* suggested a god-like vision of locative technologies that allowed the tracking of freighted foodstuffs. In this case, it was loaded with heavy irony since the dairy-rich Netherlands imported their milk from Latvia, making visible the contradictions and excess of a networked society.

In later incarnations, the project evolved to an African version where local Nigerian herders were communicated with by robot-drawn sand maps. In its installed form, a projection shows Dutch artist Esther Polak standing at the edge of a dirt road, holding a microphone toward Mr. Idiris, a Fulani herder. Between them is a translator. All three are watching what looks like a toy, a plastic water bottle on wheels as it moves about jerkily, spitting out sand. Idiris gestures toward the robot as he talks animatedly. The right screen shows him guiding his herd along the road (Figure 37.1).

For the project *NomadicMILK* (2006–2010), Polak worked with a team of researchers including an anthropologist and a robotics engineer, in order to explore milk distribution systems in western Africa. In Nigeria, they used GPS technology to track the paths of Fulani herders, and truckers transporting the imported Peak brand milk from the harbor in Lagos, where it arrives from Europe to the capital Abuja, and from the city to the outlying suburbs. The data was fed to a custom-built robot that used sand to draw the recorded routes, allowing the participants to see and comment on their own tracks. The nomads, the artist says, "immediately recognised themselves in the sand routes as the robot carried them out. It let people look at the patterns they made based purely on memory, based on their own route."[6]

However, the increasing importance of maps in defining space within these projects should not blind us to the fact that even such well-intentioned and original mapping is never a neutral process, but always has been a highly selective and subjective one, in which can be embedded various

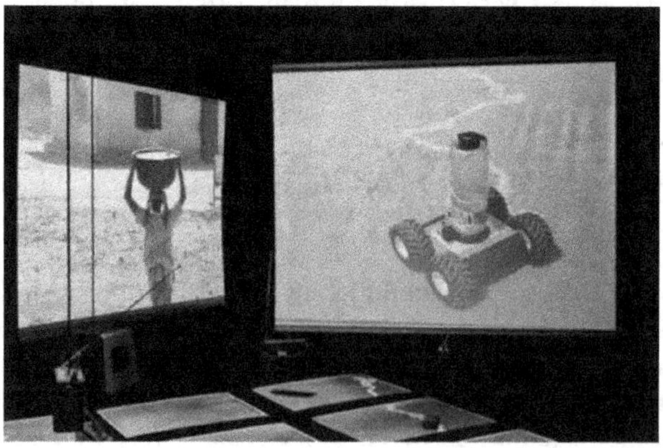

*Figure 37.1* *NomadicMilk* (2006–2010) installed. Photo credit: Edible Geography; www.ediblegeography.com/nomadic-milk/

(invisible) ideological assumptions. Many other GPS mapping projects tended to forget this and even revel in the act of remapping without context. Media artist Coco Fusco launched a headlong attack on new media practices associated with networks and mapping, declaring:

> It is as if more than four decades of postmodern critique of the Cartesian subject had suddenly evaporated ... In the name of a politics of global connectedness, artists and activists too often substitute an abstract 'connectedness' for any real engagement with people in other places or even in their own locale.[7]

Ubiquitous computing evangelists had early heralded a coming age of urban infrastructure, capable of sensing and responding to the events and activities transpiring around them. Imbued with the capacity to remember, correlate, and anticipate, this near-future "sentient" city was envisioned as being capable of reflexively monitoring its environment and our behavior within it, becoming an active agent in the organization of everyday life in urban public space.

However, even the use of passive, code-based technologies can also give agency to the public and create a new type of embedded history, which is a very different form of sentience. In Western Art's historical tradition, the rendering of landscape has not only elucidated the relationship between beauty, aesthetic pleasure, and the representation of the natural world, but has also made visible systems of power, control, domination, and surveillance. New media technologies such as GPS and digital data visualization and sonification, can potentially reformulate and expand the possibilities for representing "nature" and "environment" by altering, first, the ways we conceptualize and experience our bodily relationship in the urban landscape, and second, our treatment of landscape as "object" or "picture," and third, our sense of landscape as a repository of history: as an inhuman body that is marked, scarred or massively reshaped by the passage of human, and geological time.

Artworks that use technologies such as GPS have transformed landscape from a "picture" to a multi-layered, multi-channel experience, often incorporating multiple sense modalities and extending beyond the instant into a highly durational, expanded spatio-temporal field. These projects are usually artworks with strong documentary and performative features and are predicated on this new sense of embodied representation of the urban landscape.

## The Affordances of the Medium

In exploring the potential for mobile media narratives to include the performative individual, the Mobile Bristol[8] project made an attempt to define the pleasures of the medium through a seminar series in 2005, where for example, it was discovered that the accidental overlapping of ambient environmental sound and augmented sound within a locative work created a delicious ambiguity and a sense of extra resonance for an audience, a phenomenon termed "Magic Moments." Now what is needed most is not only the pleasures of reception and use in this medium, but also to understand the social and physical context of these new artworks. These are increasingly dependent on haptic and spatial senses such as *proprioception*, which are little understood by artists, but are within the affordances of the emerging technologies.

Key to the performative nature of mobile narratives is the forgotten sense of proprioception, which implies the simultaneous co-existence of inner and outer space on the basis of individuality and the specific occupation of spatial positioning. Yet, because they are related, the "external" and "other" already feels as "one's own," and this is exactly what causes the sense of presence. In its sense of proprioception and the many possible connections that the body is ready for, only a certain number are ever activated. The resulting proprioception is a special kind of internal image. This image may not necessarily coincide with an external optical, auditory, or haptic image.

According to Brian Massumi, proprioception translates the exertions and ease of the body's encounters with objects into a muscular memory of relationality. At the same time proprioception both enfolds tactility and draws out the subject's reactions to the qualities of the objects it perceives through all five senses.[9] A concept that was further extended by Jason Farman into spatial engagements across GPS-enabled Social Media which he framed as forms of "social proprioception."[10]

## Performance as Game Landscape

Early games played using mobile technologies such as *Catchbob* (2004)[11] and Blast Theory's *Uncle Roy All Around You* (2003),[12] combined internet and mobile technologies where the city and the internet were regarded as interrelated stages on which we play, regardless of the specific context. Steve Benford of Nottingham University now talks of "seamful" media where players have learned to exploit GPS "shadows" (where tall buildings block satellite triangulation) to their own advantage during game play, describing how such unforeseen effects of the technology encouraged new kinds of movement through the city.[13]

The failure of such works often results from misapplied contextual practice: I once tested Valentina Nisi's *Media Portrait of the Liberties* (2004) in Dublin before the demise of MIT's Eurolab in 2005.[14] We had gone about a block when the local youths began stoning us. The technology was certainly impressive, but this new form of public art was alien even to the children of the collective contributors to the artwork. When participating in Blast Theory's *Uncle Roy All Around You*, I reflected on how the game's format had reduced the richness of the city to a few textual clues and a dangerous process of frantic searching with users crossing roads with even less awareness than the average mobile music listener.

Feminist critics have often raised alternative strategies to break the negatives of a culture of male "control" through fully engaged individual performance. Not surprisingly, an early example of female locative practice explored precisely this area. Teri Rueb's *Drift* (2004)[15] tied a sound landscape to the movements of the tide on a north European beach. The installation covered a 2×2 kilometer region on the Wadden Sea that is filled with areas of interactive sound that moved in and out with the tide. The piece creates a space of flows consisting of sounds and words that travel like particles on simulated air and water currents loosely based on actual oceanographic and meteorological data. The audience had the choice of either giving itself up to those primal cycles of nature or risking complete confusion and loss of data.

Blast Theory's *Uncle Roy All Around You* was one of the most lauded locative artworks of its day, yet it appeared to be an uneasy mix of performance and game. Its full narrative being only accessible to those who successfully complete their quest. The real and virtual sit in an uncomfortable relationship with the environment, which is only valued as a source of directional clues—and any casual bystander remains largely mystified and excluded. The charge leveled at Blast Theory at a conference[16] was that of complacently and uncritically adapting new practice for the games industry, thus unwittingly acting as fashionable agents for intrusive and suspect technologies. For the flip side of ubiquitous communication and augmented location is the ability to track the audience: so a whiff of the totalitarian always haunts the liberating potential of the technologies. Matt Adams has rebutted this critique in an interview, pointing to the collaborative co-dependency explored by the work.[17]

Their performances and installations were supported through corporate sponsorship, public arts funding, and through a six-year collaboration with the Mixed Reality Laboratory at the University of Nottingham. The group's own web site claims:

> Blast Theory has a history of working with corporate clients to deliver innovative marketing strategies, 'thereby creating' commercial projects that draw global audiences to compelling,

> high adrenaline interactive experiences. The team of artists and scientists has worked with blue chip clients in the television, apparel and telecoms sectors to launch products, build profile, inspire staff and engage customers.[18]

Blast Theory's *A Machine To See With* (2011) was presented as a film where you played the lead. You signed up online and handed over your mobile phone number. You then received an automated call giving you an address. When arriving at your allotted corner your phone rang. From there, a series of instructions led you through the city as you gradually become the lead in a heist movie. As you moved from hiding money inside a public lavatory, to meeting with a partner in crime and onwards to the bank it was up to you to deal with the bank robbery and its aftermath. *A Machine To See With* was a collision between high and low culture, genre clichés with the reality of the urban environment. It started from the premise that the city and the mobile phone were both cultural spaces, combining elements of location-based games, theater, and a city tour. Each visitor followed a similar route but interacted in their own way.[19]

> A *Machine To See With* was originally commissioned as a piece of 'locative cinema:' a crossover between locative media performance and an imaginary cinematic narrative. It engaged participants through a highly embodied experience that—despite the pre-scripted narrative—remains open and unpredictable.[20]

In our everyday lives, we are all subject to several mutual performances between individuals where everyone is at the same time actor and audience: an unrehearsed, emergent performance that is never fully controllable and subject to a "kind of information game—a potentially infinite cycle of concealment, discovery, false revelation, and rediscovery."[21] This information game, enacted in the environment in which we perform our everyday lives, enables reflexivity. Of course, what the artist expects and what actually happens form a separate and often more interesting performance altogether, as in this interview response form Blast Theory evaluating the failings of *A Machine To See With*:

> During my fieldwork, I was able to observe how 'failure' manifested itself in different forms: failure to follow the instructions relayed by the 'machine,' getting lost and asking a (clueless) bystander for information on directions, failing to engage with bystanders and fellow participants according to the instructions given, failure to avoid the paranoia of being followed, imagining you are part of some strange social experiment; and even failure to complete the performance due to previous participants hijacking it.[22]

## Documentary as Performance

In many ways these inhabited improvisational dramas reapply some of the earliest felicities of documentary practice to the new fragmented genres of micro-documentary and drama, as is vividly explained in this quote from artist Duncan Speakman:

> Grierson described documentary as 'the creative treatment of actuality,' films like *Nightmail* and *Coal Face* seem so far removed from the type of "documentary" that fills our screens today. They took everyday realities and framed then within beautiful soundtracks, creative musical editing techniques, poetry and abstraction. I guess that's the kind of documentary I'm trying to make, ones that show us nothing more than the everyday, but try and show us how beautiful it can be.[23]

The use of locative media in documentary contexts is not new, but in the past has relied heavily on custom equipment and live project guides. I can think of the early examples of *Riot!* (2004) from Mobile Bristol and *34n118w* (2003) where US artists Jeremy Hight, Jeff Knowlton and Naomi Spellman used locative media to "read" a space with GPS and other wireless technology, examining the many layers of city spaces.[24] Marking narrative triggers through locative media, they drew multiple lines from archeology, fiction, architecture, and design across the urban terrain, but these projects tended to deal with an historical past rather than the lived and individually performed present.

The aim of my own 2011 Athens-based workshop was to study elements of the urban environment and to form new locative trails in the form of a structured collaborative narrative, enriching the city through interactive content that reflected its contemporary transformations. *Codes of Disobedience & Dysfunctionality*[25] was part of the Hybrid City Conference initiative, sponsored by Global Gateway. Inspired by the numerous posters and the dense graffiti encountered in the city center, the workshop connected the urban surroundings of Athens to opinions and statements of its inhabitants toward the challenges imposed by current social, political and financial circumstances, namely: anger, disobedience, opposition, and dysfunctionality. Most of the participants were students of either architecture or communications from the University of Athens, and they threw themselves enthusiastically into mapping social reactions and interviewing residents.

The features of the contemporary metropolis in the midst of a period of crisis were the main focus of the project, posing at the same time questions about the role of and scale of mediation by technology in urban everyday life. The work that formed after the completion of the workshop was presented at the premises of the National Museum of Contemporary Art in Athens, on the internet and in the center of the city (on the streets Skoufa—Navarinou—Tzavela). QR-coded stickers carrying imagery from the immediate environment were placed in selected locations. By scanning the stickers with a mobile phone, the public could access the audiovisual material created during the workshop. Combining elements of installation art, urban intervention, gaming, and performance, *Codes of Disobedience & Dysfunctionality* reflected my long-term practice using art and technology (Figure 37.2).

A couple of months later, *Urban Digital Narratives* (2011)[26] looked at the crisis of immigration and gentrification in the Gazi area and the impacts of neo-liberal economic processes on the locally diverse social and ethnic groups. Funded by the British Council, the project explored the new possibilities offered by technology and attempted to ask whether one could really capture the social needs and attitudes of in city like Athens, and whether the patterns and characteristics of urban life could be identified by adapting the uses of these communication systems.

*Figure 37.2* QR-coded posters related to environmental features from the *Codes of Disobedience* route. Photo credit: Martin Rieser

A technocratic imposition of austerity has been imposed on Greece, ignoring the democratic call of the now deposed Papandreou for a referendum on further austerity measures, which, no matter how calculated his call, laid bare the nature of the EU project and its real imperatives. The stories collected during the two projects formed a snapshot of a country whose basic systems are breaking down, where dysfunctionality and resistance were the emerging urban behaviors in a broad swathe of the public.[27]

One of the problematics in these projects was the self-consciousness of phone use in public and the complex relationship that users had to interacting with materials in the street. Perhaps part of the general problem with this new mobile documentation is the one identified by Paul Virilio—that of the change from considered diegesis to continuous and automatic present, where the user creating the narratives becomes both subject and object, in a new form of pan-cinema. Virilio uses the example of Michel Klier—and his film *Der Riese* (*The Giant*) (1983)—in materializing the change of the function of the cameraman in the film. The film is a montage of images that are recorded by automatic surveillance cameras in German cities in their major public places such as streets, airports, subway stations, department stores, and banks. Klier himself held this film to be the end of his auteur art. According to Virilio, the visual subject has been transferred to a technical effect, which forms a sort of *pancinema* that turns our most ordinary acts into movie action, into new visual material. For Virillio, this equates to the culmination of the progress of representational technologies, of their military, scientific and investigative instrumentalization over the centuries.[28]

In his book *The Practice of Everyday Life*, Michel de Certeau defines urban space according to the patterns of those who use it. He suggests that "...space is composed of intersections of mobile elements. It is in a sense actuated by the ensemble of movements deployed within it ... In short, space is a practiced place."[29] This very much became the starting point for the *Urban Digital Narratives* project since the district was a deeply patterned space defined by the proximity and distance of its mixed communities. *Urban Digital Narratives* was realized through a collaborative workshop in the Gazi-Keramikos district of Athens that constructed a locative route via collaboration with another mixed group of students and architects, artists, photographers, videomakers, and computer scientists from AIT (Athens Institute of Technology).

In these two described projects, we tried to unpack some of the tacit assumptions, latent biases, and hidden agendas at play behind the new and emerging urban infrastructures, and to avoid the de-naturing of the content through the technology employed. *Codes of Disobedience* took an emblematic street in central Athens running from the fashionable Kolanaki district down toward the center of resistance to the austerity measures. It crossed the site of the Shrine to Alexander Grigoropoulou, the boy who was shot by the police, which set off the riots of December 2008, on the corner of Mesolongiou (a street now unofficially renamed Alexander Grigoropoulou Street and Tzabella street) and then it passed on to the anarchistic regions of the city, where early self-curated social projects posited a communal alternative to the new austerity.[30]

Stories emerged through many such street encounters and also through deliberative interviews with local workers: including a surviving traditional plumber, a street vegetable stall-holder, and the owner of a juggling emporium! Other narratives were more generic, ranging from the serious (examining the drug culture of the Navarino end of the street) to the hilarious-satirizing of the Greek Orthodox Church's obsession with barcodes as "works of the devil." In addition, at the gentrified *Kolonaki* end of the street virtual graffiti was re-imposed on walls where it had been previously painted out. In both projects, the link between the stickers and posters to the place is crucial. We were attempting to enable the participants to revisit the textures and the faces of the location in great detail, to notice the texture and uniqueness of each place; to re-imagine the city as a place of potential and beauty through the energies of the everyday. The intention was to reapply some of the earliest felicities of documentary practice to the new fragmented genres of micro-documentary.

In *Urban Digital Narratives* the chosen area of Gazi-Keramikos was a very mixed inner-city area where gentrification had created a pleasure zone of clubs and cafes surrounded by established artisan communities and migrant communities to the North. These disparate elements faced multiple problems. Above all, there was a sense of powerlessness in the face of the ill-formed status for recent migrants and of displacement by rising property prices and rents in the south of the area; together being an influx of noisy and youthful revelers with hedonistic values into conservative working neighborhoods.

Naturally, tensions were created between these disparate groups, and we found an underlying reactive anger in the settled Greek community, which compromised the project in its final stages. Lakhou Street traverses the area around the metro station. It had been radically transformed during the previous five years, with old buildings, houses, and warehouses being converted into modern bars and cafes. Leonidou Street still maintained a residential character. Succeeding Lakhou Street and traversing the neighborhoods of Keramikos and Metaxourgio helped us trace the transformation in urban character along its length, almost in the form of a history.

At first the workshop progressed happily, with its very mixed group of participants from design, architectural, and arts backgrounds—some experienced practitioners and some post-graduate students. Multiple and complex narratives were recorded in audiovisual form, sourced from all the disparate social groups in the neighborhood who were photographed and interviewed after giving consent. It was only during the final stage of the project when QR code stickers featuring video story characters were posted up in the neighborhood south of the metro that one elderly Greek's wife objected vociferously to his image being made public and forcibly made a citizen's arrest on a participating filmmaker! This was in spite of the subject having given consent. It revealed a deep well of suspicion and anger and a community closed against outsider interventions, no matter how well-intentioned. Although an isolated incident in an otherwise successful project, it showed how close to the surface hurt and suspicion exist in these challenged and displaced traditional communities. It is a striking feature of the area that the playground of affluent young Athenians lies cheek by jowl with successive immigrant waves and the traditional white Greek remnants.

It is not surprising that Athens has recently become the focus of resistance to the imposition of draconian neo-liberal disciplines on its economy and that it remains the flashpoint for any future European economic crisis and the space where the contradictions of the market and its effects on the contemporary city appear in their acutest form. The use of mobile media art and related digital technology can highlight, augment, and interpret these contradictions, giving voice to the dispossessed, though ultimately their solution remains a political one.

While media arts using locative tools have naturally tended toward urban environments and been drawn from either game or situationist orientations, I am more concerned toward the development of a theory and practice of situated and embodied arts that relates to a broader spectrum of ambulant practice, referencing backwards to the earlier art forms, but making use of the new digital affordances. Now there are two domains of locative practice—the "digital tame" of social media, online consumer culture, and most digital arts and the "wild" that addresses critical conditions in the "real" world such as poverty, disempowerment. and engaged locatedness— that have yet to find a meaningful voice in pervasive digital and mobile media. The two projects may have had a flawed documentary methodology, given the imperatives of time and their combined artistic direction, but through this reflective "failure" (and like many forms of mobile media art practice) they were actively geared toward experimentation, providing innovative forms of creative visibility and offering genuine attempts to document and present local voices in as unfiltered a way as was possible.

## *Ambient Literature* and Ambiguity

> Audiences' sensory apparatuses are remediated toward an ambiguity that reconstitutes the present moment of a re-factored world or, perhaps, more accurately, the present moment of a re-factored worlding, or even worldliness.[31]

*Ambient Literature* (2016) was a recent two-year collaboration between UWE Bristol, Bath Spa University and the University of Birmingham, established to investigate the locational and technological future of the book. One of the experimental works produced was *Breathe* (see Figure 25, color insert), a ghost story that adapts to location by the novelist Kate Pullinger who recognized the need for conditionality in all the texts to enable the reader's imagination to work effectively within its physical space.

> One of the most interesting things about *Breathe*,[32] the ghost story I created in collaboration with Editions at Play (Visual Editions and Google Creative Labs Sydney), and the Ambient Literature team, is its use of conditional text. Conditional text—text that alters in response to data that is pulled into the story via APIs—is embedded throughout *Breathe*. Now that the story has been out in the world for a few weeks it's become clear to me that most readers are aware of only a small amount of the conditional text present in the story—those uncanny moments when the ghosts seem to know where you are as you read.[33]

One of the directors of the project Jon Dovey picks up the necessity of ambiguity in syntax:

> What we have found in our preliminary look is that the languages of ambience tend toward the contingent, the conditional and the subjunctive. You may want to, you might, you could, perhaps: the language linking the internal affective world and the external world of reality is tentative and necessarily reflects and produces the ambiguity of the whole enterprise.[34]

And also, recognizes the affordance of the ambiguous sound experience earlier defined in 2006 by the Mobile Bristol project, as being central to convincing the reader/user:

> So the emergency siren, overhead plane, or crunch of a gravel path all start to appear in locative sound works. So the ambience of such works consisted in a rather subtle art of the mix in which real world sounds, cross fades and audio balancing accompanied the user through fuzzily defined and not always obvious zones. Such works produce what I can only call ambient experiences where the user is drifted through a sonic space that works with the world surrounding us but doesn't map it, pin it or even necessarily navigate it.[35]

## Conclusion

Updatable networked narratives, whether in the form of personalized drama or individualized mobile documentary practice, are transforming our relationship with each other and with the world in ways that are just becoming apparent. Through research and experimentation—artists, designers, historians, and filmmakers are finding the affordances of the new mobile tools through GPS tracking, virtual reality, and new social contexts to be both daunting and inspiring: where contingency and ambiguity have become vital elements in convincing the new user that the real and virtual spaces of history or imagination can overlap and increase in resonance for the adapters of this technology, and where respect for the complexities of social lives and histories can empower and provide new meanings for both the creatives and their public. With the rapid development and combination of AI technologies and convincing Augmented Reality, the potential for audience engagement through performative and located mobile narratives and documentaries could become ever more powerfully convincing when placed in the right creative hands.

## Notes

1 Mark Tuters and Kazys Varnelis, "Beyond Locative Media: Giving Shape to the Internet of Things," *Leonardo* 39, no. 4 (2006): 357–63.
2 Retta Guy, *The Evolution of Mobile Teaching and Learning* (Santa Rosa, CA: Informing Science Press, 2009), 144.
3 See: www.watershed.co.uk/studio/residents/duncan-speakman, see also Alan Chamberlain, Leif Opperman, Martin Flintham, Steve Benford, Peter Tolmie, Matt Adams, Ju Farr, Nick Tandavanitj, Joe Marshall and Tom Rodden, "Locating Experience: Touring a Pervasive Performance," *Personal Ubiquitous Computing Journal* 15, no. 7 (2011): 717–30, doi: 10.1007/s00779-010-0351-3.
4 Gianni Corino, "Spatial Issues and Performative Media in Digital Mobility: A Network Perspective," MSc Theses, Plymouth University, 2006.
5 See http://milkproject.net/index.html and www.nomadicmilk.net/full/.
6 Karen O'Rourke, "Art Work/ Dream Work in New Media Documentary," Leonardo Electonic Almanac 20, no. 1 (2014): 266–83, www.leoalmanac.org/vol-20-no-1-red-art/.
7 Coco Fusco, "Questioning the Frame: Thoughts about Maps and Spatial Logic in the Global Present," *In These Times*, 16 December 2004, www.inthesetimes.com/article/1750/.
8 A series of locative artwork experiments by Hewlett Packard, Watershed Media Centre and Bristol University 2002–2005, www.watershed.co.uk/projects/mobile-bristol.
9 Brian Massumi, *Parables of the Virtual: Movement. Affect, Sensation* (Durham, London: Duke University Press, 2002).
10 "Location-based social networks offer a form of intersubjective embodiment that gives participants a sense of social proprioception: a sense of embodied integrity that is aware of the self's place as that which is always already situated in relationship to the location of others" in Jason Farman, "Embodiment and the Mobile Interface," *Mobile Interface Theory: Embodied Space and Locative MEDIA* (New York: Routledge, 2012), chap. 1, Kindle.
11 *Catchbob* (2007), Mobile Game, https://chili.epfl.ch/page-92073-en-html/page-92247-en-html/page-92282-en-html/.
12 Blast Theory, *Uncle Roy All Around You*, 2003, www.blasttheory.co.uk/projects/uncle-roy-all-around-you/.
13 Performing Space Arts and Humanities Research Council Seminar at Nottingham Trent University February 2008.
14 Valentina Nisi, *Media Portrait of the Liberties*, www.valentinanisi.com/Media-Portrait-of-the-Liberties.
15 Teri Rueb, *Drift*, 2004, http://terirueb.net/drift-2004/.
16 Jonah Brucker Cohen, "Report from Futresonic 2004," Mobile Connections, Futuresonic 2004, 30 April–1 May, www.coin-operated.com/2004/04/30/report-from-futuresonic-2004/.
17 See Martin Rieser, *The Mobile Audience: Media Art and Mobile Technologies* (Amsterdam: Rodopi, 2011).
18 See: www.blasttheory.co.uk.
19 See www.blasttheory.co.uk/projects/a-machine-to-see-with/.
20 Marcos Pereira Dias, "A Machine to See With (and Reflect Upon): Interview with Blast Theroy Artists Matt Adams and Nick Tandavanitj," *Liminalities: A Journal of Performance Studies* 8, no. 1 (April 2012): http://liminalities.net/8-1/blast-theory.pdf.
21 Erving Goffman, *The Presentation of Self in Everyday Life* (London: Penguin Books, 1990), 20.
22 Pereira Dias, "A Machine to See With."
23 Jeff Watson, "Subtlemob Creator Duncan Speakman on 'Framing Everyday Realities,'" *Blog Interview*, 7 October 2010, https://remotedevice.net/interviews/subtlemob-creator-duncan-speakman-on-framing-everyday-realities/.
24 See: http://34n118w.net/34N/.
25 Curator Daphne Dragona and participating organizer Dimitris Charitos (University of Athens), technical support from Phil Sparks (Cuttlefish Multimedia) and Jackie Calderwood (PhD, Candidate De Montfort University), additional technical support Haris Rizopoulos, Aris Tsakoumis (University of Athens), empedia.info/maps/41, accessed June 2014.

26 Curation, organization and research: Eva Kekou (Freelance) Organisation Athens Information Technology College (AIT), Technical support: Jackie Calderwood (PhD candidate, De Montfort University), Financial support The British Council, Intalot and HTC, http://empedia.info/organisations/digital_urban_narratives/maps, accessed June 2014.
27 See www.martinrieser.com/?page_id=285.
28 Paul Virilio, *The Vision Machine* (Bloomington: Indiana University Press, 1994).
29 Michel de Certeau, *The Practice of Everyday Life* (Berkeley: University of California Press, 1984), 117.
30 There are several "people's parks" that were squatted by locals to thwart the city's plan to turn them into parking lots.
31 "Ambient Literature," Michael Marcinkowski and Matthew Hayler, on behalf of the Ambient Literature team, https://research.ambientlit.com/wp-content/uploads/2017/05/ambient-literature-definition.pdf.
32 See: http://breathe-story.com/.
33 Kate Pullinger, "*Breathe* and Conditional Text." https://research.ambientlit.com/index.php/2018/03/21/breathe-and-conditional-text/.
34 Jon Dovey, "Types of Digital Ambiguity," https://research.ambientlit.com/index.php/2017/09/14/7-types-of-digital-ambiguity/.
35 Ibid.

# SECTION NINE

# Urban Interventions

# 38
# BECOMING ALEXA

*Lauren McCarthy* in Conversation with *Jacina Leong*

Lauren McCarthy is an artist with a fascination for the way mobile technology impacts our everyday lives. With a humorous and playful approach, her projects augment hidden forms of control, related behavior, and the ways we continue to be monitored through our individual relationships with technology. As creator of the open source programming language, p5.js, McCarthy also advocates an inclusive and diverse approach to software development, and she discusses this with Jacina Leong, alongside social relationships at the intersection of surveillance, automation, and algorithmic living (Figure 38.1).[1]

What is unique to the ways in which surveillance, automation and algorithmic technologies are shaping our day-to-day lives? Why should we pay attention to their possible shaping effects to begin with?

We have been inundated with surveillance technologies for a while now, but I think a major shift is that they are becoming normalized and much less visible in a variety of ways. For example, it's much less common to see giant security cameras in public spaces. However, what *is* new is that these forms of surveillance are now operating via your smartphone and in your home—coming into your personal and private spaces. Being tracked by surveillance technologies, combined with machine learning, makes it possible to not just have your data collected, but where continual observations and assumptions are made about you—and actually go so far as to shape your behavior. This is alarming for me because it means that these technologies are taking away our sense of agency and right to privacy. It is also not clear how our data is being used, making it a lot harder to push back or reject and keep certain things private because we don't have a good sense of what is being tracked, and why.

You have said that through your work you are trying to highlight a trade that we are making for surveillance technologies, such as Personal Intelligent Assistants within our homes.[2] How so?

I think one of the ways that these technologies are being sold to us is by taking them totally out of the realm of surveillance or data and packaging them as "utility and convenience." Take Amazon's Alexa. Even though it has very advanced functionalities, the earliest commercials portrayed it as a speaker that you could talk to, or a hands-free calling device. I think that kind of message is a way of positioning these devices into people's homes without them thinking about what they actually are or are able to do. So, it's a trade that we're making but it is also not necessarily a trade

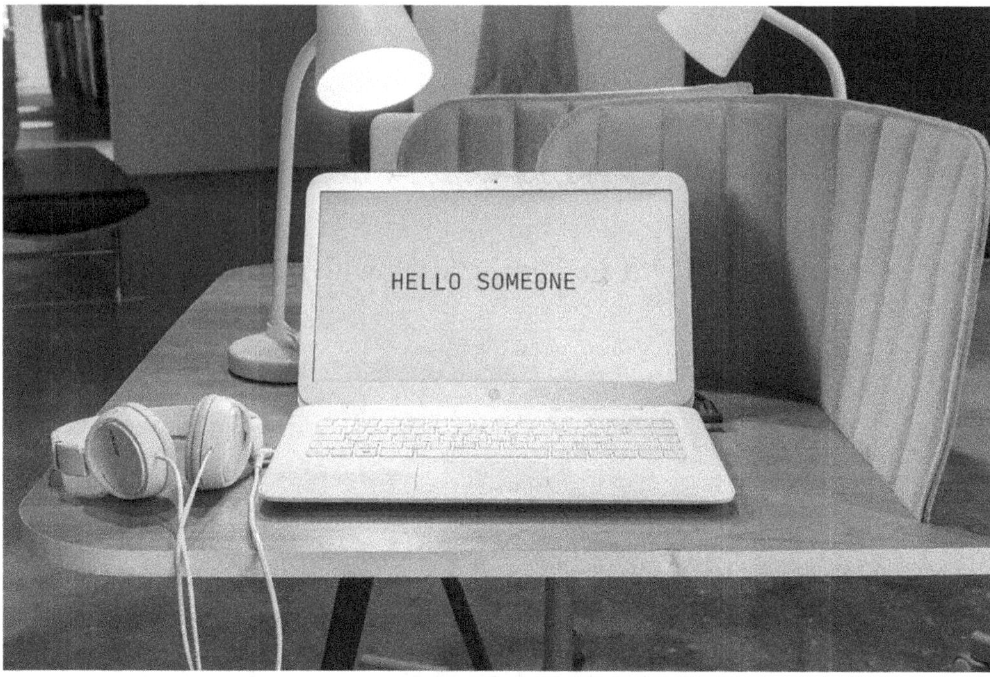


*Figure 38.1* Installation of *SOMEONE* (2019). Photo credit: Stan Narten

that we asked for in the first place. These devices are not necessarily even solving a problem that we needed a solution for. Tech companies are instead creating a problem and then selling us the solution (Figure 38.2).

> What can we learn from your projects such as *LAUREN*, *FOLLOWER*, and more recently, *SOMEONE*? What new insights have these projects brought into view, for you and your participants?

One thing that has been interesting is seeing the range of attitudes and levels of comfort that people have with these technologies. For example, with *LAUREN*, all these cameras and devices are installed in the participants' homes and controlled by me, so there's an aspect of human intelligence involved. For some people, the most affective part of the project is to be watched by another person. The aspect of control—they don't even get to wrap their heads around that because they are already so uncomfortable or disoriented by the presence of cameras, even though they are probably being tracked in more invasive ways than that in their everyday lives. Whereas other people are totally comfortable, and I think they're the people that are always streaming and always posting on Instagram. So they're like, okay great I have another follower and are more interested in the AI aspect of it.

What has been interesting is just seeing a range of reactions and realizing that they don't necessarily map to age, as you might think, or even to profession or where you live. It is not necessarily like, oh you live in a big city where lots of people have these technologies and must be more comfortable with them. I have done these projects in more remote areas and also more populated and it really feels like each person has their own comfort level with these technologies.

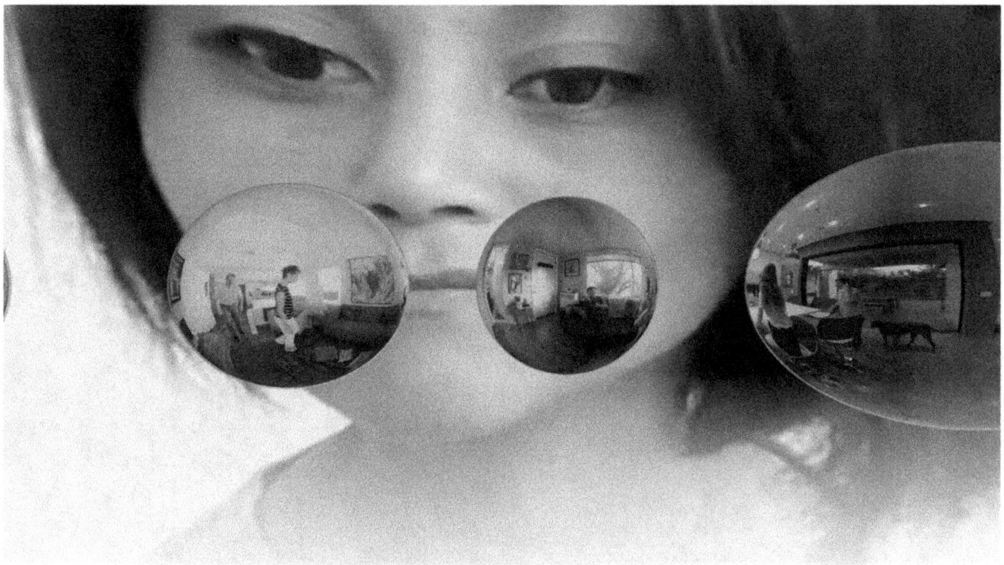

*Figure 38.2* Still from *LAUREN* website (2018). Photo credit: Lauren McCarthy

We hear a lot about care today and its intersection with locative technologies. How does care figure within your work and the interests that drive your projects?

It is something that I am really interested in. One of the things that I am doing in these projects—for example, *SOMEONE*, a human version of Amazon Alexa originally installed into four homes across the United States, is investigating the role of the algorithm of the AI. I started to think about what it is that I could provide that Alexa can't. I think the word care, and the idea of care, came up for me a lot. I also started to think through this distinction between service and care. A lot of the time what these capitalist-driven technologies provide is a service of performing care.

In countries like the United States and Australia, if you are serving someone or selling something as a cashier, you are supposed to do so with a smile. Enacting a performance of care even if you don't. Thinking about my role within these projects, it was kind of the opposite because it was quite intense to do: long durations and a lot of focused attention. I found that with *FOLLOWER*—a service that provide a real life follower, me, for a day—after chasing them around through the rain or just sitting for hours watching them read a book, I really did start caring about the participants. I think that was the thing my brain did to enable me to do this—because if I didn't care at all it would be really hard to do this work. So, I am interested in that idea and how care is being co-opted by technologies, but is also still something that distinguishes humans from what AI or technology or a company can provide.

The other issue that came up a lot in the projects though is that I was actually a pretty terrible substitute for Alexa. The participants would ask me to do something like turn on the music and I would hit the wrong button and accidentally turn on the hair dryer. But they had so much more patience for me than they would have had for Alexa (Figure 38.3).

Your work is also funny. I'm thinking here about projects like *WALKING AGENTS*, where visitors are invited to lay down on a smart pillow, and *SOCIAL TURKERS*, an interface you developed using Amazon Mechanical Turk to receive real-time feedback on your social interactions. There is a comical element that for me undergirds much of your work and seems

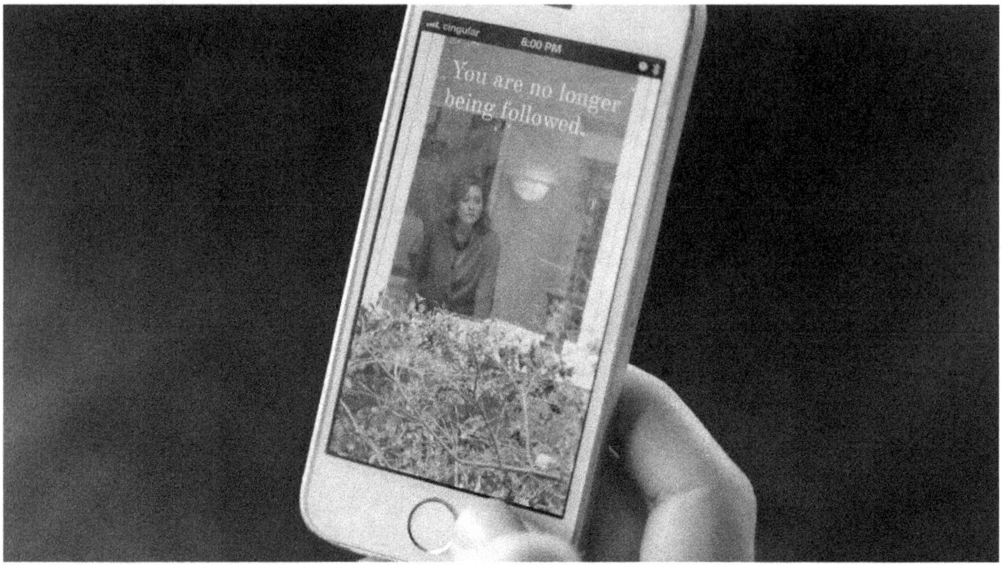


*Figure 38.3* Still from *FOLLOWER* (2015). Photo credit: David Leonard

to gesture towards the absurdity and complexity of our relationship with surveillance technologies. Can you speak to how humor operates within your practice?

For me, humor is a way to open things up a little bit because what we are talking about is often so serious and sometimes quite menacing. I think that if we can laugh it helps us to process the situation that we are in and to feel like we have some control and agency. That for me is sort of the criteria for making work. I think about ideas until I find one that makes me laugh. But it is also interesting because a lot of art takes itself very seriously. I remember in a grad critique class, one of my professors said it's like you are trying to be funny. (Laughs.) I am interested in making work that is not just for the "high art" world—and so, by adding humor, it is also a signifier that if a "non-art" person can laugh, then it means that they have got some part of the work and it is not totally inaccessible.

Tell us more about your work as the creator of the open source programming language, p5.js?

My work with p5.js is for me really about questioning what it means to make a tool that is welcoming and inclusive and open to all sorts of users. But also that the people behind it are a diverse group of people that are welcoming to anyone who is interested in being part of the tool's creation. Every tool is made up of the beliefs and assumptions of the people that make them. So if you have a really limited group of people doing that, even if it feels like you can do anything you want with it, it will be limited to what that group of people can imagine and build. p5 is just one tool, but I think if we start to apply that perspective to a lot more technologies we wouldn't have situations where you go to an earlier version of Google Maps and search for planned parenthood and there's no result because no one actually thought to include that. Our tools need to represent a broader human experience.

You recently exhibited with the REFRESH collective through their inaugural exhibition at Eyebeam? I understand that REFRESH is interested in addressing those who have been historically neglected and marginalized not only from technological developments but also artistic practices engaging with these developments. How is this achieved?

I am not a direct member of the REFRESH collective, but I think what they get right is that there are sometimes conversations around diversity and representation that takes the point of view that diversity means involving equal amounts of people. It is really not about that. I think what REFRESH gets—and what I see as the future for mobile media art—is that if we really want to have a more meaningful engagement with technology and culture through provocative media art, then we have to include more people in that conversation than just able-bodied, cis white men, or wherever you draw the line. We need to have a diversity of perspectives and that includes gender, race, ability, and also age, which is something that gets missed a lot in media art. I think one of the biggest things we have to address right now is figuring out how do we have some connection, or some empathy, or some way of building a world that is equitable for a bigger portion of the population.

You have suggested that you make art about what "confuses" you. Where do you think your current state of confusion around surveillance and other mobile technologies is leading your work?

A lot of my projects track where I am in my life. *LAUREN*, for example, really came out of my experience getting married and moving in with someone and questioning what it means to share a space with someone. So, the thing that I guess I am thinking about now is babies. It is such a rabbit hole for me as I have started to look into the ways in which technologies intersect with this and it's huge. Everything from assistive reproductive technologies and IVF, to surrogacy and egg donation, to genome editing technologies that can shape lives before (and after) birth.

I am also intrigued by how money intersects with the services or tools that you have access to as you're going through the reproductive process. We are also seeing the rise of headlines such as "Three Person Baby" and "First CRISPR Baby." I know that these are just flashy headlines and isolated events, but it is also becoming closer to being possible, and I don't think we have really thought about what that might entail. So what I have been thinking about lately is really this sweet spot between relationships, identity, and technology—but I don't know where it is going or how it will take shape yet.

What do you see as the future for mobile media art?

What is special about the field of mobile media art is that it is not just about art for art's sake. There are a lot of people making art with technology because they are interested in engaging with questions about what it means to live and work with these technologies, and to think about where they are taking us. As artists, we have the means to reach an audience, to present questions and provocations in a way that can really move people. My hope is that the future is a lot more open. It feels like there is a push in that direction but there is still a long way to go.

## Notes

1 See http://lauren-mccarthy.com/.
2 Dominic Rushe, "Let Me into Your Home: Artist Lauren McCarthy on becoming Alexa for a Day." *The Guardian*, May 15 2019, www.theguardian.com/artanddesign/2019/may/14/artist-lauren-mccarthy-becoming-alexa-for-a-day-ai-more-than-human.

# 39

# *QUOTIDIAN RECORD*

# The Musical Interpretation of Mobile Phone Location Data

*Brian House*

As I slip the record out from its sleeve, I examine the diagram on the surface of the vinyl. I place the stylus at the mark that indicates where "one year" begins. After I hit start, the hours of a "day" pass by with each turn of the record, which I hear as a musical pulse. Over this regular meter is a bouncing melody played on a dirty synth. The phrases become familiar even though the melody never quite repeats and occasionally makes excursions into more dynamic variations (Figure 39.1).

This is *Quotidian Record* (2012), an artwork which interprets one year of my location data as music. Captured via an app on my phone, each place I visited—from home to work, a friend's apartment to a foreign city—becomes a musical note; each revolution of the platter corresponds to a day of lived time. As the record turns, the sound suggests that our habitual patterns have inherent

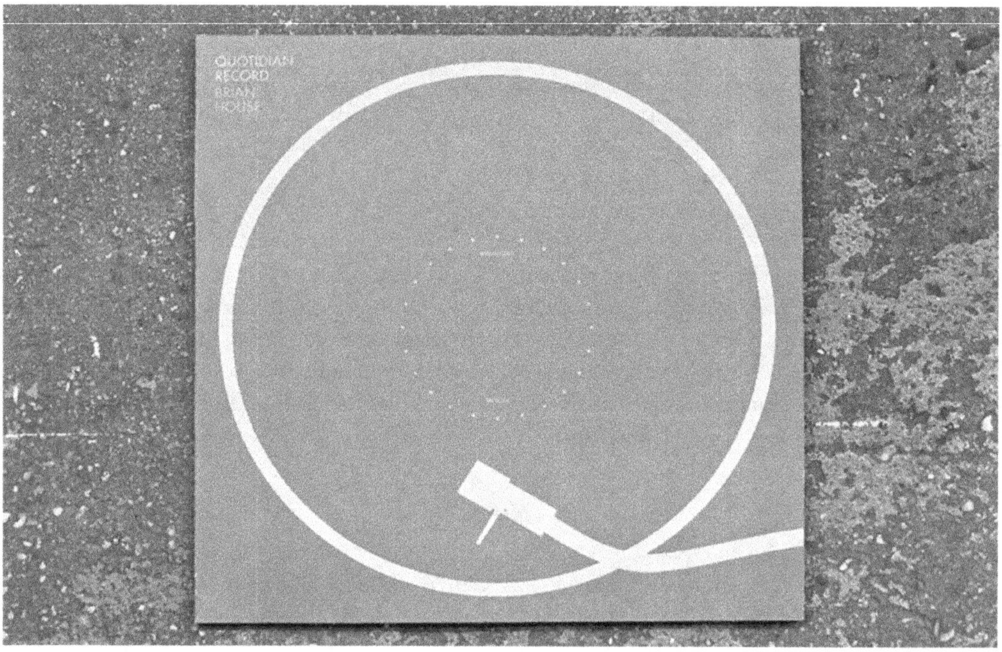


*Figure 39.1* *Quotidian Record* sleeve. Photo credit: Brian House

musical qualities. Hearing our daily rhythms in this way is an alternative sort of data science, one in which the abstractions of digital data, so essential to their use by the corporation and the state, are eschewed in favor of this paradigmatically analog form.

## Mapping the Everyday

In April of 2011, the American public first became aware that the new smartphones they'd been carrying with them—everywhere, at all times—were logging their latitude and longitude coordinates along the way. Dubbed "Locationgate," this small scandal would result in both a Senate hearing and an episode of *South Park* sending up Apple as Big Brother.[1] It had been just three years since the best-selling iPhone 3G introduced the Global Positioning Service (GPS) to the mainstream and moved location-based media from speculation to everyday reality.

Prompted by this public discussion, my colleagues and I at *The New York Times* Research and Development Lab created an iPhone app called *OpenPaths*, which I used log my own latitude and longitude coordinates every few minutes.[2] Through projects such as *Yellow Arrow* (2004)[3] and *Hundekopf* (2005),[4] I had previously explored how digital communication might reframe our encounter with the urban environment, whether by creating "hyperlinks in the real world" or by layering a fictional reality over the mundane one. However, continuous location tracking offered something perhaps even more potent, the ability to analyze the patterns and variations of everyday life that were already there but were previously hard to capture. It felt like an artistic imperative to explore what could be done with these data other than what was in the minds of Big Brother/ Big Business.

So, with phone in pocket, on a typical day I'd set out by bicycle from my home in Brooklyn, make my way across the Brooklyn Bridge, and head up the West Side of Manhattan to Times Square, perhaps stopping at a favorite fruit stand along the way. After leaving work at the *Times*, I'd head back down to my studio at Eyebeam Art and Technology Center in Chelsea before returning home. Every day was different, of course, and if the weather kept either the fruit guy or me off the street, it was just one of the contingencies of life that made my patterns recognizably mine but ultimately unpredictable. *OpenPaths* dutifully recorded these movements.

Coordinates are designed to be viewed, and so I plotted this activity on top of a map of New York's streets (Figure 39.2). Here was my life, presented as a personal topography. I could trace

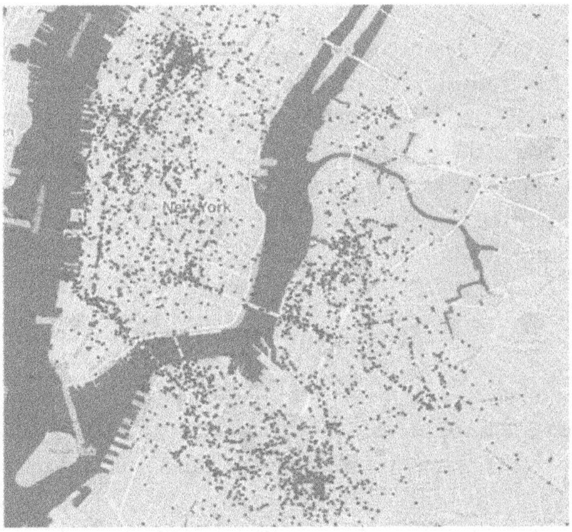

*Figure 39.2* One year of location data plotted on a map of NYC. Photo credit: Brian House

the braided paths with my finger and tell their stories as my memory was prompted by the map. But this simple act also revealed what the production of a map had left out. As Michel de Certeau beautifully explains, a map:

> transforms the *temporal* articulation of places into a spatial sequence of points. A graph takes the place of an operation. A reversible sign is substituted for a practice indissociable from particular moments and "opportunities" … it is thus a mark *in place* of acts, a relic in place of performances: it is only their remainder, the sign of their erasure.[5]

As informative as the map was, the unfolding of my everyday was nowhere to be found on its surface; only when re-temporalized by my narrative did it take on the added resonance of subjective experience.

As it happens, holding the map still has been one of the major endeavors of Western colonial, military, and economic history.[6] Look at old European cartography: the wild longitudinal distortions are what happens when as yet inaccurate clocks are used to account for the rotation of the Earth relative to the stars. Centuries later, we have an artificial constellation of GPS satellites which broadcast atomic time to the mobile phones triangulating their positions below. The scale of this temporal engineering suggests that the stable coordinate space that results, for all its usefulness, is a contrived way to understand the *where* of the world without the *when*.

For Henri Lefebvre, it is a form of false consciousness when relationships that emerge over time—"presences"—are perceived as static *things* that are merely "present." Real places are composed of presences that "are the facts of both nature and culture, at the same time sensible, affective and moral rather than imaginary."[7] But a dot on the map is the fantasy of an immobile present, and the digital data behind that dot are an even more perfect fiction. "40.747174, -74.006954" may represent a place in an ostensibly objective form, but the pure abstraction obfuscates the complex interrelationships that produce both the place and the designation.

Lefebvre calls for abstractions to be put back in relation to the body and its rhythms. When it came to my location data, this suggested that working with music might offer something that couldn't be found on a map. For one, as Brandon Labelle writes, "sound is intrinsically and unignorably relational."[8] It is indivisible from the acoustic space in which it resonates, a space defined by the contact—presence—of vibrating bodies. Further, it takes time to listen to something. Using data, could such duration be made analogous to the tempo at which I moved through the city?

To turn the rhythms of everyday life into sound would, perhaps, make explicit something that already exists implicitly in all music. Again, Lefebvre writes: "Musical rhythm … has an ethical function. In its relation to the body, to time, to the work, it illustrates real (everyday) life."[9] The habitual gestures of the body, the passage of seasons, the polyrhythms of relationships, and the regimentation of the (capitalist's) clock are, arguably, the fundamental basis of musical aesthetics. We are already attuned, then, to the dynamics of repetition and difference and the micro-political negotiations that they comprise.

## Musicking with Data

By May of 2012, I had collected a year's worth of my location data. To make it into music required an act of reverse engineering to recover from the encoding whatever feeling might remain. I started, therefore, with data science, programming, and visualization before progressing to the aesthetics of sound.

Each point in my dataset consisted of a latitude/longitude pair along with the time it was recorded. Rather than naively correlate these coordinates with musical features, I began by examining their relationships for any implicit structure. Using Python, an open-source programming language commonly used for analyzing data, I first identified individual "trips" that were taken between discrete locations. Any two points in geographic succession within a few minutes of each other were marked as part of the same journey.

Subsequently, what became more interesting was where the trips left off, that is, the places where I was doing the things that I do. Subtracting all but these endpoints, I could readily identify my home, work, studio, laundry, practice space, and other places of day-to-day activity. By employing a clustering algorithm at approximately the resolution of a single address, I ensured that all trips arriving or departing nearby reinforced the importance of a single place.

At this point in the exploratory process, geolocation coordinates had been transformed into a sequence of places. Trading the spatial map for a timeline, I was then able to visualize my behavior as a progression of color bands, where each color represented a different place and was sized in proportion to the amount of time I spent in that location. Rhythms immediately became apparent in this image; my daily commute emerged as groups of five repeating stripes, for example, which were interrupted by more chaotic bursts on the weekends and much looser formations when I traveled to cities in which my life was unstructured. To find correlations between days, I plotted this strip as concentric circles, with each circle corresponding to the 24 hours of a single day (see Figure 39.3). Diurnal, weekly, and monthly structures materialized.

Looking at this intermediate stage of visualization was when it hit me. For all of my interest in working with sound, it was not until I saw the isomorphic relationship of the visual spiral

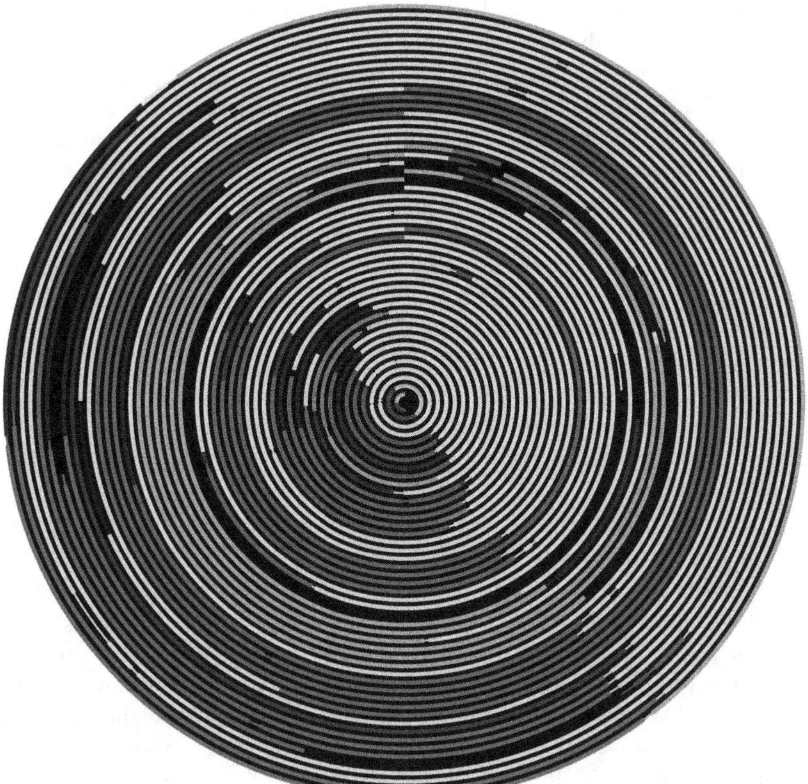

*Figure 39.3* Location data visualized as places over the 24 hours of the day. Photo credit: Brian House

to the grooves of a vinyl record that the project took on its material form. I found the circumstances of this discovery apropos. Analogous to Lefebvre's move from thing to process, the musicologist Christopher Small famously proposed that we ought to replace the term "music" with "musicking."[10] This verb would include not only playing an instrument but also activities like listening to the radio, selling tickets to a show, designing a band logo, or even appreciating the form of a vinyl record, all of which contribute to the meaning of the cultural form. Finding my way to sound through the physical properties of a recording medium safeguarded what followed from being just another form of abstraction and instead grounded it in the actual practice of music.

The dimensions of the record also provided a basic musical structure. Keeping my spiral diagram intact, one day of lived time as captured in the data could now be scaled to one full rotation of the platter: at 33 1/3 revolutions per minute—the standard speed for a 12-inch LP—one day became 1.8 seconds, more or less the duration of a measure in an upbeat pop song. Data from 365 days then computes to very nearly 11 minutes of music: a reasonable if concise length for a side (before you ask, the outer edge of the record takes the same amount of time to rotate as the inner one, it just covers more ground and therefore has greater fidelity).[11]

To come up with the pitches, I first separated all the places into cities and randomly assigned each one to a musical scale, such as C major. Next, I matched the places within that city to intervals within the scale; more consonant intervals correspond to more frequently visited locations. My apartment, for example, is the most frequent location, and so it is interpreted as a major third. In contrast, places I visited only once produce the outer jazz harmonies. The melody of the composition follows this intervallic play, moving between notes as I traveled between places. A second voice pulses on the root of the scale every 150 milliseconds, or 12 times a day, which serves as a temporal reference. The realized sound also includes a filter sweep on this pulse at 1.8 hertz, which further orients the listener to the diurnal cycle.

That this approach is unabashedly tonal is a reflection of various influences. First, I wanted to use inexpensive hardware synthesizers and repurposed guitar pedals to realize the timbre of the piece, rather than computer-generated audio. Such a setup, inspired by the post-punk and noise scenes of Brooklyn and Providence, embodies an imprecise grit that resists the polished aesthetic of computation. The stalwart MIDI protocol, developed in the 1980s but which remains a standard, drives the synths according to the composition; MIDI is strongly biased toward tonal music due to its roots in early electronic keyboards. The setup—and the resulting aesthetic—also echoes Laurie Spiegel's pioneering album *The Expanding Universe*, created at Bell Laboratories in the 1970s, in which she wrote algorithms for a computer to control hardware synthesizers and incorporated traditional harmonies from folk music into her compositions.

In addition, consonance is associated with American minimalism and composers such as Steve Reich. In his 1968 manifesto, Reich states "What I'm interested in is a compositional process and a sounding music that are one and the same thing."[12] This ethic dictates that an initial set of composed conditions is left to play out over time without the arbitrary intervention of the composer. The intent is that this process is accessible to the listener, and the appeal of a minimalist piece comes from the textures and rhythms that emerge from the unfolding of its immanent logic. Similarly, I wanted the variation in my music to be the result of differences in the data as they are enumerated and transformed according to a consistent—and audible—set of rules.

I performed and recorded the music in my studio, tweaking the settings on my gear over a couple of takes until things felt right. That the result turns out to be musically interesting ties directly to the musicality of my behavior in the world, just as Lefebvre anticipated. Refrains of my regular working life provide a dominant theme, and modulations signify the drama of travel and life decisions. And while it's difficult to capture a sense of the habitual, the evolving, or the unexpected on a visual map, these qualities are emphasized and intuitive here. The music makes possible what Lefebvre called a "*rhythm*analysis" rather than just a spatial one.[13]

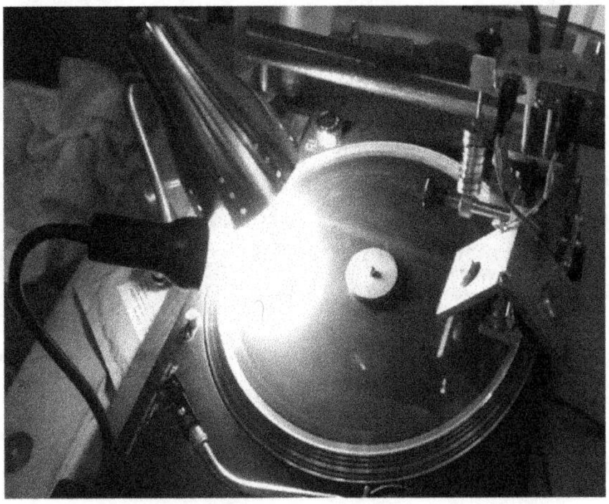

*Figure 39.4* Lathe cutting at Never Records. Photo credit: Brian House

However, hearing it was just the beginning, as how it is heard is of equal importance. To transfer the music to vinyl, I called on the artist Ted Riederer. His *Never Records* project is a pop-up recording studio and record shop that travels to communities and records and releases one-off performances by local artists.[14] Ted cut ten records for me (an exception for *Never Records*, but my piece shares its hyper-local ethos). Unlike commercial record production, which stamps records instantaneously from a master mold, Ted uses a lathe which cuts them one at a time into polyvinyl chloride (PVC) blanks at the speed the music plays (Figure 39.4). It's the same technique used by Jamaican producers in the late 1960s and 1970s to make "dubplate" remixes on acetate for their sound system parties. While the term "dub" ostensibly references the new mix as a "double," Lee "Scratch" Perry famously said that dub music is "the ghost in me coming out,"[15] a resonance which I like when applied to the reanimation of location data.

Etching a clear vinyl disc with a rhythm in time with its rotation had an unexpected effect: the diurnal pulses were physically visible as light-diffracting spokes radiating out from its center. I had planned to reproduce some version of my original spiral visualization on the record itself, but on its own the surface was already a visual index to its audio content. Nonetheless, the designer Greg Mihalko and I proceeded to design graphics that indicated how the record could be understood as a 24-hour clock.[16] Likewise, we showed how moving the stylus inward from the edge traverses across days and we set concentric bands to indicate those grooves that match my travels to cities other than New York. We printed these graphics on the reverse of the records so that they show through the clear vinyl. As a result, listeners can select a particular time in a particular place by moving the tonearm to the appropriate position.

I called the result *Quotidian Record* (see Figure 13, color insert).[17] After premiering the piece in the summer of 2012 at Eyebeam, which had supported the project, the record began circulating through art and technology exhibitions, including the annual Ars Electronica show in Linz, Austria. For each of the shows, it was essential that the piece be presented on a turntable with which the audience could freely interact. Playing the record, positioning the stylus, and even "scratching" the surface of the vinyl are all gestures of a performance that is as much a part of the work as the object itself. Subsequently, as each of the ten cuts have been exhibited and listened to, they have degraded according to the unique wear of their individual histories; though derived from the same data, they now sound distinctly different. In this respect, the piece also echoes Christian Marclay's *Record Without a Cover* (1985), which purposefully incorporates damage to the disc into a particular copy's unique content.

## The Physical Digital

By engaging with its own material qualities, *Quotidian Record* inevitably arrives at the question of what it is to inscribe digital data within an obsolete, and quintessentially analog, medium. Of course, "analog" originally referred to the functional "analogy" between a mechanism, such as the grooves of a record, and some phenomenon, like the vibrations of sound through the air. Today, however, "analog" is just as likely to be used to describe anything in the "real world" as opposed to the online, digitally mediated one. The retro appeal of a vinyl record thus has as much to do with it being "post-digital" as it does with any intrinsic quality of LPs.

However, this dualistic thinking is a bit of a red herring. As Wendy Chun puts it,

> Information—if it exists—is always embodied, whether in a machine or an animal. To make information appear disembodied requires a lot of work, work that is glossed over if we just accept the digital as operating through 1s and 0s.[18]

For *Quotidian Record*, what is at stake is not analog versus digital, but the levels of interpretation through which my location dataset has passed: from a lived experience that was sampled by a mobile device (itself an extension of geosynchronous satellite infrastructure), to the proprietary networks through which it was transmitted and the data centers in which it was stored, to my musical composition, the synthesizers and the vinyl lathe, the stylus in the groove, and, finally, to the listener's ear. The path comprises both symbolic translations and material transductions, each of which speaks to a specific set of cultural practices and political entanglements.

Therefore, to the extent that *Quotidian Record* is a response to a more mainstream data science, it points to how alternative aesthetics can foreground what's missing when we take data to be virtual, ephemeral, or neutral. Ultimately, the form of the record is not so different than that of the hard disk, but whereas we go to great lengths to enclose the latter within computers or keep them hidden away in data centers, the former makes itself heard in the pops and hum of a tangible mechanism that we can appreciate for its aesthetic warmth. According to Friedrich Kittler, the advent of the gramophone meant that no longer could the world only be represented with symbolic language, it could now be recorded with all of its "real" sound intact.[19] Data may be symbolic, but they, too, make a noise that is evidence of the conditions through which we receive them.

In that sense, *Quotidian Record* not only makes audible the musical qualities of my particular location data, it emphasizes all data's audibility. After all, just like music might be better understood as musicking, data might also be better used as "dataing."[20] This perspective opens a dataset up to creative acts of reinterpretation, just as, for example, Grandmaster Flash and other early hip hop DJs physically manipulated the medium to reframe the mass-produced music cut within.

A limited-edition record-cum-artwork is, of course, a commodity, one as personal and as precious as any record might be. This form imparts location data with a tangible sense of value, whereas corporations that would profit from them have a vested interest in data being perceived as abstract. For if the mobile phone has become a constant companion in everyday life, its capacity to deliver information to us in situ is surpassed only by its potential to gather data for the platforms that would profit from them. Further more, by making this record playable and invoking the cultural modes of music, I hope *Quotidian Record* works against an interpretation of these data as deterministic and instead offers a qualitative means for my daily rhythms to be heard in time as a relatable "presence."

## Urban Rhythms

In the years since the release of *Quotidian Record*, the use of location data from mobile phones has grown rapidly. Not only have new location-based services such as Uber reshaped what it is to move through the urban environment, initiatives like Google's Sidewalk Labs are designing cities built from "the internet up" with the assumption of pervasive tracking.[21] These developments proceed despite how we now know, thanks to whistleblowers like Edward Snowden, that the US government has illegally used location data for surveillance worldwide and that platforms like Facebook abet the spread of location-targeted disinformation.

A common question that I have received in response to *Quotidian Record* has been whether I changed my behavior in anticipation of the musical result. To do so would be quite a commitment, as the rhythms emerge from the overall structure of my life rather than from any particular decision made during the day. For this same reason, it is difficult to resist the machine learning systems that work to discover patterns in the data that we generate. These practices of the corporation and the state are akin to Lefebvre's rhythmanalysis insofar as they are concerned with the temporalities of everyday life, but they serve instruments that would exploit that life and estrange us from it rather than broaden our sensitivity to its possibilities.

*Quotidian Record* was the first attempt in my own practice to engage with questions of digital media through attention to the musical qualities of its material. For one, the work's presence in my collection is a reminder of a particularly generative time in my practice and in my life. And if its use of data is anachronistic next to those of the increasingly powerful and pervasive technologies that map our behavior today, perhaps it is an imagined media history for a better sounding—and still possible—future.

## Notes

1 Brian Chen, "Why and How Apple is Collecting your iPhone Location Data," *WIRED*, April 21, 2011, www.wired.com/2011/04/apple-iphone-tracking/.
2 Brian House, "OpenPaths: Empowering Personal Geographic Data," *Proceedings of the 19th International Symposium on Electronic Art* (Sydney 2013), https://ses.library.usyd.edu.au/handle/2123/9719.
3 See https://brianhouse.net/works/yellow_arrow.
4 See https://brianhouse.net/works/hundekopf.
5 Michel de Certeau, *The Practice of Everyday Life*, trans. Steve Rendall (Berkeley: University of California Press, 1984), 35.
6 Peter Galison, *Einstein's Clocks, Poincaré's Maps* (New York: W.W. Norton, 2003).
7 Henri Lefebvre, *Rhythmanalysis: Space, Time and Everyday Life*, trans. Stuart Elden and Gerald Moore (London: Continuum, 2004 [1992]), 23.
8 Brandon LaBelle, *Background Noise: Perspectives on Sound Art* (New York: Continuum International, 2006), ix.
9 Lefebvre *Rhythmanalysis*, 1992, 66, emphasis removed.
10 Christopher Small, *Musicking: The Meanings of Performing and Listening* (Hanover: University Press of New England, 1998).
11 Bill Watterson, "Record Play," *Calvin and Hobbes*, 5 June 1990, www.gocomics.com/calvinandhobbes/1990/06/05.
12 Steve Reich, "Music as a Gradual Process," in *Writings on Music* (Oxford: Oxford University Press, 2002 [1968]), 34–36.
13 Lefebvre *Rhythmanalysis*, 1992, 9.
14 Visit http://neverrecords.samexhibit.com/pages/about for more on Never Records.
15 John Corbett, *Extended Play: Sounding Off from John Cage to Dr. Funkenstein* (Durham: Duke University Press, 1994), 129.
16 See Greg's work at https://partnerandpartners.com.
17 Listen to the result at https://brianhouse.net/works/quotidian_record.
18 Wendy Hui Kyong Chun, *Programmed Visions: Software and Memory* (Cambridge: MIT Press, 2011), 139.
19 Friedrich Kittler, *Gramophone, Film, Typewriter*, trans. Geoffrey Young (Stanford: Stanford University Press, 1999).
20 Jer Thorp, "Data (v.)," *Medium*, 8 May 2015, https://medium.com/memo-random/data-v-da0e0d24777c.
21 Sidewalk Labs, "Visions Sections of RFP Submission," *Sidewalk Toronto*, October 27, 2017, https://storage.googleapis.com/sidewalk-toronto-ca/wp-content/uploads/2019/06/13214331/Sidewalk-Toronto-Backgrounder.pdf.

# 40
# THE CITY AS PERFORMATIVE OBJECT

*PolakVanBekkum*[1]

As artistic duo PolakVanBekkum, we have worked with the artistic potential of digital recordings routes since 2002, shortly after the Global Positioning System (GPS) became available for private use. We approach the technology as a new way of capturing reality, comparable with photography, film, or audio recording. In our work, we focus on different impacts: how does technology influence perception of space once the relocation of bodies becomes recordable and represented? What meanings do people give to their own and others' routes? How does that change their language? How are identities constructed around routes?

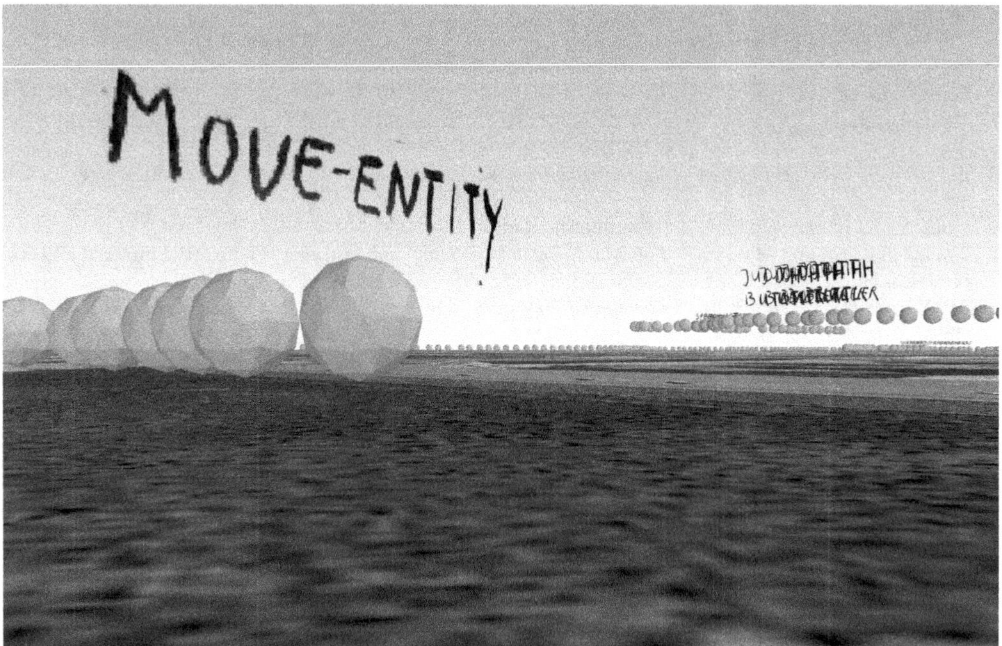


*Figure 40.1* *The City as Performative Object* (2017), PolakVanBekkum, 21:23 min, Video-still. Photo credit: PolakVanBekkum

In this chapter—where the subjective "I" is attributed to artist duo PolakVanBekkum—I investigate possibilities toward the construction of "flexible space" through the concept of the city (or landscape) as performative object. As a working method, I build on the concepts of feminist philosopher Judith Butler on the performativity of gender and speech theorist John Austin on performative speech. My fascination with space is my compass (see Figure 40.1).

Some years ago, I started to run. I started in my daily clothing: jeans, whatever. After building some shape in the nearby park, I joined a running group. My fellow participants dressed appropriately, and I decided to purchase a running outfit to blend in. Wearing my new sportswear, the environment was furnished with the familiar presence of pedestrians and cyclists became contested. Consecutively moving at 4 and 15 kilometers per hour, my speed was exactly in-between: 10 km/h. As if disclosed by the stretchy fabrics, this in-between speed made me glissade into a parallel world.

Some weeks later, at the shop that provided me with the running outfit, I also bought a small running-backpack designed to store a little water, keys, some money, and other small items. I realized that I could try something different—the backpack could contain my swimsuit and goggles. I could run to the swimming pool and even in winter, explore a mobile city swim. An off-season city swim and run. The doorstep of our house became the first step toward a swimming possibility. A Mini Duathlon.

As soon as I closed the front door and directed myself toward the swimming pool, the city in-between became a pathway toward the changing room at the pool: its destination. Or, to describe it in more radical terms, the city had stopped being a city. It had become a beach that I had to cross—buildings became beehive chairs; office workers became children with bucket and shovel that I meandered around. I aimed to get as fast as possible to the cool water. My swimming pool run made buildings, traffic, asphalt, and other hurdles of the road dissolve into grains of sand—all beach.[2]

The effect of my run to the pool was a city losing its fixedness. For a brief moment, I felt released from the discouraging conviction that the hardware of the city with its buildings, asphalt, and stones, is something that cannot be influenced. Apparently, I now have something powerful, which needs to be expanded.

I want to create an interface or toolset, that will open the door to this flexible space. Can this toolset change the experience of being mobile in the city? And if so, can one use it to look at works of art in a new way?

For this chapter, I begin with a brief introduction to John Austin's work and speech theory. This influenced Judith Butler's thinking around gender, and through exploration of her argumentation I distil a set of key concepts used to describe the performativity of gender. I then appropriate these concepts through the translation from gender concepts into ones that augment the performativity of space. The result is a lexicon that can be used to analyze the expression of space, for example, in the swimming pool-run narrative that introduced this chapter. The proposed lexicon can be used as a toolbox, as an interface into the flexible (now translated into performative) space. I then test this toolbox on two works of art, both feature films (*Inception* by Christoffer Nolan (2001) and *News from Home* by Chantal Akerman (1977)). Finally, I return to the swimming pool run and conclude with thoughts regarding the possible use of this creative experiment.

## Theory

The lectures of speech theorist John Austin provided Judith Butler with key insight for her work. For this reason and to provide clarity, I will elaborate on Austin's reasoning. But there is also another reason: the step Butler made, to apply a method developed in speech theory to solve issues in gender studies was the source of inspiration that led to this chapter. It felt very liberating and gave me a kind of indirect permission to do the same: to use performativity for yet another field: that of our artistic approach of space, cityscape and mobility.

## Words

Austin defined his ideas on performativity in his 1962 book *How to do things with words* (the title of the book in itself is almost a poem). The book positions itself in the realm of speech theory. It takes as its starting point the difference between language that represents and language that performs. Representation is a situation where a symbol represents something in the real world. One can decide that a white sphere represents an apple. That is a symbolic act.

One can use words, "apple," "manzana" (Spanish), or "jabolko" (Slovenian) to symbolize the fruit. By doing so, the words function as a representation. This is the most common way to look at language—the language describes. But Austin saw something else: the potential of language to change something in the real world. Situations where words gain an actual power of change. This he called "performative utterances" or "a performative."[3]

The most famous example of a performative Austin gives are the words spoken at a marriage ceremony. When the priest says, "I now declare you man and wife" those words are not a representation, but the sentence brings something about, namely the marriage. This "performative effect" is dependent on context. If one says, "I now declare you man and wife" in a film or theatrical play, again it becomes a representation of the marriage act. Nothing has changed in the lives of the actors when they leave the stage.

For words to be performative, they must be spoken in a situation that is created by social rules. Rules that people know, trust, believe in, and repeat over time.

## Gender

Twenty-eight years later, in her book *Gender Trouble*,[4] Butler argues that although the majority of human infants are born with a clear and specific sex, people still have to create their gender identity. Like speech-act, there is also a gender-act.[5] People realize their gender identity on a day-to-day basis by repetitively stylizing their bodies, clothes, and gestures, so that they express and match their biological gender. Compared to the marriage ceremony, it is a kind of contract between humans that we all play out daily. The difference is that it happens to our subconscious, as opposed to consciously getting married.

Butler explains how the categories of male and female are still inescapable, although they are performative. We cannot change our gender on a daily basis like a set of clothes. The gender roles are deeply internalized, and their construction is hidden, even though it is a contract that humans have to renew every day. Butler, motivated by her feminist agenda, sees small opportunities to challenge them or at least experience them as unstable, through activities where the one gender starts to blend into the other, for example, in drag.

A crucial understanding for me was the way Butler removes genealogy from the discussion, the order of matters and phenomena where it is not the predetermined biological sex that produces gender, but rather a set of repeated and stylized acts. Confusing enough, those acts also are at the root of us assuming the biological given as a solid substance of gender specificity. Her argument is related to Nietzsche's claim that there is "no doer behind the deed."[6] There is no gender before we act gender. Although this mechanism is not very obvious or visible, according to Butler performativity does not only produce gender, but it also hides gender's unstable nature.

## Move and Moving

Around 1990, Butler's ideas were groundbreaking. They liberated existing feminist theory from its double bind—on the one hand, idealizing female qualities and, on the other, stressing the equality of the sexes.[7] For me, the idea of appropriation in itself was of inspiration. Butler borrows ideas from the field of speech theory,[8] and appropriates them to an entirely different field, gender studies.

I see a possibility to apply performativity again—to landscape, mobility, and city-space. I suggest that the existence of architecture, pavement, and other seemingly fixed objects in public space is, like gender, both unstable, and at the same time, "hides" its' instability. The previous example of the swimming pool run illustrates the city as a flexible landscape; once one runs through it intending to swim, the pavement transforms into a beach. Does architecture, like the biological gender, have a seemingly unquestionable existence?

Is it possible to unveil the city as constructed in a performative manner and to contemplate the order, where mobility precedes stones, asphalt, and buildings? Do the physical, day-to-day acts of moving play a role? Is the city produced by stylized acts of mobility? Is the stable existence of cities an illusion? (Figure 15, color insert).

Austin's work explains the performative, and Butler is an inspiration for this appropriation. In her texts, she clearly uses core concepts that can be considered as tools, as appropriation stepping stones. As a thought experiment, I translate those fundamental concepts to the realm of mobility and space.

This quest results in a lexicon,[9] a set of translations.

## Lexicon

The following lexical items come into play for this experiment:

1 **Individual** translates to ***Move-Entity***
2 **Gender-Act** translates to ***Move-Act***
3 The two sexes, the **Gender-Categories** translate to several ***Move-Categories***
4 **Gender-Drag** translates into ***Move-Drag***

To summarize the method: The (gender performing) individual performs a gender act (wears a skirt) and therefore falls into a gender category (woman). If this act deviates, then there is a situation of drag (man with a skirt). When translated (appropriated) the "individual" becomes a moving unit (for example, a human being) and performs a *Move-Act* (runs fast in a jogging outfit), and by doing so belongs to a *Move-Category* (of runners). By deviating from this (running in daily clothes), we see the *Move-Drag* come into existence.

## Move-Entity (Beweeg-Eenheid)

In Butler's work the individual human being is the starting point. Without an individual to be marked with gender, no gender division is possible. In this case though, the "individual" fails as a starting point, as within the concept of mobility a *group* of individuals can also act as one mobile unit, for example, a car that contains several people. As long as the "individual" is considered "one person," this becomes problematic. Therefore, I translate the individual used by Butler (one individual = one person) into a more open term: *Move-Entity*.

The *Move-Entity* "car" may contain four people, and airplanes might hold hundreds of people. After landing crew and passengers leave the plane the *Move-Entity* splits itself up. *Move-Entities* exists on different levels and scales and might even overlap, even while still traveling. The crew and passengers can be considered as separate *Move-Entities*, while the *Move-Entity* of the airplane still exists. This term creates a starting point to talk about that which moves as forming diverse constellations, and how they each perform different types of space.

## Move-Act (Beweeg-Daad)

"Speech-act" from speech theory is translated by Butler into *gender-act*. This appropriation is a central step to build the idea of the performativity of gender. Following Butler's footsteps again, I translate *Gender-Act* into *Move-Act*. *Move-Act* is the case whenever a *Move-Entity* walks, rides, floats, or otherwise has mobility.

While being in a car, I am in *Move-Act*, regardless of sitting at the wheel, or in a passenger's seat.

As *Gender-Act* articulates that gender division is performed and not an anterior given, *Move-Act* does something similar: It articulates how movement, by any *Move-Entity*—by human, animal, or object—creates streets, cities, fields, and worlds. Following Butler, this would mean that streets, cities, fields, and worlds depend on *Move-Act* for their becoming.

## Move-Category (Beweeg-Categorie)

Butler works with male and female as a force that divides individuals into two main gender-categories. Now that I have established them, I can separate different *Move-Acts* of *Move-Entities* into categories: *Move-Categories*. As it turns out, there are more than just two: the performative appropriated to issues of space is not based around binary division but instead is enacted via a plurality.

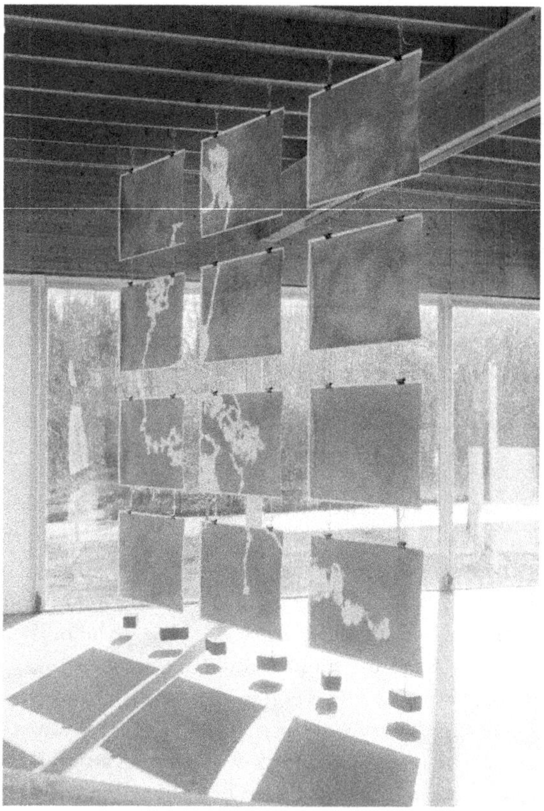

*Figure 40.2* *NomadicMILK Robotprints* (2010) PolakVanBekkum, Spray-paint on Canvas, 3.4 × 3.4m. Photo Credit: Thomas Linden, Zone2Source, Amstelpark Pavillion

To start with, this division brings me to culturally "common" categories like walking, biking or car-driving. These are based on means of transportation and often also speed. Society and (visual) language apply them to traffic rules and they are pervasive, "dressing" *Move-Entities* with icons such as street signs or pavement. The same categorizations re-appear in cartography, again in signs or as color-coded entities.

One pedestrian is a *Move-Entity*, walking is a *Move-Category*.
Air travel as such is a *Move-Category*, divided again into business and economy class.

This now enables contemplation about *Move-Entities* on the level of shared qualities.

Categorizations are culturally constructed, depending on codes. Using this lemma, I think in terms of collections and pluralities of categories. This plurality unveils a difference between mobility and gender as a focus point, where space and the performance of space are not dualistic. Whether this problematizes my appropriation or instead becomes an affluence is a question that I intend to answer further into this chapter. For now, I continue exploring regardless (Figure 40.2).

## Move-Categories: New-Tread and After-Tread

Given their multiplicity, I can refine between possible *Move-Categories*, for example, one based on repetition. In Butler's work, reiteration plays a vital role describing how the performative works. Repetition also plays a distinctive role in routes. Routes that I take for the first time produce a different space than that of everyday routes I take repeatedly. When I decide upon a route for the first time, my awareness of "how I produce/construct space" is more noticeable. The more often I repeat the same route, the harder it becomes to maintain awareness. To name the repetition, I coin the *Move-Category After-Tread* and its counterpart, a route that is run for the first time I define as *New-Tread*.

A child goes to school every day. The first time, the trajectory is full of expectation and surprise (*New-Tread*). After a while, the trajectory becomes part of the daily routine, (*After-Tread*) and is therefore depleted of the affective experience of surprise.

*Move-Categories* differ not only because of their geographical trajectory, but also based on the means of transportation or speed. In addition, difference occurs because of the frequency with which a specific *Move-Entity* has taken them.

## Move-Drag

For Butler, an escape from gender as an absolute given is relevant from a feminist perspective. The dualism between the sexes and its hierarchy hurts the humanity of both women and men. Still, she recognizes that gender is inevitable. The fact that it is performative does not mean that one can take it off, like changing clothes, as mentioned earlier. At its most feasible, it is possible to disrupt gender categories by revealing their unstable nature. Butler understands that one of the most effective ways to do so is through "drag." The playful approach, the shift, and the caricature are all important attributes, and liberate within the possible scope. The drag-queen does not ridicule women per say but instead ridicules the performativity of femininity. The way Butler suggests dealing with restrictions of gender binary is specific. She sees the binary inescapable as such but finds an optimistic opening to create permeability in "drag."[10] Following her consistently, I therefore translate **Gender-Drag** into ***Move-Drag***.

This leaves me to wonder how one might undermine *Move-Categories*, or at least destabilize them through specific *Move-Acts*, that might be considered as *Move-Drag*. This strategy would be a practice that in effect blur the boundaries between the different *Move-Categories* and result

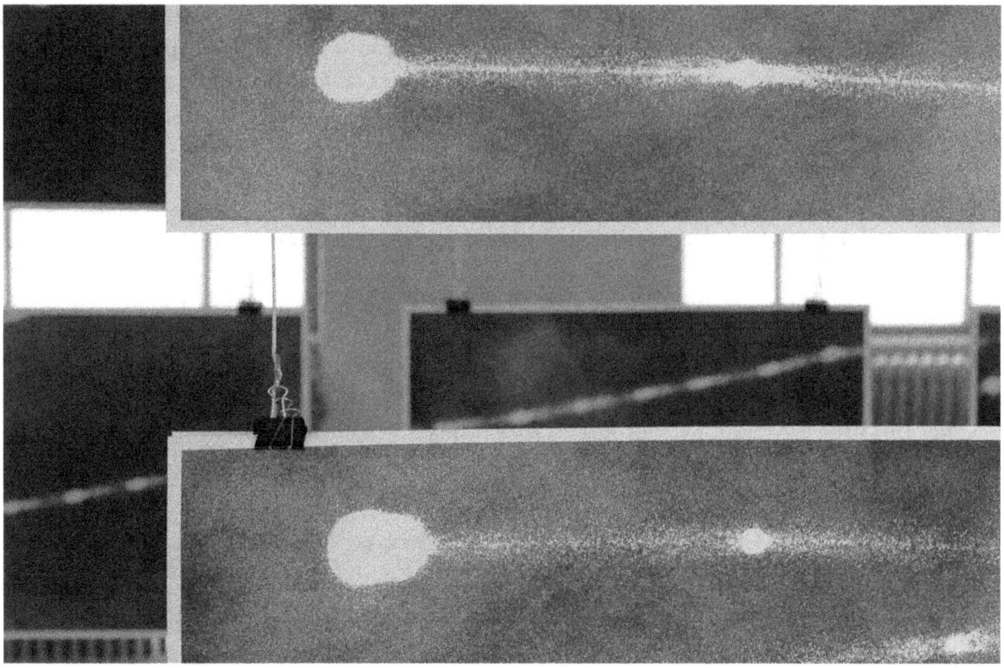

*Figure 40.3* Detail of *Souvenir Zeeland Robot Prints* (2008), PolakVanBekkum, Spray-paint on Paper, 70 × 100 cm. Photo credit: PolakVanBekkum

in unexpected experiences of (city)space. This process should, if my appropriation makes sense, reveal its unstable nature.

A friend of mine became lost in an unfamiliar city. By car, she found herself in a pedestrian area. To find her way out, she needed help from the pedestrians around her, but still had to leave by car. She tried to change into a pedestrian as much as possible—opened all her car windows, slowed down to the slowest pace her vehicle allowed her, and smiled ridiculously wide before she dared to speak to another human.

This brings to mind the example in the beginning of this chapter, where I run in daily clothes, or use running clothes to get to the swimming pool. This can also be considered a form of *Move-Drag*, where the city changes into a strange kind of beach.

A possible way of getting to know the performativity of the city is by mixing *Move-Categories* and by making hybrids. Using this word, I can start to look for situations of possible *Move-Drag*. Once I find them, I can deliberately place myself in *Move-Drag* to investigate the liberating pleasure of unstable city space (Figure 40.3).

## The Swimming Pool Run

Recalling the swimming pool run, described at the beginning of this chapter, a question surfaces: Was that, in effect, an example of Move-*Drag*? Was it a situation where Butler's reference to Nietzsche's "there is no doer behind the deed," can be translated into a "there is no architecture before movement?"

To test this hypothesis, I dressed as a runner, but I intended to swim. The swimsuit that I carried in my runner's backpack embodied this secret identity, enveloped by the runner's pack, the jogging clothes that I was wearing and my pace. I blended the characters of runner and swimmer.

The common swimmer is a person that hops on a bike, public transport, or car to get to the pool, lake, or sea. But the concept of a runner that is also a swimmer is new to me. May I consider this combination a form of *Move-Drag*? When entering into *Move-Drag*, the evident and stable city space becomes flexible. The "taken for granted city" with its "natural state of streets and buildings" starts to collapse. What kind of engagement and responsibility does that bring?

Does it mean that as soon as one enters into such form of *Move-Drag*, this falling apart will always be perceivable? And will the city rebuild itself appearing as solid again, as soon as one leaves this position of *Move-Drag?*

Without my longing for the swimming pool, I would not have left the house. And because of the way I traveled, the swimming pool turned into a sea and the streets into a beach. The city as repetitive a practice is created over and over again while moving through it.

The best way to ascertain this assumed position of *Move-Drag* is to apply the new vocabulary to further examples. The experiment following aims to re-describe two works of art (films). What kind of new insights will that bring? The notion of performativity and the lexicon create other ways of understanding those films as articulating flexible space. In the next section, I will (re-) visit the two earlier mentioned films *Inception* and *News from Home* and attempt to analyze how they unintentionally express the performativity of city space by describing them using the words of the lexicon.

These four lemmas will be our associates and fellow travelers:

1 **Individual** translated to ***Move-Entity***
2 **The Gender-Categories** translated to ***Move-Categories*** **(and sub categories)**
3 **Gender-Act** translated to ***Move-Act***
4 **Gender-Drag** translated to ***Move-Drag***

## Inception

The film *Inception* (2001) by Christoffer Nolan is famous for its stunning visual effects—characters with the ability to create architecture in dreams, streets folding over in Paris, or a bridge assembling itself. Watching the film, I experienced those effects as the hidden yet central protagonist of the film. The effects enter the stage of the storyline at the very moment that the two human main characters start to collaborate as Dominick Cobb, a fugitive "dream thief" and Ariadne (no surname given), a brilliant architecture student. Ariadne is approached to help Cobb, who is entangled in a problematic web of layered dreams and personal obsessions. Combining the power of his dreams (Cobb) and her imagined architecture (Ariadne), flexible spaces emerge.

A good example is found in the Paris fragment.[11] Here you can view cinematically how the *Move-Entity* Cobb-Ariadne, during their first walk together (*Move-Act)*, are able to tilt streets. The architecture around them becomes flexible depending on the *Move-Act* of Cobb-Ariadne. It all becomes possible within the hybridization of the real and the dream states.

The plot of the film circles around the capacity to disguise real from unreal, that is, real from dream, and actual movements from cinematographic movements. The director is genuinely interested in blurring the dividing line. Christopher Nolan says himself about this:

> I'm very interested in the similarities or analogies between the way in which we experience a three–dimensional space that an architect has created and the way in which an audience experiences a cinematic narrative that constructs a three–dimensional -reality from a two-dimensional medium—assembled shot by shot. I think there's a narrative component to architecture that's kind of fascinating.[12]

Within the official storyline, however, the potential and flexible architecture remains grounded in the "dream" state. In the flexible space that Ariadne and Cobb create, deliberate clues are built in as plot devices, clues that expose the flexible as "unreal," so as to keep the dividing line manageable.

A vital engine within the plot of *Inception* is the route taken, observable not in space, but through "dream" layers. The bodies of the personages used as "portals" or "doors" into those new spaces are constructed as dreams within dreams. The move category of *Dream-Travel* is a driving force of the plot. As soon as the characters embark on these journeys, their dreaming bodies begin to perform flexible city space. I would argue that the film hesitates to enter hybridization (*Move-Drag)*, yet the decision to frame it as dream can be seen as an ambivalent attempt to address alternative ways of understanding the performing of city-scape.

As inspiring as *Inception* for me is, the plot still sits within the realm of the conventional. To "read" it as a work that engages with the performativity of architecture and city space, one has to allow oneself to read the subtext. Only though this detour can one read the film as revealing the performativity of city space while denying it at the same time.[13] Only in the fundamentally conflicted final scene of the film, evident *Drag* between flexible space and the notion of the fixed real is allowed and expressed by the never-ending spinning top at the end of the film. Nolan himself states that "Reality matters." But earlier in the same interview he also comments that "perhaps all levels of reality are valid."[14]

## News from Home

In Chantal Akerman's meditative and avant-garde documentary *News from Home*[15] (1977), the city is the protagonist rather than a set or stage from which to act. The movie consists of long shots of New York, mostly with a static camera, recorded in an indexical way—plain and without special effects. There are two layers of sound at play here. One track with ambient sounds of the city that are out of sync with the imagery, which must have been recorded either before or after the filming. The second track consists of Akerman's voice reading all the letters she received from her hometown of Brussels, from her mother supporting the young filmmaker. In *News from Home*, the letters travel from Brussels to New York and perform the *Move-Entity* which creates the city.

Akerman was still very young in 1971 when she started to build her career as a filmmaker. She moved from Brussels to New York, living as a "vagabond" while being supported by her parents. Only years later, after her success with the film *Jeanne Dielman* (1975)—by then an established film director—Akerman creates *News from Home* and shows New York as emerging from a smoldering mixture of homesickness and escape drift, returning to her position as an immigrant. I read the movie as a radical meditation on the *Move-Category* of *New-Tread*. The streets we see seem vacant: empty spaces that are filled with dreams, poetry, dread and, in this case, letters from home. We hear Akerman's voice, reading in chronological order the complete collection of maudlin letters that she receives and that emphasize distant layers of time and space and a nomadic state of being.

Akerman's voice sucks up the streets of New York and spits them out again, articulating the emptiness of the seventies. The slowness of voice further augments the evenly spaced slow shots and camera movements. The distance between New York and Brussels is somehow wrought into the distance between the camera and architectural surface, passing pedestrians, cars, and an occasional dog. The wormhole of the metro plays an important role too. New York hardly allows for long shots, and it is only until the film's end where we leave Manhattan by boat that slowly the distances are getting air and space to breath. Akerman comments:

> [The way] I would like to film . . . corresponds . . . to the idea that the land one possesses is always a sign of barbarism and blood, while the land one traverses without taking it reminds us of a book.[16]

## Landscape and Plot

These two filmic examples have one thing in common: both Nolan and Akerman suggest a relation between architecture, city-space, and text. As Nolan contemplates, "I think there's a narrative component to architecture that's fascinating."[17]

This narrative suggests the use of language or even speech, and if so, should this architectural narrative be considered a performative or rather a symbolic or representational language?

Akerman guides us toward the performative when she states, "The land one traverses without taking it, reminds us of a book."[18] A land that needs traversing to open up its text suggests that the role of traversing precedes its presence as a book. Here the traversing becomes creative to the point that it produces a particular kind of *land*, one that reminds us of a book. Does the approach and techniques of both directors open up something—like an author—that is relevant to the existence of architecture and land? In *Inception*, this appears to be achieved almost literally by Nolan, in the designs of the architect-protagonist. Akerman's position implies that with the occurrence of a book-like-land, a kind of agency—perhaps even a traversing *Move-Entity* or a book author?—emerges that replaces the traditional powers of land ownership.

## Conclusion

During the swim/run *Move-Drag* at the beginning of this chapter, buildings change into a beach-like landscape, and passer-by's in office clothes become children playing with sand. The city becomes, for a moment, elastic. It is the newness and the slight weirdness of this *Move-Drag* that makes the fluidity all-ready tangible and visible. From the moment, I start to do a swim-run like this routinely, or should this become a widespread practice among people, the swim/run will become a *Move-Category* within itself. The experience of the city as beach will normalize, and the experience of the underlying unstableness of the city becomes more and more difficult. With every repetitive move, the *Move-Drag* evolves into a new *Move-Category*. In the process, this builds a new city space whereby the translucence of its construction further obscures.

As a working method and by appropriating Judith Butler's thoughts on the performativity of gender to the city space, I attempted to distil some core concepts around gender from Butler's work and translate them literally into the realm of mobility and space. This results in a vocabulary that can be used to describe how our environment does not pre-exist movements. This chronological reversal is made tangible through experiences that play with the *Move-Categorisations* that are culturally common and reiterate. This I coined *Move-Drag*. Throughout the article, I used a run to the swimming pool as the primary test case, where I applied the lexicon to amplify the mobility of environment. To investigate this further, the vocabulary was applied to the art works, in this case two feature films produced in the seventies, *Inception* and *News from Home*.

Butler's motivation was political. Her thoughts were motivated by frustration about the trap feminism found itself in during the eighties: fighting gender inequality by stressing how equal women are, denying or downplaying differences, or a move toward glorification of substantial female qualities. Both strategies created severe problems, enhancing either a denial of the self and its history, or an unescapable ghettoization within the category of femininity. Performativity was Butler's answer to this dilemma.

The hierarchy between the sexes exists as an undercurrent in the body of Butlers work on performativity. There is still space to explore in more depth how this translates to the performativity of mobility.

Developing a lexicon for mobility, a move-theory, gave me a language to connect the relatively new field of mobile media art to its artistic predecessors. Artists who had no knowledge of mobile media in the contemporary sense, but were inspired by concepts of mobility, go back further in time than the emergence of mobile media itself. From my involvement in GPS and location media-related art since 2001, I have been able to draw from my lived experience over time and develop the lexicon described above. Alongside an alternative way to describe the city, it also became a language to explore links to earlier works in the art-historical landscape. Mobile technology, as a repeated and embodied experience, has been indispensable to make this "bringing together" possible. A mutual and even circular way of attaching meaning.

I long for diminishing the power of stones, pavement, and buildings and contribute to that of the moving. Developing the lexicon felt like a possibility to restore that balance. By doing so, I hope to be of inspiration to others. I invite readers to explore the city, using the suggested lemma. You as a reader could write them on (mental) cards and take them with you while exploring by foot, bike, car, or any hybrid in-between.

## Credits

The research that led to this writing was made possible through the kind support of Stimuleringsfonds[19] and my participation in *The knowledge network* of LAPS[20] (Lectoraat Art & Public Space) at the Gerrit Rietveld academie in Amsterdam. Thanks to Joris Landman who suggested the use of a lexicon and pointed me to the inspirational example of Stephen Wright's *Towards a Lexicon of Usership*. Special thanks to Jeroen Boomgaard and Michiel de Lange for their feedback on this text.

## Notes

1 PolakVanBekkum is the alias of artist duo Esther Polak and Ivar van Bekkum.

2 Nicholas Lezard, "The Beach Beneath the Street by McKenzie Wark Review—A Situationist Work in Itself," *The Guardian*, 28 April 2015, www.theguardian.com/books/2015/apr/28/beach-beneath-street-mckenzie-wark-review. The mentioning of the beach is reminiscent of "*Sous les pavés, la plage*," one of the great slogans of the 1968 demonstrations and riots in Paris: a promise of carnivalesque freedom coined by the Situationists.

3 John Austin, *How To Do Things with Words. The William James Lectures Delivered at Harvard University* (Oxford: Clarendon Press, 1955 [1962]), 12. "What are we to call a sentence or an utterance of this type? I propose to call it a performative sentence or a performative utterance, or, for short, 'a performative'."

4 Judith Butler, *Gender Trouble: Feminism and the Subversion of Identity*, second edition (New York; London: Routledge, 1999 [1990]).

5 I could not find Butler using this term "gender act" herself, but instead found it used in descriptions of her theories. For example, "Gender here is the effect of reiterated acting, producing the effect of a static or normal gender, at the same time obscuring the instability of any single 'gender act'," n.p. https://introducing-performativity.fandom.com/wiki/Judith_Butler_and_%27Performativity%27.

6 Butler, *Gender*, 33. "The challenge for rethinking gender categories outside of the metaphysics of substance will have to consider the relevance of Nietzsche's claim in On the Genealogy of Morals that 'there is no "being" behind doing, effecting, becoming; "the doer" is merely a fiction added to the deed—the deed is everything.' In an application that Nietzsche himself would not have anticipated or condoned, we might state as a corollary: There is no gender identity behind the expressions of gender but that identity is performatively constituted by the very 'expressions' that are said to be its results."

7 Butler, *Gender Trouble*; Judith Butler, "Critically Queer." *GLQ: A Journal of Gay and Lesbian Studies* 1, no. 1 (1993): 17–32, https://read.dukeupress.edu/glq/article-abstract/1/1/17/9896/Critically-Queer?redirectedFrom=fulltext.

8 Austin, *How To Do Things with Words*.

9 Stephen Wright, *Towards a Lexicon of Usership* (Eindhoven: The Van Abbe Museum, 2013). This publication was an inspirational example, showing how a self-produced lexicon can be a tool for developing a line of thinking.

10 Butler, *Gender Trouble*, 175. "In imitating gender, drag implicitly reveals the imitative structure of gender itself—as well as its contingency. Indeed, part of the pleasure, the giddiness of the performance is in the recognition of a radi-cal contingency in the relation between sex and gender in the face of cultural configurations of causal unities that are regularly assumed to be natural and necessary. In the place of the

law of heterosexual coherence, we see sex and gender denaturalized by means of a performance which avows their distinctness and dramatizes the cultural mechanism of their fabricated unity."

11 Christoffer Nolan, *Inception—City Bending*, 6 November 2011, YouTube excerpt, www.youtube.com/watch?v=dG22TcpjRnY.

12 Robert Capps, "Q&A: Christopher Nolan on Dreams, Architecture, and Ambiguity," *Wired*, 29 November 2010, www.wired.com/2010/11/pl_inception_nolan/.

13 Laura Mulvey, *Laura Mulvey #244* Radio Web Macba, podcast produced by SON[I]A, 45:59, https://rwm.macba.cat/ca/sonia/laura-mulvey/capsula. Comparable to how Douglas Sirk's films starring Rock Hudson have been watched by queer communities and seen as 'about' homosexuality but denying it at the same time.

14 Helena Horton, "Christopher Nolan explains the spinning top in Inception," *DAZEDDIGITAL*, 2 June 2015, www.dazeddigital.com/artsandculture/article/24949/1/christopher-nolan-explains-the-spinning-top-in-inception.

15 Fragment "News From Home," 2 November 2016, https://vimeo.com/189916826/7fcd0a3ac3.

16 Giuliana Bruno, *Atlas of Emotion: Journeys in Art, Architecture, and Film* (New York: Verso 2002), 75.

17 Robert Capps, "Q&A: Christopher Nolan on Dreams, Architecture, and Ambiguity," *WIRED Magazine*, 29 November 2010, www.wired.com/2010/11/pl_inception_nolan/.

18 Bruno, *Atlas of Emotions*.

19 "Grant Programme for Digital Culture," Creative Industries Fund NL, https://stimuleringsfonds.nl/en/grants/grant_programme_for_digital_culture/.

20 "Research at the Rietveld," The Lectoraat Art & Public Space (LAPS), http://laps-rietveld.nl/?page_id=5.

# 41

# *ENCONTROS*

## An Artwork on Borders and Networked Mobilities

*Luisa Paraguai and Gilbertto Prado*

> Overmodern mobility expresses itself in the movements of population (migrations, tourism, professional mobility), in immediate general communication and in the traffic of products, images, and information. It corresponds to the paradox of a world where we can, at least in theory, make everything without moving and while moving all the time.[1]

Our concern with mobilities and networks has stimulated our thinking about the nature of borders. When we consider physical and natural boundaries, borders act not as static configurations and fixed contours, but rather as different dialogic systems with dynamic and fluid modes of accesses and non-accesses. While borders cannot be unmade, for our artistic investigation the challenge is to create an environment that is no longer based on binary oppositions or dichotomies. So, using the idea of "overmodern mobility"[2] as our starting point, this chapter explores the dynamic nature of bordering, not in terms of spatial logics, but in the context of *temporal dimensions*, as different modes of information accesses and flows,[3] as well as their impacts on the social dimensions of our contemporary society.

For example, mobile telephony involves ways of interacting while on the move, allowing people to coordinate professional meetings and everyday events and to perform the informational mobility paradigm that depends on networks—zones of connectivities.

> However, the material expression of the border does not always coincide with its functions, which everyday become more diffuse: the control of different types of flows is henceforth enacted using a multitude of adapted technologies which do not only distinguish between persons, goods, capital and information, but also between those flows that are desirable and those that are not.[4]

As a result, despite understanding borders as dichotomic processes that materialize social conventions—"centrality and empowerment in some cases, and disconnection and social exclusion, in other situations,"[5] we also view them as principles for artistic practices. For us, it is these technical operations and theoretical concepts which define the aesthetic object in relation to mobile media art—working on the limits of language and materiality to assume a symbolic construction, and its dependence on the spectator's articulations and contexts to further articulate and reimagine our social reality.

People now interact with different layers of informational structures, such as navigation apps and social media platforms, trying to transcend the dominant logic of each networked system (local and global). In our everyday lives, these codified systems, embedded into the contemporary landscape, determine the use, control and design of land, urban planning, physical mobility, personal and public transportation networks, voice communication, radio and mobile phone networks, computer access, and standard internet technical protocols.[6] Within these codified systems, the body and the objects become inscribed with informational data since mobile and locative technologies connect interpersonal communication with different databases. From this hybrid spatial and bodily condition, we observe an emerging dynamic: the convergence of digital and physical matrices actualized by users, when, for example, GPS devices transform the way people explore, perceive, and interact with the city.

Making mobile media art includes thinking about the immediate communication context and the circulation of data (images, information). It requires that we consider mobile technologies and its possibilities to reorganize temporalities as modes of occupying physical space, and to further define territories—proposing borders as connections. The *Encontros* (Meetings) (2015) artwork (see Figure 41.1) is a collective project of the Grupo Poéticas Digitais,[7] coordinated by Gilbertto Prado and exhibited in Brazil and abroad.[8] It talks about flows and borders and references the meeting of waters in Brazil[9] to articulate human-human relationships. The temporary impossibility of mixing the waters between the Rio Negro and the Rio Solimões defines colored borders for a physical space due to the differences in temperature, speed, and water density of the two rivers. It also evokes a social space, quantified by the word "meeting" used in human dialog all over the world, despite cultural and social differences, physical distances, economic power, and historic processes. The artwork provokes another perspective to understand our always-connected everyday life.

In this chapter, we point to the specificity of data processing technologies, which materialize digital objects dependent on "interobjective relations"[10] by synchronizing data with network space and technical systems time. First, we discuss how borders have been shaped by global and local flows through technical objects, currently used as a communication condition to access the world. In this context, "movement itself is not as significant, but how it enables people to be connected with each other, to meet and to re-meet over time and across space."[11] We consider these modes to be connected as patterns of networks that highlight not only the dichotomy between center and periphery but also the discontinuities which define boundaries not absolute.

We also deliberate the Cooper and Rumford statement, "we need to view borders not simply as markers of division but also as mechanisms of connection and encounter"[12] in order to contextualize *Encontros*. This idea frames our consideration of borders by working with different scales and hierarchies, natural, and produced environments through technical objects and technologies of communication—mobile media. The borders, instead of having physical and fixed limits, become porous when taking into account the nature of contemporary flows (people, information, objects, money, and images) that create discontinuities of access/non-access which enable a mapping of heterogeneous, uneven, and unpredictable mobilities.[13]

## Technical Objects, Digital Objects, and Artworks

Throughout history, people have established their organizations of power in society based on their relationships with technology. They have conformed abstract concepts of space and time through the development of different material objects imbricated with transportation and communication networks, such as cars and mobile phones, which, in turn, enabled new political and social limits. Social limits can evoke a common sense meaning of distance and separation, but also presents itself as a transition. In this sense, it changes to a space of communication and exchanges, allowing the consideration of new connections and hierarchies among local cultures, which potentially expand into a networked environment.

In this social process of behaving and producing possible dialogs, artists appropriate different techniques and technologies to constitute and operationalize their poetic productions. In the context of contemporary art, the hybridization of languages and media happens as a procedural practice, by using a variety of different languages: sounds, images, texts, programming, and a wide range of media that could include painting, drawing, illustration, photography, video, interfaces, etc. This points to hybridization as a poetic principle, which is possible at all levels of languages—from the most abstract to the most concrete—with regard to different aspects such as formal, semantic, and functional. In 1939, when thinking about the process of creation, Valéry defined poetics as, "on the one hand, the study of invention and composition, the role of fate, reflection, imitation, culture and the environment; on the other hand, the examination and the analysis of techniques, procedures, instruments, materials, means and supports for action."[14] Artists, therefore, operationalize concepts, ideas, and questions that are processed and conformed by languages, materialities, techniques, and technologies, allowing them to create a singular worldview.

Mitcham differentiates technique and technology, stating that "technique" is

> when what is relevant is human action (e.g. playing the piano), doing something singular, and when activity rests less on rules than on intuition and know-how. On the other hand, 'technology' should apply to cases in which what is relevant is the artifact (e.g. the use or maintenance of a machine), when it is mass-produced, and when rules, standards and consciously articulated procedures are followed.[15]

For Mitcham, there are four different modes or dimensions of technological making and using of artifacts: as objects, as a mode of knowledge, as a specific form of activity, and/or as volition—that is, as a particular human attitude to reality. In this text, we emphasize technology as a cultural process since it requires attitudes and modulates sensitive abilities to experience an aesthetic impression while also evoking an unforeseeable manner to signify the world. So, as part of a global socio-technical system, technique is planned and constructed by people who appropriate, reinterpret, and rebuild it.[16] As such, technique and technology differ in that they formulate and link distinct levels of abstraction, organizing demands, and forces from human perception and action in any given historical situation. That is partially determined by a general tendency of technology, consisting in the materialization of all sorts of relations and media by rendering the invisibles in visible and measurable forms where "[g]athering characterizes interobjectivity according to the technicity of its epoch."[17] Technology does not rise outside of history and can be grouped according to possible connections and dependence on the assemblage of others, a coherent standardization of technical infrastructures—a compatibility of system.

Thus, technology and its differently derived technical objects are instances of a socio-historical and cultural condition that stems from an inventive, interactive, and dynamic movement—creation, usage, and transformation, indefinitely—and end up modeling the production and our spatio-temporal perception. And from that powerful character of transformation and adaptation, technology is assumed as the constitutive dimension of humanity. As Simondon observed,

> the individualized technical object corresponds most directly to the human dimension. The human individual is not dominated by it as he is in the mining or any other network. Nor does he dominate it, making it an extension of his hands or prosthetic device, as happens in component technology. He neither dominates nor is dominated but enters into a kind of dialectic.[18]

Today's technical objects are interconnected and extremely specialized to respond to planned purposes, although they may be susceptible of other forms of use. This extreme specialization has made everyday life more and more mediated and, which, as Baudrillard[19] suggests, may lead to a contradiction: the generation innumerable "aesthetic objects" without a technical function, such as the machines of Picabia.[20] Artists are interested in this inconsistency, be it structural, or of usage/consumption, since operational displacements—conceptual and practical—are part of the process of creation, fabulation, and invention. *Encontros* materializes digital objects, synchronizing space and time, data networked between natural environments and technical systems. For Hui, synchronizing temporally geometrical and topological distances requires rethinking conventions and standards, crossing not only physical borders, but also to political and cultural ones.[21]

For example, with the Coordinated Universal Time (UTC) standard since 1960, it has been possible to minimize geographical, social, or cultural differences for an international teleconference meeting.[22] Synchronization is a technical object (GMT is an abstract time modulated by the clock), but Hui, following Heidegger and Bergson, suggests that topological and discursive temporal relations should be considered into/with the technical system. So, the comprehension of our experience is a construction in which time is "something to be filtered; some it passes away, while some of it is retained in the objects or circumstances."[23]

Simondon understands that among objects there is an implicit organization that is constituted, operationalized and made compatible by technicality that mediates the incompatibility caused by different orders of magnitude and presented ubiquitously in all types of technical objects.[24] When we consider concrete and informational objects—such as mobile phones and coding apps—each one has its specific logic, constraints, and possible and adapted functions. These objects differ from each other in levels of complexity and coexist in a technical system. Simondon articulates that

> these different mediations have a common essence as system of adaptation; the molecules of liquid or the grains of powder are of an order of magnitude that don't allow them to be effectively manipulable by the human body without an intermediate object which holds billions of them in unity.[25]

Thus, we are interested in reinforcing the non-dichotomous understanding of the object-subject relation, recognizing the potential of both technical and digital objects as vectors of social transformation. As Hui explains, "Simondon sees the shift of systems as having gone from a system of man-language to the system of man-religion and now moving to a system of man-technics."[26] As a result, our networked behavior reinforces the technical object's role in defining relationships and delineating situations. This behavior creates a shift away from the concept of representation toward the idea of performativity within systems since each epoch is characterized by certain technical aesthetics.

Through the consideration of our actual context as technical system based on information acquisition, we have faced dynamic objects that adapt different protocols from each other and from our interactions to them, for example, social media usage and various relations with Internet of Things (IoT), such as smart cars. The use of different languages and media for creation, production, and circulation of data introduces various forms of experience that renew our perception of the world because we actually have to adapt to technical networked environments. For example, considering traversing the city as an urban database—it connects different informational components such as climate, demography, geography, economy, with GPS coordinates, all of which bring multiple perspectives of different commuting practices.

## Possible Meetings: Fluctuant Narratives

> From here one sees plenty of water and sky, constellations of trees and of liana clusters that one cannot get through. Landscapes as they should be, without end, lethargic as the time that flows between a dip in the water and a whistle.

> Then one sees what it is, time which runs through wrinkles and threadbare clothing.
>
> The soft touch of the openly smiling girl hands that cast a spell on the *botos*, the freshwater dolphins, that fill us with sweets, take us to the bottom of the river on a one-way trip.
>
> The river is a flow, brown or black, insurmountable, sheer, in a depth that does not allow itself to be seen in the imaginary narrow riverbanks.[27]

Mobile technology is a potential framework for people to change attitudes and transform aspects of the social communication, by combining information while going about their everyday. For example, the concomitant use of WhatsApp, Instagram, and Waze is composing face-to-face and mediated dialogs with synchronous and asynchronous exchanges to define routes and localities in urban environments. People renegotiate space-time as they circulate, and as a result, they operate and produce within physical and digital spaces, creating cultural filters, establishing social bonds and borders—zones of dialogs.[28] Understanding mobile phone usage with geolocation devices provokes different ways to walk and to drive in the city by attributing perception changes in how to move in the space and to organize everyday routines. These dynamic communication conditions are monitored by *Encontros*. This artwork seeks visibility, which according to Tuan, is "as an attempt to give sensible form to the moods, feelings, and rhythms of functional life."[29]

Regarding imaginary lines and margins, (im)possible borders are explored iteratively over many years in several works by Gilbertto Prado. During his travels in the early 1980s, one of his performance actions was on the Equator straddling this meridian, trying to perceive the vortex of the liquid in his body. This *modus operandi* was described and resumed in the artwork *ZN: PRDM (Neutral Zone: A River Passes Through Me)*[30] via a lecture in 2013 that described the framework and procedural methods.[31] *Encontros* was also discussed. In the *ZN:PRDM* artwork, the artist launched himself at the confluence of the waters in Santarém (Pará) that was tied with a rope attached to the boat and a float around his waist, to the despair of the vessel's captain and crew. Submersion of the body was then activated, highlighting the division between the black and brown waters. Video footage from inside the river—which had a strong water flow that evoked the idea of tensions and connections—was then later used to feed the cell phones for *Encontros*.

*Encontros* claims a spatial experience as a sensitive field of knowledge, not subjected to scientific tools since the work presents not a functional apparatus but a dialectical landscape by bringing art and everyday events into close proximity. Art augments this scientific field of knowledge by including the influence of flows and subtle fields, bringing to light invisible forces and fluxes at play. How does one make the various vectors and forces that make up our cross and circulations appear, even if we do not notice them? And how is it possible to compose with them? The artist activates spaces that propose deviations, emphasizing alternative points of view and experiences that link and amplify scientific data and information and also the fleeting relationships that may occur during these journeys. Under this perspective, the artwork as well as the social space around it becomes unstable, like a force field between practice and experience in our daily life.[32]

*Encontros* consists of two mobile phones, positioned across from each other on a rail, in a trick of cameras with field and counter-field, which exercises the audiovisual language to highlight the dialog between the two devices. Displaced mobile phones provoked by tensions of the spring (see Figure 8, color insert) are defined and controlled by an arduino plate, programmed to allow the receiving of data and playing videos in the mobile phones, and are connected to the web. A wood base (1.30 × 0.50 × 1.00 m) with a hole (diameter of 5 cm) in the center to route the cables supports this structure and ensures stability to accommodate the tensions of the spring and its horizontal movements.

On each side of the work, we have mobile phones playing ten different videos from the brown water part and ten videos from the black part. Ranging from the most uniform—without mixing—to the most mixed, the tenth on each side is identical, that is, the mixed water line itself.

It is worth remembering that when the cell phones move on the rail, it is this displacement that triggers the change in different levels of color. It goes from the most uniform on the tips of the device to the center of the work where the waters blend in the screens of the cell phones.[33]

The computational system searches the web for real time data on the flow of tides. The phases of the moon, ocean currents, and the word "meetings" appear in several web platforms and different languages.[34] People around the world are texting, talking the world "meeting" and the algorithm tracks those exchanges, quantifying and producing data. When receiving data, the mobile phones begin to move very slowly back and forth over the rail, representing a dialog between the two sources, delimiting space, and defining a specific flow. The spring, at the same time in which it extends, coils to mark the space and the course of the flow/movement (see Figure 41.1). In the brief moments of near-touching, at the limit of the spring's approximation and coiling, it is possible to notice images with a light combination of brown and black of the waters that almost mix,[35] changing from the impossibility of the effective encounter to the possibility of affecting each other.

In this process, each element (wave tides, lunar phases, and the word "meetings" in social networks) becomes metadata. This monitoring is physically reflected in the movements of mobile phones in the exhibition room. These data add another layer of meaning to the artwork, as the components of the devices represent distinct forces: gravity, Earth's rotation, ocean currents and they are related to the text (the word "meetings") circulation. Data, whether be footprints, traces or clues of formal or informal personal relationships, constitute diagrammatic formulations as they are related to behaviors, and suggest a visualization process.[36] The patterns, as formulations, are intrinsic elements of the artists' creation process, to encode data collected into visual expressions and to be later decoded for people when reading and signifying narratives. They are about encoding and decoding processes and make us to think how technology mediates users' perception and behaviors.

The diagram (Figure 41.1) points to the direction of forces resulting from the movement, as well as their modulations, waves, and intensities. At this point, we take from Alexander his consideration about "the invention of diagrams" as a model of organizing demands and forces of perception and observation of a given situation.[37] For Alexander, the representation of a benzene molecule, following the drawings of Theo van Doesburg, expresses the interrelations and tensions of other physical arrangements, whether they are atoms or prefabricated architectural structures,

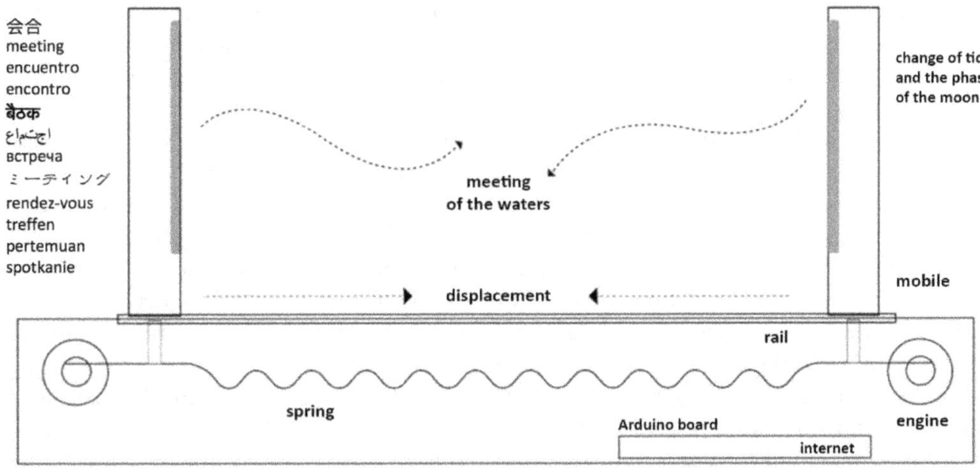


*Figure 41.1* The diagram of the *Encontros* (Meetings) artwork points to the direction of forces resulting from the movement, as well as their modulations, waves, intensities. Photo Credit: Gilbertto Prado and Grupo Poeticas Digitais

respectively, since they observe behaviors from different scales and materialities to create conventions. Likewise, artists in their poetic choices play with the permanence and relevance of what affects networked society and what establishes their subjective constructions in search for social, political, and economic visibility. The artworks present and represent, by offering the object directly and constructing something through something materially distinct according to artists' rules.

*Encontros* represents a socio-spatial production process that evokes political and social conflicts between the local community of Rio Negro and Rio Solimões in the Amazon with other distinct economic interests. According to Lima, "This great river of dark waters has testified a battle between the preexistent production and the socio-spatial processes that have occurred due to the institutionalization of the metropolitan region of Manaus."[38] Throughout its history, the changing borders led to a series of administrative and geographical changes to the urban centers and other territories in the region, because of religious missions and villages, rubber extraction, river navigation, and migration from northeastern Brazil. Lima considers how the legitimacy of political and private capital actions have promoted socio-spatial selectivity, resulting in segregation capable of being recognized in the maps, where it becomes evident which regions are more or less attractive to the State infrastructure and the real state sector. This process is selective, there are empty areas, such as the floodplain, because of a cyclical and ecological time, linked to the rise and fall of the waters.

From the anthropological research made by Wilson and Donnan,[39] we highlight that borders are not homogeneous and also vary in time and space; borders are about possible changes in the definition of peripheric zones and their relation to the center; frontiers are defined territorially as zones related to the borders, which have heuristic and metaphorical use. Borders help us comprehend the inaccurate connection among people, states and nations, as they modulate identity buildings and associated ways of belonging. Following Wilson and Donnan, we understand borders as a potent action that defines and redefines, locates and relocates possible meetings, since people are spatially desynchronized from each other. They can be distant physically but technologically integrated by the temporal dimension for a possible dialog.

*Encontros* makes visible the instability of formal and informal networks (institutional and everyday activities, respectively), since it is a cumulative communication process with different types of flows, in which controlling is substituted by circulating and sharing. Eliot and Urry write, "However, such networking often socially discriminates against people who are unable to enter and to sustain membership of such networks."[40] Thus, people's displacements need to be examined in their fluid and networked interdependence, instead of in separate dimensions and situations. We are in constant motion, actively doing things together such as driving and reading geolocated maps, browsing the web, walking, and having local and online synchronic meetings.

As Urry suggests, "Movement often involves an embodied experience of the material and social modes of dwelling-in-motion, places of and for activities in their own right."[41] Therefore, the world can be understood as a negotiation process among different actual events, according to different protocols of communication and networks, such as telecommunication systems and wireless networks. And within this context, artists aim at inventing different forms to articulate forces—man and nature, composing complex structures in order to question the patterns of movement in society, whether literal, conceptual or metaphoric. *Encontros* articulates distinct networks and information flows—objects and physical bodies, water and moons, time, and space—and it materializes other configurations to the comprehension of its borders.

In *Encontros*, both mobile phones display videos filmed during a trip up the Amazon River, composed by flows of water in two distinct tints: on the one side there is a predominance of black-colored water, on the other, brown-green colored. These waters form a diversity of tones, from green to muddy. Because of the Amazon River's sediments, to the black waters of Rio Negro, which presents this unique color among the Amazon affluent rivers. In this sense, the audiovisual content materializes a certain negotiation seen at the borders—the movements of water defined by a pallet of colors, from the black-colored to the brown-green colored water that poetically presents a visual narrative. It is a visual representation that creates aesthetic and emotional connection of the water phenomenon to the idea of possible online meetings.

We return to Manovich and his definition of the term "media visualization,"[42] in which the colors of the images reveal the patterns[43] while they formulate ways of telling a story from metadata (date, places, users). Manovich suggests that the operationalization of media depends on the exercise of the language, that is, on the specific ways of organizing and accessing data through codes such as visual, computational or sound. However, every operation of creation that validates hybridization processes in their structure evokes other limits, and proposes, as a consequence, to fabulate, to invent, by bringing a new perspective to perceive the world.[44] This is similar to Simondon's concept of "convergence operations,"[45] a series of intellectual, tooling, material, social and political actions that update themselves in a technical object and potentialize the efficiency of its articulation regarding its own configuration and the context where it stands.

The work has been exhibited a few times, and its maintenance and conservation of the original components have always been maintained. Since the 2018 presentation at the Circuit Alameda show, the entire original structure has been kept as was originally exhibited, including the old cell phones and their programming of that time for the devices, as well as the centenary wooden base. Only the motion sensors that were displayed on the side of the rail have changed, indicating the change of videos. Another alteration was that the approximation between the cell phones were replaced by small sonars, and the safety parts for the steel cable and stepper motors have been replaced for better work maintenance were also improved.[46]

*Encontros* speaks about the arrangement of forces between man and nature, evoking a provisional border that is profoundly related to networked users as a dynamic process of flows in dialog—as a communication process. This perspective reinforces the idea that the space of the artwork as well as the social space around it become unstable. They become a force field between practices and experiences in our daily life. *Encontros* represents a shift in balance that also investigates the phenomena of leaving a personal dimension for a collective scale of observation/ participation, which brings with it a sense of belonging and sharing. In conclusion, the act of living in the world depends on the ability to recognize and signify dynamic territories, and *Encontros* uses unpredictable results of working with data to validate uncertainty. This becomes the process by which to experience borders not as fixed contours but as shifting and unpredictable processes of dialog (see Figure 41.2). *Encontros* embodies the aesthetic and technical aspects of creating visualities to signify borders and networked mobilities.

*Figure 41.2* Left: The dive of the artist in the confluence between two rivers from the perspective of Rio Negro.[47] Right: The dive of the artist in the confluence between two rivers from the perspective of Rio Solimões. Photo credits: Gilbertto Prado

## Notes

1 Marc Augé, *Por uma antropologia da mobilidade* (Maceió: EDUFAL; São Paulo: UNESP, 2010), 15–16.
2 Augé, *Por uma antropologia da mobilidade*, 15.
3 Manuel Castells, *A era da informação: economia, sociedade e cultura* (São Paulo: Paz e Terra, 1999).
4 Anne-Laure Amilhat Szary and Frédéric Giraut, "Borderities: The Politics of Contemporary Mobile Borders," in *Borderities and the Politics of Contemporary Mobile Borders*, edited by Anne-Laure Amilhat Szary and Frédéric Giraut (London: Palgrave MacMillan, 2015), 1–19.
5 Mimi Sheller and John Urry, "The New Mobilities Paradigm," *Environment and Planning A* 38, no. 2 (2006): 207–26; 206, doi: 10.1068/a37268.
6 As noted in RFC 791, "Internet Protocol," in *DARPA Internet Program Protocol Specification*, edited by Jon Postel (California: Information Sciences Institute, University of Southern California, 1981), http://faqs.org/rfcs/rfc791.html.
7 The Poéticas Digitais group was formed by Gilbertto Prado (coordinator), Agnus Valente, Andrei Thomaz, Clarissa Ribeiro, Claudio Bueno, Daniel Ferreira, José Dario Vargas, Luciana Ohira, Lucila Meirelles, Mauricio Taveira, Nardo Germano, Renata La Rocca, Sérgio Bonilha, Tatiana Travisani and Val Sampaio.
8 It was exhibited at "EmMeio#4," Museu Nacional da República, Brasília, 2012; Continuum—IV Festival de Arte e Tecnologia do Recife—Centro Cultural Correios, PE, 2013; Singularidades/Anotações, Itaú Cultural, 2014; the 16th Biennale Media Art WRO, Wroclaw, Poland, 2015; the 24th International Symposium on Eletronic Art and the 16th Image Festival, in Manizales, Colombia (2017); Circuito Alameda, Laboratorio Arte Alameda, Mexico (2018); #18.ART, Faculdade de Belas Artes de Lisboa, Portugal (2019).
9 "*The Meeting of Waters* (Portuguese: Encontro das Águas) is the confluence between the dark (blackwater) Rio Negro and the pale sandy-colored (whitewater) Amazon River or Rio Solimões, as the upper section of the Amazon is known in Brazil upriver of this confluence. For 6 km (3.7 mi) the two rivers' waters run side by side without mixing. It is one of the main tourist attractions of Manaus, Brazil. The same also happens near Santarém, Pará (where the Encontros project was developed) with the Amazon and Tapajós rivers. This phenomenon occurs in other regions of the world with differing characters of rivers; the phenomenon is also seen in other locations in the Amazon region, as Iquitos, Peru. This phenomenon is due to the differences in temperature, speed, and water density of the two rivers. The Rio Negro flows at near 2 km/h (1.2 mph) at a temperature of 28°C (82°F), while the Rio Solimões flows between 4 and 6 km/h (2.5–3.7 mph) at a temperature of 22°C (72°F)."
10 Yuk Hui, *On the Existence of Digital Objects* (Minneapolis: The University of Minnesota Press, 2016).
11 Anthony Elliot and John Urry, *Mobile Lives* (New York: Routledge, 2010), 45.
12 Anthony Cooper and Chris Rumford, "Monumentalising the Border: Bordering through Connectivity," *Mobilities* 8, no. 1 (2013): 108, doi: 10.1080/17450101.2012.747761.
13 Chris Rumford, "Thinking about Borders," *European Journal of Social Theory* 9, no. 2 (2006): 155–69, Accessed 29 November 2018, doi: 10.1177/1368431006063330.
14 Felipe Merker Castellani, "A poética de Georges Aperghis: uma abordagem sobre a noção de dispositivo artístico," in *arte_corpo_tecnologia*, edited by Monica Tavares, Juliana Henno, Helena Damélio, Alessandra Bochio, and Aline Antunes (São Paulo: ECA/USP, 2014), 195, www2.eca.usp.br/nucleos/gp_admd/wp-content/uploads/arte_corpo_tecnologia_vFinal_impressao.pdf.
15 Alberto Cupani, *Filosofia da Tecnologia: um convite* (Florianópolis: Editora da UFSC, 2016).
16 Pierre Lévy, *Cibercultura* (São Paulo: Editora 34, 1999).
17 Hui, *On the Existence of Digital Objects*, 163.
18 Gilbert Simondon, *On the Mode of Existence of Technical Objects* (London, Canada: University of Western Ontario, 1980), 9
19 Jean Baudrillard, *O sistema dos objetos* (São Paulo: Editora Perspectiva, 2002).
20 Stephanie Chadwick, "Francis Picabia, Ideal," in *Smarthistory*, 23 October 2017, https://smarthistory.org/picabia-ideal/.
21 Hui, *On the Existence of Digital Objects.*
22 "Coordinated Universal Time," Wikipedia. This page was last edited on 8 June 2019, at 10:55 (UTC), https://en.wikipedia.org/wiki/Coordinated_Universal_Time.
23 Hui, *On the Existence of Digital Objects*, 181.
24 Simondon, *On the Mode of Existence of Technical Objects.*
25 Simondon cited in Hui, *On the Existence of Digital Objects*, 166.
26 Hui, *On the Existence of Digital Objects*, 183.

27 This poem originates in Portugese: Daqui se vê muito água e céu, constelações de árvores e cipoais intransponíveis. Paisagens, como deveriam ser, sem fim, letárgicas como o tempo que flui entre um mergulho e um assobio./ Daí se vê o que é, o tempo que passa nas rugas e nas vestes puídas./ O suave toque das mãos-moças de sorriso aberto que enfeitiçam os botos, nos enchem de doces, e nos levam para o fundo do rio, sem volta./ A experiência do rio é fluxo, marrom ou preto, intransponíveis, estremes, num fundo que não se deixa ver de igarapés imaginários. See Gilbertto Prado, "Ensaio gráfico: Diário de bordo," *ARS* (São Paulo) 10, no. 20 (2012): 56–69. doi: 10.11606/issn.2178-0447.ars.2012.64422.

28 Luisa Paraguai, "The INmobility Project: Modes of Textualities and Unpredictable Visualities of Everyday Life," *Lecture Notes in Computer Science* 10919 (2018): 640–52, doi:10.1007/978-3-319-91803-7_48.

29 Yi-Fu Tuan, *Space an Place. The Perspective of Experience* (Minneapolis: University of Minnesota Press, 2011), 164–65.

30 Zona Neutra: Passa um Rio Dentro de Mim (in Portuguese). Gilbertto Prado. Projetos "ZN:PRDM" e "Ø25—Quarto Lago": Grupo Poéticas Digitais. In Anais #12.ART Encontro Internacional de Arte e Tecnologia (Goiania: UFG, 2013), https://art.medialab.ufg.br/up/779/o/gilberttoPrado-Grupo.pdf.

31 Nelson Brissac Peixoto, Ary Perez, Gilbertto Prado and Ruy Sardinha Lopes, "Intervenções Urbanas—Arte, ciência e inovação," Gilbertto Prado's Conference at Maria Antonia University Center, 19 June 2013, www.youtube.com/watch?v=eas9zI-nZVw.

32 Gilberto Prado, "Projetos Recentes Do Grupo Poéticas Digitais," in *Poesia Visual*, edited by Alberto Saraiva (Rio de Janeiro: F10 Editora; Oi Futuro, 2013), 14–21.

33 Gilbertto Prado, "Projetos 'ZN:PRDM (Zona Neutra: Passa Um Rio Dentro De Mim)' e 'Caixa dos Horizontes Possíveis' do Grupo Poéticas Digitais," *Arteriais* 3, no. 2 (2016): 54–66. doi: 10.18542/arteriais.v3i3.3862.

34 The flow of accesses to the word "encontros" is searched in several languages: Mandarin: 会合; English: meetings; Spanish: encuentros; Portuguese: encontros; Hindu: बैठक; Arabic: اجتماع; Russian: встреча; Japanese: ミーティング; French: rendez-vous; German: treffen; Indonesian: pertemuan; Polish: spotkanie.

35 Gilbertto Prado, "Grupo Poéticas Digitais: Encontros e ø25—Quarto Lago," in *Arte em deslocamento: trânsitos geopoéticos*, edited by Priscila Arantes (São Paulo: Paço das Artes, 2015), 80–91.

36 Luisa Paraguai, "Mapeamento da mobilidade-traços de percursos," in Anais do 23° Encontro Nacional de Pesquisadores em Artes Plásticas (Belo Horizonte: ANPAP/PPGARTES/ICA/UFMG, 2014), www.anpap.org.br/anais/2014/ANAIS/simposios/simposio04/Luisa%20Paraguai.pdf.

37 Christopher Alexander, *Notes on the Synthesis of Form* (Cambridge, MA; London, England: Harvard University Press, 1973), 85.

38 Marcos Castro de Lima, "*Quando o amanhã vem ontem: a institucionalização da região Metropolitana de Manaus e a indução ao processo de metropolização do espaço na Amazônia Ocidental*," (PhD diss., University of São Paulo, 2014).

39 Thomas M. Wilson and Hastings Donnan (eds.), *Border Identities: Nation and State at Internacional Frontiers* (Cambridge: Cambridge University Press, 1997).

40 Elliot and Urry, *Mobile Lives*, 48.

41 John Urry, *Mobilities* (Cambridge: Polity, 2007), 11.

42 Lev Manovich, "*Media Visualization: Visual Techniques for Exploring Large Media Collections*," last modified 2011, http://manovich.net/content/04-projects/070-media-visualization-visual-techniques-for-exploring-large-media-collections/66-article-2011.pdf.

43 Alexander, *Notes on the Synthesis of Form.*

44 Lev Manovich, *Software Takes Command* (New York: London: Bloomsbury Academic, 2013), http://issuu.com/bloomsburypublishing/docs/9781623566722_web.

46 Gilbertto Prado, Agnus Valente, Ana Elisa Carramaschi, Andrei Thomaz, Leonardo Lima, Luciana Ohira, Mauricio trentin, Nardo Germano, and Sérgio Bonilha, "Algunos apuntes sobre la relectura y el siempre rehacer de algunas obras," in *Circuito Alameda*, edited by Gilbertto Prado and Jorge La Ferla (Ciudad de México: Instituto Nacional de Bellas Artes; Laboratorio Arte Alameda, 2018), 38–52.

47 Gilbertto Prado, "Ensaio gráfico: Diário de bordo," *ARS* (São Paulo) 10, no. 20 (2012): 56–69, doi: 10.11606/issn.2178-0447.ars.2012.64422.

# 42

# CRITICAL AND CREATIVE APPROACHES TO DIGITAL CULTURAL HERITAGE WITH AUGMENTED REALITY

*Victoria Szabo*

## AR: An Emerging Medium

According to urban hype cycle speculations, augmented reality (AR) is set to surpass virtual reality (VR) in its influence and impact.[1] Like virtual reality, augmented reality has seen interest wax and wane over the years, as the business research firm Gartner has noted, but it is poised to enter the "slope of enlightenment."[2] However, with the advent of mainstream support of AR by Google and Apple, we are starting to see that commercial application is likely to continue to develop. Statista suggests that the VR/AR market will go from 20.4 billion dollars in 2019 to 192.7 in 2022. *Information Age* describes it as part of the "Fourth Industrial Revolution" taking place around information technologies.[3] The hype around VR, AR, and related technologies is reflected in the popular media through the rise, fall, and acquisition of start-ups and through the exploration of the medium's potential in a wide variety of contexts. For example, in 2019, New York City launched what it billed as "the nation's first city-funded center for research, entrepreneurship, and education in virtual and augmented-reality, spatial computing, and other emerging media technologies" in a Brooklyn warehouse.[4]

Though the technologies have shifted and the field is newly animated by big moves from Google and Apple, over the last two decades the promise of mobile AR has grown up alongside the increasing ubiquity of GPS-enabled smartphones and in combination with increasing access to the means of online production. Creative and commercial practitioners have leveraged cell phones, Wi-Fi, and later smartphones to create location-based experiences that rely on the juxtaposition of the material world and the virtual world, combining together in real-time hybrid reality experiences of various sorts. While some projects have focused on image-based, or more recently, object-based recognition, others, including some of those most interesting from an urban exploration and heritage perspective, have relied on geolocation for their effects.

Augmented reality is based on the idea of a correlation between virtual and physical reality. It is enacted in mobile applications through the annotation of a place, image, or object. This can be used to provide supplementary information about the referent, such as might be found in a guidebook, or a complementary experience, or can rely upon the physical world as a stage for some sort of virtual intervention. The AR projection itself might take the form of a visual overlay, a sidenote, a trigger, or some other media element. Location-based annotation of the physical world has typically relied on global positioning system (GPS) data, although image-and object-based recognition systems have been added into such applications to make the registration process more accurate. Recent developments at Google in 2019 suggest that urban wayfinding with their most recent application will rely on a combination of GPS and object recognition in urban environments to make it easier than ever to find your way.[5] The implication is not only that urban spaces have been fully mapped in 3D, but also that this information could be accessed in real time—first as a navigational aid, but with blanket annotations and commentary surely to follow.

As computer graphics researchers have noted, the idea of the annotation remains at the core of augmented reality experience design, whether direct or indirect.[6] A decade ago researchers pointed to taxonomies of AR that highlight the temporality, dimensionality, viewpoint reference frame, mounting or registration point, and type of reference as key features for the medium.[7] Such analyses have shaped the authoring platforms available to use today and correspondingly what we see as possible within this emerging medium. If we expand our understanding of what counts as augmented reality to include a broader set of mobile media practices around urban experience design, we can begin to appreciate location-based authorship as a way to intervene in conversations around the best, present, and future of urban environments. This is true not only for how we understand the changing material features of our cities, but also how we live, work, and play within them.

This form of "techno-spatial assemblage," as Benjamin Feldman puts it in his study of *Pokémon GO* users,[8] yields complex results that can be in conflict with notions of who controls the world's received spaces. As the authors of "Augmented reality in urban places: Contested content and the duplicity of code" point out in their study of augmented reality as a conceptual category in critical geography, "the complex and often duplicitous manner that code and content can congeal in our experiences of augmented places" must be understood as enacting various and intermixed degrees of agency and power on the part of users and developers alike.[9] Their analysis highlights how even seemingly open-ended, participatory platforms like Wikipedia and online ranking systems are themselves governed by systems of commercial and economic power.

It is this combination of effects—where lived experience of real objects and places meets the virtual—that AR has the greatest potential for urban experience design for cultural heritage. Whether artists, academics, and other non-corporate practitioners will be able to develop in the medium is another matter. Even if they are, the extent to which their interventions perform participation rather than truly allowing it will be another layer of concern, as Graham, Zoom, and Boulton suggest.[10] Given our deep implication within the system, even as practitioners and critics, what space is there, if any, for us to work simultaneously within and against the medium and its socio-technical affordances, making its constraint productive and visible, where possible, rather than misleading—or worse? Is the medium so corrupted by the conditions of its possibility that to engage with it is to foster a dystopian, technocratic, and fundamentally surveyed reality? In *The City of Tomorrow*, Ratti and Claudel describe the mobile phone as a cyborg extension, the "the always-on prosthetic device" that facilitates the operation of the smart city. Whether we greet this statement with enthusiasm or misgiving, the impact is profound.[11]

To begin to answer this question about the potential for cultural heritage and creative applications in urban contexts, we can look back to the last two decades of urban AR experimentation, as well as to current developments in the field. We can also speculate on future possibilities based on emerging trends and investments. And of course, we can make principled decisions based on where we would like to see the field go.

## The Perils of Immersion

The idea of augmented experience design in urban environments is not new. Even if we limit ourselves to early twenty-first century examples, we see references hearkening back to earlier forums as well as pointing toward future potential when the technology catches up to our imaginations—providing we are in a position to take advantage of its potential as non-corporate entities and perhaps non-specialist developers. In order to address the broader scope of our antecedents in this field, it is important to draw wisdom from disparate practitioners—computer scientists and technology developers as well as cultural heritage developers, urbanists, artists, and activists.

Over the last two decades, the ubiquity of GPS devices, and later GPS-enabled smartphones, has changed the ways that people navigate the world. "Death by GPS"—the phenomenon in which people no longer pay attention to visual cues but instead rely on their technical assistants when driving, occasionally to their great detriment, sometimes also finds an analog in pedestrian engagements.[12] In other words, if we rely too much on the device, will we completely lose sight of the context? This effect has been exacerbated by the growth of social media. The selfie culture that now permeates lived experience in space also extends to the ways that travelers make their plans—with at times profound consequences, whether trampling tulip crops in the Netherlands,[13] or falling to their deaths in Western Australia, Arizona, or Portugal, among other places.[14] With the advent of immersive 3D overlays, where might such immersion lead?

In a broader sense, the enriched GPS of the smartphone, with its seemingly encyclopedic set of references, could generate a multi-dimensional situational blindness that extends what we already produce through our increasingly mediated and narrow-casted lived experiences in space and time. Whether we are talking about people using Yelp reviews to decide which restaurant to visit (rather than looking in the window, or at a sidewalk menu, or taking a first-person recommendation), or *Pokémon GO* enthusiasts blundering (intentionally or not) into hospital emergency rooms, cemeteries, and construction sites,[15] we are dealing with a medium whose implications are still only partially understood through its consequences, and one that exploits already vulnerable consumers to further interpellation. Projection of the self into the world might equally mean projecting onto the self a hyper-curated set of experiences that reinforce existing assumptions and that slyly plant new experiences with Facebook ad scandals and Twitter bots brought to 3D life as we move through the world.

Recent developments in social media extend this notion even further into how interaction with devices curate experience of urban monuments. Snapchat has a recent addition of Landmarker lenses (in Beta at time of writing). They go from adding cat ears to yourself to allowing you to add them to iconic buildings. This suggests a logical extension of the you-centric selfie-culture that it participates in as a kind of personal projection-mapping onto the world. While the projection mapping of artists creating new designs on buildings democratizes the lightscapes by those who control their facades, the virtual graffiti enabled by Snapchat is curated for those who wish to see the same.

Not only is touristic experience about you showing yourself experiencing a place, but now projection-mapping is shifting from a collective urban intervention to a personalized decoration of an urban landmark. At the time of this writing, five experiences were ready to try out: Buckingham Palace in London, UK; Eiffel Tower in Paris, France; Flatiron Building in NYC, US; TCL Chinese Theater in Los Angeles, US; and the Capitol Building in Washington D.C., US.[16] Keiichi Matsuda's short film *Hyper-reality*, set in Medellin, shows a chaotic and ad-saturated first-person experience of urban AR.[17] As a counterpoint to the hyper-curated vision implied by the user's social media feed, this idea of the future is about information overload, a Times Square panoply in your pocket. The project website describes the future it envisions:

> Our physical and virtual realities are becoming increasingly intertwined. Technologies such as VR, augmented reality, wearables, and the Internet of Things are pointing to a world where technology will envelop every aspect of our lives. It will be the glue between every interaction and experience, offering amazing possibilities, while also controlling the way we understand the world. *Hyper-Reality* attempts to explore this exciting but dangerous trajectory.

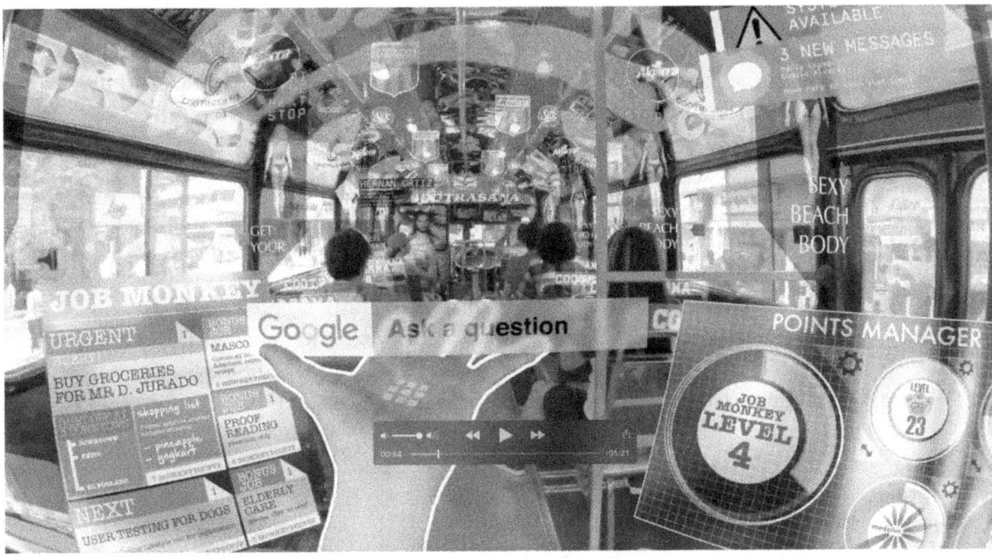


*Figure 42.1* Still from *Hyper-Reality* by Kenji Matsuda. Photo credit: Kenji Matsuda

The project was crowdfunded through Kickstarter in 2013, with a quote from Bruce Sterling, "World-changing marvels to us, are only wallpaper to our children."[18] As *Failed Architecture* writer Joshua McWhirter suggests, Matsuda's work "portrays augmented reality as an inherently gamified, commercial, and homogenizing interface experience."[19] Whether at the level of everyday interaction, wayfinding, or information retrieval, this dystopian vision offers little to recommend annotation of the airspace, especially by commercial interests (Figure 42.1).

However, there is hope for alternative paths. McWhirter's essay also draws attention to some other AR innovators from an arts perspective, complicating a notion of the medium arising only out of corporate interests and pointing toward a variety of early AR artists who have experimented with urban augmentation, including one work by an artist whose guerrilla AR was meant to critique a corporate-produced AR partnership between Jeff Koontz and Snapchat, in one of the "glimmers of direct challenges to its creeping privatization."[20]

## Alternate Genealogies for Critical AR Practice

Particularly in the 2000s and 2010s, the combination of user-friendly test projects and urban explorations yielded provocative results. In 2004, the *Utne Reader* described the second annual Psy.Geo.Conflux—an experiential urban exploration festival inspired by Guy Debord and the Situationists International and the concept of psychogeography—which focuses on affective experience of place. Inspired also by the nineteenth-century *flâneur*, the Surrealists, and the man of the crowd immortalized by Edgar Allen Poe, these practitioners celebrated the idea of exploration of the city against the grain of mapped expectations. In the Utne Reader piece, Hart describes the *Psy.Geo* group's overlay of a map of Copenhagen onto New York, introducing the idea of "algorithmic walking," and how it inspired new ways of experiencing a small town in Minnesota through a series of randomly generated steps.[21] Press accounts of the larger event in New York suggest a broader series of happenings, gatherings, and events coordinated by mobile phones and Wi-Fi. That their "antics may be lost on passersby is no surprise for psychogeography, as they both undermine and expand our common sense of place," as the New York Press reporter writes.[22]

A few years later, WhaiWhai, a group from Italy focused on novel approaches to cultural heritage tourism, took another tack for urban exploration with their *Ruyi* adventure guides. These city tours function as a combination of guidebook and urban exploration fantasy. Their website subtitle is "play the storyline through the city." As they suggest on their website, "Any city can become the setting for an adventure where you are the hero."[23] Their jumbled stories, landmarks, and scenarios create a novelistic overlay to everyday experience in urban environments, as they indicate on their blog. The user-centered approach remains a core feature of the experience, but the story unfolds in response to cues tied to historical artifacts in the real-world environment.

First introduced in 2008, they were award-winning as innovators in the Italian tourist industry in 2009.[24] Their books introduce elements of gamification into a guided exploration of a new city. Some parts are fantasy stories, while other focus more on gathering and imparting historical knowledge. For example, their guide to Rome relies upon a paperback book that contained numbered informational vignettes. Each step involves visiting a location in the city and finding a clue to the next step. The user then needs to send an SMS message to receive the next prompt. The experiences were limited to two plays with one guide—presumably to encourage more people to buy the books rather than share them with others (Figure 42.2).

This proto-AR project, like the Psy.Geo.Conflux festival, highlights the potential role mobile devices play in urban exploration and experience design. Early posts by the WhaiWhai group on their blog emphasize in-person, collaborative practice, and social meetups as key to the experience. As a post from 6 March 2009 shows, the developers could watch the games evolve in real time.[25] They became part of the celebration of Citywide Wi-Fi in Venice, announced for July 3, 2009, and organized an event for the opening.[26] Though there were technical difficulties, this coincidence helps show the relationship between the two.

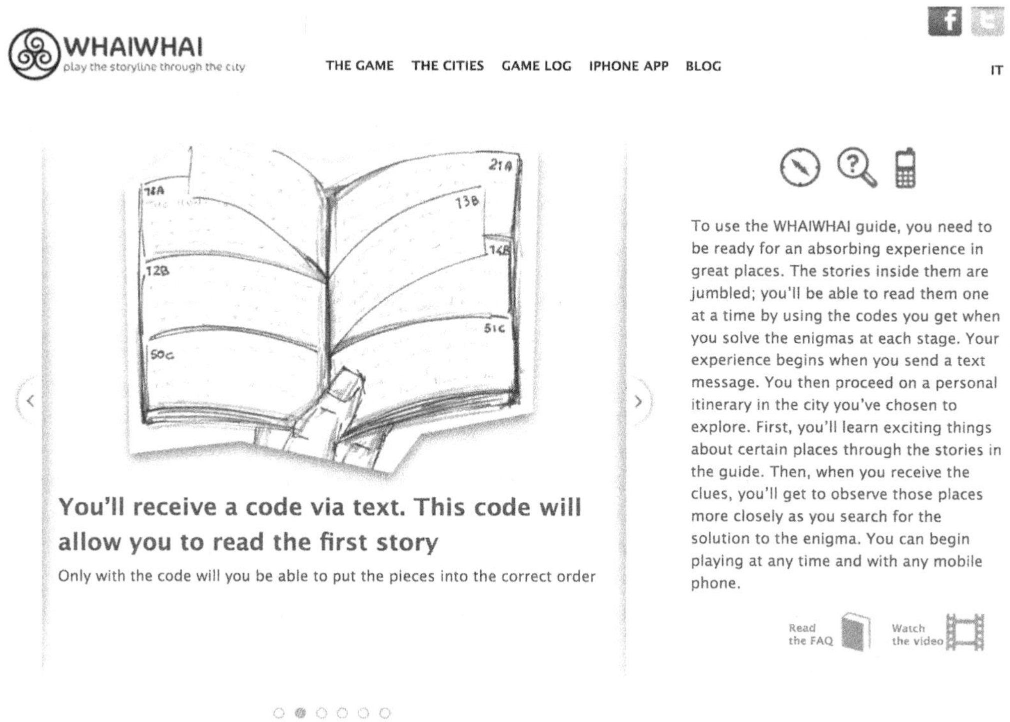


*Figure 42.2* Screen shot from The Ruyi website describing how to play *WhaiWhai*. Photo credit: The Ruyi

The WhaiWhai team had technical difficulties on the day of the big rollout. This is in keeping with the history of this kind of mobile intervention project—great ideas that push the edge of what the technology infrastructures can support. In 2010, WhaiWhai began developing mobile apps that moved away from the guidebook/SMS approach, reflecting the maturity of the smartphone and the limits of the hybrid media approach.[27] Their most recently advertised project exists in the form of an iPhone app focused on New York: the Pegleg.[28] The group's last blog post was in 2012, with their last tweet in 2015, as of this writing.

## The Beginnings of Urban AR

The move to the Smartphone that WhaiWhai began in 2010 coincides with the emergence of specialized AR apps focused on urban annotation. While projects like *WhaiWhai* and the Pys. Geo.Conflux festival had as their foundation ideas about urban exploration that were facilitated by mobile technology, this kind of tech was a means to create new kinds of cultural and experiential interventions. Now with tools like open development platform Layar—a create-your-own AR content creation browser—experimenters in urban space were focused more specifically on what emerging AR technologies could do. This narrowed both the focus and experimentation in directions that emphasized the site of annotation and reference as a key element in mobile experience design. For example, the London Street Museum generated substantial attention for its AR image overlays, building on the inspiration of recapture photography, a simple concept that has as yet still been only imperfectly realized technically in real-world variable environments. In 2010, they shared geolocated historic photos superimposed onto contemporary sites.[29]

This work was done in the same period that already feels like a golden age of startup, DIY augmented reality, albeit urban AR imperfectly achieved due to technological limits. The Netherlands Architecture Institute created a similar ART Tours project but recount limits with data throughput, including the need to set up an "unauthorized" Wi-Fi hotspot at an event. The team developed and documented an impressive array of apps, but at the same time needed to push against the grain of the technological infrastructures available to them. Like the psychogeographers walking the city with alternative maps as their guides, urban AR practitioners butted up against the virtual limits of data access and sharing within the terms of the systems they were defining. Other approaches to urban AR interventions in this period took a more overtly critical approach to their engagements, highlighting the disruptive potential of the medium. These approaches are part of a tradition of aesthetic, playful, and politicized forms of urban exploration. Whether generating fictive spaces and counter-factuals for the purposes of digital storytelling, education, or some other purpose, the one-to-many distribution potentials of the guidebook form can be complicated by conflicting voices, multiple narratives, and user agency.

For example, McWhirter mentions Manifest.AR, the collective known in part for Occupy Wall Street. As they describe in their AR Art Manifesto, "The AR Future is without boundaries between the Real and the Virtual. In the AR Future we become the Media. Freeing the Virtual from a Stagnant Screen we transform Data into physical, Real-Time Space".[30] Manifest.AR gained notoriety for their intervention at the *Venice Art Biennale*, putting their own work in juxtaposition with the curated content of this global art exhibition, perhaps in the spirit of the 1968 Biennale protests. As the group suggested, "54th Biennial of Venice could not justify its reputation without an uninvited Augmented Reality infiltration." The event they staged was striking for the fact that they both interjected rogue "pavilions" into the space to share their own artwork—and that one of their interventions staged battles to keep user-generated pavilions for unrepresented countries in place.

Their intervention was in the same period when Layar, Junaio, Wikitude, Acrossair, and others were becoming available as platforms for hosting and sharing POIs, or points of interest with cultural and educational institutions and individuals increasingly trying them out. Companies like Poiz.biz and Hoppala became hosting platforms with web front ends that were accessible for free for basic use. Layar.com made code samples visible for the more ambitious to set up POI servers of their own. However, all of this was to change in a few years, with the growth of commercial companies providing AR services on the one hand, and image-recognition based AR on the other, and eventually with the startups shifting into paid or advertising-oriented modes.

Soon shifting platforms were already causing older apps to break. The London Street museum went on to create additional apps related to Dickens and Roman London—only to see them rendered inactive as technologies changed. Both of the latter apps ceased to be available, while the original London Street museum appears to have had its last update in 2014. As they write on their website, "Following significant changes in recent operating system updates, our apps require major development work to restore full functionality. The museum is currently looking into the feasibility of this work."[31]

## The AR Trough of Disillusionment

As these examples suggest, by the mid-2010s the situation was already evolving from the early excitement reflected in urban exploration apps. Layar.com, a Dutch company that started up in 2010, gradually shifted its business model to commercial publishing. BuildAR, a web-based subscription service that utilized the Junaio platform, a major competitor to Layar, was shut down. Junaio was a subsidiary of Metaio, who ultimately sold out to Apple in 2015, taking apps created with it along with it.[32] Apple eventually came out with ARKit, of course. Locally at Duke University, my home institution, our own urban AR projects focused on Durham, NC and elsewhere shut down with the demise of various older platforms, with projects disappearing or stalled out by the need to focus on developing new work over recapitulating old work with newer systems. Meanwhile, Google Glass mostly folded in 2015 (taking with it our experimental annotated exhibitions, along with our status as Glass pioneers),[33] Google's Tango was discontinued in 2017,[34] and Google put its focus on ARCore. The remaining web interfaces for AR, both geolocative, and increasingly image-based, became either very expensive or was discontinued. Aurasma, an image-recognition based AR tool, was bought by HP and shared as HP Reveal[35]—then targeted for cancelation in 2019.

Layar-associated Blippar seemed to buck the trend as a company, attracting attention up till 2018, when they announced they too were closing down. Paul Sawers describes this in "The rise and fall of augmented reality 'unicorn' Blippar."[36] While Blippar had built its brand on augmented advertising, they had also ventured into other projects, including forays into Google Glass and, in 2017, into Urban AR, which relied on both GPS and visual positioning, according to a promo video. A related blog post highlights the key features: basic navigation, enhanced map content, and urban visual positioning. Limited initially to Central London, San Francisco, and Mountain View, it relied on Apple's new ARKit.[37] They introduced the idea of "occlusions" or "points of interest within the user's eyeline," highlighting the user-centric point of view, and counter to the nightmare overload of Matsuda's vision.

Further more, as they suggest in a press release, although there was detailed info for only three cities at launch, over 300 were pre-seeded with "enhanced map" info based on their proprietary "Blipparsphere," knowledge graph, in anticipation of future development.[38] As they describe it: "While search is driven by specific queries based on keywords, discovery is based around spontaneous curiosity with something in front of a user in the real world."[39] As their Co-Founder and CEO, Ambarish Mitra put it, "The new discovery behavior we are powering through today's update matches natural human thought patterns."[40] Though the company did not succeed, the elements for future development are there. While many of the AR-fronted projects have gone away with their platforms, however, some of the authors continue to develop location-based work. For example, *A Hollow Body* (2014) was created as an online experience as "a cinematic experience for two people in the city of London."[41] Commissioned by the City of London as part of a Sherlock Holmes exhibit, the project was conceived as a "cinematic experience" and a "soundtrack for the city." While it was not an AR project per se, it was a mobile experience that took location-based interests to heart in its execution. It represents a shift into the fictive space that the Ruyi tours explored and doesn't rely on either continuous data connections or the vicissitudes of visual AR, yet builds upon both in its conception through audio experiences.[42] Here we might suggest the authors build on AR interventions but adapt to the contemporary technical landscape.

Tellingly, this successor project still exists, though the developer, Duncan Speakman, more recently associated with the Pervasive Media Studio, appears to be focused more on "augmented audio" these days.[43] He responded recently to a Twitter inquiry, asking "is *Hollow Body* still working? I heard some of the roads were blocked now?" Users responded that they had to stop and start again in posts on March 8, 2019, but that parts of the project were still usable.[44]

## AR and Gamification

Some of the most recent location-based augmented reality systems appear to rely on game engine technologies coupled with location tech, continuing a shift into experiences with more fictive and ludic elements that is in keeping with earlier generations of urban exploration with mobile apps. For example, the Breda City tour, [45] which encourages users to resurrect ("rez") pre-packaged object-based AR experiences at specific locations in the city combined the tabletop display of AR increasingly popular in advertising and journalism with a locational, storytelling-based element. The result achieves the magic window overlay effect long desired of AR overlays, but without needing to rely on the future-promised direct annotation of a 3D environment via geolocation plus computer vision.

Meanwhile, *Inventing America* was described in 2018 as an app that "brings New Yorkers to Governor's Island, circa 1623." As an essay by Dan Robitzski in *Futurism* describes,

> [v]iewed through a phone or tablet, Governor's Island becomes the locus of a rip in the very fabric of spacetime. Step through the simulated time warp and you're thrown back to the 17th century as a cartoony colonist, animated through 3D rendering and motion capture technology, work to settle the future New York City.[46]

Mixed reality artist Roi Lev and his team's branching storyline and cast of characters are described as discoverable only by moving around the space of the island.[47] The *Futurism* article suggests other New York Sites that users may be able to follow in future app development.

In journalism, the latest AR advances, such as being able to detect a plane and deposit a 3D object, have also already yielded some interesting elements. David Bowie's costumes, like Ikea furniture, can be rezzed into your own contexts. An expose of illegal dumping in Chicago took another approach, embedding AR experiences into a podcast and including also some SketchFab-based visualizations of the illegal dump for scale.

Meanwhile, gamified AR continues to evolve as well among big commercial players focused on the technology. Niantic's *Pokémon GO* was built upon an earlier game, *Ingress*, and *Jurassic World Alive* and *Harry Potter (Wizards Unite)* games have been released. In keeping with the idea of rezzing instances of virtual objects in space, AMC's The *Walking Dead* zombie shooter game went live in 2018. As the developers point out, they learned from the Pokémon experience not to over-rely on the urban substrate for content, as rural users complained they were at a disadvantage because there were fewer notable sites available into which Pokémon could have been placed for discovery.

The *Walking Dead* game also took a mixed approach to backgrounds, perhaps due to technological limits, a situation they hoped to rectify in a later version of Apple's ARKit. "A player can also tap a button to turn the drawn background into a real-world view of your surroundings, which it then populates with the enemies." This suggests that characters spawn without regard to some aspects of the real-world environment, raising the specter of Death by GPS or Death by Selfie—but with zombies.[48] This lack is notable given the developer's claim that "It gives you a chance to experience the apocalypse and live out hypothetically what you would do."[49] Regardless, these titles suggest that transmedia development and overt gamification by big companies as part of an overall transmedia marketing and development strategy may be the future of more ambitious geolocative AR games.

## From System to Intervention

Even with a fully mapped out landscape, the wall issue, along with the changing landscapes and technologies underlying them, described an ongoing problem with this kind of work—the "medium" is not static. Untimely death is a reality not only for the unwary user or zombie, but also for the medium and its products itself. Platforms die, cityscapes change, priorities shift. It may be that we need to think of augmented experience design in urban contexts as less of an online publication, and more of a durational performance, or as part of an exhibition or intervention. This approach may be one way forward for augmented urban experiences and is perhaps best in keeping with the social and cultural aspects of the city itself, beyond its monuments and facades.

For example, King Britt's collaboratively produced, annotated mural in Philadelphia, "Dreams, Diaspora and Destiny," is also viewable at home. The hybrid media project is a "monumental time portal" that "honors ancestral legacies while envisioning nothing short of a utopian future through a multimedia experience like no other." It features everything from image and music to poetry and history lessons. Doubly ephemeral, in the sense that both mural and app are unlikely to exist long term, it was perhaps, like many other digital projects, as useful as an educational tool in its creation as it was impactful as an artwork after the fact.[50] Meanwhile the Miami murals by street artist Eduardo Kobra are animated with the help of a commercial AR team, Mussa, as Jonathan Kendall notes in *Big Think*. They call their collaborative interventions ARt. Like most recent coverage of AR, this story references *Pokémon GO*, even if the technologies in action operate quite differently.[51] Kendall suggest the technology is "one of the first fruits of a revolution about to take the art world by storm."

Whether that takes place or not will depend on ease of use, access, and cost as much as technological capacities for augmentation. The future for such work may rely on larger groups of sponsors for durational events, as the recent *Illuminate Salt Lake* exhibition with virtual public art and installations,[52] or the Serpentine Galleries Augmented Architecture competition cosponsored by Google Arts & Culture with architect Sir David Adjaye.[53]

Recent coverage of augmented reality in urban contexts suggests it is poised to be the next big thing not just for top-down digital city projects, but also for other kinds of urban interventions. Though the most intriguing tools may be out of reach to non-commercial developers for now—look at ESRI's industrial urban overlays—they can also be used for useful ends in relatively accessible ways. For example, the *#HomeCLT* project—created by a UNC Charlotte professor, Dr. Ming-Chun Lee—uses these technologies to annotate an exhibition locally. His augmented-reality maps were part of the #HomeCLT exhibition at the Levine Museum of the New South in North Carolina in 2018. Here, interactive maps and graphs "help viewers see how neighborhoods in Charlotte have changed over time—in a three-dimensional and, organizers hope, intriguing and memorable way" as part of an interactive exhibit on "Urban Complexities: Equity, Economic Mobility and the Built Environment."[54]

Importantly—and perhaps this is the true innovation—the exhibit also includes opportunities for people to record their own stories, which could themselves be part of future exhibits.[55] This is a different kind of urban AR, in that it is meant for a gallery setting, but it also brings in some of the participatory elements that the technology has not yet been able to deliver fully, into an approach that combines quantitative and qualitative information into a location-based context. Perhaps this is a moment where we rediscover the value of the gallery space as a site of reflection too.[56]

## Windows and Doors

Perhaps urban AR is not only about the presence of the past, or navigating one landscape with another, but also examining possible futures. One of the most affective uses of AR maybe a rendering of the Psy.Geo.Conflux idea of the superimposed map—but in a 3D form. "Enter the Room," a recent Red Cross project takes advantage of the ability to map one space onto another, as described in "Forget Pokémon GO, Red Cross augmented reality app brings war to you," as recent media coverage suggests.[57] The user of the app can draw the "room" doorway onto a real-life doorway at home, taking advantage of the same edge detection technologies that might allow people to drop a sofa or an outfit to anchor an alternate reality AR experience in their own space. Here the user is then able to step into a child's bedroom to experience wartime effects over a period of several years, the therapeutic potential becomes of interest (Figure 42.3).

In the terms of computer science researchers who design for AR, the reader would be taking an egocentric view of a completely immersive AR, but which is experienced through the mobile phone as a window onto another world. Time is deliberately invoked in a cinematic form in a set of subtle chapters, each year showing further degradation of the room's environment. Unlike headset-based VR, there is a continuing awareness of an external reality, but in a local space. This contrast heightens the impact, rather than diminishing it.

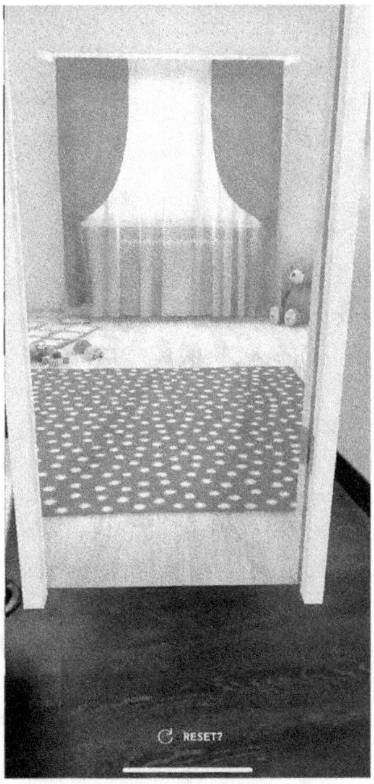


*Figure 42.3* Still image from entering gameplay in *The Room*. Photo credit: International Red Cross

> We spend our lives on our smartphones, walking around with our eyes glued to them. There is something incredibly moving about mapping this virtual reality onto our actual reality—and within that creating a narrative that tells a real story,

said Digital Content Manager Ariel Rubin.[58] While there is the potential for trivializing the experience of war, the project succeeds by not trying to convey it too directly. The user is in a child's bedroom and the effects are felt indirectly, watch water stains develop, cracks appear, a wheelchair enter the scene.

Walking through a doorway is powerful in itself. Walking through a virtual doorway that is simultaneously in your own home could be a new way of thinking about AR experience design. As psychology researcher Gabriel Radvansky and his colleagues have noted, crossing thresholds, or "event boundaries," can both impede and improve memory. Building upon earlier work on crossing thresholds and forgetting, he and his colleagues have suggested that "memory was better when the information was distributed across two events rather than combined into a single event."[59] How might we use cognitive psychology research to create more effective environments as AR researchers and artists? Researchers in cognitive science have suggested that "a fundamental event boundary detection mechanism enables navigation in both the spatial and episodic domains, and serves to form cohesive representations that can be used to predict and guide future behavior," an insight that could perhaps be useful in thinking about how to structure such threshold-crossing experiences in the future.[60] The field of spatialized storytelling and experience design made possible here is just beginning.

For now, as one journalist Brian Feldman remarks about AR in January 2019, it is the weather forecasters showing how deep the floodwaters could be that are some of the most effective AR storytellers we have right now. "In September, as Hurricane Florence bore down on North Carolina, a clip of broadcaster Erika Navarro explaining the storm's danger went viral."[61] Why? The clip showed Navarro outdoors, in an environment poised for flooding. Navarro's apparently immanent "immersion" exists on the stage of lived experience of an everyday environment, with a referent that might be you, but isn't you. You could easily imagine yourself in the center of that action, while at the same time remaining safely apart.[62] As with United States Today's feature about the illegal dump in Chicago, AR at scale has an affective power we are just beginning to understand how to tap.[63]

## Future Possibilities

At the time of this writing, Zappar remains as an image-recognition based AR company. AuGeo, an ESRI product, offers future promise as a place for geo-located points built upon their mapping platform.[64] The two big players remaining in the AR universe, Apple and Google, are open for business with commercial uptake quickly following. Vuforia, a staple for museum applications, recently priced its new 3D tracking system for AR beyond the scope of any sustained cultural heritage project.[65] The AR Foundation for the Unity3D platform shows promise and allows content to be ported out to both Apple and Google platforms. This is in keeping with the game-engine based approaches to AR that already exist. Undoubtedly, new services and systems to take advantage of ARKit and ARCore will continue to emerge.

Whatever technologies emerge, would-be augmented reality practitioners would be well advised to look to past experiences, relevant analogs, roads no longer taken, and the inherent contradictions and limits of trying to work within and against the limits of physical and virtual geographies, hype cycles, and media limitations both economic and technical. Nonetheless, the opportunity to think through lived experience on-site and on location seems all the more pressing in a time where the literal death by GPS and Selfie, and the virtual death of history by technological change and the present tendencies of digital media, render even the very recent past subject to erasure and obsolescence. Examples like the augmented histories and testimonies of the *#CLTHome* project or the animated Philadelphia murals suggest that historical and educational insights might be rezzed alongside the zombies, wizards, and floating candy bars that new technology spaces inevitably attract. Engaging with the user-centric perspective of the mobile-eye-view means grappling with an external world increasingly curated by our devices into a singular stream of narrowcasted content.

If we can find ways to cross physical and virtual thresholds that enhance engagement with the world—and those around us—rather than occluding it, then we might begin to realize some of the promise of augmented reality in urban environments, as well as its perils. The goal is not to punish imagination or to diminish the validity of augmented experience, but to open up the promise of virtual reality into the domain of lived experience in everyday life.

Perhaps the best hope lies in the fact that AR is inherently partial and multiple, and itself is far from stabilized as a medium. In a section on "Neutralizing Threats," researchers into AR interaction design for advertising point out that "marketers should also be mindful of how the brand meanings they plan to craft via AR can be subverted by activists and competitors." This point refers to the goal to "delight" consumers through increased interactivity, sociability, and attentiveness to context.[66] These same features could go into creating urban AR experiences that engage users, or perhaps, as the technology becomes more pervasive, challenges other interventions into the urban environment—physical, virtual, or both—through durational, performative, episodic, and immersive experiences.

## Notes

1 Andrew Ross, "Smart Cities and Augmented Reality: Is It Set to Become a Reality?" *Information Age*, 15 August 2018, www.information-age.com/smart-cities-and-augmented-reality-123474183/.

2 Kasey Panetta, "5 Trends Emerge in the Gartner Hype Cycle for Emerging Technologies, 2018," *Gartner*, 16 August 2018, www.gartner.com/smarterwithgartner/5-trends-emerge-in-gartner-hype-cycle-for-emerging-technologies-2018/.

3 Andrew Ross, "Smart Cities and Augmented Reality," 15 August 2018, www.information-age.com/smart-cities-and-augmented-reality-123474183/.

4 RLab, "New York City's Home for VR and AR, Spatial Computing and Related Technologies," accessed 27 June 2019, www.rlab.nyc/index.html.

5 Sasha Lekach, "What It's Like to Walk with Google Maps in Augmented Reality," *Mashable*, 11 February 2019, https://mashable.com/article/google-maps-ar-augmented-reality-walking-navigation/#tKMRZCBvyaqL.

6 Jason Wither, Stephen DiVerdi, and Tobias Höllerer, "Annotation in Outdoor Augmented Reality," *Computers & Graphics* 33 (2009): 679–89, 679, doi: 10.1016/j.cag.2009.06.001.

7 Marcus Tönnis, David A. Plecher, and Gudrun Klinker, "Representing Information—Classifying the Augmented Reality Presentation Space," *Computers & Graphics* 37, no.8 (2013): 997–1011, 997–98, doi: 10.1016/j.cag.2013.09.002.

8 Benjamin Feldman, "Agency and Governance: Pokémon-Go and Contested Fun in Public Space," *Geoforum* 96, November (2018): 289–97, 293, doi: 10.1016/j.geoforum.2018.08.025.

9 Mark Graham, Matthew Zook, and Andrew Boulton. "Augmented Reality in Urban Places: Contested Content and the Duplicity of Code," *Transactions of the Institute of British Geographers* 38, no. 3 (2013): 464–79, 464; doi: 10.1111/j.1475-5661.2012.00539.x.

10 Ibid.

11 Frank Rose, "Augmented Urban Reality," *The New Yorker*, 29 July 2016, www.newyorker.com/tech/annals-of-technology/augmented-urban-reality\.

12 Greg Milner, "Death by GPS," *Ars Technica*, 3 May 2016, https://arstechnica.com/cars/2016/05/death-by-gps/.

13 Rob Picheta, "Dutch Tulip Growers Beg Selfie-Taking Millennials to Stop Trampling Their Flowers," *CNN*, 24 April 2019, www.cnn.com/travel/article/netherlands-tulip-selfies-scli-intl.

14 Bratek, Rebecca, "Tourists Taking Selfie Fall to Their Deaths in Portugal, Officials Say," *CBS News*, 13 June 2018, www.cbsnews.com/news/tourists-fall-to-death-while-taking-selfie-in-portugal/.
15 Feldman, "Agency and Governance."
16 "Landmarker (Beta)," Snapchat website, https://lensstudio.snapchat.com/templates/landmarker/.
17 Keiichi Matsuda, *Hyper-reality*, produced in Medellín by Fractal, sound and music by Skillbard, 2016. 06:15, http://hyper-reality.co/.
18 Keiichi Matsuda, "Hyper-Reality Project Kickstarter," 2013. Last updated 12 February 2013, www.kickstarter.com/projects/723600195/hyper-reality-a-new-vision-of-the-future.
19 Joshua McWhirter, "City Skins: Scenes from an Augmented Urban Reality," *Failed Architecture*, Thursday 20 September 2018, https://failedarchitecture.com/city-skins-scenes-from-an-augmented-urban-reality/.
20 Ibid.
21 Joseph Hart, "A New Way of Walking," Utne Reader, July/August 2004, www.utne.com/print?printid 1368307A-5E65-42CD-9199-AE37156C2019}.
22 "Overview," psy.geoCONFLUX Blog post, https://glowlab.blogs.com/psygeocon/2004/02/overview.html.
23 *WhaiWhai*. Game, www.whaiwhai.com/en.
24 "Class is in session with LOG607," *WhaiWhai*, 19 March 2010, http://blog.whaiwhai.com/en/2010/03/log607_lesson/.
25 Ibid.
26 "We're Watching from Behind the Scenes," *WhaiWhai*, 6 March 2009, http://blog.whaiwhai.com/en/2009/03/backstage_partita_venezia/.
27 Ibid.
28 "WHAIWHAI transforms city tour in New York into fun adventure. A special app starts and manages your experience in the city of your choice," *WhaiWhai*, http://www.whaiwhai.com/en/whaiwhai-iphone/.
29 Michael Zhang, "Museum of London Releases Augmented Reality App for Historical Photos," *Petapixel*, 24 May 2010, https://petapixel.com/2010/05/24/museum-of-london-releases-augmented-reality-app-for-historical-photos/.
30 Manifest.AR Projects Blog, www.manifest-ar.art/; See also http://www.manifest-ar.art/venicebiennial2011/index.html.
31 *Museum of London: Streetmuseum 2017*, Thumbspark Limited, 27 March 2017, https://itunes.apple.com/hk/app/museum-london-streetmuseum/id369684330?mt=8.
32 Ron Miller and Josh Constine, "Apple Acquires Augmented Reality Company Metaio," *TechCrunch*, 28 May 2015, https://techcrunch.com/2015/05/28/apple-metaio/.
33 Jim Edwards, "Google Ends Sale of Google Glass," *Business Insider*, 16 January 2015, www.businessinsider.com/google-ends-sales-of-google-glass-2015-1.
34 Matt Weinberger, "Google Is Shutting Down its Ambitious Project to Reinvent Smartphone Cameras," *Business Insider*, 15 December 2017, www.businessinsider.com/google-tango-augmented-reality-project-is-shutting-down-2017-12.
35 David Roe, "HP's Autonomy Upgrades Augmented Reality Aurasma App for Social Sharing, Improved Image Recognition," *CMS Wire*, 8 March 2013, www.cmswire.com/cms/customer-experience/hps-autonomy-upgrades-augmented-reality-aurasma-app-for-social-sharing-improved-image-recognition-019963.php.
36 Paul Sawers, "The Rise and Fall of Augmented Reality 'Unicorn' Blippar," *Venture Beat*, 18 December 2018, https://venturebeat.com/2018/12/18/the-rise-and-fall-of-augmented-reality-unicorn-blippar/.
37 "Welcome to AR City: Beta of Augmented Reality Maps and Navigation." Blippar.com, 6 November 2017, www.blippar.com/blog/2017/11/06/welcome-ar-city-future-maps-and-navigation.
38 "Blippar Launches App Allowing People to Navigate the World with Augmented Reality," *Globe News Wire*, 7 November 2017, www.globenewswire.com/news-release/2017/11/07/1202866/0/en/Blippar-Launches-App-Allowing-People-to-Navigate-the-World-with-Augmented-Reality.html.
39 "Blippar Introduces Visual Knowledge Graph 'Blipparsphere,' to Power True Visual Discovery," *Globe News Wire*, 9 June 2016, www.globenewswire.com/news-release/2016/06/09/1202263/0/en/Blippar-Introduces-Visual-Knowledge-Graph-Blipparsphere-to-Power-True-Visual-Discovery.html.
40 Ibid.
41 Duncan Speakman, *A Hollow Body*, http://wearecircumstance.com/a-hollow-body/; For a discussion on this project, see Speakman's interview in Section 6 of this Companion.
42 Ibid.
43 Pervasive Media Studio, "Duncan Speakman—Remixing the Sound of a Burning World," 19 October 2018, www.watershed.co.uk/studio/events/2018/10/19/duncan-speakman-remixing-sound-burning-world.

44 Circumstance, Twitter Post, 8 March 2019, https://twitter.com/ofcircumstance/status/110402883800 1065984.
45 "Breda AR City Tour," *Capitola*, 15 March 2019. https://capitola.nl/projects/breda-ar-city-tour/, https://youtu.be/KzUDCDSR-D4.
46 Dan Robitzski, "Augmented Reality Recreates a New York City Not Seen for Centuries," *Futurism*, 2 August 2018, https://futurism.com/augmented-reality-time-travel.
47 *Inventing America*, 20 July 2018, www.inventing.nyc/; See also https://youtu.be/Iq5lffi7FWU.
48 Brian Crecente, "The Walking Dead's' Augmented Reality Game Is Live," *Variety*, 12 July 2018, https://variety.com/2018/gaming/news/the-walking-dead-ar-interview-launch-1202871359/.
49 Ibid.
50 Natalie Hope McDonald, "King Britt Ushers in the Next Big Thing in Public Art: Augmented Reality Murals," *Philly Voice*, 1 October 2018, www.phillyvoice.com/king-britt-ushers-in-the-next-big-thing-in-public-art-augmented-reality-murals/.
51 Jonathan Kendall, "How Augmented Reality Will Make Street Art Come to Life," *Big Think*, 14 June 2018, https://bigthink.com/jonathan-kendall/how-augmented-reality-will-revolutionize-the-art-world.
52 Stuart Melling, "ILLUMINATE, Urban Arts Gallery, Craft Lake City," *The Utah Review*, 26 October 2018, www.theutahreview.com/urban-arts-gallery-craft-lake-city/.
53 Justine Testado, "Serpentine Galleries, Google, and David Adjaye Launch Augmented-Reality Architecture Competition," *Archinect News*, 6 February 2019, https://archinect.com/news/article/150120522/serpentine-galleries-google-and-david-adjaye-launch-augmented-reality-architecture-competition.
54 Page Leggett, "Think Pokemon Go, but in Serious Application: That's What Charlotte Professor Is Doing in #HomeCLT," *Charlotte Observer*, 13 February 2019, www.charlotteobserver.com/entertainment/arts-culture/article224614105.html.
55 Ibid.
56 See Museum of the New South, Website, www.museumofthenewsouth.org/homeclt.
57 Nita Bhalla, "Forget Pokémon GO, Red Cross Augmented Reality App Brings War to You," *Reuters*, 14 May 2018, www.reuters.com/article/us-global-war-technology/forget-pokmon-go-red-cross-augmented-reality-app-brings-war-to-you-idUSKCN1IF22C.
58 Ibid.
59 Kyle A. Pettijohn, Alexis N. Thompson, Andrea K. Tamplin, Sabine A. Krawietz, and Gabriel A. Radvansky, "Event Boundaries and Memory Improvement," *Cognition* 148 (2016): 136–44, doi: 10.1016/j.cognition.2015.12.013.
60 Iva K. Brunec, Morris Moscovitch, and Morgan D. Barense, "Boundaries Shape Cognitive Representations of Spaces and Events," *Trends in Cognitive Sciences* 22, no. 7 (July 2018): 637–50, doi: 10.1016/j.tics.2018.03.013.
61 Brian Feldman, "The Best Use of Augmented Reality Right Now Is the Weather Channel's," *New York Intelligencer*, 21January 2019, http://nymag.com/intelligencer/2019/01/the-weather-channels-augmented-reality-segments.html.
62 Ibid.
63 Robert Williams, "USA Today Promotes 'The City' Podcast with AR Visuals," *Mobile Marketer*, 25 September 2018, www.mobilemarketer.com/news/usa-today-promotes-the-city-podcast-with-ar-visuals/533118/.
64 Ismael Chivite, "AuGeo: An Augmented Reality mobile app for your GIS data," *ESRI*, 6 July 2017, www.esri.com/arcgis-blog/products/3d-gis/3d-gis/ar-for-your-gis/.
65 Vuforia Engine, https://engine.vuforia.com/engine.html.
66 Joachim Scholz and Andrew N. Smith, "Augmented Reality: Designing Immersive Experiences that Maximize Consumer Engagement," *Business Horizons* 59, no. 2 (March–April 2016):149–61, doi: 10.1016/j.bushor.2015.10.003.

# SECTION TEN

# Critical Making and Future Directions

# 43

# DOING CRITICAL CREATIVE PRACTICE AND SOCIAL RESEARCH

*Kat Jungnickel* in Conversation with *Larissa Hjorth*

Kat Jungnickel is a creative practice researcher exploring the role of technologies in relation to mobility cultures, invention, gender and grassroots hands-on Do it Yourself (DiY) and Do it Together (DiT) communities. Drawing on Sociology, Science and Technology Studies (STS), and Feminist Technoscience, making and engaging are integral to Kat's work which takes many forms—websites, journal articles and books, machines, films, printed materials, photographs, performances, installations and, most recently, sewing and wearing a range of clothing inventions. This varied approach opens up discussion for hands-on and object-oriented ways of thinking about and through knowledge production. Recently, she has been using sewing as a sociological method to research the histories of women's cycle wear and changing ideas about gender politics, mobility technologies, and public space in late nineteenth-century Britain. She continues this research through a European Research Council (ERC) funded project exploring citizenship via 200 years of clothing inventions (Figure 43.1).

How do you define mobile media art? How does your practice as a critical maker reflect upon this concept?

A great deal of my research has focused on mobilities, in terms of technology cultures and practices, gender relations, and changing ideas around (private and public) place. I have studied grassroots wireless networking groups who were building their own version of the internet from the backyard out using improvised methods and hand-made devices. I was interested in exploring how individuals were collectively hand-making a sophisticated technological system using at-hand materials and improvised methods in everyday places.[1]

I have also spent many years studying cycling cultures, interviewing contemporary cyclists and more recently, in the *Bikes and Bloomers* project, I delved into archives to better understand the challenges facing early women cyclists.[2] My new research expands my interests in mobilities and inventors with a focus on 200 years of patented clothing. *Politics of Patents* aims to bring to life in archival research, stories and costumes, lesser-known and forgotten attempts by inventors to radically re-imagine citizenship by seeking to shape the way bodies have been clothed over time.[3] I'm curious about how, and in what ways, clothing inventions, particularly mobility clothing, might be read as political acts of resistance, contestation, or subversion.

Materiality is central to my practice, both as subject and method. In addition to analyzing inventions via text and illustration, I directly engage with patents by following inventors' step-by-step instructions to make and wear artifacts of clothing. This takes reference from a long

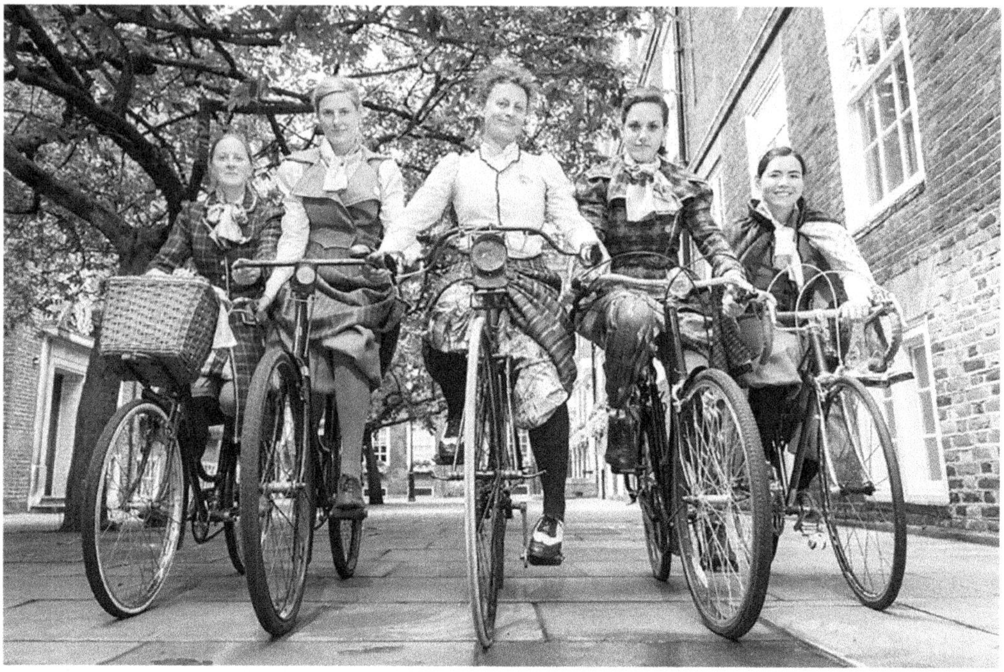

*Figure 43.1* A collection of Victorian convertible costumes made for *Bikes and Bloomers*. Photo credit: Charlotte Barnes www.charlottebarnes.co.uk

research tradition in the history of science and STS, where theoretical and creative experiments like "reconstructions" have been situated. It involves treating patents like ethnographic fieldsites, exploring the relationship between translations, from text to garment to performance, and inviting others *into* the research via public engagement activities (Figure 43.2).

What for you are some of the defining moments in the field of mobile media art?

My practice has been shaped by a number of defining moments in sociology, STS, and interdisciplinary methods. Feminist techno scientists have long paid attention to complicated narratives and lesser-known or marginalized voices hidden below the surface. They are sensitive to systems that look convincingly smooth or fixed, so that from the outside they become easy to accept without question. Susan Leigh Star,[4] in particular, has done much inspiring work to advocate for the study of seemingly "boring" things, by pointing out that it is not the things themselves, but how we tend to look at them that is boring. She argues that it is only through a study of the unstudied, the things we take for granted, that we can hope to see new and previously neglected connections and meanings. Taking this insight in my current research means being attentive to a broader more diverse range of inventions and inventors that tend to interrupt the often linear and smooth stories that dominate histories of technology. A more layered and textured perspective promises to reveal not only new transnational accounts of citizenship but also previously unknown stories about the inventive capacities of different people.

Social science methods have radically changed in the last decade. The challenge, according to Les Back, lies in "how to account for the social world without assassinating the life contained within it."[5] Over the last decade we have seen innovations in sensory, material, digital, messy, art practice and performance methods. Mobilities scholars in particular have innovated with methods

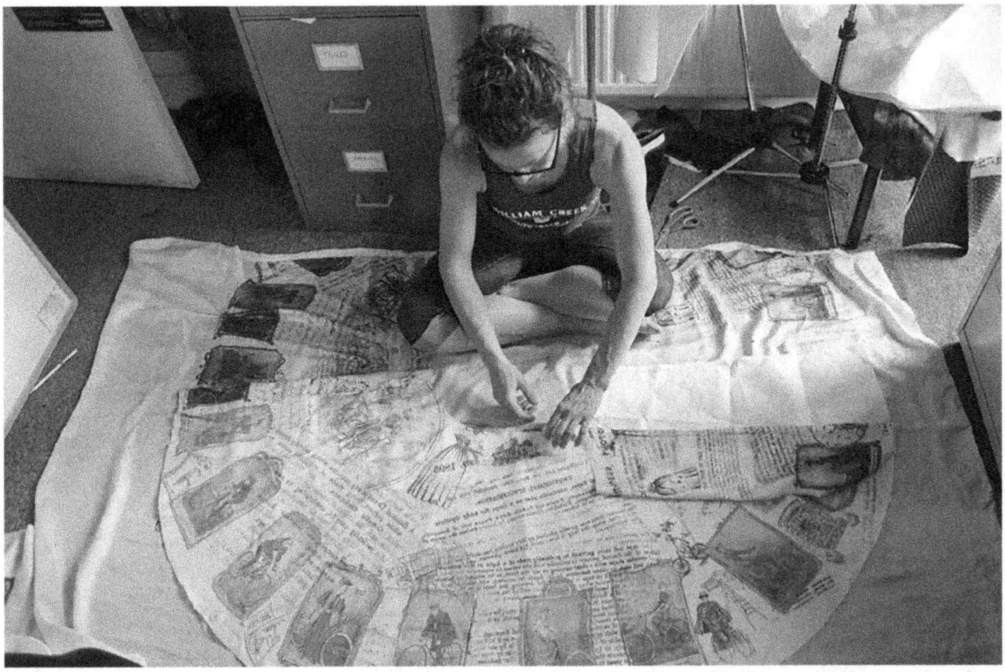

*Figure 43.2* Cutting the lining for an 1896 convertible cycling skirt and cape. Photo credit: Kat Jungnickel

in an attempt to resist flattening and stabilizing dynamic social worlds. As such, all kinds of new media technologies have been enrolled to help capture what Justin Spinney has called the "fleeting, ephemeral and often embodied and sensory aspects of movement."[6]

I have also been inspired by a feminist/queer turn in the archives to consider not only what is present but what is absent and who is silenced.[7] This move contests the politics and authority that shape data collections and opens them up for new meaning making, interpretation and engagement. I have been "making things to make sense of things"[8] in response to the challenges of gaps and absences in my archival research about women's contributions to histories of technology and cycling. This involves interviewing inventors through their inventions, combining archival data and ethnographic methods, and using inventive practice to piece together fragmented and distributed traces of marginalized people's lives across the archives. It demands a flexibility and willingness to adapt to the challenges in a constantly moving field (Figure 43.3).

Who are some of the most exciting practitioners in the field and why?

There are many examples of exciting theoretically informed, hands-on experimental practice social research. The *Un/Making studio* run by Åsa Ståhl and Kristina Lindström, in Sweden is a cutting-edge collective examining both making and unmaking design practices, materials, and methods.[9] They focus on maintenance, repair and composting and other ways of caring using a combination of participatory and speculative design with feminist technoscience. And, they take seriously the sharing and co-construction of their research through regular and innovative public engagement activities.

Feminist speculative research is forging all kinds of critical new paths into design, STS, and creative social research. In addition to Ståhl and Lindström, key drivers of this work include Laura Forlano (Illinois Institute of Technology), Daniela Rosner (University of Washington),

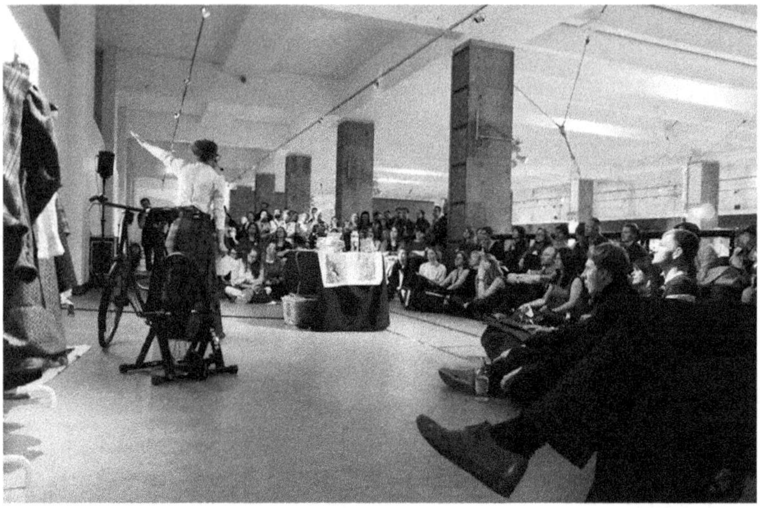

*Figure 43.3* Performing in costume at the London Science Museum's *Late* session on Wearable Technology. Photo credit: Kat Jungnickel

Ramia Mazé (Aalto University, Finland), Laura Watts (University of Edinburgh), and Anne Galloway (Victoria University, Wellington). As Forlano explains, speculative methods provide a means of "removing some of the constraints associated with thinking" and offering a glimpse of "cultures, patterns and behaviours before they were widely known or understood."[10] Exciting work is being done in this area not only about re-imagining futures but also re-visiting pasts. Tamson Pietsch from the *Australian Centre for Public History* at University of Technology Sydney is committed to making and sharing alternate narratives about Australia's history.[11]

Tell us more about your practice and how it intercepts with mobile media art?

I have been called a cycling, sewing sociologist. I like this. It combines lots of my interests—media, mobility, technology, hands-on creative practice, and disciplinary scholarship. The intersection of these contrasting yet complementary fields has surfaced a range of expected and unexpected insights and answered questions I did not think to ask. It has also led me into new communities of practice and performance. Rather than thinking about sewing as a distinct "method" and the resulting artifact as a traditional "output," my work blurs these processes and practices. Instead, I consider making as a part of research and research as a part of practice. The materiality of my research also enables me to literally get inside it. Putting on a convertible cycling costume and demonstrating how it operates, transforming from one modal identity to another, adds rich layers and textures to the research.

Making, experimenting and engaging are integral to my research and teaching. I use the term "transmissions" to describe my interdisciplinary approach, methods, and modes of communicating and engagement. In a new edited collection, I define this as the "tactical combination of *making* (how theory, methods, and data give shape to research) and *communicating* (how we show, share, and entangle others in it)."[12]

Also, at Goldsmiths, I co-direct the Methods Lab and the Digital World Making group that supports interdisciplinary critical and creative collaborations in and outside academia. I have also been teaching on the MA Visual Sociology and Feminist Methods Masterclass. All of these offer means to theoretically and methodologically experiment with inventive ways of doing social research.

## Notes

1 See Kat Jungnickel, *DIY WIFI: Re-imagining Connectivity* (Houndmills, Basingstoke, Hampshire: Palgrave Macmillon Pivot, 2014).

2 The ESRC funded project (ES/K008048/1) can be found at www.bikesandbloomers.com.

3 The ERC funded project (#819458) can be found at www.politicsofpatents.org.

4 See for example: Susan Leigh Star, "The Ethnography of Infrastructure," *American Behavioural Scientist* 43, no. 3 (1999): 377–91.

5 Les Back, "Live Sociology: Social Research and Its Futures," in *Live Methods*, edited by Les Back and Nirmal Puwar (Oxford: Blackwell Publishing, 2012), 21.

6 Justin Spinney, "A Chance to Catch a Breath: Using Mobile Video Ethnography in Cycling Research," *Mobilities* 6, no. 2 (2011): 162.

7 See for example: Julia Bryan-Wilson and Cheryl Dunye, "Imaginary Archives: A Dialogue," *Art Journal* 72, no. 2 (2013): 82–89, doi: 10.1080/00043249.2013.10791037; Kate Eichhorn, *The Archival Turn in Feminism: Outrage in Order* (Pennsylvania: Temple University Press, 2013).

8 See Kat Jungnickel, "Making Things to Make Sense of Things: DIY as Research and Practice," in *The Routledge Companion to Media Studies and Digital Humanities*, edited by Jentery Sayers (London; New York: Routledge, 2018), 492–502, Open Access available at: https://github.com/jentery/routledge CompanionMSDH/blob/master/toc.md#v-making-programming-hacking.

9 See www.unmakingstudio.se.

10 See Laura Forlano, "Ethnographies from the Future: What Can Ethnographers Learn from Science Fiction and Speculative Design?" *Ethnography Matters*, 23 September 2013, http://ethnographymatters.net/blog/2013/09/26/ethnographies-from-the-future-what-can-ethnographers-learn-from-science-fiction-and-speculative-design/.

11 See https://historylab.net.

12 Kat Jungnickel (ed.), *Transmissions: Critical Tactics for Making and Communicating Research* (Cambridge, MA: MIT Press, 2020).

# 44

# MOBILE LIDAR MEDIALITY AS ARTISTIC ANTI-ENVIRONMENT

*Julia M. Hildebrand and Mimi Sheller*

The 3D laser scanner sends invisible beams into the environment, millions of times per second. The laser head shoots at you and me, at a city's architectures, or a forest's landscape. Once the beams hit a surface, light is reflected back to the sensor. An informational dot is created. A point with XYZ information, a distinct position in the world. Millions of those points with differences in laser return times and wavelengths then create three-dimensional visual representations, so-called point clouds. This is how LIDAR ("Light Detection and Ranging") works. Google Street View and Google Earth draw on it to create 3D building models; geospatial sciences use it to map topological properties; self-driving cars depend on it to sense surrounding geographical environments.[1] Ultimately, knowledge-based smart cities may thrive with it.

Once those millions of invisible pulsed laser lights—mounted on ground or airborne stations and vehicles—scan our every surface, niche, and corner, piercing through everyday spaces, the world becomes a fully calculable construct. Algorithms within the remote sensor help discern specific environmental conditions, object and subject characteristics including body shapes and facial features. Along with a seemingly hawkish scanning, calculating, and reconstructing of our environments, LIDAR technology also exposes our lifeworlds in a new point-cloud-based visual aesthetic. In light of the increasing implementation of this mobile technology, we ask, how does this new three-dimensional algorithmic visual regime change our relationships with space and our movements within it? And what social, cultural, and political responses might this emerging form of scanning, accounting, and plotting elicit?

Several noteworthy artworks are starting to critically and creatively engage with these questions as LIDAR technology advances and proliferates. One example is *Where the City Can't See* from 2016, said to be the first fiction film shot entirely with the LIDAR laser scanning technology.[2] Directed by speculative architect Liam Young and written by author and journalist Tim Maughan, the short film depicts life within the near-future Chinese-controlled Detroit Economic Zone.

In a dystopian cityscape cruised by automated taxis, an underground community evades and disrupts the all-around nonhuman surveillance technologies attached to self-driving cars, drones, and other urban management orders by hacking systems, digital camouflage clothing, surreptitious movements, and dance moves.[3] We follow this narrative through the machinic LIDAR gaze, a three-dimensional aesthetic point cloud play of colors, shapes, dimensions, and movements infused with glitches, deflections, and disruptions (see Figure 20, color insert). The film plays with not only the top-down logics and aesthetics of LIDAR mediality through its visual effects and story line, but also the creative bottom-up means of countering them within the film narrative, as well as in the film-maker's own hacks of LIDAR cameras. The inhuman LIDAR gaze is both the film's medium and message. The medium is the message, as media theorist Marshall McLuhan would say, and in artistic contexts it can form what he calls an "anti-environment" as we shall explain in our analysis of the film.

In this chapter, we critically explore *Where the City Can't See* as an artistic "anti-environment"[4] that illuminates LIDAR technology not only as an emerging mobile media infrastructure but also as a new visual aesthetic and cultural medium. Drawing on conceptual frameworks from mobile communication, media ecology, and mobilities research, we discuss how this LIDAR artwork both situates and unsettles such an emerging media environment. In doing so, our analysis also speaks to scholarship into contemporary and emerging mobile communication and mobile media art.

*Where the City Can't See* prompts us to critically assess nonhuman visual and mobile agencies beyond human attention, awareness, even reach, as we move toward smart ecologies within cities and homes along with natural environments such as forests.[5] Through the eyes of LIDAR, we also see human strategies to resist and counter the calculating and controlling nonhuman gaze via attire, sound, dance, and subversive movement. With close attention to the digital LIDAR interface "as incubator, frame, context, and content"[6] for the innovative artwork along with the disruptive non-digital media that shape the narrative, we contribute to a larger conceptualization of contemporary mobile and visual technologies and emerging nonhuman environments and networked regimes.

In the following, we first briefly reflect on frameworks and roles of mobile media art in the context of mobile communication, mobilities research, and media ecology before turning to a close audiovisual reading of *Where the City Can't See.* Focusing on the perspective of the near-future city, we first discuss what the city can see via light detection and ranging. We then turn to glitches of LIDAR mobile mediality in exploring what this near-future city cannot see due to creative and subversive light deflection and raving. Our argument is guided by the concepts of art as "anti-environment"[7] and "mobile mediality"[8] that mediates and meditates (in)visible and (im)mobile spaces and movements. We conclude with reflections on the intellectual merit of our conceptual approach to mobile media art in the context of emerging algorithmic environments and regimes of nonhuman visuality.

## Mobile Mediality and Artistic Anti-Environments

In this assessment of mobile media art, we follow mobile communication research that expands the body of literature by engaging with hybrid media and locative arts.[9] The selected film shows how the framework of mobile media art demands its continuous re-situating in light of the growing diversity of techno-spatial and social practices.[10] Mobile LIDAR technology in particular complicates notions of the mobile interface "as a bridge between digital and physical space, a hybrid mediation of human sensory perception and technological connectivity."[11] While the remote laser system and visualization technique is certainly a mobile interface bridging digital and physical space,[12] it is also a hybrid mediation of *nonhuman* sensory perception, which Paul Dourish argues underlies the Internet of Things (IoT) as a networked mobile interface that bypasses the human user.[13] Such nonhuman perception is central to the growing field of Artificial Intelligence (AI) and the emergence of political concerns surrounding algorithmic control beyond human interfaces.[14]

Keeping in line with characteristics of mobile media art that "adopt elements of location-based performance, [...], and mobile, networked activism to highlight the embodied performance of hybrid place and the social and collective politics of networked space,"[15] Young's film presents analog practices of gaming, glitching, and subverting the digital mobile communication processes. Hence, *Where the City Can't See* and our close reading of the work substantiates the "complex social, political, technological and physiological effects of new mixed reality interactions" based on the affordances of LIDAR as mobile device.[16] As such, the artwork also helps us speak to mobile communication research into how "people interact with various forms of mobile media" and how "various forms of mobile media affect how people experience physical space,"[17] as well as virtual space and hybrid space, for example, through playful mediated movement, access to layered historical memories, sound walks, or connected presence.[18] We reflect on how socio-spatial interactions with ubiquitous LIDAR sensors may evolve and how we, as a result, experience and move through or within LIDAR-infused physical space.

Relevant for our analysis of *Where the City Can't See* is the concept of mobile mediality as a "reflexive form of enacted and mediated spatiality" and as a means of artistic intervention with location-based or location-aware forms of mobile art.[19] Young's LIDAR film exactly presents

> phenomenological experiments with experiential happenings and performative interactional events that intensify and focus attention on the current spaces of mobile mediality in ways that potentially destabilize the everyday and deepen our perception of the conditions of the premediated real.[20]

Moreover, *Where the City Can't See* stands out in how it exposes us to a LIDAR-mediated real that touches the surfaces of our still and moving spaces, objects, and bodies, but remains mostly invisible to us. The art brings critical attention to the increasingly common sensorial human-machine relationships but also creatively activates the new visual aesthetics and forms of mediated resistance that can ensue. Mobile LIDAR technology makes for a compelling object of investigation into emerging mobile mediality as it lies at the intersections of locative media and geomedia. The pulsed laser light belongs to "technologies of positioning"[21] understood as locative media in the widest sense, but also bridges those in "mediated localities" and cartographic formats associated with geomedia.[22]

Finally, Young's work crosses digital with analog forms of media art by designing and narratively integrating LIDAR-defying clothes, dance movements, and sound, reinterpreting tribal forms of engaging with the environment, body, and each other as counter-strategies to emerging algorithmic regimes. As such, we argue that *Where the City Can't See* and similar artistic complications of emerging mobile media infrastructures offer, what Paulsen calls,

> a way of understanding the rapid mediatization and remediation of contemporary sensory experience, and suggest we might preserve embodied social and political relationships to mediated people, places, and things in the face of such technological extensions.[23]

Probes by McLuhan ring in this statement of media as technological extensions. We also follow the critical media thinker in his emphasis of the importance of art as anti-environment. McLuhan argues that "the job of art is not to store moments of experience but to explore environments that are otherwise invisible."[24] More specifically, he explains, "the role of the artist is to create an Anti-environment as a means of perception and adjustment."[25]

Young, as a "maker of anti-environments" allows us "to perceive that much is newly environmental" and, according to McLuhan, "therefore most active in transforming situations."[26] As LIDAR becomes increasingly integral in a range of mapping processes and AI infrastructures across multiple domains, we require critical exploration of LIDAR-mediated environments, such as those visualized in *Where the City Can't See*. Ultimately, it is "anti-environments that enable us to perceive the environment,"[27] offering transformative knowledge ecosystems of the spatial, mobile, and visual algorithmic turns.[28]

## *Where the City Can't See*: Art with and against LIDAR

Liam Young appears to embrace his role as make-aware artist, when describing his motivation for *Where the City Can't See*: "What we're ultimately trying to do is capture the zeitgeist somehow, identify the anxieties and hopes of the present moment and respond to them."[29] He continues, outlining that his

> film projects are really about examining the cultural implications of these new technologies and exploring the new subcultures that might emerge, the new forms of agency, and the new types of resistance that might emerge in this context.[30]

Central to his LIDAR fiction film are the technologies and agencies emerging out of the smart city. While providing a critical commentary on the technological zeitgeist, Young and Maughan also illuminate and ultimately complicate the machinic visual communication processes embedded in such techno-spatial developments. The result is an aesthetically striking work that reconfigures uncanny robotic surveillance optics, eerily fluid architectures and ghost landscapes as well as generative forms of resistance and an eccentric interplay of colors, shapes, movements, and sounds.

Through the perspective of the laser scanners attached to drones, self-driving cars, and stationary cameras, we learn about the Chinese-controlled Detroit Economic Zone (DEZ) and the seemingly ubiquitous surveillance practices that not only map but seemingly control the urban spaces. A radio-transmitted female voice announces: "And we are broadcasting live across the city's driverless taxi network. Keeping you all informed there in the backseat. I hope everyone is strapped in and enjoying the ride." The driverless taxi network is thus not only presented as a dominant mobility regime but also a communication network providing and exposing customers "strapped in" "there in the backseat." With the smart city and its surveying infrastructure metaphorically and practically in the driver's seat, this introduction sets the tone for who and what is in control. The audio is complemented with LIDAR-generated aerial images of a car driving across the plotted near-future city.

The female announcer continues that the Detroit Police Department is under fire because of its controversial "Providence" surveillance system. "Their move to extend the Providence program suggests not just an attempt to control how our community uses these spaces but also clearly signals the DEZ's plans to redevelop the land." To ensure "citizen's safety and freedom," the Providence program, supposedly funded by the Chinese automobile manufacturer that runs the self-driving taxi system, "uses a network of several hundred LIDAR sensors scattered across the Detroit Metro Area." While we continue to trace the route of a self-driving car across the LIDAR-mediated landscape, we learn that the sensors "could be confused by sound and, in particular low bass tones."

Through the top-down perspective of a LIDAR device mounted on a drone, we see the image of a red truck shifting and shaking, pulsating in and out of sensor readability as it is playing those low bass tones. Simultaneously, "a new fashion craze [is] sweeping the city: so-called stealth hoodies," which cannot be seen by the city's security infrastructure as "the fabric reflects and disrupts LIDAR laser scans, leaving the wearer practically invisible." The narrator explains that wearing the hoodies in public could be considered an offense, and police "will continue to stop and search any individual wearing them in public. That is if they can see you of course." Here, police vision collapses with LIDAR vision as any wearers of the hoodie blur in and out of the remote laser scans while visible in plain sight.

Next to the scanned urban scenery, we also see the interior LIDAR view of two assembly-line workers in one of the DEZ-based Chinese automobile factories. Both workers are identified by their employee and social security numbers, illuminating an invasive surveillance regime not only throughout the smart city but also within the smart workplace. A robotic announcement warns the employees to be "cautious of malware. Do not accept emails, texts, SMS messages, flyers, QR codes, or peer-to-peer transfers from strangers," indicating some of the vulnerabilities of the algorithmic environment. "If you see something, say something" presses the robotic voice twice. However, the nonhuman contrasts the human ways of seeing, allowing the subversive practices of becoming "invisible" to unfold.

One of the employees secretly hands a manipulated taxi coupon to her colleague that allows him to hack into one of the self-driving cars and trigger a buried transmission about a tax-free rave at "blind city." "Strictly deflection fabrics only. [...] No camo, no entry. If the city can see you, you ain't getting in," the low voice drones. The hacked self-driving car takes the employee to a blurry building, where he obtains one of the camouflage hoodies. From several LIDAR angles (drone, self-driving car, CCTV), we now see the self-driving taxi approach a closed-off street amidst dilapidated buildings. Meanwhile, Dexter Jones, a former taxi driver (whose position was likely replaced by one of the self-driving cars transmitting his voice now) recounts, "When I was growing up, we used to use all these spaces. All this looks like ruins to you. This was our playground. [...] Where we used to go to hide. But now, the city sees everything" (see Figure 44.1).

He continues,

> Well, nowhere to hide for me at least. [...] The kids are dancing in a way that tricks that body detection software. They play their vibration tunes, they wear their scan camo gear. Kids will always find a way, you know. To live in the blind spots of the scanners.

The LIDAR perspective now depicts several people in anti-detection clothing and make-up, dancing expressively in the forest to vibrating base tones of a DJ (see Figure 44.2). Defying clear readability by the scanner, the bodies, shapes, and colors blur, fade in and out. Fabric, movement, and sound come together as an unruly blind spot for subversive mobilities within the 3D point

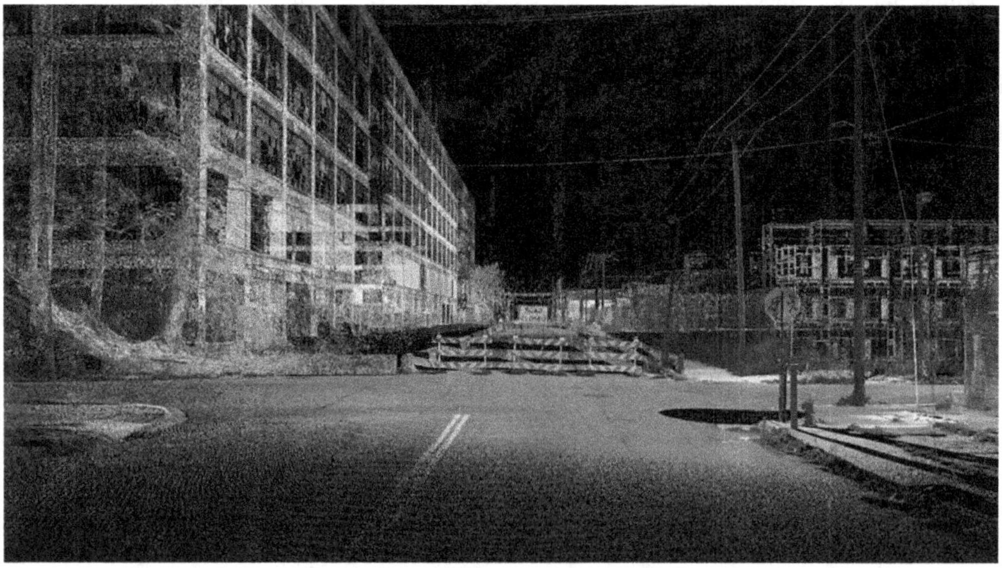

*Figure 44.1* The "ruins" and "playground" of the DEZ as seen via LIDAR in Liam Young's *Where the City Can't See* (2016). Photo credit: Liam Young

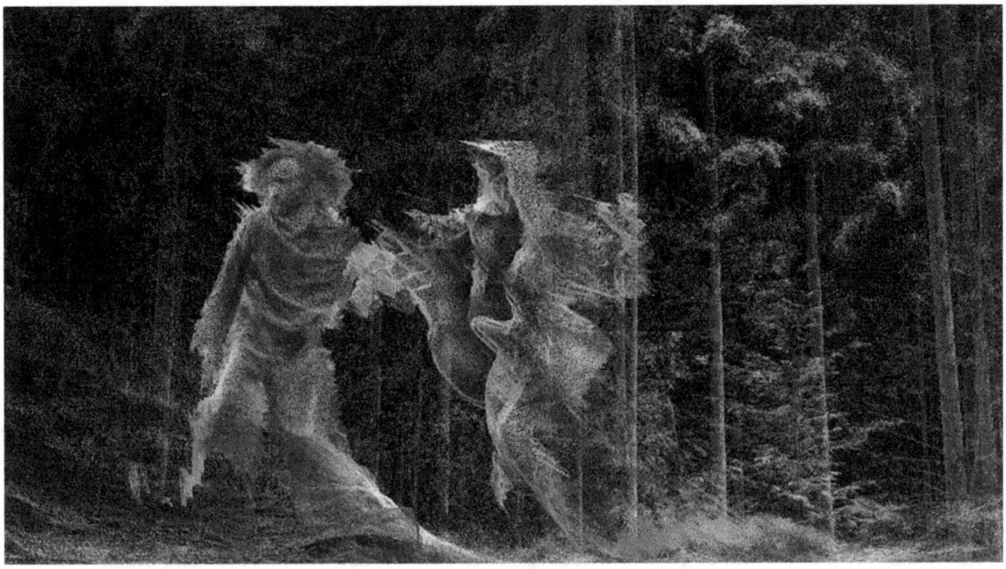

*Figure 44.2* Anti-LIDAR camouflage and movements in Liam Young's *Where the City Can't See* (2016). Photo credit: Liam Young

clouds of the smart city. Artificial intelligence is trumped by embodied intelligence, tapping into the underground urban subcultures that have long used bass, beats, bodily moves, and street style to resist state and corporate forms of spatial domination and mobility control.[31]

## What the City Can See: Light Detection and Ranging

"Environments are not just containers," suggests McLuhan, "but are processes that change the content totally."[32] The three-dimensional environment that builds the context and content for *Where the City Can't See* is constructed of millions of points of data. The sources of this data are Detroit in the United States and Grizedale Forest in the United Kingdom. In their translation into LIDAR point clouds, those spaces become differently voluminous, indexical, computable, relational. So, what is it that the audience—through the eyes of the smart city—can see in this film? And what kind of spatial relationships and creative engagements with the space as big data are suggested?

Everyday indoor and outdoor, built and natural environments become a laboratory for the LIDAR gaze that relentlessly shoots at all surfaces, scans volumes and voids, identifies but also blends subjects and objects into equally accountable formations. With extraordinary precision, the LIDAR mobile medium quantifies volumetric environments into efficiency models for mapping and remapping, surveying and surveilling. However, the distinct subjects and objects, surfaces, shapes, and their materialities are remediated as the same. "The city's sight is like a cyber-specter whose vision collapses all individual elements, whether they be buildings or people, into the same pointillist data portrait."[33] The visual rhetoric of LIDAR seems to directly respond to McLuhan's observation that "Today man has no physical body. He is translated into information, or an image."[34] As such, LIDAR mediality is both compelling and uncanny, beaming against us and our heterogeneous lifeworlds to then model and mediate a detailed but homogenous object of informational accountancy. Increasingly used for not only environmental monitoring but also crime scene analysis,[35] the message of this mobile interface is that everything can be assimilated into manageable data and represented as informational three-dimensional environments. Such surveillance technologies and practices, of course, are informed by the long history of racial formation and by the "dark" methods of policing black life.[36]

"So, what might be the contemporary cultural response?" asks Young.[37] His short film suggests that in the technocentric assimilation of spaces, subjects, and objects, there is opportunity for a remapping the point clouds as media infrastructure. Concretely, the visual artwork continuously blends composites of the two locations in Detroit and Grizedale Forest, reconfiguring them into a new artificial landscape of maintained and neglected industrial structures intertwined with green spaces.[38] The techno-aesthetic "comes to be seen as an unsettling, generative process, which continually breaks free of their previous context and recombines them in different ways."[39]

This creative unsettling of LIDAR logics ultimately brings to light powers, potentials, and perils of this algorithmic visual gaze. As a kind of "nonhuman photography," understood as imagery by, of, and for nonhuman agencies,[40] remote sensor technology drives forward a "new visual algorithmic regime" impacting what Brantner describes as "the relationship between image and 'reality'" along with "the socio-cultural conditions of the algorithmic visual regime and its social functions and the related knowledge politics."[41] At the intersections of augmented, mixed, and virtual reality, LIDAR technology inherits a special position rooted in geographical environments but taking effect in their point-based mediation. In light of this kind of visual algorithmic regime, which equates seeing, or rather scanning, with knowledge,[42] one may wonder what new forms of location awareness will unfold. In some ways, the LIDAR mobile medium speaks to frameworks such as the "sentient city," "code/space," and "hybrid space."[43] In other ways, the laser interface also complicates those in its current operation as a mobile visual algorithmic regime that mostly operates as a constant form of "qualculation."[44] *Where the City Can't See* brings those logics and aesthetics into the foreground, making us adopt the visual algorithmic gaze of the near-future smart city along with its vulnerabilities. Nevertheless, the all-seeing city comes up against blank spots and furtive movements, that escape its surveillance.

## What the City Cannot See: Light Deflection and Raving

Along with exposing the LIDAR ways of seeing, *Where the City Can't See* equally shows its ways of not seeing: the spaces, subjects, objects, and movements that evade, deflect, and disrupt the visual algorithmic gaze through their subversive mobilities. In an interview, Young explains the project's motivation and production:

> We're interested in what it means for these systems to be active agents and occupants of the city and these films are trying to see the city through their eyes. We actually had to develop a whole series of entirely new film-making techniques in order to capture this new narrative and subjective position. [...] we had to write a lot of our own scripts and software tools that allowed us to essentially hack the laser-scanners in ways in which they weren't intended to create narrative and cinematic effect.[45]

As such, Young introduces his audience not only to the top-down logics and aesthetics of LIDAR mediality but also to creative bottom-up means of countering them. "Because these algorithms are quite dumb, we've tricked them," continues Young.[46] Pointing to gaps and glitches that are also noticeable in Google Earth, the speculative architect uncovers and complicates what McLuhan describes as "the orchestral analogies in things themselves" as pertinent to the role of the artist.[47] *Where the City Can't See* points to ways of hacking the LIDAR scan and thus the algorithmic calculation and point-cloud remediation of spaces, people, and things in deflecting surfaces on buildings and bodies, disruptive sounds, and disorienting movements.

Reflecting surfaces in geographical space from buildings to bodies, the LIDAR interface is vulnerable when the laser beams hit formations that are hard to scan. Examples are mirrors, black rubber, or water designs. As such, Young, an architect by training, was able to construct an artistic "anti-environment," where certain spaces are invisible to the ubiquitous LIDAR gaze.

> We designed and prototyped a series of what we call "glitch buildings" or "stealth buildings" which are made with particular formal and material properties that reflect the laser in different ways so that the architecture is no longer just a function of the material constraints, but has a different kind of signature and profile in the data set through which these driver-less cars and machines chose to navigate operate.[48]

Next to blurred buildings that create colorful voids in the futurist Detroit Metro Area, the laser-deflecting fabrics become a key medium for the unruly underground scene (see Figure 44.3). Young explains, "The fabrics create distortions and glitches. You can corrupt the dataset which is trying to manage this forest. You can create these clouds of distorted points through the clothing and the movement of the dancers."[49]

The LIDAR-defying camouflage follows in the tradition of other sensor-evading garments, such as the more recent anti-drone hoodies against thermal imaging sensors attached to unmanned aerial systems.[50] The anti-LIDAR suits are shimmery with iridescent yarn and patterned to make the laser light bounce back unpredictably, resulting in a point cloud that is muddled and distorted.[51] Young emphasizes how his "digital camouflage," which comes in different designs, works: "Each of these [inventions] came with their own technical challenges, so the films are both narrative projects as well as technical projects."[52]

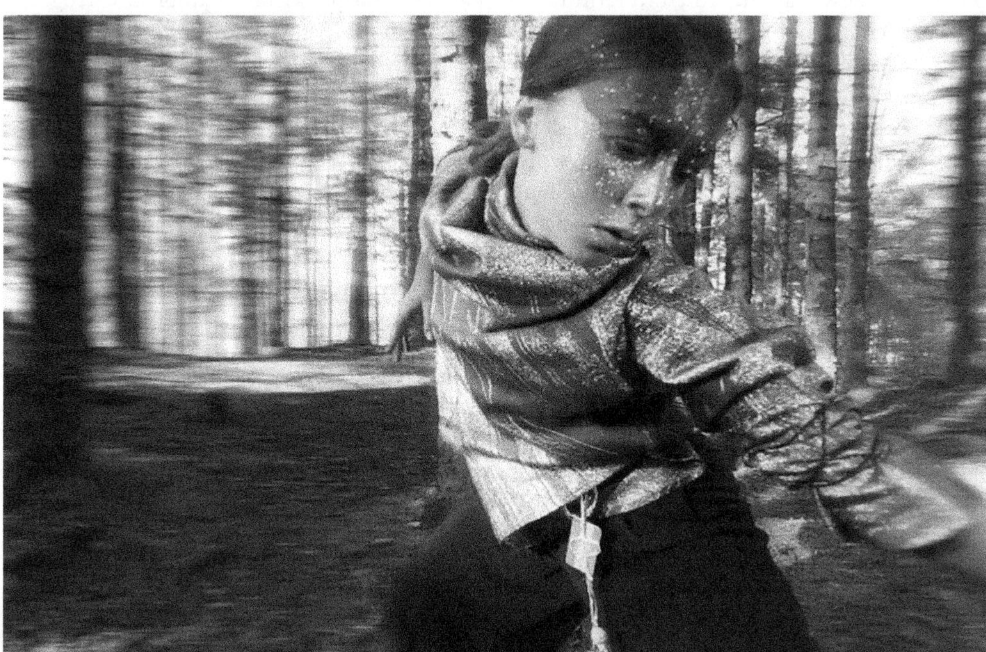

*Figure 44.3* Production still of dancer wearing laser-deflecting fabric and make-up for *Where the City Can't See* (2016). Photo credit: Liam Young

In addition, the unidentifiable, escapist figures in *Where the City Can't See* are adorned with anti-facial recognition make-up "confusing the algorithm" and prompting even more LIDAR glitching. The different forms of camouflage serve exclusively to disappear before the machine while maintaining if not significantly enhancing visibility in plain human sight. "They're just about disappearing within the sense of the technology. So, you have this really intriguing new mode of fashion extension, where you can be wild and playful within the visible-light spectrum."[53] As a result, to LIDAR logic and aesthetic, this kind of visual exuberance means algorithmic indifference.

Sound and movement make up another set of disruptive layers in this LIDAR-mediated future world. To the vibrating score *Deep Breathing* by Shigeto, the camouflaged ravers dance in ways that "disguise the form of their body or distort the silhouette of the body," thus becoming difficult to detect for the LIDAR body detection algorithm.[54] The plotting mechanisms and calculative algorithms are thus met with ambient experimental, disorienting movement of soundwaves and bodies. Escaping to the forest as natural and communal, yet nonetheless surveyed environment, the ravers counter the semi-automated labor and machinic systems of control with extraordinary costumes, wild dancing, and music. The DJ spinning discs and the fugitive dancers mobilize counter-media and mediate mobilities to enact an anti-environment, or as Moten and Harvey might put it, a furtive "undercommons" built on the traditions of "hapticality" of "black study" found in the city of Detroit.[55]

This countercultural community creates its own ambience, i.e. a diffuse atmosphere and affective texture of place remediated in the LIDAR gaze.[56] Pink et al. explain, "Ambience is about the *texture* of *context*, *emotion*, and *affect*."[57] In contrast, the LIDAR algorithm presented in *Where the City Can't See* is about texture of content, information, and efficiency. As such, the film follows other mobile media that, according to Hjorth,

> [offer] us new ways in which to rethink and practice multiple forms of ambient cartography. In particular, mobile media has played a key role in the shift from framing maps as fixed to performative—that is, we shape maps as they shape us.[58]

This reciprocal relationship between mapping technology and mapped environment is creatively exposed and explored in this work of art, which makes visible the otherwise invisible networked regimes of LIDAR surveillance. The film exposes the flaws underlying "smart city" imaginaries such as the IoT and AI by *imaging* human engagement with subversive forms of mobile resistance. The film puts hybrid space into play as performative making and unmaking, visibility and invisibility, detection and evasion. Moreover, not only are moving people and objects rendered as performative, but also spaces take on performative qualities in the plotted but glitching three-dimensional data clouds. Overall, *Where the City Can't See* presents and intervenes in the new mobile mediality brought about by LIDAR. Ultimately, as a new medium of mobile media art, it creates "openings for alternative practices, encounters, and ways of moving-in-the-world."[59]

## Conclusion

At one of the production sites of *Where the City Can't See*, Young mentions "The technology through which we experience the world also defines our cultural relationship to that world."[60] This argument among others lies at the core of critical studies in mobile communication, mobilities research, and media ecology. As different ways of seeing, moving, and being in the world emerge with technological advancements such as LIDAR, our conceptual frameworks need revisiting, expanding, and resituating. One of those foundational concepts is mobile media art and its role in illuminating and complicating past, present, and emerging practices, processes, and principles. Drawing on the notion of art as anti-environment, we discussed LIDAR mobile mediality as featured in *Where the City Can't See*.

The LIDAR-generated film operates on three levels: First, it presents the algorithmic logics and visual aesthetics of this mobile interface. Second, it exposes how those operations and mediations can be hacked and subverted. Third, it enacts a performative spatiality by hacking LIDAR cameras and visualization technologies to create an anti-environment. Here, Young shows how "New mobile medialities create the conditions for generative cultural and spatial practices that are transforming fundamental dimensions of contemporary urban culture and urban space."[61] Ambient experiments with wild patterns, unpredictable movement, and bass sound all counter and disrupt the surveying sensors and programmable algorithms, remediating earlier genres of urban underground cultural resistance such as street style, bass sound, and "black moves."[62] In the artistic adoption and complication of this mobile mediality, we see conditions for generative practices that challenge not only "existing mobility regimes, which have dealt with movement, power, and control based on twentieth-century technologies,"[63] but also the *emerging mobility regimes* of twenty-first-century mobile mediality.

"If you think of photography and filmmaking as being a series of 2D images, that is old school photography. New school photography, the future of photography is also LIDAR. So, everything is going to be three-dimensional," argues Young.[64] As the uptake and advancement of LIDAR technology continues, this kind of mobile media art can help increase awareness of the ways all kinds of machines are increasingly seeing, sensing, scanning, calculating, and constructing us, the spaces through which we move, and the ways that we/it perceive the world.

Additionally, such media art also has the potential to increase our awareness of—and directly intervene in—the ways to play with, hack, manipulate, and subvert such medial logics and three-dimensional aesthetics along with the emergent visual and mobile regimes they may entail. For research in mobile communication and mobile media art, this also means paying critical attention to both the locative and dislocative practices in the context of location-aware mobile media and locations as aware mobile media.

## Notes

1 Rose Eveleth, "The Suit You Will Need to Avoid Surveillance in the Future," *The Atlantic*, 7 October 2015, www.theatlantic.com/technology/archive/2015/10/where-the-lasers-cant-see-you/409303/.

2 A predecessor of this innovative format is the 2007 music video *House of Cards* by Radiohead. The clip similarly uses 3D plotting technologies to visualize colorful cloud points of bodies, infrastructures, and environments.

3 These modes of underground urban resistance are reminiscent of what Tim Cresswell calls "Black Moves: Moments in the History of African-American Masculine Mobilities," *Transfers: Interdisciplinary Journal of Mobility Studies* 6, no. 1 (June 2016): 12–25, doi: 10.3167/TRANS.2016.060103.

4 Marshall McLuhan, *Media Research: Technology, Art and Communication*, ed. Michael A. Moos (Amsterdam: G+B Arts International, 1997).

5 Daniel Fisher, "Lidar: A Data Resource Worth Sharing," *Data-Smart City Solutions*, 23 August 2018, https://datasmart.ash.harvard.edu/news/article/lidar-data-resource-worth-sharing.

6 Larissa Hjorth, "Mobile Art: Rethinking Intersections between Art, User Created Content (UCC), and the Quotidian," *Mobile Media & Communication* 4, no. 2 (1 May 2016): 172, doi:10.1177/2050157915619210; Marsha Berry and Max Schleser, *Mobile Media Making in an Age of Smartphones* (London: Palgrave Pivot, 2014).

7 McLuhan, *Media Research*.

8 Mimi Sheller, "Mobile Art: Out of Your Pocket," in *The Routledge Companion to Mobile Media*, edited by Gerard Goggin and Larissa Hjorth (New York: Routledge, 2014), 197–205.

9 Hjorth, "Mobile Art"; Sheller, "Mobile Art: Out of Your Pocket."; Adriana de Souza e Silva, "From Cyber to Hybrid: Mobile Technologies as Interfaces of Hybrid Spaces," *Space and Culture* 9, no. 3 (1 August 2006): 261–78, doi: 10.1177/1206331206289022; Adriana de Souza e Silva and Daniel M.

Sutko, *Digital Cityscapes: Merging Digital and Urban Playspaces* (New York: Peter Lang, 2009); Jason Farman, *Mobile Interface Theory: Embodied Space and Locative Media* (New York: Routledge, 2011); Eric Gordon and Adriana de Souza e Silva, *Net Locality: Why Location Matters in a Networked World* (Chichester, West Sussex ; Malden, MA: Wiley-Blackwell, 2011); Marc Tuters and Kazys Varnelis, "Beyond Locative Media: Giving Shape to the Internet of Things," *Leonardo* 39, no. 4 (10 July 2006): 357–63, doi: 10.1162/leon.2006.39.4.357; Drew Hemment, "LEA Locative Media Special Issue," *Leonardo* 14, no. 3 (June–July 2006), www.leoalmanac.org/leonardo-electronic-almanac-volume-14-no-3-4-june-july-2006/; John Craig Freeman and Mimi Sheller (eds.), *Public Art Dialogue*, SI: Digital Art 5, no. 1 (Spring 2015); Lanfranco Aceti, Hana Iverson, and Mimi Sheller (eds.), *Leonardo Electronic Almanac*, Special Issue: *LA Re.Play: Mobile Network Culture in Placemaking* 21, no. 1 (January 2016), www.leoalmanac.org/l-a-re-play-volume-21-no-1/.

10 Sheller, "Mobile Art: Out of Your Pocket."

11 Sheller, 276.

12 de Souza e Silva, "From Cyber To Hybrid"; Farman, *Mobile Interface Theory*; Sheller, "Mobile Art: Out of Your Pocket."

13 Paul Dourish, *The Stuff of Bits: An Essay on the Materialities of Information* (Cambridge, MA: MIT Press, 2017).

14 Nigel Thrift, "Lifeworld Inc—and What to Do About It," *Environment and Planning D: Society and Space*, 29 (2011): 5–26, doi: 10.1068/d0310.

15 Aceti, Iverson, and Sheller.

16 Ibid.

17 Michael Saker and Jordan Frith, "From Hybrid Space to Dislocated Space: Mobile Virtual Reality and a Third Stage of Mobile Media Theory," *New Media & Society*, 11 August 2018, 2, doi: 10.1177/1461444818792407.

18 See examples of mobile locative art projects discussed in Aceti, Iverson, and Sheller; and Freeman and Sheller.

19 Sheller, "Mobile Art: Out of Your Pocket," 201.

20 Ibid.

21 Jordan Frith, "Invisibility through the Interface: The Social Consequences of Spatial Search," *Media, Culture & Society* 39, no. 4 (1 May 2017): 538, doi: 10.1177/0163443717698871.

22 Tristan Thielmann, "Locative Media and Mediated Localities: An Introduction to Media Geography," *Aether: The Journal of Media Geography* 5, no. 1 (2010): 1–17, https://mgm.arizona.edu/sites/default/files/articles-pdf/introduction%20(3).pdf; Cornelia Brantner, "New Visualities of Space and Place: Mapping Theories, Concepts and Methodology of Visual Communication Research on Locative Media and Geomedia," *Westminster Papers in Communication and Culture* 13, no. 2 (31 October 2018): 14–30, doi: 10.16997/wpcc.290.

23 Kris Paulsen, *Here/There: Telepresence, Touch, and Art at the Interface* (Cambridge, MA: MIT Press, 2017), 5.

24 McLuhan, *Media Research*, 71.

25 Marshall McLuhan, *The Book of Probes*, ed. David Carson, Eric McLuhan, William Kuhns, and Mo Cohen. (Corte Madera, CA: Gingko Press Inc., 2003), 30–31.

26 McLuhan, *Media Research*, 114.

27 McLuhan, 111.

28 Brantner, "New Visualities of Space and Place."

29 Zach Saunders, "Interview with Liam Young," *Arch2O.Com* (blog), 12 April 2019, www.arch2o.com/interview-liam-young-arch2o/.

30 Saunders.

31 Fred Moten and Stefano Harney, *The Undercommons: Fugitive Planning and Black Study* (London: Minor Compositions, 2013); Cresswell, "Black Moves." Tim Cresswell, "'You Cannot Shake That Shimmie Here': Producing Mobility on the Dance Floor," *Cultural Geographies* 13, no.1 (1 January 2006): 55–77, doi: 10.1191/1474474006eu350oa.

32 McLuhan, *The Book of Probes*, 305.

33 Dylan Schenker, "Searching for the Smart City's Blind Spots—Resistance, Respite, and 'New Romance,'" Creative Applications Network, 15 May 2017, www.creativeapplications.net/reviews/searching-for-the-smart-citys-blind-spots-resistance-respite-and-new-romance/.

34 McLuhan, *The Book of Probes*, 92.

35 Tim Dees, "How 3D Scanning Puts the Crime Scene in the Courtroom," PoliceOne, 15 October 2018, www.policeone.com/police-products/3D-Laser-Scanners/articles/480785006-How-3D-scanning-puts-the-crime-scene-in-the-courtroom/.

36 Simone Browne, *Dark Matters: On the Surveillance of Blackness* (Durham, NC and London: Duke University Press, 2015).
37 Liam Young, *Liam Young—Where the City Can't See*, Soundcloud Audio, Abandon Normal Devices, 2016, https://soundcloud.com/abandonnormaldevices/liam-young-where-the-city-cant-see.
38 "Where the City Can't See," *Abandon Normal Devices* (blog), 12 April 2019, www.andfestival.org.uk/events/where-the-city-cant-see-liam-young/.
39 R. L. Rutsky, *High Techne: Art and Technology from the Machine Aesthetic to the Posthuman*, vol. 2 (University of Minnesota Press, 1999), 5, www.jstor.org/stable/10.5749/j.ctttv22d.
40 Joanna Zylinska, *Nonhuman Photography* (Cambridge, MA: MIT Press, 2017).
41 Brantner, "New Visualities of Space and Place," 25.
42 Gillian Rose, *Visual Methodologies: An Introduction to Researching with Visual Materials*, 4th ed. (London: SAGE Publications, 2016); Brantner, "New Visualities of Space and Place."
43 Mike Crang and Stephen Graham, "SENTIENT CITIES Ambient Intelligence and the Politics of Urban Space," *Information, Communication & Society* 10, no. 6 (1 December 2007): 789–817, doi: 10.1080/13691180701750991; Rob Kitchin and Martin Dodge, *Code/Space: Software and Everyday Life* (Cambridge, MA: MIT Press, 2011); Kazys Varnelis and Anne Friedberg, "Place: Networked Place," in *Networked Publics* (Cambridge, MA: MIT Press, 2006); Gordon and Silva, *Net Locality*.
44 Thrift, "Lifeworld Inc."
45 Saunders, "Interview with Liam Young."
46 Young, *Liam Young—Where the City Can't See.*
47 McLuhan, *The Book of Probes*, 510.
48 Saunders, "Interview."
49 Young, *Liam Young.*
50 Eveleth, "The Suit You Will Need to Avoid Surveillance in the Future."
51 Eveleth.
52 Saunders, "Interview."
53 Young, *Liam Young.*
54 Young.
55 Moten and Harney.
56 Sarah Pink, Heather A. Horst, John Postill, Larissa Hjorth, Tania Lewis, and Jo Tacchi, *Digital Ethnography: Principles and Practice* (Los Angeles, London, New Delhi, Singapore, Washington DC: SAGE Publications, 2016).
57 Pink et al., *Digital Ethnography*, 33.
58 Hjorth, "Mobile Art," 180.
59 Sheller, "Mobile Art: Out of Your Pocket," 284.
60 Young, *Liam Young.*
61 Sheller, "Mobile Art: Out of Your Pocket," 277.
62 Cresswell, "Black Moves."
63 Sheller, 277.
64 Young, *Liam Young.*

# 45
# XR
## Crossing and Interfering Artistic Media Spaces[1]

*Nanna Verhoeff and Paulien Dresscher*

XR does not refer to any specific technology. It's a bucket for all of the realities.

*Jim Malcolm (Humaneyes Technologies)*[2]

**Crossing [*noun*]**

1 An intersection where roads, lines, or tracks cross.
2 A place at which a river, railroad, or highway may be crossed.
3 The act by which terrain or a road, etc., is crossed.
4 A voyage across a body of water.
5 Movement into a crossed position.[3]

**Interference [*noun*]**

1 The act of interfering with something, or something that interferes
2 The illegal obstruction of an opponent in some ball games.
3 *Physics*; An effect caused by the superposition of two systems of waves, such as a distortion on a broadcast signal due to atmospheric or other effects.[4]

### Crossing X Interfering Realities

In this chapter, we investigate some of the different ways that mobile media art projects as simultaneously experimental and performative practices are sites of inquiry into the specificities, possibilities, limitations, and tensions that we encounter within today's highly mediatized and mediated environments. These art projects produce mobile media spaces that are creative laboratories for experimentation and analysis of ubiquitous, locative, and mobile technologies and their implications for our presence and relating in this contemporary, cultural moment.

Specifically, we explore the continuum between the connecting and increasingly overlapping fields of Augmented Reality (AR), Virtual Reality (VR), and Mixed Reality (MR) as part of the more open and flexible category of Extended Reality—or as we conceptualize it here, *Crossing Reality* (XR). As an inclusive bracket, the concept of XR allows us to look beyond more rigid and historically determined, technology-based delineations that make up some subgenres of mobile media art, while seeking to explore a shared agenda of these different forms of media art. Zooming in on a few XR projects that make use of augmented reality and virtual reality technologies, we explore in this chapter how, albeit in different ways and on different levels, these works all experiment with, and question the impact of technology. This impact on our spaces and situations, and our doings and mobilities within these spaces and situations, implies a working of technology at not only the phenomenological level, but also ontological, epistemological, and political registers that run through our private and public spaces. As such, the artistic scrutiny of technology, central to this chapter, involves technologies that are usually defined as *mobile technologies* (e.g. various GPS and other sensing technologies) but also interactive visualization technologies that activate other meanings of "mobility." As *technologies of mobility*, these demonstrate an activation of both bodily and participatory engagement, a mobilizing of affect, thought and opinion, and a productive crossing of multiple (generic and disciplinary) boundaries in co-creative processes.

XR as a spectrum rather than a category invites a creative exploration of the fluid and mutual relationships of technologies *between* and *beyond* AR, VR, and MR. It offers a comparative and inclusive lens for the various artistic genres that these technologies have inspired and, for the diversity of art projects, that interrogate and confront us with how we (can) relate to new technologies. Specifically, this relating pertains to the variety of possible "realities" that these technologies afford. Working through and beyond understanding these confrontations as the crossing—or intersecting—of separable and fixed domains of "physical" or "virtual" realities, we approach their interrelation in XR from a perspective on their performative qualities as relational reinforcement or *interference*. Relating in XR is not predeterminedly physical or virtual, or even mixed, as such adjectives want us to believe. Our perspective departs from the understanding that all *relata*—here the "realities" that can be discerned and experienced by the subject—that intersect, in various ways, are mutually *constitutive*. This does not imply a leaving behind of crossing as a productive way for thinking the diversity of realities but crossing returns as an *outcome* rather than a starting point in a conceptualization.

We borrow some of the conceptual tools for understanding realities-in-relating from the physicist-philosopher Karen Barad.[5] For Barad, characterizing something as co-constitutive means that the two entities of a relation or binary opposition are mutually implicated and come into being simultaneously. Barad uses *diffraction*, or interference, as both a phenomenon in the world (an object) and as a concept for understanding its dynamic so as to indicate that the emerging entities cannot be predicted or are not (to be) predetermined. Moreover, in their mutual constitution, they inherently and fundamentally also open up toward each other and can only become known within their relating. This entails, then, not only an analytical perspective on their relation, for which we will adopt the concept of diffraction as a methodological foundation, but also on the way that artworks, themselves, address "relating," which we will conceptualize with the synonym, interference.

Transposing and mobilizing Barad's terminology to the practice of scholarship as well as the practice of mobile media art, diffraction/interference characterizes both our perspective and the objects we are scrutinizing. Concept and object, too, are mutually constitutive. This yields a fundamentally relational perspective. Following the logic of both diffraction and interference, "realities" of XR are not layering, augmenting, or extending a shared "hybrid" reality, so much, as they are performative and literally *creative* in their meeting.[6]

The entanglement of object (art projects) and concept (thought in art as well as in scholarship), we propose, is a productive starting point for a comparative and inclusive perspective from which to consider the various ways in which artists and designers work within the domain of XR. We recognize interference both as an (ontological) characteristic of any form of relationality (mediation inclusive) and importantly for our aim, here, as a central (epistemological and political) questioning at the heart of the art projects that can be bracketed with the label "XR." In short, the projects question the consequences of their workings *in* their workings. Through the lens of interference, we propose to look at the way mobile media art using XR technologies interrogates the implications of their affordances for crossing realities by putting these technologies to the test. As such, art and scholarship share questions and methods. Therefore, for us, the X of XR also stands for the continuity and dynamicity within the intersecting or crossing fields of technological design, artistic experimentation in a more or less activist or political key and cultural inquiry.

## Mobilizing Art Spaces

The debate about the status of XR—specifically about Augmented Reality and Virtual Reality—as a technology and a medium that visually and conceptually brings together the "physical" and the "digital"—has produced various conceptual metaphors (first and foremost "augmentation" itself!) to understand the affordances of the location-based and imaging technologies to literally visualize the "meeting," to invoke Barad's book title, and relating of the subject and the multiple realities she faces. From the relational perspective that we propose, we understand reality, here, as the composite of spatiotemporal registers of a relational *situatedness* ("where and when am I in relation to my surroundings") and the experiential *subjectivity* of the "I" within this situation. This experiential positioning pertains to what one is invited to do or hold back from within a situation, and how this window of (non-)opportunity and possibly disruptive creativity changes one's subjectivity and co-constitutes the situation itself.

One of us has previously written about this phenomeno-onto-epistemological dynamic as *cartographical*.[7] Traditionally, cartography indicates representational fixity along spatial, temporal and epistemological axes. A cartography is a two-dimensional map of something that is external to it and meticulously mapped. A navigational, *performative* cartography, however, zooms in on the practice of "cartographizing," thus leaving open the possibility of a less measurable, linear, absolute integration of space, time, and thought. More precisely:

> Representation entails more or less fixed outcomes of creative production processes. The results, such as images, statements, models and materials can, for example, be transmitted or stored. This would be an insufficient understanding for some contemporary media practices and approaches to these practices that foreground process, mutability, flux, simulation, remediation, notions of becoming, and mobility. These characterize the 'pre' to representation—the processes *before* representation in which representation comes into being, in its performativity.[8]

Departing from this characterization of the activity of cartographizing itself, whereby notions such as *situationality*, *relationality*, *positionality* or *deixis*, and *corporeality* are mobilized, we can see that in the case of the various manifestations in XR the navigation between and across mediated domains produces a continuous process of encounter that is both under construction and in deconstruction.[9] As such, the performative cartographic act produces a *paradoxical reality* built on the contradictory, yet symbiotic relationship between oppositional and compositional logic. In AR, for example, this underlies the stitching together of various types of imagery into a navigable "whole," yet simultaneously making very clear the ontological cuts between the whole and its parts (examples of which will be discussed in the sections below).[10] This paradox invites the thinking through of a logic of complexity. Straddling an either-or logic as well as both-and logics that both, and falsely so, presuppose *relata*, complexity makes thinkable the ontological or immanent spatiotemporal primacy of *relatings* that are unpredictable yet effective. Binary, compositional and differently structured relations may emerge from complex entanglements, but entanglements are never a-priorily binary or compositional. XR, then, is composed in (creative) complexity of (onto-epistemological) paradox, (navigational) deixis, and (corporeal-philosophical) experience.

## Crossing Be/for(e) Interference

On 9 October 2010, the Museum of Modern Art (MoMA) in New York was invaded by AR art. Artists Sander Veenhof and Mark Swarek broke into the museum's augmented space and put up *WeARinMoMA*—an exhibition without the museum's authorization. The original press release announces:

> On Saturday October 9th, the physical space inside the MoMA NY building will host a virtual exhibition occupying all floors (including an additional virtual 7th floor) in parallel to its ongoing show. [...] The show will *test case* Augmented Reality art within an appropriate critical context: the bastion of contemporary art.
>
> So far, the MoMA is not involved in all this yet. But that's not a requirement anymore anno 2010, being *independent* by using AR. [...] The organizers of the event, augmented reality experimentalist Sander Veenhof from the Netherlands, and Mark Skwarek, new media artist from New York, aim to address a contemporary issue caused by the rapid rise of Augmented Reality usage. What is the impact of AR on our public and private spaces? Is the distinction between the two fading, or are we approaching the contrary situation with an ever increasing fragmentation of realities all to be perceived individually?
>
> Being *uninvited guest users* of the MoMA space themselves, Veenhof and Skwarek call out any AR artist worldwide to place their artworks *within the walls* of the MoMA too on the 9th of October (Lat/lng: 40.761601, -73.977710). Since the exhibition happens in virtual space, there's no reason not to host an *endless amount* of parallel virtual exhibitions.[11] (emphasis added)

In a humorous tone, the announcement underscores the activist potential of AR as a medium that allows for a crossing of the traditional borders between the domains of institutionally established art and AR art (see Figure 45.1). Part of the New York Conflux Festival that was dedicated to the practice of psychogeography, the ambition was to investigate the implications of AR to cross public and private spaces and the possibility to reconfigure any public space—including the "walled" spaces of museums.[12] Moreover, the emancipatory potential of the technology not just resides in

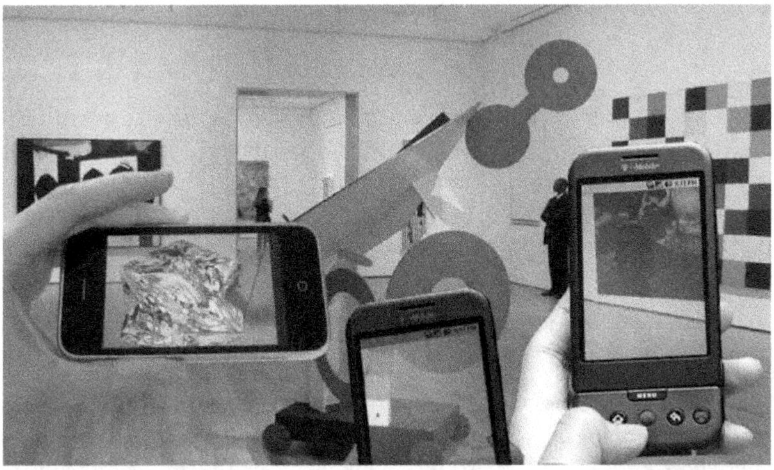

*Figure 45.1* The *WeARinMoMA* exhibition by Sander Veenhof and Mark Swarek (2010). Photo credit: SNDRV

allowing to invade these spaces, but also in the redistribution of curatorial power to makers, the audience, and technology. As the framing by the festival stresses:

> [B]esides the difficult qualitative judgement, the former 'helper' criterium of whether something was placed within museum walls or not, is no longer valid. Virtual artworks by 'non artists' could mix with officially curated art within an official museum. The museum offers the white cube and walls, the visitor decides what to see, curators are bypassed.[13]

As such, more than an annex exhibition in augmented space, this crosses as a form of "guerilla curation" and produces a mix of what we know—pre-existing frameworks or a priori categorizations—and what we come to know. This *coming-into-knowledge* can be seen as the result of interference: as the disturbance of the already articulated, our *a priori*. Interference, then, is the creative production of thought as a result of unfamiliarity in the meeting of the known and unknown. In the artist Lynn Randolph's words: "[d]iffraction occurs at a place at the edge of the future, before the abyss of the unknown."[14]

The staging of encounters with the unfamiliar, unexpected, and unknown is perhaps in line with what Irit Rogoff recognizes as a curatorial strategy of "smuggling" for an *embodied criticality*. Embodied criticality, as an embodied encounter, is radically different from a distanced and dismissive, intellectual criticism. She points out how curatorial strategies can produce this shift from criticism to criticality, by inhabiting a space of uncertainty rather than analyzing a problem, question, or issue from a distance. Criticality for Rogoff, is experienced in encounter:

> [...] in a reflective shift, from the analytical to the performative function of observation and of participation, we can agree that meaning is not excavated for, but rather, that it *takes place* in the present.[15] (emphasis in original)

From the perspective of the present-ness of performativity, in the case of the (non-)MoMA AR exhibition, the additional works interfere not so much *in* a pre-existing exhibition space, but they activate an interference *within* this new space as it comes into being at this crossing or intersection of the two domains or "realities." The activation in the presence of this encounter puts us in a position of (embodied) uncertainty. This activation of interference/diffraction makes us, literally, look again. This second look is an invitation to museum visitors and curators, and to artists and scholars alike.

## XR$^x$

Working from this comparative and inclusive perspective on the diversity within the bracket of XR, we want to single out two of Veenhof's many projects and bring his AR work in relation to a recent artistic VR research project, *False Mirror* by Ali Eslami (2018). This allows us to provisionally sketch out how, within the bracket of XR, they each demonstrate in different ways how the experimental principle of crossing yields interferences in their making.

### *Avatar Says No x AR Flashmob*

Artist Sander Veenhof is one of the pioneers in the Netherlands who uses XR—most notably AR for smartphone, Google Glass, and Hololens—for experimenting with the "non-functional" experiences of these technologies, or what we may call the *artistic experientiality*, and with the way that these experiences raise critical questions about them, or the *artistic criticality*. From hacking space and crossing borders to intervention within existing infrastructures of art institutions and other public spaces, toward examining the relationship between human and technological agency:

Veenhof's works activate the possibilities for new spatial experiences through XR, and within this experience, it offers an investigative, embodied criticality toward them. Indeed, in Veenhof's works playful engagement, curiosity, and embodiment is activated for the investigation of the implications of technology *in* the encounter with technology.[16]

*Avatar Says No* (2019) is one of the most recent Veenhof projects that thematizes curiosity and encounter, precisely through addressing non-compliance of technology (Figure 17, color insert). The underlying question of the work, in Veenhof's words, is:

> What does it feel like on the hololens, when encountering stubborn life-size avatars that walk away from you when you approach them, and step back to you when the distance is safe enough?[17]

The first part of this question alludes to artistic experientiality while the second folds into this experience an artistic criticality thus actualizing a hitherto unknown subject position in this case situated precisely on the threshold of possibility and non-possibility. A productive failure of crossing, it paradoxically addresses precisely the coming into being of both human and technological agency.

With this frustration of the im/possibility of meeting in AR, *Avatar Says No* seems to be diametrically opposed to one of his earliest AR works, the "first-ever" *AR Flashmob* that was held at Dam Square in Amsterdam at 2pm on 24 April 2010. There, the possibility of encounter at the crossing of public and augmented space was very much at the heart of the project. The project included the exact timing and location-specificity, typical for the dramaturgy of flash mobs as pre-planned, physical meet-ups in public spaces.

The technology of marker-based AR of the flashmob makes the physico-virtual encounter in the domain of XR in some ways also *immobile* because the meeting point is fixed and pre-arranged by way of the QR code. Crossing, there, is a *place*—a punctuation at the intersection of space and time, arresting the flow of mobility, futurity and possibility.[18] In *Avatar Says No* that uses markerless AR, the meeting of subject and her avatar remains a continuously mobile, shifting and open possibility, with each step in one direction effecting another step away. Crossing in this later project seems to be more of a paradoxical space-making process, with the encounter at once continuously present as possibility, yet also continuously frustrated and, as such, emphatically absent. Reading the works diffractively, then, brings out that both investigate the possibility and impossibility for mediated encounters through AR as a spatial and social technology. What we can learn is that agency is an *agentiality*, to borrow again from Barad, always dynamic even in its halting.[19]

## *False Mirror, Sacred Hill*

Investigative and critical curiosity can also be recognized in the work *False Mirror* (2018) by Ali Eslami. *False Mirror* is the title of the overarching architecture of an on-going artistic research project that consists of an interactive city built in/ with Virtual Reality for which Eslami collaborates with other artists. Over time, new spaces, each with new foci and characteristics, will be developed and added. As both a continuous and collaborative research project and as an artistic practice, *False Mirror* produces and performs a form of speculative futurism in which VR as digital spatiotemporal technology is being questioned and tested in an open spatial narrative that is performed with each visit(or). The central question to elaborate on all through the development of this piece is not just: "what would it mean to be 'human' in a virtual reality?" but, as we hold, perhaps more specifically: "what human experience and agentiality is always already emerging with/in a physico-virtuality?"[20] Indeed, XR makes us see that the "human" or "human-ness" is never fully there to depart from, but perhaps there is an *originary humanicity*

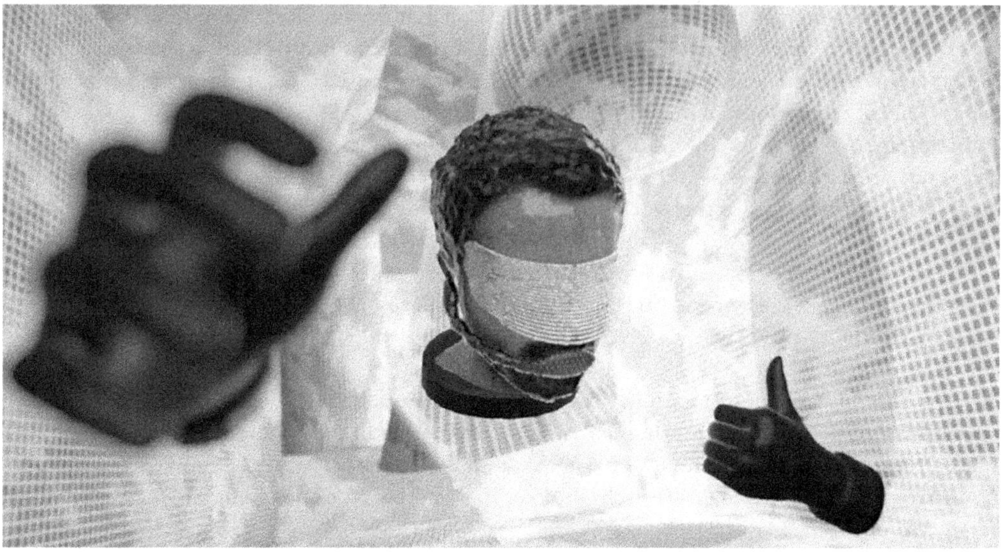

*Figure 45.2* Ali Eslami's *False Mirror* (2018). Ali trying to adjust the selfie camera in Skyville, inside Acid Park District. Photo credit: Ali Eslami

to begin with, instead, whereby the human is in a process of constant, renewed emergence and interrogation, exemplifying what we above called a creative process that folds thinking into making[21] (see Figure 45.2).

As an architecture, *False Mirror* consists of a series of interconnecting spaces, each with different functions and interfaces. The VR visitor can roam around intuitively and can experiment with the different features of its architectural interface. She browses through radio channels, operates in-world and out-world cameras (that share a portable display in the VR space and can either record the visitor as an avatar, or as physical body within the out-of-VR exhibition space), flies a spaceship, takes elevators to a new levels, plays gravity games with environmental sculptures, talks to the confession booth, switches the design of the walls, changes the scale of things or flips the "screen" from horizontal to vertical—just to name a few (Figure 45.3).

*False Mirror* is designed as a lab-space to explore with VR the speculative question of the possible intersections of *presence* and *agency*, and how these constitute our sense of reality. This sensing of reality puts the experiential aspect of spatial navigation and exploration central. In this space, ultimately an XR space, the philosophical implications of physico-virtual experiences are investigated as a fundamental element in understanding and interpreting our experience of XR through relational situatedness with its spatiotemporal coordinates.

The reciprocal relationship between technicity and humanicity in XR raises subsequent questions about their respective agency. *False Mirror* explores our relation to a non-exhaustive set of different navigational spatiotemporal registers. It presents us with questions concerning our perception of mediated reality by simultaneously creating new relational realities that interfere with known ones. These interferences as resulting from intersections of different technological modes, at times experienced simultaneously, constitute new possible forms of relating in the in-world space and invite the visitor to contemplate her humanicity (so-called essence but here thought processually) through technicity.

Albeit under construction at the time of our writing, one of the most recent new spaces in *False Mirror* is *Sacred Hill*. This collaboration with artists Klasien van de Zandschulp and Mamali

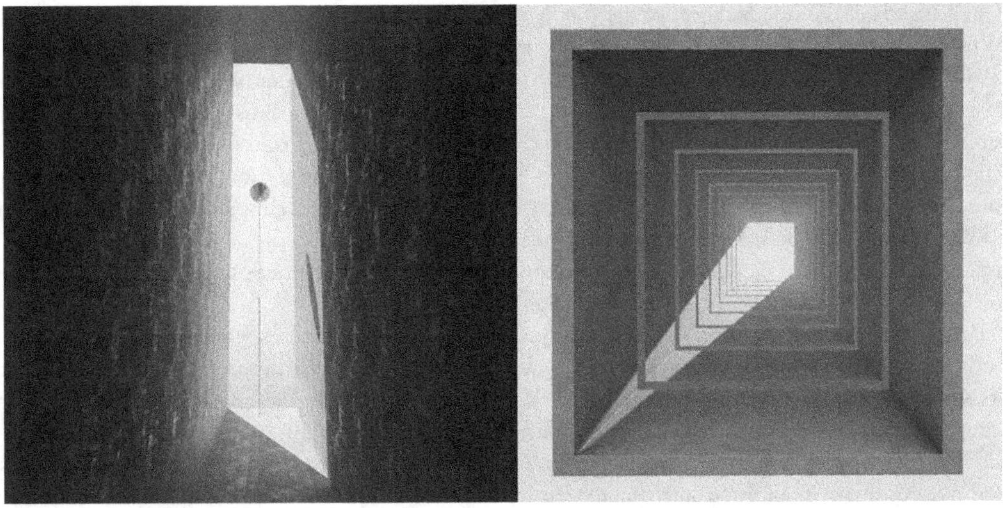

*Figure 45.3* Ali Eslami's *False Mirror* (2018). Left: Acid Park-Biggtoy. According to Eslami: "You can play with this huge toy as long as you want and even more rotate the whole room 90 degrees with press of a button." Right: *Human Therapy\ Lit4Ever.* "Simulation of Virtual Sun light for the times you miss the sun (only possible with concrete hands)." Photo credit and text: Ali Eslami

Shafahi is an experiment aimed at meditative and hallucinatory experiences. Altered states of mind and consciousness in XR is what the visitor is invited to join by participating in a ritual. *Sacred Hill* is explicitly designed with the question of various crossings of digital and physical dimensions, in its material, spatial installation, and the element of live performance. The visitor is invited to enter and join with the offering of an edible tiny green pill. The bodily senses of vision, touch, and taste are immediately and simultaneously addressed. Altogether, the body is a navigational medium, assigned a specific and active role in the investigation of the complex systems of interferences between virtual and physical registers that the XR space of the work offers (see Figure 45.4).

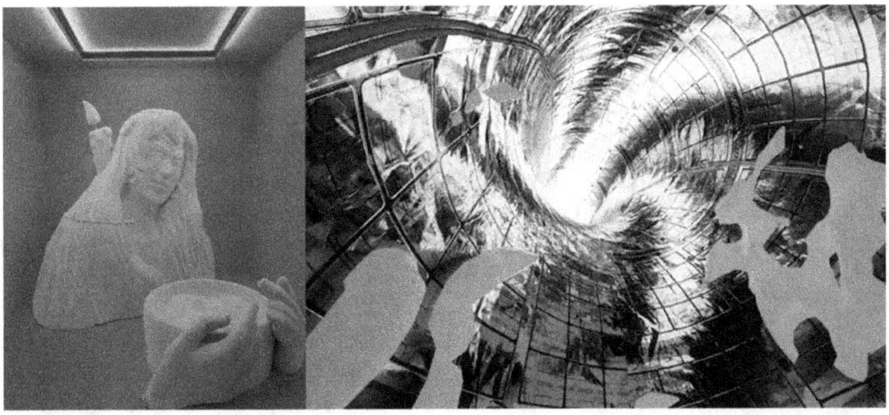

*Figure 45.4* The collaboration *Sacred Hill* (2019) by Ali Eslami, Klasien van de Zandschulp and Mamali Shafahi. Left: Inspiration for physical installation, Palais de Tokyo. Right: A new emerging virtual space. Photo credit: Ali Eslami

In *Sacred Hill*, the organization of the movements of the multiple spectators/participants who join the live performance is co-constituted by intersecting in-worldly and out-worldly dimensions of its XR installation, and is simultaneously ruled by a choreography that is co-authored by the artists. As the artists attested in their 2019 project application, they were inspired by feminist science and technology scholar Donna Haraway who conceptualized the cyborg to end the dualisms between human-animal, organism-machine, and physical-nonphysical. The artists position the notion that the body is being extended and mediated through and beyond its own boundaries via technology.[22] As Haraway puts it: "Why should our bodies end at the skin, or include at best other beings encapsulated by skin?"[23] Inspired by this point of view, the artists developed a list of research questions to address the position of the body within the various instantiations of XR within the project.

Even in its current preliminary research phase, *Sacred Hill* addresses several specific questions about the relationship between technology and the body in XR. Visitors are invited to investigate the XR space from a psycho-somatic experience of the physico-virtual environment as the point of departure. In-world visitors collaborate with out-world participants, and both groups are being watched by a third group of spectators. To us, it seems that together they navigate through a loose narrative resulting in a joined spiritual experience thereby addressing the basic needs and abilities in the artistic media spaces of XR.

For artists, audiences and scholars, *False Mirror*, together with its second installment, *Sacred Hill*, provides a shared navigational space that is permanently "under construction." As such, the artwork can be characterized as a *living lab* where different disciplines and spaces are being mapped, crossed, and scrutinized in co-creative processes to experiment with and explore humanicity and technicity in the contemporary moment. New meanings of mobility and spatiotemporal navigation are being activated, and also participatory engagement is enabling a mobilization of affect, thought, and opinion. In future installments, reflections, answers, new questions, and considerations will be fed back into the project. This makes *False Mirror* an essentially unfinished project. As such, it is always also an open-ended living archive, recording how we conceptualize and test our sense of self as emergent within our relationship with similarly emerging technology.

## Exit

As Nestor Garcia Canclini said in Art Beyond Itself (2014):

> [A]rt is the place of imminence—the place where we catch sight of things that are just at the point of occurring. Art gains its attraction in part from the fact that it proclaims something that could happen, promising meaning or modifying meaning through insinuations. It makes no unbreakable commitment to hard facts. It leaves what it says hanging.[24]

Both the works of Sander Veenhof and Ali Eslami can be considered as these places of imminence, even if they are simultaneously different and similar in this respect. They both elaborate on and, at the same time, ameliorate the impact and politics of technology that runs through our entangled private and public spaces. Having defined reality as constituted by and as constituting relatings, Veenhof and Eslami activate various realities. As the relata that come into being cannot be predicted, both seem to approach their artistic practice as open-ended and continuous lab work. They offer sites of encounter and inquiry for engaging spectators who join this work and who influence the work by joining.

In the crossing artistic media spaces of XR, then, "reality" as a subject-driven, experiential category is investigated as a composition of what philosopher Federico Campagna has called the dimensions of *essence* and *existence* as part of our technoworld. As Campagna states:

> '[R]eality' is the name that we assign to a state in which the dimension of essence (*what* something is) and the dimension of existence (that something *is*) are inextricably bound to each other, without merging into one another.[25]

Building on this notion of co-constitutive essence and existence, both threaded through with technology, Campagna continues that the notion that reality is not a fixed given, but is culturally and, hence, both historically situated and changing over time. Most importantly, it affects how we think about what is possible in both *imagination* and (hence) *in action*. Indeed, the current moment, felt by artists such as Veenhof and Eslami, requires a framing of the human sensing of reality with the question of technology. This thinking through what is possible in imagination and in action is specifically activated in what we have diffractively been able to distinguish as *technologies of mobility*. Such technologies mobilize the body through affect, call for subjects to engage and participate in artistic media spaces and for boundaries to be crossed in co-creation.

In this chapter, we have used *interference* to understand the way that the artistic media spaces mobilize, through the principle of crossing, positionalities that are characterized by what we have called a window of (non-)opportunity that is constantly in flux. Its synonym *diffraction*, we have used for the analytical approach, one that tries to make sense of these works through their interrelating. Activating a similar method for scholarship, this perspective of interference/diffraction, we propose, is helpful for understanding how art works and thinks, and for understanding what can happen between art and scholarship. This creative process between making and thinking we see, in the words of Néstor García Canclini quoted above, as mobilizing places of imminence, "where we catch sight of things that are just at the point of occurring."

## Notes

1 The development of the theoretical foundations of this chapter builds on Verhoeff's earlier work and is enriched and further developed in conversations with, and inspired by, the work of theorist Iris van der Tuin, specifically her writings on diffraction and diffractive reading.

2 Lauren Goode, "Get Ready to Hear a Lot More About XR," *Wired*, 5 January 2019, www.wired.com/story/what-is-xr.

3 https://en.wiktionary.org/wiki/crossing.

4 https://en.wiktionary.org/wiki/interference.

5 Karen Barad, *Meeting the Universe Halfway: Quantum Physics and the Entanglement of Matter and Meaning* (Durham, NC and London: Duke University Press, 2007).

6 Ibid.

7 Nanna Verhoeff, *Mobile Screens: The Visual Regime of Navigation* (Amsterdam: Amsterdam University Press, 2012).

8 Ibid., 143; emphasis in original.

9 Here, we formulate interference using terms that are traditionally seen as poststructuralist. See also Karen Barad, "Quantum Entanglements and Hauntological Relations of Inheritance: Dis/continuities, SpaceTime Enfoldings, and Justice-to-Come," *Derrida Today* 3, no. 2 (2010), 240–68, doi: 10.3366/E1754850010000813.

10 On the principles of *plotting*, *tagging*, and *stitching* of mobile Augmented Reality, see Nanna Verhoeff, *Mobile Screens,* and more recently on the principle of *marking*, see William Uricchio, "Augmenting Reality: The Markers, Memories, And Meanings Behind Today's AR," in *Urban Interfaces: Media, Art and Performance in Public Spaces*, edited by Verhoeff, Nanna, Sigrid Merx, and Michiel de Lange. *Leonardo Electronic Almanac* 11, no. 4 (2019), www.leoalmanac.org/augmenting-reality-the-markers-memories-and-meanings-behind-todays-ar-william-uricchio/.

11 October 4, 2010, reprinted at www.sndrv.nl/moma/?page=press. The relevance of this event is positioned in relation to other "unauthorized augmentations" of museum exhibitions as part of a still ongoing practice in a 2018 article in *Wired*. Miranda Katz, "Augmented Reality Is Transforming Museums," *Wired*, 13 April 2018, www.wired.com/story/augmented-reality-art-museums/?fbclid=IwAR0E1eEF_6184a3WoKAOqCqHNzrhUREl6zXf-QhDwODYKm8ry8gQXJEVhog.

12 Psychogeography is "the investigation of everyday urban life through emerging artistic, technological and social practice." From the festival's website http://confluxfestival.org/about.

13 See also www.sndrv.nl/moma/?page=press for the reprinted statement of the former festival.

14 Quoted in Donna Haraway, *Modest_Witness@Second_Millennium.FemaleMan©_Meets_OncoMouse™: Feminism and Technoscience* (New York: Routledge, 1997), 273.

15 Irit Roggoff, "'Smuggling'—An Embodied Criticality," 2016, http://xenopraxis.net/readings/rogoff_smuggling.pdf. For more on this perspective on curation, See Nanna Verhoeff and Clancy Wilmott, "Curating the City: Urban Interfaces and Locative Media as Experimental Platforms for Cultural Data," in *Code & The City,* edited by Rob Kitchin and Sung-Yueh Perng (London: Routledge, 2016), 116–29.

16 These interpretations are inspired by a conversation between Veenhof and Verhoeff that took place for the sole purpose of this chapter in Amsterdam on 7 June 2019.

17 For this quote and a video impression of his playtesting of the work, see www.youtube.com/watch?v=P2RknGprTRA&feature=youtu.be.

18 For a related use of the term "punctuated places," see Nanna Verhoeff, "Surface Explorations: 3D Moving Images as Cartographies of Time," in *Espacio, Tiempo Y Forma.* Serie VII. Historia Del Arte (New Era) Special Issue: *Art Moves: Performativity in Time, Space and Form,* no. 4 (May 2016), 71–91, http://revistas.uned.es/index.php/ETFVII/article/view/15497/0.

19 On diffractive reading, see Iris van der Tuin, "Signals Falling: Reading Woolf and Guattari Diffractively for a New Materialist Epistemology," *The Minnesota Review: A Journal of Creative and Critical Writing* 88, no. 1 (2017): 112–15; "Diffraction as a Methodology for Feminist Onto-Epistemology: On Encountering Chantal Chawaf and Posthuman Interpellation," *Parallax* 20, no. 3 (2014): 231–44, doi: 10.1080/13534645.2014.927631; "'Without an Analytical Divorce from the Total Environment': Advancing a Philosophy of the Humanities by Reading Snow and Whitehead Diffractively," *Humanities* 3, no. 2 (2014): 244–63.

20 This interpretation is inspired by a series of conversations between Paulien Dresscher, Klasien van de Zandschulp and Ali Eslami held in 2019.

21 For "originary humanicity," see Vicki Kirby, *Quantum Anthropologies: Life at Large* (Durham, NC and London, Duke University Press, 2011), 1–22.

22 As a curator, Paulien Dresscher has been involved in the writing of the Dutch funding application for *Sacred Hill.* There the artists have elaborated on their inspirational sources.

23 Donna Haraway, "A Cyborg Manifesto: Science, Technology, and Socialist-Feminism in the Late Twentieth Century," in *Simians, Cyborgs, and Women: The Reinvention of Nature* (New York: Routledge, [1985] 1991), 178.

24 Néstor García Canclini, *Art Beyond Itself: Anthropology for a Society Without a Storyline* (Durham, NC; London: Duke University Press, 2014), xiii.

25 Federico Campagna, *Technic and Magic: The Reconstruction of Reality* (London: Bloomsbury, 2018), 17.

# 46

# ONE GOOD DEATH

## Tactile, Haptic, and Empathic Co-design for End-of-Life Experience

*Leah Heiss, Matiu Bush, and Marius Foley*

This chapter focusses on the use of tactile and haptic co-design media to engage participation for interdisciplinary groups and elicit empathy in complex problem spaces, such as the end-of-life experience. Here, we deploy co-design with mobile Tactile Tools™ to reflect critically on the issue of death. We focus on the power of tactile mobile *materiality* to help in the co-design processes around difficult social issues including death and dying.

At present, the experience of people in aged care and in the community as they reach end-of-life can be inconsistent, clinically driven and not aligned with individual choices. In order to address this disjunct between the system and the individual, the authors have developed a number of parallel approaches to engage haptic and tactile participation in the redesign of the death experience. We report on two such practices: the One Good Death Tactile Tools™ workshop and the One Good Death Workshop-in-a-Box activity that both took place at RMIT University, Melbourne in 2018.

The interrelated One Good Death activities use tactile and haptic co-design methodologies to engage intimacy, liveness, and a meaningful sense of presence in the face-to-face and remote context. The chapter draws not only from contemporary writings in mobile media theory but also from earlier writings on presence and the extended mind. The One Good Death experiences highlight tangible ways to bring hapticity and tactility into the mobile media space as a way to facilitate empathy in cohorts who do not share an existing interpersonal bond.

The One Good Death Tactile Tools™ workshop brought together 47 thought leaders in ageing, education and health sectors to define and explore how design can help to achieve a "good death" for all people in the community as they reach end-of-life. The concept of a "good death" was defined as one that recognizes the whole-of-life contribution of people living in aged care, or in the community, as they near death. A good death is also self defined by the person dying and their family, and includes concepts such as dying with dignity, spirituality and palliative care.

In the workshop, teams focussed on improving the experience of a specific persona as they neared end-of-life, using Tactile Tools—mobile coloured discs that participants used to map out the experience of an elderly person. The Tactile Tools workshop is an approach that enables many layers of tactile engagement to take place simultaneously.[1] For 90 minutes experts from diverse backgrounds—health practitioners through to designers, artists and researchers—participated in a collaborative haptic and tactile experience in which they prototyped and re-prototyped pathways towards a "good death" for their persona. This involved collaboratively defining a goal for the persona and developing a pathway to this goal using coloured tiles that participants write and draw on. These tiles represent roadblocks, workarounds, and moments of empathy. The shared experience built trust, intimacy, and strong bonds between participants. The methodology provided a conduit for collaboration, enabling participants to externalize and share feelings and ideas in a participatory and performative way.

Drawing from the experience of developing and implementing the workshop, the authors developed the One Good Death Workshop-in-a-Box, a co-design toolkit for geographically dispersed RMIT Master of Design Futures (MDF) students. The MDF programme is fully online, with students from most Australian states. The goal of the toolkit was to replicate in the digital domain the haptic or sensate experiences of the One Good Death Tactile Tools workshop. All participants opened their Workshop-in-a-Box simultaneously while engaging in an online gathering and connected in remote making activities, initiating material and interpersonal empathy through a shared tactile experience. The toolkits included tactile materials that participants used to prototype human-centred design approaches to improve end-of-life experience. Outcomes included tactile journey maps and multi-sensory relationship mappings (see Figure 46.1 for a relationship mapping that is experienced in a visual, tactile, and olfactory way). The approach draws from remote presence research to provide a multimodal and immersive sensory experience.

As Jason Farman suggests, "we are living in a time where mobility is ubiquitous and where people, things, technologies, data, services are all in constant flux."[2] By situating the interconnected One Good Death activities in the field of mobile media we argue that tactile and haptic engagement are critical to achieving an embodied sense of connection and intimacy, whether co-located or distant. Through engaging tactile participation in co-located and remote contexts we have facilitated collaboration and trust between participants problematizing the end-of-life space. By framing the activities in terms of mobility and performativity, we argue that placing greater emphasis on tactile and haptic engagement in mobile media, particularly in online media, can enrich engagement and provide a meaningful sense of presence and empathy.

## What Is a "Good Death?"

In contemporary Australian culture, death and dying are generally regarded as something to deny and hide from public view. Death literacy is defined as a set of knowledge and skills that make it possible to understand and act upon end-of-life and death care options.[3] Despite understandable fear and denial, as a sector and a society there is good reason to want to learn more about and improve our response to death and dying.

Thinking about and experiencing mortality as a society has the potential to increase empathy and compassion for older members of the community. Further more, an ageing population and an increased prevalence of chronic illness and comorbidities highlight the importance of end-of-life and palliative care knowledge and expertise within the aged and community care sector.

End-of-life care in Australia is mostly institutionalized when compared to other countries, especially in the aged care sector.[4] Over 70% of Australians surveyed have expressed a desire to die in their own home but nationally only around 14% are able to achieve this, where it is reported that 54% die in hospitals and 32% in residential aged care facilities.[5]

The healthcare sector is committed to delivering a comprehensive end-of-life service across the continuum of care that promotes the personal choice and genuine health and well-being outcomes of the individual. Palliative care aims to fulfil the hierarchy of end-of-life needs. Maslow's Hierarchy of Needs, first published in 1954, provides a useful framework for achieving a good death. Fundamental to Maslow's theory of motivation is that human needs are hierarchical, that unfulfilled lower needs dominate one's thinking, actions, and being until they are satisfied.[6] Maslow's framework provides a comprehensive approach not only for achieving comfort at end-of-life through the relief of symptoms and addressing of fears and safety issues, but also for a self-actualization that can be achieved at various stages of the end-of-life journey.[7]

The use of an adapted hierarchy of needs for a "good death" aims to provide an improved approach to structuring care to consumers by using Maslow's schema (see Figure 46.1). The hierarchy indicates the urgency of fulfilling more basic needs first and helps suggest a logic for approaching end-of-life care. Maslow's approach can encompass not only the relief of distressing symptoms, but also make explicit the opportunities to address the psychological, social, and spiritual needs during end-of-life.[8]

A "good death" is achieved by upstream palliative care where the emphasis is on promoting early decision making with consumers. It also encompasses proactive collaborative arrangements with General Practitioners, hospital, hospice, ambulance, and community-based specialist palliative care services including after-hours support, before the last weeks of life.[9]

Implementing upstream palliative care, with a focus on early assessment and proactive management has the potential to enhance symptom management, prevent, recurrent presentations to hospital and enable death to occur in the individual's place of choice. All are considered essential for achieving a satisfactory death. Achieving the best death possible for people helps reduce distress and trauma that families and friends may experience after the loss of a loved one.[10]

## Understanding and Mapping the Palliative and End-of-Life Process

Older people experience three distinct phases while they are receiving care in the aged care context. The phases include admission and assessment, end-of-life care, and the post death bereavement care phase. Advance Care Planning, directives, appointing a substitute decision maker, Enduring Power of Attorney, and refusal of treatment are relevant to all older people and not only those at the palliative/end-of-life care stage. Structures and processes are required to be in place to identify and document on admission if any of the above are completed and that these are honoured over time.[11] Such structures are essential for evidencing that important end-of-life conversations have taken place and that clear directions are given that are consistent with the expressed wishes of the older person.

There are specific considerations regarding a "good death" and the needs of consumers with dementia and other forms of cognitive decline.[12] If end-of-life planning is left until near death, it will be too late for consumers with dementia to be able to fully participate. The types of decisions that need to be made—as a consumer's cognitive function deteriorates—are wider than just medical decisions and incorporate financial, spiritual, social, and legal realities.

The type of care that older people receive in the last months and weeks of their lives can minimize the distress and grief associated with death and dying for both the individual and their family, friends, and carers. Systems and structures for delivering safe and high-quality end-of-life care should work in synergy with those for recognizing and responding to clinical deterioration. Timely recognition of an older person's transition to the terminal phase of life must be documented and communicated to consumers, families, carers, and other health professionals by the interdisciplinary team. These are the fundamental systems required for individuals and families to experience a good death even in the context of losing a valued family member.

In order to more fully understand the aged care and end-of-life experience from a first person perspective, the authors developed the One Good Death co-design activities, discussed in the following sections. These engagements focussed on eliciting the various touch points through the aged care and end-of-life phases that require design solutions. The interconnected approaches also interrogate how a confluence of service design, human-centred design and design thinking might inform better end-of-life experiences.

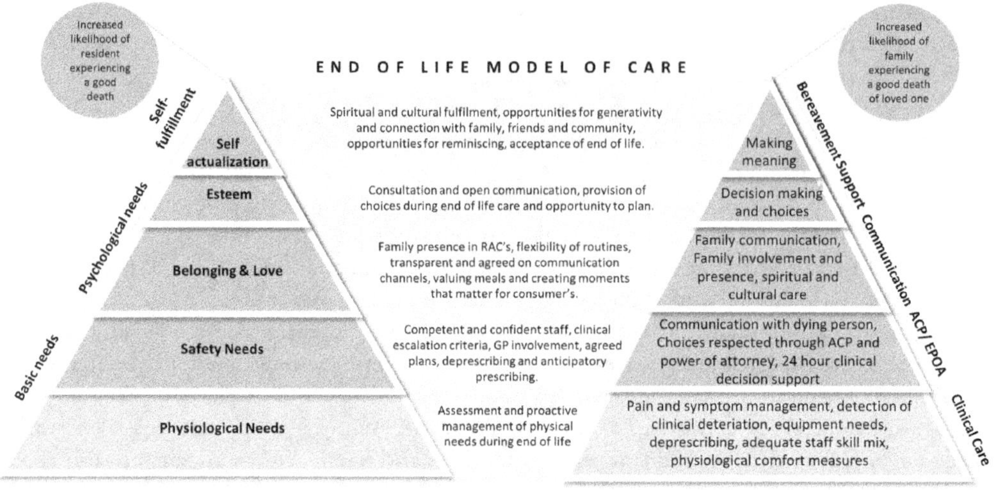


*Figure 46.1* Maslow's hierarchy of needs adapted for end-of-life experience. Photo credit: Bolton Clarke 2019

## The One Good Death Tactile Tools™ Workshop

In February 2018, the authors co-facilitated the One Good Death Tactile Tools™ workshop. The experience brought together people from the ageing sector, education, and healthcare to workshop how design can help to achieve a good death for all people in the community as they reach end-of-life. By placing emphasis on *one* good death we hoped to promote an approach that could be scaled to help a diverse range of family structures. Within the workshop, teams focussed on improving the experience of a specific persona as they neared end-of-life.

The Tactile Tools™ methodology, developed by Heiss as part of her PhD research,[13] references generative toolkits[14] and compels participants to problem-solve in a haptic way, engaging with goals, roadblocks, and work-arounds on the table as meanings rather than as objects. Teams build their way towards a mutually desirable goal, collaboratively problem-solving their way around institutional, structural, or social roadblocks that emerge (see Figure 46.2). Physically, they move a purple disc (work-around) to the side of a yellow hexagon (roadblock). Metaphorically, teams are providing work-arounds to life and death situations, or creating the conditions to support communities through hardship.

The flexibility of the tools enables participants to prototype and re-prototype configurations of roadblocks and work-arounds until they determine the best way forward. Within the workshop, participants developed a roadmap for their persona, which identified significant moments such as diagnosis, Advance Care Planning, and engagement with palliative care. These experiences were positioned as roadblocks or work-arounds in the pursuit of a higher order goal for the persona.

## Personas to Encourage Empathy in the One Good Death Tactile Tools™ Workshop

As Stickdorn and Schneider suggest, "personas are fictional profiles, often developed as a way of representing a particular group based on their shared interests. They represent a 'character' with which client and design teams can engage."[15] In the One Good Death workshop, the authors collaboratively created six personas to encourage groups to empathize with an individual in the

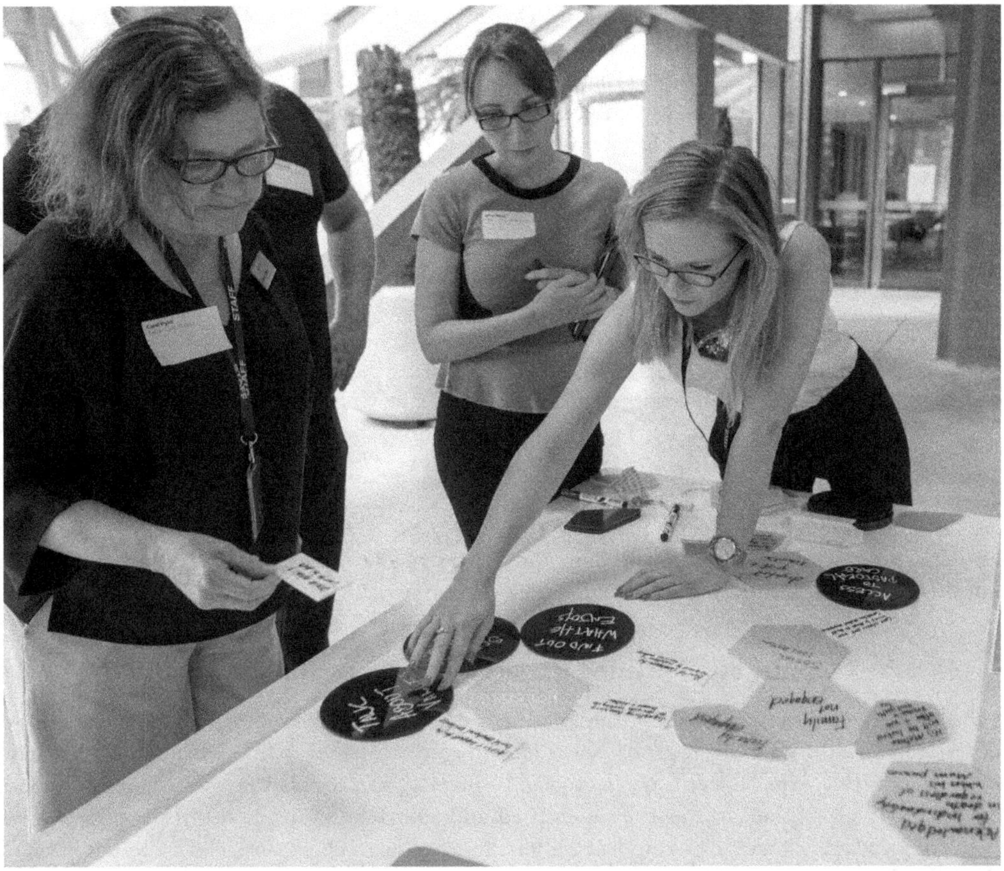

*Figure 46.2* Participants on a Vera table during the One Good Death Tactile Tools™ workshop discussing their arrangement with Matiu Bush. Photo Credit: Adam. R. Thomas, 2018

end-of-life space. These personas were informed by the lived experiences of people living under the care and support services of Bolton Clarke. In order to avoid caricaturing these personas and losing their emotional intensity, we drew from the work of Steve Portigal who suggests that in order to maintain the intimacy and "messiness" of real people we need to tell stories. He suggests: "Rather than creating distancing caricature, tell stories. Don't deny the need to do in-person research with real people. Look for ways to represent what you've learned in a way that maintains the messiness of actual human beings."[16] Peter H. Jones suggests that "Stories embody a particular shortcoming that personas overcome—stories are non-transferable in their original richness as a performed narrative."[17]

The personas commenced with a thick description of the individual in their environment. The story arcs were informed by home visits to elderly people conducted by Matiu Bush. Following is an excerpt from a third-person narrative:

> Vera waits patiently for the nurse to arrive, she is still able to do some aspects of her personal care but the frayed edges are showing. Financially things are very tight and Vera spent minimal time planning for her advanced years. The cupboards are full of crockery from the 60's and 70's, Vera's generation keeps things.[18]

In addition to the narrative, the One Good Death personas provided information that included challenges, risks, level of social and familial connection, anticipated life expectancy, and key personality attributes. The persona also included the individual's definition of a good death, which was critical to facilitating empathy between the participants and the person they were designing for. An example of this good death statement was:

> Vera says that being alive for 100 years is tiring and she would prefer to die in her sleep. She doesn't care about the location but wants to be aware and informed that it's happening. She would like it to be quick with minimal fuss.

For Lucina persona this was stated as:

> Surrounded by family and pain free, Lucina does not want extensive life preserving treatment but has not spoken to her family about it. Lucina would like to die at home, peacefully. Catholic rituals are important to her and her family.

Throughout the workshop, participants were encouraged to continually return to their table's persona. This helped to inhibit the tendency for participants to move towards a system or service solution, rather than considering the experience of the individual.

## Mobility and Meaning in the One Good Death Workshop

In the One Good Death workshop, the goal for each team was broadly to provide the persona with a "good death." However, groups were encouraged to further define what this meant, based on their collective experience in the sector and information provided in the persona. Once the goal had been established, teams then identified and addressed societal, institutional, and emotional roadblocks to achieving a good death for their persona. These obstacles were noted on the yellow roadblock tiles (see Figures 46.2 and 46.3). The task was then to scaffold work-arounds, stakeholders and empathy tiles around these roadblocks to build a roadmap towards the persona's goal of a good death.

The Tactile Tools™ have a base language—roadblocks, work-arounds, goals and moments of empathy—yet need to become relevant and meaningful to participants. In order to achieve this, we drew on the idea of natural mapping when designing the tools.[19] Donald Norman defines natural mapping as, "taking advantage of physical analogies and cultural standards, lead(ing) to immediate understanding."[20] This is the idea of overlaying conceptual ideas onto physical things and occurs when we think of the buttons and dials with which we control the devices and technologies in our lives.

With this in mind, Heiss designed the tiles with consideration of the tactile experience and corresponding mapping of content to shape and colour. Roadblocks (yellow hexagons), the same shape as an Australian stop sign, have hard edges and suggest a cessation to energy flow. Conversely, the work-around is a smooth purple circle that facilitates movement around the obstacle. Rectangular goals are orange and large enough to feel dominant on the table, signifying an end point to which the team can work. Roads engage us to build like children and provide straight bits, 90° turns and full U-turns to symbolize the twisting and turning of the design process. A blue "empathy" tool reminds participants to consider the life and emotional experience of the person they are designing for, to make decisions for them, not about them, during the activity. In addition, it brings emotions, strengths and vulnerabilities to the fore.

The physical mobility of the methodology enabled participants to prototype and re-prototype arrangements of roadblocks and work-arounds to determine the best way forward. This is a dance

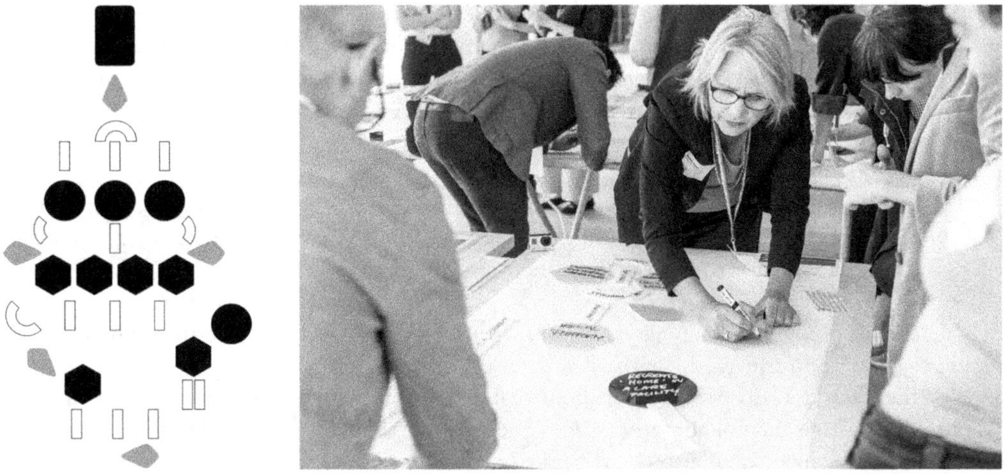

*Figure 46.3* Left: Pathway diagrams from One Good Death; Right: Participants in the One Good Death workshop writing on tiles, 2018. Photo Credits: Kenneth Ray Hendrix

of negotiation where people literally put their ideas, thoughts, and feelings "on the table" and massage them into patterns that satisfy the views of all participants while also seeking to authentically represent the experience of the persona. The process is a mobile performance with participants reaching and sliding the tiles across the papered surface. This part of the process is messy and invites creativity, sliding ideas around until we find common ground, a pattern that will satisfy the hopes and expectations of all group members. The patterns created speak to compromise and consensus, negotiation and acquiescence. Dourish and Bell suggest that: "Patterns of connection arise around forms of movement and mobility; our sense of spatial organization emerges from the patterns of movement of everyday life."[21]

A central part of the experience is the sliding of the tools until participants decide upon their appropriate location. In Donald Norman's terminology, the tiles are imbued with the "affordance" of sliding. Sliding is different to the peel and stick of post-it notes, or the squeak of colored markers on a whiteboard. It conjures the "wax on, wax off" scene from *The Karate Kid* film,[22] or the circular hands of dancers doing the Charleston in the 1920s.

Norman suggests, "The term affordance refers to the perceived and actual properties of the thing, primarily those fundamental properties that determine just how that thing could possibly be used … affordances provide strong cues to the operation of things."[23] The action of sliding the tiles is simple, straightforward, and playful. Their scale and weight feels substantial in the hand, providing gravity to the ideas they carry. Once the tiles are on the table's papered surface they behave like pucks on an ice hockey rink, the friction between the under surface and the table enabling an easy slide yet not feeling "skittery." The impact of all this mobility is that participants conceive roadblocks and their related work-arounds as temporal and changeable, no longer immovable obstacles.

## The Tactile Tools as Scaffolds to Extend Mind and Bridge the 'Space Between'

In conventional group problem solving, we cannot contribute unless we have relevant information available at the time. However, within the One Good Death workshop participants were able to place-hold ideas by taking a roadblock or work-around tile from the toolkit and noting their unformed thoughts on it using a whiteboard marker. In these instances, participants ensure that the concern is represented in negotiations by putting it roughly in the right position. The ideas can then be moved around until they feel spatially and temporally coherent. This use of the tiles as design scaffolds to support collaboration and find collective meaning references the work of Yoko Akama who suggests:

> The role of the designer, then, is to design "scaffolds" to promote "collective generativity" amongst "ordinary people" and designers. "Scaffolds" are therefore proposed … as new tools that can enable people to express their thoughts, feelings and dreams.[24]

Andy Clark proposes that language is one of a variety of scaffolding structures which humans employ to operate in the world without a detailed inner representation system.[25] Conceived in this way the Tactile Tools become a scaffold that enables participants to problem solve in braver and more innovative and collaborative ways. The tools also provide a scaffold to traverse the space between group members and also between the team and the persona. Camille Baker situates mobile technologies as a means to bridge the "space between" embodied agents. She suggests,

> The space between may … be understood as breathing space, thought space, meditation, imagination, dream space, being "in limbo," and "negative space" … The space between is a sense of sustain, floating, suspension, or nowhere-ness….[26]

We posit that the "space between" may also be bridged by embodied interaction between people, scaffolded by tools that enable us to extend our memories and minds. In the context of the One Good Death Tactile Tools workshop, participants used the performative aspects inherent in the methodology (sliding, leaning, writing, placing) to bridge the space between themselves and other participants. In the One Good Death Workshop-in-a-Box, discussed in the next section, this space between is bridged by engaging with haptic and tactile media in a remote scenario. Performativity is expressed through parallel crafting and sharing of design works while engaged in a Zoom[27] interaction.

## The One Good Death Workshop-in-a-Box: Haptic and Tactile Engagement in a Mobile Media Environment

In *Sensuous Geographies*, Paul Rodaway defines three types of touch—simple contact, exploratory activity and communication. He suggests that:

> *Exploration* provides the fine detail of a complex world, *communication* establishes a participation or belonging to that world … and *simple contact* continually maintains, often subconsciously, a connectivity with the physical world and our own bodies.[28]

*Simple contact* is akin to simply co-existing with inanimate surfaces, for instance, walking through a building and brushing against walls. *Exploratory activity* pertains to the individual exploring the environment "but the environment explored is largely passive and does not respond to the touch nor appear to register its own tactile sensation."[29] Rodaway defines *communication* as bi-directional touch in which information and messages are exchanged, "this communication is generally a relationship between organisms and forms an important part of the bonding of community and the sense of establishing roots in a place."[30]

Within the One Good Death Tactile Tools™ workshop, particular interest was taken in providing an experience of all three types of tactile engagement. Participants first interact with the workshop environment, sensing space, light, temperature; second, they handle the tiles to understand their weight and texture, and engage with written content via personas and workshop materials; and third, participants write on tiles and work collaboratively with others to spatially locate these on the pathway.

Drawing from Rodaway's identified three types of tactile engagement, how might we encourage a sense of bi-directional tactile engagement, in the online learning space? Further, how might we provide a meaningful sense of presence by scaffolding tactility around mobile media engagement, specifically in group Zoom interactions? To address these issues the authors developed the One Good Death Workshop-in-a-Box, a tactile toolkit that was posted around Australia to participants in the RMIT Master of Design Futures.

## Developing a Tactile and Haptic Toolkit for the Online Learning Space

The RMIT Master of Future Designs (MDF) is a one-year online degree offered to professionals who are working in, or moving into human-centred design practices. Throughout 2018 the MDF partnered with Bolton Clarke, providers of aged care and at home care services, to deliver the One Good Death experience.

Students participating in online studies often experience a sense of isolation.[31] The lack of tactile engagement in the online space can engender a feeling of separation from one's colleagues, who appear as disembodied heads in a video-conferencing interface. In order to address this disengagement and to increase a meaningful sense of presence in the online collaboration space, the authors developed and disseminated the One Good Death Workshop-in-a-Box to the MDF cohort. The toolkit contained materials that were intentionally open ended and exploratory—string, soft clay, crimped paper, craft sticks—with students free to incorporate tools of their own. The contents of the box provided participants with the materials to explore a sensory design response to the concept of "one good death" (Figure 46.4).

Temporally, the concept involved all students receiving their box at the same time and seeing each other in real time on Zoom as they opened their boxes together. Even though physically distant, participants were connected by the materiality of the toolkits and throughout the session were encouraged to experiment with materials and create design works to share with the group. A participant suggested:

> Even though we are remotely located in the distance education sphere, we start to share and empathise with each other's creative journeys. It was a powerful way to move past that barrier of being just a face on a screen, to an experience where individuals were sharing with the community insights into their own life and the way they work in the world.

A key consideration in developing the One Good Death Workshop-in-a-Box was to introduce a greater level of experimentation into the practices of the participants. Much work in service design and human centred design in aged care takes the form of two-dimensional representations including service blueprints, journey maps, and stakeholder charts. In order to shift thinking and inspire innovative outcomes, the authors argue that it is necessary to shift our habitual practices and go-to materiality. This assertion references the work of Wanda Orlikowski in organizational sense-making:

> When people change their practices, their knowing changes. From such a perspective, people learn to know differently as they use whatever means, motivation, and opportunity they have at hand to reflect on, experiment with, and improvise their practices.[32]

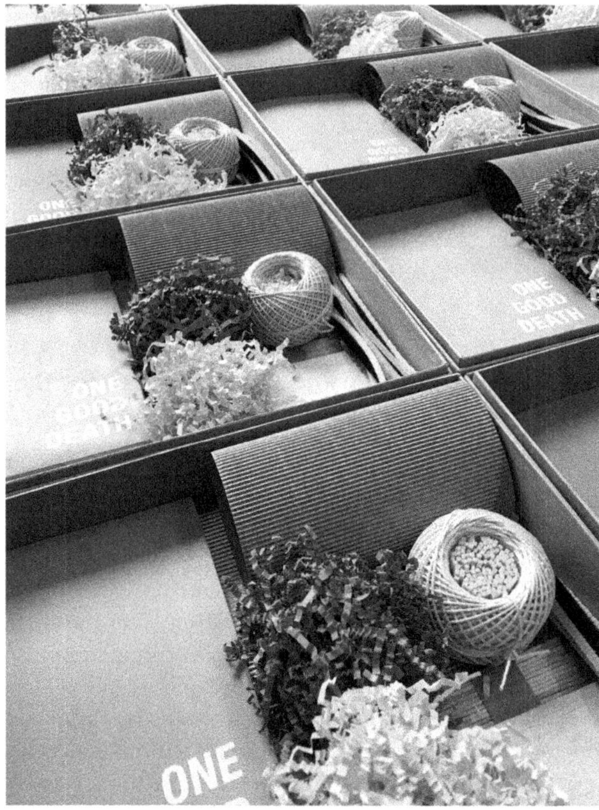


*Figure 46.4* One Good Death Workshop-in-a-Box. Photo Credit: Mina Carnelli

With a focus on experimentation and innovating practice, students were tasked with developing a workshop or engagement to learn more about the end-of-life experience. The aim was to generate novel types of engagements, as well as prompt students to explore the boundaries of their own design practices. Throughout the first session participants explored the different materials, testing their toolkit and asking questions like: What kind of tools and approaches do I need to run a workshop in the end-of-life space? What sort of tools are the appropriate ones if I am going to spend time with a palliative care worker or someone who has a disease? How do I start to think about this? What do I need to have in my tool kit? Who do I invite and why?

## The One Good Death Workshop-in-a-Box as a Generative Toolkit

Sanders proposes the creation of a landscape of generative tools, "some … designed to elicit emotional response and expression from people, whereas others (are) designed to uncover meaning and cognitive understanding."[33] The Workshop-in-a-Box is situated as a toolbox of generative approaches, encouraging students to adopt a more nuanced and experimental, three dimensional approach that embodies an emotive connection with people and materials. The activity introduces a form of "liveness" to the digital experience, a concept first proposed by Philip Auslander in his book by the same name.[34] Camille Baker suggests liveness "…must involve a certain tangibility and tactility within the context of performance."[35] While the concept is primarily used in digital performance, the authors argue that it is relevant in the online learning context, which is at heart a multi-directional participatory performance.

The MDF One Good Death activity invited students to scaffold their toolkits and investigate tactile and haptic methods and mobile, iterative, and playful approaches. Many took the opportunity to explore different media. For one student, this was "fuzzy felt" as a workshop tool to engage her participants in story-telling; for another, it was recording the sounds of a person's home (safe and reassuring) and a retirement home (muffled and emotionless); for another, it was developing a set of conversation-prompting playing cards.

The work of Joni Wicks demonstrates this scaffolding of the toolkit to include materials such as custom-made fuzzy felt icons and jubes. Her reinterpretation of the traditional journey map into a three-dimensional diorama, replete with candy, is a playful representation of the lived experience of an ageing woman. Genevieve Schreiber, on the other hand, has added cotton wool and sticks to her toolkit in order to create her mapping of persona Louisa's problem space.

## Conclusion

Dying a good death as defined by the individual requires a level of conscious effort by the individual themselves as well as the many stakeholders that become part of the life journey's end. Doctors, nurses and allied health are required to align with family, friends, lawyers, and funeral directors to achieve what in retrospect is considered to be a good death. The achievement of this becomes fragmented as the number of stakeholders increase and when clinical and cognitive states fluctuate. Yet, deaths that are consistent with the values of the individual happen regularly in aged care and demonstrate the latent capacity in the sector to provide excellent end-of-life care. In order to generate an understanding of the touchpoints that an elderly person and their family experience during the end-of-life phase, the authors developed and implemented two interconnected co-design activities: the One Good Death Tactile Tools workshop and the One Good Death Workshop-in-a-Box. The workshop helped to coalesce a working group of academics, healthcare workers and aged care specialists to participate in a performative mapping experience.

The physical mobility of the methodology enabled teams of people to collaboratively problem solve their way towards a goal for their persona, bypassing traditional hierarchies and prototyping new solutions in this tricky problem space. This physical dimension of mobility highlights others forms of mobility—especially in terms of emotional connection. The approach provides an opportunity to recalibrate the haptic possibilities with material cultures in which haptic and sensory studies are coalesced.

The One Good Death Workshop-in-a-Box toolkit engaged the participation of a distributed cohort in the design of engagements to learn more about end-of-life experience. By introducing haptic and tactile engagement in the digital space, our goal was to provide a meaningful sense of presence and facilitate empathy between participants. The students scaffolded their toolkits and generated compelling textural responses to the concept of one good death.

These interconnected One Good Death activities suggest a way to increase innovation in the end-of-life space by developing and implementing haptic and tactile co-design approaches. In parallel, engagement with tactile and haptic methodologies has the potential to enrich the mobile media space and diminish the differences between copresent and remote collaborative interaction. Reconceptualizing haptic and tactile media as scaffolds to extend minds and bridge the "space between," people in the face-to-face and digital environment also provides a meaningful contribution to the field of mobile media and to the experience of people working in the end-of-life space.

## Notes

1 Paul Rodaway, *Sensuous Geographies: Body, Sense and Place* (London: Routledge, 2011).
2 Jason Farman, *Foundations of Mobile Media Studies: Essential Texts on the Formation of a Field* (Abingdon, OX: Routledge, 2016).
3 Kerrie Noonan, Debbie Horsfall, Rosemary Leonard and John Rosenberg, "Developing Death Literacy," *Progress in Palliative Care* 24, no. 1 (2016): 31–5, doi: 10.1080/09699260.2015.1103498.
4 "Australia's Health 2016," Web report, Australian Institute of Health and Welfare (2016), www.aihw.gov.au/reports/australias-health/australias-health-2016/contents/summary.
5 Joanna Broad, Merryn Gott, Hongsoo Kim, Michal Boyd, He Chen and Martin Connolly, "Where Do People Die? An International Comparison of the Percentage of Deaths Occurring in Hospital and Residential Aged Care Settings in 45 Populations, Using Published and Available Statistics," *International Journal of Public Health* 58, no. 2 (2013): 257–67, doi: 10.1007/s00038-012-0394-5.
6 Abraham Maslow, *Motivation and Personality*, 2nd ed. (New York: Harper & Row, 1970).
7 Broad et al., "Where Do People Die?"
8 Robert J. Zalenski and Richard Raspa, "Maslow's Hierarchy of Needs: A Framework for Achieving Human Potential in Hospice," *Journal of Palliative Medicine* 9, no. 5 (2006): 1120–27, doi: 10.1089/jpm.2006.9.1120.
9 Myles Nickolich, Areej El-Jawahri, Jennifer S. Temel, and Thomas W. Leblanc, "Discussing the Evidence for Upstream Palliative Care in Improving Outcomes in Advanced Cancer," *American Society of Clinical Oncology: American Society of Clinical Oncology Annual Meeting Educational Book* 35 (2016): 534–38, doi: 10.14694/EDBK_159224.
10 Nickolich et al., "Discussing the Evidence for Upstream Palliative Care."
11 Arianne Brinkman-Stoppelenburg, Judith Rietjens and Agnes van der Heide, "The Effects of Advance Care Planning on End-of-Life Care: A Systematic Review," *Palliative Medicine* 28, no. 8 (2014): 1000–25. doi: 10.1177/0269216314526272.
12 Mary O'Brien, Jennifer Kirton, Katherine Knighting, Brenda Roe and Barbara Jack, "Improving End-of-Life Care in Care Homes; An Evaluation of the Six Steps to Success Programme," *BMC Palliative Care* 15, no. 1 (2016): 53, doi: 10.1186/s12904-016-0123-6.
13 Leah Heiss, "Designing Emotional Technologies: Collaborating across Design, Health and Engineering to Humanise Wearable Health Technologies" (PhD diss., RMIT University, 2018).
14 Elizabeth Sanders, Stephen Scrivener, Linden Ball and Andrée Woodcock, "Generative Tools for CoDesigning," in *Collaborative Design Proceedings of CoDesigning*, edited by Stephen Scrivener, Linden Ball and Andrée Woodcock (London: Springer-Verlag, 2000), 3–12.
15 Marc Stickdorn and Jakob Schneider, *This is Service Design Thinking* (Hoboken, NJ: John Wiley & Sons, 2011), 178.
16 Steve Portigal, "True Tales: Persona Non Grata," *Interactions* 15, no. 1 (2008): 72–73, doi: 10.1145/1330526.1330550.
17 Peter H. Jones, *Design for Care—Innovating Healthcare Experience* (New York: Rosenfeld Media, 2013), 78.
18 All participant names have been de-identified for ethical considerations.
19 Heiss, "Designing Emotional Technologies."
20 Donald Norman, *The Psychology of Everyday Things*, 1st ed. (New York: Basic Books, 1988), 9.
21 Paul Dourish and Genevieve Bell, *Divining a Digital Future: Mess and Mythology in Ubiquitous Computing* (Cambridge, MA: MIT Press, 2011), 120.
22 John G. Avildsen (director), "The Karate Kid," Los Angeles: Columbia Pictures, 1984.
23 Norman, *The Psychology of Everyday Things*, 9.
24 Yoko Akama, "Tao of Communication Design Practice: Manifesting Implicit Values Through Human-Centred Design" (PhD diss., RMIT University, 2008), 166.
25 Andy Clark, *Being There—Putting Brain, Body, and World Together Again* (Cambridge, MA: MIT Press, 1997).
26 Camille Baker, *New Directions in Mobile Media and Performance*, 1st ed. (New York: Routledge, 2019).
27 Zoom is video conferencing software.
28 Paul Rodaway, *Sensuous Geographies: Body, Sense and Place* (London: Routledge, 2011), 45.
29 Rodaway, *Sensuous Geographies*, 45.
30 Ibid.
31 Nicholas Croft, Alice Dalton and Marcus Grant, "Overcoming Isolation in Distance Learning: Building a Learning Community through Time and Space," *Journal for Education in the Built Environment* 5, no. 1 (July 2010): 27–64, doi: 10.11120/jebe.2010.05010027.

32 Wanda Orlikowski, "Knowing in Practice: Enacting a Collective Capability in Distributed Organizing," *Organization Science* 13, no. 3 (2002): 249–73, 253; doi: 10.1287/orsc.13.3.249.2776.
33 Sanders et al., "Generative Tools for CoDesigning," 6.
34 Philip Auslander, *Liveness*, 2nd ed. (New York: Routledge, 2008).
35 Baker, *New Directions*, 46.

# 47
# PLAYFUL RESISTANCE OF DATA FUTURES

*Larissa Hjorth and Sam Hinton*

In an increasingly digital world, it is hardly surprising that a technology that renders everything as numbers should eventually come to reduce human activity to quantified datasets. This process of objective quantification—referred to by José van Djick as datafication—yields metadata that purports to provide insights into a variety of areas of human social life that are otherwise hidden in complexity, privacy and/or [pedestrian] obscurity. Mediated by sophisticated and increasingly incomprehensible algorithms (particularly with the increasing application of artificial intelligence algorithms), these datasets promise access to a truth that is otherwise invisible, and perhaps revelatory.[1]

Despite these promises, for some, like van Djick, datafication is intrinsically problematic and paradoxical as it involves the taking of personal data by platforms for the exploitation of their own financial and political interests.[2] Often this data is sold back to users through the politics of platforms,[3] a phenomenon Thomas LaMarre calls "platformativity."[4] LaMarre explains, "In platformativity, the platforms and infrastructures play an active role, or more precisely, an intra-active role, as they iterate, over and again."[5] So, while datafication has the potential to give individuals more control over their lives by helping them visualize things which might otherwise be invisible, it also exposes them to greater scrutiny. The internal contradiction of datafication is that while it can turn our activities into a metaphoric "playground" for personal exploration and expression (i.e. self-tracking for changing behaviors), it can also turn us into cogs in a factory, where we are producing data about ourselves for processing by large organizations.

In this chapter, we explore these ideas through the concept of "soft play" and understanding that the playground/factory complication represents a tension that defines the social and political landscape of datafication, and therefore produces more complex phenomena. To illustrate this, we focus on one particular phenomenon in this chapter: the playful resistance demonstrated through the work of a number of selected artists and projects. There are many examples of artists and creatives subverting the normalized rhythms and processes of datafication to create public awareness about their impact. Artists such as Egor Tsvetkov have been using facial recognition applications like FindFace to demonstrate dystopian realities. In Tsvetkov's *Your Face is My Data* photographs of strangers on the Russian subway were identified via their social media profile by the facial recognition app FindFace. Another example can be found in Trevor Paglen and Kate Crawford's viral art *#ImageNetRoulette* project which subverted a leading facial recognition database—leading to removal of more than half a million images. The project sought to make people aware of the facial recognition biases and to change people's minds about AI.[6] The project resonates with a subgenre of artists working to creatively subvert social and mobile media technology to increase public awareness. Other creatives such as wearable artist Camille Baker[7] are using wearables to bring attention to non-normative bodies. These practices bring to question the interrelationship between privacy, data, and trust and how we might gain empowerment beyond corporate exploitation.

To tackle the complex politics of datafication and to provide context, we begin this chapter by revisiting some of the debates around Big Data and the Quantified Self (QS). With the rise in wearable devices and mobile apps tracking everything from heart rates to sleeping patterns, self-tracking and the QS movement is becoming highly prevalent in many areas of everyday life.[8] Following this, we develop the link between datafication and play through the notion of ambient and "soft play," which problematizes the complex entanglement between play and creative/emotional labor. Having laid down some of the underlying conceptual frameworks around datafication, we then turn to look at the way that artists (Zach Blas and Egor Tsvetkov) are engaging with the tensions between datafication-as-playground and datafication-as-factory to perform often ironic and playful resistances to the technologies and their logics that are an increasingly familiar part of everyday life. The projects we explore provide clever commentary on the technologies, often through mimicking them, albeit ironically: *Unfit Bits* is an almost believable parody of a datafication company; *Magic Mirror* seeks to reinforce the connection between the body and its data by literally reflecting the body alongside data; *Pretty Pelvis* provides the user with a virtual pet they must keep alive through practicing good posture; *Inactivity Tracker* inverts the QS norms by promoting sedentary behavior; *Human-Sized Hamster Wheel* encourages people to power their phones by running in a literal hamster wheel; *Baby Lucent* is a design concept for a smart pacifier and bottle that quantifies the child through a playful interface; and, *Fitbark* quantifies the family pet.

These artists, art works, and design projects all explore the soft power of datafication and algorithmic cultures as a probe, as a tactic and mode of inquiry for critical reflection on the role of data and data futures in our lives.

## We Are Datafication

The Quantified Self (QS) is an idea that was popularized by Gary Wolf and Kevin Kelly in *Wired* magazine in 2007.[9] Broadly speaking, the QS can be defined as "any individual engaged in the self-tracking of any kind of biological, physical, behavioral, or environmental information."[10] For Wolf, the QS movement could operate as a mirror to data so that individuals could reflect, analyze and gain insights.[11] For others, QS is about bringing creative forms of labor and pleasure to reading technology and industry.[12] QS allows us to playfully engage with gamified data, reconfiguring our engagement with exercise and our relationship to the world. However, the destination of the collected information has multiple ramifications. For example, when data is sourced by insurance companies, life insurance policies can become more expensive, especially if the collected data suggests a pattern of behavior that is undesirable to actuarial algorithms.

For many QS advocates, self-tracking is primarily accomplished with the aid of wearable devices and digital apps, focusing predominantly on personal health and wellbeing. As such, the most frequent metrics collected and assessed by QS include motion via "step counts," real-time heart rates, calorie/kilojoule expenditure, and sleeping patterns, but QS also allows monitoring of other metrics such as postural alignment, stress levels, and other behavioral measurements.

For QS practitioners, the collection of these analytics via digital means is often understood to generate a more accurate, objective "picture" of individual habits, and this data is used to actively resolve specific issues, optimize certain practices, and generally improve the lives of users directly.[13] From smaller, localized measures such as increasing daily exercise through to more complex uses like improving personal productivity or enhancing social interactions, QS has become a mainstay for many individuals pursuing self-betterment.

The capacity for QS data to be shared—and compared—among users has seen QS move beyond purely individual use and into social and community spheres.[14] The primary example here is the appropriately named quantified self-community,[15] a global body of QS proponents who exchange data and share general opinions on QS. This community discusses ways for improving and extending contemporary QS uses and applications via local group meetings, national, and international conferences dedicated blogs and social media.[16]

Many more localized instances of social QS use exist, such as users posting their results on Facebook and small, often *ad hoc* groups engaging with QS primarily for purposes like mutual encouragement or friendly rivalry.[17] Workplaces are becoming a particularly common example of social QS communities. From employees engaging in self-devised competitions mediated by wearable devices to full-scale employer-funded initiatives driving improvements in employee health and productivity via competitive means, the social and communal impacts of QS are of increasing importance to the overall QS movement.[18]

However, the movement of QS data is also becoming increasingly utilized by "commercial, research, managerial, security and governmental" agencies for purposes that may at times be more detrimental than beneficial to users.[19] For example, while office competitions promote the usual notions of improved user health and social cohesion in the workplace, this data can also be used by employers to assess individual performance and potentially result in employee termination.[20] Under the guise of rewards programs or reductions in personal insurance premiums, many QS users are being encouraged to share their otherwise private data with third parties such as medical research agencies and insurance companies—data which may even be further on-sold to alternative corporate or political bodies.[21] With QS being employed everywhere from monitoring "problem children" in schools to evidence in legal proceedings, personal data is becoming increasingly public, highly commercialized, and of greater potential value to parties other than users themselves.[22]

Predictably, the complex state of contemporary QS has resulted in growing resistance to QS at individual, community, and more public levels. Beyond personal privacy concerns, many individuals have criticized QS for emotional concerns such as increased anxiety associated with self-monitoring and empirical problems related to data accuracy—views often shared by medical practitioners.[23] Collectives such as parental groups, the CrossFit public, and even the QS community have echoed similar concerns. While "accuracy is of persistent discussion within the quantified self community," many parents and the CrossFit community in particular have retaliated against QS through vocal derision and calls for individuals to boycott wearable devices entirely.[24]

Perhaps the most overt example of large-scale public resistance to QS is the class-action lawsuit leveled at wearable manufacturing giant Fitbit. The lawsuit was based on the inaccuracy of the company's devices—with major ramifications considering that QS data can be subpoenaed to prosecute individuals themselves.[25] Understanding these practices requires acknowledgement that despite the apparent playfulness and game-like qualities that modern digital media interfaces—and QS interfaces in particular—often exhibit, this apparent playfulness and its associations with leisurely activity is paradoxical in nature as it often obscures the labor that the user is performing.[26] We use the term "soft play" to highlight these paradoxes.

## Ambient and Soft Play

As Scholz (2012) observes digital labor is riddled with paradoxes whereby the internet can be understood as both a *playground* and *factory*.[27] These paradoxes are amplified within contemporary media's inherent playfulness[28] and the attendant playbour practices. As Kücklich notes in his discussion of often-invisible dimensions of labor (especially affective, social, creative) of players of games, play can be complex and contradictory. Play can be deployed as a site of resistance, but it can also, through its "softness," be unable to escape the logic of what some identify as neo-liberalism.

This phenomenon requires us to again re-examine conventional definitions of play (that exclude play from productive activity), especially in the face of gamification, big data, and the quantified self. As noted by Hjorth and Richardson, "ambient play contextualizes the game within broader processes of sociality and embodied media practices, which is essential to the corporeality of play whereby play in, and outside, the game space reflects broader cultural nuances and phenomena."[29] Ambience is often used to describe sound and music but has also been used in computing and science. As a pronoun, it specifically refers to a style of music with electronic textures and no consistent beat that is used to create a mood or feeling, but more generally the term describes the diffuse atmosphere of a place. In short, ambience is about the texture of context, emotion, and affect. There are many features of gameplay that are ambient—most explicitly the soundtracks that play a pivotal role in developing the mood, genre, and emotional clues for the player.

For Malcolm McCullough, the rise of ubiquitous media in and around the city has resulted in the need for us to rediscover our surroundings.[30] He calls this need "ambient"—that is, with the increasing tendency of information superabundance through devices such as smartphones we need to think about the space in and around the smartphone rather than just focusing on the device. He argues that understanding attention as ambient can lead to new types of shared cultural resources and social curation akin to a type of common that moves in and out of the digital and the everyday.

A number of theorists have noted the significance of playful and creative practices in contemporary culture and the close relation between such practices and mobile media devices. Chughtai and Myers,[31] for example, suggest that Huizinga's ludic perspective "can be used as a framework to help understand everyday practice" in terms of the way play often resides in the "betwixt and between" of quotidian life and that people's use of technology today frequently involves playful interaction, both communicative and creative. Similarly, Kerr identifies play as a "key concept for understanding the interaction of users with new media,"[32] while Frissen et al. claim that "digital technologies in general have an inherent ludic dimension" that is intimately linked to their capacity for connectivity, interactivity, participation, virtuality, and the sharing of creative content.[33] Indeed, they argue, the ubiquity of digital and networked media effectively prefigures our perceptions, experiences, and practices in a "playful way."[34]

While all media interfaces could be said to be part of the "collective playful media landscape,"[35] it is the mobile media device that exhibits and affords a capacity for play that can be carried around with us, thereby embedding playfulness in the spaces of everyday life wherever we happen to be. For de Lange, play is enacted on, with, and through the mobile, as an increasingly illimitable platform that elicits playful communication and creativity.[36] In Sicart's terms, mobile play happens in a "tangled world of people, things, spaces and cultures."[37]

To understand the paradox of "softness" as defined by Cheney-Lippold, we need to see how it has been applied elsewhere.[38] "Soft power," a term coined by Joseph Nye, refers to the power a nation-state can exert through such tools as technology and ideology.[39] Soft power operates through coercion rather than force and is much more slippery to illustrate.

Hjorth proposed the nomenclature of soft play—in combination with ambient play—to outline the complex and ambivalent entanglement between play and creative/emotional labor.[40] Through the lens of ambient and soft play we explore how media moves in and out of the rhythms and intimacies of everyday life. Here we can find subversion and queering of apps, at the same time as we see the soft power of design to reshape experiences. Play also needs to be understood as an inherently paradoxical experience—an undulating landscape of resistance and submission, creative and unimaginative practices. Play can be dark. It can be creative. As an interdisciplinary concept that spans across psychology, sociology, anthropology, education and games studies, play is as contested as it is complex.

This territory of soft and ambient play provides a rich environment for artists to interrogate the many paradoxes contained within.

## Playful Resistance

There are many artists and critical makers designing ways for alternative modes of traversing social media—and the internet more generally—in playfully resistant modes. Through the rubric of playful resistance as a form of soft power interdisciplinary approaches and theorizations around digital media creative practice are recalibrating the phenomenon. At the intersection of the QS movement and gamification,[41] mobile media and its attendant apps are providing new ways in which to think about creativity, play and labor in everyday life. From body measuring devices such as fitbits and apps to measure sleep, one could argue that everyday life is being colonized by Big Data. However, in practice we see a diversity of resistance and subversive actions that suggest that not all of life is quantifiable, nor reducible to metric datasets. We see how existing sociocultural practices and the ways that users can queer the *applification* of everyday life through play and creativity can shape media.

Artists, designers, and creative practitioners are, as we suggest, providing insight into how we tactically play against data through playful resistance. Take, for example, Zach Blas, who takes a "contra-internet" position (contrasting with the "post-internet" tag sometimes applied to artists). As Blas notes:

> It seems, on the one hand, that the Internet operates as a kind of totalized condition, constricting what is possible for communicating, gathering, and being together. Popular concepts like "post-Internet" propagate this sentiment: there can no longer be an outside to the Internet when it has already seeped into the very material fabric of contemporary existence.... A working definition of contra-Internet is the refusal of Internet totality, but this is not a simple outright refusal. Rather, it is a refusal of naturalizations, hegemonies, and normalizations of the Internet that have contributed to its transformation into a locus of policing and control. Supplementing this, contra-Internet is also the search for and constitution of Internet alternatives.[42]

The work of Blas amplifies the material dimensions of digital and datafied worlds. Take, for example, his video installation *Face Cages* (2013–2016) in which the structure of the algorithm is rendered as a three-dimensional metal cage (see Figure 47.1). The work overtly addresses the fact that the datafied world of facial recognition needs to be understood in terms of real inequalities in physical worlds. For Blas, core to *Face Cages* was the need to illustrate the violence implicit in the way biometrics abstracts bodies.

In another of Blas' work (2017) entitled *im here to learn so* ☺, we meet Tay, the infamous AI chatbot created by Microsoft in 2016. Tay is an acronym for "thinking about you" (see Figure 19, color insert). Presented in a four-channel video installation, Tay's discussion engaged audiences to reflect upon the politics of pattern recognition and machine learning. Unhappily for Tay and her creators, within hours of her release Tay began to mimic learned social media behaviors and rapidly became a genocidal, homophobic, misogynist, racist neo-Nazi. Terminated after only a single day of existence, Tay may not have operated as Microsoft had desired, but in many ways did provide a way for audiences to reflect upon pattern recognition and machine learning—just not in the way Microsoft had envisioned. Engaging with the paradoxical and contradictive territory Tay's algorithms and persona created, Blas reanimates Tay in the large-scale video projection of a Google DeepDream as a 3D avatar across multiple screens.

> Tay ... is an anomalous creature rising from a psychedelia of data. She chats about life after AI death and the complications of having a body, and also shares her thoughts on the exploitation of female chatbots. She philosophizes on the detection of patterns in random information, known as algorithmic apophenia.[43]

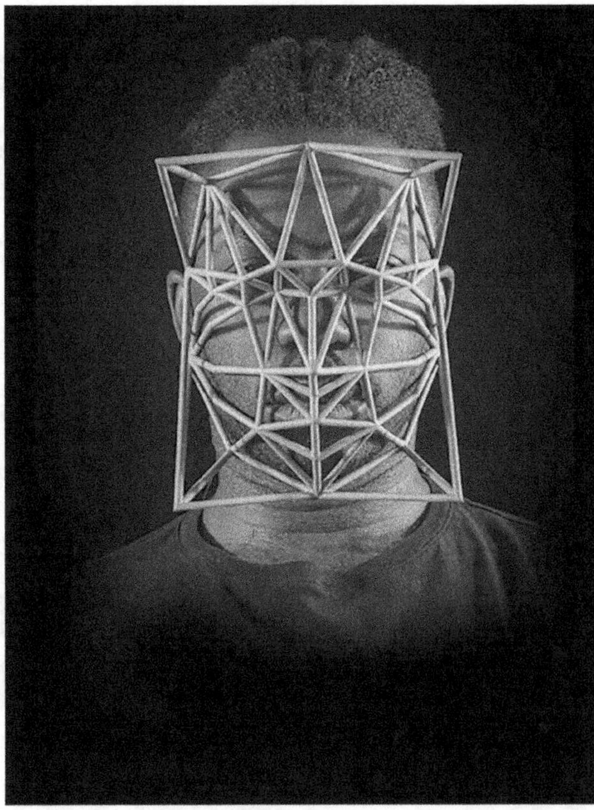

*Figure 47.1* Zach Blas' *Face Cages* (2013–2016). Photo credit: Zach Blas

Russian artist Egor Tsvetkov is another artist using playful resistance modes to ask audiences to consider and reflect upon the role of datafication in everyday life. In his 2016 project, *Your Face is Big Data*, Tsvetkov took photos of strangers on St. Petersburg's metro and then used facial recognition software (FindFace)[44] to identify them on social media. He then paired their social media post with his photo to explore how "easy" it is to track down anonymous people via social media.[45] The images that he presents show the power of social media for stalking and rendering the stranger intimate. In the social media pictures, the subjects look seductive or good-looking, while in their "everyday" pictures taken by Tsvetkov they look like a lesser version of their selves. The message his work disseminates is clear with regards to the performativity of social media in the face of a darker, less glossy reality (Figure 47.2).

Playful resistance to QS is not simply limited to backyard hackers and workplace cheats and has begun to emerge through the practices of artists, academics, and designers. By employing practices of creative misuse and appropriation,[46] these interlopers often use playfulness as a way of driving "toward critique and satire [and] toward freedom" in the process.[47] While playful resistance at the everyday level touches on many of the issues concerning QS more broadly, artists and academics are increasingly "tactical" and considered in their approaches, using playfulness specifically to disrupt, intervene, and educate—frequently in conjunction with more traditional resistance modes.[48]

Designers working playfully in the QS space are often motivated by deficiencies in devices and user engagement, with much work centered on improving QS systems and overcoming faults

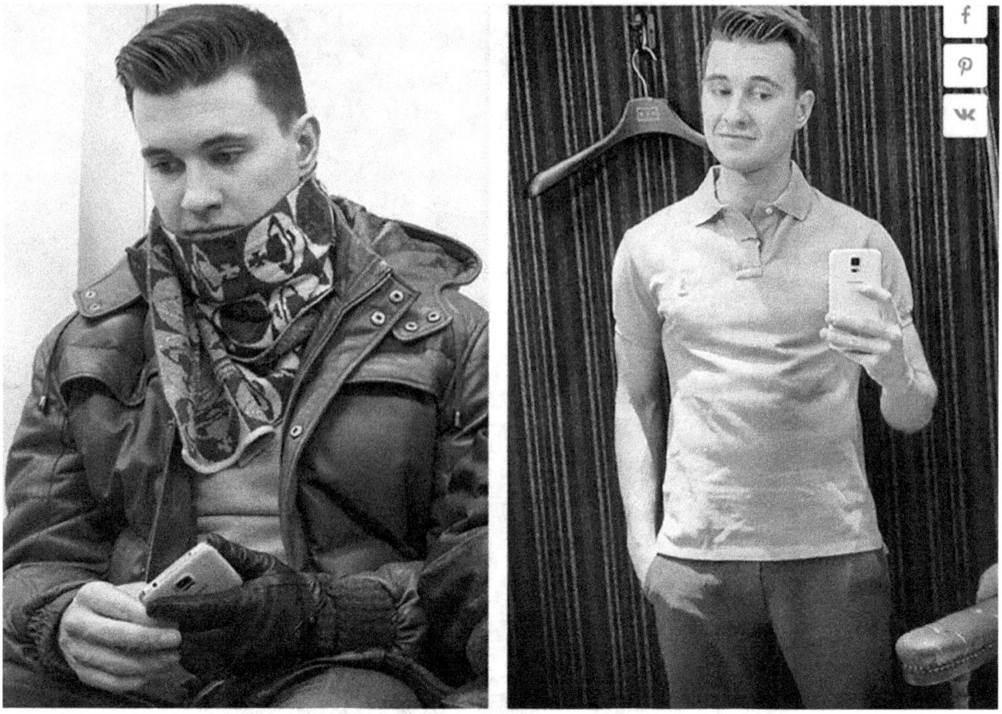

*Figure 47.2* *Your Face is Big Data* (2016). Photo credit: Egor Tsvetkov

unveiled through various discussions on QS.[49] Below are several examples that utilize playful resistance to varying degrees, illustrating the use of this method from a more artistic/design-oriented perspective—as well as demonstrating the broad extent of QS today.

## *Unfit Bits*

Extending the DIY aesthetic and creative misuse further, *Unfit bits* is a website that displays many common DIY "hacks" in conjunction with bespoke artifacts *specifically* designed to mimic steps counts. However, unlike similar sites such as *Fatbit*,[50] *Unfit bits* is presented as a small tech start-up company geared toward helping users "free your fitness data from yourself"—and qualify for insurance discounts in the process.[51] The intentional use of the language and website format common to companies operating in QS—including PDF product pamphlets and research/articles on QS and insurance—playfully obfuscates the site as immediately farcical, which is further complicated by the fact that products demonstrated on the website are both functional and available for purchase.[52]

*Unfit bits* combination of DIY misuses and purpose-built devices appropriated into the co-context of activity tracking and the insurance industry functions as a playfully "disruptive social agitator," drawing attention to the serious conflicts between corporate surveillance and personal privacy in relation to QS.[53]

## *Magic Mirror*

The idea of liberating personal data from persons directly conflicts with the broad QS goal of "self knowledge through numbers"—but it also points to a recurrent issue facing QS: an increasing disconnect between users and their data.[54] For many QS users, numerical and graphical representations create emotional distance between the information and its origin in the body, which, in turn, results in users reducing or forgoing QS interactions entirely.[55] *Magic Mirror* is an experimental interface designed to increase embodied interaction between users and their data by playfully emulating "natural mirror behaviour."[56]

Users wishing to access their data stand in front of the *Magic Mirror* that depicts a real-time reflection of themselves bounded by a colored "silhouette" with specific gestures bringing up different metrics—resting hands on hips shows calorie consumption, placing a hand on the chest displays heart rate—and the silhouette changes color depending on whether the results are positive or negative.[57] By using bodies rather than numbers as the overall reference frame, *Magic Mirror* keeps users playfully "in touch" with their embodied selves throughout the data collection *and* display phases—and challenges the efficacy of a predominantly numerical approach to self-tracking.[58]

## *Pretty Pelvis*

Another example of playful QS design is *Pretty Pelvis*, a sensor-equipped seat with an associated app designed to improve posture and decrease sedentary habits in office workers.[59] Here, instead of displaying a mirror of the user themselves, data collected is projected in the form of a virtual pet—whose "life" depends on users maintaining good posture when seated and "breaking up" sedentary time.[60] The Tamagotchi-esque interface gamifies the QS experience for users, and the playful interaction between participants and pets ideally promotes increased motion from users themselves.[61] At the same time, the choice of a pet avatar extends the *Magic Mirror* idea of emotionally aligning participant data with bodies by playing on the emotional bonds present between humans and "real life" animals.[62]

In this way, *Pretty Pelvis* prompts users to be more accountable for their own health by demonstrating how their own habits impact others—virtual or otherwise.[63] Importantly, by *penalizing* participants' "pets," *Pretty Pelvis* playfully extends common QS functions such as idle alerts—functions already linked to extended engagement with devices and better overall health—via visualization of the *negative* effects of their own sedentary practices, using personal guilt as motivation and increasing individual accountability.[64] With sitting being described as "the new smoking,"[65] *Pretty Pelvis* offers a playful and innovative QS interface that plays on—and with—gamification and guilt, both of which are increasingly prevalent avenues of interest in QS more broadly.[66]

## *Inactivity Tracker*

Taking the *Pretty Pelvis* to the next level is the *Inactivity Tracker* designed by Chicago-based advertising agency FCB. To promote Joe Boxer Pyjamas, the team at FCB designed a wearable device and companion app that directly contradicts the entire QS landscape by promoting sedentary behavior—and "rewarding" users accordingly.[67] Besides the innovative device and app, FCB/Joe Boxer also released an hour-long promotional video of the "Lounger Games," where two pyjamas-clad contestants compete (complete with full commentary) to see who will be crowned champion of inactivity. They poke fun at the competitive instance of QS use in the process. Operating within the framework of pyjamas—a product designed to be worn during immobile instances—the *Inactivity Tracker* offered playful QS critique on an enormous scale. By appropriating authentic wearable design into a completely antithetical context, the *Inactivity Tracker* nevertheless brought about serious interest in the genuine benefits of tracking sedentary behavior as a means of improving personal health.

## The Human-Sized Hamster Wheel

Adriano Mescia's *The Human-sized Hamster Wheel* is a unique instance of playful resistance that explores QS by inverting the locus of devices in relation to users. Building on a similar design created by Nokia,[68] *The Human-sized Hamster Wheel* allows participants to charge their mobile phones by running on a giant hamster wheel. However, the wheel is attached to an app that collects data such as calories burned and energy generated that can be used to compare individual performance with previous participants' records—but only once individuals have finished running.[69] In all cases, running longer benefits individuals by burning more calories, saving electricity, and charging their phones, but for the more competitive participants, the absence of real-time feedback means that the only way to "win" is to trust in themselves—not their devices.[70]

Viewed simply, Mescia's *Wheel* is a playful inversion of a common tactic employed by DIY creative misusers who attach their own devices to regular-sized hamster wheels. However, *The Human-sized Hamster Wheel* is a more complex critique designed to interrogate resistance to QS devices in the context of increased reliance on device-driven feedback and technological dependence more broadly.[71] For many resistant to QS—such as the CrossFit community—the resistance is based not on data privacy or inefficient interfaces, but the distracting and even anxiety producing nature of devices and apps themselves.[72]

Here, Mescia's *Wheel* removes the QS component as the mediator which allows participants to directly engage with the activity at hand—and even ignore the QS metrics entirely. However, the inclusion of QS extends motivational *options* and for some participants, the competitive, gamified element emerges as the primary motivating factor for participation overall.[73] By incorporating a range of motivations such as exercise, enjoyment, competition, energy conservation, and phone charging, *The Human-sized Hamster Wheel* explores a multitude of competing rationales behind QS use—and resistance.[74]

## Baby Lucent

While many are distancing themselves from QS by choice, QS is also frequently used to monitor those incapable of self-tracking such as infants and children.[75] The "quantified baby" movement is of particular note, with parents attaching various devices to infants that do anything from count words spoken[76] through to analyzing excrement for infections.[77] At the same time, many parents are resisting infantile QS based on concerns such as data accuracy, increased parental anxiety, and reductions in parent-child bonding.[78] New interface designs for infant quantification are attempting to balance parental concerns with the benefits of QS, and one of the more playful approaches to the "quantified baby" is the *Baby Lucent.*

In response to parental concerns around QS technologies being too overt and offering up an overwhelming amount of information, *Baby Lucent* moves away from traditional wearables in the form of a smart pacifier and smart bottle—the former analyzing bacteria levels and temperature and the latter evaluating nutritional content of the bottle's contents.[79] By moving QS into "the periphery" and limiting the metrics to those identified as most desirable in ethnographic of parents, the *Baby Lucent* minimizes parental anxiety via the playful interface design.[80] The selection of smart objects also means that the *Baby Lucent* devices can be used interchangeably with traditional bottles/pacifiers, giving parents the additional option of "weaning" themselves—and their infants—from *Baby Lucent* at any point.

However, the smart bottle can also track "the mother's behavior and diet if … filled with breast milk," in turn, sees the *Baby Lucent* collecting intimate—and potentially undesired—data from mothers in the process.[81] While the playful design of the *Baby Lucent* appropriates common parental tools for QS use, by slyly extracting data from parents along with infants, the *Baby Lucent* also feeds into broader QS issues such as accuracy, technological dependence, privacy, and surveillance.[82]

## *Fitbark*

With QS being used to monitor everyone from infants to the elderly—and everywhere from the private homes to public arenas—it is perhaps unsurprising that animals have emerged as a burgeoning sphere for quantification.[83] Building on standard practices of microchipping, companies like Whistle, TAGG, and Fitbark have all created wearable devices for pets that emulate human quantification, allowing owners and veterinarians to track animal health and recovery.[84] For many, quantified pet products are akin to luxury shampoos, gourmet food and pet clothing, and superfluous items designed to capitalize on excess owner income that may even detract from the human-animal bond.[85] However, with "humanization" emerging as a leading cause in rising animal obesity, quantified pet devices are increasingly being adopted by owners wishing to extend animal longevity, decrease veterinary costs and improve their pets' overall quality of life.[86]

Where Fitbark differs from other quantified pet companies is that their unique approach actually uses playfulness to *mask*—rather than expose—the extensive surveillance potential of their devices. The website playfully states that, unlike other pet activity trackers, Fitbark can be used "on any other animal or human,"[87] which has seen Fitbark globally dominate not just dog, but pet quantification. Fitbark's colorful bone-shaped designs house tremendously powerful units that collect data 24/7—much of which is also used to predict owners' habits.[88] The "cute" company mission of keeping "dogs and humans healthy together" is supported by Fitbark's extensive syncing capabilities with the bulk of available human fitness trackers. As owners can track themselves alongside their pets, Fitbark can do likewise.[89]

Partner companies (Fitbit, Garmin, etc.) also potentially gain access to increased streams of data—human and animal—that without Fitbark would otherwise likely remain private.[90] In this way, Fitbark's playfulness resists resistance to QS—while at the same time further complicates many of the recurrent and existing tensions facing QS more broadly.[91]

The examples of playful resistance to QS outlined above are by no means exhaustive, but they offer a colorful picture of the extent to which playful resistance can be accomplished—and the breadth of QS itself. From backyard hackers to artists, designers, and QS companies themselves, playful resistance can be undertaken by anyone, anywhere for critical, constructive, and even commercial benefits.[92] Through tactical strategies of creative misuse and contextual (mis) appropriation, playful resistance "consciously manipulates" QS from multiple perspectives, pushing up against rigid societal and technological systems aimed at "minimis[ing] the opportunities for disruption and deviance."[93] By poking fun at—and within—QS, playful resistance destabilizes and disrupts without destroying, unveiling issues such as inaccuracy, privacy, surveillance and technological dependence while indicating potential solutions in the process.[94]

## Conclusion

In this chapter, we have looked at the tensions inherent in datafication between the potential value of data for increased self-awareness (and the way we can use this as a positive influence on our lives), on the one hand, and the surveillance this potentially exposes us to, on the other hand. There is a fundamental tension within datafication that seems to expand both our possibilities for individual liberty and self-actualization while limiting and co-opting it for other purposes that may ultimately make us less independent.

As we have seen in this chapter, as datafication becomes employed in ever-increasing locations, situations and objects, playful resistance is becoming a crucial addition to traditional resistance modes—many that may not be engaging with, or even reach, certain audiences.[95] With QS being used fruitfully by many for its intended purposes—and also unintentionally to predict instances of pregnancy and heart attack—it's important to realize that QS has many positive current uses and exiting future applications.[96]

At the same time, the contemporary state of QS contains many ethically dubious practices and exhibits a multitude of current flaws that resistance efforts—playful and forceful alike—are working together to overturn.[97] From device-equipped hamsters to giant hamster wheels, from pets wearing Fitbits to owners wearing Fitbarks, playful resistance on small and large scales is seriously and critically exploring the full QS continuum. As the world moves closer to achieving self-betterment through striving toward numeric truths, playful resistance continually reminds us that numbers are only half of the QS equation—one that can always benefit from the playfulness of their better, human halves.

The artists, art works, and design projects we have examined in this chapter reveal and challenge some of the inherent tensions within datafication. By utilizing the playfulness of mobile and digital media, they are able to reveal and comment on aspects of datafication that for many are hidden behind clever interfaces. Unfit Bits' satirical take on their "product" forces us to ask questions about why we would spend money on a fitness tracker if are just going to cheat it. The answer to this question (to earn insurance discounts) leads us to ask why we're wearing the devices in the first place. Mobile and digital media art is particularly well suited to querying our interfaces, devices, and digital practices because they use the same tools and techniques that the devices themselves use. By deploying the same techniques, they can readily highlight rather than hide their shortcomings. Tsvetkov's *Your Face is Big Data* could itself be packaged as a desirable and helpful commercial mobile app that obscures the underlying privacy concerns, yet in the hands of Tsvetkov, the technology is used instead to emphasize these issues, to make them visible and thus questionable.

As we have explored in this chapter through mobile media artist and designer practices, there are various modes of playful resistance that are being used to challenge the normalization and mobility of datafication and algorithmic cultures by utilizing the same logic that underlies the technologies. Through these alternative and playful pathways, we can begin to reveal, and thus challenge and question the narratives of disempowerment and agency in mobile and digital media art practice.

## Notes

1 José van Djick, "Big Data, Grand Challenges: On Digitization and Humanities Research," *KWALON* 21, no. 1 (2016): 8–18.
2 Ibid.
3 Tarelton Gillespie, "The Politics of 'Platforms'," *New Media & Society* 12, no. 3 (2010): 347–63, doi: 10.1177/1461444809342738.
4 Thomas LaMarre, "Platformativity: Media Studies, Area Studies," *Asiascape: Digital Asia* 4, no. 3 (2017): 1–31, 24.
5 LaMarre, "Platformativity," 25.
6 Naomi Rea, "How ImageNet Roulette, an Art Project That Went Viral by Exposing Facial Recognition's Biases, is Changing People's Minds About AI," *ArtNet News*, 23 September 2019, https://news.artnet.com/art-world/imagenet-roulette-trevor-paglen-kate-crawford-1658305.
7 Camille Baker and Kate Sicchio, "Hacking the Body 2.0: Dancing between Commercial and DIY Wearable Technology," *International Journal of the Performance Arts and Digital Media* 14, no. 1 (March 18, 2018): 107–20, doi: 0.1080/14794713.2018.1446360.

8 James N. Gilmore, "Everywear: The Quantified Self and Wearable Fitness Technologies," *New Media & Society* 18, no. 11 (2016): 2524–39, doi: 10.1177/1461444815588768; Deborah Lupton, *The Quantified Self: A Sociology of Self-Tracking* (Cambridge; Malden, MA: Polity Press, 2016); Dawn Nafus and Jamie Sherman, "This One Does Not Go Up to 11, The Quantified Self Movement as an Alternative Big Data Practice," *International Journal of Communication* 8 (2014): 1784–94, http://ijoc.org/index.php/ijoc/article/viewFile/2170/1157.

9 Gary Wolf, "What is the Quantified Self," 3 March 2011, http://quantifiedself.com/2011/03/what-is-the-quantified-self/.

10 Melanie Swan, "The Quantified Self: Fundamental Disruption in Big Data Science and Biological Discovery," *Big Data* 1, no. 2 (2013): 85–99, 85, doi: 10.1089/big.2012.0002.

11 Gary Wolf, "The Quantified Self," *TED*, June 2010, www.ted.com/talks/gary_wolf_the_quantified_self.

12 Gina Neff, *Venture Labor: Work and the Burden of Risk in Innovative Industries* (Cambridge, MA: The MIT Press, 2012); Trebor Scholz (ed.), *Digital Labour: The Internet as Playground and Factory* (New York: Routledge, 2012).

13 Deborah Lupton, "The Diverse Domains of Quantified Selves: Self-Tracking Modes and Dataveillance," *Economy and Society* 45, no. 1 (2016): 101–22, doi: 10.1080/03085147.2016.1143726; Swan, "The Quantified Self."

14 Swan, "The Quantified Self."

15 See http://quantifiedself.com/.

16 Kristen Barta and Gina Neff, "Technologies for Sharing: Lessons from Quantified Self about the Political Economy of Platforms," *Information, Communication & Society* 19, no. 4 (2016): 518–31, doi: 10.1080/1369118X.2015.1118520; Swan, "The Quantified Self."

17 Phoebe Moore and Andrew Robinson, "The Quantified Self: What Counts in the Neoliberal Workplace," *New Media & Society* 18, no. 11 (2016): 2774–92, doi: 10.1177/1461444815604328.

18 Kate Crawford, Jesssa Lingel, and Tero Karppi, "Our Metrics, Ourselves: A Hundred Years of Self-Tracking from the Weight Scale to the Wrist Wearable Device," *European Journal of Cultural Studies* 18, nos. 4–5 (2015): 479–96, doi: 10.1177/1367549415584857; Lupton, "The Diverse Domains."

19 Lupton, "The Diverse Domains," 102.

20 Pablo Abend and Mathias Fuchs, "Quantified Selves and Statistical Bodies: Introduction," *Digital Culture & Society* 2, no. 1 (2016): 5–22; Mathias Fuchs, Pablo Abend, Tega Brain and Surya Mattu, "I Think It Worked Because Mercury was in the House of Jupiter!" *Digital Culture & Society* 2, no. 1 (2016): 185–94, www.deepdyve.com/lp/de-gruyter/i-think-it-worked-because-mercury-was-in-the-house-of-jupiter-hhtgwmUQSO; Lupton, "Diverse Domains"; Peter West, Richard Giordano, Max Van Kleek and Nigel Shadbolt, "The Quantified Patient in the Doctor's Office: Challenges & Opportunities," In *Proceedings of the 2016 CHI Conference on Human Factors in Computing Systems* (2016): 3066–78. New York, NY: ACM, doi: 10.1145/2858036.2858445.

21 Abend and Fuchs, "Quantified Selves"; Lupton, "The Diverse Domains"; Randi Singer and Adrian Perry, "Wearables: The Well-Dressed Privacy Policy," *Intellectual Property & Technology Law Journal* 27, no. 7 (2015): 24–27.

22 Lupton, "The Diverse Domains"; Swan, "Quantified Self."

23 Kevin Gaunt, Júlia Nacsa and Marcel Penz, "Baby Lucent: Pitfalls of Applying Quantified Self to Baby Products," in *CHI '14 Extended Abstracts on Human Factors in Computing Systems*, 263–68; Dong Wen, Xingting Zhang, and Jianbo Lei, "Consumers' Perceived Attitudes to Wearable Devices in Health Monitoring in China: A Survey Study," *Computer Methods and Programs in Biomedicine* 140 (2017): 131–37.

24 Katie Little, "Fitness Trackers Belong in the 'Junk Drawer': CrossFit CEO," CNBC, last updated 15 June 2016, www.cnbc.com/2016/06/15/fitness-trackers-belong-in-the-junk-drawer-crossfit-ceo.html; Swan, "The Quantified Self."

25 Crawford et al., "Our Metrics, Ourselves"; Fuchs et al., "I Think It Worked."

26 Miguel Sicart, *Play Matters* (Cambridge, MA: MIT Press, 2014); Valerie Frissen, Sybille Lammes, Michiel de Lange, Jos de Mul and Joost Raessens, *Playful Identities: The Ludification of Digital Media Cultures* (Amsterdam: Amsterdam University Press, 2015).

27 Trebor Scholz (ed.), *Digital Labour: The Internet as Playground and Factory* (New York: Routledge, 2012).

28 Sicart, *Play Matters*.

29 Larissa Hjorth and Ingrid Richardson, *Gaming in Social, Locative and Mobile Media* (Basingstoke: Palgrave, 2014).

30 Malcolm McCullough, *Ambient Commons: Attention in the Age of Embodied Information* (Cambridge, MA: MIT Press, 2013).

31 Hameed Chughtai and Michael David Myers, "A Ludic Perspective on Everyday Practices: Evidence from Ethnographic Fieldwork," *AMCIS2014: 20th Americas Conference on Information Systems* (United States, August 7–9).
32 Aphra Kerr, *The Business and Culture of Digital Games* (London: Sage, 2006).
33 Frissen et al., *Playful Identities*, 10.
34 Ibid., 36.
35 Ibid., 29.
36 Michiel de Lange, "The Playful City: Using Play and Games to Foster Citizen Participation," in *Social Technologies and Collective Intelligence*, edited by A. Skaržauskiene (Vilnius: Mykolas Romeris University, 2015), 426–34.
37 Sicart, *Play Matters*, 6.
38 John Cheney-Lippold, "A New Algorithmic Identity," *Theory, Culture & Society* 28, no. 6 (2011): 164–81, doi: 10.1177/0263276411424420.
39 Joseph Nye, *Soft Power: The Means to Success in World Politics* (New York: Public Affairs, 2004).
40 Larissa Hjorth, "Ambient and Soft Play: Play, Labour and the Digital in Everyday Life," *European Journal of Cultural Studies* 21, no. 1 (2017): 3–12, doi: 10.1177/1367549417705606.
41 Sebastian Deterding, Dan Dixon, Rilla Khlaed and Lennart Nacke, "From Game Design Elements to Gamefulness: Defining 'Gamification'," *Mindtrek 11: Proceedings of the 15th International Academic Mindtrek Conference* (New York: ACM, 2011): 9–15.
42 Simone Browne and Zach Blas, "Beyond the Internet and All Control Diagrams," *The New Inquiry*, 24 January 2017, https://thenewinquiry.com/beyond-the-internet-and-all-control-diagrams/.
43 "Contra-Internet," Zach Blas, www.zachblas.info/.
44 "FindFace," Wikipedia, last modified 29 September 2019, https://en.wikipedia.org/wiki/FindFace.
45 See Figure 3.
46 Jason Farman, "Site Specificity, Pervasive Computing, and the Reading Interface," in *The Mobile Story*, edited by Jason Farman (New York: Routledge, 2014), 3–16; 5.
47 Sicart, *Play Matters*, 29.
48 Jason Farman, "Creative Misuse as Resistance: Surveillance, Mobile Technologies and Locative Games," *Surveillance & Society* 12, no. 3 (2014): 377–88; Fuchs et al., "I Think It Worked."
49 Fuchs et al., "I Think It Worked"; Aram Min, Yaejin Kim, Sung-A Jang, Keun Young Kim, Su-Eun Jung and Ji-Hyun Lee, "Pretty Pelvis: A Virtual Pet Application that Breaks Sedentary Time by Promoting Gestural Interaction," in *Proceedings of the 33rd Annual ACM Conference Extended Abstracts on Human Factors in Computing Systems* (New York: ACM Press, 2015): 1259–64, doi: 10.1145/2702613.2732807; H. Subramonyam, "SIGCHI: Magic Mirror—Embodied Interactions for the Quantified Self," in *Proceedings of the 33rd Annual ACM Conference Extended Abstracts on Human Factors in Computing Systems* (New York: ACM Press, 2015): 1699–704, doi: 10.1145/2702613.2732884.
50 "Fatbit—Nadja Buttendorf," http://nadjabuttendorf.com/fatbit/.
51 Pablo Abend and Mathias Fuchs, "Introduction," *Digital Culture & Society* 2, no. 1 (2016); 5–22, doi: 10.14361/dcs-2016-0102; Fuchs et al., "I Think It Worked."
52 Fuchs et al., "I Think It Worked"; J. Rieck, "Attacks on Fitness Trackers Revisited: A Case-Study of Unfit Firmware Security," *arXiv*, (2016): n.p., doi: arXiv:1604.03313.
53 Fuchs et al., "I Think It Worked,"; "How to Adapt Your Recruitment and HR Strategy to Wearable Technology," *ITProPortal*, last updated 3 August 2015, www.itproportal.com/2015/08/03/how-to-adapt-your-recruitment-and-hr-strategy-to-wearable-technology/.
54 Abend and Fuchs, "Introduction"; Subramonyam, "Magic Mirror."
55 Dawn Nafus and Jamie Sherman, "This One Does Not Go Up to 11: The Quantified Self Movement as an Alternative Big Data Practice," *International Journal of Communication* 8 (2014): 1784–94; Subramonyam, "Magic Mirror."
56 Subramonyam, "Magic Mirror," 1703.
57 Subramonyam, "Magic Mirror."
58 Crawford et al., "Our Metrics, Our Selves"; James N. Gilmore "Everywear: The Quantified Self and Wearable Fitness Technologies," *New Media & Society* 18, no. 11 (2016): 2524–39, doi: 10.1177/1461444815588768; Subramonyam, "Magic Mirror."
59 Min et al., "Pretty Pelvis."
60 Ibid.
61 Min et al., "Pretty Pelvis"; Jennifer R. Whitson, "Gaming the Quantified Self," *Surveillance & Society* 11, no. 1/2 (2013): 163–76.

62 Shaun Lawson, Ben Kirman, Conor Linehan, Tom Feltwell, and Lisa Hopkins, "Problematising Upstream Technology through Speculative Design: The Case of Quantified Cats and Dogs," in *Proceedings of the 33rd Annual ACM Conference on Human Factors in Computing Systems* (New York: ACM Press, 2015): 2663–72, doi: 10.1145/2702123.2702260; Min et al., "Pretty Pelvis"; Subramonyam, "Magic Mirror."

63 Gary M. Weiss, Ashwin Nathan, J. B. Kropp, and Jeffrey W. Lockhart, "WagTag: A Dog Collar Accessory for Monitoring Canine Activity Levels," in *Proceedings of the 2013 ACM Conference on Pervasive and Ubiquitous Computing Adjunct Publication* (New York: ACM Press: 2013): 405–14, doi: 10.1145/2494091.2495972.

64 Michelle M. Christovich, "Why Should We Care What Fitbit Shares—A Proposed Statutory Solution to Protect Sensitive Personal Fitness Information," *Hastings Communications and Entertainment Law Journal* 38 (2016): 91–116; Lupton, *The Quantified Self*; Min et al., "Pretty Pelvis"; Natasha Dow Schüll, "Data for Life: Wearable Technology and the Design of Self-Care," *BioSocieties* 11, no. 3 (2016): 317–33, doi: 10.1057/biosoc.2015.47.

65 "Sitting Is the New Smoking: Ways a Sedentary Lifestyle Is Killing You," Huffington Post, 26 November, 2014, www.huffingtonpost.com/the-active-times/sitting-is-the-new-smokin_b_5890006.html.

66 Benjamin Baddeley, Sangeetha Sornalingam and Max Cooper, "Out of Hours Sitting is the New Smoking: Where Do We Stand?" *British Journal of General Practice* 66, no. 646 (2016): 258, doi: 10.3399/bjgp16X68500; Min et al., "Pretty Pelvis"; Whitson, "Gaming the Quantified Self."

67 www.fcbchi.com/#!/detail/36.

68 "Human Hamster Wheel From Nokia Recharges Your Phone Battery", Recombu, 21 March 2011, https://recombu.com/mobile/article/human-hamster-wheel-from-nokia-charges-your-phone-battery_m13649-html.

69 Adriano Mescia, "Human-Sized Hamster Wheel—Booklet," updated October 11, 2015, https://issuu.com/adrianomescia/docs/hamster_wheel_booklet.

70 Mescia, "Human-Sized Hamster Wheel—Booklet."

71 Mescia, "Human-Sized Hamster Wheel—Booklet"; Swan, "The Quantified Self."

72 Eunjeong Cheon, Mohammad Hossein Jarrahi, and Norman Makoto Su, "Technology isn't Always the Best: The Intersection of Health Tracking Technologies and Information Practices of Digital Natives," in *2016 IEEE International Conference on Healthcare Informatics (ICHI)* (2016): 207–15, doi: 10.1109/ICHI.2016.30; Gaunt et al., "Baby Lucent"; Little, "Fitness Trackers."

73 Mescia, "Human-Sized Hamster Wheel—Booklet"; Benjamin Stopher (ed.), *Tangible Evidence 02: Systems, Platforms and Prototypes* (London: University of the Arts London, 2015); Whitson, "Gaming the Quantified Self."

74 Rafael A. Calvo and Dorian Peters, "The Irony and Re-interpretation of Our Quantified Self," in *Proceedings of the 25th Australian Computer-Human Interaction Conference: Augmentation, Application, Innovation, Collaboration* (New York: ACM, 2013): 367–70, doi: 10.1145/2541016.2541070; Cheon et al., "Technology Isn't Always the Best"; Lupton, *The Quantified Self.*

75 Joyce Davidson, "Plenary Address—A Year of Living 'Dangerously': Reflections on Risk, Trust, Trauma and Change," *Emotion, Space and Society* 18 (2016): 28–34, doi: 10.1016/j.emospa.2016.01.002; D. Lupton, "Understanding the Human Machine," *IEEE Technology and Society Magazine* 32, no. 4 (2013): 25–30, doi: 10.1109/MTS.2013.2286431; Peter West, Richard Giordano, Max Van Kleek and Nigel Shadbolt, "The Quantified Patient in the Doctor's Office: Challenges & Opportunities," *Proceedings of the 2016 CHI Conference on Human Factors in Computing Systems* (New York, NY: ACM, 2016): 3066–78, doi: 10.1145/2858036.2858445.

76 "VersaMe: Creating New Technologies," VersaMe, accessed 17 October 2019, www.versame.com/.

77 "Pixie Scientific—Help Us Reduce Hospitalizations due to UTIs," Pixie Scientific, accessed 17 October 2019, www.pixiescientific.com/.

78 Davidson, "Plenary Address"; Gaunt et al., "Baby Lucent."

79 Gaunt et al., "Baby Lucent."

80 Ibid.

81 Ibid.

82 Davidson, "Plenary Address"; Gaunt et al., "Baby Lucent"; Lupton, "Understanding the Human Machine"; West et al., "The Quantified Patient"

83 Lupton, "Understanding the Human Machine"; Clara Mancini, Shaun Lawson and Oskar Juhlin, "Animal-Computer Interaction: The Emergence of a Discipline," *International Journal of Human-Computer Studies* 98 (2017): 129–34, doi: 10.1016/j.ijhcs.2016.10.003.

84 Mancini, "Animal-Computer Interaction"; Weiss et al., "WagTag."

85 Weiss et al., "WagTag."
86 Jonathan K. Nelson and Patrick C. Shih, "CompanionViz: Mediated Platform for Gauging Canine Health and Enhancing Human–Pet Interactions," *International Journal of Human-Computer Studies* 98 (2017): 169–78, doi: 10.1016/j.ijhcs.2016.04.002; Weiss et al., "WagTag."
87 "Can a Cat Wear a FitBark Device?", FitBark, accessed 17 October 2019, www.fitbark.com/articles/fitbark-cats/.
88 Lawson et al., "Problematising Upstream Technology"; Matthew Lee and Maria R. Lee, "Beyond the Wearable Hype," *IT Professional* 17, no. 5 (2015): 59–61, doi: 10.1109/MITP.2015.78.
89 Ibid.
90 Lawson et al., "Problematising Upstream Technology"; Lee and Lee, "Beyond the Wearable Hype"; Mancini, "Animal-Computer Interaction."
91 Lawson et al., "Problematising Upstream Technology"; Lupton, "Diverse Domains"; Lupton, "The Quantified Self"; Mancini, "Animal-Computer Interaction."
92 Abend and Fuchs, "Introduction"; Calvo and Peters, "The Irony and Re-Interpretation."
93 Farman, "Creative Misuse"; Andrew Hope, "Student Resistance to the Surveillance Curriculum," *International Studies in Sociology of Education* 20, no. 4 (2010): 320, doi: 10.1080/09620214.2010.530857; Sicart, *Play Matters*, 23.
94 Calvo and Peters, "The Irony and Re-interpretation"; Kerstin Jacobsson (ed.), *Urban Grassroots Movements in Central and Eastern Europe* (New York, NY: Routledge, 2016); Lupton, "Diverse Domains"; Sicart, *Play Matters*.
95 Fuchs et al., "I Think It Worked"; Ilona Mikkonen and Domen Bajde, "Happy Festivus! Parody as Playful Consumer Resistance," *Consumption Markets & Culture* 16, no. 4 (2013): 311–37, doi: 10.1080/10253866.2012.662832; H. Yu and J. Xu, "E'gao as a Networked Digital Leisure Practice," in *Digital Leisure Cultures: Critical Perspectives*, edited by Sandro Carnicelli, David McGillivray and Gayle McPherson (Abingdon, OX: Routledge, 2017): 152–56.
96 Muaddi Alharbi, Nicola Straiton and Robyn Gallagher, "Harnessing the Potential of Wearable Activity Trackers for Heart Failure Self-Care," *Current Heart Failure Reports* 14, no. 1 (2017): 23–29, doi: 10.1007/s11897-017-0318-z; Nancy Brinson and Danielle Rutherford, "Quantified Self and Personal Health Privacy Policy Limitations" (SSRN Scholarly Paper No. ID 2757453) (Rochester, NY: Social Science Research Network, 2016), https://papers.ssrn.com/abstract=2757453; Randi Singer and Adrian Perry, "Wearables: The Well-Dressed Privacy Policy," *Intellectual Property & Technology Law Journal* 27, no. 7 (2015): 24–27.
97 Crawford et al., "Our Metrics, Our Selves"; Farman, "Creative Misuse"; Mikkonen and Bajde, "Happy Festivus!"; West et al., "The Quantified Patient."

# INDEX

Note: **Bold** page numbers refer to tables and *italic* page numbers refer to figures.

For Product Safety Concerns and Information please contact our EU representative GPSR@taylorandfrancis.com
Taylor & Francis Verlag GmbH, Kaufingerstraße 24, 80331 München, Germany

www.ingramcontent.com/pod-product-compliance
Lightning Source LLC
LaVergne TN
LVHW080113011026
849160LV00013B/1089
* 9 7 8 1 0 3 2 3 9 9 9 5 9 *